SOUTH AMERICA

Pages 72–73

75

74

58–59

56–57

60–61

64–65

68

66

67

62–63

69

70

NORTH AMERICA

Pages 48–49

50–51

47

AFRICA

AUSTRALASIA

Pages 32–33

34

35

C000142932

Copenhagen 83
Amsterdam 81 Stockholm 83
Brussels 81 Moscow 83
London 78 Hamburg 82
Paris 79 Berlin 82 Beijing 84 Seoul 85 Tokyo 85
Barcelona 80 Vienna 81 Shanghai 84 Osaka 85
Madrid 80 Rome Istanbul 80
Geneva 82 80 Athens 83 Jerusalem 88 Delhi 87 Hong Kong 84
Milan 82 Cairo 88 Calcutta 87 Bangkok 84
Bombay 87 Singapore 87

Ottawa 89 Montreal 89
San Francisco Toronto 89 Boston 89
91 Chicago 89 New York 90
Los Angeles 91 Washington 91

Mexico City 92

Nairobi 88

São Paulo 92 Rio de Janeiro 92
Santiago 92 Buenos Aires 92

Perth 86
Melbourne 86 Sydney 86
Auckland 86

CITY PLANS

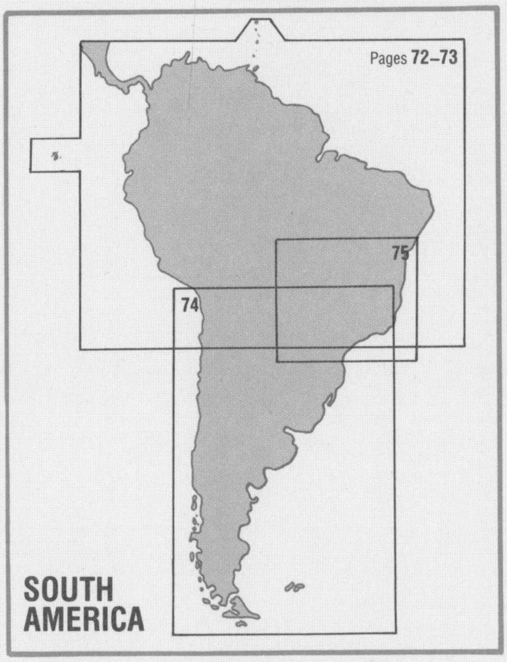

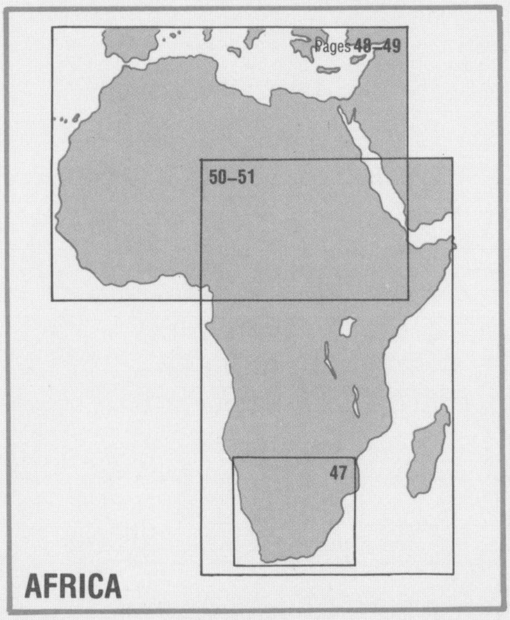

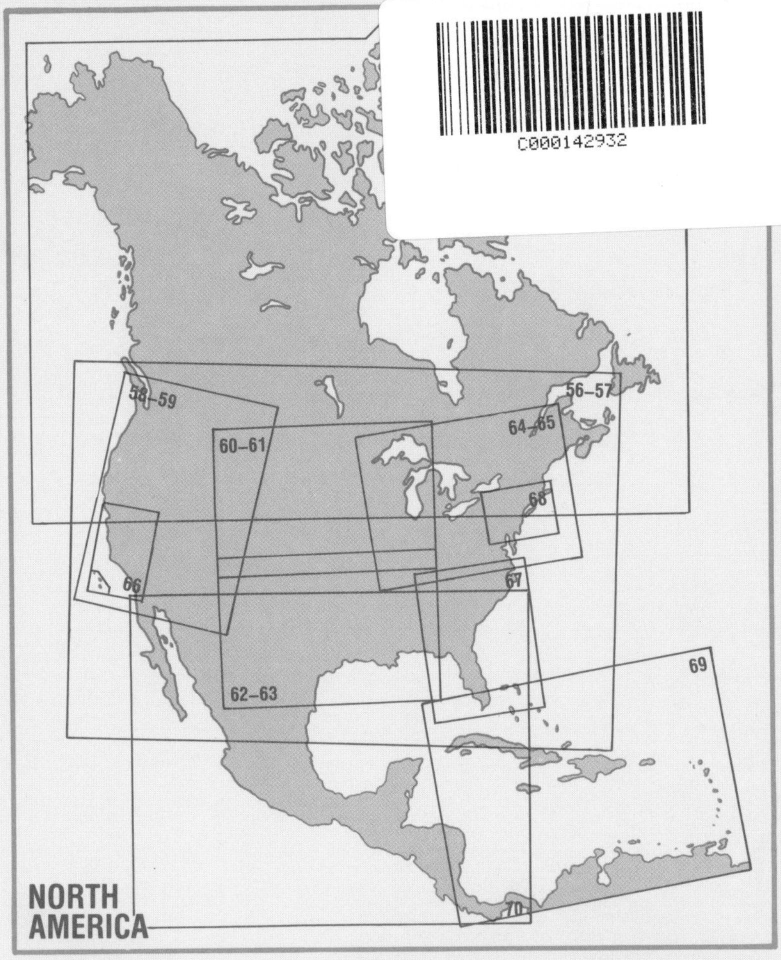

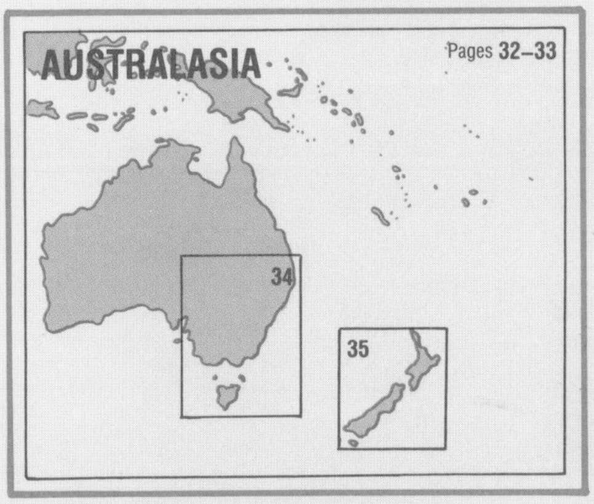

To Anne

Christmas 1994

With love

Dad

THE TIMES ATLAS OF THE WORLD

FAMILY EDITION

TIMES BOOKS
A Division of HarperCollins*Publishers*

Published in 1995 by
TIMES BOOKS
HarperCollins*Publishers*
77-85 Fulham Palace Road
Hammersmith
London W6 8JB

First edition 1988
Reprinted 1988
Reprinted with revisions 1989, 1990, 1991
Second edition 1992
Reprinted with revisions 1993 (twice)
Third edition 1995

Maps and index prepared by
Bartholomew,
HarperCollins*Publishers*,
Edinburgh

Geographical Dictionary prepared by
Professor B.W. Atkinson

Physical Earth Maps
Duncan Mackay

Design
Ivan Dodd

Printed and bound in Italy by
L.E.G.O. SpA

The Publishers would like to extend their grateful thanks to the following:

Mrs J. Candy, Geographical Research Associates, Maidenhead
Flag information provided and authenticated by the Flag Institute, Chester
Mr P.J.M. Geelan, Place-name consultant
Mr Michael Hendrie, Astronomy Correspondent, *The Times*, London
Mr H.A.G. Lewis OBE, Geographical consultant to *The Times*

British Library Cataloguing in Publication Data.
A catalogue record for
this book is available
from the British Library.

ISBN 0-7230-0712-8

This, *The Times Atlas of the World, Family Edition,* has been extensively revised since it was first published in 1988. This is the third edition of this popular atlas. It is a reference work for use in the home, office or school, for those who travel the world and those, like Francis Bacon, who journey only "in map and chart".

An index of no fewer than 30,000 entries, keyed to the main map plates, will aid those who, whilst familiar with the name of a place, are uncertain of just where it lies on a map.

It is by no means always easy to ascertain the correct title and status of a country as distinct from its everyday name used on maps. The list of states and territories gives in addition to name, title and status, the population and area, the national currency, the major religions and the national flag.

Maps, being an efficient way of storing and displaying information, are used to amplify the list of states and territories and the geographical comparisons of the continents, oceans, lakes and islands. They form the basis of the section on earthquakes, volcanoes, economic minerals, vegetation, temperature, rainfall and population.

Maps are also, by nature, illustrative and a 14-page section shows the world's major physical features in the way they appear from space but with the names of the features added.

Amongst the statistical data contained in the Atlas is a listing of the major metropolitan areas with their populations. For the past several decades there has been, throughout the world, an accelerating flow of people from the land to towns and cities and especially the major cities, some of which now contain the bulk of the national population. Growth in air travel has turned those same cities into centres of tourism. Influx of population and the demands of tourism have enhanced the status of the cities. Generous space has, therefore, been allocated to maps of the major cities and their environs.

Geographical names in this Atlas are given in their anglicized (conventional) form where such a form is in current use. Other names are given in their national Roman alphabet or else converted into English by transliteration (letter to letter) or transcription (sound to sound). Because Roman alphabet letters, sometimes modified, are pronounced in a variety of ways, a brief guide to pronunciation has been included. The whole is supplemented by a dictionary of geographical terms.

In the names, in the portrayal of international boundaries and in the list of states and territories, the aim has been to show the situation as it pertains in the area at the time of going to press. This must not be taken as an endorsement by the publishers of the status of the territories concerned. The aim throughout has been to show things as they are. In that way the Atlas will best serve the reader to whom, it is hoped, it will bring interest, benefit and continuing pleasure.

H.A.G. Lewis, OBE
Geographical Consultant to *The Times*

CONTENTS

INTRODUCTORY SECTION

States & Territories of the World *4–43*

Geographical Comparisons: *44–47*
Continents, metropolitan areas, mountain heights, islands, oceans, seas, rivers, drainage basins and lakes.

Physical Earth
North America *48*
Central America *50*
Antarctica & South America *52*
Africa *54*
Europe *56*
Asia *58*
Australasia *60*

Solar System *62*

The Earth *63*

Earthquakes & Volcanoes *64*
Economic Minerals

Temperature: January & July *65*

Annual Rainfall *66*
Natural Vegetation

Population Density *67*
Population Change

Time Zones *68*

Front Endpaper:
Locator guide to World Maps and City Plans

Rear Endpaper:
Table of distances between the major Cities of the World

THE MAPS

Key to Symbols on maps *1*
Nations of the World 1:70M *2,3*
Nations of Europe 1:15M *4,5*
England Wales 1:2M *6,7*
Scotland 1:2M *8*
Ireland 1:2M *9*
British Isles & the North Sea 1:5M *10,11*
Scandinavia & the Baltic 1:7.5M *12*
Netherlands Belgium 1:2.5M *13*
France 1:5M *14*
Spain Portugal 1:5M *15*
Italy & the Balkans 1:5M *16,17*
Germany & Central Europe 1:5M *18,19*
Eastern Europe 1:10M *20,21*
Nations of Asia & Australasia 1:40M *22,23*
Northern Asia 1:20M *24,25*
Eastern Asia 1:20M *26,27*
Japan Korea 1:5M *28,29*
South-East Asia, Mainland 1:10M *30*
Central China 1:10M *31*
Australia & South West Pacific 1:20M *32,33*
South-East Australia 1:7.5M *34*
New Zealand 1:5M *35*
Indian & Pacific Oceans 1:60M *36,37*
South Asia & Middle East 1:20M *38,39*
Turkey Syria Iraq Iran 1:7.5M *40,41*
Northern India 1:7.5M *42,43*
The Ganges Plain 1:4M *43*
Southern India 1:7.5M *44*
Israel Lebanon Cyprus 1:2.5M *45*
Nations of Africa 1:40M *46*
South Africa 1:7.5M *47*
Northern Africa 1:15M *48,49*
Central & Southern Africa 1:15M *50,51*
Atlantic Ocean 1:60M *52*
Nations of North America 1:35M *53*
Canada 1:15M *54,55*
United States of America 1:12.5M *56,57*
Western USA 1:5M *58,59*
North Central USA 1:5M *60,61*
South Central USA 1:5M *62,63*
USA & Canada: The Great Lakes 1:5M *64,65*
California & Hawaii 1:2.5M & 1:5M *66*
Florida & South East USA 1:5M *67*
USA: Atlantic Seaboard 1:2.5M *68*
Caribbean 1:10M *69*
Mexico & Central America 1:15M *70*
Nations of South America 1:35M *71*
Northern South America 1:15M *72,73*
Southern South America 1:15M *74*
South East Brazil 1:7.5M *75*
Polar Regions 1:40M *76*

CITY PLANS

Key to symbols on city plans *77*
London *78*
Paris *79*
Rome Madrid Barcelona *80*
Vienna Amsterdam Brussels *81*
Hamburg Berlin Geneva Milan *82*
Copenhagen Stockholm Athens Moscow *83*
Beijing Shanghai Bangkok Hong Kong *84*
Tokyo Seoul Osaka *85*
Perth Sydney Melbourne Auckland *86*
Delhi Calcutta Bombay Singapore *87*
Jerusalem Istanbul Cairo Nairobi *88*
Montreal Ottawa Toronto Chicago Boston *89*
New York Manhattan *90*
Washington San Francisco Los Angeles *91*
Mexico City São Paulo Santiago Rio de Janeiro Buenos Aires *92*

INDEX

Guide to Pronunciation *93*
Geographical Dictionary *94–99*
Abbreviations used on the maps *100*
Abbreviations used in the Index *101*
Index to the maps *101–156*
Acknowledgements *156*

AFGHANISTAN

STATUS: Islamic State
AREA: 652,225 sq km (251,773 sq miles)
POPULATION: 16,433,000
ANNUAL NATURAL INCREASE: 2.5%
CAPITAL: Kabul
LANGUAGE: Pushtu, Dari
RELIGION: 90% Sunni, 9% Shi'a Muslim, Hindu, Sikh and Jewish minorities
CURRENCY: Afghani (AFA)
ORGANIZATIONS: Col. Plan, UN

Afghanistan is a mountainous landlocked country in southwest Asia with a climate of extremes. In summer the lowland southwest reaches a temperature of over 40°C (104°F); in winter this may drop to -26°C (-15°F) in the northern mountains. The country is one of the poorest in the world with barely 10 per cent of the land suitable for agriculture. Main crops are wheat, fruit and vegetables. Sheep and goats are the main livestock. Mineral resources are rich but underdeveloped with natural gas, coal and iron ore deposits predominating. The main industrial area was centred on Kabul, but both Kabul and the rural areas have been devastated by civil war.

ÅLAND

STATUS: Self-governing Island Province of Finland
AREA: 1,505 sq km (581 sq miles)
POPULATION: 24,993
CAPITAL: Mariehamn

ALBANIA

STATUS: Republic
AREA: 28,750 sq km (11,100 sq miles)
POPULATION: 3,363,000
ANNUAL NATURAL INCREASE: 1.7%
CAPITAL: Tirana (Tiranë)
LANGUAGE: Albanian (Gheg, Tosk)
RELIGION: 70% Muslim, 20% Greek Orthodox, 10% Roman Catholic
CURRENCY: lek (ALL)
ORGANIZATIONS: UN

Albania is situated on the eastern seaboard of the Adriatic. With the exception of a coastal strip, most of the territory is mountainous and largely unfit for cultivation. The climate is Mediterranean along the coast, but cooler inland. Average temperatures in July reach 25°C (77°F) and there is 1,400 mm (55 inches) of rainfall annually. The country possesses mineral resources, notably chrome which is a major export, and deposits of coal, oil and natural gas. After decades of self-imposed political and economic isolation Albania shook off its own peculiar variant of communism in 1990. Administrative chaos and a massive fall in production ensued resulting in acute food shortages and widespread emigration. The country is one of the poorest in Europe with a backward rural economy and nearly half the labour force unemployed.

ALGERIA

STATUS: Republic
AREA: 2,381,745 sq km (919,355 sq miles)
POPULATION: 26,600,000
ANNUAL NATURAL INCREASE: 2.7%
CAPITAL: Algiers (Alger, El-Djezaïr)
LANGUAGE: 83% Arabic, French, Berber
RELIGION: Muslim
CURRENCY: Algerian dinar (DZD)
ORGANIZATIONS: Arab League, OAU, OPEC, UN

Physically the country is divided between the coastal Atlas mountain ranges of the north and the Sahara to the south. Algeria is mainly hot, with negligible rainfall, but along the Mediterranean coast temperatures are more moderate, with most rain falling during the mild winters. Arable land occupies small areas of the northern valleys and coastal strip, with wheat, barley and vines the leading crops. Sheep, goats and cattle are the most important livestock. Although oil from the southern deserts dominates the economy, it is now declining and natural gas output has increased dramatically. A virtual civil war has existed between the army and Islamic extremists which has caused the economy to deteriorate.

AMERICAN SAMOA

STATUS: Unincorporated Territory of USA
AREA: 197 sq km (76 sq miles)
POPULATION: 132,726
CAPITAL: Pago Pago

ANDORRA

STATUS: Principality
AREA: 465 sq km (180 sq miles)
POPULATION: 59,000
CAPITAL: Andorra la Vella
LANGUAGE: Catalan, Spanish, French
RELIGION: Roman Catholic majority
CURRENCY: French franc (FRF), Andorran peseta (ADP)
ORGANIZATIONS: UN

Andorra, a tiny state in the Pyrenees between France and Spain, achieved fuller independence from these countries in 1993. The climate is alpine with a long winter, which lasts for six months, a mild spring and a warm summer. Tourism is the main occupation, with Andorra becoming an important skiing centre during the winter. Tobacco and potatoes are the principal crops, sheep and cattle the main livestock. Other important sources of revenue are the sale of hydro-electricity, stamps, duty-free goods and financial services.

ANGOLA

STATUS: Republic
AREA: 1,246,700 sq km (481,225 sq miles)
POPULATION: 10,770,000
ANNUAL NATURAL INCREASE: 2.9%
CAPITAL: Luanda
LANGUAGE: Portuguese, tribal dialects
RELIGION: mainly traditional beliefs, Roman Catholic and Protestant minorities
CURRENCY: new kwanza (AOK)
ORGANIZATIONS: OAU, UN

Independent from the Portuguese since 1975, Angola is a large country south of the equator in southwest Africa. Much of the interior is savannah plateaux with average rainfall varying from 250 mm (10 inches) in the south to 1,270 mm (50 inches) in the north. Most of the population is engaged in agriculture producing cassava, maize and coffee. Most consumer products and textiles are imported. Angola possesses vast wealth in the form of diamonds, oil, iron ore, copper and other minerals. Apart from the production of oil, which is the biggest export, the economy has collapsed as a result of many years of civil war.

ABBREVIATIONS

The following abbreviations have been used. Codes given in brackets following the name of a currency are those issued by the International Standards Organization.

ANZUS	Australia, New Zealand, United States Security Treaty
ASEAN	Association of Southeast Asian Nations
Caricom	Caribbean Community and Common Market
CACM	Central American Common Market
CIS	Commonwealth of Independent States
Col. Plan	Colombo Plan
Comm.	Commonwealth
CSCE	Council for Security and Co-operation in Europe
ECOWAS	Economic Community of West African States
EEA	European Economic Area
EFTA	European Free Trade Association
EU	European Union
G7	Group of seven industrialized nations:– (Canada, France, Germany, Italy, Japan, UK, USA)
Mercosur	Common Market of the Southern Cone
NAFTA	North American Free Trade Agreement
NATO	North Atlantic Treaty Organization
OAS	Organization of American States
OAU	Organization of African Unity
OECD	Organization for Economic Co-operation and Development
OPEC	Organization of Petroleum Exporting Countries
UN	United Nations
WEU	Western European Union

ANGUILLA

STATUS: UK Dependent Territory
AREA: 115 sq km (60 sq miles)
POPULATION: 8,960
CAPITAL: The Valley

ANTIGUA AND BARBUDA

STATUS: Commonwealth State
AREA: 442 sq km (171 sq miles)
POPULATION: 65,962
ANNUAL NATURAL INCREASE: 1.0%
CAPITAL: St John's (on Antigua)
LANGUAGE: English
RELIGION: Anglican Christian majority
CURRENCY: E Caribbean dollar (XCD)
ORGANIZATIONS: Caricom, Comm., OAS, UN

The country consists of two main islands in the Leeward group in the West Indies. Tourism is the main activity. Local agriculture is being encouraged to reduce food imports and the growth of sea island cotton is making a comeback. The production of rum is the main manufacturing industry; there is also an oil refinery.

ARGENTINA

STATUS: Republic
AREA: 2,766,889 sq km (1,068,302 sq miles)
POPULATION: 33,101,000
ANNUAL NATURAL INCREASE: 1.3%
CAPITAL: Buenos Aires
LANGUAGE: Spanish
RELIGION: 90% Roman Catholic, 2% Protestant, Jewish minority
CURRENCY: peso (ARP)
ORGANIZATIONS: Mercosur, OAS, UN

Relief is highest in the west in the Andes mountains, where altitudes exceed 6,000 m (19,500 ft). East of the Andes there are fertile plains known as the Pampas. In the northern scrub forests and grasslands of the Chaco hot tropical conditions exist. Central Argentina lies in temperate latitudes, but the southernmost regions are cold, wet and stormy. The economy of Argentina was long dominated by the produce of the rich soils of the Pampas, beef and grain. Agricultural products still account for some 40 per cent of export revenue, with grain crops predominating, despite a decline due to competition and falling world prices. Beef exports also decreased by over 50 per cent between 1970 and 1983, due to strong competition from western Europe. Industry is now the chief export earner. Industrial activity includes petrochemicals, steel, cars, and food and drink processing. There are oil and gas reserves and an abundant supply of hydroelectric power.

ARMENIA

STATUS: Republic
AREA: 30,000 sq km (11,580 sq miles)
POPULATION: 3,686,000
ANNUAL NATURAL INCREASE: 1.2%
CAPITAL: Yerevan
LANGUAGE: Armenian, Russian
RELIGION: Russian Orthodox, Armenian Catholic
CURRENCY: dram
ORGANIZATIONS: CIS, UN

Armenia is a country of rugged terrain, with most of the land above 1,000 m (3,300 feet). The climate, much influenced by altitude, has continental tendencies. Rainfall, although occurring throughout the year, is heaviest in summer. Agriculture is dependent upon irrigation and the main crops are vegetables, fruit and tobacco. Conflict over the disputed area of Nagornyy Karabakh, an enclave of Armenian Orthodox Christians within the territory of Azerbaijan, is casting a cloud over the immediate future of the country.

ARUBA

STATUS: Self-governing Island of Netherlands Realm
AREA: 193 sq km (75 sq miles)
POPULATION: 68,897
CAPITAL: Oranjestad

ASCENSION

STATUS: Island Dependency of St Helena
AREA: 88 sq km (34 sq miles)
POPULATION: 1,117
CAPITAL: Georgetown

ASHMORE AND CARTIER ISLANDS

STATUS: External Territory of Australia
AREA: 3 sq km (1.2 sq miles)
POPULATION: no permanent population

AUSTRALIA

STATUS: Federal Nation
AREA: 7,682,300 sq km (2,965,370 sq miles)
POPULATION: 17,662,000
ANNUAL NATURAL INCREASE: 1.6%
CAPITAL: Canberra
LANGUAGE: English
RELIGION: 75% Christian, Aboriginal beliefs, Jewish minority
CURRENCY: Australian dollar (AUD)
ORGANIZATIONS: ANZUS, Col. Plan, Comm., OECD, UN

The Commonwealth of Australia was founded in 1901. The British Monarch, as head of state, is represented by a governor-general. It is the sixth largest country in the world in terms of area. The western half of the country is primarily arid plateaux, ridges and vast deserts. The central-eastern area comprises lowlands of river systems draining into Lake Eyre, while to the east is the Great Dividing Range. Climate varies from cool temperate to tropical monsoon. Rainfall is high only in the northeast, where it exceeds 1,000 mm (39 inches) annually, and decreases markedly from the coast to the interior which is hot and dry. Over 50 per cent of the land area comprises desert and scrub with less than 250 mm (10 inches) of rain a year. The majority of the population live in cities concentrated along the southeast coast. Australia is rich in both agricultural and natural resources. It is the world's leading producer of wool, which together with wheat, meat, sugar and dairy products accounts for over 40 per cent of export revenue. There are vast reserves of coal, oil, natural gas, nickel, iron ore, bauxite and uranium ores. Gold, silver, lead, zinc and copper ores are also exploited. Minerals now account for over 30 per cent of Australia's export revenue. New areas of commerce have been created in eastern Asia, particularly in Japan, to counteract the sharp decline of the traditional European markets. Tourism is becoming a large revenue earner and showed a 200 per cent growth between 1983 and 1988. This has slowed recently, although the Olympics Games, due to be held in Sydney in the year 2000, are expected to attract an additional 1.5 million overseas visitors.

AUSTRALIAN CAPITAL TERRITORY
STATUS: Federal Territory
AREA: 2,432 sq km (939 sq miles)
POPULATION: 299,000
CAPITAL: Canberra

NEW SOUTH WALES
STATUS: State
AREA: 801,430 sq km (309,350 sq miles)
POPULATION: 6,009,000
CAPITAL: Sydney

NORTHERN TERRITORY
STATUS: Territory
AREA: 1,346,200 sq km (519,635 sq miles)
POPULATION: 168,000
CAPITAL: Darwin

QUEENSLAND
STATUS: State
AREA: 1,727,000 sq km (666,620 sq miles)
POPULATION: 3,113,000
CAPITAL: Brisbane

SOUTH AUSTRALIA
STATUS: State
AREA: 984,380 sq km (79,970 sq miles)
POPULATION: 1,462,000
CAPITAL: Adelaide

TASMANIA
STATUS: State
AREA: 68,330 sq km (26,375 sq miles)
POPULATION: 472,000
CAPITAL: Hobart

VICTORIA
STATUS: State
AREA: 227,600 sq km (87,855 sq miles)
POPULATION: 4,462,000
CAPITAL: Melbourne

WESTERN AUSTRALIA
STATUS: State
AREA: 2,525,500 sq km (974,845 sq miles)
POPULATION: 1,678,000
CAPITAL: Perth

AUSTRIA
STATUS: Federal Republic
AREA: 83,855 sq km (32,370 sq miles)
POPULATION: 7,910,000
ANNUAL NATURAL INCREASE: 0.6%
CAPITAL: Vienna (Wien)
LANGUAGE: German
RELIGION: 89% Roman Catholic, 6% Protestant
CURRENCY: schilling (ATS)
ORGANIZATIONS: Council of Europe, EEA, EFTA, OECD, UN

Austria is an alpine, landlocked country in central Europe. The mountainous Alps which cover 75 per cent of the land consist of a series of east-west ranges enclosing lowland basins. The climate is continental with temperatures and rainfall varying with altitude. About 25 per cent of the country, in the north and northeast, is lower foreland or flat land containing most of Austria's fertile farmland. Half is arable and the remainder is mainly for root or fodder crops. Manufacturing and heavy industry, however, account for the majority of export revenues, particularly pig-iron, steel, chemicals and vehicles. Over 70 per cent of the country's power is hydro-electric. Tourism and forestry are also important to the economy.

AZERBAIJAN
STATUS: Republic
AREA: 87,000 sq km (33,580 sq miles)
POPULATION: 7,398,000
ANNUAL NATURAL INCREASE: 1.0%
CAPITAL: Baku
LANGUAGE: 83% Azeri, 6% Armenian, 6% Russian
RELIGION: 83% Muslim, Armenian Apostolic, Orthodox
CURRENCY: manat
ORGANIZATIONS: CIS, UN

Azerbaijan gained independence on the break-up of the USSR in 1991. It is a mountainous country that has a continental climate, greatly influenced by altitude. Arable land accounts for less than 10 per cent of the total area, with raw cotton and tobacco the leading products. Major reserves of oil and gas exist beneath and around the Caspian Sea, which are as of yet fully undeveloped. The country includes two autonomous regions: Nakhichevan, which it is cut off by a strip of intervening Armenian territory and the enclave of Nagornyy Karabakh, over which long standing tensions escalated into conflict in 1992.

AZORES
STATUS: Self-governing Island Region of Portugal
AREA: 2,335 sq km (901 sq miles)
POPULATION: 237,100
CAPITAL: Ponta Delgada

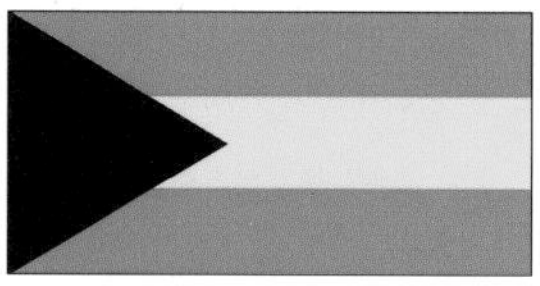

BAHAMAS
STATUS: Commonwealth Nation
AREA: 13,865 sq km (5,350 sq miles)
POPULATION: 262,000
ANNUAL NATURAL INCREASE: 1.9%
CAPITAL: Nassau
LANGUAGE: English
RELIGION: Anglican Christian majority, Baptist and Roman Catholic minorities
CURRENCY: Bahamian dollar (BSD)
ORGANIZATIONS: Caricom, Comm., OAS, UN

About 700 islands and over 2,000 coral sand cays (reefs) constitute the sub-tropical Commonwealth of the Bahamas. The island group extends from the coast of Florida to Cuba and Haiti in the south. Only 29 islands are inhabited. Most of the 1,000 mm (39 inches) of rainfall falls in the summer. The tourist industry is the main source of income and, although fluctuating through recession, still employs over 70 per cent of the working population. Recent economic plans have concentrated on reducing imports by developing fishing and domestic agriculture. Other important sources of income are ship registration (the world's fourth largest open-registry fleet), income generated by offshore finance and banking, and export of rum, salt and cement.

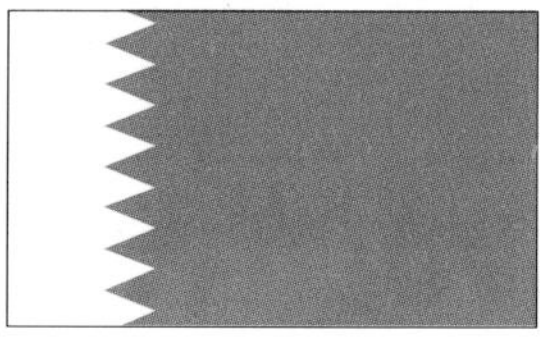

BAHRAIN
STATUS: State
AREA: 661 sq km (225 sq miles)
POPULATION: 539,000
ANNUAL NATURAL INCREASE: 3.2%
CAPITAL: Manama (Al Manāmah)
LANGUAGE: Arabic, English
RELIGION: 60% Shi'a and 40% Sunni Muslim, Christian minority
CURRENCY: Bahraini dinar (BHD)
ORGANIZATIONS: Arab League, UN

The sheikdom is a barren island in the Persian Gulf with less than 80 mm (3 inches) rainfall a year. Summer temperatures average 32°C (89°F). Bahrain was the first country in the Arabian peninsula to strike oil, in 1932. Oil still accounts for 60 per cent of revenue and gas is becoming increasingly important. Lower oil prices and decreased production is now causing the government to diversify the economy with expansion of light and heavy industry and chemical plants, and the subsequent encouragement of trade and foreign investment.

BANGLADESH
STATUS: Republic
AREA: 144,000 sq km (55,585 sq miles)
POPULATION: 118,700,000
ANNUAL NATURAL INCREASE: 2.2%
CAPITAL: Dhaka, (Dhākā, Dacca)
LANGUAGE: Bengali (Bangla), Bihari, Hindi, English
RELIGION: 85% Muslim, Hindu, Buddhist and Christian minorities
CURRENCY: taka (BDT)
ORGANIZATIONS: Col. Plan, Comm., UN

Bangladesh is one of the poorest and most densely populated countries of the world. Most of its territory, except for bamboo-forested hills in the southeast, comprises the vast river systems of the Ganges and Brahmaputra which drain from the Himalayan mountains into the Bay of Bengal, frequently changing course and flooding the flat delta plain. This land is, however, extremely fertile and attracts a high concentration of the population. The climate is tropical, and agriculture is dependent on monsoon rainfall. When the monsoon fails there is drought. Eighty-two per cent of the population are farmers, the main crops being rice and jute. Bangladesh is the world's leading supplier of jute, which accounts for 25 per cent of the country's exports. The main industry and number one export is clothing . Natural gas reserves, under the Bay of Bengal, are beginning to be exploited.

BARBADOS

STATUS: Commonwealth State
AREA: 430 sq km (166 sq miles)
POPULATION: 259,000
ANNUAL NATURAL INCREASE: 0.3%
CAPITAL: Bridgetown
LANGUAGE: English
RELIGION: Anglican Christian majority, Methodist and Roman Catholic minorities
CURRENCY: Barbados dollar (BBD)
ORGANIZATIONS: Caricom, Comm., OAS, UN

The former British colony of Barbados in the Caribbean is the most eastern island of the Antilles chain. The gently rolling landscape of the island is lush and fertile, the temperature ranging from 25–28°C (77–82°F) with 1270–1900 mm (50–75 inches) of rainfall per year. Sugar and its by-products, molasses and rum, are traditional cash crops. These are being overtaken in importance by tourism which provides an occupation for one-third of the population. This is a growth sector, although it has suffered recently from world recession. An oilfield supplies one-third of domestic oil requirements.

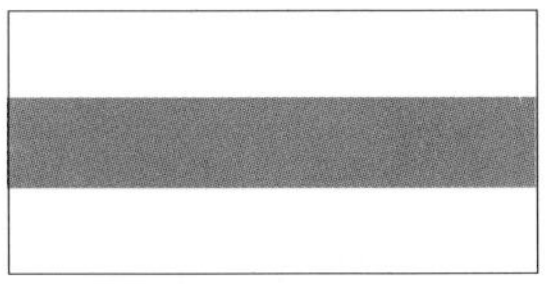

BELARUS

STATUS: Republic
AREA: 208,000 sq km (80,290 sq miles)
POPULATION: 10,280,000
ANNUAL NATURAL INCREASE: 0.5%
CAPITAL: Minsk
LANGUAGE: Belorussian, Russian
RELIGION: Roman Catholic, Uniate
CURRENCY: rouble
ORGANIZATIONS: CIS, UN

Belarus achieved independence in 1991. The country is mainly flat with forests covering more than one-third of the area. Swamps and marshlands cover large areas but, when drained, the soil is very fertile. The climate is continental with fairly cold winters (-7°C or 20°F). Grain, flax, potatoes and sugar beet are the main crops but livestock production accounts for more than half the value of agricultural output. Large areas of Belarus are thinly populated; most people live in the central area. The republic is comparatively poor in mineral resources and suffered terrible devastation during the Second World War. Post-war industrialization has been based on imported raw materials and semi-manufactured goods, concentrating on the production of trucks, tractors, agricultural machinery and other heavy engineering equipment. However, these industries are heavily reliant on imported Russian energy and output has declined since independence.

BELGIUM

STATUS: Kingdom
AREA: 30,520 sq km (11,780 sq miles)
POPULATION: 10,020,000
ANNUAL NATURAL INCREASE: 0.3%
CAPITAL: Brussels (Bruxelles/Brussel)
LANGUAGE: French, Dutch (Flemish), German
RELIGION: Roman Catholic majority, Protestant and Jewish minorities
CURRENCY: Belgium franc (BEF)
ORGANIZATIONS: Council of Europe, EEA, EU, NATO, OECD, UN, WEU

Over two-thirds of Belgium comprises the Flanders plain, a flat plateau covered by fertile wind-blown loess which extends from the North Sea coast down to the forested mountains of the Ardennes in the south. The climate is mild, maritime temperate with 720–1200 mm (28–47 inches) of rainfall a year. Over half the country is intensively farmed – cereals, root crops, vegetables and flax are the main crops and the country is nearly self-sufficient in meat and dairy products. Belgium's tradition as an industrialized nation dates back to the 19th century and Flanders has historically been famed for its textiles. The main industries now are metal-working (including motor vehicle assembly), chemicals, iron and steel, textiles, food and drink processing and diamonds. In recent years many companies have embarked on high-technology specialization including computer software, micro-electronics and telecommunications. Belgium is a trading nation, exporting more than half its national production. Most trade passes through the port of Antwerp, and an efficient communications network links it with the rest of Europe.

BELIZE

STATUS: Commonwealth Nation
AREA: 22,965 sq km (8,865 sq miles)
POPULATION: 230,000
ANNUAL NATURAL INCREASE: 2.6%
CAPITAL: Belmopan
LANGUAGE: English, Spanish, Maya
RELIGION: 60% Roman Catholic, 40% Protestant
CURRENCY: Belizean dollar (BZD)
ORGANIZATIONS: CARICOM, Comm., OAS, UN

Bordering the Caribbean Sea, in Central America, sub-tropical Belize is dominated by its dense forest cover. Principal exports are sugar cane, citrus concentrates and bananas. Since independence from Britain in 1973 the country has developed agriculture to lessen reliance on imported food products. Other commodities produced include tropical fruits, vegetables, fish and timber.

BENIN

STATUS: Republic
AREA: 112,620 sq km (43,470 sq miles)
POPULATION: 5,010,000
ANNUAL NATURAL INCREASE: 3.2%
CAPITAL: Porto Novo
LANGUAGE: French, Fon, Adja
RELIGION: majority traditional beliefs, 15% Roman Catholic, 13% Muslim
CURRENCY: CFA franc (W Africa) (XOF)
ORGANIZATIONS: ECOWAS, OAU, UN

Benin, formerly Dahomey, is a small strip of country descending from the wooded savannah hills of the north to the forested and cultivated lowlands fringing the Bight of Benin. The economy is agricultural, with palm oil, cotton, cocoa, coffee, groundnuts and copra as main exports. The developing offshore oil industry has proven reserves of over 20 million barrels.

BERMUDA

STATUS: Self-governing UK Crown Colony
AREA: 54 sq km (21 sq miles)
POPULATION: 74,837
CAPITAL: Hamilton

BHUTAN

STATUS: Kingdom
AREA: 46,620 sq km (17,995 sq miles)
POPULATION: 600,000
ANNUAL NATURAL INCREASE: 2.2%
CAPITAL: Thimphu
LANGUAGE: Dzongkha, Nepali, English
RELIGION: Mahayana Buddhist, 30% Hindu
CURRENCY: ngultrum (BTN), Indian rupee (INR)
ORGANIZATIONS: Col. Plan, UN

Bhutan is a small country in the Himalayan foothills between China and India, and to the east of Nepal. Rainfall is high at over 3000 mm (118 inches) a year but temperatures vary between the extreme cold of the northern ranges to a July average of 27°C (81°F) in the southern forests. Long isolated, the economy of Bhutan is dominated by agriculture and small local industries. All manufactured goods are imported.

BOLIVIA

STATUS: Republic
AREA: 1,098,575 sq km (424,050 sq miles)
POPULATION: 7,832,396
ANNUAL NATURAL INCREASE: 2.5%
CAPITAL: La Paz
LANGUAGE: Spanish, Quechua, Aymara
RELIGION: Roman Catholic majority
CURRENCY: Boliviano (BOB)
ORGANIZATIONS: OAS, UN

Bolivia, where the average life expectancy is 51 years, is one of the world's poorest nations. Landlocked and isolated, the country stretches from the eastern Andes across high cool plateaux before dropping to the dense forest of the Amazon basin and the grasslands of the south-east. Bolivia was once rich, its wealth based on minerals (in recent decades tin) but in 1985 world tin prices dropped and the industry collapsed. Oil and gas and agriculture now dominate the economy. Crops include soya, cotton, coca (cocaine shrub), sugar and coffee. Mining is still important, with the emphasis on zinc.

BOSNIA-HERZEGOVINA

STATUS: Republic
AREA: 51,130 sq km (19,736 sq miles)
POPULATION: 2,900,000
ANNUAL NATURAL INCREASE: 0.2%
CAPITAL: Sarajevo
LANGUAGE: Serbo-Croat
RELIGION: Muslim, Christian
CURRENCY: dinar
ORGANIZATIONS: UN

Bosnia-Herzegovina achieved independence in April 1992, but international recognition did not spare the Republic from savage ethnic warfare between Muslims, Serbs and Croats. Partitioning of the country into a new federation acceptable to all warring parties appears to be a necessity for peace. Before the war Bosnia's economy was based predominantly on agriculture – sheep rearing and the cultivation of vines, olives and citrus fruits. The country is mainly mountainous with the Sava valley in the north being the only lowland of consequence. The climate is Mediterranean towards the Adriatic, but continental and cooler inland.

BOTSWANA

STATUS: Republic
AREA: 582,000 sq km (224,652 sq miles)
POPULATION: 1,291,000
ANNUAL NATURAL INCREASE: 3.4%
CAPITAL: Gaborone
LANGUAGE: Setswana, English
RELIGION: traditional beliefs majority, Christian minority
CURRENCY: pula (BWP)
ORGANIZATIONS: Comm., OAU, UN

The arid high plateau of Botswana, with its poor soils and low rainfall, supports little arable agriculture, but over 2.3 million cattle graze the dry grasslands. Diamonds are the chief export, providing 80 per cent of export earnings. Copper, nickel, potash, soda ash, salt and coal are also important. The growth of light industries around the capital has stimulated trade with neighbouring countries.

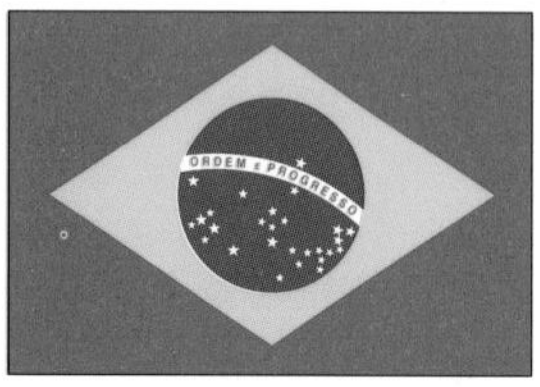

BRAZIL

STATUS: Federal Republic
AREA: 8,511,965 sq km (3,285,620 sq miles)
POPULATION: 156,275,000
ANNUAL NATURAL INCREASE: 2.2%
CAPITAL: Brasília
LANGUAGE: Portuguese
RELIGION: 90% Roman Catholic, Protestant minority
CURRENCY: cruzeiro real (BRC),URV
ORGANIZATIONS: Mercosur, OAS, UN

Brazil is the largest country in South America with the Amazon basin tropical rain forest covers roughly a third of the country. It is one of the world's leading agricultural exporters, with coffee, soya beans, sugar, bananas, cocoa, tobacco, rice and cattle major commodities. Brazil is an industrial power but with development limited to the heavily populated urban areas of the eastern coastal lowlands. Mineral resources, except for iron ore, do not play a significant role in the economy at present, but recent economic policies have concentrated on developing the industrial base – road and rail communications, light and heavy industry and expansion of energy resources, particularly hydro-electric power harnessed from the three great river systems. Unlike other South American countries Brazil still has a serious inflation rate, introducing the 'real', on 1 July 1994 (the fifth new currency in a decade), in an attempt to slow the rate down.

BRITISH ANTARCTIC TERRITORY

STATUS: UK Dependent Territory
AREA: 1,544,000 sq km (599,845 sq miles)
POPULATION: no permanent population

BRITISH INDIAN OCEAN TERRITORY

STATUS: UK Dependency comprising the Chagos Archipelago
AREA: 5,765 sq km (2,225 sq miles)
POPULATION: 266,000

BRUNEI

STATUS: Sultanate
AREA: 5,765 sq km (2,225 sq miles)
POPULATION: 270,000
ANNUAL NATURAL INCREASE: 3.2%
CAPITAL: Bandar Seri Begawan
LANGUAGE: Malay, English, Chinese
RELIGION: 65% Sunni Muslim, Buddhist and Christian minorities
CURRENCY: Brunei dollar (BND)
ORGANIZATIONS: ASEAN, Comm, UN

The Sultanate of Brunei is situated on the northwest coast of Borneo. Its tropical climate is hot and humid with annual rainfall ranging from 2500 mm (98 inches) on the narrow coastal strip to 5000 mm (197 inches) in the mountainous interior. Oil and gas reserves, mostly offshore, are the basis of the Brunei economy. Half the oil and nearly all the natural gas (in liquefied form) are exported to Japan.

BULGARIA

STATUS: Republic
AREA: 110,910 sq km (42,810 sq miles)
POPULATION: 8,467,000
ANNUAL NATURAL INCREASE: 0.0%
CAPITAL: Sofia (Sofiya)
LANGUAGE: Bulgarian, Turkish
RELIGION: Eastern Orthodox majority, Muslim minority
CURRENCY: lev (BGL)
ORGANIZATIONS: Council of Europe, EFTA, OIEC, UN

Bulgaria exhibits great variety in its landscape. In the north, the land from the plains of the Danube slope upwards into the Balkan mountains (Stara Planina), which run east-west through central Bulgaria. The Rhodope mountains dominate the west, with the lowlands of Thrace and the Maritsa valley in the south. Climate is continental with temperatures ranging from -5°C (23°F) in winter to 28°C (82°F) in summer. The economy is based on agricultural products, with cereals, tobacco, cotton, fruits and vines dominating. Wine is a particularly successful export. Nuclear power is the main domestic power source, however the reactors are becoming elderly and other sources of energy are being sought, in particular oil and gas in the Black Sea. The heavy industry sector, which thrived in close association with the former USSR, is declining.

BURKINA

STATUS: Republic
AREA: 274,122 sq km (105,811 sq miles)
POPULATION: 9,490,000
ANNUAL NATURAL INCREASE: 2.8%
CAPITAL: Ouagadougou
LANGUAGE: French, Moré (Mossi), Dyula
RELIGION: 60% animist, 30% Muslim, 10% Roman Catholic
CURRENCY: CFA franc (W Africa) (OXF)
ORGANIZATIONS: ECOWAS, OAU, UN

Situated on the southern edge of the Sahara, Burkina, previously known as Upper Volta, is a poor, landlocked country with thin soils supporting savannah grasslands. Frequent droughts, particularly in the north, seriously affect the economy, which is mainly subsistence agriculture with livestock herding, and the export of groundnuts and cotton. There is virtually no industry. Some minerals are exported and manganese exports began in 1993.

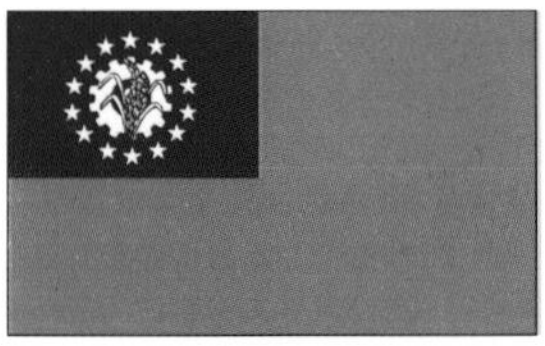

BURMA (MYANMAR)

STATUS: Union of states and divisions
AREA: 678,030 sq km (261,720 sq miles)
POPULATION: 42,330,000
ANNUAL NATURAL INCREASE: 2.2%
CAPITAL: Rangoon (Yangon)
LANGUAGE: Burmese
RELIGION: 85% Buddhist. Animist, Muslim, Hindu and Christian minorities
CURRENCY: kyat (BUK)
ORGANIZATIONS: Col. Plan, UN

Much of Burma (renamed Myanmar by its military leaders in 1989) is covered by tropical rainforest divided by the central valley of the Irrawaddy, the Sittang and the Salween rivers. The western highlands are an extension of the Himalaya mountains; hills to the east and south

are a continuation of the Yunnan plateau of China. The economy is based on the export of rice and forestry products. The irrigated central basin and the coastal region to the east of the Irrawaddy delta are the main rice-growing areas. Hardwoods, particularly teak, cover the highlands. There is potential for greater exploitation of tin, copper, gold, oil and natural gas deposits.

BURUNDI

STATUS: Republic
AREA: 27,835 sq km (10,745 sq miles)
POPULATION: 5,786,000
ANNUAL NATURAL INCREASE: 2.9%
CAPITAL: Bujumbura
LANGUAGE: French, Kirundi, Swahili
RELIGION: 60% Roman Catholic, animist minority
CURRENCY: Burundi franc (BIF)
ORGANIZATIONS: OAU, UN

This small central African republic is densely populated and one of the world's poorest nations. Although close to the equator, temperatures are modified because of altitude. Coffee is the main export, followed by tea, cotton and manufactured goods. The country has a history of ethnic fighting between the Hutu farming people, who make up 85 per cent of the population, and the Tutsi, originally pastoralists, who have dominated the army and the running of the country. Massacres of thousands of people in 1993-4 resulted from ethnic war, ignited by a Hutu election victory marking an end to 31 years of Tutsi domination.

CAMBODIA

STATUS: Kingdom
AREA: 181,000 sq km (69,865 sq miles)
POPULATION: 12,000,000
ANNUAL NATURAL INCREASE: 2.7%
CAPITAL: Phnom Penh
LANGUAGE: Khmer
RELIGION: Buddhist majority, Roman Catholic and Muslim minorities
CURRENCY: reil (KHR)
ORGANIZATIONS: Col. Plan, UN

Cambodia, in southeast Asia, is mostly a lowland basin. Over 70 per cent of the country is covered by the central plain of the Mekong river. The climate is tropical, with average annual temperatures exceeding 25°C (77°F). Monsoon rainfall occurs from May to October. These provide ideal conditions for the country's rice production and fish harvesting. The economy has been damaged since the 1970s by almost constant civil war. Power shortages hamper industrial development, the roads are badly damaged and land mines buried in the countryside make farming hazardous.

CAMEROON

STATUS: Republic
AREA: 475,500 sq km(183,545 sq miles)
POPULATION: 12,198,000
ANNUAL NATURAL INCREASE: 3.0%
CAPITAL: Yaoundé
LANGUAGE: English, French
RELIGION: 40% Christian, 39% traditional beliefs, 21% Muslim
CURRENCY: CRA franc (C Africa) (XAF)
ORGANIZATIONS: OAU, UN

Cameroon, in west Africa, is situated between the Gulf of Guinea in the south and the shores of Lake Chad in the north. In the south, coastal lowlands rise to densely forested plateaux, whereas further northwards savannah takes over, and aridity increases towards the Sahara. Oil products, once the main export, have declined in importance and now agricultural products account for most export revenue. Coffee, cocoa, bananas and avocados are the main cash crops. Mineral resources are underdeveloped but Cameroon is one of Africa's main producers of bauxite (aluminium ore) and aluminium is smelted at Edea.

CANADA

STATUS: Commonwealth Nation
AREA: 9,922,385 sq km (3,830,840 sq miles)
POPULATION: 28,866,000
ANNUAL NATURAL INCREASE: 1.4%
CAPITAL: Ottawa
LANGUAGE: English, French
RELIGION: 46% Roman Catholic, Protestant and Jewish minorities
CURRENCY: Canadian dollar (CAD)
ORGANIZATIONS: Col. Plan, Comm., G7, OAS, OECD, NATO, NAFTA, UN

Canada is the world's second largest country stretching from the great barren islands of the Arctic north to the vast grasslands of the central south, and from the Rocky Mountains in the west to the farmlands of the Great Lakes in the east. This huge area experiences great climatic differences but basically a continental climate prevails with extremes of heat and cold particularly in the central plains. The Arctic tundra of the far north provides summer grazing for caribou. Further south coniferous forests grow on the thin soils of the ancient shield landscape and on the extensive foothills of the Rocky Mountains. In contrast, the rich soils of the central prairies support grasslands and grain crops. The Great Lakes area provides fish, fruit, maize, root crops and dairy products; the prairies produce over 20 per cent of the worlds wheat; and the grasslands of Alberta support a thriving beef industry. Most minerals are mined and exploited in Canada with oil and natural gas, iron ore, bauxite, nickel, zinc, copper, gold and silver the major exports. Recently, diamonds have been discovered in the Northwest Territories. The country's vast rivers provide huge amounts of hydro-electric power but most industry is confined to the Great Lakes and St Lawrence margins. The principal manufactured goods for export are steel products, motor vehicles and paper for newsprint. The USA is Canada's main trading partner, taking 80 per cent of exports. Following a free trade agreement (NAFTA) in 1993 between the USA, Canada and Mexico, even closer economic ties will be made with the USA.

ALBERTA

STATUS: Province
AREA: 661,190 sq km (255,220 sq miles)
POPULATION: 2,672,000
CAPITAL: Edmonton

BRITISH COLUMBIA

STATUS: Province
AREA: 948,565 sq km (366,160 sq miles)
POPULATION: 3,570,000
CAPITAL: Victoria

MANITOBA

STATUS: Province
AREA: 650,090 sq km (250,935 sq miles)
POPULATION: 1,117,000
CAPITAL: Winnipeg

NEW BRUNSWICK

STATUS: Province
AREA: 73,435 sq km (28,345 sq miles)
POPULATION: 751,000
CAPITAL: Fredericton

NEWFOUNDLAND AND LABRADOR

STATUS: Province
AREA: 404,520 sq km (156,145 sq miles)
POPULATION: 581,000
CAPITAL: St John's

NORTHWEST TERRITORIES

STATUS: Territory
AREA: 3,379,685 sq km (1,304,560 sq miles)
POPULATION: 63,000
CAPITAL: Yellowknife

NOVA SCOTIA

STATUS: Province
AREA: 55,490 sq km (21,420 sq miles)
POPULATION: 925,000
CAPITAL: Halifax

ONTARIO

STATUS: Province
AREA: 1,068,630 sq km (412,490 sq miles)
POPULATION: 10,795,000
CAPITAL: Toronto

PRINCE EDWARD ISLAND

STATUS: Province
AREA: 5,655 sq km (2,185 sq miles)
POPULATION: 132,000
CAPITAL: Charlottetown

QUEBEC

STATUS: Province
AREA: 1,540,680 sq km (594,705 sq miles)
POPULATION: 7,226,000
CAPITAL: Quebec

SASKATCHEWAN

STATUS: Province
AREA: 651,900 sq km (251,635 sq miles)
POPULATION: 1,002,000
CAPITAL: Regina

YUKON TERRITORY

STATUS: Province
AREA: 482,515 sq km (186,250 sq miles)
POPULATION: 33,000
CAPITAL: Whitehorse

CANARY ISLANDS

STATUS: Island Provinces of Spain
AREA: 7,275 sq km (2,810 sq miles)
POPULATION: 1,493,784
CAPITAL: Las Palmas (Gran Canaria) and Santa Cruz (Tenerife)

CAPE VERDE

STATUS: Republic
AREA: 4,035 sq km (1,560 sq miles)
POPULATION: 350,000
ANNUAL NATURAL INCREASE: 2.7%
CAPITAL: Praia
LANGUAGE: Portuguese, Creole
RELIGION: 98% Roman Catholic
CURRENCY: Cape Verde escudo (CVE)
ORGANIZATIONS: ECOWAS, OAU, UN

Independent since 1975, the ten inhabited volcanic islands of the republic are situated in the Atlantic 500 km (310 miles) west of Senegal. Rainfall is low but irrigation encourages growth of sugar cane, coffee, coconuts, fruit (mainly bananas) and maize. Fishing accounts for about 70 per cent of export revenue and all consumer goods are imported.

CAYMAN ISLANDS

STATUS: UK Dependent Territory
AREA: 259 sq km (100 sq miles)
POPULATION: 29,000
CAPITAL: George Town

CENTRAL AFRICAN REPUBLIC

STATUS: Republic
AREA: 624,975 sq km (241,240 sq miles)
POPULATION: 3,173,000
ANNUAL NATURAL INCREASE: 2.7%
CAPITAL: Bangui
LANGUAGE: French, Sango (national)
RELIGION: Animist majority, Christian minority
CURRENCY: CFA franc (C Africa) (XAF)
ORGANIZATIONS: OAU, UN

The republic is remote from both east and west Africa. It has a tropical climate with little variation in temperature. Savannah covers the rolling plateaux with rainforest in the southeast. To the north lies the Sahara Desert. Most farming is at subsistence level with a small amount of crops grown for export – cotton, coffee, groundnuts and tobacco. Hardwood forests in the southwest provide timber for export. Diamonds are the major export, accounting for over half of foreign earnings.

CHAD

STATUS: Republic
AREA: 1,284,000 sq km (495,625 sq miles)
POPULATION: 6,288,000
ANNUAL NATURAL INCREASE: 2.5%
CAPITAL: Ndjamena
LANGUAGE: French, Arabic, local languages
RELIGION: 50% Muslim, 45% animist
CURRENCY: CRA franc (C Africa) (XAF)
ORGANIZATIONS: OAU, UN

Chad is a vast state of central Africa stretching deep into the Sahara. The economy is based on agriculture but only the south, with 1,000 mm (39 in) of rainfall, can support crops for export – cotton, rice and groundnuts. Severe droughts, increasing desertification and border disputes have severely restricted development. Life expectancy at birth is still only 43 years. Salt is mined around Lake Chad where the majority of the population live.

CHANNEL ISLANDS

STATUS: British Crown Dependency
AREA: 194 sq km (75 sq miles)
POPULATION: 145,796
CAPITAL: St Hélier (Jersey)
St Peter Port (Guernsey)

CHILE

STATUS: Republic
AREA: 751,625 sq km (290,125 sq miles)
POPULATION: 13,813,000
ANNUAL NATURAL INCREASE: 1.7%
CAPITAL: Santiago
LANGUAGE: Spanish
RELIGION: 85% Roman Catholic, Protestant minority
CURRENCY: Chilean peso (CLP)
ORGANIZATIONS: OAS, UN

Chile is a long narrow country on the west coast of South America, stretching through 38° of latitude from the Atacama desert of the north to the sub-polar islands of Tierra del Fuego. Apart from a coastal strip of lowland, the country is dominated by the Andes mountains. Most energy is provided by hydro-electric power. The economy is based upon the abundance of natural resources with copper (the world's largest reserve), iron ore, nitrates, gold, timber, coal, oil and gas. Light and heavy industries are based around Concepción and Santiago. Traditional major exports are copper, fishmeal and cellulose. In the early 1990s farm production increased dramatically and food products now account for 29 per cent of export earnings.

CHINA

STATUS: People's Republic
AREA: 9,597,000 sq km (3,704,440 sq miles)
POPULATION: 1,154,887,381
ANNUAL NATURAL INCREASE: 1.3%
CAPITAL: Beijing (Peking)
LANGUAGE: Mandarin Chinese, regional languages
RELIGION: Confucianist, Buddhist, Taoist, Christian and Muslim minorities
CURRENCY: yuan (CNY)
ORGANIZATIONS: UN

The land of China is one of the most diverse on Earth and has vast mineral and agricultural resources. The majority of the people live in the east where the economy is dictated by the great drainage basins of the Yellow River (Huang He) and the Yangtze (Chang Jiang). Here, intensively irrigated agriculture produces one-third of the world's rice as well as wheat, maize, sugar, cotton, soya beans and oil seeds. Pigs are reared and fish caught throughout China. The country is basically self-sufficient in foodstuffs.

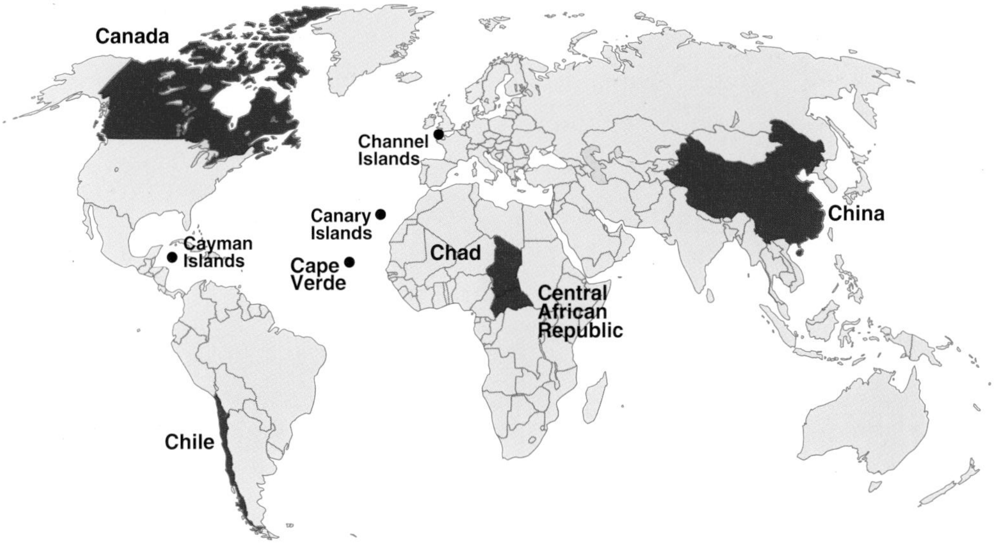

Western and northern China are much less densely populated as cultivation is restricted to oases and sheltered valleys. In the southwest, the Tibetan plateau averages 4,900 m (16,000 ft) and supports scattered sheep herding. To the north are Sinkiang and the desert basins of Tarim (Tarim Pendi) and Dzungaria, and bordering Mongolia the vast dry Gobi desert. In the far north only in Manchuria does a more temperate climate allow extensive arable cultivation, of mainly wheat, barley and maize.

The natural mineral resources of China are immense, varied and under-exploited. The Yunnan plateau of the southeast is rich in tin, copper, and zinc; Manchuria possesses coal and iron ore; and oil is extracted from beneath the Yellow Sea. The main industrial centres concentrate on the production of iron, steel, cement, light engineering and textile manufacturing.

With a population of over one billion, China has made tremendous efforts since the late 1970s to erase the negative economic effects of the collectivization policy implemented from 1955, and the cultural revolution of the late 1960s. In 1978 the Chinese leader, Deng Xiaoping, launched an economic revolution (creating special economic zones and encouraging foreign investment). The country is now experiencing phenomenal economic growth, a new consumer revolution and waves of entrepreneurial activities. A growing inequality in living standards between the rural provinces and the richer urban areas has led to a surge of migrants from the countryside to the cities.

ANHUI (ANHWEI)

STATUS: Province
AREA: 139,900 sq km (54,000 sq miles)
POPULATION: 57,600,000
CAPITAL: Hefei

BEIJING (PEKING)

STATUS: Municipality
AREA: 17,800 sq km (6,870 sq miles)
POPULATION: 10,900,000

FUJIAN (FUKIEN)

STATUS: Province
AREA: 123,000 sq km (47,515 sq miles)
POPULATION: 30,800,000
CAPITAL: Fuzhou

GANSU (KANSU)

STATUS: Province
AREA: 530,000 sq km (204,580 sq miles)
POPULATION: 22,900,000
CAPITAL: Lanzhou

GUANGDONG (KWANGTUNG)

STATUS: Province
AREA: 231,400 sq km (89,320 sq miles)
POPULATION: 64,400,000
CAPITAL: Guangzhou (Canton)

GUANGXI (KWANGSI-CHUANG)

STATUS: Autonomous Region
AREA: 220,400 sq km (85,075 sq miles)
POPULATION: 43,200,000
CAPITAL: Nanning

GUIZHOU (KWEICHOW)

STATUS: Province
AREA: 174,000 sq km (67,165 sq miles)
POPULATION: 33,200,000
CAPITAL: Guiyang

HAINAN

STATUS: Province
AREA: 34,965 sq km (13,500 sq miles)
POPULATION: 6,700,000
CAPITAL: Haikou

HEBEI (HOPEI)

STATUS: Province
AREA: 202,700 sq km (78,240 sq miles)
POPULATION: 62,200,000
CAPITAL: Schijiazhuang

HEILONGJIANG (HEILUNGKIANG)

STATUS: Province
AREA: 710,000 sq km (274,060 sq miles)
POPULATION: 35,800,000
CAPITAL: Harbin

HENAN (HONAN)

STATUS: Province
AREA: 167,000 sq km (64,460 sq miles)
POPULATION: 87,600,000
CAPITAL: Zhengzhou

HUBEI (HUPEH)

STATUS: Province
AREA: 187,500 sq km (72,375 sq miles)
POPULATION: 55,100,000
CAPITAL: Wuhan

HUNAN
STATUS: Province
AREA: 210,500 sq km (81,255 sq miles)
POPULATION: 62,100,000
CAPITAL: Changsha

JIANGSU (KIANGSU)
STATUS: Province
AREA: 102,200 sq km (39,450 miles)
POPULATION: 68,400,000
CAPITAL: Nanjing (Nanking)

JIANGXI (KIANGSI)
STATUS: Province
AREA: 164,800 sq km (63,615 sq miles)
POPULATION: 38,700,000
CAPITAL: Nanchang

JILIN (KIRIN)
STATUS: Province
AREA: 290,000 sq km (111,940 sq miles)
POPULATION: 25,100,000
CAPITAL: Changchun

LIAONING
STATUS: Province
AREA: 230,000 sq km (88,780 sq miles)
POPULATION: 39,900,000
CAPITAL: Shenyang

NEI MONGOL (INNER MONGOLIA)
STATUS: Autonomous Region
AREA: 450,000 sq km (173,700 sq miles)
POPULATION: 21,800,000
CAPITAL: Hohhot

NINGXIA HUI (NINGHSIA HUI)
STATUS: Autonomous Region
AREA: 170,000 sq km (65,620 sq miles)
POPULATION: 4,800,000
CAPITAL: Yinchuan

QINGHAI (CHINGHAI)
STATUS: Province
AREA: 721,000 sq km (278,305 sq miles)
POPULATION: 4,500,000
CAPITAL: Xining

SHAANXI (SHENSI)
STATUS: Province
AREA: 195,800 sq km (75,580 sq miles)
POPULATION: 33,600,000
CAPITAL: Xian (Xi'an)

SHANDONG (SHANTUNG)
STATUS: Province
AREA: 153,300 sq km (59,175 sq miles)
POPULATION: 83,430,000
CAPITAL: Jinan

SHANGHAI
STATUS: Municipality
AREA: 5,800 sq km (2,240 sq miles)
POPULATION: 13,400,000

SHANXI (SHANSI)
STATUS: Province
AREA: 157,100 sq km (60,640 sq miles)
POPULATION: 29,400,000
CAPITAL: Taiyuan

SICHUAN (SZECHWAN)
STATUS: Province
AREA: 569,000 sq km (219,635 sq miles)
POPULATION: 109,000,000
CAPITAL: Chengdu

TIANJIN (TIENTSIN)
STATUS: Municipality
AREA: 4,000 sq km (1,545 sq miles)
POPULATION: 9,100,402

XINJIANG UYGUR (SINKIANG-UIGHUR)
STATUS: Autonomous Region
AREA: 1,646,800 sq km (635,665 sq miles)
POPULATION: 15,600,000
CAPITAL: Urumchi (Ürümqi)

XIZANG (TIBET)
STATUS: Autonomous Region
AREA: 1,221,600 sq km (471,540 sq miles)
POPULATION: 2,300,000
CAPITAL: Lhasa

YUNNAN
STATUS: Province
AREA: 436,200 sq km (168,375 sq miles)
POPULATION: 37,800,000
CAPITAL: Kunming

ZHEJIANG (CHEKIANG)
STATUS: Province
AREA: 101,800 sq km (39,295 sq miles)
POPULATION: 42,000,000
CAPITAL: Hangzhou

CHRISTMAS ISLAND
STATUS: External Territory of Australia
AREA: 135 sq km (52 sq miles)
POPULATION: 1,275

COCOS (KEELING) ISLANDS
STATUS: External Territory of Australia
AREA: 14 sq km (5 sq miles)
POPULATION: 647

COLOMBIA
STATUS: Republic
AREA: 1,138,915 (439,620 sq miles)
POPULATION: 13,813,000
ANNUAL NATURAL INCREASE: 1.8%
CAPITAL: Bogotá
LANGUAGE: Spanish, Indian languages
RELIGION: 95% Roman Catholic, Protestant and Jewish minorities
CURRENCY: Colombian peso (COP)
ORGANIZATIONS: OAS, UN

Colombia is bounded by both the Caribbean Sea and Pacific Ocean. The northernmost peaks of the Andes chain runs from north to south through its western half and the eastern plains, beyond the Andes, contain the headwaters of the Amazon and Orinoco rivers. Almost half of Colombia is covered by the Amazon jungle. Colombia has a tropical climate and temperatures that vary with climate. The fertile river valleys in the uplands produce most of the famous Colombian coffee. Bananas, tobacco, cotton, sugar and rice are grown at lower altitudes. Coffee has always been the major export crop, but manufacturing industry and oil, coal, gold and precious stones are becoming more dominant in the economy. An oil boom is predicted following the discovery of new oil fields at Cusiana and Cupiagua. Immense illegal quantities of cocaine are exported to the US and elsewhere.

COMOROS
STATUS: Federal Islamic Republic
AREA: 1,860 sq km (718 sq miles)
POPULATION: 585,000
ANNUAL NATURAL INCREASE: 3.7%
CAPITAL: Moroni
LANGUAGE: French, Arabic, Comoran
RELIGION: Muslim majority, Christian minority
CURRENCY: Comoro franc (KMF)
ORGANIZATIONS: OAU, UN

The Comoro Islands, comprising Grand Comore, Anjouan, and Móheli, are situated between Madagascar and the east African coast. The climate is tropical and humid all year round, with a moderate average annual rainfall ranging from 1,000–1140 mm (40–45 inches). Less than half the land is cultivated and the country is dependent on imports for food supplies. The island's economy is based on the export of vanilla, copra, cloves and ylang-ylang essence (exported for the French perfume industry). Mangoes, coconuts and bananas are grown around the coastal lowlands. Timber and timber products are important to local development. There is no manufacturing of any importance.

CONGO
STATUS: Republic
AREA: 342,000 sq km (132,010 sq miles)
POPULATION: 2,690,000
ANNUAL NATURAL INCREASE: 3.3%
CAPITAL: Brazzaville
LANGUAGE: French, Kongo, Teke, Sanga
RELIGION: 50% traditional beliefs, 30% Roman Catholic, Protestant and Muslim minorities
CURRENCY: CFA franc (C Africa) (XAF)
ORGANIZATIONS: OAU, UN

The Congo, Africa's first communist state still has strong economic ties with the west, especially France, its former colonial ruler. Situated on the coast of west Africa, it contains over two-thirds swamp and forest, with wooded savannah on the highlands of the Bateké plateau near the Gabon border. Its climate is hot and humid with average rainfall of 1220–1280 mm (48–50 inches). Over 60 per cent of the population is employed in subsistence farming, while sugar, coffee, palm oil and cocoa are all exported. Timber and timber products are major exports but the main source of export revenue is oil from offshore oilfields. Mineral resources are considerable, including industrial diamonds, gold, lead and zinc. Manufacturing industry is concentrated in the major towns and is primarily food processing and textiles.

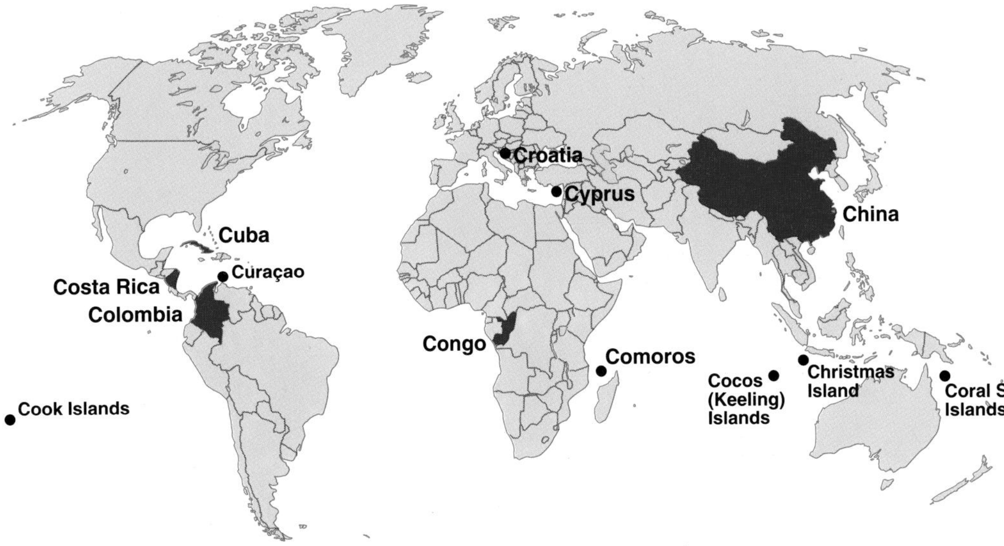

COOK ISLANDS

STATUS: Self-governing Territory Overseas in Free Association with New Zealand
AREA: 233 sq km (90 sq miles)
POPULATION: 18,617
CAPITAL: Avarua on Rarotonga

CORAL SEA ISLANDS

STATUS: External Territory of Australia
AREA: 22 sq km (8.5 sq miles)
POPULATION: no permanent population

COSTA RICA

STATUS: Republic
AREA: 50,900 sq km (19,650 sq miles)
POPULATION: 3,099,000
ANNUAL NATURAL INCREASE: 2.5%
CAPITAL: San José
LANGUAGE: Spanish
RELIGION: 95% Roman Catholic
CURRENCY: Costa Rican colón (CRC)
ORGANIZATIONS: CACM, OAS, UN

Costa Rica is a narrow country, situated between Nicaragua and Panama, with both a Pacific and a Caribbean coastline. Its coastal regions experience hot, humid, tropical conditions, but in upland areas its climate is more equable. The mountain chains that run the length of the country form the fertile uplands where coffee is grown and cattle are kept. Bananas, grown on the Pacific coast, and coffee are the major cash crops for export. Although gold, silver, iron ore and bauxite are mined, the principal industries are food processing and the manufacture of textiles and chemicals, fertilizers and furniture.

CROATIA

STATUS: Republic
AREA: 56,540 sq km (21,825 sq miles)
POPULATION: 4,764,000
ANNUAL NATURAL INCREASE: 0.4%
CAPITAL: Zagreb
LANGUAGE: Serbo-Croat
RELIGION: Roman Catholic majority
CURRENCY: kuna
ORGANIZATIONS: UN

Croatia is an oddly shaped country which runs in a narrow strip along the Adriatic coast and extends inland in a broad curve. Its climate varies from Mediterranean along the coast to continental further inland. Once part of the Yugoslavian Federation, Croatia achieved recognition as an independent nation in 1992 following the 1991 civil war between Serb and Croat factions. The conflict left the country with a damaged economy, disruption of trade, loss of tourist revenue and a huge reconstruction bill. Traditionally the fertile plains of central and eastern Croatia have been intensively farmed, producing surplus crops, meat and dairy products. The mountainous and barren littoral has been developed for tourism. Croatia used to be the most highly developed part of Yugoslavia, concentrating on electrical engineering, metal working, machine building, chemicals and rubber. Economic recovery is dependent upon political stability and an accommodation with the Serbs over the UN-supervised areas still under ethnic Serb control.

CUBA

STATUS: Republic
AREA: 114,525 sq km (44,205 sq miles)
POPULATION: 10,870,000
ANNUAL NATURAL INCREASE: 1.0%
CAPITAL: Havana (Habana)
LANGUAGE: Spanish
RELIGION: Roman Catholic majority
CURRENCY: Cuban peso (CUP)
ORGANIZATIONS: OIEC, UN

Cuba, the largest of the Greater Antilles islands, dominates the entrance to the Gulf of Mexico. It consists of one large and over 1,500 small islands, and is a mixture of fertile plains, mountain ranges and gentle countryside. Temperatures range from 22–28°C (72–82°F) and an there is an average annual rainfall of 1,200 mm (47 inches). Sugar, tobacco and nickel are the main exports. Being a communist state, most of Cuba's trade has been with the former USSR and in the three years following the collapse of the Soviet Union the Cuban economy contracted by over 30 per cent (having lost its principal market for sugar, which it had bartered for oil, food and machinery). The economy was already suffering from US sanctions. Severe shortages of food, fuel and basic necessities were tolerated and in 1993 the government was forced to permit limited private enterprise and the use of American dollars.

CURAÇAO

STATUS: Self-governing Island of the Netherlands Antilles
AREA: 444 sq km (171 sq miles)
POPULATION: 707,000

CYPRUS

STATUS: Republic (Turkish unilateral declaration of independence in northern area)
AREA: 9,250 sq km (3,570 sq miles)
POPULATION: 725,000
ANNUAL NATURAL INCREASE: 1.1%
CAPITAL: Nicosia
LANGUAGE: Greek, Turkish, English
RELIGION: Greek Orthodox majority, Muslim minority
CURRENCY: Cyprus pound (CYP), Turkish lira (TL)
ORGANIZATIONS: Comm., Council of Europe, UN

Cyprus is a prosperous Mediterranean island. The summers are very hot (38°C or 100°F) and dry, and the winters warm and wet. About two-thirds of the island is under cultivation and citrus fruit, potatoes, barley, wheat and olives are produced. Sheep, goats and pigs are the principal livestock. Copper is mined but the mining industry is declining. The main exports are manufactured goods, clothing and footwear, fruit, wine and vegetables. Tourism is an important source of foreign exchange.

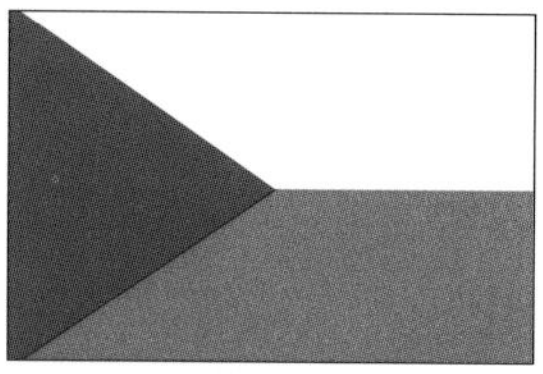

CZECH REPUBLIC

STATUS: Federal Republic
AREA: 127,870 sq km (49,360 sq miles)
POPULATION: 10,330,000
ANNUAL NATURAL INCREASE: 0.3%
CAPITAL: Prague (Praha)
LANGUAGE: Czech
RELIGION: 40% Roman Catholic, 55% no stated religion
CURRENCY: Czech crown or koruna (CSK)
ORGANIZATIONS: Council of Europe, OIEC, UN

Following the break up of Czechoslovakia, the Czech Republic came into being in January 1993. It is a country that lies at the heart of central Europe and has a diversity of landscapes. In Bohemia, to the west of the country, the upper Elbe drainage basin is surrounded by mountains. Moravia, separated from Bohemia by hills and mountains, is a lowland area centred on the town of Brno. The climate is temperate but with continental characteristics. Rain falls mainly in spring and autumn. This is historically one of the most highly industrialized regions of Europe, whose heavy industry once specialized in producing arms for the Soviet Union. Now the main products include cars, aircraft, tramways and locomotive diesel engines. There are raw materials (coal, minerals and timber) and a nuclear power station is being built to replace some polluting coal-fired stations.

DENMARK

STATUS: Kingdom
AREA: 43,075 sq km (16,625 sq miles)
POPULATION: 5,181,000
ANNUAL NATURAL INCREASE: 0.1%
CAPITAL: Copenhagen (København)
LANGUAGE: Danish
RELIGION: 94% Lutheran, Roman Catholic minority
CURRENCY: Danish krone (DKK)
ORGANIZATIONS: Council of Europe, EU, NATO, OECD, UN

Denmark is the smallest of the Scandinavian countries. It consists of the Jutland Peninsula and over 400 islands of which only one quarter are inhabited. The country is low-lying with a mixture of fertile and sandy soils, generally of glacial origin. Climate is temperate, with rainfall all the year round. Denmark's economy stems traditionally from agriculture and dairy products; bacon and sugar are still particularly important. An extensive fishing industry is centred on the shallow lagoons along the western coastline. Danish North Sea oil and gas provide self-sufficiency in energy and gas exports began in 1991. Food processing, beer, pharmaceuticals and specialist biotechnological equipment contribute to the industrial sector which provides 75 per cent of Danish exports.

DJIBOUTI

STATUS: Republic
AREA: 23,000 sq km (8,800 sq miles)
POPULATION: 467,000
ANNUAL NATURAL INCREASE: 2.9%
CAPITAL: Djibouti
LANGUAGE: French, Somali, Dankali, Arabic
RELIGION: Muslim majority, Roman Catholic minority
CURRENCY: Djibouti franc (DJF)
ORGANIZATIONS: Arab League, OAU, UN

Situated at the mouth of the Red Sea, Djibouti consists almost entirely of low-lying desert. There are mountains in the north of which Musa Ālī Terara reaches 2,063 m (6,768 feet). Its climate is very hot all year with annual temperatures between 25–35°C (78–96°F). The annual rainfall is as low as 130 mm (5 inches). The land is barren so Djibouti's economy must rely on activities based on its deep natural port and position along a major shipping route. It therefore acts as a trade outlet for Ethiopia, as well as serving Red Sea shipping. Main exports are cattle and hides.

DOMINICA

STATUS: Commonwealth State
AREA: 751 sq km (290 sq miles)
POPULATION: 72,000
ANNUAL NATURAL INCREASE: -0.3%
CAPITAL: Roseau
LANGUAGE: English, French patois
RELIGION: 80% Roman Catholic
CURRENCY: East Caribbean dollar (XCD)
ORGANIZATIONS: Comm., OAS, UN

Dominica is located in the Windward Islands of the east Caribbean. It is mountainous and forested with a coastline of steep cliffs. Tropical rainforest covers nearly half of the island. The climate is tropical with average temperatures exceeding 25°C (77°F) and has abundant rainfall. Bananas are the major export, followed by citrus fruits, coconuts and timber. Coffee and cocoa production is developing. Tourism is the most rapidly expanding industry.

DOMINICAN REPUBLIC

STATUS: Republic
AREA: 48,440 sq km (18,700 sq miles)
POPULATION: 7,471,000
ANNUAL NATURAL INCREASE: 1.9%
CAPITAL: Santo Domingo
LANGUAGE: Spanish
RELIGION: 90% Roman Catholic, Protestant and Jewish minorities
CURRENCY: Dominican peso (DOP)
ORGANIZATIONS: OAS, UN

The Dominican Republic is situated on the eastern half of the Caribbean island of Hispaniola. The landscape is dominated by a series of mountain ranges, thickly covered with rainforest, reaching up to 3,000 m (9,843 feet). To the south there is a coastal plain where the capital, Santo Domingo, lies. Minerals, in particular nickel, are important but agricultural products account for 70 per cent of export earnings. The traditional dependence on sugar has diminished, with coffee, tobacco and newer products including cocoa, fruit and vegetables gaining importance.

ECUADOR

STATUS: Republic
AREA: 461,475 sq km (178,130 sq miles)
POPULATION: 10,741,000
ANNUAL NATURAL INCREASE: 2.5%
CAPITAL: Quito
LANGUAGE: Spanish, Quechua, other Indian languages
RELIGION: 90% Roman Catholic
CURRENCY: sucre (ECS)
ORGANIZATIONS: OAS, UN

Ecuador falls into two distinctive geographical zones, the coastal lowlands which border the Pacific Ocean and inland, the Andean highlands. The highlands stretch about 400 km (250 miles) north-south, and here limited quantities of maize, wheat and barley are cultivated. Ecuador's main agricultural export, bananas, coffee and cocoa, are all grown on the fertile coastal lowlands. The rapidly growing fishing industry, especially shrimps, is becoming more important. Large resources of crude oil have been found in the thickly-forested lowlands on the eastern border and Ecuador has now become South America's second largest oil producer after Venezuela. Mineral reserves include silver, gold, copper and zinc.

EGYPT

STATUS: Republic
AREA: 1,000,250 sq km (386,095 sq miles)
POPULATION: 55,163,000
ANNUAL NATURAL INCREASE: 2.4%
CAPITAL: Cairo (El Qâhira)
LANGUAGE: Arabic, Berber, Nubian, English, French
RELIGION: 80% Muslim (mainly Sunni), Coptic Christian minority
CURRENCY: Egyptian pound (EGP)
ORGANIZATIONS: Arab league, OAU, UN

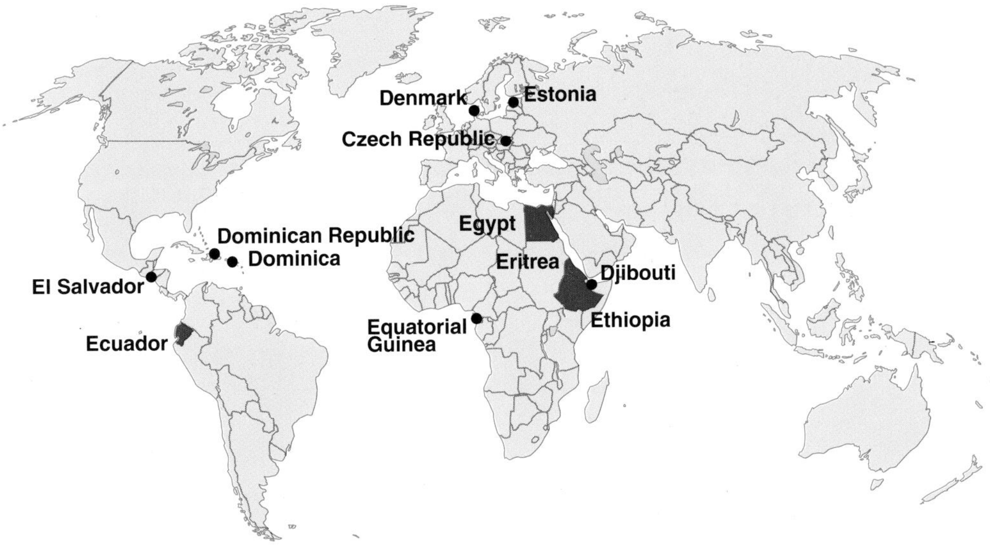

The focal point of Egypt, situated on the Mediterranean coast of northeast Africa, is the fertile, irrigated Nile river valley, sandwiched between two deserts. Egypt is virtually dependent on the Nile for water as average rainfall varies between only 200 mm (8 inches) in the north and zero in the deserts. Cotton and Egyptian clover are the two most important crops, with increasing cultivation of cereals, fruits, rice, sugar cane and vegetables. Agriculture is concentrated around the Nile flood plain and delta. In spite of this, however, Egypt has to import over half the food it needs. Buffalo, cattle, sheep, goats and camels are the principal livestock. Tourism is an important source of revenue together with the tolls from the Suez Canal. Major industries include the manufacture of cement, cotton goods, iron and steel, and processed foods. The main mineral deposits are phosphates, iron ore, salt, manganese and chromium. Egypt has sufficient oil and natural gas reserves for its own needs and exports crude oil. Gas is now replacing oil in Egyptian power stations in order to release more crude oil for export.

EL SALVADOR

STATUS: Republic
AREA: 21,395 sq km (8,260 sq miles)
POPULATION: 5,048,000
ANNUAL NATURAL INCREASE: 1.8%
CAPITAL: San Salvador
LANGUAGE: Spanish
RELIGION: 80% Roman Catholic
CURRENCY: El Salvador colón (SVC)
ORGANIZATIONS: CACM, OAS, UN

El Salvador is a small, densely populated country on the Pacific coast of Central America. Most of the population live around the lakes in the central plain. Temperatures range from 24–26°C (75–79°F) with an average annual rainfall of 1,780 mm (70 inches). Coffee provides about 50 per cent of export revenue. Other products include sugar, cotton, bananas and balsam. Industry has expanded considerably with the production of textiles, shoes, cosmetics, cement, processed foods, chemicals and furniture. Geothermal and hydro-electric resources are being developed and there are copper deposits as yet unexploited.

EQUATORIAL GUINEA

STATUS: Republic
AREA: 28,050 sq km (10,825 sq miles)
POPULATION: 369,000
ANNUAL NATURAL INCREASE: 2.3%
CAPITAL: Malabo
LANGUAGE: 85% Fang, Spanish, Bubi, other tribal languages
RELIGION: 96% Roman Catholic, 4% Animist
CURRENCY: CFA franc (C Africa) (XAF)
ORGANIZATIONS: OAU, UN

Independent from Spain since 1968, Equatorial Guinea consists of two separate regions – a mainland area with a tropical, humid climate and dense rainforest but little economic development, and the volcanic island of Bioko. Agriculture is the principal source of revenue. Cocoa and coffee from the island plantations are the main exports with wood products, fish and processed foods manufactured near the coast on the mainland.

ERITREA

STATUS: Republic
AREA: 91,600 sq km (35,370 sq miles)
POPULATION: 3,500,000
CAPITAL: Asmara (Āsmera)
LANGUAGE: Arabic, native languages, English
RELIGION: 50% Christian, 50% Muslim
CURRENCY: Ethiopian birr
ORGANIZATIONS: OAU, UN

Eritrea gained formal recognition of its independence from Ethiopia in 1993. The landscape consists of an arid coastal plain, which borders the Red Sea, and the highlands of the central area, which rise to over 2000 m (6,562 feet). There are few natural resources, with what industry there is being concentrated around Asmara. The consequences of continuing drought and the protracted civil war will affect the population and economy for some time to come.

ESTONIA

STATUS: Republic
AREA: 45,100 sq km (17,413 sq miles)
POPULATION: 1,516,000
ANNUAL NATURAL INCREASE: 0.2%
CAPITAL: Tallinn
LANGUAGE: Estonian, Russian
RELIGION: Lutheran, Roman Catholic
CURRENCY: kroon (EKR)
ORGANIZATIONS: Council of Europe, UN

With the mainland situated on the southern coast of the Gulf of Finland and encompassing a large number of islands, Estonia is the smallest and most northerly of the Baltic States. The generally flat and undulating landscape is characterised by extensive forests and many lakes. The climate is temperate. Agriculture, mainly livestock production, woodworking and textiles are also important. The economy is currently undergoing a transformation from central planning and state-ownership to a free market system based on private enterprise. Incorporated into the Soviet Union in 1940, Estonia regained its independence in 1991.

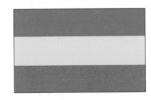

ETHIOPIA

STATUS: Republic
AREA: 1,023,050 sq km (394,895 sq miles)
POPULATION: 51,980,000
ANNUAL NATURAL INCREASE: 3.4%
CAPITAL: Addis Ababa (Ādīs Ābeba)
LANGUAGE: Amharic, English, Arabic
RELIGION: Ethiopian Orthodox, Muslim and animist
CURRENCY: birr (ETB)
ORGANIZATIONS: OAU, UN

Ethiopia's landscape consists of heavily dissected plateaux and plains of arid desert. Rainfall in these latter areas is minimal and unreliable, and drought and starvation are ever-present problems. Farming, in the high rural areas, accounts for 90 per cent of export revenue with coffee as the principal crop and main export together with fruit and vegetables, oil-seeds, hides and skins. Gold is mined on a small scale. The most important industries are cotton textiles, cement, canned foods, construction materials and leather goods. These are concentrated around the capital. In recent years the economy has been devastated by almost constant civil war.

FAEROES

STATUS: Self-governing Island Region of Denmark
AREA: 1,399 sq km (540 sq miles)
POPULATION: 47,000
CAPITAL: Tórshavn

FALKLAND ISLANDS

STATUS: UK Crown Colony
AREA: 12,175 sq km (4,700 sq miles)
POPULATION: 2,121
CAPITAL: Stanley

FIJI

STATUS: Republic
AREA: 18,330 sq km (7,075 sq miles)
POPULATION: 758,275
ANNUAL NATURAL INCREASE: 1.8%
CAPITAL: Suva
LANGUAGE: Fijian, English, Hindi
RELIGION: 51% Methodist Christian, 40% Hindu, 8% Muslim
CURRENCY: Fiji dollar (FJD)
ORGANIZATIONS: Col. Plan, UN

A country of some 320 tropical islands, of which over 100 are inhabited, the Republic of Fiji is located in Melanesia, in the south-central Pacific Ocean. The islands range from tiny coral reefs and atolls to the two largest Vanua Levu and Viti Levu, which are mountainous and of volcanic origin. The climate is tropical with temperatures ranging from 16–33°C (60–90°F) and annual rainfall being 236 mm (60 inches). Fiji's economy is geared to production of sugar cane, which provides 45 per cent of export revenue. Coconuts, bananas and rice are grown and livestock raised. Main industries are sugar processing, gold-mining, copra processing and fish canning. Tourism is also an important revenue earner.

FINLAND

STATUS: Republic
AREA: 337,030 sq km (130,095 sq miles)
POPULATION: 5,076,000
ANNUAL NATURAL INCREASE: 0.4%
CAPITAL: Helsinki
LANGUAGE: Finnish, Swedish
RELIGION: 87% Evangelical Lutheran, Eastern Orthodox minority
CURRENCY: markka (Finnmark) (FIM)
ORGANIZATIONS: Council of Europe, EEA, EFTA, OECD, UN

Finland is a flat land of lakes and forests. Over 70 per cent of the land supports coniferous woodland with a further 10 per cent being water. The Saimaa lake area is Europe's largest inland water system. Its soils are thin and poor on ice-scarred granite plateaux. Most of Finland's population live in towns in the far south because of the harsh northern climate. In the north temperatures can range from -30°C (-22°F) in the winter to 27°C (81°F) in summer. The Baltic Sea can freeze for several miles from the coast during winter months. There is 600 mm (24 inches) of rain per annum throughout the country. Forestry products (timber, pulp and paper) once dominated the economy (80 per cent in 1980) but now account for 40 per cent of the export total and engineering, in particular shipbuilding and forest machinery, is almost equal in importance. Finland is virtually self-sufficient in basic foodstuffs. The country depends heavily on imported energy, producing only 30 per cent of its total consumption (20 per cent by its four nuclear power stations).

FRANCE

STATUS: Republic
AREA: 543,965 sq km (209,970 sq miles)
POPULATION: 57,800,000
ANNUAL NATURAL INCREASE: 0.6%
CAPITAL: Paris
LANGUAGE: French
RELIGION: 90% Roman Catholic. Protestant, Muslim, Jewish minorities
CURRENCY: French franc (FRF)
ORGANIZATIONS: Council of Europe, EEA, EU, G7, NATO, OECD, UN, WEU

France encompasses a great variety of landscapes, ranging from mountain ranges, high plateaux to lowland plains and river basins. The Pyrenees, in the southwest, form the border with Spain and the Jura mountains, in the west, form a border with Switzerland. The highest mountain range is the Alps, south of the Jura. The Massif Central is the highest of the plateaux, which also include the Vosges bordering the plain of Alsace, and Armorica occupying the granite moors of the Brittany peninsula. The French climate is moderated by proximity to the Atlantic, and is generally mild. The south has a Mediterranean climate with hot dry summers, the rest of the country has rain all year round. (Paris has an average annual rainfall of 600 mm or 24 inches). Much of the French countryside is agricultural and it is estimated that one-third of the population derives an income from the land. France is self-sufficient in cereals, dairy products, meat, fruit and vegetables, and is a leading exporter of wheat, barley and sugar beet. Wine is also a major export. Over the past years there has been a steady drift of labour, mainly of younger people from the countryside to the industrialized areas. France is the fourth industrial power in the world after USA, Japan and Germany. It has reserves of coal, oil and natural gas, and is one of the world's leading producers of iron ore. It has large steel-making and chemical refining industries. Its vehicle, aeronautical and armaments industries are among the world's most important. Leading light industries are fashion, perfumes and luxury goods. Most of its heavy industry is concentrated in the major industrial zone of the northeast. In the past, sources of energy have been provided from its reserves of fossil fuels, however in recent years other sources have increased in importance, such as nuclear power using uranium from French mines, tidal power, and hydro-electricity. Tourism is an important source of income, that will be further encouraged by the opening of the Channel Tunnel.

FRENCH GUIANA

STATUS: Overseas Department of France
AREA: 91,000 sq km (35,125 sq miles)
POPULATION: 114,808
CAPITAL: Cayenne

FRENCH POLYNESIA

STATUS: Overseas Territory of France
AREA: 3,940 sq km (1,520 sq miles)
POPULATION: 199,031
CAPITAL: Papeete

GABON

STATUS: Republic
AREA: 267,665 sq km (103,320 sq miles)
POPULATION: 1,012,000
ANNUAL NATURAL INCREASE: 2.7%
CAPITAL: Libreville
LANGUAGE: French, Bantu dialects, Fang
RELIGION: 60% Roman Catholic.
CURRENCY: CFA franc (C Africa) (XAF)
ORGANIZATIONS: OAU, OPEC, UN,

Gabon, which lies on the equator, consists of the Ogooué river basin covered with tropical rain forest. It is hot and wet all year with average annual temperatures of 25°C (77°F). It is one of the most prosperous states in Africa with valuable timber (mahogany, ebony and walnut) and mineral (manganese and uranium) resources. State-run plantations growing oil palms, bananas, sugar cane and rubber are also important. Gabon's economy, however, is heavily dependent on its oil industry. It is the third largest producer in sub-Saharan Africa after Nigeria and Angola. France supplies nearly half the country's imports and French influence is evident everywhere.

GAMBIA, THE

STATUS: Republic
AREA: 10,690 sq km (4,125 sq miles)
POPULATION: 1,026,000
ANNUAL NATURAL INCREASE: 3.2%
CAPITAL: Banjul
LANGUAGE: English, Madinka, Fula, Wolof

RELIGION: 90% Muslim,
Christian and animist minorities
CURRENCY: dalasi (GMD)
ORGANIZATIONS: Comm., ECOWAS, OAU, UN

The Gambia is the smallest country in Africa. An enclave within Senegal, it is 470 km (292 miles) long, averages 24 km (15 miles) wide and occupies land bordering the Gambia river. The climate has two distinctive seasons. November to May is dry but July to October sees monsoon rainfall of up to 1,300 mm (51 inches). The temperatures average about 23–27°C (73–81°F) throughout the year. Groundnuts and subsidiary products are the mainstay of the economy but tourism is developing rapidly. The production of cotton, livestock, fish and rice is increasing to change the present economic reliance on groundnuts.

GEORGIA

STATUS: Republic
AREA: 69,700 sq km (26,905 sq miles)
POPULATION: 5,471,000
ANNUAL NATURAL INCREASE: 0.5%
CAPITAL: Tbilisi
LANGUAGE: 70% Georgian, 8% Armenian, 6% Russian, 6% Azeri
RELIGION: Orthodox Christian
CURRENCY: coupon
ORGANIZATIONS: CIS

Georgia, covering part of the southern Caucasus, is a mountainous country with forests covering one-third of its area. The climate ranges from sub-tropical on the shores of the Black Sea, to perpetual ice and snow on the Caucasian crests. Rich deposits of coal are mainly unexploited. Cheap oil and gas imports, hydro-electric power and minerals, in particular rich manganese deposits, have led to industrialization successfully concentrated on metallurgy and machine-building. With the exception of the fertile plain to the east, agricultural land is in short supply and difficult to work. This is partly compensated by the cultivation of labour-intensive and profitable crops such as tea, grapes, tobacco and citrus fruit. The break-up of the Soviet Union brought independence for Georgia in 1991. The question of regional autonomy for the Abkhaz, Adzhar and South Ossetian minorities has repeatedly led to violent ethnic conflict in recent years, causing economic collapse.

GERMANY

STATUS: Federal Republic
AREA: 356,840 sq km (137,740 sq miles)
POPULATION: 81,051,000
ANNUAL NATURAL INCREASE: 0.6%
CAPITAL: Berlin
(seat of government Berlin/Bonn)
LANGUAGE: German
RELIGION: 45% Protestant
40% Roman Catholic
CURRENCY: Deutsch-mark (DM)
ORGANIZATIONS: Council of Europe, EEA, EU, G7, NATO, OECD, UN, WEU

Germany has three main geographical regions: the Northern plain, stretching from the rivers Oder and Neisse in the east to the Dutch border; the central uplands with elevated plateaux intersected by river valleys and relieved by isolated mountains, gradually rising to peaks of up to nearly 1500 m (5000 feet) in the Black Forest: finally the Bavarian Alps stradling the Austrian border. With exception of the Danube, all German river systems run northwards into the North or the Baltic Seas. The climate is mainly continental with temperatures ranging from -3°–1°C (27–34°F) in January to 16°–19°C (61°–66°F) in July. Only in the north-western corner of the country does the climate become more oceanic in character. Germany on the whole has large stretches of very fertile farmland.

Politically, the division of Germany, a product of the post-1945 Cold War between the victorious Allies against Hitler, was rapidly overcome after the collapse of communism in Eastern Europe, and the unification of the two German states was effected in 1990. Economically, the legacy of 40 years of socialist rule in the East ensures that, in terms of both structure and performance, Germany will encompass two vastly different halves for a long time to come. Having lost its captive markets in what used to be the Soviet Bloc, the eastern economy then all but collapsed under the weight of superior western competition. The task of reconstruction is proving more difficult, more protracted and, most of all, more costly than expected. In the West, the Ruhr basin, historically the industrial heartland of Germany, with its emphasis on coal mining and iron and steel works, has long since been overtaken by more advanced industries elsewhere, notably in the Rhine-Main area and further south in the regions around Stuttgart and Munich. The rapidly expanding services sector apart, the German economy is now dominated by the chemical, pharmaceutical, mechanical engineering, motor and high-tech industries. To lessen the country's dependence on oil imports, an ambitious nuclear energy programme has been adopted. Although poor in minerals and other raw materials with the exception of lignite and potash, Germany has managed to become one of the world's leading manufacturers and exporters of vehicles, machine tools, electrical and electronic products and of consumer goods of various description, in particular textiles. But the massive balance of trade surplus West Germany used to enjoy has now disappeared due to the sucking in of imports by, and the redistribution of output to, the newly acquired territories in the East.

GHANA

STATUS: Republic
AREA: 238,305 sq km (91,985 sq miles)
POPULATION: 15,959,000
ANNUAL NATURAL INCREASE: 3.3%
CAPITAL: Accra
LANGUAGE: English, tribal languages
RELIGION: 42% Christian
CURRENCY: cedi (GHC)
ORGANIZATIONS: Comm., ECOWAS, OAU, UN

Ghana, the west African state once known as the Gold Coast, gained independence from Britain in 1957. The landscape varies from tropical rainforest to dry scrubland, with the terrain becoming hillier to the north, culminating in a plateau averaging some 500 m (1,600 feet). The climate is tropical with the annual rainfall ranging from over 2,000 mm (79 inches) on the coast to less than 1,000 mm (40 inches) inland. The temperature averages 27°C (81°F) all year. Cocoa is the principal crop but although most Ghanaians farm, there is also a thriving industrial base around Tema, where local bauxite is smelted into aluminium. Tema has the largest artificial harbour in Africa. In recent years gold production has surged, Ghana having some of the world's richest gold deposits. Besides gold, Ghana's major exports are cocoa and timber. Principal imports are fuel, food and manufactured goods. Offshore oil has yet to be economically developed.

GIBRALTAR

STATUS: UK Crown Colony
AREA: 6.5 sq km (2.5 sq miles)
POPULATION: 31,000

GREECE

STATUS: Republic
AREA: 131,985 sq km (50,945 sq miles)
POPULATION: 10,269,074
ANNUAL NATURAL INCREASE: 0.4%
CAPITAL: Athens (Athínai)
LANGUAGE: Greek
RELIGION: 97% Greek Orthodox
CURRENCY: drachma (GRD)
ORGANIZATIONS: Council of Europe, EC, NATO, OECD, UN

Greece is a mountainous country and over one-fifth of its area comprises numerous islands, 154 of which are inhabited. The climate is Mediterranean with temperatures averaging 28°C (82°F) in summer. The mountains experience some heavy snowfall during winter. Poor irrigation and drainage mean that much of the agriculture is localized. The main products of olives, fruit and vegetables, cotton, tobacco and wine are exported. The surrounding seas are important, providing two-thirds of Greece's fish requirements and supporting an active merchant fleet. Athens is the main manufacturing base and at least one quarter of the population lives there. Greece is a very popular tourist destination which helps the craft industries – tourism is a prime source of national income.

GREENLAND

STATUS: Self-governing Island Region of Denmark
AREA: 2,175,600 sq km (836,780 sq miles)
POPULATION: 55,558
CAPITAL: Godthåb (Nuuk)

GRENADA

STATUS: Commonwealth State
AREA: 345 sq km (133 sq miles)
POPULATION: 95,343
ANNUAL NATURAL INCREASE: -0.2%
CAPITAL: St George's
LANGUAGE: English, French patois
RELIGION: Roman Catholic majority
CURRENCY: E Caribbean dollar (XCD)
ORGANIZATIONS: Caricom, Comm., OAS, UN

The Caribbean island of Grenada, whose territory includes the southern Grenadines, is the most southern of the Windward Islands. It is mountainous and thickly forested, with a settled warm climate and an average temperature of 27°C (81°F). Rainfall varies with altitude, ranging from 760 mm (30 inches) to 3,560 mm (140 inches) on the higher ground. The island is famous for its spices and nutmeg is the main export. Cocoa and bananas are also important, together with some citrus fruits and vegetables. Tourism is important and continues to expand.

GUADELOUPE

STATUS: Overseas Department of France
AREA: 1,780 sq km (687 sq miles)
POPULATION: 406,000
CAPITAL: Basse-Terre

GUAM

STATUS: External Territory of USA
AREA: 450 sq km (174 sq miles)
POPULATION: 139,000
CAPITAL: Agaña

GUATEMALA

STATUS: Republic
AREA: 108,890 sq km (42,030 sq miles)
POPULATION: 9,745,000
ANNUAL NATURAL INCREASE: 2.9%
CAPITAL: Guatemala City (Guatemala)
LANGUAGE: Spanish, Indian languages
RELIGION: 75% Roman Catholic, 25% Protestant
CURRENCY: quetzal (GTQ)
ORGANIZATIONS: CACM, OAS, UN

The central American country of Guatemala has both a Pacific and a Caribbean coastline. The mountainous interior, with peaks reaching up to 4,000 m (13,120 feet), covers two-thirds of the country while to the north there is the thickly forested area known as the Petén. The northern lowland and the smaller coastal plains have a hot tropical climate, but the central highlands are more temperate. A rainy season lasts from May to October. Annual rainfall reaches up to 5,000 mm (200 inches) in some lowland areas but decreases to an average of 1,150 mm (45 inches) in the mountains. Agricultural products form the bulk of Guatemala's exports, notably coffee, sugar cane, cotton and bananas, but there is also a substantial industrial base. Manufacturing includes textiles, paper and pharmaceuticals. Mineral resources include nickel, antimony, lead, silver and in the north crude oil.

GUINEA

STATUS: Republic
AREA: 245,855 sq km (94,900 sq miles)
POPULATION: 6,116,000
ANNUAL NATURAL INCREASE: 2.8%
CAPITAL: Conakry
LANGUAGE: French, Susu, Manika
RELIGION: 85% Muslim 10% animist, 5% Roman Catholic
CURRENCY: Guinea franc (GNF)
ORGANIZATIONS: ECOWAS, OAU, UN

Guinea, a former French colony, is situated on the west African coast. Its drowned coastline, lined with mangrove swamps, contrasts strongly with its interior highlands containing the headwaters of the Gambia, Niger and Senegal rivers. Agriculture occupies 80 per cent of the workforce, the main exports being coffee, bananas, pineapple and palm products. Guinea has some of the largest resources of bauxite (aluminium ore) in the world as well as gold and diamonds. Bauxite accounts for 80 per cent of export earnings.

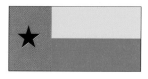

GUINEA-BISSAU

STATUS: Republic
AREA: 36,125 sq km (13,945 sq miles)
POPULATION: 1,006,000
ANNUAL NATURAL INCREASE: 1.9%
CAPITAL: Bissau
LANGUAGE: Portuguese, Creole, Guinean dialects
RELIGION: Animist and Muslim majority, Roman Catholic minority
CURRENCY: Guinea-Bissau peso (GWP)
ORGANIZATIONS: ECOWS, OAU, UN

Guinea-Bissau, on the west African coast, was once a centre for the Portuguese slave trade. The coast is swampy and lined with mangroves, and the interior consists of a low-lying plain densely covered with rain forest. The coast is hot and humid with annual rainfall of 2,000–3,000 mm (79–118 inches) a year, although the interior is cooler and drier. Eighty per cent of the country's exports comprise groundnut oil, palm kernels and palm oil. Fish, fish products and coconuts also make an important contribution to trade.

GUYANA

STATUS: Co-operative Republic
AREA: 214,970 sq km (82,980 sq miles)
POPULATION: 808,000
ANNUAL NATURAL INCREASE: 0.3%
CAPITAL: Georgetown
LANGUAGE: English, Hindi, Urdu, Amerindian dialects
RELIGION: Christian majority, Muslim and Hindu minorities
CURRENCY: Guyana dollar (GYD)
ORGANIZATIONS: Caricom, Comm., UN

Guyana, formerly the British colony of British Guiana, borders both Venezuela and Brazil. Its Atlantic coast, the most densely-populated area, is flat and marshy, while towards the interior the landscape gradually rises to the Guiana Highlands – a region densely covered in rainforest. The climate is tropical, with hot, wet and humid conditions, which are modified along the coast by sea breezes. Agriculture, dominated by sugar and rice, is the basis of the economy. Bauxite deposits provide a valuable export and in the mid-1990s gold production increased.

HAITI

STATUS: Republic
AREA: 27,750 sq km (10,710 sq miles)
POPULATION: 6,764,000
ANNUAL NATURAL INCREASE: 2.0%
CAPITAL: Port-au-Prince
LANGUAGE: French, Creole
RELIGION: 80% Roman Catholic, Voodoo folk religion minority
CURRENCY: gourde (HTG)
ORGANIZATIONS: OAS, UN

Haiti occupies the western part of the island of Hispaniola in the Caribbean. It is the poorest country in Central America. The country is mountainous with three main ranges, the highest reaching 2,680 m (8,793 feet). Agriculture is restricted to the plains which divide the ranges. The climate is tropical. Ninety per cent of the workforce are farmers and traditional exports have been coffee, sugar, cotton, and cocoa. In the early to mid-1990s national poverty worsened as a result of UN embargoes imposed against an illegal military regime. Thousands of Haitians fled the country. New sanctions in 1994 threatened to bring an end to all manufacturing and exporting activities.

HEARD AND McDONALD ISLANDS

STATUS: External Territory of Australia
AREA: 412 sq km (159 sq miles)
POPULATION: no permanent population
CAPITAL: Edmonton

HONDURAS

STATUS: Republic
AREA: 112,085 sq km (43,265 sq miles)
POPULATION: 5,462,000
ANNUAL NATURAL INCREASE 3.1%
CAPITAL: Tegucigalpa
LANGUAGE: Spanish, Indian dialects
RELIGION: Roman Catholic majority
CURRENCY: lempira (HNL) or peso
ORGANIZATIONS: CACM, OAS, UN

The central American republic of Honduras is a poor, sparsely populated country which consists substantially of rugged mountains and high plateaux with, on the Caribbean coast, an area of hot and humid plains, densely covered with tropical vegetation. These low-lying plains are subject to high annual rainfall, averaging 2,500 mm (98 inches), and it is in this region that bananas and coffee, accounting for over half the nation's exports, are grown. Other crops include sugar, rice, maize, beans and tobacco. There has been growth in new products such as shrimps, melons and tomatoes. Most industries are concerned with processing local products. Lead and zinc are exported.

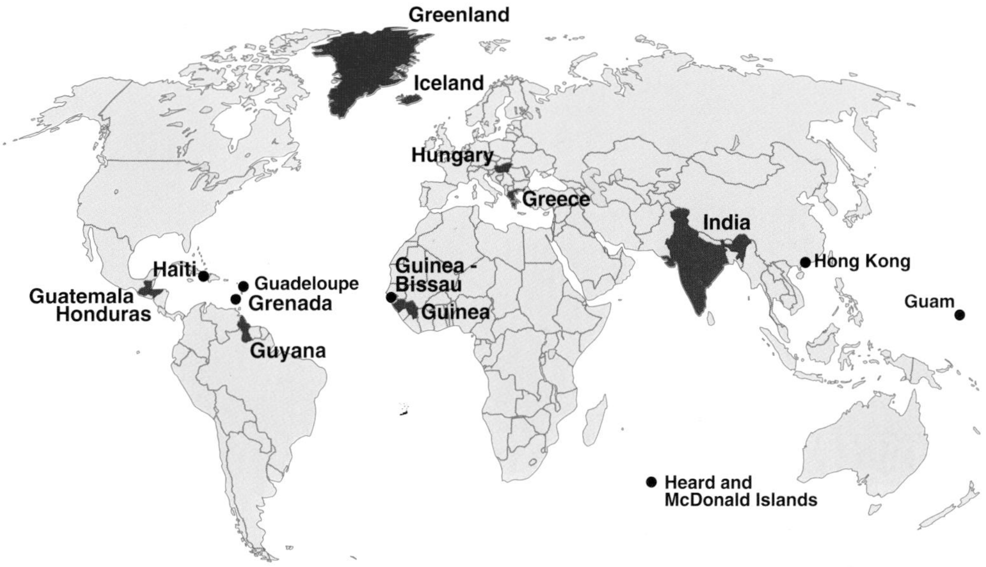

HONG KONG

STATUS: UK Dependent Territory
AREA: 1,067 sq km (412 sq miles)
POPULATION: 5,920,000

HUNGARY

STATUS: Republic
AREA: 93,030 sq km (35,910 sq miles)
POPULATION: 10,289,000
ANNUAL NATURAL INCREASE: -0.6%
CAPITAL: Budapest
LANGUAGE: Hungarian (Magyar)
RELIGION: 60% Roman Catholic, 20% Hungarian Reformed Church, Lutheran and Orthodox minorities
CURRENCY: forint (HUF)
ORGANIZATIONS: Council of Europe,OIEC, UN

Hungary is situated in the heartland of Europe. Its geomorphology consists mainly of undulating fertile plains with the highest terrain in the northeast of the country. The country is bisected north to south by the Danube. It has a humid continental climate, with warm summers that can become very hot on the plains, averaging 20°C (68°F), and cold winters, averaging 0°C (32°F). There is an annual rainfall of 500–750 mm (20–30 inches). Bauxite is Hungary's only substantial mineral resource, and less than 15 per cent of the gross national product is now derived from agriculture. The massive drive for industrialization has fundamentally transformed the structure of the economy since 1945. Both capital and consumer goods industries were developed, and during the 1980s engineering accounted for more than half the total industrial output. After a series of more or less unsuccessful attempts to introduce market elements into what essentially remained a centrally planned and largely state-owned economy, the communist regime finally gave up in 1989/90. However, their democratically elected successors have yet to prove that privatization and free competition will eventually bring general prosperity as well as political stability to what is now a profoundly troubled society.

ICELAND

STATUS: Republic
AREA: 102,820 sq km (39,690 sq miles)
POPULATION: 260,000
ANNUAL NATURAL INCREASE: 1.2%
CAPITAL: Reykjavík
LANGUAGE: Icelandic
RELIGION: 93% Evangelical Lutheran
CURRENCY: Icelandic krona (ISK)
ORGANIZATIONS: Council of Europe, EEA, EFTA, NATO, OECD, UN

One of the most northern islands in Europe, Iceland is 798 km (530 miles) away from Scotland, its nearest neighbour. The landscape is entirely volcanic – compacted volcanic ash has been eroded by the wind and there are substantial ice sheets and lava fields as well as many still active volcanoes, geysers and hot springs. The climate is mild for its latitude, with average summer temperatures of 9–10°C (48–50°F), and vegetation is sparse. Fishing is the traditional mainstay of the economy. An average of some 1,540,000 tonnes of fish are landed each year and 80 per cent of Iceland's exports consist of fish and fish products. Tourism is becoming an increasing source of income.

INDIA

STATUS: Federal Republic
AREA: 3,166,830 sq km (1,222,395 sq miles)
POPULATION: 870,000,000
ANNUAL NATURAL INCREASE: 2.1%
CAPITAL: New Delhi
LANGUAGE: Hindi, English, regional languages
RELIGION: 83% Hindu, 11% Muslim
CURRENCY: Indian rupee (INR)
ORGANIZATIONS: Col. Plan, Comm., UN

Occupying most of the Indian subcontinent, India is second only to China in the size of its population. This vast country contains an extraordinary variety of landscapes, climates and resources. The Himalayas, in the north, are the world's highest mountain range with many peaks reaching over 6,000 km (19,685 feet). The Himalayan foothills, are covered with lush vegetation, water is in abundant supply (rainfall in Assam reaches 10,700 mm or 421 inches in a year) and the climate is hot, making this region a centre for tea cultivation. To the south lies the vast expanse of the Indo-Gangetic plain, 2,500 km (1,550 miles) east-west, divided by the Indus, Ganges and Brahmaputra rivers. This is one of the world's most fertile regions, although it is liable to flooding, and failure of monsoon rainfall (June to September) can result in severe drought. In the pre-monsoon season the heat becomes intense – average temperatures in New Delhi reach 38°C (110°F). Rice, wheat, cotton, jute, tobacco and sugar are the main crops. To the south lies the Deccan plateau, bordered on either side by the Eastern and Western Ghats, and in the northwest lies the barren Thar Desert. India's natural resources are immense – timber, coal, iron ore and nickel – and oil has been discovered in the Indian Ocean. There has been a rapid expansion of light industry, notably in the food processing sector, and the manufacturing of consumer goods. Nevertheless, 70 per cent of the population live by subsistence farming. Main exports by value are precious stones and jewelry, engineering goods, clothing, leather goods, chemicals and cotton. Tourism is a valuable source of revenue.

INDONESIA

STATUS: Republic
AREA: 1,919,445 sq km
(740,905 sq miles)
POPULATION: 187,870,000
ANNUAL NATURAL INCREASE: 1.8%
CAPITAL: Jakarta
LANGUAGE: Bahasa Indonesian, Dutch
RELIGION: 88% Muslim, 9% Christian,
Hindu and Buddhist minorities
CURRENCY: rupiah (IDR)
ORGANIZATIONS: ASEAN, Col. Plan,
OPEC, UN

Indonesia consists of thousands of islands in equatorial southeast Asia which include Kalimantan (the central and southern parts of Borneo), Sumatera, Irian Jaya (the western part of New Guinea), Sulawesi (Celebes) and Java. The climate is tropical: hot (temperatures averaging 24°C or 75°F per year), humid and subject to monsoons. Most of its people live along the coast and river valleys of Java, leaving parts of the other islands virtually uninhabited. It is a Muslim nation and has the fourth largest population in the world. Over three-quarters of the people farm and live in small villages. Oil and gas, manufactured goods and coal are the chief exports. Indonesia is also a leading supplier of forest products, palm oil, rubber, spices, tobacco, tea, coffee and tin. With the use of modern techniques, the country has achieved self-sufficiency in rice.

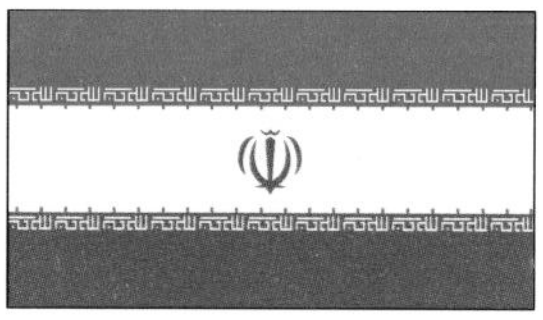

IRAN

STATUS: Republic
AREA: 1,648,000 sq km (636,130 sq miles)
POPULATION: 56,964,000
ANNUAL NATURAL INCREASE: 3.7%
CAPITAL: Tehran
LANGUAGE: Farsi, Kurdish, Arabic,
Baluchi, Turkic
RELIGION: Shi'a Muslim majority, Sunni Muslim
and Armenian Christian minorities
CURRENCY: Iranian rial (IRR)
ORGANIZATIONS: Col. Plan, OPEC, UN

Iran is a large mountainous country north of The Gulf. The climate is one of extremes with temperatures ranging from -20–55°C (-4–131°F) and rainfall varying from 2,000 mm (79 inches) to almost zero. Iran is rich in oil and gas and the revenues have been used to improve communications and social conditions generally. The war with Iraq between 1980 and 1988 seriously restricted economic growth and particularly affected the Iranian oil industry in The Gulf. Oil is the source of 85 per cent of Iran's revenue and thus when world oil prices fall, as in the early–mid 1990s, the economy suffers. Agricultural conditions are poor, except around the Caspian Sea, and wheat is the main crop though fruit (especially dates) and nuts are grown and exported. The main livestock is sheep and goats. Iran has substantial mineral deposits relatively underdeveloped

---

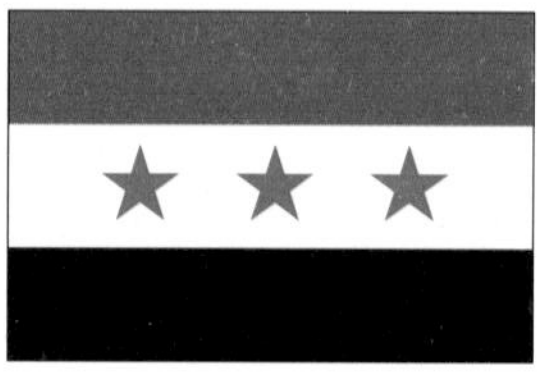

IRAQ

STATUS: Republic
AREA: 438,317 sq km (169,235 sq miles)
POPULATION: 19,410,000
ANNUAL NATURAL INCREASE: 3.3%
CAPITAL: Baghdad
LANGUAGE: Arabic, Kurdish, Turkoman
RELIGION: 50% Shi'a, 45% Sunni Muslim
CURRENCY: Iraqi dinar (IQD)
ORGANIZATIONS: Arab League, OPEC, UN

Iraq is mostly desert, marsh and mountain, but there are substantial areas of fertile land between the Tigris and the Euphrates. The two great rivers join and become the Shatt al-Arab which flows into The Gulf. The climate is arid with rainfall of less than 500 mm (20 inches) and summers are very hot (averaging 35° or 95°F). Iraq has a short coastline with Basra the only port. Light industry is situated around Baghdad, and there are major petro-chemical complexes around the Basra and Kirkuk oilfields. The war with Iran (1980–8) and the Gulf conflict (1991) wrecked the economy with exports of oil and natural gas, formerly accounting for 95 per cent of export earnings, severely restricted by sanctions. Meanwhile, Arabs living in the Tigris-Euphrates marsh regions are being deprived of their livelihood as the marshes are drained in government reclamation schemes.

IRELAND (EIRE)

STATUS: Republic
AREA: 68,895 sq km (26,595 sq miles)
POPULATION: 3,548,000
ANNUAL NATURAL INCREASE: -0.1%
CAPITAL: Dublin (Baile Átha Cliath)
LANGUAGE: Irish, English
RELIGION: 95% Roman Catholic, 5% Protestant
CURRENCY: punt or Irish pound (IEP)
ORGANIZATIONS: Council of Europe, EEA, EU,
OECD, UN

The Irish Republic, forming 80 per cent of the island of Ireland, is a lowland country of wide valleys, lakes and marshes, but with some hills of significance, such as the Wicklow Mountains, south of Dublin and Macgillicuddy's Reeks, in the southwest. The Irish climate is maritime and influenced by the Gulf Stream. Temperatures average 5°C (40°F) in winter to 16°C (60°F) in summer, with annual rainfall at about 1,400 mm (55 inches) in the west and half that in the east. There is much rich pastureland and livestock farming predominates. Meat and dairy produce is processed in the small market towns where there are also breweries and mills. Large-scale manufacturing, in which food processing, electronics and textiles have shown recent growth, is centred around Dublin, the capital and main port. The Irish Republic possesses reserves of oil and natural gas, peat and deposits of lead and zinc. A large zinc mine at Galmoy is expected to come into production in 1996.

ISRAEL

STATUS: State
AREA: 20,770 sq km (8,015 sq miles)
POPULATION: 5,287,000
ANNUAL NATURAL INCREASE: 2.7%
CAPITAL: Jerusalem
LANGUAGE: Hebrew, Arabic, Yiddish
RELIGION: 85% Jewish, 13% Muslim
CURRENCY: shekel (ILS)
ORGANIZATIONS: UN

Israel, in the eastern Mediterranean littoral, contains a varied landscape – a coastal plain, interior hills, a deep valley extending from the river Jordan to the Dead Sea, and the Negev semi-desert in the south. Efficient water management is crucial as two-thirds of rainfall, which falls mostly in the mild winters, is lost by evaporation. Fuel needs to be imported (mainly oil from Egypt). Economic development in Israel is the most advanced in the Middle East. Manufacturing, particularly diamond finishing, electronics and science based products are important, although Israel also has flourishing agriculture specializing in exporting fruit, flowers and vegetables to western Europe. The only viable mineral resources are phosphates in the Negev and potash from the Dead Sea.

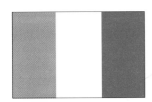

ITALY

STATUS: Republic
AREA: 301,245 sq km (116,280 sq miles)
POPULATION: 56,767,000
ANNUAL NATURAL INCREASE: 0.2%
CAPITAL: Rome (Roma)
LANGUAGE: Italian, German, French
RELIGION: 90% Roman Catholic
CURRENCY: Italian lira (ITL)
ORGANIZATIONS: Council of Europe, EEA, EU, G7, NATO, OECD, UN, WEU

Italy, separated from the rest of Europe by the great divide of the Alps, thrusts southeastwards into the Mediterranean Sea, in its famous boot-shaped peninsula. Including the large islands of Sicily and Sardinia, over 75 per cent of the landscape is either hill or mountain. The north is dominated by the plain of the river Po rising to the high Alps. Further along the peninsula the Apennine mountains run from north to south. Climate varies with altitude, but generally there is a Mediterranean regime in the south; in the north the climate becomes more temperate. Agriculture flourishes with cereals, vegetables, olives, and cheese the principal products and Italy is the world's largest wine producer. Tourism is a major source of revenue. In spite of the lack of mineral and power resources, Italy has become a trading nation with a sound industrial base. Manufacturing of textiles, cars, machine tools, textile machinery and engineering, mainly in the north, is expanding rapidly and accounts for nearly 50 per cent of the work force. This is increasing the imbalance between the north and south where the average income is far less per head, and where investment is lacking.

IVORY COAST (CÔTE D'IVOIRE)

STATUS: Republic
AREA: 322,465 sq km (124,470 sq miles)
POPULATION: 12,910,000
ANNUAL NATURAL INCREASE: 4.0%
CAPITAL: Yamoussoukro
LANGUAGE: French, tribal languages
RELIGION: 65% traditional beliefs, 23% Muslim, 12% Roman Catholic
CURRENCY: CFA franc (W Africa) (XOF)
ORGANIZATIONS: ECOWAS, OAU, UN,

Independent from the French since 1960, the Ivory Coast rises from low plains in the south to plateaux in the north. The climate is tropical with rainfall in two wet seasons in the south. Much of the population is engaged in subsistence agriculture. The two chief exports are cocoa and coffee. Other products include cotton, timber, fruit and tobacco. Gold mining began in 1990, diamonds are extracted and by 1995 the Ivory Coast is expected to become self-sufficient in oil and gas from the offshore fields.

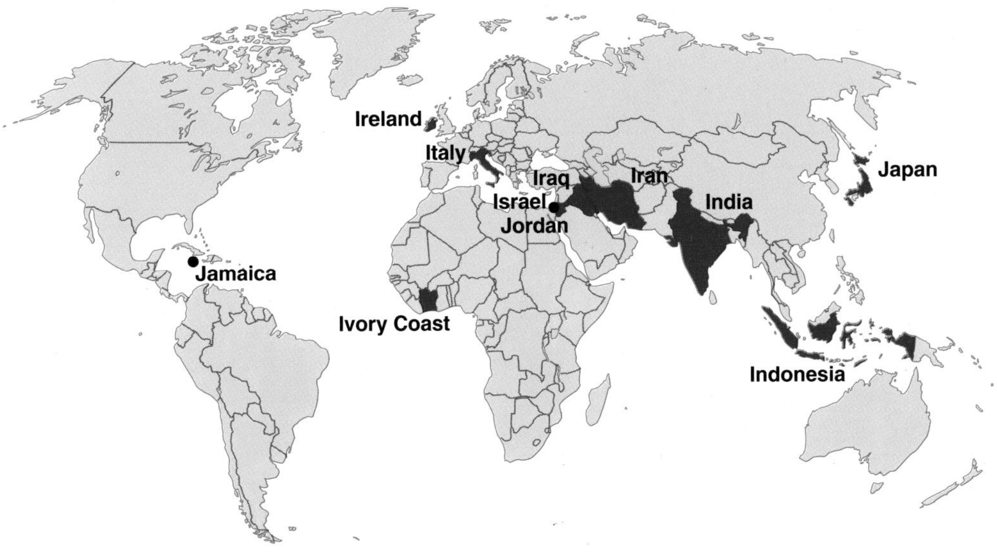

JAMAICA

STATUS: Commonwealth State
AREA: 11,425 sq km (4,410 sq miles)
POPULATION: 2,469,000
ANNUAL NATURAL INCREASE: 0.8%
CAPITAL: Kingston
LANGUAGE: English, local patois
RELIGION: Anglican Christian majority. Rastafarian minority
CURRENCY: Jamaican dollar (JMD)
ORGANIZATIONS: Caricom, Comm., OAS, UN

Jamaica, part of the Greater Antilles chain of islands in the Caribbean, is formed from the peaks of a submerged mountain range. The climate is tropical with an annual rainfall of over 5,000 mm (197 inches) on the high ground. There is a plentiful supply of tropical fruits such as melons, bananas and guavas. Principal crops include sugar cane, bananas, cocoa and coffee. Jamaica is rich in bauxite which, with the refined product alumina, is the main export. Major industries are food processing, textiles, cement and agricultural machinery. Since 1988 tourism has developed rapidly and is now the biggest single source of foreign earnings.

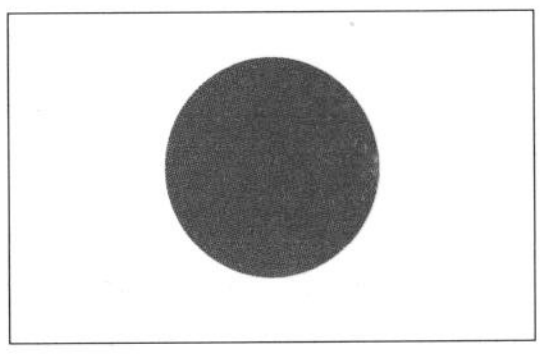

JAPAN

STATUS: Constitutional monarchy
AREA: 369,700 sq km (142,705 sq miles)
POPULATION: 123,653,000
ANNUAL NATURAL INCREASE: 0.4%
CAPITAL: Tokyo (Tōkyō)
LANGUAGE: Japanese
RELIGION: Shintoist, Buddhist, Christian minority
CURRENCY: yen (JPY)
ORGANIZATIONS: Col. Plan, G7, OECD, UN

Japan consists of the main islands of Hokkaido, Honshu, Shikoku and Kyushu which stretch over 1,600 km (995 miles). The land is mountainous and heavily forested with small, fertile patches and a climate ranging from harsh to tropical. The highest mountain is Mt Fuji (Fuji-san) at 3,776 m (12,388 feet). The archipelago is also subject to monsoons, earthquakes, typhoons and tidal waves. Very little of the available land is cultivable. Most food has to be imported but the Japanese both catch and eat a lot of fish. The Japanese fishing fleet is the largest in the world. Japan is a leading economic power. Because of the importance of trade, industry has grown up around the major ports especially Yokohama, Osaka and Tokyo, the capital. The principal exports are motor vehicles, chemicals, iron and steel products and electronic, electric and optical equipment. Japan relies heavily on imported fuel and raw materials and is developing the country's nuclear power resources to reduce this dependence. Production of coal, oil and natural gas is also being increased. In the early–mid 1990s, after four decades of phenomenal growth, industrial output declined as Japan experienced its worst recession for half a century.

JORDAN

STATUS: Kingdom
AREA: 90,650 sq km (35,000 sq miles)
POPULATION: 4,291,000
ANNUAL NATURAL INCREASE: 5.8%
CAPITAL: Amman ('Ammān)
LANGUAGE: Arabic
RELIGION: 90% Sunni Muslim, Christian and Shi'ite Muslim minorities
CURRENCY: Jordanian dinar (JOD)
ORGANIZATIONS: Arab League, UN

Jordan, one of the few kingdoms in the Middle East, is mostly desert, but has fertile pockets. The climate is predominantly arid. Temperatures rise to 49°C (120°F) in the eastern valleys but it is cooler and wetter in the west. Fruit and vegetables account for 20 per cent of Jordan's exports and phosphate, the most valuable mineral, accounts for over 40 per cent of export revenue. Amman is the manufacturing centre, processing bromide and potash from the Dead Sea. Other important industries are food processing and textiles.

KAZAKHSTAN

STATUS: Republic
AREA: 2,717,300 sq km (1,048,880 sq miles)
POPULATION: 17,035,000
ANNUAL NATURAL INCREASE: 1.0%
CAPITAL: Alma-Ata
LANGUAGE: Kazakh, Russian
RELIGION: Muslim majority, Orthodox minority
CURRENCY: tenge
ORGANIZATIONS: CIS, UN

Stretching across central Asia, Kazakhstan is Russia's southern neighbour. Consisting of lowlands, hilly plains and plateaux, with small mountainous areas, the country has a continental climate with hot summers (30°C or 86°F in July) alternating with equally extreme winters. Exceptionally rich in raw materials, extractive industries have played a major role in the country's economy. Vast oil and gas reserves near the Caspian Sea are now being exploited. Rapid industrialization in recent years has focused on iron and steel, cement, chemicals, fertilizers and consumer goods. Although three-quarters of all agricultural land is used for pasture, the nomadic ways of the Kazakh people have all but disappeared. Economic development during the Soviet period brought a massive influx of outside labour which swamped the indigenous population. The proportion of Kazakhs employed in the industrial sector has, until recently, been small, but with the move to towns and better training, the balance is starting to be redressed. Since Kazakhstan's independence in 1991, its economic prospects appear favourable; but the Soviet legacy includes many environmental problems, such as the ruthless exploitation of the Aral Sea for irrigation.

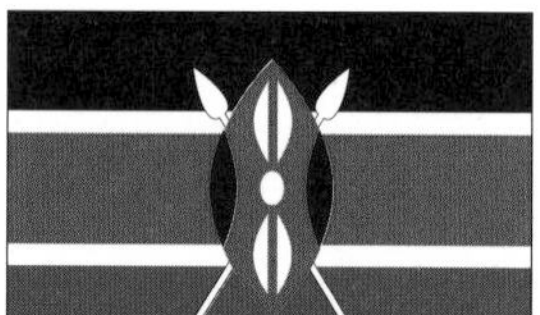

KENYA

STATUS: Republic
AREA: 582,645 sq km (224,900 sq miles)
POPULATION: 25,700,000
ANNUAL NATURAL INCREASE: 3.5%
CAPITAL: Nairobi
LANGUAGE: Kiswahili, English, Kikuyu, Luo
RELIGION: majority traditional beliefs, 25% Christian, 6% Muslim
CURRENCY: Kenya shilling (KES)
ORGANIZATIONS: Comm., OAU, UN

Kenya lies on the equator but as most of the country is on a high plateau the temperatures range from 10–27°C (50–81°F). Rainfall varies from 760–2,500 mm (30–98 inches) depending on altitude. Arable land is scarce but agriculture is the only source of livelihood for over three-quarters of the population. Tea, coffee, flowers and vegetables are the main products for export. Tea, however, has replaced coffee as the chief export and is second only to tourism as a source of foreign revenue. Manufacturing, centred at Nairobi and Mombasa, is dominated by food processing.

KIRGHIZIA (KYRGYZSTAN)

STATUS: Republic
AREA: 198,500 sq km (76,620 sq miles)
POPULATION: 4,502,000
ANNUAL NATURAL INCREASE: 1.7%
CAPITAL: Bishkek
LANGUAGE: Kirghizian, Russian
RELIGION: Muslim
CURRENCY: som
ORGANIZATIONS: CIS, UN

Located in the heart of Asia, to the south of Kazakhstan, Kirghizia is a mountainous country. Traditionally an agrarian-based economy with stock-raising prevalent, the country underwent rapid industrialization during the Soviet period becoming a major producer of machinery and, more recently, producing consumer goods. Valuable mineral deposits include gold, silver, antimony, mercury with the gold deposits believed to be among the world's largest. The cultivation of cotton, sugar beet, tobacco and opium poppies is expanding and provides the basis for a growing processing industry. Independence came unexpectedly in 1991, although Kirghizia had long wanted to control its own affairs.

KIRIBATI

STATUS: Republic
AREA: 717 sq km (277 sq miles)
POPULATION: 72,298
ANNUAL NATURAL INCREASE: 2.1%
CAPITAL: Bairiki (on Tarawa Atoll)
LANGUAGE: I-Kirbati, English
RELIGION: Christian majority
CURRENCY: Australian dollar (AUD)
ORGANIZATIONS: Comm., UN

Kiribati consists of 16 Gilbert Islands, eight Phoenix Islands, three Line Islands and Ocean Island. These four groups are spread over 5 million sq km (1,930,000 miles) in the central and west Pacific. The temperature is a constant 27°–32°C (80–90°F). The islanders grow coconut, breadfruit, bananas and babia (a coarse vegetable). Copra is a major export and fish, particularly tuna, accounts for one-third of total exports. Main imports are machinery and manufactured goods.

KOREA, NORTH

STATUS: Republic
AREA: 122,310 sq km (47,210 sq miles)
POPULATION: 22,618,000
ANNUAL NATURAL INCREASE: 1%
CAPITAL: P'yŏngyang
LANGUAGE: Korean
RELIGION: Chundo Kyo, Buddhism, Confucianism, Daoism
CURRENCY: North Korean won (KPW)
ORGANIZATIONS: OIEC, UN

High, rugged mountains and deep valleys typify North Korea. Climate is extreme with severe winters and warm, sunny summers. Cultivation is limited to the river valley plains where rice, millet, maize and wheat are the principal crops. North Korea, rich in minerals including iron ore and copper, has developed a heavy industrial base. Industry has, however, since the early 1990s, been severely curtailed, firstly by the loss of Soviet aid following the break-up of the Soviet Union and then by losing imports through its isolationist policies and secretive nuclear industries. Its coal supplies, the main energy source for factories, are running out. Complete economic collapse is only salvaged by remittances from Koreans in Japan.

KOREA, SOUTH

STATUS: Republic
AREA: 98,445 sq km (38,000 sq miles)
POPULATION: 44,190,000
ANNUAL NATURAL INCREASE: 1.9%
CAPITAL: Seoul (Sŏul)
LANGUAGE: Korean
RELIGION: 26% Mahayana Buddhism, 22% Christian, Confucianism, Daoism, Chundo Kyo
CURRENCY: won (KPW)
ORGANIZATIONS: Col. Plan, UN

The terrain of South Korea, although mountainous, is less rugged than that of North Korea. The flattest parts lie along the west coast and the extreme south of the peninsula. Its climate is continental, with an average temperature range of -5°C (23°F) in winter to 27°C (81°F) in summer. The majority of the population live in the arable river valleys and along the coastal plain. Agriculture is very primitive, with rice the principal crop. Tungsten, coal and iron ore are the main mineral deposits. Despite having to import oil and industrial materials, the country is a major industrial nation producing iron and steel, textiles, aircraft, chemicals, machinery, vehicles and, in recent years, specializing in electronics and computers. South Korea, with Japan, leads the world in ship-building.

KUWAIT

STATUS: State
AREA: 24,280 sq km (9,370 sq miles)
POPULATION: 1,500,000
ANNUAL NATURAL INCREASE: -2.3%
CAPITAL: Kuwait (Al Kuwayt)
LANGUAGE: Arabic, English
RELIGION: 95% Muslim, 5% Christian and Hindu

CURRENCY: Kuwaiti dinar (KWD)
ORGANIZATIONS: Arab League, UN

Kuwait comprises low, undulating desert, with summer temperatures as high as 52°C (126°F). Since the discovery of oil, Kuwait has been transformed into one of the world's wealthiest nations, exporting oil to Japan, France, the Netherlands and the UK since 1946. The natural gas fields have also been developed. Other industries include fishing (particularly shrimp), food processing, chemicals and building materials. In agriculture, the aim is to produce half the requirements of domestic vegetable consumption by expanding the irrigated area. The invasion and attempted annexation of Kuwait by Iraq in 1990–1 had severe effects on the country's economy, but by 1994 the oil industry was restored to its pre-Gulf war efficiency.

LAOS

STATUS: Republic
AREA: 236,725 sq km (91,375 sq miles)
POPULATION: 4,469,000
ANNUAL NATURAL INCREASE: 2.9%
CAPITAL: Vientiane (Viangchan)
LANGUAGE: Lao, French, tribal languages
RELIGION: Buddhist majority, Christian and animist minorities
CURRENCY: kip (LAK)
ORGANIZATIONS: Col. Plan, UN

Laos is a landlocked, mostly mountainous and forested country in Indo-China. Temperatures range from 15°C (59°F) in winter, to 32°C (90°F) before the rains, and 26°C (79°F) during the rainy season from May to October. Most of the sparse population are subsistence farmers growing rice, maize, sweet potatoes and tobacco. Mineral resources include tin, iron ore, gold, bauxite and lignite. The major exports are coffee, tin and teak. Almost constant warfare since 1941 has hindered any possible industrial development, and Laos has become one of the world's poorest countries.

LATVIA

STATUS: Republic
AREA: 63,700 sq km (24,590 sq miles)
POPULATION: 2,577,000
ANNUAL NATURAL INCREASE: 0.0%
CAPITAL: Riga
LANGUAGE: Latvian, Lithuanian, Russian
RELIGION: Lutheran, Roman Catholic and Orthodox minorities
CURRENCY: roublis (Latvian rouble), lats
ORGANIZATIONS: UN

Latvia is situated on the shores of the Baltic Sea and the Gulf of Riga. Forests cover more than a third of the total territory, a second third being made up of meadows and marsh, and there are some 4,000 lakes. Farmland supports dairy and meat production and grain crops. The country possesses no mineral resources of any value. Industrial development has been sustained by a massive influx of Russian labour since Latvia's incorporation into the Soviet Union in 1940. Under the Soviets, Latvia was assigned the production of consumer durables such as refrigerators and motorcycles as well as ships, rolling stock and power generators. Latvia regained its independence in 1991. The main industries are now radio engineering, electronics, engineering, instruments and industrial robots.

LEBANON

STATUS: Republic
AREA: 10,400 sq km (4,015 sq miles)
POPULATION: 2,838,000
ANNUAL NATURAL INCREASE: 2.3%
CAPITAL: Beirut (Beyrouth)
LANGUAGE: Arabic, French, English
RELIGION: 62% Shi'a and Sunni Muslim, 38% Roman Catholic and Maronite Christian
CURRENCY: Lebanese pound (LBP)
ORGANIZATIONS: Arab League, UN

Physically, Lebanon can be divided into four main regions: a narrow coastal plain; a narrow, fertile interior plateau; the west Lebanon (Jebel Liban) and the Anti-Lebanon (Jebel esh Sharqi) mountains. It has a Mediterranean climate. Trade and tourism have been severely affected by civil war for 17 years from 1975. Agriculture accounts for nearly half of employment and cement, fertilisers, jewelry, sugar and tobacco products are all manufactured on a small scale.

LESOTHO

STATUS: Kingdom
AREA: 30,345 sq km (11,715 sq miles)
POPULATION: 1,836,000
ANNUAL NATURAL INCREASE: 2.7%
CAPITAL: Maseru
LANGUAGE: Sesotho, English
RELIGION: 80% Christian
CURRENCY: loti (LSL), S African rand (ZAR)
ORGANIZATIONS: Comm., OAU, UN

Lesotho, formerly Basutoland, is completely encircled by South Africa. This small country is rugged and mountainous, with southern Africa's highest mountain, Thabana Ntlenyana (3,482 m or 11,424 feet) to be found in the east of the Drakensberg. From these peaks the land slopes westwards in the form of dissected plateaux. The climate is generally sub-tropical although influenced by altitude; rainfall, sometimes variable, falls mainly in the summer months. Because of the terrain, agriculture is limited to the lowlands and foothills. Sorghum, wheat, barley, maize, oats and legumes are the main crops. Cattle, sheep and goats graze on the highlands.

LIBERIA

STATUS: Republic
AREA: 11,370 sq km (42,990 sq miles)
POPULATION: 2,580,000
ANNUAL NATURAL INCREASE: 3.1%
CAPITAL: Monrovia
LANGUAGE: English, tribal languages
RELIGION: traditional beliefs, Christian, 5% Muslim
CURRENCY: Liberian dollar (LRD)
ORGANIZATIONS: ECOWAS, OAU, UN

The west African republic of Liberia is the only nation in Africa never to have been ruled by a foreign power. The hot and humid coastal plain with its savannah vegetation and mangrove swamps rises gently towards the Guinea Highlands, and the interior is densely covered by tropical rainforest. Until the civil war, which ravaged the country, broke out in 1989 the country enjoyed some prosperity from its rubber plantations, rich iron ore deposits, diamonds and gold. Liberia has the world's largest merchant fleet due to its flag of convenience register and this is the only source of revenue relatively unscathed by the war.

LIBYA

STATUS: Republic
AREA: 1,759,540 sq km (679,180 sq miles)
POPULATION: 4,875,000
ANNUAL NATURAL INCREASE: 3.6%
CAPITAL: Tripoli (Ţarābulus)
LANGUAGE: Arabic, Italian, English
RELIGION: Sunni Muslim
CURRENCY: Libyan dinar (LYD)
ORGANIZATIONS: Arab League, OAU, OPEC, UN

Libya is situated on the lowlands of north Africa which rise southwards from the Mediterranean Sea. Ninety-five per cent of its territory is hot, dry desert or semi-desert with average rainfall of less then 130 mm (5 inches). The coastal plains, however, have a more moist Mediterranean climate with annual rainfall of around 200–610 mm (8–24 inches). In these areas, a wide range of crops are cultivated including grapes, groundnuts, oranges, wheat and barley. Only 30 years ago Libya was classed as one of the world's poorest nations but the exploitation of oil has transformed Libya's economy and now accounts for over 95 per cent of its exports.

LIECHTENSTEIN

STATUS: Principality
AREA: 160 sq km (62 sq miles)
POPULATION: 30,000
ANNUAL NATURAL INCREASE: 1.1%
CAPITAL: Vaduz
LANGUAGE: Alemannish, German
RELIGION: 87% Roman Catholic
CURRENCY: franken (Swiss franc)(CHF)
ORGANIZATIONS Council of Europe, EFTA, UN

Situated in the central Alps between Switzerland and Austria, Liechtenstein is one of the smallest states in Europe. Its territory is divided into two zones – the flood plains of the Rhine to the north and Alpine mountain ranges to the southeast, where cattle are reared. Liechtenstein's other main sources of revenue comprise light industry, chiefly the manufacture of precision instruments, and also textile production, food products, tourism, postage stamps and a fast-growing banking sector.

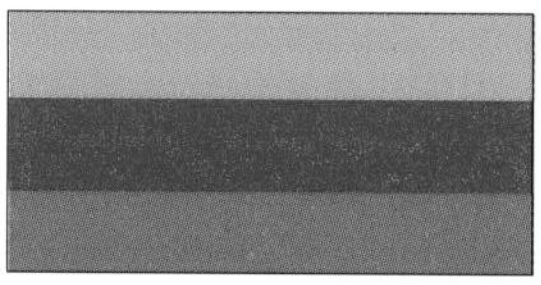

LITHUANIA

STATUS: Republic
AREA: 65,200 sq km (25,165 sq miles)
POPULATION: 3,742,000
ANNUAL NATURAL INCREASE: 0.7%
CAPITAL: Vilnius
LANGUAGE: Lithuanian, Russian, Polish
RELIGION: 80% Roman Catholic
CURRENCY: litas
ORGANIZATIONS: Council of Europe, UN

Lithuania is one of the three small ex-Soviet states lying on the shores of the Baltic Sea. The country consists of a low-lying plain with many lakes. Its climate is transitional, ranging between the oceanic type of western Europe and continental conditions. Temperatures range between -5–-3°C (24–28°F) in winter to 17–18°C (62–66°F) in summer. There is on average 510 mm–610 mm (20–24 inches) of rainfall per year. Agriculture is dominated by beef and dairy produce; major crops are potatoes and flax. There is a large fishing industry. Industrial products include paper, chemicals, electronics and electrical goods. After almost 50 years' involuntary incorporation into the Soviet Union, Lithuania regained its independence in 1991. The economy is still linked to ex-Soviet countries and the change to a market economy is slow.

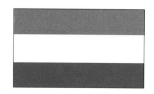

LUXEMBOURG

STATUS: Grand Duchy
AREA: 2,585 sq km (998 sq miles)
POPULATION: 395,200
ANNUAL NATURAL INCREASE: 0.8%
CAPITAL: Luxembourg
LANGUAGE: Letzeburgish, French, German
RELIGION: 95% Roman Catholic
CURRENCY: Luxembourg franc (LUF)
Belgian Franc (BEF)
ORGANIZATIONS: Council of Europe, EEA, EU, NATO, OECD, UN, WEU

The Grand Duchy of Luxembourg is situated between France, Belgium and Germany. The climate is mild and temperate with rainfall ranging from 700–1,000 mm (28–40 inches) a year. Just over half the land is arable, mainly cereals, dairy produce and potatoes. Wine is produced in the Moselle valley. Iron ore is found in the south and is the basis of the thriving steel industry. Other industries are textiles, chemicals and pharmaceutical products. Banking and financial services are growing sectors.

MACAU (MACAO)

STATUS: Chinese Territory under Portuguese Administration
AREA: 16 sq km (6 sq miles)
POPULATION: 374,000
CAPITAL: Macau

MACEDONIA
Former Yugoslav Republic of,

STATUS: Republic
AREA: 25,715 sq km (9,925 sq miles)
POPULATION: 2,066,000
ANNUAL NATURAL INCREASE: 1.1%
CAPITAL: Skopje
LANGUAGE: Macedonian, Albanian
RELIGION: Orthodox
CURRENCY: denar
ORGANIZATIONS: UN, Council of Europe (non-voting member)

The landlocked Balkan state of the Former Yugoslav Republic of Macedonia is a rugged country crossed from north to south by the Vardar valley. The climate is continental with fine hot summers but bitterly cold winters. The economy is basically agricultural. Cereals, tobacco, fruit and vegetables are grown and livestock raised. Heavy industries include chemicals and textiles, which are the county's major employers. Following a Greek economic blockade in 1994, heavy industry – which had already declined through the loss of markets in other former Yugoslav republics – suffered further collapse.

MADAGASCAR

STATUS: Republic
AREA: 594,180 sq km (229,345 sq miles)
POPULATION: 12,827
ANNUAL NATURAL INCREASE: 3.1%
CAPITAL: Antananarivo
LANGUAGE: Malagasy, French, English
RELIGION: 47% animist, 48% Christian, 2% Muslim
CURRENCY: Malagasy franc (MGF)
ORGANIZATIONS: OAU, UN

Madagascar, the world's fourth largest island, is situated 400 km (250 miles) east of the Mozambique coast. The terrain consists largely of a high plateau with steppe and savannah vegetation and desert in the south. Much of the hot humid east coast is covered by tropical rainforest – here rainfall reaches 1,500–2,000 mm (59–79 inches) per annum. Although farming is the occupation of about 85 per cent of the population, only 3 per cent of the land is cultivated. Coffee and vanilla are the major exports, and the shellfish trade is growing rapidly. Much of Madagascar's unique plant and animal life are under increasing threat due to widespread deforestation, caused by the rapid development of forestry and soil erosion.

MADEIRA

STATUS: Self-governing Island Region of Portugal
AREA: 796 sq km (307 sq miles)
POPULATION: 253,400
CAPITAL: Funchal

MALAWI

STATUS: Republic
AREA: 94,080 sq km (35,315 sq miles)
POPULATION: 8,823,000
ANNUAL NATURAL INCREASE: 3.4%

CAPITAL: Lilongwe
LANGUAGE: Chichewa, English
RELIGION: traditional beliefs majority, 10% Roman Catholic, 10% Protestant
CURRENCY: kwacha (MWK)
ORGANIZATIONS: Comm., OAU, UN

Malawi is located at the southern end of the east African Rift Valley. The area around Lake Malawi is tropical and humid with swampy vegetation. In the highlands to the west and southeast conditions are cooler. Malawi has an intensely rural economy – 96 per cent of the population work on the land. Maize is the main subsistence crop, and tea, tobacco, sugar and groundnuts are the main exports. Malawi has deposits of both coal and bauxite, but they are under-exploited at present. Manufacturing industry concentrates on consumer goods and building and construction materials. All energy is produced by hydro-electric power.

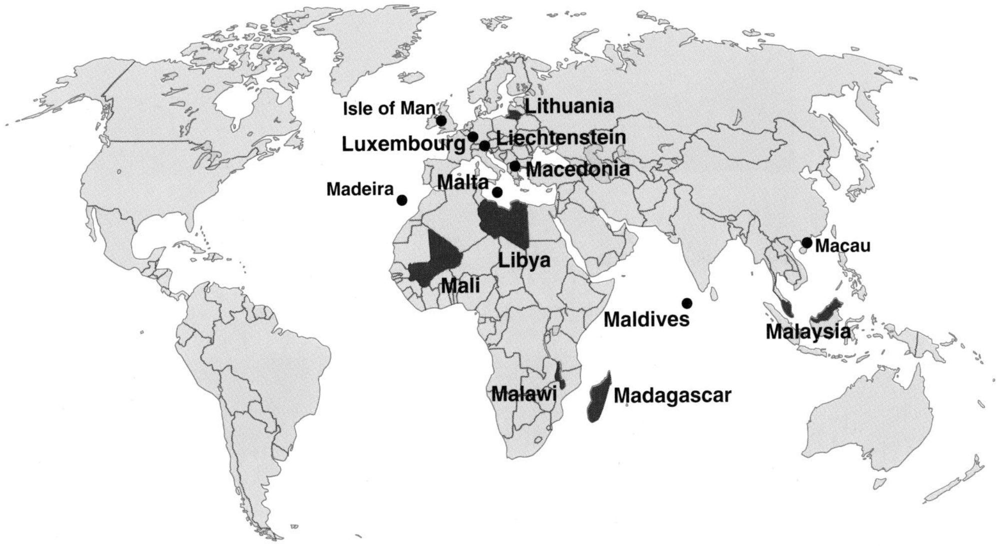

MALAYSIA

STATUS: Federation
AREA: 332,665 sq km (128,405 sq miles)
POPULATION: 18,606,000
ANNUAL NATURAL INCREASE: 2.5%
CAPITAL: Kuala Lumpur
LANGUAGE: 58% Bahasa Malaysian, English, Chinese
RELIGION: 53% Muslim, 25% Buddhist, Hindu, Christian and animist minorities
CURRENCY: Malaysian dollar or ringgit (MYR)
ORGANIZATIONS: ASEAN, Col. Plan, Comm., UN

The Federation of Malaysia consists of two separate parts; west Malaysia is located on the Malay Peninsula, while east Malaysia consists of Sabah and Sarawak on the island of Borneo 700 km (435 miles) across the South China Sea. Despite this distance, both areas share a similar landscape, which is mountainous and covered with lush tropical rainforest. The climate is tropical, hot and humid all the year round, with annual average rainfall of 2,500 mm (98 inches). At one time the economy was dominated by tin, rubber and timber. Now manufactured goods, in particular electronics, account for over two-thirds of the nation's exports in terms of value. Malaysia is rich in natural resources and other major exports include crude oil, timber, palm oil, pepper, rubber and tin. The fast-growing industrial sector demands increased power supplies which are being met by new power stations and hydro-electric power projects.

PENINSULAR MALAYSIA

STATUS: State
AREA: 131,585 sq km (50,790 sq miles)
POPULATION: 15,286,098
CAPITAL: Kuala Lumpur

SABAH

STATUS: State
AREA: 76,115 sq km (29,380 sq miles)
POPULATION: 1,736,902
CAPITAL: Kota Kinabalu

SARAWAK

STATUS: State
AREA: 124,965 sq km (48,235 sq miles)
POPULATION: 1,583,000
CAPITAL: Kuching

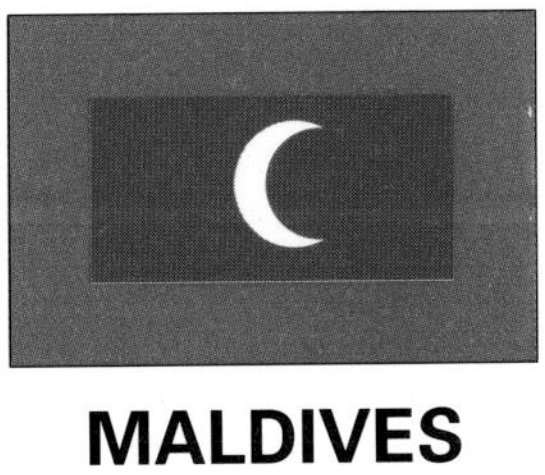

MALDIVES

STATUS: Republic
AREA: 298 sq km (115 sq miles)
POPULATION: 238,363
ANNUAL NATURAL INCREASE: 3.3%
CAPITAL: Male
LANGUAGE: Dhivehi
RELIGION: Sunni Muslim majority
CURRENCY: rufiyaa (MVR)
ORGANIZATIONS: Col. Plan, Comm., UN

The Maldives are one of the world's poorest nations. They consist of a series of coral atolls stretching 885 km (550 miles) across the Indian Ocean. Although there are 2,000 islands, only about 215 are inhabited. The main island, Male, is only 1½ miles long. Fishing is the main activity and fish and coconut fibre are both exported. Most staple foods have to be imported but coconuts, millet, cassava, yams and fruit are grown locally. Tourism is developing and this is now the main source of revenue.

MALI

STATUS: Republic
AREA: 1,240,140 sq km (478,695 sq miles)
POPULATION: 9,818,000
ANNUAL NATURAL INCREASE: 2.8%
CAPITAL: Bamako
LANGUAGE: French, native languages
RELIGION: 65% Muslim, 30% traditional beliefs, 1% Christian
CURRENCY: CFA franc (W Africa) (XOF)
ORGANIZATIONS: ECOWAS, OAU, UN

Mali is one of the world's most underdeveloped countries. Over half the area is barren desert. South of Timbuktu (Tombouctou) the savannah-covered plains support a wide variety of wildlife. Most of the population live in the Niger valley and grow cotton, oil seeds and groundnuts. Fishing is important. Mali has few mineral resources, although a gold mine opened in 1994. Droughts have taken their toll of livestock and agriculture. Main exports are cotton, groundnuts and livestock.

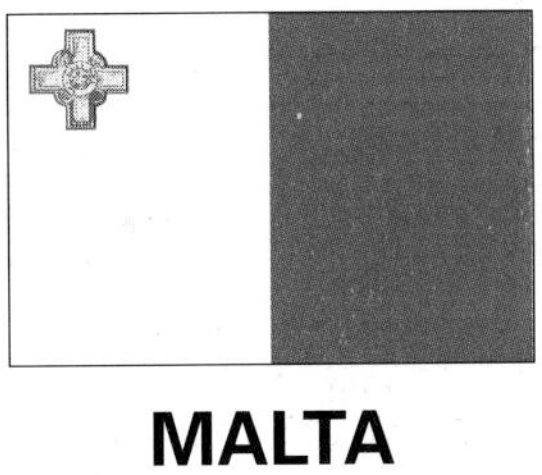

MALTA

STATUS: Republic
AREA: 316 sq km (122 sq miles)
POPULATION: 364,593
ANNUAL NATURAL INCREASE: 0.7%
CAPITAL: Valletta
LANGUAGE: Maltese, English, Italian
RELIGION: Roman Catholic majority
CURRENCY: Maltese lira (MTL)
ORGANIZATIONS: Comm., Council of Europe, UN

Malta lies about 96 km (60 miles) south of Sicily, and consists of three islands; Malta, Gozo and Comino. It has a Mediterranean climate with summer temperatures averaging 25°C (77°F). About 40 per cent of the land is under cultivation with wheat, potatoes, tomatoes and vines the main crops. The large natural harbour at Valletta has made it a major transit port, and shipbuilding and repair are traditional industries. Principal exports are machinery, beverages, tobacco, flowers, wine, leather goods and potatoes. Tourism and light manufacturing are booming sectors of the economy.

MAN, ISLE OF

STATUS: British Crown Dependency
AREA: 588 sq km (227 sq miles)
POPULATION: 71,000
CAPITAL: Douglas

MARSHALL ISLANDS

STATUS: Self-governing state in Compact of Free Association with USA
AREA: 605 sq km (234 sq miles)
POPULATION: 48,000
CAPITAL: Majuro
LANGUAGE: English, local languages
RELIGION: Roman Catholic majority
CURRENCY: US dollar (USD)
ORGANIZATIONS: UN

The Marshall Islands, formerly UN Trust Territory under US administration, consist of over 1,000 atolls and islands which in total account for only 181 sq km (70 sq miles) but are spread over a wide area of the Pacific. The climate is hot all year round with a heavy rainfall averaging 4,050 mm (160 inches). Fishing, subsistence farming and tourism provide occupation for most. The economy is heavily dependent on grants from the USA for use of the islands as military bases.

MARTINIQUE

STATUS: Overseas Department of France
AREA: 1,079 sq km (417 sq miles)
POPULATION: 373,000
CAPITAL: Fort-de-France

MAURITANIA

STATUS: Islamic Republic
AREA: 1,030,700 sq km (397,850 sq miles)
POPULATION: 2,143,000
ANNUAL NATURAL INCREASE: 2.7%
CAPITAL: Nouakchott
LANGUAGE: Arabic, French
RELIGION: Muslim
CURRENCY: ouguiya (MRO)
ORGANIZATIONS: Arab League, ECOWAS, OAU, UN

Situated on the west coast of Africa, Mauritania consists of savannah, steppes and vast areas of the Sahara desert. It has high temperatures, low rainfall and frequent droughts. There is very little arable farming except in the Senegal river valley where millet and dates are grown. Most Mauritanians raise cattle, sheep, goats or camels. The country has only one railway which is used to transport the chief export, iron ore, from the mines to the coast at Nouadhibou. Mauritania has substantial copper reserves which are mined at Akjoujt. A severe drought during the last decade decimated the livestock population and forced many nomadic tribesmen into the towns. Coastal fishing contributes nearly 50 per cent of foreign earnings. Exports are almost exclusively confined to iron ore, copper and fish products.

MAURITIUS

STATUS: Republic
AREA: 1,865 sq km (720 sq miles)
POPULATION: 1,098,000
ANNUAL NATURAL INCREASE: 1.1%
CAPITAL: Port Louis
LANGUAGE: English, French Creole, Hindi, Bhojpuri
RELIGION: 51% Hindu, 31% Christian, 17% Muslim
CURRENCY: Mauritian rupee (MUR)
ORGANIZATIONS: Comm., OAU, UN

Mauritius is a mountainous island in the Indian Ocean. It has a varied climate with temperatures ranging from 7–36°C (45–97°F) and annual rainfall of between 1,530–5,080 mm (60–200 inches). The economy of Mauritius once depended wholly on sugar. Although this is still important, with tea as a second crop, earnings from the manufacturing of clothing now surpass those from sugar. Tourism and financial services are also expanding.

MAYOTTE

STATUS: 'Territorial collectivity' of France
AREA: 376 sq km (145 sq miles)
POPULATION: 85,000
CAPITAL: Dzaoudzi

MEXICO

STATUS: Federal Republic
AREA: 1,972,545 sq km (761,400 sq miles)
POPULATION: 89,538,000
ANNUAL NATURAL INCREASE: 1.8%
CAPITAL: Mexico City
LANGUAGE: Spanish
RELIGION: 96% Roman Catholic
CURRENCY: Mexican peso (MXP)
ORGANIZATIONS: NAFTA, OAS, OECD, UN

Mexico consists mainly of mountain ranges and dissected plateaux. The only extensive flat lands are in the Yucatan Peninsula. Temperature and rainfall are modified by altitude – the north is arid but the south is humid and tropical. Mexico has one of the world's fastest growing populations and, with extreme poverty in many rural areas, migration to the cities continues to be prevalent. One-third of the land is used for livestock ranching and only 20 per cent farmed. Communal farms were abolished in 1991 and peasants are encouraged, with private ownership, to vary crops from the traditional corn and beans. Mexico has great mineral wealth, e.g. silver, strontium and gold, but much is still unexploited. There are considerable reserves of oil, natural gas, coal and uranium. Ten years ago petroleum products accounted for 70 per cent of exports. Now oil accounts for 30 per cent and the major exports are manufactured goods from an industrial base of vehicle production, steel, textiles, breweries and food processing. Other exports are coffee, fruit, vegetables and shrimps. Tourism brings in important foreign revenue. Trading should be enhanced by Mexico's decision to join the USA and Canada in the North American Free Trade Association (NAFTA).

MICRONESIA
Federated States of,

STATUS: Self-governing Federation of States in Compact of Free Association with USA
AREA: 702 sq km (271 sq miles)
POPULATION: 109,000
ANNUAL NATURAL INCOME: 2.4%
CAPITAL: Palikir
LANGUAGE: English, eight indigenous languages
RELIGION: Christian majority
CURRENCY: US dollar (USD)
ORGANIZATIONS: UN

Micronesia, a former UN Trust Territory administered by the USA, is a federation of 607 islands and atolls spread over some 3,200 km (2,000 miles) of the Pacific. Being near the equator, the climate is hot and humid all year round with a high annual rainfall of 9,300 mm (194 inches). Subsistence farming and fishing are the traditional occupations while income is derived from the export of phosphates and copper, a growing tourist industry and revenue from foreign fleets fishing within its territorial waters.

MOLDOVA

STATUS: Republic
AREA: 33,700 sq km (13,010 sq miles)
POPULATION: 4,356,000
ANNUAL NATURAL INCREASE: 0.6%
CAPITAL: Kishinev
LANGUAGE: Moldovan, Russian, Romanian
RELIGION: Orthodox
CURRENCY: rouble
ORGANIZATIONS: CIS, UN

A country of hilly plains, Moldova enjoys a warm and dry climate with relatively mild winters. Temperatures range from 5–7°C (23–26°F) during winter , to 20–23°C (68°–72°F) for summer and rainfall averages 305–457mm (12–18 inches) per year. It has very fertile soil, so arable farming dominates agricultural output with viticulture, fruit and vegetables especially important. Sunflower seeds are the main industrial crop; wheat and maize the chief grain crops. Traditionally, food processing has been the major industry but recently light machine building and metal working industries have been expanding. Moldova, part of the Soviet Union between 1939 and 1991, has close ethnic, linguistic and historical ties with neighbouring Romania. Any moves towards re-unification have been fiercely resisted by the Russian minority in the eastern region of Trans-Dniester.

MONACO

STATUS: Principality
AREA: 1.6 sq km (0.6 sq miles)
POPULATION: 28,000
ANNUAL NATURAL INCREASE: 1.4%
CAPITAL: Monaco-ville
LANGUAGE: French, Monegasque, Italian, English
RELIGION: 90% Roman Catholic
CURRENCY: French franc (FRF)
ORGANIZATIONS: UN

The tiny principality is the world's smallest independent state after the Vatican City. It occupies a rocky peninsula on the French Mediterranean coast near the Italian border and is backed by the Maritime Alps. The climate is Mediterranean. It comprises the towns of Monaco, la Condamine, Fontvieille and Monte Carlo. Most revenue comes from tourism, casinos, light industry and financial services. Land has been reclaimed from the sea to extend the area available for commercial development.

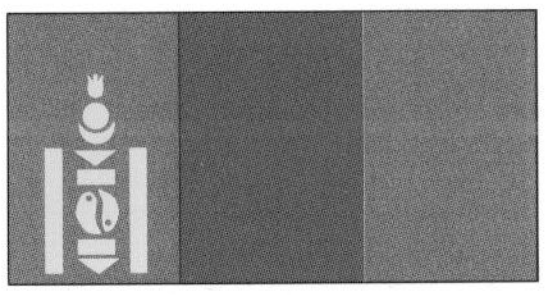

MONGOLIA

STATUS: People's Republic
AREA: 1,565,000 sq km (604,090 sq miles)
POPULATION: 2,310,000
ANNUAL NATURAL INCREASE: 2.8%
CAPITAL: Ulan Bator (Ulaanbaatar)
LANGUAGE: Khalkha Mongolian
RELIGION: some Buddhist Lamaism
CURRENCY: tugrik (MNT)
ORGANIZATIONS: OIEC, UN

Situated between China and the Russian Federation, Mongolia has one of the lowest population densities in the world. Much of the country consists of a high undulating plateau reaching 1,500 m (4,920 feet) covered with grassland. To the north, mountain ranges reaching 4,231 m (13,881 feet) bridge the border with the Russian Federation, and to the south is the vast Gobi desert. The climate is very extreme with January temperatures falling to -34°C (-29°F). Mongolia is predominantly a farming economy, based on rearing cattle and horses. Its natural resources include some oil, rich coal deposits, iron ore, gold , tin and copper. About half the country's exports originate from the Erdanet copper mine. The break-up of the Soviet Union in 1991 brought an end to a partnership whereby Mongolia supplied raw materials in exchange for aid. A year later communism was abandoned. The country is now forced to reform its economy, but is isolated and in need of investment.

MONTSERRAT

STATUS: UK Crown Colony
AREA: 106 sq km (41 sq miles)
POPULATION: 11,000
CAPITAL: Plymouth

MOROCCO

STATUS: Kingdom
AREA: 710,895 sq km
(274,414 sq miles)
POPULATION: 26,318,000
ANNUAL NATURAL INCREASE: 2.5%
CAPITAL: Rabat
LANGUAGE: Arabic, French, Spanish, Berber
RELIGION: Muslim majority, Christian
and Jewish minorities
CURRENCY: Moroccan dirham (MAD)
ORGANIZATIONS: Arab League, UN

One-third of Morocco consists of the Atlas Mountains, reaching 4,165 m (13,665 feet). Beyond the coastal plains and the mountains lies the Sahara. The north of the country has a Mediterranean climate with some winter rainfall, but elsewhere conditions are mostly desert like and arid. Agriculture has diversified in recent years and as well as tomatoes and citrus fruits exports now include a variety of fruit and vegetables. Morocco has considerable phosphate deposits, which in value account for a quarter of total exports. Manufacturing industries include textiles, leather, food processing and chemicals and a growing mechanical and electronic sector. Income from tourism and remittances from Moroccans abroad are the main sources of foreign revenue.

MOZAMBIQUE

STATUS: Republic
AREA: 784,755 sq km
(302,915 sq miles)
POPULATION: 14,872,000
ANNUAL NATURAL INCREASE: 2.7%
CAPITAL: Maputo
LANGUAGE: Portuguese, tribal languages
RELIGION: majority traditional beliefs,
15% Christian, 15% Muslim
CURRENCY: metical (MZM)
ORGANIZATIONS: OAU, UN

The ex-Portuguese colony of Mozambique consists of a large coastal plain, rising towards plateaux and mountain ranges which border Malawi, Zambia and Zimbabwe. The highlands in the north reach 2,436 m (7,992 feet). The climate is tropical on the coastal plain, although high altitudes make it cooler inland. Over 90 per cent of the population are subsistence farmers cultivating coconuts, cashews, cotton, maize and rice. Cashew nuts and shrimps are the main exports. Mozambique also acts as an entrepôt, handling exports from South Africa, and landlocked Zambia and Malawi. Natural resources include large reserves of coal, also iron ore, copper, bauxite, gold and offshore gas, but most are unexploited.

NAMIBIA

STATUS: Republic
AREA: 825,419 sq km
(318,614 sq miles)
POPULATION: 1,534,000
ANNUAL NATURAL INCREASE: 3.1%
CAPITAL: Windhoek
LANGUAGE: Afrikaans, German, English,
regional languages
RELIGION: 90% Christian
CURRENCY: Namibian dollar, SA rand
ORGANIZATIONS: Comm., OAU, UN

The southwest African country of Namibia is one of the driest in the world. The Namib desert, on the coast, has less than 50 mm (2 inches) average rainfall per year, the Kalahari, to the northeast, has 100–250 mm (4–10 inches). The vegetation is sparse. Maize and sorghum are grown in the northern highlands and sheep are reared in the south. Namibia, however, is rich in mineral resources, with large deposits of lead, tin and zinc, and the world's largest uranium mine. The rich coastal waters are the basis of a successful fishing industry.

NAURU

STATUS: Republic
AREA: 21.2 sq km (8 sq miles)
POPULATION: 9,919
ANNUAL NATURAL INCREASE: -0.3%
CAPITAL: Yaren
LANGUAGE: Nauruan, English
RELIGION: Nauruan Protestant majority
CURRENCY: Australian dollar (AUD)
ORGANIZATIONS: Comm. (special member)

Nauru, a small island only 19 km (12 miles) in circumference, is situated in the Pacific, 2,100 km (1,3000 miles) northeast of Australia. The flat coastal lowlands, encircled by coral reefs, rise gently to a central plateau. The country was once rich in phosphates which were exported to Australia and Japan. However these deposits will soon become exhausted.

NEPAL

STATUS: Kingdom
AREA: 141,415 sq km (54,585 sq miles)
POPULATION: 20,577,000
ANNUAL NATURAL INCREASE: 2.6%
CAPITAL: Katmandu (Kathmandu)
LANGUAGE: Nepali, Maithir, Bhojpuri
RELIGION: 90% Hindu, 5% Buddhist, 3% Muslim
CURRENCY: Nepalese rupee (NPR)
ORGANIZATIONS: Col. Plan, UN

Nepal is a Himalayan kingdom sandwiched between China and India. Some of the highest mountains in the world, including Everest, are to be found along its northern borders. The climate changes sharply with altitude from the mountain peaks southwards to the Tarai plain. Central Kathmandu varies between 2–30°C (35–86°F). Most rain falls between June and October and can reach 2,500 mm (100 inches). Agriculture concentrates on rice, maize, cattle, buffaloes, sheep and goats. The small amount of industry processes local products, with carpets and clothing showing particular economic growth.

NETHERLANDS

STATUS: Kingdom
AREA: 41,160 sq km (15,890 sq miles)
POPULATION: 15,269,000
ANNUAL NATURAL INCREASE: 0.7%
CAPITAL: Amsterdam
(seat of Government: The Hague)
LANGUAGE: Dutch
RELIGION: 40% Roman Catholic,
30% Protestant, Jewish minority
CURRENCY: gulden (guilder or florin) (NLG)
ORGANIZATIONS: Council of Europe, EEA, EU, NATO, OECD, UN, WEU

The Netherlands is exceptionally low-lying, with about 25 per cent of its territory being reclaimed from the sea. The wide coastal belt consists of flat marshland, mud-flats, sand-dunes and dykes. Further inland, the flat alluvial plain is drained by the Rhine, Maas and Ijssel. A complex network of dykes and canals prevents the area from flooding. To the south and east the land rises. Flat and exposed to strong winds, the Netherlands has a maritime climate with mild winters and cool summers. The Dutch are the leading world producers of dairy goods and also cultivate crops such as cereals, sugar beet and potatoes. Lacking mineral resources, much of the industry of the Netherlands is dependent on natural gas. Most manufacturing industry has developed around Rotterdam, where there are oil refineries, steel-works and chemical and food processing plants.

NETHERLANDS ANTILLES

STATUS: Self-governing Part of Netherlands Realm
AREA: 993 sq km (383 sq miles)
POPULATION: 191,311
CAPITAL: Willemstad

NEW CALEDONIA

STATUS: Overseas Territory of France
AREA: 19,105 sq km (7,375 sq miles)
POPULATION: 164,173
CAPITAL: Nouméa

NEW ZEALAND

STATUS: Commonwealth Nation
AREA: 265,150 sq km (102,350 sq miles)
POPULATION: 3,470,000
ANNUAL NATURAL INCREASE: 0.7%
CAPITAL: Wellington
LANGUAGE: English, Maori
RELIGION: 35% Anglican Christian, 22% Presbyterian, 16% Roman Catholic
CURRENCY: New Zealand dollar (NZD)
ORGANIZATIONS: ANZUS, Col. Plan, Comm., OECD, UN

New Zealand consists of two main and several smaller islands, lying in the south Pacific Ocean. South Island is mountainous, with the Southern Alps running along its length. It has many glaciers and a coast line that is indented by numerous sounds and fjords. On the more heavily populated North Island, mountain ranges, broad fertile valleys and volcanic plateaux predominate. The overall climate is temperate, with an annual average temperature of 9°C (40°F) on South Island and 15°C (59°F) on the North Island. In terms of value the chief exports are meat, dairy produce and forestry products, followed by wood, fruit and vegetables. In the mineral sector there are deposits of coal, iron ore, oil and natural gas. Hydro-electric and geothermal power are well developed. Manufacturing industries are of increasing importance and in the early 1990s tourism expanded rapidly.

NICARAGUA

STATUS: Republic
AREA: 148,000 sq km (57,130 sq miles)
POPULATION: 4,130,000
ANNUAL NATURAL INCREASE: 2.8%
CAPITAL: Managua
LANGUAGE: Spanish
RELIGION: Roman Catholic
CURRENCY: cordoba (NIO)
ORGANIZATIONS: CACM, OAS, UN

Nicaragua, the largest of the Central American republics, is situated between the Caribbean and the Pacific. Active volcanic mountains run parallel with the western coast. The south is dominated by Lakes Managua and Nicaragua. Climate is tropical, with average daily temperatures in excess of 25°C (77°F) throughout the year. On the west coast wet summer months contrast with a dry period from December to April. Agriculture is the main occupation with cotton, coffee, sugar cane and fruit the main exports. Gold, silver and copper are mined.

NIGER

STATUS: Republic
AREA: 1,186,410 sq km (457,955 sq miles)
POPULATION: 8,252,000
ANNUAL NATURAL INCREASE: 3.2%
CAPITAL: Niamey
LANGUAGE: French, Hausa and other native languages
RELIGION: 85% Muslim, 15% traditional beliefs
CURRENCY: CFA franc (W Africa) (XOF)
ORGANIZATIONS: ECOWAS, OAU, UN

Niger is a vast landlocked southern republic. Apart from savannah in the south and in the Niger valley, most of the vast country lies within the Sahara desert. Rainfall is low, and decreases from 560 mm (22 inches) in the south to near zero in the north. Temperatures are above 35°C (95°F) for much of the year. Most of the population are farmers, particularly of cattle, sheep, and goats. Recent droughts have affected both cereals and livestock. The only significant export is uranium. and phosphates, coal, and tungsten are also mined. The economy depends largely on foreign aid.

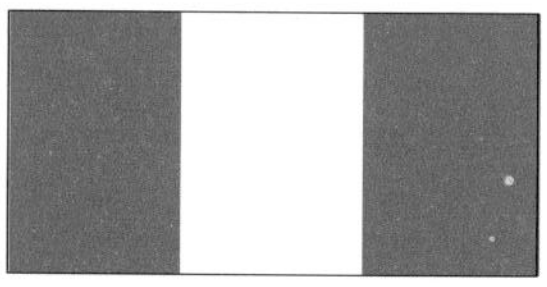

NIGERIA

STATUS: Federal Republic
AREA: 923,850 sq km (356,605 sq miles)
POPULATION: 88,515,000
ANNUAL NATURAL INCREASE: 2.9%
CAPITAL: Abuja

LANGUAGE: English, Hausa, Yoruba, Ibo
RELIGION: Muslim majority, 35% Christian, animist minority
CURRENCY: naira (NGN)
ORGANIZATIONS: Comm., ECOWAS, OAU, OPEC, UN

The most populous nation in Africa, Nigeria is bounded to the north by the Sahara and to the west, east and southeast by tropical rainforest. The southern half of the country is dominated by the Niger and its tributaries, the north by the interior plateaux. Temperatures average 32°C (90°F) with high humidity. From a basic agricultural economy, Nigeria is only slowly being transformed by the vast oil discoveries in the Niger delta and coastal regions, which account for 95 per cent of exports. Gas reserves are relatively underdeveloped.

NIUE

STATUS: Self-governing Territory Overseas in Free Association with New Zealand
AREA: 259 sq km (100 sq miles)
POPULATION: 2,267
CAPITAL: Aloli

NORFOLK ISLAND

STATUS: External Territory of Australia
AREA: 36 sq km (14 sq miles)
POPULATION: 1,977
CAPITAL: Kingston

NORTHERN MARIANA ISLANDS

STATUS: Self-governing Commonwealth of USA
AREA: 471 sq km (182 sq miles)
POPULATION: 45,200
CAPITAL: Saipan

NORWAY

STATUS: Kingdom
AREA: 323,895 sq km (125,025 sq miles)
POPULATION: 4,305,000
ANNUAL NATURAL INCREASE: 0.4%
CAPITAL: Oslo
LANGUAGE: Norwegian, Lappish
RELIGION: 92% Evangelical Lutheran Christian
CURRENCY: Norwegian krone (NOK)
ORGANIZATIONS: Council of Europe, EEA, EFTA, NATO, OECD, UN

Norway is a mountainous country stretching from 58° to 72°N. The climate along its indented western coast is modified by the Gulf Stream, with high rainfall and relatively mild winters. Temperatures average -3.9°C (25°F) in January and 17°C (63°F) in July. Rainfall may be as high as 1,960 mm (79 inches). Most settlements are scattered along the fjords, the coast and around Oslo in the south. Norway is rich in natural resources. Oil and natural gas predominate in exports, but are supplemented by metal products, timber, pulp and paper, fish and machinery. The advanced production of hydro-electric power has helped develop industry, particularly chemicals, metal products and paper.

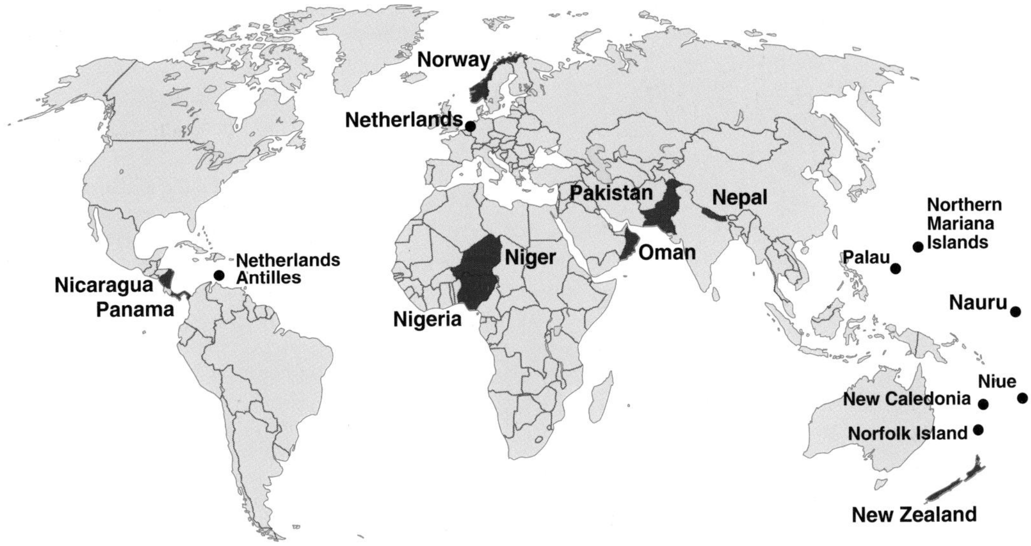

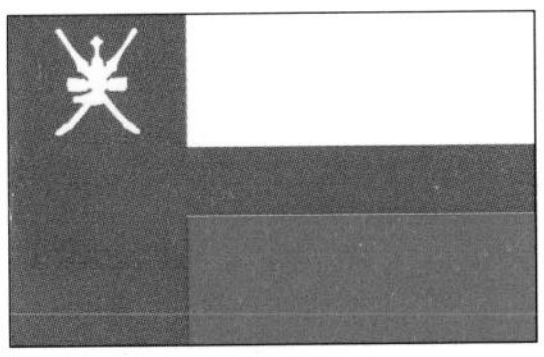

OMAN

STATUS: Sultanate
AREA: 271,950 sq km (104,970 sq miles)
POPULATION: 1,637,000
ANNUAL NATURAL INCREASE: 3.8%
CAPITAL: Muscat (Masqaţ)
LANGUAGE: Arabic, English
RELIGION: 75% Ibadi Muslim, 25% Sunni Muslim
CURRENCY: rial Omani (OMR)
ORGANIZATIONS: Arab League, UN

The Sultanate of Oman occupies the northeast coast of the Arabian peninsula, with an enclave overlooking the Strait of Hormuz. Its desert landscape consists of a coastal plain and low hills rising to plateau in the interior, and has two fertile areas; Batinah in the north and Dhofar in the south. Copper ores are being mined and exported and oil provides over 95 per cent of export revenue. New discoveries of gas suggest that this will eventually supplant oil in importance.

PAKISTAN

STATUS: Republic
AREA: 803,940 sq km (310,320 sq miles)
POPULATION: 119,107,000
ANNUAL NATURAL INCREASE: 3.1%
CAPITAL: Islamabad
LANGUAGE: Urdu, Punjabi, Sindhi, Pushtu, English
RELIGION: 90% Muslim
CURRENCY: Pakistan rupee (PKR)
ORGANIZATIONS Col. Plan, Comm., UN

The landscape of Pakistan is dominated by the river Indus which flows south through the country flanked by the plateau of Balochistan and the Sulaiman mountains to the west and the Thar desert to the east. The climate is arid with temperatures averaging 27°C (80°F). Rainfall can be less than 127 mm (5 inches) in the southwest and only in the northern mountains does it reach appreciable amounts; 900 mm (36 inches). Over 50 per cent of the population are engaged in agriculture which is confined to the irrigated areas near rivers. Main crops are wheat, cotton, maize, rice and sugar cane. There are many types of low-grade mineral deposits, such as coal and copper, which are little developed. Main industries are textiles, food processing and oil refining but these only contribute about 20 per cent to the economy.

PALAU

STATUS: Self-governing state in Compact of Free Association with USA
AREA: 497 sq km (192 sq miles)
POPULATION: 15,450
CAPITAL: Babelthuap

PANAMA

STATUS: Republic
AREA: 78,515 sq km (30,305 sq miles)
POPULATION: 2,535,000
ANNUAL NATURAL INCREASE: 2.1%
CAPITAL: Panama City (Panamá)
LANGUAGE: Spanish, English
RELIGION: Roman Catholic majority
CURRENCY: balboa (PAB), US dollar (USD)
ORGANIZATIONS: OAS, UN

Panama is situated at the narrowest part of central American isthmus. Mountain ranges, reaching heights exceeding 3,000 m (9,800 feet), run the country's length. Much of its tropical forest has now been cleared, but some remains towards the border with Colombia. Its climate is tropical with little variation throughout the year. The average temperature is around 27°C (80°F). There is a rainy season from April to December. Most of its foreign income is earned from revenues derived from the Panama Canal and from a large merchant fleet that is registered in its name. Petroleum products, bananas and shrimps are the main exports.

PAPUA NEW GUINEA

STATUS: Commonwealth Nation
AREA: 462,840 sq km (178,655 sq miles)
POPULATION: 4,056,000
ANNUAL NATURAL INCREASE: 2.3%
CAPITAL: Port Moresby
LANGUAGE: English, Pidgin English,
RELIGION: Pantheist, Christian minority
CURRENCY: kina (PGK)
ORGANIZATIONS: Col. Plan, Comm., UN

Papua New Guinea (the eastern half of New Guinea and neighbouring islands) is a mountainous country. It has an equatorial climate with temperatures of 21–32°C (70–90°F) and annual rainfall of over 2,000 mm (79 inches). The country is rich in minerals, in particular copper, gold and silver, but development is restricted by rainforest and lack of roads. Exports include coconuts, cocoa, coffee, rubber, tea and sugar. Logging was once dominant but exports are now being reduced in order to preserve forest resources.

PARAGUAY

STATUS: Republic
AREA: 406,750 sq km (157,055 sq miles)
POPULATION: 4,500,000
ANNUAL NATURAL INCREASE: 2.9%
CAPITAL: Asunción
LANGUAGE: Spanish, Guarani
RELIGION: 90% Roman Catholic
CURRENCY: guarani (PYG)
ORGANIZATIONS: OAS, UN

Paraguay is a landlocked country in South America with hot rainy summers, when temperatures reach over 27°C (80°F), and mild winters with an average temperature of 18°C (64°F). Lush, fertile plains and heavily forested plateau east of the River Paraguay contrast with the scrubland of the Chaco to the west. Cassava, cotton, soya beans and maize are the main crops but the rearing of livestock – cattle, horses, pigs and sheep – and food processing, dominate the export trade. The largest hydro-electric power dam in the world is at Itaipú, constructed as a joint project with Brazil, and another massive hydro-electric development is being constructed at Yacyreta in conjunction with Argentina.

PERU

STATUS: Republic
AREA: 1,285,215 sq km (496,095 sq miles)
POPULATION: 22,454,000
ANNUAL NATURAL INCREASE: 2.1%
CAPITAL: Lima
LANGUAGE: Spanish, Quechua, Aymara
RELIGION: Roman Catholic majority
CURRENCY: new sol (PES)
ORGANIZATIONS: OAS, UN

Peru exhibits three geographical regions. The Pacific coastal region is very dry but with fertile oases producing cotton, sugar, fruit and fodder crops. This is the most prosperous and heavily populated area and includes the industrial centres around Lima. In the ranges and plateaux of the Andes and in the Amazon lowlands to the northeast, the soils are thin with the inhabitants depending on cultivation and grazing. Poor communications have hindered the development of Peru and there are great differences between the rich and poor. Peru has rich mineral deposits of copper, gold, lead, zinc and silver and there are oil and gas reserves in the interior.

PHILIPPINES

STATUS: Republic
AREA: 300,000 sq km (115,800 sq miles)
POPULATION: 65,650,000
ANNUAL NATURAL INCREASE: 2.3%
CAPITAL: Manila
LANGUAGE: Filipino (Tagalog), English, Spanish, Cebuano
RELIGION: 90% Christian, 7% Muslim
CURRENCY: Philippine peso (PHP)
ORGANIZATIONS: ASEAN, Col. Plan, UN

The Philippine archipelago consists of some 7,000 islands and is subject to earthquakes and typhoons. It has a monsoonal climate, with up to 6,350 mm (250 inches) of rainfall per annum in some areas. This once supported tropical rain forest but, apart from Palawan island, this has now been destroyed. Fishing is important but small farms dominate the economy, producing rice and copra for domestic consumption and other coconut and sugar products for export. Main exports are textiles, fruit and electronic products. Remittances from Filipinos working overseas are important to the economy. There is high unemployment and the extent of poverty is widespread.

PITCAIRN ISLAND

STATUS: UK Dependent Territory
AREA: 45 sq km (17.25 sq miles)
POPULATION: 71
CAPITAL: Adamstown

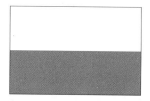

POLAND

STATUS: Republic
AREA: 312,685 sq km (120,695 sq miles)
POPULATION: 38,310,000
ANNUAL NATURAL INCREASE: 0.4%
CAPITAL: Warsaw (Warszawa)
LANGUAGE: Polish
RELIGION: 90% Roman Catholic
CURRENCY: zloty (PLZ)
ORGANIZATIONS: Council of Europe, OIEC, UN,

Much of Poland lies in the north European plain, south of the Baltic Sea. It is a land of woods and lakes, gently rising southwards from the coast towards the Tartry mountains in the south and Sudety mountains in Silesia. The climate is continental with short, warm summers and long severe winters, when average temperatures can drop below freezing point (32°F). Rainfall occurs mainly in the summer months and averages between 520 and 730 mm (21–29 inches). Both agriculture and natural resources play an important part in the economy and Poland is nearly self-sufficient in cereals, sugar beet and potatoes. There are large reserves of coal, copper, sulphur and natural gas. Its major industries are ship-building in the north and the production of machinery, transport equipment, metals and chemicals in the major mining centres of the south. Manufacturing industries in both the private and public sectors are expanding rapidly and the government is committed to a programme of economic reforms and privatization.

PORTUGAL

STATUS: Republic
AREA: 91,630 sq km (35,370 sq miles)
POPULATION: 9,846,000
ANNUAL NATURAL INCREASE: -0.7%
CAPITAL: Lisbon (Lisboa)
LANGUAGE: Portuguese
RELIGION: Roman Catholic majority
CURRENCY: escudo (PTE)
ORGANIZATIONS: Council of Europe, EEA, EU, NATO, OECD, UN, WEU

Portugal occupies the western Atlantic coast of the Iberian Peninsula. The river Tagus, on whose estuary is Lisbon, divides the country physically. In the north the land lies mainly above 4,000 m (1,220 feet) with plateaux cut by westward flowing rivers. Here, the climate is modified by westerly winds and the Gulf Stream. This is reflected in the lush mixed deciduous/coniferous forests. Land to the south is generally less than 300 m (1,000 feet) and the climate becomes progressively more arid further south, with Mediterranean scrub predominating in the far south. A quarter of the population are farmers growing vines, olives, wheat and maize. Wines, cork and fruit are important exports. In industry the chief exports are textiles, clothing, footwear and wood products. Mineral deposits include coal, copper, kaolinite and uranium. Tourism is an important source of revenue, with many visitors coming to the Algarve region in the far south of the country.

PUERTO RICO

STATUS: Self-governing Commonwealth of USA
AREA: 8,960 sq km (3,460 sq miles)
POPULATION: 3,580,000
CAPITAL: San Juan

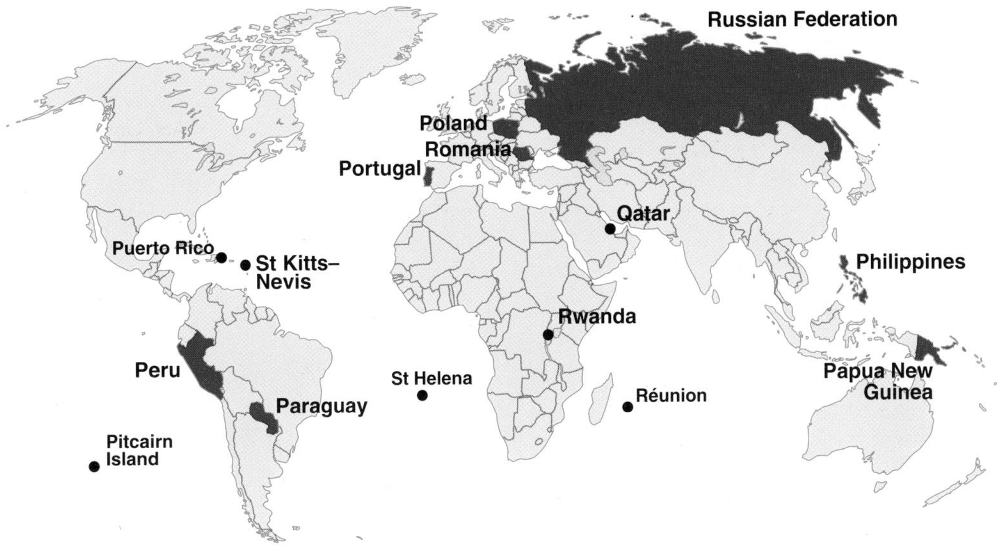

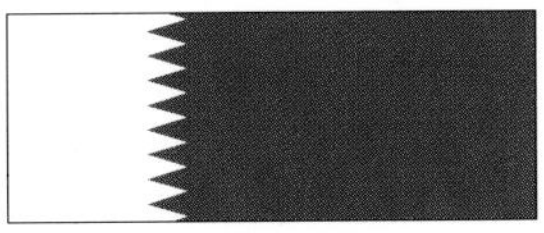

QATAR

STATUS: State
AREA: 11,435 sq km (4,415 sq miles)
POPULATION: 453,000
ANNUAL NATURAL INCREASE: 6%
CAPITAL: Doha (Ad Dawḩah)
LANGUAGE: Arabic, English
RELIGION: Muslim
CURRENCY: Qatari riyal (QAR)
ORGANIZATIONS: Arab League, OPEC, UN

The country occupies all of the Qatar peninsula in the Gulf and is a land of flat, arid desert. July temperatures average 37°C (98°F) and annual rainfall averages 62mm (2.5 inches). The main source of revenue is from the exploitation of oil and gas reserves. The North Field gas reserves are the world's largest single field and the development of these has a high priority.

RÉUNION

STATUS: Overseas Department of France
AREA: 2,510 sq km (969 sq miles)
POPULATION: 624,000
CAPITAL: Saint-Denis

ROMANIA

STATUS: Republic
AREA: 237,500 sq km (91,699 sq miles)
POPULATION: 22,767,000
ANNUAL NATURAL INCREASE: 0.1%
CAPITAL: Bucharest (Bucureşti)
LANGUAGE: Romanian, Magyar
RELIGION: 85% Romanian Orthodox,
CURRENCY: leu (ROL)
ORGANIZATIONS: Council of Europe, OIEC, UN

Romania is dominated by the great curve of the Carpathians, flanked by rich agricultural lowlands and has a continental climate. Forced industrialization has taken the economy from one based on agriculture to one dependent on heavy industry, notably chemicals, metal processing and machine-building. Since the fall of the communist dictatorship in 1989, most land has been privatized and there has been a re-emergence of Romania's traditional agriculture, with exports of cereals, fruit and wine. There are natural resources including oil, gas and minerals but industrial reform is slow and the economy is sluggish. Living standards are among the lowest in Europe.

RUSSIAN FEDERATION

STATUS: Federation
AREA: 17,078,005 sq km (6,592,110 sq miles)
POPULATION: 148,673,000
ANNUAL NATURAL INCREASE: 0.5%
CAPITAL: Moscow (Moskva)
LANGUAGE: Russian
RELIGION: Russian Orthodox, Jewish and Muslim minorities
CURRENCY: rouble
ORGANIZATIONS: CIS, UN

Covering much of east and northeast Europe and all of north Asia, the Russian Federation (Russia) displays an enormous variety of landforms and climates. The Arctic deserts of the north give way to tundra wastes and taiga which cover two-thirds of the country. In the far south, beyond the steppes, some areas assume subtropical and semi-desert landscapes. The majority of the population live west of the north-south spine of the Urals but in recent decades there has been a substantial migration eastwards to the Siberian basin in order to exploit its vast natural resources. Massive oil fields off the east coast of Sakhalin north of Japan and also in the Russian Arctic (Timan Pechora basin) are now to be developed. Russia's extraordinary wealth of natural resources was a key factor in the country's speedy industrialization during the Soviet period. Heavy industry still plays a decisive role in the economy, while light and consumer industries have remained relatively under-developed. Agricultural land covers one-sixth of Russia's territory but there remains great potential for increase through drainage and clearance. By the mid-1980s the Soviet system was finally acknowledged to have reached an impasse, and the failure of the *perestroika* programme for reform precipitated the disintegration of the Soviet Union, which finally broke up in 1991. A transition from a state-run Communist economy to a market economy is taking place. Between 1992 and 1994 70 per cent of state-owned enterprises were privatized and farms are also starting to be re-organized.

RWANDA

STATUS: Republic
AREA: 26,330 sq km (10,165 sq miles)
POPULATION: 7,526,000
ANNUAL NATURAL INCREASE: 3%
CAPITAL: Kigali
LANGUAGE: French, Kinyarwanda (Bantu), tribal languages
RELIGION: 50% animist, 50% Christian (mostly Roman Catholic)
CURRENCY: Rwanda franc (RWF)
ORGANIZATIONS: OAU, UN

Small and isolated, Rwanda supports a high density of population on the mountains and plateaux east of the Rift Valley. It has a tropical climate with a dry season between June and August. Agriculture is basically subsistence with coffee the major export. Tin is mined and there are major natural gas reserves. Since 1990 a civil war has raged between the Tutsi and Hutu tribes, creating many thousands of casualties and well over one million refugees. The country has become reliant on foreign aid, and will require a massive international relief effort to avert disease and famine.

ST HELENA

STATUS: UK Dependent Territory
AREA: 122 sq km (47 sq miles)
POPULATION: 5,564
CAPITAL: Jamestown

ST KITTS-NEVIS

STATUS: Commonwealth State
AREA: 262 sq km (101 sq miles)
POPULATION: 40,618
ANNUAL NATURAL INCREASE: -0.4%
CAPITAL: Basseterre
LANGUAGE: English
RELIGION: Christian (mostly Protestant)
CURRENCY: E Caribbean dollar (XCD)
ORGANIZATIONS: CARICOM, Comm., OAS, UN

St Kitts-Nevis, in the Leeward Islands, comprises two volcanic islands: St Kitts and Nevis. The climate is tropical with temperatures of 16–33°C (61–91°F) and an average annual rainfall of 1,400 mm (55 inches). Main exports are sugar, molasses and cotton. Tourism is an important industry.

ST LUCIA

STATUS: Commonwealth State
AREA: 616 sq km (238 sq miles)
POPULATION: 136,000
ANNUAL NATURAL INCREASE: 1.9%
CAPITAL: Castries
LANGUAGE: English, French patois
RELIGION: 82% Roman Catholic
CURRENCY: E. Caribbean dollar (XCD)
ORGANIZATIONS: Caricom, Comm., OAS, UN

Independent since 1979 this small tropical Caribbean island in the Lesser Antilles grows coconuts, cocoa and fruit. Bananas account for over 40 per cent of export earnings. Main industries are food and drink processing and all consumer goods are imported. Tourism is a major growth sector.

ST PIERRE AND MIQUELON

STATUS: Territorial Collectivity of France
AREA: 241 sq km (93 sq miles)
POPULATION: 6,392
CAPITAL: St Pierre

ST VINCENT AND THE GRENADINES

STATUS: Commonwealth State
AREA: 389 sq km (150 sq miles)
POPULATION: 107,598
ANNUAL NATURAL INCREASE: 0.9%
CAPITAL: Kingstown
LANGUAGE: English
RELIGION: Christian
CURRENCY: E. Caribbean dollar (XCD)
ORGANIZATIONS: Caricom, Comm., OAS, UN

St Vincent in the Lesser Antilles comprises a forested main island and the northern part of the Grenadines. It has a tropical climate. Most exports are foodstuffs: arrowroot, sweet potatoes, coconut products and yams, but the principal crop is bananas. Some sugar cane is grown for the production of rum and other drinks. Tourism is well-established.

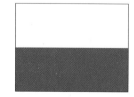

SAN MARINO

STATUS: Republic
AREA: 61 sq km (24 sq miles)
POPULATION: 24,003
ANNUAL NATURAL INCREASE: 1.2%
CAPITAL: San Marino
LANGUAGE: Italian
RELIGION: Roman Catholic
CURRENCY: Italian lira (ITL), San Marino coinage
ORGANIZATIONS: Council of Europe, UN

An independent state within Italy, San Marino straddles a limestone peak in the Apennines south of Rimini. The economy is centred around tourism and the sale of postage stamps. Most of the population are farmers growing cereals, olives and vines and tending herds of sheep and goats.

SÃO TOMÉ AND PRÍNCIPE

STATUS: Republic
AREA: 964 sq km (372 sq miles)
POPULATION: 124,000
ANNUAL NATURAL INCREASE: 2.3%
CAPITAL: São Tomé
LANGUAGE: Portuguese, Fang
RELIGION: Roman Catholic majority
CURRENCY: dobra (STD)
ORGANIZATIONS: OAU, UN

This tiny state, independent from Portugal since 1975, comprises two large and several small islands near the equator, 200 km (125 miles) off west Africa. The climate is tropical with temperatures averaging 25°C (77°F) and rainfall of between 1,000–5,000 mm (40–197 inches). Cocoa (which provides 90 per cent of revenue), coconuts and palm oil are the main crops grown on the rich volcanic soil. Other foods and consumer goods are imported.

SAUDI ARABIA

STATUS: Kingdom
AREA: 2,400,900 sq km (926,745 sq miles)
POPULATION: 16,900,000
ANNUAL NATURAL INCREASE: 3.5%
CAPITAL: Riyadh (Ar Riyāḑ)
LANGUAGE: Arabic
RELIGION: 90% Sunni Muslim, 5% Roman Catholic
CURRENCY: Saudi riyal (SAR)
ORGANIZATIONS: Arab League, OPEC, UN

Saudi Arabia occupies the heart of the vast arid Arabian Peninsula. The country is mostly desert and there are no rivers which flow all year round. To the west, the Hejaz and Asir mountains fringe the Red Sea but even here rainfall rarely exceeds 380 mm (15 inches). Temperatures rise beyond 44°C (111°F) in the summer. The interior plateau slopes gently eastwards down to the Gulf and supports little vegetation. The southeast of the country is well named as the 'Empty Quarter'; it is almost devoid of population. Only in the coastal strips and oases are cereals and date palms grown. Oil is the most important resource – Saudi Arabia has a quarter of the world's known oil reserves – and export commodity and economic development is dependent on its revenue.

SENEGAL

STATUS: Republic
AREA: 196,720 sq km (75,935 sq miles)
POPULATION: 7,970,000
ANNUAL NATURAL INCREASE: 3.0%
CAPITAL: Dakar
LANGUAGE: French, native languages
RELIGION: 94% Sunni Muslim, animist minority
CURRENCY: CFA franc (W Africa) (XOF)
ORGANIZATIONS: ECOWAS, OAU, UN

Senegal is a flat, dry country cut through by the Gambia, Casamance and Senegal rivers. Rainfall rarely exceeds 580 mm (23 inches) on the wetter coast. The interior savannah supports varied wildlife but little agriculture. Cultivation is mainly confined to the south where groundnuts account for nearly half of the agricultural output. Cotton and millet are also grown, but frequent droughts have reduced their value as cash crops. Phosphate mining, ship-repairing, textiles, petroleum products and food processing are the major industries. Both tourism and fishing are becoming increasingly important.

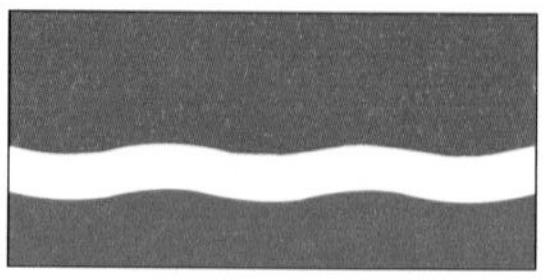

SEYCHELLES

STATUS: Republic
AREA: 404 sq km (156 sq miles)
POPULATION: 72,000
ANNUAL NATURAL INCREASE: 0.8%
CAPITAL: Victoria
LANGUAGE: English, French, Creole
RELIGION: 92% Roman Catholic
CURRENCY: Seychelles rupee (SCR)
ORGANIZATIONS: Comm., OAU, UN

This archipelago in the Indian Ocean comprises over 100 granite or coral islands. Main exports are copra, coconuts and cinnamon and in recent years tea and tuna. All domestic requirements, including most foodstuffs, have to be imported. Tourism has developed rapidly in the 1990s and is now the dominant sector in the economy.

SIERRA LEONE

STATUS: Republic
AREA: 72,325 sq km (27,920 sq miles)
POPULATION: 4,376,000
ANNUAL NATURAL INCREASE: 2.4%
CAPITAL: Freetown
LANGUAGE: English, Krio Temne, Mende
RELIGION: 52% animist, 39% Muslim and 8% Christian

CURRENCY: leone (SLL)
ORGANIZATIONS: Comm., ECOWAS, OAS, UN

Sierra Leone, a former British colony, has a coast dominated by swamps but is essentially a flat plain some 70 miles wide which extends to interior plateaux and mountains. Three-quarters of the population are employed in subsistence farming. Cash crops include cocoa and coffee but the main source of revenue is from minerals. Diamonds, gold, bauxite and iron ore are mined but the most important export is now rutile (titanium ore). Manufacturing in the form of processing local products has developed around Freetown.

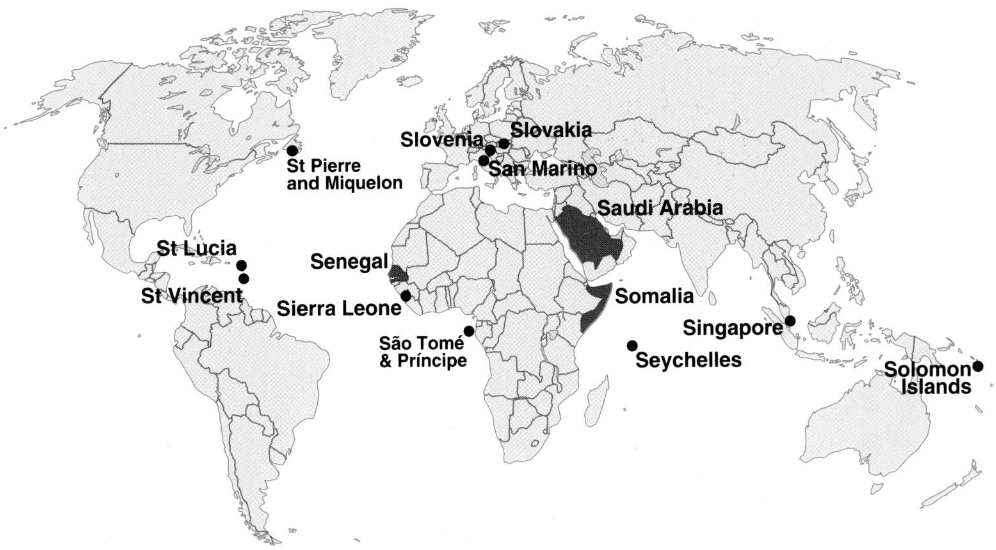

SINGAPORE

STATUS: Republic
AREA: 616 sq km (238 sq miles)
POPULATION: 2,874,000
ANNUAL NATURAL INCREASE: 1.2%
CAPITAL: Singapore
LANGUAGE: Malay, Chinese (Mandarin), Tamil, English
RELIGION: Daoist, Buddist, Muslim, Christian and Hindu
CURRENCY: Singapore dollar (SGD)
ORGANIZATIONS: ASEAN, Col. Plan, Comm., UN

The republic of Singapore, independent from Britain since 1959, has been transformed from an island of mangrove swamps into one of the world's major entrepreneurial centres. The island, connected to Peninsular Malaysia by a man-made causeway, has a tropical, humid climate with 2,240 mm (96 inches) of rain per year. With few natural resources, Singapore depends on manufacturing precision goods, electronic products, financial services and activities associated with its port, which is one of the world's largest.

SLOVAKIA

STATUS: Republic
AREA: 49,035 sq km (18,932 sq miles)
POPULATION: 5,320,000
ANNUAL NATURAL INCREASE: 0.4%
CAPITAL: Bratislava
LANGUAGE: Slovak, Hungarian
RELIGION: Roman Catholic
CURRENCY: Slovak crown or koruna
ORGANIZATIONS: Council of Europe, UN

On 1 January 1993 Czechoslovakia ceased to exist and Slovakia and the Czech Republic came into being. Slovakia's geomorphology is dominated by the Tatry mountains in the north. Bratislava, the capital, lies in the extreme southwest, on the north bank of the Danube. Natural resources include iron ore, copper, antimony, mercury, magnesite and oil. Under Communism large manufacturing complexes developed, many of which specialized in arms and tanks. The end of the Cold War in 1989 brought a collapse in demand for these products. This, and a decline in trade with the Czech Republic, has forced Slovakia to restructure existing industry and look to new developments such as aluminium smelting and car assembly.

SLOVENIA

STATUS: Republic
AREA: 20,250 sq km (7,815 sq miles)
POPULATION: 1,990,000
ANNUAL NATURAL INCREASE: 0.7%
CAPITAL: Ljubljana
LANGUAGE: Slovene
RELIGION: Roman Catholic
CURRENCY: Slovenian tolar (SLT)
ORGANIZATIONS: Council of Europe, UN

The northernmost republic of the former Yugoslav federation, Slovenia, has always been one of the key gateways from the Balkans to central and western Europe. Much of the country is mountainous, its heartland and main centre of population being the Ljubljana basin. The climate generally shows continental tendencies, with warm summers and cold winters, when snow is plentiful on the ground. The small coastal region has a Mediterranean regime. Extensive mountain pastures provide profitable dairy-farming, but the amount of cultivable land is restricted. There are large mercury mines in the northwest and, in recent decades, this area has also developed a broad range of light industries. Combined with tourism, this has given the country a well-balanced economy. After a brief military conflict Slovenia won its independence in 1991.

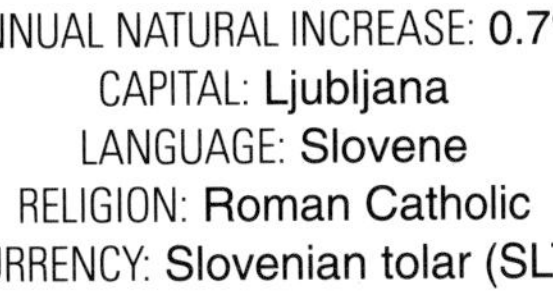

SOLOMON ISLANDS

STATUS: Commonwealth Nation
AREA: 29,790 sq km (11,500 sq miles)
POPULATION: 349,500
ANNUAL NATURAL INCREASE: 2.9%
CAPITAL: Honiara
LANGUAGE: English, Pidgin English, native languages
RELIGION: 95% Christian
CURRENCY: Solomon Islands dollar (SBD)
ORGANIZATIONS: Comm., UN

Situated in the South Pacific Ocean the Solomon Islands consist of a 1400 km (870 miles) archipelago of six main and many smaller islands. The mountainous large islands are covered by tropical rain forest reflecting the high temperatures, on average 22–34°C (72–95°F) and heavy rainfall, about 3,050 mm (120 inches). The main crops are coconuts, cocoa and rice, with copra, timber and palm oil being the main exports. Mineral deposits include reserves of bauxite, gold and phosphate, mined on the small island of Bellona south of Guadalcanal. Once a British protectorate, the Solomons became independent in 1978.

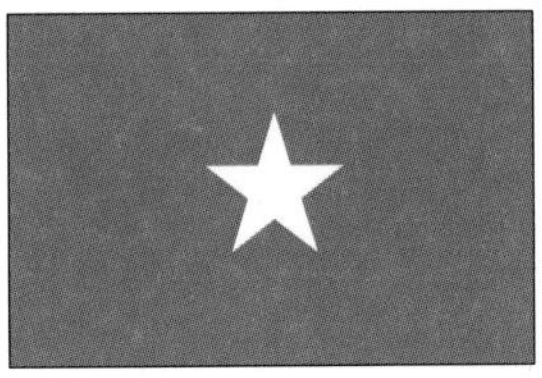

SOMALIA

STATUS: Republic
AREA: 6300,000sq km (243,180 sq miles)
POPULATION: 7,497,000
ANNUAL NATURAL INCREASE: 3.0%
CAPITAL: Mogadishu (Muqdisho)
LANGUAGE: Somali, Arabic, English, Italian
RELIGION: Muslim, Roman Catholic minority
CURRENCY: Somali shilling (SOS)
ORGANIZATIONS: UN, Arab League, OAU

Independent since 1960, Somalia is a hot and arid country in northeast Africa. The semi-desert of the northern mountains contrasts with the plains of the south where the bush country is particularly rich in wildlife. Most of the population are nomadic, following herds of camels, sheep, goats and cattle. Little land is cultivated but cotton, maize, millet and sugar cane are grown. Bananas are a major export. Iron ore, gypsum and uranium deposits are as yet unexploited. Five years of inter-clan warfare and a lack of coherent government have led to the collapse of the economy.

SOUTH AFRICA

STATUS: Republic
AREA: 1,220,845 sq km (471,369 sq miles)
POPULATION: 37,600,000
ANNUAL NATURAL INCREASE: 2.4%
CAPITAL: Pretoria (administrative) Cape Town (legislative)
LANGUAGE: Afrikaans, English, various African languages
RELIGION: mainly Christian, Hindu, Jewish and Muslim minorities
CURRENCY: rand (ZAR)
ORGANIZATIONS: Comm., OAU, UN

The interior of South Africa consists of a plateau of over 900 m (2,955 feet) drained by the Orange and Limpopo rivers. Surrounding the plateau is a pronounced escarpment below which the land descends by steps to the sea. Rainfall in most areas is less than 500 mm (20 inches) and the land is increasingly drier towards the west. Agriculture is limited by poor soils but sheep and cattle are extensively grazed. Main crops are maize, wheat, sugar cane, vegetables, cotton and vines. Wine is an important export commodity. South Africa abounds in minerals. Diamonds, gold, platinum, silver, uranium, copper, manganese and asbestos are mined and nearly 80 per cent of the continent's coal reserves are in South Africa. Manufacturing and engineering is concentrated in the southern Transvaal area and around the ports. In 1994 the first ever multiracial elections were held resulting in Nelson Mandela coming to power. In a post-apartheid era, economic sanctions have been lifted, boosting exports, but the country faces adaptation, beginning with a rush of complicated land-ownership claims.

EASTERN CAPE

STATUS: Province
AREA: 174,405 sq km (67,338 sq miles)
POPULATION: 5,900,000
CAPITAL: East London

EASTERN TRANSVAAL

STATUS: Province
AREA: 73,377 sq km (28,311 sq miles)
POPULATION: 2,600,000
CAPITAL Nelspruit

KWAZULU-NATAL

STATUS: Province
AREA: 90,925 sq km (35,106 sq miles)
POPULATION: 8,000,000
CAPITAL: Durban

NORTHERN CAPE

STATUS: Province
AREA: 369,552 sq km (142,684 sq miles)
POPULATION: 700,000
CAPITAL: Kimberley

NORTHERN TRANSVAAL

STATUS: Province
AREA: 121,766 sq km (47,014 sq miles)
POPULATION: 4,700,000
CAPITAL: Pietersburg

NORTH WEST

STATUS: Province
AREA: 120,170 sq km (46,398 sq miles)
POPULATION: 3,300,000
CAPITAL: Klerksdorp

ORANGE FREE STATE

STATUS: Province
AREA: 123,893 sq km (47,835 sq miles)
POPULATION: 2,500,000
CAPITAL: Bloemfontein

PRETORIA-WITWATERSRAND-VEREENIGING (PWV)

STATUS: Province
AREA: 18,078 sq km (6,980 sq miles)
POPULATION: 6,500,000
CAPITAL: Johannesburg

WESTERN CAPE

STATUS: Province
AREA: 128,679 sq km (49,683 sq miles)
POPULATION: 3,400,000
CAPITAL: Cape Town

SOUTHERN AND ANTARCTIC TERRITORIES

STATUS: Overseas Territory of France
AREA: 439,580 sq km (169,680 sq miles)
POPULATION: 180

SOUTH GEORGIA AND THE SOUTH SANDWICH ISLANDS

STATUS: UK Dependent Territory
AREA: 3,755 sq km (1,450 sq miles)
POPULATION: no permanent population

SPAIN

STATUS: Kingdom
AREA: 504,880 sq km (194,885 sq miles)
POPULATION: 39,166,000
ANNUAL NATURAL INCREASE: 0.5%
CAPITAL: Madrid
LANGUAGE: Spanish (Castilian), Catalan, Basque, Galician
RELIGION: Roman Catholic
CURRENCY: Spanish peseta (ESP)
ORGANIZATIONS: Council of Europe, EEA, EU, NATO, OECD, UN, WEU

Spain occupies most of the Iberian Peninsula, from the Bay of Biscay and the Pyrenees mountains in the north, to the Strait of Gibraltar in the south. It includes in its territory the Balearic Islands in the Mediterranean Sea, and the Canary Islands in the Atlantic. The mainland of Spain is mostly plateaux, often forested in the north, but becoming more arid and open further south. Climate is affected regionally by latitude and proximity to the Atlantic Ocean and Mediterranean Sea. Although the climate and terrain are not always favourable, agriculture is important to the Spanish economy. Wheat and other cereals such as maize, barley and rice are cultivated while grapes, citrus fruits and olives are important cash crops. Textile manufacturing in the northeast and steel, chemicals, consumer goods and vehicle manufacturing in the towns and cities have proved a magnet for great numbers of the rural population. The main minerals found are coal, iron ore, uranium and zinc. Tourism is of vital importance to the economy.

SRI LANKA

STATUS: Republic
AREA: 65,610 sq km (25,325 sq miles)
POPULATION: 17,405,000
ANNUAL NATURAL INCREASE: 1.5%
CAPITAL: Colombo
LANGUAGE: Sinhala, Tamil, English
RELIGION: 70% Buddhist, 15% Hindu, Roman Catholic and Muslim minorities
CURRENCY: Sri Lanka rupee (LKR)
ORGANIZATIONS: Col. Plan, Comm., UN

The island of Sri Lanka is situated only 19 km (12 miles) from mainland India. The climate is tropical along the coastal plain and temperate in the central highlands. Annual rainfall averages only 1,000 mm (39 inches) in the north and east while the south and west receive over 2,000 mm (79 inches). The traditional economy of Sri Lanka is based on agriculture in which rubber, coffee, coconuts and particularly tea are dominant. The nation is also self-sufficient in rice. In recent years, however, manufacturing, especially of clothing and textiles, has become the main export earner. Gemstones and tourism are also important, but the tourist industry has suffered because of the activities of Tamil separatists.

SUDAN

STATUS: Republic
AREA: 2,505,815 sq km (967,245 sq miles)
POPULATION: 24,941,000
ANNUAL NATURAL INCREASE: 3.0%
CAPITAL: Khartoum
LANGUAGE: Arabic, tribal languages
RELIGION: 60% Sunni Muslim, animist and Christian
CURRENCY: Sudanese pound (SDP)
ORGANIZATIONS: Arab League, OAU, UN

Sudan, in the upper Nile basin, is Africa's largest country. The land is mostly flat and infertile with a hot, arid climate. The White and Blue Niles are invaluable, serving not only to irrigate cultivated land but also as a potential source of hydro-electric power. Subsistence farming accounts for 80 per cent of Sudan's total production. Major exports include cotton, groundnuts, sugar cane and sesame seed. The principal activity is nomadic herding with over 40 million cattle and sheep and 14 million goats. However, economic activity has been damaged by the effects of drought and civil war.

Sweden
Switzerland
Spain
Syria
Sudan
Surinam
Sri Lanka
Swaziland
South Africa
South Georgia and the
● Sandwich Islands
Southern and
● Antarctic Territories

SURINAM

STATUS: Republic
AREA: 163,820 sq km (63,235 sq miles)
POPULATION: 438,000
ANNUAL NATURAL INCREASE: 2.5%
CAPITAL: Paramaribo
LANGUAGE: Dutch, English, Spanish,
Surinamese (Sranang Tongo), Hindi
RELIGION: 45% Christian, 28% Hindu,
20% Muslim
CURRENCY: Surinam guilder (SRG)
ORGANIZATIONS: OAS, UN

Independent from the Dutch since 1976, Surinam is a small state lying on the northeast coast in the tropics of South America. Physically, there are three main regions: a low-lying, marshy coastal strip; undulating savannah; densely forested highlands. Rice growing takes up 75 per cent of all cultivated land; sugar and pineapples are also grown, while cattle rearing for both meat and dairy products has been introduced. Bauxite accounts for 90 per cent of Surinam's foreign earnings. Timber resources offer great potential but as yet are largely untapped.

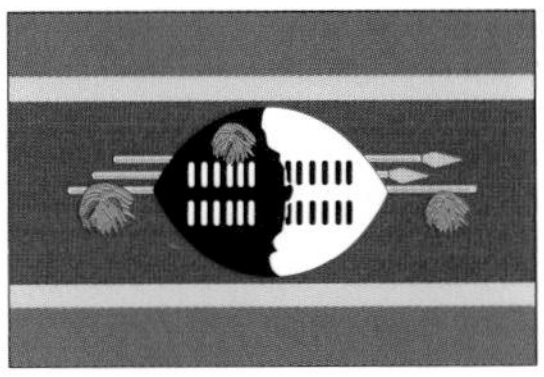

SWAZILAND

STATUS: Kingdom
AREA: 17,365 sq km (6,705 sq miles)
POPULATION: 823,000
ANNUAL NATURAL INCREASE: 3.4%
CAPITAL: Mbabane
LANGUAGE: English, Siswati
RELIGION: 60% Christian, 40% traditional beliefs
CURRENCY: lilangeni (SZL),
South African rand (ZAR)
ORGANIZATIONS: Comm., OAU, UN

Landlocked Swaziland in southern Africa, is a sub-tropical, savannah country. It is divided into four main regions: the High, Middle and Low Velds and the Lebombo Mountains. Rainfall is abundant, promoting good pastureland for the many cattle and sheep. Major exports include sugar, meat, citrus fruits, textiles, wood products and asbestos.

SWEDEN

STATUS: Kingdom
AREA: 449,790 sq km (173,620 sq miles)
POPULATION: 8,721,000
ANNUAL NATURAL INCREASE: 0.2%

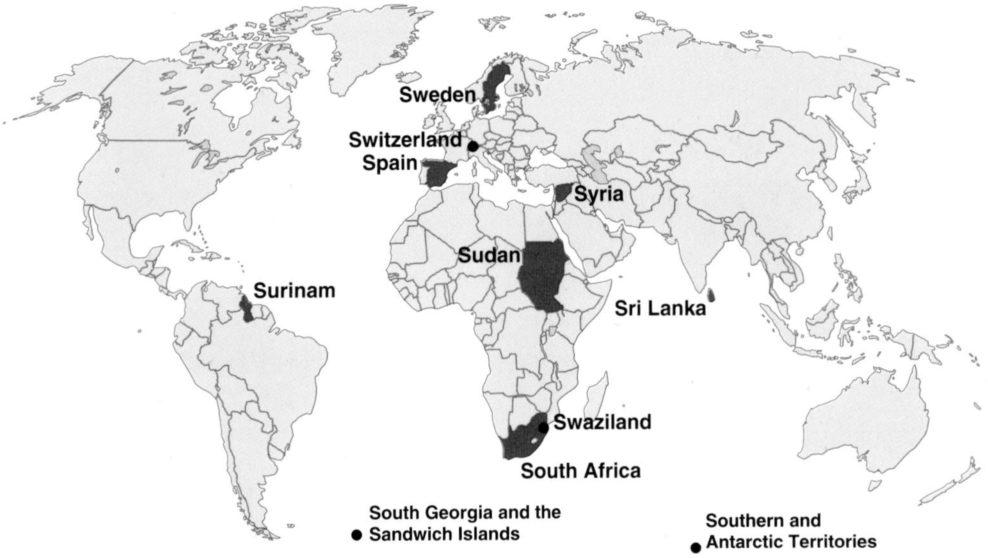

CAPITAL: Stockholm
LANGUAGE: Swedish, Finnish, Lappish
RELIGION: 95% Evangelical Lutheran
CURRENCY: Swedish krona (SED)
ORGANIZATIONS: Council of Europe, EEA, EFTA,
OECD, UN

Glacial debris, glacier-eroded valleys and thick glacial clay are all dominant features of Sweden. Physically, Sweden comprises four main regions: Norrland, the northern forested mountains; the Lake District of the centre south; the southern uplands of Jönköping; the extremely fertile Scania plain of the far south. Summers are short and hot with long, cold winters. Temperatures vary with latitude; in the south from -3–18°C (27–64°F) and in the north from -14–14°C (7–57°F). Annual rainfall varies between 2,000 mm (79 inches) in the southwest, to 500 mm (20 inches) in the east. Over half the land area is forested resulting in a thriving timber industry, but manufacturing industry, particularly cars and trucks, metal products and machine tools, is well established. Mineral resources are also rich and plentiful – iron ore production alone exceeds 17 million tons a year. There are also deposits of copper, lead and zinc.

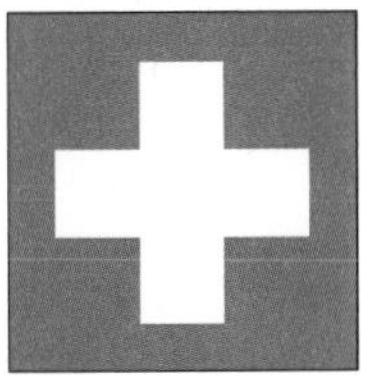

SWITZERLAND

STATUS: Federation
AREA: 41,285 sq km (15,935 sq miles)
POPULATION: 6,908,000
ANNUAL NATURAL INCREASE: 0.3%
CAPITAL: Bern (Berne)
LANGUAGE: German, French, Italian, Romansch
RELIGION: 48% Roman Catholic,
44% Protestant, Jewish minority
CURRENCY: Swiss franc (CHF)
ORGANIZATIONS: Council of Europe, EFTA,
OECD

Switzerland is a landlocked, mountainous country of great scenic beauty, situated in western Europe. The Alps traverse the southern half of the country, in which are to be found some of Europe's highest peaks. In the north the Jura mountains form a natural border with France.

Winters are cold with heavy snowfall in the highest regions. Summers are mild with an average July temperature of 18–19°C (64–66°F). Most rain falls in the summer months. Agriculture is based mainly on dairy farming. Major crops include hay, wheat, barley and potatoes. Industry plays a major role in Switzerland's economy, centred on metal engineering, watchmaking, food processing, textiles and chemicals. The high standard of living enjoyed by the Swiss owes much to the tourist industry. The financial services sector, especially banking, is also of great importance. Switzerland's history of neutrality has made it an attractive location for the headquarters of several international organizations.

SYRIA

STATUS: Republic
AREA: 185,680 sq km (71,675 sq miles)
POPULATION: 13,400,000
ANNUAL NATURAL INCREASE: 3.6%
CAPITAL: Damascus, (Dimashq, Esh Sham)
LANGUAGE: Arabic
RELIGION: 65% Sunni Muslim, Shi'a Muslim
and Christian minorities
CURRENCY: Syrian pound (SYP)
ORGANIZATIONS: Arab League, UN

Syria is situated in the heart of the Middle East. Its most fertile areas lie along the coastal strip on the Mediterranean Sea which supports the bulk of its population, and in the depressions and plateaux of the northeast which are cut through by the rivers Orontes and Euphrates. In the south the Anti-Lebanon mountains (Jebel esh Sharqi) is bordered to the east by the Syrian desert. While the coast has a Mediterranean climate with dry hot summers and mild winters, the interior becomes increasingly hot and arid – average summer temperatures in the desert reach 43°C (109°F). Rainfall varies between 220–400 mm (9–16 inches). Cotton is Syria's main export crop, and wheat and barley are also grown. Cattle, sheep and goats are the main livestock. Although traditionally an agriculturally-based economy, the country is rapidly becoming industrialized as oil, natural gas, salt, gypsum and phosphate are being exploited.

TAHITI

STATUS: Main Island of French Polynesia
AREA: 1,042 sq km (402 sq miles)
POPULATION: 199,031

TAIWAN

STATUS: Island 'Republic of China'
AREA: 35,990 sq km
(13,890 sq miles)
POPULATION: 20,600,000
ANNUAL NATURAL INCREASE: 1.5%
CAPITAL: Taipei (T'ai-pei)
LANGUAGE: Mandarin Chinese, Taiwanese
RELIGION: Buddhist majority, Muslim,
Daoist and Christian minorities
CURRENCY: New Taiwan dollar (TWD), yuan (CNY)
ORGANIZATIONS: none listed

Taiwan is separated from mainland China by the Taiwan Strait (the former Formosa Channel) in which lie the Pescadores. Two-thirds of Taiwan is mountainous, the highest point is 3,950 m (12,959 feet). The flat to rolling coastal plain in the western part of the island accommodates the bulk of the population and the national commerce, industry and agriculture. The climate is tropical marine, with persistent cloudy conditions. The monsoon rains fall in June to August, with an annual average of 2,600 mm (102 inches). Main crops are rice, tea, fruit, sugar cane and sweet potatoes. Industry has been founded on textiles but in recent years electronic products have gained in importance. The Taiwanese economy is inevitably influenced by its large neighbour and is likely to benefit from improving Chinese performance.

TAJIKISTAN

STATUS: Republic
AREA: 143,100 sq km (55,235 sq miles)
POPULATION: 5,465,000
ANNUAL NATURAL INCREASE: 3.0%
CAPITAL: Dushanbe
LANGUAGE: Tajik, Uzbek, Russian
RELIGION: Sunni Muslim
CURRENCY: Russian rouble
ORGANIZATIONS: CIS, UN

Situated in the mountainous heart of Asia, more than half the territory of Tajikistan lies above 3,000 m (10,000 feet). The major settlement areas lie within the Fergana valley in the west. The climate varies from continental to subtropical according to elevation and shelter. Extensive irrigation, without which agriculture would be severely limited, has made it possible for cotton growing to develop into the leading branch of agriculture, and on that basis textiles have become the largest industry in the country. Tajikistan is rich in mineral and fuel deposits, the exploitation of which became a feature of economic development during the Soviet era. Preceding full independence in 1991 there was an upsurge of sometimes violent Tajik nationalism as a result of which many Russians and Uzbeks have left the country.

TANZANIA

STATUS: Republic
AREA: 939,760 sq km (362,750 sq miles)
POPULATION: 27,829,000
ANNUAL NATURAL INCREASE: 3.5%
CAPITAL: Dodoma
LANGUAGE: Swahili, English
RELIGION: 40% Christian, 35% Muslim
CURRENCY: Tanzanian shilling
ORGANIZATIONS: Comm., OAU, UN

Much of this east African country consists of high interior plateaux covered by scrub and grassland, bordered to the north by the volcanic Kilimanjaro region and Lake Victoria, to the west by Lake Tanganyika, by highlands to the south and by the Indian Ocean in the east. Despite its proximity to the equator, the altitude of much of Tanzania means that temperatures are reduced, and only on the narrow coastal plain is the climate truly tropical. Average temperatures vary between 19–28°C (67–82°F), and annual rainfall is around 570–1,060 mm (23–43 inches). The economy is heavily based on agriculture and subsistence farming is the main way of life for most of the population, although coffee, cotton, sisal, cashew nuts and tea are exported. Industry is limited, but gradually growing in importance, and involves textiles, food processing and tobacco. Tourism could be a future growth area.

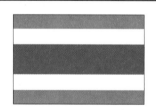

THAILAND

STATUS: Kingdom
AREA: 514,000 sq km (198,405 sq miles)
POPULATION: 57,800,000
ANNUAL NATURAL INCREASE: 1.9%
CAPITAL: Bangkok (Krung Thep)
LANGUAGE: Thai
RELIGION: Buddhist, 4% Muslim
CURRENCY: baht (THB)
ORGANIZATIONS: ASEAN, Col. Plan, UN

Thailand is a land of flat undulating plains and mountains, consisting of the plains of the Chao Phraya and Mae Nam Mun river systems, fringed by mountains, a plateau in the northeast drained by the tributaries of the Mekong river, and the northern half of the Malay peninsula. From May to October, monsoon rains are heavy with an annual average rainfall of 1,500 mm (59 inches). The climate is tropical with temperatures reaching 36°C (97°F) and much of the country is forested. The central plain is well-served with irrigation canals which supply the paddy fields for rice cultivation; Thailand is the world's leading exporter of this crop. Maize, cassava, sugar and rubber also contribute to the economy. Tin production has declined in importance in recent years and has, in part, been replaced by a small scale petro-chemical industry. Other industries of importance include textiles and clothing. Tourism, which grew at a record rate during the 1980s, has since levelled out after the military coup of 1991.

TOGO

STATUS: Kingdom
AREA: 699 sq km (270 sq miles)
POPULATION: 130,000
ANNUAL NATURAL INCREASE: 3.5%
CAPITAL: Lomé
LANGUAGE: French, Kabre, Ewe
RELIGION: Christian
CURRENCY: pa'anga (TOP)
ORGANIZATIONS: Comm.

Togo, formerly a German protectorate and French colony, is situated between Ghana and Benin in west Africa. A long narrow country, it has only 65 km (40 miles) of coast. The interior consists of mountains and high infertile tableland. The climate is tropical with an average temperature of 27°C (81°F). Most of Togo's farmers grow maize, cassava, yams, groundnuts and plantains, and the country is virtually self-sufficient in food stuffs. Phosphates account for half of export revenue. Cotton, cocoa and coffee are also exported.

TOKELAU ISLANDS

STATUS: Overseas Territory of New Zealand
AREA: 10 sq km (4 sq miles)
POPULATION: 1,577
CAPITAL: none, each island has its own
administration centre

TONGA

STATUS: Kingdom
AREA: 699 sq km (270 sq miles)
POPULATION: 103,000
ANNUAL NATURAL INCREASE: 0.4%
CAPITAL: Nuku'alofa
LANGUAGE: Tongan, English
RELIGION: Christian
CURRENCY: pa'anga (TOP)
ORGANIZATIONS: Comm.

Tonga consists of an archipelago of 169 islands in the Pacific 180 km (112 miles) north of New Zealand. There are seven groups of islands, but the most important are Tongatapu, Ha'apai and Vava'u. All the islands are covered with dense tropical vegetation, and temperatures range from 11–29°C (52–84°F). Main exports are coconut products and bananas.

TRINIDAD & TOBAGO

STATUS: Republic
AREA: 5,130 sq km (1,980 sq miles)
POPULATION: 1,265,000
ANNUAL NATURAL INCREASE: 1.7%
CAPITAL: Port of Spain
LANGUAGE: English, Hindi, French, Spanish
RELIGION: 60% Christian, 25% Hindu, 6% Muslim
CURRENCY: Trinidad and Tobago dollar (TTD)
ORGANIZATIONS: Caricom, Comm., OAS, UN

Trinidad and Tobago, the southernmost Caribbean islands of the Lesser Antilles lie only 11 and 30 km (7 and 19 miles) respectively from the Venezuelan coast. Both islands are mountainous, the Northern Range of Trinidad reaching 940 m (3,084 feet) with its highest parts retaining tropical forest cover. The country has a humid, tropical climate with temperatures averaging 25°C (76°F) per annum. Rain falls mostly between June and December and varies between 1,300–3,000 mm (51–118 inches) annually. Sugar was once the mainstay of the economy but oil is now the leading source of revenue accounting for over 70 per cent of export revenue. There is also a petro-chemical industry based on significant gas reserves.

TRISTAN DA CUNHA

STATUS: Dependency of St Helena
AREA: 98 sq km (38 sq miles)
POPULATION: 295

TUNISIA

STATUS: Republic
AREA: 164,150 sq km (63,360 sq miles)
POPULATION: 8,401,000
ANNUAL NATURAL INCREASE: 2.0%
CAPITAL: Tunis
LANGUAGE: Arabic, French
RELIGION: Muslim
CURRENCY: Tunisian dinar (TND)
ORGANIZATIONS: Arab League, OAU, UN

Tunisia, on the southern shores of the Mediterranean is largely an arid, desert country of northern Africa. The eastern limits of the Atlas mountain range extend into northern parts of the country, which are separated from the Sahara desert to the south by a lowland belt of salt pans, called the Chott El Jerid. Average annual temperatures are in the range 10–27°C (50–81°F) and rainfall averages 380–500 mm (15–20 inches) in the north, but drops to virtually nothing in the south. The majority of the population live along the northeast coast. Wheat, barley, olives and citrus fruit are the main crops and oil, natural gas and sugar refining are the main industries. The tourist industry is expanding and is becoming increasingly important to the economy.

TURKEY

STATUS: Republic
AREA: 779,450 sq km (300,870 sq miles)
POPULATION: 59,869,000
ANNUAL NATURAL INCREASE: 2.2%
CAPITAL: Ankara
LANGUAGE: Turkish, Kurdish
RELIGION: 98% Sunni Muslim, Christian minority
CURRENCY: Turkish lira (TRL)
ORGANIZATIONS: Council of Europe, NATO, OECD, UN

Turkey has always occupied a strategically important position linking Europe and Asia. It is a rugged, mountainous country particularly in the east. The central Anatolian plateau is bordered in the north by the Pontine mountains (Anadolu Dağlari) and in the south by the Taurus mountains (Toros Dağlari) which converge in the east, crowned by Mt Ararat (Büyük Ağri). Thrace, in European Turkey is flatter with rolling hills. Coastal regions exhibit Mediterranean conditions with short mild winters with some rainfall and long hot, dry summers. The interior is relatively arid with average rainfall in some places less than 250 mm (10 inches). The main crops are wheat and barley, but tobacco, olives, sugar beet, tea and fruit are also grown, and sheep, goats and cattle are raised. Turkey is becoming increasingly industrialized; textiles account for a third of exports and the car industry is developing. The nation now leads the Middle East in the production of iron, steel, chrome, coal and lignite. Tourism is a rapidly growing industry.

TURKMENISTAN

STATUS: Republic
AREA: 488,100 sq km (188,405 sq miles)
POPULATION: 3,714,000
ANNUAL NATURAL INCREASE: 2.5%
CAPITAL: Ashkhabad
LANGUAGE: Turkmen, Russian, Uzbek
RELIGION: Muslim
CURRENCY: manat
ORGANIZATIONS: CIS, UN

Situated in the far south of the former Soviet Union, Turkmenistan is a desert land except for the lowlands in the west along the Caspian shore, the mountains along its southern borders and the valley of Amudar'ya river in the north. The continental climate is responsible for great fluctuations in temperature, both during the day and throughout the year. Traditionally nomads, the Turkmen tribes under the Soviet regime, turned from pastoral farming to cotton-growing, made possible by extensive irrigation. Turkmenistan enjoys substantial natural resources, principally oil and gas but also potassium, sulphur and salt.

TURKS & CAICOS ISLANDS

STATUS: UK Dependent Territory
AREA: 430 sq km (166 sq miles)
POPULATION: 11,696
CAPITAL: Cockburn Town

TUVALU

STATUS: Special membership of the Commonwealth
AREA: 24.6 sq km (9.5 sq miles)
POPULATION: 10,090
ANNUAL NATURAL INCREASE: 1.5%
CAPITAL: Funafuti
LANGUAGE: Tuvaluan, English
RELIGION: 98% Protestant
CURRENCY: Australian dollar (AUD), Tuvaluan coinage
ORGANIZATIONS: Comm., (special member)

Tuvalu consists of nine dispersed coral atolls, north of Fiji, in the Pacific Ocean. The climate is tropical; hot, with heavy annual rainfall exceeding 3,000 mm (118 inches). Fish is the staple food but coconuts and bread-fruit are cultivated. The sale of postage stamps abroad is, however, the largest source of revenue.

UGANDA

STATUS: **Republic**
AREA: **236,580 sq km (91,320 sq miles)**
POPULATION: **18,674,000**
ANNUAL NATURAL INCREASE: **3.1%**
CAPITAL: **Kampala**
LANGUAGE: **English, tribal languages**
RELIGION: **62% Christian, 6% Muslim**
CURRENCY: **Uganda shilling (UGS)**
ORGANIZATIONS: **Comm., OAU, UN**

Uganda is bordered in the west by the great Rift Valley and the Ruwenzori mountain range which reaches 5,220 m (16,765 feet). In the east it is bordered by Kenya and Lake Victoria, from which the Nile flows northwards. Most of the country is high plateau with savannah vegetation although the lands around Lake Victoria have been cleared for cultivation and have become the most populated and developed areas. The climate is warm (21–24°C or 70–75°F), and rainfall ranges from 750–1,500 mm (30–59 inches) per annum. The Ugandan economy is firmly based on agriculture with a heavy dependence on coffee, the dominant export crop, and cotton. Fishing, from the waters of Lake Victoria is also important for local consumption.

UKRAINE

STATUS: **Republic**
AREA: **603,700 sq km (233,030 sq miles)**
POPULATION: **52,194,000**
ANNUAL NATURAL INCREASE: **0.3%**
CAPITAL: **Kiev (Kiyev)**
LANGUAGE: **Ukrainian, Russian**
RELIGION: **Russian Orthodox, Roman Catholic (Uniate)**
CURRENCY: **karbovanets (coupon)**
ORGANIZATIONS: **CIS, UN**

Ukraine consists mainly of level plains and mountainous border areas. The landscape is, however, diverse, with marshes, forests, wooded and treeless steppe. Deposits of 'black earth', among the most fertile soils, cover about 65 per cent of Ukraine. Grain, potatoes, vegetables and fruits, industrial crops (notably sugar beets and sunflower seeds) and fodder crops are grown. Food processing is important to the economy, and southern regions are renowned for wines. Ukraine is rich in mineral resources, such as iron ore, coal and lignite, and has large reserves of petroleum and gas. Extensive mining, metal production, machine-building, engineering and chemicals dominate Ukrainian industry, most of it located in the Donetsk basin and the Dneiper lowland. These two regions account for four-fifths of the urban population. Despite its natural wealth and industrial development, Ukraine has failed to respond to the economic needs of its independent status and has experienced sharp declines in agricultural and industrial output.

UNITED ARAB EMIRATES (UAE)

STATUS: **Federation of seven Emirates**
AREA: **75,150 sq km (29,010 sq miles)**
POPULATION: **2,083,000**
ANNUAL NATURAL INCREASE: **3.1%**
CAPITAL: **Abu Dhabi (Abū Ẓabī)**
LANGUAGE: **Arabic, English**
RELIGION: **Sunni Muslim**
CURRENCY: **UAE dirham (AED)**
ORGANIZATIONS: **Arab League, OPEC, UN**

The United Arab Emirates (UAE), comprising seven separate emirates, are stretched along the southeastern coast of the Gulf. It is a country covered mostly by flat deserts with the highest land in the Hajar mountains of the Musandam Peninsula. Summer temperatures reach 40°C (104°F); meagre rains of 130 mm (5 inches) fall mainly in the winter. Only the desert oases are fertile, producing fruit and vegetables. The economic wealth of the UAE is founded on its huge reserves of hydrocarbons, mainly within the largest Emirate, Abu Dhabi, with smaller supplies in three others – Dubai, Sharjah and Ras al Khaimah. Natural gas and oil are the major exports for which Japan and the Far East are the major markets. Revenue gained from these has allowed the economy to grow rapidly, with there being huge investment in the service industries. It has a population that is overwhelmingly made up of foreign immigrants.

ABU DHABI

STATUS: **Emirate**
AREA: **64,750 sq km (24,995 sq miles)**
POPULATION: **670,175**

AJMAN

STATUS: **Emirate**
AREA: **260 sq km (100 sq miles)**
POPULATION: **64,318**

DUBAI

STATUS: **Emirate**
AREA: **3,900 sq km (1,505 sq miles)**
POPULATION: **419,104**

FUJAIRAH

STATUS: **Emirate**
AREA: **1,170 sq km (452 sq miles)**
POPULATION: **54,425**

RAS AL KHAIMAH

STATUS: **Emirate**
AREA: **1,690 sq km (625 sq miles)**
POPULATION: **116,470**

SHARJAH

STATUS: **Emirate**
AREA: **2,600 sq km (1,005 sq miles)**
POPULATION: **268,722**

UMM AL QAIWAIN

STATUS: **Emirate**
AREA: **780 sq km (300 sq miles)**
POPULATION: **29,229**

UNITED KINGDOM OF GREAT BRITAIN & NORTHERN IRELAND (UK)

STATUS: **Kingdom**
AREA: **244,755 sq km (94,475 sq miles)**
POPULATION: **57,998,400**
ANNUAL NATURAL INCREASE: **0.3%**
CAPITAL: **London**
LANGUAGE: **English, Welsh, Gaelic**
RELIGION: **Protestant majority, Roman Catholic, Jewish, Muslim, Hindu minorities**
CURRENCY: **pound sterling (GBP)**
ORGANIZATIONS: **Col. Plan, Comm., Council of Europe, EEA, EU, G7, NATO, OECD, UN, WEU**

The United Kingdom, part of the British Isles, is situated off the northwest European coast, separated from France by the English Channel. It includes the countries of England and Scotland, the principality of Wales, and the region of Northern Ireland in the north of the island of Ireland.

In broad terms Britain can be divided into the upland regions of Wales, Northern England and Scotland, characterized by ancient dissected and glaciated mountain regions, and the lowland areas of southern and eastern England where low ranges of chalk, limestone and sandstone hills are interspersed with wide clay vales. The highest point in the United Kingdom is Ben Nevis in the Grampians of Scotland at 1,344 m (4,409 feet).

The climate of the British Isles is mild, wet and variable. Summer temperatures average 13–17°C (55–63°F) and winter temperatures 5–7°C (41–45°F). Annual rainfall varies between 640–5,000 mm (26–200 inches) with the highest rainfall in the Lake District and the lowest in East Anglia.

Although only a tiny percentage of the nation's workforce is employed in agriculture, farm produce is important to both home and export markets. Seventy-six per cent of the total UK land area is farmland. The main cereal crops are wheat, barley and oats. Potatoes, sugar beet and green vegetable crops are widespread.

About 20 per cent of the land is permanent pasture for raising dairy and beef stock and 28 per cent, mainly hill and mountain areas, is used for rough grazing of sheep. The best fruit-growing areas are the southeast, especially Kent, East Anglia and the central Vale of Evesham. Fishing supplies two-thirds of the nation's requirements but overfishing and encroachment into territorial waters by other countries have created problems.

The major mineral resources of the UK are coal, oil and natural gas. Over two-thirds of deep-mined coal came from the Yorkshire and East Midlands fields and substantial reserves remain. However, the coal industry, which had already been in slow decline for some 30 years, collapsed rapidly in 1993–4 when many of the remaining pits were closed. The number of employees fell from 208,000 in 1983 to 18,000 in early 1994 and by mid-1994 only 16 deep coal mines remained in operation, compared with 50 pits two years earlier.

Before the 1970s Britain relied on imports from the Middle East for its oil supplies, but in 1975 supplies of oil and gas from the vast North Sea oil fields began to provide both self-sufficiency and enough to export. Some of the older fields are now nearly worked out and operating costs for these are rising. The major Scott Field came on-stream in 1993 and in 1994 approval was granted for the development of the Fife and Birch oil fields and the Armada gas fields.

Wind farms as a source of energy, often the subject of controversy with environmentalists, contribute less than 1 per cent of Britain's electricity.

Although the UK is an industrialized nation, the traditional mainstays of heavy industry such as coal, iron and steel and shipbuilding no longer figure prominently in the economy. Concurrent with the decline of heavy industry, there has been a substantial growth of light industries. High technology and electronic products predominate, as well as pharmaceuticals, motor parts and food processing. Tourism is an essential part of the economy, especially in London, and in five years up to 1993 the number of visitors to the UK rose by 22 per cent. Financial services is another expanding sector, the 'City' of London having the greatest concentration of banks in the world.

The UK is a trading nation. The balance of trade has changed during the last 30 years because of increasingly closer economic ties with Europe and the move towards a Single European Market. Consequently, trading with Commonwealth nations, particularly Australia, has assumed lower priority. In terms of value, the most important exports from the UK are machinery, chemicals and transport equipment, followed by food, beverages and tobacco, petroleum products, iron and steel.

The transport network in the UK is highly developed. Out of 362,357 km (225,164 miles) of public roads, 9 per cent are motorways and 13 per cent are other major roads. The railway network covers over 16,730 km (10,395 miles) and carries over 150 million tonnes of freight annually. The opening of the Channel Tunnel in 1994 has connected the motorway and rail networks of Britain with those of northern France and southern Belgium. The inland waterway system totals only 563 navigable kilometres (350 miles) but has potential to carry more than its present 4 million tonnes of goods annually.

ENGLAND

STATUS: Constituent Country
AREA: 130,360 sq km (50,320 sq miles)
POPULATION: 48,208,100
CAPITAL: London

NORTHERN IRELAND

STATUS: Constituent Region
AREA: 14,150 sq km (5,460 sq miles)
POPULATION: 1,573,282
CAPITAL: Belfast

SCOTLAND

STATUS: Constituent Country
AREA: 78,750 sq km (30,400 sq miles)
POPULATION: 4,998,567
CAPITAL: Edinburgh

WALES

STATUS: Principality
AREA: 20,760 sq km (8,015 sq miles)
POPULATION: 2,891,500
CAPITAL: Cardiff

UNITED STATES OF AMERICA (USA)

STATUS: Federal Republic
AREA: 9,363,130 sq km (3,614,170 sq miles)
POPULATION: 255,020,000
ANNUAL NATURAL INCREASE: 0.9%
CAPITAL: Washington D.C.
LANGUAGE: English, Spanish
RELIGION: Christian majority, Jewish minority
CURRENCY: US dollar (USD)
ORGANIZATIONS: ANZUS, Col. Plan, G7, NAFTA, NATO, OAS, OECD, UN

The United States of America is the world's fourth largest country after Canada, China and Russia with the world's fourth largest population. The 19th and 20th centuries have brought 42 million immigrants to its shores, and the population of the USA now has the highest living standard of any country in the world. The large land area covers a huge spectrum of different landscapes, environments and climates. The eastern coast of New England, where the European settlers first landed, is rocky, mountainous and richly wooded. South of New England is the Atlantic coastal plain, rising to the west towards the Appalachian mountain system. Beyond the Appalachians lie the central lowlands, a large undulating plain cut through by the Mississippi and Ohio rivers. Further west lie the Great Plains crossed by the Missouri, Red and Arkansas rivers and rising gently towards the mighty Rocky Mountains, a spine of mountains running south from Alaska. Beyond these lie the Great Valley of California, the coastal ranges and the Pacific coast.

Climatic variety within the United States is enormous, ranging from the Arctic conditions of Alaska to the desert of the southwest – winter temperatures in Alaska plummet to -28°C (-19°F); in Florida they maintain a steady 19°C (66°F). The centre of the continent is dry, but both the northwest Pacific and the New England Atlantic coast are humid with heavy rainfall. Many areas of the USA fall prey to exceptional, often disastrous, weather conditions: the northeastern seaboard is susceptible to heavy blizzards, the southern lowlands are vulnerable to spring thaw flooding and the Mississippi valley is prone to tornadoes.

The natural vegetation of the USA reflects its climatic diversity. The northwest coast is rich in coniferous forest, while the Appalachian mountain region is well endowed with hardwoods. In the arid southwest, vegetation is limited to desert scrub whereas the Gulf and South Atlantic coast are fringed with swampy wetlands. The central lowlands are endowed with rich black-earth soils (the agricultural heartland), gradually supplanted, towards the Rockies, by tall-grass prairie. The northeastern states of Illinois, Iowa, Indiana and Nebraska form the 'corn belt', which produces 45 per cent of the world's corn. Further west wheat supplements corn as the main crop. The northeastern states are predominantly dairy country, and the south is famous for cotton and tobacco. Rice is grown in Texas, California and Louisiana, and fruit and vegetables in Florida.

The USA consumes 25 per cent of all the world's energy resources but is well endowed with energy reserves. There are substantial coal resources, particularly in the Appalachians. The great rivers have been harnessed extensively for hydro-electric power. Oil and natural gas fields are found in Texas, Alaska, Louisiana and California and new deep-sea exploratory drilling is underway in the Gulf of Mexico. Oil production, however, has declined steadily since 1983.

The industrial base is diverse, the main industries being steel, motor vehicles, aerospace, chemicals, computers, electronics, telecommunications and consumer goods. The service industries (encompassing tourism and finance) are by far the biggest source of employment in the United States.

ALABAMA

STATUS: State
AREA: 131,485 sq km (50,755 sq miles)
POPULATION: 4,136,000
CAPITAL: Montgomery

ALASKA

STATUS: State
AREA: 1,478,450 sq km (570,680 sq miles)
POPULATION: 587,000
CAPITAL: Juneau

ARIZONA

STATUS: State
AREA: 293,985 sq km (113,480 sq miles)
POPULATION: 3,832,000
CAPITAL: Phoenix

ARKANSAS
STATUS: State
AREA: 134,880 sq km (52,065 sq miles)
POPULATION: 2,399,000
CAPITAL: Little Rock

CALIFORNIA
STATUS: State
AREA: 404,815 sq km (156,260 sq miles)
POPULATION: 30,867,000
CAPITAL: Sacramento

COLORADO
STATUS: State
AREA: 268,310 sq km (103,570 sq miles)
POPULATION: 3,470,000
CAPITAL: Denver

CONNECTICUT
STATUS: State
AREA: 12,620 sq km (4,870 sq miles)
POPULATION: 3,281,000
CAPITAL: Hartford

DELAWARE
STATUS: State
AREA: 5,005 sq km (1,930 sq miles)
POPULATION: 689,000
CAPITAL: Dover

DISTRICT OF COLUMBIA
STATUS: Federal District
AREA: 163 sq km (63 sq miles)
POPULATION: 589,000
CAPITAL: Washington D.C.

FLORIDA
STATUS: State
AREA: 140,255 sq km (54,1405 sq miles)
POPULATION: 13,488,000
CAPITAL: Tallahassee

GEORGIA
STATUS: State
AREA: 150,365 sq km (58,040 sq miles)
POPULATION: 6,751,000
CAPITAL: Atlanta

HAWAII
STATUS: State
AREA: 16,640 sq km (6,425 sq miles)
POPULATION: 1,160,000
CAPITAL: Honolulu

IDAHO
STATUS: State
AREA: 213,445 sq km (82,390 sq miles)
POPULATION: 1,067,000
CAPITAL: Boise

ILLINOIS
STATUS: State
AREA: 144,120 sq km (55,630 sq miles)
POPULATION: 11,631,000
CAPITAL: Springfield

INDIANA
STATUS: State
AREA: 93,065 sq km (35,925 sq miles)
POPULATION: 5,662,000
CAPITAL: Indianapolis

IOWA
STATUS: State
AREA: 144,950 sq km (55,950 sq miles)
POPULATION: 2,812,000
CAPITAL: Des Moines

KANSAS
STATUS: State
AREA: 211,805 sq km (81,755 sq miles)
POPULATION: 2,523,000
CAPITAL: Topeka

KENTUCKY
STATUS: State
AREA: 102,740 sq km (39,660 sq miles)
POPULATION: 3,755,000
CAPITAL: Frankfort

LOUISIANA
STATUS: State
AREA: 115,310 sq km (44,510 sq miles)
POPULATION: 4,287,000
CAPITAL: Baton Rouge

MAINE
STATUS: State
AREA: 80,275 sq km (30,985 sq miles)
POPULATION: 1,235,000
CAPITAL: Augusta

MARYLAND
STATUS: State
AREA: 25,480 sq km (9,835 sq miles)
POPULATION: 4,908,000
CAPITAL: Annapolis

MASSACHUSETTS
STATUS: State
AREA: 20,265 sq km (7,820 sq miles)
POPULATION: 5,998,000
CAPITAL: Boston

MICHIGAN
STATUS: State
AREA: 147,510 sq km (56,940 sq miles)
POPULATION: 9,437,000
CAPITAL: Lansing

MINNESOTA
STATUS: State
AREA: 206,030 sq km (79,530 sq miles)
POPULATION: 4,480,000
CAPITAL: St Paul

MISSISSIPPI
STATUS: State
AREA: 122,335 sq km (47,220 sq miles)
POPULATION: 2,614,000
CAPITAL: Jackson

MISSOURI
STATUS: State
AREA: 178,565 sq km (68,925 sq miles)
POPULATION: 5,193,000
CAPITAL: Jefferson City

MONTANA
STATUS: State
AREA: 376,555 sq km (145,350 sq miles)
POPULATION: 824,000
CAPITAL: Helena

NEBRASKA
STATUS: State
AREA: 198,505 sq km (76,625 sq miles)
POPULATION: 1,606,000
CAPITAL: Lincoln

NEVADA
STATUS: State
AREA: 284,625 sq km (109,865 sq miles)
POPULATION: 1,327,000
CAPITAL: Carson City

NEW HAMPSHIRE
STATUS: State
AREA: 23,290 sq km (8,990 sq miles)
POPULATION: 1,111,000
CAPITAL: Concord

NEW JERSEY
STATUS: State
AREA: 19,340 sq km (7,465 sq miles)
POPULATION: 7,789,000
CAPITAL: Trenton

NEW MEXICO
STATUS: State
AREA: 314,255 sq km (121,300 sq miles)
POPULATION: 1,581,000
CAPITAL: Sante Fe

NEW YORK
STATUS: State
AREA: 122,705 sq km (47,365 sq miles)
POPULATION: 18,119,000
CAPITAL: Albany

NORTH CAROLINA
STATUS: State
AREA: 126,505 sq km (48,830 sq miles)
POPULATION: 6,843,000
CAPITAL: Raleigh

NORTH DAKOTA
STATUS: State
AREA: 179,485 sq km (69,280 sq miles)
POPULATION: 636,000
CAPITAL: Bismarck

OHIO
STATUS: State
AREA: 106,200 sq km (40,995 sq miles)
POPULATION: 11,016,000
CAPITAL: Columbus

OKLAHOMA
STATUS: State
AREA: 177,815 sq km (68,635 sq miles)
POPULATION: 3,212,00
CAPITAL: Oklahoma City

OREGON
STATUS: State
AREA: 249,115 sq km (96,160 sq miles)
POPULATION: 2,977,000
CAPITAL: Salem

PENNSYLVANIA
STATUS: State
AREA: 116,260 sq km (44,875 sq miles)
POPULATION: 12,009,000
CAPITAL: Harrisburg

RHODE ISLAND
STATUS: State
AREA: 2,730 sq km (1,055 sq miles)
POPULATION: 1,005,000
CAPITAL: Providence

SOUTH CAROLINA
STATUS: State
AREA: 78,225 sq km (30,195 sq miles)
POPULATION: 3,603,000
CAPITAL: Columbia

SOUTH DAKOTA
STATUS: State
AREA: 196,715 sq km (75,930 sq miles)
POPULATION: 711,000
CAPITAL: Pierre

TENNESSEE
STATUS: State
AREA: 106,590 sq km (41,145 sq miles)
POPULATION: 5,024,000
CAPITAL: Nashville

TEXAS
STATUS: State
AREA: 678,620 sq km (261,950 sq miles)
POPULATION: 17,656,000
CAPITAL: Austin

UTAH
STATUS: State
AREA: 212,570 sq km (82,050 sq miles)
POPULATION: 1,813,000
CAPITAL: Salt Lake City

VERMONT
STATUS: State
AREA: 24,015 sq km (9,270 sq miles)
POPULATION: 570,000
CAPITAL: Montpelier

VIRGINIA
STATUS: State
AREA: 102,835 sq km (39,695 sq miles)
POPULATION: 6,377,000
CAPITAL: Richmond

WASHINGTON
STATUS: State
AREA: 172,265 sq km (66,495 sq miles)
POPULATION: 5,136,000
CAPITAL: Olympia

WEST VIRGINIA
STATUS: State
AREA: 62,470 sq km (24,115 sq miles)
POPULATION: 1,812,000
CAPITAL: Charleston

WISCONSIN
STATUS: State
AREA: 140,965 sq km (54,415 sq miles)
POPULATION: 5,007,000
CAPITAL: Madison

WYOMING
STATUS: State
AREA: 251,200 sq km (96,965 sq miles)
POPULATION: 466,000
CAPITAL: Cheyenne

URUGUAY
STATUS: Republic
AREA: 186,925 sq km (72,155 sq miles)
POPULATION: 3,131,000
ANNUAL NATURAL INCREASE: 0.6%
CAPITAL: Montevideo
LANGUAGE: Spanish
RELIGION: Roman Catholic
CURRENCY: Uruguayan peso (UYP)
ORGANIZATIONS: Mercosur, OAS, UN

Uruguay is a small country on the southeast coast of south America. Geographically it consists firstly of a narrow plain, fringed with lagoons and dunes, skirting along the coast and the estuary of the river Plate. Further inland, rolling grassland hills are broken by minor ridges of the Brazilian highlands, which reach heights of no more than 500 m (1,600 feet). The climate is temperate and rainfall is spread evenly throughout the year at about 100 mm (4 inches) per month. Monthly temperatures average in the range of 10–22°C (50–72°F). The land has good agricultural potential, however most is given over to the grazing of sheep and cattle. The economy relies heavily on the production of meat and wool with 87 per cent of the area devoted to farming. Uruguay has no oil or gas reserves, and most of its energy requirements are obtained from hydro-electricity.

UZBEKISTAN
STATUS: Republic
AREA: 447,400 sq km (172,695 sq miles)
POPULATION: 20,708,000
ANNUAL NATURAL INCREASE: 2.4%
CAPITAL: Tashkent
LANGUAGE: Uzbek, Russian, Turkish
RELIGION: Muslim
CURRENCY: som
ORGANIZATIONS: CIS, UN

Established in 1924 as a constituent republic of the Soviet Union, Uzbekistan became an independent state in 1991. The majority of the country consists of flat, sun-baked lowlands with mountains in the south and east. The climate is markedly continental and very dry with an abundance of sunshine and mild, short winters. The southern mountains are of great economic importance, providing ample supplies of water for hydro-electric plants and irrigation schemes. The mountain regions also contain substantial reserves of natural gas, oil, coal, iron and other metals. With its fertile soils (when irrigated) and good pastures, Uzbekistan is well situated for cattle raising and the production of cotton. It is also the largest producer of machines and heavy equipment in central Asia, and has been specializing mainly in machinery for cotton cultivation and harvesting, for irrigation projects, for road-building and textile processing. During the Soviet period the urban employment market became increasingly dominated by Russians and other outsiders. The gradual emergence of better educated and better trained Uzbeks has generated fiercely nationalist sentiments.

VANUATU
STATUS: Republic
AREA: 14,765 sq km (5,700 sq miles)
POPULATION: 154,000
ANNUAL NATURAL INCREASE: 2.4%
CAPITAL: Port-Vila
LANGUAGE: Bislama (national), English, French, Melanesian languages
RELIGION: Christian
CURRENCY: vatu (VUV)
ORGANIZATIONS: Comm., UN

Vanuatu is a chain of some 80 densely forested, mountainous, volcanic islands, situated in the Melanesian south Pacific. Its climate is tropical, with a high rainfall and a continuous threat of cyclones. Copra, cocoa and coffee are grown mainly for export, with fish, pigs and sheep as well as yams, taro, manioc and bananas important only for home consumption. Manganese is the only mineral with deposits of economic value. Tourism is becoming important, particularly with Australian and Japanese visitors.

VATICAN CITY

STATUS: Ecclesiastical State
AREA: 0.44 sq km (0.17 sq miles)
POPULATION: 1,000
LANGUAGE: Italian, Latin
RELIGION: Roman Catholic
CURRENCY: Italian lira (ITL), Papal coinage
ORGANIZATIONS: none

The Vatican City, the headquarters of the Roman Catholic Church, is the world's smallest independent state. It is entirely surrounded by the city of Rome, occupying a hill to the west of the river Tiber. It has been the papal residence since the 5th century and a destination for pilgrims and tourists from all over the world. Most income is derived from voluntary contributions (Peter's Pence), tourism and interest on investments. The only industries are those connected with the Church.

VENEZUELA

STATUS: Republic
AREA: 912,045 sq km (352,050 sq miles)
POPULATION: 20,410,000
ANNUAL NATURAL INCREASE: 2.5%
CAPITAL: Caracas
LANGUAGE: Spanish
RELIGION: Roman Catholic
CURRENCY: bolivar (VEB)
ORGANIZATIONS: OAS, OPEC, UN

Venezuela, one of the richest countries of Latin America, is divided into four topographical regions: the continuation of the Andes in the west; the humid lowlands around Lake Maracaibo in the north; the savannah-covered central plains (Llanos), and the extension of the Guiana Highlands covering almost half the country. The climate varies between tropical in the south to warm temperate along the northern coasts. The majority of the population live along the north coast. Venezuela's economy is built around oil production in the Maracaibo region; over three-quarters of export revenue comes from oil. Bauxite and iron ore are also important. The majority of employment is provided by industrial and manufacturing sectors of the economy.

VIETNAM

STATUS: Republic
AREA: 329,566 sq km (127,246 sq miles)
POPULATION: 69,306,000
ANNUAL NATURAL INCREASE: 2.3%
CAPITAL: Hanoi
LANGUAGE: Vietnamese, French, Chinese
RELIGION: Buddhist
CURRENCY: dong (VND)
ORGANIZATIONS: OIEC, UN

Situated on the eastern coast of the Indo-Chinese peninsula of southeastern Asia, Vietnam is predominantly a rugged, mountainous country. The north-south oriented mountainous spine separates two major river deltas: the Red River (Hong river) in the north and the Mekong in the south. Monsoons bring 1,500 mm (59 inches) of rain every year and temperatures average 15°C (59°F) annually. Rainforest still covers some of the central mountainous areas, but most has been cleared for agriculture and habitation. Rice is grown extensively throughout the north (Vietnam is the world's third largest exporter after the USA and Thailand) along with coffee and rubber in other parts of the country. Vietnam possesses a wide range of minerals including coal, lignite, anthracite, iron ore and tin. Industry is expanding rapidly, but decades of warfare and internal strife have impeded development. The US government has lifted its 20-year-old trade embargo, which will further help strengthen Vietnam's trade position.

VIRGIN ISLANDS (UK)

STATUS: UK Dependent Territory
AREA: 153 sq km (59 sq miles)
POPULATION: 16,749
CAPITAL: Road Town

VIRGIN ISLANDS (USA)

STATUS: External Territory of USA
AREA: 345 sq km (133 sq miles)
POPULATION: 101,809
CAPITAL: Charlotte Amalie

WALLIS & FUTUNA ISLANDS

STATUS: Self-governing Overseas Territory of France
AREA: 274 sq km (106 sq miles)
POPULATION: 14,100
CAPITAL: Mata-Uta

WESTERN SAHARA

STATUS: Territory in dispute, administered by Morocco
AREA: 266,000 sq km (102,675 sq miles)
POPULATION: 250,000
CAPITAL: Laayoune

WESTERN SAMOA

STATUS: Commonwealth State
AREA: 2,840 sq km (1,095 sq miles)
POPULATION: 170,000
ANNUAL NATURAL INCREASE: 0.5%
CAPITAL: Apia
LANGUAGE: English, Samoan
RELIGION: Christian
CURRENCY: tala (dollar) (WST)
ORGANIZATIONS: Comm., UN

Western Samoa constitutes a 160 km (100 mile) chain of nine south Pacific islands. The two largest islands, Savaii and Upolu, are mountainous and volcanic. Annual rainfall averages 2,500 mm (100 inches) per year and temperatures average 26°C (79°F) for most months. Only four of the islands are populated – Savaii, Upolu, Manono and Apolima. Main exports are copra, timber, coffee, cocoa and fruit. Western Samoa has some light industries, such as food processing, textiles and cigarette manufacture and a tourist trade is developing. Remittances from citizens abroad are, however, also very important to the economy.

YEMEN

STATUS: Republic
AREA: 527,970 sq km (328,065 sq miles)
POPULATION: 11,092,084
ANNUAL NATURAL INCREASE: 4.4%
CAPITAL: San'a (Şan'ā')
LANGUAGE: Arabic
RELIGION: Sunni and Shi'a Muslim
CURRENCY: Yemeni dinar and rial
ORGANIZATIONS: Arab League, UN

The Yemen Arab Republic and the People's Democratic Republic of Yemen were unified in 1990 to form a single state with its capital at San'a. Situated in the southern part of the Arabian Peninsula the country comprises several contrasting physical landscapes. The north is mainly mountainous and relatively wet with rainfall reaching 890 mm (35 inches) in inland areas which helps to irrigate the cereals, cotton, fruits and vegetables grown on the windward mountain sides and along the coast. The south coast stretches for 1,100 km (685 miles) from the mouth of the Red Sea to Oman. These southern regions are generally arid except along the coastal plain where irrigation schemes support some agriculture and away from the coast in the Hadhramaut valley where sufficient rainfall occurs for cereal cultivation. To the north of the Hadhramaut lies the uninhabited Arabian Desert. The population, most of whom are subsistence farmers or nomadic herders of sheep and goats, are concentrated in western regions. Until recently the only mineral exploited commercially was salt but since the discovery of oil in 1984 and 1991, that commodity is making an important contribution to the economy. Otherwise, industrial activity is limited to small scale manufacturing.

YUGOSLAVIA
Federal Republic of,

STATUS: Federation of former Yugoslav Republics of Serbia and Montenegro

AREA: 102,170 sq km (39,435 sq miles)
POPULATION: 10,479,000
ANNUAL NATURAL INCREASE: 0.8%
CAPITAL: Belgrade (Beograd)
LANGUAGE: Serbo-Croat, Albanian and Hungarian
RELIGION: Orthodox Christian, 10% Muslim
CURRENCY: new Yugoslav dinar (YUD)
ORGANIZATIONS: UN (suspended)

Serbia and Montenegro are the last remaining elements of the Federal Republic of Yugoslavia. Until 1918, they were separate kingdoms. Union of the two, including Vojvodina, followed by unification with lands freed from the Turkish and Austro-Hungarian Empires, resulted in the creation of the Kingdom of Serbs, Croats and Slovenes, a name which was changed to the Kingdom of Yugoslavia in 1929. Yugoslavia became a Socialist Federal Republic in 1945. Economic difficulties from 1980 onwards, combined with regional and ethnic factors, culminated in the secession of Slovenia and Croatia in 1992. International recognition of their sovereignty did not deter Serbia, with the Serb-dominated army at its disposal, from armed incursion to secure areas inhabited by Serbians. Macedonia's claim for recognition was not so well received internationally because of Greek objection to the name Macedonia. Yet, it has ceased to be a part of Yugoslavia. No such impediment stood in the way of recognizing the independence of Bosnia-Herzegovina. Armed conflict intensified in this ethnically complex republic as rival factions fought to support their kinsfolk.

The climate is essentially continental with hot summers and cold winters. Agriculture, which is largely in private hands, features cotton and cereal cultivation on the fertile plains of Vojvodina in the north, livestock production in central Serbia and fruit and tobacco growing in Kosovo in the south. Industry, however, which had accounted for 80 per cent of economic wealth, has suffered severely from the effects of civil war and United Nations sanctions. Inflation is rife and only the black market flourishes.

MONTENEGRO

STATUS: Constituent Republic
AREA: 13,810 sq km (5,330 sq miles)
POPULATION: 664,000
CAPITAL: Podgorica

SERBIA

STATUS: Constituent Republic
AREA: 88,360 sq km (34,105 sq miles)
POPULATION: 9,815,000
CAPITAL: Belgrade (Beograd)

ZAIRE

STATUS: Republic
AREA: 2,345,410 sq km (905,330 sq miles)
POPULATION: 39,882,000
ANNUAL NATURAL INCREASE: 3.3%
CAPITAL: Kinshasa
LANGUAGE: French, Lingala, Kiswahili, Tshiluba, Kikongo

RELIGION: 46% Roman Catholic, 28% Protestant, traditional beliefs
CURRENCY: zaire (ZRZ)
ORGANIZATIONS: OAU, UN

Zaire, formerly the Belgian Congo, lies astride the Equator and is Africa's third largest country after Sudan and Algeria. It is dominated by the drainage basin of the Zaire, Kasai, and Oubangui rivers, which join to flow into the Atlantic. The land gradually rises from these basins to the south and east, culminating in the Chaine des Mitumba or Mitumbar mountains. On its eastern border the great Rift Valley forms a natural boundary with Uganda and Tanzania. Tropical rainforest covers most of the basin. Zaire's climate is equatorial with both high temperatures, averaging 27°C (80°F) throughout the year, and high rainfall of about 1,500–2,000 (59–79 inches). The majority of the population is engaged in shifting agriculture. Cassava, cocoa, coffee, cotton, millet, rubber and sugar cane are grown. Although the nation possesses mineral wealth, particularly copper which alone has provided 40 per cent of foreign earnings, political turmoil has reduced the country to bankruptcy. The copper mines are closed and diamonds are the only source of income. Zaire faces expulsion from the IMF because of debt arrears.

ZAMBIA

STATUS: Republic
AREA: 752,615 sq km (290,510 sq miles)
POPULATION: 8,638,000
ANNUAL NATURAL INCREASE: 3.5%
CAPITAL: Lusaka
LANGUAGE: English, African languages
RELIGION: 75% Christian, animist minority
CURRENCY: kwacha (ZMK)
ORGANIZATIONS: Comm., OAU, UN

Mineral-rich Zambia, is situated in the interior of southern central Africa. Its geography consists mainly of high rolling plateaux, with mountains to the north and northeast. In the south is the Zambezi river basin and the man-made reservoir of Lake Kariba, which forms Zambia's border with Zimbabwe. Altitude moderates the potentially tropical climate so that the summer temperature averages only 13–27°C (55–81°F). The north receives over 1,250 mm (49 inches) of rain per annum, the south less. Most of the country is grassland with some forest in the north. Farming is now mainly at subsistence level, as droughts have had an adverse effect on many crops, but some cattle rearing still takes on importance in the east. Copper remains the mainstay of the country's economy although reserves are fast running out. Lead, zinc, cobalt, cotton, groundnuts and tobacco are also exported. Wildlife is diverse and abundant and contributes to expanding tourism.

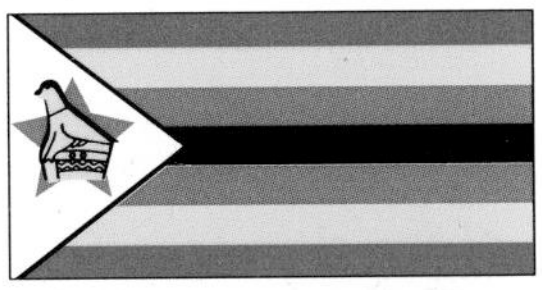

ZIMBABWE

STATUS: Republic
AREA: 390,310 sq km (150,660 sq miles)
POPULATION: 10,402,000
ANNUAL NATURAL INCREASE: 3.0%
CAPITAL: Harare
LANGUAGE: English, native languages
RELIGION: 58% Christian, traditional beliefs
CURRENCY: Zimbabwe dollar (ZWD)
ORGANIZATIONS: Comm., OAU, UN

Landlocked Zimbabwe (formerly southern Rhodesia) in south central Africa consists predominantly of rolling plateaux and valleys. A broad ridge of upland plateaux (the high veld) crosses east-west over the greater part of the country reaching heights of 1,200–1,500 m (3,940–4,920 feet). There are lowland areas (the low veld) formed by the valleys of the Zambezi and Limpopo rivers, in the north and south respectively. The climate varies with altitude and distance from the ocean. Rainfall across the country averages between 600-1,000 mm (24-39 inches). The exploitation of mineral deposits have traditionally supported the economy although recent years have seen a shift in the decline of chrome and coal and a rise in the importance of platinum, nickel and asbestos. Maize is the most important crop as it is the staple food of a large proportion of the population. Tobacco, tea, sugar cane and fruit are also grown. Manufacturing industry is slowly developing and now provides a wide range of consumer products.

CONTINENTS

land area □ = 1 000 000 sq kms / 386 000 sq miles

North and Central America
25 349 000
9 785 000

South America
17 611 000
6 798 000

Antarctica
13 340 000
5 149 240

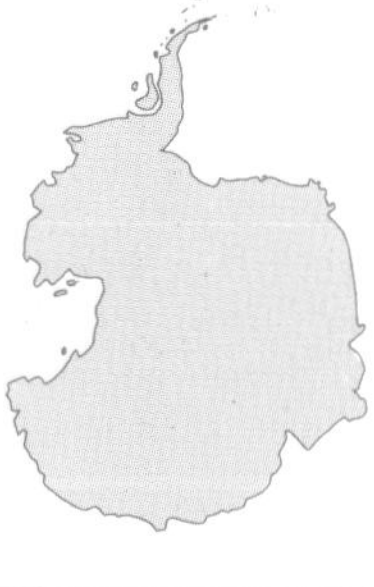

Europe
10 498 000
4 052 000

Asia
43 608 000
16 833 000

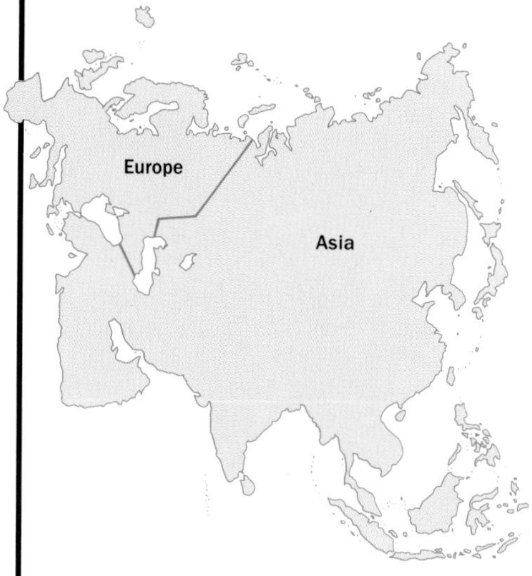

Africa
30 335 000
11 709 000

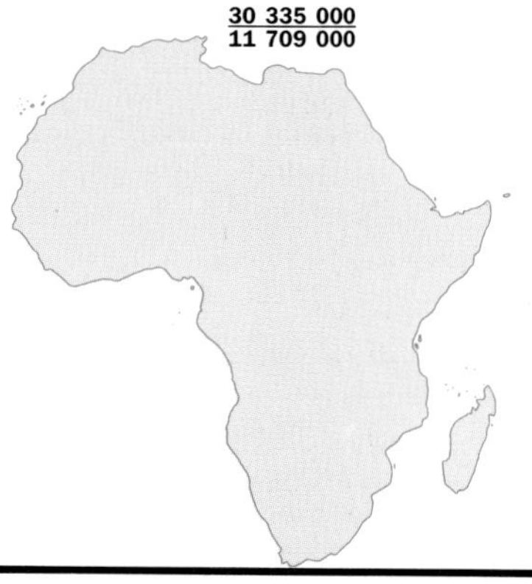

Australasia
8 923 000
3 444 278

METROPOLITAN AREAS

Population	*City*	*Country*
2,500,000	**Adibjan**	*Ivory Coast*
1,891,000	**Addis Ababa**	*Ethiopia*
3,297,655	**Ahmadabad**	*India*
3,380,000	**Alexandria**	*Egypt*
3,033,000	**Algiers**	*Algeria*
1,151,300	**Alma-Ata**	*Kazakhstan*
1,091,338	**Amsterdam**	*Netherlands*
3,022,236	**Ankara**	*Turkey*
1,390,000	**Anshan**	*China*
3,096,775	**Athens**	*Greece*
3,051,000	**Atlanta**	*USA*
896,700	**Auckland**	*New Zealand*
4,044,000	**Baghdad**	*Iraq*
1,779,500	**Baku**	*Azerbaijan*
2,414,000	**Baltimore**	*USA*
4,086,548	**Bangalore**	*India*
5,876,000	**Bangkok**	*Thailand*
1,625,542	**Barcelona**	*Spain*
10,900,000	**Beijing (Peking)**	*China*
1,500,000	**Beirut**	*Lebanon*
1,168,454	**Belgrade**	*Yugoslavia*
3,461,905	**Belo Horizonte**	*Brazil*
3,446,000	**Berlin**	*Germany*
2,310,900	**Birmingham**	*UK*
5,025,989	**Bogotá**	*Colombia*
12,571,720	**Bombay**	*India*
4,497,000	**Boston**	*USA*
1,803,478	**Brasília**	*Brazil*
950,339	**Brussels**	*Belgium*
2,350,984	**Bucharest**	*Romania*
2,992,000	**Budapest**	*Hungary*
12,200,000	**Buenos Aires**	*Argentina*
13,300,000	**Cairo**	*Egypt*
10,916,000	**Calcutta**	*India*
320,000	**Canberra**	*Australia*
2,350,157	**Cape Town**	*South Africa*
4,092,000	**Caracas**	*Venezuela*
3,210,000	**Casablanca**	*Morocco*
2,214,000	**Changchun**	*China*
1,362,000	**Changsha**	*China*
1,148,000	**Chelyabinsk**	*Russian Federation*
3,004,000	**Chengdu**	*China*
7,498,000	**Chicago**	*USA*
3,010,000	**Chongqing**	*China*
1,342,679	**Copenhagen**	*Denmark*
2,543,000	**Dalian**	*China*
4,135,000	**Dallas – Fort Worth**	*USA*
2,913,000	**Damascus**	*Syria*
1,657,000	**Dar-es-Salaam**	*Tanzania*
8,375,000	**Delhi**	*India*
4,285,000	**Detroit**	*USA*
6,105,160	**Dhaka**	*Bangladesh*
915,516	**Dublin**	*Republic of Ireland*
2,720,400	**Essen – Dortmund**	*Germany*
1,420,000	**Fushun**	*China*
383,900	**Geneva**	*Switzerland*
2,846,720	**Guadalajara**	*Mexico*
3,620,000	**Guangzhou (Canton)**	*China*
1,669,000	**Hamburg**	*Germany*
1,412,000	**Hangzhou**	*China*
3,056,146	**Hanoi**	*Vietnam*
2,840,000	**Harbin**	*China*
2,099,000	**Havana**	*Cuba*
3,924,435	**Ho Chi Minh (Saigon)**	*Vietnam*
5,812,000	**Hong Kong**	*UK colony*
3,437,000	**Houston**	*USA*
4,280,000	**Hyderabad**	*India*
6,407,215	**Istanbul**	*Turkey*
9,000,000	**Jakarta**	*Indonesia*
608,000	**Jerusalem**	*Israel*
1,327,000	**Jilin**	*China*
2,415,000	**Jinan**	*China*
1,916,063	**Johannesburg**	*South Africa*
1,300,000	**Kābul**	*Afghanistan*
7,702,000	**Karachi**	*Pakistan*
1,947,000	**Khartoum**	*Sudan*
2,616,000	**Kiev**	*Ukraine*
3,505,000	**Kinshasa**	*Zaire*
1,711,000	**Kuala Lumpur**	*Malaysia*
5,689,000	**Lagos**	*Nigeria*
4,092,000	**Lahore**	*Pakistan*
1,566,000	**Lanzhou**	*China*
6,483,901	**Lima**	*Peru*
1,742,000	**Lisbon**	*Portugal*
9,277,687	**London**	*UK*
11,420,000	**Los Angeles**	*USA*
5,361,468	**Madras**	*India*
2,909,792	**Madrid**	*Spain*
2,578,900	**Manchester**	*UK*
8,475,000	**Manila – Quezon City**	*Philippines*
1,594,967	**Medellín**	*Colombia*
3,178,000	**Melbourne**	*Australia*
20,200,000	**Mexico City**	*Mexico*
1,814,000	**Miami**	*USA*
2,583,000	**Minneapolis – St Paul**	*USA*
1,633,000	**Minsk**	*Belarus*
2,521,697	**Monterrey**	*Mexico*
1,383,660	**Montevideo**	*Uruguay*
3,127,100	**Montréal**	*Canada*
8,957,000	**Moscow**	*Russian Federation*
1,236,000	**Munich**	*Germany*
2,095,000	**Nagoya**	*Japan*
1,503,000	**Nairobi**	*Kenya*
1,415,000	**Nanchang**	*China*
2,265,000	**Nanjing**	*China*
16,972,000	**New York**	*USA*
1,442,000	**Novosibirsk**	*Russian Federation*
1,106,000	**Odessa**	*Ukraine*
8,520,000	**Osaka-Kobe**	*Japan*
473,344	**Oslo**	*Norway*
921,000	**Ottawa**	*Canada*
9,318,000	**Paris**	*France*
4,941,000	**Philadelphia**	*USA*
2,287,000	**Phoenix**	*USA*
2,404,000	**Pittsburgh**	*USA*
3,015,960	**Pôrto Alegre**	*Brazil*
1,214,174	**Prague**	*Czech Republic*
3,797,566	**Pusan**	*South Korea*
2,230,000	**Pyôngyang**	*North Korea*
645,000	**Quebec**	*Canada*
2,060,000	**Qingdao**	*China*
1,281,849	**Quito**	*Ecuador*
3,295,000	**Rangoon**	*Burma*
2,859,469	**Recife**	*Brazil*
910,200	**Riga**	*Latvia*
9,871,165	**Rio de Janeiro**	*Brazil*
1,500,000	**Riyadh**	*Saudi Arabia*
2,723,327	**Rome**	*Italy*
1,388,000	**Sacramento**	*USA*
2,472,131	**Salvador**	*Brazil*
2,549,000	**San Deigo**	*USA*
5,240,000	**San Francisco**	*USA*
1,390,000	**San Juan**	*Puerto Rico*
4,628,000	**Santiago**	*Chile*
2,055,000	**Santo Domingo**	*Dominican Repub*
15,199,423	**São Paulo**	*Brazil*
10,627,000	**Seoul**	*South Korea*
13,341,896	**Shanghai**	*China*
4,763,000	**Shenyang**	*China*
2,874,000	**Singapore**	*Singapore*
1,221,000	**Sofia**	*Bulgaria*
2,507,000	**St Louis**	*USA*
5,004,000	**St Petersburg**	*Russian Federatio*
1,669,840	**Stockholm**	*Sweden*
2,473,272	**Surabaya**	*Indonesia*
3,700,000	**Sydney**	*Australia*
2,228,000	**Taegu**	*South Korea*
2,720,000	**Taipei**	*Taiwan*
2,199,000	**Taiyuan**	*China*
452,000	**Tallinn**	*Estonia*
2,094,000	**Tashkent**	*Uzbekistan*
1,400,000	**Tbilisi**	*Georgia*
6,773,000	**Tehran**	*Iran*
1,135,800	**Tel Aviv**	*Israel*
9,100,000	**Tianjin**	*China*
11,609,735	**Tokyo**	*Japan*
3,893,400	**Toronto**	*Canada*
2,062,000	**Tripoli**	*Libya*
1,603,600	**Vancouver**	*Canada*
1,565,000	**Vienna**	*Austria*
593,000	**Vilnius**	*Lithuania*
1,655,700	**Warsaw**	*Poland*
4,293,000	**Washington DC**	*USA*
325,700	**Wellington**	*New Zealand*
652,000	**Winnipeg**	*Canada*
3,921,000	**Wuhan**	*China*
2,859,000	**Xian**	*China*
1,202,000	**Yerevan**	*Armenia*
726,770	**Zagreb**	*Croatia*
2,460,000	**Zibo**	*China*

MOUNTAIN HEIGHTS

metres	feet		
8,848	29,028	**Everest (Qomolangma Feng)**	*China–Nepal*
8,611	28,250	**K2 (Qogir Feng) (Godwin Austen)**	*India – China*
8,598	28,170	**Kangchenjunga**	*India–Nepal*
8,481	27,824	**Makalu**	*China–Nepal*
8,217	26,958	**Cho Oyu**	*China–Nepal*
8,167	26,795	**Dhaulagiri**	*Nepal*
8,156	26,758	**Manaslu**	*Nepal*
8,126	26,660	**Nanga Parbat**	*India*
8,078	26,502	**Annapurna**	*Nepal*
8,088	26,470	**Gasherbrum**	*India–China*
8,027	26,335	**Xixabangma Feng (Gosainthan)**	*China*
7,885	25,869	**Distaghil Sar**	*Kashmir, India*
7,820	25,656	**Masherbrum**	*India*
7,817	25,646	**Nanda Devi**	*India*
7,788	25,550	**Rakaposhi**	*India*
7,756	25,446	**Kamet**	*China–India*
7,756	25,447	**Namjagbarwa Feng**	*China*
7,728	25,355	**Gurla Mandhata**	*China*
7,723	25,338	**Muztag**	*China*
7,719	25,325	**Kongur Shan (Kungur)**	*China*
7,690	25,230	**Tirich Mir**	*Pakistan*
7,556	24,790	**Gongga Shan**	*China*
7,546	24,757	**Muztagata**	*China*
7,495	24,590	**Pik Kommunizma**	*Tajikistan*
7,439	24,406	**Pik Pobedy (Tomur Feng)**	*Kirghizia–China*
7,313	23,993	**Chomo Lhari**	*Bhutan–Tibet*
7,134	23,406	**Pik Lenina**	*Kirghizia*
6,960	22,834	**Aconcagua**	*Argentina*
6,908	22,664	**Ojos del Salado**	*Argentina–Chile*
6,872	22,546	**Bonete**	*Argentina*
6,800	22,310	**Tupungato**	*Argentina–Chile*
6,770	22,221	**Mercedario**	*Argentina*

metres	feet		
6,768	22,205	**Huascarán**	*Peru*
6,723	22,057	**Llullaillaco**	*Argentina–Chile*
6,714	22,027	**Kangrinboqê Feng (Kailas)**	*Tibet, China*
6,634	21,765	**Yerupaja**	*Peru*
6,542	21,463	**Sajama**	*Bolivia*
6,485	21,276	**Illampu**	*Bolivia*
6,425	21,079	**Coropuna**	*Peru*
6,402	21,004	**Illimani**	*Bolivia*
6,310	20,702	**Chimborazo**	*Ecuador*
6,194	20,320	**McKinley**	*USA*
5,959	19,551	**Logan**	*Canada*
5,896	19,344	**Cotopaxi**	*Ecuador*
5,895	19,340	**Kilimanjaro**	*Tanzania*
5,800	19,023	**Sa. Nevada de Sta. Marta (Cristobal Colon)**	*Columbia*
5,775	18,947	**Bolivar**	*Venezuela*
5,699	18,697	**Citlaltépetl (Orizaba)**	*Mexico*
5,642	18,510	**El'brus**	*Russian Federation*
5,601	18,376	**Damāvand**	*Iran*
5,489	18,008	**Mt St. Elias**	*Canada*
5,227	17,149	**Mt Lucania**	*Canada*
5,199	17,057	**Kenya (Kirinyaga)**	*Kenya*
5,165	16,945	**Ararat (Büyük Ağri Daği)**	*Turkey*
5,140	16,860	**Vinson Massif**	*Antarctica*
5,110	16,763	**Stanley (Margherita)**	*Uganda–Zaire*
5,029	16,499	**Jaya (Carstensz)**	*Indonesia*
5,005	16,421	**Mt Bona**	*USA*
4,949	16,237	**Sandford**	*USA*

metres	feet		
4,936	16,194	**Mt Blackburn**	*Canada*
4,808	15,774	**Mont Blanc**	*France–Italy*
4,750	15,584	**Klyuchevskaya Sopka**	*Russian Federation*
4,634	15,203	**Monte Rosa (Dufour)**	*Italy–Switzerland*
4,565	14,979	**Meru**	*Tanzania*
4,545	14,910	**Dom (Mischabel group)**	*Switzerland*
4,533	14,872	**Ras Dashen**	*Ethiopia*
4,528	14,855	**Kirkpatrick**	*Antarctica*
4,508	14,790	**Wilhelm**	*Papua, New Guinea*
4,507	14,786	**Karisimbi**	*Rwanda–Zaire*
4,477	14,688	**Matterhorn**	*Italy–Switzerland*
4,418	14,495	**Whitney**	*USA*
4,398	14,431	**Elbert**	*USA*
4,392	14,410	**Rainier**	*USA*
4,351	14,275	**Markham**	*Antarctica*
4,321	14,178	**Elgon**	*Kenya–Uganda*
4,307	14,131	**Batu**	*Ethiopia*
4,169	13,677	**Mauna Loa**	*USA, Hawaii*
4,165	13,644	**Toubkal**	*Morocco*
4,095	13,435	**Cameroon (Caméroun)**	*Cameroon*
4,094	13,431	**Kinabalu**	*Malaysia*
3,794	12,447	**Erebus**	*Antarctica*
3,776	12,388	**Fuji**	*Japan*
3,754	12,316	**Cook**	*New Zealand*
3,718	12,198	**Teide**	*Canary Is*
3,482	11,424	**Thabana Ntlenyana**	*Lesotho*
3,482	11,424	**Mulhacén**	*Spain*
3,415	11,204	**Emi Koussi**	*Chad*
3,323	10,902	**Etna**	*Italy, Sicily*
2,743	9,000	**Mt Balbi**	*Bougainville, Papua New Guinea*
2,655	8,708	**Gerlachovsky stit (Tatra)**	*Czech Republic*
2,230	7,316	**Kosciusko**	*Australia*

ISLANDS

land area ☐ = 10 000 sq kms / 3 860 sq miles

Europe

Iceland 102 820 / 39 690

Ireland 83 045 / 32 055

Great Britain 229 870 / 88 730

Sardinia 24 090 / 9 300

Spitsbergen 39 045 / 15 070

Sicily 25 710 / 9 925

Asia

Sakhalin 76 400 / 29 490

Hokkaido 78 460 / 30 285

Hainan 34 000 / 13 125

Novaya Zemlya 82 620 / 31 890

Honshu 230 455 / 88 955

Luzon 104 690 / 40 410

Kyushu 42 010 / 16 215

Taiwan 35 990 / 13 890

Celebes 189 040 / 72 970

Sri Lanka 65 610 / 25 325

Borneo 757 050 / 292 220

Mindanao 94 630 / 36 530

Timor 33 915 / 13 090

Sumatra 524 100 / 202 300

Java 134 045 / 51 740

Central and South America

Hispaniola 78 460 / 30 285

Cuba 114 525 / 44 205

Tierra del Fuego 47 000 / 18 140

Africa

Madagascar 594 180 / 229 355

Australasia

Tasmania 68 330 / 26 375

N. Island 114 690 / 44 270

New Britain 36 500 / 14 090

New Zealand

S. Island 150 460 / 58 080

New Guinea 808 510 / 312 085

North America

Ellesmere I. 212 690 / 82 100

Greenland 2 175 600 / 839 780

Newfoundland 95 830 / 36 990

Victoria I. 212 200 / 81 910

Banks I. 67 000 / 25 860

Prince of Wales I. 33 230 / 12 825

Devon I. 54 030 / 20 855

Melville I. 42 400 / 16 365

Vancouver I. 32 135 / 12 405

Axel Heiberg I. 40 870 / 15 775

Baffin I. 476 070 / 183 760

Somerset I. 24 270 / 9 370

Southampton I. 40 650 / 15 690

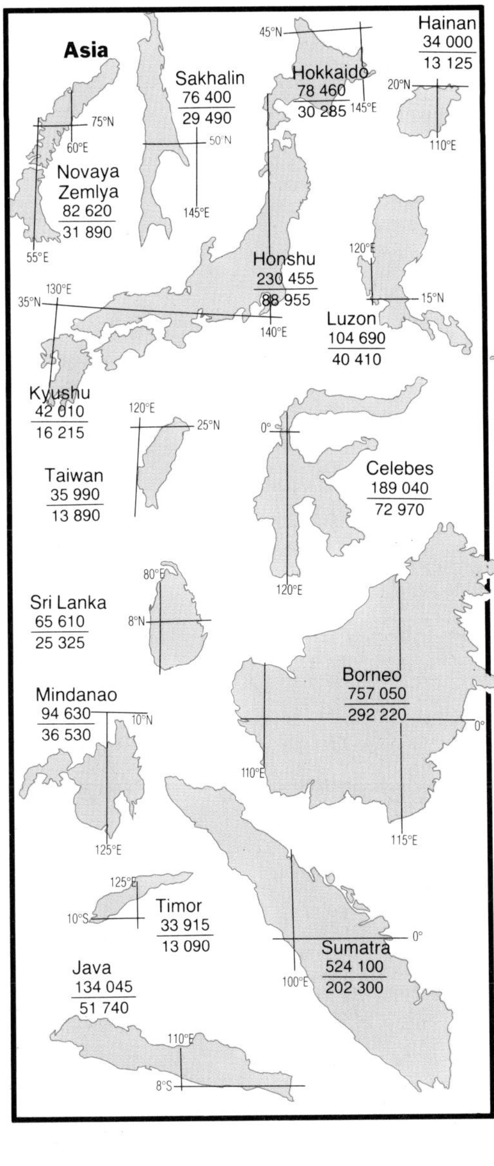

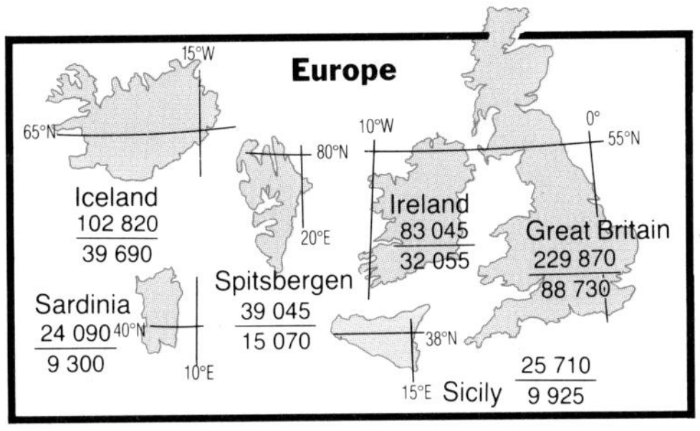

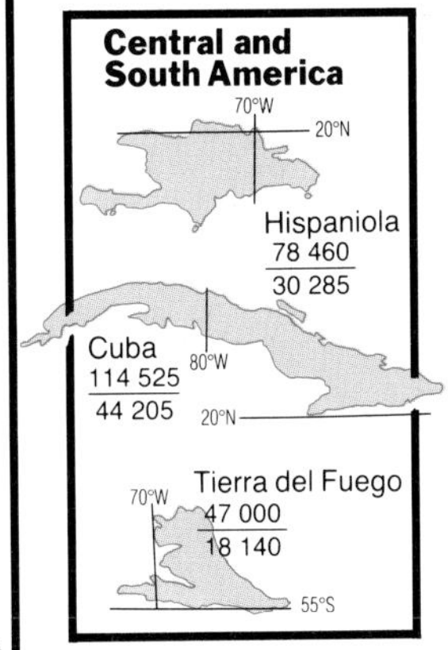

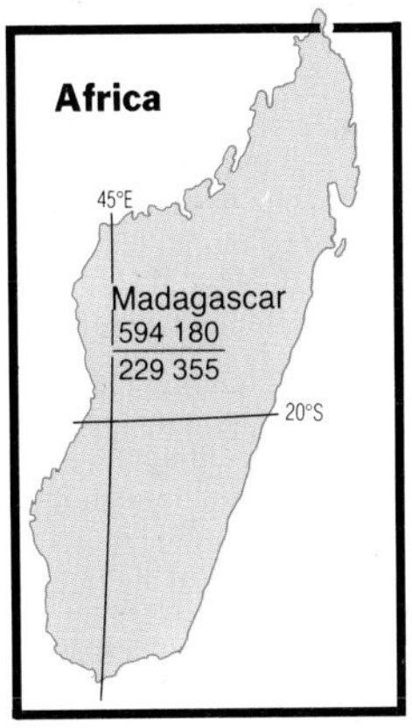

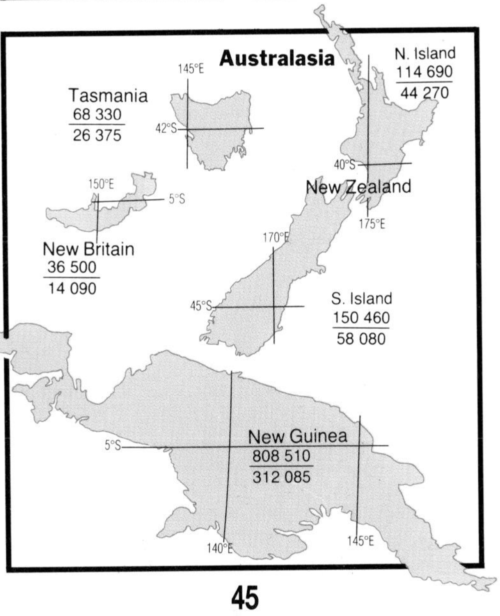

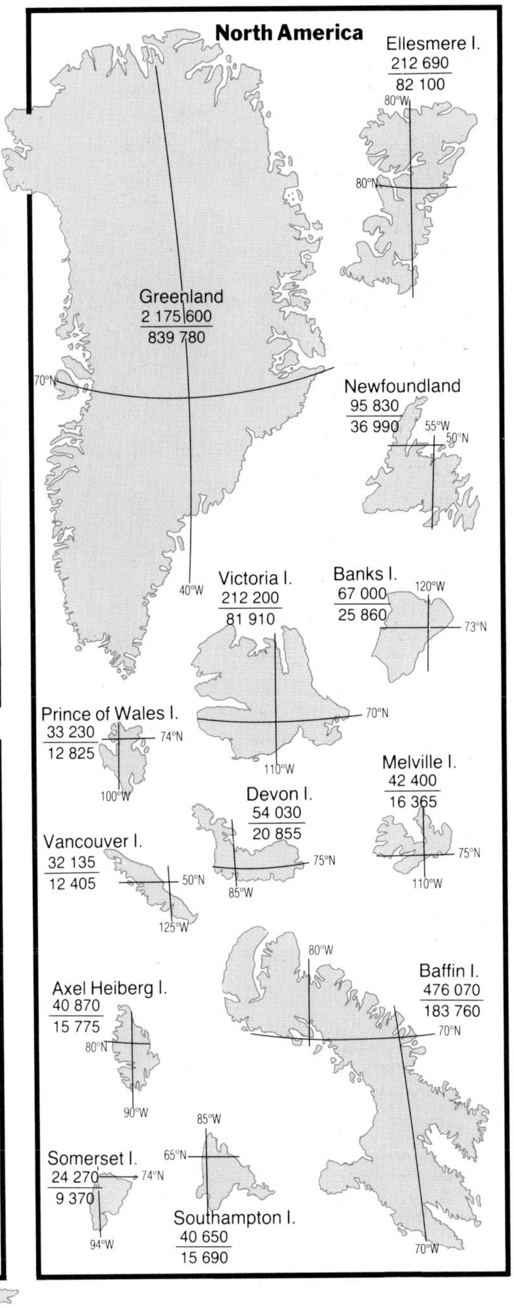

OCEANS AND SEAS

water area ▨ = $\dfrac{1\ 000\ 000}{386\ 000}$ sq km / sq miles

OCEAN FACTS AND FIGURES

The area of the Earth covered by sea is estimated to be 361,740,000 sq km (139,670,000 sq miles), or 70.92% of the total surface. The mean depth is estimated to be 3554 m (11,660 ft), and the volume of the oceans to be 1,285,600,000 cu. km (308,400,000 cu. miles).

INDIAN OCEAN

Mainly confined to the southern hemisphere, and at its greatest breadth (Tasmania to Cape Agulhas) 9600 km. Average depth is 4000 m; greatest depth is the Amirante Trench (9000 m).

ATLANTIC OCEAN

Commonly divided into North Atlantic (36,000,000 sq km) and South Atlantic (26,000,000 sq km). The greatest breadth in the North is 7200 km (Morocco to Florida) and in the South 9600 km (Guinea to Brazil). Average depth is 3600 m; the greatest depths are the Puerto Rico Trench 9220 m, S. Sandwich Trench 8264 m, and Romansh Trench 7728 m.

PACIFIC OCEAN

Covers nearly 40% of the world's total sea area, and is the largest of the oceans. The greatest breadth (E/W) is 16,000 km and the greatest length (N/S) 11,000 km. Average depth is 4200 m; also the deepest ocean. Generally the west is deeper than the east and the north deeper than the south. Greatest depths occur near island groups and include Mindanao Trench 11,524 m, Mariana Trench 11,022 m, Tonga Trench 10,882 m, Kuril-Kamchatka Trench 10,542 m, Philippine Trench 10,497 m, and Kermadec Trench 10,047 m.

Comparisons (where applicable)	greatest distance N/S (km)	greatest distance E/W (km)	maximum depth (m)
Indian Ocean	—	9600	9000
Atlantic Ocean	—	9600	9220
Pacific Ocean	11,000	16,000	11,524
Arctic Ocean	—	—	5450
Mediterranean Sea	960	3700	4846
S. China Sea	2100	1750	5514
Bering Sea	1800	2100	5121
Caribbean Sea	1600	2000	7100
Gulf of Mexico	1200	1700	4377
Sea of Okhotsk	2200	1400	3475
E. China Sea	1100	750	2999
Yellow Sea	800	1000	91
Hudson Bay	1250	1050	259
Sea of Japan	1500	1100	3743
North Sea	1200	550	661
Red Sea	1932	360	2246
Black Sea	600	1100	2245
Baltic Sea	1500	650	460

EARTH'S SURFACE WATERS

Total volume	c.1400 million cu. km
Oceans and seas	1370 million cu. km
Ice	24 million cu. km
Interstitial water (in rocks and sediments)	4 million cu. km
Lakes and rivers	230 thousand cu. km
Atmosphere (vapour)	c.140 thousand cu. km

to convert metric to imperial measurements:
1 m = 3.281 feet
1 km = 0.621 miles
1 sq km = 0.386 sq miles

Red Sea
438 000
169 000

Indian Ocean
73 481 000
28 364 000

Arctic Ocean
14 056 000
5 426 000

Baltic Sea
422 000
163 000

Hudson Bay
1 233 000
476 000

North Sea
575 000
222 000

Black Sea
461 000
178 000

Gulf of Mexico
1 544 000
596 000

Mediterranean Sea
2 505 000
967 000

Caribbean Sea
1 943 000
750 000

Atlantic Ocean
82 217 000
31 736 000

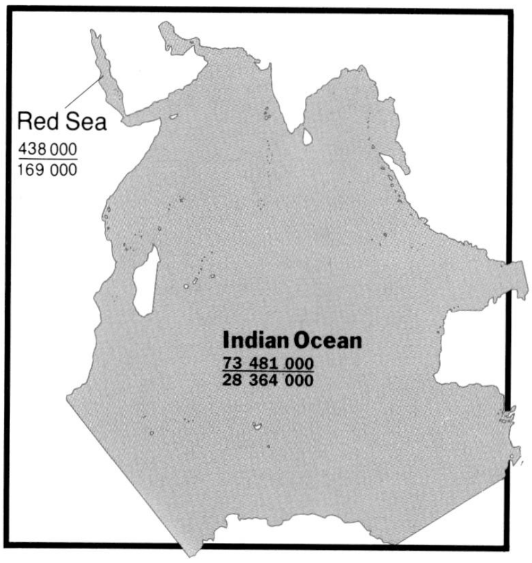

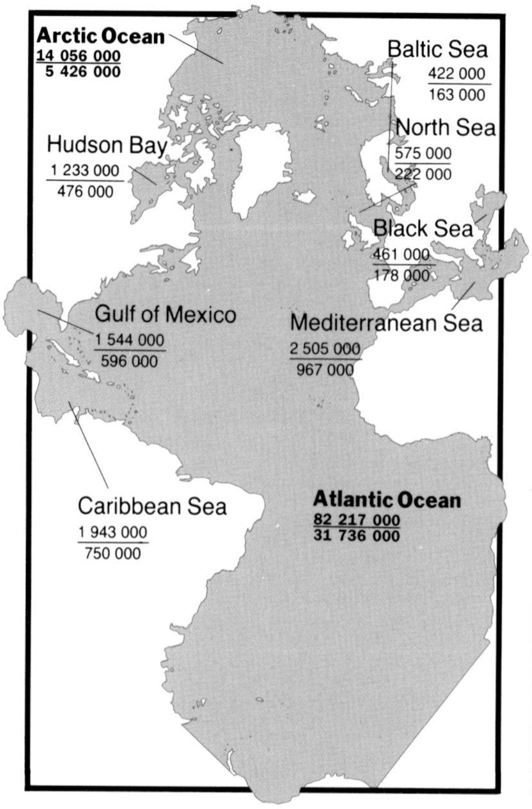

FEATURES OF THE OCEAN BASIN

The majority of land drainage occurs in the Atlantic, yet this is the most saline ocean due to interchange of waters with its marginal seas. The continental margins (21% of ocean floors) are the most important economic areas.

	PACIFIC	ATLANTIC	INDIAN	WORLD
AVERAGE OCEAN DEPTH (metres)				
OCEAN AREA (million sq km)	180	107	74	361
LAND AREA DRAINED (million sq km)	19	69	13	101
AREA AS PERCENTAGE OF TOTAL				
Continental margin	15.8	27.9	14.8	20.6
Ridges, rises and fracture zones	38.4	33.3	35.6	35.8
Deep ocean floor	42.9	38.1	49.3	41.9
Island arcs and trenches	2.9	0.7	0.3	1.7

(Average ocean depth scale: 3000, 3500, 4000)

Sea of Japan
1 008 000
389 000

Sea of Okhotsk
1 528 000
590 000

Yellow Sea
404 000
156 000

East China Sea
1 248 000
482 000

Bering Sea
2 269 000
876 000

South China Sea
2 318 000
895 000

Pacific Ocean
165 384 000
63 838 000

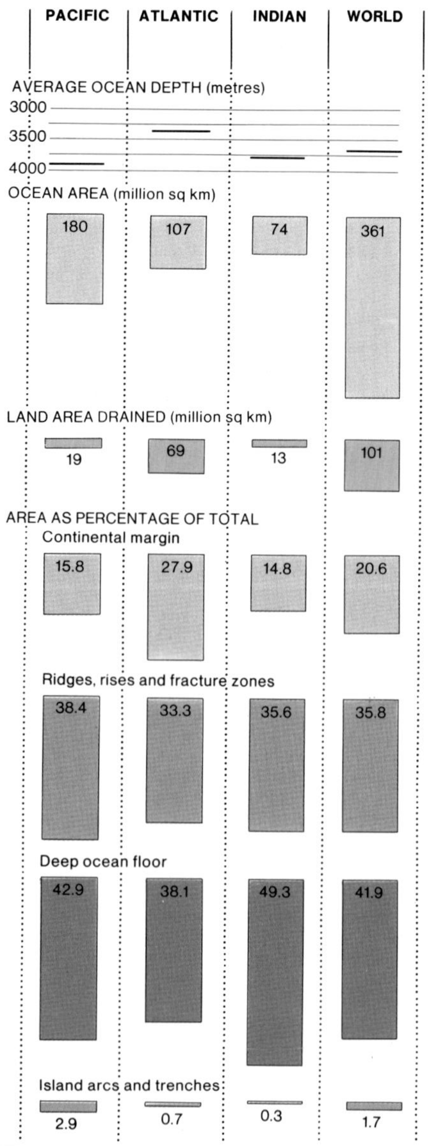

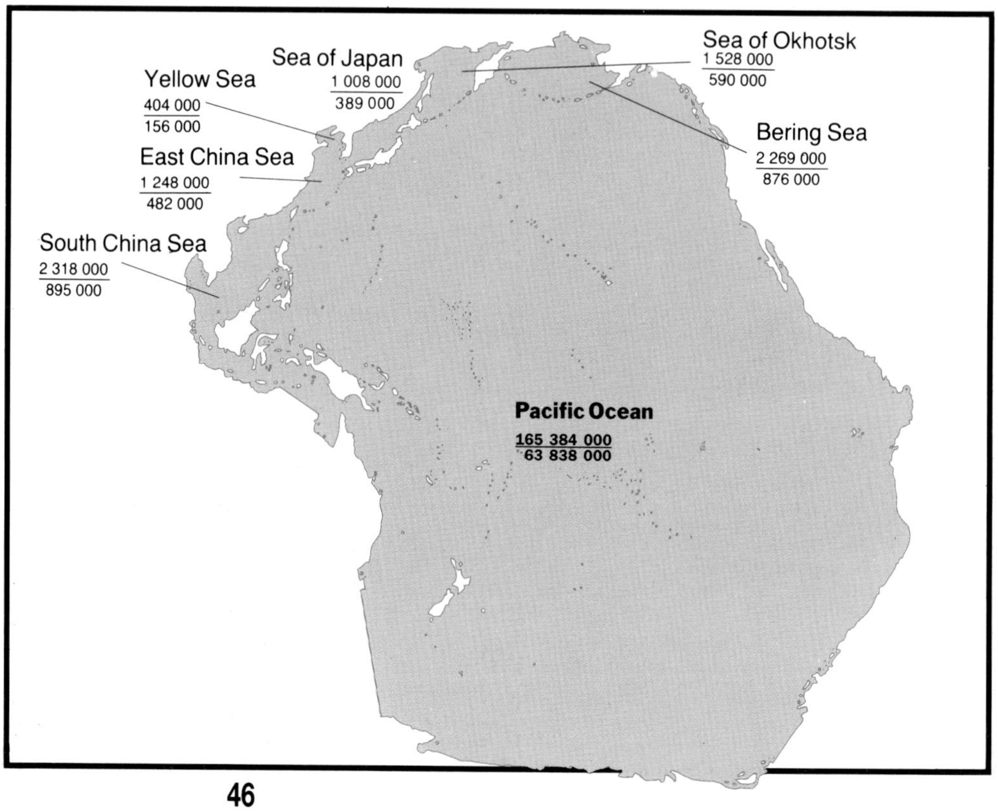

RIVER LENGTHS

km	miles		
6,695	4,160	**Nile**	Africa
6,515	4,050	**Amazon**	South America
6,380	3,965	**Yangtze (Chang Jiang)**	Asia
6,019	3,740	**Mississippi-Missouri**	North America
5,570	3,460	**Ob'-Irtysh**	Asia
5,550	3,450	**Yenisei-Angara**	Asia
5,464	3,395	**Yellow River (Huang He)**	Asia
4,667	2,900	**Congo (Zaire)**	Africa
4,500	2,800	**Paraná**	South America
4,440	2,775	**Irtysh**	Asia
4,425	2,750	**Mekong**	Asia
4,416	2,744	**Amur**	Asia
4,400	2,730	**Lena**	Asia
4,250	2,640	**Mackenzie**	North America
4,090	2,556	**Yenisei**	Asia
4,030	2,505	**Niger**	Africa
3,969	2,466	**Missouri**	North America
3,779	2,348	**Mississippi**	North America
3,750	2,330	**Murray-Darling**	Australasia
3,688	2,290	**Volga**	Europe
3,218	2,011	**Purus**	South America
3,200	1,990	**Madeira**	South America
3,185	1,980	**Yukon**	North America
3,180	1,975	**Indus**	Asia
3,078	1,913	**Syrdar'ya**	Asia
3,060	1,901	**Salween**	Asia
3,058	1,900	**St Lawrence**	North America
2,900	1,800	**São Francisco**	South America
2,870	1,785	**Rio Grande**	North America
2,850	1,770	**Danube**	Europe
2,840	1,765	**Brahmaputra**	Asia
2,815	1,750	**Euphrates**	Asia
2,750	1,710	**Pará-Tocantins**	South America
2,750	1,718	**Tarim**	Asia
2,650	1,650	**Zambezi**	Africa
2,620	1,630	**Amudar'ya**	Asia
2,620	1,630	**Araguaia**	South America
2,600	1,615	**Paraguay**	South America
2,570	1,600	**Nelson-Saskatchewan**	North America

RIVER LENGTHS & DRAINAGE BASINS

2,534	1,575	**Ural**	Asia
2,513	1,562	**Kolyma**	Asia
2,510	1,560	**Ganges (Ganga)**	Asia
2,500	1,555	**Orinoco**	South America
2,490	1,550	**Shabeelle**	Africa
2,490	1,550	**Pilcomayo**	South America
2,348	1,459	**Arkansas**	North America
2,333	1,450	**Colorado**	North America
2,285	1,420	**Dneper**	Europe
2,250	1,400	**Columbia**	North America
2,150	1,335	**Irrawaddy**	Asia
2,129	1,323	**Pearl River (Xi Jiang)**	Asia
2,032	1,270	**Kama**	Europe
2,000	1,240	**Negro**	South America
1,923	1,195	**Peace**	North America
1,899	1,186	**Tigris**	Asia
1,870	1,162	**Don**	Europe
1,860	1,155	**Orange**	Africa
1,809	1,124	**Pechora**	Europe
1,800	1,125	**Okavango**	Africa
1,609	1,000	**Marañón**	South America
1,609	1,095	**Uruguay**	South America
1,600	1,000	**Volta**	Africa
1,600	1,000	**Limpopo**	Africa
1,550	963	**Magdalena**	South America
1,515	946	**Kura**	Asia
1,480	925	**Oka**	Europe
1,480	925	**Belaya**	Europe
1,445	903	**Godavari**	Asia
1,430	893	**Senegal**	Africa
1,410	876	**Dnester**	Europe
1,400	875	**Chari**	Africa
1,368	850	**Fraser**	North America
1,320	820	**Rhine**	Europe
1,314	821	**Vyatka**	Europe
1,183	735	**Donets**	Europe
1,159	720	**Elbe**	Europe
1,151	719	**Kizilirmak**	Asia

1,130	706	**Desna**	Europe
1,094	680	**Gambia**	Africa
1,080	675	**Yellowstone**	North America
1,049	652	**Tennessee**	North America
1,024	640	**Zelenga**	Asia
1,020	637	**Duena**	Europe
1,014	630	**Vistula (Wisła)**	Europe
1,012	629	**Loire**	Europe
1,006	625	**Tagus (Tejo)**	Europe
977	607	**Tisza**	Europe
925	575	**Meuse (Maas)**	Europe
909	565	**Oder**	Europe
761	473	**Seine**	Europe
354	220	**Severn**	Europe
346	215	**Thames**	Europe
300	186	**Trent**	Europe

DRAINAGE BASINS

sq km	sq miles		
7,050,000	2,721,000	**Amazon**	South America
3,700,000	1,428,000	**Congo**	Africa
3,250,000	1,255,000	**Mississippi-Missouri**	North America
3,100,000	1,197,000	**Paraná**	South America
2,700,000	1,042,000	**Yenisei**	Asia
2,430,000	938,000	**Ob'**	Asia
2,420,000	934,000	**Lena**	Asia
1,900,000	733,400	**Nile**	Africa
1,840,000	710,000	**Amur**	Asia
1,765,000	681,000	**Mackenzie**	North America
1,730,000	668,000	**Ganges-Brahmaputra**	Asia
1,380,000	533,000	**Volga**	Europe
1,330,000	513,000	**Zambezi**	Africa
1,200,000	463,000	**Niger**	Africa
1,175,000	454,000	**Yangtze**	Asia
1,020,000	394,000	**Orange**	Africa
980,000	378,000	**Yellow River**	Asia
960,000	371,000	**Indus**	Asia
945,000	365,000	**Orinoco**	South America
910,000	351,000	**Murray-Darling**	Australasia
855,000	330,000	**Yukon**	North America
815,000	315,000	**Danube**	Europe
810,000	313,000	**Mekong**	Asia
225,000	86,900	**Rhine**	Europe

INLAND WATERS

water surface area ■ = $\frac{1\,000 \text{ sq km}}{386 \text{ sq miles}}$

deepest point $\frac{229 \text{ metres}}{751 \text{ feet}}$

North and Central America

L.Superior
83270 _393_
32140 _1289_

L.Huron
60700 _229_
23430 _751_

L.Ontario
19230 _237_
7425 _778_

L.Michigan
58020 _281_
22395 _922_

L.Erie
25680 _64_
9915 _210_

L.de Nicaragua
8270 _70_
3190 _230_

Great Bear Lake
31790 _319_
12270 _1047_

L.Athabasca
8080 _91_
3120 _299_

Great Slave Lake
28440 _140_
10980 _459_

Nettilling Lake
5250
2030

L.Winnipeg
24510 _21_
9460 _69_

Reindeer Lake
6390
2470

Africa

L.Victoria
68800 _100_
26560 _328_

L.Tanganyika
32900 _1435_
13860 _4708_

L.Nyasa (Malawi)
22490 _706_
8680 _2316_

L.Turkana (Rudolf)
4250 _73_
1640 _240_

L.Chad
10-26000 _4-7_
4-10000 _13-23_

L.Albert
6410 _48_
2475 _158_

L.Mweru
4920 _14_
1900 _46_

Europe

L.Onega
9600 _124_
3705 _407_

L.Vänern
5580 _98_
2155 _322_

L.Ladoga
18390 _230_
7100 _755_

Asia

Caspian Sea (salt)
371 000 _980_
143 205 _3215_

L.Balkhash
17 400 _26_
6 715 _85_

L.Baikal
30 500 _1741_
11 775 _5712_

D.-ye Orūmīyeh
5900 _15_
2280 _49_

Issyk-Kul
6200 _702_
2395 _2303_

Qinghai Hu
2300 _38_
890 _125_

Poyang Hu
5000
1930

South America

L.Titicaca
8340 _304_
3220 _997_

Australasia

L.Eyre (salt)
0 - 8900 _0-20_
0 - 3435 _0-66_

L.Torrens (salt)
5780
2230

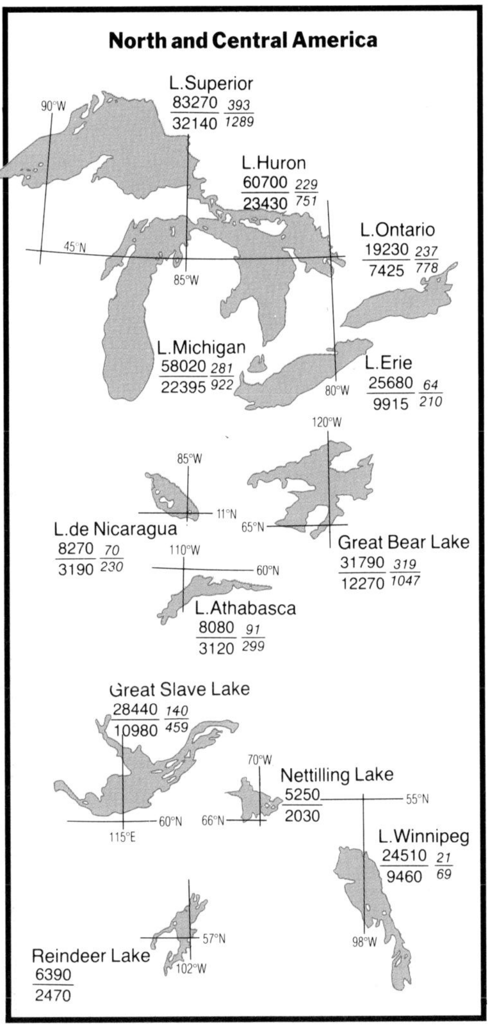

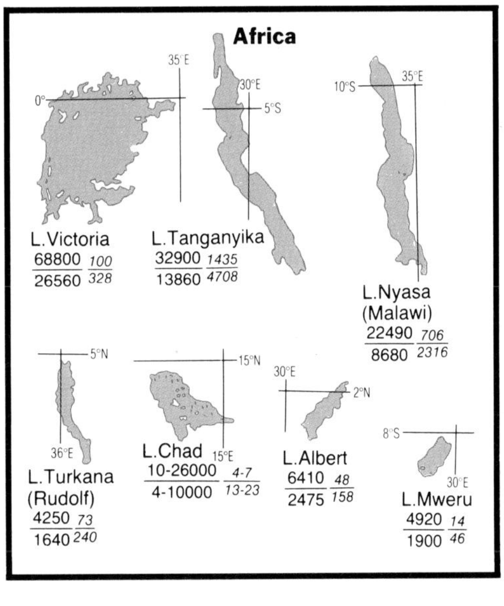

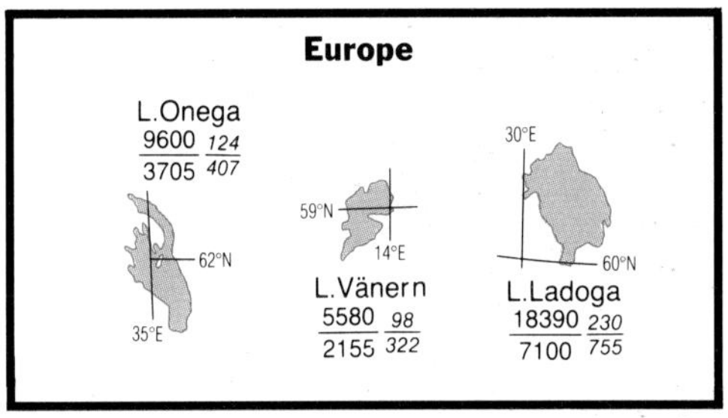

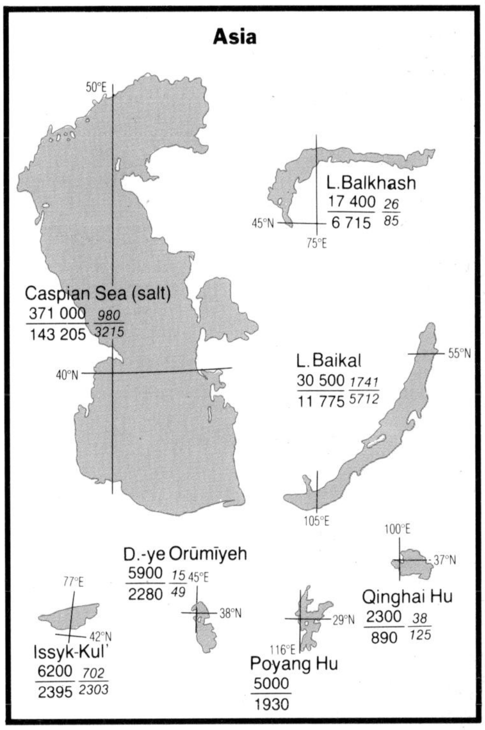

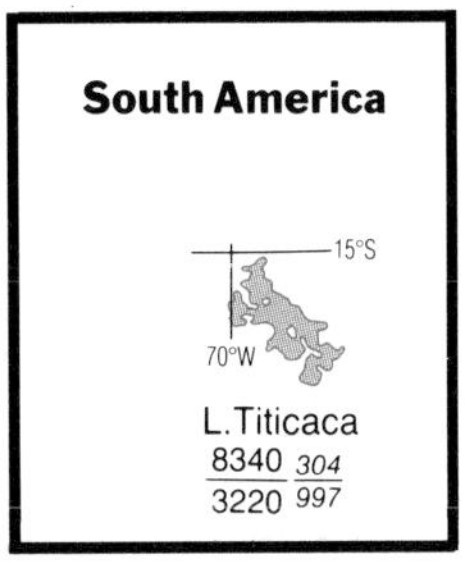

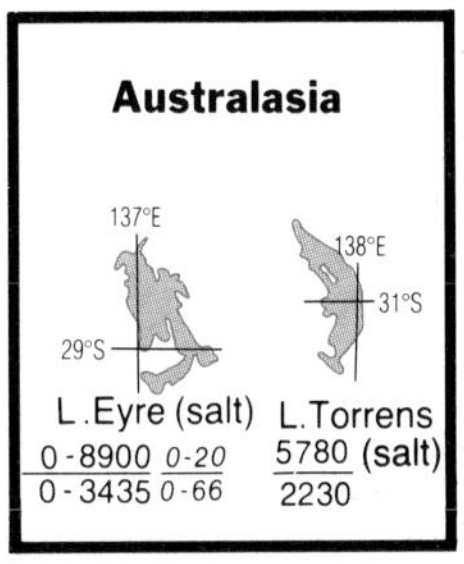

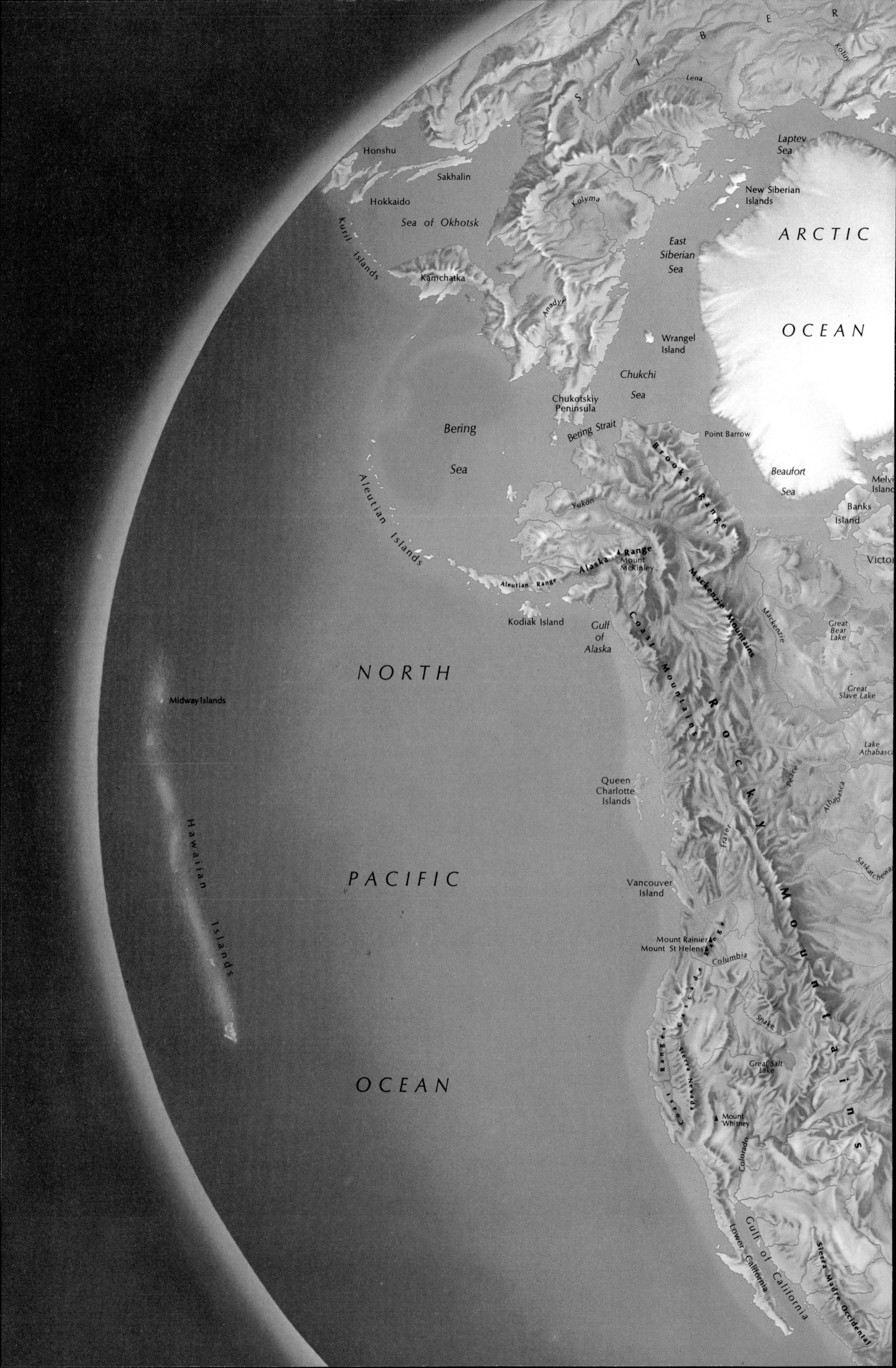
S I B E R
Lena
Kolyma
Laptev Sea
Honshu
Sakhalin
Hokkaido
Sea of Okhotsk
Kuril Islands
New Siberian Islands
ARCTIC
East Siberian Sea
Kamchatka
Anadyr
OCEAN
Wrangel Island
Chukchi Sea
Chukotskiy Peninsula
Bering Sea
Bering Strait
Point Barrow
Brooks Range
Beaufort Sea
Banks Island
Aleutian Islands
Yukon
Alaska Range
Mount McKinley
Aleutian Range
Mackenzie Mountains
Mackenzie
Great Bear Lake
Kodiak Island
Gulf of Alaska
Coast Mountains
NORTH
Midway Islands
Great Slave Lake
ROCKY MOUNTAINS
Lake Athabasca
Peace
Athabasca
Queen Charlotte Islands
Fraser
Hawaiian Islands
PACIFIC
Vancouver Island
Mount Rainier
Mount St Helens
Cascade Range
Columbia
Snake
Coast Ranges
Sierra Nevada
Great Salt Lake
OCEAN
Mount Whitney
Colorado
Gulf of California
Lower California
Sierra Madre Occidental

Kara Sea
Novaya Zemlya
Barents Sea
Severnaya Zemlya
Franz Josef Land
North Cape
SCANDINAVIA
Baltic Sea
Black Sea
Limit of permanent pack ice
Bear Island
Svalbard
Norwegian Sea
NORTH POLE
Wandell Sea
Jan Mayen
North Sea
Mediterranean Sea
Greenland Sea
Lincoln Sea
Denmark Strait
BRITISH ISLES
Bay of Biscay
Ellesmere Island
Greenland
Iceland
Axel Heiburg Island
Queen Elizabeth Islands
NORTH AFRICA
Parry Islands
Devon Island
Baffin Bay
Somerset Island
Prince of Wales Island
Davis Strait
Cape Farewell
Madeira
Baffin Island
Nettiling Lake
NORTH
Canary Islands
Foxe Basin
Labrador Sea
Azores
Southampton Island
Hudson Strait
Cape Chidley
Hudson Bay
Labrador
Churchill
Reindeer Lake
Southern Indian Lake
Nelson
La Grande Rivière
Laurentian Highlands
Newfoundland
Cape Race
ATLANTIC
James Bay
Rupert
Lake Winnipeg
Nova Scotia
Lake Manitoba
St Lawrence
Lake of the Woods
Lake Superior
Cape Cod
Lake Huron
Lake Ontario
Missouri
Mississippi
Lake Michigan
Lake Erie
Appalachian Mountains
Great Plains
Platte
Ohio
Bermuda
OCEAN
Cape Hatteras
Ozark Plateaus
Arkansas
Tennessee
Savannah
Red River
Florida
The Bahamas
West Indies
Rio Grande
Sierra Madre Oriental
Gulf of Mexico
Caribbean Sea
Yucatan
Orinoco

Mississippi
Florida
GULF
OF
MEXICO
Sierra Madre Occidental
Gulf of California
Lower California
Rio Grande
Sierra Madre Oriental
Gulf of Campeche
Yucatan
Popocatépetl
Sierra Madre del Sur
Islas Revillagigedo
Gulf
of
Honduras
Lake
Nicaragua
Isthmus of
Gulf of Panama
Clipperton
Island
PACIFIC
Isla del Coco
Isla de Malpelo
Galapagos Islands
Cotopaxi
Chimborazo
OCEAN

Bermuda
NORTH ATLANTIC OCEAN
Sargasso Sea
BAHAMAS
WEST INDIES
Hispaniola
Puerto Rico
ANTILLES
ARIBBEAN SEA
LESSER ANTILLES
Trinidad
Gulf of Darien
Lake Maracaibo
LLANOS
Orinoco
Roraima
Guiana Highlands
Occidental
Cordillera Oriental
Cauca
Magdalena
Branco
Mouths of the Amazon
Negro
Japurá
Putumayo
Amazon
Xingu
Tocantins
Tapajós
Juruá
Marañón
Purus
Madeira
Ucayali
Parnaíba
Araguaia
São Francisco
Madre de Dios
MATO GROSSO
Brazilian Highlands
Lake Titicaca
Ancohuma
Lake Poopó
Salar de Uyuni
Atacama Desert
GRAN CHACO
Paraguay
Paraná
Pilcomayo

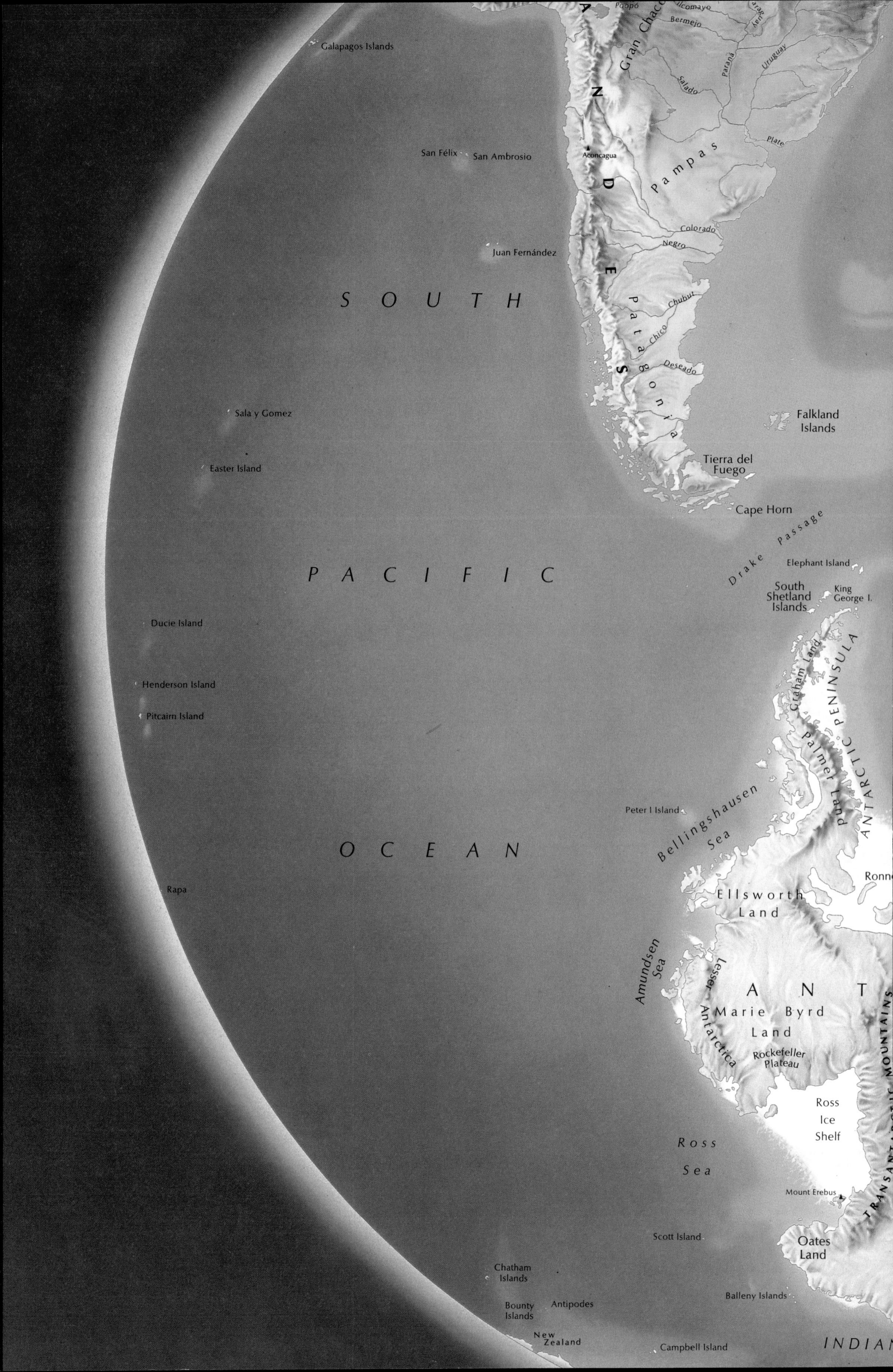
Galapagos Islands
Poopó
Ilcomayo
Bermejo
Gran Chaco
Paraná
Uruguay
Salado
Plate
San Félix
San Ambrosio
Aconcagua
Pampas
A N D E S
Colorado
Negro
Juan Fernández
Chubut
Chico
Patagonia
Deseado
S O U T H
Sala y Gomez
Falkland Islands
Easter Island
Tierra del Fuego
Cape Horn
Drake Passage
Elephant Island
P A C I F I C
South Shetland Islands
King George I.
Ducie Island
Graham Land
ANTARCTIC PENINSULA
Henderson Island
Pitcairn Island
Palmer Land
Peter I Island
Bellingshausen Sea
O C E A N
Rapa
Ellsworth Land
Amundsen Sea
Lesser Antarctica
A N T
Marie Byrd Land
Rockefeller Plateau
Ross Ice Shelf
Ross Sea
Mount Erebus
TRANSANTARCTIC MOUNTAINS
Scott Island
Oates Land
Chatham Islands
Balleny Islands
Bounty Islands
Antipodes
New Zealand
Campbell Island
INDIAN

St Helena
Tristan da Cunha
SOUTH
Gough Island
Cunene
Kalahari
Desert
Orange River
Cape
of
Good Hope
Limpopo
South Georgia
South
Sandwich
Islands
South Orkney
Islands
ATLANTIC
Bouvet Island
Madagascar
Weddell
Sea
Lazarev
Sea
Limit of permanent pack ice
Prince Edward
Islands
Queen Maud Land
OCEAN
ce Shelf
Îles Crozet
ARCTICA
Enderby Land
Antarctica
SOUTH POLE
Greater
Îles Kerguelen
Macdonald Islands
Heard Island
St Paul
Amsterdam Island
George V
Land
Wilkes Land
OCEAN

Azores
Strait of Gibraltar
Chott Melrhir
El Jerid
Mediterr
Gulf of Sirte
Madeira
ATLAS MOUNTAINS
Canary Islands
Libyan
NORTH ATLANTIC OCEAN
Hoggar
Tibesti
S A H A R A
Lac Faguibine
Sénégal
Niger
Cape Verde Islands
Cape Verde
S A H E L
Lake Chad
Gambia
Lake Volta
Benue
Adamawa Highlands
Grain Coast
Ivory Coast
Gold Coast
Slave Coast
Bight of Benin
Mouths of the Niger
Sanaga
Ubangi
Uele
Bioko
Gulf of Guinea
Zaire
Príncipe
São Tomé
St Paul Rocks
Pagalu
Lac Mai-Ndombe
Congo
Kasai
Cuango
Ascension
SOUTH AMERICA
Bie Plateau
S O U T H
St Helena
Cubango
Okavango
Cunene
Etosha Pan
Okavango
A T L A N T I C
Lake Ngami
Walvis Bay
Namib Desert
Kalahar
Desert
O C E A N
Orange River
Great Karoo
Cape of Good Hope

Cyprus
Euphrates
Tigris
Daryācheh-ye-Namak
Zagros Mountains
Hindu Kush
Karakoram
Plateau of Iran
Plateau of Tibet
H I M A L A Y A S
Dead Sea
Nile Delta
Sinai
Gulf of Aqaba
Qattâra Depression
Gulf of Suez
Nile
Persian Gulf
Helmand
Brahmaputra
The Great Oasis
Lake Nasser
R E D S E A
ARABIAN PENINSULA
Makran
Indus
Thar Desert
Gulf of Oman
Al Liwā'
Umm as Samim
Ganges (Ganga)
Nubian Desert
Maşīrah
Narmada
ARABIAN SEA
AR RUB AL KHĀLĪ
Godavari
Deccan
Krishna
Hadhramaut
White Nile
Blue Nile
Bab el Mandeb
Lake Tana
Danakil Desert
Gulf of Aden
Socotra
Ethiopian Plateau
Laccadive Islands
Ogaden
Shabeelle
Ceylon
Maldive Islands
Lake Turkana
Lake Kyoga
Lake Albert
Mt Stanley
Jubba
Mount Kenya
Tana
Lake Edward
Lake Victoria
Lake Kivu
Rift Valley
I N D I A N
Lake Natron
Kilimanjaro
Lake Eyasi
Seychelles
Pemba Island
Zanzibar
Amirante Islands
Lake Tanganyika
Chagos Archipelago
Coëtivy Island
Lake Rukwa
Mafia Island
Lake Mweru
Aldabra Islands
Providence Islands
Lake Bangweulu
Agalega Islands
Lake Nyasa
Comoro Islands
Mozambique Channel
Madagascar
O C E A N
Lake Chilwa
Zambezi
Tromelin
Lake Kariba
Rodrigues
Mauritius
Réunion
Limpopo
Vaal
Drakensberg

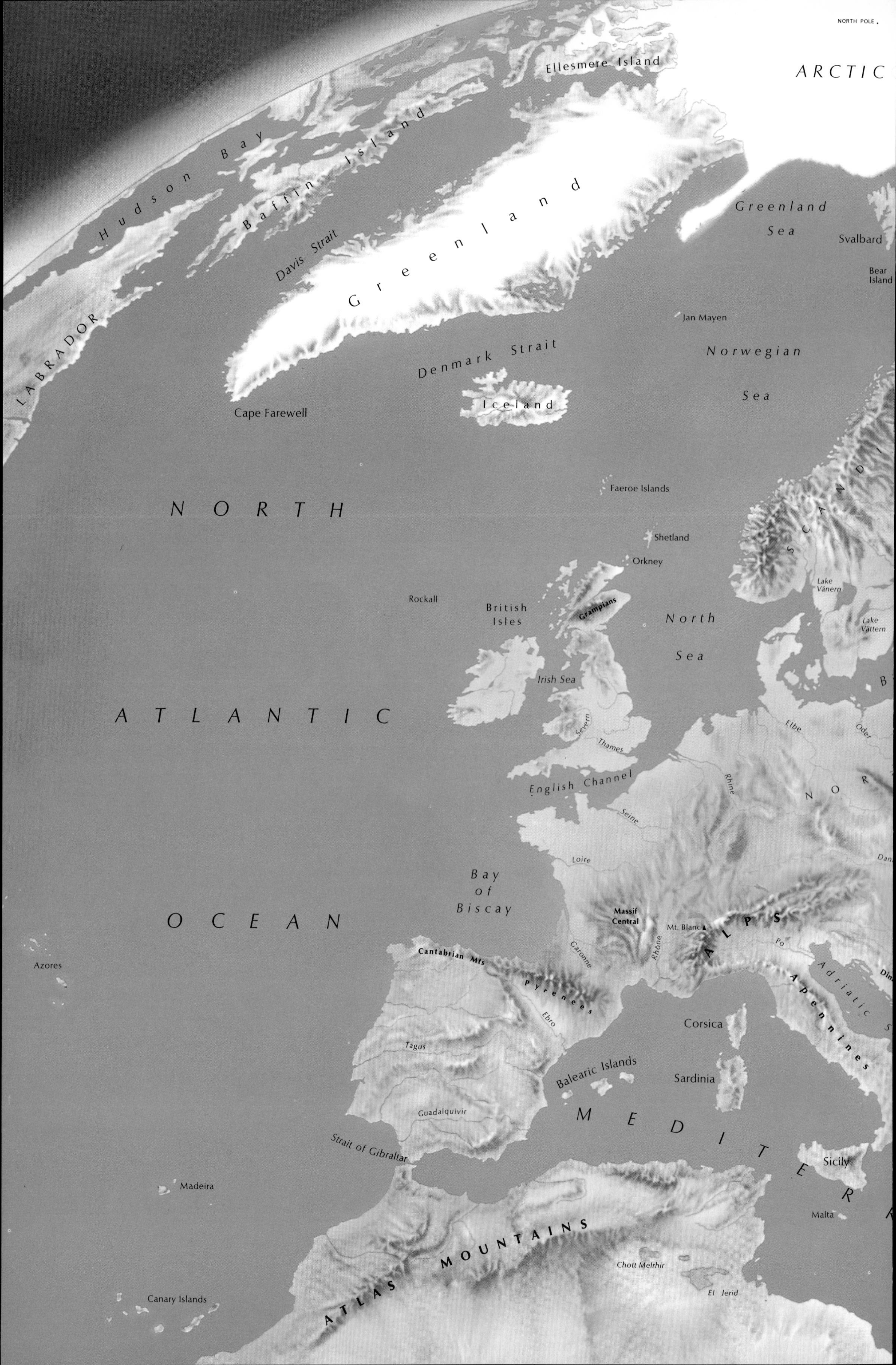
NORTH POLE
ARCTIC
Ellesmere Island
Hudson Bay
Baffin Island
Davis Strait
Greenland
Greenland Sea
Svalbard
Bear Island
LABRADOR
Jan Mayen
Denmark Strait
Norwegian Sea
Iceland
Cape Farewell
Faeroe Islands
NORTH
Shetland
Orkney
Rockall
British Isles
Grampians
North Sea
Lake Vänern
Lake Vättern
Irish Sea
ATLANTIC
Severn
Thames
Elbe
Oder
English Channel
Rhine
Seine
Loire
Bay of Biscay
Massif Central
Mt. Blanc
ALPS
OCEAN
Azores
Cantabrian Mts
Garonne
Rhône
Po
Adriatic
Apennines
Pyrenees
Ebro
Corsica
Tagus
Balearic Islands
Sardinia
Guadalquivir
MEDITER
Strait of Gibraltar
Sicily
Madeira
Malta
ATLAS MOUNTAINS
Chott Melrhir
El Jerid
Canary Islands

CEAN
Severnaya Zemlya
Limit of permanent pack ice
Franz Josef Land
Kara Sea
sbergen
Novaya Zemlya
Barents Sea
rth Cape
Lena
CENTRAL SIBERIAN PLATEAU
Nizhnyaya Tunguska
Lena
Yenisey
WEST SIBERIAN PLAIN
Angara
Lake Baikal
Pechora
URAL MOUNTAINS
Ob'
Ob'
White Sea
Severnaya Dvina
Irtysh
of Bothnia
Lake Onega
Lake Ladoga
Gulf of Finland
EUROPEAN PLAIN
Volga
Central Russian Uplands
Dvina
KIRGHIZ STEPPE
Lake Balkhash
Ural
Aral Sea
Syrdar'ya
Volga
Caspian Sea
Kyzylkum
Dnieper
Don
CARPATHIANS
Dniester
ungarian Plain
Tisza
Sea of Azov
Caucasus
Amudar'ya
Karakumy
Black Sea
Danube
Balkan Mountains
Rhodope
Thrace
Bosporus
Araxes
Lake Van
Lake Urmia
Sea of Marmara
Elbruz Mts
Daryācheh-ye-Namak
Dardanelles
ASIA MINOR
Kizil Irmak
Tuz Gölü
Pindus
Aegean Sea
Zagros Mountains
Taurus
Plateau of Iran
Mesopotamia
Tigris
Euphrates
Cyprus
Crete
ANEAN SEA
Jordan
Syrian Desert
Dead Sea
Persian Gulf
Gulf of Oman

Baltic Sea
Lake Ladoga
Lake Onega
Pechora
NORTH EUROPEAN PLAIN
Kheta
CENTRAL SIBERIAN PLATEAU
Ural Mountains
Ob
Yenisey
Nizhnyaya Tunguska
WEST SIBERIAN PLAIN
Dnieper
Volga
Tobol
Angara
Lena
Don
Ural
Ishim
Ozero Tengiz
Black Sea
Caucasus
Kirghiz Steppe
Caspian Sea
Ustyurt Plateau
Aral Sea
Irtysh
Lake Baikal
Yablonovy
Hövsgöl Nuur
Selenga
Syrdar'ya
Ozero Zaysan
ALTAI
Kyzylkum
Amudar'ya
Lake Balkhash
Ozero Alakol'
Ebi Nor
Kerulen
MONGOL
Karakumy
Ili
Dzungaria
Issyk Kul
Tian Shan
Bosten Hu
GOBI
Pik Kommunizma
Tarim
Plateau of Iran
Pamirs
Lop Nur
Yellow River (Huang He)
Hindu Kush
Takla Makan
Ordos
Karakoram
K2
Kunlun Shan
Altun Shan
Qaidam Pendi
Helmand
Qinghai Hu
HIMALAYA
Plateau of Tibet
Chenab
Moron Us He (Chang Jiang)
Yellow River (Huang He)
Yalong He
Tongtian He
Qin Ling
Indus
Sutlej
Indo-Gangetic Plain
Salween
Thar Desert
Brahmaputra
Red Basin
Lancang Jiang
Everest
Kangchenjunga
Dongting Hu
Yangtze Kiang (Chang Jiang)
Ganges (Ganga)
Narmada
Khasi Hills
Naga Hills
Nan Ling
Arabian Sea
Mahanadi
Pearl River (Xi Jiang)
Deccan
Western Ghats
Arakan
Mouths of the Ganges
Red River (Song Hong)
Godavari
Irrawaddy
Salween
INDOCHINA
Gulf of Tongking
Krishna
Bay of Bengal
Eastern Ghats
Hainan
Laccadive Islands
Gulf of Martaban
Chao Phraya
Paracel Islands
Cauvery
Mekong
Andaman Islands
Andaman Sea
Palk Strait
Maldive Islands
Ceylon
Kra Isthmus
Gulf of Thailand
Nicobar Islands
Mouths of the Mekong
Malay Peninsula
INDIAN OCEAN

Nunivak Island
Anadyr
Kolyma
Yana
Indigirka
Verkhoyanskiy Khrebet
Lena
Bering Sea
Aleutian Islands
Komandorskiye Ostrova
Kamchatka
Sea of Okhotsk
Aldan
Khr. Dzhugdzhur
Kuril Islands
Sakhalin
Tatarskiy Proliv
Greater Khingan Range
Hulun Nur
Manchuria
Amur
Ussuri
Sikhote Alin
Songhua
Oz Khanka
Hokkaido
NORTH PACIFIC OCEAN
Midway Islands
Sea of Japan
Changbai Shan
Honshu
Korea
Bo Hai
Yellow River (Huang He)
Great Plain of China
Yellow Sea
Korea Strait
Shikoku
Kyushu
Yangtze Kiang (Chang Jiang)
East China Sea
Bonin Islands
Poyang Hu
Volcano Islands
Ryukyu Islands
Taiwan Strait
Taiwan
Marianas
Marshall Islands
PHILIPPINES
South China Sea
Guam
Kiribati
Luzon
Caroline Islands
Mindoro
Samar
Panay
Negros
Palawan
Sulu Sea
Mindanao
New Ireland

Nicobar Islands
South China Sea
Malay Peninsula
Strait of Malacca
Sumatra
Borneo
Celebes Sea
Makassar Strait
Celebes
Moluccas
Halmahera
Seram
NORT
Java Sea
Banda Sea
Java
Bali
Sumbawa
Flores
Sumba
Timor
Arafura Sea
EAST INDIES
Christmas Island
Timor Sea
Cocos-Keeling Island
Arnhem Land
Victoria
Barkly Tablela
Kimberley Plateau
Fitzroy
Tanami Desert
INDIAN
Great Sandy Desert
Lake Mackay
Macdonnell Ranges
Ashburton
Gibson Desert
Simpso Deser
Gascoyne
Lake Amadeus
Finke
Murchison
Great Victoria Desert
Lake Eyre
Lake Barlee
Lake Moore
Lake Torrens
Nullarbor Plain
Lake Gairdner
Great Australian Bight
Spencer Gulf
OCEAN
Amsterdam Island
St Paul
Kerguelen
Heard Island
Macdonald Islands
ANTARCTICA

PACIFIC OCEAN
MICRONESIA
Marshall Islands
SOUTH
POLYNESIA
MELANESIA
Admiralty Islands
New Ireland
Bismarck Sea
New Guinea
New Britain
Nauru
Banaba
Kiribati
Bougainville
Solomon Islands
Tokelau Islands
Tuvalu
Torres Strait
Great Barrier Reef
Cape York Peninsula
Santa Cruz Islands
PACIFIC
ulf of
entaria
Coral Sea
Vanuatu
Samoan Islands
Fiji
Tahiti
Flinders
Great Dividing Range
New Caledonia
Tonga
OCEAN
Diamantina
Cooper Creek
Fraser Island
Warrego
Culgoa
Barwon
Lake Frome
Darling
Norfolk Island
Lord Howe Island
Kermadec Islands
Murray
Lachlan
Murrumbidgee
Murray
Murray
Mount Kosciusko
Australian Alps
Tasman Sea
King Island
Bass Strait
Flinders Island
Tasmania
New Zealand
Cook Strait
Chatham Islands
Foveaux Strait
Stewart Island
Bounty Islands
Antipodes Islands
Auckland Islands
Campbell Island
Macquarie Island

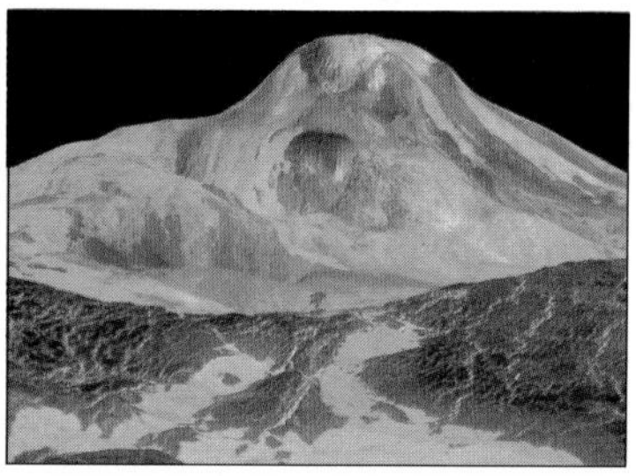

Far left The Caloris basin of Mercury is the largest impact feature on the planet.

Left Radar mapping of Venus has provided this computer-generated image of the volcano, Maat Mons.

Top right Io (left) and Europa are clearly visible as they cross the face of Jupiter.

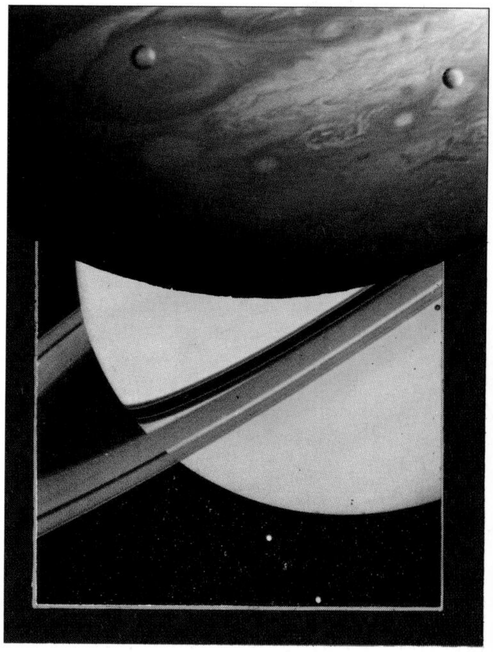

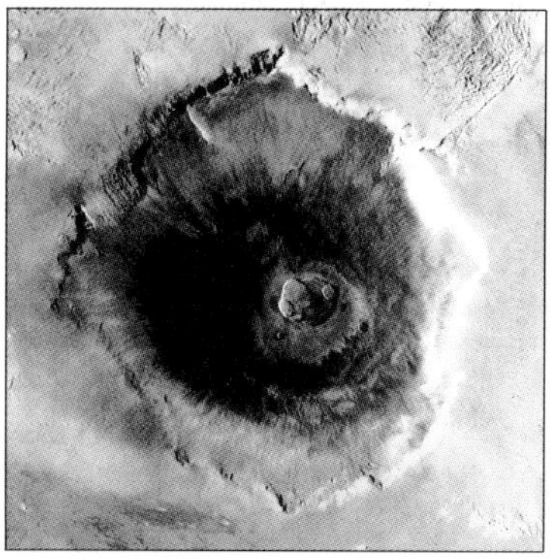

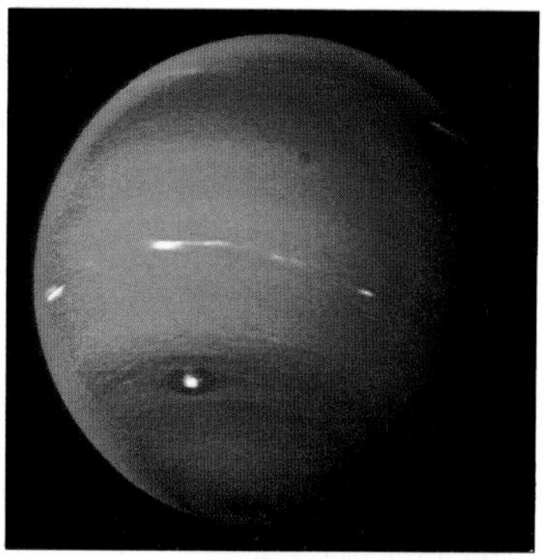

Far left Olympus Mons on Mars is the largest known volcano in the solar system. It is 550 km across at the base and more than 26 km high.

Right The rings of Saturn lie in the equatorial plane and consist of countless ice-covered particles, perhaps up to several metres across.

Left Voyager 2 produced this false-colour image of Neptune in August 1989. A planet-wide haze (red) and white clouds are visible.

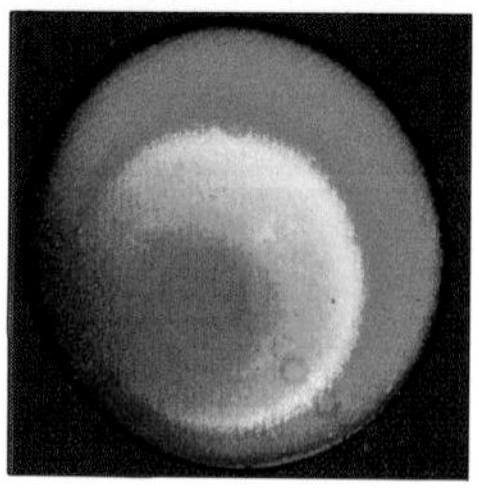

Left This image of Uranus in false-colour was taken from 9.1 million km by Voyager 2. The atmosphere is deep, cold and remarkably clear, but the false colours enhance the polar region. Here, the suggestion is that a brownish haze of smog is concentrated over the pole.

Current theory suggests that the solar system condensed from a primitive solar nebula of gas and dust during an interval of a few tens of millions of years about 4600 million years ago. Gravity caused this nebula to contract, drawing most of its mass into the centre. Turbulence gave the original cloud a tendency to rotate faster and faster, forcing the remainder of the cloud into a disc shape.

The centre of the cloud heated up as it compressed, and so eventually became hot enough for the Sun to begin to shine, through nuclear energy released at its core. Meanwhile the surrounding disc of cloud cooled, allowing material to condense into solid form. Particles stuck together as they collided and progressively larger bodies were built up. These swept up most of the debris to form the planets, which now orbit the Sun.

EARTHLIKE PLANETS

Mercury is the nearest planet to the Sun, spinning three times for every two orbits around the Sun. It has an exceptionally large metallic core which may be responsible for Mercury's weak magnetic field. Mercury is an airless world subject to vast extremes of temperature, from −180°C (−292°F) at night to 430°C (806°F) near the middle of its long day. The Mariner 10 space probe, during the mid-1970s, revealed the surface to be dominated by heavily cratered areas.

Venus has a dense atmosphere with a surface pressure 90 times that of the Earth. Made up of 96% carbon dioxide, the lower layers are rich in sulphur dioxide while sulphuric acid droplets populate the higher clouds. The clouds maintain a mean surface temperature of about 480°C (896°F). The hidden surface has been mapped by radar from orbiting probes and shows a rugged surface with some volcanoes, possibly still active.

Mars has a thin atmosphere of about 96% carbon dioxide mixed with other minor gasses. The polar caps consist of semi-permanent water-ice and solid carbon dioxide. Day and night surface temperatures vary between about −120°C (−184°F) and −20°C (−4°F). Mars has two small satellites, Phobos and Deimos, each less than about 25km (15.5 miles) across, probably captured asteroids.

Mars also shows evidence of erosional processes. The effect of winds is seen in the form of the deposition of sand dunes. Dust storms frequently obscure the surface. The large channels, such as the 5000km (3107 miles) long Valles Marineris, may have been cut by flowing water. Water is abundant in the polar caps and may be widespread, held in as permafrost.

GAS GIANTS

Jupiter has at least 16 satellites and a debris ring system about 50,000km (31,070 miles) above the cloud tops. The outer atmosphere is all that can be directly observed of the planet itself. It is mostly hydrogen with lesser amounts of helium, ammonia, methane and water vapour. Jupiter's rapid rotation causes it to be flattened towards the poles. This rotation and heat flow from the interior cause complex weather patterns. Where cloud systems interact vast storms can occur in the form of vortices. Some last only a few days, but the most persistent of these, the Great Red Spot, has been present since it was first detected in the 17th century.

Saturn is the least dense of the planets. It has a stormy atmosphere situated above a 30,000km (18,640 miles) layer of liquid hydrogen and helium distorted by rotation.

The rings of Saturn are thought to be mostly made of icy debris, from 10m (33 ft) down to a few microns in size, derived from the break-up of a satellite. The rings are less than 1km thick.

Uranus, consisting mainly of hydrogen, was little known until Voyager 2 flew by it in 1986. The probe discovered ten new satellites and provided images of the planet's eleven icy rings of debris.

Neptune was visited by Voyager 2 in 1989. Six new satellites were discovered, one larger than Nereid, the smaller of the two known satellites. Triton, the largest satellite, was found to be smaller than previous estimates. The turbulent atmosphere is a mixture of hydrogen, helium and methane.

Pluto is now 4500 million km from the Sun, closer than Neptune until 1999, but its eccentric orbit will take it to 7500 million km by 2113. A tenuous atmosphere has been found above a surface of frozen methane. Charon, the satellite, is half Pluto's diameter.

	SUN	MERCURY	VENUS	EARTH	(MOON)	MARS	JUPITER	SATURN	URANUS	NEPTUNE	PLUTO
Mass (Earth = 1)	333 400	0.055	0.815	1 (5.97 10^{24}kg)	0.012	0.107	317.8	95.2	14.5	17.2	0.003
Volume (Earth = 1)	1 306 000	0.06	0.88	1	0.020	0.150	1 323	752	64	54	0.007
Density (water = 1)	1.41	5.43	5.24	5.52	3.34	3.94	1.33	0.70	1.30	1.64	2.0
Equatorial diameter (km)	1 392 000	4 878	12 104	12 756	3 476	6 794	142 800	120 000	52 000	48 400	2 302
Polar flattening	0	0	0	0.003	0	0.005	0.065	0.108	0.060	0.021	0
'Surface' gravity (Earth = 1)	27.9	0.37	0.88	1	0.16	0.38	2.69	1.19	0.93	1.22	0.05
Number of satellites greater than 100 km diameter	—	0	0	1	—	0	7	13	7	6	1
Total number of satellites	—	0	0	1	—	2	16	17	15	8	1
Period of rotation (in Earth days)	25.38	58.65	−243 (retrograde)	23hr 56m 4 secs	27.32	1.03	0.414	0.426	−0.74 (retrograde)	0.67	−6.39 (retrograde)
Length of year (in Earth days and years)	—	88 days	224.7 days	365.26 days	—	687 days	11.86 years	29.46 years	84.01 years	164.8 years	247.7 years
Distance from Sun (mean) Mkm	—	57.9	108.9	149.6	—	227.9	778.3	1 427	2 870	4 497	5 900

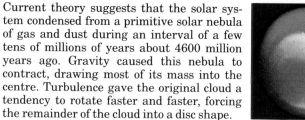

EARTH STRUCTURE

Internally, the Earth may be divided broadly into crust, mantle and core (*see right*).

The crust is a thin shell constituting only 0.2% of the mass of the Earth. The continental crust varies in thickness from 20 to 90km (12 to 56 miles) and is less dense than ocean crust. Two-thirds of the continents are overlain by sedimentary rocks of average thickness less than 2km (1.2 miles). Ocean crust is on average 7km (4.4 miles) thick. It is composed of igneous rocks, basalts and gabbros.

Crust and mantle are separated by the Mohorovičić Discontinuity (Moho). The mantle differs from the crust. It is largely igneous. The upper mantle extends to 350km (218 miles). The lower mantle has a more uniform composition. A sharp discontinuity defines the meeting of mantle and core. The inability of the outer core to transmit seismic waves suggests it is liquid. It is probably of metallic iron with other elements – sulphur, silicon, oxygen, potassium and hydrogen have all been suggested. The inner core is solid and probably of nickel-iron. Temperature at the core-mantle boundary is about 3700°C (5430°F) and 4000°–4500°C (7230°–8130°F) in the inner core.

THE ATMOSPHERE

The ancient atmosphere lacked free oxygen. Plant life added oxygen to the atmosphere and transferred carbon dioxide to the crustal rocks and the hydrosphere. The composition of air today at 79% nitrogen and 20% oxygen remains stable by the same mechanism.

Solar energy is distributed around the Earth by the atmosphere. Most of the weather and climate processes occur in the troposphere at the lowest level. The atmosphere also shields the Earth. Ozone exists to the extent of 2 parts per million and is at its maximum at 30km (19 miles). It is the only gas which absorbs ultra-violet radiation. Water-vapour and CO_2 keep out infra-red radiation.

Above 80km (50 miles) nitrogen and oxygen tend to separate into atoms which become ionized (an ion is an atom lacking one or more of its electrons). The ionosphere is a zone of ionized belts which reflect radio waves back to Earth. These electrification belts change their position dependent on light and darkness and external factors.

Beyond the ionosphere, the magnetosphere extends to outer space. Ionized particles form a plasma (a fourth state of matter, ie. other than solid, liquid, gas) held in by the Earth's magnetic field.

ORIGIN AND DEVELOPMENT OF LIFE

Primitive life-forms (blue-green algae) are found in rocks as old as 3500Ma (million years) and, although it cannot yet be proved, the origin of life on Earth probably dates back to about 4000Ma. It seems likely that the oxygen levels in the atmosphere increased only slowly at first, probably to about 1% of the present amount by 2000Ma. As the atmospheric oxygen built up so the protective ozone layer developed to allow organisms to live in shallower waters. More highly developed photosynthesising organisms led to the development of oxygen breathing animals. The first traces of multicellular life occur about 1000Ma; by 700Ma complex animals, such as jellyfish, worms and primitive molluscs, had developed.

Organisms developed hard parts that allowed their preservation as abundant fossils at about 570Ma. This coincided with a period of explosive evolution of marine life. Fishes appeared about 475Ma and by 400Ma land plants had developed. Between 340 and 305Ma dense vegetation covered the land, amphibians emerged from the sea, and by about 250Ma had given rise to reptiles and the first mammals. These expanded hugely about 65Ma.

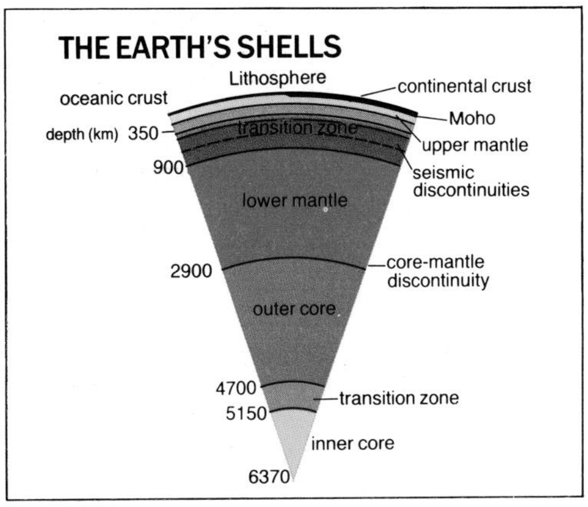

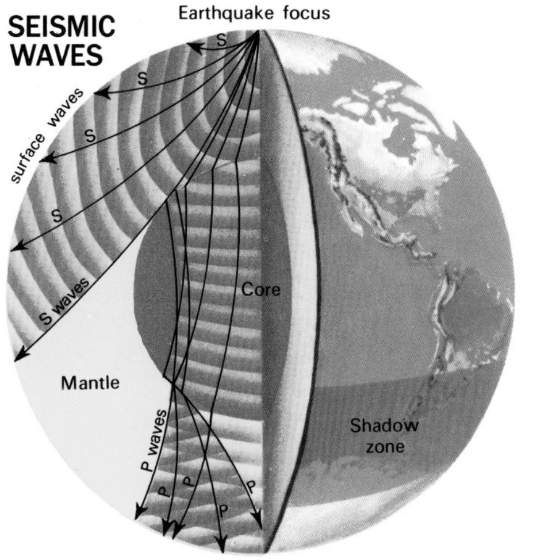

Above In an earthquake the shock generates vibrations, or seismic waves, which radiate in all directions from the focus. The slowest waves are Surface waves which transmit the bulk of the energy in shallow earthquakes.

Other waves known as body waves pass through the body of the Earth. Primary (P) waves are compressional. They are able to travel through solids and fluids and cause the particles of the Earth to vibrate in the direction of travel. Secondary (S) waves are transverse, or shear, waves. They can only pass through solids and do not penetrate the Earth's outer core.

EARTHQUAKES

Earthquakes are the manifestation of a slippage at a geological fault. The majority occur at tectonic plate boundaries. The interior of a plate tends to be stable and less subject to earthquakes. When plates slide past each other strain energy is suddenly released. Even though the amount of movement is very small the energy released is colossal. It is transferred in shock waves.

Some earthquakes originate at depths as shallow as 5km (3 miles) below the surface. Others, however, may be as deep as 700km (435 miles). The precise cause of these very deep earthquakes is not known. The point from which the earthquake is generated is the focus and the point on the surface immediately above the focus is the epicentre.

The Richter Scale is used to define the magnitude of earthquakes. Each unit represents an increase in the amount of energy released by a factor of around 30 over the preceding point on the Scale. There is no upper limit, but the greatest magnitude yet recorded is 8.9.

VOLCANOES

Almost all the world's active volcanoes, numbering 500–600 are located at convergent plate boundaries. Those are the volcanoes which give spectacular demonstrations of volcanic activity. Yet far greater volcanic activity continues unnoticed and without cessation at mid-ocean ridges where magma from the upper mantle is quietly being extruded on to the ocean floor to create new crustal material.

Chemical composition of magmas and the amount of gas they contain determine the nature of a volcanic eruption. Gas-charged basalts produce cinder cones. Violent eruptions usually occur when large clouds of lava come into contact with water to produce fine-grained ash. When andesites are charged with gas they erupt with explosive violence.

Nuées ardentes (burning clouds) are extremely destructive. They are produced by magmas which erupt explosively sending molten lava fragments and gas at great speeds down the mountain sides.

In spite of the destructiveness of many volcanoes people still live in their vicinity because of the fertile volcanic soils. Geothermal energy in regions of volcanic activity is another source of attraction.

GRAVITY AND MAGNETISM

The Earth is spheroidal in form because it is a rotating body. Were it not so it would take the form of a sphere. The shape is determined by the mass of the Earth and its rate of rotation. Centrifugal force acting outwards reduces the pull of gravity acting inwards so that gravity at the equator is less than at the poles. Uneven distribution of matter within the Earth distorts the shape taken up by the mean sea-level surface (the geoid). Today the belief is that electric currents generated in the semi-molten outer core are responsible for the magnetic field. The Earth's magnetic poles have experienced a number of reversals, the north pole becoming the south and vice-versa.

ROCK AND HYDROLOGICAL CYCLES

Right In the most familiar cycle rain falls onto the land, drains to the sea, evaporates, condenses into cloud and is precipitated onto the land again. Water is also released and recirculated. In the rock cycle rocks are weathered and eroded, forming sediments which are compacted into rocks that are eventually exposed and then weathered again.

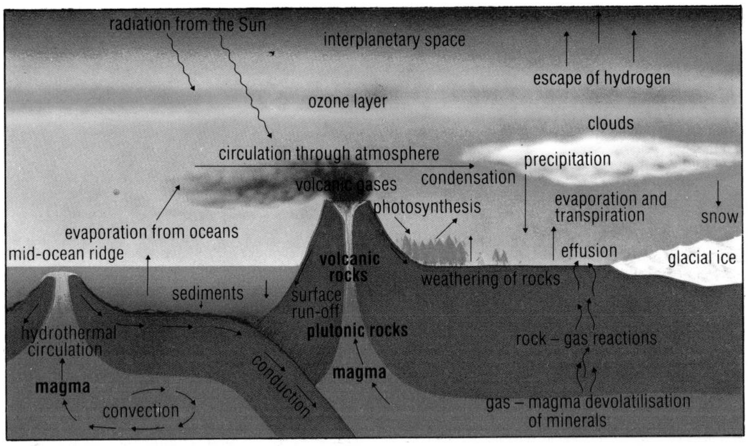

EARTHQUAKES AND VOLCANOES

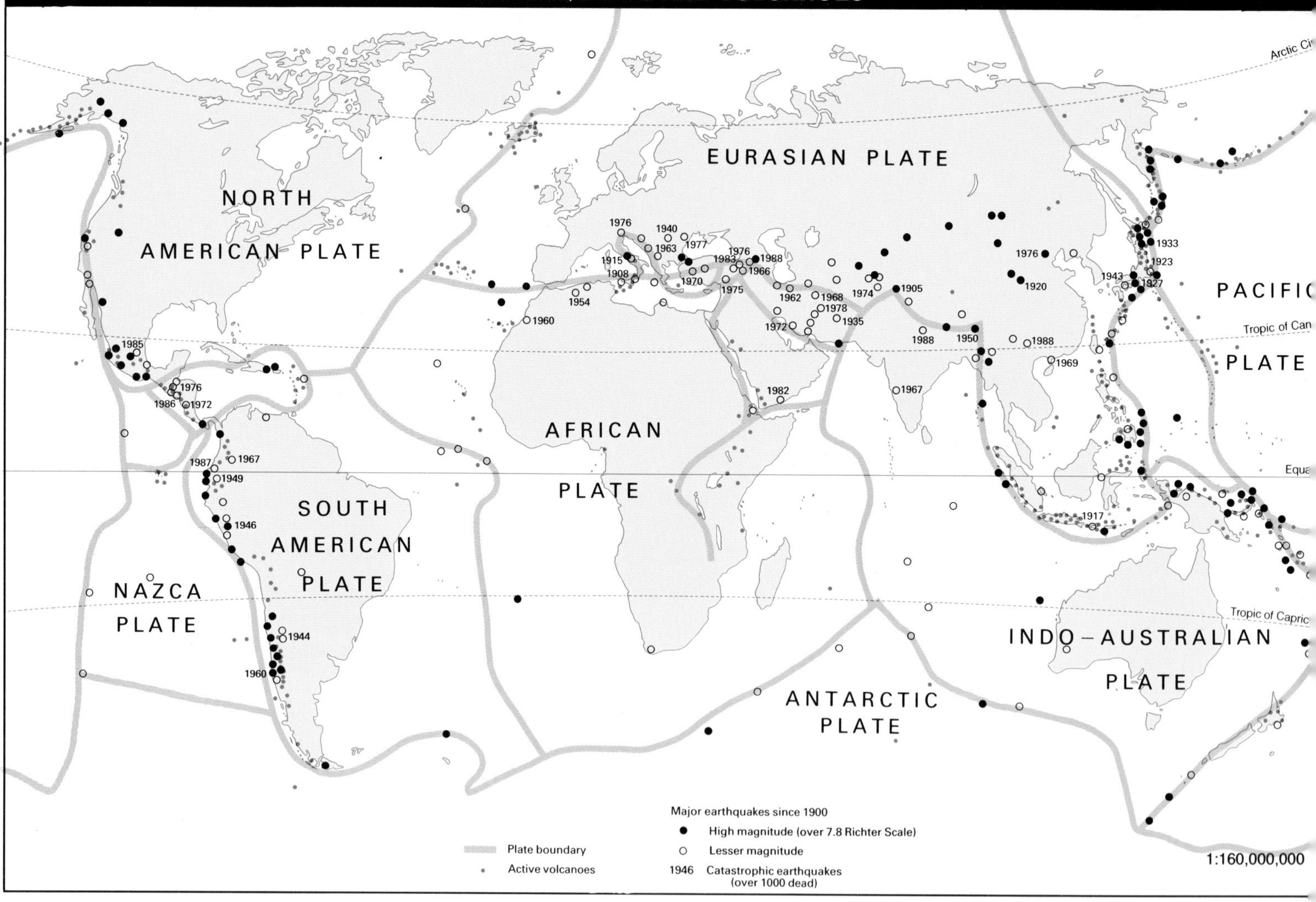

ECONOMIC MINERALS

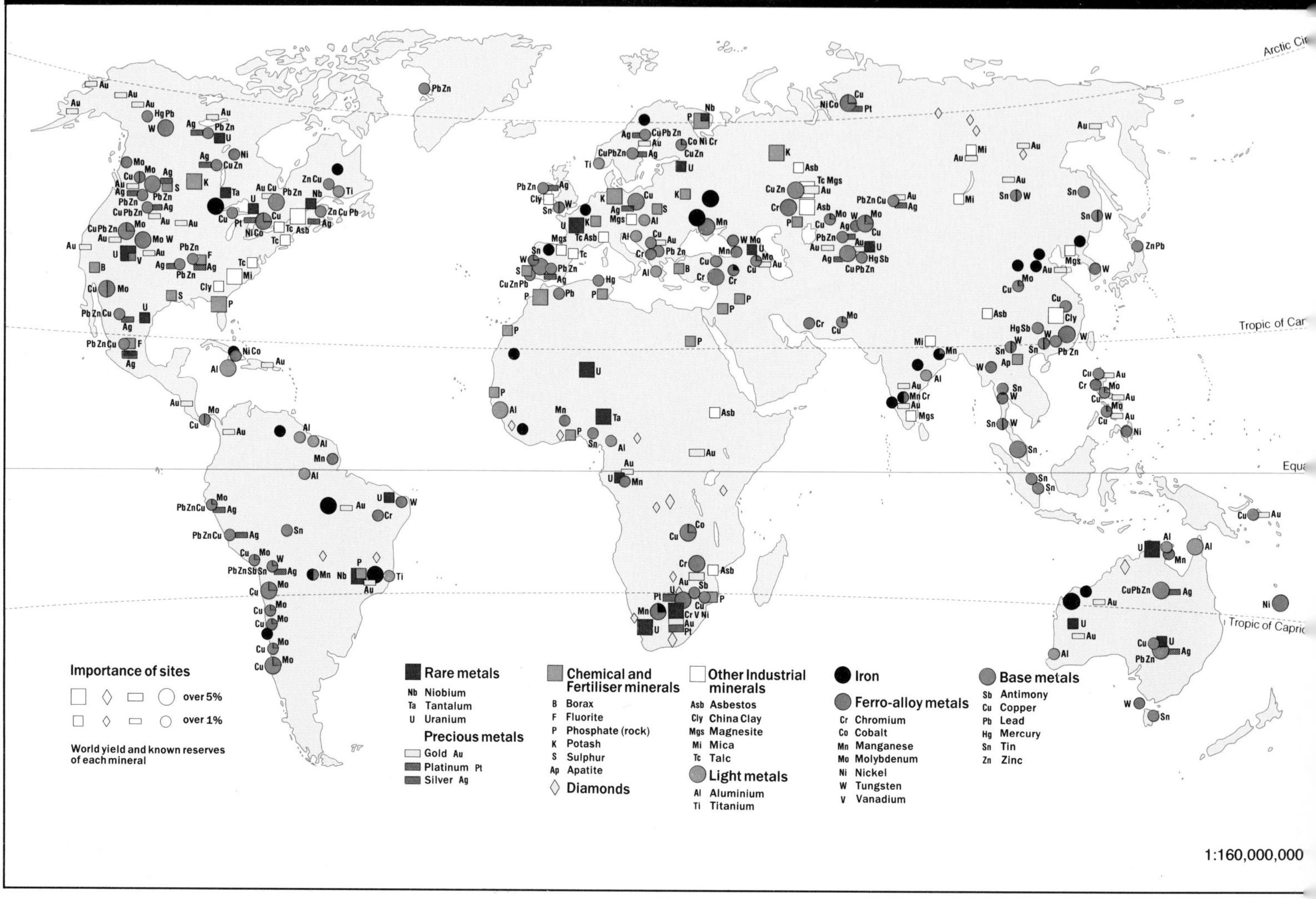

NORTH AMERICAN PLATE

EURASIAN PLATE

PACIFIC PLATE

AFRICAN PLATE

SOUTH AMERICAN PLATE

NAZCA PLATE

INDO–AUSTRALIAN PLATE

ANTARCTIC PLATE

Arctic Circle

Tropic of Cancer

Equator

Tropic of Capricorn

Major earthquakes since 1900

● High magnitude (over 7.8 Richter Scale)

○ Lesser magnitude

1946 Catastrophic earthquakes (over 1000 dead)

Plate boundary

Active volcanoes

1:160,000,000

ECONOMIC MINERALS

Arctic Circle

Tropic of Cancer

Equator

Tropic of Capricorn

Importance of sites

☐ ◇ ▭ ◯ over 5%

☐ ◇ ▭ ◯ over 1%

World yield and known reserves of each mineral

■ **Rare metals**
Nb Niobium
Ta Tantalum
U Uranium

Precious metals
☐ Gold Au
▤ Platinum Pt
▨ Silver Ag

▨ **Chemical and Fertiliser minerals**
B Borax
F Fluorite
P Phosphate (rock)
K Potash
S Sulphur
Ap Apatite

◇ **Diamonds**

☐ **Other Industrial minerals**
Asb Asbestos
Cly China Clay
Mgs Magnesite
Mi Mica
Tc Talc

● **Light metals**
Al Aluminium
Ti Titanium

● **Iron**

● **Ferro-alloy metals**
Cr Chromium
Co Cobalt
Mn Manganese
Mo Molybdenum
Ni Nickel
W Tungsten
V Vanadium

● **Base metals**
Sb Antimony
Cu Copper
Pb Lead
Hg Mercury
Sn Tin
Zn Zinc

1:160,000,000

TEMPERATURE: JANUARY

Arctic Circle
Westerlies
N.E. Trades
N.E. Trades
Tropic of Cancer
N.E. Trades
N.E. Monsoon
Doldrums
Equator
Inter-tropical Convergence Zone
S.E. Trades
S.E. Trades
S.E. Trades
Tropic of Capricorn
Westerlies
Roaring Forties
Roaring Forties

°F	-40	-30	-20	-10	0	10	20	30	40	50	60	70	80	90
°C	-40		-30		-20		-10		0		10		20	30

Prevailing Surface Wind

1:160,000,000

TEMPERATURE: JULY

Arctic Circle
Westerlies
Tropic of Cancer
N.E. Trades
S.W. Monsoon
Inter-tropical Convergence Zone
Doldrums
Equator
S.E. Monsoon
S.E. Trades
S.E. Trades
S.E. Trades
Tropic of Capricorn
Roaring Forties
Roaring Forties

°F	-40	-30	-20	-10	0	10	20	30	40	50	60	70	80	90
°C	-40		-30		-20		-10		0		10		20	30

Prevailing Surface Wind

1:160,000,000

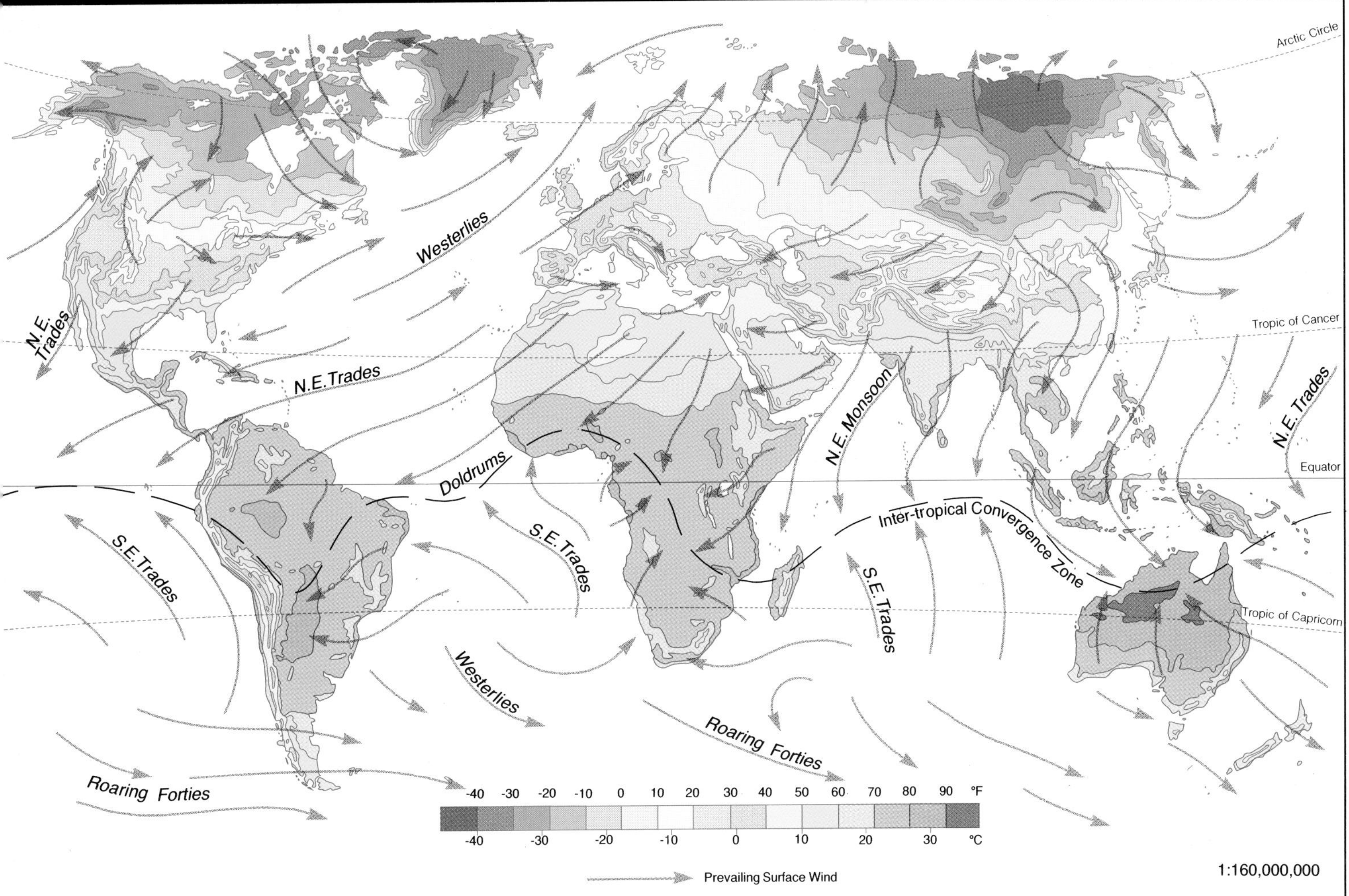

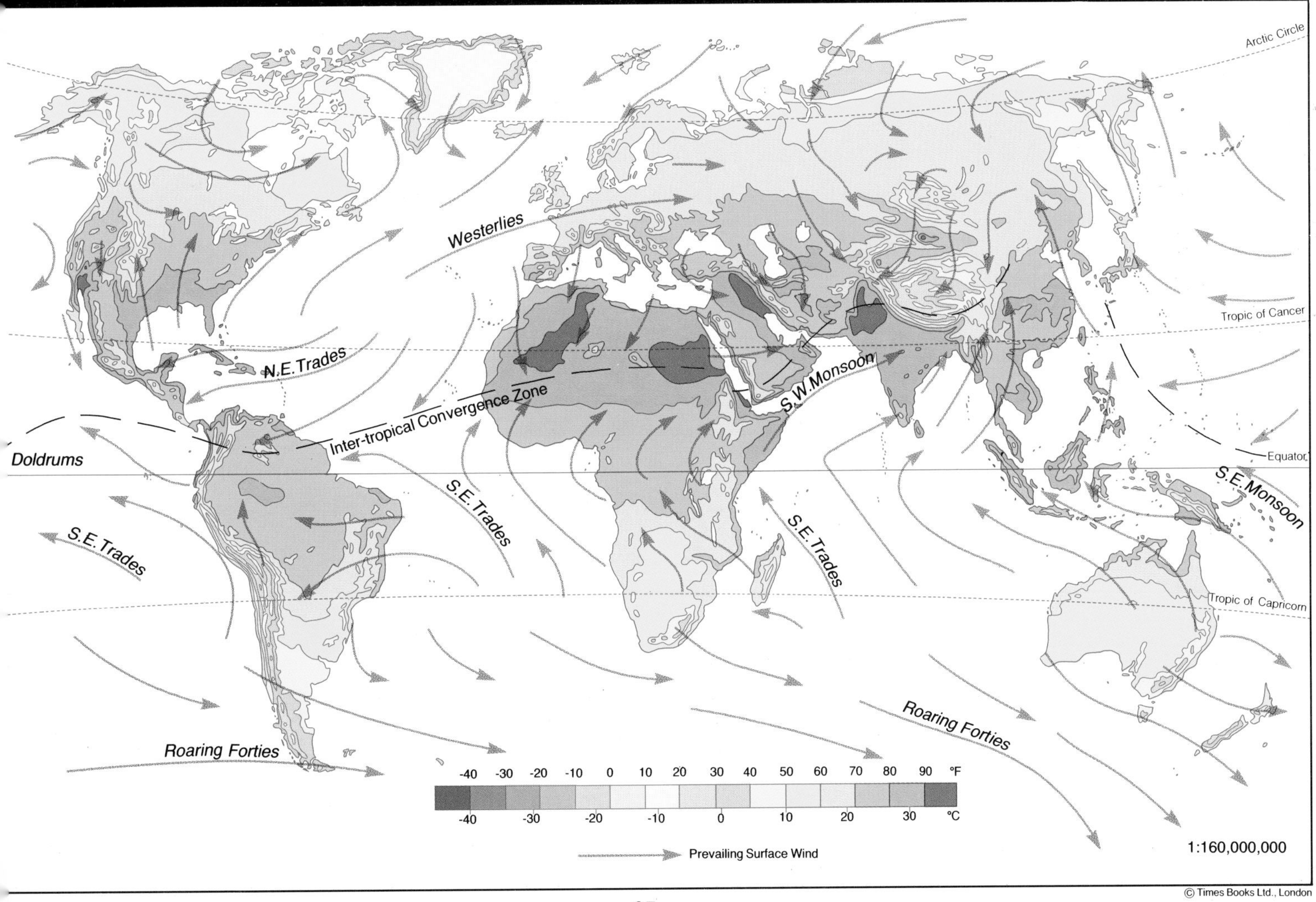

Mean Annual Precipitation

0	100	200	400	600	1000	2000	4000 millimetres
0	3·9	7·9	15·7	23·6	39·4	78·7	157·5 inches

1:160,000,000

NATURAL VEGETATION

Types of Natural Vegetation

Tundra and Mountain Vegetation	Mediterranean Scrub	Monsoon Forest
Coniferous Forest	Prairie and Steppe	Dry Tropical Forest
Mixed Forest	Savannah	Sub-Tropical Forest
Broadleaf Forest	Tropical Rain Forest	Desert

1:160,000,000

66

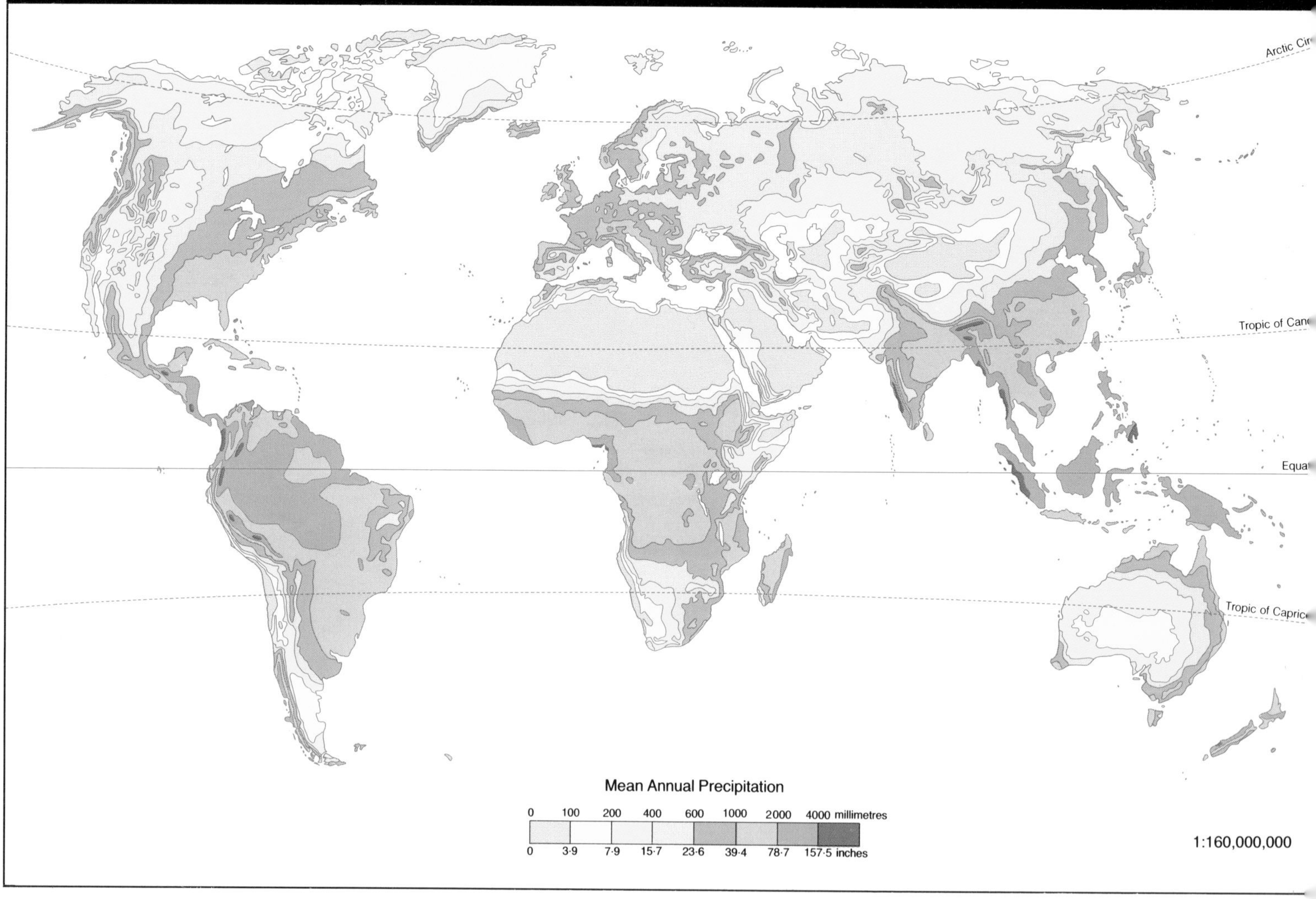

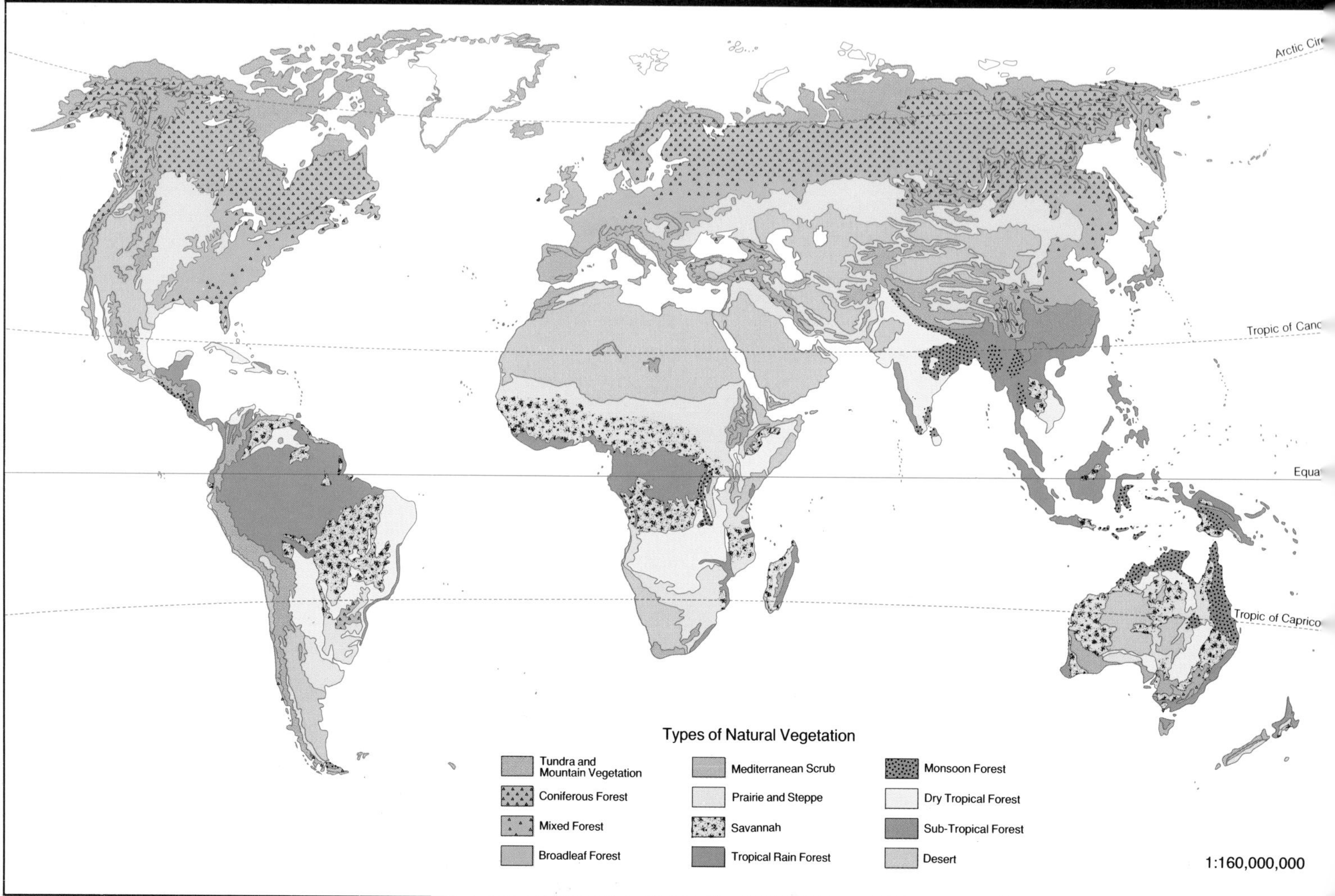

POPULATION DENSITY

Metropolitan Areas

- ■ Population over 10 million
- ● Population over 5 million
- ○ Population over 1 million

0	1	5	25	100	250	500	Persons per square mile
0	0·4	2	10	40	100	200	Persons per square kilometre

1:160,000,000

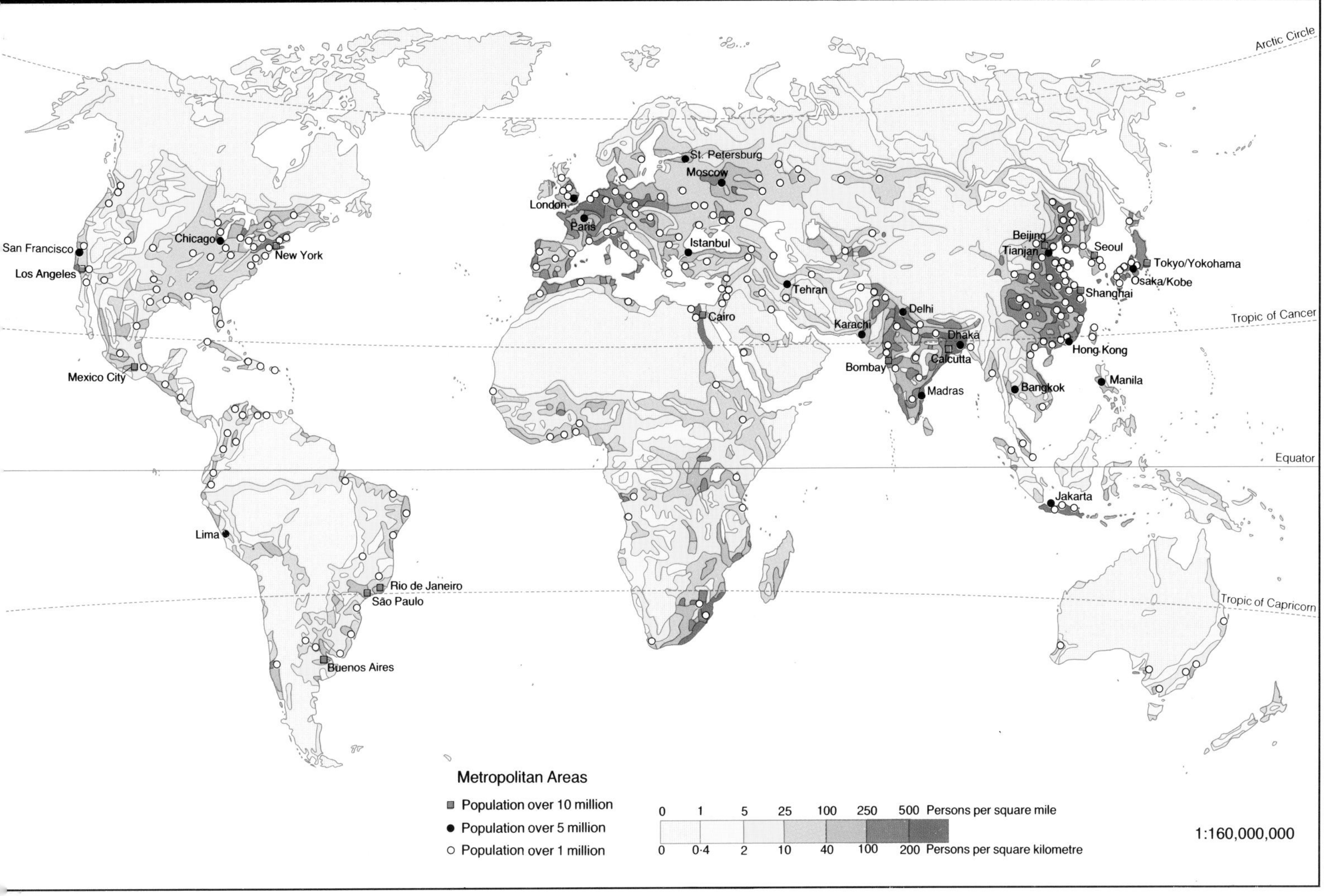

POPULATION CHANGE

Percentage Change

4
3   INCREASE
2
0

DECREASE

Estimated (x 1000 millions)

Rest of Asia
China
Africa
C. & S. America
N. America
U.S.S.R.*
Europe
Oceania

1950 60 70 80 90 2000
WORLD POPULATION GROWTH

1:160,000,000

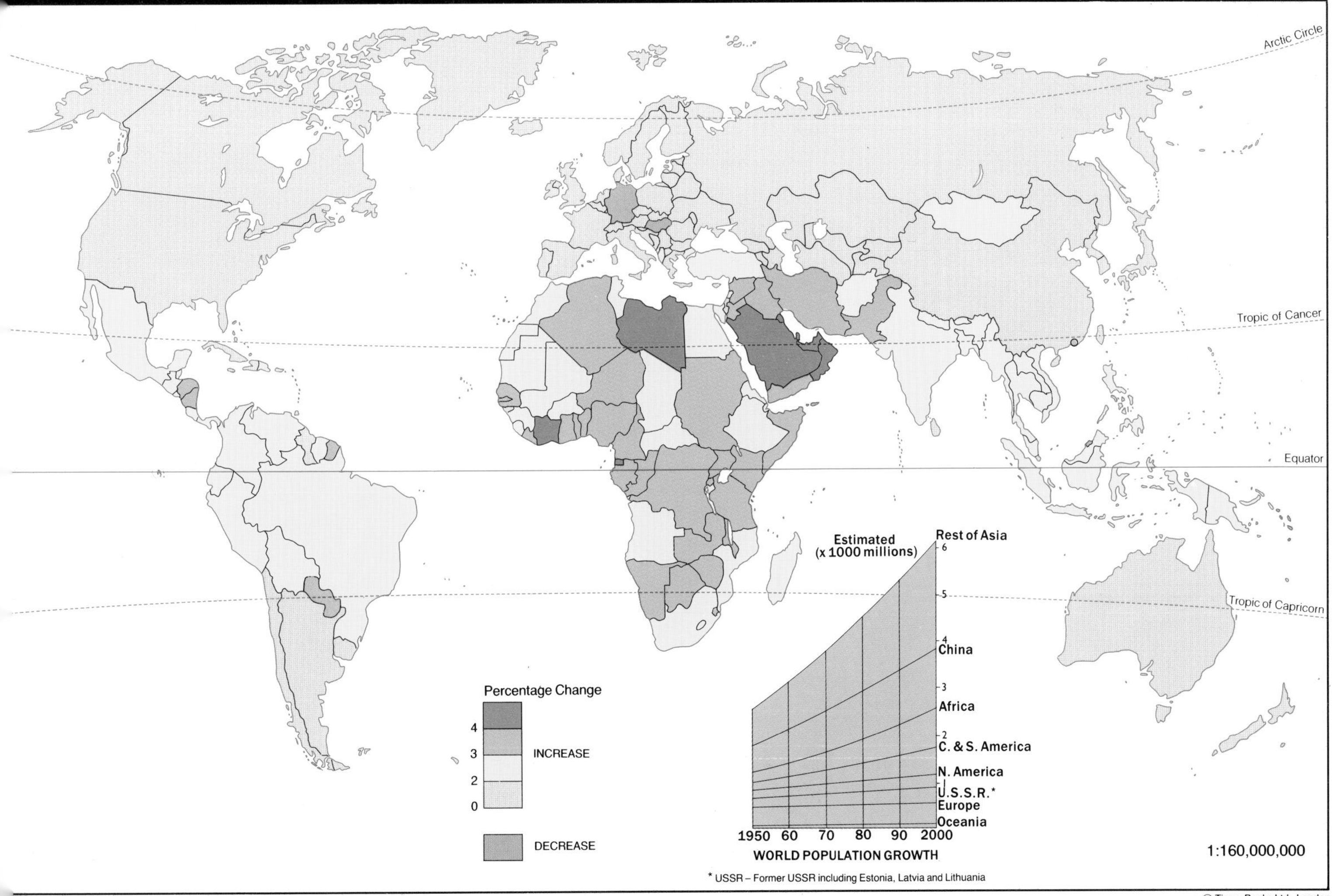

* USSR – Former USSR including Estonia, Latvia and Lithuania

© Times Books Ltd., London

TIME ZONES

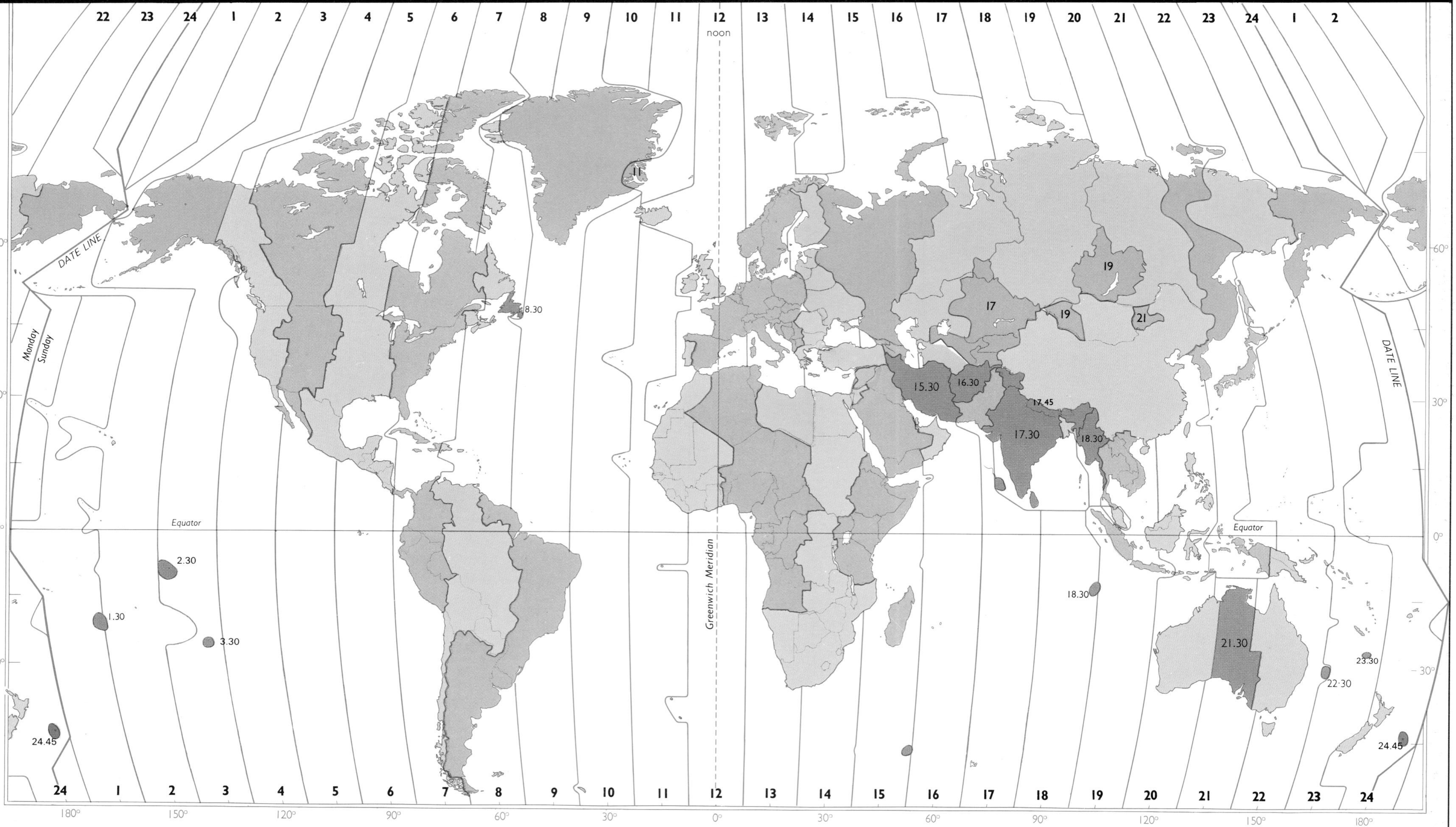

Zone times (given in bold figures at the top and bottom of map) are the Standard Times kept on land and sea compared with 12 hours (noon) Greenwich Mean Time. Daylight Saving Time (normally one hour in advance of local Standard time), which is observed by certain countries for part of the year, is not shown on the map.

1:105,000,000

This page explains the main symbols, lettering style and height/depth colours used on the reference maps on pages 2 to 76. The scale of each map is indicated at the foot of each page. Abbreviations used on the maps appear at the beginning of the index.

BOUNDARIES

	International
	International under Dispute
	Cease Fire Line
	Autonomous or State
	Administrative
	Maritime (National)
	International Date Line

COMMUNICATIONS

	Motorway/Express Highway
	Under Construction
	Major Highway
	Other Roads
	Under Construction
	Track
	Road Tunnel
	Car Ferry
	Main Railway
	Other Railway
	Under Construction
	Rail Tunnel
	Rail Ferry
	Canal
⊕	International Airport
✈	Other Airport

LAKE FEATURES

	Freshwater
	Saltwater
	Seasonal
	Salt Pan

LANDSCAPE FEATURES

	Glacier, Ice Cap
	Marsh, Swamp
	Sand Desert, Dunes

OTHER FEATURES

	River
	Seasonal River
≍	Pass, Gorge
	Dam, Barrage
	Waterfall, Rapid
	Aqueduct
	Reef
▲ 4231	Summit, Peak
. 217	Spot Height, Depth
ᵕ	Well
△	Oil Field
▲	Gas Field
Gas / Oil	Oil/Natural Gas Pipeline
Gemsbok Nat. Pk	National Park
∴ UR	Historic Site

LETTERING STYLES

CANADA	Independent Nation
FLORIDA	State, Province or Autonomous Region
Gibraltar (U.K.)	Sovereignty of Dependent Territory
Lothian	Administrative Area
LANGUEDOC	Historic Region
Loire **Vosges**	Physical Feature or Physical Region

TOWNS AND CITIES

Square symbols denote capital cities. Each settlement is given a symbol according to its relative importance, with type size to match.

■	●	**New York**	Major City
■	●	**Montréal**	City
□	○	Ottawa	Small City
■	●	Québec	Large Town
□	○	St John's	Town
□	○	Yorkton	Small Town
□	○	Jasper	Village
			Built-up-area

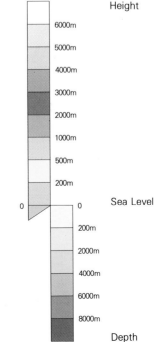

Height
6000m
5000m
4000m
3000m
2000m
1000m
500m
200m
0 — Sea Level
200m
2000m
4000m
6000m
8000m
Depth

For more information about each country refer to the States and Territories section (page number in bold type). For large scale map refer to map section (page number in italic).

AFRICA
Algeria **4** *48*
Angola **4** *51*
Benin **7** *48*
Botswana **8** *51*
Burkina **9** *48*
Burundi **9** *50*
Cameroon **9** *48-49*
Cape Verde **10** *48*
Central African Republic **10** *50*
Chad **10** *49*
Comoros **12** *51*
Congo **12-13** *50*
Djibouti **14** *50*
Egypt **14-15** *49*
Equatorial Guinea **15** *48*
Eritrea **15** *50*
Ethiopia **15** *50*
Gabon **16** *50*
Gambia, The **16 -17** *48*
Ghana **17** *48*
Guinea **18** *48*
Guinea-Bissau **18** *48*
Ivory Coast **21** *48*
Kenya **22** *50*
Lesotho **23** *51*
Liberia **23** *48*
Libya **24** *49*
Madagascar **24** *51*
Malawi **24-25** *51*
Mali **25** *48*
Mauritania **26** *48*
Mauritius **26** *51*
Morocco **27** *48*
Mozambique **27** *51*
Namibia **27** *51*
Niger **28** *48*
Nigeria **28-29** *48*
Rwanda **31** *50*
São Tomé & Príncipe **32** *48*
Senegal **32** *48*
Seychelles **32** *48*
Sierra Leone **32-33** *48*
Somalia **33** *50*
South Africa **34** *51*
Sudan **34** *49*
Swaziland **35** *51*
Tanzania **36** *50-51*
Togo **36** *48*
Tunisia **37** *48*
Uganda **38** *50*
Zaire **43** *50-51*
Zambia **43** *51*
Zimbabwe **43** *51*

AMERICA, North & Central
Antigua & Barbuda **5** *69*
Bahamas **6** *69*
Barbados **7** *69*
Belize **7** *70*
Canada **10** *54-55*
Costa Rica **13** *70*
Cuba **13** *69*
Dominica **14** *69*
Dominican Republic **14** *69*
El Salvador **15** *70*
Grenada **18** *69*
Guatemala **18** *70*
Haiti **19** *69*
Honduras **19** *70*
Jamaica **21** *69*
Mexico **26** *70*
Nicaragua **28** *70*
Panama **29** *70*
St Kitts-Nevis **31** *69*
St Lucia **32** *69*
St Vincent and the Grenadines **32** *69*
Trinidad & Tobago **37** *69*
United States of America **39-41** *56-57*

AMERICA, South
Argentina **5** *74*
Bolivia **8** *72-73*
Brazil **8** *72-73*
Chile **11** *74*
Colombia **12** *72*
Ecuador **14** *72*
Guyana **18** *73*
Paraguay **30** *74*
Peru **30** *72*
Surinam **35** *73*
Uruguay **41** *74*
Venezuela **42** *72*

ASIA
Afghanistan **4** *42*
Armenia **5** *41*
Azerbaijan **6** *41*
Bahrain **6** *41*
Bangladesh **6-7** *43*
Bhutan **8** *43*
Brunei **8** *27*

Burma **9** *30*
Cambodia **9** *30*
China **11-12** *31*
Georgia **17** *21*
India **19-20** *42-44*
Indonesia **20** *27*
Iran **20** *41*
Iraq **20** *40-41*
Israel **20** *45*
Japan **21** *28-29*
Jordan **21** *40*
Kazakhstan **22** *24*
Kirghizia **22** *24*
Korea, North **22** *28*
Korea, South **22** *28*
Kuwait **22-23** *41*
Laos **23** *30*
Lebanon **23** *45*
Malaysia **25** *30*
Maldives **25** *44*
Mongolia **27** *26*
Nepal **28** *43*
Oman **29** *38*
Pakistan **29** *42*
Philippines **30** *27*
Qatar **31** *41*
Russian Federation **31** *24-25*
Saudi Arabia **32** *40-41*
Singapore **33** *30*
Sri Lanka **34** *44*
Syria **35** *40*
Taiwan **36** *31*
Tajikistan **36** *39*
Thailand **36** *30*
Turkey **37** *40*
Turkmenistan **37** *38*
United Arab Emirates **38** *41*
Uzbekistan **41** *38*
Vietnam **42** *30*
Yemen **42** *38*
AUSTRALASIA
Australia **5-6** *32-34*
Fiji **16** *33*
Kiribati **22** *33*
Marshall Islands **26** *37*
Micronesia,
Federated States of **26** *36*
Nauru **28** *33*
New Zealand **28** *35*
Papua New Guinea **30** *32*
Solomon Islands **33** *33*
Tonga **36** *33*
Tuvalu **37** *33*
Vanuatu **41** *33*
Western Samoa **42** *33*
EUROPE
Albania **4** *17*
Andorra **4** *15*
Austria **6** *18*
Belarus **7** *19*
Belgium **7** *13*
Bosnia-Herzegovina **8** *16-17*
Bulgaria **8-9** *17*
Croatia **13** *16*
Cyprus **13** *45*
Czech Republic **14** *18-19*
Denmark **14** *11*
Estonia **15** *20*
Finland **16** *12*
France **16** *14*
Germany **17** *18*
Greece **18** *17*
Hungary **19** *18-19*
Iceland **19** *12*
Ireland **20** *9*
Italy **21** *16*
Latvia **23** *19*
Liechtenstein **24** *16*
Lithuania **24** *19*
Luxembourg **24** *13*
Macedonia **24** *17*
Malta **25** *16*
Moldova **26** *19*
Monaco **27** *14*
Netherlands **28** *13*
Norway **29** *12*
Poland **30** *18-19*
Portugal **30** *15*
Romania **31** *17*
Russian Federation **31** *20-21*
San Marino **32** *16*
Slovakia **33** *18-19*
Slovenia **33** *16*
Spain **34** *15*
Sweden **35** *12*
Switzerland **35** *16*
Ukraine **38** *21*
United Kingdom **38-39** *6-9*
Vatican City **42**
Yugoslavia **42-43** *17*

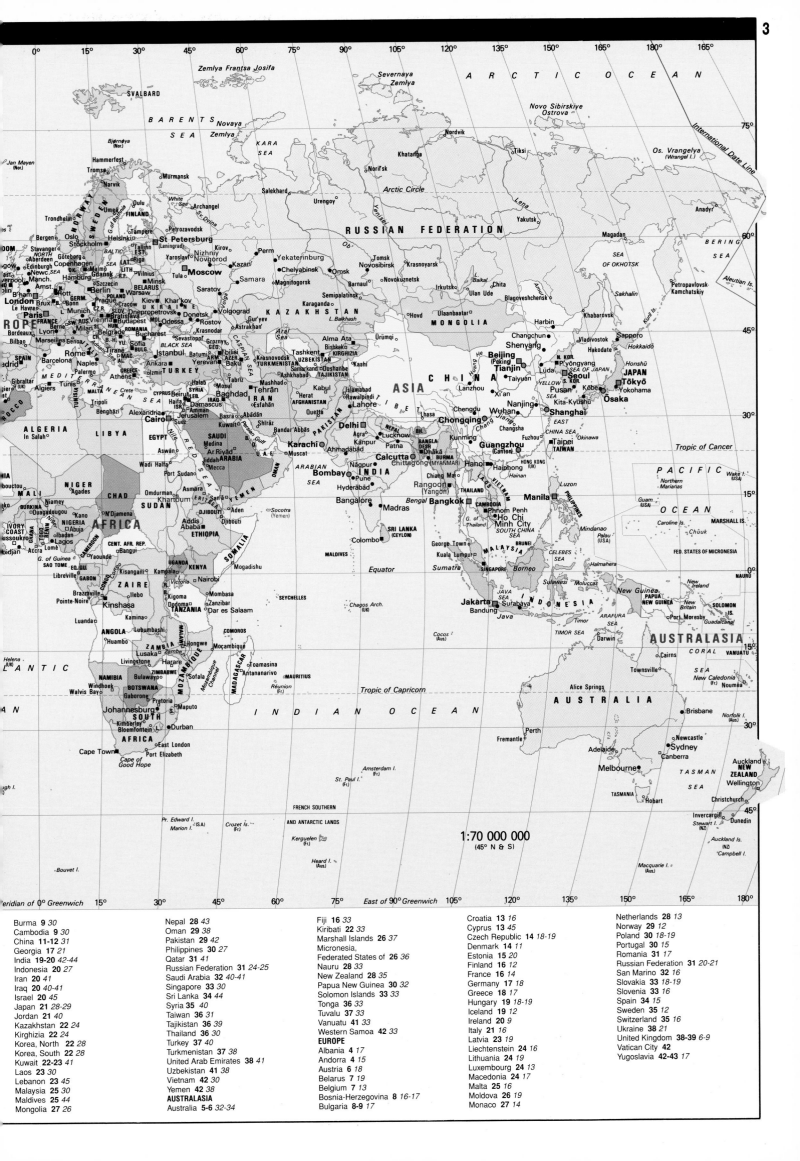

Greenland (Dan.)
Cape Farewell
Jan Mayen (Nor.)
ARCTIC
ICELAND
Reykjavík
Arctic Circle
NORWEGIAN SEA
Vesterålen
Lofoten
Narvik
Faeroes
Rockall
Shetland
Orkney
ATLANTIC OCEAN
NORWAY
SWEDEN
Trondheim
Bergen
Oslo
Stavanger
Uppsala
Västerås
Vänern
Örebro
Stockholm
Norrköping
Linköping
Borås
Göteborg
Jönköping
Öland
UNITED KINGDOM OF GREAT BRITAIN AND NORTHERN IRELAND
Dundee
Aberdeen
Glasgow
Edinburgh
NORTH SEA
Belfast
IRELAND
Dublin
Cork
Newcastle
Middlesborough
Blackpool
Liverpool
Leeds
Hull
Manchester
Sheffield
Wolverhampton
Derby
Birmingham
Leicester
Norwich
Northampton
Swansea
Cardiff
Oxford
Luton
Reading
Bristol
London
Ipswich
Isles of Scilly
Plymouth
Southampton
Brighton
English Channel
Channel Islands
DENMARK
Ålborg
Århus
Copenhagen (København)
Helsingborg
Malmö
Odense
Bornholm
Baltic
Kiel
Rostock
Lübeck
Schwerin
Hamburg
Bremerhavn
Wilhelmshaven
Groningen
Bremen
Amsterdam
The Hague 's-Gravenhage
NETHERLANDS
Rotterdam
Antwerp
Hannover
Wolfsburg
Berlin
Enschede
Hildesheim
Szczecin
Gorzow Wlkp
Poznań
Paderborn
Essen
Göttingen
GERMANY
Cottbus
Zielona Gora
Brussels (Bruxelles)
Düsseldorf
Dortmund
Boulogne
Lille
BELGIUM
Cologne (Köln)
Kassel
Leipzig
Jena
Dresden
Valenciennes
Bonn
Zwickau
Chemnitz
Wrocław
Le Havre
Amiens
Namur
Koblenz
Frankfurt
Rouen
Seine
Mainz
Offenbach
Brest
Caen
Reims
Luxembourg
LUXEMBOURG
Darmstadt
Paris
Heidelberg
Plzen
Prague (Praha)
Lorient
Rennes
Metz
Karlsruhe
Nürnberg
Erlangen
CZECH REP.
Le Mans
Angers
St. Nazaire
Orléans
Troyes
Nancy
Strasbourg
Heilbronn
Regensburg
Nantes
Loire
Stuttgart
Brno
Tours
Ulm
Augsburg
Freiburg
Mulhouse
Rhein
Munich (München)
Vienna (Wien)
Bratislava
FRANCE
Dijon
Montbéliard
Bay of Biscay
Besançon
Berne (Bern)
Basle
Zurich
Salzburg
Limoges
Clermont-Ferrand
Geneva (Genève)
SWITZERLAND
Lausanne
LIECHTENSTEIN
Innsbruck
AUSTRIA
Graz
HUNGARY
La Coruña
Bordeaux
Lyon
Bolzano
Gijón
Oviedo
Santander
Baracaldo
St-Étienne
Villeurbanne
Bergamo
Brescia
Udine
SLOVENIA
Ljubljana
Pécs
Vigo
León
Bilbao
Bayonne
Valence
Novara
Milan (Milano)
Verona
Trieste
Zagreb
Vitoria
San Sebastian
Toulouse
Pau
Rhône
Turin (Torino)
Piacenza
Padova
Venice (Venezia)
CROATIA
Oporto (Porto)
Burgos
Alessandria
Parma
Reggio
Ferrara
Valladolid
Logroño
Nîmes
Montpellier
Genoa (Genova)
La Spezia
Bologna
Ebro
Nice
MONACO
Florence (Firenze)
Rimini
BOSNIA HERZEGOVINA
PORTUGAL
Salamanca
ANDORRA
Marseilles (Marseille)
Pisa
Livorno
SAN MARINO
Ancona
Zaragoza
Sabadell
Perpignan
Toulon
Split
Sarajevo
Madrid
Alcalá de H.
Tarrasa
Corsica (Corse)
Bastia
Perugia
ADRIATIC SEA
Lisbon (Lisboa)
Tajo
SPAIN
Badalona
Barcelona
Ajaccio
ITALY
Toledo
Tarragona
Terni
Pescara
Badajoz
Castellon de la P.
Rome (Roma)
Foggia
Córdoba
Albacete
Valencia
Balearic Islands
Minorca (Menorca)
Sardinia (Sardegna)
Sassari
Olbia
Bari
Naples (Napoli)
Faro
Sevilla
Huelva
Alicante
Majorca (Mallorca)
Ibiza
TYRRHENIAN SEA
Salerno
Taranto
Madeira (Port.)
Jerez de la F.
Cádiz
Granada
Murcia
Elche
Málaga
Cartagena
Cagliari
Almería
Gibraltar (U.K.)
Ceuta (Sp.)
Tangiers (Tanger)
Tetouan
MEDITERRANEAN SEA
Cosenza
Algiers (Alger)
Palermo
Messina
Melilla (Sp.)
Oran
Rabat
Casablanca
Sicily (Sicilia)
Reggio di Calabria
Syracuse
Tunis
MOROCCO
ALGERIA
TUNISIA
MALTA
Canary Is.
Marrakech
0 200 400 600 km

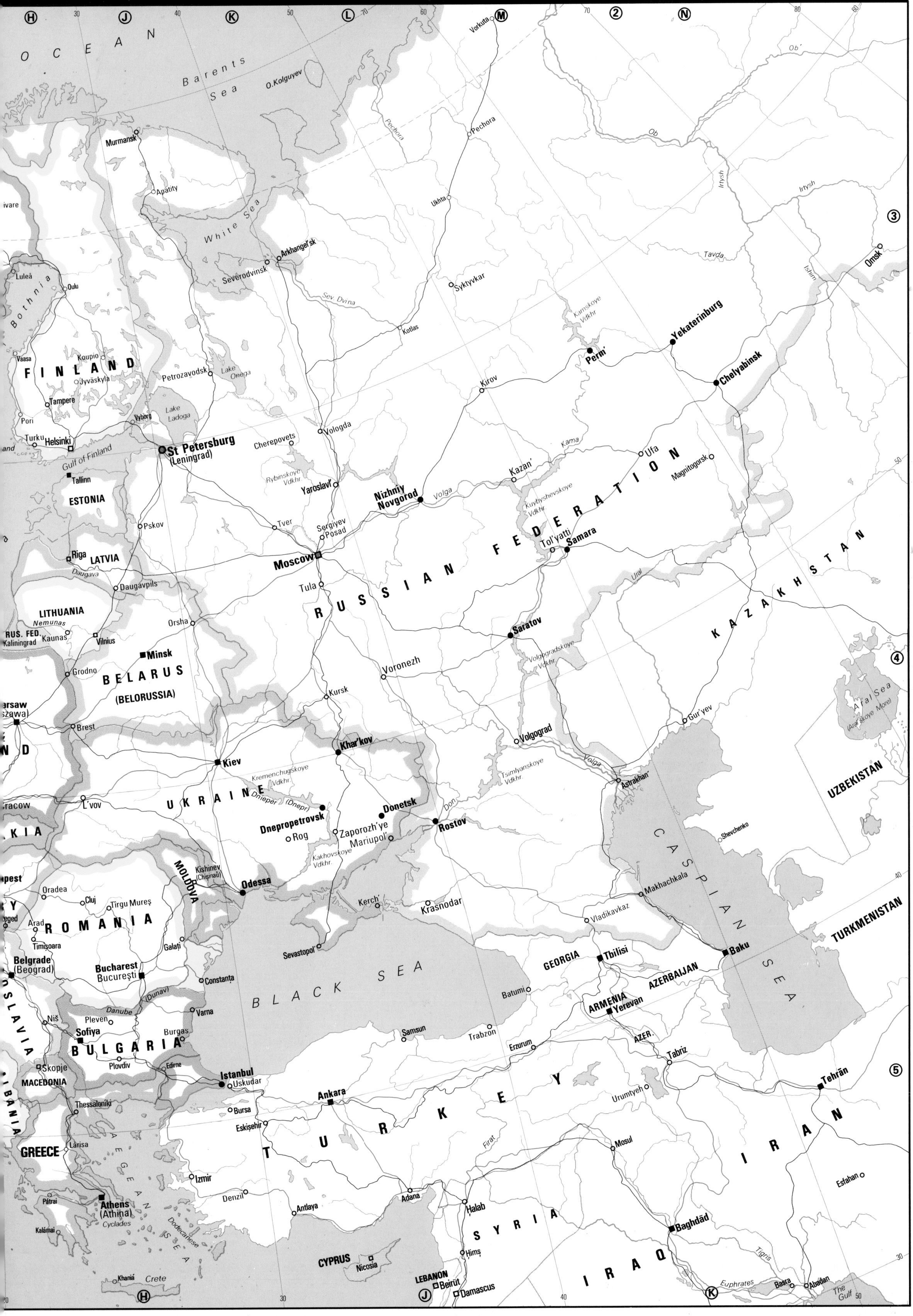

H
J
K
L
M
N
2
3
4
5
O C E A N
Barents Sea
O.Kolguyev
White Sea
Vorkuta
Pechora
Ob'
Ob
Irtysh
Tavda
Ishim
Omsk
Murmansk
Apatity
Ukhta
Arkhangel'sk
Severodvinsk
Syktyvkar
Sev. Dvina
Kotlas
Kamskoye Vdkhr
Yekaterinburg
Perm'
Chelyabinsk
Luleå
Oulu
Bothnia
Vaasa
Koupio
FINLAND
Jyväskylä
Petrozavodsk
Lake Onega
Tampere
Pori
Lake Ladoga
Vyborg
Turku
Helsinki
St Petersburg
(Leningrad)
Gulf of Finland
Tallinn
ESTONIA
Cherepovets
Vologda
Kirov
Kama
Ufa
Magnitogorsk
Rybinskoye Vdkhr
Yaroslavl'
Nizhniy Novgorod
Volga
Kazan'
Kuybyshevskoye Vdkhr
RUSSIAN FEDERATION
Pskov
Tver
Sergiyev Posad
Tol'yatti
Samara
Riga
LATVIA
Daugava
Moscow
Daugavpils
Tula
Ural
KAZAKHSTAN
LITHUANIA
Nemunas
RUS. FED.
Kaliningrad
Kaunas
Vilnius
Orsha
Saratov
Minsk
Grodno
BELARUS
(BELORUSSIA)
Volgogradskoye Vdkhr
Voronezh
Kursk
Aral Sea
(Aral'skoye More)
Warsaw
Brest
Gur'yev
Volgograd
Khar'kov
Kiev
Kremenchugskoye Vdkhr
Tsimlyanskoye Vdkhr
Astrakhan'
UZBEKISTAN
L'vov
UKRAINE
Dnieper (Dnepr)
Donetsk
Don
Rostov
Dnepropetrovsk
Krivoy Rog
Zaporozh'ye
Mariupol'
Kakhovskoye Vdkhr.
Shevchenko
CASPIAN SEA
MOLDOVA
Kishinev (Chişinău)
Odessa
Oradea
Cluj
Tirgu Mureş
Arad
ROMANIA
Timişoara
Kerch'
Krasnodar
Makhachkala
Vladikavkaz
TURKMENISTAN
Sevastopol
Galaţi
Belgrade (Beograd)
Bucharest
Bucureşti
Constanţa
BLACK SEA
GEORGIA
Tbilisi
Baku
AZERBAIJAN
Batumi
(Dunav)
Danube
Varna
ARMENIA
Yerevan
Niš
Pleven
Sofiya
Burgas
BULGARIA
Samsun
Trabzon
Erzurum
AZER.
Tabriz
Skopje
Plovdiv
Edirne
MACEDONIA
Istanbul
Uskudar
TURKEY
Urumiyeh
Tehrān
Thessaloniki
Ankara
Bursa
Eskişehir
GREECE
Lárisa
AEGEAN SEA
Firat
Mosul
IRAN
Izmir
Esfahan
Denizli
Antalya
Adana
Halab
Pátrai
Athens
(Athína)
Cyclades
Dodecanese
SYRIA
Baghdād
Kalámai
CYPRUS
Nicosia
Hims
Tigris
LEBANON
Beirūt
Damascus
IRAQ
Euphrates
Basra
Abadan
The Gulf
Khaniá
Crete
30
40
50
60
70
80

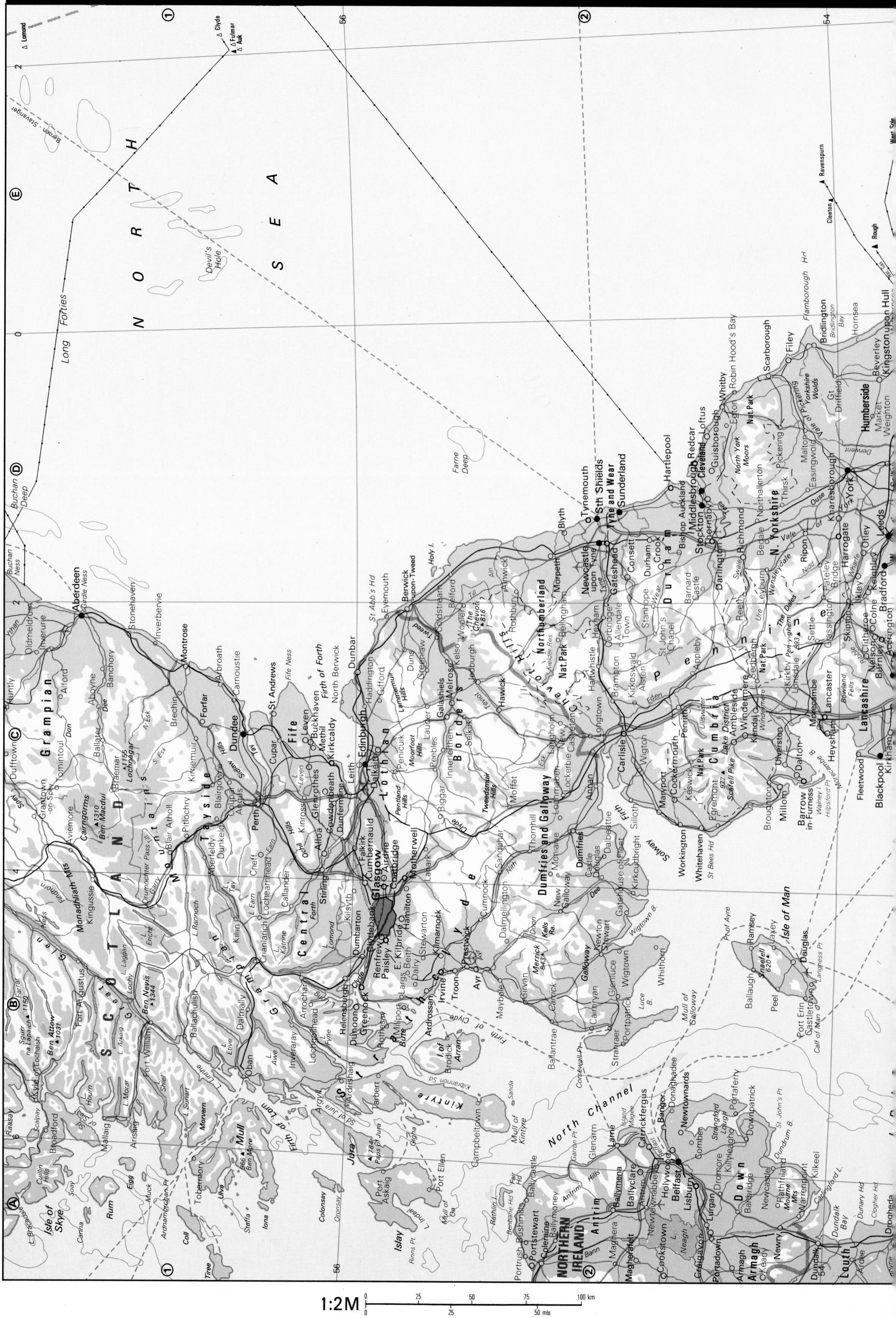

NORTH SEA
Long Forties
Devil's Hole
Buchan Deep
Buchan Ness
Farne Deep
SCOTLAND
Grampian Mountains
Grampian
Tayside
Central
Fife
Lothian
Borders
Strathclyde
Dumfries and Galloway
Northumberland
Durham
Cumbria
N. Yorkshire
Cleveland
Tyne and Wear
Humberside
Lancashire
Aberdeen
Girdle Ness
Stonehaven
Inverbervie
Montrose
Arbroath
Carnoustie
Forfar
Brechin
Dundee
Perth
St Andrews
Fife Ness
Kirkcaldy
Firth of Forth
North Berwick
Dunbar
Edinburgh
Leith
Dalkeith
Stirling
Falkirk
Glasgow
Paisley
Greenock
Dumbarton
Motherwell
Hamilton
Kilmarnock
Ayr
Irvine
Troon
Berwick-upon-Tweed
Holy I.
St Abb's Hd
Galashiels
Melrose
Hawick
Jedburgh
Kelso
The Cheviot 816
Cheviot Hills
Morpeth
Blyth
Newcastle upon Tyne
Tynemouth
Sth Shields
Sunderland
Gateshead
Durham
Hartlepool
Middlesbrough
Redcar
Stockton
Darlington
Whitby
Robin Hood's Bay
Scarborough
Filey
Flamborough Hd
Bridlington
York
Harrogate
Leeds
Bradford
Kingston upon Hull
Carlisle
Penrith
Workington
Whitehaven
Kendal
Windermere
Lancaster
Morecambe
Blackpool
Barrow in-Furness
Solway Firth
Dumfries
Isle of Man
Douglas
Ramsey
Snaefell 620
Mull of Galloway
Stranraer
North Channel
NORTHERN IRELAND
Antrim
Belfast
Lisburn
Bangor
Larne
Down
Armagh
Newry
Isle of Skye
Fort William
Ben Nevis 1344
Cairngorms
Ben Macdui 1310
Lochnagar 1155
Oban
Mull
Islay
Jura
Arran
Kintyre
Campbeltown
Firth of Clyde
Firth of Lorn
Clyde
Fulmar
Auk
Lomond
Ravenspurn
Rough
1:2M
0 25 50 75 100 km
0 25 50 mls

ENGLAND
WALES
ENGLISH CHANNEL
Bristol Channel
Cardigan Bay
St George's Channel
Celtic Sea
Strait of Dover
London
Gtr London
Birmingham
W. Mid
Manchester
Liverpool
Merseyside
Sheffield
S. Yorkshire
Leicester
Nottingham
Northampton
Derby
Coventry
Oxford
Bristol
Avon
Cardiff
Swansea
Newport
Gloucester
Southampton
Portsmouth
Bournemouth
Brighton
Plymouth
Exeter
Cambridge
Peterborough
Norwich
Ipswich
Colchester
Dover
Folkestone
Canterbury
Calais
Boulogne
Dieppe
Dublin
Wicklow
Wexford
Rosslare
Norfolk
Suffolk
Essex
Kent
Surrey
West Sussex
East Sussex
Hampshire
Isle of Wight
Dorset
Devon
Cornwall
Somerset
Wilts.
Berks.
Oxford
Buckingham
Bedford
Hertford
Northampton
Warwick
Leicester
Lincoln
Nottingham
Derby
Stafford
Shropshire
Hereford and Worcester
Gloucester
Cheshire
Clwyd
Gwynedd
Powys
Dyfed
W. Glamorgan
Mid Glamorgan
S. Glamorgan
Gwent
Isles of Scilly
Land's End
Lizard Pt
Lundy
Anglesey
Holyhead
Snowdon
The Wash
The Broads
Salisbury Plain
Cotswold Hills
Chiltern Hills
North Downs
South Downs
Dartmoor
Exmoor
Bodmin Moor
Brecon Beacons
Cambrian Mts

Herma Ness
Unst
Isbister
Fetlar
Yell
The Faither
Hillswick
St Magnus Bay
Brae
Papa Stour
Whalsay
Shetland
Bressay
Noss
Foula
Scalloway
Lerwick
W. Burra
Fitful Hd
Grutness
Sumburgh Hd
Fair Isle
at the same scale
Sula Sgeir
N. Rona
Sule Skerry
Stack Skerry
Dennis Hd.
Noup Hd.
Papa Westray
N. Ronaldsay
Westray
Sanday
Rousay
Birsay
Eday
Stronsay
Shapinsay
Auskerry
Mainland
Stromness
Kirkwall
Orkney
Rora Hd.
Scapa Flow
Burray
Hoy
S. Ronaldsay
Pentland Firth
Stroma
Dunnet Hd
John o' Groats
Duncansby Hd
C. Wrath
Thurso
Halkirk
Noss Hd.
Wick
Butt of Lewis
Durness
L. Eriboll
Tongue
Ben Hope 927
Caithness
Handa
Eddrachillis Bay
L. Naver
Ben Kilbreck 961
Lybster
Kinbrace
Stornoway
Lewis
Broad B.
Tiumpan Hd.
Lochinver
Ben More Assynt 998
Enard Bay
Inchnadamph
L. Shin
Helmsdale
Beatrice
North Minch
Lairg
Brora
Scarp
Western Isles
Oykel
Taransay
Tarbert
Sound of Shiant
Greenstone Pt
L. Broom
Ullapool
Dornoch
Dornoch Firth
Harris
Rubha Reidh
Tarbat Ness
Pabbay
Berneray
Sd of Harris
L. Ewe
Ben Dearg 1081
Tain
Rubha Hunish
Gairloch
Moray Firth
North Uist
L. Maree
L. Fannich
Ben Wyvis 1045
Alness
Invergordon
Lossiemouth
Kinnairds Hd
Lochmaddy
Little Minch
Uig
L. Snizort
Rona
Cromarty
Elgin
Banff
Fraserburgh
Monach Is
L. Torridon
Dingwall
Black Isle
Forres
Buckie
Macduff
Benbecula
Ronay
Sd of Raasay
Beauly
Nairn
Lossie
Keith
Deveron
Turriff
Peterhead
Wiay
Portree
Raasay
Highland
Inverness
Rothes
Buchan Ness
Huntly
South Uist
L. Bracadale
Scalpay
Sgurr na Lapaich 1150
Farrar
Grantown-on-Spey
Spey
Dufftown
Ythan
Oldmeldrum
Cuillin Hills
Kyle of Lochalsh
Inverurie
Lochboisdale
Isle of Skye
Broadford
Ben Attow 1031
L. Ness
Findhorn
Tomintoul
Grampian
Sd of Barra
Eriskay
Soay
Canna
Monadhliath Mts
Aviemore
Alford
Aberdeen
Girdle Ness
Castlebay
Barra
Sd of Sleat
L. Hourn
Fort Augustus
Kingussie
Cairngorms
Ben Macdui 1310
Don
Aboyne
Ballater
Dee
Banchory
Rum
Mallaig
Great Glen
SCOTLAND
L. Arkaig
L. Laggan
Braemar
Lochnagar 1155
Stonehaven
Mingulay
Eigg
L. Morar
Arisaig
L. Lochy
Drumochter Pass
Tilt
N. Esk
Barra Hd
Muck
Fort William
Ben Nevis 1344
L. Ericht
Garry
Mountains
S. Esk
Inverbervie
Shiel
Ardnamurchan Pt
Blair Atholl
Brechin
Coll
L. Sunart
Pitlochry
Kirriemuir
Montrose
Tobermory
Morvern
L. Linnhe
Ballachulish
L. Rannoch
Tayside
Forfar
Tiree
Ulva
Bridge of Orchy
Aberfeldy
Dunkeld
Blairgowrie
Arbroath
Mull
966 Ben More
L. Etive
Killin
L. Tay
Coupar Angus
Sidlaw Hills
Dundee
Carnoustie
Broughty Ferry
Staffa
Iona
Oban
Dalmally
Lochearnhead
Crieff
Perth
Tay
Stanton Banks
Grampian
Crianlarich
L. Earn
Earn
Cupar
St Andrews
L. Awe
Firth of Lorn
L. Katrine
Callander
Fife Ness
Inveraray
Ochil Hills
Kinross
Leven
Fife
Arrochar
Central
Forth
Glenrothes
Buckhaven
Methil
Lochgoilhead
Aberfoyle
Alloa
Firth of Forth
Colonsay
Argyll
L. Fyne
L. Long
L. Lomond
Stirling
Cowdenbeath
Kirkcaldy
Oronsay
Sd of Jura
Strathclyde
Helensburgh
Dunfermline
North Berwick
Dunbar
Jura
Ardrishaig
Dunoon
Clyde
Dumbarton
Kilsyth
Falkirk
Edinburgh
Leith
784 Paps of Jura
Tarbert
Greenock
Clydebank
Cumbernauld
Dalkeith
Haddington
Gifford
St Abb's Hd
Port Askaig
Rothesay
Renfrew
Paisley
Glasgow
Airdrie
Coatbridge
Livingstone
Lothian
Eyemouth
Islay
Bute
Millport
Largs
E. Kilbride
Pentland Hills
Penicuik
Lammermuir Hills
Berwick-upon-Tweed
Rinns Pt
Gigha
Beith
Hamilton
Moorfoot Hills
Duns
L. Indaal
Dalry
Stewarton
Motherwell
Greenlaw
Holy I.
Kintyre
Kilbrannan Sd
Ardrossan
Lanark
Lauder
Tweed
Port Ellen
I. of Arran
Brodick
Arran
Kilmarnock
Carstairs
Peebles
Galashiels
Coldstream
Belford
Mull of Oa
Irvine
Biggar
Innerleithen
Melrose
Kelso
Wooler
Malin Hd
Inishtrahull Sd.
Troon
Prestwick
Borders
Selkirk
Jedburgh
The Cheviot 816
Glengad Hd.
Campbeltown
Firth of Clyde
Ayr
Tweedsmuir Hills
Teviot
Sheep Haven
L. Swilly
Rathlin I.
Cumnock
Aln
Carndonagh
Benbane Hd.
Fair Hd
Maybole
Dalmellington
Sanquhar
Hawick
Alnwick
Moville
Inishowen
Portrush
Mull of Kintyre
Sanda
Nith
Moffat
Rothbury
Portstewart
Bushmills
Ballycastle
Girvan
L. Doon
Buncrana
Coleraine
Merrick 843
Kells Ra.
Thornhill
Cheviot Hills
Northumberland
Rahtmelton
Ballymoney
North Channel
Ballantrae
Carrick
Dumfries and Galloway
Esk
Langholm
Kielder Res.
Wansbeck
Letterkenny
L. Foyle
Limavady
Antrim Hills
Moniaive
New Galloway
Lochmaben
New Castleton
Lockerbie
Nat.Park
Bellingham
Morpeth
Donegal
Londonderry
Garron Pt
Corsewall Pt
Galloway
Dumfries
Newcastle upon Tyne
Bann
Antrim
Glenarm
Loch Ryan
Cairnryan
Newton Stewart
Dee
Castle Douglas
Annan
Longtown
Haltwhistle
Hexham
Tyne
Lifford
Strabane
Sperrin Mts
Maghera
Ballymena
Larne
Island Magee
Stranraer
Glenluce
Dalbeattie
Corbridge
Gateshead
Magherafelt
Ballyclare
Portpatrick
Wigtown
Gatehouse of Fleet
Solway Firth
Brampton
Allendale Town
Newton Stewart
Antrim
Carrickfergus
Wigtown B.
Kirkcudbright
Carlisle
Silloth
Wigton
Alston
Consett
Tyrone
NORTHERN IRELAND
Newtownabbey
Belfast
Luce B.
Eden
Kirkoswald
Stanhope
Wear
Durham
Crook
Omagh
Cookstown
Bangor
Donaghadee
Whithorn
Maryport
St John's Chapel
Durham
Pomeroy
L. Neagh
Holywood
Burrow Hd.
Cockermouth
Bishop Auckland
ULSTER
Fintona
Dungannon
Lisburn
Newtownards
Comber
Mull of Galloway
Workington
Whitehaven
Keswick
Cumbria Nat.Park
Penrith
Ullswater
Appleby
Barnard Castle
1:2M
0 25 50 75 100 km
0 25 50 mls

Stanton Banks
Firth of Lorn
Colonsay
Oronsay
Jura
Paps of Jura
Islay
Port Askaig
Rinns Pt
L. Indaal
Port Ellen
Mull of Oa
Gigha
Kintyre
Kilbrannon Sd
I. of Arran
Brodick
Campbeltown
Mull of Kintyre
Sanda
Inveraray
Arrochar
Lochgoilhead
L. Fyne
L. Long
Helensburgh
Dunoon
Greenock
Ardrishaig
Tarbert
Rothesay
Bute
Largs
Millport
Ardrossan
Irvine
Troon
Prestwick
Ayr
Firth of Clyde
Strathclyde
Maybole
Girvan
Ballantrae
Cairnryan
Stranraer
Glenluce
Portpatrick
Luce B.
Mull of Galloway
Corsewall Pt
North Channel
Malin Hd
Inishtrahull Sd.
Glengad Hd.
Rathlin I.
Benbane Hd
Fair Hd
Tory I.
Tory Sound
Sheep Haven
L. Swilly
Carndonagh
Moville
Inishowen
Portrush
Bushmills
Ballycastle
Portstewart
Coleraine
Ballymoney
Bloody Foreland
Gola
Errigal 752
Rathmelton
Buncrana
L. Foyle
Limavady
Aran I.
Letterkenny
Londonderry
Antrim Hills
Garron Pt.
Glenarm
Gweebarra B.
Donegal
Donegal Mts
Lifford
Strabane
Londonderry
Antrim
Ballymena
Glenties
Blue Stack 676
Sperrin Mts
Maghera
Magherafelt
Ballyclare
Larne
Island Magee
Rossan Pt.
Killybegs
Donegal
Newtown Stewart
Antrim
Carrickfergus
Belfast L.
NORTHERN IRELAND
Newtownabbey
Tyrone
Cookstown
L. Neagh
Belfast
Bangor
Holywood
Donaghadee
Newtownards
Muckros Hd
Donegal Bay
L. Derg
Omagh
Pomeroy
Bundoran
Ballyshannon
ULSTER
Lisburn
Comber
Inishmurray
Fintona
Dungannon
Lurgan
Craigavon
Strangford Lough
Benwee Hd.
Broad Haven
Melvin
L. Erne
Portadown
Killyleagh
Erris Hd.
The Mullet
Belmullet
Ballycastle
Killala B.
Sligo Bay
Enniskillen
Aughnacloy
Ballynahinch
Portaferry
Sligo
Fermanagh
Armagh
Down
Banbridge
Downpatrick
Carrowmore L.
Leitrim
Upper L. Erne
Monaghan
Armagh
Keady
Newcastle
Rathfriland
Isle of Man
Inishkea
Ballina
Ox Mts
Clones
Newry
Mourne Mts
Dundrum B.
St. John's Pt.
Peel
Blacksod B.
Mts of Mayo
Nephin 807
L. Conn
Sligo
L. Allen
Monaghan
Castleblayney
Warrenpoint
Kilkeel
Port Erin
Calf of Man
Achill Hd
Achill
Corraun Pen.
Moy
L. Oughter
Cootehill
Dundalk
Carlingford L.
Swinford
Boyle
Carrick on Shannon
Cavan
Clare I.
Clew Bay
Castlebar
Mayo
Ballaghaderreen
L. Gara
L. Boderg
Carrickmacross
Cavan
Louth
Dundalk Bay
Westport
Ballyhaunis
Claremorris
Roscommon
Castlerea
L. Sheelin
L. Bowna
REPUBLIC
Ardee
Dunany Pt
Clogher Hd
Inishturk
Inishbofin
Inishshark
Partry Mts.
CONNAUGHT
L. Mask
Longford
Boyne
Kells
Drogheda
IRISH SEA
Ballinrobe
Roscommon
Longford
L. Derravaragh
An Uaimh
Mts of Connemara
Clifden
Tuam
L. Ree
Meath
Balbriggan
Skerries
Slyne Hd
L. Corrib
Suck
Mullingar
OF
Trim
Swords
Bertraghboy B.
Galway
Athlone
Moate
Westmeath
Royal Canal
Dublin
Howth
Clara
L. Ennell
Edenderry
Galway
Athenry
Ballinasloe
Tullamore
Kildare
Liffey
Dublin
(Baile Atha Cliath)
Holyhead
Kilkieran B.
Galway B.
Black Hd
Loughrea
IRELAND
Dun Laoghaire
Holy I.
Inishmore
Aran Is
Slieve Aughty Mts.
Portumna
Shannon
Offaly
Banagher
Birr
Mountmellick
Dromhead Nua
Portarlington
Naas
Kippure 754
Bray
Inishmaan
Ballyvaghan
Gort
Slieve Bloom Mts
Kildare
Greystones
Hags Hd
Ennistimon
LEINSTER
Caernarfon Bay
Liscannor B.
Clare
Scarriff
Lough Derg
Port Laoise
Athy
Wicklow Mts 926
Wicklow
Wicklow Hd.
Mutton I.
Milltown Malbay
Ennis
Roscrea
Laois
Barrow
Lugnaquillia Mtn
Donegal Pt.
Killaloe
Nenagh
Carlow
Wicklow
Kilmichael Pt.
Kilkee
Templemore
Tullow
Arklow
Kilrush
Shannon
Thurles
Carlow
Bardsey
Loop Hd
Mouth of the Shannon
Limerick
Kilkenny
Muine Bheag
Gorey
Foynes
Tipperary
Slaney
Kerry Hd
Limerick
Rathkeale
Kilkenny
Listowel
Newcastle W.
Cashel
Thomastown
Cahore Pt
Tralee Bay
MUNSTER
Tipperary
Fethard
Nore
Enniscorthy
Abbeyfeale
Rath Luirc
Kilmallock
Galty Mts.
Carrick on-Suir
Wexford
Tralee
Castleisland
Cahir
New Ross
Dingle
Mitchelstown
Clonmel
Wexford
Blasket Sd.
Gt. Blasket
Newmarket
Kanturk
Knockmealdown Mts.
Comeragh Mts
Waterford
Rosslare
St George's Channel
Kerry
Killorglin
Fermoy
Lismore
Waterford
Dingle B.
Killarney
Mallow
Blackwater
Cappoquin
Tramore
Ballyteige Bay
Carnsore Pt
1041
Millstreet
Boggeragh Mts
Dungarvan
Waterford Harb.
Hook Hd
Saltee
Cardigan
Valencia
MacGillycuddy's Reeks
Cork
Helvick Hd.
Nat.Pk
Cahersiveen
Sneem
Kenmare
Macroom
Lee
Cork
Youghal
Mine Hd
Strumble Hd
Fishguard
Ballinskelligs B.
Kenmare River
Passage West
Midleton
Cobh
Youghal Harb.
St Davids Hd
St. Davids
Caha Mts
Bandon
Ballycotton Bay
Ramsey I.
Castletown Bere
Bantry
Dunmanway
Kinsale
Cork
St Brides B.
Haverfordwest
Dursey
Bantry Bay
Clonakilty
Skomer
Milford Haven
Dunmanus Bay
Schull
Clonakilty Bay
Old Head of Kinsale
Milford Haven
Pembroke
Tenby
Mizen Hd
Skibbereen
Caldy
Roaringwater B.
Baltimore
St Govans Hd
C. Clear
Fastnet Rock
Kinsale
Lundy
A
B
C
D
1
2
3
4
8
6
56
54
52

1:2M 0 25 50 75 100 km
0 25 50 mls

Ⓐ   Ⓑ   ①   Ⓒ   Ⓓ

N O R T H S E A

SCOTLAND

N. IRELAND

REP. OF IRELAND

WALES

ENGLAND

IRISH SEA

English Channel

BRITTANY

NORMANDY

FRANCE

Shetland · Unst · Fetlar · Yell · Lerwick · Sumburgh Hd · Foula · Fair Isle

Orkney · Kirkwall · Hoy · Scapa Flow · Stromness · Stronsay · Sanday · Westray · Rousay

Thurso · Wick · Helmsdale · Dornoch · Dingwall · Inverness · Elgin · Banff · Fraserburgh · Peterhead · Buchan Ness · Aberdeen · Stonehaven · Montrose · Arbroath · Dundee · St Andrews · Perth · Pitlochry · Braemar · Ben Macdui 1309 · Ben Nevis 1344 · Ben Lawers 1214 · Fort William · Fort Augustus · Mallaig · Kyle of Lochalsh · Portree · Ullapool

Outer Hebrides · Stornoway · Lewis · Harris · N. Uist · S. Uist · Barra · St Kilda · The Minch · Skye · Rum · Coll · Tiree · Mull · Islay · Jura · Colonsay · Oban · F. of Lorn · L. Lomond · Stirling · Greenock · Paisley · **Glasgow** · Motherwell · **Edinburgh** · Kirkcaldy · F. of Forth · Irvine · Kilmarnock · Ayr · Galashiels · Berwick-upon-Tweed · Holy I. · St Abbs Hd · Campbeltown · Arran · Girvan · Moffat · Hawick · Cheviots · Merrick 843 · White Coomb 822

Londonderry · Coleraine · Ballymena · Larne · Bangor · **Belfast** · Omagh · Enniskillen · L. Neagh · Portadown · Armagh · Newry · Monaghan · Cavan · Dundalk · Drogheda · Donegal · Donegal B. · Sligo · Ballina · Boyle · Castlebar · Roscommon · Longford · Mullingar · Athlone · **Dublin** (Baile Átha Cliath) · Dún Laoghaire · Bray · Wicklow · Arklow · Galway · Ennis · Limerick · Nenagh · Port Laoise · Carlow · Kilkenny · Clonmel · Waterford · Wexford · Rosslare · Tralee · Killarney · Tipperary · Dungarvan · Youghal · **Cork** · Bantry · Dingle · Carrauntoohill 1041

Carlisle · Penrith · Scafell Pike 977 · Kendal · Barrow-in-Furness · Morecambe · Lancaster · Blackpool · Preston · Harrogate · York · Hull · Grimsby · **Leeds** · Bradford · Huddersfield · Bolton · **Liverpool** · Birkenhead · **Manchester** · Warrington · Chester · Crewe · Stoke-on-Trent · **Sheffield** · Doncaster · Lincoln · Derby · Nottingham · Shrewsbury · Wolverhampton · **Birmingham** · Leicester · Coventry · Northampton · Peterborough · King's Lynn · Norwich · Great Yarmouth · Lowestoft · Worcester · Gloucester · Oxford · Milton Keynes · Bedford · Cambridge · Newmarket · Ipswich · Felixstowe · Colchester · Harwich · Swindon · Luton · **London** · Chelmsford · Southend-on-Sea · Reading · Windsor · Maidstone · Canterbury · Dover · **Bristol** · Bath · Weston-super-Mare · Guildford · Crawley · Brighton · Hastings · Eastbourne · Folkestone · Cardiff · Newport · Swansea · Taunton · Barnstaple · Bude · Exeter · Bournemouth · Southampton · Portsmouth · Isle of Wight · Weymouth · Torquay · Plymouth · Truro · Penzance · Land's End · Falmouth · Isles of Scilly · Newquay

Snowdon 1085 · Aberystwyth · Cardigan Bay · Builth Wells · Brecon · Carmarthen · Pembroke · Fishguard · St David's Hd · Holyhead · Anglesey · Bangor · Pwllheli

Gt Fisher Bank · Great Fisher Bank · Dogger Bank · Long Forties · Viking Bank

Calais · Dunkirk · Boulogne · St-Omer · Béthune · Lille · Roubaix · Tourcoing · Lens · Douai · Arras · Valenciennes · Amiens · Abbeville · Dieppe · Le Tréport · Le Havre · Fécamp · Bolbec · Rouen · Beauvais · Compiègne · Senlis · Cherbourg · Caen · Lisieux · Évreux · Mantes · Versailles · **Paris** · Rambouillet · Chartres · Étampes · Fontainebleau · Melun · Provins · Rennes · St-Malo · Dinan · St-Brieuc · Morlaix · Brest · Quimper · Lorient · Le Mans · Laval · Alençon · Argentan

Amsterdam · Leiden · The Hague ('s-Gravenhage) · Rotterdam · Dordrecht · Utrecht · Den Helder · Alkmaar · Haarlem · Zaanstad · Hoorn · Antwerp (Antwerpen) · **Brussels** (Bruxelles) · Gent · Bruges · Oostende · Vlissingen · Zeebrugge · Leuven · Mechelen · Namur · Charleroi

1:5M

0   50   100   150   200 km

0   50   100 mls

NORWAY
Oslo
Lillestrøm
Drammen
Kongsberg
Notodden
Horten
Moss
Sarpsborg
Fredrikstad
Halden
Skien
Porsgrunn
Larvik
Kragerø
Risør
Tvedestrand
Arendal
Grimstad
Kristiansand
Mandal
Lindesnes
Flekkefjord
Hønefoss
Rjukan
Odda
Voss
Myrdal
Geilo
Hamar
Kongsvinger
Skagerrak
SWEDEN
Stockholm
Uppsala
Västerås
Enköping
Sala
Avesta
Hedemora
Säter
Ludvika
Norrtälje
Kapellskär
Rimbo
Östhammar
Mariehamn
Ålands Hav
Södertälje
Nynäshamn
Eskilstuna
Strängnäs
Köping
Örebro
Kumla
Karlskoga
Kristinehamn
Karlstad
Arvika
Säffle
Åmål
Vänern
Mälaren
Hjälmaren
Katrineholm
Nyköping
Oxelösund
Norrköping
Finspång
Motala
Askersund
Linköping
Mariestad
Lidköping
Skövde
Vänersborg
Trollhättan
Uddevalla
Vättern
Mjölby
Tranås
Atvidaberg
Falköping
Jönköping
Huskvarna
Göteborg
Borås
Mölndal
Kungsbacka
Eksjö
Nässjö
Vetlanda
Hultsfred
Västervik
Oskarshamn
Mönsterås
Värnamo
Varberg
Falkenberg
Halmstad
Ljungby
Växjö
Nybro
Kalmar
Borgholm
Öland
Älmhult
Båstad
Ängelholm
Hässleholm
Helsingborg
Landskrona
Lund
Malmö
Ystad
Trelleborg
Simrishamn
Kristianstad
Karlshamn
Ronneby
Karlskrona
Hanöbukten
Gotland
Visby
Klintehamn
Hemse
Burgsvik
Fårö
Gotska Sandön
BALTIC SEA
DENMARK
Copenhagen (København)
Skagen
Frederikshavn
Hirtshals
Hjørring
Ålborg
Thisted
Nykøbing
Skive
Hobro
Randers
Viborg
Holstebro
Herning
Silkeborg
Århus
Grenå
Horsens
Vejle
Fredericia
Kolding
Varde
Esbjerg
Jylland (Jutland)
Kattegat
Odense
Fyn
Svendborg
Nyborg
Korsør
Sjælland
Roskilde
Køge
Næstved
Vordingborg
Nakskov
Lolland
Nykøbing
Falster
Møn
Helsingør
Hillerød
Bornholm
Rønne
Haderslev
Åbenrå
Sønderborg
Als
Rødbyhavn
GERMANY
SCHLESWIG-HOLSTEIN
Flensburg
Schleswig
Kiel
Rendsburg
Neumünster
Husum
Heide
Itzehoe
Lübeck
Travemünde
Puttgarden
Fehmarn
Oldenburg
Cuxhaven
Hamburg
Bremerhaven
Wilhelmshaven
Emden
Bremen
Oldenburg
NIEDERSACHSEN
Hannover
Celle
Wolfsburg
Braunschweig
Hildesheim
Salzgitter
Osnabrück
Bielefeld
Münster
Göttingen
Kassel
Lüneburg
Uelzen
Stendal
Salzwedel
MECKLENBURG-VORPOMMERN
Rostock
Warnemünde
Wismar
Schwerin
Stralsund
Sassnitz
Rügen
Greifswald
Neubrandenburg
Anklam
Prenzlau
Berlin
Potsdam
Brandenburg
Frankfurt an-der-O.
Cottbus
Magdeburg
Dessau
SACHSEN-ANHALT
Halle
Leipzig
Dresden
SACHSEN
Chemnitz
Zwickau
Gera
Jena
Erfurt
Weimar
THÜRINGEN
Eisenach
Plauen
Hof
Fulda
Marburg
Giessen
HESSEN
Frankfurt
Wiesbaden
Mainz
Darmstadt
Offenbach
Würzburg
Schweinfurt
Bamberg
Bayreuth
Erlangen
Fürth
Nürnberg
Regensburg
Ingolstadt
Augsburg
Munich (München)
Landshut
Passau
Ulm
Stuttgart
Karlsruhe
Heilbronn
Heidelberg
Mannheim
Ludwigshafen
Worms
Kaiserslautern
Saarbrücken
Trier
Koblenz
Bonn
Cologne (Köln)
Düsseldorf
Duisburg
Essen
Dortmund
Wuppertal
Hagen
Siegen
NORDRHEIN-WESTFALEN
RHEINLAND-PFALZ
BADEN-WÜRTTEMBERG
BAYERN
Freiburg
Tübingen
Reutlingen
Pforzheim
Offenburg
Strasbourg
Nancy
Colmar
Luxembourg
Groningen
Zwolle
Enschede
Apeldoorn
Arnhem
POLAND
Warsaw (Warszawa)
Gdańsk
Gdynia
Sopot
Elbląg
Olsztyn
Słupsk
Koszalin
Kołobrzeg
Szczecin
Świnoujście
Stargard Szczeciński
Gorzów Wlkp.
Piła
Bydgoszcz
Toruń
Grudziądz
Włocławek
Płock
Poznań
Gniezno
Konin
Łódź
Kalisz
Wrocław
Opole
Legnica
Zielona Góra
Częstochowa
Katowice
Gliwice
Bytom
Sosnowiec
Cracow
Kaliningrad (Königsberg)
RUS. FED.
LITHUANIA
Klaipėda
LATVIA
Liepāja
Ventspils
ESTONIA
Saaremaa
Hiiumaa
Gulf of Riga
Gulf of Gdańsk
CZECH REP.
Prague (Praha)
Plzeň
Karlovy Vary
Ústí
Liberec
Hradec Králové
Pardubice
Olomouc
Ostrava
Brno
České Budějovice
Vienna (Wien)
Linz
Salzburg
St Pölten
Bratislava
SLOVAKIA
Budapest
Győr
Žilina
Trenčín
Nitra

Inset: Iceland

Arctic Circle

ICELAND

Bolungarvik, Ísafjörður, Drangajökull, Siglufjörður, Ólafsfjörður, Grímsey, Bakkaflói, Dalvík, Húsavík, Akureyri, Njarðvík, Seyðisfjörður, Neskaupstaður, Eskifjörður, Reyðarfjörður, Snæfell 1833, Biargtangar, Breiðafjörður, Stykkishólmur, Húnaflói, Blönduós, Sauðárkrókur, Glama 845, Oddáðahraun, Langjökull, Hofsjökull, Tungnafells-jökull, Vatnajökull, Öræfajökull 2119, Faxaflói, Akranes, Reykjavík, Kópavogur, Hafnarfjörður, Keflavík, Grindavík, Selfoss, Þjórsá, Mýrdalsjökull, Ingólfshöfði, Vestmannaeyjar, Surtsey

Inset: Faeroes (Faerøerne) (Den.)

Streymoy, Vágar, Tórshavn, Sandoy, Suðuroy

at the same scale 7W

Main map

ARCTIC OCEAN

BARENTS SEA

NORWEGIAN SEA

BALTIC SEA

North Sea

Skagerrak, Kattegat

Gulf of Bothnia, Gulf of Finland, Gulf of Riga

NORWAY, SWEDEN, FINLAND, DENMARK, GERMANY, POLAND, ESTONIA, LATVIA, LITHUANIA, BELARUS (BELORUSSIA), RUSSIAN FEDERATION, RUS. FED.

Major cities: Oslo, Bergen, Stavanger, Trondheim, Kristiansand, Stockholm, Göteborg, Malmö, Uppsala, Norrköping, Helsinki (Helsingfors), Turku, Tampere, Oulu, Copenhagen, Hamburg, Berlin, Bremen, Lübeck, Rostock, Kiel, Gdańsk (Danzig), Gdynia, Szczecin, Poznań, Warsaw, Bydgoszcz, Toruń, Kaliningrad, Klaipėda, Šiauliai, Kaunas, Vilnius, Riga, Liepāja, Daugavpils, Tallinn, Narva, Pskov, Novgorod, St Petersburg (Leningrad), Murmansk, Minsk, Murmansk

Nordkapp, Hammerfest, Tromsø, Narvik, Bodø, Kiruna, Rovaniemi, Kemi, Luleå, Umeå, Sundsvall, Östersund, Lillehammer, Hamar, Drammen, Kristiansund, Ålesund, Molde

1:7.5M

0   100   200   300 km
0   50   100   150 mls

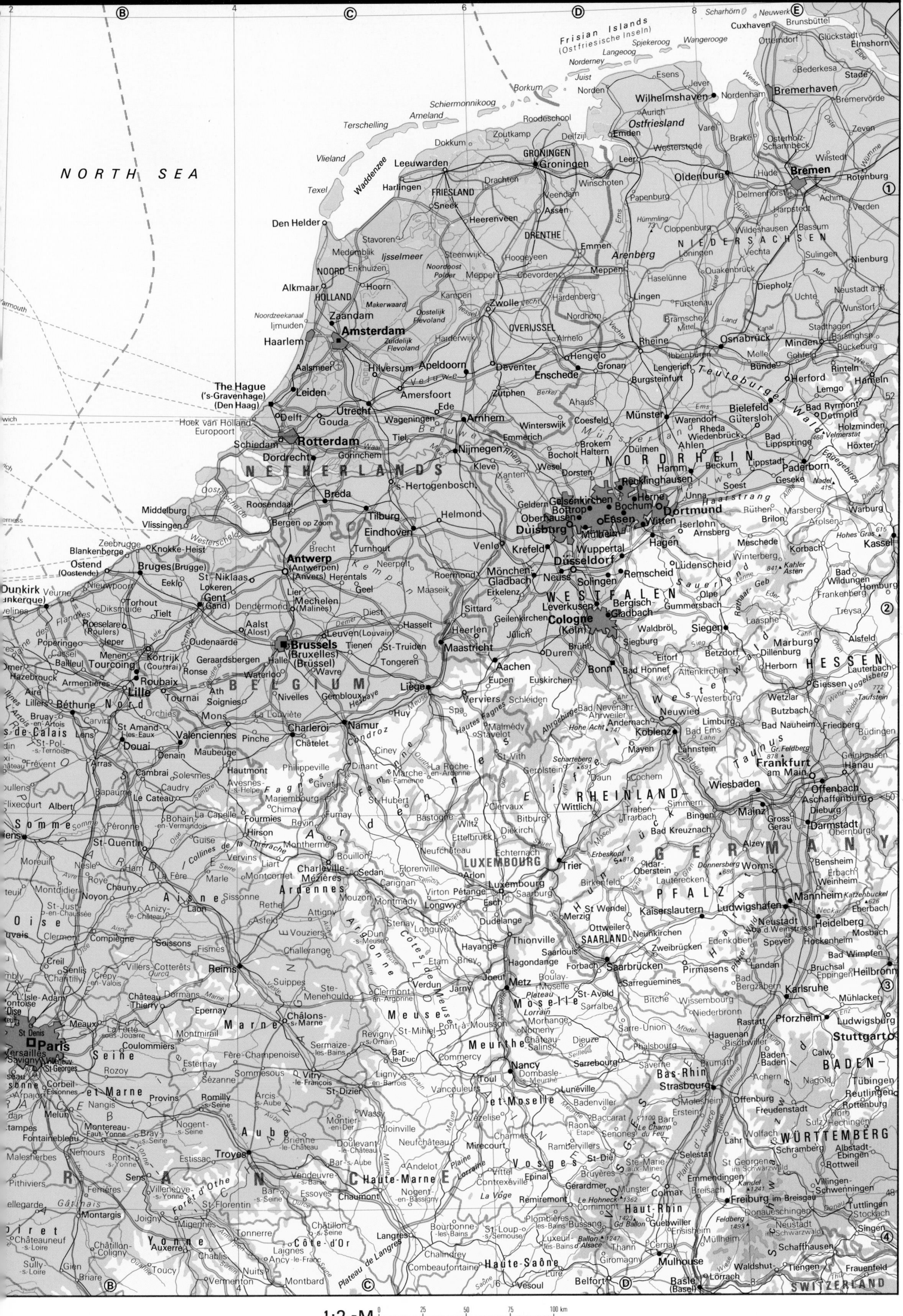
NORTH SEA
Frisian Islands (Ostfriesische Inseln)
Borkum
Juist
Norderney
Langeoog
Spiekeroog
Wangerooge
Scharhörn
Neuwerk
Schiermonnikoog
Ameland
Terschelling
Vlieland
Texel
Waddenzee
Cuxhaven
Brunsbüttel
Otterndorf
Glückstadt
Elmshorn
Bederkesa
Stade
Bremerhaven
Bremervörde
Nordenham
Wilhelmshaven
Jever
Esens
Norden
Aurich
Ostfriesland
Emden
Leer
Varel
Brake
Osterholz-Scharmbeck
Zeven
Wilstedt
Bremen
Rotenburg
Oldenburg
Delmenhorst
Achim
Verden
Hude
Harpstedt
Wildeshausen
Bassum
Papenburg
Cloppenburg
NIEDERSACHSEN
Löningen
Vechta
Sulingen
Nienburg
Hümmling
Haselünne
Quakenbrück
Diepholz
Uchte
Neustadt a. R.
Wunstorf
Meppen
Arenberg
Lingen
Fürstenau
Bramsche
Stadthagen
Osnabrück
Minden
Bückeburg
Rinteln
Hameln
Bünde
Melle
Herford
Lemgo
Bad Pyrmont
Detmold
Bielefeld
Gütersloh
Teutoburger Wald
Rheine
Ibbenbüren
Lengerich
Burgsteinfurt
Münster
Warendorf
Rheda-Wiedenbrück
Bad Lippspringe
Paderborn
Holzminden
Höxter
Ahlen
Beckum
Lippstadt
Geseke
Hamm
NORDRHEIN
Soest
Unna
Haarstrang
Rüthen
Marsberg
Brilon
Warburg
Arolsen
Kassel
Hohes Gras
Korbach
Meschede
Arnsberg
Iserlohn
Dortmund
Witten
Bochum
Herne
Recklinghausen
Gelsenkirchen
Bottrop
Oberhausen
Essen
Mülheim
Duisburg
Krefeld
Wuppertal
Hagen
Düsseldorf
Remscheid
Solingen
Lüdenscheid
Winterberg
Kahler Asten
Bad Wildungen
Homburg
Frankenberg
Treysa
WESTFALEN
Leverkusen
Bergisch-Gladbach
Cologne (Köln)
Gummersbach
Olpe
Rothaar-Geb.
Sauerland
Laasphe
Marburg
Alsfeld
Siegen
Waldbröl
Siegburg
Eitorf
Betzdorf
Dillenburg
Herborn
HESSEN
Lauterbach
Vogelsberg
Taufstein
Giessen
Westerwald
Wetzlar
Butzbach
Friedberg
Büdingen
Bad Nauheim
Gelnhausen
Hanau
Frankfurt am Main
Offenbach
Aschaffenburg
Taunus
Gr. Feldberg
Wiesbaden
Mainz
Gross-Gerau
Darmstadt
Dieburg
Limburg
Bad Ems
Lahnstein
Koblenz
Neuwied
Altenkirchen
Bad Honnef
Bonn
Brühl
Euskirchen
Düren
Jülich
Geilenkirchen
Erkelenz
Mönchengladbach
Neuss
Rhine
Ruhr
Groningen
GRONINGEN
Roodeschool
Delfzijl
Zoutkamp
Dokkum
Leeuwarden
Harlingen
FRIESLAND
Drachten
Sneek
Heerenveen
Winschoten
Veendam
Assen
DRENTHE
Emmen
Hoogeveen
Coevorden
Steenwijk
Stavoren
Medemblik
Enkhuizen
IJsselmeer
Noordoost Polder
Meppel
NOORD HOLLAND
Alkmaar
Hoorn
Den Helder
Markerwaard
Kampen
Zwolle
Hardenberg
Nordhorn
OVERIJSSEL
Almelo
Hengelo
Gronau
Enschede
Oostelijk Flevoland
Zuidelijk Flevoland
Harderwijk
Noordzeekanaal
IJmuiden
Zaandam
Amsterdam
Haarlem
Aalsmeer
Hilversum
Apeldoorn
Deventer
Veluwe
Zutphen
Amersfoort
Leiden
The Hague ('s-Gravenhage) (Den Haag)
Delft
Utrecht
Gouda
Hoek van Holland
Europoort
Schiedam
Rotterdam
Dordrecht
Gorinchem
Ede
Wageningen
Arnhem
Tiel
Betuwe
Nijmegen
Emmerich
Winterswijk
Bocholt
Coesfeld
Dülmen
Haltern
Brokem
Borken
Ahaus
Kleve
Xanten
Wesel
Dorsten
NETHERLANDS
's-Hertogenbosch
Breda
Roosendaal
Tilburg
Helmond
Eindhoven
Bergen op Zoom
Middelburg
Vlissingen
Oosterschelde
Westerschelde
Venlo
Geldern
Roermond
Maaseik
Sittard
Heerlen
Maastricht
Aachen
Eupen
Zeebrugge
Blankenberge
Knokke-Heist
Ostend (Oostende)
Bruges (Brugge)
Eeklo
St-Niklaas
Lokeren
Gent (Gand)
Dendermonde
Antwerp (Antwerpen) (Anvers)
Brecht
Turnhout
Herentals
Geel
Kempen
Neerpelt
Lier
Mechelen (Malines)
Diest
Hasselt
Aalst (Alost)
Leuven (Louvain)
Tienen
St-Truiden
Tongeren
Brussels (Bruxelles) (Brüssel)
Halle
Wavre
Waterloo
Nivelles
Gembloux
Hesbaye
Liège
Verviers
Spa
Hautes Fagnes
Malmédy
Stavelot
Schleiden
St-Vith
Dunkirk (Dunkerque)
Veurne
Nieuwpoort
Diksmuide
Torhout
Tielt
Roeselare (Roulers)
Poperinge
Ieper
Menen
Kortrijk (Courtrai)
Oudenaarde
Geraardsbergen
Ronse
Ath
Soignies
Tournai
BELGIUM
Mons
La Louvière
Charleroi
Châtelet
Namur
Huy
Condroz
Ciney
Dinant
Philippeville
Givet
Famenne
Marche-en-Famenne
La Roche-en-Ardenne
Ardennes
Eifel
Gerolstein
Daun
Cochem
Mayen
Andernach
Hohe Acht
Ahrweiler
Bad Neuenahr
Scharteberg
Wittlich
Bitburg
Traben-Trarbach
RHEINLAND-PFALZ
Hunsrück
Simmern
Bingen
Bad Kreuznach
Alzey
Worms
Erbeskopf
Idar-Oberstein
Donnersberg
Kaiserslautern
Ludwigshafen
Mannheim
Bensheim
Weinheim
Heidelberg
Neustadt a.d. Weinstrasse
Speyer
Hockenheim
Landau
Pirmasens
Zweibrücken
Bad Bergzabern
Bruchsal
Eppingen
Heilbronn
Bad Wimpfen
Mosbach
Eberbach
Katzenbuckel
Karlsruhe
Mühlacker
Pforzheim
Ludwigsburg
Stuttgart
Calw
BADEN-WÜRTTEMBERG
Baden-Baden
Rastatt
Nagold
Tübingen
Reutlingen
Rottenburg
Freudenstadt
Horb
Hechingen
Albstadt-Ebingen
Schramberg
Rottweil
Villingen-Schwenningen
Tuttlingen
Donaueschingen
Stockach
Singen
Schwarzwald
Titisee-Neustadt
Freiburg im Breisgau
Feldberg
Kandel
Emmendingen
Lahr
Offenburg
Achern
Schaffhausen
Waldshut-Tiengen
Frauenfeld
SWITZERLAND
Basle (Basel)
Lörrach
Müllheim
St Georgen
Wolfach
Saarlouis
Saarbrücken
SAARLAND
Merzig
St Wendel
Ottweiler
Neunkirchen
Trier
LUXEMBOURG
Luxembourg
Echternach
Diekirch
Ettelbruck
Wiltz
Clervaux
Esch
Dudelange
Arlon
Bastogne
Neufchâteau
St-Hubert
Bouillon
Florenville
Virton
Pétange
Longwy
Chimay
Mariembourg
Fagne
Avesnes-s-Helpe
Hautmont
Maubeuge
Valenciennes
Denain
Douai
Cambrai
Caudry
Solesmes
Le Cateau
Fourmies
Hirson
La Capelle
Bohain-en-Vermandois
Guise
Thiérache
Vervins
Revin
Monthermé
Charleville-Mézières
Sedan
Carignan
Montmédy
Mouzon
Rethel
Attigny
Vouziers
Stenay
Dun-s-Meuse
Argonne
Côtes de Meuse
Longuyon
Thionville
Hayange
Briey
Etain
Hagondange
Metz
Boulay-Moselle
Forbach
Sarreguemines
St-Avold
Bitche
Wissembourg
Niederbronn
Haguenau
Bischwiller
Saverne
Bas-Rhin
Strasbourg
Erstein
Molsheim
Sélestat
Colmar
Haut-Rhin
Guebwiller
Ensisheim
Mulhouse
Cernay
Thann
Belfort
Giromagny
Ballon d'Alsace
Gd Ballon
Le Hohneck
Munster
Gérardmer
Remiremont
Plombières-les-Bains
Bussang
Luxeuil-les-Bains
Vosges
St-Dié
Senones
Raon
Baccarat
Rambervillers
Épinal
Charmes
Mirecourt
Vittel
Contrexéville
Lunéville
Badonviller
Sarrebourg
Phalsbourg
Dieuze
Château-Salins
Sarre-Union
Morhange
Nomeny
Pont-à-Mousson
Moselle
Lorraine
Nancy
Dombasle-s-Meurthe
Toul
Meurthe-et-Moselle
Vaucouleurs
Commercy
St-Mihiel
Verdun
Jarny
Meuse
Bar-le-Duc
Revigny-s-Ornain
Ligny-en-Barrois
Clermont-en-Argonne
Ste-Menehould
Châlons-s-Marne
Marne
Sermaize-les-Bains
Vitry-le-François
St-Dizier
Wassy
Joinville
Montier-en-Der
Neufchâteau
Doulevant-le-Château
Andelot
Bar-s-Aube
Vendeuvre-s-Barse
Haute-Marne
Chaumont
Nogent-en-Bassigny
Langres
Plateau de Langres
Bourbonne-les-Bains
Chalindrey
Combeaufontaine
Haute-Saône
Vesoul
Lure
St-Loup-s-Semouse
Montbard
Châtillon-s-Seine
Côte-d'Or
Laignes
Ancy-le-Franc
Essoyes
Bar-s-Seine
Troyes
Aube
Brienne-le-Château
Arcis-s-Aube
Romilly-s-Seine
Nogent-s-Seine
Estissac
Sens
Pont-s-Yonne
Bray-s-Seine
Villeneuve-s-Yonne
Forêt d'Othe
St-Florentin
Joigny
Auxerre
Migennes
Tonnerre
Chablis
Yonne
Noyers
Vermenton
Toucy
Briare
Gien
Sully-s-Loire
Châteauneuf-s-Loire
Châtillon-Coligny
Montargis
Gâtinais
Nemours
Pithiviers
Malesherbes
Fontainebleau
Ferrières
Montereau-Faut-Yonne
Melun
Provins
Nangis
Seine-et-Marne
Corbeil-Essonnes
Sézanne
Sommesous
Fère-Champenoise
Esternay
Coulommiers
Montmirail
Épernay
Dormans
Château-Thierry
Reims
Suippes
Fismes
Soissons
Villers-Cotterêts
Crépy-en-Valois
Senlis
Chantilly
Creil
Compiègne
Noyon
Chauny
Laon
Aisne
Sissonne
Marle
Montcornet
La Fère
Ham
St-Quentin
Péronne
Somme
Nesle
Roye
Montdidier
Moreuil
St-Just-en-Chaussée
Clermont
Oise
Beauvais
L'Isle-Adam
Pontoise
Meaux
La Ferté-s-Jouarre
Paris
St Denis
Versailles
Savigny
Villeneuve-St-Georges
Rozoy
Étampes
Chelles
Albert
Bapaume
Arras
Doullens
Frévent
St-Pol-s-Ternoise
St Amand-les-Eaux
Pas-de-Calais
Lens
Béthune
Lillers
Aire
Bruay-en-Artois
Lille
Roubaix
Tourcoing
Armentières
Bailleul
Cassel
Hazebrouck
Flandres
Orchies
Carvin
Nord
Pinche
Fougères
1:2.5M
0 25 50 75 100 km
0 25 50 mls

1:5M
0 50 100 150 200 km
0 50 100 mls

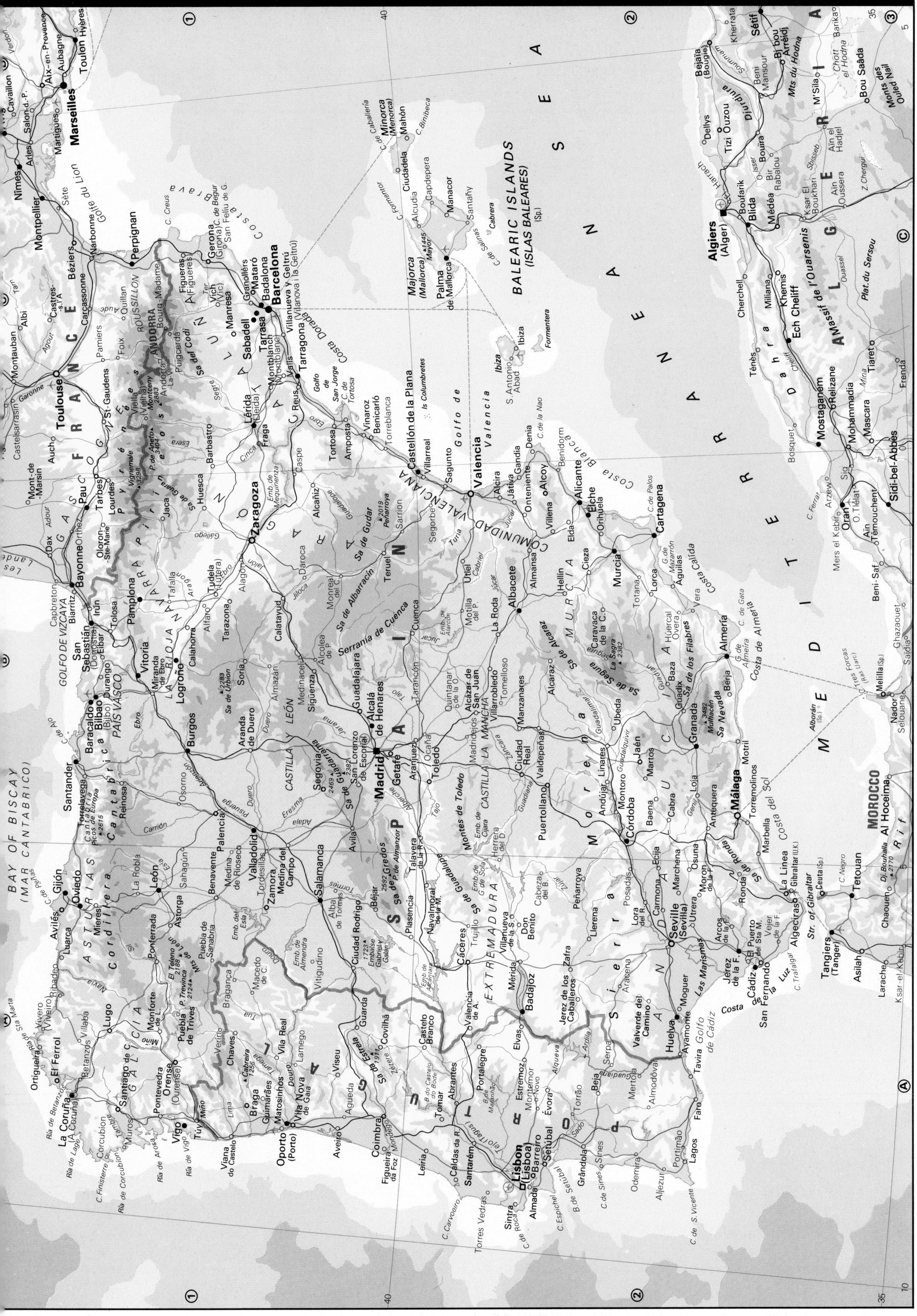
BAY OF BISCAY
(MAR CANTABRICO)
GOLFO DE VIZCAYA
BALEARIC ISLANDS
(ISLAS BALEARES)
(Sp.)
MEDITERRANEAN SEA
MOROCCO
ALGERIA
FRANCE
SPAIN
PORTUGAL
ANDORRA
Madrid
Lisboa
(Lisboa)
Barcelona
Valencia
Zaragoza
Seville
(Sevilla)
Málaga
Granada
Córdoba
Bilbao
(Bilbo)
Oporto
(Porto)
Salamanca
Valladolid
Burgos
Toledo
Murcia
Alicante
Cartagena
Almería
Cádiz
Gibraltar
Tangiers
(Tanger)
Tetouan
Algiers
(Alger)
Oran
Toulouse
Marseilles
Montpellier
Perpignan
Bayonne
Pamplona
Santander
Oviedo
Gijón
León
La Coruña
(A Coruña)
Vigo
Coimbra
Faro
Huelva
Badajoz
Cáceres
Mérida
Albacete
Cuenca
Teruel
Castellón de la Plana
Tarragona
Lérida
(Lleida)
Gerona
(Girona)
Palma
de Mallorca
Majorca
(Mallorca)
Minorca
(Menorca)
Ibiza
Formentera
Pyrénées
Cordillera Cantabrica
Sierra Morena
Sa Nevada
Costa Brava
Costa Dorada
Costa Blanca
Costa del Sol
Costa de la Luz
Golfo de Valencia
Golfo de Cádiz
Str. of Gibraltar
CASTILLA Y LEÓN
CASTILLA-LA MANCHA
EXTREMADURA
ANDALUCÍA
CATALUÑA
ARAGÓN
GALICIA
ASTURIAS
PAÍS VASCO
NAVARRA
LA RIOJA
MURCIA
COMUNIDAD VALENCIANA
1:5M
0 50 100 150 200 km
0 50 100 mls

A
B
C
1
2
3
5
10
15
40
FRANCE
SWITZERLAND
GERMANY
AUSTRIA
SLOVENIA
CROATIA
ITALY
ALGERIA
TUNISIA
MONACO
SAN MARINO
LIECHTENSTEIN
CORSICA (CORSE)
SARDINIA (SARDEGNA)
SICILY (SICILIA)
TYRRHENIAN SEA
Ligurian Sea
ADRIATIC
MEDITERRANEAN
Malta Channel
Sicilian Channel
Strait of Bonifacio
Str. de Messina
G. di Venezia
G. di Genova
Côte d'Azur
Alpi Dolomitiche
Mte Blanc 4808
Mte Rosa
Matterhorn 4477
Jungfrau 4158
Gran Paradiso 4061
Mte Viso 3841
Ortles 3905
Marmolada 3342
Grossglockner 3798
Etna 3323
Mte Corno 2912
Mte Cinto 2710
Mte Cimone 2165
Mte Amiata 1738
Vesuvio 1277
Mte Pollino 2248
Munich
Vienna
Zürich
Basle (Basel)
Berne (Bern)
Geneva (Genève)
Lausanne
Lyon
Marseilles
Nice
Grenoble
Turin (Torino)
Milan (Milano)
Genoa (Genova)
Venice (Venezia)
Trieste
Bologna
Florence (Firenze)
Pisa
Livorno
Perugia
Ancona
Pescara
Rome (Roma)
Naples (Napoli)
Salerno
Foggia
Bari
Cosenza
Messina
Reggio di Calabria
Palermo
Catania
Syracuse (Siracusa)
Agrigento
Trapani
Marsala
Cagliari
Sassari
Olbia
Ajaccio
Bastia
Innsbruck
Salzburg
Graz
Klagenfurt
Ljubljana
Zagreb
Rijeka (Fiume)
Split (Spalato)
Zadar
Bizerte
Tunis
Sousse
Kairouan
Annaba (Bône)
Constantine
Valletta
Malta
Gozo

1:5M
0 50 100 150 200 km
0 50 100 mls

H U N G A R Y
R O M A N I A
Y U G O S L A V I A
S E R B I A
MONTENEGRO
K o s o v o
M A C E D O N I A
A L B A N I A
B U L G A R I A
G R E E C E
T U R K E Y
UKRAINE
MOLDOVA
(MOLDAVIA)
BLACK
SEA
AEGEAN
SEA
IONIAN SEA
IONIAN ISLANDS
(Iónioi Nísoi)
Sea of Marmara
Sea of Crete
Mirtoan Sea
Strait of Otranto
CYCLADES
(Kikládhes)
DODECANESE
(Dhodhekánisos)
Budapest
Miskolc
Nyíregyháza
Debrecen
Szeged
Pécs
Kecskemét
Szolnok
Székesfehérvár
Satu Mare
Baia Mare
Oradea
Cluj-Napoca
Tîrgu Mureş
Arad
Timişoara
Sibiu
Braşov
Suceava
Iaşi
Bacău
Galaţi
Brăila
Ploieşti
Bucharest
(Bucureşti)
Constanţa
Craiova
Piteşti
Kishinev
(Chişinău)
Tiraspol'
Odessa
Izmail
Belgrade
(Beograd)
Novi Sad
Niš
Sarajevo
Mostar
Podgorica
Priština
Skopje
Sofia
(Sofiya)
Plovdiv
Varna
Burgas
Ruse
Pleven
Stara Zagora
Edirne
İstanbul
Üsküdar
Bursa
Balıkesir
İzmir
(Smyrna)
Denizli
Tiranë
Durrës
Shkodër
(Scutari)
Vlorë
Thessaloníki
(Salonica)
Lárisa
Vólos
Ioánnina
Pátrai
Athens
(Athína)
Piraiévs
Corinth
(Kórinthos)
Tripolis
Kalámai
Khaniá
Iráklion
Crete
(Kríti)
Corfu
(Kérkira)
Kefallinía
Zákinthos
(Zante)
Euboea
(Évvoia)
Lésvos
Khíos
Sámos
Rhodes
(Ródhos)
Kárpathos
Brindisi
Lecce
Gallipoli
Peloponnese
Khalkidhikí
Stara Planina
Rodopi Planina
Carpaţii Meridionali
(Transylvanian Alps)
Mţii Apuseni
Danube
E
F
G

GERMANY & CENTRAL EUROPE
NORTH SEA
DENMARK
SWEDEN
Kattegat
BALT
Jylland (Jutland)
Göteborg
Mölndal
Kungsbacka
Borås
Jönköping
Huskvarna
Nässjö
Eksjö
Hultsfred
Vetlanda
Värnamo
Växjö
Oskarsha
Nybro
Kalmar
Ljungby
Älmhult
Varberg
Falkenberg
Halmstad
Båstad
Markaryd
Ängelholm
Hässleholm
Karlshamn
Ronneby
Karlskrona
Kristianstad
Helsingør
Helsingborg
Landskrona
Lund
Malmö
Ystad
Simrishamn
Trelleborg
Hanöbukten
Bornholm
Rønne
Hirtshals
Skagen
Hjørring
Frederikshavn
Åby
Ålborg
Læsø
Thisted
Limfjorden
Nykøbing
Hadsund
Skive
Hobro
Anholt
Holstebro
Viborg
Randers
Grenå
Herning
Silkeborg
Århus
Skjern
Samsø
Horsens
Varde
Vejle
Hillerød
Copenhagen (København)
Kalundborg
Roskilde
Esbjerg
Kolding
Fredericia
Odense
Sjælland
Køge
Haderslev
Assens
Fyn
Nyborg
Korsør
Næstved
Rømø
Sylt
Westerland
Åbenrå
Als
Svendborg
Vordingborg
Sønderborg
Flensburg
Nakskov
Lolland
Falster
Møn
Rødbyhavn
Nykøbing
Husum
Schleswig
SCHLESWIG-HOLSTEIN
Kieler Bucht
Kiel
Oldenburg
Puttgarden
Fehmarn
Gedser
Sassnitz
Heide
Rendsburg
Neumünster
Stralsund
Rügen
Mecklenburger Bucht
Warnemünde
Greifswald
Cuxhaven
Itzehoe
Neustadt
Travemünde
Lübeck
Rostock
Ostfriesische Ins.
Terschelling
Ameland
Vlieland
Texel
Wilhelmshaven
Elmshorn
Wismar
Świnoujście
Kołobrzeg
Koszalin
Karlino
Białogard
Ustka
Sławno
Leeuwarden
Harlingen
Emden
Stade
Bremerhaven
Hamburg
Malchin
Anklam
Świdwin
Szczecinek
Den Helder
Groningen
Leer
Schwerin
Neubrandenburg
Goleniów
Szczecin
Stargard Szczecinski
IJsselmeer
Sneek
Heerenveen
Oldenburg
Lauenburg
MECKLENBURG-VORPOMMERN
Neustrelitz
Prenzlau
Ludwigslust
Lüneburg
Alkmaar
Hoorn
Assen
Bremen
Rotenburg
Pritzwalk
Wałcz
Piła
Jastrow
Zaanstad
Emmen
NIEDERSACHSEN
Meppen
Kampen
Zwolle
Uelzen
Wittenberge
Neuruppin
Oder (Odra)
Choszczno
Haarlem
Amsterdam
Harwich
The Hague ('s-Gravenhage) (Den Haag)
Leiden
Hilversum
Deventer
Hengelo
Lingen
Diepholz
Nienburg
Salzwedel
Myślibórz
Krzyż
Noteć
Rotterdam
Utrecht
Amersfoort
Apeldoorn
Enschede
Rheine
Osnabrück
Minden
Langenhagen
Celle
Oranienburg
Eberswalde
Gorzów Wlkp.
Dordrecht
Arnhem
Coesfeld
Hannover
Wolfsburg
Stendal
Rathenow
Nauen
Berlin
Kostrzyn
Skwierzyna
Pniewy
Poznań
Vlissingen
Nijmegen
Bocholt
Münster
Bielefeld
Hildesheim
Braunschweig
Brandenburg
Potsdam
Fürstenwalde
Słubice
Frankfurt an-der-Oder
NETHERLANDS
Breda
Tilburg
's-Hertogenbosch
NORDRHEIN-
Gütersloh
Salzgitter
Genthin
Burg
Magdeburg
BRANDENBURG
Luckenwalde
Świebodzin
Oostende
Zeebrugge
Eindhoven
Wesel
Haltern
Hamm
Lippe
GERMANY
Bruges
Antwerp (Antwerpen) (Anvers)
Venlo
Duisburg
Dortmund
Paderborn
SACHSEN-ANHALT
Wittenberg
Spree
Gubin
Zielona Góra
Gent
Mechelen
Krefeld
Essen
Aschersleben
Bernburg
Dessau
Cottbus
Nowa Sól
Leszno
Kortrijk
Brussels (Bruxelles) (Brüssel)
Hasselt
Hagen
Wuppertal
Ruhr
Münden
Göttingen
Bitterfeld
Zary
Głogów
Tourcoing
Leuven
Maastricht
Mönchen-gladbach
Düsseldorf
Kassel
Nordhausen
Halle
Torgau
Finsterwalde
Szprotawa
Lille
Roubaix
WESTFALEN
Korbach
Heiligenstadt
Leipzig
Riesa
Elsterwerda
Béthune
Tournai
Soignies
St-Truiden
Aachen
Cologne (Köln)
Siegen
Mühlhausen
Weissenfels
Wurzen
Bolesławiec
Wołów
Douai
Arras
Valenciennes
Mons
Namur
Liège
Bonn
Bad-Godesberg
Bad Hersfeld
Fulda
Eisenach
Erfurt
Naumburg
Meissen
Bautzen
Legnica
Cambrai
Denain
Maubeuge
Charleroi
BELGIUM
Euskirchen
Marburg
Jena
Zeitz
Dresden
Görlitz
Fourmies
Marche
Andernach
Giessen
Alsfeld
Thüringer Wald
THÜRINGEN
Gera
SACHSEN
Chemnitz
Zittau
Jelenia Góra
Świdnica
Wałbrzych
Dzierżoniów
St-Quentin
Ardennes
Koblenz
Limburg
HESSEN
Zwickau
Elbe
Ústí n.L.
Liberec
Bastogne
Bitburg
Mosel
Frankfurt am Main
Plauen
Erzgebirge
Most
Teplice
Jablonec n.N.
Sněžka 1603
Bielawa
Kłodzko
Oise
Charleville-Mézières
Compiègne
Laon
LUXEMBOURG
Wiesbaden
Mainz
Offenbach
Hof
Chomutov
Mladá Boleslav
Sedan
Arlon
Bingen
Bad-Kreuznach
Schweinfurt
Coburg
Ohře
Brandýs-nad-L.
Hradec Králové
Soissons
Aisne
Longwy
Trier
RHEINLAND-PFALZ
Darmstadt
Aschaffenburg
Cheb
Karlovy Vary
Kladno
Prague (Praha)
Kolín
Pardubice
Château-Thierry
Reims
Thionville
Luxembourg
Worms
Würzburg
Bamberg
Bayreuth
CZECH REP.
Kutná Hora
Zabreh
Épernay
Verdun
SAAR-LAND
Saarlouis
Ludwigshafen
Mannheim
Kitzingen
Weiden
Plzeň
Berounka
Benešov
Svitavy
Metz
Kaiserslautern
Saarbrücken
Pirmasens
Heidelberg
Erlangen
Fürth
Brdy
Sézanne
Châlons-s.-M.
Sarreguemines
Speyer
Ansbach
Nürnberg
Amberg
Havlíčkův Brod
Českomoravská Vysočina
Olomouc
Provins
Vitry-l.-F.
Karlsruhe
Heilbronn
Crailsheim
Klatovy
Tábor
Prostějov
Romilly-s.-S.
St-Dizier
Sarrebourg
Pforzheim
BADEN-
Cham
Parsberg
Jihlava
Troyes
CHAMPAGNE
Toul
Nancy
Rastatt
Stuttgart
Ludwigsburg
Esslingen
BAYERN
Písek
Třebíč
Brno
FRANCE
Bar-s.-A.
LORRAINE
Strasbourg
Baden-Baden
Heidenheim
Donauwörth
Regensburg
Rachel 1452
České Budějovice
Třebon
Sens
Joigny
Chaumont
Épinal
St Dié
Offenburg
Tübingen
Ingolstadt
Donau
Kaplice
Gmünd
Znojmo
Mikulov
Hodonín
Auxerre
Châtillon
Vosges
Schwarzwald
Reutlingen
Schwäbische Alb
Ulm
Augsburg
Landshut
Passau
Horn
Hollabrunn
Langres
Colmar
WÜRTTEMBERG
Biberach
Schärding
Freistadt
Avallon
BOURGOGNE
Freiburg
Tuttlingen
Landsberg
Dachau
Munich (München)
Mühldorf
Inn
Linz
Stockerau
Klosterneuburg
Vienna (Wien)
Bratislava
Vesoul
Belfort
Mulhouse
Lörrach
Ravensburg
Memmingen
Starnberg
Vöcklabruck
Wels
St Pölten
Mödling
Dijon
Saône
Yonne
Montbéliard
Besançon
Basle (Basel)
Schaffhausen
Konstanz
Friedrichshafen
Kempten
Rosenheim
Salzburg
Gmunden
Steyr
Hainfeld
Wr. Neustadt
Beaune
Dôle
Olten
Zürich
Winterthur
Lindau
Füssen
Bad Tölz
Bad Ischl
Mariazell
Autun
Doubs
St Gallen
Dornbirn
Garmisch-P.
Kufstein
Dachstein 2996
Liezen
Neunkirchen
Sopron
Le Creusot
Chalon-s.-S.
Biel
Neuchâtel
LIECHTENSTEIN
Feldkirch
Innsbruck
Kitzbühel
Hochkönig 2938
Eisenerz
Montceau-l.-M.
Lons-l.-S.
Pontarlier
Luzern
Berne (Bern)
Zug
Schwyz
Vaduz
Bludenz
Landeck
Brenner 1370
Radstadt
Leoben
Bruck an der Mur
Digoin
Fribourg
Thun
Interlaken
AUSTRIA
Wildspitze 3774
Grossglockner 3798
Badgastein
Mur
Judenburg
Gleisdorf
Szombathely
Mâcon
Lausanne
Vevey
SWITZERLAND
Jungfrau 4158
Chur
Arosa
Merano
Brunico
Lienz
Graz
St Claude
L. Léman
Montreux
St Gotthard 2112
Roanne
Bourg
Bellegarde
Geneva (Genève)
Brig
Sion
Simplon 2009
St Moritz
Ortles 3899
Bolzano
Cortina d'A.
Spittal
Wolfsberg
Leibnitz
Zalaegerszeg
Tarare
Villefranche
Rhône
Bellinzona
Villach
Klagenfurt
Lyon
Villeurbanne
Annecy
Martigny
Matterhorn 4477
Domodossola
L. Maggiore
Edolo
Tarvisio
Jesenice
Drava
Maribor
Nagykanizsa
St-Chamond
Chambéry
Aix-l.-B.
Mont Blanc 4808
Col du Gd St Bernard 2469
Aosta
Lugano
Sondrio
L. di Como
Trento
Marmolada 3342
Alpi Dolomitiche
Gemona
Kranj
Velenje
Varazdin
St-Étienne
Loire
Vienne
Albertville
Varese
Como
Lecco
ITALY
Belluno
Udine
Ljubljana
Celje
Koprivnica
Annonay
Voiron
Gran Paradiso 4061
Biella
Busto Arsizio
Bergamo
Lovere
Rovereto
Bassano
Piave
Gorizia
SLOVENIA
Brežice
Bjelovar
Romans-s.-I.
Grenoble
Ivrea
Novara
Monza
Monfalcone
Zagreb
Virovitica
Bourg
DAUPHINÉ
Massif du Pelvoux
Col du Mt Cenis 2803
Vercelli
Milan (Milano)
Brescia
L. di Garda
Vicenza
Treviso
Mestre
Trieste
Postojna
Novo Mesto
Daruvar
Aubenas
Valence
Briançon
Corps
Susa
Turin (Torino)
Lodi
Verona
Padova
Venice (Venezia)
Koper
Karlovac
Sisak
Pavia
Casale Monf.
Cremona
Mantova
Adige
G. di Venezia
Rijeka (Fiume)
Vrbovsko
Kupa
Montélimar
Gap
Mte Viso 3841
Asti
Piacenza
Alessandria
Rovigo
Chioggia
Poreč
Rovinj
Istra
Ogulin
Una
CROATIA
1:5M
0 50 100 150 200 km
0 50 100 mls

Gulf of Riga
Gotland
Visby
Klintehamn
Burgsvik
Ventspils
Roja
Valmiera
Cēsis
Gulbene
Ostrov
Kholm
Selizharovo
Pytalovo
Andreapol'
Riga
Ogre
Ērgli
Tukums
Jūrmala
Kuldīga
Sakasleja
Jelgava
Dobele
Saldus
LATVIA
Kārsava
Opochka
Loknya
Toropets
Nelidovo
Rzhev
Velikiye-Luki
Zap. Dvina
Rezekne
Daugava
Jekabpils
Līvāni
Zilupe
Sebez
Pustoshka
Liepāja
Mazeikiai
Joniškis
Birzai
Akhiste
Nevel
Il'yino
Zharkovskiy
Belyy
Tupik
Usvyaty
Velizh
RUSSIAN FEDERATION
Telšiai
Šiauliai
Pasvalys
Daugavpils
Zarasai
Druya
Radviliškis
Panevežys
Novopolotsk
Polotsk
Gorodok
Demidov
Safonovo
Yartsevo
Klaipeda
Priekule
Kelme
Utena
Vidzy
Ulla
Vitebsk
Rudnya
Smolensk
Yel'nya
LITHUANIA
Šilute
Kedainiai
Ukmerge
Postavy
Glubokoye
Taurage
Jonava
Pabrade
Lepel'
Pochinok
Sovetsk
Nemunas
Kaunas (Kovno)
Kaisiadorys
Svir
M'adel
Tolochin
Orsha
Dnepr
Courland Lagoon
Svetlogorsk
RUS. FED.
Vilnius
Vileyka
Gorki
Roslavl'
Władysławowo
Gulf of Gdańsk (Z. Gdańska)
Kaliningrad (Königsberg)
Talpaki
Chernyakhovsk
Pregolya
Gusev
Marijampole
Smorgon'
Molodechno
Borisov
Krupki
Shklov
Mstislavl'
Gdynia
Sopot
Gdańsk (Danzig)
Alytus
Zhodino
Mogilev
Elblag
Braniewo
Bartoszyce
Varena
Minsk
Krichev
Klimovichi
Tczew
Kętrzyn
Suwałki
Druskininkai
Lida
Rakov
BELARUS
Cherven'
Bykhov
Slavgorod
Kletnya
Starogard Gdański
Malbork
Gizycko
Ełk
Augustów
Dzerzhinsk
(BELORUSSIA)
Olsztyn
Ostróda
Grajewo
Grodno
Novogrudok
Marjina Gorki
Osipovichi
Dovsk
Unecha
Kwidzyn
Szczytno
Sokółka
Mosty
Bobruysk
Rogachev
Chechersk
Klintsy
Grudziądz
Nidzica
Slonim
Baranovichi
Slutsk
Dnepro
Zhlobin
Novozybkov
Chełmno
Brodnica
Ostrołęka
Łomża
Białystok
Volkovysk
Soligorsk
L'uban
Gomel
Dobrush
Toruń
Mława
Zambrów
Bielsk Podlaski
Ivacevichi
Ozarichi
Rechitsa
Ciechanów
Ostrów Mazowiecka
Inowrocław
Sierpc
Pułtusk
POLAND
Pruzhany
Bereza
Kalinkovichi
Mozyr
Shchors
Gorodnya
Repki
Włocławek
Płock
Nowy Dwór Maz.
Wisła (Vistula)
Bug
Luninec
Zhitkovichi
Pripyat'
Nizmennost'
Gostynin
Warsaw (Warszawa)
Siedlce
Pinsk
Kutno
Sochaczew
Brest
Kobrin
Stolin
Yel'sk
Narovl'a
Chernigov
Mena
Koło
Łowicz
Mińsk M.
Biala Podlaska
Łuków
Borzna
Łódź
Pabianice
Zgierz
Pruszków
Piaseczno
Otwock
Mabrita
Ratno
Lyubeshov
Dubrovica
Ovruch
Chernobyl
Nezhin
Kalisz
Ostrów Wlkp.
Żyrardów
Skierniewice
Włodawa
Sarny
Olevsk
Nosovka
Zduńska Wola
Tomaszów Maz.
Radom
Dęblin
Puławy
Manevichi
Bobrovica
Piotrków Tryb.
Lublin
Chełm
Kovel'
Korosten'
Malin
Kiev
Priluki
Wieluń
Końskie
Skarżysko-Kamienna
Starachowice
Kiverci
Kostopol'
Brovary
Yagotin
Warta
Radomsko
Kraśnik
Krasnystaw
Vladimir Volynskiy
Lutsk
Novograd V.
Radomyshl'
Kluczbork
Kielce
Ostrowiec
Zamość
Novovolynsk
Rovno
Korec
Boyarka
Vasil'kov
Pereyaslav
Opole
Częstochowa
Sandomierz
Jędrzejów
Stalowa Wola
Dubno
Slavuta
Zhitomir
Korostyshev
Fastov
Zawiercie
Busko Zdrój
Tarnobrzeg
Tomaszów Lubelski
Chervonograd
Shepetovka
Polonnye
Belaya Tserkov'
Zolotonosha
Bytom
Gliwice
Zabrze
Chorzów
Rybnik
Dabrowa-Gorn
Sosnowiec
Katowice
Cracow (Kraków)
Mielec
Rava Russkaya
Brody
Kremenets
Berdichev
Kazatin
Mironovka
Cherkassy
Smela
Rzeszów
Dębica
Tarnów
Jarosław
Goryn'
Starokonstantinov
UKRAINE
Karviná
Bielsko-Biala
Oświęcim
Bochnia
Przemyśl
Gorodok
L'vov
Zolochev
Bazaliya
Khmel'nitskiy
Kalinovka
Zhashkov
Zvenigorodka
Cieszyn
Zywiec
Myślenice
Jasło
Nowy Sącz
Sanok
Sambor
Berezhany
Ternopol
Letichev
Vinnitsa
Tal'noye
Novomirgorod
Beskidy Zachodnie
Drogobych
Khodorov
Terebovlya
Podol'skaya
Pridneprovskaya Vozv.
Čadca
Zakopane
Borislav
Stryy
Gorodok
Chortkov
Zhmerinka
Bratslav
Gaysin
Uman
Žilina
Tatry
Gerlachovsky 2655
Bardejov
Kalush
Ivano-Frankovsk
Dunayevtsy
Kamenets Podolskiy
Mogilev Podol'skiy
Tul'chin
Martin
Ružomberok
Prešov
Ulyanovka
SLOVAKIA
Michalovce
Trenčín
Banská Bystrica
Košice
Uzhgorod
Nadvornaya
Kolomyya
Khotin
Dnestr
Kodyma
Pervomaysk
Rožňava
Svalyava
Chernovtsy
Yedintsy
Soroki
Piešťany
Zvolen
Mukachevo
Yasinya
Goverla 2058
Storozhinets
Balta
Nitra
Lučenec
Kazincbarcika
Kisvárda
Khust
Ryskany
Kotovsk
Voznesensk
Levice
Ózd
Rakhov
Dorohoi
Rybnitsa
Nové Zámky
Salgótarján
Eger
Miskolc
Nyíregyháza
Mátészalka
Sighetu Marmației
Carpathian Mts
Rădăuți
Botoșani
Bel'tsy
MOLDOVA (MOLDAVIA)
Veselinovo
Vác
Gyöngyös
Satu Mare
Baia Mare
Borșa
Suceava
Orgeyev
Dubossary
Zhovten'
Berezovka
Esztergom
Hajdúböszörmény
Újfehértó
Carei
Mtii Rodnei
Vatra Dornei
Fălticeni
Iași
Kalarash
Kishinev (Chișinău)
Tiraspol'
Razdel'naya
Budapest
Hatvan
Debrecen
Marghita
Bistrița
Mtii Călimani
Pietrosu 2303
Pașcani
Bendery
Odessa
Székesfehérvár
Karcag
Szolnok
Berettyóújfalu
Oradea
Zalău
Dej
Bicaz
Piatra-Neamt
Roman
Hiiși
Kotovsk
Veszprém
Dunaújváros
Cegléd
Nagykőrös
Kecskemét
HUNGARY
Reghin
Gheorgheni
Vaslui
Belgorod Dnestrovskiy
Siófok
Salonta
Cluj-Napoca
Vlădeasa 1836
Bacău
Komrat
Békéscsaba
Orosháza
Turda
Luduș
Tirgu Mureș
Mtii Apuseni
Miercurea-Ciuc
Onești
Bîrlad
Paks
K'félegyháza
Kiskunhalas
Tîrnăveni
Sighișoara
Kagul
Artsiz
Sarata
Dombóvár
Hódmező'hely
Sîntana
Bihor 1849
Mediaș
Nemira 1649
Adjud
Kaposvár
Szekszárd
Baja
Szeged
Makó
Arad
Mtii Zarandului
Alba Iulia
Sebeș
Rupea
Făgăraș
Sfîntu Gheorghe
Focșani
Tecuci
Bolgrad
Prut (Prutul)
Black Sea
Pécs
Subotica
Lipova
Deva
Orăștie
Sibiu
Reni
Izmail
Kiliya
Vilkovo
Senta
Sombor
Kikinda
Timișoara
Hunedoara
Lugoj
Cindrelu 2245
Moldoveanu 2543
Brașov
Galați
Brăila
Tulcea
Sulina
Vojvodina
Vrbas
Bečej
ROMANIA
Carpații Meridionali (Transylvanian Alps)
Rîmnicu Sărat
Buzău
Apatin
Osijek
Zrenjanin
Caransebeș
Peleaga 2509
Reșița
Deta
Babadag
Vukovar
Novi Sad
Cîmpina
Mizil
L. Razim
Dakovo
Vinkovci
Vršac
Oravița
Tîrgu Jiu
Rîmnicu Vîlcea
Tîrgoviște
Ploiești
Urziceni
Hîrșova

RUSSIAN FEDERATION

Major cities and features:

Chelyabinsk, Yekaterinburg, Perm, Izhevsk, Kazan, Samara, Tol'yatti, Nizhniy Novgorod (Gorki), MOSCOW (Moskva), St Petersburg (Leningrad), Archangel, Murmansk, Severodvinsk, Syktyvkar, Kirov, Vologda, Yaroslavl', Ivanovo, Rybinsk, Cherepovets, Kostroma, Podolsk, Tula, Ryazan', Saransk, Ul'yanovsk

Regions: URAL, Ural Mts, Severnyy Ural, Sredniy Ural, Timanskiy Kряж, Komi, Tatarstan, Udmurt, Chuvash, Mari El, Mordovian, Karelian R., Zapadno Sibirskaya Nizmennost', Bol'shezemel'skaya Tundra

Seas and water: BARENTS SEA (Barentsovo More), Pechorskoye More, WHITE SEA (Beloye More), Norwegian Sea, Gulf of Finland, Gulf of Bothnia, BALTIC SEA, Gulf of Riga, Lake Ladoga, Lake Onega, Lake Peipus, Novaya Zemlya, Kolguyev, Kol'skiy Poluostrov

Other countries: FINLAND, Helsinki, Tampere, Turku, Oulu; NORWAY, Narvik, Tromsø; SWEDEN, Stockholm, Uppsala, Göteborg; ESTONIA, Tallinn, Tartu; LATVIA, Riga, Daugavpils; LITHUANIA, Vilnius, Kaunas, Klaipeda; BELORUSSIA, Minsk; POLAND, Warsaw (Warszawa), Gdańsk, Gdynia; Kaliningrad

Scale: 1:10M

0	100	200	300	400 km
0	100	200 mls		

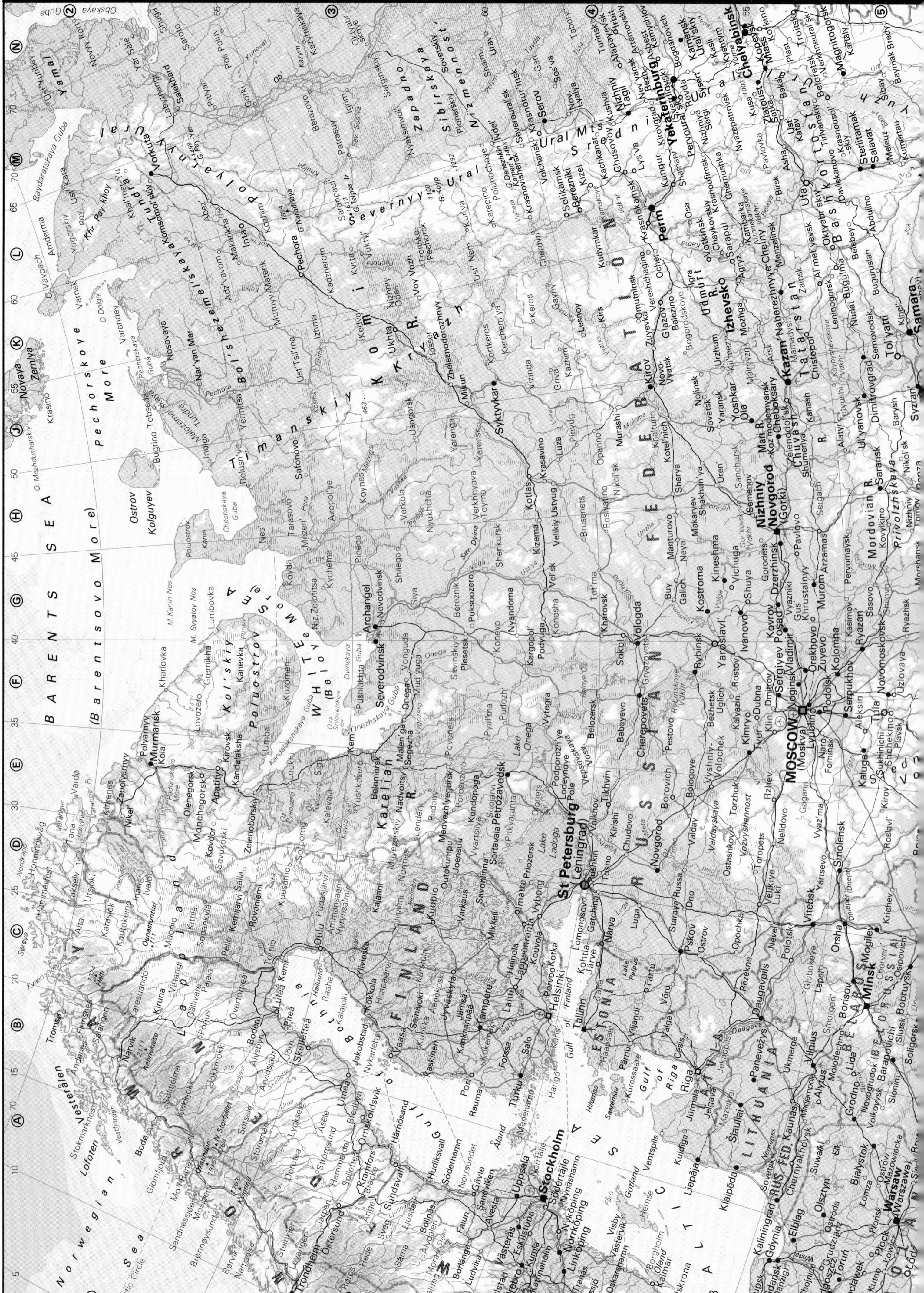

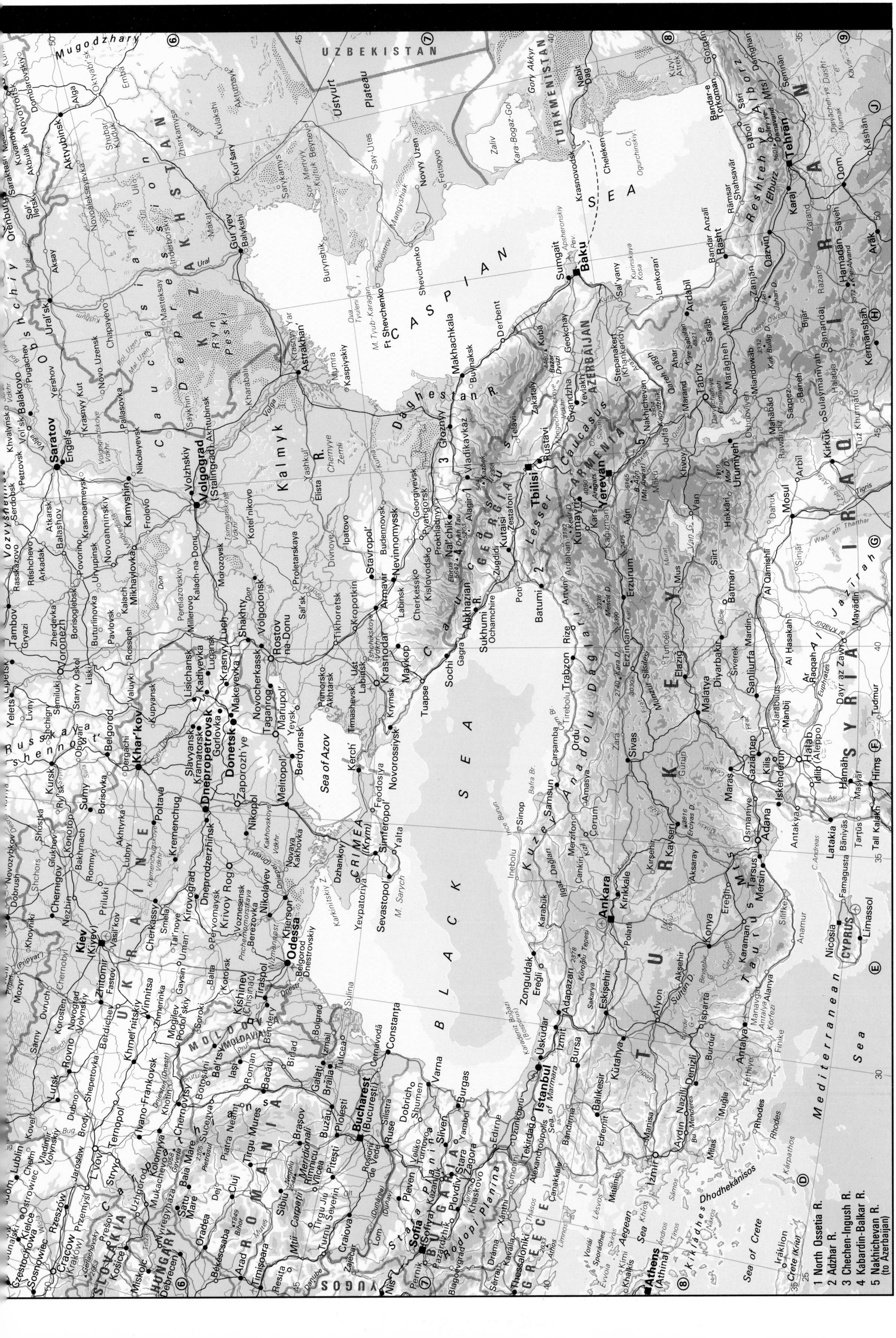
BLACK SEA
CASPIAN SEA
Sea of Azov
Mediterranean Sea
Aegean Sea
Sea of Crete
UZBEKISTAN
TURKMENISTAN
KAZAKHSTAN
UKRAINE
MOLDOVA (MOLDAVIA)
ROMANIA
BULGARIA
HUNGARY
SLOVAKIA
GREECE
TURKEY
SYRIA
IRAQ
IRAN
GEORGIA
ARMENIA
AZERBAIJAN
CYPRUS
CRIMEA (Krym)
Caspian Depression
Kalmyk R.
Daghestan R.
Abkhazian R.
Caucasus
Lesser Caucasus
Anadolu Dağlari
Taurus Mts
Reshteh-ye Alborz (Elburz Mts)
Ustyurt Plateau
Mugodzhary
Kiev (Kiyev)
Khar'kov
Odessa
Dnepropetrovsk
Donetsk
Volgograd (Stalingrad)
Saratov
Rostov na-Donu
Astrakhan'
Gur'yev
Ural'sk
Aktyubinsk
Baku
Tbilisi
Yerevan
Tehran
Ankara
Istanbul
Bucharest (Bucureşti)
Sofia (Sofiya)
Athens (Athina)
Kishinev (Chişinău)
Krasnodar
Makhachkala
Tabrīz
Mosul
Halab (Aleppo)
Nicosia
1 North Ossetia R.
2 Adzhar R.
3 Chechen-Ingush R.
4 Kabardin-Balkar R.
5 Nakhichevan R. (to Azerbaijan)

ICELAND

ARCTIC OCEAN

Greenland (Den.)

Barents Sea

Svalbard

Zemlya Frantsa Iosifa

Severnaya Zemlya

Novaya Zemlya

Novosibirskiye Ostrova

Arctic Circle

IRELAND

Edinburgh

Dublin

London

UNITED KINGDOM

PORT.

SPAIN

FRANCE

Paris

Marseilles

Corsica

Sardinia

Rome

ITALY

Sicily

Tunis

NETH.

DENMARK

GERMANY

SWITZ.

AUSTRIA

SLOV.

CROATIA

BOS. HERZ.

YUG.

ALB. MAC.

GREECE

Athens

Crete

NORWAY

Oslo

Faeroes (Den.)

S W E D E N

Stockholm

Copenhagen

Baltic Sea

Helsinki

FINLAND

Tallinn

Riga

Vilnius

EST.

LAT.

LITH.

RUS. FED.

Murmansk

White Sea

L. Onega

St Petersburg (Leningrad)

Yaroslavl'

Arkhangel'sk

Ladoga

Moscow

Minsk

BELARUS (BELORUSSIA)

Warsaw

POLAND

CZECH REP.

SLOVAKIA

HUNGARY

ROMANIA

Bucureşti

BULGARIA

Istanbul

Ankara

TURKEY

Black Sea

Kiev

UKRAINE

Dnepropetrovsk

Khar'kov

Odessa

MOLD.

Rostov

Voronezh

Nizhniy Novgorod

Kazan'

Perm

Volga

Saratov

Samara

Ufa

Volgograd

Astrakhan'

Ural'sk

Yekaterinburg

Chelyabinsk

Omsk

R U S S I A N   F E D E R A T I O N

Ob'

Yenisey

Noril'sk

Vorkuta

Yakutsk

Lena

Krasnoyarsk

Bratsk

Novosibirsk

Barnaul

Semipalatinsk

Karaganda

L. Baikal

Irkutsk

Ulan-Ude

K A Z A K H S T A N

Aral'sk

Aral Sea

L. Balkhash

Ulaanbaatar (Ulan Bator)

M O N G O L I A

INNER MONGOLIA

LIBYA

Alexandria

Cairo

EGYPT

Aswān

Nile

SUDAN

Khartoum

RED SEA

ERITREA

Asmara

DJIBOUTI

Aden

G. of Aden

ETHIOPIA

Ādīs Abeba

SOMALIA

Mogadishu (Muqdisho)

KENYA

Mombasa

Equator

TANZANIA

Dar es Salaam

MOZAMBIQUE

COMOROS

MADAGASCAR

Antananarivo

Aldabra Is (Sey.)

SEYCHELLES

CYPRUS

LEB.

Beirut

Damascus

SYRIA

ISRAEL

Jerusalem

Amman

JOR.

Adana

Halab

Mosul

Yerevan

Tbilisi

GEO.

ARM.

AZER.

Baku

Caspian Sea

Tabrīz

Tehrān

Mashhad

Esfahān

Baghdād

IRAQ

Basra

Abādān

Kermān

IRAN

KUWAIT

BAHRAIN

QATAR

Abū Dhabi

U.A.E.

Riyadh

Makkah

SAUDI ARABIA

San'ā

YEMEN

OMAN

Muscat

Socotra (Yemen)

ARABIAN SEA

Persian Gulf

UZBEKISTAN

Ashkhabad

TURKMENISTAN

Tashkent

KIRGHIZIA

Bishkek

Oz. Issyk Kul'

Alma Ata

TAJIKISTAN

Dushanbe

Herat

Kabul

AFGHANISTAN

Islamabad

Lahore

Kashmir

PAKISTAN

Karachi

Hyderābād

Indus

Delhi

Agra

Jaipur

Kānpur

Lucknow

Allahabad

Ahmadābād

Bombay

Nagpur

Godāvari

Krishna

Hyderabad

Bangalore

Madras

Madurai

Jaffna

Colombo

Kandy

SRI LANKA

MALDIVES

Laccadive Is. (Ind.)

I N D I A

Jabalpur

Ganga

Patna

Kathmandu

NEPAL

Thimphu

BHUTAN

Brahmaputra

BANGLA-DESH

Dhāka

Calcutta

Chittagong

Imphal

Bay of Bengal

Andaman Is (Ind.)

Nicobar Is (Ind.)

INDIAN OCEAN

Chagos Arch. (U.K.)

Ürümqi

C H I N A

TIBET

SINKIANG

Qinghai Hu

Lhasa

Lanzhou

Chengdu

Chongqing

Kunming

Guiyang

Changsha

Wuhan

Zhengzhou

Xi'an

Taiyuan

Beij...

Tianjin

Guangzho...

Chang Jiang

BURMA (MYANMAR)

Mandalay

Chiang Mai

Rangoon (Yangon)

Moulmein

Irrawaddy

THAILAND

Bangkok

Hanoi

Haiphong

Da Nang

LAOS

Vientiane

CAMBODIA

Phnom Penh

Ho Chi Minh City (Saigon)

Surat Thani

Kota Bharu

George Town

Medan

Kuala Lumpur

SINGAPORE

M A L A Y

S U M A T R A

Padang

Palembang

Jakarta

Christmas (Aust.)

Cocos Is (Aust.)

1:40M

0   400   800   1200   1600 km

0   400   800 mls

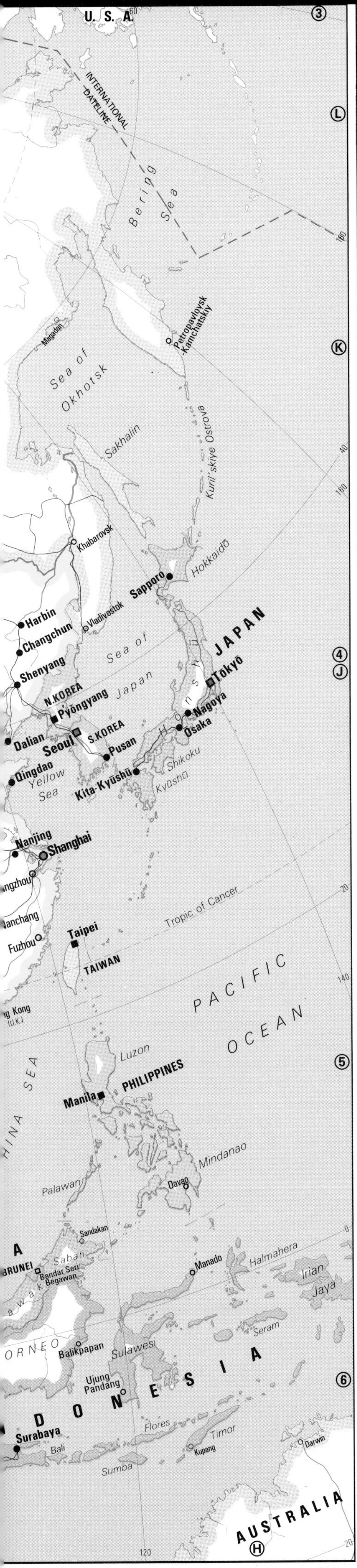

U. S. A.
INTERNATIONAL DATELINE
Bering Sea
Magadan
Petropavlovsk Kamchatskiy
Sea of Okhotsk
Sakhalin
Kuril'skiye Ostrova
Khabarovsk
Hokkaidō
Sapporo
Harbin
Changchun
Vladivostok
Shenyang
Sea of Japan
JAPAN
Honshū
Tōkyō
N.KOREA
Pyŏngyang
Nagoya
Dalian
Seoul
S.KOREA
Ōsaka
Pusan
Shikoku
Qingdao
Yellow Sea
Kita-Kyūshū
Kyūshū
Nanjing
Shanghai
Tropic of Cancer
Nanchang
Taipei
Fuzhou
TAIWAN
PACIFIC OCEAN
Hong Kong (U.K.)
Luzon
PHILIPPINES
Manila
Mindanao
Palawan
Davao
Sandakan
Sabah
BRUNEI
Bandar Seri Begawan
Manado
Halmahera
Irian Jaya
Seram
Balikpapan
Sulawesi
Ujung Pandang
INDONESIA
Surabaya
Bali
Flores
Timor
Kupang
Darwin
Sumba
AUSTRALIA

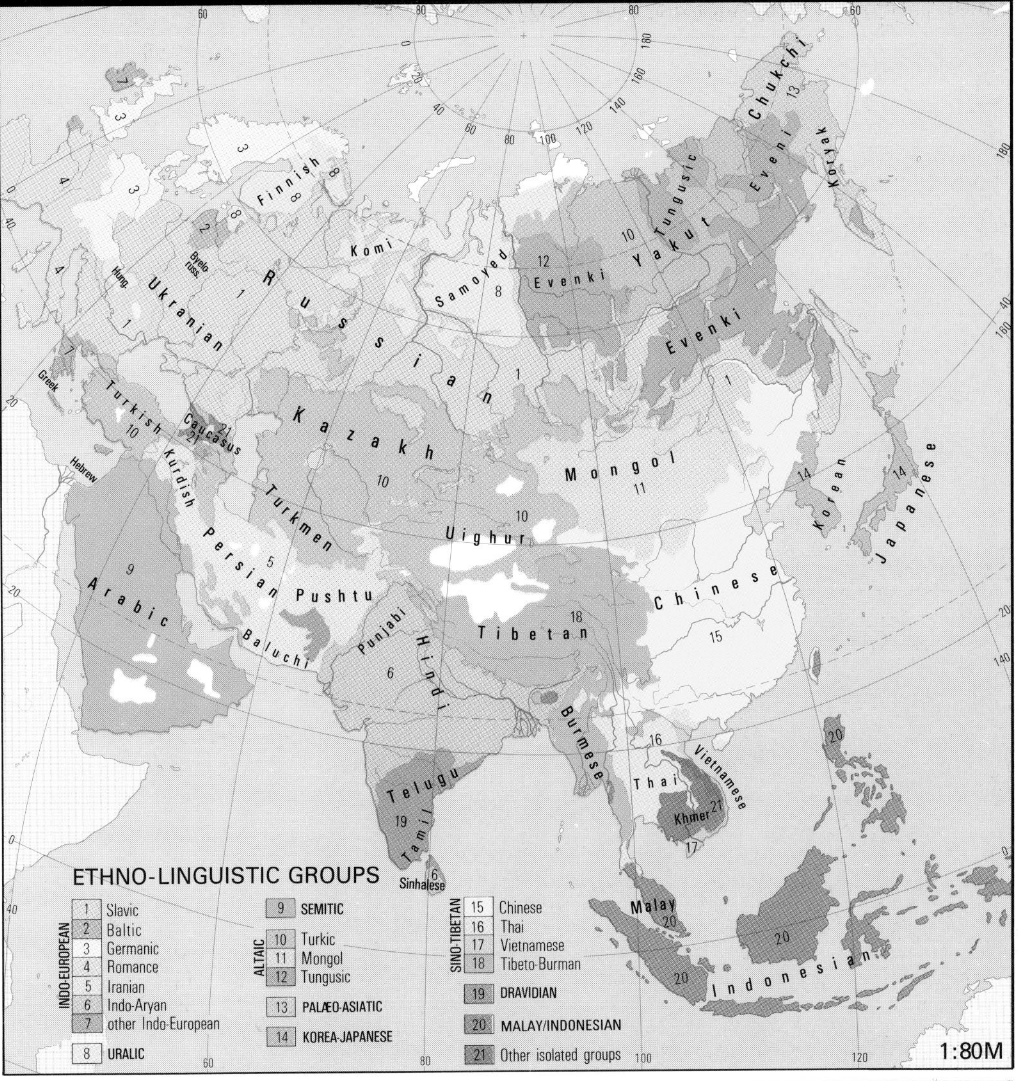

Finnish
Komi
Samoyed
Evenki
Yakut
Tungusic
Eveni
Chukchi
Koryak
Hung.
Byelo russ.
Ukranian
Russian
Greek
Turkish
Caucasus
Kurdish
Hebrew
Kazakh
Mongol
Uighur
Turkmen
Persian
Pushtu
Arabic
Baluchi
Punjabi
Hindi
Tibetan
Chinese
Korean
Japanese
Burmese
Thai
Vietnamese
Khmer
Telugu
Tamil
Sinhalese
Malay
Indonesian
ETHNO-LINGUISTIC GROUPS
INDO-EUROPEAN
1 Slavic
2 Baltic
3 Germanic
4 Romance
5 Iranian
6 Indo-Aryan
7 other Indo-European
8 URALIC
9 SEMITIC
ALTAIC
10 Turkic
11 Mongol
12 Tungusic
13 PALÆO-ASIATIC
14 KOREA-JAPANESE
SINO-TIBETAN
15 Chinese
16 Thai
17 Vietnamese
18 Tibeto-Burman
19 DRAVIDIAN
20 MALAY/INDONESIAN
21 Other isolated groups
1:80M

Manila
PHILIPPINES
Northern Marianas (U.S.A.)
Guam (U.S.A.)
PACIFIC OCEAN
MARSHALL ISLANDS
MALAYSIA
Sandakan
Davao
Palau (Belau) (U.S.A.)
FEDERATED STATES OF MICRONESIA
BRUNEI
Bandar Seri Begawan
Caroline Islands
Halmahera
Equator
Borneo
Balikpapan
Sulawesi (Celebes)
Jayapura
Irian Jaya
PAPUA NEW GUINEA
NAURU
KIRIBATI
Ujung Pandang
Seram
INDONESIA
New Guinea
SOLOMON ISLANDS
Port Moresby
TUVALU
Sumba
Timor
Arafura Sea
Wrn SAMOA
Is Wallis (Fr.)
Darwin
Timor Sea
G. of Carpentaria
Coral Sea
VANUATU
FIJI
TONGA
Cairns
Townsville
Suva
New Caledonia (Fr.)
Rockhampton
Alice Springs
Tropic of Capricorn
AUSTRALIA
Brisbane
L. Eyre
INTERNATIONAL DATELINE
L. Torrens
Darling
Kalgoorlie
Perth
Fremantle
Murray
Wollongong
Sydney
Adelaide
Canberra
Melbourne
Geelong
Bass Strait
NEW ZEALAND
North I.
Auckland
Launceston
Tasmania
Tasman Sea
Wellington
Hobart
South I.
Christchurch
Chatham I. (NZ)
Dunedin
Stewart I.
AUSTRALASIA
1:60M

NORTHERN ASIA

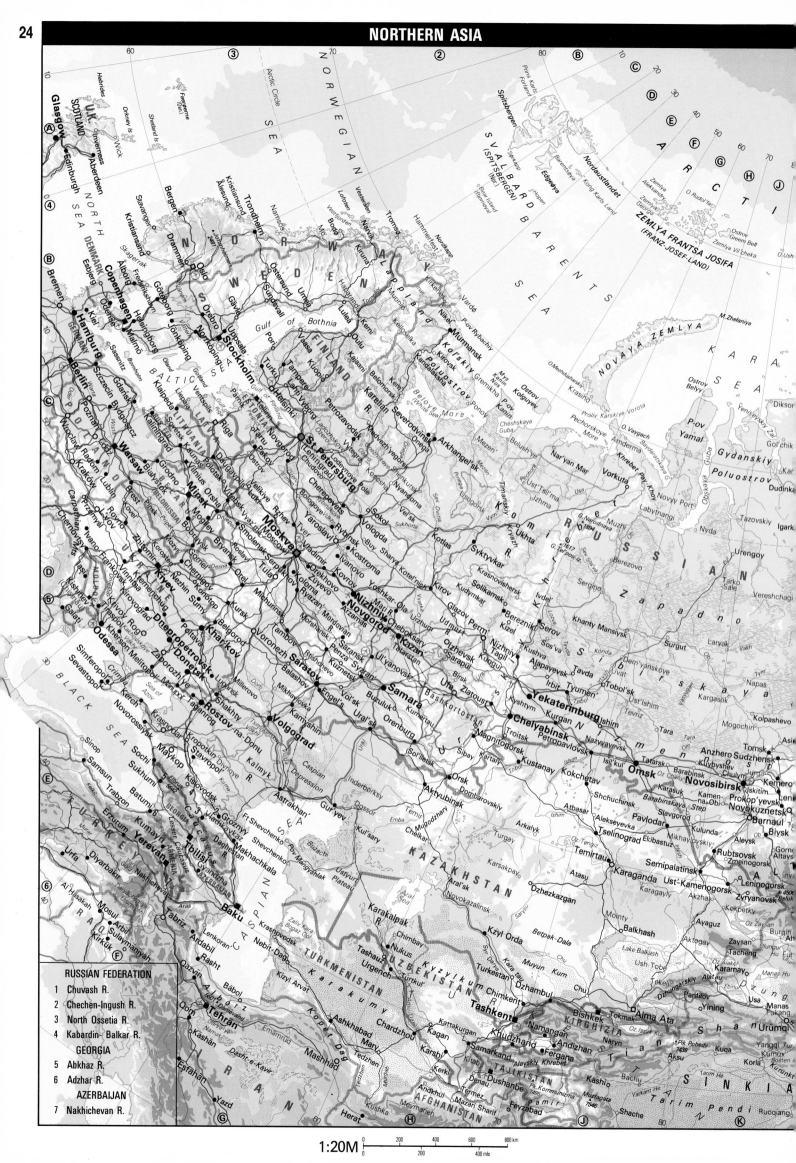

1:20M

0 200 400 600 800 km
0 200 400 mls

O C E A N
EAST SIBERIAN SEA
LAPTEV SEA
CHUKCHI SEA
BERING SEA
SEA OF OKHOTSK
SEA OF JAPAN
YELLOW SEA
Bering Str.
SEVERNAYA ZEMLYA (NORTH LAND)
Ostrov Komsomolets
Ostrov Bol'shevik
Oktyabrskoy Revolyutsii
Mys Chelyushin
NOVOSIBIRSKYE OSTROVA (NEW SIBERIAN ISLANDS)
Ostrov Kotel'nyy
Ostrov Faddeyevskiy
O. Novaya Sibir
Wrangel I.
Proliv Longa
Mys Shmidta
Chukotskiy Poluostrov
Chukotskiy Khrebet
Anadyrskoye Ploskogor'ye
Anadyrskiy Zaliv
Koryakskoye Nagor'ye
Kolymskoye Nagor'ye
Khrebet Cherskogo
Verkhoyanskiy Khrebet
Khrebet Orulgan
Poluostrov Taymyr
Gory Byrranga
Gory Putorana
Srednesibirskoye Ploskogor'ye
Sibirskoye Ploskogor'ye
Severo Baykal'skoye Nagor'ye
Patomskoye Nagor'ye
Aldanskoye Nagor'ye
Stanovoy Khrebet
Dzhugdzhur
Yablonovyy Khrebet
Da Hinggan Ling
Xiao Hinggan Ling
Sikhote-Alin'
KAMCHATKA
Sredinnyy Khrebet
Zaliv Shelikhova
SAKHALIN
Kuril Islands
Komandorskiye Ostrova
RUSSIAN FEDERATION
MONGOLIA
GOBI
INNER MONGOLIA
MANCHURIA
NORTH KOREA
SOUTH KOREA
JAPAN
HONSHU
HOKKAIDO
KYUSHU
SHIKOKU
Yakutsk
Magadan
Petropavlovsk-Kamchatskiy
Okhotsk
Anadyr'
Pevek
Bilibino
Tiksi
Khatanga
Noril'sk
Mirnyy
Lensk
Olekminsk
Aldan
Neryungri
Bratsk
Irkutsk
Ulan Ude
Chita
Krasnoyarsk
Kansk
Achinsk
Abakan
Kyzyl
Blagoveshchensk
Khabarovsk
Komsomol'sk-na-Amure
Vladivostok
Nakhodka
Yuzhno-Sakhalinsk
Ulaanbaatar
Erdenet
Choybalsan
Hohhot
Baotou
Beijing (Peking)
Tianjin (Tientsin)
Shenyang
Harbin
Changchun
Jilin
Qiqihar
Dalian
Anshan
Fushun
Jinan
Qingdao
Taiyuan
Yinchuan
Lanzhou
Datong
Shijiazhuang
P'yŏngyang
Seoul (Sŏul)
Taegu
Pusan
Kwangju
Inch'ŏn
Ch'ŏngjin
Tokyo
Yokohama
Nagoya
Osaka
Kyōto
Kobe
Hiroshima
Fukuoka
Kita-Kyūshū
Kagoshima
Sapporo
Hakodate
Aomori
Sendai
Niigata
Akita
Morioka
Lake Baikal
Lena
Yenisey
Kolyma
Indigirka
Amur
Aldan
Vilyuy
Olenek
Khrebet Dzhagdy
Tukuringra
Gora Munku Sardyk 3492
Ala Shan
Qilian Shan
Lang Shan
Ordos
Hami
Dunhuang
Yumen
Erenhot
Bayan Obo
GREAT WALL
Korea Bay
Bo Hai
La Pérouse Strait
Tsugaru-kaikyō
Korea Strait
Zaliv Petra Velikogo
Proliv Tatarskiy

SEA OF OKHOTSK

KAMCHATKA

Kuril Islands (Kuril'skiye Ostrova)

SAKHALIN

R U S S I A N   F E D.

M A N C H U R I A

MONGOLIA

INNER MONGOLIA AUT. REGION

SINKIANG AUT. REG.

TIBET AUT. REG.

C H I N A

SEA OF JAPAN

J A P A N

HOKKAIDŌ

NORTH KOREA

SOUTH KOREA

YELLOW SEA

EAST CHINA SEA

RYUKYU ISLANDS

P A C I F I C   O C E A N

BURMA (MYANMAR)

INDIA

Tropic of Cancer

Major cities: Petropavlovsk-Kamchatskiy, Novosibirsk, Krasnoyarsk, Irkutsk, Ulaanbaatar, Khabarovsk, Vladivostok, Harbin, Changchun, Shenyang, Dalian, Beijing (Peking), Tianjin (Tientsin), Jinan, Xi'an (Sian), Chengdu, Chongqing, Kunming, Guangzhou (Canton), HONG KONG, Macau, Wuhan, Nanjing, Shanghai, Hanoi, Haiphong, Seoul (Sŏul), P'yŏngyang, Pusan, Taegu, Sapporo, Tōkyō, Yokohama, Nagoya, Kyōto, Osaka, Kōbe, Fukuoka, Kyūshū, Taipei, Kaohsiung, TAIWAN (FORMOSA)

1:20M

0	200	400	600	800 km

0	200	400 mls

PHILIPPINES
LUZON
MINDANAO
Manila
Quezon City
SOUTH CHINA SEA
SULU SEA
CELEBES SEA
MOLUCCA SEA
BANDA SEA
FLORES SEA
JAVA SEA
ARAFURA SEA
TIMOR SEA
CORAL SEA
SERAM SEA
MOLUCCAS
MALAYSIA
PENINSULAR MALAYSIA
SINGAPORE
BRUNEI
SABAH
SARAWAK
BORNEO
KALIMANTAN
SULAWESI (CELEBES)
SUMATERA
JAVA (JAWA)
INDONESIA
IRIAN JAYA
NEW GUINEA
PAPUA NEW GUINEA
AUSTRALIA
Arnhem Land
Gulf of Carpentaria
Great Barrier Reef
THAILAND
CAMBODIA
VIETNAM
INDO-CHINA
Bangkok (Krung Thep)
Phnom Penh
Ho Chi Minh City (Saigon)
Rangoon (Yangon)
Kuala Lumpur
Jakarta
Surabaya
Bandung
Semarang
Medan
Palembang
Padang
Pontianak
Banjarmasin
Balikpapan
Samarinda
Ujung Pandang (Makassar)
Manado
Kupang
Ambon
Jayapura
Port Moresby
Darwin
Davao
Zamboanga
Cebu
Iloilo
Bacolod
Kota Kinabalu
Kuching
Bandar Seri Begawan
George Town
Johor Bharu
Hainan
Spratly Islands
Palawan
Halmahera
Seram
Timor
Sumba
Flores
Bali
Lombok
Sumbawa
Bangka
Belitung
Palau (Belau)
CAROLINE ISLANDS
FEDERATED STATES OF MICRONESIA
Northern Marianas
Guam (U.S.A.)
Equator
INDIAN OCEAN
ANDAMAN SEA
Gulf of Thailand
Isthmus of Kra
Christmas I. (Aust.)
Cocos Is (Aust.)
Keeling Is
100
110
120
130
140
10
0

CHINA
Jilin
Liaoning
NORTH KOREA
SOUTH KOREA
KYŪSHŪ
Korea Bay
YELLOW SEA
(HUANG HAI)
KOREA STRAIT
(TSUSHIMA-KAIKYŌ)
Tongjosŏn-man
Liaodong Wan
Liaodong Bandao
Qian Shan
Changbai Shan
Longgang Shan
Nangnim Sanmaek
Taebaek Sanmaek
Sobaek Sanmaek
Kyongsang Sanmaek
Hamgyong Sanmaek
Changchun
Jilin
Siping
Liaoyuan
Shenyang
Fushun
Benxi
Liaoyang
Anshan
Haicheng
Yingkou
Fuxin
Jinzhou
Dandong
Dalian
Lüshun
Tonghua
Huadian
Dunhua
Yanji
Tumen
Hunchun
Ussuriysk
Vladivostok
Artem
Nakhodka
Partizansk
Yantai
Weihai
Rongcheng
Rushan
Sinŭiju
Kanggye
Hyesan
Ch'ŏngjin
Najin
Kimch'aek
Tanch'ŏn
Hamhŭng
Hŭngnam
Wŏnsan
P'yŏngyang
Namp'o
Sariwŏn
Haeju
Kaesŏng
Seoul
(Sŏul)
Inch'ŏn
Suwŏn
Ch'unch'ŏn
Kangnŭng
Wŏnju
Ch'ŏngju
Taejŏn
Andong
P'ohang
Kyŏngju
Taegu
Ulsan
Pusan
Masan
Chinju
Kunsan
Iri
Ch'ŏnju
Kwangju
Mokp'o
Yŏsu
Cheju
Halla-san 1950
Cheju do
Ullung-do
Tok-do
(Take-shima)
(Liancourt Rocks)
Tsushima
Iki
Gotō-rettō
Fukuoka
Kita-Kyūshū
Shimonoseki
Hiroshima
Yamaguchi
Sasebo
Nagasaki
Kumamoto
Ōita
Beppu
Miyazaki
Miyakonojō
Kagoshima
Kanoya
Nobeoka
Oki-shotō
Matsue
SEA
JA
H
1:5M
0 50 100 150 200 km
0 50 100 mls

RUS. FED.
Arkhipovka
Ol'ga
Vangou
Lazo
Margaritovo
continued on inset
HOKKAIDŌ
Asahikawa
Fukagawa
Akabira
Ashibetsu
Asahi dake 2290
Kutcharo-ko
Teshikaga
Nemuro
Me-akan dake
Takikawa
Sunagawa
Furano
Bibai
Iwamizawa
Yūbari
Shakotan-misaki
Furubira
Ishikari-wan
Otaru
Sapporo
Ebetsu
Kushiro
Ikeda
Obihiro
Iwanai
Kutchan
Eniwa
Chitose
Tomakomai
Mukawa
Hidaka-sammyaku
Tokachi
Suttsu
Shikotsu-ko
Oshamambe
Toya-ko
Date
Monbetsu
Taiki
Setana
Noboribetsu
Hiroo
Uchiura-wan
Muroran
Urakawa
Samani
Yakumo
Erimo-misaki
Mori
Komaga take 1133
Okushiri-tō
Esashi
Esan-misaki
Hakodate
Kikonai
Ōma-saki
Ōhata
Shiriya-saki
Matsumae
Tsugaru-kaikyō
Mutsu
Ōminato
Kodomari-misaki
Mimmaya
Mutsu-wan
Goshogawara
Noheji
Ajigasawa
Aomori
Iwaki-san 1625
Kuroishi
Towada
Henashi-zaki
Hirosaki
Towada-ko
Hachinohe
Odate
Noshiro
Kuji
Mi-zaki
Oga
Koma
Akita
Tazawa-ko
Morioka
Miyako
Tazawako
Yamada
Honjō
Hanamaki
Yokote
Tono
Kamaishi
Kitakami
Mizusawa
Ōfunato
Tobi-shima
Chokai-san 2230
Yuzawa
Yokobori
Rikuzen-Tanaka
Ichinoseki
Kesennuma
Sakata
Shinjō
Narugo
Tsuruoka
Furukawa
Obanazawa
Higashine
Ishinomaki
Murayama
Awa-shima
Tendo
Sendai
Shiogama
Hajiki-saki
Murakami
Yamagata
Natori
Sado-shima
Nagai
Kaminoyama
Ryōtsu
Aikawa
Kakuda
Niigata
Shibata
Yonezawa
Sōma
Mano-wan
Niitsu
Iide san 2105
Fukushima
Haramachi
Hegura-jima
Teradomari
Sanjō
Aizu-Wakamatsu
Kitakata
Nihommatsu
Nanatsu-jima
Suzu-misaki
Nagaoka
Inawashiro-ko
Kōriyama
Kashiwazaki
Wajima
Suzu
Ojiya
Sukagawa
Koide
Shirakawa
Taira
Iwaki
Noto-hantō
Itoigawa
Naoetsu
Takada
Tokamachi
Kuroiso
Hakui
Nanao
Arai
Shirane-san 2368
Otawara
Himi
Toyama-wan
Kurabe
Nakano
Nikko
Yaita
Imaichi
Hitachi
Hitachi-Ota
Shinminato
Takaoka
Toyama
Suzaka
Numata
Utsunomiya
Shibukawa
Mito
Katsuta
Kanazawa
Tsubata
Nagano
Kiryū
Maebashi
Ashikaga
Nakaminato
Omachi
Isesaki
Komatsu
Tsurugi
Yariga take 3180
Ueda
Oyama
Ishioka
Kaga
Komoro
Takasaki
Ota
Koga
Hoko
Matsumoto
Kumagaya
Tsuchiura
Dōgo
Saigō
Haku-san 2702
Okaya
Konosu
Katsuyama
Suwa
Fukui
Takayama
Omiya
Sawara
Ono
Chichibu
Kawagoe
Urawa
Narita
Chōshi
Sabae
Ontake-san 3063
Ina
Chino
Tōkyō
Inubo-saki
Takefu
Osaka
Enzan
Kawaguchi
Funabashi
Wakasa-wan
Shirotori
Agematsu
Hachiōji
Chiba
Hachiman
Kanayama
Kōfu
Yokohama
Kawasaki
Bōsō-hantō
Kasumi
Amino
Tsuruga
Shirani-san 3192
Fuji-Yoshida
Mobara
Kinomoto
Nakatsu-gawa
Iida
Kisarazu
Kurayoshi
Toyooka
Obama
Gifu
Kiso-sammyaku
Fujisawa
Yokosuka
Tottori
Miyazu
Maizuru
Ōgaki
Ichinomiya
Akaishi-sanchi
Fuji-san 3776
Katsuura
Ayabe
Fukuchiyama
Biwa-ko
Kasugai
Seto
Fujinomiya
Odawara
Miura
Kamogawa
Chizu
Hikone
Toyota
Shimizu
Numazu
Tateyama
Tsuyama
Kyōto
Ōtsu
Tsushima
Kuwana
Nagoya
Shizuoka
Fuji
Itō
Sagami-nada
Nojima-zaki
Niimi
Tatsuno
Nishiwaki
Uji
Yokkaichi
Okazaki
Shimada
Yaizu
Himeji
Toyonaka
Handa
Suruga-wan
Ō-shima
Takahashi
Kōbe
Nara
Tsu
Suzuka
Toyohashi
Kakogawa
Hamamatsu
Shimoda
Okayama
Akashi
Ōsaka
Nabari
Ise-wan
Ōmae-zaki
Iro-zaki
To-shima
Kurashiki
Harima-nada
Sakai
Matsusaka
Ise
Toba
Nii-jima
Onomichi
Tamano
Sumoto
Awaji-shima
Kishiwada
Izumi-Sano
Kōzu-shima
Sakaide
Hashimoto
Takamatsu
Wakayama
Nagashima
Miyake-jima
Marugame
Naruto
Kainan
Owase
Ōnohara-jima
Mikura-jima
Tokushima
Kii-sanchi
Komatsushima
Gobo
Kumano
Niihama
Anan
Shikoku-sanchi
Hiwasa
Tanabe
Shingū
Inamba-jima
Kōchi
Nankoku
Hikigawa
Aki
Kii-suidō
Tosa
Susaki
Kushimoto
Shiono-misaki
Tosa-wan
Muroto
Muroto-zaki
SHIKOKU
HONSHŪ
SEA OF JAPAN
PACIFIC OCEAN
JAPAN
145 at the same scale
Wakkanai
Sōya-misaki
Rebun-tō
Rishiri-tō
Hama-Tombetsu
Kitami-Esashi
Otoineppu
Ōmu
Okoppe
Yagishiri-tō
Teuri-tō
Nayoro
Mombetsu
M.Dokuchayevo
Shiretoko-misaki
Rudnaya
Uryū-ko
Takinoue
Saroma-ko
Abashiri-wan
O. Kunashir (Rus. Fed. admin./claimed by Japan)
Shibetsu
Engaru
Abashiri
Rausu
Rumoi
Teshio dake 1558
Kitami
Shari
Golovnino
Nemuro-kaikyō
135
140
145
40
35
45

BURMA
MYANMAR
CHINA
LAOS
THAILAND
CAMBODIA
VIETNAM
MALAYSIA
INDONESIA
SUMATERA
BORNEO
Kalimantan
SARAWAK
(Malaysia)
HAINAN
PENINSULAR MALAYSIA
MALAYA
Bay of Bengal
ANDAMAN SEA
Mergui Archipelago
GULF OF THAILAND
Gulf of Tongkin
SOUTH CHINA SEA
INDO-CHINA
Strait of Malacca
Paracel Islands
(claimed by China & Vietnam)
NICOBAR ISLANDS
(India)
Mouths of the Irrawaddy
Mouths of the Mekong
G. of Martaban
Bight of Bangkok
Isthmus of Kra
Mandalay
Rangoon
(Yangon)
Bassein
(Pathein)
Moulmein
(Mawlamyine)
Pegu
(Bago)
Pye
(Prome)
Toungoo
Henzada
Myingyan
Meiktila
Magwe
(Magway)
Taunggyi
Lashio
Hsipaw
Maymyo
Monywa
Sagaing
Shwebo
Thaton
Tavoy
(Dawei)
Mergui
Kengtung
Chiang Mai
Chiang Rai
M. Lampang
Uttaradit
M. Phitsanulok
Tak
M. Nakhon Sawan
Nakhon Ratchasima
Ubon Ratchathani
Udon Thani
Nong Khai
Vientiane
(Viangchan)
Luang Prabang
Savannakhet
Pakse
Champassak
Bangkok
Thon Buri
Nakhon Pathom
Ayutthaya
Pattaya
Chanthaburi
Battambang
Siem Reap
ANGKOR
Tonle Sap
Kompong Thom
Kompong Chhnang
Kompong Cham
Phnom Penh
Kratie
Sihanoukville
(Kompong Som)
Kampot
Hanoi
Haiphong
Hoa Binh
Nam Dinh
Ninh Binh
Thai Binh
Thanh Hoa
Vinh
Ha Tinh
Dong Hoi
Quang Tri
Hue
Da Nang
Quang Ngai
Kontum
Pleiku
Qui Nhon
Tuy Hoa
Ban Me Thuot
Nha Trang
Cam Ranh
Da Lat
Phan Rang
Phan Thiet
Vung Tau
Ho Chi Minh City (Saigon)
My Tho
Vinh Long
Can Tho
Rach Gia
Long Xuyen
Chau Phu
Quan Long
Nam Can
Con Son
Lao Cai
Ha Giang
Cao Bang
Lang Son
Dien Bien Phu
Nanning
Pingxiang
Beihai
Zhanjiang
Maoming
Haikou
Leizhou Bandao
Surat Thani
Nakhon Si Thammarat
Ranong
Chumphon
Prachuap Khiri Khan
Phuket
Ko Phuket
Trang
Songkhla
Hat Yai
Pattani
Narathiwat
Ko Samui
Ko Phangan
Alor Setar
George Town
Pinang
Butterworth
Kota Baharu
Kuala Trengganu
Taiping
Ipoh
Kuantan
Kuala Lumpur
Kelang
Seremban
Port Dickson
Melaka
(Malacca)
Johor Bharu
SINGAPORE
Banda Aceh
Sabang
Medan
Binjai
Pematangsiantar
Tebingtinggi
Sibolga
Padangsidempuan
Nias
Simeulue
Siberut
Pekanbaru
Bukittinggi
Padang
Jambi
Bangka
Kep. Riau
Kep. Lingga
Kep. Anambas
Bunguran
Kuching
Pontianak
Singkawang
Equator
Ketapang
1:10M

1:10M
0 100 200 300 400 km
0 100 200 mls

MONGOLIA
GOBI
INNER MONGOLIA AUT. REGION
(NEI MONGOL ZIZHIQU)
Badain Jaran Shamo
Mu Us Shamo
Tengger Shamo
Ningxia
Qinghai
Gansu
Shaanxi
Shanxi
Hebei
Shandong
Henan
Jiangsu
Anhui
Hubei
Sichuan
Hunan
Jiangxi
Zhejiang
Fujian
Guizhou
Yunnan
Guangxi
Guangdong
Liaoning
Jilin
CHINA
TAIWAN
VIETNAM
LAOS
KOREA BAY
BO HAI
Bohai Wan
YELLOW SEA
(HUANG HAI)
SOUTH CHINA SEA
GULF OF TONGKIN
TAIWAN STRAIT
(FORMOSA CHANNEL)
HAINAN
Beijing
(Peking)
Tianjin
(Tientsin)
Shanghai
Nanjing
(Nanking)
Wuhan
Chongqing
(Chungking)
Chengdu
Xi'an
(Sian)
Zhengzhou
Jinan
(Tsinan)
Taiyuan
Shijiazhuang
Hohhot
Baotou
Datong
Lanzhou
Xining
Yinchuan
Kunming
Guiyang
Nanning
Guangzhou (Canton)
Changsha
Nanchang
Hangzhou
Fuzhou
(Foochow)
Hefei
Shenyang
Dalian
Changchun
Qingdao(Tsingtao)
Xiamen
(Amoy)
Shantou
(Swatow)
Hong Kong
(U.K.)
Kowloon
Macau
(Port.)
Taipei
Kaohsiung
Hanoi
Haiphong
Haikou
Zhanjiang
Guilin
Liuzhou
Wuzhou
Yichang
Xiangfan
Luoyang
Kaifeng
Xuzhou
Lianyungang
Yantai
Weifang
Zibo
Tangshan
Qinhuangdao
Anshan
Fushun
Benxi
Dandong
Zhangjiakou
Baoding
Handan
Anyang
Nanyang
Wuxi
Suzhou
Ningbo
Wenzhou
Jingdezhen
Jiujiang
Huangshi
Shashi
Zhuzhou
Xiangtan
Hengyang
Shaoguan
Ganzhou
Zigong
Neijiang
Luzhou
Yibin
Dukou
Baoji
Hanzhong
Tianshui
Qin Ling
Daba Shan
Dabie Shan
Taihang Shan
Lüliang Shan
Wuling Shan
Nan Ling
Taibai Shan
Gongga Shan
Dongting Hu
Poyang Hu
Hongze Hu
Taiwan
Yu Shan
Pengho Lieh Tao
(Pescadores)
Leizhou Bandao
(Luichow Peninsula)
Red River Delta
see page 11 for details
of Chinese Provinces
1:10M
0 100 200 300 400 km
0 100 200 mls

BORNEO

Tajungselor
Tanjungredeb
Kelolokan
Samarinda
Balikpapan
Kintap
Tg Selatan
Banjarmasin
Pareparé
Ujung Pandang (Makassar)
Benthain
Kabaena
Selayar
Kep. Takabonerate

Manado
Tolitoli
Gorontalo
Belang Sea
Minahassa Peninsula
Teluk Tomini
Luwuk
Poso
Palu
Donggala
Teluk Togian
Kep. Togian
Palopo
Watampone
Teluk Bone
Kendari
Buton
Majene

SULAWESI (CELEBES)
Tanjung
Kep. Sula
Banggai

MOLUCCAS
Ternate
Halmahera
Morotai
Tubelo
Kep. Asia
Kep. Ayu
Mapia
Waigeo
Salawati
Sorong
Manokwari
Biak
Numfoor
Yapen
Sarmi
Jayapura
Aitape
Wewak

INDONESIA

Seram Sea
Seram (Amboina)
Ambon
Buru
Namlea
Piru
Bula
Kep. Gorong
Adi
Kaimana
Fakfak
Babo
Kokonau
Kep. Watubela
Kep. Kai
Dobo
Kep. Aru

IRIAN JAYA
Pegunungan Maoke
Pk. Jaya 5029
Tanahmerah
Digul
Merauke
Dolak
Tg Vals

Banda Sea
Kep. Banda

NEW GUINEA
Mt Wilhelm
Mt Hagen
Mendi
Goroka
Madang
Sepik Central Ra.
Bismarck Ra.
Ramu

PAPUA NEW GUINEA
Bulolo
Lae
Morobe
Kerema
Gulf of Papua
Mt St Mary
Kikori
Daru
Saibai I.
Kupiano
Port Moresby
Owen Stanley Ra.
Kokoda
Popondetta
D'Entrecasteaux
Samarai
Alotau

Bismarck Archipelago
Ninigo Is
Hermit Is
Admiralty Is
Mussau
Saint Matthias Group
New Hanover
Kavieng
New Ireland
Manus
Manam
Schouten Is
Talasea
New Britain
Rabaul

Bismarck Sea

Arafura Sea

Torres Strait
C. York
Pr. of Wales I.
Somerset

Flores Sea
Reo
Ruteng
Endeh
Flores
Lomblen
Alor
Wetar
Kisar
Kep. Leti
Kep. Babar
Sermata
Kep. Damar
Roma
Kep. Tanimbar

Bali
Denpasar
Lombok
Mataram
Sumbawa
Memboro
Sumba
Waingapu
Savu
Rote
Kupang
Dili
Timor

Timor Sea

INDIAN OCEAN

Java Trench
Cartier I.
Scott Reef
Rowley Shoals

Melville I.
Bathurst I.
Van Diemen G.
Clarence Str.
Darwin
Rum Jungle
Adelaide River
Burrundie
Pine Creek
Katherine
Daly
Roper
Cobourg Pen.
Croker I.
C. Arnhem
Nhulunbuy
Groote Eylandt
Wessel Is
Limmen Bight
Sir Edward Pellew Group

Gulf of Carpentaria

ARNHEM LAND
Joseph Bonaparte Gulf
Pago Mission
Wyndham
Victoria
Birdum
Daly Waters
Borroloola
Mornington
Wellesley Is
Weipa

C. Londonderry
Collier B.
C. Lévêque
King Sound
Derby
Broome
L. Argyle
Victoria River Downs
Wave Hill
Newcastle Waters
Powell Creek
Barkly Tableland
Burketown
Normanton
Croydon

Cape York Peninsula
Iron Range
Coen
Princess Charlotte B.
Cooktown
Laura
Mitchell River
Mitchell

Cairns
Innisfail
Ingham
Townsville
Ayr
Charters Towers
Bowen
Proserpine
Mackay

NORTHERN TERRITORY
Tennant Creek
Barrow Creek
Mt Isa
Camooweal
Cloncurry
Hughenden
Richmond
Selwyn
Dajarra
Winton
Clermont
Emerald
Rockhampton
Mount Morgan
Gladstone

WESTERN AUSTRALIA
Great Sandy Desert
Gibson Desert
Great Victoria Desert

Port Hedland
Shay Gap
Marble Bar
Nullagine
Wittenoom
Hamersley Ra.
Mt Bruce
Paraburdoo
Newman
L. Disappointment
L. Mackay
Macdonnell Ranges
Mt Ziel 1510
Alice Springs
Simpson Desert

Dampier
Roebourne
Onslow
Fortescue
Ashburton
North West C.
Barlee Ra.
Mt Augustus
L. Carnegie
L. Wells
Mt Aloysius 987
Tomkinson Ra.
Musgrave Ra.
Mt Woodroffe 1440
Petermann Ra.

Lake Eyre Basin
Oodnadatta
Coober Pedy
L. Eyre

QUEENSLAND
Longreach
Barcaldine
Blackall
Windorah
Charleville
Quilpie
Roma
Miles
Toowoomba
Goondiwindi

Carnarvon
Shark B.
Dirk Hartog I.
Gascoyne
Lyons
McLeod
Wiluna
Meekatharra
Cue
Sandstone
Mt Magnet
Leonora
Barlee
Muchison

SOUTH AUSTRALIA
Marree
Leigh Ck
Frome
Milparinka
Tibooburra

Geraldton
Houtman Abrolhos
Dongara
Northampton
Mullewa
L. Moore
Bencubbin
Bullfinch
Southern Cross
Kalgoorlie
Coolgardie
Norseman
Rawlinna
Forrest
Nullarbor Plain
Ooldea
Tarcoola
Penong
Ceduna
Gawler Ranges
Streaky Bay
Woomera
Port Augusta
Quorn
Peterborough
Broken Hill
Menindee
Ivanhoe

NEW SOUTH WALES
Bourke
Cobar
Nyngan
Walgett
Moree
Narrabri
Tamworth
Armidale

Perth
Fremantle
Pinjarra
Bunbury
Collie
Narrogin
Wagin
Katanning
Manjimup
Albany
Esperance
C. Pasley
Arch. of the Recherche

Moora
Goomalling
Merredin
Northam
Corrigin

C. Naturaliste
Busselton
Augusta
C. Leeuwin
Blue Knob

Great Australian Bight

Port Lincoln
Eyre Peninsula
Whyalla
Port Pirie
Wallaroo
Spencer Gulf
Iron Knob
Penong
Kingston
Naracoorte
Mount Gambier
Portland
Port Fairy
Warrnambool

Flinders I.
Investigator Str.
Kangaroo I.
Adelaide
Elizabeth
Murray Bridge
Victor Harbour

Mildura
Balranald
Hay
Griffith
Wagga Wagga
Deniliquin
Albury
Shepparton
Bendigo
Ballarat
Geelong
Melbourne
Colac
Morwell
Sale
Bairnsdale
Orbost

Cobram
Junee
Cootamundra
Goulburn
Canberra
A.C.T.
Mt Kosciusko 2230
Bombala

Dubbo
Orange
Bathurst
Lithgow
Sydney
Wollongong
Newcastle
Maitland
Cessnock
Mt Barrington
Orange

VICTORIA
Horsham
Ararat
Hamilton
Wonthaggi
Wilson's Prom.

Bass Strait
King I.
Furneaux Group
Flinders
C. Barren

C. Grim
Smithton
Burnie
Devonport
Queenstown
Launceston
St Mary's
Hobart
Geeveston
South West C.
South East C.
Mt Ossa 1617

TASMANIA

Great Barrier Reef
Great Dividing Range

1:20M
0 200 400 600 800 km
0 200 400 mls

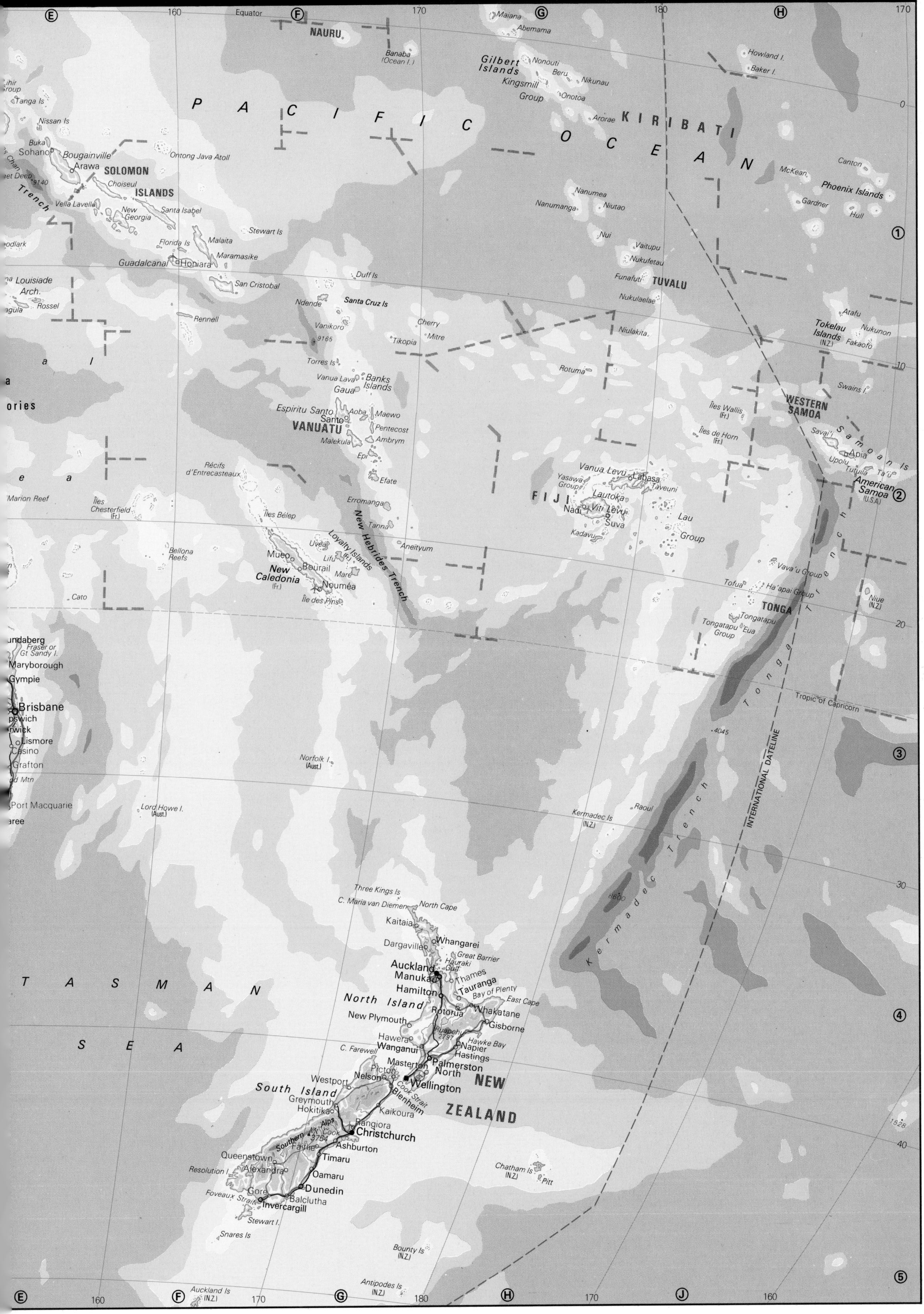
Equator
NAURU
Banaba (Ocean I.)
Maiana
Abemama
Gilbert Islands
Kingsmill Group
Nonouti
Beru
Nikunau
Onotoa
Arorae
KIRIBATI
Howland I.
Baker I.
PACIFIC OCEAN
Tanga Is
Nissan Is
Buka
Sohano
Bougainville
Arawa
SOLOMON ISLANDS
Choiseul
Ontong Java Atoll
Vella Lavella
New Georgia
Santa Isabel
Stewart Is
Florida Is
Malaita
Maramasike
Guadalcanal
Honiara
San Cristobal
Louisiade Arch.
Rossel
Rennell
Duff Is
Santa Cruz Is
Ndende
Vanikoro
9165
Cherry
Mitre
Tikopia
Torres Is
Vanua Lava
Banks Islands
Gaua
Espiritu Santo
Santo
Aoba
Maewo
Pentecost
Ambrym
VANUATU
Malekula
Epi
Efate
Erromanga
Tanna
Aneityum
New Hebrides Trench
Loyalty Islands
Récifs d'Entrecasteaux
Îles Chesterfield (Fr.)
Îles Belep
Bellona Reefs
Uvea
Lifu
Mare
Mueo
Bourail
New Caledonia (Fr.)
Nouméa
Île des Pins
Cato
Marion Reef
Nanumea
Niutao
Nanumanga
Nui
Vaitupu
Nukufetau
Funafuti
TUVALU
Nukulaelae
Niulakita
Rotuma
Canton
McKean
Phoenix Islands
Gardner
Hull
Atafu
Nukunon
Tokelau Islands (N.Z.)
Fakaofo
Swains I.
WESTERN SAMOA
Îles Wallis (Fr.)
Îles de Horn (Fr.)
Savai'i
Apia
Upolu
Tutuila
Ta'u
Samoa Is
American Samoa (U.S.A.)
Vanua Levu
Labasa
Taveuni
Yasawa Group
Lautoka
Viti Levu
Nadi
Suva
Kadavu
FIJI
Lau Group
Vava'u Group
Tofua
Ha'apai Group
TONGA
Tongatapu
'Eua
Tongatapu Group
Niue (N.Z.)
Tonga Trench
Tropic of Capricorn
4045
INTERNATIONAL DATELINE
Norfolk I. (Aust.)
Lord Howe I. (Aust.)
Kermadec Is (N.Z.)
Raoul
Kermadec Trench
Bundaberg
Fraser or Gt Sandy I.
Maryborough
Gympie
Brisbane
Ipswich
Lismore
Casino
Grafton
Port Macquarie
TASMAN SEA
Three Kings Is
C. Maria van Diemen
North Cape
Kaitaia
Whangarei
Dargaville
Great Barrier
Hauraki Gulf
Auckland
Manukau
Thames
Hamilton
Tauranga
Bay of Plenty
East Cape
North Island
Rotorua
Whakatane
Gisborne
New Plymouth
Ruapehu 2797
Hawera
Wanganui
Hawke Bay
Napier
Hastings
C. Farewell
Masterton
Palmerston North
Picton
Nelson
Wellington
NEW ZEALAND
Westport
South Island
Greymouth
Blenheim
Cook Strait
Hokitika
Kaikoura
Rangiora
Southern Alps
Mt Cook 3754
Christchurch
Fairlie
Ashburton
Timaru
Queenstown
Alexandra
Oamaru
Resolution I.
Dunedin
Gore
Balclutha
Foveaux Strait
Invercargill
Stewart I.
Snares Is
Chatham Is (N.Z.)
Pitt
Bounty Is (N.Z.)
Antipodes Is (N.Z.)
Auckland Is (N.Z.)
1526
E
F
G
H
J
1
2
3
4
5
160
170
180
0
10
20
30
40

QUEENSLAND

SOUTH AUSTRALIA

NEW SOUTH WALES

VICTORIA

TASMANIA

Lake Eyre Basin

Sturt Desert

Grey Range

Darling Downs

Great Dividing Range

New England Range

Flinders Range

Mt Lofty Ra.

Riverina

Snowy Mts

Australian Alps

Gippsland

Bass Strait

King I.

Furneaux Flinders I. Group

Banks Strait

Brisbane
Gold Coast
Toowoomba
Ipswich
Lismore
Grafton
Coff's Harbour
Armidale
Tamworth
Port Macquarie
Taree
Newcastle
Maitland
Sydney
Parramatta
Wollongong
Port Kembla
Canberra
A.C.T.
Queanbeyan
Dubbo
Orange
Bathurst
Broken Hill
Adelaide
Port Pirie
Mildura
Wagga Wagga
Albury
Wodonga
Shepparton
Bendigo
Ballarat
Melbourne
Geelong
Warrnambool
Mount Gambier
Portland
Horsham
Traralgon
Morwell
Sale
Bairnsdale
Lakes Entrance

Devonport
Burnie
Launceston
Hobart
New Norfolk

Cooper Ck

Darling

Murray

Murrumbidgee

Lachlan

Ninety Mile Beach

Wilson's Promontory

1:7.5M

0 100 200 300 km

50 100 150 mls

Three Kings Is
C. Maria van Diemen
North Cape
Ninety Mile Beach
Rangaunu B.
Doubtless B.
Ahipara B.
Tauroa Pt
Kaitaia
Bay of Islands
C.Brett
Russell
Kaikohe
Kawakawa
Hokianga Har.
Hikurangi
Whangarei
Hen & Chickens Is
Bream B.
Dargaville
Little Barrier I.
Great Barrier I.
Wellsford
Kaipara Har.
Hauraki Gulf
C.Colville
Manly
Mercury Is
Takapuna
Auckland
Mercury Bay
Coromandel Ra.
Coromandel Peninsula
Papatoetoe
Manukau
Papakura
Thames
Pukekohe
Waiuku
NORTH
Mayor I.
Paeroa
Waihi
Huntly
Te Aroha
Matakana I.
White I.
Glen Afton
Tauranga Har.
C. Runaway
Hicks Bay
Ngaruawahia
Morrinsville
Tauranga
Bay of Plenty
East C.
Hamilton
Cambridge
Te Puke
ISLAND
Te Awamutu
Whakatane
Opotiki
Raukumara Ra.
Kawhia
Putaruru
Rotorua
Kawerau
Taneatua
Otorohanga
Waitomo
Tokomaru Bay
Te Kuiti
Tolaga Bay
Mangakino
Murupara
Huiarau Ra.
N.Taranaki Bight
Ohura
Taupo
L. Taupo
Gisborne
Waitara
Taumarunui
Waikaremoana
Poverty Bay
New Plymouth
Inglewood
Mt Ngauruhoe 2291
Mt Makorako 1727
Tarawera
Mt Egmont (Mt Taranaki) 2518
C. Egmont
Stratford
Mt Ruapehu 2797
Kaimanawa Mts
Hawke Bay
Wairoa
Mahia Peninsula
Opunake
Eltham
Raetihi
Ohakune
Eskdale
Portland I.
Hawera
Waiouru
Taradale
Napier
S.Taranaki Bight
Patea
Taihape
Hastings
C. Kidnappers
Havelock North
Wanganui
Ruahine Ra.
Marton
Waipukurau
Feilding
Dannevirke
Palmerston N.
Woodville
Foxton
Pahiatua
C. Farewell
Farewell Spit
Golden Bay
C.Turnagain
Herbertville
Collingwood
Separation Pt
C.Stephens
Levin
Rocks Pt
D'Urville I.
Eketahuna
Takaka
Otaki
Tasman Mts
Tasman Bay
Paraparaumu
C.Jackson
Tararua Ra.
Masterton
Mt Hector 1529
Porirua
Motueka
The Twins 1826
Tawa
Upper Hutt
Carterton
Karamea
Karamea Bight
Nelson
Picton
Wellington
Lower Hutt
Wairarapa
Martinborough
Richmond
Blenheim
Palliser Bay
Mt Ross 983
Seddonville
Richmond Ra.
Wairau
C. Palliser
Westport
C. Foulwind
Murchison
C. Campbell
COOK STRAIT
Buller
L. Rotoroa
L. Rotoiti
Awatere
Victoria Ra.
Spenser Mts
Mt Travers 2338
Tapuaenuku 2885
Reefton
Kaikoura Ra.
Clarence
Runanga
Greymouth
Grey
Lewis Pass
Hanmer Springs
Kaikoura
Kaikoura Pen.
Hokitika
L. Brunner
Waiau
L. Sumner
Culverden
Hurunui
Cheviot
SOUTH
Ross
Arthurs Pass
Puketeraki Ra.
Waipara
Abut Hd
Rangiora
Pegasus Bay
Franz Josef Gl.
L. Coleridge
Waimakariri
Kaiapoi
Rakaia
Hornby
Christchurch
ISLAND
Mt Cook 3754
Methven
Lyttelton
SOUTHERN ALPS
Mt Sefton 3157
Lincoln
Banks Peninsula
Rangitata
Canterbury Plains
Hermitage
Akaroa
L. Ellesmere
L. Tekapo
Geraldine
Ashburton
Jackson Hd
Cascade Pt
Pollux 2542
L. Pukaki
Lake Fairlie
Pukaki
Temuka
Canterbury Bight
Young Ra.
Ohau
Awarua Pt
L. Benmore
Timaru
Mt Aspiring 3027
Wanaka
L. Hawea
Omarama
Milford Sd
L. Aviemore
Waimate
Milford Sd
Homer Tunnel
Wanaka
Hawkdun Ra.
Kurow
Mt Pyramid 2326
Dunstan Mts
Waitaki
George Sd
Arrowtown
Caswell Sd
Queenstown
Cromwell
Ranfurly
Oamaru
Clyde
Secretary I.
Fiordland Nat. Park
L. Te Anau
Wakatipu
Alexandra
Hampden
Doubtful Sd
Te Anau
Kingston
Manapouri
Manapouri
Roxburgh
Palmerston
Breaksea Sd
Mt Ward 1718
Taieri
Waikouaiti
Resolution I.
Dusky Sd
Waiau
Lumsden
Heriot
Port Chalmers
Riversdale
Otago Peninsula
Ohai
Mosgiel
Dunedin
Cameron Mts
L. Hauroko
Oreti
Tapanui
Clutha
Lawrence
Milton
Tuatapere
Winton
Gore
Puysegur Pt
Edendale
Mataura
Balclutha
Te Waewae Bay
Kaitangata
Riverton
Owaka
Invercargill
Foveaux Strait
Solander I.
Bluff
Codfish I.
Oban
Paterson Inlet
Stewart Island
Mt Allen 730
Shelter Pt
Port Pegasus
TASMAN SEA
PACIFIC OCEAN
170
175
35
40
45
A
B
C
1
2
3
1:5M
0
50
100
150
200 km
0
50
100 mls

Barents Sea

Norwegian Basin

ICELAND

Arctic Circle

EUROPE

North Sea

Sea of Okhotsk

Sakhalin

A S I A

Black Sea

Caspian Sea

Aral Sea

Sea of Japan

Vityaz Depth 10542

Kuril Trench

Mediterranean Sea

J A P A N

Japan Trench

Huang He

Chang Jiang

Red Sea

Persian Gulf

Ganga

TAIWAN

S. Honshu Ridge

Arabian Sea

Bay of Bengal

Hainan

Lyushu-Palau Ridge

Mariana Trench

NORTHERN MARIANAS

Raas Caseyr

Arabian Basin

Andaman Is

South China Sea

PHILIPPINES

Mariana Is

M I C R O

Guam

Philippine Trench

C. Johnson Depth 10497

11022 Challenger Depth

AFRICA

Carlsberg Ridge

MALDIVES

SRI LANKA (CEYLON)

Nicobar Is

Palau (Belau) (USA)

Caroline Is

FEDERATED STATES OF

MICRONESIA

Somali Basin

Maldives Ridge

Celebes Sea

6920

M E L

SEYCHELLES

Nascarene Ridge

Chagos Arch.

Sumatra

Borneo

Celebes

New Guinea

Planet Deep 9140

COMOROS

Mid Indian Basin

Ninety-East Ridge

I N D O N E S I A

Java

Arafura Sea

I N D I A N

Mozambique Channel

Mid-Indian Ridge

1737

Cocos Is

West Australian Basin

Java Trench

7450

Christmas I.

Timor

Coral Sea Basin

MADAGASCAR

Réunion

MAURITIUS

1924

Great Barrier Reef

O C E A N

Madagascar Basin

S. Madagascar Ridge

2067

Tropic of Capricorn

AUSTRALIA

Natal Basin

South West Indian Ridge

W. Australian Ridge

7102

C. Agulhas

1198

I. Amsterdam I.St Paul

South Australia Basin

Tasman Sea

Agulhas Plateau

Crozet Basin

Indian-Antarctic Ridge

Tasmania

Agulhas Basin

Is Crozet

Pr.Edward Is

Îs Kerguelen

1922

Macquarie Is

Atlantic-Indian Ridge

Kerguelen Ridge

Heard I.

Atlantic-Indian Antarctic Basin

Banzare Seamount 186

Indian-Antarctic Basin

A N T A R C T I C A

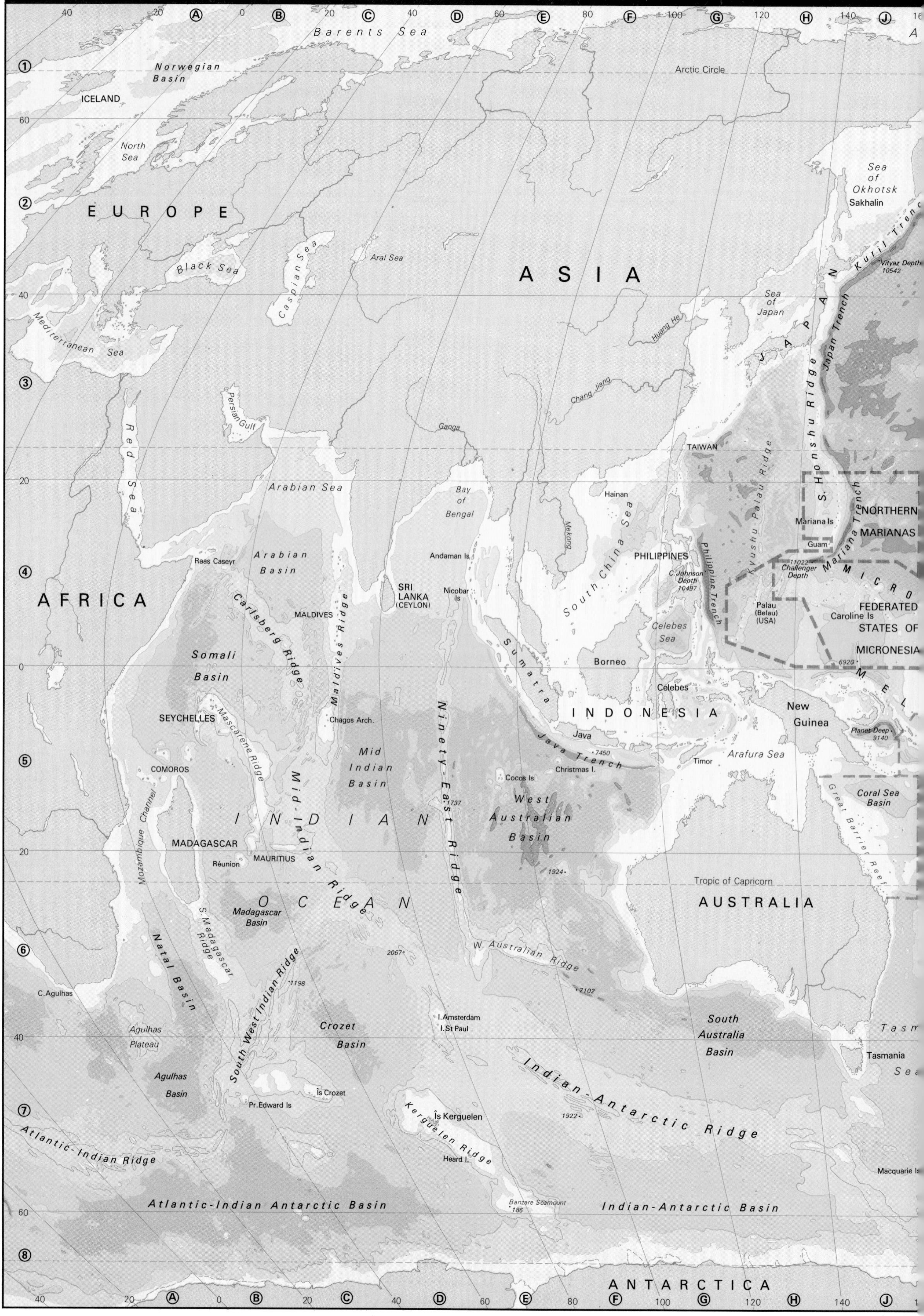

1:60M

0 600 1200 1800 2400 km

0 600 1200 mls

GREENLAND
To enhance the ocean features, the 3000m contour has been added, and over 5000m is shown by an extra tint.
ICELAND
C. Farewell
Labrador Basin
Hudson Bay
Bering Sea
Aleutian Is
Aleutian Trench
7822
Atlantic
Newfoundland
Grand Banks
Ocean
NORTH AMERICA
Emperor Seamount Chain
2926
Mendocino Seascarp
Murray Seascarp
North American Basin
Bermuda
18
104
Midway Is
Gulf of Mexico
Hawaiian Islands
Tropic of Cancer
C. Falso
CUBA
West Indies
Cayman Tr.
1477
Mid-Pacific Mountains
Is Revilla Gigedo
Clarion Fracture Zone
Middle America Trench
East Pacific Rise
Caribbean Sea
MARSHALL ISLANDS
Marshall Is
PACIFIC OCEAN
POLYNESIA
Line Is
Cocos Ridge
Equator
Is Galápagos
SOUTH AMERICA
NAURU
KIRIBATI
Phoenix Is
SOLOMON ISLANDS
TUVALU
Tokelau
Îs Marquises
6150
American Samoa
Wallis & Futuna
Wrn Samoa
French Polynesia
East Pacific Ridge
NUATU
FIJI
TONGA
Samoa
Îs de la Société
Tahiti
Îs Tuamotu
Peru Basin
S.W. Peru or Nasca Ridge
Peru-Chile Trench
Niue
Cook Is
New Caledonia
Horizon Depth 10882
Tonga Trench
Îs Tubuai
Îs Gambier
8066
5537
S. Fiji Basin
Pitcairn
1344
Sala y Gómez
S. Ambrosio
S. Félix
Easter I. (I. de Pascua)
Norfolk I. Ridge
Norfolk I.
10047
Kermadec Trench
INTERNATIONAL DATE LINE
Is Juan Fernández
N. Cape
South West Pacific Basin
NEW ZEALAND
Chatham Is
Pacific-Antarctic Ridge
Argentine Basin
New Zealand Plateau
Falkland Is
ckland Is
Campbell I.
N. Scotia Ridge
S. Georgia
6240
732
C. Horn
Scotia Sea
S. Sandwich Trench
S. Sandwich Is
South East Pacific Basin
Drake Passage
5486
S. Orkney Is
Antarctic Peninsula
Antarctic Circle
alleny Is
Scott Is
Weddell Sea
K L M N O P Q R S
180 160 140 120 100 80 60 40 20 0
1 2 3 4 5 6 7 8
60 40 20 0 20 40 60

Belgrade · Sarajevo · Split · Dubrovnik · Niksic · Shkoder · Skopje · Tiranë · Sofia · Plovdiv · Burgas · Varna · Bucharest · Ruse · Constanta · Ploiesti · Galati · Sibiu · ROMANIA · BULGARIA · YUGOS. · B.H. · MAC. · ALBANIA · GREECE · Thessaloniki · Trikkala · Olimbos · Patra · Athens (Athina) · Peloponnisos · Kalamai · Crete (Kriti) · Rhodes · Aegean Sea · Izmir · Aydin · Denizli · Antalya · Konya · Adana · Istanbul · Üsküdar · Bursa · Eskisehir · Ankara · Kayseri · Sivas · Erzurum · Malatya · Diyarbakir · Van · Gaziantep · Latakia · Halab · Hamah · Hims · Nicosia · CYPRUS · Famagusta · Beirut · Damascus · Dar'a · Haifa · Tel Aviv · Jerusalem · Amman · ISRAEL · LEBANON · JORDAN · SYRIA

BLACK SEA · Sulina · Odessa · Nikolayev · Mariupol · Melitopol · Berdyansk · Taganrog · Rostov-na-Donu · Donetsk · Shakhty · Zaporozh'ye · Krym · Simferopol · Sevastopol · Kerch · Sea of Azov · RUS. FED. · Volgograd · Astrakhan' · Kalmyk R. · Divnoye · Kropotkin · Krasnodar · Maykop · Stavropol · Kislovodsk · Groznyy · Vladikavkaz · Makhachkala · Sukhumi · Sochi · Batumi · Kutaisi · Tbilisi · GEORGIA · Gyandzha · Baku · AZERBAIJAN · ARMENIA · Yerevan · Nakhichevan · Tabriz · Ardabil · Rasht · CASPIAN SEA

KAZAK... · UZBEKISTAN · Nukus · Tashauz · Urgench · Turtkul · TURKMENISTAN · Nebit-Dag · Ashkhabad · Chardzhou · Karshi · Bukhara · Mary · Mashhad · Herat · AFGHANISTAN · Kandahar

MEDITERRANEAN SEA · Darnah · Tubruq · LIBYA · Matrûh · Alexandria · Dumyat · Port Said · Cairo · Tanta · Ismailiya · Suez · Sinai · Aqaba · El Faiyûm · Beni Suef · El Minya · Asyût · EGYPT · Farafra Oasis · El Khârga · Luxor · Aswân · L. Nasser · Wadi Halfa · Dongola · Nubian Desert · Libyan Desert · Merowe · Berber · Atbara · Port Sudan · Suakin · SUDAN · Omdurman · Khartoum · Kassala · Ed Damer · Wad Medani · Ed Dueim · El Obeid · Kosti · Sennar · Singa · SAUDI ARABIA · An Nafûd · Tabûk · Al Jawf · Taymâ' · Hâ'il · Buraydah · Unayzah · Ar Riyâd · Medina · Yanbu al Bahr · Jiddah · Makkah · At Tâ'if · Al Hufûf · Ad Dahnâ · Ar Rub' al Khâlî

Baghdad · IRAQ · Mosul · Al Hasakah · Dayr az Zawr · Arbil · Kirkûk · Sulaymâniyah · Sâmarrâ · Ar Ramâdi · Karbalâ · An Najaf · Ad Diwâniyah · Al Amârah · Basra · Kuwait · KUWAIT · Dhahran · BAHRAIN · Manâmah · QATAR · Doha · Abu Dhabi · UNITED ARAB EMIRATES · Dubai · Al Khâbûrah · Muscat · OMAN · IRAN · Tehrân · Qom · Hamadan · Kermânshâh · Arâk · Kâshân · Esfahân · Yazd · Shirâz · Kermân · Zâhedan · Bandar 'Abbâs · Ahvâz · Abâdân · Bandar Khomeyni · Bûshehr · Persian Gulf · Gulf of Oman · Makran · PAKISTAN · Karachi

YEMEN · San'â · Al Hudaydah · Ta'izz · Al Mukhâ · Aden ('Adan) · Al Mukallâ · Ash Shihr · Hadramawt · Gulf of Aden · Socotra (Suqutra) · Salâlah · Masîrah · Gulf of Masirah · ARABIAN SEA

ERITREA · Massawa (Mits'iwa) · Asmara · Adigrat · Adwa · Aseb · Djibouti · DJIBOUTI · Berbera · Hargeysa · SOMALIA · Ceerigaabo · Raas Xaafuun · Ras Dashan · Gonder · L. Tana · ETHIOPIA · Âdis Âbeba · Debre Mark'os · Nazrêt · Dirê Dawa · Harêr · Jima · Gore · Dembi Dolo · Negele · Moyale · Dolo · Shebele · SUDAN · ZAIRE · UGANDA · Juba · Rumbek · Nimule · Malakal · L. Albert · L. Rudolf · KENYA · Wajir · Garissa · Kirinyaga (Mt Kenya) · Nairobi · Kampala · Entebbe · Jinja · Kisumu · Nakuru · Eldoret · Kitale · Mt Elgon · RWANDA · Kigali · BURUNDI · Bujumbura · Butare · Gitega · TANZANIA · Lake Victoria · Bukoba · Mwanza · Mbeya · Arusha · Moshi · Kilimanjaro 5895 · Muqdisho (Mogadishu) · Marka · Baraawe · Kismaayo · Gulf of Aden · Somali Basin · INDIAN OCEAN · Equator · Tropic of Cancer

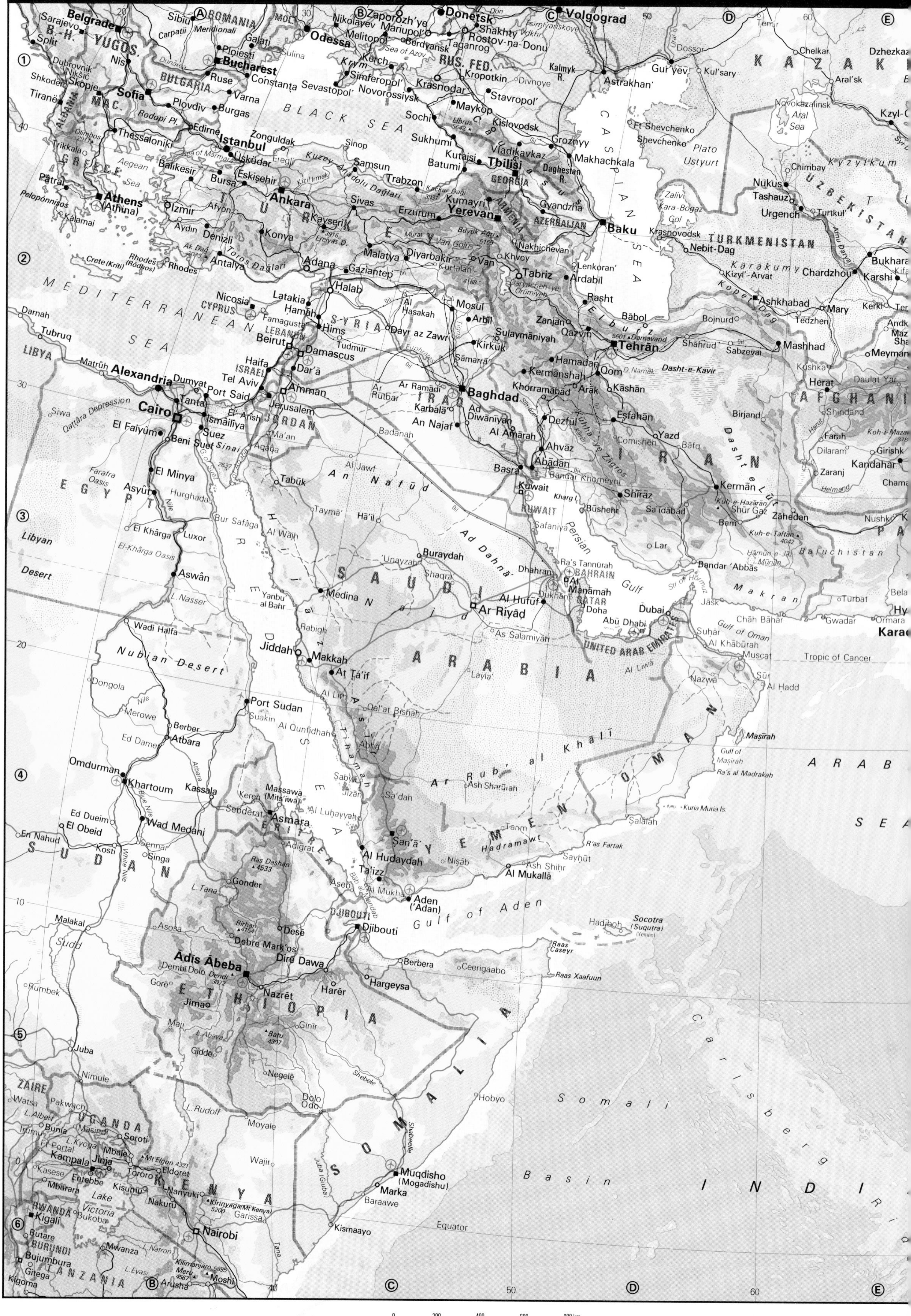

1:20M · 0 200 400 600 800 km · 0 200 400 mls

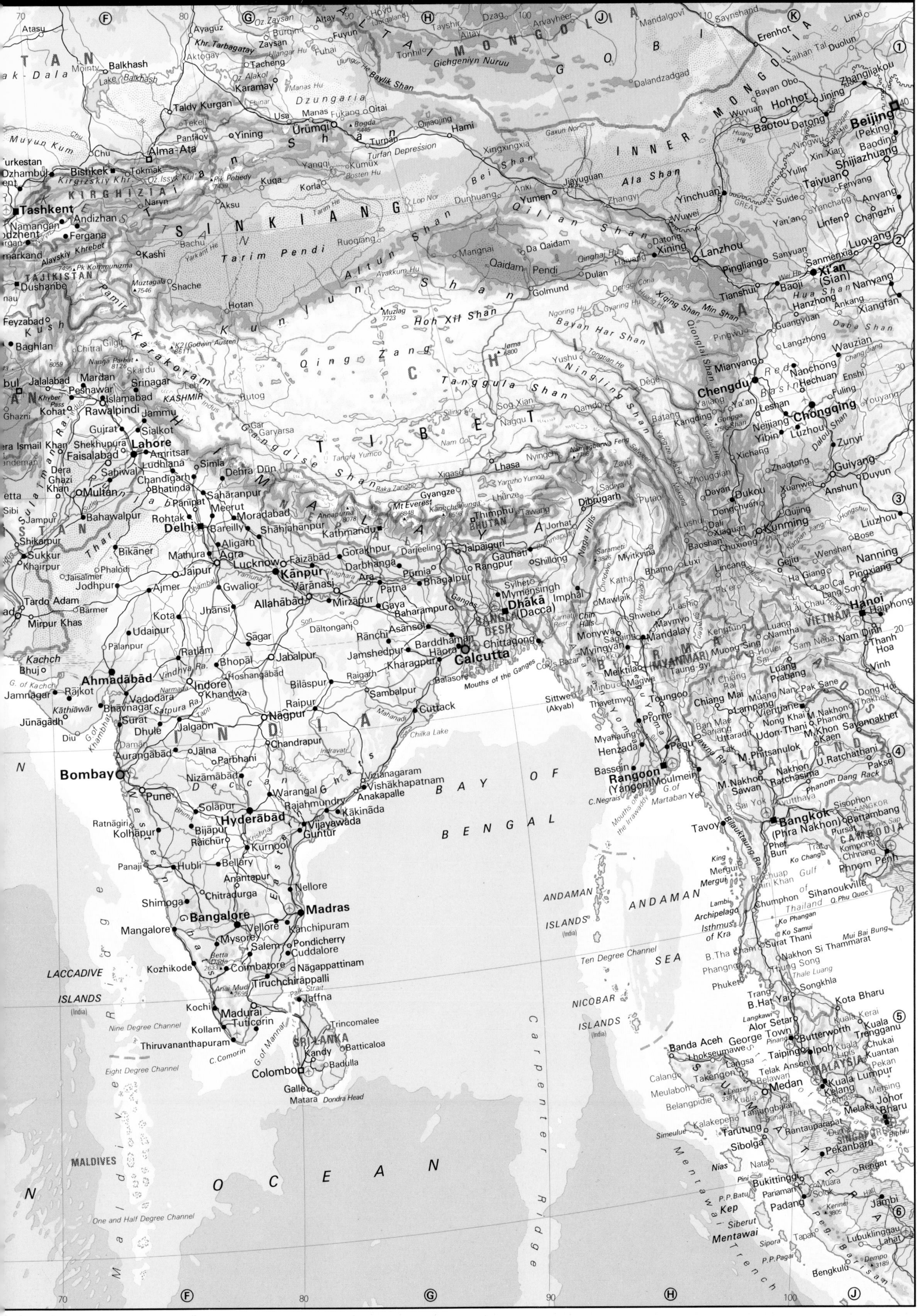
MONGOLIA
G O B I
INNER MONGOLIA
SINKIANG
Tarim Pendi
Kunlun Shan
Altun Shan
Qilian Shan
Tian Shan
Dzungaria
Turfan Depression
Qaidam Pendi
Qing Zang
TIBET
Tanggula Shan
Hoh Xil Shan
Bayan Har Shan
Gangdise Shan
HIMALAYA
Karakoram
KASHMIR
Mt Everest
Hindu Kush
CHINA
INDIA
Deccan
Western Ghats
Eastern Ghats
Thar
BHUTAN
BANGLADESH
BURMA (MYANMAR)
THAILAND
VIETNAM
CAMBODIA
LAOS
MALAYSIA
SINGAPORE
SUMATERA
SRI LANKA
BAY OF BENGAL
ANDAMAN SEA
ANDAMAN ISLANDS (India)
NICOBAR ISLANDS (India)
LACCADIVE ISLANDS (India)
MALDIVES
INDIAN OCEAN
Maldive Ridge
Carpenter Ridge
Mentawai Trench
Gulf of Thailand
Mouths of the Ganges
Mouths of the Irrawaddy
Ten Degree Channel
Nine Degree Channel
Eight Degree Channel
One and Half Degree Channel
Lake Balkhash
Beijing (Peking)
Xi'an (Sian)
Chengdu
Chongqing
Kunming
Lanzhou
Ürümqi
Lhasa
Kashi
Alma-Ata
Bishkek
Tashkent
Dushanbe
Kabul
Islamabad
Rawalpindi
Lahore
Delhi
Agra
Kanpur
Lucknow
Kathmandu
Calcutta
Dhaka (Dacca)
Ahmadabad
Bombay
Pune
Hyderabad
Bangalore
Madras
Colombo
Rangoon (Yangon)
Mandalay
Bangkok (Phra Nakhon)
Hanoi
Phnom Penh
Kuala Lumpur
Medan
Padang
Nanning
Guiyang
Taiyuan
Hohhot
Baotou
Lanzhou
Xining
Yinchuan

Haskovo Edirne Kırklareli İğneada Br. BLACK SEA Inebolu Ince Br. Sinop Zestafoni Ozurgety Batumi Akhalsikh
Babaeski Karadeniz Boğazı Bosporus Zonguldah Bartın Kuzey Anadolu Dağları Boyabat Bafra Br. Samsun
Uzunköprü Çorlu Istanbul Üsküdar Ereğli Kastamonu Terme Ünye Cam Br. Ordu Trabzon Çayeli Rize Artvin Ardahan
Tekirdağ Sea of Marmara Izmit Adapazarı Karabük Ilgaz Dağları Tosya Merzifon Giresun Tirebolu
Evros Gelibolu Gemlik Düzce Bolu Iskilip Amasya Yeşil Taşova Niksar
Eceabat Biga Bandırma Iznik Köroğlu Tepesi 2378 Çankırı Çorum Turhal Gümüşhane Mescit D. 3236 Sarıkamış Horasan
Çanakkale Gönen Bursa Inegöl Bilecik Kalecik Delice Tokat Kelkit Bayburt Kağızman
Edremit Balıkesir Eskişehir Ankara Kırıkkale Yozgat Sorgun Yıldızeli Sivas Zara Refahiye Erzincan Aşkale Erzurum Eleşkirt
Mitilíni Ayvalık Tavşanlı Kütahya Polatlı Sivrihisar Balâ Hirfanlı Brj Boğazlıyan Şarkışla Kangal Divriği Munzur Silsilesi 2160 Malazgirt Patnos
Lésvos Bergama Akhisar Emirdağ Kulu Kırşehir Gemerek Tunceli Bingöl Suphan D. 4058
Manisa Uşak Afyon Bolvadin TURKEY Kızıl Keban Br. Muş Van
Çeşme Turgutlu Izmir (Smyrna) Alaşehir Sandıklı Cihanbeyli Tuz Gölü Nevşehir Kayseri Gürün Elazığ Palu Tatvan
Khíos Sámos Ikaría Ephesus Aydın Nazilli Saraykoy Akşehir Kadınhanı Eğirdir G. Aksaray Erciyas D. 3916 Elbistan Ergani Silvan Bitlis
Bü Menderes Söke Denizli Beyşehir G. Konya Niğde Bor Göksun Malatya Atatürk Barajı Diyarbakır Dicle Batman Siirt
Milas Muğla Burdur Isparta Beyşehir Karapınar Ala D. Feke Seyhan Gölbaşı Adıyaman Hilvan Siverek Midyat Cizre
Dodecanese Köyceğiz Korkuteli Perge Çarşamba Ereğli Kahramanmaraş Besni Sirnak
Kos Fethiye Antalya Akseki Karaman Taurus Mts Pozantı Kozan Ceyhan Gaziantep Nizip Sanliurfa Mardin Nusaybin
Rhodes Manavgat Alanya Tarsus Adana Osmaniye Ceylanpınar Akçakale Al Qāmishlī
Rhodes (Ródhos) Finike Bey D. Antalya Körfezi Caga Tepe Mersin Ceyhan Kilis Jarābulus Ra's al 'Ayn Al Hasakah Zākhō
GREECE Kastellorizon Gelidonya Br. Silifke Incekum Br. Karataş Iskenderun Kor. Iskenderun Antakya A'zāz Al Bāb Manbij Buhayrat al Asad J. 'Abd al 'Aziz 920 Sinjār Tall 'Afar
Kárpathos Anamur Samandağı Idlib Aleppo (Halab) Ar Raqqah Al Khābūr Al Jazīrah Al Badī Al Hadr
Crete C. Andreas Latakia (Al Lādhiqīyah) Jisr ash Shughūr Ma'arret an Nu'mān As Sabkhah
C. Arnauti Nicosia Famagusta Bāniyās Masyāf Hamāh SYRIA Dayr az Zawr Mayādīn
CYPRUS Mt Troödos 1951 Larnaca C. Greco Ţartūs As Salamīyah Tall Kalakh Hims As Sukhnah
Limassol Tripoli (Trâblous esh Sham) 3088 Tudmur Al Bū Kamāl Euphrates Al Qā'im 'Anah Hadīthah
Mediterranean Sea Beirut (Beyrouth) Ba'albek Jebel esh Sharqi An Nabk Al Qaryatayn Tulūl ash Shāmīyah Al Qutayfah Sab' Bi'ār Muhaywir W. Hawrān
LEBANON Zahle Saida Damascus (Dimashq) Tyr 'Akko (Acre) Al Qunayţirah Az Zilaf Ar Rutbah IRAQ W. al Ghadaf
Haifa Zefat As Suwaydā' ISRAEL Dar'ā Şalkhad Badiyat ash Sham
Nazareth Irbid Netanya Mafraq Nablus Zarqa JORDAN Tel Aviv-Yafo Ashdod Amman Al Azraq Nukhayb
Baltīm Matrûh Râs el Kenâyis Alexandria (El Iskandarîya) Rashîd Dumyât Port Saïd (Bûr Sa'îd) Gaza Jerusalem 392 Dead Sea Turayf W. al Mirah Al Widyan
El Mahalla el Kubra El Mansûra Hebron Al Hadīthah An Nabk Al Harrah Al Hamad Wādī as Sirhān
Libyan Plateau Damanhûr El 'Alamein Tanta Ismâ'iliya Suez Canal El 'Arîsh Beersheba Karak Qatrāna Al Jalāmīd Badanah
W. el Natrûn Benha Zagâzîg Bitter Lakes Negev Safi Ardh es Suwwān Al 'Isāwīyah W. Ar'ar
Qattâra Depression El Giza Cairo (El Qâhira) Suez (El Suweis) W. el Brûk El Kuntilla Wādī Araba Shaubak Bāyir Al Jafr Ad Duwayd
Qara -133 Helwân Nakhl Ma'ān Naqb Ishtar Sakākah
Birkat Qârûn 'Ain Sukhna El Tîh Elat Aqaba Al Mudawwara At Tubayq Al Jawf
El Faiyûm Beni Suef 1274 SINAI Haql Mughayra Al 'Urayq
El Fashn Biba El Igma Gulf of 'Aqaba J. al Lawz 2578 Al Bi'r Al Hawjā'
Bawîti Beni Mazar Maghâgha Râs Ghârib Dahab G. Katherina 2637 Tabūk
Bahariya Oasis El Harra El Minya Sahra esh Sharqiya El Tûr Gulf of Suez Al Qalībah An Nafūd
Nile Mallawi Râs Muhammad Jubbah
Dairût Al Muwaylih Taymā' Hā'il
Farâfra Manfalût Asyût W. Qena Hurghada Dubā Harrat al 'Uwayrid Hijaz
EGYPT Abu Tig Tahta Akhmîm Bûr Safâga Jabal Shammar
Sohâg Girga El Balyana Dishna Qena Quseir Al 'Ulā SAUDI ARABIA
Mût Balât Qus Luxor El Khârga RED SEA Al Wajh Khaybar Hulayfah 'Uqlat aş Şuqūr
El-Khârga Oasis Isna Marsa Alam Umm Lajj
Bârîs Idfu W. Sha'it Ra's Abu Madd
Saad el Aali (Aswân High Dam) Aswân G. Hamâta Medina (Al Madīnah)
Libyan Desert Berenice Râs Banâs Yanbu'al Bahr
Badr Hunayn
Khazzan an-Nasr (Lake Nasser) Râs Abû Dâra Rābigh Harrat Kishb

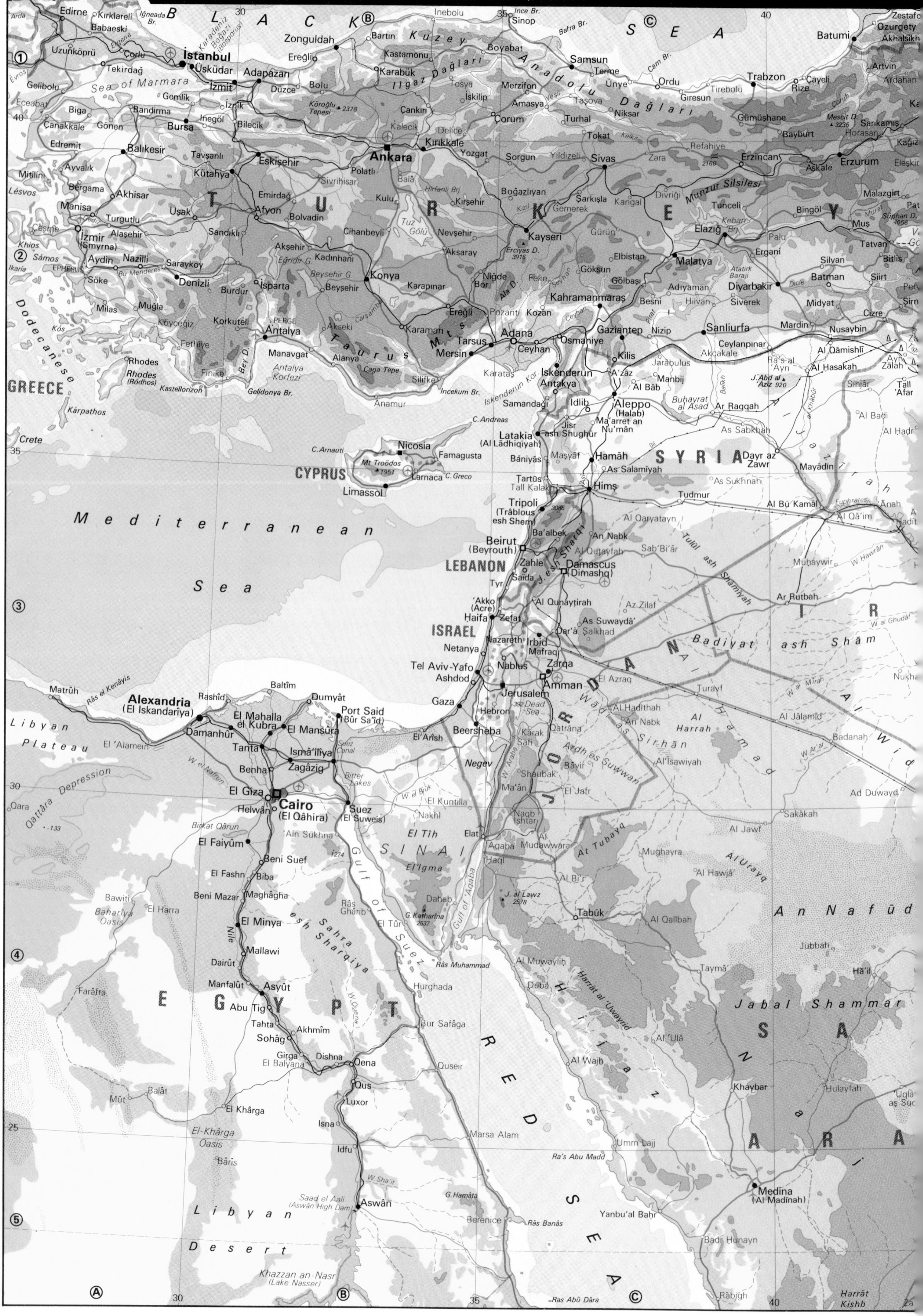

1:7.5M 0 100 200 300km 0 50 100 150 mls

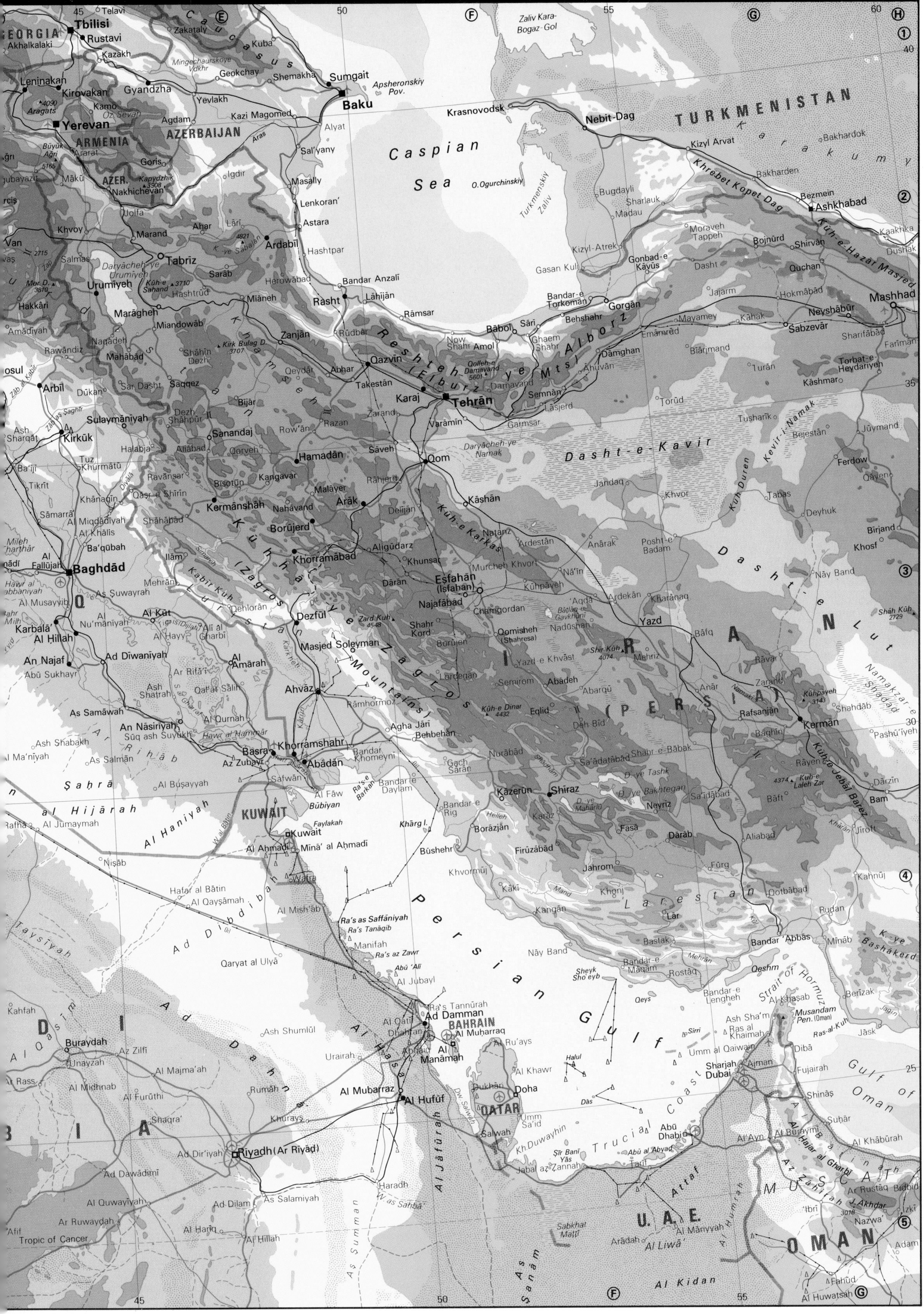
GEORGIA
Tbilisi
Rustavi
Telavi
Akhalkalaki
Zakataly
Kuba
Kazakh
Caucasus
Mingechaurskoye Vdkhr
Geokchay
Shemakha
Sumgait
Apsheronskiy Pov.
Baku
Leninakan
Kirovakan
Gyandzha
Yevlakh
Aragats
Kamo
Oz Sevan
Yerevan
Agdam
Kazi Magomed
ARMENIA
AZERBAIJAN
Aras
Alyat
Sal'yany
Goris
Mākū
AZER.
Nakhichevan
Kapydzhik
Masally
Lenkoran'
Astara
Igdir
Jolfa
Khvoy
Marand
Ahar
Lārī
Ardabīl
Hashtpar
Tabrīz
Salmās
Daryācheh-ye Urūmīyeh
Kūh-e Sahand
Sarāb
Urumīyeh
Hakkâri
Hashtrūd
Herowābād
Bandar Anzalī
Rasht
Lāhījān
Rāmsar
Mīāneh
Marāgheh
Miandowāb
Amādīyah
Naqadeh
Mahābād
Zanjān
Kirk Bulag D.
Rūdbār
Qazvīn
Now Shahr
Āmol
Bābol
Sārī
Ghaem Shahr
Behshahr
Bandar-e Torkoman
Gorgān
Reshteh-ye Alborz (Elburz Mts)
Qolleh-ye Damāvand 5601
Damavand
Tehrān
Karaj
Takestān
Abhar
Qeydar
Saqqez
Sar Dasht
Rawāndiz
Mosul
Arbīl
Dūkān
Sulaymānīyah
Kirkūk
Tuz Khurmātū
Halabja
Bijār
Sanandaj
Dezh Shāhpūr
Qorveh
Row'ān
Razan
Zarand
Sāveh
Qom
Varāmīn
Garmsar
Semnān
Lāsjerd
Dāmghan
Āhuvān
Emāmrūd
Shāhrūd
Bīārjmand
Mayamey
Kāhak
Sabzevār
Neyshābūr
Mashhad
Sharīfābād
Farīmān
Torbat-e Heydarīyeh
Kāshmar
Tūrān
Torūd
Tusharīk
Bejestān
Jūymand
Ferdows
Qāyen
Dasht-e-Kavīr
Daryācheh-ye Namak
Kevīr-i-Namak
Kūh Duren
Tabas
Deyhuk
Bīrjand
Khosf
Dasht-e Lut
Nāy Band
Shāh Kūh 2729
Hamadān
Kangavar
Ravānsar
Bīsotūn
Kermānshāh
Qasr-e Shīrīn
Khānaqīn
Malāyer
Arāk
Nahāvand
Borūjerd
Rāhjerd
Delījān
Kāshān
Kūh-e Karkas
Natanz
Ardestān
Anārak
Posht-e Badām
Jandaq
Khvor
Tikrīt
Sāmarrā'
Al Miqdādīyah
Al Khālis
Ba'qūbah
Shāhābād
Ilām
Aligūdarz
Khorramābād
Khunsar
Dārān
Esfahān (Isfahān)
Murcheh Khvort
Nā'īn
Kūhpāyeh
Ardekān
Kharānaq
Yazd
Bāfq
Najafābād
Chamgordan
Bātlāq-e Gavkhūnī
'Aqdā
Nadūshan
Baghdād
Fallūjah
Mehrān
As Suwayrah
Kabīr Kūh
Kūhhā-ye Zāgros (Zagros Mountains)
Dehlorān
Al Kūt
Al Nu'mānīyah
Al Musayyib
Karbalā'
Al Hillah
An Najaf
Abū Sukhayr
Ad Dīwānīyah
Al Hayy
Alī al Gharbī
Dezfūl
Zard Kūh 4548
Shahr Kord
Borūjen
Qomisheh (Shahresa)
Shīr Kūh 4074
Mehrīz
Yazd-e Khvāst
Masjed Soleyman
Al 'Amārah
Ar Rifā'ī
Qal'at Sālih
Ash Shatrah
Ahvāz
Lordegān
Semīrom
Ābādeh
Abarqū
Rāmhormoz
Kūh-e Dīnar 4432
Eqlīd
Deh Bīd
As Samāwah
Al Qurnah
An Nāsirīyah
Sūq ash Suyūkh
Hawr al Hammār
Agha Jārī
Behbehān
Basra
Khorramshahr
Abādān
Az Zubayr
Bandar Khomeynī
Ash Shabakh
Al Ma'nīyah
As Salmān
Ar Rihāb
Sahrā
al Hijārah
Al Busayyah
Safwān
Al Fāw
Būbīyan
Ra's-e Barkan
Bandar-e Daylam
Gach Sārān
Nūrābād
Sa'ādatābād
Shahr-e Bābak
Kāzerūn
Shīrāz
D.-ye Tashk
D.-ye Bakhtegan
Neyrīz
Sa'īdābād
Rafsanjān
Kermān
Zarand
Rāvar
Bāghīn
Rāyen
Kūh-e Laleh Zar 4374
Kūhhā-ye Jebal Barez
Bam
Dārzīn
Bāft
Jīroft
Pashū'īyeh
Shahdāb
Namakzār-e Shahdād
Kūhpāyeh 3143
KUWAIT
Faylakah
Kuwait
Al Ahmadī
Mīnā' al Ahmadī
Rafhā
Al Jumaymah
Al Haniyah
Wādī al Bātin
Khārg I.
Bandar-e Rīg
Borāzjān
Būshehr
Fīrūzābād
Fasā
Dārāb
Jahrom
Fūrg
Alīābād
Nisāb
Hafar al Bātin
Al Qaysūmah
Al Mish'āb
Khvormūj
Kākī
Kangān
Khonj
Lārestān
Lār
Qotbābād
Kahnūj
Rūdān
Bandar 'Abbās
Mīnāb
Kūh-e Bashākerd
Bastak
Ad Dibdibah
Ra's as Saffānīyah
Ra's Tanāqib
Manīfah
Ra's az Zawr
Abū 'Alī
Al Jubayl
Qaryat al Ulyā
Persian Gulf
Nāy Band
Bandar-e Maqām
Rostāq
Qeshm
Sheyk Sho'eyb
Qeys
Strait of Hormuz
Bandar-e Lengheh
Al Khasab
Musandam Pen. (Oman)
Bīrīzak
Jāsk
Ra's Tannūrah
Ad Damman
BAHRAIN
Al Muharraq
Al Manāmah
Al Qatīf
Dhahran
Abqaiq
Ash Shumlūl
Al Ru'ays
Sīrrī
Ash Sha'm
Ras al Khaimah
Umm al Qaiwain
Ras-al-Kuh
Dibā
Kahfah
Buraydah
Unayzah
Az Zilfī
Ar Rass
Al Midhnab
Al Majma'ah
Al Furūthī
Rumāh
Ad Dahnā
Al Hasā
Uraira
Al Mubarraz
Al Hufūf
Al Khawr
Dukhān
Doha
QATAR
Halul
Dās
Sharjah
Dubai
Ajmān
Fujairah
Gulf of Oman
Shināş
Suhār
Shaqrā'
Khurays
Umm Sa'īd
Salwah
Kh. Duwayhin
Trucial Coast
Abū Dhabi
Al Ayn
Al Buraymī
Al Hajar al Gharbī
Al Khābūrah
Ad Dir'iyah
Riyadh (Ar Riyād)
Ad Dawādimī
Jabal az Zannah
Şīr Banī Yās
Abū al Abyad
Tarīf
Attaf
Ar Rustāq
Bidbid
Ibrī
J. Akhdar 3018
Izkī
Nizwa'
Haradh
Al Quwayīyah
Ad Dilam
As Salamīyah
W. as Sahbā'
Al Jāfūrah
U.A.E.
Sabkhat Matti
Al Māriyyah
Arādah
Al Liwā'
Ar Ruwaydah
Al Hariq
Al Hillah
Afīf
Tropic of Cancer
As Summan
As Sanām
Al Kidan
OMAN
Adam
Fahūd
Al Huwatsah
MUSCAT
TURKMENISTAN
Karakumy
Krasnovodsk
Zaliv Kara-Bogaz-Gol
Nebit-Dag
Kizyl Arvat
Bakhardok
Bakharden
Khrebet Kopet Dag
Bezmein
Ashkhabad
Caspian Sea
O. Ogurchinskiy
Turkmenskiy Zaliv
Bugdayli
Sharlauk
Madau
Kizyl-Atrek
Gasan Kuli
Gonbad-e Kāvūs
Moraveh Tappeh
Bojnūrd
Shīrvān
Dasht
Quchan
Jajarm
Hokmābād
Kūh-e Hazār Masjed
Kaakhka
Dushak
IRAN (PERSIA)
IRAQ
SAUDI ARABIA
45
50
55
60
40
35
30
25
E
F
G
H
1
2
3
4
5

TURKMENISTAN
UZBEK.
TAJIKISTAN
CHINA
AFGHANISTAN
PAKISTAN
BALOCHISTĀN
SINDH
KHAIRPUR
BAHAWALPUR
PUNJAB
N.W. FRONTIER PROV.
JAMMU AND KASHMĪR
HIMĀCHAL PRADESH
HARYĀNA
RĀJASTHĀN
GUJARĀT
MADHYA PRADESH
MAHĀRĀSHTRA
THAR DESERT
INDIAN DESERT
HINDU KUSH
KARAKORAM
Ladākh Range
Zāskār Mountains
Siwalik
Sulaiman Range
Kirthar Range
Arāvalli Range
Sātpura Range
Vindhya Range
Malwa Plateau
Makran Coast Range
Central Makran Ra.
Toba and Kakar Ranges
Salt Ra.
Rann of Kachchh
Kāthiāwār
Gulf of Khambhāt
G. of Kachchh
Mouths of the Indus
Tropic of Cancer
ARABIAN SEA
Kabul
Islamabad
Delhi
New Delhi
Karachi
Lahore
Bombay
Ahmadābād
Hyderabad
Peshawar
Rawalpindi
Quetta
Kandahar
Srinagar
Jaipur
Agra
Indore
Bhopāl
Nāgpur
Pune (Poona)
Multan
Faisalabad
1:7.5M
0 100 200 300 km
0 50 100 150 mls

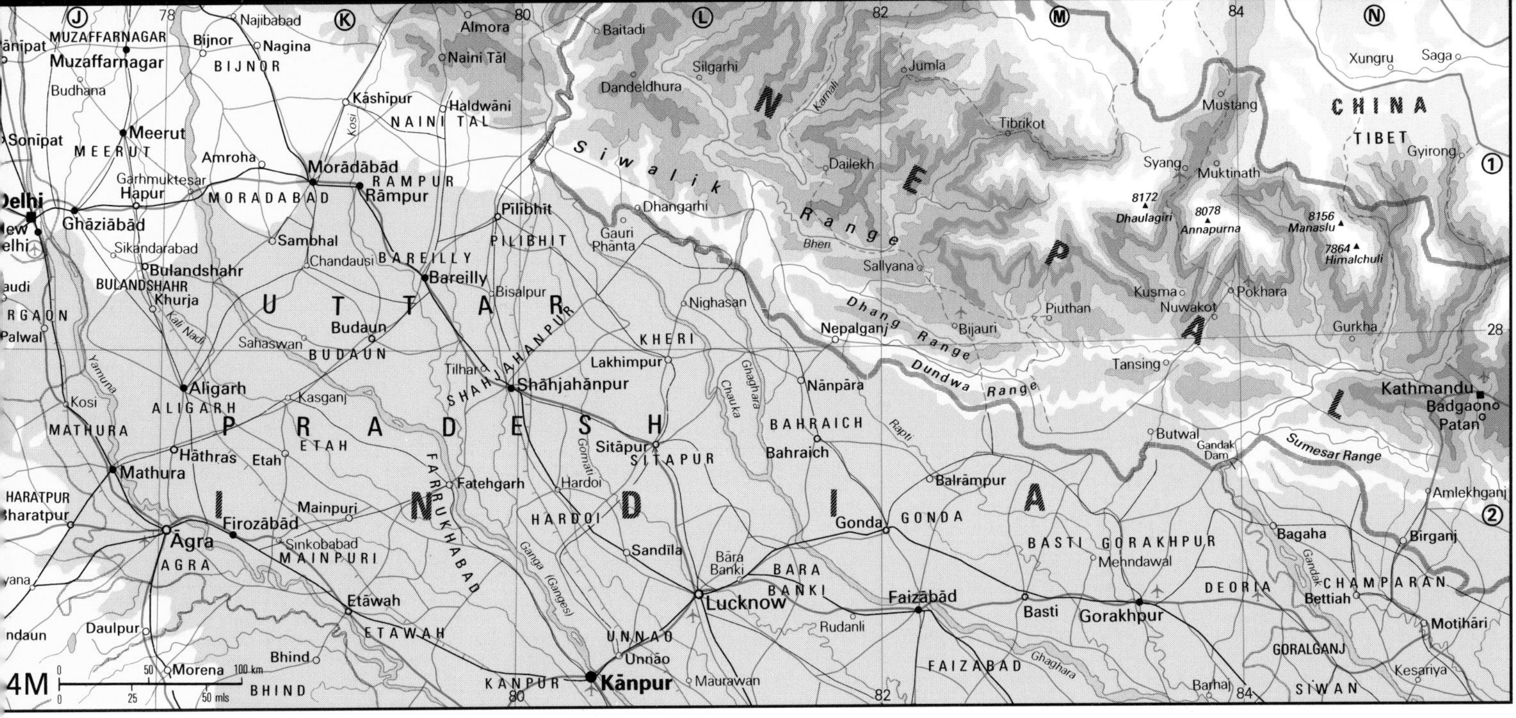
UTTAR PRADESH
INDIA
NEPAL
CHINA
TIBET
Siwalik Range
Dhang Range
Dundwa Range
Sumesar Range
Delhi
Ghāziābād
Meerut
Muzaffarnagar
MUZAFFARNAGAR
Bijnor
BIJNOR
Najibabad
Nagina
Almora
Naini Tāl
NAINI TAL
Haldwāni
Kāshipur
Sonipat
MEERUT
Hapur
Garhmuktesar
Amroha
Morādābād
MORADABAD
Rāmpur
RAMPUR
Pilibhit
PILIBHIT
Sambhal
Chandausi
Bareilly
BAREILLY
Sikandarabad
Bulandshahr
BULANDSHAHR
Khurja
Budaun
BUDAUN
Sahaswan
Aligarh
ALIGARH
Kasganj
Mathura
MATHURA
Hāthras
Etah
ETAH
Agra
AGRA
Firozābād
Mainpuri
MAINPURI
Sinkobabad
Fatehgarh
FARRUKHABAD
Etāwah
ETAWAH
Daulpur
Morena
Bhind
BHIND
Kānpur
KANPUR
Unnāo
UNNAO
Maurawan
Lucknow
BARA BANKI
Bāra Banki
Sandīla
Hardoi
HARDOI
Sitāpur
SITAPUR
Shāhjahānpur
SHAHJAHANPUR
Tilhar
Lakhimpur
KHERI
Bisalpur
Gauri Phanta
Dhangarhi
Nighasan
Nānpāra
Bahraich
BAHRAICH
Nepalganj
Bijauri
Sallyana
Dailekh
Jumla
Silgarhi
Dandeldhura
Baitadi
Tibrikot
Mustang
Syang
Muktinath
Dhaulagiri
8172
Annapurna
8078
Manaslu
8156
Himalchuli
7864
Kusma
Nuwakot
Pokhara
Piuthan
Gurkha
Tansing
Butwal
Gandak Dam
Kathmandu
Badgaon
Patan
Amlekhganj
Birganj
Xungru
Saga
Gyirong
Balrāmpur
Gonda
GONDA
BASTI
GORAKHPUR
Mehndawal
Basti
Gorakhpur
Faizābād
FAIZABAD
Rudanli
DEORIA
Bagaha
CHAMPARAN
Bettiah
Motihāri
GORALGANJ
SIWAN
Kesariya
Barhaj
Ghaghara
Rapti
Gomati
Ganga (Ganges)
Yamuna
Kali Nadi
Karnali
Chauka
Gandak
Bheri
Kosi
4M
50 100 km
25 50 mls
78
80
82
84
28
J
K
L
M
N
1
2

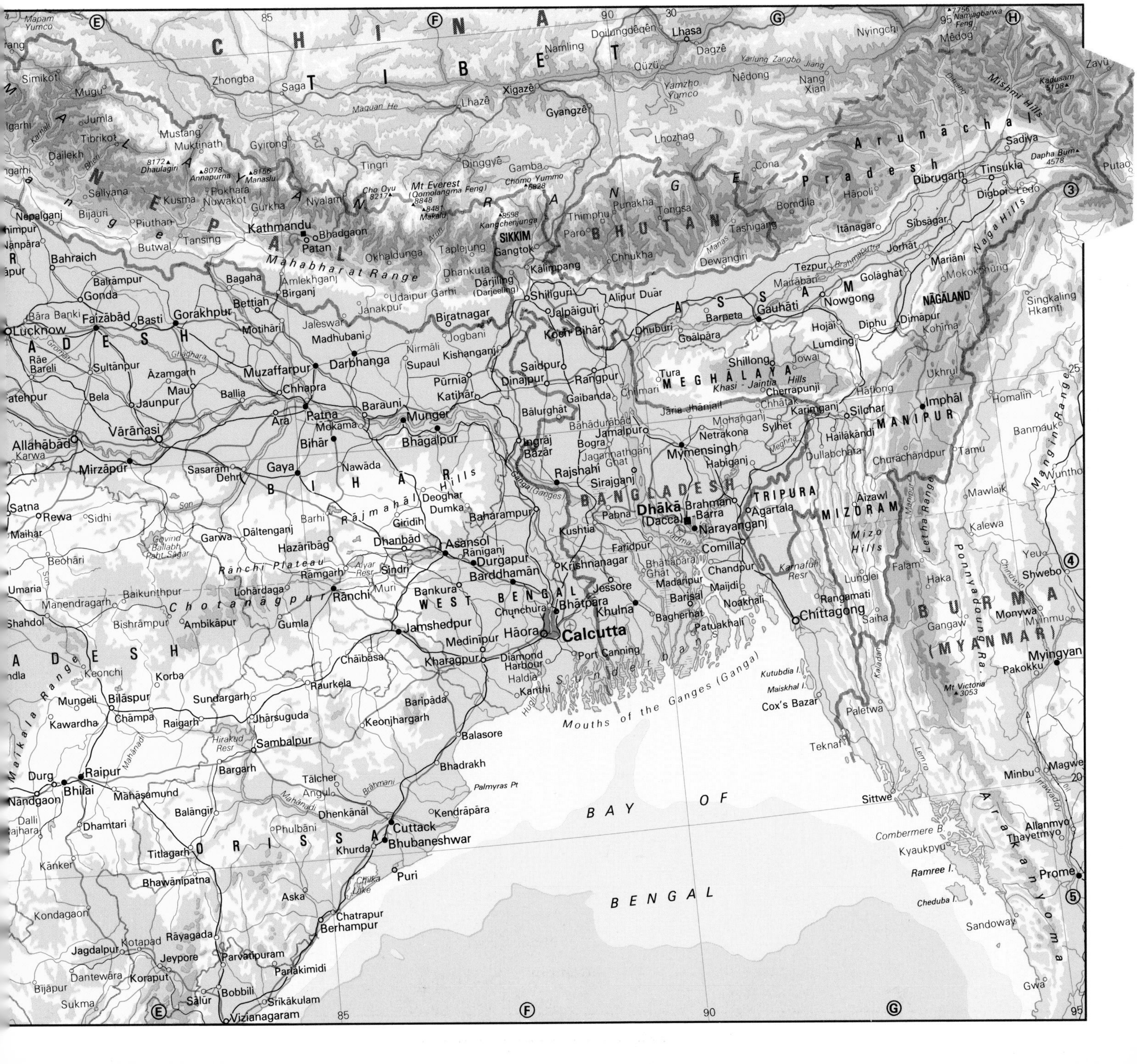
CHINA
TIBET
NEPAL
BHUTAN
SIKKIM
BANGLADESH
BURMA (MYANMAR)
Arunāchal Pradesh
NĀGĀLAND
MANIPUR
MIZORAM
TRIPURA
MEGHĀLAYA
ASSAM
BIHAR
WEST BENGAL
ORISSA
PRADESH
Mahabharat Range
Rājmahāl Hills
Rānchi Plateau
Chotanāgpur
Khasi - Jaintia Hills
Mizo Hills
Naga Hills
Mishmi Hills
Letha Range
Ponnyadaung Ra.
Mangin Range
Arakan Yoma
Maikala Range
Sundarbans
Mouths of the Ganges (Ganga)
BAY OF BENGAL
Mt Everest (Qomolangma Feng)
8848
Makalu
8481
Cho Oyu
8217
Kangchenjunga
8598
Chomo Yummo
6828
Namjagbarwa Feng
7756
Kadusam
5109
Dapha Bum
4578
Mt Victoria
3053
Lhasa
Xigazê
Gyangzê
Lhazê
Saga
Zhongba
Tingri
Dinggyê
Gamba
Namling
Qüxü
Dagzê
Nêdong
Nang Xian
Nyingchi
Mêdog
Zayü
Yamzho Yumco
Yarlung Zangbo Jiang
Maquan He
Lhozhag
Cona
Kathmandu
Bhadgaon
Patan
Pokhara
Gurkha
Nyalam
Kusma
Nuwakot
Butwal
Tansing
Piuthan
Mustang
Muktinath
Gyirong
Jumla
Tibrikot
Dailekh
Simikot
Mugu
Sallyana
Nepalganj
Bijauri
Okhaldunga
Taplejung
Dhankuta
Biratnagar
Janakpur
Udaipur Garhi
Gangtok
Dārjiling (Darjeeling)
Kālimpang
Shiliguri
Jalpāiguri
Alipur Duār
Koch Bihār
Thimphu
Paro
Punakha
Tongsa
Tashigang
Chhukha
Dewangiri
Bomdila
Itānagar
Hāpoli
Dibrugarh
Tinsukia
Sadiya
Digboi
Ledo
Sibsāgar
Jorhāt
Golāghāt
Mariāni
Mokokchūng
Tezpur
Mangaldai
Gauhāti
Barpeta
Nowgong
Dhuburi
Goālpāra
Hojāi
Lumding
Diphu
Dimāpur
Kohima
Singkaling Hkamti
Shillong
Jowai
Tura
Cherrapunji
Chhātak
Hāflong
Silchar
Karimganj
Imphāl
Ukhrul
Homalin
Hailākāndi
Churachāndpur
Tamu
Banmauk
Aizawl
Lunglei
Agartala
Sylhet
Mymensingh
Netrakona
Habiganj
Jamālpur
Bogra
Rājshāhi
Pabna
Sirajganj
Dhāka (Dacca)
Narāyanganj
Comilla
Brahmanbaria
Chandpur
Faridpur
Jessore
Khulna
Barisāl
Bagherhat
Patuakhali
Noakhāli
Maijdi
Chittagong
Rangamati
Cox's Bazar
Kutubdia I.
Maiskhal I.
Teknaf
Paletwa
Sittwe
Kyaukpyu
Ramree I.
Cheduba I.
Sandoway
Gwa
Combermere B.
Kalewa
Mawlaik
Yeu
Shwebo
Monywa
Myinmu
Myingyan
Pakokku
Gangaw
Falam
Haka
Minbu
Magwe
Allanmyo
Thayetmyo
Prome
Saiha
Kaladan
Lemro
Manipur
Bahraich
Balrāmpur
Gonda
Bāra Banki
Faizābād
Basti
Gorakhpur
Lucknow
Rāe Bareli
Sultānpur
Āzamgarh
Mau
Jaunpur
Bela
Allahābād
Karwa
Vārānasi
Mirzāpur
Ballia
Chhapra
Ara
Patna
Mokāma
Bihār
Gaya
Nawāda
Sasarām
Dehri
Motihāri
Bettiah
Bagaha
Amlekhganj
Birganj
Jaleswar
Madhubani
Darbhanga
Muzaffarpur
Barauni
Munger
Bhāgalpur
Nirmāli
Supaul
Kishanganj
Jogbani
Pūrnia
Katihār
Saidpur
Dinājpur
Rangpur
Gaibanda
Chilmari
Bālurghāt
Ingrāj Bāzār
Deoghar
Dumka
Giridih
Dhanbād
Asansol
Raniganj
Durgāpur
Barddhamān
Bāharampur
Kushtia
Krishnanagar
Bhātpāra
Chunchura
Hāora
Calcutta
Port Canning
Diamond Harbour
Haldia
Kānthi
Medinīpur
Kharagpur
Bankura
Jamshedpur
Chāibāsa
Rānchi
Muri
Sindri
Ramgarh
Hazāribāg
Dāltenganj
Garwa
Lohārdaga
Gumla
Rewa
Sidhi
Satna
Maihar
Beohāri
Umaria
Baikunthpur
Manendragarh
Bishrāmpur
Ambikāpur
Shahdol
Keonchi
Korba
Bilāspur
Mungeli
Chāmpa
Kawardha
Raigarh
Sundargarh
Jhārsuguda
Raurkela
Baripāda
Keonjhargarh
Balasore
Bhadrakh
Sambalpur
Hirakud Resr
Bargarh
Tālcher
Angul
Dhenkānāl
Cuttack
Bhubaneshwar
Kendrāpāra
Palmyras Pt
Khurda
Puri
Chilka Lake
Aska
Chatrapur
Berhampur
Parlākimidi
Srikākulam
Bobbili
Sālūr
Vizianagaram
Pārvatipuram
Koraput
Jeypore
Rāyagada
Kotapad
Jagdalpur
Dantewāra
Bijāpur
Sukma
Kondagaon
Bhawānipatna
Titlagarh
Kānker
Balāngir
Phulbāni
Mahāsamund
Dhamtari
Raipur
Bhilai
Durg
Nāndgaon
Dalli Rajhara
Mahānadi
Brahmani
Son
Gomati
Ghaghara
Ganga (Ganges)
Padma
Meghna
Jāria Jhānjail
Manas
Brahmaputra
Arun
Karnaphuli Resr
Alyar Resr
Gevind Ballabh Pant Sāgar
Mapam Yumco
85
90
95
25
20
30
E
F
G
H
3
4
5

A
B
C
D
E
1
2
3
4
15
20
10
75
80
85
95
Tropic of Cancer
GUJARĀT
Mahesāna
Himatnagar
Kadi
Gāndhinagar
Ahmadābād
Nadiād
Petlād
Vadodara
Jambusar
Bhāvnagar
Bharūch
Pālitāna
Mahuva
Sūrat
Navsāri
Valsād
Damān
(G.D. & D.)
Silvassa
Gulf of Khambhat
Dāhod
Godhra
Jhābua
Dabhoi
Rājpipla
Bānswāra
Jaora
Ratlām
Ujjain
Dewās
Indore
Mhow
Dhār
Barwāh
Sanāwad
Barwāni
Khargon
Sendwha
Nandurbār
Burhānpur
Khandwa
Harda
Hoshangābād
Shājāpur
Shujālpur
Vidisha
Bhopāl
Sihora
Umaria
Jabalpur
Shahdol
Narsimhapur
MADHYA PRADESH
Vindhya Range
Sātpura Range
Mahadeo Hills
Maikala Range
Mandla
Nainpur
Seoni
Bālāghāt
Tirodi
Gondia
Chhindwāra
Betūl
Achalpur
Manendragarh
Baikunthpur
Chota Nagpur
Bishrāmpur
Ambikāpur
Keonchi
Korba
Mungeli
Bilāspur
Chāmpa
Kawardha
Raigarh
Lohārdaga
Rāmgarh
Rānchi
Sindri
Muri
Bankura
Gumla
Jamshedpur
Chāibāsa
Raurkela
Sundargarh
Jhārsuguda
Baripāda
Keonjhargarh
Hirakud Resr
Sambalpur
Balasore
Bhadrakh
Bargarh
Tālcher
Angul
Brāhmani
Mahanadi
Dhenkānāl
Kendrāpāra
Balāngir
Mahāsamund
Raipur
Bhilai
Durg
Raj Nāndgaon
Dalli Rajhara
Dhamtari
Kānker
Titlāgarh
ORISSA
Phulbāni
Cuttack
Bhubaneshwar
Khurda
Puri
Chilka Lake
Aska
Chatrapur
Berhampur
Bhawānipatna
Kondagaon
Kotapad
Rāyagada
Jagdalpur
Jeypore
Koraput
Dantewāra
Parvatipuram
Parlākimidi
Sukma
Bijāpur
Bobbili
Sālūr
Eastern Ghats
Srīkākulam
Vizianagaram
Vishākhapatnam
Anakāpalle
Narsipatnam
Tuni
Kākināda
Yanam
Bhadrāchalam
Kottagūdem
Rājahmundry
Bhīmavaram
Elūru
Vijayawada
Machilīpatnam
Tenāli
Guntūr
Chilakalūrupet
Bāpatla
Chīrāla
Ongole
Kandukūr
Kavali
Nellore
Penner
Gūdūr
Sri Kālahasti
Pulicat L.
Tirupati
Venkatagiri
Madras
Coromandel Coast
BAY OF BENGAL
Tāpi
Kāmthi
Tumsar
Bhandāra
Nāgpur
Umred
Wardha
Hinganghāt
Amrāvati
Akot
Akola
Khāmgaon
Malkāpur
Buldāna
Bhusāwal
Jalgaon
Amalner
Dhule
Malegaon
Chālisgaon
Mehekar
Kāranja
Wāshim
Yavatmāl
Rājura
Chandrapur
Penganga
Manmād
Nāsik
Deolāli
Aurangābād
Kopargaon
Jālna
Hingoli
Pusad
Ādilābād
Sangamner
Godāvari
MAHĀRĀSHTRA
Thāne
Kalyān
Bombay
Ahmadnagar
Bīr
Parbhani
Purna
Nānded
Nirmal
Belampalli
Sironcha
Mancherāl
Jagtial
Nizāmābād
Bodhan
Parli
Lonāvale
Pune (Poona)
Daund
Alībāg
Udgir
Lātūr
Karimnagar
Siddipet
Warangal
Godāvari
Yellandu
Sabari
Mahād
Wai
Bārāmati
Phaltan
Srīvardhan
Barsi
Koyna Resr
Sātāra
Pandharpur
Solāpur
Manjra
Bīdar
Sangāreddi
Bhongir
Chiplūn
Karād
Vite
Homnābād
Akalkot
Gulbarga
Hyderābād
Ratnāgiri
Shahābād
Tāndūr
Nalgonda
Suriapet
Khammam
Sāngli
Miraj
Kolhāpur
Ichalkaranji
Bijāpur
Yādgir
Nārāyanpet
Mahbūbnagar
ANDHRA PRADESH
Krishna
Shorāpur
Jamkhandi
Mācherla
Wanparti
Rāichur
Nallamala Range
Narasarāopet
Mālvan
Vengurla
Bāgalkot
Guledagudda
Belgaum
Gajendragarh
Kurnool
Ādoni
Tungabhadra
Nandyāl
Dhone
Goa, Daman & Diu
Panaji
Madgaon
KARNĀTAKA
Gadag
Koppal
Hubli
Dandeli
Hospet
Bellary
Guntakal
Gooty
Giddalūr
Kani Giri
Kārwār
Hāveri
Swāmihalli
Tādpatri
Proddatūr
Kumta
Sirsi
Rānibennur
Hirihar
Kotturu
Rāyadurg
Anantapur
Dāvangere
Kalyandurg
Dhamavaram
Cuddapah
Bhatkal
Jog Falls
Shimoga
Chitradurga
Kadiri
Bhadrāvati
Tarikere
Hindupur
Coondapoor
Bhadra Resr
Sira
Kadūr
Arsikere
Tumkūr
Chik Ballāpur
Chittoor
Arakkonam
Udupi
Kārkal
Chikmagalūr
Hassan
Tiptūr
Dod Ballāpur
Kolār
ARABIAN SEA
Mangalore
Bangalore
Kolār Gold Fields
Vellore
Kānchipuram
Hole Narsipur
Mandya
Ambūr
Kāsaragod
Madikeri
Krishnagiri
Javadi Hills
Tiruppattūr
Mysore
Tiruvannāmalai
Tindivanam
Nanjangūd
Dharmapuri
Cannanore
Tellicherry
Mahe
Chāmrājnagar
Stanley Resr
Villupuram
Pondicherry
Badagara
Mettūr
Salem
Cuddalore
Doda Betta 2636
Lakshadweep
(Laccadive Islands)
(India)
Kozhikode
Ootacamund
Coonoor
Nilgiri Hills
Erode
Vriddhāchalam
Chidambaram
Beypore
Coimbatore
TAMIL NĀDU
Kumbakonam
Androth
Ponnāni
Shoranūr
Pālghāt
Tiruppur
Cauvery
Kāraikāl
Nāgappattinam
Malabar Coast
Trichūr
Pollāchi
Tiruchchirāppalli
Thanjāvūr
Mannārgudi
Anaimalai Hills
Palani
Dindigul
Pudukkottai
Pt Calimera
Kodikkarai
Kalpeni
Bodināyakkanūr
Kochi
Ernākulam
Vembanad L.
Kambam
Madurai
Palk Strait
Pt Pedro
Kottayam
Alleppey
Virudunagar
Aruppukkottai
Paramakkudi
Jaffna
Rājapālaiyam
Rāmanāthapuram
Nine Degree Channel
Kāyankulam
Puliyangudi
Tenkāsi
Adam's Bridge
Talaimannar
Mannar
Mullaittvu
Kollam
Tirunelveli
Tuticorin
Palayankottai
Gulf of Mannār
Vavuniya
SRI LANKA
Trincomalee
Thiruvananthapuram
Tiruchchendūr
Havankulam
Anuradhapura
Minicoy
Nāgercoil
Kanniyākumari
C.Comorin
Puttalam
Dambulla
Batticaloa
CEYLON
Eight Degree Channel
Chilaw
Kurunegala
Matale
Negombo
Kandy
Colombo
Gampola
Badulla
Adam's Pk 2243
Nuwara-Eliya
Dehiwala-Mt Lavinia
Moratuwa
Ratnapura
Opanake
MALDIVES
Ambalangoda
Galle
Hambantota
Matara
Dondra Hd
Preparis I.
Preparis South Channel
Gt Coco I.
(Burma)
Coco Channel
North Andaman
Karen
Middle Andaman
ANDAMAN ISLANDS
(India)
Ritchie's Archipelago
South Andaman
N. Sentinel
Port Blair
Rutland
Duncan Passage
Palalankwe
Little Andaman
Ignoitijala
Ten Degree Channel
Car Nicobar
Batti Malv
Chaura
Tillanchong
Teressa
Camorta
Katchall
Nancowry
NICOBAR ISLANDS
(India)
Sombrero Channel
Little Nicobar
Great Nicobar
Bananga
at the same scale
1:7.5M
0
100
200
300 km
50
150 mls

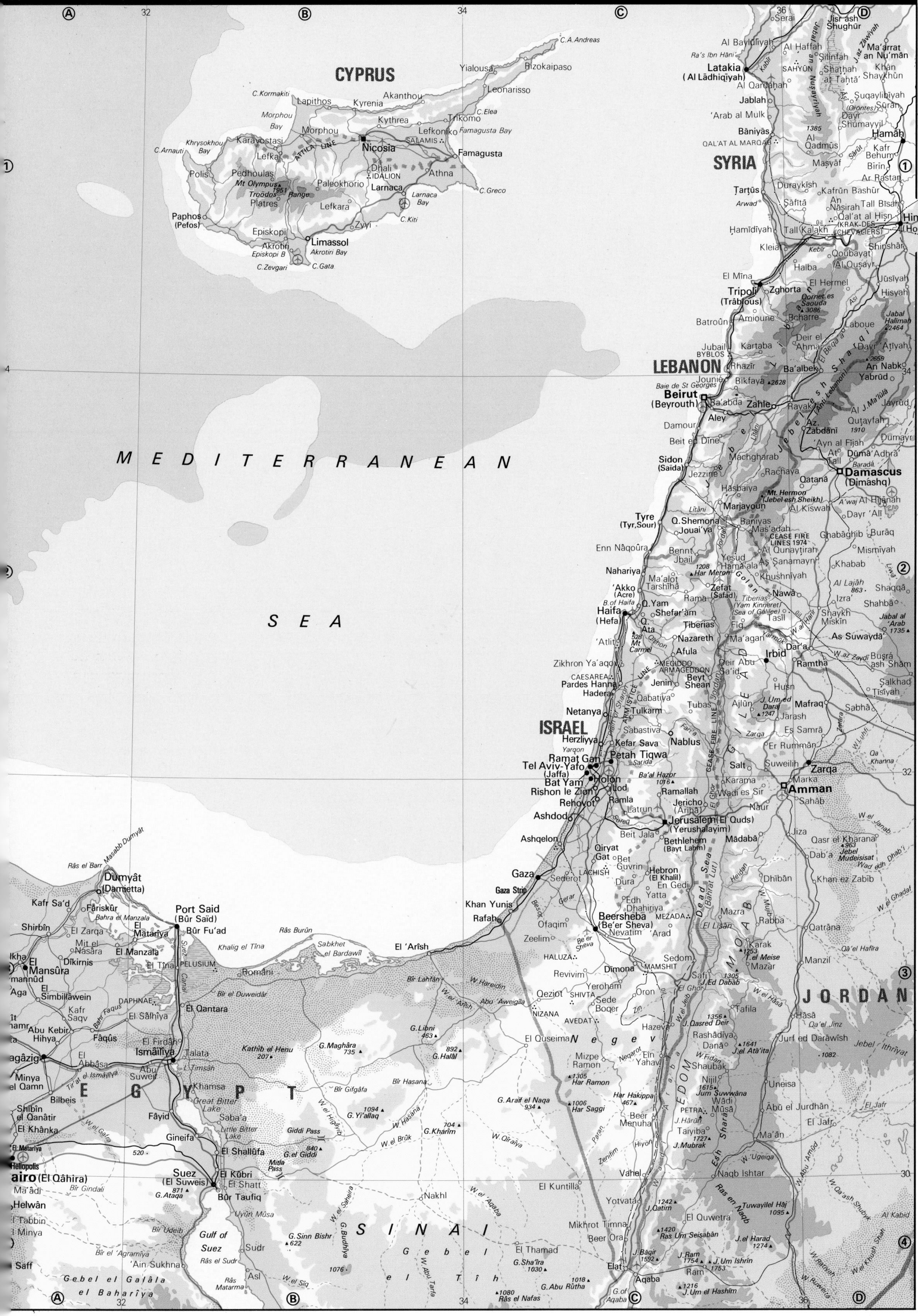

1:2.5M
0 25 50 75 100 km
0 25 50 mls

A 30 B 20 10 C 0 D 10 E F 20 G 30 H 40 J 50 K 60 L 70 M

NORWAY FINLAND
Oslo SWEDEN Helsinki
Stockholm Tallinn St Petersburg (Leningrad) Nizhniy Novgorod Magnitogorsk
EST. Volga
Edinburgh North DENMARK Göteborg LAT. Riga Samara
IRELAND Sea Copenhagen Baltic Sea LITH. RUSSIAN FEDERATION KAZAKHSTAN
Dublin Hamburg Gdansk RUS. FED. Vilnius Minsk Moscow Ural Lake Balkha
UNITED KINGDOM NETH. Berlin BELARUS (BELORUSSIA) Syr Darya
London The Hague GERMANY Wisla Warsaw Khar'kov Volgograd Aral Sea UZBEKISTAN Tashkent
Brussels BELG. Bonn POLAND Kiev Amu Darya
Lux. Prague Cracow UKRAINE Volga
Paris CZECH REP. SLOVAKIA Rostov Don TURKMENISTAN Ashkhabad
Berne SWITZ. Munich Vienna Bratislava MOLD. Odessa Caspian Sea
Bordeaux FRANCE AUSTRIA HUNGARY Budapest ROMANIA Black Sea GEO. Tbilisi AZER. Baku Mashhad
Milan SL. Belgrade Bucharest Istanbul ARM. Tabriz AFGHANISTAN
Marseilles ITALY CR. B.-H. YUG. Sofia BULGARIA Tehrān
Corsica Sarajevo Ankara
Madrid Barcelona Rome Naples Tiranë MAC. Skopje GREECE TURKEY IRAN
Lisbon PORTUGAL SPAIN Sardinia Adriatic Sea Athens Nicosia SYRIA Baghdād
Oporto Ebro Balearic Is. Mediterranean Sea CYPRUS LEB. Damascus IRAQ Shīrāz
Tajo Sicily Crete Beirut ISR. Amman Basra
Madeira (Port.) Tangiers Algiers Skikda Annaba Tunis Malta Jerusalem JORDAN KUWAIT Kuwait Persian Gulf
Rabat Fès Oran Constantine TUNISIA Tripoli Alexandria Port Said SAUDI BAHRAIN Abu Dhabi
Canary Is. (Sp.) Casablanca Oujda Sfax Misrātah Cairo Suez El Faiyūm ARABIA QATAR Doha UNITED ARAB EMIRATES Muscat
La Ayoun Marrakesh Agadir MOROCCO Béchar Touggourt Benghāzi Tobruk El Minya Tabuk Medina Riyadh OMAN
Tarfaya Bir Moghrein Ouargla Ghadamis Asyūt Nile Riyadh
Tropic of Cancer ALGERIA Ghāt LIBYA EGYPT Aswān L. Nasser Mecca (Makkah) Jiddah Kuria Muria Is.
Western Sahara Timimoun In Salah Sabhā Wadi Halfa RED SEA
Zouérate F'dérik Reggane Tamanrasset Port Sudan YEMEN San'ā Socotra (Yemen)
Nouâdhibou Atar SAHARA Atbara Aden Gulf of Aden
MAURITANIA Tombouctou Omdurman Khartoum Kassala Asmara DJIBOUTI Djibouti
Nouakchott Agadez NIGER L. Chad CHAD Wad Medani ERITREA Hargeysa
St-Louis Senegal NIGER Zinder Ndjamena El Obeid Blue Nile Dire Dawa
Dakar Kayes MALI Niamey Kano SUDAN Wad Medani Ādīs Ābeba Jimma SOMALIA
THE GAMBIA Banjul Tambacounda BURKINA Ouagadougou Kaduna Maiduguri White Nile Wau ETHIOPIA Mogadishu (Muqdisho)
GUINEA BISSAU Bissau Bamako Bobo Dioulasso Jos NIGERIA Juba Gulu L. Turkana Marka
GUINEA Mamou Kankan BENIN Ilorin Niger Abuja CENTRAL Bangassou UGANDA Kismaayo
Conakry SIERRA LEONE Kumasi TOGO Ogbomosho Enugu AFRICAN REPUBLIC Kampala L. Albert Nairobi INDIAN
Freetown Bo IVORY COAST GHANA Porto Novo Onitsha Ngaoundéré Bangui Kisangani Entebbe KENYA Seychelles Amirante Is.
Monrovia Bouaké Accra Lagos Aba Garoua Zaire (Congo) Goma L. Edward Lake Victoria Mombasa SEYCHELLES OCEAN
LIBERIA Yamoussoukro Lomé Port Harcourt CAMEROON Boundi Bambari Kindu RWANDA Kigali Mwanza SEYCHELLES Aldabra Is.
Buchanan Abidjan Douala Yaoundé Bangui Mbandaka BURUNDI Bujumbura Arusha Dodoma
Gulf of Guinea Bioco (Malabo) EQUAT. GUINEA Bata Libreville Congo ZAIRE Kigoma Kalemie TANZANIA Dar es Salaam Farquhar Is.
Ascension (U.K.) Príncipe SÃO TOMÉ & PRINCIPE Bandundu Ilebo Lake Tanganyika Zanzibar
São Tomé GABON Brazzaville Kikwit Mbuji Mayi L. Mweru Mbala Mbeya Ruvuma COMOROS
Annobon (Eq. Gl) Lambaréné CONGO Kinshasa Kananga Kamina L. Bangweulu Lilongwe Lake Nyasa Pemba Antseranana Tromelin (Fr.)
Equator Pointe Noire Matadi Kasai Kolwezi Likasi MALAWI Lichinga Mayotte (Fr.) Antananarivo
Cabinda (Ang.) Luanda Malanje Kuito Lubumbashi Ndola Lilongwe Nampula Mahajanga MADAGASCAR
SOUTH Lobito Cubango Kasai ZAMBIA Lusaka Blantyre Zomba Moçambique Toamasina
ATLANTIC St Helena (U.K.) Namibe Lubango ANGOLA Zambezi Livingstone Harare MOZAMBIQUE Quelimane Mozambique Channel MAURITI
Huambo Kunene L. Kariba Hwange ZIMBABWE Mutare Sofala (Beira) Fianarantsoa Réunion (Fr.)
OCEAN Tsumeb Otjiwarongo Gweru Bulawayo Limpopo Inhambane Toliara
Walvis Bay Windhoek BOTSWANA Francistown Serowe Limpopo Xai Xai
NAMIBIA Gaborone Pietersburg Maputo
Tropic of Capricorn Lüderitz Keetmanshoop Johannesburg Mbabane SWAZILAND
Grünau Kimberley Pretoria
Welkom Bloemfontein Maseru LESOTHO Pietermaritzburg
SOUTH AFRICA Orange Durban
Bitterfontein East London
Paarl Worcester Port Elizabeth
Cape Town Mossel Bay

Tristan da Cunha (U.K.)

1:40M 0 400 800 1200 1600 km / 0 400 800 mls

SOUTH AFRICA
NAMIBIA
BOTSWANA
ZIMBABWE
MOZAMBIQUE
LESOTHO
SWAZILAND
ATLANTIC
OCEAN
INDIAN
OCEAN
NORTHERN TRANSVAAL
EASTERN TRANSVAAL
NORTH WEST
ORANGE FREE STATE
KWAZULU
NATAL
NORTHERN CAPE
WESTERN CAPE
EASTERN CAPE
Kalahari
Desert
Central Kalahari Game Reserve
Gemsbok National Park
Kalahari Gemsbok Nat. Park
Kruger National Park
Tropic of Capricorn
Pretoria
Johannesburg
Soweto
Durban
Pietermaritzburg
Bloemfontein
Kimberley
Port Elizabeth
East London
Cape Town
Windhoek
Gaborone
Maputo
Maseru
Mbabane
Upington
Lüderitz
Walvis Bay
Swakopmund
Keetmanshoop
Welkom
Pietersburg
Nelspruit
Mafikeng
Beaufort West
George
Knysna
Mossel Bay
Graaff-Reinet
Grahamstown
Richard's Bay
Port Shepstone
Orange
Vaal
Limpopo
Molopo
Great Karoo
Little Karoo
Drakensberg
C. Agulhas
Cape of Good Hope
Table Mtn.

1:7.5M 0 100 200 300 km
0 50 100 150 mls

40N 30W

Azores (Açores) (Portugal)
at the same scale

Flores
São Jorge
Faial
Pico
Terceira
Angra Do Heroismo
São Miguel
Ponta Delgada
Formigas
Santa Maria

Madeira (Portugal)
Porto Santo
Funchal
Deserta Grande

Canary Islands (Islas Canarias) (Spain)
Santa Cruz De La Palma
La Palma
Gomera
Hierro
Tenerife
Santa Cruz De Tenerife
Las Palmas De Gran Canaria
Gran Canaria
Lanzarote
Arrecife
Fuerteventura
Pto Del Rosario

PORTUGAL
Lisbon (Lisboa)
Beja
Faro
C. de S. Vincente
Huelva
Cádiz
Tangier (Tanger)
Larache

SPAIN
Badajoz
Ciudad Real
Córdoba
Seville (Sevilla)
Granada
Málaga
Almería
Murcia
Alicante
Albacete
Cartagena
BALEARIC ISLANDS (Islas Baleares)
Ibiza
MEDITERRANEAN

Sardinia (Sardegna)
Cagliari

Gibraltar (U.K.)
Ceuta (Sp)
Tetouan
Melilla (Sp.)
Al Hoceima
Oran
Mostaganem
Algiers (Alger)
Cherchell
Blida
Tizi Ouzou
Bejaïa (Bougie)
Skikda (Philippeville)
La Galite
Annaba (Bône)
Bizerte
Tunis

MOROCCO
Casablanca (Dar-el-Beida)
El Jadida
Rabat
Kenitra
Meknès
Fès
Safi
Essaouira
Marrakech
Agadir
Tiznit
Ksar-El-Kebir
Taza
Oujda
Tlemcen
Sidi-bel-Abbès
Mascara
Tiaret
Saïda
Djelfa
Laghouat
Ghardaïa

TUNISIA
Constantine
Souk Ahras
Sétif
Batna
Biskra
Touggourt
Ouargla
El Oued
Gafsa
Gabès
Sfax
Kairouan
Sousse

ALGERIA
Béchar
Adrar
In Salah
Reggane
Timimoun
El Golea
El Gassi
Ghadames
Ghat
Djanet
Tamanrasset
Hoggar
Tahat 2918 (Ahaggar)
In Ecker
Idelès

Tropic of Cancer

Tanezrouft
Tessalit
Bidon 5 (Ruins)
Silet
Abalessa

WESTERN SAHARA
Dakhla
Laâyoune
Smara
Bir Moghrein
Zouérate
Fdérik
Tourine
Atar
Chinguetti
Ouadâne

MAURITANIA
Nouadhibou
Nouakchott
Rosso
Akjoujt
Tidjikja
Tichitt
Néma
Tombouctou
Aïoun El Atrouss
Kiffa
Kaédi

MALI
Tombouctou
Gao
Gourma Rharous
Bourem
Ansongo
Kidal
Aguelhok

NIGER
Agadez
Tahoua
In Guezzam
Iférouane

SENEGAL
St-Louis
Dakar
Thiès
Diourbel
Kaolack
Tambacounda
Linguère

THE GAMBIA
Banjul

GUINEA-BISSAU
Bissau

GUINEA
Conakry
Labé
Kankan
Mamou
Kindia

SIERRA LEONE
Freetown
Makeni
Bo
Kenema

LIBERIA
Monrovia
Buchanan
Greenville
Harper

IVORY COAST (CÔTE D'IVOIRE)
Abidjan
Yamoussoukro
Bouaké
Man
Daloa

BURKINA
Ouagadougou
Bobo Dioulasso
Koudougou

GHANA
Accra
Kumasi
Sekondi
Takoradi
Cape Coast
Tamale

MALI
Bamako
Ségou
Mopti
Sikasso
San

BENIN

NIGERIA
Lagos
Ibadan
Abuja
Kano
Kaduna
Zaria
Katsina
Sokoto
Maiduguri
Ilorin
Ogbomosho
Oshogbo
Ife
Abeokuta
Benin City
Enugu
Onitsha
Aba
Port Harcourt
Calabar
Makurdi
Jos
Bauchi
Minna
Lafia

Niamey
Maradi
Zinder

Bight of Benin

CAMEROON
Douala
Yaoundé
Mt Cameroon 4095

EQUATORIAL GUINEA
Malabo
Bata

S.TOME & PRINCIPE
Libreville

GABON

Bight of Biafra

GULF OF GUINEA

CAPE VERDE
25W
Sto Antão
S Vicente
S Nicolau
Sal
Boa Vista
Maio
S Tiago
Fogo
Brava
Praia
at the same scale

1:15M
0 200 400 600 km
0 100 200 300 mls

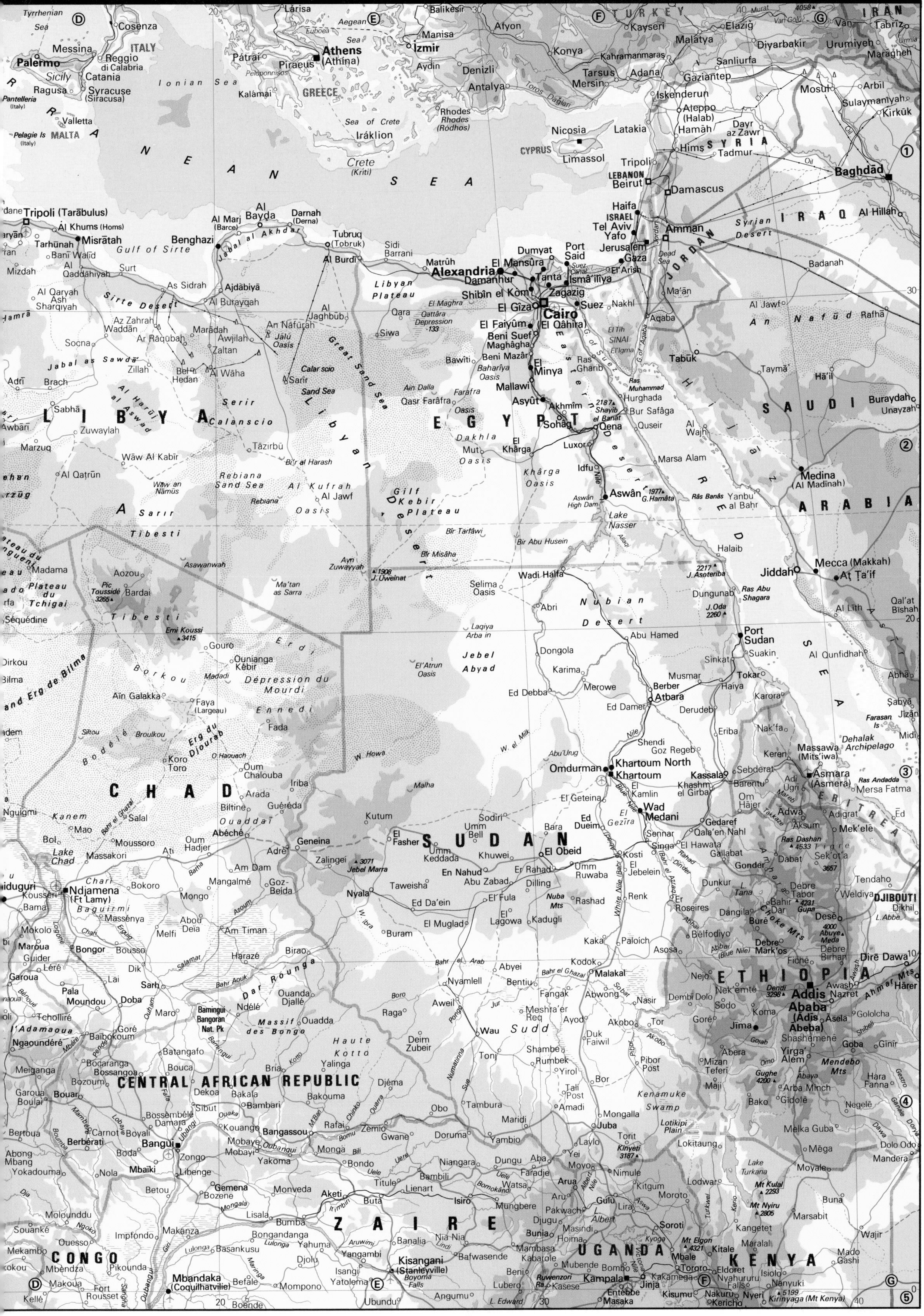

Tyrrhenian Sea
Cosenza
Messina
ITALY
Reggio di Calabria
Palermo
Sicily
Catania
Ragusa
Syracuse (Siracusa)
Pantelleria (Italy)
Valletta
Pelagie Is (Italy)
MALTA
Larisa
Aegean Sea
Euboea
Athens (Athína)
Pátrai
Piraeus
Peloponnisos
Ionian Sea
Kalámai
GREECE
Sea of Crete
Iráklion
Crete (Kriti)
Balikesir
Manisa
Izmir
Aydin
Afyon
Denizli
Antalya
Toros Dağlari
Rhodes
Rhodes (Ródhos)
TURKEY
Kayseri
Konya
Kahramanmaraş
Tarsus
Mersin
Adana
Elaziğ
Malatya
Diyarbakir
Sanliurfa
Gaziantep
Iskenderun
Van
IRAN
Tabriz
Urumiyeh
Maragheh
Mosul
Arbil
Sulaymaniyah
Kirkuk
Aleppo (Halab)
Hamah
Dayr az Zawr
Hims
SYRIA
Tadmur
Nicosia
CYPRUS
Limassol
Latakia
Tripoli
LEBANON
Beirut
Damascus
Baghdad
Haifa
ISRAEL
Tel Aviv Yafo
Jerusalem
Amman
JORDAN
Syrian Desert
IRAQ
Al Hillah
Gaza
El 'Arish
Dead Sea
MEDITERRANEAN SEA
Tripoli (Tarābulus)
Al Khums (Homs)
Misrātah
Tarhūnah
Banī Walīd
Mizdah
Al Qaddāhiyah
Benghazi
Al Marj (Barce)
Al Bayda
Darnah (Derna)
Jabal al Akhdar
Gulf of Sirte
Surt
Tubruq (Tobruk)
Al Burdī
Sidi Barrani
Matrûh
Alexandria
Damanhûr
El Mansûra
Dumyat
Port Said
Suez Canal
Tanta
Ismâ'ilîya
Zagazig
Shibîn el Kôm
El Gîza
Cairo (El Qâhira)
Suez
Nakhl
Aqaba
Badanah
Ma'ān
Al Jawf
An Nafūd
Rafhā
As Sidrah
Ajdābiyā
Al Burayqah
Al Qaryah Ash Sharqiyah
Sirte Desert
Az Zahrah
Waddān
Ar Rāqūbah
Marādah
Awjilah
Zaltan
Jaghbūb
An Nāfūrah
Jālū Oasis
Siwa
Qara
Qattâra Depression -133
El Maghra
Libyan Plateau
Great Sand Sea
Socna
Jabal as Sawdā'
Zillah
Bel Hedan
Al Wāha
Calar scio Sand Sea
Sarīr
Adrī
Brach
El Faiyûm
Beni Suef
Maghâgha
Beni Mazâr
El Minya
Mallawi
Asyût
Bawîti
Baharîya Oasis
Farafra Oasis
Ain Dalla
Qasr Farâfra
El Tih
SINAI
El'Igma
G. of Suez
G. of Aqaba
Ras Gharib
Ras Muhammad
Hurghada
Tabūk
Taymā'
Hā'il
Buraydah
Unayzah
SAUDI ARABIA
Al Hārūj al Aswad
Sabhā
LIBYA
Serir Calanscio
Zuwaylah
Marzuq
Wāw Al Kabīr
Tāzirbū
Bi'r al Harash
Al Qatrūn
Rebiana Sand Sea
Wāw an Nāmūs
Al Kufrah Oasis
Al Jawf
Rebiana
Sarir
Tibesti
Libyan Desert
Gilf Kebir Plateau
Dakhla Oasis
Mut
El Khârga
Khârga Oasis
EGYPT
Akhmîm
Sohâg
Qena
Luxor
Eastern Desert
2187 Shayib el Banat
Bur Safâga
Quseir
Al Wajh
Hijaz
Idfu
Nile
Aswân
Aswân High Dam
1977 G. Hamâta
Marsa Alam
Râs Banâs
Yanbu' al Bahr
Medina (Al Madīnah)
Lake Nasser
Allaqi
Bir Tarfâwi
Bir Abu Husein
Bir Misâha
Ayn Zuwayyah
1908 J. 'Uweinat
Wadi Halfa
Halaib
RED SEA
2217 J. Asoteriba
Jiddah
Mecca (Makkah)
At Ta'if
Madama
Plateau du Djado
Plateau du Tchigai
Séguédine
Aozou
Pic Toussidé 3265
Bardai
Asawanwah
Ma'tan as Sarra
Selima Oasis
Abri
Nubian Desert
Dungunab
Ras Abu Shagara
J. Oda 2260
Qal'at Bishah
Al Līth
Emi Koussi 3415
Gouro
Erdi
Ounianga Kébir
Laqiya Arba in
Dongola
Abu Hamed
Port Sudan
Suakin
Al Qunfidhah
Dirkou
Bilma
Grand Erg de Bilma
Borkou
Madadi
Dépression du Mourdi
El 'Atrun Oasis
Jebel Abyad
Karima
Merowe
Sinkat
Musmar
Tokar
Haiya
Abhā
Aïn Galakka
Faya (Largeau)
Ennedi
Ed Debba
Berber
Atbara
Ed Damer
Derudeb
Karora
Şabyā
Jīzān
Fada
Siltou
Broulkou
Erg du Djourab
Bodélé
Koro Toro
O. Haouach
W. Howa
W. el Milk
Nile
Shendi
Goz Regeb
Eriba
Nak'fa
Farasan Is
Dehalak Archipelago
Massawa (Mits'iwa)
Oum Chalouba
Iriba
Abu 'Urug
Omdurman
Khartoum North
Khartoum
Kassala
Sebderat
Keren
Asmara (Asmera)
Ras Andadda
Mersa Fatma
CHAD
Arada
Malha
El Geteina
Blue Nile
Biltine
Guéréda
Kamlin
Khashm el Girba
Barentu
Agordat
Adi Ugri
Mareb
ERITREA
Nguigmi
Kanem
Ouaddaï
Salal
Kutum
Sodiri
Wad Medani
El Gezira
Om Hajer
Adwa
Adigrat
Mek'ele
Takkaze
Mao
Bahr el Ghazal
Abéché
El Fasher
Umm Bell
Bara
Ed Dueim
Sennar
Gedaref
Qala'en Nahl
Aksum
Bol
Moussoro
Oum Hadjer
Adré
Geneina
Zalingei
3071 Jebel Marra
SUDAN
El Obeid
Kosti
Singa
El Hawata
Ras Dashan 4533
Tigre
Sek'ot'a
3657
Lake Chad
Massakori
Ati
Batha
Am Dam
Umm Keddada
Khuwei
Er Rahad
Umm Ruwaba
El Jebelein
Rahad
Dinder
Gallabat
Gonder
Dabat
Maiduguri
Ndjamena (Ft Lamy)
Chari
Bokoro
Mangalmé
Goz Beïda
En Nahud
Abu Zabad
Dilling
Nyala
Taweisha
Dunkur
L. Tana
Amhara
Debre Tabor
Tendaho
Kousseri
Bama
Baguirmi
Mongo
Ed Da'ein
El Fula
Nuba Mts
Rashad
Renk
White Nile (Bahr el Abiad)
Bahr el Azraq
Er Roseires
Bahir Dar
4231 Guna
Weldiya
DJIBOUTI
Dikhil
L. Abbe
Massenya
Azoum
Abou Deïa
Am Timan
Buram
El Muglad
El Lagowa
Kadugli
Dangila
Choke Mts
Burē
Desē
4000 Abuye Meda
Mokolo
Marouà
Guider
Logone
Bongor
Bousso
Melfi
Harazé
Birao
Kaka
Paloich
Asosa
Belfodiyo
Abbai (Blue Nile)
Debre Mark'os
Debre Birhan
Dirē Dawa
Léré
Lai
Dik
Salamat
Dar Rounga
Bahr el Arab
Abyei
Kodok
Malakal
Bahr el Ghazal
Fichē
Awash
Garoua
Pala
Moundou
Sarh
Doba
Bahr Aouk
Ouanda Djallé
Nyamlell
Bentiu
Fangak
Sobat
Abwong
Nasir
Nejo
Nek'emtē
ETHIOPIA
Dembi Dolo
Sodo
Dendi 3288
Addis Ababa (Adis Abeba)
Nazret
Ahmar Mts
Harer
Bénoué
Tcholliré
Maro
Ndélé
Bamingui Bangoran Nat. Pk
Massif des Bongo
Ouadda
Raga
Aweil
Jur
Meshra'er Req
Ayod
Akobo
Tor
Gorē
Koma
Jima
Asela
Gololcha
Shashemenē
Shibeli
Adamaoua
Ngaoundéré
Baibokoum
Goré
Wau
Sudd
Duk Faiwil
Deim Zubeir
Haute Kotto
Pongo
Boro
Abera
Gojeb
Omo
Yirga 'Alem
Abaya
Goba
Ginir
Mendebo Mts
Batangafo
Bodaranga
Bossangoa
Bouca
Bria
Kotto
Yalinga
Tonj
Shambe
Rumbek
Pibor Post
Mizan Teferi
Gughe 4200
Hara Fanna
Gestro
Meiganga
Bozoum
CENTRAL AFRICAN REPUBLIC
Djéma
Yirol
Bor
Maji
Arba Minch
Garoua Boulai
Bouar
Dekoa
Bakala
Bambari
Bakouma
Tali Post
Amadi
Kenamuke Swamp
Bako
Gīdolē
Genale
Negelē
Sibut
Ouaka
Obo
Tambura
Mongalla
Lotikipi Plain
Dawa
Bossembélé
Damara
Bouar
Mambéré
Kouango
Bangassou
Rafai
Chinko
Zemio
Mbomu
Gwane
Doruma
Yambio
Maridi
Juba
Torit
Melka Guba
Dolo Odo
Bertoua
Berbérati
Carnot
Boyali
Lobaye
Bangui
Ubangi
Mobaye
Mobayi
Oubangui
Mongà
Bili
Uele
Niangara
Dungu
Aba
Laylo
Yei
Kinyeti 3187
Lokitaung
Mēga
Mandera
Abong Mbang
Yokadouma
Nola
Boda
Mbaïki
Zongo
Libenge
Yakoma
Bondo
Bambili
Faradje
Moyo
Nimule
Lake Turkana
Moyale
Betou
Gemena
Bozene
Monveda
Aketi
Titule
Lienart
Bomokandi
Watsa
Arua
Albert Nile
Kitgum
Lodwar
Mt Kulal 2293
Dja
Mongala
Itimbiri
Buta
Isiro
Mungbere
Gulu
Lira
Aswa
Moroto
Turkwel
Kerio
Mt Nyiru 2805
Buna
Moloundou
Ngoko
Souanké
Lisala
Bumba
ZAIRE
Pakwach
Djugu
Masindi
Albert
Soroti
Marsabit
Kangetet
Ouesso
Impfondo
Makanza
Bongandanga
Lulonga
Yahuma
Aruwimi
Banalia
Nia Nia
Lindi
Bunia
Hoima
Kyoga
Mt Elgon 4321
Kitale
Maralal
Wajir
Mekambo
CONGO
Pikounda
Lulonga
Basankusu
Djolu
Yangambi
Kisangani (Stanleyville)
Bafwasende
Mambasa
Kabarole
UGANDA
Mbale
KENYA
Mado Gashi
Mbendza
Mbandaka (Coquilhatville)
Maringa
Isangi
Boyoma Falls
Beni
Ruwenzori Ra.
Mubende
Kampala
Tororo
Eldoret
Nyahururu Falls
Isiolo
Nanyuki
Makoua
Fort Rousset
Sangha
Befale
Mompono
Yatolema
Lubero
Kasese
Kakamega
Entebbe
Jinja
Kisumu
Nakuru
Nyeri
5199 Kirinyaga (Mt Kenya)
Kellé
Boende
Ubundu
Angumu
L. Edward
Masaka
Kericho

SAUDI ARABIA
YEMEN
RED SEA
Gulf of Aden
ERITREA
DJIBOUTI
ETHIOPIA
SOMALIA
SUDAN
LIBYA
CHAD
NIGER
NIGERIA
CAMEROON
CENTRAL AFRICAN REPUBLIC
UGANDA
KENYA
RWANDA
BURUNDI
TANZANIA
ZAIRE
CONGO
GABON
INDIAN
Lake Victoria
Lake Chad
Equator
1:15M
0 200 400 600 km
0 100 200 300 mls

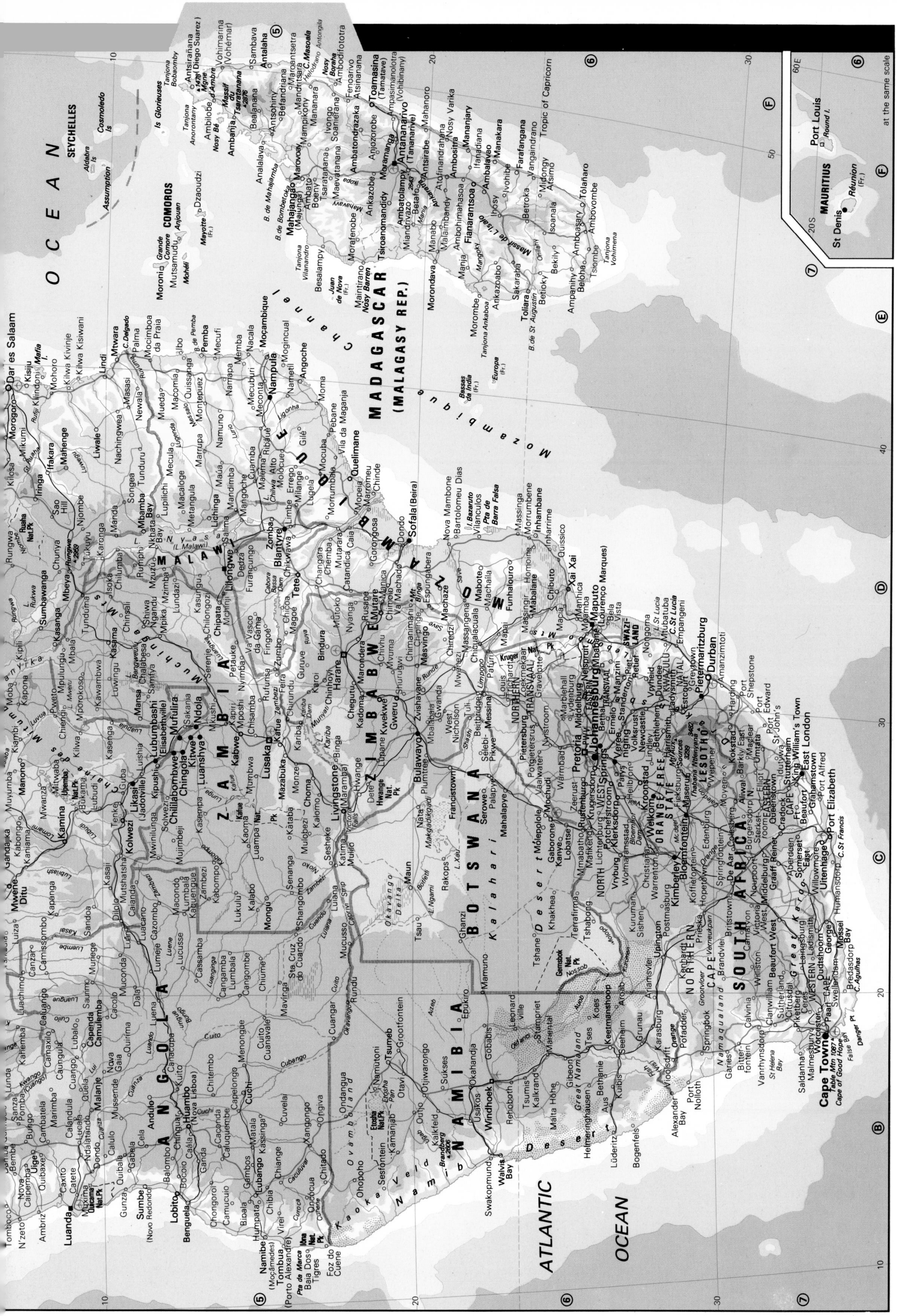
OCEAN
ATLANTIC
OCEAN
Mozambique Channel
SEYCHELLES
COMOROS
MADAGASCAR
(MALAGASY REP.)
MAURITIUS
Port Louis
Réunion
(Fr.)
St Denis
at the same scale
ANGOLA
ZAMBIA
MALAWI
MOZAMBIQUE
ZIMBABWE
BOTSWANA
NAMIBIA
SOUTH AFRICA
LESOTHO
SWAZILAND
Kalahari Desert
Namib Desert
Luanda
Lobito
Benguela
Huambo
(Nova Lisboa)
Namibe
(Moçâmedes)
Lubango
Lusaka
Kitwe
Ndola
Livingstone
Lilongwe
Blantyre
Zomba
Harare
Bulawayo
Gweru
Mutare
Maputo
(Lourenço Marques)
Beira
Sofala
Quelimane
Nampula
Moçambique
Dar es Salaam
Mtwara
Windhoek
Walvis Bay
Swakopmund
Lüderitz
Gaborone
Francistown
Maun
Pretoria
Johannesburg
Bloemfontein
Kimberley
Maseru
Durban
Pietermaritzburg
East London
Port Elizabeth
Cape Town
Cape of Good Hope
C. Agulhas
Antananarivo
(Tananarive)
Toamasina
(Tamatave)
Mahajanga
(Majunga)
Antsiranana
(Diego Suarez)
Fianarantsoa
Toliara
Tropic of Capricorn
Moroni
Dzaoudzi
Mayotte
(Fr.)
Europa
(Fr.)
Bassas da India
(Fr.)
Juan de Nova
(Fr.)
Lake Malawi
Okavango Delta
Kruger Nat. Pk
Gemsbok Nat. Pk
10
20
30
40
50
B
C
D
E
F
5
6
7

To enhance the ocean features, the 3000m contour has been added, and over 5000m is shown by an extra tint.

NORTH AMERICA

SOUTH AMERICA

EUROPE

AFRICA

ANTARCTICA

Baffin Bay

GREENLAND

Greenland Basin

Bear Island

Barents Sea

N.Cape

Norwegian Basin

Denmark Strait

ICELAND

Arctic Circle

Hudson Bay

Labrador Sea

C.Farewell

Faeroes

Shetland Is

Rockall

North Sea

Land's End

Baltic Sea

Black Sea

Newfoundland

Grand Banks

Newfoundland Basin

Mid-Atlantic Ridge

N. E. Atlantic Basin

Azores

Mediterranean Sea

Mississippi

North American Basin

Bermuda

Madeira

Nile

Gulf of Mexico

Canary Basin

Canary Is

Tropic of Cancer

West Indies

Cayman Tr.

Puerto Rico Trench
·9220

Cape Verde Basin

Cape Verde Is

C.Vert

Caribbean Sea

Cocos Ridge

Guyana Basin

Niger

Guinea Basin

Bioco
Príncipe

Equator

São Tomé

Zaire

Galapagos Is

Amazon

Rocas

Fernando de Noronha

Romanche Gap
7856

Ascension

Brazil Basin

Mid-Atlantic Ridge

St Helena

Angola Basin

Peru-Chile Trench

S.W.Peru or Nazca Ridge

Martin Vaz

Trindade

Tropic of Capricorn

·8066
·7635

Rio Grande Rise
·637

Walvis Ridge

Cape Basin

C.Agulhas

I.San Ambrosia
I.San Felix

·6081

Tristan da Cunha

Is Juan Fernandez

Argentine Basin

Gough I.

Discovery Tablemount
411

Agulhas Plateau

Falkland Is

S.Georgia

S.Sandwich Tr.
8264·

Crozet Plateau

Prince Edward Is

N.Scotia Ridge

Atlantic-Indian Ridge

Bouvet I.

Is Crozet

C.Horn

Scotia Sea

S.Sandwich Is

Pacific-Antarctic Ridge

Drake Passage

S.Orkney Is

Atlantic-Indian Antarctic Basin

Is Kergu

Antarctic Penin.

Weddell Sea

Maud Seamount
·1199

South East Pacific Basin

Antarctic Circle

Peter 1st I.

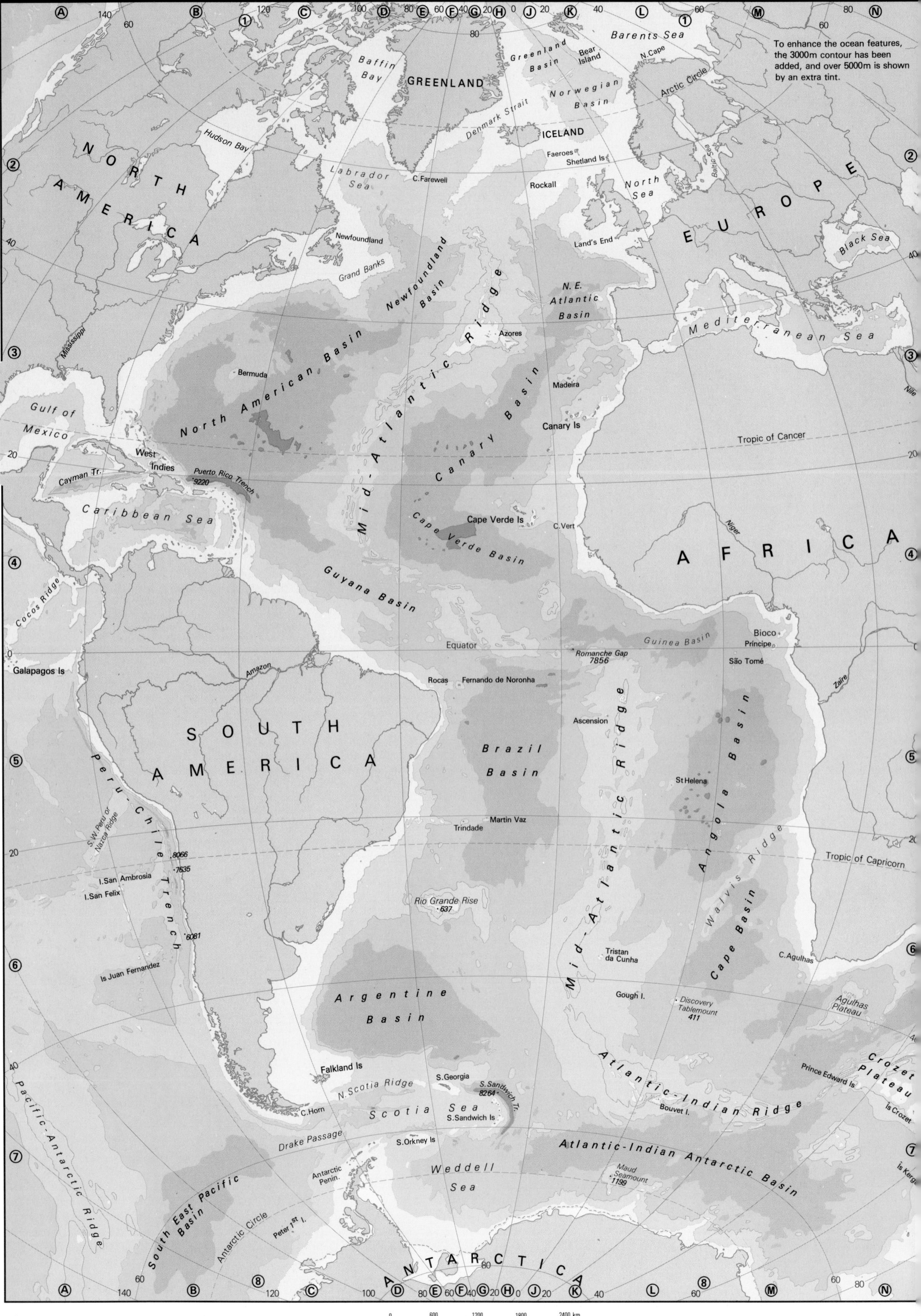

1:60M

0   600   1200   1800   2400 km
0   600   1200 mls

③ ② ① Ⓐ Ⓡ ① ②

Ⓑ Ⓠ

Chukchi Ⓒ Ⓟ

Sea Ⓓ Ⓞ

60 Ⓔ Ⓝ

180 170 Ⓕ Ⓖ Ⓗ Ⓙ Ⓚ Ⓛ Ⓜ 70 80

Arctic
Ocean

G R E E N L A N D
(KALAALLIT NUNAAT)
(Denmark)

Bering Strait

Ellesmere I.

Thule

ICELAND
Reykjavik

B e r i n g

S e a

Aleutian Islands

A L A S K A

Yukon

Prudhoe Bay

Anchorage

Fairbanks

Dawson

Whitehorse

Juneau

Alexander
Arch.

Prince Rupert

Q. Charlotte
Is

Vancouver I.

Victoria ● Vancouver

● Seattle

● Portland

Columbia

Beaufort
Sea

Mackenzie

Inuvik

Banks
I.

Victoria
I.

Great
Bear L.

Resolute

Devon I.

Queen
Elizabeth Islands

Baffin
Bay

Denmark Strait

Gothab
(Nuuk)

Yellowknife

Hay River

Great
Slave L.

Uranium City

Athabasca

Dawson
Creek

Prince
George

Fraser

Peace

Edmonton

Calgary

C A N A D A

Saskatchewan

Saskatoon

Medicine Hat

Regina

L.
Athabasca

L.
Winnipeg

Arctic Circle

Churchill

Hudson

Bay

James
Bay

Moosonee

Southampton
I.

Hudson
Strait

Inukjuak

Chibougamau

Schefferville

Churchill
Falls

Goose Bay

L a b r a d o r

S e a

Newfoundland

Anticosti
I.

St
John's

Charlottetown

Sept Îles

P A C I F I C

San Francisco ●
Sacramento ●

Reno

Salt Lake
City

Winnipeg

Kenora

Great Falls

Butte

Snake

Fargo

Duluth

Thunder
Bay

L. Superior

Sault
Ste Marie

Sudbury

Quebec

Montréal

Ottawa

Fredericton

Moncton
St. John

Halifax

Minneapolis ● St Paul

Milwaukee ●

Chicago ●

U N I T E D   S T A T E S

Omaha

Denver

O F   A M E R I C A

Colorado

Los Angeles ○

San Diego ○
Tijuana

San
Bernadino

Phoenix

Tucson

Pueblo

Amarillo

Kansas City ●

St Louis ●

Wichita

Oklahoma
City

L. Michigan

Detroit ●

Indianapolis ●

Cincinatti ●

Huron

L. Erie

Cleveland ●

Toronto

Buffalo ●

L. Ontario

New York

Boston

Baltimore ● Philadelphia

Washington ●

Newport News
Norfolk

Nashville

Memphis ●

A T L A N T I C

O C E A N

Bermuda
(U.K.)

⑤

Albuquerque

El Paso

Ciudad Juárez

Hermosillo

Chihuahua

M E X I C O

Fort Worth

Dallas ●

Austin

San
Antonio

Red

Jackson

Baton
Rouge

Mississippi

Birmingham

Mobile

Tallahassee

Atlanta ●

Charleston

Savannah

Jacksonville

Houston ●

New ●
Orleans

Corpus
Christi

Gulf of Mexico

Tampa

Miami ●

THE

BAHAMAS

Nassau

Sargasso
Sea

⑥

Tropic of Cancer

Rio Grande

Monterrey

Torreón

Durango

Mazatlán

Guadalajara ●

México □

Veracruz

Tampico

Mérida

Habana ■

C U B A

Guantánamo

JAMAICA

Kingston

HAITI
Port-au-
Prince

DOMINICAN
REP.
Santo
Domingo

Pto Rico (U.S.A.)
San Juan

ST KITTS-NEVIS

ANTIGUA &
BARBUDA

DOMINICA

⑦

Revilla Gigedo Is.
(Mex.)

O C E A N

Acapulco

BELIZE
Belmopan

CARIBBEAN   SEA

ST LUCIA

ST VINCENT &
THE GRENADINES

BAR-
BADOS

GRENADA

GUATEMALA

Guatemala

S.Salvador

EL SALVADOR

HONDURAS

Tegucigalpa

NICARAGUA

Managua

Netherlands
Antilles

TRINIDAD
& TOBAGO

Sta
Marta

Clipperton
(Fr.)

COSTA
RICA

S.José

P A N A M A

Panamá

Barranquilla

Maracaibo

Caracas ■

Cd
Guayana

⑧

Equator

I. del Coco
(C.R)

Malpelo
(Col.)

Buenaventura

Medellín

Cali

Bogotá ●

C O L O M B I A

Orinoco

V E N E Z U E L A

Quito
ECUADOR

PERU

B R A Z I L

Negro

Galapagos Is
(Ecu.)

Ⓖ Ⓗ Ⓙ Ⓚ Ⓛ Ⓜ

1:35M

0 250 500 750 1000 1250 km

ARCTIC OCEAN

BEAUFORT SEA

BERING SEA

St. Lawrence I.

Bering Str.

ALASKA

Brooks Range

Endicott Mts

North Slope

Alaska Range

Mt. McKinley

Anchorage

Kuskokwim

Aleutian Ra.

Kodiak Island

Gulf of Alaska

YUKON TERRITORY

Mackenzie Mountains

Selwyn Mountains

Whitehorse

Ogilvie Mts

Dawson

NORTHWEST TERRITORIES

Inuvik

Tuktoyaktuk

Banks Island

Victoria Island

Prince of Wales Island

Melville Island

Parry Islands

Great Bear Lake

Great Slave Lake

Yellowknife

Ft Simpson

Ft Providence

Hay River

Fort Smith

Wood Buffalo Nat Pk

Lake Athabasca

BRITISH COLUMBIA

Queen Charlotte Islands

Prince Rupert

Kitimat

Prince George

Williams Lake

Kamloops

Vancouver

Vancouver Island

Victoria

Nanaimo

New Westminster

Kelowna

Penticton

COAST MOUNTAINS

ROCKY MOUNTAINS

ALBERTA

Edmonton

Calgary

Red Deer

Lethbridge

Medicine Hat

Banff

Jasper Nat Pk

Grande Prairie

Peace River

Ft McMurray

SASKATCHEWAN

Saskatoon

Regina

Prince Albert

Moose Jaw

Swift Current

North Battleford

MANITOBA

Winnipeg

The Pas

Flin Flon

Thompson

Churchill

Lake Winnipeg

Reindeer Lake

PACIFIC OCEAN

Seattle

Tacoma

Olympia

Portland

Spokane

WASHINGTON

OREGON

Vancouver

Coeur d'Alene

MONTANA

Great Falls

Helena

Missoula

Butte

Billings

IDAHO

Boise

Idaho Falls

Pocatello

WYOMING

Casper

NORTH DAKOTA

Bismarck

Fargo

Grand Forks

Minot

SOUTH DAKOTA

Pierre

Rapid City

Names underlined indicate Province/State capitals

1:15M

0   200   400   600 km

0   100   200   300 mils

GREENLAND
(KALAALLIT NUNAAT)
(Denmark)
ICELAND
DENMARK STRAIT
BAFFIN BAY
DAVIS STRAIT
Labrador Sea
NEWFOUNDLAND
HUDSON STRAIT
HUDSON BAY
Ungava Bay
Foxe Basin
Baffin Island
Ellesmere Island
Devon Island
Lancaster Sound
Melville Peninsula
Southampton Island
QUEBEC
ONTARIO
LAKE SUPERIOR
MICHIGAN
L. MICHIGAN
HURON
L. Ontario
L. Erie
James Bay
Gulf of Saint Lawrence
ATLANTIC OCEAN
NEW BRUNSWICK
NOVA SCOTIA
PRINCE EDWARD I.
MAINE
VERMONT
NEW HAMPSHIRE
MASS.
CONN.
NEW YORK
WISCONSIN
Labrador
Newfoundland
Cape Breton I.
Arctic Circle
Reykjavík
Godthåb (Nuuk)
Cape Farewell (Kap Farvel)
St John's
Halifax
Québec
Montréal
Ottawa
Toronto
Boston
Providence
Hartford
Buffalo
Detroit
Milwaukee
Duluth
Thunder Bay
Sault Ste Marie
St Paul
Churchill
Iqaluit
Frobisher Bay
Goose Bay
Sept-Îles
Sydney
Charlottetown
Fredericton
Saint John
Sudbury
Kingston
Hamilton
Rochester
Syracuse
Albany
Springfield
Worcester
New Bedford
New Haven
Long Island
Madison
Lansing
Flint
Windsor

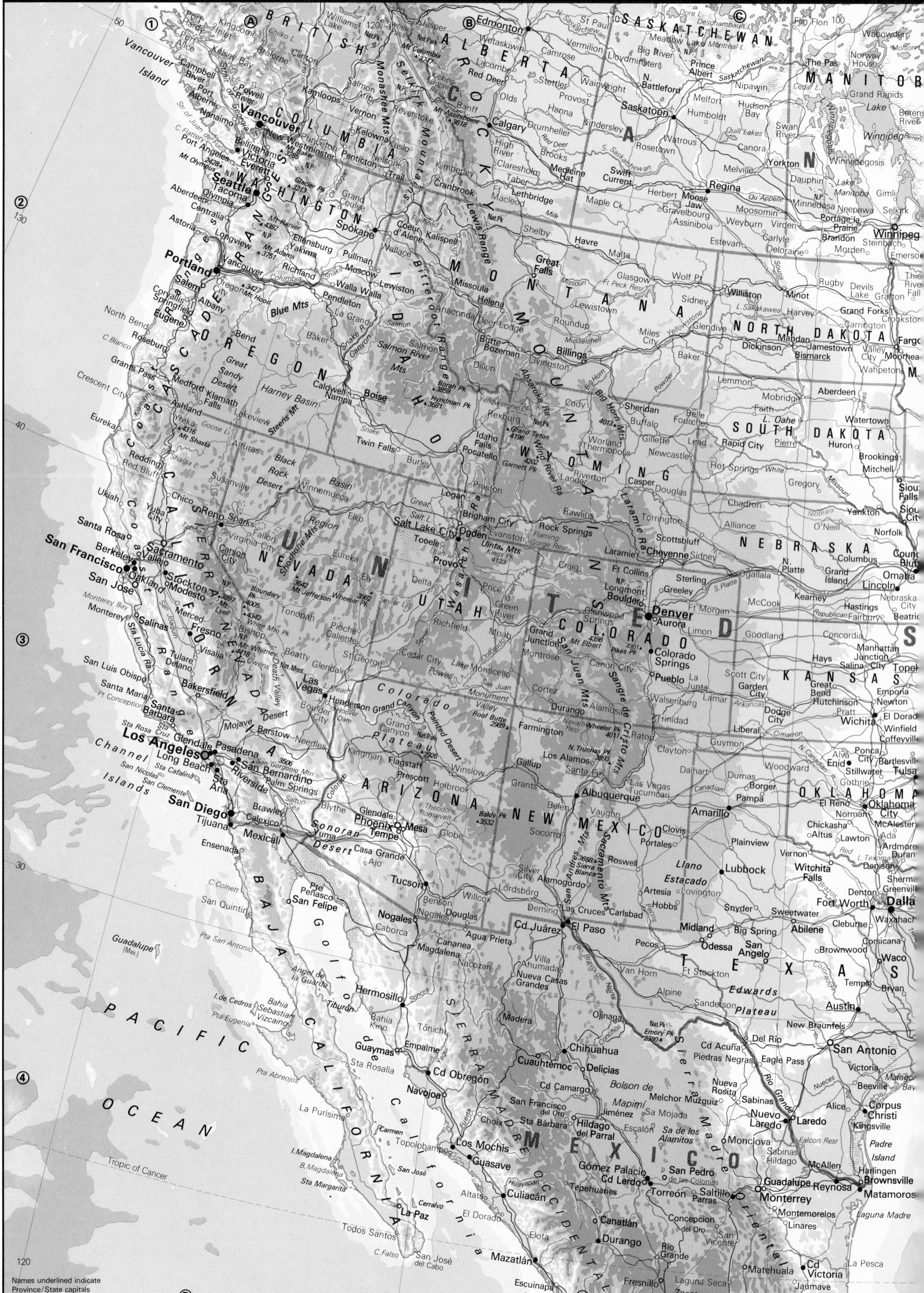

Names underlined indicate Province/State capitals

James Bay
ONTARIO
QUEBEC
LAKE SUPERIOR
LAKE HURON
LAKE MICHIGAN
L. ONTARIO
LAKE ERIE
UNITED STATES
MICHIGAN
WISCONSIN
MINNESOTA
IOWA
ILLINOIS
INDIANA
OHIO
PENNSYLVANIA
NEW YORK
VERMONT
NEW HAMPSHIRE
MAINE
MASS.
CONN.
R.I.
N.J.
DEL.
MD
D.C.
WEST VIRGINIA
VIRGINIA
KENTUCKY
TENNESSEE
NORTH CAROLINA
SOUTH CAROLINA
GEORGIA
ALABAMA
MISSISSIPPI
LOUISIANA
ARKANSAS
MISSOURI
FLORIDA
NEW BRUNSWICK
NOVA SCOTIA
PRINCE EDWARD I.
APPALACHIAN MOUNTAINS
Ozark Plateau
Gulf of St Lawrence
Bay of Fundy
ATLANTIC OCEAN
GULF OF MEXICO
THE BAHAMAS
CUBA
Straits of Florida
Chicago
Detroit
Toronto
Montréal
Ottawa
Québec
Boston
New York
Philadelphia
Baltimore
Washington D.C.
Pittsburgh
Cleveland
Buffalo
Cincinnati
Indianapolis
Columbus
Louisville
St Louis
Kansas City
Milwaukee
St Paul
Minneapolis
Duluth
Thunder Bay
Sault Ste Marie
Sudbury
Halifax
Saint John
Fredericton
Charlottetown
Nashville
Memphis
Knoxville
Atlanta
Birmingham
Montgomery
Jackson
New Orleans
Baton Rouge
Shreveport
Little Rock
Houston
Galveston
Mobile
Pensacola
Tallahassee
Jacksonville
Savannah
Charleston
Columbia
Charlotte
Raleigh
Richmond
Norfolk
Orlando
Tampa
St Petersburg
Miami
Key West
Nassau
Havana (La Habana)
Matanzas
Cienfuegos
Camagüey
Holguín
Great Abaco
Eleuthera
Andros
Great Exuma
Long I.
Cat I.
San Salvador
Crooked
Great Inagua
Caicos Is
Mt Mitchell 2037
Mt Washington 1916
C. Hatteras
C. Cod
C. Canaveral
Long Island
Delaware Bay
Chesapeake Bay
Albemarle Sound
Apalachee Bay
L. Okeechobee
The Everglades
Florida Keys
Mississippi
Ohio
Missouri
Tennessee
30
40
50
60
70
80
90

1:5M

0 50 100 150 200 km

0 50 100 mls

UTAH
NEVADA
ARIZONA
CALIFORNIA
COLORADO
PLATEAU
GREAT BASIN
SIERRA NEVADA
MOJAVE DESERT
SONORA
BAJA CALIFORNIA
MEXICO
PACIFIC OCEAN
Painted Desert
Grand Canyon
Lake Powell
Lake Mead
Death Valley
San Joaquin Valley
Sacramento Valley
Diablo Range
Santa Lucia Range
San Bernardino Mts
Panamint Range
Shoshone Mts
Monitor Range
Schell Creek Range
Egan Range
Black Mts
Channel Islands
Gulf of Santa Catalina
G. de California
Salton Sea
Colorado
Salt Lake City
Provo
Orem
Grand Junction
Moab
Reno
Carson City
Sparks
Las Vegas
Henderson
Boulder City
Sacramento
San Francisco
Oakland
San Jose
Stockton
Fresno
Bakersfield
Los Angeles
Long Beach
Anaheim
Santa Ana
Riverside
San Bernardino
Pasadena
San Diego
Tijuana
Mexicali
Phoenix
Mesa
Tempe
Scottsdale
Glendale
Tucson
Flagstaff
Prescott
Yuma
Nogales
Kingman
Needles
Barstow
Santa Barbara
Ventura
Oxnard
San Luis Obispo
Salinas
Monterey
Santa Cruz
Modesto
Merced
Visalia
Lancaster
Palm Springs
El Centro
Ensenada
Yosemite Nat. Park
Kings Canyon Nat. Park
Sequoia Nat. Park
Zion Nat. Pk
Bryce Canyon N.P.
Capitol Reef Nat. Pk
Canyonlands Nat. Pk
Arches N.P.
Petrified Forest Nat. Park
Grand Canyon Nat. Park
Mt Whitney 4418
Humphreys Peak 3826
Mt Lemmon 2915
Mt Graham 3265
Baldy Peak 3533
Mt Peale 3857
Wheeler Peak 3982
Boundary Peak 4005
White Mtn Peak 4342
Telescope Peak 3368
Charleston Peak 3633
San Jacinto Peak 3301
Mt San Antonio 3068
Pt Conception
Pt Arena
Pt Pinos
Monterey Bay
40
35
120
115
110
3
4
B
C
D
E

CANADA

ALBERTA · SASKATCHEWAN · MANITOBA

MONTANA

NORTH DAKOTA

SOUTH DAKOTA

WYOMING

ROCKY MOUNTAINS

NEBRASKA

UTAH

COLORADO

KANSAS

Major cities and features:

Great Falls, Helena, Bozeman, Billings, Havre, Malta, Glasgow, Wolf Point, Williston, Minot, Bismarck, Mandan, Jamestown, Aberdeen, Pierre, Rapid City, Sheridan, Buffalo, Casper, Cheyenne, Scottsbluff, North Platte, Denver, Aurora, Boulder, Fort Collins, Greeley, Colorado Springs, Pueblo, Grand Junction, Durango, Dodge City

Fort Peck Reservoir, Lake Sakakawea, Lake Oahe, Yellowstone Nat. Park, Grand Teton Nat. Park, Rocky Mtn. Nat. Park, Black Hills, Badlands

Granite Peak 3901, Cloud Peak 4016, Gannett Peak 4202, Kings Peak 4114, Longs Peak 4345, Mt Elbert 4399, Mt Harvard 4378, Pikes Peak 4301, Mt Evans 4348, Blanca Peak 4364

1:5M

0 50 100 150 200 km
0 50 100 mils

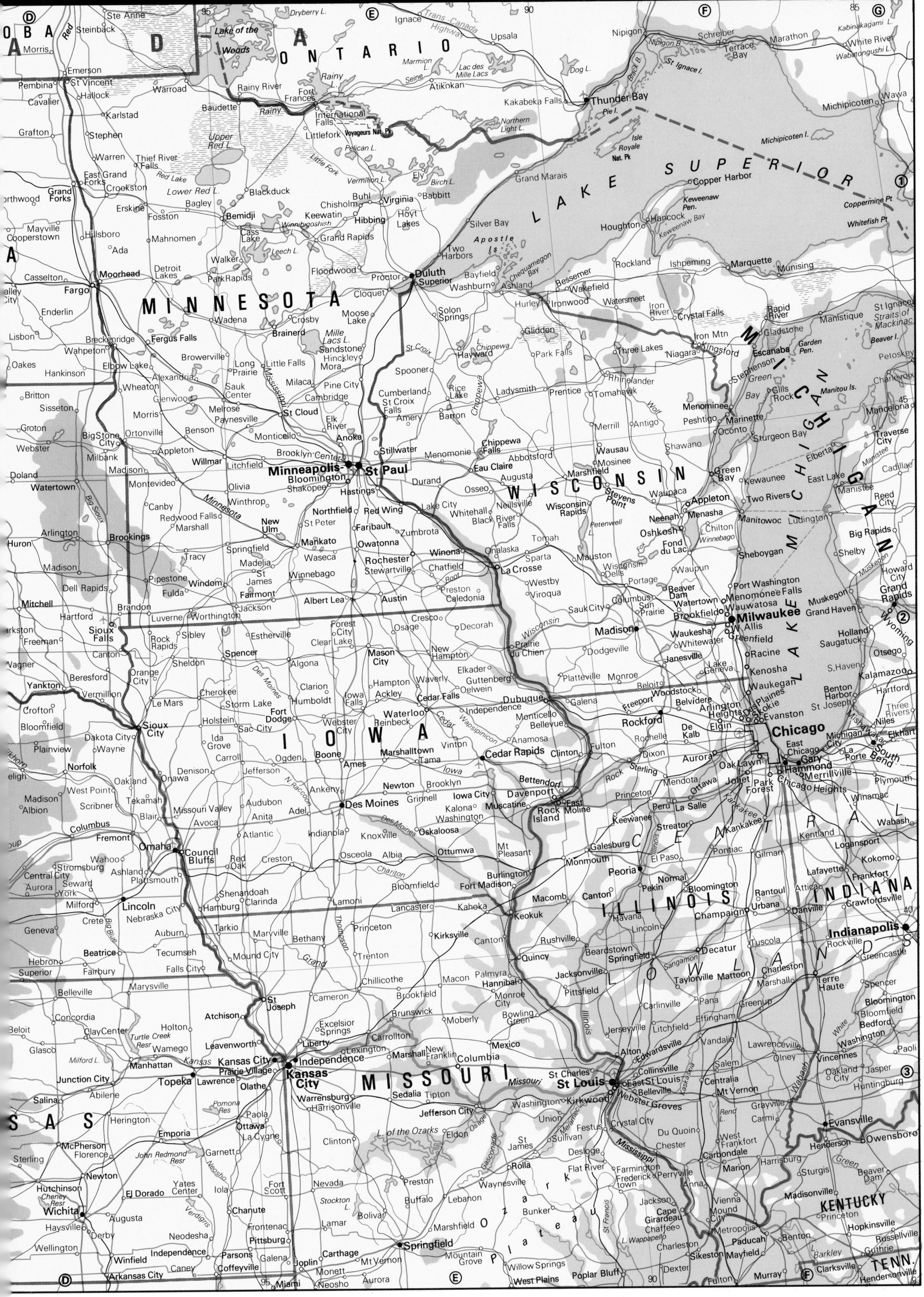
ONTARIO
LAKE SUPERIOR
MINNESOTA
WISCONSIN
IOWA
ILLINOIS
MISSOURI
INDIANA
KENTUCKY
TENN.
LAKE MICHIGAN
MICHIGAN
CENTRAL LOWLAND
Ozark Plateau
Lake of the Woods
Thunder Bay
Isle Royale Nat. Pk
Voyageurs Nat. Pk
International Falls
Duluth
Superior
Minneapolis
St Paul
Rochester
St Cloud
Mankato
Moorhead
Fargo
Grand Forks
Sioux Falls
Sioux City
Omaha
Council Bluffs
Lincoln
Des Moines
Cedar Rapids
Waterloo
Dubuque
Davenport
Rock Island
La Crosse
Eau Claire
Wausau
Green Bay
Appleton
Oshkosh
Madison
Milwaukee
Racine
Kenosha
Chicago
Gary
Hammond
Rockford
Peoria
Springfield
Champaign
Decatur
Bloomington
Indianapolis
Terre Haute
Evansville
Owensboro
St Louis
Kansas City
Independence
St Joseph
Topeka
Jefferson City
Columbia
Springfield
Joplin
Wichita
Marquette
Escanaba
Muskegon
Grand Rapids
Kalamazoo
South Bend
Paducah
Cape Girardeau

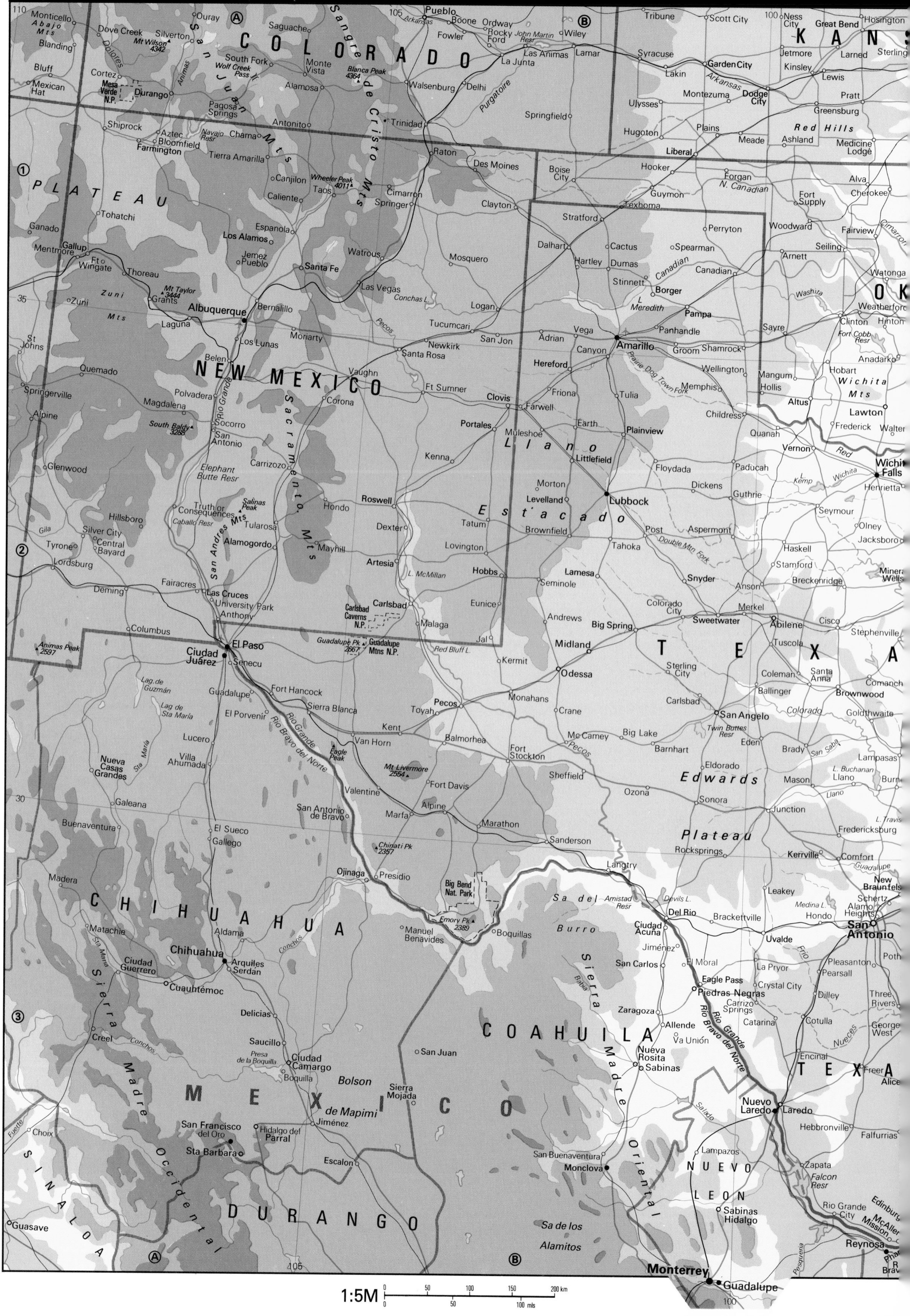
COLORADO
NEW MEXICO
TEXAS
KANS
OK
CHIHUAHUA
COAHUILA
MEXICO
DURANGO
SINALOA
NUEVO LEON
PLATEAU
Llano Estacado
Edwards Plateau
Sangre de Cristo Mts
San Juan Mts
Sacramento Mts
San Andres Mts
Zuni Mts
Abajo Mts
Red Hills
Wichita Mts
Sierra Madre Occidental
Sierra Madre Oriental
Sa del Burro
Sa de los Alamitos
Bolson de Mapimi
Monticello
Blanding
Bluff
Mexican Hat
Dove Creek
Silverton
Ouray
Mt Wilson 4342
Cortez
Mesa Verde N.P.
Durango
Saguache
South Fork
Wolf Creek Pass
Monte Vista
Alamosa
Blanca Peak 4364
Pagosa Springs
Antonito
Pueblo
Boone
Ordway
Fowler
Rocky Ford
John Martin Resr
Wiley
Las Animas
Lamar
La Junta
Walsenburg
Delhi
Purgatoire
Trinidad
Springfield
Tribune
Scott City
Syracuse
Garden City
Lakin
Ness City
Great Bend
Hosington
Larned
Sterling
Jetmore
Kinsley
Lewis
Arkansas
Montezuma
Dodge City
Pratt
Ulysses
Greensburg
Hugoton
Plains
Meade
Ashland
Medicine Lodge
Liberal
Shiprock
Aztec
Bloomfield
Farmington
Navajo Resr
Chama
Tierra Amarilla
Raton
Des Moines
Boise City
Hooker
Forgan
N. Canadian
Guymon
Texhoma
Alva
Cherokee
Fort Supply
Canjilon
Wheeler Peak 4011
Cimarron
Caliente
Taos
Springer
Clayton
Tohatchi
Ganado
Espanola
Los Alamos
Mentmore
Gallup
Ft Wingate
Thoreau
Mt Taylor 3444
Grants
Jemez Pueblo
Santa Fe
Watrous
Las Vegas
Conchas L.
Mosquero
Logan
Stratford
Perryton
Dalhart
Cactus
Spearman
Hartley
Dumas
Canadian
Stinnett
Borger
L. Meredith
Pampa
Woodward
Fairview
Seiling
Arnett
Watonga
Weatherford
Clinton
Hinton
Fort Cobb Resr
Zuni
St Johns
Laguna
Albuquerque
Bernalillo
Moriarty
Los Lunas
Belen
Tucumcari
San Jon
Newkirk
Santa Rosa
Pecos
Adrian
Vega
Amarillo
Panhandle
Canyon
Groom
Shamrock
Sayre
Anadarko
Quemado
Springerville
Alpine
Magdalena
Polvadera
Vaughn
Corona
Ft Sumner
Clovis
Hereford
Friona
Farwell
Tulia
Prairie Dog Town Fork
Wellington
Memphis
Mangum
Hollis
Hobart
Altus
Lawton
Childress
Quanah
Frederick
Walter
Vernon
Red
Wichita Falls
Henrietta
South Baldy 3288
Socorro
San Antonio
Elephant Butte Resr
Carrizozo
Portales
Muleshoe
Earth
Plainview
Kenna
Littlefield
Floydada
Paducah
Glenwood
Truth or Consequences
Caballo Resr
Salinas Peak
Tularosa
Hondo
Roswell
Morton
Levelland
Lubbock
Dickens
Guthrie
L. Kemp
Seymour
Olney
Jacksboro
Hillsboro
Silver City
Gila
Tyrone
Central
Bayard
Lordsburg
Alamogordo
Dexter
Mayhill
Artesia
Tatum
Lovington
Brownfield
Post
Tahoka
Aspermont
Double Mtn Fork
Haskell
Stamford
Deming
Fairacres
Las Cruces
University Park
Anthony
L. McMillan
Carlsbad
Carlsbad Caverns N.P.
Hobbs
Eunice
Lamesa
Seminole
Snyder
Anson
Breckenridge
Mineral Wells
Colorado City
Andrews
Big Spring
Sweetwater
Merkel
Abilene
Cisco
Columbus
Animas Peak 2597
El Paso
Ciudad Juárez
Senecu
Guadalupe Pk 2667
Guadalupe Mtns N.P.
Malaga
Jal
Red Bluff L.
Kermit
Midland
Odessa
Tuscola
Stephenville
Sterling City
Coleman
Santa Anna
Comanche
Brownwood
Ballinger
Lag. de Guzmán
Lag de Sta María
Guadalupe
Fort Hancock
Sierra Blanca
El Porvenir
Rio Grande
Rio Bravo del Norte
Toyah
Pecos
Monahans
Crane
Carlsbad
San Angelo
Colorado
Goldthwaite
Kent
Van Horn
Balmorhea
Mc Camey
Big Lake
Twin Buttes Resr
Barnhart
Eden
Brady
San Saba
Lampasas
Lucero
Eagle Peak
Fort Stockton
Nueva Casas Grandes
Villa Ahumada
Sta María
Mt Livermore 2554
Fort Davis
Sheffield
Eldorado
L. Buchanan
Llano
Mason
Burnet
Galeana
Valentine
Ozona
Sonora
Buenaventura
San Antonio de Bravo
Marfa
Alpine
Marathon
Junction
L. Travis
Fredericksburg
El Sueco
Gallego
Chinati Pk 2357
Sanderson
Rocksprings
Kerrville
Comfort
Guadalupe
Langtry
Madera
Ojinaga
Presidio
Big Bend Nat. Park
Amistad Resr
Devils L.
New Braunfels
Schertz
Medina L.
Leakey
Del Rio
Alamo Heights
Hondo
Brackettville
San Antonio
Matachie
Emory Pk 2389
Boquillas
Ciudad Acuña
Manuel Benavides
Aldama
Uvalde
Frio
Jiménez
Chihuahua
Conchos
Ciudad Guerrero
Arquiles Serdán
San Carlos
El Moral
La Pryor
Pleasanton
Poth
Pearsall
Cuauhtémoc
Eagle Pass
Piedras Negras
Crystal City
Carrizo Springs
Dilley
Three Rivers
Delicias
Zaragoza
Catarina
Cotulla
Creel
Allende
Va Unión
Nueces
George West
Saucillo
Presa de la Boquilla
Ciudad Camargo
San Juan
Nueva Rosita
Sabinas
Encinal
Freer
Alice
Boquilla
Sierra Mojada
Nuevo Laredo
Laredo
Hebbronville
Falfurrias
Choix
Fuerte
San Francisco del Oro
Hidalgo del Parral
Jiménez
Salado
Sta Barbara
Escalon
San Buenaventura
Monclova
Lampazos
Zapata
Falcon Resr
Rio Grande City
Edinburg
McAllen
Mission
Sabinas Hidalgo
Guasave
Reynosa
Monterrey
Guadalupe
Pesqueria
1:5M
0 50 100 150 200 km
0 50 100 mls

GULF OF MEXICO
ARKANSAS
LOUISIANA
MISSISSIPPI
ALABAMA
TENNESSEE
KENTUCKY
Ozark Plateau
Boston Mts
Ouachita Mts
Memphis
Little Rock
Shreveport
Dallas
Fort Worth
Houston
Galveston
Beaumont
Baton Rouge
New Orleans
Jackson
Vicksburg
Mobile
Pensacola
Birmingham
Nashville
Evansville
Springfield
Tulsa
Oklahoma City
Wichita
Austin
Waco
Corpus Christi
Brownsville
Matamoros
Fort Smith
Texarkana
Monroe
Alexandria
Lake Charles
Lafayette
Biloxi
Gulfport
Meridian
Tuscaloosa
Tupelo
Pine Bluff
Jonesboro
Paducah
Mississippi Delta
Matagorda I.
Galveston Bay
Mobile Bay
Breton Sound
L. Pontchartrain
Atchafalaya Bay
Terre Bonne Bay
Timbalier Bay
Baffin Bay
Laguna Madre
Mississippi
Arkansas
Red
Brazos
Trinity
Tennessee
D
E
C
1
2
3
30
35
90
95

LAKE SUPERIOR

LAKE MICHIGAN

LAKE HURON

LAKE ERIE

MINNESOTA

WISCONSIN

MICHIGAN

ONTARIO

IOWA

ILLINOIS

INDIANA

OHIO

MISSOURI

KENTUCKY

WEST VIRGINIA

TENNESSEE

ARKANSAS

CUMBERLAND PLATEAU

ALLEGHENY PLATEAU

Thunder Bay

Duluth
Superior

St Paul

St Louis

Milwaukee

Chicago

Detroit

Cleveland

Indianapolis

Columbus

Cincinnati

Madison

Grand Rapids

Lansing

Toledo

Fort Wayne

Nashville

1:5M

0   50   100   150   200 km

0   50   100 mls

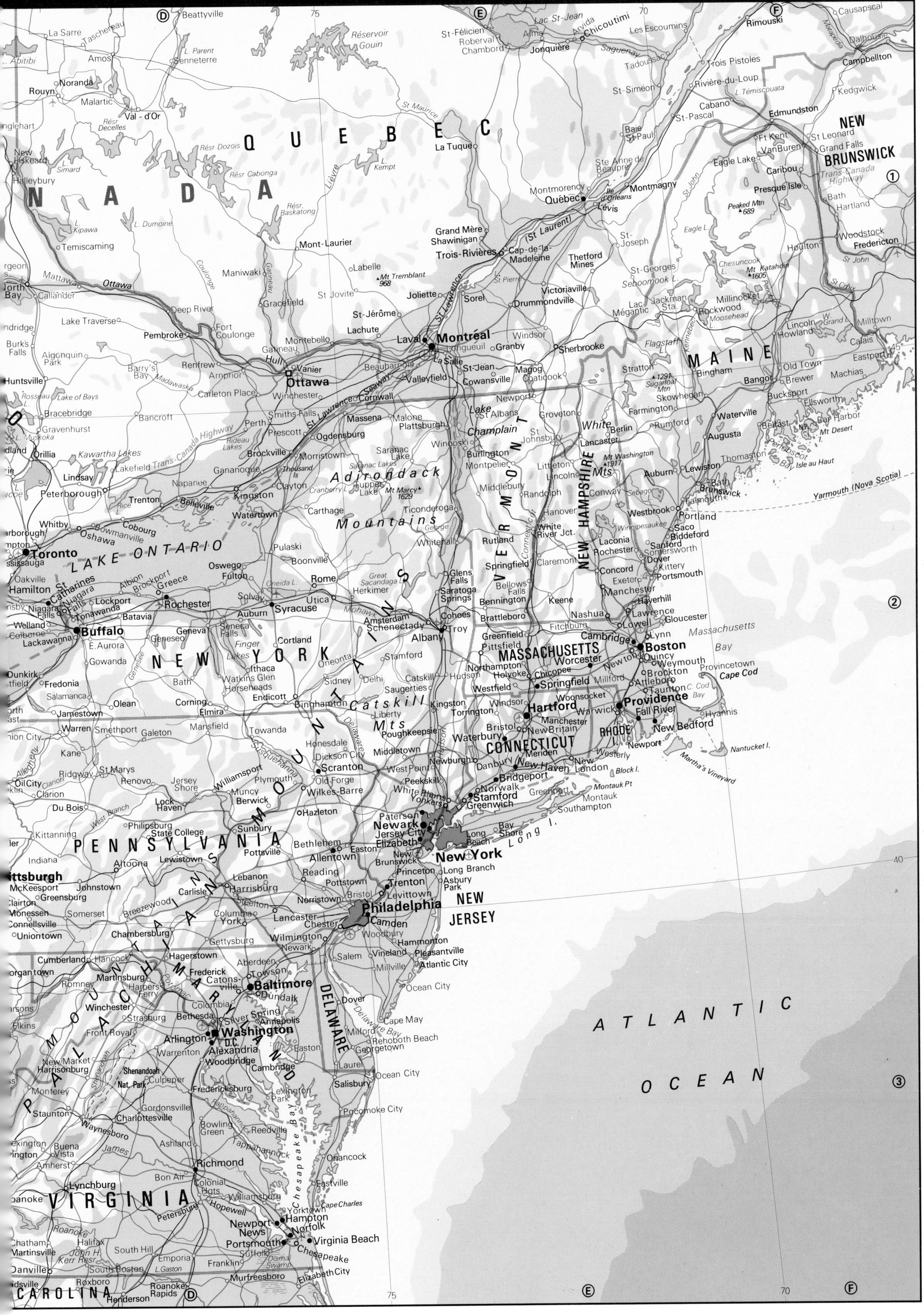
Beattyville
La Sarre
Taschereau
Réservoir Gouin
St-Félicien
Roberval
Chambord
Lac St-Jean
Alma
Jonquière
Chicoutimi
Les Escoumins
Rimouski
Causapscal
Matapedia
Dalhousie
Campbellton
L. Parent
Senneterre
Amos
Abitibi
Saguenay
Tadoussac
Trois Pistoles
Rivière-du-Loup
L. Témiscouata
Kedgwick
Noranda
Rouyn
Malartic
Val - d'Or
Résr Decelles
St Maurice
St-Siméon
Cabano
St-Pascal
Edmundston
NEW BRUNSWICK
Q U E B E C
C A N A D A
Résr Dozois
Résr Cabonga
La Tuque
L. Kempt
Lièvre
Baie St Paul
Ft Kent
St Leonard
Grand Falls
Van Buren
Eagle Lake
Caribou
Trans Canada Highway
Ste Anne de Beaupré
Montmorency
Québec
Ile d'Orléans
Montmagny
Lévis
Presque Isle
Bath
Hartland
Peaked Mtn 689
St John
Eagle L.
New Liskeard
L. Simard
Haileybury
Résr. Baskatong
L. Kipawa
L. Dumoine
Temiscaming
Mont-Laurier
Grand Mère
Shawinigan
Trois-Rivières
St Laurent
Cap-de-la-Madeleine
Thetford Mines
St-Joseph
Woodstock
Fredericton
Houlton
Chesuncook L.
Mt Katahdin 1605
Mattawa
Ottawa
North Bay
Callander
Maniwaki
Gatineau
Coulonge
Labelle
Mt Tremblant 968
St Jovite
Joliette
St Lawrence
Sorel
St Pierre
Victoriaville
Drummondville
St-Georges
Seboomook L.
Millinocket
Rockwood
Moosehead L.
Deep River
Gracefield
St-Jérôme
Lac Mégantic
Jackman Sta.
Kennebec
Lake Traverse
Pembroke
Fort Coulonge
Lachute
Montebello
Laval
Montréal
Longueuil
Granby
Windsor
Sherbrooke
Flagstaff L.
Lincoln
Howland
Grand L.
Milltown
Calais
Eastport
St Croix
Burk's Falls
Algonquin Park
Barry's Bay
Madawaska
Renfrew
Arnprior
Gatineau
Hull
Vanier
Ottawa
Beauharnois
La Salle
St-Jean
Magog
Coaticook
Valleyfield
Cowansville
Stratton
Bingham
MAINE
Old Town
Machias
Bangor
Brewer
Huntsville
Rosseau L.
Lake of Bays
Carleton Place
Winchester
Cornwall
Seaway
Newport
Sugarloaf Mtn 1291
Skowhegan
Bucksport
Ellsworth
Bracebridge
Gravenhurst
L. Muskoka
Bancroft
Perth
Smiths Falls
St Lawrence
Massena
Malone
Plattsburgh
Lake Champlain
St Albans
Groveton
White Mts
Berlin
Farmington
Rumford
Waterville
Augusta
Belfast
Bar Harbor
Mt Desert I.
Orillia
Kawartha Lakes
Rideau Lakes
Trans-Canada Highway
Prescott
Ogdensburg
Saranac Lake
Winooski
Burlington
St Johnsbury
Lancaster
Mt Washington 1917
Auburn
Lewiston
Thomaston
Penobscot Bay
Isle au Haut
Lindsay
Lakefield
Brockville
Morristown
Saranac Lakes
Adirondack
Montpelier
Littleton
Lincoln
Bath
Brunswick
Peterborough
Gananoque
Thousand Is
Napanee
Kingston
Clayton
Cranberry L.
Tupper Lake
Mt Marcy 1629
Middlebury
Randolph
Conway
Sebago L.
Falmouth
Portland
Yarmouth (Nova Scotia)
Rice L.
Trenton
Belleville
Carthage
Ticonderoga
Hanover
Westbrook
Whitby
Cobourg
Bowmanville
Oshawa
Watertown
Mountains
L. George
White River Jct.
Winnipesaukee L.
Saco
Biddeford
Toronto
LAKE ONTARIO
Pulaski
Whitehall
Rutland
Connecticut
Laconia
Sanford
Rochester
Somersworth
Dover
Kittery
Portsmouth
Oakville
Hamilton
St Catharines
Niagara Falls
Oswego
Fulton
Boonville
Rome
Great Sacandaga L.
Glens Falls
Springfield
Claremont
Concord
Exeter
Manchester
Haverhill
Lockport
Brockport
Albion
Greece
Rochester
Tonawanda
Oneida L.
Solvay
Syracuse
Utica
Herkimer
Saratoga Springs
Bellows Falls
Bennington
Keene
Nashua
Lawrence
Gloucester
Batavia
Buffalo
Welland
Colborne
Lackawanna
Auburn
Seneca Falls
Geneva
Mohawk
Amsterdam
Schenectady
Cohoes
Troy
Albany
Brattleboro
Fitchburg
Lowell
Lynn
Massachusetts Bay
E. Aurora
Geneseo
Finger Lakes
Cortland
Greenfield
Pittsfield
MASSACHUSETTS
Cambridge
Boston
Quincy
Weymouth
Gowanda
NEW YORK
Oneonta
Stamford
Northampton
Holyoke
Worcester
Newton
Brockton
Provincetown
Cape Cod
Dunkirk
Fredonia
Genesee
Ithaca
Watkins Glen
Horseheads
Bath
Sidney
Delhi
Catskill
Hudson
Chicopee
Springfield
Milford
Attleboro
Taunton
C. Cod Bay
Salamanca
Olean
Corning
Endicott
Binghamton
Catskill Mts
Westfield
Woonsocket
Providence
Hyannis
Jamestown
Elmira
Liberty
Kingston
Torrington
Windsor
Hartford
Warwick
Fall River
Warren
Smethport
Galeton
Mansfield
Towanda
Delaware
Poughkeepsie
Bristol
New Britain
Manchester
RHODE I.
New Bedford
Kane
Honesdale
Dickson City
Scranton
Middletown
Hudson
Waterbury
CONNECTICUT
Westerly
Newport
Nantucket I.
Martha's Vineyard
Allegheny
Ridgway
St Marys
Renovo
Jersey Shore
Williamsport
Susquehanna
Plymouth
Old Forge
Wilkes-Barre
West Point
Newburgh
Danbury
Meriden
New Haven
New London
Block I.
Oil City
Clarion
Muncy
Berwick
Peekskill
White Plains
Yonkers
Bridgeport
Norwalk
Stamford
Greenwich
Greenport
Montauk Pt
Montauk
Southampton
Du Bois
Lock Haven
Hazleton
Paterson
Newark
Jersey City
Elizabeth
Long Beach
Bay Shore
Long I.
Kittanning
West Branch
Philipsburg
State College
Sunbury
PENNSYLVANIA
Bethlehem
Easton
New Brunswick
New York
Indiana
Altoona
Lewistown
Pottsville
Allentown
Long Branch
Pittsburgh
McKeesport
Johnstown
Lebanon
Reading
Princeton
Trenton
Asbury Park
Greensburg
Carlisle
Harrisburg
Pottstown
Norristown
Bristol
Levittown
NEW JERSEY
Monessen
Somerset
Breezewood
Steelton
Columbia
York
Lancaster
Philadelphia
Camden
Connellsville
Uniontown
Chambersburg
Chester
Woodbury
Gettysburg
Wilmington
Hammonton
Newark
Salem
Vineland
Pleasantville
Cumberland
Hancock
Hagerstown
Aberdeen
Millville
Atlantic City
Morgantown
Frederick
Martinsburg
Catonsville
Towson
Baltimore
Romney
Harpers Ferry
Potomac
Dundalk
DELAWARE
Ocean City
Winchester
Columbia
Dover
Strasburg
Bethesda
Silver Spring
Annapolis
Cape May
Delaware Bay
Front Royal
Arlington
Washington D.C.
Alexandria
MARYLAND
Milford
Rehoboth Beach
Georgetown
Warrenton
Woodbridge
Easton
Cambridge
Laurel
New Market
Harrisonburg
Shenandoah Nat. Park
Culpeper
Ocean City
Monterey
Fredericksburg
Lexington Park
Salisbury
Rappahannock
Gordonsville
Charlottesville
Staunton
Waynesboro
Bowling Green
Reedville
Pocomoke City
Chesapeake Bay
Lexington
Buena Vista
Ashland
James
Tappahannock
Onancock
Amherst
Richmond
Bon Air
Eastville
Lynchburg
Colonial Hgts
Williamsburg
Cape Charles
VIRGINIA
Hopewell
Petersburg
Yorktown
Hampton
Newport News
Norfolk
Roanoke
Virginia Beach
Portsmouth
Chatham
Halifax
Martinsville
John H. Kerr Resr
South Hill
Suffolk
Chesapeake
Dismal Swamp
Emporia
Danville
South Boston
L. Gaston
Franklin
Roxboro
Roanoke Rapids
Murfreesboro
Elizabeth City
CAROLINA
Henderson
ATLANTIC OCEAN
APPALACHIAN MOUNTAINS
75
70
40
45

1:2.5M 0 25 50 75 100 km 0 25 50 mls

NEVADA

PACIFIC OCEAN

San Francisco · Oakland · Berkeley · San Jose · Sacramento · Stockton · Modesto · Fresno · Bakersfield · **Los Angeles** · **San Diego**

Sierra Nevada

San Joaquin Valley

Death Valley National Monument

Mojave Desert

Yosemite National Park

Kings Canyon National Park

Sequoia National Park

Coast Ranges

Santa Cruz Mts · Gabilan Ra · Santa Lucia Range · La Panza Ra. · Temblor Ra · Panamint Ra

Monterey Bay · Santa Barbara Channel · Channel Islands · Gulf of Santa Catalina

Mt Whitney 4418 · Mt Dana 3978 · Mt Ritter 4010 · Mt Lyell 3997 · Arc Dome 3589

Santa Catalina · San Clemente

USA, HAWAII

PACIFIC OCEAN

Kauai · Niihau · Oahu · Honolulu · Pearl City · Molokai · Lanai · Maui · Kahoolawe · Hawaii

Mauna Kea 4201 · Mauna Loa 4169 · Hawaii Volcanoes Nat. Park · Kilauea Crater 1243

Hanalei · Kapaa · Lihue · Koloa · Waialua · Wahiawa · Kaneohe · Kailua · Kaunakakai · Lanai City · Wailuku · Kahului · Hana · Hawi · Kapaau · Honokaa · Waimea · Hilo · Pahoa · Kalapana · Pahala · Naalehu · Milolii · Kailua · Kiholo · Kawaihae

20 N · 160 · 155

1:5M

1:2.5M

KENTUCKY
VIRGINIA
TENNESSEE
NORTH CAROLINA
SOUTH CAROLINA
GEORGIA
ALABAMA
FLORIDA
ATLANTIC
OCEAN
GULF OF MEXICO
THE BAHAMAS
CUMBERLAND PLATEAU
APPALACHIAN MTS
BLUE RIDGE
Great Smoky Mts
Great Smoky Mts Nat. Park
Mt Mitchell 2037
Mt Rogers 1743
Clinch Mountains
Bowling Green
Russellville
Springfield
Gallatin
Hendersonville
Nashville
Lebanon
Cookeville
Murfreesboro
Franklin
McMinnville
Shelbyville
Manchester
Tullahoma
Fayetteville
Chattanooga
Cleveland
Knoxville
Oak Ridge
Crossville
Harriman
Maryville
Gatlinburg
Athens
Dayton
Morristown
Greeneville
Kingsport
Bristol
Elizabethton
Johnson City
Middlesboro
Corbin
Harlan
Big Stone Gap
Abingdon
Galax
Hillsville
Martinsville
Danville
Chatham
Halifax
South Boston
South Hill
Emporia
Franklin
Suffolk
Portsmouth
Chesapeake
Winston-Salem
Greensboro
High Point
Durham
Burlington
Chapel Hill
Raleigh
Cary
Rocky Mt
Wilson
Tarboro
Greenville
Williamston
Washington
Elizabeth City
Kitty Hawk
Manteo
Cape Hatteras
Pamlico Sound
Albemarle Sd
New Bern
Havelock
Morehead City
Cape Lookout
Jacksonville
Wilmington
Carolina Beach
Cape Fear
Fayetteville
Goldsboro
Kinston
Lumberton
Whiteville
Asheville
Morganton
Hickory
Statesville
Salisbury
Lexington
Thomasville
Asheboro
Kannapolis
Concord
Gastonia
Charlotte
Shelby
Albemarle
Hendersonville
Brevard
Franklin
Murphy
Greenville
Spartanburg
Gaffney
Easley
Anderson
Rock Hill
Lancaster
Chester
Columbia
Sumter
Florence
Darlington
Camden
Orangeburg
Aiken
Myrtle Beach
Conway
Georgetown
Charleston
Cape Romain
Walterboro
Beaufort
Hilton Head
Savannah
Windsor Forest
St Catherines I.
Atlanta
Marietta
Decatur
Roswell
Athens
Gainesville
Rome
Dalton
Macon
Augusta
Columbus
Albany
Valdosta
Waycross
Brunswick
Jesup
Statesboro
Dublin
Milledgeville
Warner Robins
Tifton
Thomasville
Bainbridge
Americus
Moultrie
Douglas
Birmingham
Huntsville
Gadsden
Anniston
Montgomery
Dothan
Enterprise
Auburn
Opelika
Phenix City
Troy
Tallahassee
Panama City
Fort Walton Beach
Jacksonville
Jacksonville Beach
Fernandina Beach
St Augustine
Lake City
Gainesville
Palatka
Ocala
Daytona Beach
Ormond Beach
New Smyrna Beach
Sanford
Orlando
Winter Park
Titusville
Cape Canaveral
Merritt Island
Cocoa
Melbourne
Palm Bay
Vero Beach
Fort Pierce
Stuart
Lakeland
Tampa
St Petersburg
Clearwater
Dunedin
Largo
Pinellas Park
Bradenton
Sarasota
Port Charlotte
Punta Gorda
Fort Myers
Naples
Cape Coral
Okeechobee
Lake Okeechobee
West Palm Beach
Palm Beach
Riviera Beach
Boca Raton
Delray Beach
Boynton Beach
Pompano Beach
Ft Lauderdale
Hollywood
Miami
Miami Beach
Hialeah
Coral Gables
Homestead
Florida City
Key Largo
Islamorada
Marathon
Key West
Florida Keys
The Everglades
Everglades National Park
Straits of Florida
Freeport City
Grand Bahama
Great Abaco
Nassau
New Providence
Andros
Great Bahama Bank
Bimini Is.
Berry Is.
1:5M
50 100 150 200 km
50 100 mls

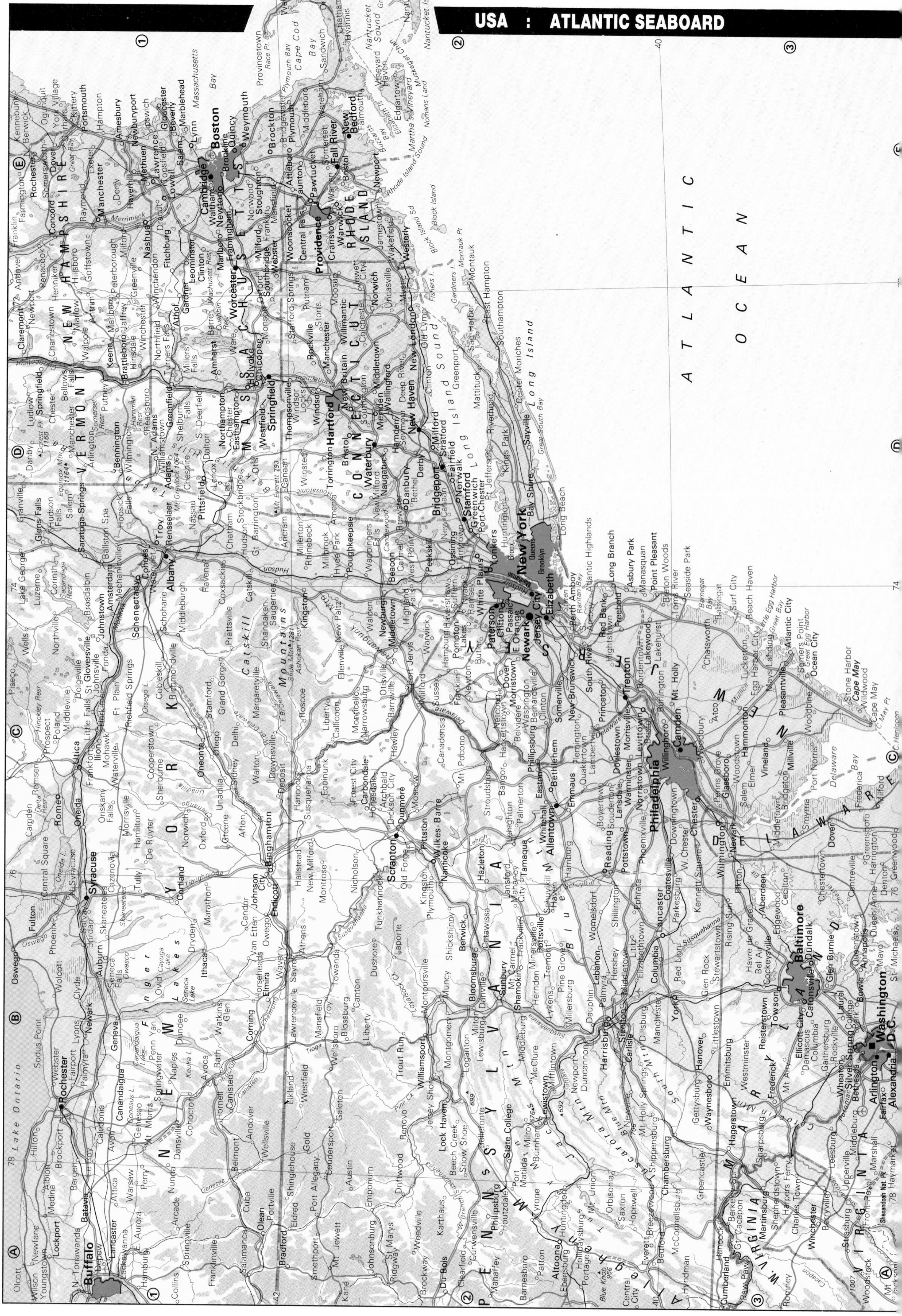
ATLANTIC OCEAN
NEW HAMPSHIRE
VERMONT
MASSACHUSETTS
RHODE ISLAND
CONNECTICUT
NEW YORK
PENNSYLVANIA
NEW JERSEY
DELAWARE
MARYLAND
W. VIRGINIA
VIRGINIA
Lake Ontario
Long Island Sound
Long Island
Cape Cod Bay
Massachusetts Bay
Catskill Mountains
Finger Lakes
Boston
Providence
Hartford
Springfield
Albany
New York
Newark
Philadelphia
Baltimore
Washington D.C.
Buffalo
Rochester
Syracuse
Binghamton
Scranton
Allentown
Harrisburg
Trenton
Wilmington
1:2.5M
0 25 50 75 100 km
0 25 50 mls

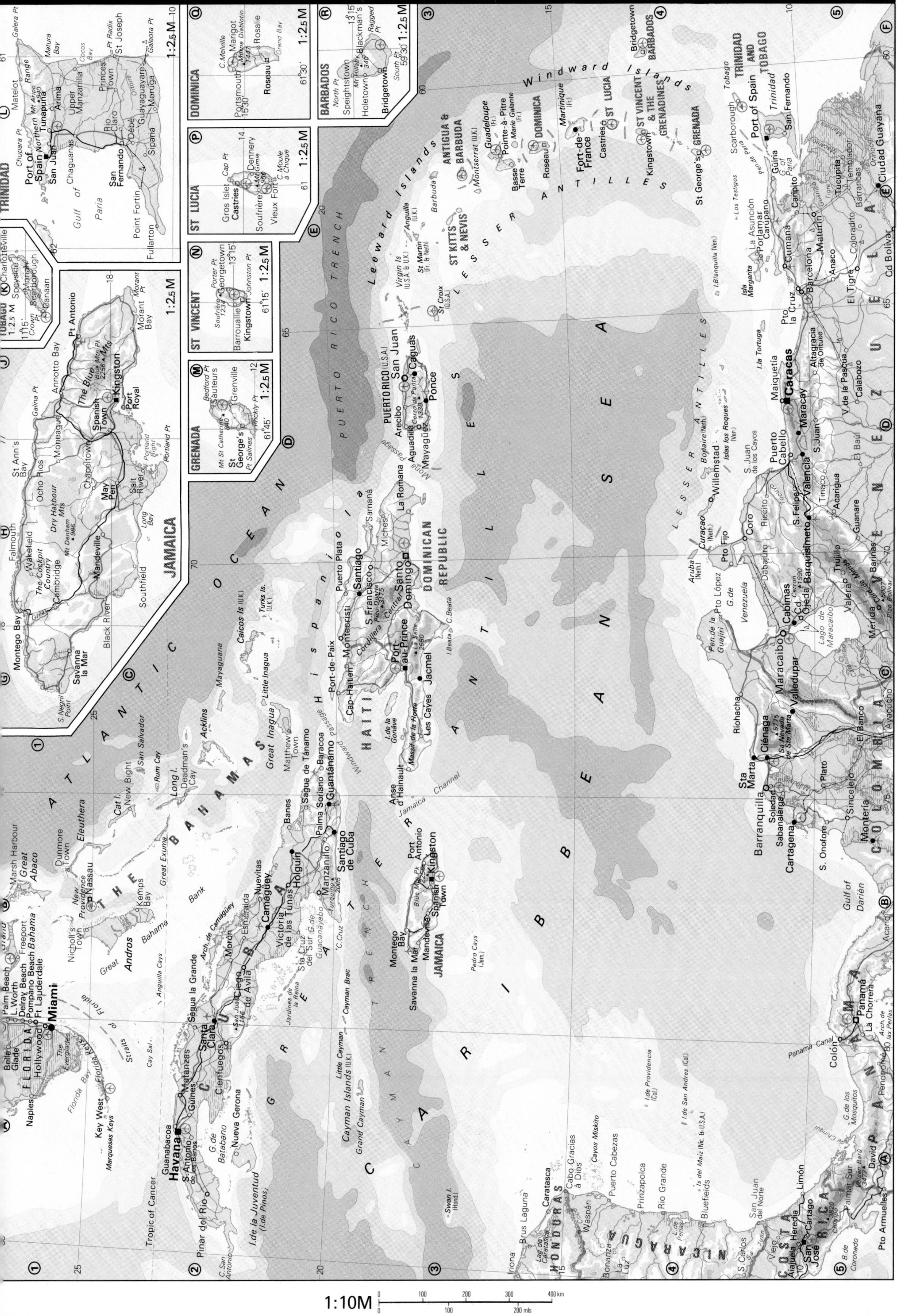
TRINIDAD
TOBAGO
JAMAICA
1:2.5M
GRENADA
ST VINCENT
ST LUCIA
DOMINICA
BARBADOS
ATLANTIC OCEAN
CARIBBEAN SEA
PUERTO RICO TRENCH
CAYMAN TRENCH
Leeward Islands
Windward Islands
LESSER ANTILLES
GREATER ANTILLES
THE BAHAMAS
CUBA
HAITI
DOMINICAN REPUBLIC
PUERTO RICO (U.S.A.)
ANTIGUA & BARBUDA
ST KITTS & NEVIS
ST VINCENT & THE GRENADINES
TRINIDAD AND TOBAGO
VENEZUELA
COLOMBIA
PANAMA
COSTA RICA
NICARAGUA
HONDURAS
FLORIDA
Miami
Havana
Nassau
Kingston
Port-au-Prince
Santo Domingo
San Juan
Caracas
Port of Spain
Panamá
Tropic of Cancer
Straits of Florida
Jamaica Channel
Windward Passage
Mona Passage
Panama Canal
Gulf of Darién
G. de Venezuela
Lago de Maracaibo

1:10M
0 100 200 300 400 km
0 100 200 mls

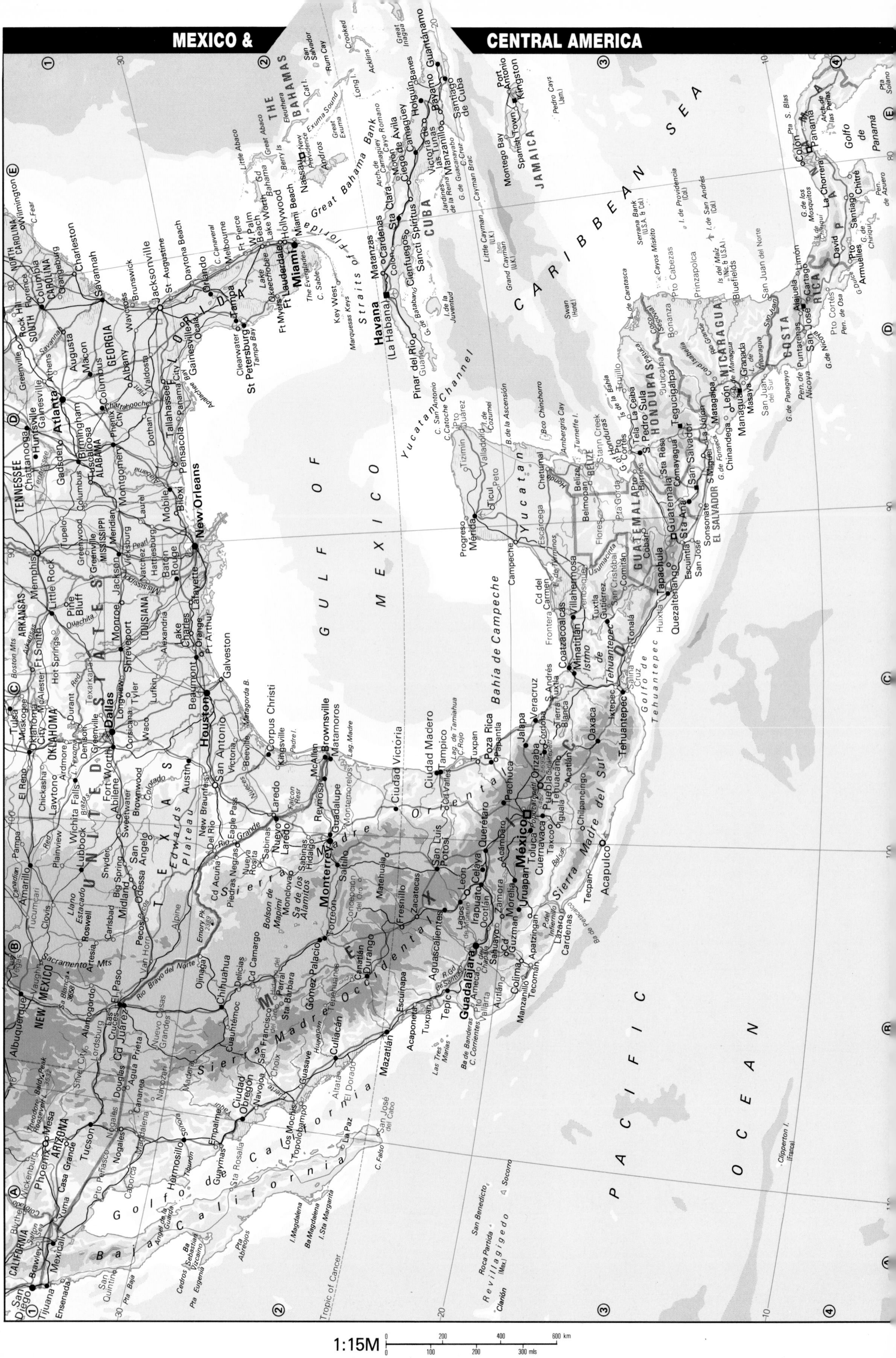
GULF OF MEXICO
CARIBBEAN SEA
PACIFIC OCEAN
UNITED STATES
TEXAS
Edwards Plateau
FLORIDA
CUBA
JAMAICA
THE BAHAMAS
MEXICO
Sierra Madre Occidental
Sierra Madre Oriental
Sierra Madre del Sur
Golfo de California
Baja California
Bahía de Campeche
Yucatan
Yucatan Channel
Straits of Florida
Great Bahama Bank
Golfo de Tehuantepec
Istmo de Tehuantepec
GUATEMALA
BELIZE
HONDURAS
EL SALVADOR
NICARAGUA
COSTA RICA
PANAMA
Golfo de Panamá
Tropic of Cancer
Revillagigedo
Clipperton I. (France)
Mexico
Guadalajara
Monterrey
Houston
Dallas
New Orleans
Miami
Havana (La Habana)
Atlanta

1:15M 0 200 400 600 km 0 100 200 300 mls

U.S.A.
Miami
THE BAHAMAS
Gulf of Mexico
Habana
Tropic of Cancer
Mérida
CUBA
Guantanamo
DOMINICAN REP.
Santiago
MEXICO
BELIZE
Belmopan
Santiago de Cuba
HAITI
JAMAICA
Kingston
Port-au-Prince
Santo Domingo
Pto Rico (U.S.A.)
San Juan
ANTIGUA & BARBUDA
ST KITTS-NEVIS
Guadeloupe (Fr.)
GUATEMALA
Guatemala
HONDURAS
Tegucigalpa
S.Salvador
EL SALVADOR
NICARAGUA
DOMINICA
Martinique (Fr.)
CARIBBEAN SEA
ST LUCIA
ST VINCENT & THE GRENADINES
BARBADOS
GRENADA
Neth. Antilles
Curaçao
Managua
COSTA RICA
S.José
Sta Marta
Barranquilla
Cartagena
Maracaibo
Caracas
Port of Spain
TRINIDAD & TOBAGO
Barcelona
Barquisimeto
Colón
Panamá
PANAMA
Cd. Bolivar
Orinoco
Cd. Guayana
S.Cristóbal
VENEZUELA
Medellín
Georgetown
GUYANA
Paramaribo
Cayenne
I. del Coco (C.R.)
Manizales
Bogotá
SURINAM
FR. GUIANA
Malpelo (Col.)
Buenaventura
Cali
COLOMBIA
Boa Vista
Popayán
S.Lorenzo
Pasto
Branco
Macapá
I. de Marajó
S.Pedro e S.Paulo (Braz.)
Quito
Equator
Galapagos Is (Ecu.)
ECUADOR
Putumayo
Negro
Amazon
Guayaquil
Manaus
Santarém
Belém
Iquitos
Amazon
Juruá
Xingu
Tocantins
São Luís
Piura
Tapajós
Codó
Sobral
Fortaleza
Rocas
I. Fernando de Noronha (Braz.)
Teresina
Marañón
Ucayali
Purus
Madeira
Chiclayo
Natal
Trujillo
PERU
Pto Velho
João Pessoa
Chimbote
Rio Branco
Araguaia
Recife
Juazeiro
BRAZIL
Maceió
Callao
Lima
Huancayo
Pto Maldonado
Alagoinhas
Aracajú
Salvador
Cuzco
Cáceres
Cuiabá
Goiânia
Brasília
São Francisco
Ilhéus
Arequipa
La Paz
BOLIVIA
Montes Claros
SOUTH PACIFIC OCEAN
Oruro
Cochabamba
Sucre
Sta Cruz
Arica
Corumbá
Corinto
Belo Horizonte
Iquique
Campo Grande
Ribeirao Prêto
Juiz de Fora
Vitória
Dourados
PARAGUAY
Campinas
Campos
Rio de Janeiro
Concepción
São Paulo
Santos
Antofagasta
Asunción
Foz do Iguacu
Ponta Grossa
Curitiba
Trindade (Braz.)
Tropic of Capricorn
Salta
Salado
Paraná
S.Félix (Chile)
S.Miguel de Tucumán
Resistencia
Posadas
Florianópolis
CHILE
Uruguay
Paraná
Pto Alegre
Córdoba
Rivera
Pelotas
Santa Fe
Paraná
Paysandu
Rio Grande
Mendoza
URUGUAY
Viña del Mar
Valparaíso
Rosario
SOUTH ATLANTIC OCEAN
Santiago
Juan Fernández Is. (Chile)
Buenos Aires
Montevideo
R. de la Plata
Talca
ARGENTINA
Concepción
Mar del Plata
Colorado
Bahía Blanca
Temuco
Negro
Valdivia
Pto Montt
Chico
Cmd. Rivadavia
G.San Jorge
Deseado
Falkland Is (U.K.)
Stanley
Rio Gallegos
Pto Natales
Punta Arenas
Tierra del Fuego
Cape Horn
S.Georgia (U.K.)
S.Shetland Is (U.K.)
S.Orkney Is (U.K.)
S.Sandwich Is (U.K.)
ANTARCTICA

1:35M
0 250 500 750 1000 1250 km
0 250 500 750 mls

PACIFIC OCEAN
COLOMBIA
VENEZUELA
ECUADOR
PERU
BOLIVIA
CHILE
ARGENTINA
PANAMA
COSTA RICA
NICARAGUA
AMAZONAS
RONDÔNIA
ACRE
S E L V A S
LLANOS
CORDILLERA DE LOS ANDES
Neth. Antilles
ST LUCIA
ST VINCENT & THE GRENADINES
GRENADA
Martinique
Caracas
Bogotá
Quito
Lima
La Paz
Medellín
Cali
Barranquilla
Cartagena
Maracaibo
Valencia
Guayaquil
Cuenca
Iquitos
Trujillo
Chiclayo
Piura
Arequipa
Cuzco
Puno
Arica
Tacna
Iquique
Antofagasta
Calama
Oruro
Cochabamba
Santa Cruz
Sucre
Potosí
Tarija
Salta
Jujuy
Rio Branco
Pôrto Velho
Leticia
Tabatinga
Ciudad Bolívar
Ciudad Guayana
Panamá
San José
Managua
Tegucigalpa
Lago Titicaca
Salar de Uyuni
Desierto de Atacama
Tropic of Capricorn
GALAPAGOS ISLANDS
ISLAS GALÁPAGOS
(ARCHIPIÉLAGO DE COLÓN)
(Equ.)
at the same scale
Islas Juan Fernández
(Chile)
Alejandro Selkirk
Robinson Crusoe
Sta Clara
Isabela
Fernandina
Santa Cruz
San Salvador
San Cristóbal
Baquerizo Moreno
Santa María
Española
Pinta
Marchena
Genovesa
Culpepper
Wenman

1:15M
0 200 400 600 km
0 100 200 300 mls

ATLANTIC OCEAN
BARBADOS
Bridgetown
TRINIDAD AND TOBAGO
GUYANA
SURINAM
FRENCH GUIANA
Georgetown
New Amsterdam
Paramaribo
Nieuw Amsterdam
Marienburg
Nieuw Nickerie
Totness
Albina
Sinnamary
I. du Diable (Devil's I.)
Kourou
Cayenne
Cabo Orange
Oiapoque
Apoera
Witagron
Julianatop 1280
Linden
Bartica
Suddie
Charity
Mabaruma
Serra Tumucumaque
AMAPÁ
Amapá
Ilha de Maracá
Macapá
Pto Santana
Sa do Navio
C. Maguarinho
I. de Marajó
B. de Marajó
Salinópolis
Bragança
Capanema
Belém
Abaetetuba
Cametá
Oriximiná
Óbidos
Amazonas
Monte Alegre
Santarém
Manaus
Itacoatiara
Altamira
Aveiro
Itaituba
Parque Nacional Amazonia
Pimenta
Tucuruí
Tocantins
PARÁ
Xingu
Jacareacanga
S. Félix
Serra do Cachimbo
Cachimbo
Equator
B. de São Marcos
Alcântara
Pinheiro
São Luís
Rosário
Parnaíba
Camocim
Acaraú
Monção
Chapadinha
Bacabal
Coroatá
Codó
Caxias
Itapipoca
Sobral
Caucaia
Fortaleza (Ceará)
Sta Quitéria
Piripiri
Campo Maior
Teresina
Nova Russas
Canindé
Aracati
Quixadá
Crateús
Castelo
Morada Nova
CEARÁ
Areia Branca
Macau
Mossoró
Pta do Calcanhar
Natal
Rocas
I. Fernando de Noronha
MARANHÃO
Marabá
Imperatriz
Grajaú
Pto Franco
Carolina
Araguaína
Balsas
Floriano
Oeiras
PIAUÍ
Picos
Mombaça
Tauá
Iguatu
Acopiara
RIO GRANDE DO NORTE
Patu
Caicó
Sousa
Patos
J. do Norte
Crato
PARAÍBA
Cabedelo
João Pessoa
Campina Grande
Salgueiro
Sa Talhada
Limoeiro
Caruaru
Olinda
Recife (Pernambuco)
Jaboatão
Palmares
Garanhuns
Palmeira dos Índ.
Barreiros
PERNAMBUCO
Paulistana
Ouricuri
S. Raimundo Nonato
Petrolina
Juàzeiro
Cach. de P. Afonso
ALAGOAS
Maceió
Propriá
Arapiraca
SERGIPE
Penedo
Aracajú
Estância
C. do Araguaia
TOCANTINS
São Félix
Ilha do Bananal
Barragem de Sobradinho
Barra
Sen. do Bonfim
Jacobina
BAHIA
Lagarto
Serrinha
Alagoinhas
Barreiras
Ibotirama
R. de Jacuípe
Feira de S.
Cachoeira
Castro Alves
Salvador (Bahia)
B. de T. os Santos
Iaçu
Bom Jesus da Lapa
Chapada Diamantina
Valença
Jequié
Caetité
Vitória da Conquista
Itabuna
Ilhéus
Ipiaú
BRAZIL
MATO GROSSO
Pto Artur
Sa Formosa
Sa dos Caiabis
GOIÁS
Uruaçu
Aruanã
Planalto de Mato Grosso
Cuiabá
Cáceres
Fatima du Sul
Rondonópolis
Aragarças
Goiás
Céres
Jaraguá
Formosa
Pirenópolis
Brasília
Anápolis
Goiânia
Iporá
São Francisco
Januária
Porteirinha
Montes Claros
Salinas
Itapetinga
Canavieiras
Belmonte
Pôrto Seguro
Araçuaí
Sa do Chifre
Serra do Espinhaço
Rio Verde
Caldas Novas
Paracatu
Pirapora
João Pinheiro
Mineiros
Jataí
Itumbiara
Catalão
Araguari
Patos de Minas
Curvelo
Corinto
Diamantina
Teófilo Otôni
Nanuque
Itamaraju
Gov. Valadares
Coxim
Corumbá
Pto Suárez
MATO GROSSO DO SUL
Uberlândia
MINAS GERAIS
Araxá
Iturama
Uberaba
Sete Lagoas
Itabira
Belo Horizonte
Caratinga
Cnl. Fabriciano
ESPÍRITO SANTO
São Mateus
Linhares
Colatina
Vitória
Vila Velha
Cachoeiro de Itapemirim
Campo Grande
Aquidauana
Três Lagoas
Rubinéia
Fernandópolis
S. José do R. Prêto
Barretos
Franca
Passos
Divinópolis
Manhuaçu
Cariacica
Ponte Nova
Jardim
Araçatuba
Catanduva
Ribeirão Prêto
S. João del Rei
Lafaiete
Carangola
Barbacena
Itaperuna
Campos
S. João da Barra
Pto Murtinho
Dourados
Pres. Epitácio
Tupã
SÃO PAULO
Araraquara
São Carlos
Poços de Caldas
Lavras
Juiz de Fora
Pres. Prudente
Marília
Bauru
Limeira
Volta Redonda
Nova Friburgo
Petrópolis
Magé
Niterói
Rio de Janeiro
Ponta Porã
Paranavaí
Assis
Ourinhos
Piracicaba
Campinas
Barra Mansa
Concepción
Horqueta
PARAGUAY
Umuarama
Maringá
Londrina
Apucarana
Jacarèzinho
Sorocaba
Jundiaí
São Paulo
Itapeva
Itapetininga
Santos
São Vicente
Itanhaém
Iguape
C. Mourao
Goio-Erê
Guaíra
Toledo
Cascavel
PARANÁ
Castro
Juquiá
Itararé
Asunción
Luque
San Pedro
Pedro J. Caballero
Fte Olimpo

55

BOLIVIA

BRAZIL

MATO GROSSO DO SUL

MINAS GERAIS

SÃO PAULO

PARAGUAY

PARANÁ

SANTA CATARINA

GRAN CHACO

RIO GRANDE DO SUL

URUGUAY

ARGENTINA

La Pampa

Chubut

Santa Cruz

PATAGONIA

ATLANTIC OCEAN

FALKLAND ISLANDS (ISLAS MALVINAS) (U.K.)

West Falkland
East Falkland
Stanley

South Georgia (U.K.)

Ilo
Pta Coles
Tacna
Aiquile
Arica
Iquique
Tocopilla
Pedro de Valdivia
Mejillones
Antofagasta
Taltal
Chañaral
Caldera
Copiapó
Huasco
Vallenar
La Serena
Coquimbo
Ovalle
Punitaqui
Illapel
Los Vilos
Quillota
Viña del Mar
Valparaiso
S. Antonio
Santiago
S. Bernardo
Rancagua
Pichilemu
S. Fernando
Curicó
Constitución
Talca
Linares
S. Carlos
Cauquenes
Tomé
Talcahuano
Concepción
Coronel
Lebu
Los Angeles
Angol
Carahue
Temuco
Toltén
Loncoche
Valdivia
Los Lagos
La Unión
Osorno
Pto Varas
Puerto Montt
Ancud
I. de Chiloé
Castro
Achao
Esquel
Pto Aisén
Coihaique
Sarmiento

Oruro
Huanuni
Sajama 6542
Sabaya
Poopó
Uyuni
Salar de Uyuni
Vol. Ollagüe 5870
Ollagüe
Ujina
Chuquicamata
Calama
Tocorpuri 5833
Ojos del Salado 6908
Pissis 6858
Llullaillaco 6723
 Co. del Toro 6380
Olivares
Mercedario 6770
Aconcagua 6960
Tupungato 6800
Vol. Maipo 5290
Vol. Peteroa 4090
Vol. Domuyo 4800
Vol. Lanin 3140

Santa Cruz
Valle Grande
Llanos de Chiquitos
San José de Chiquitos
Pto Suárez
Corumbá
Mayor P. Lagerenza
Fte Olimpo
Aquidauana
Campo Grande
Três Lagoas
Jardim
Panorama
Pto Murtinho
Dourados
Filadelfia
Concepción
Pedro J. Caballero
Ponta Porã
Araçatuba
Marília
Bauru
Tupã
Presidente Prudente
Assis
Ourinhos
Londrina
Maringá
Apucarana
Itapeva
Jacarezinho
Sorocaba
Jundiaí
Campinas
São Paulo
Santos
São Vicente
Rio de Janeiro
Itanhaém
Barra Mansa
Volta Redonda

Oruro
Sucre
Potosí
Tarabuco
Camargo
Cotagaita
Tupiza
La Quiaca
Abra Pampa
Humahuaca
Tilcara
S. Salvador de Jujuy
Jujuy
Ledesma
Orán
Embarcación
Tartagal
Yacuíba
Villa Montes
Camiri
Pozo Colorado
Concepción
Horqueta
Formosa
Pres. R.S. Peña
S.J. Bautista
Pilar
Resistencia
Barranqueras
Corrientes
Empedrado
Posadas
Encarnación
Misiones
S. Miguel d'Oeste
União de Vitória
Guaíra
São Miguel
Cascavel
Foz do Iguaçu
Pto Pres. Stroessner
Guarapuava
Ponta Grossa
Curitiba
Paranaguá
São Francisco do Sul
Joinville
Blumenau
Itajaí
Florianópolis
I. de Sta Catarina
Imbituba
Tubarão
Criciúma
Ararangua
Lajes
Vacaria
Caxias do Sul
Bento Gonçalves
N. Hamburgo
Canoas
Gravataí
Porto Alegre
Pelotas
Rio Grande

Salta
Cachi
Metán
Cafayate
Campo Gallo
S. Miguel de Tucumán
Tucumán
Catamarca
Londres
Tinogasta
Santiago del Estero
Añatuya
Catamarca
La Rioja
Chilecito
Chepes
Jáchal
S. Agustín
S. Juan
Mendoza
San Luis
San Rafael
Gral Alvear
Telén
Sta Rosa
Gral Acha
Gral Pico
Guaminí
Carhué
Cnl Pringles
Balcarce
Tres Arroyos
Bahía Blanca
Punta Alta
Claromecó
Miramar
Necochea
Mar del Plata
Va Gesell
Ayacucho
Tandil
Azul
Las Flores
Dolores
Chascomús
Buenos Aires
La Plata
Avellaneda
Mercedes
Colonia
Montevideo
Maldonado
Punta del Este
Rocha
Minas
Treinta y Tres
Chui
Florida
Trinidad
Durazno
Melo
Bagé
Livramento
Rivera
Artigas
Salto
Paysandú
Concordia
Concepción
Paraná
Santa Fe
Rafaela
San Francisco
Córdoba
Alta Gracia
Villa María
Río Cuarto
Venado Tuerto
Rufino
Lincoln
Junín
Pergamino
San Nicolás
Rosario
Bell Ville

Reconquista
Vera
Goya
Mercedes
Paso de los Libres
Uruguaiana
Alegrete
Santa Maria
Cruz Alta
Passo Fundo
Erechim
Sto Angelo
S. Borja
Cachoeira do Sul
Encruzilhada

S. Antonio Oeste
Viedma
Carmen de Patagones
Choele Choel
Gral Roca
Neuquén
Zapala
Las Plumas
Trelew
Gaimán
Rawson
Pto Madryn
Pto Pirámides
Las Heras
Caleta Olivia
Comodoro Rivadavia
Camarones
C. Dos Bahías
Pto Deseado
Puerto Santa Cruz
San Julián
Río Gallegos
Río Turbio
Calafate
Bahía Grande
Pta Médanosa

Cochrane
Pen. de Taitao
Archipiélago de las Chones
Wellington
Madre de Dios
Hanover
Pto Natales
Arch. de la Reina Adelaida
Punta Arenas
Desolación
Santa Inés
Isla Grande de Tierra del Fuego
Tierra del Fuego
Río Grande
Ushuaia
I. de los Estados
Hoste
C. de Hornos (C Horn)
Is Wollaston
Londonderry
Is Diego Ramírez

Tropic of Capricorn

1:15M
0 200 400 600 km
0 100 200 300 mls

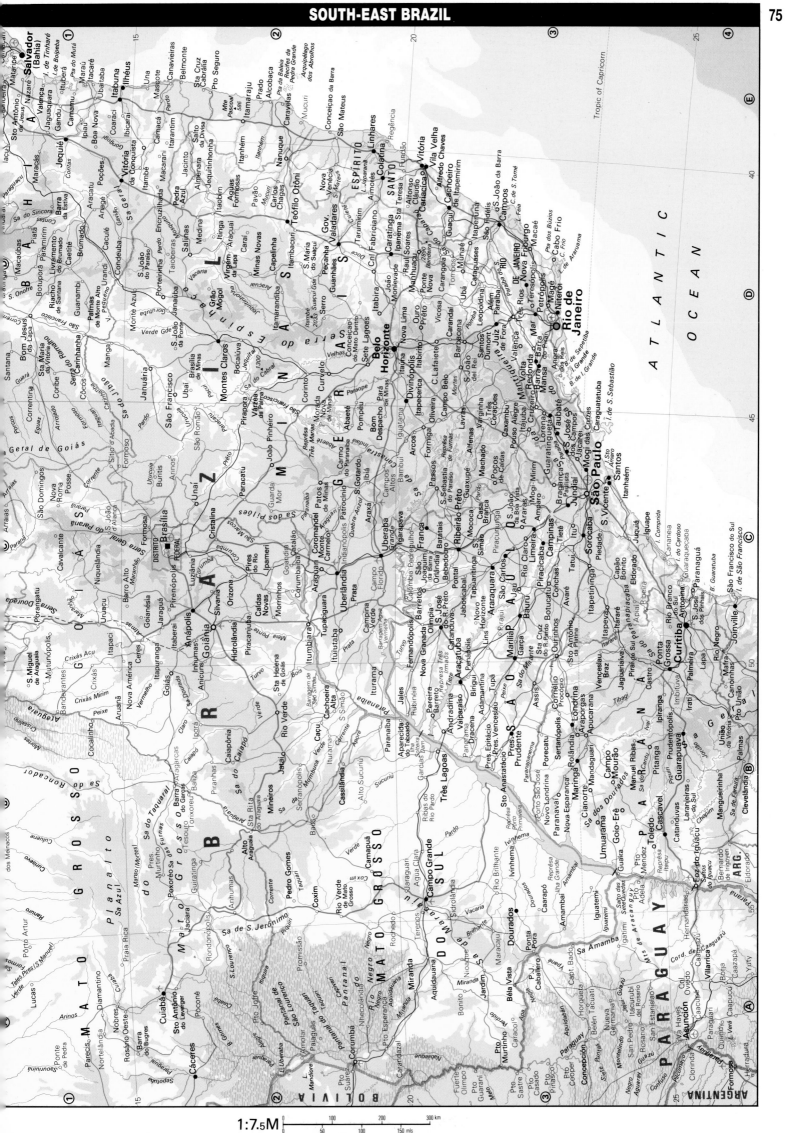

1:7.5M
0 100 200 300 km
0 50 100 150 mls

Northern Polar Region (top map)

Portland, Seattle, Vancouver, Prince Rupert, Juneau, Vaduz, Anchorage, Mt McKinley *6194, Yukon, Teller, Vankarem, Ayan, Blagoveshchensk, CHINA

U.S.A., Calgary, Edmonton, Saskatoon, Fairbanks, Dawson, Alaska (U.S.A.), Chukchi Sea, Pevek, Ambarchik, Ust Nera, Skovorodino, Chul'man, Chita, Ulan

ROCKY MTS, CANADA, Norman Wells, Inuvik, Prudhoe Bay, Barrow, Beaufort Sea, Kolyma, Polyarn'yy, Verkhoyansk, Yakutsk, Aldan, Irkutsk

Gt Bear L., Coppermine, Yellowknife, Gt Slave L., Mackenzie, Banks I., Victoria I., McClure Str., Wrangel I. (O. Vrangel'ya), East Siberian Sea, Zhigansk, Oz. Baykal, Ust Kut

Flin Flon, L. Athabasca, Tree Limit, Bering Str., Novosibirskiye Ostrova, Laptev Sea, Lena, Tiksi, Ust Kut

L. Winnipeg, Churchill, Southampton I., Hudson Bay, Foxe Basin, Resolute, Queen Elizabeth Islands, N. Magnetic Pole (1990), North Pole, Severnaya Zemlya, Nordvik, Khatanga, RUSSIAN FEDERATION

James B., Fort George, Inukjuak, Baffin I., Eureka, Ellesmere I., Alert, Lincoln Sea, Zemlya Frantsa Iosifa, Novaya Zemlya, Kara Sea, Dikson, Dudinka, Noril'sk, Turukhansk, Novosibirsk, Barn

Schefferville, Hebron, Nain, Pond Inlet, Thule, Nares Str., Nord, Svalbard (Spitsbergen), average minimum extent of sea ice, Nadym, Salekhard, Berezovo, Tobol'sk, Omsk

Labrador Sea, Godhavn (Qeqertarsuaq), Sondre Stromfjord, Godthåb (Nuuk), Greenland (Kalaallit Nunaat) (Den.), Greenland Sea, Barents Sea, Vorkuta, Serov, Yekaterinburg, Perm', Ufa, Magnitogorsk

Gulf of St Lawrence, Newfoundland, Gander, Julianehåb (Qaqortoq), Ammassalik (Angmagssalik), Watkins Bjerge 3700, Scoresbysund, Bjørnøya (Bear I.) (Nor.), Jan Mayen (Nor.), Nordkapp, Tromsø, Murmansk, Arkhangel'sk, Mezen, White Sea, Sev. Dvina, Kotlas, Kirov, Orsk, Aktyubinsk

K. Farvel, Denmark Strait, Norwegian Sea, Arctic Circle, NORWAY, SWEDEN, Narvik, Oulu, Umeå, FINLAND, Kazan', Samara

ATLANTIC OCEAN, Reykjavik, ICELAND, St Petersburg (Leningrad), Yaroslavl', Nizhniy Novgorod

Southern Polar Region (bottom map)

ATLANTIC OCEAN, Antarctic Circle

Falkland Is (U.K.), Scotia Sea, Orcadas (Arg.), S. Orkney Is (U.K.), Signy (U.K.), Sanae (S.Afr.), Maitri (India), Prinsesse Astrid Kyst, Georg Forster (Germany), Novolazarevskaya (Former USSR), Asuka (Japan), Prinsesse Ragnhild Kyst, Syowa (Jap.), Molodezhnaya (Former USSR), Enderby Land, INDIAN OCEAN

ARGENTINA, S. Shetland Is (U.K.), King George I., Graham Land, Georg Von Neumayer (Germany), Halley (U.K.), Coats Land, Dronning Maud Land, Mawson (Aust.), Heard I. (Aust.)

Tierra del Fuego, CHILE, Palmer Arch., Antarctic Peninsula, General Belgrano II (Arg.), Mac. Robertson Land, Pt Charles Mts *3355, C. Darnley, Amery Ice Shelf

Drake Passage, Alexander I., Charcot I., Palmer Land, Ronne Ice Shelf, Berkner I., Pensacola Mts, GREATER ANTARCTICA, American Highland, Lambert Gl., Zhongshan (China), Davis (Aust.)

PACIFIC OCEAN, Bellingshausen Sea, Ellsworth Land, Siple (U.S.), Vinson Massif 4897, Transantarctic Mts, South Pole, Amundsen-Scott (U.S.), Queen Mary Land, Mirnyy (Former USSR)

Peter I Øy (Nor.), Thurston I., LESSER ANTARCTICA, Mt Seelig 3022, Q Maud Mts, Vostok (Former USSR), Shackleton Ice Shelf, Knox Coast

Amundsen Sea, Walgreen Coast, Mt Sidley 4181, Marie Byrd Land, Mt Kirkpatrick *4528, Mt Markham *4351, Ross Ice Shelf, Wilkes Land, Casey (Aust.), C. Poinsett

Siple I., Roosevelt I., C. Colbeck, Scott (N.Z.), McMurdo (U.S.), Cape Evans (Greenpeace), Ross Sea, Victoria Land, George V Land, Terre Adélie

C. Adare, Leningradskaya (Former USSR), S. Magnetic Pole (1990), Dumont d'Urville (Fr.), Oates Land, Balleny Is, Sturge I., Scott I.

Antarctic Research Stations

1. Commandante Ferraz (Brazil)
2. Henryk Arctowski (Poland)
3. Teniente Jubany (Argentina)
4. King Sejong (Korea)
5. Artigas (Uruguay)
6. Teniente Rodolfo Marsh (Chile)
7. Bellingshausen (Former USSR)
8. Great Wall (China)
9. Captain Arturo Prat (Chile)
10. Esperanza (Argentina)
11. General Bernardo O'Higgins (Ch.)
12. Marambio (Argentina)
13. Palmer (USA)
14. Faraday (UK)
15. General San Martin (Argentina)
16. Rothera (UK)

King George Island (inset map): 0 10 20 30km

1:40M 400 800 1200 1600 km / 400 800 mls

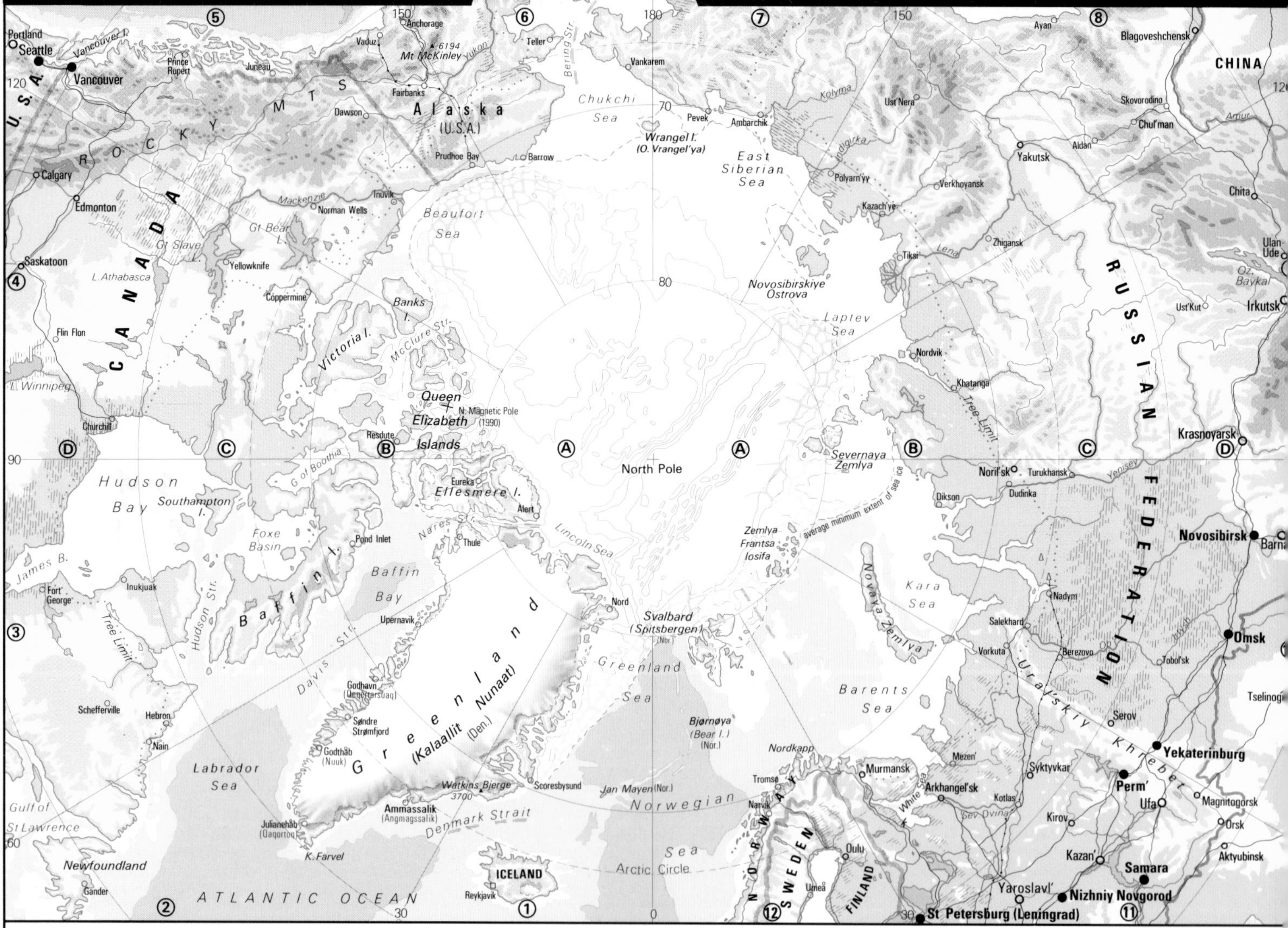

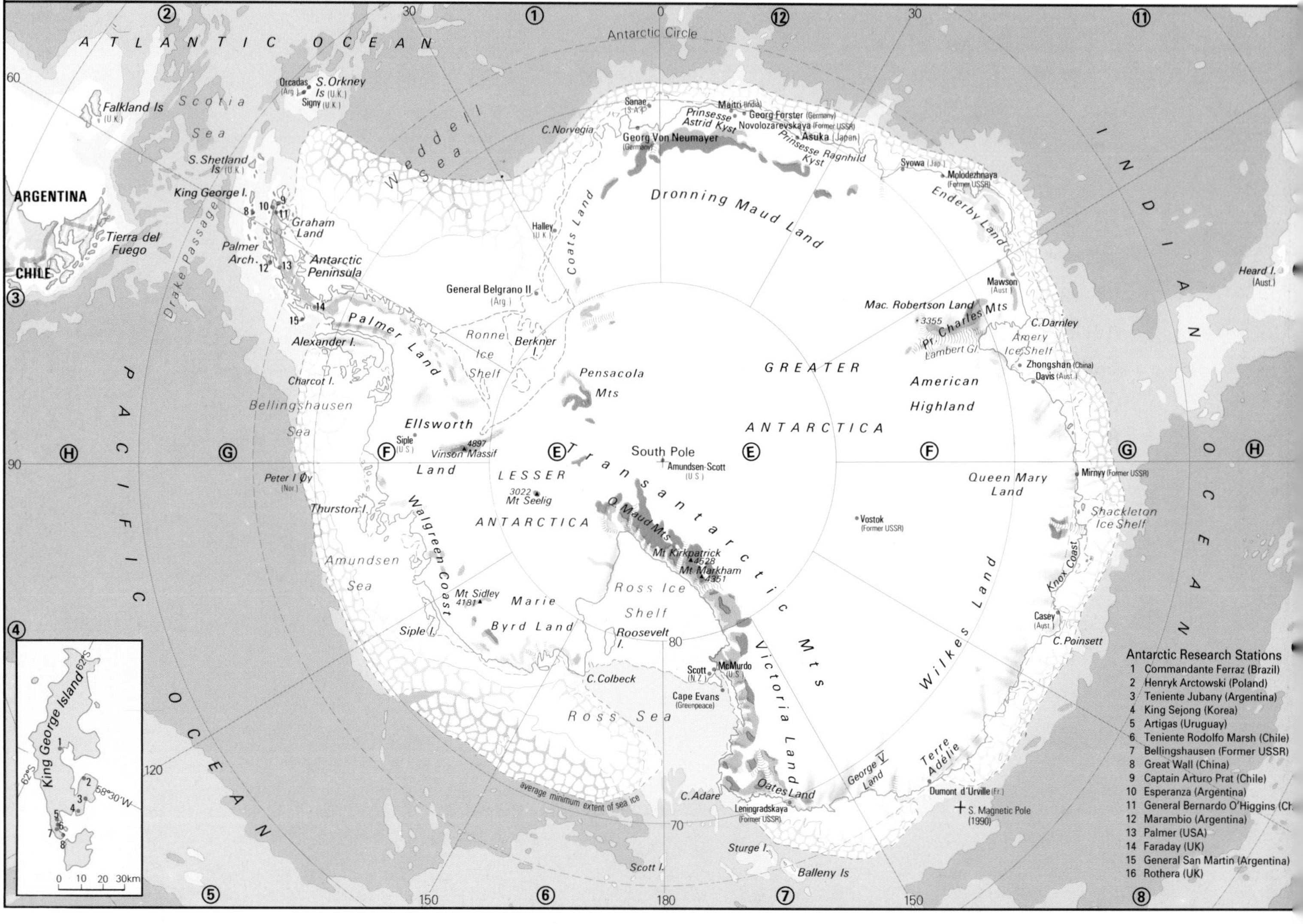

KEY TO SYMBOLS ON CITY PLANS

- International Boundary
- State Boundary
- Department Boundary
- City Limits
- Borough, District Boundary
- Military Zones
- Armistice, Ceasefire Line
- Demilitarised Zone
- Main Railways
- Other Railways
- Projected Railways
- Underground Railway
- Aerial Cableway, Funicular
- Metro Stations
- Special Highway
- Main Road
- Secondary Road
- Other Road, Street
- Track
- Road Tunnel
- Bridge, Flyover

- Seaway
- Canals
- Drainage Canal
- Waterfalls, Rapids
- Important Buildings
- Historic Walls
- Airports
- Car Ferry
- Racecourses
- Stadium
- Cemetery, Churches
- Woodland, Park
- Jungle
- Mangrove Swamp
- Farmland
- Built-up Area

Amsterdam 81
Athens 83
Auckland 86
Bangkok 84
Barcelona 80
Beijing 84
Berlin 82
Bombay 87
Boston 89
Brussels 81
Buenos Aires 92
Cairo 88
Calcutta 87
Chicago 89
Copenhagen 83
Delhi 87
Geneva 82
Hamburg 82
Hong Kong 84
Istanbul 88
Jerusalem 88
London 78
Los Angeles 91
Madrid 80
Manhattan 90
Melbourne 86
Mexico City 92
Milan 82
Montreal 89
Moscow 83
Nairobi 88
New York 90
Osaka 85
Ottawa 89
Paris 79
Perth 86
Rio de Janeiro 92
Rome 80
San Francisco 91
Santiago 92
São Paulo 92
Seoul 85
Shanghai 84
Singapore 87
Stockholm 83
Sydney 86
Tokyo 85
Toronto 89
Vienna 81
Washington 91

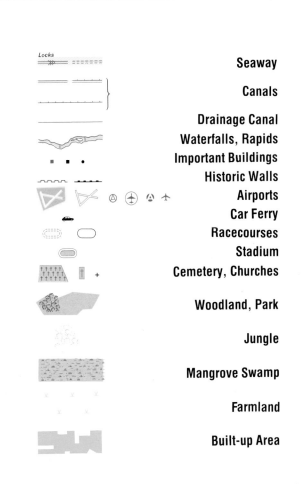

LONDON
Borough names underlined
0 1 2 3km
BARNET
HARINGEY
WALTHAM FOREST
REDBRIDGE
NEWHAM
GREENWICH
LEWISHAM
SOUTHWARK
LAMBETH
WANDSWORTH
MERTON
KINGSTON UPON THAMES
RICHMOND
HOUNSLOW
EALING
BRENT
CAMDEN
HACKNEY
ISLINGTON
TOWER HAMLETS
CITY OF WESTMINSTER
KENSINGTON AND CHELSEA
HAMMERSMITH
RIVER THAMES
CITY OF LONDON
TOTTENHAM
HORNSEY
HAMPSTEAD
WILLESDEN
WEMBLEY
ACTON
CHISWICK
FULHAM
CHELSEA
BATTERSEA
WANDSWORTH
WIMBLEDON
PADDINGTON
MARYLEBONE
ST PANCRAS
HOLBORN
FINSBURY
SHOREDITCH
STOKE NEWINGTON
BETHNAL GREEN
STEPNEY
POPLAR
WEST HAM
EAST HAM
LEYTON
WALTHAMSTOW
WANSTEAD
BERMONDSEY
DEPTFORD
CAMBERWELL
ELTHAM

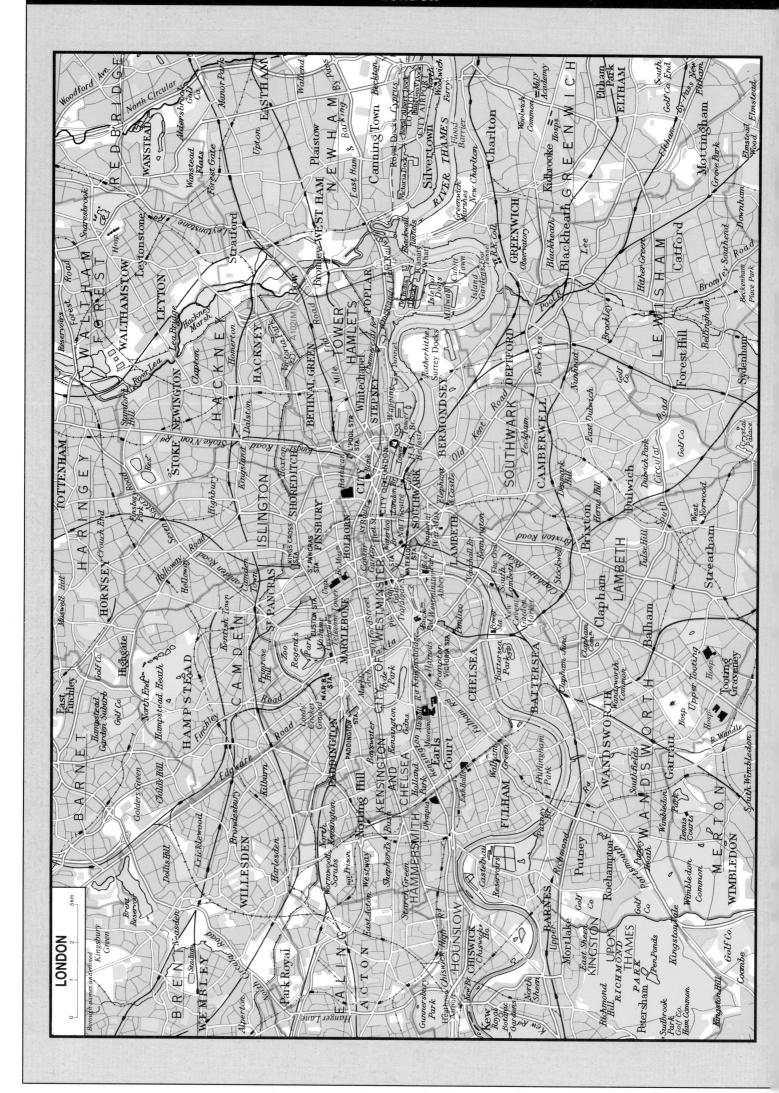

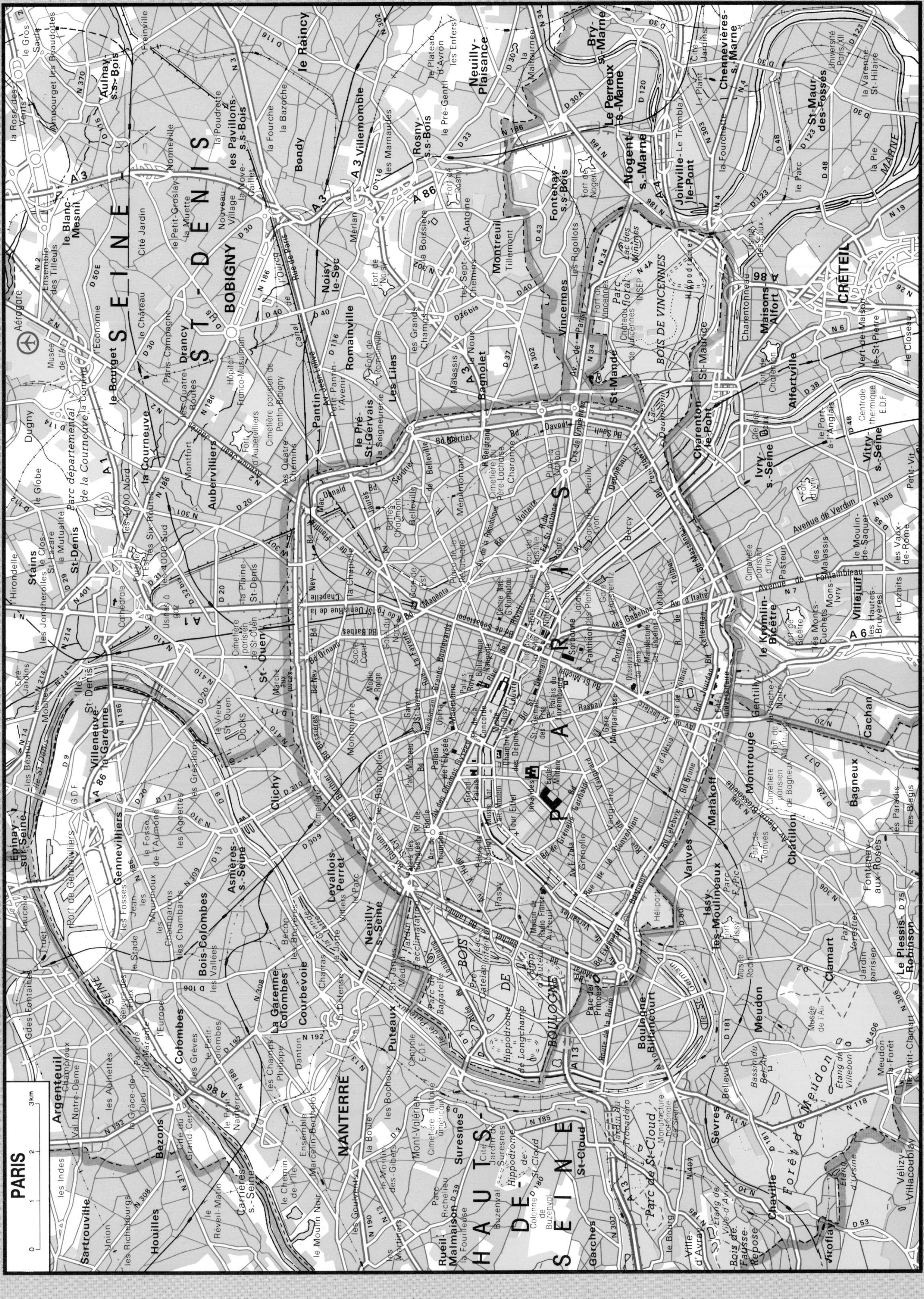
PARIS
0 1 2 3km
HAUTS-DE-SEINE
SEINE-ST-DENIS
PARIS
St-Denis
Aubervilliers
la Courneuve
le Bourget
Drancy
BOBIGNY
Pantin
Noisy-le-Sec
Romainville
les Lilas
le Pré-St-Gervais
Bagnolet
Montreuil
Vincennes
St-Mandé
Fontenay-s.-Bois
Nogent-s.-Marne
le Perreux-s.-Marne
Bry-s.-Marne
Neuilly-Plaisance
Rosny-s.-Bois
Villemomble
le Raincy
Bondy
les Pavillons-s.-Bois
Aulnay-s.-Bois
le Blanc-Mesnil
Dugny
Stains
Joinville-le-Pont
St-Maur-des-Fossés
Chennevières-s.-Marne
CRÉTEIL
Maisons-Alfort
Alfortville
Charenton-le-Pont
St-Maurice
Ivry-s.-Seine
Vitry-s.-Seine
Villejuif
le Kremlin-Bicêtre
Gentilly
Cachan
Bagneux
Montrouge
Malakoff
Châtillon
Vanves
Issy-les-Moulineaux
Clamart
Fontenay-aux-Roses
le Plessis-Robinson
Meudon
Sèvres
Chaville
Viroflay
Vélizy-Villacoublay
Ville-d'Avray
St-Cloud
Garches
Boulogne-Billancourt
Suresnes
Rueil-Malmaison
NANTERRE
Puteaux
Courbevoie
La Garenne-Colombes
Colombes
Bois-Colombes
Asnières-s.-Seine
Gennevilliers
Villeneuve-la-Garenne
Épinay-s.-Seine
Clichy
Levallois-Perret
Neuilly-s.-Seine
St-Ouen
Argenteuil
Bezons
Sartrouville
Houilles
Carrières-s.-Seine
BOIS DE BOULOGNE
BOIS DE VINCENNES
Forêt de Meudon
Parc de St-Cloud
SEINE
MARNE

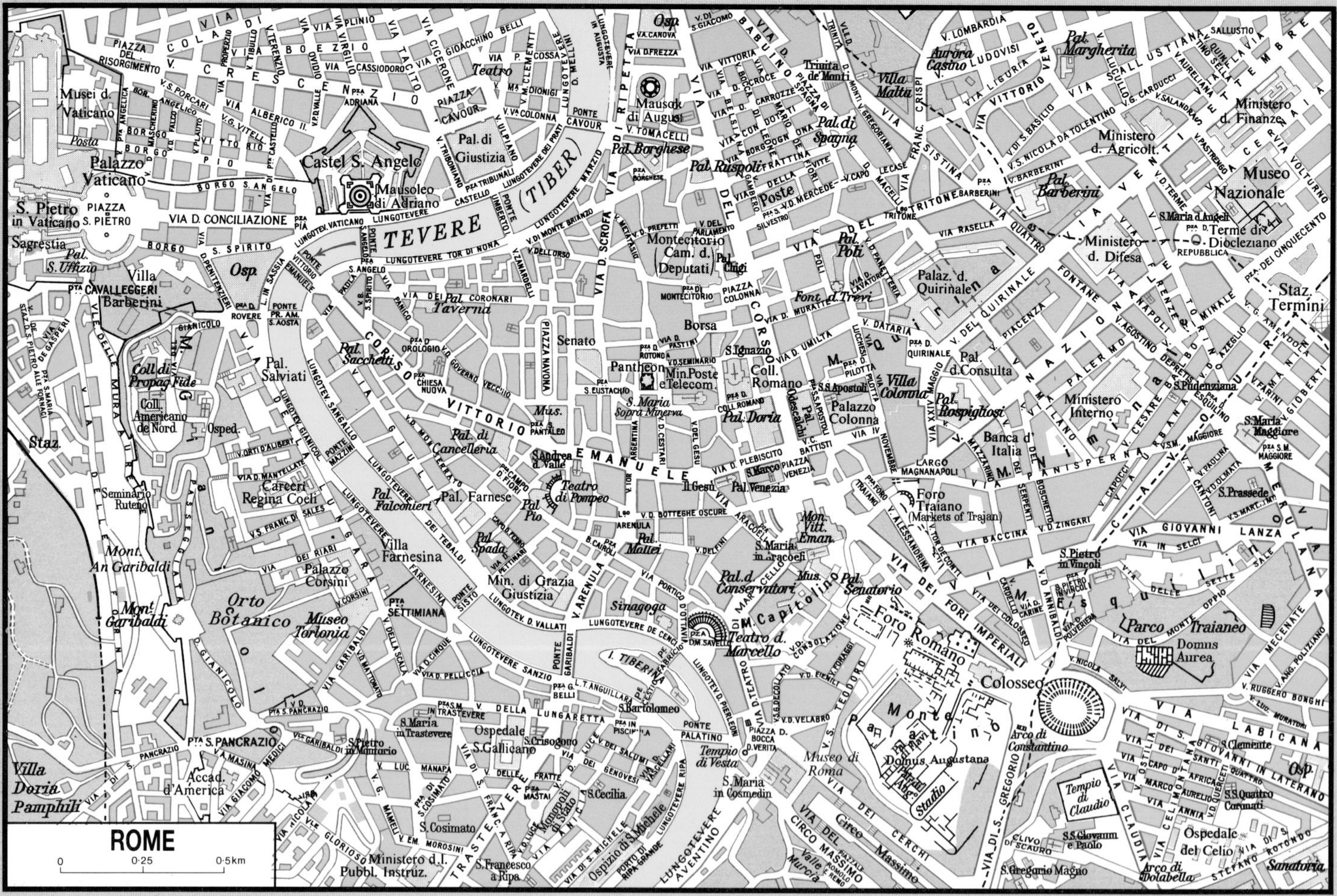
ROME
0
0·25
0·5km
Musei d. Vaticano
Palazzo Vaticano
S. Pietro in Vaticano
PIAZZA S. PIETRO
Sagrestia
Pal. S. Uffizio
Villa Barberini
PIAZZA DEL RISORGIMENTO
Castel S. Angelo
Mausoleo di Adriano
VIA D. CONCILIAZIONE
TEVERE
(TIBER)
Pal. di Giustizia
PIAZZA CAVOUR
Mausoleo di Augusto
Pal. Borghese
Pal. Ruspoli
Trinità de' Monti
Pal. di Spagna
Villa Malta
Aurora Casino
Pal. Margherita
Ministero d. Finanze
Ministero d. Agricolt.
Museo Nazionale
Terme di Diocleziano
Staz. Termini
Ministero d. Difesa
Pal. Barberini
Palaz. d. Quirinale
Font. d. Trevi
Pal. Poli
Montecitorio Cam. d. Deputati
Pal. Chigi
Borsa
Pantheon
Senato
Pal. Taverna
Pal. Sacchetti
PIAZZA NAVONA
Mus.
Pal. di Cancelleria
S. Andrea d. Valle
Teatro di Pompeo
Pal. Farnese
Pal. Falconieri
Pal. Spada
Villa Farnesina
Palazzo Corsini
Orto Botanico
Museo Torlonia
Mont. Garibaldi
Carceri Regina Coeli
Seminario Ruteno
Coll. Americano del Nord
Coll. di Propag. Fide
Pal. Salviati
Osped.
Osp.
Staz.
Villa Doria Pamphili
Accad. d'America
S. Pietro in Montorio
S. Maria in Trastevere
Ospedale S. Gallicano
S. Crisogono
S. Cecilia
S. Cosimato
Ministero d. I. Pubbl. Instruz.
S. Francesco a Ripa
Ospizio di S. Michele
I. TIBERINA
S. Bartolomeo
Sinagoga
Teatro d. Marcello
Tempio di Vesta
S. Maria in Cosmedin
Museo di Roma
Circo Massimo
Pal. d. Conservatori
Mus. Capitolino
Pal. Senatorio
Foro Romano
Mon. Vitt. Eman.
S. Maria in Aracoeli
Il Gesù
Pal. Venezia
Pal. Mattei
Pal. Doria
S. Maria Sopra Minerva
S. Ignazio
Coll. Romano
Min. Poste e Telecom.
Palazzo Colonna
Villa Colonna
Pal. Rospigliosi
Pal. d. Consulta
Banca d' Italia
Ministero Interno
Foro Traiano (Markets of Trajan)
S. Pietro in Vincoli
Parco Traianeo
Domus Aurea
Colosseo
Arco di Constantino
Monte Palatino
Domus Augustana
Stadio
Tempio di Claudio
S.S. Giovanni e Paolo
S. Gregorio Magno
Ospedale del Celio
Arco di Dolabella
S. Clemente
S.S. Quattro Coronati
S. Maria Maggiore
S. Pudenziana
S. Prassede
Sanatoria
VIA VITTORIO VENETO
CORSO VITTORIO EMANUELE
VIA DEL CORSO
VIA CAVOUR
VIA NAZIONALE
VIA XX SETTEMBRE
VIA GIOVANNI LANZA
VIA LABICANA
VIA DEI FORI IMPERIALI
LUNGOTEVERE
VIA ARENULA
VIA DEL TRITONE

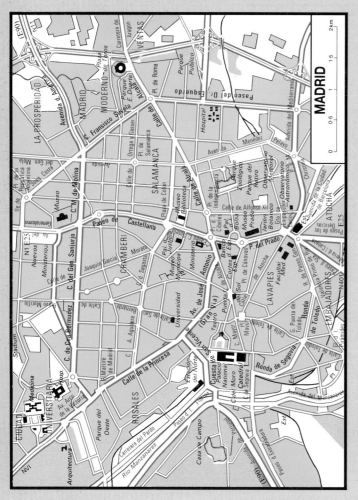

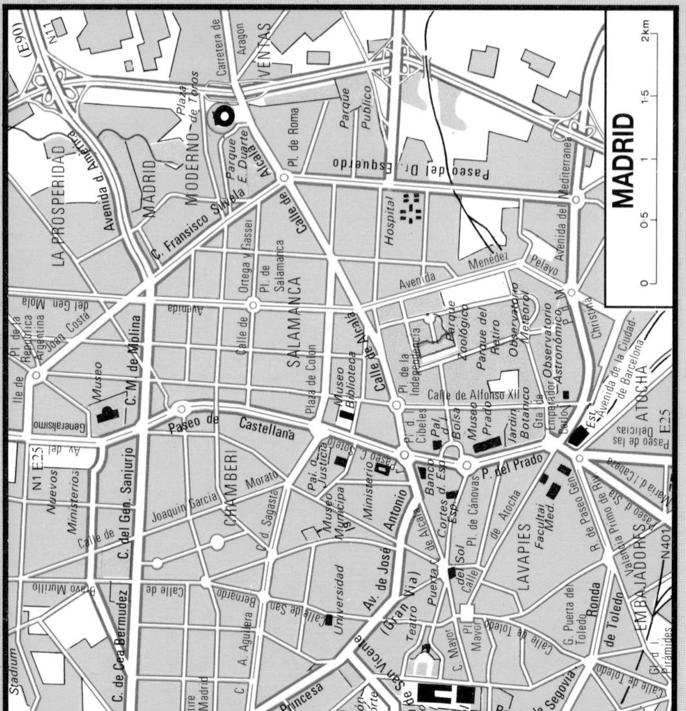
MADRID
0
0·5
1
1·5
2km
LA PROSPERIDAD
MADRID MODERNO
VENTAS
Plaza de Toros
Parque E. Duarte
SALAMANCA
Paseo del Dr. Esquerdo
Hospital
Avenida del Mediterraneo
Parque Zoologico
Parque del Retiro
Observatorio Astronómico
Jardin Botanico
Museo Prado
Plaza de Colón
Paseo de Castellana
Calle de Alcalá
Calle de Alfonso XII
CHAMBERI
Museo
Generalisimo
Nuevos Ministerios
Joaquín García Morato
Bernardo
Universidad
Av. de José Antonio (Gran Via)
Puerta del Sol
Banco de Esp.
Cortes
Ministerio
Museo Municipal
Museo Justicia
LAVAPIES
Facultad Med.
Ronda de Toledo
Ronda de Segovia
EMBAJADORES
ATOCHA
Est.
Palacio Nacional
Catedral
Estación del Norte
Cuesta de San Vicente
Calle de la Princesa
ROSALES
Parque del Oeste
Casa de Campo
Río Manzanares
Carretera del Pardo
CIUDAD UNIVERSITARIA
Medicina
Arquitectura
Stadium
Hosp.
Av. Arco de la Victoria
C. de Cea Bermudez
Avenida del Manzanares
N VI
N I
E 25
E 90
N 401

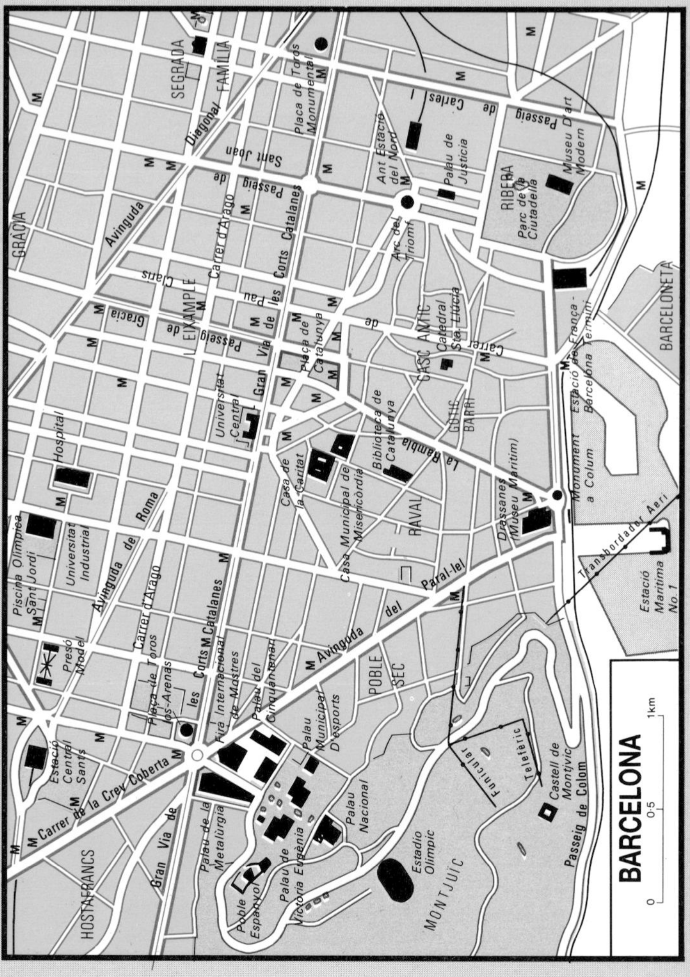
BARCELONA
0
0·5
1km
SAGRADA FAMILIA
GRACIA
Avinguda Diagonal
Sant Joan
Plaça de Toros Monumental
Passeig de Carles
Passeig de Gràcia
Gran Via de les Corts Catalanes
Carrer d'Aragó
Plaça de Catalunya
L'EIXAMPLE
Universitat Central
Hospital
Ant. Estació del Nord
Palau de Justicia
Arc del Triomf
RIBERA
Parc de la Ciutadella
Museu d'art Modern
BARCELONETA
Estació de França
CASC ANTIC
Catedral
Sta. Lucia
GOTIC
BARRI
La Rambla
RAVAL
Biblioteca de Catalunya
Casa Municipal de Misericòrdia
Casa de la Caritat
Drassanes (Museu Marítim)
Monument a Colom
Transbordador Aeri
Estació Marítima No. 1
Avinguda del Paral·lel
POBLE SEC
Avinguda de Roma
Universitat Industrial
Piscina Olímpica Sant Jordi
Presó Model
Plaça de Toros les Arenas
Fira Internacional de Mostres
Palau del Cinquantenari
Palau Municipal d'Esports
Estació Central Sants
Carrer de la Creu Coberta
HOSTAFRANCS
Palau de la Metal·lúrgia
Palau de Victòria Eugènia
Poble Espanyol
Palau Nacional
Estadio Olímpic
MONTJUIC
Castell de Montjuïc
Funicular
Teleferic
Passeig de Colom

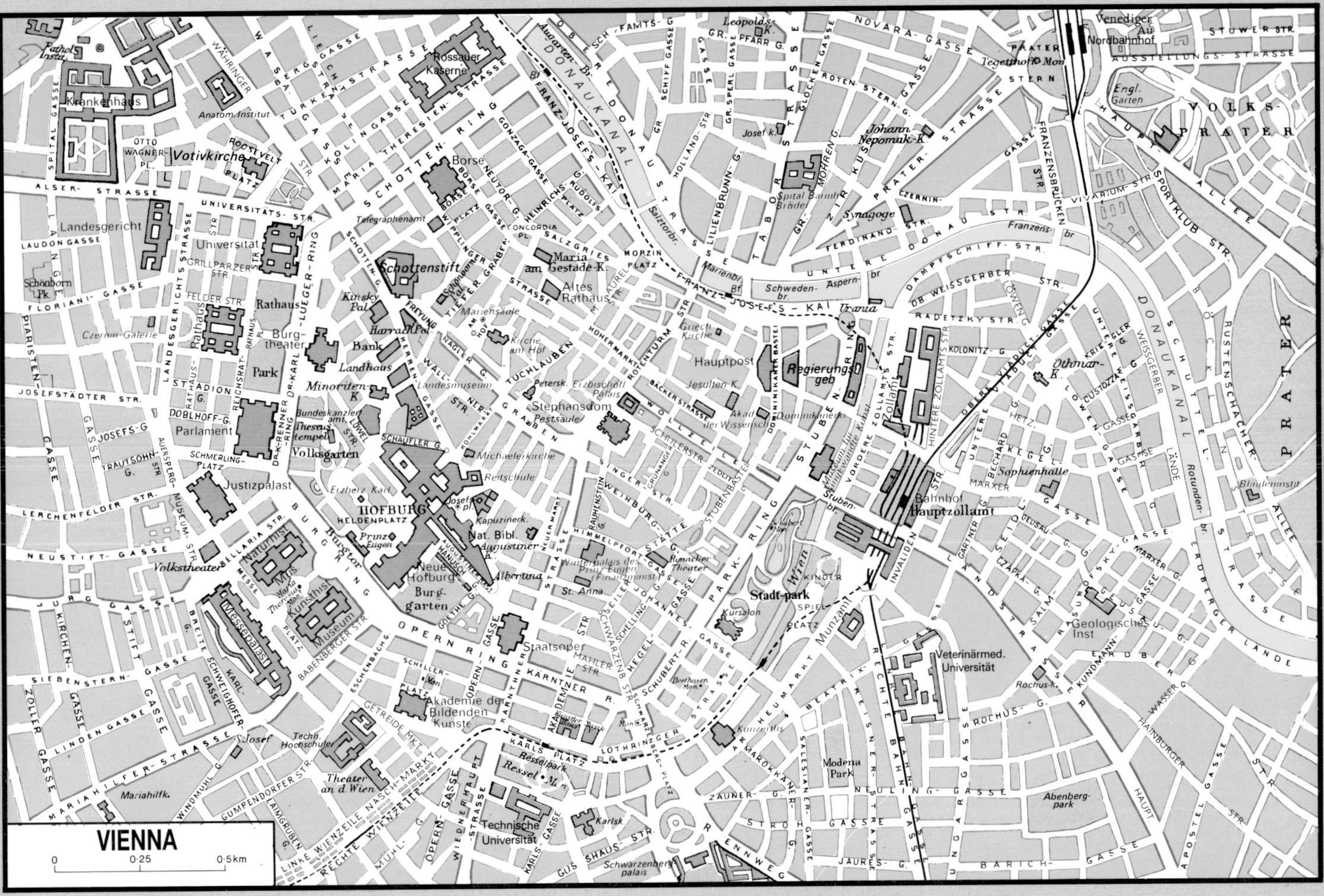
VIENNA
0 0·25 0·5km
HOFBURG
Rathaus
Parlament
Volksgarten
Stephansdom
Staatsoper
Stadt-park
PRATER
DONAUKANAL
Votivkirche
Universität
Burg-theater
Justizpalast
Westbahnhof
Bahnhof Hauptzollamt
Veterinärmed. Universität
Technische Universität

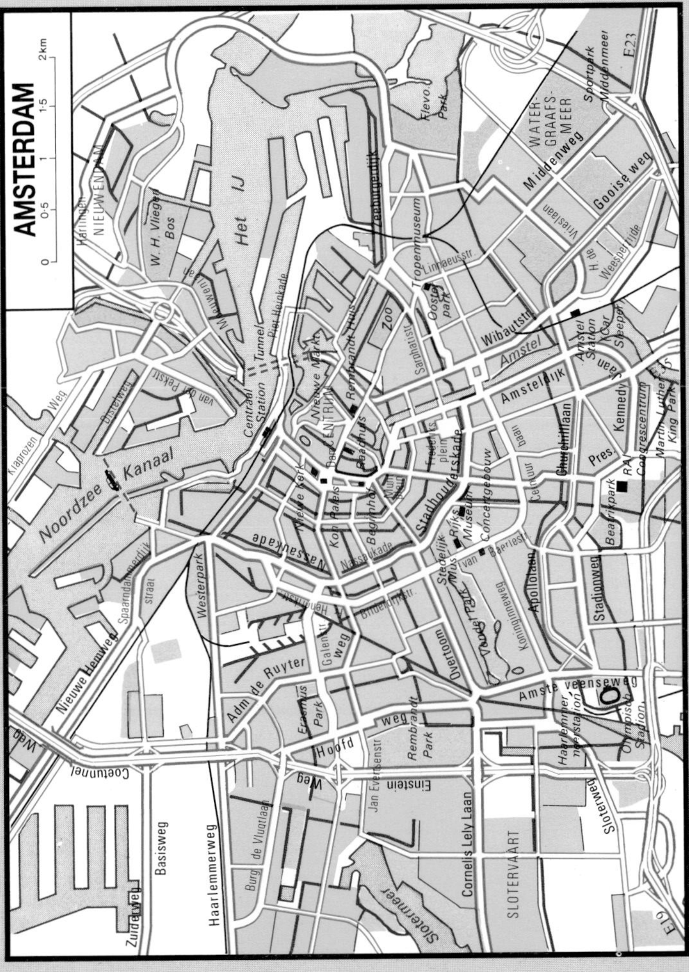
AMSTERDAM
0 0·5 1 1·5 2km
Het IJ
Noordzee Kanaal
Centraal Station
Amstel
Vondel Park
Rijks Museum
Concertgebouw
Stadhouderskade
Westerpark
Sloterdijk

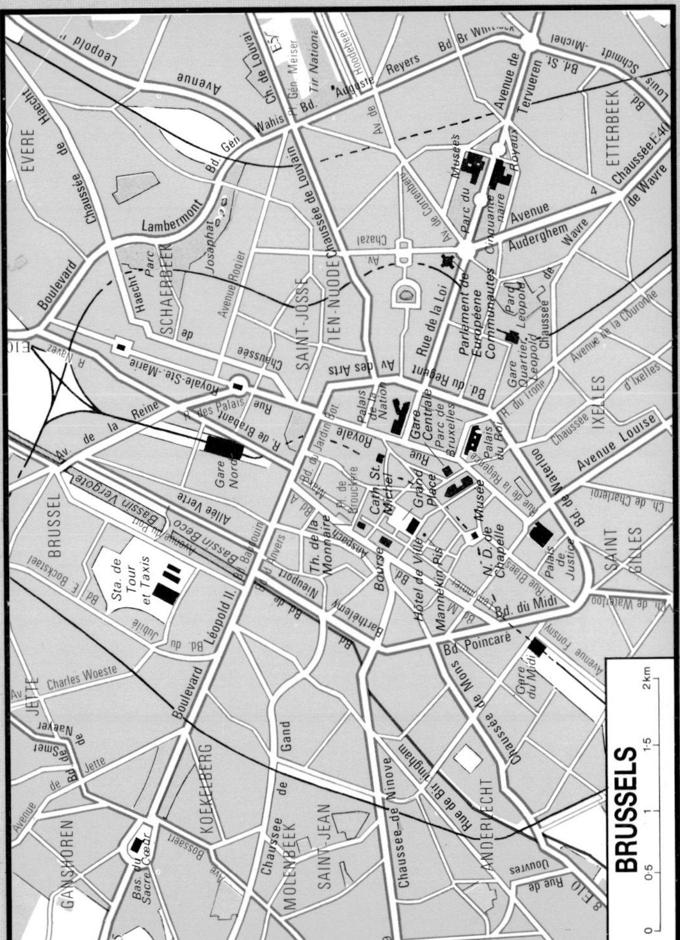
BRUSSELS
0 0·5 1 1·5 2km
Gare Centrale
Gare du Nord
Gare du Midi
Grand Place
Palais Royale
Parc de Bruxelles
Palais de Justice
Parc du Cinquantenaire
SCHAERBEEK
ETTERBEEK
IXELLES
SAINT GILLES
ANDERLECHT
KOEKELBERG
MOLENBEEK SAINT-JEAN
Avenue Louise
Boulevard Léopold II

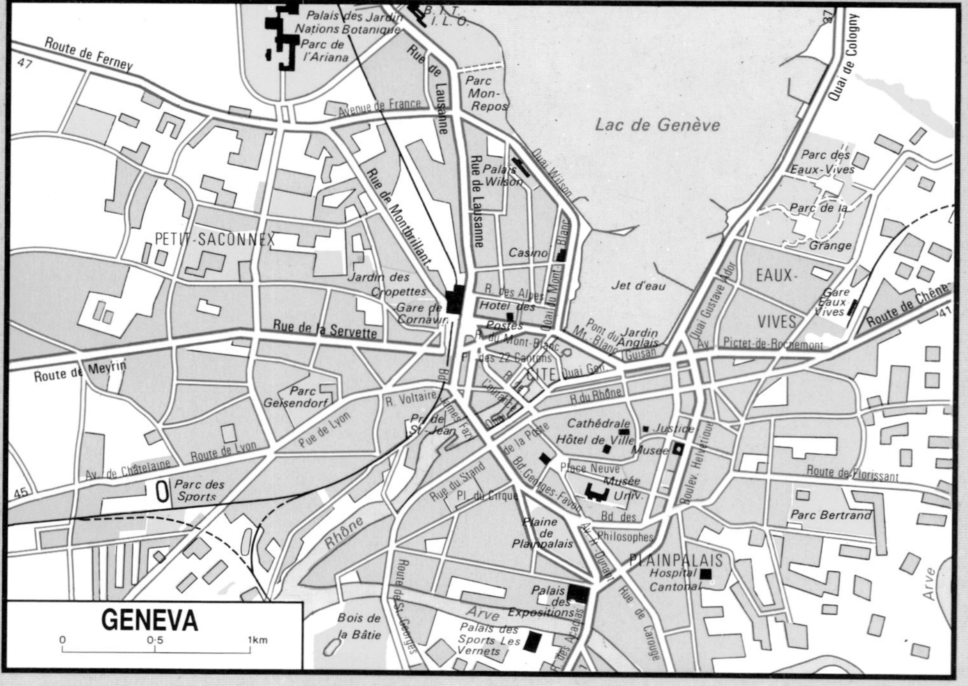
GENEVA
0 0·5 1km
Lac de Genève
Route de Ferney
Palais des Nations
Jardin Botanique
Parc de l'Ariana
B.I.T. I.L.O.
Parc Mon-Repos
Avenue de France
Rue de Lausanne
Rue de Montbrillant
Palais Wilson
Quai Wilson
Casino
PETIT-SACONNEX
Jardin des Cropettes
Gare de Cornavin
Hôtel des Postes
Rue de la Servette
Route de Meyrin
Parc Geisendorf
R. Voltaire
Jet d'eau
Jardin Anglais
Pont du Mont-Blanc
Quai Gustave Ador
Parc des Eaux-Vives
Parc de la Grange
EAUX-VIVES
Gare Eaux Vives
Route de Chêne
Quai de Cologny
Pictet-de-Rochemont
CITÉ
R. du Rhône
Cathédrale
Hôtel de Ville
Justice
Musée
Place Neuve
Musée
Univ.
Bd des Philosophes
Plaine de Plainpalais
PLAINPALAIS
Hospital Cantonal
Route de Florissant
Parc Bertrand
Palais des Expositions
Palais des Sports Les Vernets
Arve
Rhône
Bois de la Bâtie
Parc des Sports
Av. de Châtelaine
Route de Lyon
Rue de Lyon
Route de Carouge
Route de St. Georges

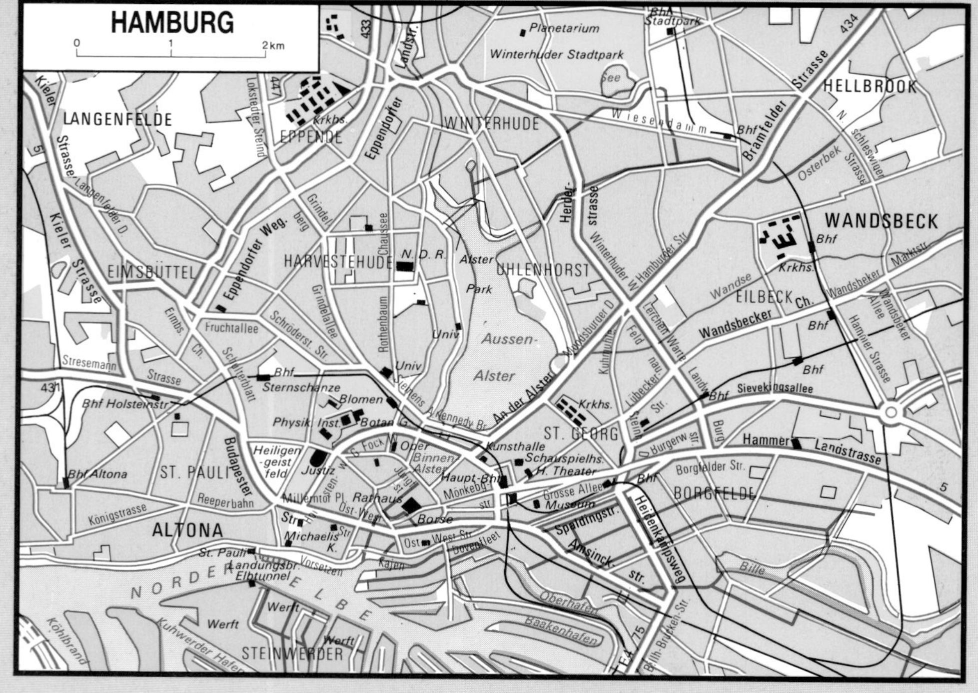
HAMBURG
0 1 2km
LANGENFELDE
Kieler Strasse
EPPENDORF
Eppendorfer Landstr.
Planetarium
Winterhuder Stadtpark
WINTERHUDE
Bramfelder Strasse
HELLBROOK
WANDSBECK
Wandsbeker Chaussee
EILBECK
EIMSBÜTTEL
Eppendorfer Weg
HARVESTEHUDE
N.D.R.
Alster Park
UHLENHORST
Aussen-Alster
Univ.
Sternschanze
Blomen
Physik. Inst.
Botan. G.
Heiligen geist feld
Justiz
Oper
Binnen Alster
Kunsthalle
Schauspielhs.
Haupt-Bhf
Rathaus
Börse
ST. GEORG
Sievekingsallee
Hammer Landstrasse
BORGFELDE
Heidenkampsweg
Bhf Holstenstr.
Bhf Altona
ST. PAULI
Budapester
Reeperbahn
ALTONA
Königstrasse
Michaelis K.
St. Pauli Landungsbr.
Elbtunnel
NORDERELBE
Werft
STEINWERDER
Baakenhafen
Oberhafen
Bille

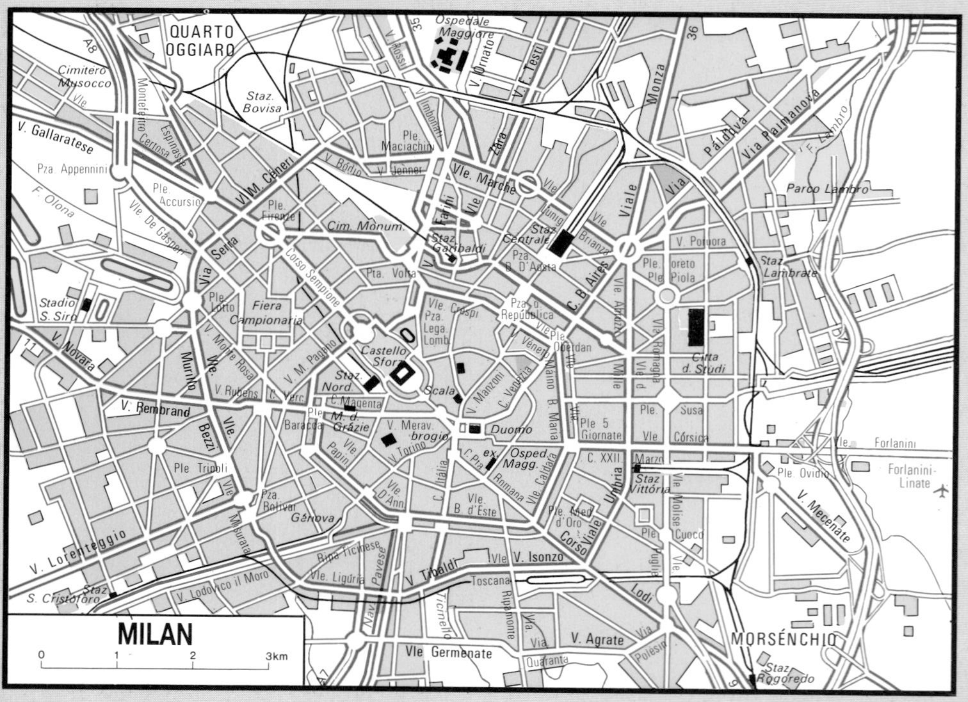
MILAN
0 1 2 3km
QUARTO OGGIARO
Cimitero Musocco
Staz. Bovisa
Ospedale Maggiore
V. Gallaratese
Monza
Via Palmanova
Parco Lambro
Staz. Lambrate
Cim. Monum.
Staz. Garibaldi
Staz. Centrale
Fiera Campionaria
Castello Sforz.
Scala
Duomo
Staz. Nord
Città d. Studi
Osped. Magg.
Stadio S. Siro
V. Novara
V. Lorenteggio
Ple Tripoli
Staz. Vittoria
Forlanini-Linate
V. Mecenate
MORSÉNCHIO
Staz. Rogoredo
Staz. S. Cristoforo
Vle Germenate
V. Agrate

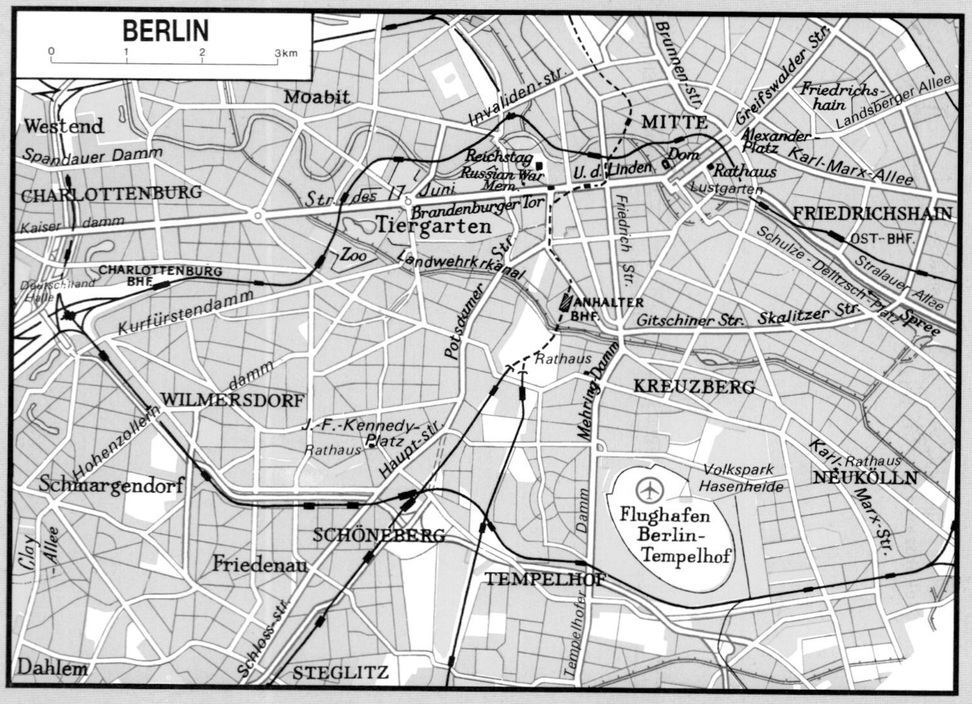
BERLIN
0 1 2 3km
Moabit
Westend
Spandauer Damm
CHARLOTTENBURG
Kaiserdamm
CHARLOTTENBURG BHF
Invaliden-str.
Brunnen-str.
MITTE
Greifswalder Str.
Friedrichshain
Landsberger Allee
Alexander Platz
Karl-Marx-Allee
Reichstag
Russian War Mem.
U. d. Linden
Dom
Rathaus
Lustgarten
Str. des 17. Juni
Brandenburger Tor
Tiergarten
Zoo
Landwehrkanal
FRIEDRICHSHAIN
OST-BHF.
Stralauer Allee
Spree
Friedrich Str.
Potsdamer Str.
ANHALTER BHF.
Gitschiner Str.
Skalitzer Str.
Kurfürstendamm
WILMERSDORF
Hohenzollerndamm
Schmargendorf
J.-F.-Kennedy-Platz
Rathaus
Haupt-str.
Mehringdamm
KREUZBERG
Volkspark Hasenheide
Karl-Marx-Str.
NEUKÖLLN
Flughafen Berlin-Tempelhof
SCHÖNEBERG
Friedenau
TEMPELHOF
Tempelhofer Damm
Clay-Allee
Dahlem
Schloss-str.
STEGLITZ

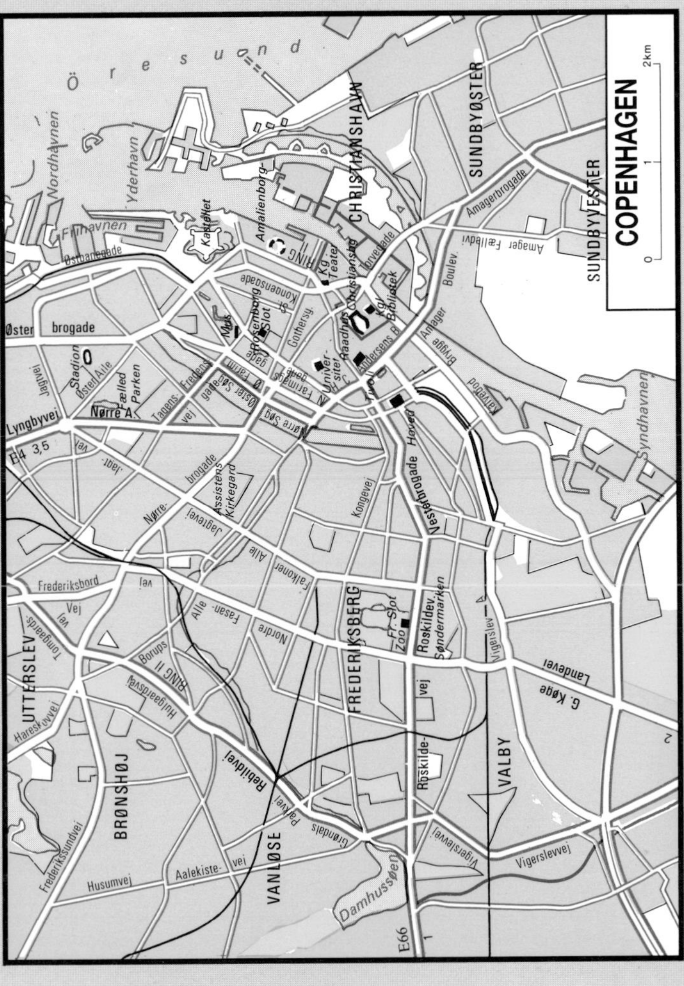
COPENHAGEN

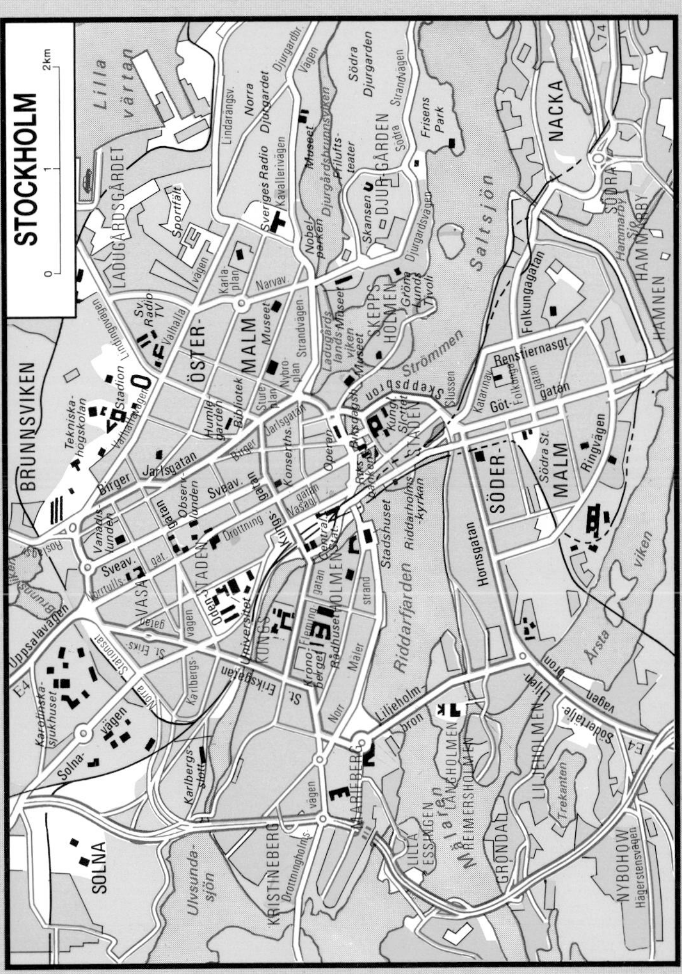
STOCKHOLM

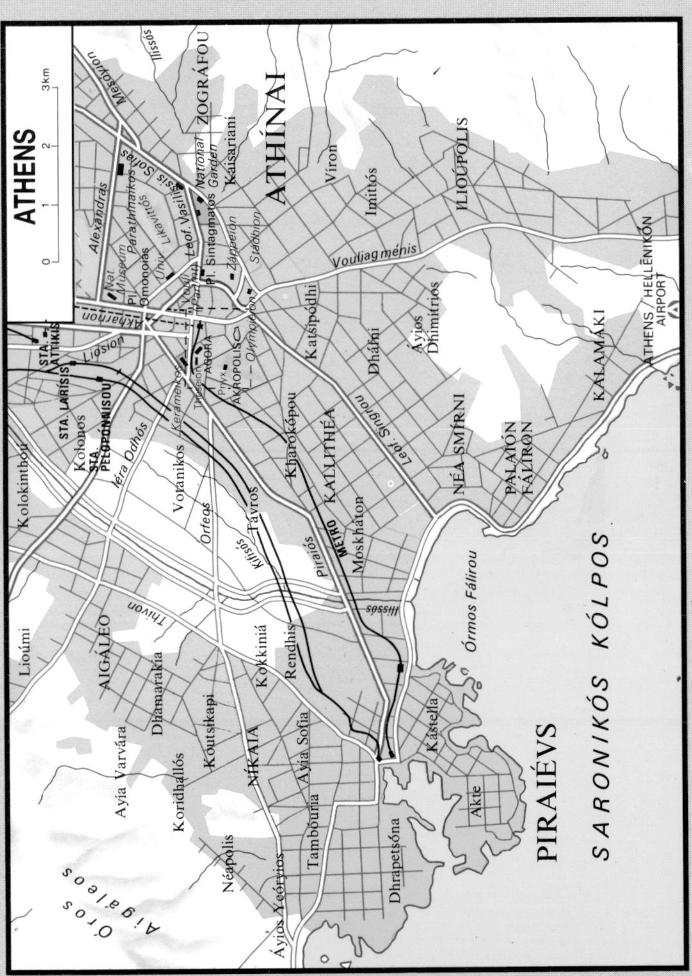
ATHENS

MOSCOW
1. Red Square
2. Mausoleum (Lenin)
3. S. Basils Cath. (Museum)
4. National Hotel
5. Karl Marx Statue

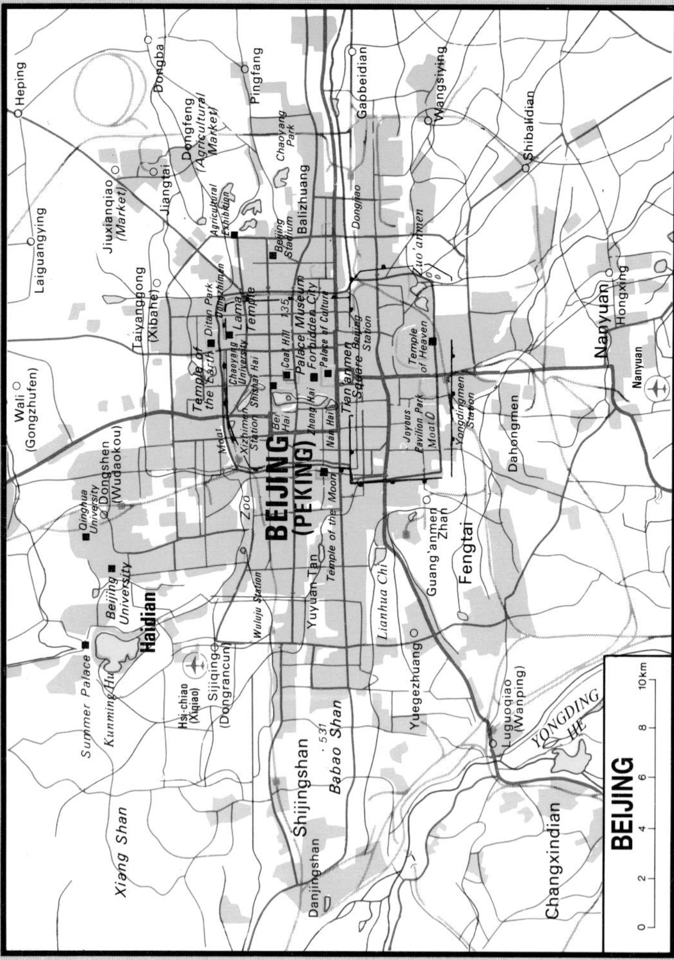
BEIJING
0 2 4 6 8 10km
BEIJING (PEKING)
Haidian
Fengtai
Nanyuan
Shijingshan
Changxindian
Summer Palace
Xiang Shan
Babao Shan
Forbidden City
Temple of Heaven
Tiananmen Square
Beijing University
Yongding He

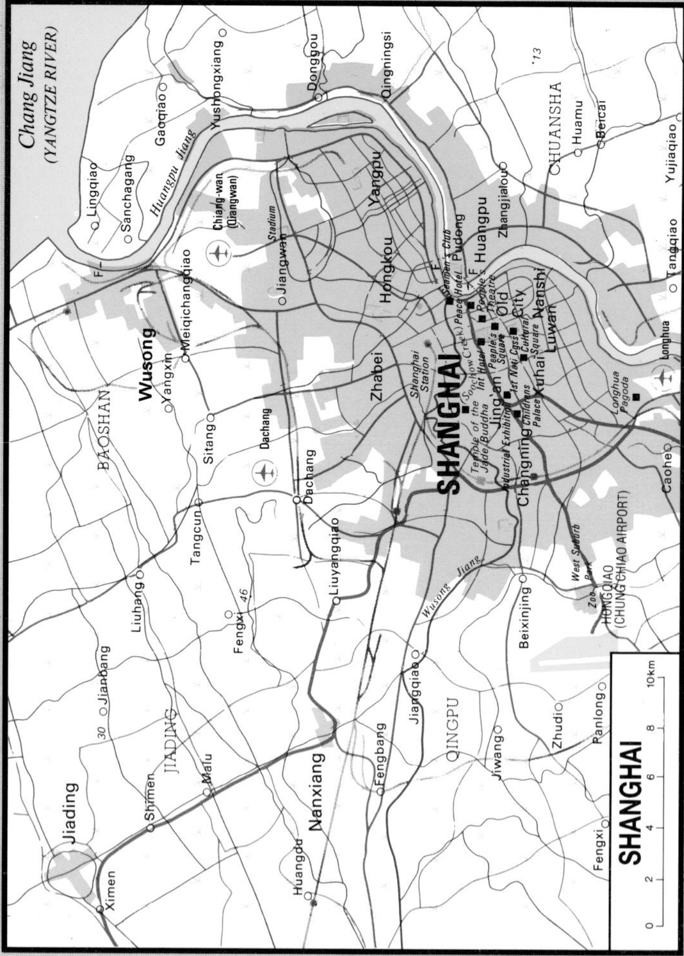
SHANGHAI
0 2 4 6 8 10km
SHANGHAI
Chang Jiang (YANGTZE RIVER)
Huangpu Jiang
Wusong
Dachang
Jiading
Nanxiang
Hongkou
Yangpu
Zhabei
Huangpu
Nanshi
Luwan
Xuhui
Jing'an
Changning
Putuo
Hongqiao (Chung Chiao Airport)
Longhua Pagoda
Baoshan
Jiading
Qingpu
Chuansha

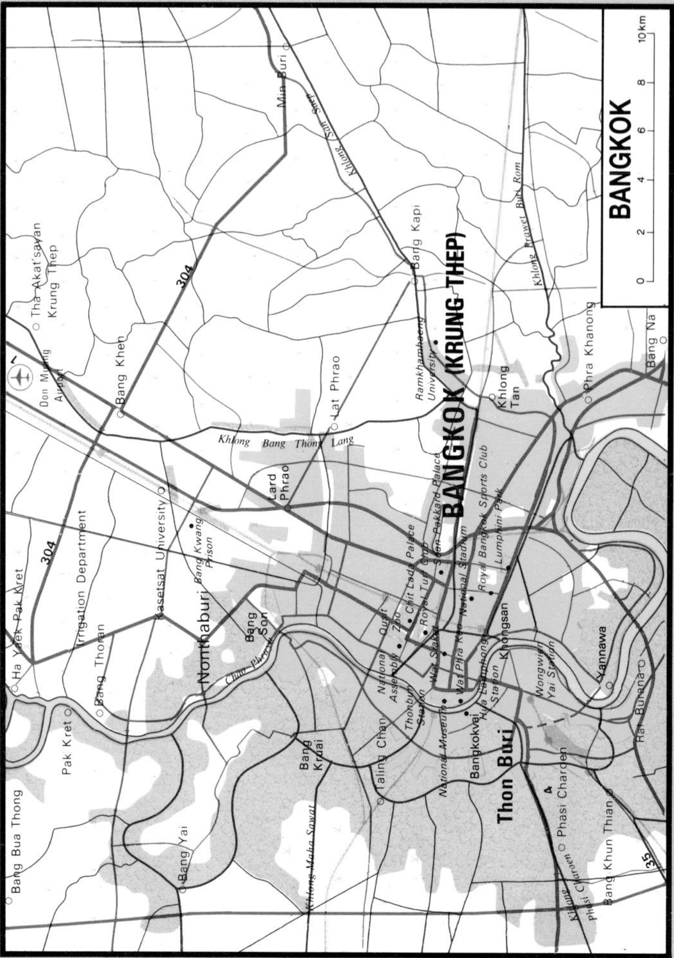
BANGKOK
0 2 4 6 8 10km
BANGKOK (KRUNG THEP)
Thon Buri
Nonthaburi
Don Muang Airport
Bang Kapi
Bang Khen
Lat Phrao
Phra Khanong
Chao Phraya
Grand Palace
Lumphini Park
Royal Bangkok Sports Club
Irrigation Department
Kasetsart University

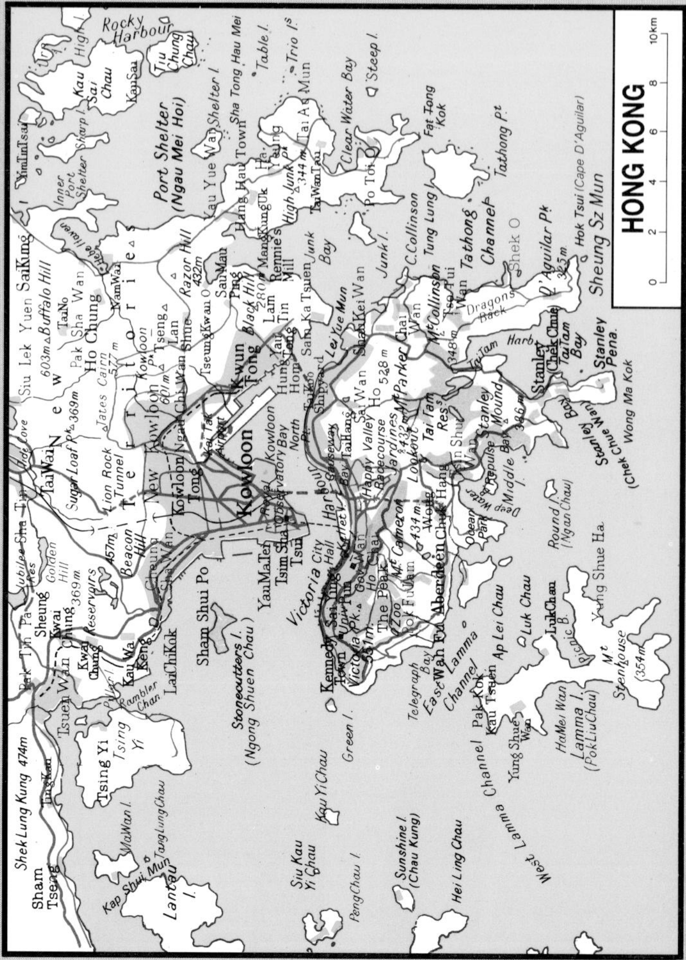
HONG KONG
0 2 4 6 8 10km
Kowloon
Victoria
New Territories
Tsuen Wan
Sha Tin
Kwun Tong
Tsing Yi
Lantau I.
Lamma I.
Aberdeen
Stanley
Victoria Peak
Kai Tak Airport
Port Shelter
Clear Water Bay
Tolo Channel
Sai Kung
Lamma Channel
Stonecutters I.

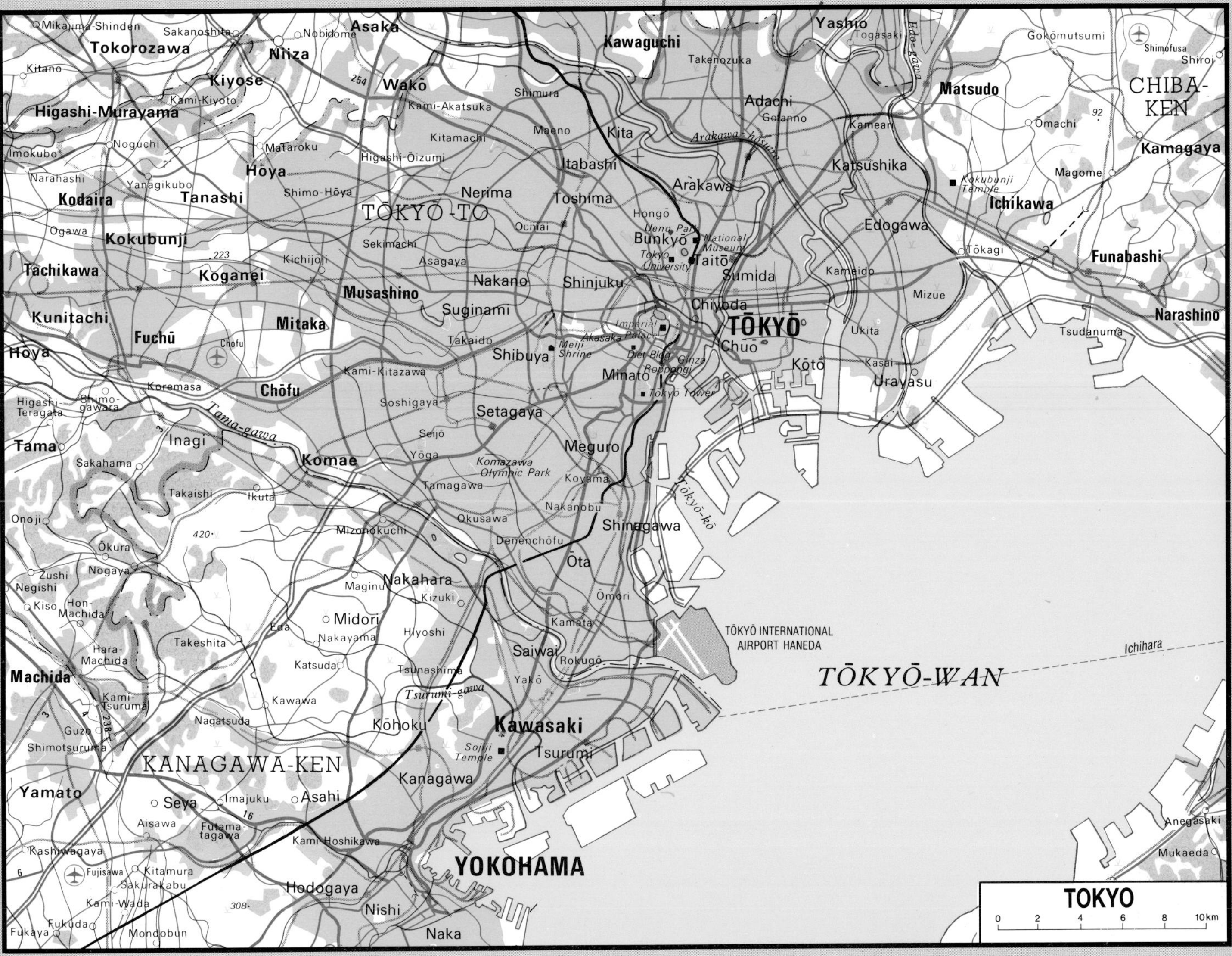
Mikajima-Shinden
Sakanoshita
Nobidome
Asaka
Kawaguchi
Yashio
Togasaki
Edo-gawa
Gokōmutsumi
Shimofusa
Shiroi
Tokorozawa
Niiza
Takenozuka
Kitano
Kiyose
Wakō
Shimura
Matsudo
CHIBA-KEN
Kami-Kiyoto
Kami-Akatsuka
Adachi
Higashi-Murayama
Gotanno
Maeno
Kita
Kameari
Ōmachi
92
Noguchi
Kitamachi
Arakawa-hōsuiro
Imokubo
Mataroku
Higashi-Ōizumi
Kamagaya
Narahashi
Hōya
Itabashi
Katsushika
Yanagikubo
Arakawa
Magome
Kokubunji Temple
Kodaira
Tanashi
Shimo-Hōya
Nerima
Toshima
Ichikawa
TŌKYŌ-TO
Hongō
Ogawa
Ochiai
Ueno Park
Edogawa
Kokubunji
Sekimachi
Bunkyō
National Museum
Tōkagi
223
Kichijōji
Asagaya
Tokyo University
Taitō
Funabashi
Tachikawa
Koganei
Kameido
Sumida
Musashino
Nakano
Shinjuku
Mizue
Chiyoda
Imperial Palace
Kunitachi
Mitaka
Suginami
TŌKYŌ
Narashino
Ukita
Tsudanuma
Fuchū
Chōfu
Takaido
Akasaka Palace
Chūō
Meiji Shrine
Hōya
Shibuya
Diet Bldg
Ginza
Kōtō
Kasai
Kami-Kitazawa
Roppongi
Minato
Urayasu
Koremasa
Chōfu
Tokyo Tower
Higashi-Teragata
Shimo-gawara
Soshigaya
Setagaya
Tama-gawa
Seijō
Tama
Inagi
Meguro
Komae
Yōga
Sakahama
Komazawa Olympic Park
Koyama
Takaishi
Tamagawa
Ikuta
Tōkyō-kō
Nakanobu
Onoji
Okusawa
Shinagawa
420
Mizonokuchi
Ōkura
Denenchōfu
Ōta
Nogaya
Zushi
Nakahara
Negishi
Maginu
Ōmori
Kiso
Hon-Machida
Kizuki
Midori
Kamata
TŌKYŌ INTERNATIONAL AIRPORT HANEDA
Eda
Nakayama
Hiyoshi
Ichihara
Takeshita
Saiwai
Hara-Machida
Katsuda
Rokugō
Tsunashima
TŌKYŌ-WAN
Machida
Yakō
Kami-Tsuruma
Tsurumi-gawa
Kawawa
Kōhoku
Kawasaki
Guzo
Nagatsuda
238
Sōjiji Temple
Tsurumi
Shimotsuruma
KANAGAWA-KEN
Kanagawa
Yamato
Seya
Imajuku
Asahi
16
Anegasaki
Aisawa
Futama-tagawa
Kashiwagaya
Kami-Hoshikawa
Mukaeda
Fujisawa
Kitamura
YOKOHAMA
Sakurakabu
Hodogaya
Kami-Wada
308
Nishi
Fukuda
Fukaya
Mondobun
Naka
TOKYO
0 2 4 6 8 10km

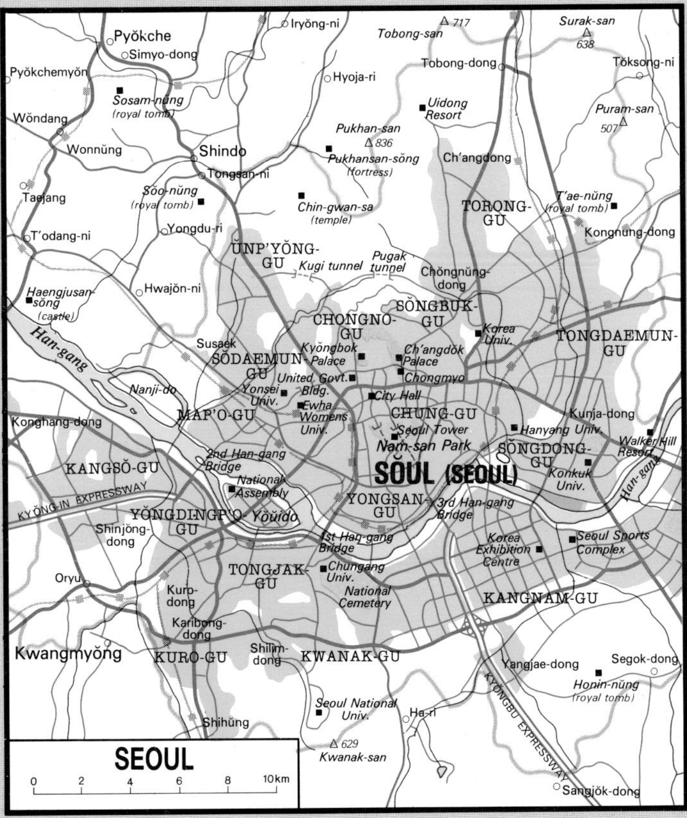
Pyŏkche
Iryŏng-ni
717
Surak-san
Simyo-dong
Tobong-san
638
Pyŏkchemyŏn
Hyoja-ri
Tobong-dong
Tŏksong-ni
Sosam-nŭng (royal tomb)
Uidong Resort
Puram-san
Wŏndang
507
Pukhan-san
836
Wonnŭng
Shindo
Pukhansan-sŏng (fortress)
Ch'angdong
Tongsan-ni
Sŏo-nŭng (royal tomb)
T'ae-nŭng (royal tomb)
Taejang
Chin-gwan-sa (temple)
TORONG-GU
Yongdu-ri
Kongnŭng-dong
T'odang-ni
UNP'YŎNG-GU
Pugak tunnel
Kugi tunnel
Chŏngnŭng-dong
Hwajŏn-ni
Haengjusan-sŏng (castle)
SŎNGBUK-GU
CHONGNO-GU
Korea Univ.
TONGDAEMUN-GU
Han-gang
Susaek
Kyŏngbok Palace
Ch'angdŏk Palace
SŎDAEMUN-GU
United Govt. Bldg.
Chongmyo
Yonsei Univ.
Nanji-do
Ewha Womens Univ.
City Hall
MAP'O-GU
CHUNG-GU
Kunja-dong
Konghang-dong
Seoul Tower
Hanyang Univ.
Walker Hill Resort
Nam-san Park
SŎNGDONG-GU
2nd Han-gang Bridge
KANGSŎ-GU
National Assembly
SŎUL (SEOUL)
Konkuk Univ.
KYŎNGIN EXPRESSWAY
YONGSAN-GU
3rd Han-gang Bridge
YŎNGDŬNGP'O-GU
Yŏŭido
Shinjŏng-dong
1st Han-gang Bridge
Korea Exhibition Centre
Seoul Sports Complex
Oryu
TONGJAK-GU
Chungang Univ.
National Cemetery
KANGNAM-GU
Kurp-dong
Karibong-dong
Shilim-dong
KWANAK-GU
Kwangmyŏng
KURO-GU
Segok-dong
Yangjae-dong
KYŎNGBU EXPRESSWAY
Honin-nŭng (royal tomb)
Seoul National Univ.
He-ri
Shihŭng
629
Kwanak-san
Sangjŏk-dong
SEOUL
0 2 4 6 8 10km

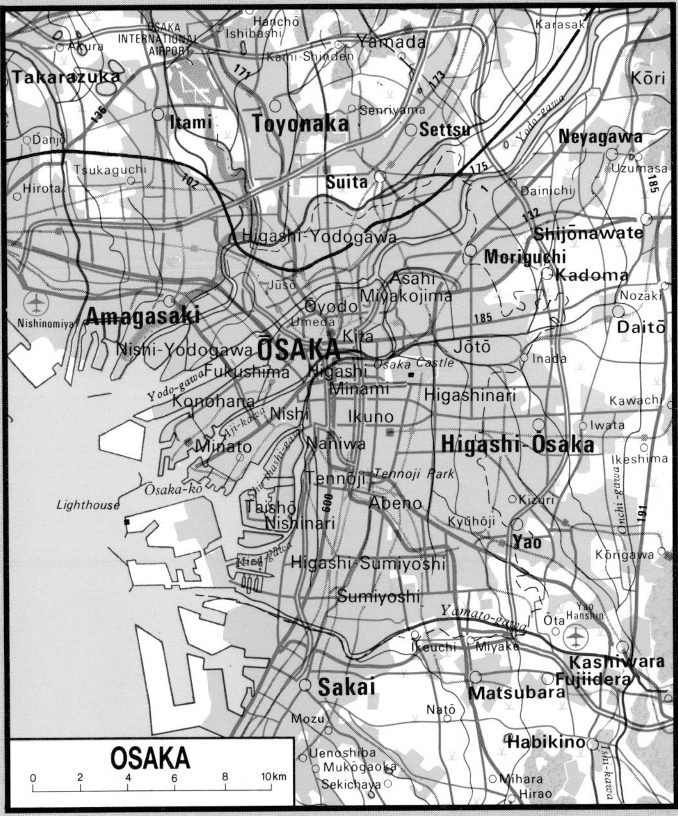
OSAKA INTERNATIONAL AIRPORT
Hanchō
Ishibashi
Karasaki
Ikura
Yamada
Kami-Shinden
Takarazuka
171
Kōri
Senriyama
136
Itami
Toyonaka
Settsu
Yodo-gawa
Neyagawa
Danjo
Uzumasa
Tsukaguchi
175
185
Hirota
102
Suita
Dainichi
Higashi-Yodogawa
Shijōnawate
Moriguchi
Kadoma
Jūsō
Asahi
Miyakojima
Nishinomiya
Amagasaki
Oyodo
Nozaki
Umeda
Kita
Daitō
185
Jōtō
Nishi-Yodogawa
ŌSAKA
Ōsaka Castle
Fukushima
Higashi
Inada
Yodo-gawa
Minami
Konohana
Higashinari
Kawachi
Nishi
Ikuno
Iwata
Minato
Naniwa
Higashi-Ōsaka
Ikeshima
Ōsaka-kō
Tennōji
Tennoji Park
Lighthouse
Taishō
Abeno
Kizuri
Nishinari
Kyūhōji
Yao
Higashi-Sumiyoshi
Kōngawa
Sumiyoshi
Yamato-gawa
Yao Hanshin
Ikeuchi
Miyake
Ōta
Kashiwara
Sakai
Matsubara
Fujiidera
Natō
Mozu
Habikino
Uenoshiba
Mukogaoka
Mihara
Sekichaya
Hirao
Ishi-kawa
OSAKA
0 2 4 6 8 10km

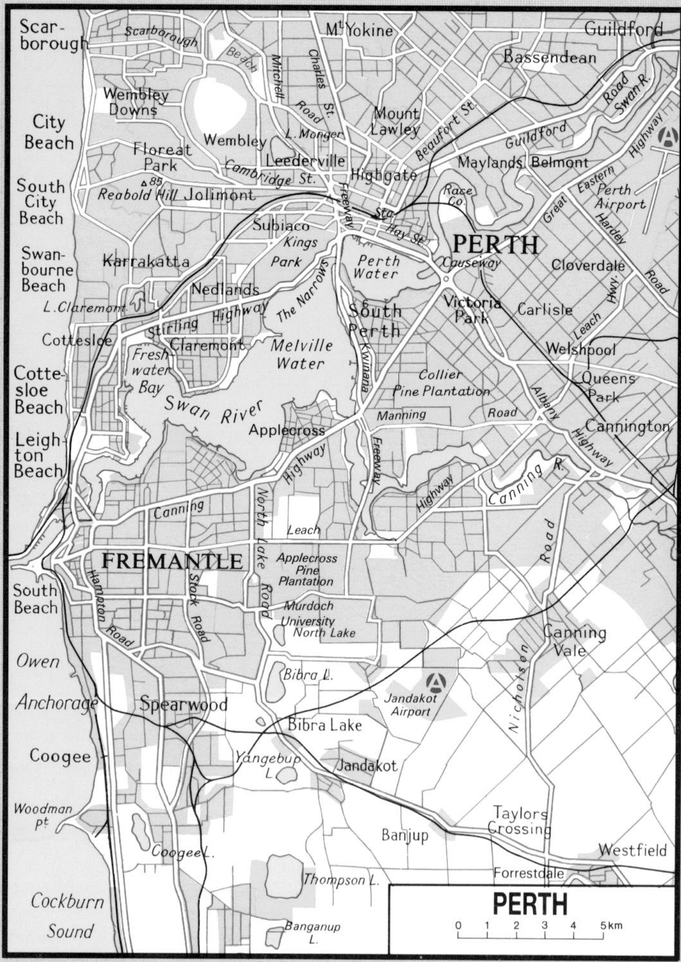
PERTH
0 1 2 3 4 5km
Scarborough
Mt Yokine
Guildford
Bassendean
Wembley Downs
City Beach
Floreat Park
Wembley
Mount Lawley
Maylands
Belmont
Leederville
Highgate
South City Beach
Reabold Hill
Jolimont
Subiaco
Swanbourne Beach
Karrakatta
Kings Park
PERTH
Perth Water
Causeway
Cloverdale
Perth Airport
Nedlands
L.Claremont
South Perth
Victoria Park
Carlisle
Cottesloe
Claremont
Melville Water
Welshpool
Freshwater Bay
Cottesloe Beach
Swan River
Collier Pine Plantation
Queens Park
Leighton Beach
Applecross
Manning
Cannington
Canning R.
FREMANTLE
Leach
Applecross Pine Plantation
South Beach
Murdoch University
North Lake
Canning Vale
Owen Anchorage
Spearwood
Bibra L.
Bibra Lake
Jandakot Airport
Coogee
Yangebup L.
Jandakot
Woodman Pt
Taylors Crossing
Banjup
Westfield
Coogee L.
Forrestdale
Thompson L.
Cockburn Sound
Banganup L.

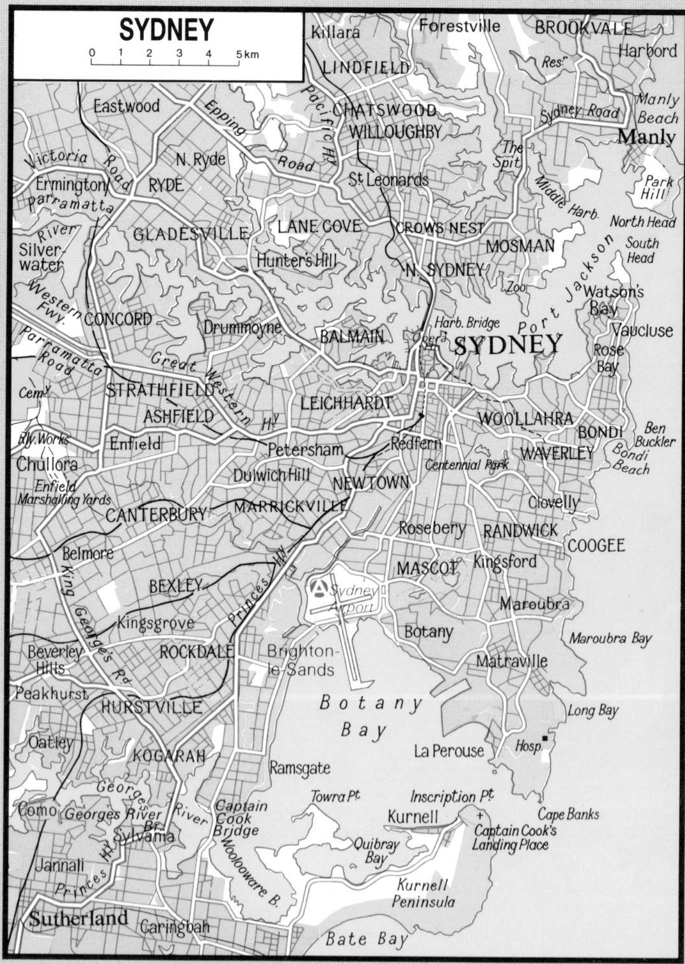
SYDNEY
0 1 2 3 4 5km
Killara
Forestville
BROOKVALE
Harbord
LINDFIELD
Res^r
Eastwood
CHATSWOOD
WILLOUGHBY
Manly Beach
Manly
N. Ryde
Ermington
RYDE
St Leonards
The Spit
Parramatta River
GLADESVILLE
LANE COVE
CROWS NEST
North Head
Silverwater
Hunters Hill
MOSMAN
South Head
N. SYDNEY
Watson's Bay
CONCORD
Drummoyne
BALMAIN
Harb. Bridge
SYDNEY
Vaucluse
Rose Bay
STRATHFIELD
Cem^y
ASHFIELD
LEICHHARDT
WOOLLAHRA
BONDI
Ben Buckler
Chullora
Enfield
Petersham
Redfern
WAVERLEY
Bondi Beach
Enfield Marshalling Yards
Dulwich Hill
NEWTOWN
Centennial Park
CANTERBURY
MARRICKVILLE
Clovelly
Rosebery
RANDWICK
COOGEE
Belmore
MASCOT
Kingsford
BEXLEY
Sydney Airport
Maroubra
Kingsgrove
Botany
Maroubra Bay
Beverley Hills
ROCKDALE
Brighton-le-Sands
Matraville
Peakhurst
HURSTVILLE
Botany Bay
Long Bay
Oatley
KOGARAH
La Perouse
Ramsgate
Hosp.
Towra Pt
Inscription Pt
Como
Georges River
Sylvania
Captain Cook Bridge
Kurnell
Cape Banks
Captain Cook's Landing Place
Quibray Bay
Jannali
Kurnell Peninsula
Sutherland
Caringbah
Bate Bay

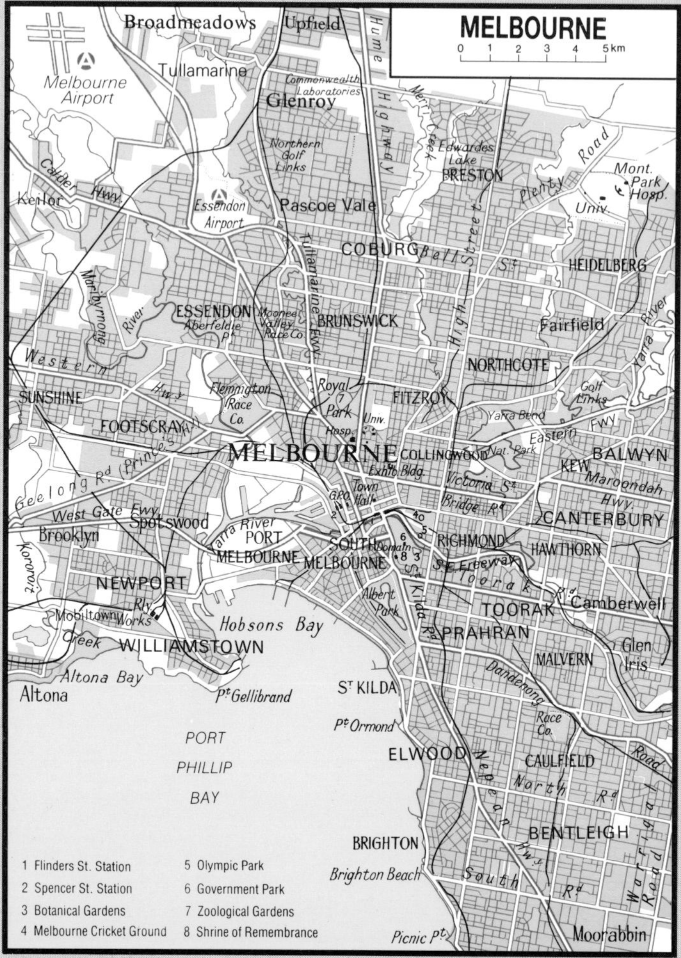
MELBOURNE
0 1 2 3 4 5km
Broadmeadows
Upfield
Tullamarine
Melbourne Airport
Commonwealth Laboratories
Glenroy
Hume Highway
Edwardes Lake
RESERVOIR
Plenty Road
Mont. Park Hosp.
Keilor
Calder Hwy
Essendon Airport
Pascoe Vale
Univ.
COBURG
Bell St
HEIDELBERG
Maribyrnong River
ESSENDON
Moonee Valley Race Co.
BRUNSWICK
Fairfield
Western Hwy
NORTHCOTE
Yarra River
SUNSHINE
Flemington Race Co.
Royal Park
FITZROY
Golf Links
FOOTSCRAY
Univ. Hosp.
Yarra Bend
MELBOURNE
COLLINGWOOD
Exhib. Bldg.
KEW
BALWYN
Geelong Rd
West Gate Fwy
Spotswood
Victoria St.
Maroondah Hwy.
Brooklyn
PORT MELBOURNE
SOUTH MELBOURNE
RICHMOND
Bridge Rd
CANTERBURY
HAWTHORN
Kororoit
NEWPORT
Toorak Rd.
Albert Park
TOORAK
Camberwell
Mobiltown
Rly. Works
Hobsons Bay
PRAHRAN
Glen Iris
WILLIAMSTOWN
MALVERN
Altona Bay
Dandenong Rd
Altona
Pt Gellibrand
St KILDA
Pt Ormond
Race Co.
PORT PHILLIP BAY
ELWOOD
CAULFIELD
North Rd
BRIGHTON
BENTLEIGH
Brighton Beach
South Rd
Warrigal Road
Picnic Pt
Moorabbin
1 Flinders St. Station
2 Spencer St. Station
3 Botanical Gardens
4 Melbourne Cricket Ground
5 Olympic Park
6 Government Park
7 Zoological Gardens
8 Shrine of Remembrance

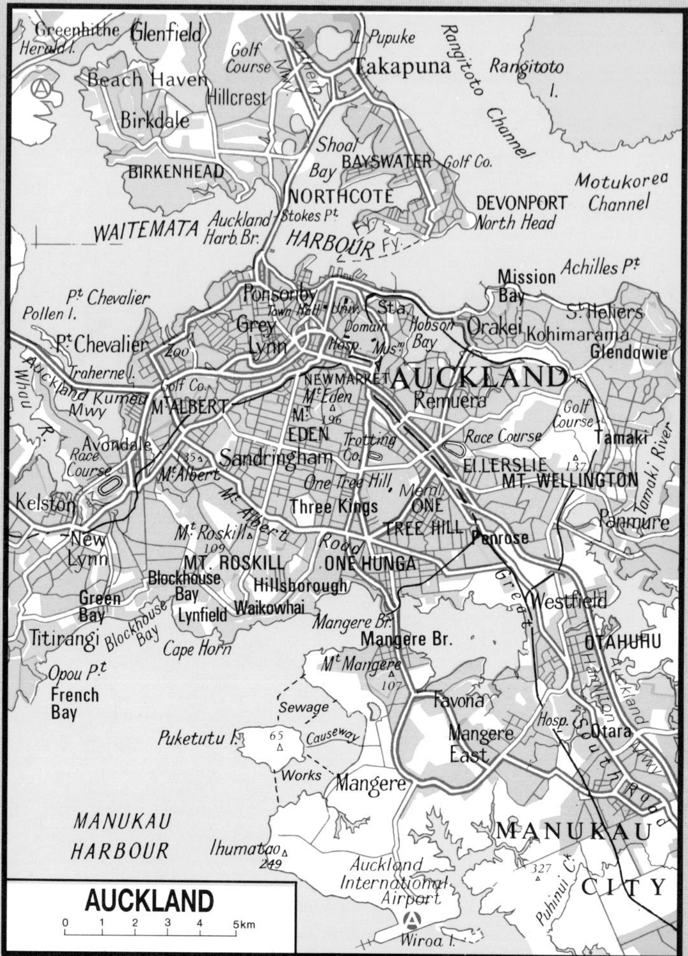
AUCKLAND
0 1 2 3 4 5km
Greenhithe
Herald I.
Glenfield
Golf Course
Pupuke
Takapuna
Rangitoto Channel
Rangitoto I.
Beach Haven
Hillcrest
Birkdale
Shoal Bay
BAYSWATER
Golf Co.
BIRKENHEAD
NORTHCOTE
Motukorea Channel
DEVONPORT
North Head
WAITEMATA
Auckland Harb. Br.
Stokes Pt
HARBOUR
Achilles Pt
Mission Bay
Pt Chevalier
Ponsonby
St Heliers
Pollen I.
Univ.
Hobson Bay
Orakei
Kohimarama
Pt Chevalier
Grey Lynn
Domain
Glendowie
Traherne I.
Zoo
NEWMARKET
AUCKLAND
Whau R.
Golf Co.
Mt Eden
Remuera
Kumeu Mwy
Mt ALBERT
Mt EDEN
Golf Course
Avondale
Race Course
Trotting Co.
Race Course
Tamaki
Sandringham
ELLERSLIE
MT. WELLINGTON
Kelston
Mt Albert
One Tree Hill
Tamaki River
Three Kings
ONE TREE HILL
Panmure
New Lynn
Mt Roskill
MT. ROSKILL
ONEHUNGA
Penrose
Green Bay
Blockhouse Bay
Hillsborough
Westfield
Lynfield
Waikowhai
Titirangi
Mangere Br.
OTAHUHU
Cape Horn
Mangere Br.
Mt Mangere
Opou Pt
French Bay
Favona
Sewage Works
Puketutu I.
Causeway
Mangere East
Hosp.
Otara
Mangere
MANUKAU HARBOUR
Ihumatao
MANUKAU CITY
Auckland International Airport
Wiroa I.

DELHI
0 1 2 3 4km
Wazirabad
Azadpur
West Yamuna Canal
Grand Trunk Road
Karnal Road
Hospital
Wazirpur
Univ.
Civil Lines
Keth Wara
Rampur
Jhil
Shastrinagar
Asoka Pillar
Alipur Rd
Yamuna
SABZI MANDI
Kashmir Gate
G.P.O.
Najafgarh
Sta.
Salim Garh
SADAR BAZAR
Chandni Chauk
Red Fort
Jain Temple
OLD
Jami Masjid
CITY
DARYA GANJ
Kirtinagar
Patel Rd
Karol Bagh
Ajmer Gate
Pusa Rd
PAHAR GANJ
Sta.
Kalan Masjid
Hosp.
Delhi Gate
Asoka Pillar
Agricultural Research Inst.
Library
Town Hall
FIROZABAD
NEW DELHI
Park
Legislative Bldgs.
Rashtrapati Bhavan
Raj Path
Stadium
Secretariat
Curzon Rd
India Gate
Purana Kila
Naraina
Ring Road
Mus.
INDRAPRASTHA
Upper Ridge Rd
Kitchener Rd
Race Course
Lodi Tombs
Humayun's Tomb
Lodi Road
New Cantonment
Safdar Jang's Tomb
Airport
Mathura Rd
Gurgaon Road
Aliganj
Lajpatnagar
Ring Road
Mehrauli Road
Vasant Vihar
Ramakrishnapuram
Qutb Minar

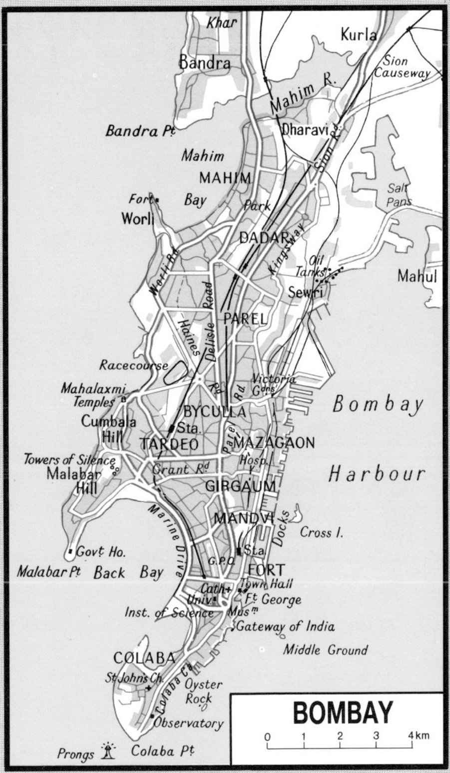
BOMBAY
0 1 2 3 4km
Khar
Kurla
Bandra
Sion Causeway
Mahim R.
Bandra Pt
Dharavi
Mahim
MAHIM
Salt Pans
Fort
Worli
Bay
Park
DADAR
Kingsway
Oil Tanks
Mahul
Sewri
PAREL
Haines Rd
Delisle Road
Racecourse
Mahalaxmi Temples
Victoria Gdns.
Bombay
BYCULLA
Cumbala Hill
Sta.
TARDEO
MAZAGAON
Towers of Silence
Malabar Hill
Grant Rd
Hosp.
Harbour
GIRGAUM
MANDVI
Docks
Cross I.
Marine Drive
Sta.
Govt Ho.
G.P.O.
FORT
Malabar Pt
Back Bay
Town Hall
Cath.
Ft George
Univ.
Inst. of Science
Mus.
Gateway of India
Middle Ground
COLABA
St. John's Ch.
Colaba Causeway
Oyster Rock
Observatory
Prongs
Colaba Pt

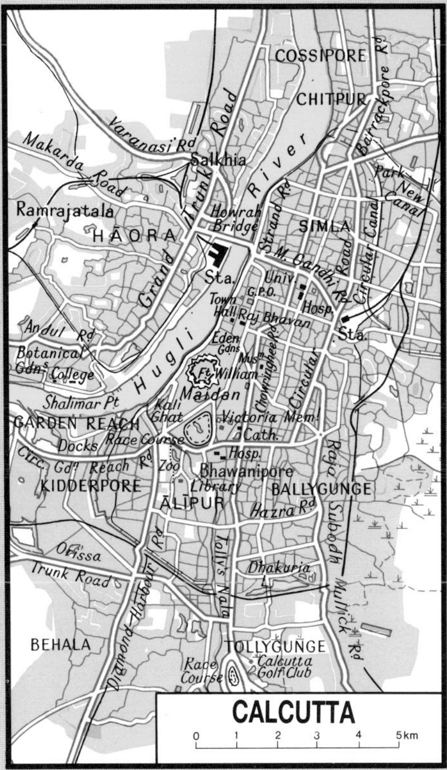
CALCUTTA
0 1 2 3 4 5km
COSSIPORE
CHITPUR
Barrackpore Rd
Varanasi Rd
Makarda Road
Salkhia
River
Park
New Canal
Ramrajatala
HAORA
Howrah Bridge
Strand Rd
SIMLA
Grand Trunk Road
M. Gandhi Rd
Circular Canal
Sta.
Univ.
G.P.O.
Town Hall
Hosp.
Raj Bhavan
Sta.
Andul Rd
Botanical Gdns.
College
Hugli
Eden Gdns.
Mus.
Ft William
Maidan
Shalimar Pt
Kali Ghat
Victoria Mem.
GARDEN REACH
Race Course
Cath.
Docks
Garden Reach Rd
Zoo
Hosp.
KIDDERPORE
Bhawanipore
Library
BALLYGUNGE
ALIPUR
Hazra Rd
Orissa Trunk Road
Diamond Harbour Rd
Tolly's Nala
Dhakuria
Raja Subodh Mullick Rd
BEHALA
TOLLYGUNGE
Calcutta Golf Club
Race Course

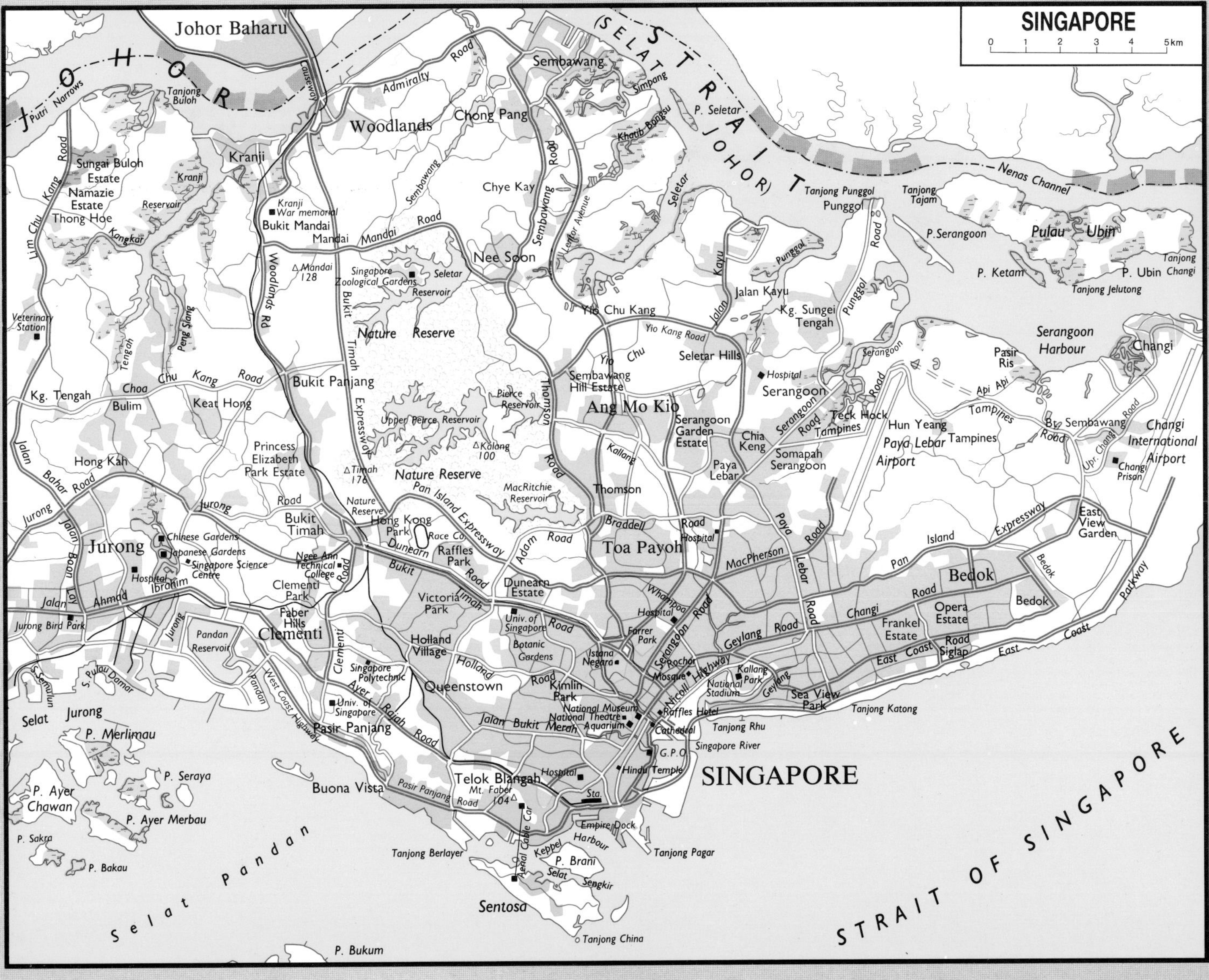
SINGAPORE
0 1 2 3 4 5km
Johor Baharu
JOHOR
Putri Narrows
Causeway
SELAT JOHOR
STRAIT
Tanjong Buloh
Admiralty Road
Sembawang
Simpang
P. Seletar
Woodlands
Chong Pang
Khaub Bangsu
Sungai Buloh Estate
Kranji
Namazie Estate
Thong Hoe
Reservoir
Lim Chu Kang Road
Kangkar
Chye Kay
Sembawang Road
Nenas Channel
Tanjong Punggol
Punggol
Tanjong Tajam
Kranji War memorial
Bukit Mandai
Mandai
Mandai Road
Seletar
P. Serangoon
Pulau Ubin
Nee Soon
Lentor Avenue
Punggol Road
Tanjong Changi
Mandai 128
Singapore Zoological Gardens
Seletar Reservoir
P. Ketam
P. Ubin
Tanjong Jelutong
Woodlands Rd
Bukit Timah Expressway
Jalan Kayu
Kg. Sungei Tengah
Veterinary Station
Peng Siang
Tengah
Nature Reserve
Yio Chu Kang
Yio Kang Road
Seletar Hills
Serangoon Harbour
Changi
Pasir Ris
Kg. Tengah
Choa Chu Kang Road
Bukit Panjang
Sembawang Hill Estate
Hospital
Serangoon
Bulim
Keat Hong
Pierce Reservoir
Ang Mo Kio
Teck Hock
Tampines
Upper Peirce Reservoir
Thomson Road
Serangoon Garden Estate
Hun Yeang
Tampines
Sembawang
Changi International Airport
Jalan Bahar
Hong Kah
Princess Elizabeth Park Estate
Kalong 100
Chia Keng
Paya Lebar Airport
Changi Prison
Timah 176
Nature Reserve
Somapah Serangoon
Paya Lebar
MacRitchie Reservoir
Pan Island Expressway
Thomson
Jurong
Bukit Timah
Nature Reserve
Hong Kong Park
Race Co.
Braddell Road
Hospital
Island Expressway
East View Garden
Chinese Gardens
Japanese Gardens
Singapore Science Centre
Hospital
Ngee Ann Technical College
Raffles Park
Dunearn Road
Adam Road
Toa Payoh
MacPherson
Paya Lebar Road
Pan
Bedok
Jalan Ahmad Ibrahim
Clementi Park
Bukit Timah
Victoria Park
Dunearn Estate
Whampoa
Bedok
Parkway
Jurong Bird Park
Faber Hills
Clementi
Pandan Reservoir
Holland Village
Univ. of Singapore
Botanic Gardens
Hospital
Farrer Park
Serangoon Road
Geylang Road
Changi Road
Frankel Estate
Opera Estate
Siglap
East Coast Road
Istana Negara
Rochor
Mosque
Nicoll Highway
National Stadium
Kallang Park
Sea View Park
Tanjong Katong
Singapore Polytechnic
Holland Road
Kimlin Park
West Coast Highway
Queenstown
National Museum
National Theatre
Aquarium
Raffles Hotel
Cathedral
Tanjong Rhu
Singapore River
Selat Jurong
Univ. of Singapore
Pasir Panjang
Ayer Rajah Road
Jalan Bukit Merah
G.P.O.
P. Merlimau
Hindu Temple
SINGAPORE
P. Seraya
Buona Vista
Telok Blangah
Hospital
Mt. Faber 104
Sta.
P. Ayer Chawan
P. Ayer Merbau
Pasir Panjang Road
Empire Dock
Keppel Harbour
P. Sakra
P. Bakau
Selat Pandan
Tanjong Berlayer
Aerial Cable Car
P. Brani
Selat Sengkir
Tanjong Pagar
STRAIT OF SINGAPORE
Sentosa
Tanjong China
P. Bukum

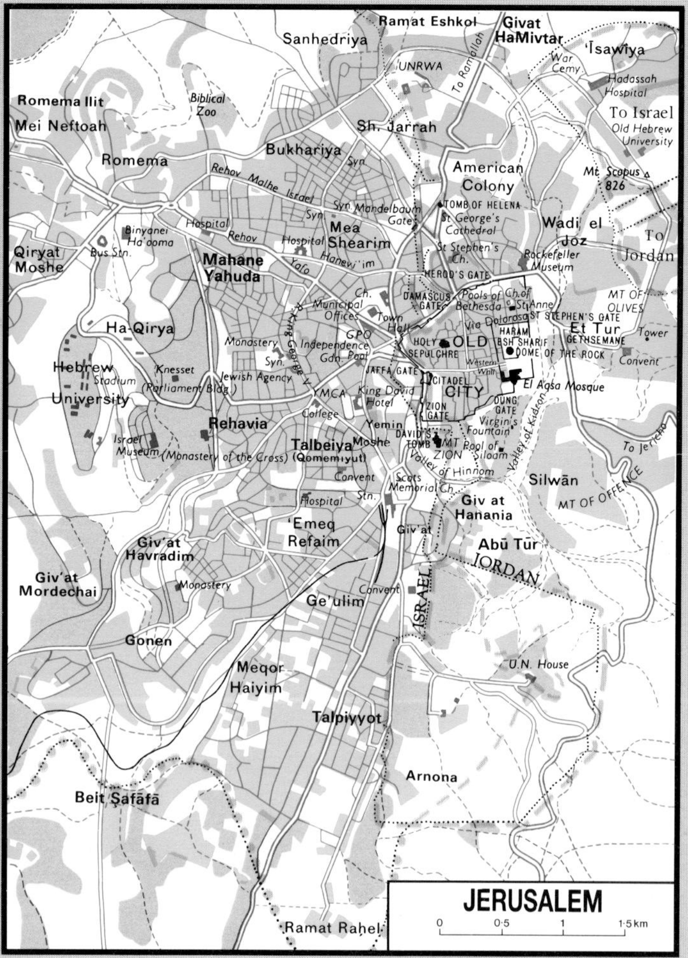
JERUSALEM
0 0·5 1 1·5km
Ramat Eshkol
Givat HaMivtar
Sanhedriya
'Isawiya
UNRWA
To Ramallah
War Cemy
Hadassah Hospital
To Israel
Old Hebrew University
Romema Ilit
Biblical Zoo
Mei Neftoah
Sh. Jarrah
Romema
Bukhariya
American Colony
Mt. Scopus 826
Mandelbaum Gate
TOMB OF HELENA
St. George's Cathedral
Mea Shearim
Wadi el Joz
To Jordan
Binyanei Ha'ooma
Hospital
Qiryat Moshe
Bus Stn.
Mahane Yahuda
St. Stephen's Ch.
Rockefeller Museum
HEROD'S GATE
DAMASCUS GATE
Pools of Bethesda
St. Anne
MT OF OLIVES
Municipal Offices
Via Dolorosa
ST STEPHEN'S GATE
Ha-Qirya
GPO
OLD
HARAM ESH SHARIF
GETHSEMANE
Tower
Monastery
Independence Gdn.
HOLY SEPULCHRE
DOME OF THE ROCK
Convent
Hebrew University
Knesset
Jewish Agency
JAFFA GATE
CITADEL
CITY
El Aqsa Mosque
Stadium
(Parliament Bldg.)
YMCA
King David Hotel
ZION GATE
DUNG GATE
Rehavia
Yemin
DAVID'S TOMB
Virgin's Fountain
Valley of Kidron
Israel Museum
(Monastery of the Cross)
Talbeiya
(Qomemiyut)
Moshe
MT ZION
Pool of Siloam
To Jericho
Convent
Scots Memorial Ch.
Valley of Hinnom
Silwān
Hospital
Giv at Hanania
MT OF OFFENCE
'Emeq Refaim
Abū Tūr
Giv'at Havradim
Giv'at Mordechai
Monastery
JORDAN
ISRAEL
Convent
Ge'ulim
Gonen
Meqor Haiyim
U.N. House
Talpiyyot
Arnona
Beit Şafāfā
Ramat Rahel

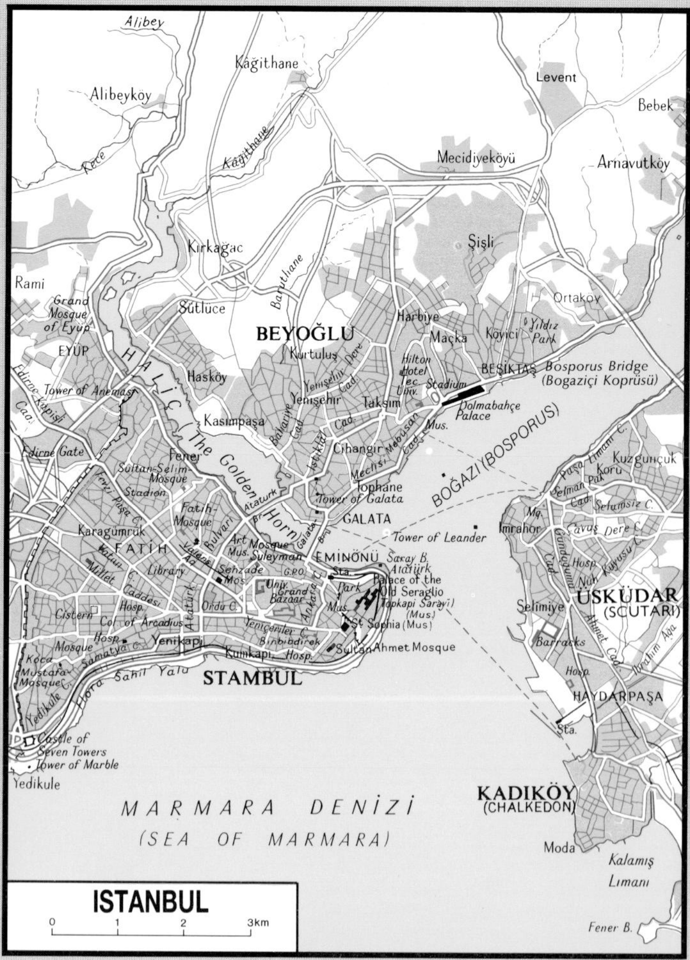
ISTANBUL
0 1 2 3km
Alibey
Kâğithane
Alibeykoy
Levent
Bebek
Kâğithane
Mecidiyeköyü
Arnavutköy
Kirkağac
Şişli
Rami
Ortaköy
Grand Mosque of Eyüp
Sütlüce
BEYOĞLU
Harbiye
Yildiz Park
EYÜP
Kurtuluş
Maçka
Köyici
Hasköy
Hilton Hotel
Stadium
BEŞİKTAŞ
Bosporus Bridge (Bogaziçi Koprüsü)
Tower of Ankara
Yenişehir
Taksim
Dolmabahçe Palace
HALİÇ (The Golden Horn)
Kasımpaşa
Mus.
Cihangir
BOĞAZİ (BOSPORUS)
Kuzguncuk
Fener
Edirne Gate
Sultan-Selim Mosque
Tophane
Tower of Galata
GALATA
Fatih Mosque
FATIH
Karagümrük
Art Mus.
Mosque Suleyman
EMINÖNÜ
Tower of Leander
Imrahor
Library
Sehzade Mos.
Univ.
Grand Bazaar
Palace of the Old Seraglio (Topkapi Sarayi) (Mus)
Selimiye
ÜSKÜDAR (SCUTARI)
Cistern
Col. of Arcadius
St. Sophia (Mus)
Barracks
Yenikapi
Kumkapi
Sultan Ahmet Mosque
Hosp.
STAMBUL
HAYDARPAŞA
Koca Mustafa Mosque
Sta.
Castle of Seven Towers
Tower of Marble
Yedikule
MARMARA DENİZİ (SEA OF MARMARA)
KADIKÖY (CHALKEDON)
Moda
Kalamış Limanı
Fener B.

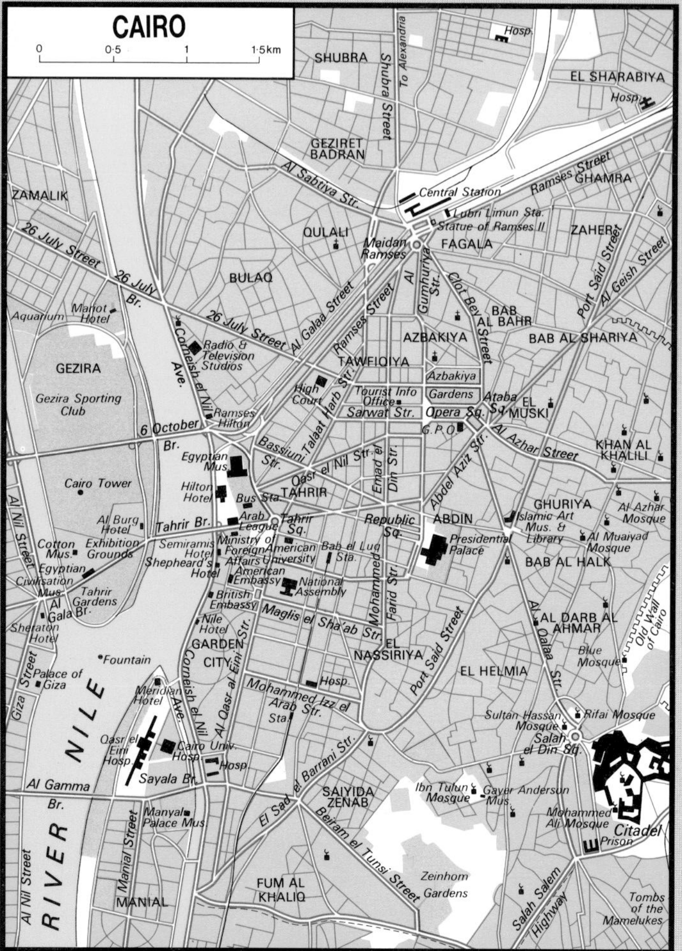
CAIRO
0 0·5 1 1·5km
SHUBRA
Hosp.
To Alexandria
EL SHARABIYA
Shubra Street
GEZIRET BADRAN
ZAMALIK
Al Sabtiya Str.
Central Station
Ramses Street
GHAMRA
Lutfi Limun Sta.
Statue of Ramses II
QULALI
Maidan Ramses
ZAHER
FAGALA
26 July Street
BULAQ
Port Said Street
Al Geish Street
26 July Br.
Aquarium
Marriot Hotel
BAB AL BAHR
Radio & Television Studios
AZBAKIYA
BAB AL SHARIYA
GEZIRA
TAWFIQIYA
Azbakiya Gardens
High Court
Tourist Info Office
Gezira Sporting Club
Ramses Hilton
Opera Sq.
Ataba Sq.
EL MUSKI
6 October Br.
G.P.O.
Al Azhar Street
KHAN AL KHALILI
Egyptian Mus.
Cairo Tower
Hilton Hotel
TAHRIR
Al Burg Hotel
Tahrir Br.
Tahrir Sq.
ABDIN
GHURIYA
Al Azhar Mosque
Islamic Art Mus. & Library
Presidential Palace
Cotton Mus.
Exhibition Grounds
Semiramis Hotel
Ministry of Foreign Affairs
American University
Al Muaiyad Mosque
Egyptian Civilisation Mus.
Shepheard's Hotel
American Embassy
National Assembly
BAB AL HALK
Tahrir Gardens
British Embassy
Gala Br.
Sheraton Hotel
AL DARB AL AHMAR
GARDEN CITY
Nile Hotel
Blue Mosque
Fountain
EL NASSIRIYA
EL HELMIA
Palace of Giza
Meridien Hotel
Hosp.
Sultan Hassan Mosque
Rifai Mosque
Qasr el Eini Hosp
Cairo Univ.
Salah el Din Sq.
RIVER NILE
Sayala Br.
Al Gamma Br.
SAIYIDA ZENAB
Ibn Tulun Mosque
Gayer Anderson Mus.
Mohammed Ali Mosque
Citadel
Prison
Manyal Palace Mus.
Zeinhom Gardens
FUM AL KHALIQ
MANIAL
Salah Salem Highway
Tombs of the Mamelukes

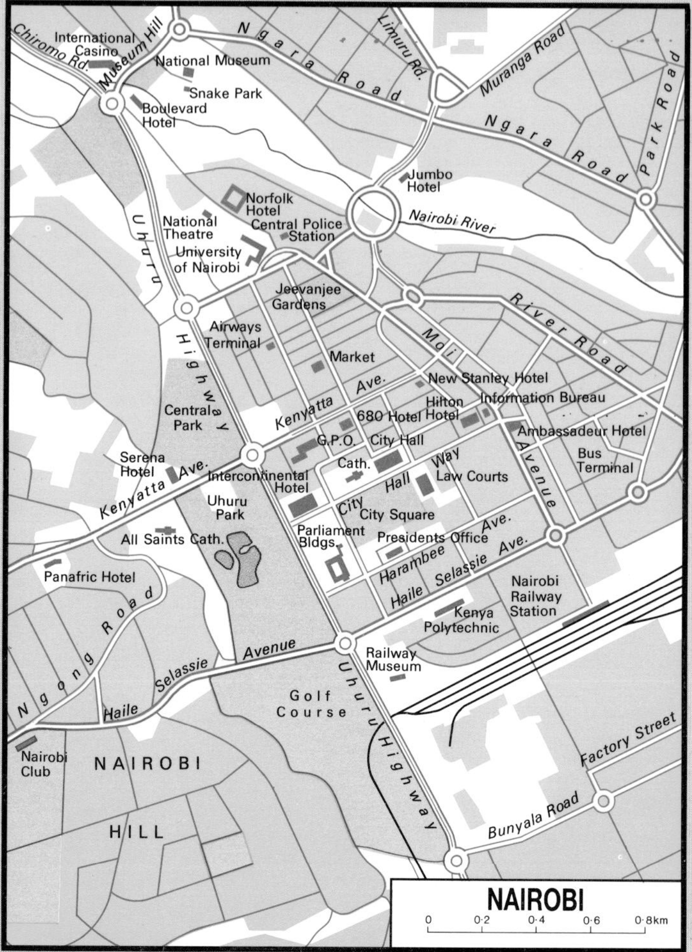
NAIROBI
0 0·2 0·4 0·6 0·8km
International Casino
Chiromo Rd.
Museum Hill
National Museum
Ngara Road
Limuru Rd.
Muranga Road
Snake Park
Boulevard Hotel
Park Road
Jumbo Hotel
Norfolk Hotel
National Theatre
Central Police Station
Nairobi River
University of Nairobi
Uhuru Highway
Jeevanjee Gardens
River Road
Airways Terminal
Moi Avenue
Market
New Stanley Hotel
Hilton Hotel
Information Bureau
Kenyatta Ave.
680 Hotel
Central Park
Ambassadeur Hotel
G.P.O.
City Hall
Serena Hotel
Cath.
Way
Bus Terminal
Intercontinental Hotel
Law Courts
Uhuru Park
City Square
All Saints Cath.
Parliament Bldgs.
Presidents Office
Harambee Ave.
Panafric Hotel
Haile Selassie Ave.
Nairobi Railway Station
Kenya Polytechnic
Ngong Road
Railway Museum
Golf Course
Nairobi Club
NAIROBI HILL
Factory Street
Bunyala Road

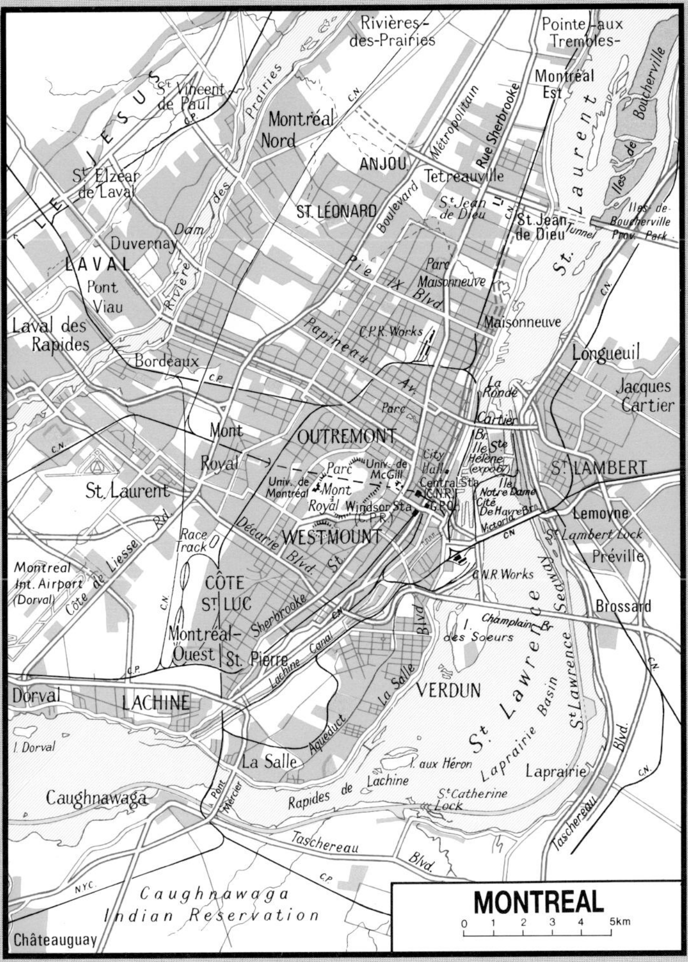
MONTREAL
0 1 2 3 4 5km
Rivières-des-Prairies
Pointe-aux-Trembles
Montréal Est
Montréal Nord
ANJOU
Tetreauville
ST. LÉONARD
St. Jean de Dieu
Îles de Boucherville Prov. Park
St. Vincent de Paul
St. Elzéar de Laval
Duvernay
LAVAL
Pont Viau
Laval des Rapides
Bordeaux
Maisonneuve
Parc Maisonneuve
C.P.R. Works
Longueuil
Jacques Cartier
Mont Royal
OUTREMONT
St. Laurent
Univ. de Montréal
Univ. de McGill
Central Sta.
Windsor Sta.
WESTMOUNT
ST. LAMBERT
Lemoyne
Préville
Brossard
Montreal Int. Airport (Dorval)
CÔTE ST. LUC
Montréal-Ouest
St. Pierre
Race Track
C.N.R. Works
Champlain Br.
I. des Soeurs
VERDUN
Dorval
LACHINE
I. Dorval
La Salle
I. aux Héron
Rapides de Lachine
St. Catherine Lock
Laprairie
Laprairie Basin
St. Lawrence Seaway
St. Lawrence
Caughnawaga
Caughnawaga Indian Reservation
Châteauguay
Taschereau Blvd.
Lachine Canal

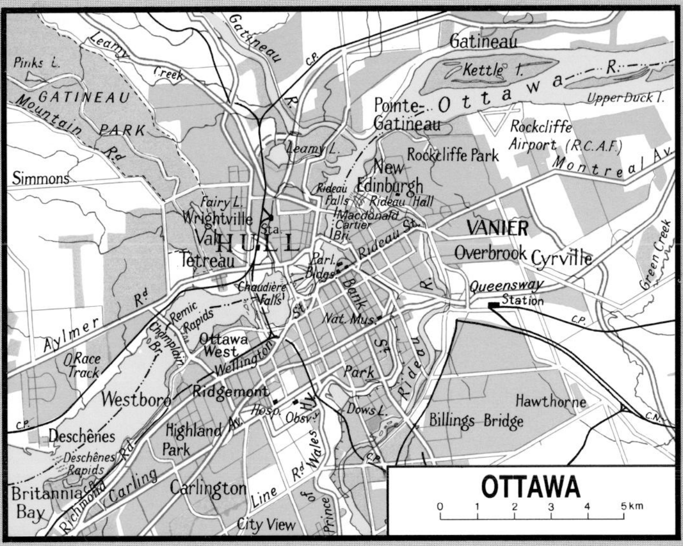
OTTAWA
0 1 2 3 4 5km
Gatineau
Kettle I.
Ottawa R.
Upper Duck I.
Pinks L.
Leamy Creek
GATINEAU PARK
Mountain Rd
Pointe-Gatineau
Rockcliffe Airport (R.C.A.F.)
Rockcliffe Park
Montreal Av.
Simmons
Leamy L.
New Edinburgh
Rideau Hall
Fairy L.
Wrightville
Val Tetreau
HULL
VANIER
Overbrook
Cyrville
Green Creek
Parl. Bldgs.
Chaudière Falls
Queensway Station
Aylmer Rd
Remic Rapids
Ottawa West
Nat. Mus.
Race Track
Wellington
Park
Westboro
Ridgemont
Dows L.
Hawthorne
Billings Bridge
Deschênes
Deschênes Rapids
Highland Park
Britannia Bay
Richmond Rd
Carling
Carlington
Line Rd
Prince of Wales
City View

TORONTO
0 1 2 3 4 5km
Downsview Airport
York Mills
SCARBOROUGH
NORTH YORK
Downsview
Lawrence Ave.
Eglinton Ave.
Wilson
Freeway
Sunnybrook Park Hosp.
Macdonald-Cartier
Lawrence Ave. W.
Dufferin
Avenue Rd
Yonge St.
Don R.
Weston
North Fairbank
Pkwy.
O'Connor Drive
Kingston Rd
YORK
Bathurst
EAST YORK
St. Clair Av.
Casa Loma
Danforth Av.
Lambton Mills
Humber R.
Riverdale Park
Royal Ont. Mus.
Parl. Bldgs.
Zoo
Univ. of Toronto
City Hall
Queen St.
Race Track
Bloor
TORONTO
Old Fort York
Gardiner Expy.
Union Sta.
High Park
Lake Shore Blvd.
Exhibition Park
Toronto Harbour
Q. Elizabeth Way
Humber Bay
Toronto I. Airport
Ashbridges Bay Park
Mimico
Gibraltar Pt.
Island Park
LAKE ONTARIO
Lake Shore Blvd.

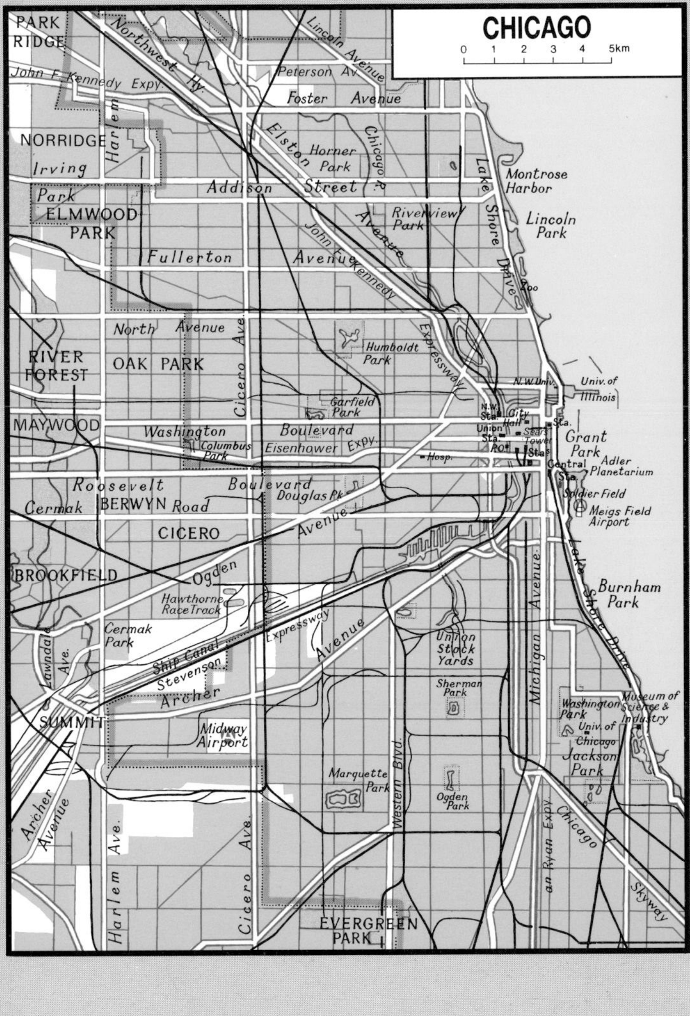
CHICAGO
0 1 2 3 4 5km
PARK RIDGE
Northwest Hy.
Lincoln Avenue
John F. Kennedy Expy.
Peterson Av.
Foster Avenue
NORRIDGE
Irving Park
Harlem
Elston
Horner Park
Chicago R.
Lake Shore Drive
Montrose Harbor
Addison Street
ELMWOOD PARK
Riverview Park
Lincoln Park
Fullerton Avenue
John F. Kennedy
Zoo
North Avenue
RIVER FOREST
OAK PARK
Cicero Ave.
Humboldt Park
Expressway
Univ. of Illinois
MAYWOOD
Garfield Park
Washington
Columbus Park
Boulevard
Eisenhower Expy.
Grant Park
Adler Planetarium
Roosevelt
Cermak
BERWYN
Road
Boulevard
Douglas Pk.
Soldier Field
Meigs Field Airport
CICERO
Avenue
BROOKFIELD
Ogden
Hawthorne Race Track
Burnham Park
Cermak Park
Expressway
Avenue
Union Stock Yards
Lawndale Ave.
Ship Canal
Stevenson
Archer
Sherman Park
Michigan Avenue
Washington Park
Museum of Science & Industry
Univ. of Chicago
Jackson Park
SUMMIT
Midway Airport
Marquette Park
Western Blvd.
Ogden Park
Archer Avenue
Harlem Ave.
Cicero Ave.
Dan Ryan Expy.
Chicago Skyway
EVERGREEN PARK

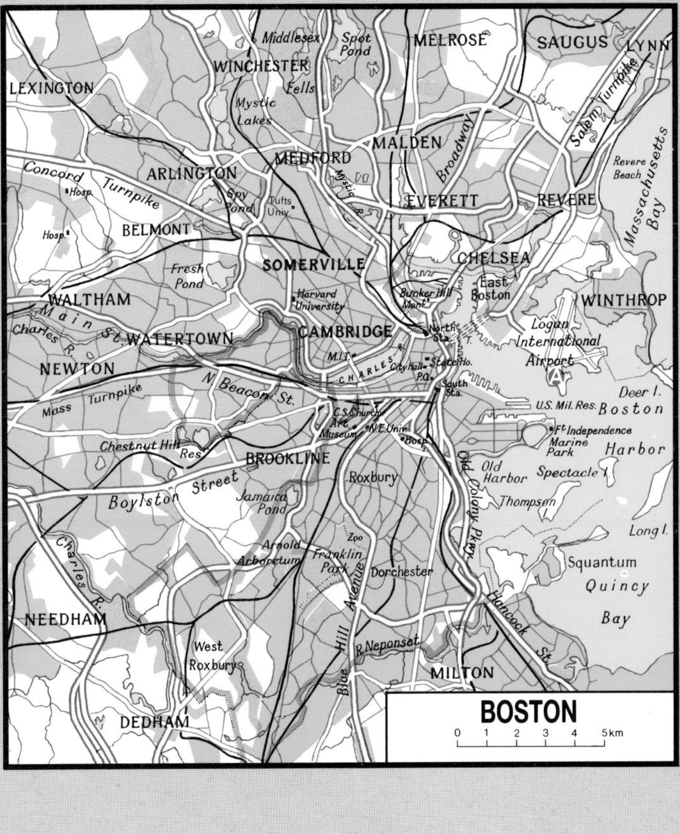
BOSTON
0 1 2 3 4 5km
Middlesex Fells
Spot Pond
MELROSE
SAUGUS
LYNN
WINCHESTER
LEXINGTON
Mystic Lakes
Salem Turnpike
MEDFORD
MALDEN
Broadway
Revere Beach
Massachusetts Bay
Concord Turnpike
ARLINGTON
Hosp.
Spy Pond
Tufts Univ.
EVERETT
REVERE
BELMONT
CHELSEA
Fresh Pond
SOMERVILLE
Bunker Hill Mont.
East Boston
WALTHAM
Harvard University
WINTHROP
Main St.
Charles R.
WATERTOWN
CAMBRIDGE
Logan International Airport
M.I.T.
City Hall
State Ho.
South Sta.
North Sta.
NEWTON
Mass. Turnpike
Beacon St.
Deer I.
U.S. Mil. Res.
Boston Harbor
Chestnut Hill Res.
BROOKLINE
Ft. Independence Marine Park
Old Harbor
Spectacle I.
Boylston Street
Jamaica Pond
Roxbury
Thompson
Old Colony Pkwy.
Long I.
Arnold Arboretum
Zoo
Franklin Park
Dorchester
Squantum
Quincy Bay
Charles R.
NEEDHAM
Blue Hill Avenue
R. Neponset
Hancock St.
West Roxbury
MILTON
DEDHAM

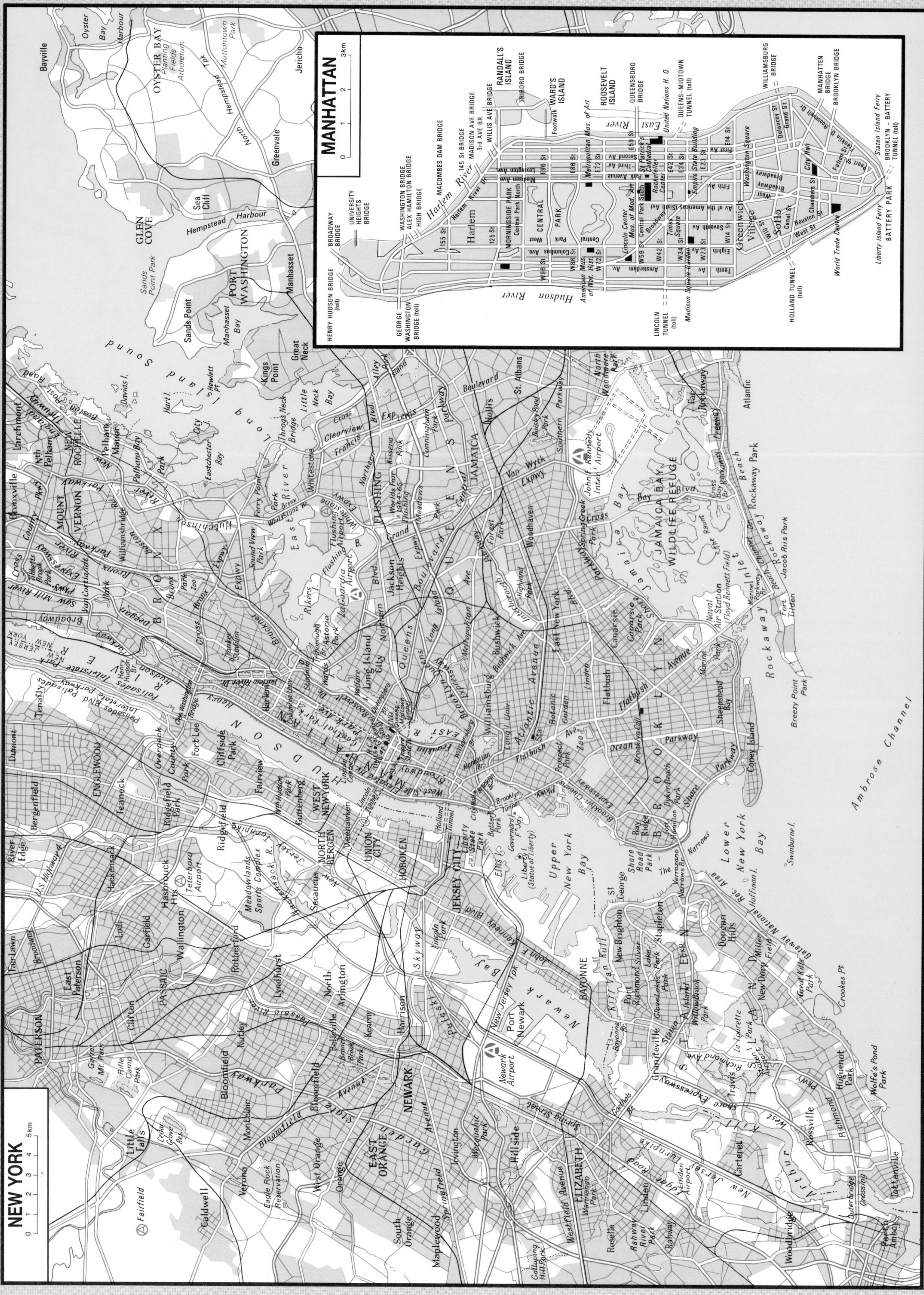
NEW YORK
0 1 2 3 4 5km
MANHATTAN
0 1 2 3km
NEWARK
JERSEY CITY
HOBOKEN
UNION CITY
ELIZABETH
BAYONNE
PATERSON
PASSAIC
EAST ORANGE
ENGLEWOOD
MOUNT VERNON
NEW ROCHELLE
FLUSHING
JAMAICA
QUEENS
BRONX
BROOKLYN
STATEN ISLAND
HUDSON
JAMAICA BAY WILDLIFE REFUGE
GLEN COVE
PORT WASHINGTON
OYSTER BAY
Long Island Sound

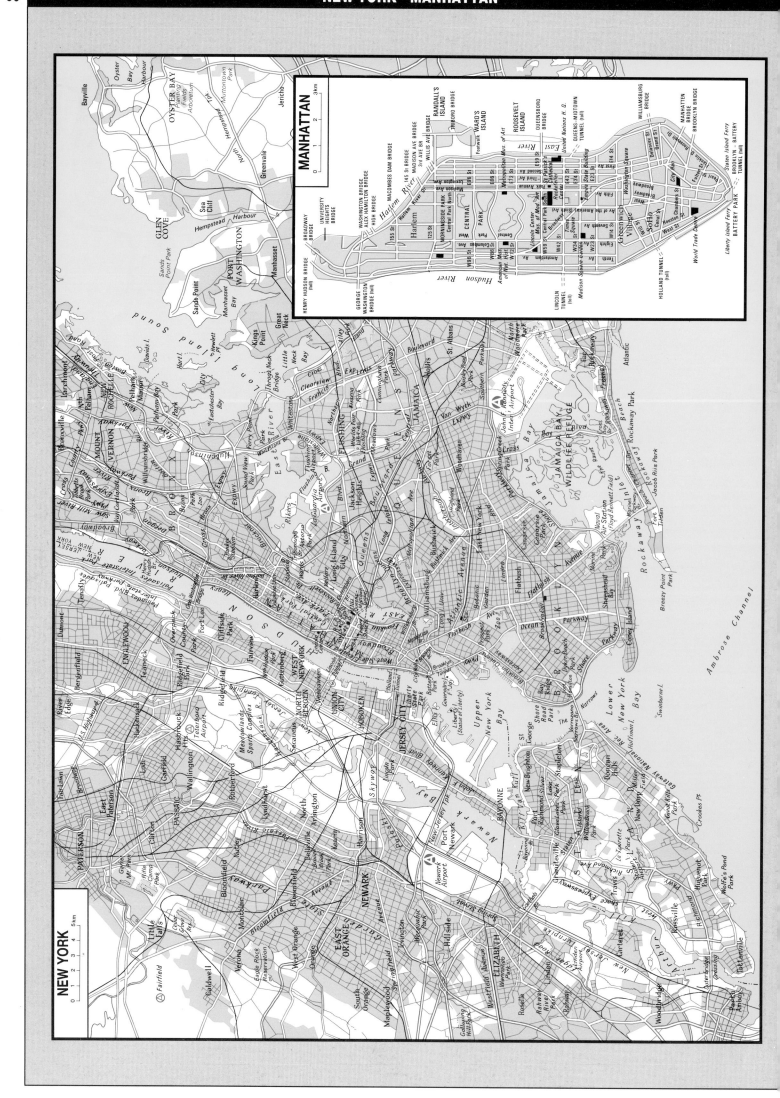

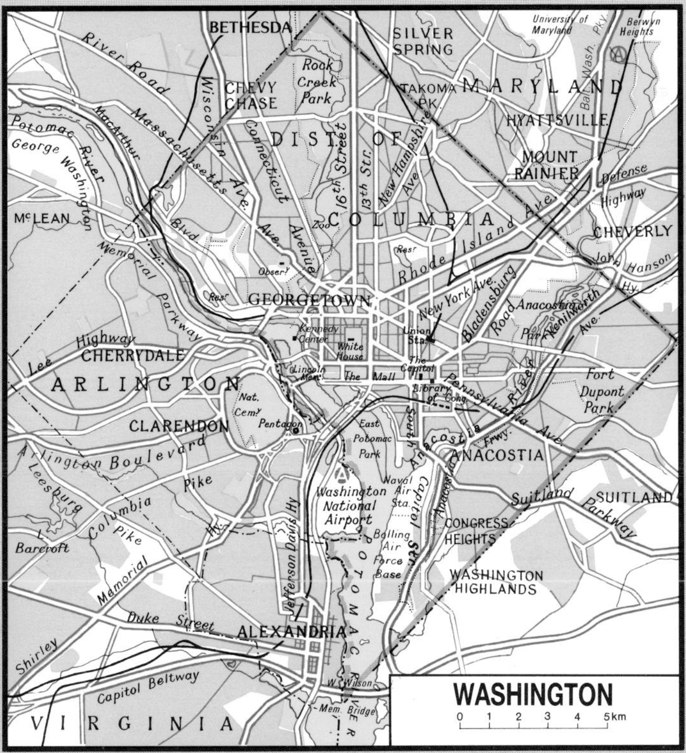
WASHINGTON
0 1 2 3 4 5km
BETHESDA
SILVER SPRING
University of Maryland
Berwyn Heights
River Road
CHEVY CHASE
Rock Creek Park
TAKOMA PK
MARYLAND
HYATTSVILLE
Potomac River
George Washington
MacArthur
Massachusetts Ave.
Wisconsin Ave.
Connecticut Ave.
DIST. OF COLUMBIA
16th Str.
13th Str.
New Hampshire Ave.
MOUNT RAINIER
Defense Highway
McLEAN
CHEVERLY
Memorial Parkway
Rhode Island Ave.
John Hanson Hy.
GEORGETOWN
New York Ave.
Bladensburg Road
Anacostia
Kenilworth Ave.
Highway
CHERRYDALE
Lee
ARLINGTON
White House
The Mall
Union Sta.
Fort Dupont Park
Nat. Cem.
Pentagon
CLARENDON
Arlington Boulevard
Pennsylvania Ave.
ANACOSTIA
Leesburg Pike
Columbia Pike
East Potomac Park
Naval Air Sta.
Suitland Parkway
SUITLAND
Barcroft
Washington National Airport
Bolling Air Force Base
CONGRESS HEIGHTS
WASHINGTON HIGHLANDS
Memorial
Jefferson Davis Hy.
POTOMAC RIVER
Duke Street
ALEXANDRIA
Shirley
Capitol Beltway
W. Wilson Mem. Bridge
VIRGINIA

SAN FRANCISCO
0 5 10 15km
Anselmo
San Rafael
San Pablo
El Sobrante
Concord
Ross
Kentfield
RICHMOND-SAN RAFAEL BRIDGE
San Pablo Ridge
San Pablo Res.
Pleasant Hill
Cowell
Larkspur
San Quentin
Richmond
Briones Res.
Mill Valley
Corte Madera
El Cerrito
Charles Lee Tilden Regional Park
Orinda Village
Walnut Creek
Muir Woods Nat. Monument
Albany
Orinda
Lafayette
Saranap
Tiburon
University of California
Lafayette Reservoir
Belvedere
Angel Island State Park
Berkeley
CALDECOTT TUNNEL
Alamo
Sausalito
GOLDEN GATE BRIDGE
Alcatraz I.
Treasure Island
Piedmont
Moraga
Golden Gate
Oakland
Danville
SAN FRANCISCO
OAKLAND BAY BRIDGE
Redwood Regional Park
Upper San Leandro Reservoir
San Ramon
Golden Gate Park
Richmond
Univ. of San Francisco
Mission
Alameda N.A.S.
Alameda
Sunset
Mt. Davidson
929
Oakland International Airport
San Leandro
Lake Chabot
Lake Merced
Zoological Gardens
Naval Shipyard
Castro Valley
State Univ
Daly City
Brisbane
San Francisco Bay
San Lorenzo
Hayward
South San Francisco
Pacifica
Mt. Eden
San Bruno
San Francisco International Airport
SAN MATEO BRIDGE
Union City
Shelter Cove
Point San Pedro
San Pedro Valley
San Andreas Lake
Millbrae
Niles
Burlingame
Hillsborough
Alameda Cr.
San Francisco State Fish and Game Refuge
San Mateo
Foster City
Coyote Hills Reg. Park
Fremont
Newark
Montara
Bair Island
Moss Beach
Belmont
El Granada
Crystal Springs Res.
Greco Is.
San Carlos
DUMBARTON BRIDGE
Redwood City
Menlo Park

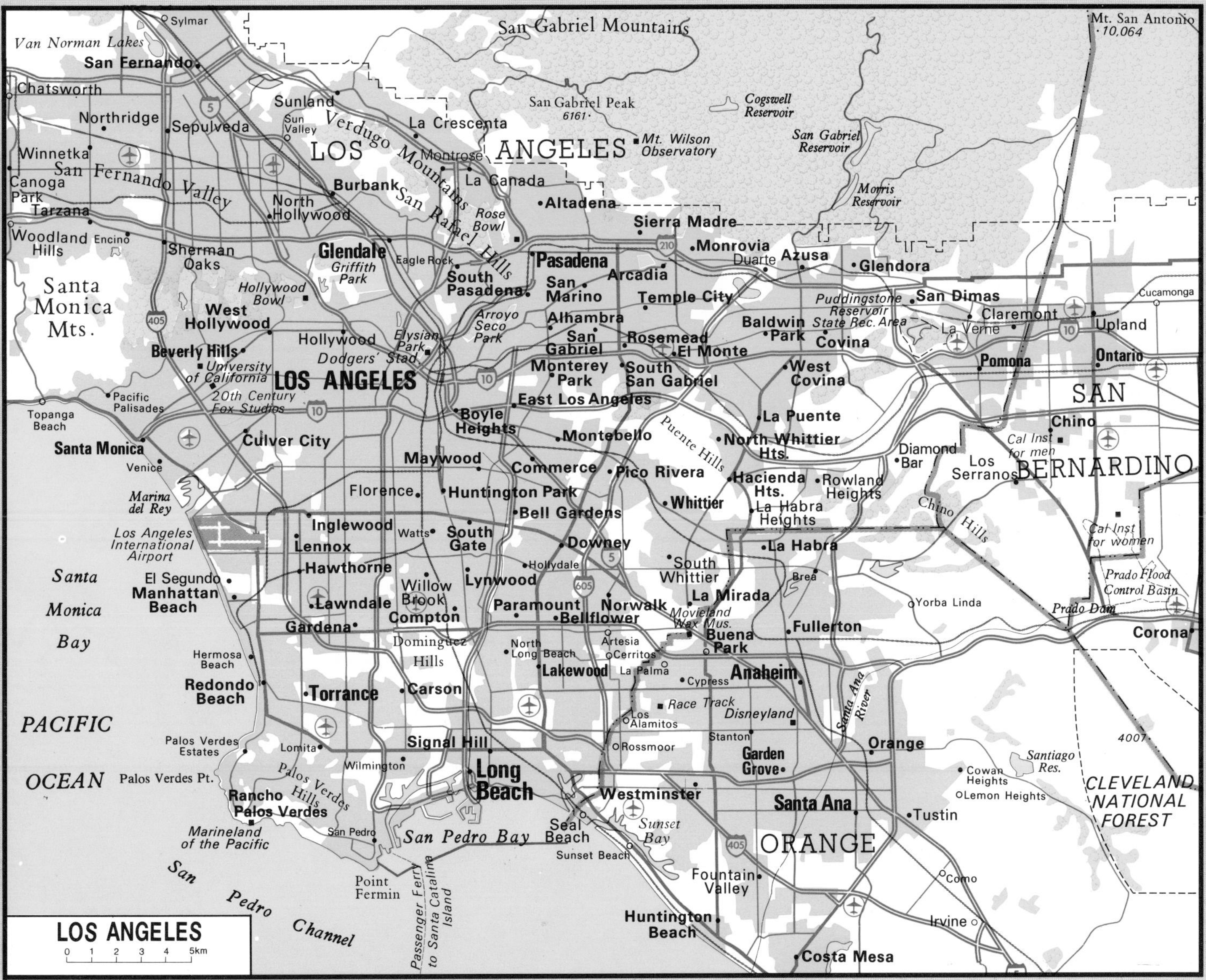
LOS ANGELES
0 1 2 3 4 5km
Sylmar
San Gabriel Mountains
Mt. San Antonio 10,064
Van Norman Lakes
San Fernando
Chatsworth
Sunland
San Gabriel Peak 6161
Cogswell Reservoir
Northridge
Sepulveda
Sun Valley
Verdugo Mountains
La Crescenta
Mt. Wilson Observatory
San Gabriel Reservoir
Winnetka
San Fernando Valley
LOS ANGELES
Montrose
Canoga Park
Burbank
San Rafael Hills
La Canada
Morris Reservoir
Tarzana
North Hollywood
Altadena
Rose Bowl
Sierra Madre
Woodland Hills
Encino
Sherman Oaks
Glendale
Griffith Park
Eagle Rock
Pasadena
Monrovia
Duarte
Azusa
Glendora
Santa Monica Mts.
Hollywood Bowl
South Pasadena
San Marino
Arcadia
Temple City
Puddingstone Reservoir State Rec. Area
San Dimas
Cucamonga
West Hollywood
Arroyo Seco Park
Alhambra
Baldwin Park
Claremont
La Verne
Upland
Hollywood
Elysian Park
San Gabriel
Rosemead
Covina
Beverly Hills
Dodgers' Stad.
El Monte
Pomona
Ontario
University of California
LOS ANGELES
Monterey Park
South San Gabriel
West Covina
SAN
Pacific Palisades
20th Century Fox Studios
East Los Angeles
Topanga Beach
Boyle Heights
La Puente
Chino
Santa Monica
Culver City
Montebello
Puente Hills
North Whittier Hts.
Cal Inst for men
Venice
Maywood
Commerce
Pico Rivera
Diamond Bar
Los Serranos
BERNARDINO
Marina del Rey
Florence
Huntington Park
Hacienda Hts.
Rowland Heights
Whittier
La Habra Heights
Chino Hills
Los Angeles International Airport
Inglewood
Watts
South Gate
Bell Gardens
Cal Inst for women
Lennox
Downey
La Habra
Hawthorne
Hollydale
South Whittier
Santa Monica Bay
El Segundo
Willow Brook
Lynwood
Brea
Prado Flood Control Basin
Manhattan Beach
Lawndale
Paramount
Norwalk
La Mirada
Yorba Linda
Prado Dam
Compton
Bellflower
Movieland Wax Mus.
Gardena
Buena Park
Fullerton
Corona
Hermosa Beach
Dominguez Hills
North Long Beach
Artesia
Cerritos
Lakewood
La Palma
Anaheim
Redondo Beach
Cypress
Torrance
Carson
Race Track
Disneyland
Santa Ana River
PACIFIC OCEAN
Los Alamitos
Palos Verdes Estates
Lomita
Signal Hill
Stanton
Orange
4007
Rossmoor
Garden Grove
Santiago Res.
Wilmington
Long Beach
Cowan Heights
Palos Verdes Pt.
Palos Verdes Hills
Westminster
Lemon Heights
CLEVELAND NATIONAL FOREST
Rancho Palos Verdes
Santa Ana
Tustin
Seal Beach
Sunset Bay
Marineland of the Pacific
San Pedro
San Pedro Bay
Sunset Beach
ORANGE
San Pedro Channel
Point Fermin
Passenger Ferry to Santa Catalina Island
Fountain Valley
Como
Huntington Beach
Irvine
Costa Mesa

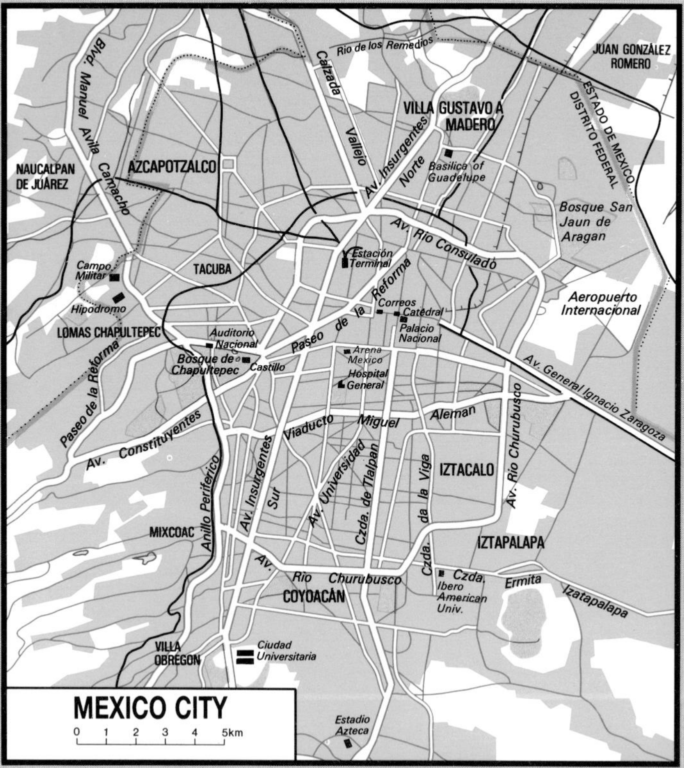
MEXICO CITY
0 1 2 3 4 5km
Rio de los Remedios
JUAN GONZÁLEZ ROMERO
VILLA GUSTAVO A. MADERO
ESTADO DE MEXICO
DISTRITO FEDERAL
Blvd. Manuel Avila Camacho
Calzada Vallejo
Av. Insurgentes Norte
NAUCALPAN DE JUÁREZ
AZCAPOTZALCO
Basilica of Guadelupe
Bosque San Jaun de Aragan
Av. Rio Consulado
Estación Terminal
TACUBA
Campo Militar
Hipodromo
LOMAS CHAPULTEPEC
Paseo de la Reforma
Correos
Catedral
Palacio Nacional
Aeropuerto Internacional
Auditorio Nacional
Bosque de Chapultepec
Castillo
Arena Mexico
Hospital General
Av. General Ignacio Zaragoza
Av. Constituyentes
Viaducto Miguel Aleman
Av. Insurgentes Sur
Av. Universidad
Czda. de Tlalpan
Czda. de la Viga
Av. Rio Churubusco
IZTACALO
Anillo Periferico
MIXCOAC
IZTAPALAPA
Av. Rio Churubusco
COYOACÁN
Czda. Ermita Izatapalapa
Ibero American Univ.
VILLA OBREGON
Ciudad Universitaria
Estadio Azteca

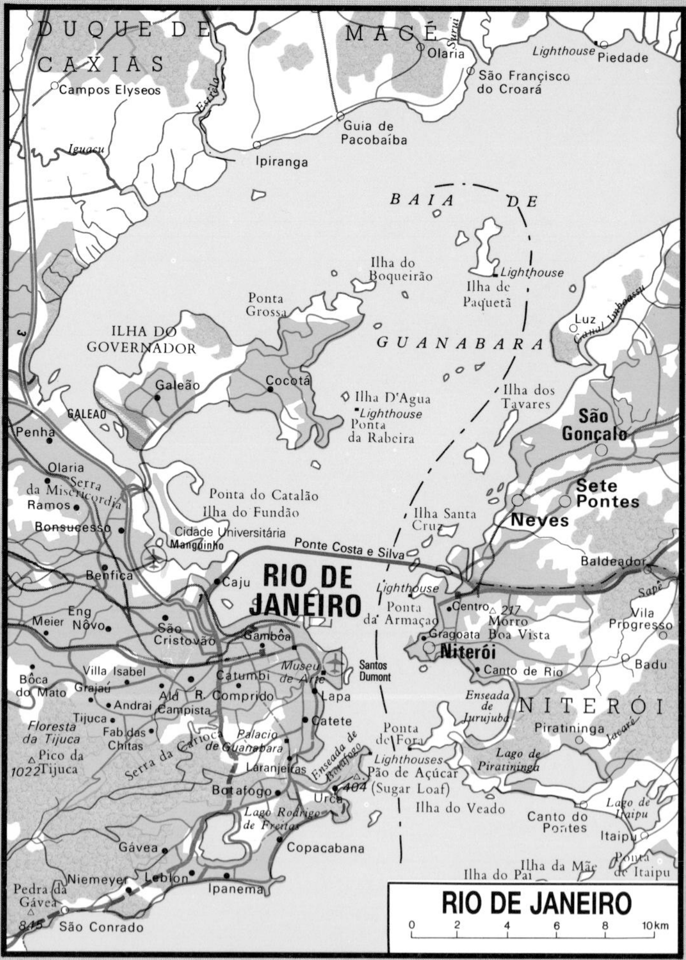
DUQUE DE CAXIAS
Campos Elyseos
MAGÉ
Olaria
Lighthouse
Piedade
São Francisco do Croará
Guia de Pacobaiba
Ipiranga
BAIA DE GUANABARA
Ilha do Boqueirão
Lighthouse
Ilha de Paquetá
Ponta Grossa
ILHA DO GOVERNADOR
Luz
Galeão
Cocotá
Ilha D'Agua
Lighthouse
Ponta da Rabeira
Ilha dos Tavares
São Gonçalo
GALEAO
Penha
Olaria
Serra da Misericordia
Ramos
Ponta do Catalão
Ilha do Fundão
Cidade Universitária
Manguinho
Bonsucesso
Ilha Santa Cruz
Sete Pontes
Neves
Ponte Costa e Silva
Baldeador
Benfica
Caju
RIO DE JANEIRO
Lighthouse
Ponta da Armação
Centro
217 Morro Boa Vista
Vila Progresso
Meier
Eng. Nôvo
São Cristovão
Gamboa
Gragoata
Niterói
Villa Isabel
Catumbi
Museu de Arte
Santos Dumont
Canto de Rio
Badu
Bôca do Mato
Grajaú
Andrai
Ald. Campista
R. Comprido
Lapa
Enseada de Jurujuba
NITERÓI
Tijuca
Floresta da Tijuca
Fab. das Chitas
Serra da Carioca
Palacio de Guanabara
Catete
Ponta de Fora
Piratininga
Pico da 1022 Tijuca
Laranjeiras
Enseada de Botafogo
Lighthouses
Pão de Açúcar
404 (Sugar Loaf)
Lago de Piratininga
Botafogo
Urca
Lago Rodrigo de Freitas
Ilha do Veado
Canto do Pontes
Lago de Itaipu
Itaipu
Gávea
Copacabana
Niemeyer
Leblon
Ipanema
Pedra da Gávea
842
São Conrado
Ilha da Mãe
Ilha do Pai
Ponta de Itaipu
RIO DE JANEIRO
0 2 4 6 8 10km

Cemitério de Vila Nova Cachoeirinha
TUCURUVI
GUARULHOS
PIRITUBA
SANTANA
NOSSA SENHORA DO O
CASA VERDE
LIMÃO
Rio Tietê
VILA JAGUARA
Aeroporto de Marte
Canal do Rio Tietê
VILA GUILHERME
VILA MARIA
CANGAIBA
LAPA
Est. Lapa
Est. Barra Funda
Bom Retiro
PENHA DE FRANÇA
Barra Funda
Pari
Est. da Luz
TATUAPE
PERDIZES
Sta. Cecilia
Sta. Ifigenia
Biblioteca Municipal
BELENZINHO
VIA MATILDE
VILA MADALENA
Consolação
SÉ
Catedral
Brás
Av. Radial Leste
Rio Pinheiros
Bela Vista
Mooca
Cemitério de Vila Formosa
Cidade Universitária
PINHEIROS
Cerqueira Cesar
Liberdade
Cambuci
ALTO DA MOOCA
VILA FORMOSA
BUTANTÃ
JARDIM AMÉRICA
Aclimação
Av. Sapopemba
Professor Francisco Morato
Jockey Clube
JARDIM PAULISTA
Vila Mariana
Monumento
Museu
VILA PRUDENTE
Est. Ipiranga
Parque Ibirapuera
IPIRANGA
Av. do Estado
INDIANÓPOLIS
Via Anchieta
SÃO CAETANO DO SUL
SANTO ANDRÉ
SAÚDE
Est. de Utinga
JABAQUARA
SAO PAULO
0 1 2 3 4 5km

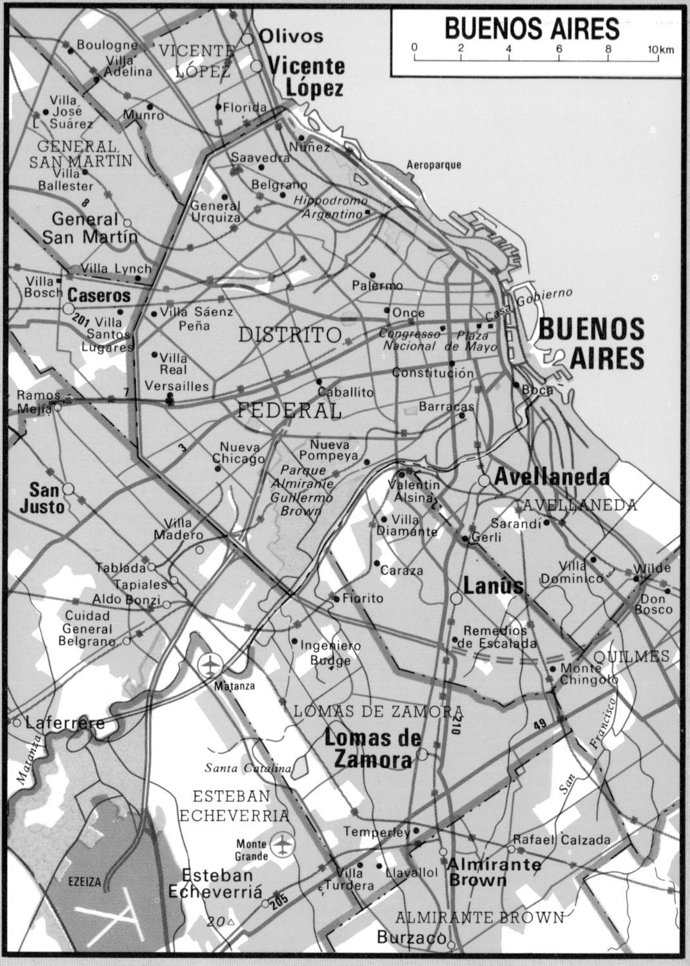
BUENOS AIRES
0 2 4 6 8 10km
Olivos
Boulogne
Villa Adelina
VICENTE LÓPEZ
Vicente López
Villa José Suárez
Munro
Florida
GENERAL SAN MARTIN
Núñez
Villa Ballester
Saavedra
Aeroparque
Belgrano
Hipodromo Argentino
General Urquiza
General San Martin
Villa Lynch
Palermo
Villa Bosch
Caseros
Once
Villa Sáenz Peña
Casa de Gobierno
Villa Santos Lugares
DISTRITO FEDERAL
Congresso Nacional
Plaza de Mayo
BUENOS AIRES
Villa Real
Versailles
Constitución
Ramos Mejía
Caballito
Boca
Barracas
Nueva Chicago
Nueva Pompeya
Parque Almirante Guillermo Brown
San Justo
Valentin Alsina
Avellaneda
AVELLANEDA
Villa Diamante
Sarandí
Gerli
Villa Madero
Tablada
Tapiales
Caraza
Villa Dominico
Wilde
Aldo Bonzi
Lanús
Don Bosco
Fiorito
Cuidad General Belgrano
Remedios de Escalada
Ingeniero Budge
QUILMES
Monte Chingolo
Matanza
Laferrere
LOMAS DE ZAMORA
Lomas de Zamora
Santa Catalina
ESTEBAN ECHEVERRIA
Monte Grande
Temperley
Rafael Calzada
EZEIZA
Esteban Echeverriá
Villa Turdera
Llavallol
Almirante Brown
ALMIRANTE BROWN
Burzaco

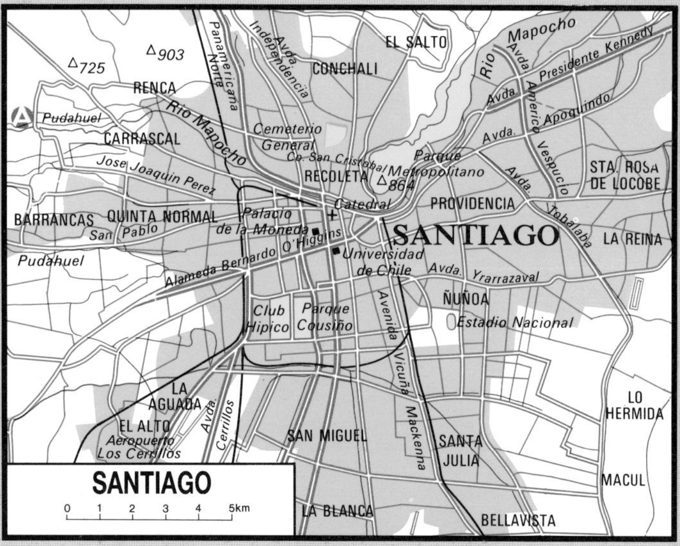
Panamericana Norte
Avda. Independencia
EL SALTO
Rio Mapocho
Avda. Presidente Kennedy
903
725
CONCHALI
RENCA
Pudahuel
Rio Mapocho
Avda. Americo Vespucio
Avda. Apoquindo
CARRASCAL
Cemeterio General
Co. San Cristobal
Parque Metropolitano
Jose Joaquin Perez
RECOLETA
864
STA. ROSA DE LOCOBE
BARRANCAS
QUINTA NORMAL
San Pablo
Palacio de la Moneda
Catedral
PROVIDENCIA
Tobalaba
SANTIAGO
LA REINA
Pudahuel
Alameda Bernardo O'Higgins
Universidad de Chile
Avda. Yrrarrazaval
ÑUÑOA
Club Hipico
Parque Cousiño
Estadio Nacional
Avenida Vicuña Mackenna
LA AGUADA
Avda. Cerrillos
LO HERMIDA
EL ALTO
Aeropuerto Los Cerrillos
SAN MIGUEL
SANTA JULIA
MACUL
SANTIAGO
0 1 2 3 4 5km
LA BLANCA
BELLAVISTA

The roman alphabet is used world-wide. Yet the sounds of Latin from which it was inherited were far too few to allow the alphabet to be applied unaltered to the languages of the world. As a result numerous modifications have been made by adding supplementary letters, by changing the original letters or by adding accents or other diacritical signs.

This brief guide is intended to give no more than an indication of the English language equivalents of the more important letters or combinations of letters in the various alphabets used in the Atlas. An English word is added in brackets to illustrate the sound intended.

FRENCH
There are four nasal vowels:
am an aen em en aon ã
aim ain en eim ein im in ẽ
om on õ
um un ẽũ
ã ẽ õ ẽũ are like a in hart; e in met; o in corn; oo in book pronounced nasally.
au, eau = o (no); é = ay (lay); è, ê, = e (met);
oi oî = wa (wand)
c + a = k; c + e or i = ç = s (sit)
ch = sh (fresh); g + a, o or u = g (got)
g + e or i = j = zh†; gn = ni (onion)
gu = g (got); gü = gw (iguana)
ll = l or y; qu = k; th = t
u = between e in few and oo in too

SPANISH
c + a, o or u = k; c + e or i = th (thin) or s (sit)
ch = ch (cheese); g + a, o or u = g (got)
g + e or i = kh*; gu + a, o or u = gw (iguana)
gu + e or i = g (got); j = kh*; ñ = ny (canyon);
ll = y (yes)
qu + a, o or u = kw (quick); qu + e or i = k (kite)
y = y (yes); z = th (thin) or z depending on dialect

ITALIAN
c + a, o or u = k; c + e or i = ch (cheese)
ch = k
g + a, o or u = g (got); g + e or i = j (jet)
gh = g (got); gli = lli (million)
qu = kw (quick); z = ts or dz

ROMANIAN
ă = a in relative
â = i in ravine
c + a, o or u = k
c + e or i = ch (cheese); ch = k
g + a, o or u = g (got); g + e or i = j (jet)
ş = sh (fresh); ţ = ts (sits)

PORTUGUESE
ã, ãe = French ẽ
õa, õe = French õ
c + a, o or u = k; c + e or i = s
ç = s; ch = sh (fresh)
ih = lli (million)
x = sh (fresh); z = z but = zh when final

GERMAN
ä = e (met); au = ow (down)
äu = oy (boy); c = ts (sits)
ch = kh*; ei, ey = eye (= y in why)
eu = oy (boy); g = g (got)
ie = ie (retrieve); j = y (yes)
ö = oo (book); s = z but s when final
sch = sh (fresh); sp, st = shp, sht
ü = French u; v = f; w = v; z = ts (sits)

DUTCH
aa ee are long vowels
c + e or i or z = s, otherwise k
ij = eye (= y in why)

SCANDINAVIAN
å = aw (law); ä = e (met)
ø = oo (book); øj = oy (boy)
j = y (yes)

ICELANDIC
ð = dh = th (then)
hv = kw; ll = tl; þ = th

FINNISH
ay = eye (= y in why)
j = y; y = French u; w = v

HUNGARIAN
a = aw (law); cs = ch (cheese); ccs = chch;
gy = d + y (dew)
j = y; ny = ny (canyon)
s = sh (fresh); ss = shsh
sz = s (sit); ty = t + y (yes)
zs = zh†
ai = e (met); av = au or av
dh = th (then); th = th (thin)
kh = kh*; oi = i (ravine)
ou = oo (too)

TURKISH
c = j (jet); ç = ch (cheese)
ö = oo (book); ş = sh
ü = French u
ı and i = i (ravine)

RUSSIAN
ay = a + y (yes)
e = e or ye
ë = yaw; ëy = yoy
ch = ch (cheese); sh = sh (fresh)
sh ch = sh ch (fresh cheese)
ts = ts (sits)
ya = ya (yam); z = z (zoo)
zh = zh (measure)
' = sound of y (yes)
" = silent

OTHER SLAVONIC

§S-C	Pol	Cz		
c	c	c	=	ts (sits)
	ć		=	ts + y (yes)
č	cz	č	=	ch (cheese)
ć			=	t + y (yes)
đ		ď	=	d + y (yes)
		ě	=	e (mother)
h	ch	ch	=	kh*
j	j	j	=	y (yes)
	ł		=	w (wood)
nj	ń	ň	=	ny (canyon)
		ř	=	rzh*
š	sz	š	=	sh (fresh)
		ť	=	t + y (yes)
ž	ż, rz, ź	ž	=	zh*

ARABIC
long vowels have a macron (bar), ā
dh = th (then)
h = h (hat); j = (jet)
gh = French r, pronounce as g (got)
kh = kh* q = g (got)
' and ' are best treated as glottal stops
ḍ ḥ ṣ ṭ ẓ = d, h, s, t, z
Note: 1. in Egypt and Sudan g = g (got)
2. in NW Africa Dj = j (jet)
ou = w (wadi)

FARSI (IRAN)
Can be read as Arabic above. Stress is on the last syllable.

SOMALI
long vowels are aa, ee, ii, oo, uu
c is silent = glottal stop
dh = th (then)
g = g (got); q = k (kite)
sh = sh (fresh); w = w (wadi)
x = kh*

MALAY – INDONESIAN
As English except
c = ch (cheese)

CHINESE (PINYIN)
q = ch (church); c = ts (sits)
x = hs = h + s

† zh = s in measure;
* kh = ch in Scottish loch
= German ch in achtung

§ **S-C** = Serbo-Croat
Pol = Polish
Cz = Czech

A

ABLATION The loss of water from ice and snow surfaces, by melting and run-off, calving of icebergs, evaporation and snow-blowing.

ABRASION The wearing down or away of rocks by friction.

ABSOLUTE HUMIDITY The amount of water vapour in a specified amount of air, frequently expressed as grams of water vapour per kilogram of dry air containing the vapour.

ABYSSAL Usually applied to the very deep parts of the oceans, over 3km below the surface.

ACCRETION The growth of objects by collection of additional material, usually of smaller size. Ice particles in the atmosphere can grow by this process.

ACID PRECIPITATION Rain and snow with a pH of less than 5.6.

ADVECTION Movement of a property in air and water by their motion. Usually applied to horizontal rather than vertical motion.

AEOLIAN Related to winds. Thus aeolian geomorphology is concerned with the processes whereby wind removes, distributes and deposits materials of the earth's surface.

AGGLOMERATE A rock made of small pieces of lava that have been fused by heat.

AGGRADATION The building up of a land surface by deposition of material by wind, water or ice.

AGGREGATE A loose collection of rock fragments.

ALLUVIAL PLAIN A plain, usually at low altitude, made of alluvium.

ANTICYCLONE An extensive region of relatively high atmospheric pressure, usually a few thousand kilometres across, in which the low level winds spiral outwards, clockwise in the northern hemisphere and anticlockwise in the southern hemisphere.

ARCHIPELAGO A sea or lake containing numerous islands, such as the area between Sumatra and the Philippines.

ARTESIAN WELL A well which taps water held under pressure in rocks below the surface. The pressure results in a well water level higher than the highest part of the water-bearing rocks.

ATOLL A coral reef surrounding a lagoon found in the tropical oceans.

AURORA BOREALIS (Northern Lights) Flashing lights in the atmosphere some 400km above polar regions caused by solar particles being trapped in the earth's magnetic field.

AVALANCHE The sudden and rapid movement of ice, snow, earth and rock down a slope.

AZIMUTH Horizontal angle between two directions.

B

BADLANDS Highly dissected landscapes, usually associated with poorly consolidated materials and sparse vegetation cover.

BAR A usually sandy feature, lying parallel to the coast and frequently underwater.

BARCHAN A crescentic sand dune whose horns point in the direction of dune movement.

BAROGRAPH An instrument for recording atmospheric pressure. The output is a graph of pressure changes through time.

BAROMETER An instrument for measuring atmospheric pressure. The reading is either by measuring the height of a column of mercury or by the compression or expansion of a series of vacuum chambers.

BARRIER REEF A coral reef characterized by the presence of a lagoon or body of water between it and the associated coastline.

BASALT A fine-grained and dark coloured igneous rock.

BASE LEVEL The lower limit to the operation of erosional processes generating on land – usually defined with reference to the role of running water. Sea level is the most general form of base level.

BASIN An area of land encompassing the water flow into any specific river channel – hence usually known as a drainage basin.

BATHOLITH A large mass of intrusive igneous rock.

BATHYMETRY Measurement of water depth.

BAUXITE The main ore of aluminium.

BEACH A coastal accumulation of various types of sediment, usually sands and pebbles.

BEAUFORT SCALE A scale of wind speed devised by Admiral Sir Francis Beaufort based on effects of winds on ships. Later modified to include land-based phenomena.

BENCH MARK A reference point used in the measurement of land height in topographic surveying.

BENTHIC Relating to plants, animals and other organisms that inhabit the floors of lakes, seas and oceans.

BERGSCHRUND The crevasse existing at the head of a glacier because of the movement of glacier ice away from the rock wall.

BIGHT A bend in a coast forming an open bay, or the bay itself.

BIOMASS The mass of biological material present per plant or animal, per community or per unit area.

BIOME A mixed community of plants and animals occupying a large area of continental size.

BIOSPHERE The zone at the interface of the earth's surface, ocean and atmosphere where life is found.

BIOTA The entire collection of species or organisms, plants and animals found in a given region.

BISE A cold, dry northerly to north-easterly wind occurring in the mountains of Central Europe in winter.

BLACK EARTH A black soil rich in humus, found extensively in temperate grasslands such as the Russian Steppes.

BLOW HOLE Vertical shaft leading from a sea cave to the surface. Air and water are frequently forced through it by advancing seas.

BORE A large solitary wave which moves up funnel-shaped rivers and estuaries.

BOREAL A descriptive term, usually of climate and forest, to characterize conditions in middle to high latitudes.

BOURNE A river channel on chalk terrain that flows after heavy rain.

BUTTE A small, flat-topped and often steep-sided hill standing isolated on a flat plain. *(see picture below)*

C

CALDERA A depression, usually several kilometres across.

CALVING The breaking away of a mass of ice from a floating glacier or ice shelf to form an iceberg.

CANYON A steep sided valley, usually found in semi-arid and arid areas.

CAPE An area of land jutting out into water, frequently as a peninsula or promontory.

CARDINAL POINTS The four principal compass points, north, east, south and west.

CATARACT A large waterfall over a precipice.

CHINOOK A warm, dry wind that blows down the eastern slopes of the Rocky Mountains of North America.

Above Butte, Monument Valley, Arizona USA. This type of flat-topped, steep sided hill is characteristic of the arid plateau region of the western United States.

CIRQUE OR CORRIE A hollow, open downstream but bounded upstream by a curved, steep headwall, with a gently sloping floor. Found in areas that have been glaciated.

CLIMATE The long-term atmospheric characteristics of a specified area.

CLOUD A collection of a vast number of small water droplets or ice crystals or both in the atmosphere.

COL A pass or saddle between two mountain peaks.

COLD FRONT A zone of strong horizontal temperature gradient in the atmosphere moving such that, for the surface observer, cold air replaces warm.

CONDENSATION The process of formation of liquid water from water vapour.

CONFLUENCE The 'coming together' of material

flows, most usually used in fluids such as the atmosphere and oceans.

CONGLOMERATE A rock which comprises or contains rounded pebbles more than about 2mm in diameter.

CONTINENTAL DRIFT The movement of continents relative to each other. (See *Plate Tectonics*)

CONTINENTAL SHELF A portion of the continental crust below sea level that slopes gently seaward forming an extension of the adjacent coastal plain separated from the deep ocean by the steeply sloping continental slope.

CONTINENTAL SLOPE Lies on the seaward edge of the continental shelf and slopes steeply to the ocean floor.

CONTOUR A line on a map that joins points of equal height or equal depth.

CONVECTION CURRENT A current resulting from convection which is a mode of mass transport within a fluid (especially heat) resulting in movement and mixing of properties of that fluid.

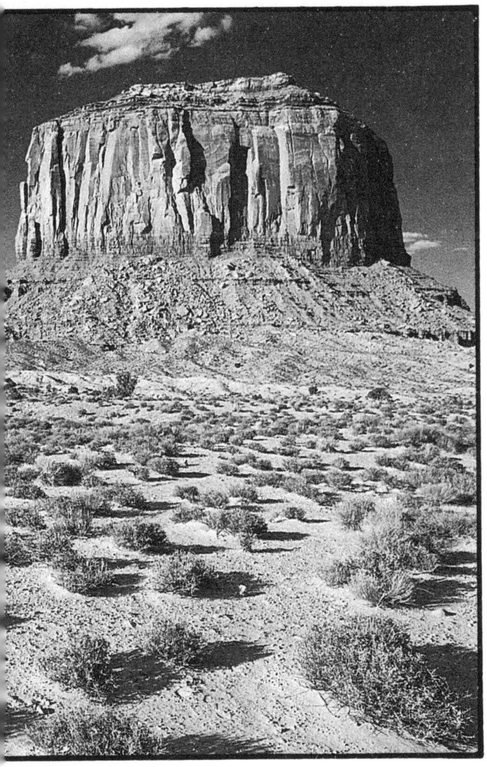

CONVERGENCE The opposite of divergence which is the outflowing mass of fluid. Hence convergence is the inflowing of such mass.

CORAL REEF Large structures fringing islands and coastlines consisting mostly of corals and algae.

CORDILLERA A system of mountain ranges consisting of a number of more or less parallel chains of mountain peaks – such as in the Rocky Mountains.

CRATER A depression at the top of a volcano where a vent carrying lava and gasses reaches the surface.

CRATON A continental area that has experienced little internal deformation in the last 600 million years.

CREVASSE A deep fissure in the surface of a body of ice.

CYCLONE A region of relatively low atmospheric pressure about 2000 km across around which air rotates anticlockwise in the northern hemisphere and clockwise in the southern.

D

DATUM LEVEL Something (such as a fixed point or assumed value) used as a basis for calculating or measuring. Frequently a height of ground relative to which other heights are assessed.

DECLINATION Angular distance north or south from the equator measured along a line of longitude.

DECIDUOUS FOREST Forest in which the trees shed their leaves at a particular time, season or growth stage. The most common manifestation is the shedding in winter.

DEFLATION The process whereby the wind removes fine materials from the surface of a beach or desert.

DEGRADATION The lowering and often flattening of a land surface by erosion.

DELTA Accumulations of sediment deposited at the mouths of rivers. The Nile and Mississippi deltas are two famous examples.

DENUDATION The laying bare of underlying rocks or strata by the removal of overlying material.

DEPOSITION The laying down of material, which, in geomorphological terms, was previously carried by wind, liquid water or ice.

DEPRESSION See *cyclone*

DESALINIZATION To take out the salt content of a material. Usually applied to the extraction of salt from sea water to give fresh water.

DESERT An area in which vegetation cover is sparse or absent and precipitation is low in amount. Deserts can be hot or cold.

DISCHARGE The volume of flow of fluid in a given time period.

DISSECTED PLATEAU A relatively flat, high level area of land which has been cut by streams.

DIURNAL Occurring everyday or having a daily cycle.

DIVERGENCE A spreading of material. Frequently found in high pressure areas (anticyclones) in the atmosphere where air spirals outwards from the centre.

DOLDRUMS A zone of light, variable winds and low atmospheric pressure near or slightly north of the equator.

DRAINAGE The flow of material (usually a fluid) over the earth's surface due to the force of gravity. Most familiarly seen as rivers.

DRIFT ICE Ice bodies drifting in ocean currents.

DROUGHT Dryness caused by lack of precipitation, most easily seen in the hot, dry desert areas of the world.

DROWNED VALLEY A valley which has been filled with water due to a rise of sea level relative to the level with which the river mouth was previously in accord.

DRUMLIN A depositional landform, usually made of glacially-derived material, which has been streamlined by the passage of overlying ice.

DRY VALLEY A valley which is seldom, if ever, occupied by a stream channel.

DUNE An accumulation of sand deposited and shaped by wind.

DUST Solid particles carried in suspension by the atmosphere.

DYKE A sheet-like intrusion of igneous rock, usually oriented vertically, which cuts across the structural planes of the host rocks.

E

EARTH PILLAR A pinnacle of soil or other unconsolidated material that is protected from erosion by the presence of a stone at the top.

EARTHQUAKE A series of shocks and tremors resulting from the sudden release of pressure along active faults and in areas of volcanic activity.

EBB TIDE Tide receding to or at its lowest point.

ECLIPSE, LUNAR The total or partial obscuring of the Moon by the Earth lying on a line between the Moon and the Sun.

ECLIPSE, SOLAR The total or partial obscuring of the Sun by the Moon lying on a line between the Sun and the Earth.

ECOLOGY A branch of science that studies the relations of plants and animals with each other and with their non-living environment.

ECOSYSTEM An entity within which ecological relations operate.

EPICENTRE The point on the earth's surface which lies directly above the focus of an earthquake.

EQUINOX The time of year when the sun is directly overhead at noon at the equator.

ERG A sand desert.

EROSION The group of processes whereby debris is loosened or dissolved and removed from any part of the earth's surface.

ERRATIC A rock that has been carried to its present location by a glacier.

ESCARPMENT A linear land form with one steep side (scarp slope) and one less steep side (dip slope).

ESKER A sinuous ridge of coarse gravel which has been deposited by a meltwater stream normally flowing underneath a glacier.

ESTUARY The sections of a river which flow into the sea and are influenced by tidal currents.

EVAPORATION The diffusion of water vapour into the atmosphere from freely exposed water surfaces.

EXFOLIATION The weathering of a rock by the peeling off of surface layers.

F

FATHOM A unit of length equal to six feet, most usually used in measuring depth of water.

FAULT A crack or fissure in rock, resulting from tectonic movement.

FAUNA Animals or animal life of an area.

FEN A low lying area partially covered by water which is characterized by accumulations of peat.

FJORD A glacially eroded valley whose floor is occupied by the sea.

FIRTH A sea inlet, particularly in Scotland.

FLORA Plants or plant life in an area.

FLUVIOGLACIAL The activity of rivers which are fed by water melted from glaciers.

FOG An accumulation of water droplets or ice crystals in the atmosphere such that visibility is reduced to 1km or less.

FÖHN WIND A strong, gusty, warm, down-slope wind which occurs on the lee side of a mountain range.

FOLD A bend in rock strata resulting from movement of the crustal rocks.

FOOD CHAIN The transfer of food from one type of organism to another in a sequence.

FORD A shallow part of a river that allows easy crossing.

FRACTURE The splitting of material into parts: usually concerned with geological materials.

FRAZIL ICE Fine spikes of ice in suspension in water, usually associated with the freezing of sea water.

FRONT A transition zone between air of different density, temperature and humidity.

FROST A situation resulting from air temperatures falling to 0°C – either in the air (air frost) or at the ground (ground frost).

FUMAROLE A small, volcanic vent through which hot gasses are emitted.

G

GABBRO A basic igneous rock, usually coarse grained and dark grey to black in colour.

GEEST Ancient alluvial sediments which still cover the land surfaces on which they were originally deposited.

GEODESY The determination of the size and shape of the earth by survey and calculation.

GEOID The shape of the earth at mean sea level.

GEOLOGY Science that deals with the nature and origin of the earth's rocks and sediments.

GEOMORPHOLOGY Science that deals with the nature and origin of landforms of the earth's surface.

GEOSYNCLINE A very large depression, tens or hundreds of kilometres across and up to ten kilometres deep, the floor of which is built up by sedimentation.

GEYSER A spring of geothermally heated water that erupts intermittently due to pressures beneath the surface. Old Faithful in Yellowstone National Park, USA, is the most famous example.

GLACIATION The incursion of ice into (or over) a landscape resulting in a whole suite of glacial processes operating thereupon.

GLACIER A large body of ice, in a valley or covering a much larger area. The largest are found in polar regions.

GLEN Valley. Term especially used in Scotland.

GNEISS A coarse-grained igneous rock that has been metamorphosed.

GONDWANALAND A large continent which it is thought was split very early in geological time to form parts of Africa, Australia, Antarctica, South America and India.

GORGE A deep and narrow section of a river valley, usually with very steep sides.

GRAVEL Loose, rounded fragments of rock.

GREAT CIRCLE A circle formed on the surface of the earth by the intersection of a plane through the centre of the earth with the surface. Lines of longitude and the Equator are great circles.

GROUND FROST See *frost*

GROUND WATER All water (gaseous, liquid or solid) lying below the earth's surface and not chemically combined with the minerals present.

GROYNE A man-made barrier running across a beach and into the sea; constructed to reduce erosion of the beach by longshore currents.

GULF A part of the sea that is partly or almost completely enclosed by land.

GULLY A linear depression worn in the earth by running water after rains.

GUYOT A flat-topped mountain on the sea floor which does not reach the sea surface.

GYRE Large circulations of water in the world's oceans, involving the major currents.

H

HAFF A coastal lagoon separated from the open seas by a sand spit.

HAIL Solid precipitation which falls as ice particles from cumulonimbus clouds. Contrasts markedly with snow.

HEMISPHERE Half of the earth, usually thought of in terms of its surface. The most familiar are the northern and southern hemispheres, bounded by the Equator.

HORIZON Apparent junction of earth and sky.

HORSE LATITUDE The latitude belts over the oceans at latitudes of 30–35° where winds are predominantly calm or light and weather is often hot and dry.

HOT SPOT A small area of the earth's crust where an unusually high heat flow is associated with volcanic activity.

HOT SPRING An emission of hot water at the land surface.

HURRICANE A severe cyclone occurring in the tropics, characterized by high wind speeds and heavy precipitation.

HYDROLOGICAL CYCLE The continuous movement of all forms of water (vapour, liquid and solid) on, in and above the earth.

HYDROSPHERE The earth's water – saline, fresh, gaseous, liquid and solid.

HYGROMETER A device for measuring the relative humidity of the atmosphere.

HYPSOGRAPHIC CURVE A generalized profile of the earth and ocean floors which represents the proportions of the area of the surface at various altitudes above or below a datum.

I

ICEBERG A large floating mass of ice detached from a glacier, usually tens of metres deep and can be several kilometres across.

ICE-CAP A dome-shaped glacier with a generally outward flow of ice.

ICE FLOE A piece of floating ice which is not attached to the land and is usually 2–3 metres thick.

ICE SHELF A floating sheet of ice attached to an embayment in the coast.

IGNEOUS ROCK Rock formed when molten material solidifies, either within the earth's crust or at the surface.

INSELBERG A large, residual hill which overlooks a surrounding eroded plain.

INSOLATION The amount of solar radiation received over a specified area and a specified time.

INTERNATIONAL DATE LINE An arbitary line, roughly along the 180° longitude line, east and west of which the date differs by one day.

INVERSION (temperature)
An increase of temperature with height.

IRRIGATION The supply of water to land by artificial means. Usually to improve agricultural productivity.

ISLAND ARC A chain of islands with an arcuate plan form. The islands are usually volcanic in origin.

ISOBAR A line drawn on diagrams joining equal values of atmospheric pressure. A particular kind of isopleth.

ISOPLETH A line drawn on diagrams joining equal values of the plotted element.

ISOSTASY The condition of balance between the rigid crustal elements of the earth's surface and the underlying, denser and more mobile material.

Above Limestone towers in the world's most spectacular karst region – Li River near Guilin, Guangxi Province, China. The towers are the result of erosional processes.

ISTHMUS A narrow strip of land which connects two islands or two large land masses.

J

JOINT A fracture or crack in a rock.

JUNGLE An area of land overgrown with dense vegetation, usually in the tropics.

K

KAME An irregular mound of stratified sediment deposited by, in association with stagnant ice.

KARST Limestone areas which have distinctive landforms such as caves, sinks and frequently a lack of surface water. *(see picture above)*

KELP A mass of large brown seaweeds.

KETTLE HOLE An enclosed depression resulting from the melting of buried ice.

KNOT A measure of speed – one nautical mile per hour (1.15 mi hr^{-1}; 0.85 km hr^{-1}).

KOPJE A small hill or rock outcrop; term used particularly in South Africa.

KRILL Small marine animals, resembling shrimps.

L

LACCOLITH A mass of intrusive rock, usually with a horizontal base and causing the doming of overlying strata.

LAGOON A shallow pool separated from a larger body of water by a bar or reef.

LANDSAT An unmanned satellite that carries sensors to record the resources of the earth.

LANDSLIDE The movement downward under the influence of gravity of a mass of rock debris.

LATERITE A red clay formed by the weathering of rock that consists especially of compounds of iron and aluminium.

LAURASIA The northern part of Pangaea, a super-continent thought to have been broken up by continental drift.

LAVA Molten rock material that emerges from volcanoes and volcanic fissures.

LEACHING The downward movement of water through soil resulting in the removal of water-soluble materials from upper layers and their accumulation in lower layers.

LEEWARD To the lee (downwind, downstream) of an obstacle lying in a flow.

LEVEE A broad, long ridge running parallel and adjacent to a river on its flood-plain.

LIGNITE A brownish black coal in which the texture of the original wood is distinct.

LITHOSPHERE The earth's crust and a portion of the upper mantle that together comprise a layer of strength relative to the more easily deformable layer below.

LITTORAL A coastal region.

LLANOS An open grassy plain in S. America.

LOAM A crumbly soil consisting of a mixture of clay, silt and sand.

LOCH A lake or narrow sea inlet in Scotland.

LOESS Unconsolidated and frequently unstratified material deposited after transport by wind.

LONGSHORE CURRENT A current that runs along a coast. It may result in longshore drift, the transport of beach material along the coast.

LOW See *cyclone*

LUNAR MONTH The period of time between two successive new moons, being about 29½ days.

M

MAGMA Fused, molten rock material beneath the earth's crust from which igneous rocks are formed.

MAGNETIC ANOMALIES Areas with local surface variations in the earth's magnetic field relative to large-scale values.

MAGNETIC FIELD The field of force exerted by the earth by virtue of its being like a giant magnet. Its most familiar manifestation is in the behaviour of a compass.

MAGNETIC REVERSAL The reversal of the earth's magnetic field, such that a north-seeking compass points toward the South Pole. Such reversals have occurred in geological time.

MANTLE The zone within the earth's interior extending from 25 to 70km below the surface to a depth of 2900km.

MAP PROJECTION A mathematical device for representing a portion of all of the earth's curved surface on a flat surface.

MAP SCALE A measure of the ratio of distances represented on a map to their true value.

MAQUIS Scrub vegetation of evergreen shrubs characteristic of the western Mediterranean.

MARL A fine grained mixture of clay and silt with a high proportion of calcium carbonate.

MASSIF A large mountainous area, often quite distinct, containing several individual substantial mountains.

MEANDER A sinuously winding portion of a river channel; also applied to similar forms within larger flows, such as the atmosphere and oceans.

MEAN SEA LEVEL The level of the sea determined from a mean of the tidal ranges over periods of several months to several years.

METAMORPHIC ROCKS Rocks in which their composition, structure and texture have been significantly altered by the action of heat and pressure greater than that produced normally by burial.

METEOROLOGY The study of the workings of the atmosphere.

MILLIBAR A unit of pressure, most widely used in meteorology. The average pressure exerted by the atmosphere on the surface of the earth is just over 1013 millibars.

MISTRAL A cold, dry, north or northwest wind affecting the Rhone Valley.

MONSOON A wind regime with marked seasonal reversal in direction, most famously found in the Indian sub-continent.

MORAINE A landform resulting from the deposition of till by glaciers, taking on several distinctive forms depending upon the location and mode of deposition.

N

NADIR A point that is vertically below the observer.

NASA National Aeronautics and Space Administration (USA).

NEAP TIDE A tide of minimum height occurring at the first and third quarter of the moon.

NÉVÉ Snow that is being compacted into ice, as found in the birth place of glaciers.

NUNATAK A mountain completely surrounded by an ice cap or ice sheet.

O

OASIS An area within a desert region where there is sufficient water to sustain animal and plant life throughout the year.

OCEAN BASIN A large depression in the ocean floor analogous to basins on land.

OCEANIC CRUST The portion of the earth's surface crust comprising largely sima (silica-magnesia rich rocks) about 5km thick. Underlies most of the world's oceans.

OCEAN RIDGE A ridge in the ocean floor, sometimes 150 to 1500 km wide and hundreds of metres high.

OCCLUSION The coming together of warm and cold fronts in cyclones in the latest stages of its evolution.

OROGENESIS The formation of mountains, such as the Andes and Rocky Mountains. The mechanism is still uncertain but is probably related to plate tectonics.

OUTWASH PLAIN Stratified material deposited by glacio-fluvial waters beyond the ice margin.

OXBOW LAKE A lake, usually curved in plan, occupying an abandoned section of meandering river.

P

PACK ICE Ice formed on sea surface when water temperatures fall to about −2°C and floating free under the influence of currents and wind.

PAMPAS An extensive, generally grass-covered plain of temperate South America east of the Andes.

PANGAEA The name given to a postulated continental landmass which split up to produce most of the present northern hemisphere continents.

PASS A narrow passage over relatively low ground in a mountain range.

PEDIMENT A smooth, erosional land surface typically sloping from the foot of a high-land area to a local base level.

PELAGIC The part of an aquatic system that excludes its margins and substrate; it is essentially the main part of the water body.

PENEPLAIN The supposed end land form resulting from erosional processes wearing down an initially uplifted block.

PENUMBRA A region of partial darkness in a shadow surrounding the region of total darkness (umbra), such as seen in an eclipse.

PERIHELION The point in its orbit about the sun that a planet is closest to the sun.

PIEDMONT GLACIER A glacier which spreads out into a lobe as it flows onto a lowland.

PILLOW LAVA Lava that has solidified, probably under water, in rounded masses.

PLACER DEPOSIT A sediment, such as in the bed of a stream, which contains particles of valuable minerals.

PLAIN Extensive area of level or rolling treeless country.

PLANKTON Small freshwater and marine organisms that tend to move with water currents and comprise the food of larger and higher order organisms.

PLATE TECTONICS A theory which holds that the earth's surface is divided into several major rigid plates which are in motion with respect to each other and the underlying mantle. Continental drift results from plate motion and earthquakes, volcanoes and mountain-building tend to occur at the plate boundaries.

PLUTONIC ROCK Rock material that has formed at depth where cooling and crystallization have occurred slowly.

POLAR WANDERING The movements of the North and South Poles throughout geological time relative to the positions of the continents.

POLDER A low lying area of land that has been reclaimed from the sea or a lake by artificial means and is kept free of water by pumping.

PRECIPITATION The deposition of water from the atmosphere in liquid and solid form. Rain, snow, hail and dew are the most familiar forms.

PRAIRIE An extensive area of level or rolling, almost treeless grassland in North America.

PRESSURE GRADIENT The change per unit distance of pressure, perhaps most frequently met in atmospheric studies. The cause of winds.

Q

QUARTZ A crystalline mineral consisting of silicon dioxide that is a major constituent of many rocks.

QUICKSAND Water-saturated sand that is semi-liquid and cannot bear the weight of heavy objects.

R

RADAR A device that transmits radio waves and locates objects in the vicinity by analysis of the waves reflected back from them (radio detection and ranging).

RADIATION The transmission of energy in the form of electromagnetic waves and requiring no intervening medium.

RAIN SHADOW An area experiencing relatively low rainfall because of its position on the leeward side of a hill.

RAISED BEACH An emerged shoreline represented by stranded marine deposits and wave cut platforms, usually backed by former cliffs.

RANGE An open region over which livestock may roam and feed, particularly in North America.

RAVINE A narrow, steep sided valley usually formed by running water.

REEF A rocky construction found at or near sea-level; coral reefs are perhaps the most familiar type.

RELATIVE HUMIDITY The amount of water vapour in an air sample relative to the amount the sample could hold if it were saturated at the same temperature; expressed as a percentage.

REMOTE SENSING The observation and measurement of an object without touching it.

RHUMB LINE An imaginary line on the surface of the earth which makes equal oblique angles with all lines of longitude so that it forms a spiral coiling round the poles but never reaching them. This would be the course sailed by a ship following a single compass direction.

RIA An inlet of the sea formed by the flooding of river valleys by rising sea or sinking land. Contrast to fjords which are drowned glacial valleys.

RIFT VALLEY A valley formed when the area between two parallel faults sinks.

RIVER TERRACE A step like land form in the flood plain of rivers due to the river incising further into the plain and leaving remnants of its former flood plain at levels higher than the present level of the river channel.

ROARING FORTIES The area between 40° and 50°S, so called because of the high speeds of the winds occurring there. Sometimes applied to the winds themselves.

RUN-OFF The section of the hydrological cycle connecting precipitation to channel flow.

S

SALINITY The presence of salts in the waters and soils of arid, semi-arid and coastal areas.

SALT-MARSH Vegetated mud-flats found commonly on many low-lying coasts in a wide range of temperate environments.

SANDBANK A large deposit of sand, usually in a river or coastal waters.

SANDSTORM A wind storm driving clouds of sand, most usually in hot, dry deserts.

SAVANNAH A grassland region of the tropics and sub-tropics.

SCHIST Medium to coarse-grained crystalline metamorphic rock.

SEA-FLOOR SPREADING The phenomenon when tectonic plates move apart.

SEAMOUNT A mountain or other area of high relief on the sea-floor which does not reach the surface.

SEASAT A satellite especially designed to sense remotely wind and sea conditions on the oceans.

SEDIMENTARY ROCK Rock composed of the fragments of older rocks which have been eroded and the debris deposited by wind and water, often as distinct strata.

SEISMIC WAVE Wave resulting from the movements of materials in earthquakes.

SEISMOLOGY Science that deals with earthquakes and other vibrations of the earth.

SHALE A compacted sedimentary rock, usually with fine-grained particles.

SHALLOW-FOCUS EARTHQUAKE An earthquake with a focus (or centre) at a shallow level relative to the earth's surface.

SIAL The part of the earth's crust with a composition dominated by minerals rich in silicon and aluminium.

SIDEREAL DAY A period of complete rotation of the earth on its axis, about 23 hours 56 minutes.

SILL A tabular sheet of igneous rock injected along the bedding planes of sedimentary and volcanic formations.

SILT An unconsolidated material of small particles ranging in size from about 2 to 60 micrometres.

SIMA The part of the earth's crust with a composition dominated by minerals rich in silicon and magnesium.

SOIL CREEP The slow movement downslope of soil, usually resulting in thinning of soils on the upper reaches and accumulations on the lower.

SOLIFLUCTION The slow movement downslope of water saturated, seasonally thawed materials.

SOLSTICE The days of maximum declination of the sun measured relative to the equator. When the midday sun is overhead at 23½°N it gives the longest day in the northern hemisphere and the shortest day in the southern. The reverse applies when the sun is overhead at 23½°S.

Above On May 18 1980, Mt St Helens demonstrated a plinian eruption (a kind first described by Pliny the Elder). The apparent smoke cloud is pulverised ash.

SPIT Usually linear deposits of beach material attached at one end to land and free at the other.

SPRING TIDE A tide of greater than average range occurring at or around the times of the new and full moon.

SQUALL A sudden, violent wind, often associated with rain or hail; frequently occurs under cumulonimbus clouds.

STALACTITE A deposit of calcium carbonate, rather like an icicle, hanging from the roof of a cave.

STALAGMITE A deposit of calcium carbonate growing up from the floor of a cave due to the constant drip of water from the roof.

STANDARD TIME The officially established time, with reference to Greenwich Mean Time, of a region or country.

STEPPE Mid-latitude grasslands with few trees, most typically found in USSR.

STORM SURGE Changes in sea level caused by extreme weather events, notably the winds in storms.

STRAIT A narrow passage joining two large bodies of water.

STRIAE Scratches of a rock surface due to the passage over it of another rock of equal or greater hardness.

SUBDUCTION ZONE An area where the rocks comprising the sea floor are forced beneath continental rocks at a plate margin to be reincorporated in the magma beneath the earth's crust.

SUBSEQUENT RIVER A stream which follows a course determined by the structure of the local bedrock.

SUBSIDENCE Usually applied to the sinking of air in the atmosphere or the downward movement of the earth's surface.

SUBSOIL The layer of weathered material that underlies the surface soil.

SUDD Floating vegetable matter that forms obstructive masses in the upper White Nile.

SUNSPOT Relatively dark regions on the disk of the sun with surface temperature of about 4500K compared to the more normal 6000K of the rest of the surface.

SURGE A sudden excess over the normal value, usually of a flow of material (soil, ice, water).

SWELL A long, perturbation (usually wavelike) of a water surface that continues beyond its cause (eg a strong wind).

T

TAIGA The most northerly coniferous forest of cold temperature regions found in Canada, Alaska and Eurasia.

TECTONIC Concerned with the broad structures of the earth's rocks and the processes of faulting, folding and warping that form them.

TETHYS OCEAN An ocean formed in the Palaeozoic Era which extended from what is now the Mediterranean Sea eastwards as far as South-east Asia.

THERMOCLINE A layer of water or a lake or sea that separates an upper, warmer, oxygen-rich zone from a lower, colder, oxygen-poor zone and in which temperature decreases by 1°C for every metre of increased depth.

THRUST FAULT A low-angle reverse fault.

THUNDERSTORM A cloud in which thunder and lightning occur, usually associated with heavy precipitation and strong winds.

TIDAL BORE A large solitary wave that moves up funnel-shaped rivers and estuaries with the rising tide, especially spring tides.

TIDAL CURRENT The periodic horizontal motions of the sea, generated by the gravitational attraction of the moon and sun, typically of $1ms^{-1}$ on continental shelves.

TIDE The regular movements of the seas due to the gravitational attraction of the moon and sun, most easily observed as changes in coastal sea levels.

TOPOGRAPHY The configuration of a land surface, including its relief and the position of its natural and man-made features.

TOR An exposure of bedrock usually as blocks and boulders, forming an abrupt, steep sided culmination of a more gentle rise to the summits of hills. Famous tors exist on Dartmoor.

TORNADO A violent, localized rotating storm with winds of $100ms^{-1}$ circulating round a funnel cloud some 100m in diameter. Frequent in mid-western USA.

TRADE WIND Winds with an easterly component which blow from the subtropic high pressure areas around 30° toward the equator.

TROPICAL CYCLONE See *hurricane*

TROPOSPHERE The portion of the earth's atmosphere between the earth's surface and a height about 15–20km. This layer contains virtually all the world's weather. Mean temperatures decrease and mean wind speeds increase with height in the troposphere.

TSUNAMI Sea-surface waves caused by submarine earthquakes and volcanic activity. Popularly called tidal waves.

TURBULENCE Chaotic and apparently random fluctuations in fluid flow, familiarly seen in the behaviour of smoke, either from a cigarette, a chimney or a volcano.

TUNDRA Extensive, level, treeless and marshy regions lying polewards of the taiga.

TYPHOON A term used in the Far East to describe tropical cyclones or hurricanes.

U

UMBRA A region of total shadow, especially in an eclipse.

UPWELLING The upward movement of deeper water towards the sea surface.

V

VARVE A sediment bed deposited in a body of water within the course of one year.

VOE An inlet or narrow bay of the Orkney or Shetland Islands.

VOLCANIC ASH Ash emitted from a volcano.

VOLCANO An opening through which magma, molten rock ash or volatiles erupts onto the earth's surface. Also used to describe the landform produced by the erupted material. *(see picture below left)*

W

WADI An ephemeral river channel in deserts.

WARM FRONT An atmospheric front whereby, as it passes over an individual on the ground, warm air replaces cold.

WATERFALL A vertical or very steep descent of water in a stream.

WATERSHED A boundary dividing and separating the areas drained by different rivers.

WATERSPOUT A funnel-shaped, rotating cloud that forms occasionally over water when the atmosphere is very unstable. Akin to tornadoes which occur over land.

WATER TABLE The level below which the ground is wholly and permanently saturated with water.

WAVE HEIGHT The vertical extent of a wave.

WAVE LENGTH The horizontal extent of a wave, most easily seen as the distance along the direction of wave movement between crests or troughs.

WAVE PERIOD The time taken for a complete cycle of the oscillation occurring within a wave.

WAVE VELOCITY The velocity of a wave form, best seen by concentrating on one part of the wave such as its crest or trough.

WEATHERING The alteration by physical, chemical and biological processes of rocks and sediments in the top metres of the earth's crust. So called because this material is exposed to the effects of atmospheric and atmospherically related conditions.

WEATHER ROUTEING Choosing a route for a ship or aeroplane to minimise the deleterious effects of weather.

WESTERLIES Winds with a westerly component occurring between latitudes of about 35° and 60°. The whole regime forms a 'vortex' around each of the poles and forms a major element in world climate.

WHIRLWIND A general term to describe rotating winds of scales up to that of a tornado, usually a result of intense convection over small areas.

WILLY-WILLY Australasian term for a tropical cyclone or hurricane.

WINDSHEAR The variation of speed or direction or both of wind over a distance.

Y

YARDANG A desert landform, usually but not always, of unconsolidated material, shaped by and lying roughly along the direction of the wind.

Z

ZENITH A point that is vertically above the observer: the opposite of nadir.

ZOOPLANKTON One of the three kinds of plankton, including mature representatives of many animal groups such as Protozoa and Crustacea.

ABBREVIATIONS	FULL FORM	ENGLISH FORM
A		
a.d.	an der	on the
Akr.	Ákra, Akrotírion	cape
Appno	Appennino	mountain range
Arch.	Archipelago	
	Archipiélago	archipelago
B		
B.	1. Bahía, Baía,	bay
	Baie, Bay, Bucht,	
	Bukhta, Bugt	
	2. Ban	village
	3. Barrage,	dam
	4. Bir, Bîr, Bi'r	well
Bol.	Bol'sh, -oy	big
Br.	1. Branch	branch
	2. Bridge, Brücke	bridge
	3. Burun	cape
Brj	Baraj, -i	dam
C		
C.	Cabo, Cap, Cape	cape
Can.	Canal	canal
Cd	Ciudad	town
Chan.	Channel	channel
Ck	Creek	creek
Co., Cord.	Cordillera	mountain chain
D		
D.	1. Dağ, Dagh, Dağı,	
	Dağları	mountain, range
	2. Daryācheh	lake
Dj.	Djebel	mountain
Dr.	doctor	doctor
E		
E.	East	east
Emb.	Embalse	reservoir
Escarp.	Escarpment	escarpment
Estr.	Estrecho	strait
F		
F.	Firth	estuary
Fj.	Fjord, Fjörður	fjord
Ft	Fort	fort
G		
G.	1. Gebel	mountain
	2. Göl, Gölü	lake
	3. Golfe, Golfo, Gulf	Gulf
	4. Gora, -gory	mountain, range
	5. Gunung	mountain
Gd, Gde	Grand, Grande	grand
Geb.	Gebirge	mountain range
Gl.	Glacier	glacier
Grl	General	general
Gt, Gtr	Great, Groot, -e,	
	Greater	greater
H		
Har.	Harbour, Harbor	harbour
Hd	Head	head
I		
I.	Ile, Ilha, Insel,	island
	Isla, Island, Isle	
	Isola,	
	Isole	islands
In.	1. Inner	inner
	2. Inlet	inlet
Is	Iles, Ilhas, Islands,	islands
	Isles, Islas	
Isth.	Isthmus	isthmus
J		
J.	Jabal, Jebel,	mountain
K		
K.	1. Kaap, Kap, Kapp	cape
	2. Kūh(hā)	mountain(s)
	3. Kólpos	gulf
Kep.	Kepulauan	islands
Khr.	Khrebet	mountain range
Kör.	Körfez, -i	gulf, bay
L		
L.	Lac, Lago, Lagoa,	lake
	Lake, Liman, Limni,	
	Loch, Lough	
Lag.	Lagoon, Laguna,	lagoon
	Lagune, Lagoa	
Ld.	Land	land
Lit.	Little	little

ABBREVIATIONS	FULL FORM	ENGLISH FORM
M		
M.	1. Muang	town
	2. Mys	cape
m	metre, -s	metre(s)
Mal.	Malyy	small
Mf	Massif	mountain group
Mgne	Montagne(s)	mountain(s)
Mt	Mont, Mount	mountain
Mte	Monte	mountain
Mti	Monti	mountains, range
Mtn	Mountain	mountain
Mts	Monts, Mountains,	mountains
	Montañas, Montes	
N		
N.	1. Neu-, Ny-	new
	2. Noord, Nord,	north
	Norte, North, Norra,	
	Nørre	
	3. Nos	cape
Nat.	National	national
Nat. Pk	National Park	national park
Ndr	Nieder	lower
N.E.	North East	north east
N.M.	National Monument	national monument
N.P.	National Park	national park
N.W.	North West	north west
O		
O.	1. Oost, Ost	east
	2. Ostrov	island
Ø	-øy	island
Oz.	Ozero, Ozera	lake(s)
P		
P.	1. Pass, Passo	pass
	2. Pic, Pico, Pizzo	peak
	3. Pulau	island
Pass.	Passage	passage
Peg.	Pegunungan	mountains
Pen.	Peninsula, Penisola	peninsula
Pk	1. Park	park
	2. Peak, Pik	peak
Plat.	Plateau, Planalto	plateau
Pov	Poluostrov	peninsula
Pr.	Prince	prince
P.P.	Pulau-pulau	islands
Pres.	Presidente	president
Promy	Promontory	promontory
Pt	Point	point
Pta	1. Ponta, Punta	point
	2. Puerta	pass
Pte	Pointe	point
Pto	Porto, Puerto	port
R		
R.	Rio, Río,	river
	River, Rivière	
Ra.	Range	range
Rap.	Rapids	rapids
Res.	Reserve, Reservation	reserve, reservation
Resp.	Respublika	Republic
Resr	Reservoir	reservoir
S		
S.	1. Salar, Salina	salt marsh
	2. San, São	saint
	3. See	sea, lake
	4. South, Sud	south
s.	sur	on
Sa	Serra, Sierra	mountain range
Sd	Sound, Sund	sound
S.E.	South East	south east
Sev.	Severo-, Severnaya,	north
	-nyy	peak
Sp.	Spitze	saint
St	Saint	saint
Sta	Santa	saint
Ste	Sainte	saint
Sto	Santo	strait
Str.	Strait	south west
S.W.	South West	
T		
T.	Tall, Tell	hill, mountain
Tg	Tanjung	cape
Tk	Teluk	bay
Tr.	Trench, Trough	trench, trough
U		
U.	Uad	wadi
Ug	Ujung	cape
Upr	Upper	upper

ABBREVIATIONS	FULL FORM	ENGLISH FORM
V		
V.	1. Val, Valle	valley
	2. Ville	town
Va	Villa	town
Vdkhr.	Vodokhranilishche	reservoir
Vol.	Volcán, Volcano,	volcano
	Vulkan	
Vozv.	Vozvyshennost'	upland
W		
W.	1. Wadi	wadi
	2. Water	water
	3. Well	well
	4. West	west
Y		
Yuzh.	Yuzhno-, Yuzhnyy	south
Z		
Z	1. Zaliv	gulf, bay
	2. Zatoka	
Zap.	Zapad-naya, Zapadno-,	western
	Zapadnyy	
Zem.	Zemlya	country, land

Introduction to the index

In the index, the first number refers to the page, and the following letter and number to the section of the map in which the index entry can be found.
For example, 14C2 **Paris** means that Paris can be found on page 14 where column C and row 2 meet.

Abbreviations used in the index

Arch	Archipelago
B	Bay
C	Cape
Chan	Channel
Gl	Glacier
I(s)	Island(s)
Lg	Lagoon
L	Lake
Mt(s)	Mountain(s)
P	Pass
Pass	Passage
Pen	Peninsula
Plat	Plateau
Pt	Point
Res	Reservoir
R	River
S	Sea
Sd	Sound
Str	Strait
UAE	United Arab Emirates
UK	United Kingdom
USA	United States of America
V	Valley

A

18B2 **Aachen** Germany
13C1 **Aalsmeer** Netherlands
13C2 **Aalst** Belgium
12K6 **Äänekoski** Finland
31A3 **Aba** China
48C4 **Aba** Nigeria
50D3 **Aba** Zaïre
41E3 **Abādān** Iran
41F3 **Abādeh** Iran
48B1 **Abadla** Algeria
75C2 **Abaeté** Brazil
75C2 **Abaeté** *R* Brazil
73J4 **Abaetetuba** Brazil
31D1 **Abagnar Qi** China
59E3 **Abajo Mts** USA
48C4 **Abakaliki** Nigeria
25L4 **Abakan** Russian Federation
48C3 **Abala** Niger
48C2 **Abalessa** Algeria
72D6 **Abancay** Peru
41F3 **Abarqū** Iran
29E2 **Abashiri** Japan
29E2 **Abashiri-wan** *B* Japan
27H7 **Abau** Papua New Guinea
50D3 **Abaya, L** Ethiopia
50D2 **Abbai** *R* Ethiopia/Sudan
50E2 **Abbe, L** Djibouti/Ethiopia
14C1 **Abbeville** France
63D3 **Abbeville** Louisiana, USA
67B2 **Abbeville** S Carolina, USA
58B1 **Abbotsford** Canada
64A2 **Abbotsford** USA
42C2 **Abbottabad** Pakistan
40D2 **'Abd al 'Azīz, Jebel** *Mt* Syria
20J5 **Abdulino** Russian Federation
50C2 **Abéché** Chad
48B4 **Abengourou** Ivory Coast
18B1 **Åbenrå** Denmark
48C4 **Abeokuta** Nigeria
50D3 **Abera** Ethiopia
7B3 **Aberaeron** Wales
7C4 **Aberdare** Wales
66C2 **Aberdeen** California, USA
65D3 **Aberdeen** Maryland, USA
63E2 **Aberdeen** Mississippi, USA
47C3 **Aberdeen** South Africa
8D3 **Aberdeen** Scotland
56D2 **Aberdeen** S Dakota, USA
56A2 **Aberdeen** Washington, USA
54J3 **Aberdeen L** Canada
7B3 **Aberdyfi** Wales
8D3 **Aberfeldy** Scotland
8C3 **Aberfoyle** Scotland
7C4 **Abergavenny** Wales
7B3 **Aberystwyth** Wales
20L2 **Abez'** Russian Federation
50E2 **Abhā** Saudi Arabia
41E2 **Abhar** Iran
48B4 **Abidjan** Ivory Coast
61D3 **Abilene** Kansas, USA
62C2 **Abilene** Texas, USA
7D4 **Abingdon** England
64C3 **Abingdon** USA
55K4 **Abitibi** *R* Canada
55L5 **Abitibi,L** Canada
21G7 **Abkhazian Republic** Georgia
42C2 **Abohar** India
48C4 **Abomey** Benin
50B3 **Abong Mbang** Cameroon
50B2 **Abou Deïa** Chad
8D3 **Aboyne** Scotland
41E4 **Abqaiq** Saudi Arabia
15A2 **Abrantes** Portugal
70A2 **Abreojos, Punta** *Pt* Mexico
50D1 **'Abri** Sudan
32A3 **Abrolhos** *I* Australia
75E2 **Abrolhos, Arquipélago dos** *Is* Brazil
56B2 **Absaroka Range** *Mts* USA
41F5 **Abū al Abyaḍ** *I* UAE
41E4 **Abū 'Alī** *I* Saudi Arabia
45D3 **Abu 'Amūd, Wadi** Jordan
45C3 **Abu 'Aweigīla** *Well* Egypt
41F5 **Abū Dhabi** UAE
45C3 **Ābū el Jurdhān** Jordan
50D2 **Abu Hamed** Sudan
48C4 **Abuja** Nigeria
45A3 **Abu Kebir Hihya** Egypt
72E5 **Abunã** Brazil
72E6 **Abunã** *R* Bolivia/Brazil
45C4 **Abu Rûtha, Gebel** *Mt* Egypt
41D3 **Abú Sukhayr** Iraq
45B3 **Abu Suweir** Egypt
45B4 **Abu Tarfa, Wadi** Egypt
35B2 **Abut Head** *C* New Zealand
40B4 **Abu Tig** Egypt
50D2 **Abu'Urug** *Well* Sudan
50D2 **Abuye Meda** *Mt* Ethiopia
50C2 **Abu Zabad** Sudan
50D3 **Abwong** Sudan
18B1 **Åby** Denmark
50C3 **Abyei** Sudan
65F2 **Acadia Nat Pk** USA
70B2 **Acámbaro** Mexico
69B5 **Acandí** Colombia
70B2 **Acaponeta** Mexico
70B3 **Acapulco** Mexico
73L4 **Acaraú** Brazil
72E2 **Acarigua** Venezuela
70C3 **Acatlán** Mexico
48B4 **Accra** Ghana
6C3 **Accrington** England
42D4 **Achalpur** India
74B6 **Achao** Chile
13E3 **Achern** Germany
9A3 **Achill Hd** *Pt* Irish Republic
10A3 **Achill I** Irish Republic
13E1 **Achim** Germany
25L4 **Achinsk** Russian Federation
16D3 **Acireale** Sicily, Italy
61E2 **Ackley** USA
69C2 **Acklins** *I* The Bahamas
72D6 **Acobamba** Peru
74B4 **Aconcagua** *Mt* Chile
73L5 **Acopiara** Brazil
Açores *Is* = **Azores**
A Coruña = **La Coruña**
Acre = **'Akko**
72D5 **Acre** *State* Brazil
66C3 **Acton** USA
63C2 **Ada** USA
15B1 **Adaja** *R* Spain
41G5 **Adam** Oman
50D3 **Adama** Ethiopia
75B3 **Adamantina** Brazil
50B3 **Adamaoua** *Region* Cameroon/Nigeria
50B3 **Adamaoua, Massif de l'** *Mts* Cameroon
68D1 **Adams** USA
44B4 **Adam's Bridge** India/Sri Lanka
56A2 **Adams,Mt** USA
44C4 **Adam's Peak** *Mt* Sri Lanka
'Adan = **Aden**
21F8 **Adana** Turkey
21E7 **Adapazarı** Turkey
76F7 **Adare,C** Antarctica
34B1 **Adavale** Australia
41E4 **Ad Dahnā'** *Region* Saudi Arabia
41F4 **Ad Damman** Saudi Arabia
41D5 **Ad Dawādimī** Saudi Arabia
41E4 **Ad Dibdibah** *Region* Saudi Arabia
41E5 **Ad Dilam** Saudi Arabia
41E5 **Ad Dir'iyah** Saudi Arabia
50D3 **Addis Ababa** Ethiopia
41D3 **Ad Dīwanīyah** Iraq
40D3 **Ad Duwayd** Saudi Arabia
61E2 **Adel** USA
32C4 **Adelaide** Australia
67C4 **Adelaide** Bahamas
76G3 **Adelaide** *Base* Antarctica
54J3 **Adelaide Pen** Canada
27G8 **Adelaide River** Australia
66D3 **Adelanto** USA
38C4 **Aden** Yemen
38C4 **Aden,G of** Somalia/Yemen
48C3 **Aderbissinat** Niger
45D2 **Adhrā'** Syria
27G7 **Adi** *I* Indonesia
16C1 **Adige** *R* Italy
50D2 **Adigrat** Ethiopia
42D5 **Adilābād** India
58B2 **Adin** USA
65E2 **Adirondack Mts** USA
50D2 **Adi Ugrī** Eritrea
40C2 **Adıyaman** Turkey
17F1 **Adjud** Romania
54E4 **Admiralty I** USA
55K2 **Admiralty Inlet** *B* Canada
32D1 **Admiralty Is** Papua New Guinea
44B2 **Ādoni** India
14B3 **Adour** *R* France
48B2 **Adrar** Algeria
48C2 **Adrar** *Mts* Algeria
48A2 **Adrar** *Region* Mauritius
48A2 **Adrar Soutouf** *Region* Morocco
50C2 **Adré** Chad
49D2 **Adri** Libya
64C2 **Adrian** Michigan, USA
62B1 **Adrian** Texas, USA
16C2 **Adriatic S** Italy/Yugoslavia
50D2 **Adwa** Ethiopia
25P3 **Adycha** *R* Russian Federation
48B4 **Adzopé** Ivory Coast
20K2 **Adz'va** *R* Russian Federation
20K2 **Adz'vavom** Russian Federation
17E3 **Aegean Sea** Greece
38E2 **Afghanistan** *Republic* Asia
50E3 **Afgooye** Somalia
41D5 **'Afif** Saudi Arabia
48C4 **Afikpo** Nigeria
12G6 **Åfjord** Norway
48C1 **Aflou** Algeria
50E3 **Afmado** Somalia
48A3 **Afollé** *Region* Mauritius
68C1 **Afton** New York, USA
58D2 **Afton** Wyoming, USA
45C2 **Afula** Israel
21E8 **Afyon** Turkey
45A3 **Aga** Egypt
50B2 **Agadem** Niger
48C3 **Agadez** Niger
48B1 **Agadir** Morocco
42D4 **Agar** India
43G4 **Agartala** India
58B1 **Agassiz** Canada
48B4 **Agboville** Ivory Coast
40E1 **Agdam** Azerbaijan
29C3 **Agematsu** Japan
14C3 **Agen** France
41E3 **Agha Jārī** Iran
48B4 **Agnibilékrou** Ivory Coast
14C3 **Agout** *R* France
42D3 **Āgra** India
41D2 **Ağrı** Turkey
16D2 **Agri** *R* Italy
16C3 **Agrigento** Sicily, Italy
26H5 **Agrihan** *I* Marianas
17E3 **Agrínion** Greece
16C2 **Agropoli** Italy
20J4 **Agryz** Russian Federation
55N3 **Agto** Greenland
75B3 **Agua Clara** Brazil
69D3 **Aguadilla** Puerto Rico
70B1 **Agua Prieta** Mexico
75A3 **Aguaray Guazú** Paraguay
70B2 **Aguascalientes** Mexico
75D2 **Aguas Formosas** Brazil
75C2 **Agua Vermelha, Barragem** Brazil
15A1 **Agueda** Portugal
48C3 **Aguelhok** Mali
48A2 **Agüenit** *Well* Morocco
15B2 **Águilas** Spain
72B5 **Aguja, Puerta** Peru
36C7 **Agulhas Basin** Indian Ocean
51C7 **Agulhas,C** South Africa
36C6 **Agulhas Plat** Indian Ocean
Ahaggar = **Hoggar**
21H8 **Ahar** Iran
13D1 **Ahaus** Germany
35B1 **Ahipara B** New Zealand
13D2 **Ahlen** Germany
42C4 **Ahmadābād** India
44A2 **Ahmadnagar** India
50E3 **Ahmar Mts** Ethiopia
67C1 **Ahoskie** USA
13D2 **Ahr** *R* Germany
13D2 **Ahrgebirge** *Mts* Germany
12G7 **Åhus** Sweden
41F2 **Āhuvān** Iran
41E3 **Ahvāz** Iran
69A4 **Aiajuela** Costa Rica
14C3 **Aigoual, Mount** France
29C3 **Aikawa** Japan
67B2 **Aiken** USA
31A5 **Ailao Shan** *Upland* China
75D2 **Aimorés** Brazil
16B3 **Aïn Beïda** Algeria
48B1 **Ain Beni Mathar** Morocco
49E2 **Ain Dalla** *Well* Egypt
15C2 **Aïn el Hadjel** Algeria
50B2 **Aïn Galakka** Chad
15C2 **Aïn Oussera** Algeria
48B1 **Aïn Sefra** Algeria
40B4 **'Ain Sukhna** Egypt
60D2 **Ainsworth** USA
15B2 **Aïn Témouchent** Algeria
29B4 **Aioi** Japan
48B2 **Aïoun Abd el Malek** *Well* Mauritius
48B3 **Aïoun El Atrouss** Mauritius
72E7 **Aiquile** Bolivia
48C3 **Aïr** *Desert Region* Niger
8D4 **Airdrie** Scotland
13B2 **Aire** France
6D3 **Aire** *R* England
13C3 **Aire** *R* France
55L3 **Airforce I** Canada
54E3 **Aishihik** Canada
13B3 **Aisne** *Department* France
14C2 **Aisne** *R* France
27H7 **Aitape** Papua New Guinea
19F1 **Aiviekste** *R* Latvia
14D3 **Aix-en-Provence** France
14D2 **Aix-les-Bains** France
43F4 **Aiyar Res** India
17E3 **Aíyion** Greece
17E3 **Aíyna** *I* Greece
43G4 **Āīzawl** India
51B6 **Aizeb** *R* Namibia
29D3 **Aizu-Wakamatsu** Japan
16B2 **Ajaccio** Corsica, Italy
16B2 **Ajaccio, G d'** Corsica, Italy
49E1 **Ajdābiyā** Libya
29E2 **Ajigasawa** Japan
45C2 **Ajlūn** Jordan
41G4 **Ajman** UAE
42C3 **Ajmer** India
59D4 **Ajo** USA
15B1 **Ajo, Cabo de** *C* Spain
17F3 **Ak** *R* Turkey
29D2 **Akabira** Japan
29C3 **Akaishi-sanchi** *Mts* Japan
44B2 **Akalkot** India
45B1 **Akanthou** Cyprus
35B2 **Akaroa** New Zealand
29B4 **Akashi** Japan
21K5 **Akbulak** Russian Federation
40C2 **Akçakale** Turkey
48A2 **Akchar** *Watercourse* Mauritius
50C3 **Aketi** Zaïre
41D1 **Akhalkalaki** Georgia
40D1 **Akhalsikhe** Georgia
17E3 **Akharnái** Greece
49E1 **Akhdar, Jabal al** *Mts* Libya
41G5 **Akhdar, Jebel** *Mt* Oman
40A2 **Akhisar** Turkey
19F1 **Akhiste** Latvia
49F2 **Akhmîm** Egypt
21H6 **Akhtubinsk** Russian Federation
21E5 **Akhtyrka** Ukraine
29B4 **Aki** Japan
55K4 **Akimiski I** Canada
29E3 **Akita** Japan
48A3 **Akjoujt** Mauritius
45C2 **'Akko** Israel
54E3 **Aklavik** Canada
48B3 **Aklé Aouana** *Desert Region* Mauritius
50D3 **Akobo** Ethiopia
50D3 **Akobo** *R* Ethiopia/Sudan
42B1 **Akoha** Afghanistan
42D4 **Akola** India
42D4 **Akot** India
55M3 **Akpatok I** Canada
17E3 **Ákra Kafirévs** *C* Greece
17E4 **Ákra Líthinon** *C* Greece
17E3 **Ákra Maléa** *C* Greece
12A2 **Akranes** Iceland
17F3 **Ákra Sídheros** *C* Greece
17E3 **Ákra Spátha** *C* Greece
17E3 **Ákra Taínaron** *C* Greece
57E2 **Akron** USA
45B1 **Akrotiri** Cyprus
45B1 **Akrotiri B** Cyprus
42D1 **Aksai Chin** *Mts* China
21E8 **Aksaray** Turkey
21J5 **Aksay** Kazakhstan
42D1 **Aksayquin Hu** *L* China
40B2 **Akşehir** Turkey
40B2 **Akseki** Turkey
25N4 **Aksenovo Zilovskoye** Russian Federation
26E1 **Aksha** Russian Federation
39G1 **Aksu** China
50D2 **Aksum** Ethiopia
24J5 **Aktogay** Kazakhstan
21K6 **Aktumsyk** Kazakhstan
21K5 **Aktyubinsk** Kazakhstan
12B1 **Akureyri** Iceland
Akyab = **Sittwe**
24K5 **Akzhal** Kazakhstan
63E2 **Alabama** *R* USA
57E3 **Alabama** *State* USA
67A2 **Alabaster** USA
40C2 **Ala Dağları** *Mts* Turkey
21G7 **Alagir** Russian Federation
73L5 **Alagoas** *State* Brazil
73L6 **Alagoinhas** Brazil
15B1 **Alagón** Spain
41E4 **Al Ahmadi** Kuwait
70D3 **Alajuela** Costa Rica
54B3 **Alakanuk** USA
24K5 **Alakol, Ozero** *L* Kazakhstan/Russian Federation
12L5 **Alakurtti** Russian Federation
27H5 **Alamagan** *I* Pacific Ocean
41E3 **Al Amārah** Iraq
59B3 **Alameda** USA
59C3 **Alamo** USA
62A2 **Alamogordo** USA
62C3 **Alamo Heights** USA
62A1 **Alamosa** USA
12H6 **Åland** *I* Finland
21E8 **Alanya** Turkey
67B2 **Alapaha** *R* USA
42L4 **Alapayevsk** Russian Federation
15B2 **Alarcón, Embalse de** *Res* Spain
40A2 **Alaşehir** Turkey
26D3 **Ala Shan** *Mts* China
54C3 **Alaska** *State* USA
54D4 **Alaska,G of** USA
54C3 **Alaska Range** *Mts* USA
16B2 **Alassio** Italy
20H5 **Alatyr'** Russian Federation
34B2 **Alawoona** Australia
41G5 **Al'Ayn** UAE
39F2 **Alayskiy Khrebet** *Mts* Tajikistan
25R3 **Alazeya** *R* Russian Federation
14D3 **Alba** Italy
15B2 **Albacete** Spain
15A1 **Alba de Tormes** Spain
40D2 **Al Badi** Iraq
17E1 **Alba Iulia** Romania
17D2 **Albania** *Republic* Europe
32A4 **Albany** Australia
67B2 **Albany** Georgia, USA
64B3 **Albany** Kentucky, USA
65E2 **Albany** New York, USA
56A2 **Albany** Oregon, USA
55K4 **Albany** *R* Canada
15B1 **Albarracin, Sierra de** *Mts* Spain
41G5 **Al Bātinah** *Region* Oman
27H8 **Albatross B** Australia
49E1 **Al Bayḍa** Libya
45C1 **Al Baylūlīyah** Syria
67B1 **Albemarle** USA
67C1 **Albemarle Sd** USA
15B1 **Alberche** *R* Spain
13B2 **Albert** France
54G4 **Alberta** *Province* Canada
27H7 **Albert Edward** *Mt* Papua New Guinea
47C3 **Albertinia** South Africa
50D3 **Albert,L** Uganda/Zaïre
57D2 **Albert Lea** USA
50D3 **Albert Nile** *R* Uganda
58D1 **Alberton** USA
14D2 **Albertville** France
14C3 **Albi** France
61E2 **Albia** USA
73H2 **Albina** Surinam
64C2 **Albion** Michigan, USA
61D2 **Albion** Nebraska, USA
65D2 **Albion** New York, USA
40C4 **Al Bi'r** Saudi Arabia
15B2 **Alborán** *I* Spain
12G7 **Ålborg** Denmark
13E3 **Albstadt-Ebingen** Germany
40D3 **Al Bū Kamāl** Syria
56C3 **Albuquerque** USA
41G5 **Al Buraymī** Oman
49D1 **Al Burayqah** Libya
49E1 **Al Burdī** Libya
32D4 **Albury** Australia
41E3 **Al Buşayyah** Iraq
15B1 **Alcalá de Henares** Spain
16C3 **Alcamo** Sicily, Italy
15B1 **Alcañiz** Spain
73K4 **Alcântara** Brazil
15A2 **Alcántara, Embalse de** *Res* Spain
15B2 **Alcaraz** Spain

Alcaraz, Sierra de

Animas Peak

15B2 **Alcaraz, Sierra de** *Mts* Spain
15B2 **Alcázar de San Juan** Spain
15B2 **Alcira** Spain
75E2 **Alcobaça** Brazil
15B1 **Alcolea de Pinar** Spain
15B2 **Alcoy** Spain
15C2 **Alcudia** Spain
46J8 **Aldabra Is** Indian Ocean
62A3 **Aldama** Mexico
25O4 **Aldan** Russian Federation
25P4 **Aldan** *R* Russian Federation
25O4 **Aldanskoye Nagor'ye** *Upland* Russian Federation
7E3 **Aldeburgh** England
14B2 **Alderney** *I* Channel Islands
7D4 **Aldershot** England
48A3 **Aleg** Mauritius
75A2 **Alegre** *R* Brazil
74E3 **Alegrete** Brazil
25Q4 **Aleksandrovsk Sakhalinskiy** Russian Federation
24J4 **Alekseyevka** Kazakhstan
20F5 **Aleksin** Russian Federation
18D1 **Älem** Sweden
75D3 **Além Paraíba** Brazil
14C2 **Alençon** France
66E5 **Alenuihaha Chan** Hawaiian Islands
21F8 **Aleppo** Syria
55M1 **Alert** Canada
14C3 **Alès** France
16B2 **Alessandria** Italy
24B3 **Ålesund** Norway
54C4 **Aleutian Ra** *Mts* USA
37L2 **Aleutian Trench** Pacific Ocean
54E4 **Alexander Arch** USA
47B2 **Alexander Bay** South Africa
67A2 **Alexander City** USA
76G3 **Alexander I** Antarctica
35A3 **Alexandra** New Zealand
74J8 **Alexandra,C** South Georgia
55L2 **Alexandra Fjord** Canada
49E1 **Alexandria** Egypt
57D3 **Alexandria** Louisiana, USA
57D2 **Alexandria** Minnesota, USA
57F3 **Alexandria** Virginia, USA
17F2 **Alexandroúpolis** Greece
45C2 **Aley** Lebanon
24K4 **Aleysk** Russian Federation
41D3 **Al Fallūjah** Iraq
15B1 **Alfaro** Spain
17F2 **Alfatar** Bulgaria
41E4 **Al Fāw** Iraq
75C3 **Alfensas** Brazil
17E3 **Alfiós** *R* Greece
75D3 **Alfonso Cláudio** Brazil
8D3 **Alford** Scotland
75D3 **Alfredo Chaves** Brazil
7D3 **Alfreton** England
41E4 **Al Furūthi** Saudi Arabia
21K6 **Alga** Kazakhstan
15A2 **Algeciras** Spain
Alger = Algiers
48B2 **Algeria** *Republic* Africa
16B2 **Alghero** Sardinia, Italy
15C2 **Algiers** Algeria
61E2 **Algona** USA
65D1 **Algonquin Park** Canada
38D3 **Al Ḥadd** Oman
40D3 **Al Ḥadīthah** Iraq
40C3 **Al Ḥadīthah** Saudi Arabia
40D2 **Al Ḥaḍr** Iraq
45D1 **Al Haffah** Syria
41G5 **Al Ḥajar al Gharbī** *Mts* Oman
40C3 **Al Hamad** *Desert Region* Jordan/Saudi Arabia
41E4 **Al Haniyah** *Desert Region* Iraq
41E5 **Al Ḥarīq** Saudi Arabia
40C3 **Al Harrah** *Desert Region* Saudi Arabia
49D2 **Al Harūj al Aswad** *Upland* Libya
41E4 **Al Hasa** *Region* Saudi Arabia
40D2 **Al Ḥasakah** Syria
40C4 **Al Hawjā'** Saudi Arabia
41E3 **Al Hayy** Iraq
45D2 **Al Hijānah** Syria
41D3 **Al Ḥillah** Iraq
41E5 **Al Ḥillah** Saudi Arabia
15B2 **Al Hoceima** Morocco
50E2 **Al Ḥudaydah** Yemen
41E4 **Al Hufūf** Saudi Arabia
41F5 **Al Humrah** *Region* UAE
41G5 **Al Huwatsah** Oman
41E2 **Alīābad** Iran
41G4 **Aliabad** Iran
17E2 **Aliákmon** *R* Greece
41E3 **Alī al Gharbī** Iraq
44A2 **Alībāg** India
15B2 **Alicante** Spain
56D4 **Alice** USA
16D3 **Alice, Punta** *Pt* Italy
32C3 **Alice Springs** Australia
16C3 **Alicudi** *I* Italy
42D3 **Aligarh** India
41E3 **Aligūdarz** Iran
42B2 **Ali-Khel** Afghanistan
17F3 **Alimniá** *I* Greece
43F3 **Alīpur Duār** India
64C2 **Aliquippa** USA
40C3 **Al' Isawiyah** Saudi Arabia
47D3 **Aliwal North** South Africa
49E2 **Al Jaghbūb** Libya
40D3 **Al Jālamīd** Saudi Arabia
49E2 **Al Jawf** Libya
40C4 **Al Jawf** Saudi Arabia
40D2 **Al Jazīrah** *Desert Region* Iraq/Syria
15A2 **Aljezur** Portugal
41E4 **Al Jubayl** Saudi Arabia
41D4 **Al Jumaymah** Saudi Arabia
45D4 **Al Kabid** *Desert* Jordan
41D4 **Al Kahfah** Saudi Arabia
41E4 **Al Kāmil** Oman
40D2 **Al Khābūr** *R* Syria
41G5 **Al Khābūrah** Oman
41D3 **Al Khālis** Iraq
41G4 **Al Khaṣab** Oman
41F4 **Al Khawr** Qatar
49D1 **Al Khums** Libya
41F5 **Al Kidan** *Region* Saudi Arabia
45D2 **Al Kiswah** Syria
18A2 **Alkmaar** Netherlands
49E2 **Al Kufrah Oasis** Libya
41E3 **Al Kūt** Iraq
Al Lādhiqīyah = Latakia
43E3 **Allahābād** India
45D2 **Al Lajāh** *Mt* Syria
54C3 **Allakaket** USA
30B2 **Allanmyo** Burma
67B2 **Allatoona L** USA
47D1 **Alldays** South Africa
65D2 **Allegheny** *R* USA
57F3 **Allegheny Mts** USA
67B2 **Allendale** USA
6C2 **Allendale Town** England
9B2 **Allen, Lough** *L* Irish Republic
35A3 **Allen,Mt** New Zealand
65D2 **Allentown** USA
44B4 **Alleppey** India
14C2 **Aller** *R* France
60C2 **Alliance** USA
50E1 **Al Līth** Saudi Arabia
41F5 **Al Liwā'** *Region* UAE
8D3 **Alloa** Scotland
34D1 **Allora** Australia
65E1 **Alma** Canada
64C2 **Alma** Michigan, USA
60D2 **Alma** Nebraska, USA
39F1 **Alma Ata** Kazakhstan
15A2 **Almada** Portugal
41E4 **Al Majma'ah** Saudi Arabia
41F4 **Al Manāmah** Bahrain
41D3 **Al Ma'nīyah** Iraq
59B2 **Almanor,L** USA
15B2 **Almansa** Spain
41F5 **Al Māriyyah** UAE
49E1 **Al Marj** Libya
75C2 **Almas** *R* Brazil
15B1 **Almazán** Spain
13E2 **Alme** *R* Germany
13D1 **Almelo** Netherlands
75D2 **Almenara** Brazil
15A1 **Almendra, Embalse de** *Res* Spain
15B2 **Almería** Spain
15B2 **Almería, Golfo de** Spain
20J5 **Al'met'yevsk** Russian Federation
18C1 **Älmhult** Sweden
41D4 **Al Midhnab** Saudi Arabia
41E3 **Al Miqdādīyah** Iraq
17E3 **Almirós** Greece
41E4 **Al Mish'āb** Saudi Arabia
15A2 **Almodôvar** Portugal
42D3 **Almora** India
41E4 **Al Mubarraz** Saudi Arabia
40C4 **Al Mudawwara** Jordan
41F4 **Al Muḥarraq** Bahrain
38C4 **Al Mukallā** Yemen
50E2 **Al Mukhā** Yemen
41D3 **Al Musayyib** Iraq
40C4 **Al Muwayliḥ** Saudi Arabia
8C3 **Alness** Scotland
6D2 **Aln, R** England
41E3 **Al Nu'mānīyah** Iraq
6D2 **Alnwick** England
27F7 **Alor** *I* Indonesia
30C4 **Alor Setar** Malaysia
Alost = Aalst
32E2 **Alotau** Papua New Guinea
32B3 **Aloysius,Mt** Australia
64C1 **Alpena** USA
16C1 **Alpi Dolomitiche** *Mts* Italy
59E4 **Alpine** Arizona, USA
62B2 **Alpine** Texas, USA
58D2 **Alpine** Wyoming, USA
16B1 **Alps** *Mts* Europe
49D1 **Al Qaddāhiyah** Libya
45D1 **Al Qadmūs** Syria
40D3 **Al Qā'im** Iraq
40C4 **Al Qalībah** Saudi Arabia
40D2 **Al Qāmishlī** Syria
45D1 **Al Qardāḥah** Syria
49D1 **Al Qaryah Ash Sharqiyah** Libya
40C3 **Al Qaryatayn** Syria
41D4 **Al Qasīm** *Region* Saudi Arabia
41E4 **Al Qaṭīf** Saudi Arabia
49D2 **Al Qatrūn** Libya
41E4 **Al Qayṣāmah** Saudi Arabia
15A2 **Alquera** *Res* Portugal/Spain
40C3 **Al Qunayṭirah** Syria
50E2 **Al Qunfidhah** Saudi Arabia
41E3 **Al Qurnah** Iraq
45D1 **Al Quṣayr** Syria
45D2 **Al Quṭayfah** Syria
41E5 **Al Quwayīyah** Saudi Arabia
18B1 **Als** *I* Denmark
14D2 **Alsace** *Region* France
13D3 **Alsace, Plaine d'** France
18B2 **Alsfeld** Germany
6C2 **Alston** England
12J5 **Alta** Norway
74D4 **Alta Gracia** Argentina
69D5 **Altagracia de Orituco** Venezuela
26B2 **Altai** *Mts* Mongolia
67B2 **Altamaha** *R* USA
73H4 **Altamira** Brazil
16D2 **Altamura** Italy
26D1 **Altanbulag** Mongolia
70B2 **Altata** Mexico
24K5 **Altay** China
25L5 **Altay** Mongolia
24K4 **Altay** *Mts* Russian Federation
13D2 **Altenkirchen** Germany
75B2 **Alto Araguaia** Brazil
51D5 **Alto Molócue** Mozambique
7D4 **Alton** England
64A3 **Alton** USA
65D2 **Altoona** USA
75B2 **Alto Sucuriú** Brazil
7C3 **Altrincham** England
39G2 **Altun Shan** *Mts* China
58B2 **Alturas** USA
62C2 **Altus** USA
40C4 **Al'Ulā** Saudi Arabia
40C4 **Al Urayq** *Desert Region* Saudi Arabia
62C1 **Alva** USA
63C2 **Alvarado** USA
12G6 **Älvdalen** Sweden
63C3 **Alvin** USA
12J5 **Älvsbyn** Sweden
49D2 **Al Wāha** Libya
40C4 **Al Wajh** Saudi Arabia
42D3 **Alwar** India
40D3 **Al Widyān** *Desert Region* Iraq/Saudi Arabia
31A2 **Alxa Youqi** China
31B2 **Alxa Zuoqi** China
41E2 **Alyat** Azerbaijan
12J8 **Alytus** Lithuania
13E3 **Alzey** Germany
50D3 **Amadi** Sudan
41D2 **Amādīyah** Iraq
55L3 **Amadjuak L** Canada
12G7 **Åmål** Sweden
25N4 **Amalat** *R* Russian Federation
17E3 **Amaliás** Greece
42C4 **Amalner** India
75A3 **Amambaí** Brazil
75B3 **Amambaí** *R* Brazil
75A3 **Amamba, Serra** *Mts* Brazil/Paraguay
26F4 **Amami** *I* Japan
26F4 **Amami gunto** *Arch* Japan
73H3 **Amapá** Brazil
73H3 **Amapá** *State* Brazil
62B1 **Amarillo** USA
21F7 **Amasya** Turkey
73H4 **Amazonas** *R* Brazil
72E4 **Amazonas** *State* Brazil
42D2 **Ambāla** India
44C4 **Ambalangoda** Sri Lanka
51E6 **Ambalavao** Madagascar
50B3 **Ambam** Cameroon
51E5 **Ambanja** Madagascar
25S3 **Ambarchik** Russian Federation
72C4 **Ambato** Ecuador
51E5 **Ambato-Boeny** Madagascar
51E5 **Ambatolampy** Madagascar
51E5 **Ambatondrazaka** Madagascar
18C3 **Amberg** Germany
70D3 **Ambergris Cay** *I* Belize
43E4 **Ambikāpur** India
51E5 **Ambilobe** Madagascar
6C2 **Ambleside** England
51E6 **Amboasary** Madagascar
51E5 **Ambodifototra** Madagascar
51E6 **Ambohimahasoa** Madagascar
Amboina = Ambon
27F7 **Ambon** Indonesia
51E6 **Ambositra** Madagascar
51E6 **Ambovombe** Madagascar
27E6 **Amboyna Cay** *I* S China Sea
51E5 **Ambre, Montagne d'** *Mt* Madagascar
51B4 **Ambriz** Angola
33F2 **Ambrym** *I* Vanuatu
50C2 **Am Dam** Chad
20L2 **Amderma** Russian Federation
70B2 **Ameca** Mexico
18B2 **Ameland** *I* Netherlands
68D2 **Amenia** USA
58D2 **American Falls** USA
58D2 **American Falls Res** USA
59D2 **American Fork** USA
76F10 **American Highland** *Upland* Antarctica
37L5 **American Samoa** *Is* Pacific Ocean
67B2 **Americus** USA
18B2 **Amersfoort** Netherlands
47D2 **Amersfoort** South Africa
61E1 **Amery** USA
76G10 **Amery Ice Shelf** Antarctica
61E2 **Ames** USA
68E1 **Amesbury** USA
17E3 **Amfilokhía** Greece
17E3 **Amfissa** Greece
25P3 **Amga** Russian Federation
25P3 **Amgal** *R* Russian Federation
26G2 **Amgu** Russian Federation
26G1 **Amgun'** *R* Russian Federation
50D2 **Amhara** *Region* Ethiopia
55M5 **Amherst** Canada
68D1 **Amherst** Massachusetts, USA
65D3 **Amherst** Virginia, USA
44B3 **Amhūr** India
16C2 **Amiata, Monte** *Mt* Italy
14C2 **Amiens** France
29C3 **Amino** Japan
45C1 **Amioune** Lebanon
46K8 **Amirante Is** Indian Ocean
62B3 **Amistad Res** Mexico
43F3 **Amlekhganj** Nepal
7B3 **Amlwch** Wales
40C3 **Amman** Jordan
7C4 **Ammanford** Wales
12K6 **Ämmänsaari** Finland
55P3 **Ammassalik** Greenland
28A3 **Amnyong-dan** *C* N Korea
41F2 **Amol** Iran
17F3 **Amorgós** *I* Greece
55L5 **Amos** Canada
Amoy = Xiamen
51E6 **Ampanihy** Madagascar
75C3 **Amparo** Brazil
51E5 **Ampasimanolotra** Madagascar
15C1 **Amposta** Spain
42D4 **Amrāvati** India
42C4 **Amreli** India
42C2 **Amritsar** India
43K1 **Amroha** India
36E6 **Amsterdam** *I* Indian Ocean
18A2 **Amsterdam** Netherlands
47E2 **Amsterdam** South Africa
65E2 **Amsterdam** USA
50C2 **Am Timan** Chad
24H5 **Amu Darya** *R* Uzbekistan
55J2 **Amund Ringnes I** Canada
54F2 **Amundsen G** Canada
76E **Amundsen-Scott** *Base* Antarctica
76F4 **Amundsen Sea** Antarctica
27E7 **Amuntai** Indonesia
26F1 **Amur** *R* Russian Federation
25N2 **Anabar** *R* Russian Federation
66C4 **Anacapa Is** USA
72F2 **Anaco** Venezuela
56B2 **Anaconda** USA
58B1 **Anacortes** USA
62C1 **Anadarko** USA
25T3 **Anadyr'** Russian Federation
25T3 **Anadyr'** *R* Russian Federation
25U3 **Anadyrskiy Zaliv** *S* Russian Federation
25T3 **Anadyrskoye Ploskogor'ye** *Plat* Russian Federation
17F3 **Anáfi** *I* Greece
75D1 **Anagé** Brazil
40D3 **'Ānah** Iraq
59C4 **Anaheim** USA
44B3 **Anaimalai Hills** India
44C2 **Anakāpalle** India
51E5 **Analalava** Madagascar
27D6 **Anambas, Kepulauan** *Is* Indonesia
64A2 **Anamosa** USA
21E8 **Anamur** Turkey
29B4 **Anan** Japan
44B3 **Anantapur** India
42D2 **Anantnag** India
73J7 **Anápolis** Brazil
41G3 **Anār** Iran
41F3 **Anārak** Iran
27H5 **Anatahan** *I* Pacific Ocean
74D3 **Añatuya** Argentina
28B3 **Anbyŏn** N Korea
54D3 **Anchorage** USA
72E7 **Ancohuma** *Mt* Bolivia
72C6 **Ancón** Peru
16C2 **Ancona** Italy
68D1 **Ancram** USA
74B6 **Ancud** Chile
74B6 **Ancud, Golfo de** *G* Chile
13C4 **Ancy-le-Franc** France
72D6 **Andahuaylas** Peru
12F6 **Åndalsnes** Norway
15A2 **Andalucia** *Region* Spain
67A2 **Andalusia** USA
39H4 **Andaman Is** India
75D1 **Andaraí** Brazil
13C3 **Andelot** France
12H5 **Andenes** Norway
18B2 **Andernach** Germany
64B2 **Anderson** Indiana, USA
63D1 **Anderson** Missouri, USA
67B2 **Anderson** S Carolina, USA
54F3 **Anderson** *R* Canada
72C5 **Andes, Cordillera de los** *Mts* Peru
44B2 **Andhra Pradesh** *State* India
17E3 **Andikíthira** *I* Greece
24J5 **Andizhan** Uzbekistan
24H6 **Andkhui** Afghanistan
28B3 **Andong** S Korea
15C1 **Andorra** *Principality* SW Europe
15C1 **Andorra-La-Vella** Andorra
7D4 **Andover** England
68E1 **Andover** New Hampshire, USA
68B1 **Andover** New York, USA
75B3 **Andradina** Brazil
19G1 **Andreapol'** Russian Federation
40B2 **Andreas,C** Cyprus
62B2 **Andrews** USA
16D2 **Andria** Italy
17E3 **Ándros** *I* Greece
57F4 **Andros** *I* The Bahamas
67C4 **Andros Town** Bahamas
44A3 **Androth** *I* India
15B2 **Andújar** Spain
51B5 **Andulo** Angola
48C3 **Anéfis** Mali
48C4 **Anécho** Togo
33F3 **Aneityum** *I* Vanuatu
25M4 **Angarsk** Russian Federation
20A3 **Ånge** Sweden
70A2 **Angel de la Guarda** *I* Mexico
12G7 **Ängelholm** Sweden
34C1 **Angellala Creek** *R* Australia
66B1 **Angels Camp** USA
27G7 **Angemuk** *Mt* Indonesia
14B2 **Angers** France
13B3 **Angerville** France
30C3 **Angkor** *Hist Site* Cambodia
10C3 **Anglesey** *I* Wales
63C3 **Angleton** USA
Angmagssalik = Ammassalik
51E5 **Angoche** Mozambique
74B5 **Angol** Chile
64C2 **Angola** Indiana, USA
51B5 **Angola** *Republic* Africa
52J5 **Angola Basin** Atlantic Ocean
14C2 **Angoulême** France
48A1 **Angra do Heroismo** Azores
75D3 **Angra dos Reis** Brazil
69E3 **Anguilla** *I* Caribbean Sea
69B2 **Anguilla Cays** *Is* Caribbean Sea
43F4 **Angul** India
50C4 **Angumu** Zaïre
18C1 **Anholt** *I* Denmark
31C4 **Anhua** China
26F2 **Anhui** China
31D3 **Anhui** *Province* China
75B2 **Anhumas** Brazil
28A3 **Anhŭng** S Korea
54C3 **Aniak** USA
75C2 **Anicuns** Brazil
62A1 **Animas** *R* USA
62A2 **Animas Peak** *Mt* USA

61E2 **Anita** USA
26H2 **Aniva, Mys** *C* Russian Federation
13B3 **Anizy-le-Château** France
14B2 **Anjou** *Region* France
51E5 **Anjouan** *I* Comoros
51E5 **Anjozorobe** Madagascar
28B3 **Anju** N Korea
31B3 **Ankang** China
21E8 **Ankara** Turkey
51E5 **Ankaratra** *Mt* Madagascar
51E6 **Ankazoabo** Madagascar
51E5 **Ankazobe** Madagascar
61E2 **Ankeny** USA
18C2 **Anklam** Germany
30D3 **An Loc** Vietnam
31B4 **Anlong** China
31C3 **Anlu** China
64B3 **Anna** USA
16B3 **'Annaba** Algeria
40C3 **An Nabk** Saudi Arabia
40C3 **An Nabk** Syria
40D4 **An Nafūd** *Desert* Saudi Arabia
49E2 **An Nāfūrah** Libya
41D3 **An Najaf** Iraq
8D4 **Annan** Scotland
65D3 **Annapolis** USA
43E3 **Annapurna** *Mt* Nepal
64C2 **Ann Arbor** USA
45D1 **An Nāsirah** Syria
41E3 **An Nāsirīyah** Iraq
14D2 **Annecy** France
30D3 **An Nhon** Vietnam
31A5 **Anning** China
67A2 **Anniston** USA
48C4 **Annobon** *I* Equatorial Guinea
14C2 **Annonay** France
69J1 **Annotto Bay** Jamaica
31D3 **Anqing** China
31B2 **Ansai** China
18C3 **Ansbach** Germany
69C3 **Anse d'Hainault** Haiti
31E1 **Anshan** China
31B4 **Anshun** China
60D2 **Ansley** USA
62C2 **Anson** USA
27F8 **Anson B** Australia
48C3 **Ansongo** Mali
64C1 **Ansonville** Canada
64C3 **Ansted** USA
21F8 **Antakya** Turkey
51F5 **Antalaha** Madagascar
21E8 **Antalya** Turkey
21E8 **Antalya Körfezi** *B* Turkey
51E5 **Antananarivo** Madagascar
76G1 **Antarctic Circle** Antarctica
76G3 **Antarctic Pen** Antarctica
15B2 **Antequera** Spain
62A2 **Anthony** USA
48B1 **Anti-Atlas** *Mts* Morocco
55M5 **Anticosti, Ī. de** Canada
64B1 **Antigo** USA
69E3 **Antigua** *I* Caribbean Sea
Anti Lebanon = Sharqi, Jebel esh
59B3 **Antioch** USA
33G5 **Antipodes Is** New Zealand
63C2 **Antlers** USA
74B2 **Antofagasta** Chile
75C4 **Antonina** Brazil
62A1 **Antonito** USA
9C2 **Antrim** Northern Ireland
68E1 **Antrim** USA
9C2 **Antrim** *County* Northern Ireland
9C2 **Antrim Hills** Northern Ireland
51E5 **Antsirabe** Madagascar
51E5 **Antsirañana** Madagascar
51E5 **Antsohiny** Madagascar
28B2 **Antu** China
30D3 **An Tuc** Vietnam
13C2 **Antwerp** Belgium
Antwerpen = Antwerp
9C3 **An Uaimh** Irish Republic
28A3 **Anui** S Korea
42C3 **Anūpgarh** India
44C4 **Anuradhapura** Sri Lanka
Anvers = Antwerp
54B3 **Anvik** USA
25L5 **Anxi** China
31C2 **Anyang** China
31A3 **A'nyêmaqên Shan** *Mts* China
25S3 **Anyuysk** Russian Federation
24K4 **Anzhero-Sudzhensk** Russian Federation
16C2 **Anzio** Italy
33F2 **Aoba** *I* Vanuatu
29E2 **Aomori** Japan
16B1 **Aosta** Italy
48B3 **Aouker** *Desert Region* Mauritius
48C2 **Aoulef** Algeria
50B1 **Aozou** Chad
74E2 **Apa** *R* Brazil/Paraguay
57E4 **Apalachee B** USA
67B3 **Apalachicola** USA
67A3 **Apalachicola B** USA
72D3 **Apaporis** *R* Brazil/Colombia
75B3 **Aparecida do Taboado** Brazil
27F5 **Aparri** Philippines
17D1 **Apatin** Croatia
20E2 **Apatity** Russian Federation
70B3 **Apatzingan** Mexico
18B2 **Apeldoorn** Netherlands
33H2 **Apia** Western Samoa
75C3 **Apiaí** Brazil
73G2 **Apoera** Surinam
34B3 **Apollo Bay** Australia
67B3 **Apopka,L** USA
73H7 **Aporé** *R* Brazil
64A1 **Apostle Is** USA
57E3 **Appalachian Mts** USA
16C2 **Appennino Abruzzese** *Mts* Italy
16B2 **Appennino Ligure** *Mts* Italy
16D2 **Appennino Lucano** *Mts* Italy
16D2 **Appennino Napoletano** *Mts* Italy
16C2 **Appennino Tosco-Emilliano** *Mts* Italy
16C2 **Appennino Umbro-Marchigiano** *Mts* Italy
6C2 **Appleby** England
61D1 **Appleton** Minnesota, USA
64B2 **Appleton** Wisconsin, USA
21J7 **Apsheronskiy Poluostrov** *Pen* Azerbaijan
74F2 **Apucarana** Brazil
72E2 **Apure** *R* Venezuela
72D6 **Apurimac** *R* Peru
40C4 **'Aqaba** Jordan
40B4 **'Aqaba,G of** Egypt/Saudi Arabia
45C4 **'Aqaba, Wadi el** Egypt
41F3 **'Aqdā** Iran
73G8 **Aqidauana** Brazil
75A3 **Aquidabán** *R* Paraguay
74E2 **Aquidauana** Brazil
75A2 **Aquidauana** *R* Brazil
43E3 **Ara** India
67A2 **Arab** USA
45C1 **'Arab al Mulk** Syria
45C3 **'Araba, Wadi** Israel
36E4 **Arabian Basin** Indian Ocean
38E4 **Arabian Sea** SW Asia
45D2 **'Arab, Jabal al** *Mt* Syria
73L6 **Aracajú** Brazil
75A3 **Aracanguy,Mts de** Paraguay
73L4 **Aracati** Brazil
75D1 **Aracatu** Brazil
73H8 **Araçatuba** Brazil
15A2 **Aracena** Spain
73K7 **Araçuaí** Brazil
45C3 **'Arad** Israel
21C6 **Arad** Romania
50C2 **Arada** Chad
41F5 **'Arādah** UAE
32C1 **Arafura S** Indonesia/Australia
73H7 **Aragarças** Brazil
21G7 **Aragats** *Mt* Armenia
15B1 **Aragon** *R* Spain
15B1 **Aragón** *Region* Spain
75C1 **Araguaçu** Brazil
73H6 **Araguaia** *R* Brazil
73J5 **Araguaína** Brazil
73J7 **Araguari** Brazil
75C2 **Araguari** *R* Brazil
29C3 **Arai** Japan
45C3 **Araif el Naqa, Gebel** *Mt* Egypt
48C2 **Arak** Algeria
41E3 **Arāk** Iran
30A2 **Arakan Yoma** *Mts* Burma
44B3 **Arakkonam** India
24G5 **Aral S** Kazakhstan
24H5 **Aral'sk** Kazakhstan
15B1 **Aranda de Duero** Spain
10B2 **Aran I** Irish Republic
10B3 **Aran Is** Irish Republic
15B1 **Aranjuez** Spain
47B1 **Aranos** Namibia
63C3 **Aransas Pass** USA
28B4 **Arao** Japan
48B3 **Araouane** Mali
60D2 **Arapahoe** USA
74E4 **Arapey** *R* Uruguay
73L5 **Arapiraca** Brazil
75B3 **Araporgas** Brazil
74G3 **Ararangua** Brazil
73J8 **Araraquara** Brazil
75C3 **Araras** Brazil
32D4 **Ararat** Australia
41D2 **Ararat** Armenia
Ararat, Mt = Büyük Ağri Daği
75D3 **Araruama, Lagoa de** Brazil
40D3 **Ar'ar, Wadi** *Watercourse* Saudi Arabia
41D1 **Aras** *R* Turkey
41E2 **Aras** *R* Azerbaijan/Iran
29D3 **Arato** Japan
72E2 **Arauca** *R* Venezuela
72D2 **Arauea** Colombia
42C3 **Arāvalli Range** *Mts* India
33E1 **Arawa** Papua New Guinea
73J7 **Araxá** Brazil
21G8 **Araxes** *R* Iran
50D3 **Arba Minch** Ethiopia
16B3 **Arbatax** Sardinia, Italy
21G8 **Arbīl** Iraq
12H6 **Arbrå** Sweden
8D3 **Arbroath** Scotland
14B3 **Arcachon** France
68A1 **Arcade** USA
67B3 **Arcadia** USA
58B2 **Arcata** USA
66D1 **Arc Dome** *Mt* USA
20G3 **Archangel** Russian Federation
68C2 **Archbald** USA
59E3 **Arches Nat Pk** USA
13C3 **Arcis-sur-Aube** France
58D2 **Arco** USA
75C3 **Arcos** Brazil
15A2 **Arcos de la Frontera** Spain
55K2 **Arctic Bay** Canada
76C1 **Arctic Circle**
54E3 **Arctic Red** *R* Canada
54E3 **Arctic Red River** Canada
54D3 **Arctic Village** USA
76G2 **Arctowski** *Base* Antarctica
17F2 **Arda** *R* Bulgaria
21H8 **Ardabīl** Iran
21G7 **Ardahan** Turkey
12F6 **Årdal** Norway
48C2 **Ardar des Iforas** *Upland* Algeria/Mali
9C3 **Ardee** Irish Republic
41F3 **Ardekān** Iran
13C3 **Ardennes** *Department* France
18B2 **Ardennes** *Region* Belgium
41F3 **Ardestāh** Iran
40C3 **Ardh es Suwwan** *Desert Region* Jordan
15A2 **Ardila** *R* Portugal
34C2 **Ardlethan** Australia
56D3 **Ardmore** USA
8B3 **Ardnamurchan Pt** Scotland
13A2 **Ardres** France
8C3 **Ardrishaig** Scotland
8C4 **Ardrossan** Scotland
69D3 **Arecibo** Puerto Rico
73L4 **Areia Branca** Brazil
59B3 **Arena,Pt** USA
13D1 **Arenberg** *Region* Germany
12F7 **Arendal** Norway
72D7 **Arequipa** Peru
16C2 **Arezzo** Italy
16C2 **Argenta** Italy
14C2 **Argentan** France
13B3 **Argenteuil** France
71D7 **Argentina** *Republic* S America
52F7 **Argentine Basin** Atlantic Ocean
74B8 **Argentino, Lago** Argentina
14C2 **Argenton-sur-Creuse** France
17F2 **Argeş** *R* Romania
42B2 **Arghardab** *R* Afghanistan
17E3 **Argolikós Kólpos** *G* Greece
13C3 **Argonne** *Region* France
17E3 **Árgos** Greece
17E3 **Argostólion** Greece
66B3 **Arguello,Pt** USA
66D3 **Argus Range** *Mts* USA
32B2 **Argyle,L** Australia
8C3 **Argyll** Scotland
18C1 **Århus** Denmark
51C6 **Ariamsvlei** Namibia
48B3 **Aribinda** Burkina
74B1 **Arica** Chile
42C2 **Arifwala** Pakistan
Arihā = Jericho
60C3 **Arikaree** *R* USA
69L1 **Arima** Trinidad
75C2 **Arinos** Brazil
73G6 **Arinos** *R* Brazil
69L1 **Aripo,Mt** Trinidad
72F5 **Aripuanã** Brazil
72F5 **Aripuanã** *R* Brazil
8C3 **Arisaig** Scotland
45B3 **'Arîsh, Wadi el** *Watercourse* Egypt
56B3 **Arizona** *State* USA
12G7 **Årjäng** Sweden
25Q4 **Arka** Russian Federation
21G5 **Arkadak** Russian Federation
63D2 **Arkadelphia** USA
8C3 **Arkaig, L** Scotland
24H4 **Arkalyk** Kazakhstan
57D3 **Arkansas** *R* USA
57D3 **Arkansas** *State* USA
63C1 **Arkansas City** USA
29C2 **Arkhipovka** Russian Federation
25K2 **Arkipelag Nordenshelda** *Arch* Russian Federation
10B3 **Arklow** Irish Republic
15B1 **Arlanzón** *R* Spain
14C3 **Arles** France
61D2 **Arlington** S Dakota, USA
63C2 **Arlington** Texas, USA
65D3 **Arlington** Virginia, USA
58B1 **Arlington** Washington, USA
64B2 **Arlington Heights** USA
18B3 **Arlon** Belgium
Armageddon = Megiddo
9C2 **Armagh** Northern Ireland
9C2 **Armagh** *County* Northern Ireland
13B4 **Armançon** *R* France
21G7 **Armavir** Russian Federation
72C3 **Armenia** Colombia
21G7 **Armenia** *Republic* Europe
13B2 **Armentières** Belgium
32E4 **Armidale** Australia
55L3 **Arnaud** *R* Canada
40B2 **Arnauti** *C* Cyprus
62C1 **Arnett** USA
18B2 **Arnhem** Netherlands
32C2 **Arnhem,C** Australia
32C2 **Arnhem Land** Australia
66B1 **Arnold** USA
65D1 **Arnprior** Canada
13E2 **Arnsberg** Germany
47B2 **Aroab** Namibia
13E2 **Arolsen** Germany
33G1 **Arorae** *I* Kiribati
16B1 **Arosa** Switzerland
13B3 **Arpajon** France
75C1 **Arraias** Brazil
75C1 **Arraias, Serra de** *Mts* Brazil
41D3 **Ar Ramādī** Iraq
8C4 **Arran, I of** Scotland
40C2 **Ar Raqqah** Syria
49D2 **Ar Rāqūbah** Libya
14C1 **Arras** France
41D4 **Ar Rass** Saudi Arabia
45D1 **Ar Rastan** Syria
48A2 **Arrecife** Canary Islands
41E3 **Ar Rifā'ī** Iraq
41E3 **Ar Rihāb** *Desert Region* Iraq
Ar Riyād = Riyadh
8C3 **Arrochar** Scotland
75C1 **Arrojado** *R* Brazil
58C2 **Arrowrock Res** USA
35A2 **Arrowtown** New Zealand
66B3 **Arroyo Grande** USA
41F4 **Ar Ru'ays** Qatar
41G5 **Ar Rustāq** Oman
40D3 **Ar Rutbah** Iraq
41D5 **Ar Ruwaydah** Saudi Arabia
44B3 **Arsikere** India
20H4 **Arsk** Russian Federation
17E3 **Árta** Greece
28C2 **Artem** Russian Federation
25L4 **Artemovsk** Russian Federation
25N4 **Artemovskiy** Russian Federation
56C3 **Artesia** USA
35B2 **Arthurs P** New Zealand
74E4 **Artigas** Uruguay
54H3 **Artillery L** Canada
14C1 **Artois** *Region* France
19F3 **Artsiz** Ukraine
76G2 **Arturo Prat** *Base* Antarctica
21G7 **Artvin** Turkey
50D3 **Aru** Zaïre
73H6 **Aruanã** Brazil
69C4 **Aruba** *I* Caribbean Sea
27G7 **Aru, Kepulauan** *Arch* Indonesia
43F3 **Arun** *R* Nepal
43G3 **Arunāchal Pradesh** *Union Territory* India
44B4 **Aruppukkottai** India
50D4 **Arusha** Tanzania
50C3 **Aruwimi** *R* Zaïre
60B3 **Arvada** USA
26D2 **Arvayheer** Mongolia
55L5 **Arvida** Canada
12H5 **Arvidsjaur** Sweden
12G7 **Arvika** Sweden
59C3 **Arvin** USA
45C1 **Arwad** *I* Syria
20G4 **Arzamas** Russian Federation
15B2 **Arzew** Algeria
42C2 **Asadabad** Afghanistan
29B4 **Asahi** *R* Japan
29E2 **Asahi dake** *Mt* Japan
29E2 **Asahikawa** Japan
28A3 **Asan-man** *B* S Korea
43F4 **Asansol** India
49D2 **Asawanwah** *Well* Libya
20L4 **Asbest** Russian Federation
47C2 **Asbestos Mts** South Africa
65E2 **Asbury Park** USA
52H5 **Ascension** *I* Atlantic Ocean
70D3 **Ascensión, B de la** Mexico
18B3 **Aschaffenburg** Germany
18C2 **Aschersleben** Germany
16C2 **Ascoli Piceno** Italy
50E2 **Āseb** Eritrea
48C2 **Asedjrad** *Upland* Algeria
50D3 **Asela** Ethiopia
12H6 **Åsele** Sweden
17E2 **Asenovgrad** Bulgaria
13C3 **Asfeld** France
20K4 **Asha** Russian Federation
7D3 **Ashbourne** England
67B2 **Ashburn** USA
33G5 **Ashburton** New Zealand
32A3 **Ashburton** *R* Australia
40B3 **Ashdod** Israel
63D2 **Ashdown** USA
67A1 **Asheboro** USA
57E3 **Asheville** USA
34D1 **Ashford** Australia
7E4 **Ashford** England
59D3 **Ash Fork** USA
29D2 **Ashibetsu** Japan
29D3 **Ashikaga** Japan
28B4 **Ashizuri-misaki** *Pt* Japan
24G6 **Ashkhabad** Turkmenistan
62C1 **Ashland** Kansas, USA
57E3 **Ashland** Kentucky, USA
60B1 **Ashland** Montana, USA
61D2 **Ashland** Nebraska, USA
64C2 **Ashland** Ohio, USA
56A2 **Ashland** Oregon, USA
65D3 **Ashland** Virginia, USA
61E1 **Ashland** Wisconsin, USA
34C1 **Ashley** Australia
60D1 **Ashley** USA
68C2 **Ashokan Res** USA
45C3 **Ashqelon** Israel
41D3 **Ash Shabakh** Iraq
41G4 **Ash Sha'm** UAE
41D2 **Ash Sharqāt** Iraq
41E3 **Ash Shaṭrah** Iraq
38C4 **Ash Shiḥr** Yemen
41E4 **Ash Shumlūl** Saudi Arabia
64C2 **Ashtabula** USA
55M4 **Ashuanipi L** Canada
21F8 **Asi** *R* Syria
15A2 **Asilah** Morocco
16B2 **Asinara** *I* Sardinia, Italy
24K4 **Asino** Russian Federation
50E1 **Asīr** *Region* Saudi Arabia
43E5 **Aska** India
40D2 **Aşkale** Turkey
12G7 **Askersund** Sweden
45B4 **Asl** Egypt
42C1 **Asmar** Afghanistan
50D2 **Asmara** Eritrea
Āsmera = Asmara
28B4 **Aso** Japan
50D2 **Asosa** Ethiopia
50D1 **Asoteriba, Jebel** *Mt* Sudan
62B2 **Aspermont** USA
35A2 **Aspiring,Mt** New Zealand
40C2 **As Sabkhah** Syria
41E5 **As Salamiyah** Saudi Arabia
40C2 **As Salamīyah** Syria
41D3 **As Salmān** Iraq
43G3 **Assam** *State* India
41E3 **As Samāwah** Iraq
41F5 **Aş Şanām** *Region* Saudi Arabia
45D2 **Aş Şanamayn** Syria
18B2 **Assen** Netherlands
18C1 **Assens** Denmark
49D1 **As Sidrah** Libya
54H5 **Assiniboia** Canada
54G4 **Assiniboine,Mt** Canada
73H8 **Assis** Brazil
40C3 **As Sukhnah** Syria
41E5 **Aş Şumman** *Region* Saudi Arabia
51E4 **Assumption** *I* Seychelles
40C3 **As Suwaydā'** Syria
41D3 **Aş Şuwayrah** Iraq
41E2 **Astara** Azerbaijan
16B2 **Asti** Italy
17F3 **Astipálaia** *I* Greece
15A1 **Astorga** Spain
56A2 **Astoria** USA
21H6 **Astrakhan'** Russian Federation
15A1 **Asturias** *Region* Spain
76F12 **Asuka** *Base* Antarctica
74E3 **Asunción** Paraguay
26H5 **Asuncion** *I* Marianas
50D3 **Aswa** *R* Uganda
40B5 **Aswân** Egypt
49F2 **Aswân High Dam** Egypt
49F2 **Asyût** Egypt
74C2 **Atacama, Desierto de** *Desert* Chile
33H1 **Atafu** *I* Tokelau Islands

45C3 **Atā'ita, Jebel el** *Mt* Jordan
48C4 **Atakpamé** Togo
27F7 **Atambua** Indonesia
55N3 **Atangmik** Greenland
45B4 **Ataqa, Gebel** *Mt* Egypt
48A2 **Atar** Mauritius
40C2 **Atatirk Baraji** *Res* Turkey
66B3 **Atascadero** USA
24J5 **Atasu** Kazakhstan
50D2 **Atbara** Sudan
24H4 **Atbasar** Kazakhstan
57D4 **Atchafalaya B** USA
57D3 **Atchison** USA
68C3 **Atco** USA
16C2 **Atessa** Italy
13B2 **Ath** Belgium
54G4 **Athabasca** Canada
54G4 **Athabasca** *R* Canada
54H4 **Athabasca,L** Canada
67A2 **Athens** Alabama, USA
57E3 **Athens** Georgia, USA
17E3 **Athens** Greece
64C3 **Athens** Ohio, USA
68B2 **Athens** Pennsylvania, USA
67B1 **Athens** Tennessee, USA
63C2 **Athens** Texas, USA
Athína = Athens
10B3 **Athlone** Irish Republic
45B1 **Athna** Cyprus
68D1 **Athol** USA
17E2 **Áthos** *Mt* Greece
9C3 **Athy** Irish Republic
50B2 **Ati** Chad
55J5 **Atikoken** Canada
25R3 **Atka** Russian Federation
21G5 **Atkarsk** Russian Federation
63D1 **Atkins** USA
57E3 **Atlanta** Georgia, USA
64C2 **Atlanta** Michigan, USA
61D2 **Atlantic** USA
57F3 **Atlantic City** USA
68C2 **Atlantic Highlands** USA
52H8 **Atlantic-Indian Antarctic Basin** Atlantic Ocean
52H7 **Atlantic Indian Ridge** Atlantic Ocean
Atlas Mts = Haut Atlas, Moyen Atlas
48C1 **Atlas Saharien** *Mts* Algeria
54E4 **Atlin** Canada
54E4 **Atlin L** Canada
45C2 **'Atlit** Israel
57E3 **Atmore** USA
51E6 **Atofinandrahana** Madagascar
63C2 **Atoka** USA
72C2 **Atrato** *R* Colombia
41F5 **Attaf** *Region* UAE
50E1 **Aţ Ţā'if** Saudi Arabia
45D2 **At Tall** Syria
67A2 **Attalla** USA
55K4 **Attawapiskat** Canada
55K4 **Attawapiskat** *R* Canada
41D3 **At Taysīyah** *Desert Region* Saudi Arabia
64B2 **Attica** Indiana, USA
68A1 **Attica** New York, USA
13C3 **Attigny** France
45B1 **Attila Line** Cyprus
65E2 **Attleboro** Massachusetts, USA
30D3 **Attopeu** Laos
40C4 **At Tubayq** *Upland* Saudi Arabia
12H7 **Atvidaberg** Sweden
66B2 **Atwater** USA
14D3 **Aubagne** France
13C3 **Aube** *Department* France
13C3 **Aube** *R* France
14C3 **Aubenas** France
67A2 **Auburn** Alabama, USA
59B3 **Auburn** California, USA
64B2 **Auburn** Indiana, USA
65E2 **Auburn** Maine, USA
61D2 **Auburn** Nebraska, USA
65D2 **Auburn** New York, USA
58B1 **Auburn** Washington, USA
14C3 **Auch** France
33G4 **Auckland** New Zealand
37K7 **Auckland Is** New Zealand
14C3 **Aude** *R* France
55K4 **Auden** Canada
61E2 **Audubon** USA
34C1 **Augathella** Australia
9C2 **Aughnacloy** Northern Ireland
47B2 **Aughrabies Falls** South Africa
18C3 **Augsburg** Germany
32A4 **Augusta** Australia
57E3 **Augusta** Georgia, USA
63C1 **Augusta** Kansas, USA
57G2 **Augusta** Maine, USA
58D1 **Augusta** Montana, USA
64A2 **Augusta** Wisconsin, USA
19E2 **Augustów** Poland
32A3 **Augustus,Mt** Australia
47B1 **Auob** *R* Namibia
42D3 **Auraiya** India
42D5 **Aurangābād** India
48C1 **Aurès** *Mts* Algeria
16B3 **Aurès, Mt de l'** Algeria
13D1 **Aurich** Germany
14C3 **Aurillac** France
56C3 **Aurora** Colorado, USA
64B2 **Aurora** Illinois, USA
64C3 **Aurora** Indiana, USA
63D1 **Aurora** Mississippi, USA
61D2 **Aurora** Nebraska, USA
47B2 **Aus** Namibia
64C2 **Au Sable** USA
48A2 **Ausert** *Well* Morocco
8D2 **Auskerry, I** Scotland
57D2 **Austin** Minnesota, USA
59C3 **Austin** Nevada, USA
68A2 **Austin** Pennsylvania, USA
56D3 **Austin** Texas, USA
32D4 **Australian Alps** *Mts* Australia
18C3 **Austria** *Federal Republic* Europe
70B3 **Autlán** Mexico
14C2 **Autun** France
14C2 **Auvergne** *Region* France
14C2 **Auxerre** France
13A2 **Auxi-le-Château** France
14C2 **Avallon** France
66C4 **Avalon** USA
55N5 **Avalon Pen** Canada
75C3 **Avaré** Brazil
13E1 **Ave** *R* Germany
45C3 **Avedat** *Hist Site* Israel
73G4 **Aveíro** Brazil
15A1 **Aveiro** Portugal
74E4 **Avellaneda** Argentina
16C2 **Avellino** Italy
66B3 **Avenal** USA
13B2 **Avesnes-sur-Helpe** France
12H6 **Avesta** Sweden
16C2 **Avezzano** Italy
8D3 **Aviemore** Scotland
35B2 **Aviemore,L** New Zealand
14C3 **Avignon** France
15B1 **Avila** Spain
15A1 **Avilés** Spain
61D2 **Avoca** Iowa, USA
68B1 **Avoca** New York, USA
34B3 **Avoca** *R* Australia
68B1 **Avon** USA
7C4 **Avon** *County* England
7D4 **Avon** *R* Dorset, England
7D3 **Avon** *R* Warwick, England
59D4 **Avondale** USA
7C4 **Avonmouth** Wales
67B3 **Avon Park** USA
13B3 **Avre** *R* France
17D2 **Avtovac** Bosnia-Herzegovina
45D2 **A'waj** *R* Syria
29D4 **Awaji-shima** *I* Japan
50E3 **Awarē** Ethiopia
35A2 **Awarua Pt** New Zealand
50E3 **Awash** Ethiopia
50E3 **Awash** *R* Ethiopia
29C3 **Awa-shima** *I* Japan
35B2 **Awatere** *R* New Zealand
49D2 **Awbārī** Libya
50C3 **Aweil** Sudan
8C3 **Awe, Loch** *L* Scotland
49E2 **Awjilah** Libya
55J1 **Axel Heiberg I** Canada
7C4 **Axminster** England
29C3 **Ayabe** Japan
74E5 **Ayacucho** Argentina
69C5 **Ayacucho** Colombia
72D6 **Ayacucho** Peru
24K5 **Ayaguz** Kazakhstan
39G2 **Ayakkum Hu** *L* China
15A2 **Ayamonte** Spain
25P4 **Ayan** Russian Federation
72D6 **Ayaviri** Peru
21D8 **Aydın** Turkey
17F3 **Áyios Evstrátios** *I* Greece
25N3 **Aykhal** Russian Federation
7D4 **Aylesbury** England
45D2 **'Ayn al Fijah** Syria
40D2 **Ayn Zālah** Iraq
49E2 **Ayn Zuwayyah** *Well* Libya
50D3 **Ayod** Sudan
32D2 **Ayr** Australia
8C4 **Ayr** Scotland
8C4 **Ayr** *R* Scotland
6B2 **Ayre,Pt of** Isle of Man, British Islands
17F2 **Aytos** Bulgaria
30C3 **Ayutthaya** Thailand
17F3 **Ayvacık** Turkey
17F3 **Ayvalık** Turkey
43E3 **Āzamgarh** India
48B3 **Azaouad** *Desert Region* Mali
48C3 **Azaouak, Vallée de l'** Niger
48D3 **Azare** Nigeria
40C2 **A'zāz** Syria
Azbine = Aïr
48A2 **Azeffal** *Watercourse* Mauritius
21H7 **Azerbaijan** *Republic* Europe
72C4 **Azogues** Ecuador
20H2 **Azopol'ye** Russian Federation
46B4 **Azores** *Is* Atlantic Ocean
50C2 **Azoum** *R* Chad
21F6 **Azov, S of** Russian Federation/Ukraine
48B1 **Azrou** Morocco
62A1 **Aztec** USA
72B2 **Azuero,Pen de** Panama
74E5 **Azul** Argentina
75B1 **Azul, Serra** *Mts* Brazil
16B3 **Azzaba** Algeria
45D2 **Az-Zabdānī** Syria
41G5 **Az Zāhirah** *Mts* Oman
49D2 **Az Zahrah** Libya
40C3 **Az Zilaf** Syria
41D4 **Az Zilfī** Saudi Arabia
41E3 **Az Zubayr** Iraq

B

45C2 **Ba'abda** Lebanon
40C3 **Ba'albek** Lebanon
45C3 **Ba'al Hazor** *Mt* Israel
50E3 **Baardheere** Somalia
17F2 **Babadag** Romania
40A1 **Babaeski** Turkey
72C4 **Babahoyo** Ecuador
50E2 **Bāb al Mandab** *Str* Djibouti/Yemen
32B1 **Babar, Kepulauan** *I* Indonesia
50D4 **Babati** Tanzania
20F4 **Babayevo** Russian Federation
61E1 **Babbitt** USA
64C2 **Baberton** USA
54F4 **Babine L** Canada
32C1 **Babo** Indonesia
41F2 **Bābol** Iran
27F5 **Babuyan Is** Philippines
73J4 **Bacabal** Brazil
27F7 **Bacan** *I* Indonesia
21D6 **Bacău** Romania
30D1 **Bac Can** Vietnam
13D3 **Baccarat** France
34B3 **Bacchus Marsh** Australia
39F2 **Bachu** China
54J3 **Back** *R* Canada
30D1 **Bac Ninh** Vietnam
27F5 **Bacolod** Philippines
6C3 **Bacup** England
44B3 **Badagara** India
31A1 **Badain Jaran Shamo** *Desert* China
15A2 **Badajoz** Spain
15C1 **Badalona** Spain
40D3 **Badanah** Saudi Arabia
28B2 **Badaohe** China
13E3 **Bad Bergzabern** Germany
13D2 **Bad Ems** Germany
18B3 **Baden-Baden** Germany
13D3 **Badenviller** France
18B3 **Baden-Württemberg** *State* Germany
18C3 **Badgastein** Austria
66C2 **Badger** USA
18B2 **Bad-Godesberg** Germany
18B2 **Bad Hersfeld** Germany
13D2 **Bad Honnef** Germany
42B4 **Badin** Pakistan
16C1 **Bad Ischl** Austria
40C3 **Badiyat ash Sham** *Desert Region* Iraq/Jordan
18B3 **Bad-Kreuznach** Germany
60C1 **Badlands** *Region* USA
13E2 **Bad Lippspringe** Germany
13E2 **Bad Nauheim** Germany
13D2 **Bad Nevenahr-Ahrweiler** Germany
40C5 **Badr Ḩunayn** Saudi Arabia
13E2 **Bad Ryrmont** Germany
18C3 **Bad Tolz** Germany
44C4 **Badulla** Sri Lanka
13E2 **Bad Wildungen** Germany
13E3 **Bad Wimpfen** Germany
15B2 **Baena** Spain
48A3 **Bafatá** Guinea-Bissau
55L2 **Baffin B** Canada/Greenland
63C3 **Baffin B** USA
55L2 **Baffin I** Canada
50B3 **Bafia** Cameroon
48A3 **Bafing** *R* Mali
48A3 **Bafoulabé** Mali
50B3 **Bafoussam** Cameroon
41G3 **Bāfq** Iran
21F7 **Bafra Burun** *Pt* Turkey
41G4 **Bāft** Iran
50C3 **Bafwasende** Zaïre
43E3 **Bagaha** India
44B2 **Bāgalkot** India
51D4 **Bagamoyo** Tanzania
59D4 **Bagdad** USA
74F4 **Bagé** Brazil
60B2 **Baggs** USA
41D3 **Baghdād** Iraq
43F4 **Bagherhat** Bangladesh
41G3 **Bāghīn** Iran
42B1 **Baghlan** Afghanistan
61D1 **Bagley** USA
48B4 **Bagnoa** Ivory Coast
14C3 **Bagnols-sur-Cèze** France
Bago = Pegu
48B3 **Bagoé** *R* Mali
28A2 **Bag Tai** China
27F5 **Baguio** Philippines
43F3 **Bāhādurābād** Bangladesh
57F4 **Bahamas,The** *Is* Caribbean Sea
43F4 **Baharampur** India
40A4 **Baharîya Oasis** Egypt
42C3 **Bahawalnagar** Pakistan
42C3 **Bahawalpur** Pakistan
42C3 **Bahawalpur** *Division* Pakistan
Bahia = Salvador
73K6 **Bahia** *State* Brazil
74D5 **Bahía Blanca** Argentina
70D3 **Bahía, Islas de la** Honduras
56B4 **Bahia Kino** Mexico
74C6 **Bahias, Cabo dos** Argentina
50D2 **Bahir Dar** Ethiopia
45A3 **Bahra el Manzala** *L* Egypt
43E3 **Bahraich** India
38D3 **Bahrain** *Sheikhdom* Arabian Pen
41D3 **Bahr al Milh** *L* Iraq
50C3 **Bahr Aouk** *R* Chad/Central African Republic
Bahrat Lut = Dead Sea
Bahr el Abiad = White Nile
50C3 **Bahr el Arab** *Watercourse* Sudan
Bahr el Azraq = Blue Nile
50D3 **Bahr el Ghazal** *R* Sudan
50B2 **Bahr el Ghazal** *Watercourse* Chad
45A3 **Bahr Fâqûs** *R* Egypt
15A2 **Baia de Setúbal** *B* Portugal
51B5 **Baia dos Tigres** Angola
21C6 **Baia Mare** Romania
50B3 **Baïbokoum** Chad
26F2 **Baicheng** China
55M5 **Baie-Comeau** Canada
45C2 **Baie de St Georges** *B* Lebanon
55L4 **Baie-du-Poste** Canada
65E1 **Baie St Paul** Canada
55N5 **Baie-Verte** Canada
31B3 **Baihe** China
31C3 **Bai He** *R* China
41D3 **Ba'ījī** Iraq
25M4 **Baikal, L** Russian Federation
43E4 **Baikunthpur** India
Baile Atha Cliath = Dublin
17E2 **Băileşti** Romania
13B2 **Bailleul** France
31A3 **Baima** China
67B2 **Bainbridge** USA
54B3 **Baird Mts** USA
31D1 **Bairin Youqi** China
31D1 **Bairin Zuoqi** China
32D4 **Bairnsdale** Australia
43E3 **Baitadi** Nepal
28A2 **Baixingt** China
17D1 **Baja** Hungary
70A1 **Baja California** *Pen* Mexico
59C4 **Baja California** *State* Mexico
70A2 **Baja, Punta** *Pt* Mexico
20K5 **Bakal** Russian Federation
50C3 **Bakala** Central African Republic
48A3 **Bakel** Senegal
59C3 **Baker** California, USA
56C2 **Baker** Montana, USA
56B2 **Baker** Oregon, USA
55J3 **Baker Foreland** *Pt* Canada
54J3 **Baker L** Canada
54J3 **Baker Lake** Canada
56A2 **Baker,Mt** USA
56B3 **Bakersfield** USA
7D3 **Bakewell** England
41G2 **Bakharden** Turkmenistan
41G2 **Bakhardok** Turkmenistan
21E5 **Bakhmach** Ukraine
12C1 **Bakkaflói** *B* Iceland
50D3 **Bako** Ethiopia
50C3 **Bakouma** Central African Republic
21H7 **Baku** Azerbaijan
40B2 **Balâ** Turkey
7C3 **Bala** Wales
27E6 **Balabac** *I* Philippines
27E6 **Balabac Str** Malaysia/Philippines
43E4 **Bālaghāt** India
34A2 **Balaklava** Australia
21H5 **Balakovo** Russian Federation
43E4 **Balāngīr** India
21G5 **Balashov** Russian Federation
43F4 **Balasore** India
17D1 **Balaton** *L* Hungary
9C3 **Balbriggan** Irish Republic
74E5 **Balcarce** Argentina
17F2 **Balchik** Bulgaria
33F5 **Balclutha** New Zealand
63D1 **Bald Knob** USA
7D4 **Baldock** England
67B2 **Baldwin** USA
58E1 **Baldy Mt** USA
56C3 **Baldy Peak** *Mt* USA
15C2 **Balearic Is** Spain
75E2 **Baleia, Ponta da** *Pt* Brazil
55M4 **Baleine, Rivière de la** *R* Canada
27F5 **Baler** Philippines
20J4 **Balezino** Russian Federation
32A1 **Bali** *I* Indonesia
40A2 **Balıkesir** Turkey
40C2 **Balīkh** *R* Syria/Turkey
27E7 **Balikpapan** Indonesia
75B2 **Baliza** Brazil
42B1 **Balkh** Afghanistan
24J5 **Balkhash** Kazakhstan
24J5 **Balkhash, L** Kazakhstan
8C3 **Ballachulish** Scotland
8C4 **Ballantrae** Scotland
54G2 **Ballantyne Str** Canada
44B3 **Ballāpur** India
32D4 **Ballarat** Australia
8D3 **Ballater** Scotland
6B2 **Ballaugh** England
76G7 **Balleny Is** Antarctica
43E3 **Ballia** India
34D1 **Ballina** Australia
10B3 **Ballina** Irish Republic
62C2 **Ballinger** USA
9A4 **Ballinskelligis B** Irish Republic
13D4 **Ballon d'Alsace** *Mt* France
17D2 **Ballsh** Albania
68D1 **Ballston Spa** USA
9C2 **Ballycastle** Northern Ireland
9D2 **Ballyclare** Northern Ireland
9C4 **Ballycotton B** Irish Republic
9B3 **Ballyhaunis** Northern Ireland
9C2 **Ballymena** Northern Ireland
9C2 **Ballymoney** Northern Ireland
9C2 **Ballynahinch** Northern Ireland
9B2 **Ballyshannon** Irish Republic
9C3 **Ballyteige B** Irish Republic
34B3 **Balmoral** Australia
62B2 **Balmorhea** USA
42B3 **Balochistān** *Region* Pakistan
51B5 **Balombo** Angola
34C1 **Balonn** *R* Australia
42C3 **Bālotra** India
43E3 **Balrāmpur** India
32D4 **Balranald** Australia
73J5 **Balsas** Brazil
70B3 **Balsas** *R* Mexico
21D6 **Balta** Ukraine
12H7 **Baltic S** N Europe
40B3 **Baltîm** Egypt
57F3 **Baltimore** USA
43F3 **Bālurghāt** India
21J6 **Balykshi** Kazakhstan
41G4 **Bam** Iran
50B2 **Bama** Nigeria
48B3 **Bamako** Mali
50C3 **Bambari** Central African Republic
67B2 **Bamberg** USA
18C3 **Bamberg** Germany
50C3 **Bambili** Zaïre
75C3 **Bambuí** Brazil
50B3 **Bamenda** Cameroon
28A2 **Bamiancheng** China
50B3 **Bamingui** *R* Central African Republic
50B3 **Bamingui Bangoran National Park** Central African Republic
42B2 **Bamiyan** Afghanistan
33F1 **Banaba** *I* Kiribati
50C3 **Banalia** Zaïre
48B3 **Banamba** Mali
44E4 **Bananga** Nicobar Is, Indian Ocean
30C3 **Ban Aranyaprathet** Thailand
30C2 **Ban Ban** Laos
30C4 **Ban Betong** Thailand
9C2 **Banbridge** Northern Ireland
7D3 **Banbury** England
8D3 **Banchory** Scotland
70D3 **Banco Chinchorro** *Is* Mexico
65D1 **Bancroft** Canada
43E3 **Bānda** India
27C6 **Banda Aceh** Indonesia

27G7 Banda, Kepulauan Arch Indonesia
48B4 Bandama R Ivory Coast
41G4 Bandar 'Abbās Iran
21H8 Bandar Anzalī Iran
41F4 Bandar-e Daylam Iran
41F4 Bandar-e Lengheh Iran
41F4 Bandar-e Māqām Iran
41F4 Bandar-e Rig Iran
21J8 Bandar-e Torkoman Iran
41E3 Bandar Khomeynī Iran
27E6 Bandar Seri Begawan Brunei
27F7 Banda S Indonesia
75D3 Bandeira Mt Brazil
75B1 Bandeirantes Brazil
70B2 Banderas, B de Mexico
48B3 Bandiagara Mali
21D7 Bandırma Turkey
47D1 Bandolier Kop South Africa
50B4 Bandundu Zaïre
27D7 Bandung Indonesia
21H8 Baneh Iran
70E2 Banes Cuba
8D3 Banff Scotland
54G4 Banff R Canada
44B3 Bangalore India
50C3 Bangassou Central African Republic
32B1 Banggai, Kepulauan I Indonesia
27E6 Banggi I Malaysia
30D2 Bang Hieng R Laos
27D7 Bangka I Indonesia
30C3 Bangkok Thailand
30C3 Bangkok, Bight of B Thailand
39G3 Bangladesh Republic Asia
42D2 Bangong Co L China
57G2 Bangor Maine, USA
9D2 Bangor Northern Ireland
68C2 Bangor Pennsylvania, USA
7B3 Bangor Wales
30B3 Bang Saphan Yai Thailand
50B3 Bangui Central African Republic
51D5 Bangweulu, L Zambia
30C4 Ban Hat Yai Thailand
30C2 Ban Hin Heup Laos
30C1 Ban Houei Sai Laos
30B3 Ban Hua Hin Thailand
48B3 Bani R Mali
48C3 Bani Bangou Niger
49D1 Banī Walīd Libya
40C2 Bāniyās Syria
16D2 Banja Luka Bosnia-Herzegovina
27E7 Banjarmasin Indonesia
48A3 Banjul The Gambia
30B4 Ban Kantang Thailand
30D2 Ban Khemmarat Laos
30B4 Ban Khok Kloi Thailand
27H8 Banks I Australia
54E4 Banks I British Columbia, Canada
54F2 Banks I Northwest Territories, Canada
33F2 Banks Is Vanuatu
58C1 Banks L USA
35B2 Banks Pen New Zealand
34C4 Banks Str Australia
43F4 Bankura India
30B2 Ban Mae Sariang Thailand
30B2 Ban Mae Sot Thailand
43H4 Banmauk Burma
30D3 Ban Me Thuot Vietnam
9C3 Bann R Irish Republic
9C2 Bann R Northern Ireland
30B4 Ban Na San Thailand
42C2 Bannu Pakistan
30C2 Ban Pak Neun Laos
30C4 Ban Pak Phanang Thailand
30D3 Ban Pu Kroy Cambodia
30B3 Ban Sai Yok Thailand
30C3 Ban Sattahip Thailand
19D3 Banská Bystrica Slovakia
42C4 Bānswāra India
30B4 Ban Tha Kham Thailand
30D2 Ban Thateng Laos
30C2 Ban Tha Tum Thailand
10B3 Bantry Irish Republic
10A3 Bantry B Irish Republic
27C6 Banyak, Kepulauan Is Indonesia
30D3 Ban Ya Soup Vietnam
27E7 Banyuwangi Indonesia
36E7 Banzare Seamount Indian Ocean
31D2 Baoding China
31C3 Baofeng China
30C1 Bao Ha Vietnam
31B3 Baoji China
30D3 Bao Loc Vietnam
26C4 Baoshan China
31C1 Baotou China
44C2 Bāpatla India
13B2 Bapaume France
45C4 Bāqir, Jebel Mt Jordan
41D3 Ba'qūbah Iraq
17D2 Bar Montenegro, Yugoslavia
50D2 Bara Sudan
50E3 Baraawe Somalia
43E3 Bāra Banki India
28C2 Barabash Russian Federation
24J4 Barabinsk Kazakhstan/ Russian Federation
24J4 Barabinskaya Step Steppe Kazakhstan/ Russian Federation
15B1 Baracaldo Spain
69C2 Baracoa Cuba
45D2 Baradá R Syria
34C2 Baradine Australia
44A2 Barāmati India
42C2 Baramula Pakistan
42D3 Bārān India
54E4 Baranof I USA
20D5 Baranovichi Belarus
34A2 Baratta Australia
43F3 Barauni India
73K8 Barbacena Brazil
69F4 Barbados I Caribbean Sea
15C1 Barbastro Spain
47E2 Barberton South Africa
14B2 Barbezieux France
72D2 Barbosa Colombia
69E3 Barbuda I Caribbean Sea
32D3 Barcaldine Australia
Barce = Al Marj
16D3 Barcellona Sicily, Italy
15C1 Barcelona Spain
72F1 Barcelona Venezuela
32D3 Barcoo R Australia
50B1 Bardai Chad
74C5 Bardas Blancas Argentina
43F4 Barddhamān India
19E3 Bardejov Slovakia
7B3 Bardsey I Wales
64B3 Bardstown USA
42D3 Bareilly India
Barentsovo More S = Barents Sea
24D2 Barentsøya I Svalbard
20F1 Barents S Russian Federation
50D2 Barentu Eritrea
14B2 Barfleur, Pointe de France
43E4 Bargarh India
25M4 Barguzin Russian Federation
25N4 Barguzin R Russian Federation
65F2 Bar Harbor USA
43F4 Barhi India
16D2 Bari Italy
15D2 Barika Algeria
72D2 Barinas Venezuela
43F4 Baripāda India
40B5 Bârîs Egypt
42C4 Bari Sādri India
43G4 Barisal Bangladesh
27D7 Barisan, Pegunungan Mts Indonesia
27E7 Barito R Indonesia
49D2 Barjuj Watercourse Libya
31A3 Barkam China
64B3 Barkley,L USA
47D3 Barkly East South Africa
32C2 Barkly Tableland Mts Australia
13C3 Bar-le-Duc France
32A3 Barlee,L Australia
32A3 Barlee Range Mts Australia
16D2 Barletta Italy
42C3 Bārmer India
34B2 Barmera Australia
7B3 Barmouth Wales
6D2 Barnard Castle England
24K4 Barnaul Russian Federation
68C3 Barnegat USA
68C3 Barnegat B USA
68A2 Barnesboro USA
55L2 Barnes Icecap Canada
67B2 Barnesville Georgia, USA
64C3 Barnesville Ohio, USA
62B2 Barnhart USA
7D3 Barnsley England
7B4 Barnstaple England
48C4 Baro Nigeria
43G3 Barpeta India
72E1 Barquisimeto Venezuela
13D3 Barr France
73K6 Barra Brazil
8B3 Barra I Scotland
34D2 Barraba Australia
75D1 Barra da Estiva Brazil
75A2 Barra do Bugres Brazil
75B2 Barra do Garças Brazil
75D3 Barra do Piraí Brazil
51D6 Barra Falsa, Punta de Pt Mozambique
73K6 Barragem de Sobradinho Res Brazil
15A2 Barragem do Castelo do Bode Res Portugal
15A2 Barragem do Maranhão Res Portugal
8B3 Barra Head Pt Scotland
73K8 Barra Mansa Brazil
72C6 Barranca Peru
72D2 Barrancabermeja Colombia
72F2 Barrancas Venezuela
74E3 Barranqueras Argentina
72D1 Barranquilla Colombia
8B3 Barra,Sound of Chan Scotland
68D1 Barre USA
73J6 Barreiras Brazil
15A2 Barreiro Portugal
73L5 Barreiros Brazil
32D5 Barren,C Australia
73J8 Barretos Brazil
65D2 Barrie Canada
34B2 Barrier Range Mts Australia
32E4 Barrington,Mt Australia
75C2 Barro Alto Brazil
27G8 Barroloola Australia
64A1 Barron USA
69N2 Barrouallie St Vincent
54C2 Barrow USA
9C3 Barrow R Irish Republic
32C3 Barrow Creek Australia
32A3 Barrow I Australia
6C2 Barrow-in-Furness England
54C2 Barrow,Pt USA
55J2 Barrow Str Canada
7C4 Barry Wales
65D1 Barry's Bay Canada
68C2 Barryville USA
44B2 Barsi India
13E1 Barsinghausen Germany
56B3 Barstow USA
14C2 Bar-sur-Aube France
13C3 Bar-sur-Seine France
73G2 Bartica Guyana
40B1 Bartın Turkey
32D2 Bartle Frere,Mt Australia
56D3 Bartlesville USA
60D2 Bartlett USA
51D6 Bartolomeu Dias Mozambique
6D3 Barton-upon-Humber England
19E2 Bartoszyce Poland
72B2 Barú Mt Panama
42D4 Barwāh India
42C4 Barwāni India
34C1 Barwon R Australia
20H5 Barysh Russian Federation
66C1 Basalt USA
50B3 Basankusu Zaïre
Basel = Basle
16D2 Basento R Italy
26F4 Bashi Chan Philippines/ Taiwan
20J5 Bashkortostan Republic Russian Federation
27F6 Basilan Philippines
27F6 Basilan I Philippines
7E4 Basildon England
58E2 Basin USA
7D4 Basingstoke England
56B2 Basin Region USA
65D1 Baskatong, Réservoir Canada
16B1 Basle Switzerland
41E3 Basra Iraq
13D3 Bas-Rhin Department France
30D3 Bassac R Cambodia
16C1 Bassano Italy
48C4 Bassar Togo
51D6 Bassas da India I Mozambique Channel
30A2 Bassein Burma
69E3 Basse Terre Guadeloupe
60D2 Bassett USA
48C4 Bassila Benin
66C2 Bass Lake USA
32D5 Bass Str Australia
13E1 Bassum Germany
12G7 Båstad Sweden
41F4 Bastak Iran
43E3 Basti India
16B2 Bastia Corsica, Italy
18B3 Bastogne Belgium
63D2 Bastrop Louisiana, USA
63C2 Bastrop Texas, USA
48C4 Bata Equatorial Guinea
27F5 Bataan Pen Philippines
69A2 Batabanó, G de Cuba
27E7 Batakan Indonesia
42D2 Batāla India
26C3 Batang China
50B3 Batangafo Central African Republic
27F5 Batangas Philippines
26F4 Batan Is Philippines
75C3 Batatais Brazil
65D2 Batavia USA
34D3 Batemans Bay Australia
67B2 Batesburg USA
63D1 Batesville Arkansas, USA
63E2 Batesville Mississippi, USA
65F1 Bath Canada
7C4 Bath England
65F2 Bath Maine, USA
65D2 Bath New York, USA
50B2 Batha R Chad
64C1 Bathawana Mt Canada
32D4 Bathurst Australia
55M5 Bathurst Canada
54F2 Bathurst,C Canada
32C2 Bathurst I Australia
54H2 Bathurst I Canada
54H3 Bathurst Inlet B Canada
48B4 Batié Burkina
41E4 Bāṭin, Wadi al Watercourse Iraq
41F3 Bāṭlāq-e-Gavkhūnī Salt Flat Iran
34C3 Batlow Australia
40D2 Batman Turkey
16B3 Batna Algeria
57D3 Baton Rouge USA
45C1 Batroûn Lebanon
30C3 Battambang Cambodia
44C4 Batticaloa Sri Lanka
44E4 Batti Malv I Nicobar Is, Indian Ocean
7E4 Battle England
57E2 Battle Creek USA
55N4 Battle Harbour Canada
58C2 Battle Mountain USA
21G7 Batumi Georgia
30C5 Batu Pahat Malaysia
45C2 Bat Yam Israel
32B1 Baubau Indonesia
48C3 Bauchi Nigeria
61E1 Baudette USA
55N4 Bauld,C Canada
25N4 Baunt Russian Federation
73J8 Bauru Brazil
75B2 Baús Brazil
18C2 Bautzen Germany
27E7 Bawean I Indonesia
49E2 Bawîti Egypt
48B3 Bawku Ghana
30B2 Bawlake Burma
34A2 Bawlen Australia
67B2 Baxley USA
70E2 Bayamo Cuba
43J2 Bayana India
26D2 Bayandzürh Mongolia
26C3 Bayan Har Shan Mts China
31A1 Bayan Mod China
31B1 Bayan Obo China
60C2 Bayard Nebraska, USA
62A2 Bayard New Mexico, USA
25N2 Bayasgalant Mongolia
40D1 Bayburt Turkey
57E2 Bay City Michigan, USA
63C3 Bay City Texas, USA
20M2 Baydaratskaya Guba B Russian Federation
50E3 Baydhabo Somalia
18C3 Bayern State Germany
14B2 Bayeux France
64A1 Bayfield USA
40C3 Bāyir Jordan
Baykal, Ozero L = Baikal, L
26D1 Baykalskiy Khrebet Mts Russian Federation
25L3 Baykit Russian Federation
25L5 Baylik Shan Mts China/ Mongolia
20K5 Baymak Russian Federation
63E2 Bay Minette USA
14B3 Bayonne France
18C3 Bayreuth Germany
63E2 Bay St Louis USA
65E2 Bay Shore USA
65D1 Bays,L of Canada
26B2 Baytik Shan Mts China
Bayt Lahm = Bethlehem
63D3 Baytown USA
15B2 Baza Spain
19F3 Bazaliya Ukraine
21H7 Bazar-Dyuzi Mt Azerbaijan
51D6 Bazaruto, Ilha Mozambique
14B3 Bazas France
31B3 Bazhong China
45D1 Bcharre Lebanon
60C1 Beach USA
68C3 Beach Haven USA
7E4 Beachy Head England
68D2 Beacon USA
51E5 Bealanana Madagascar
58D2 Bear R USA
64A2 Beardstown USA
24C2 Bear I Barents Sea
58D2 Bear L USA
66B1 Bear Valley USA
69C3 Beata, Cabo C Dominican Republic
69C3 Beata, Isla Dominican Republic
56D2 Beatrice USA
8D2 Beatrice Oilfield N Sea
54F4 Beatton River Canada
56B3 Beatty USA
65D1 Beattyville Canada
74E8 Beauchene Is Falkland Islands
34D1 Beaudesert Australia
67B2 Beaufort USA
54D2 Beaufort S Canada/USA
47C3 Beaufort West South Africa
65E1 Beauharnois Canada
8C3 Beauly Scotland
7B3 Beaumaris Wales
59C4 Beaumont California, USA
57D3 Beaumont Texas, USA
14C2 Beaune France
14C2 Beauvais France
54D3 Beaver USA
59D3 Beaver Utah, USA
54G4 Beaver R Canada
54D3 Beaver Creek Canada
64B3 Beaver Dam Kentucky, USA
64B2 Beaver Dam Wisconsin, USA
58D1 Beaverhead Mts USA
64B1 Beaver I USA
63D1 Beaver L USA
42C3 Beāwar India
75C3 Bebedouro Brazil
7E3 Beccles England
17E1 Bečej Serbia, Yugoslavia
48B1 Béchar Algeria
57E3 Beckley USA
13E2 Beckum Germany
6D2 Bedale England
13E1 Bederkesa Germany
7D3 Bedford England
64B3 Bedford Indiana, USA
68A3 Bedford Pennsylvania, USA
7D3 Bedford County England
69M2 Bedford Pt Grenada
68B2 Beech Creek USA
54D2 Beechey Pt USA
34C3 Beechworth Australia
34D1 Beenleigh Australia
45C3 Beer Menuha Israel
45C4 Beer Ora Israel
40B3 Beersheba Israel
Be'er Sheva = Beersheba
45C3 Be'er Sheva R Israel
56D4 Beeville USA
50C3 Befale Zaïre
51E5 Befandriana Madagascar
34C3 Bega Australia
Begicheva, Ostrov I = Bol'shoy Begichev, Ostrov
15C1 Begur, C de Spain
41F3 Behbehān Iran
41F2 Behshahr Iran
42B2 Behsud Afghanistan
26F2 Bei'an China
31B5 Beihai China
31D2 Beijing China
30E1 Beiliu China
31B4 Beipan Jiang R China
31E1 Beipiao China
Beira = Sofala
40C3 Beirut Lebanon
26C2 Bei Shan Mts China
47E1 Beitbridge Zimbabwe
45C2 Beit ed Dīne Lebanon
8C4 Beith Scotland
45C3 Beit Jala Israel
28A2 Beizhen China
15A2 Beja Portugal
16B3 Béja Tunisia
15C2 Bejaïa Algeria
15A1 Béjar Spain
41G3 Bejestān Iran
19E3 Békéscsaba Hungary
51E6 Bekily Madagascar
43E3 Bela India
42B3 Bela Pakistan
68B3 Bel Air USA
44B2 Belampalli India
27F6 Belang Indonesia
27C6 Belangpidie Indonesia
20D5 Belarus Republic Europe
Belau = Palau
75A3 Béla Vista Brazil/Paraguay
47E2 Bela Vista Mozambique
27C6 Belawan Indonesia
20K4 Belaya R Russian Federation
19G3 Belaya Tserkov' Ukraine
55J2 Belcher Chan Canada
55L4 Belcher Is Canada
42B1 Belchiragh Afghanistan
20J5 Belebey Russian Federation
50E3 Beledweyne Somalia
73J4 Belém Brazil
72C3 Belén Colombia
75A3 Belén Paraguay
56C3 Belen USA
33F2 Bélep, Îles Nouvelle Calédonie
16B3 Belezma, Mts de Algeria
9C2 Belfast Northern Ireland

47E2 **Belfast** South Africa
9C2 **Belfast Lough** *Estuary* Northern Ireland
60C1 **Belfield** USA
50D2 **Bēlfodiyo** Ethiopia
6D2 **Belford** England
14D2 **Belfort** France
44A2 **Belgaum** India
18A2 **Belgium** *Kingdom* NW Europe
21F5 **Belgorod** Russian Federation
21E6 **Belgorod Dnestrovskiy** Ukraine
58D1 **Belgrade** USA
17E2 **Belgrade** Serbia, Yugoslavia
49D2 **Bel Hedan** Libya
27D7 **Belitung** *I* Indonesia
70D3 **Belize** Belize
70D3 **Belize** *Republic* Central America
25P2 **Bel'kovskiy, Ostrov** *I* Russian Federation
14C2 **Bellac** France
54F4 **Bella Coola** Canada
63C3 **Bellaire** USA
44B2 **Bellary** India
34C1 **Bellata** Australia
68B2 **Bellefonte** USA
56C2 **Belle Fourche** USA
60C2 **Belle Fourche** *R* USA
14D2 **Bellegarde** France
13B4 **Bellegarde** France
67B3 **Belle Glade** USA
55N4 **Belle I** Canada
14B2 **Belle-Ile** *I* France
55N4 **Belle Isle,Str of** Canada
55L5 **Belleville** Canada
64B3 **Belleville** Illinois, USA
61D3 **Belleville** Kansas, USA
58D2 **Bellevue** Idaho, USA
64A2 **Bellevue** Iowa, USA
58B1 **Bellevue** Washington, USA
34D2 **Bellingen** Australia
6C2 **Bellingham** England
56A2 **Bellingham** USA
76G2 **Bellingshausen** *Base* Antarctica
76G3 **Bellingshausen S** Antarctica
16B1 **Bellinzona** Switzerland
72C2 **Bello** Colombia
33E3 **Bellona Reefs** Nouvelle Calédonie
66B1 **Bellota** USA
65E2 **Bellows Falls** USA
55K3 **Bell Pen** Canada
16C1 **Belluno** Italy
74D4 **Bell Ville** Argentina
68B1 **Belmont** USA
73L7 **Belmonte** Brazil
70D3 **Belmopan** Belize
26F1 **Belogorsk** Russian Federation
51E6 **Beloha** Madagascar
73K7 **Belo Horizonte** Brazil
61D3 **Beloit** Kansas, USA
57E2 **Beloit** Wisconsin, USA
20E3 **Belomorsk** Russian Federation
20K5 **Beloretsk** Russian Federation
Belorussia = Belarus
51E5 **Belo-Tsiribihina** Madagascar
Beloye More *S* **= White Sea**
20F3 **Beloye Ozero** *L* Russian Federation
20F3 **Belozersk** Russian Federation
7D3 **Belper** England
64C3 **Belpre** USA
34A2 **Beltana** Australia
63C2 **Belton** USA
19F3 **Bel'tsy** Moldavia
24K5 **Belukha** *Mt* Russian Federation
20H2 **Belush'ye** Russian Federation
64B2 **Belvidere** Illinois, USA
68C2 **Belvidere** New Jersey, USA
24J2 **Belyy, Ostrov** *I* Russian Federation
51B4 **Bembe** Angola
48C3 **Bembéréké** Benin
57D2 **Bemidji** USA
63E1 **Bemis** USA
50C4 **Bena Dibele** Zaïre
34C3 **Benalla** Australia
8C3 **Ben Attow** *Mt* Scotland
15A1 **Benavente** Spain
8B3 **Benbecula** *I* Scotland
32A4 **Bencubbin** Australia
56A2 **Bend** USA
8C3 **Ben Dearg** *Mt* Scotland
50E3 **Bendarbeyla** Somalia
19F3 **Bendery** Moldavia
32D4 **Bendigo** Australia
18C3 **Benešov** Czech Republic
16C2 **Benevento** Italy
39G4 **Bengal,B of** Asia
49D1 **Ben Gardane** Tunisia
31D3 **Bengbu** China
49E1 **Benghazi** Libya
27D7 **Bengkulu** Indonesia
51B5 **Benguela** Angola
40B3 **Benha** Egypt
8C2 **Ben Hope** *Mt* Scotland
50C3 **Beni** Zaïre
72E6 **Béni** *R* Bolivia
48B1 **Beni Abbès** Algeria
15C1 **Benicarló** Spain
15B2 **Benidorm** Spain
15C2 **Beni Mansour** Algeria
49F2 **Beni Mazâr** Egypt
48B1 **Beni Mellal** Morocco
48C4 **Benin** *Republic* Africa
48C4 **Benin City** Nigeria
15B2 **Beni-Saf** Algeria
49F2 **Beni Suef** Egypt
60C3 **Benkelman** USA
8C2 **Ben Kilbreck** *Mt* Scotland
10C2 **Ben Lawers** *Mt* Scotland
8D3 **Ben Macdui** *Mt* Scotland
8B3 **Ben More** Scotland
8C2 **Ben More Assynt** *Mt* Scotland
35B2 **Benmore,L** New Zealand
25R2 **Bennetta, Ostrov** *I* Russian Federation
8C3 **Ben Nevis** *Mt* Scotland
65E2 **Bennington** USA
45C2 **Bennt Jbail** Lebanon
50B3 **Bénoué** *R* Cameroon
13E3 **Bensheim** Germany
56B3 **Benson** Arizona, USA
61D1 **Benson** Minnesota, USA
27F7 **Benteng** Indonesia
50C3 **Bentiu** Sudan
75A2 **Bento Gomes** *R* Brazil
63D2 **Benton** Arkansas, USA
66C2 **Benton** California, USA
64B3 **Benton** Kentucky, USA
64B2 **Benton Harbor** USA
48C4 **Benue** *R* Nigeria
8C3 **Ben Wyvis** *Mt* Scotland
31E1 **Benxi** China
Beograd = Belgrade
43E4 **Beohāri** India
28C4 **Beppu** Japan
17D2 **Berat** Albania
27G7 **Berau, Teluk** *B* Indonesia
50D2 **Berber** Sudan
50E2 **Berbera** Somalia
50B3 **Berbérati** Central African Republic
19F3 **Berdichev** Ukraine
21F6 **Berdyansk** Ukraine
64C3 **Berea** USA
48B4 **Berekum** Ghana
66B2 **Berenda** USA
40C5 **Berenice** Egypt
54J4 **Berens** *R* Canada
54J4 **Berens River** Canada
61D2 **Beresford** USA
19E3 **Berettyóújfalu** Hungary
19E2 **Bereza** Belarus
19E3 **Berezhany** Ukraine
19F2 **Berezina** *R* Belarus
20G3 **Bereznik** Russian Federation
20K4 **Berezniki** Russian Federation
21E6 **Berezovka** Ukraine
20L3 **Berezovo** Russian Federation
40A2 **Bergama** Turkey
16B1 **Bergamo** Italy
12F6 **Bergen** Norway
68B1 **Bergen** USA
13C2 **Bergen op Zoom** Netherlands
14C3 **Bergerac** France
13D2 **Bergisch-Gladbach** Germany
44C2 **Berhampur** India
25S4 **Beringa, Ostrov** *I* Russian Federation
25T3 **Beringovskiy** Russian Federation
37K2 **Bering S** Russian Federation/USA
76C6 **Bering Str** Russian Federation/USA
41G4 **Berīzak** Iran
15B2 **Berja** Spain
13D1 **Berkel** *R* Germany/ Netherlands
56A3 **Berkeley** USA
68A3 **Berkeley Spring** USA
7D4 **Berkhamsted** England
76F2 **Berkner I** Antarctica
17E2 **Berkovitsa** Bulgaria
7D4 **Berkshire** *County* England
68D1 **Berkshire Hills** USA
18C2 **Berlin** Germany
18C2 **Berlin** *State* Germany
65E2 **Berlin** New Hampshire, USA
72F8 **Bermejo** Bolivia
74E3 **Bermejo** *R* Argentina
53M5 **Bermuda** *I* Atlantic Ocean
Bern = Berne
62A1 **Bernalillo** USA
75B4 **Bernardo de Irigoyen** Argentina
68C2 **Bernardsville** USA
18C2 **Bernburg** Germany
16B1 **Berne** Switzerland
8B3 **Berneray, I** Scotland
55K2 **Bernier B** Canada
18C3 **Berounka** *R* Czech Republic
34B2 **Berri** Australia
48C1 **Berriane** Algeria
14C2 **Berry** *Region* France
66A1 **Berryessa,L** USA
57F4 **Berry Is** The Bahamas
68B3 **Berryville** USA
47B2 **Berseba** Namibia
60B3 **Berthoud P** USA
50B3 **Bertoua** Cameroon
33G1 **Beru** *I* Kiribati
65D2 **Berwick** USA
6C2 **Berwick-upon-Tweed** England
7C3 **Berwyn Mts** Wales
51E5 **Besalampy** Madagascar
14D2 **Besançon** France
19E3 **Beskidy Zachodnie** *Mts* Poland
40C2 **Besni** Turkey
45C3 **Besor** *R* Israel
67A2 **Bessemer** Alabama, USA
64B1 **Bessemer** Michigan, USA
51E5 **Betafo** Madagascar
15A1 **Betanzos** Spain
45C3 **Bet Guvrin** Israel
47D2 **Bethal** South Africa
47B2 **Bethanie** Namibia
61E2 **Bethany** Missouri, USA
63C1 **Bethany** Oklahoma, USA
54B3 **Bethel** Alaska, USA
68D2 **Bethel** Connecticut, USA
64C2 **Bethel Park** USA
65D3 **Bethesda** USA
45C3 **Bethlehem** Israel
47D2 **Bethlehem** South Africa
65D2 **Bethlehem** USA
47D3 **Bethulie** South Africa
14C1 **Béthune** France
51E6 **Betioky** Madagascar
34B1 **Betoota** Australia
50B3 **Betou** Congo
39E1 **Betpak Dala** *Steppe* Kazakhstan
51E6 **Betroka** Madagascar
55M5 **Betsiamites** Canada
64A2 **Bettendorf** USA
43E3 **Bettiah** India
42D4 **Betūl** India
13C2 **Betuwe** *Region* Netherlands
42D3 **Betwa** *R* India
7C3 **Betws-y-coed** Wales
13D2 **Betzdorf** Germany
7D3 **Beverley** England
68E1 **Beverly** USA
66C3 **Beverly Hills** USA
7E4 **Bexhill** England
40B2 **Bey Dağları** Turkey
48B4 **Beyla** Guinea
44B3 **Beypore** India
Beyrouth = Beirut
40B2 **Beyşehir** Turkey
21E8 **Beyşehir Gölü** *L* Turkey
45C2 **Beyt Shean** Israel
20F4 **Bezhetsk** Russian Federation
14C3 **Béziers** France
41G2 **Bezmein** Turkmenistan
26D1 **Beznosova** Russian Federation
43F3 **Bhadgaon** Nepal
44C2 **Bhadrāchalam** India
43F4 **Bhadrakh** India
44B3 **Bhadra Res** India
44B3 **Bhadrāvati** India
42B3 **Bhag** Pakistan
43F3 **Bhāgalpur** India
42C2 **Bhakkar** Pakistan
42D4 **Bhandāra** India
42D3 **Bharatpur** India
42C4 **Bharūch** India
43F4 **Bhātiāpāra Ghat** Bangladesh
42C2 **Bhatinda** India
44A3 **Bhatkal** India
43F4 **Bhātpāra** India
42C4 **Bhāvnagar** India
43E5 **Bhawānipatna** India
42C2 **Bhera** Pakistan
43E3 **Bheri** *R* Nepal
43E4 **Bhilai** India
42C3 **Bhīlwāra** India
44C2 **Bhīmavaram** India
42D3 **Bhind** India
42D3 **Bhiwāni** India
44B2 **Bhongir** India
42D4 **Bhopāl** India
43F4 **Bhubaneshwar** India
42B4 **Bhuj** India
42D4 **Bhusāwal** India
39H3 **Bhutan** *Kingdom* Asia
27G7 **Biak** *I* Indonesia
19E2 **Biala Podlaska** Poland
18D2 **Białogard** Poland
19E2 **Bialystok** Poland
12A1 **Biargtangar** *C* Iceland
41G2 **Biārjmand** Iran
14B3 **Biarritz** France
40B4 **Biba** Egypt
29E2 **Bibai** Japan
51B5 **Bibala** Angola
18B3 **Biberach** Germany
48B4 **Bibiani** Ghana
17F1 **Bicaz** Romania
7D4 **Bicester** England
59D3 **Bicknell** USA
48C4 **Bida** Nigeria
44B2 **Bīdar** India
41G5 **Bidbid** Oman
65E2 **Biddeford** USA
7C6 **Bideford** England
7B4 **Bideford B** England
48C2 **Bidon 5** Algeria
19E2 **Biebrza** *R* Poland
16B1 **Biel** Switzerland
18D2 **Bielawa** Poland
18B2 **Bielefeld** Germany
16B1 **Biella** Italy
19E2 **Bielsk Podlaski** Poland
30D3 **Bien Hoa** Vietnam
55L4 **Bienville, Lac** Canada
16C2 **Biferno** *R* Italy
40A1 **Biga** Turkey
17F3 **Bigadiç** Turkey
58D1 **Big Belt Mts** USA
62B3 **Big Bend Nat Pk** USA
63E2 **Big Black** *R* USA
61D2 **Big Blue** *R* USA
67B3 **Big Cypress Swamp** USA
54D3 **Big Delta** USA
8D4 **Biggar** Scotland
54H4 **Biggar Kindersley** Canada
34D1 **Biggenden** Australia
7D3 **Biggleswade** England
58D1 **Big Hole** *R* USA
60B1 **Bighorn** *R* USA
60B1 **Bighorn L** USA
60B2 **Bighorn Mts** USA
48C4 **Bight of Benin** *B* W Africa
48C4 **Bight of Biafra** *B* Cameroon
55L3 **Big I** Canada
62B2 **Big Lake** USA
48A3 **Bignona** Senegal
59C3 **Big Pine** USA
67B4 **Big Pine Key** USA
66C3 **Big Pine Mt** USA
64B2 **Big Rapids** USA
54H4 **Big River** Canada
58D1 **Big Sandy** USA
61D2 **Big Sioux** *R* USA
66D1 **Big Smokey V** USA
56C3 **Big Spring** USA
60C2 **Big Springs** USA
61D1 **Big Stone City** USA
64C3 **Big Stone Gap** USA
66B2 **Big Sur** USA
58E1 **Big Timber** USA
55J4 **Big Trout L** Canada
55K4 **Big Trout Lake** Canada
16D2 **Bihać** Bosnia-Herzegovina
43F3 **Bihār** India
43F4 **Bihār** *State* India
50D4 **Biharamulo** Tanzania
21C6 **Bihor** *Mt* Romania
48A3 **Bijagós, Arquipélago dos** *Is* Guinea-Bissau
44B2 **Bijāpur** India
44C2 **Bījāpur** India
41E2 **Bījār** Iran
43E3 **Bijauri** Nepal
17D2 **Bijeljina** Bosnia-Herzegovina
31B4 **Bijie** China
42D3 **Bijnor** India
42C3 **Bijnot** Pakistan
42C3 **Bīkāner** India
45C2 **Bikfaya** Lebanon
26G2 **Bikin** Russian Federation
50B4 **Bikoro** Zaïre
Bilbo = Bilbao
42C3 **Bilāra** India
42D2 **Bilāspur** India
43E4 **Bilāspur** India
30B3 **Bilauktaung Range** *Mts* Burma/Thailand
15B1 **Bilbao** Spain
45A3 **Bilbeis** Egypt
18D3 **Bílé** *R* Czech Republic/ Slovakia
17D2 **Bileća** Bosnia-Herzegovina
40B1 **Bilecik** Turkey
50C3 **Bili** *R* Zaïre
25S3 **Bilibino** Russian Federation
56C2 **Billings** USA
50B2 **Bilma** Niger
57E3 **Biloxi** USA
50C2 **Biltine** Chad
67C3 **Bimini Is** Bahamas
42D4 **Bīna-Etawa** India
51D5 **Bindura** Zimbabwe
51C5 **Binga** Zimbabwe
51D5 **Binga, Mt** Mozambique/ Zimbabwe
34D1 **Bingara** Australia
18B3 **Bingen** Germany
65F1 **Bingham** USA
57F2 **Binghamton** USA
40D2 **Bingöl** Turkey
31D3 **Binhai** China
15C2 **Binibeca, Cabo** *C* Spain
27D6 **Bintan** *I* Indonesia
27E6 **Bintulu** Malaysia
74B5 **Bió Bió** *R* Chile
48C4 **Bioco** *I* Equatorial Guinea
44B2 **Bīr** India
49E2 **Bîr Abu Husein** *Well* Egypt
49E2 **Bi'r al Harash** *Well* Libya
50C2 **Birao** Central African Republic
43F3 **Biratnagar** Nepal
34B3 **Birchip** Australia
61E1 **Birch L** USA
54G4 **Birch Mts** Canada
55J4 **Bird** Canada
32C3 **Birdsville** Australia
32C2 **Birdum** Australia
45A4 **Bîr el 'Agramîya** *Well* Egypt
45B3 **Bîr el Duweidâr** *Well* Egypt
43E3 **Birganj** Nepal
45B3 **Bîr Gifgâfa** *Well* Egypt
45A4 **Bîr Gindali** *Well* Egypt
45B3 **Bîr Hasana** *Well* Egypt
75B3 **Birigui** Brazil
45D1 **Bīrīn** Syria
41G3 **Bīrjand** Iran
40B4 **Birkat Qârun** *L* Egypt
13D3 **Birkenfeld** Germany
7C3 **Birkenhead** England
21D6 **Bîrlad** Romania
45B3 **Bîr Lahfân** *Well* Egypt
7C3 **Birmingham** England
57E3 **Birmingham** USA
49E2 **Bîr Misâha** *Well* Egypt
48A2 **Bir Moghrein** Mauritius
48C3 **Birnin-Kebbi** Nigeria
26G2 **Birobidzhan** Russian Federation
9C3 **Birr** Irish Republic
15C2 **Bir Rabalou** Algeria
34C1 **Birrie** *R* Australia
8D2 **Birsay** Scotland
20K4 **Birsk** Russian Federation
49E2 **Bîr Tarfâwi** *Well* Egypt
45B4 **Bîr Udelb** *Well* Egypt
25L4 **Biryusa** *R* Russian Federation
12J7 **Biržai** Lithuania
48B2 **Bir Zreigat** *Well* Mauritius
43K1 **Bisalpur** India
59E4 **Bisbee** USA
14A2 **Biscay,B of** France/Spain
67B3 **Biscayne B** USA
13D3 **Bischwiller** France
64C1 **Biscotasi L** Canada
31B4 **Bishan** China
39F1 **Bishkek** Kirgizia
56B3 **Bishop** USA
6D2 **Bishop Auckland** England
7C3 **Bishops Castle** England
7E4 **Bishop's Stortford** England
43E4 **Bishrāmpur** India
48C1 **Biskra** Algeria
56C2 **Bismarck** USA
32D1 **Bismarck Arch** Papua New Guinea
32D1 **Bismarck Range** *Mts* Papua New Guinea
32D1 **Bismarck S** Papua New Guinea
41E3 **Bīsotūn** Iran
48A3 **Bissau** Guinea-Bissau
57D1 **Bissett** Canada
54G4 **Bistcho L** Canada
17F1 **Bistrita** *R* Romania
50B3 **Bitam** Gabon
18B3 **Bitburg** Germany
13D3 **Bitche** France
40D2 **Bitlis** Turkey
17E2 **Bitola** Macedonia, Yugoslavia
18C2 **Bitterfeld** Germany
47B3 **Bitterfontein** South Africa
40B3 **Bitter Lakes** Egypt
56B2 **Bitteroot Range** *Mts* USA
48D3 **Biu** Nigeria
29D3 **Biwa-ko** *L* Japan
50E2 **Biyo Kaboba** Ethiopia
24K4 **Biysk** Russian Federation
16B3 **Bizerte** Tunisia
16D1 **Bjelovar** Croatia
48B2 **Bj Flye Ste Marie** Algeria
Bjørnøya *I* **= Bear I**
63D1 **Black** *R* USA

32D3 Blackall Australia
64B1 Black B Canada
6C3 Blackburn England
54D3 Blackburn, Mt USA
59D4 Black Canyon City USA
61E1 Blackduck USA
58D1 Black Eagle USA
58D2 Blackfoot USA
58D1 Blackfoot *R* USA
9B3 Black Hd *Pt* Irish Republic
54H5 Black Hills USA
8C3 Black Isle *Pen* Scotland
69Q2 Blackman's Barbados
59D3 Black Mts USA
7C4 Black Mts Wales
47B1 Black Nosob *R* Namibia
6C3 Blackpool England
69H1 Black River Jamaica
64A2 Black River Falls USA
56B2 Black Rock Desert USA
21D7 Black S Asia/Europe
64C3 Blacksburg USA
34D2 Black Sugarloaf *Mt* Australia
48B4 Black Volta *R* W Africa
63E2 Black Warrior *R* USA
7E4 Blackwater *R* England
10B3 Blackwater *R* Irish Republic
63C1 Blackwell USA
17E2 Blagoevgrad Bulgaria
25O4 Blagoveshchensk Russian Federation
58D1 Blaikiston,Mt Canada
58B1 Blaine USA
61D2 Blair USA
8D3 Blair Atholl Scotland
8D3 Blairgowrie Scotland
67C2 Blakely USA
74D5 Blanca, Bahía *B* Argentina
62A1 Blanca Peak *Mt* USA
16B3 Blanc, C Tunisia
34A1 Blanche *L* Australia
16B1 Blanc, Mont *Mt* France/ Italy
56A2 Blanco,C USA
55N4 Blanc Sablon Canada
7C4 Blandford Forum England
59E3 Blanding USA
13B2 Blankenberge Belgium
69E4 Blanquilla, Isla Venezuela
51D5 Blantyre Malawi
9A3 Blasket Sd Irish Republic
14B2 Blaye France
34C2 Blayney Australia
33G5 Blenheim New Zealand
15C2 Blida Algeria
64C1 Blind River Canada
34A2 Blinman Australia
65E2 Block I USA
68E2 Block Island Sd USA
47D2 Bloemfontein South Africa
47D2 Bloemhof South Africa
47D2 Bloemhof Dam *Res* South Africa
73G3 Blommesteinmeer *L* Surinam
12A1 Blönduós Iceland
64B3 Bloomfield Indiana, USA
61E2 Bloomfield Iowa, USA
61D2 Bloomfield Nebraska,USA
62A1 Bloomfield New Mexico, USA
64B2 Bloomington Illinois, USA
64B3 Bloomington Indiana, USA
61E2 Bloomington Minnesota, USA
68B2 Bloomsburg USA
68B2 Blossburg USA
55Q3 Blosseville Kyst *Mts* Greenland
47D1 Blouberg *Mt* South Africa
18B3 Bludenz Austria
57E3 Bluefield USA
72B1 Bluefields Nicaragua
60D2 Blue Hill USA
68A2 Blue Knob *Mt* USA
69J1 Blue Mountain Peak *Mt* Jamaica
68B2 Blue Mt USA
34D2 Blue Mts Australia
56A2 Blue Mts USA
69J1 Blue Mts, The Jamaica
50D2 Blue Nile *R* Sudan
54G3 Bluenose L Canada
67C2 Blue Ridge USA
57E3 Blue Ridge Mts USA
9C2 Blue Stack *Mt* Irish Republic
35A3 Bluff New Zealand
59E3 Bluff USA
32A4 Bluff Knoll *Mt* Australia
74G3 Blumenau Brazil
60D2 Blunt USA
58B2 Bly USA
6D2 Blyth England
56B3 Blythe USA
57E3 Blytheville USA
48A4 Bo Sierra Leone
27F5 Boac Philippines
75D1 Boa Nova Brazil
64C2 Boardman USA
72F3 Boa Vista Brazil
48A4 Boa Vista *I* Cape Verde
30E1 Bobai China
44C2 Bobbili India
48B3 Bobo Dioulasso Burkina
19G2 Bobrovica Ukraine
20D5 Bobruysk Belarus
67B4 Boca Chica Key *I* USA
72E5 Bôca do Acre Brazil
75D2 Bocaiúva Brazil
50B3 Bocaranga Central African Republic
67B3 Boca Raton USA
19E3 Bochnia Poland
18B2 Bocholt Germany
13D2 Bochum Germany
51B5 Bocoio Angola
50B3 Boda Central African Republic
25N4 Bodaybo Russian Federation
59B3 Bodega Head *Pt* USA
50B2 Bodélé *Desert Region* Chad
12J5 Boden Sweden
9C3 Boderg, L Irish Republic
44B2 Bodhan India
44B3 Bodināyakkanūr India
7B4 Bodmin England
7B4 Bodmin Moor *Upland* England
12G5 Bodø Norway
17F3 Bodrum Turkey
50C4 Boende Zaïre
48A3 Boffa Guinea
30B2 Bogale Burma
63E2 Bogalusa USA
34C2 Bogan *R* Australia
48B3 Bogande Burkina
40C2 Boğazlıyan Turkey
20L4 Bogdanovich Russian Federation
26B2 Bogda Shan *Mt* China
47B2 Bogenfels Namibia
34D1 Boggabilla Australia
34C2 Boggabri Australia
7D4 Bognor Regis England
34C3 Bogong *Mt* Australia
27D7 Bogor Indonesia
25Q4 Bogorodskoye Russian Federation
20J4 Bogorodskoye Russian Federation
72D3 Bogotá Colombia
25K4 Bogotol Russian Federation
43F4 Bogra Bangladesh
31D2 Bo Hai *B* China
13B3 Bohain-en-Vermandois France
31D2 Bohai Wan *B* China
18C3 Bohmer-wald *Upland* Germany
27F6 Bohol *I* Philippines
27F6 Bohol S Philippines
75E1 Boipeba, Ilha de Brazil
75B2 Bois *R* Brazil
64C1 Bois Blanc I USA
56B2 Boise USA
62B1 Boise City USA
54F3 Bois, Lac des Canada
60C1 Boissevain Canada
48A2 Bojador,C Morocco
27F5 Bojeador, C Philippines
41G2 Bojnūrd Iran
48A3 Boké Guinea
34C1 Bokhara *R* Australia
12F7 Boknafjord *Inlet* Norway
50B4 Boko Congo
30C3 Bokor Cambodia
50B2 Bokoro Chad
50C4 Bokungu Zaïre
50B2 Bol Chad
48A3 Bolama Guinea-Bissau
14C2 Bolbec France
48B4 Bole Ghana
18D2 Bolesławiec Poland
48B3 Bolgatanga Ghana
21D6 Bolgrad Ukraine
63D1 Bolivar Missouri, USA
63E1 Bolivar Tennessee, USA
72D2 Bolívar *Mt* Venezuela
72E7 Bolivia *Republic* S America
12H6 Bollnäs Sweden
34C1 Bollon Australia
50B4 Bolobo Zaïre
16C2 Bologna Italy
20E4 Bologoye Russian Federation
26G1 Bolon' Russian Federation
26G2 Bolon', Oz *L* Russian Federation
16C2 Bolsena, L di Italy
25M2 Bol'shevik, Ostrov *I* Russian Federation
20J2 Bol'shezemel'skaya Tundra *Plain* Russian Federation
25S3 Bol'shoy Anyuy *R* Russian Federation
25N2 Bol'shoy Begichev, Ostrov *I* Russian Federation
21H5 Bol'shoy Irgiz *R* Russian Federation
28C2 Bol'shoy Kamen Russian Federation
25Q2 Bol'shoy Lyakhovskiy, Ostrov *I* Russian Federation
21H6 Bol'shoy Uzen *R* Kazakhstan
56C4 Bolson de Mapimí *Desert* Mexico
7C3 Bolton England
40B1 Bolu Turkey
12A1 Bolungarvik Iceland
9A4 Bolus Hd *Pt* Irish Republic
40B2 Bolvadin Turkey
16C1 Bolzano Italy
50B4 Boma Zaïre
32D4 Bombala Australia
44A2 Bombay India
51E5 Bombetoka, Baie de *B* Madagascar
50D3 Bombo Uganda
75C2 Bom Despacho Brazil
43G3 Bomdila India
48A4 Bomi Hills Liberia
73K6 Bom Jesus da Lapa Brazil
25O4 Bomnak Russian Federation
50C3 Bomokāndi *R* Zaïre
50C3 Bomu *R* Central African Republic/Zaïre
65D3 Bon Air USA
69D4 Bonaire *I* Caribbean Sea
70D3 Bonanza Nicaragua
55N5 Bonavista Canada
16C3 Bon, C Tunisia
50C3 Bondo Zaïre
48B4 Bondoukou Ivory Coast
Bône = 'Annaba
60D2 Bonesteel USA
73G3 Bonfim Guyana
50C3 Bongandanga Zaïre
50C3 Bongo, Massif des *Upland* Central African Republic
50B2 Bongor Chad
63C2 Bonham USA
16B2 Bonifacio Corsica, France
16B2 Bonifacio,Str of *Chan* Corsica, France/ Sardinia, Italy
Bonin Is = Ogasawara Gunto
67B3 Bonita Springs USA
75A3 Bonito Brazil
18B2 Bonn Germany
58C1 Bonners Ferry USA
48C4 Bonny Nigeria
32A1 Bonthain Indonesia
48A4 Bonthe Sierra Leone
50E2 Booaaso Somalia
34B2 Booligal Australia
34D1 Boonah Australia
62B1 Boone Colorado, USA
61E2 Boone Iowa, USA
67B1 Boone North Carolina, USA
65D2 Boonville USA
34C2 Boorowa Australia
55J2 Boothia,G of Canada
55J2 Boothia Pen Canada
7C3 Bootle England
50B4 Booué Gabon
47C2 Bophuthatswana *Self governing homeland* South Africa
62B3 Boquillas Mexico
50D3 Bor Sudan
40B2 Bor Turkey
17E2 Bor Serbia, Yugoslavia
56B2 Borah Peak *Mt* USA
12G7 Borås Sweden
41F4 Borāzjān Iran
14B3 Bordeaux France
54G2 Borden I Canada
55K2 Borden Pen Canada
68C2 Bordentown USA
8D4 Borders *Region* Scotland
34B3 Bordertown Australia
15C2 Bordj bou Arréidj Algeria
48C2 Bordj Omar Driss Algeria
Borgå = Porvoo
55Q3 Borgarnes Iceland
56C3 Borger USA
12H7 Borgholm Sweden
19E3 Borislav Ukraine
21G5 Borisoglebsk Russian Federation
20D5 Borisov Belarus
21F5 Borisovka Russian Federation
75A4 Borja Paraguay
50B2 Borkou *Desert Region* Chad
13D1 Borkum *I* Germany
12H6 Borlänge Sweden
27E6 Borneo *I* Indonesia/ Malaysia
12H7 Bornholm *I* Denmark
17F3 Bornova Turkey
48D3 Bornu *Region* Nigeria
50C3 Boro *R* Sudan
25P3 Borogontsy Russian Federation
48B3 Boromo Burkina
66D3 Boron USA
20E4 Borovichi Russian Federation
32C2 Borroloola Australia
17E1 Borsa Romania
41F3 Borūjen Iran
41E3 Borūjerd Iran
18D2 Bory Tucholskie *Region* Poland
19G2 Borzna Ukraine
25N4 Borzya Russian Federation
31B5 Bose China
47D2 Boshof South Africa
17D2 Bosna *R* Bosnia-Herzegovina
17D2 Bosnia-Herzegovina *Republic* Europe
29D3 Bōsō-hantō *B* Japan
Bosporus = Karadeniz Boğazi
15C2 Bosquet Algeria
50B3 Bossangoa Central African Republic
50B3 Bossèmbélé Central African Republic
63D2 Bossier City USA
24K5 Bosten Hu *L* China
7D3 Boston England
57F2 Boston USA
57D3 Boston Mts USA
42C4 Botād India
17E2 Botevgrad Bulgaria
47D2 Bothaville South Africa
20B3 Bothnia,G of Finland/ Sweden
51C6 Botletli *R* Botswana
21D6 Botoşani Romania
51C6 Botswana *Republic* Africa
16D3 Botte Donato *Mt* Italy
60C1 Bottineau USA
13D2 Bottrop Germany
75C3 Botucatu Brazil
75D1 Botuporã Brazil
55N5 Botwood Canada
48B4 Bouaké Ivory Coast
50B3 Bouar Central African Republic
48B1 Bouârfa Morocco
50B3 Bouca Central African Republic
15C2 Boufarik Algeria
33E1 Bougainville *I* Papua New Guinea
16B3 Bougaroun, C Algeria
Bougie = Bejaïa
48B3 Bougouni Mali
15A2 Bouhalla, Djebel *Mt* Morocco
13C3 Bouillon France
15C2 Bouïra Algeria
48B2 Bou Izakarn Morocco
13D3 Boulay-Moselle France
56C2 Boulder Colorado, USA
58D1 Boulder Montana, USA
56B3 Boulder City USA
66A2 Boulder Creek USA
14C1 Boulogne France
50B3 Boumba *R* Cameroon/ Central African Republic
48B4 Bouna Ivory Coast
56B3 Boundary Peak *Mt* USA
48B4 Boundiali Ivory Coast
58D2 Bountiful USA
33G5 Bounty Is New Zealand
33F3 Bourail New Caledonia
13C4 Bourbonne-les-Bains France
48B3 Bourem Mali
14D2 Bourg France
14D2 Bourg de Péage France
14C2 Bourges France
14C3 Bourg-Madame France
14C2 Bourgogne *Region* France
34C2 Bourke Australia
7D4 Bournemouth England
15C2 Bou Saâda Algeria
50B2 Bousso Chad
48A3 Boutilimit Mauritius
52J7 Bouvet I Atlantic Ocean
60C1 Bowbells USA
32D2 Bowen Australia
59E4 Bowie Arizona, USA
63C2 Bowie Texas, USA
6C3 Bowland Fells England
57E3 Bowling Green Kentucky, USA
63D1 Bowling Green Missouri, USA
64C2 Bowling Green Ohio, USA
65D3 Bowling Green Virginia, USA
60C1 Bowman USA
65D2 Bowmanville Canada
9C3 Bowna, L Irish Republic
34D2 Bowral Australia
31D3 Bo Xian China
31D2 Boxing China
40B1 Boyabat Turkey
50B3 Boyali Central African Republic
19G2 Boyarka Ukraine
54J4 Boyd Canada
68C2 Boyertown USA
10B3 Boyle Irish Republic
9C3 Boyne *R* Irish Republic
67B3 Boynton Beach USA
50C3 Boyoma Falls Zaïre
58E2 Boysen Res USA
17D1 Bozanski Brod Bosnia-Herzegovina/Croatia
17F3 Bozca Ada *I* Turkey
17F3 Boz Dağları *Mts* Turkey
56B2 Bozeman USA
Bozen = Bolzano
50B3 Bozene Zaïre
50B3 Bozoum Central African Republic
16D2 Brač *I* Croatia
8B3 Bracadale, Loch *Inlet* Scotland
16C2 Bracciano, L di Italy
65D1 Bracebridge Canada
49D2 Brach Libya
12H6 Bräcke Sweden
62B3 Brackettville USA
67B3 Bradenton USA
6D3 Bradford England
68A2 Bradford USA
66B3 Bradley USA
62C2 Brady USA
8E1 Brae Scotland
8D3 Braemar Scotland
15A1 Braga Portugal
73J4 Bragança Brazil
15A1 Bragança Portugal
75C3 Bragança Paulista Brazil
43G4 Brahman-Baria Bangladesh
43F4 Brāhmani *R* India
43G3 Brahmaputra *R* Bangladesh/India
21D6 Brăila Romania
57D2 Brainerd USA
7E4 Braintree England
47C3 Brak *R* South Africa
47D1 Brak *R* South Africa
13E1 Brake Germany
48A3 Brakna *Region* Mauritius
54F4 Bralorne Canada
65D2 Brampton Canada
6C2 Brampton England
13D1 Bramsche Germany
72F3 Branco *R* Brazil
51B6 Brandberg *Mt* Namibia
18C2 Brandenburg Germany
18C2 Brandenburg *State* Germany
47D2 Brandfort South Africa
56D2 Brandon Canada
61D2 Brandon USA
47C3 Brandvlei South Africa
18C2 Brandýs-nad-Laben Czech Republic
19D2 Braniewo Poland
57E2 Brantford Canada
34B3 Branxholme Australia
55M5 Bras d'Or Lakes Canada
72E6 Brasiléia Brazil
73J7 Brasília Brazil
75D2 Brasília de Minas Brazil
17F1 Braşov Romania
18D3 Bratislava Slovakia
25M4 Bratsk Russian Federation
19F3 Bratslav Ukraine
65E2 Brattleboro USA
18C2 Braunschweig Germany
48A4 Brava *I* Cape Verde
56B3 Brawley USA
9C3 Bray Irish Republic
55L3 Bray I Canada
13B3 Bray-sur-Seine France
71E5 Brazil *Republic* S America
52G5 Brazil Basin Atlantic Ocean
56D3 Brazos *R* USA
50B4 Brazzaville Congo
18C3 Brdy *Upland* Czech Republic
35A3 Breaksea Sd New Zealand
35B1 Bream B New Zealand
8D3 Brechin Scotland
13C2 Brecht Belgium
61D1 Breckenridge Minnesota, USA
62C2 Breckenridge Texas, USA
7E3 Breckland England
18D3 Břeclav Czech Republic
7C4 Brecon Wales
7C4 Brecon Beacons *Mts* Wales
7B3 Brecon Beacons Nat Pk Wales
18A2 Breda Netherlands

47C3 **Bredasdorp** South Africa
12H6 **Bredbyn** Sweden
20K5 **Bredy** Russian Federation
47B3 **Breede** *R* South Africa
65D2 **Breezewood** USA
12A1 **Breiethafjörethur** *B* Iceland
13D3 **Breisach** Germany
67A2 **Bremen** USA
18B2 **Bremen** Germany
18B2 **Bremerhaven** Germany
58B1 **Bremerton** USA
13E1 **Bremervörde** Germany
59E3 **Brendel** USA
63C2 **Brenham** USA
18C3 **Brenner** *P* Austria/Italy
66B2 **Brentwood** USA
16C1 **Brescia** Italy
Breslau = Wrocław
8E1 **Bressay** *I* Scotland
14B2 **Bressuire** France
14B2 **Brest** France
19E2 **Brest** Belarus
14B2 **Bretagne** *Region* France
13B3 **Breteuil** France
63E3 **Breton Sd** USA
68C2 **Breton Woods** USA
35B1 **Brett,C** New Zealand
67B1 **Brevard** USA
34C1 **Brewarrina** Australia
65F2 **Brewer** USA
68D2 **Brewster** New York, USA
58C1 **Brewster** Washington, USA
67A2 **Brewton** USA
47D2 **Breyten** South Africa
16D1 **Brežice** Slovenia
50C3 **Bria** Central African Republic
14D3 **Briançon** France
14C2 **Briare** France
7C4 **Bridgend** Wales
8C3 **Bridge of Orchy** Scotland
67A2 **Bridgeport** Alabama, USA
59C3 **Bridgeport** California, USA
65E2 **Bridgeport** Connecticut, USA
60C2 **Bridgeport** Nebraska, USA
63C2 **Bridgeport** Texas, USA
66C1 **Bridgeport Res** USA
58E1 **Bridger** USA
60B2 **Bridger Peak** USA
68C3 **Bridgeton** USA
69R3 **Bridgetown** Barbados
55M5 **Bridgewater** Canada
68E2 **Bridgewater** USA
7C4 **Bridgwater** England
7C4 **Bridgwater B** England
6D2 **Bridlington** England
6E3 **Bridlington Bay** England
34C4 **Bridport** Australia
7C4 **Bridport** England
13C3 **Brienne-le-Château** France
13C3 **Briey** France
16B1 **Brig** Switzerland
56B2 **Brigham City** USA
34C3 **Bright** Australia
7D4 **Brighton** England
75A3 **Brilhante** *R* Brazil
13E2 **Brilon** Germany
17D2 **Brindisi** Italy
63D2 **Brinkley** USA
33E3 **Brisbane** Australia
65E2 **Bristol** Connecticut, USA
7C4 **Bristol** England
65E2 **Bristol** Pennsylvania, USA
68E2 **Bristol** Rhode Island, USA
57E3 **Bristol** Tennessee, USA
64C3 **Bristol** USA
7B4 **Bristol Chan** England/Wales
54F4 **British Columbia** *Province* Canada
55K1 **British Empire Range** *Mts* Canada
54E3 **British Mts** Canada
47D2 **Brits** South Africa
47C3 **Britstown** South Africa
61D1 **Britton** USA
14C2 **Brive** France
7C4 **Brixham** England
18D3 **Brno** Czech Republic
67B2 **Broad** *R* USA
68C1 **Broadalbin** USA
55L4 **Broadback** *R* Canada
8B2 **Broad Bay** *Inlet* Scotland
8C3 **Broadford** Scotland
9B2 **Broad Haven, B** Irish Republic
7E4 **Broadstairs** England
60B1 **Broadus** USA
60C2 **Broadwater** USA
54H4 **Brochet** Canada
54G2 **Brock I** Canada
65D2 **Brockport** USA
68E1 **Brockton** USA
65D2 **Brockville** Canada
68A2 **Brockway** USA
55K2 **Brodeur Pen** Canada
8C4 **Brodick** Scotland
19D2 **Brodnica** Poland
21D5 **Brody** Ukraine
13D2 **Brokem Haltern** Germany
60D2 **Broken Bow** Nebraska, USA
63D2 **Broken Bow** Oklahoma, USA
63D2 **Broken Bow L** USA
32D4 **Broken Hill** Australia
7C3 **Bromsgrove** England
12G5 **Brønnøysund** Norway
68D2 **Bronx** *Borough* New York, USA
27E6 **Brooke's Pt** Philippines
61E3 **Brookfield** Missouri, USA
64B2 **Brookfield** Wisconsin, USA
57D3 **Brookhaven** USA
58B2 **Brookings** Oregon, USA
56D2 **Brookings** South Dakota, USA
68E1 **Brookline** USA
61E2 **Brooklyn** USA
68D2 **Brooklyn** *Borough* New York, USA
61E1 **Brooklyn Center** USA
54G4 **Brooks** Canada
54C3 **Brooks Range** *Mts* USA
67B3 **Brooksville** USA
34D1 **Brooloo** Australia
32B2 **Broome** Australia
8C3 **Broom, Loch** *Estuary* Scotland
8D2 **Brora** Scotland
58B2 **Brothers** USA
6C2 **Broughton** England
8D3 **Broughty Ferry** Scotland
50B2 **Broulkou** *Well* Chad
19G2 **Brovary** Ukraine
61E1 **Browerville** USA
62B2 **Brownfield** USA
56D4 **Brownsville** USA
56D3 **Brownwood** USA
27F8 **Browse I** Australia
13B2 **Bruay-en-Artois** France
32A3 **Bruce,Mt** Australia
64C1 **Bruce Pen** Canada
13E3 **Bruchsal** Germany
18D3 **Bruck an der Mur** Austria
Bruges = Brugge
13B2 **Brugge** Belgium
13D2 **Brühl** Germany
45B3 **Brûk, Wadi el** Egypt
75D1 **Brumado** Brazil
13D3 **Brumath** France
58C2 **Bruneau** USA
58C2 **Bruneau** *R* USA
27E6 **Brunei** *State* Borneo
16C1 **Brunico** Italy
35B2 **Brunner,L** New Zealand
13E1 **Brunsbüttel** Germany
57E3 **Brunswick** Georgia, USA
65F2 **Brunswick** Maine, USA
61E3 **Brunswick** Mississippi, USA
74B8 **Brunswick,Pen de** Chile
34C4 **Bruny I** Australia
20G3 **Brusenets** Russian Federation
60C2 **Brush** USA
69A3 **Brus Laguna** Honduras
Brüssel = Brussels
18A2 **Brussels** Belgium
Bruxelles = Brussels
13D3 **Bruyères** France
56D3 **Bryan** USA
34A2 **Bryan,Mt** Australia
20E5 **Bryansk** Russian Federation
63D2 **Bryant** USA
59D3 **Bryce Canyon Nat Pk** USA
18D2 **Brzeg** Poland
41E4 **Būbīyan** *I* Kuwait
50D4 **Bubu** *R* Tanzania
47E1 **Bubye** *R* Zimbabwe
72D2 **Bucaramanga** Colombia
8E3 **Buchan** *Oilfield* N Sea
48A4 **Buchanan** Liberia
62C2 **Buchanan,L** USA
8E3 **Buchan Deep** N Sea
55L2 **Buchan G** Canada
10C2 **Buchan Ness** *Pen* Scotland
55N5 **Buchans** Canada
17F2 **Bucharest** Romania
66B3 **Buchon,Pt** USA
13E1 **Bückeburg** Germany
59D4 **Buckeye** USA
8D3 **Buckhaven** Scotland
8D3 **Buckie** Scotland
7D3 **Buckingham** England
65F2 **Bucksport** USA
50B4 **Buco Zau** Congo
Bucureşti = Bucharest
19D3 **Budapest** Hungary
42D3 **Budaun** India
7B4 **Bude** England
63D2 **Bude** USA
21G7 **Budennovsk** Russian Federation
43J1 **Budhana** India
45B4 **Budhîya, Gebel** Egypt
13E2 **Büdingen** Germany
17D2 **Budva** Montenegro, Yugoslavia
48C4 **Buéa** Cameroon
66B3 **Buellton** USA
72C3 **Buenaventura** Colombia
62A3 **Buenaventura** Mexico
60B3 **Buena Vista** Colorado, USA
65D3 **Buena Vista** Virginia, USA
66C3 **Buena Vista L** USA
74E4 **Buenos Aires** Argentina
74E5 **Buenos Aires** *State* Argentina
74B7 **Buenos Aires, Lago** Argentina
63D1 **Buffalo** Mississipi, USA
57F2 **Buffalo** New York, USA
60C1 **Buffalo** S Dakota, USA
63C2 **Buffalo** Texas, USA
56C2 **Buffalo** Wyoming, USA
47E2 **Buffalo** *R* South Africa
58C1 **Buffalo Hump** *Mt* USA
54G3 **Buffalo L** Canada
54H4 **Buffalo Narrows** Canada
67B2 **Buford** USA
17F2 **Buftea** Romania
19E2 **Bug** *R* Poland/Ukraine
72C3 **Buga** Colombia
41F2 **Bugdayli** Turkmenistan
20H2 **Bugrino** Russian Federation
20J5 **Bugulma** Russian Federation
20J5 **Buguruslan** Russian Federation
40C2 **Buḩayrat al Asad** *Res* Syria
58D2 **Buhl** Idaho, USA
61E1 **Buhl** Minnesota, USA
7C3 **Builth Wells** Wales
50C4 **Bujumbura** Burundi
33E1 **Buka** *I* Papua New Guinea
51C4 **Bukama** Zaïre
50C4 **Bukavu** Zaïre
38E2 **Bukhara** Uzbekistan
27D7 **Bukittinggi** Indonesia
50D4 **Bukoba** Tanzania
27G7 **Bula** Indonesia
27F5 **Bulan** Philippines
42D3 **Bulandshahr** India
51C6 **Bulawayo** Zimbabwe
17F3 **Buldan** Turkey
42D4 **Buldāna** India
26D2 **Bulgan** Mongolia
17E2 **Bulgaria** *Republic* Europe
35B2 **Buller** *R* New Zealand
34C3 **Buller,Mt** Australia
32A4 **Bullfinch** Australia
34B1 **Bulloo** *R* Australia
34B1 **Bulloo Downs** Australia
34B1 **Bulloo L** Australia
63D1 **Bull Shoals Res** USA
32D1 **Bulolo** Papua New Guinea
47D2 **Bultfontein** South Africa
27E6 **Bulu, Gunung** *Mt* Indonesia
50C3 **Bumba** Zaïre
21D8 **Bu Menderes** *R* Turkey
30B2 **Bumphal Dam** Thailand
50D3 **Buna** Kenya
32A4 **Bunbury** Australia
9C2 **Buncrana** Irish Republic
33E3 **Bundaberg** Australia
34D2 **Bundarra** Australia
13E1 **Bünde** Germany
42D3 **Bündi** India
7E3 **Bungay** England
34C1 **Bungil** *R* Australia
51B4 **Bungo** Angola
28B4 **Bungo-suidō** *Str* Japan
27D6 **Bunguran** *I* Indonesia
27D6 **Bunguran, Kepulauan** *I* Indonesia
50D3 **Bunia** Zaïre
63D1 **Bunker** USA
63D2 **Bunkie** USA
67B3 **Bunnell** USA
27E7 **Buntok** Indonesia
27F6 **Buol** Indonesia
50C2 **Buram** Sudan
43E2 **Burang** China
50E3 **Burao** Somalia
45D2 **Burāq** Syria
41D4 **Buraydah** Saudi Arabia
59C4 **Burbank** USA
34C2 **Burcher** Australia
21E8 **Burdur** Turkey
50D2 **Burē** Ethiopia
7E3 **Bure** *R* England
26G1 **Bureinskiy Khrebet** *Mts* Russian Federation
26F2 **Bureya** Russian Federation
45B3 **Bûr Fu'ad** Egypt
18C2 **Burg** Germany
17F2 **Burgas** Bulgaria
67C2 **Burgaw** USA
47D3 **Burgersdorp** South Africa
15B1 **Burgos** Spain
13D1 **Burgsteinfurt** Germany
19D1 **Burgsvik** Sweden
17F3 **Burhaniye** Turkey
42D4 **Burhānpur** India
30C2 **Buriram** Thailand
75C2 **Buritis** Brazil
32C2 **Burketown** Australia
48B3 **Burkina** *Republic* W Africa
65D1 **Burk's Falls** Canada
56B2 **Burley** USA
60C3 **Burlington** Colorado, USA
57D2 **Burlington** Iowa, USA
68C2 **Burlington** New Jersey, USA
67C1 **Burlington** North Carolina, USA
57F2 **Burlington** Vermont, USA
58B1 **Burlington** Washington, USA
39H3 **Burma** *Republic* Asia
62C2 **Burnet** USA
58B2 **Burney** USA
68B2 **Burnham** USA
7E4 **Burnham-on-Crouch** England
32D5 **Burnie** Australia
6C3 **Burnley** England
58C2 **Burns** USA
54F4 **Burns Lake** Canada
24K5 **Burqin** China
34A2 **Burra** Australia
34D2 **Burragorang,L** Australia
8D2 **Burray** *I* Scotland
34C2 **Burren Junction** Australia
34C2 **Burrinjuck Res** Australia
62B3 **Burro, Serranías del** *Mts* Mexico
8C4 **Burrow Head** *Pt* Scotland
27G8 **Burrundie** Australia
21D7 **Bursa** Turkey
40B4 **Bur Safâga** Egypt
Bûr Saïd = Port Said
45B4 **Bûr Taufiq** Egypt
64C2 **Burton** USA
7D3 **Burton upon Trent** England
12J6 **Burtrask** Sweden
34B2 **Burtundy** Australia
27F7 **Buru** *I* Indonesia
50C4 **Burundi** *Republic* Africa
60D2 **Burwell** USA
7C3 **Bury** England
25N4 **Buryat Republic** Russian Federation
21J6 **Burynshik** Kazakhstan
7E3 **Bury St Edmunds** England
28A3 **Bushan** China
41F4 **Būshehr** Iran
9C2 **Bushmills** Northern Ireland
50B4 **Busira** *R* Zaïre
19E2 **Busko Zdrój** Poland
45D2 **Buşrá ash Shām** Syria
13D4 **Bussang** France
32A4 **Busselton** Australia
16B1 **Busto Arsizio** Italy
50C3 **Buta** Zaïre
50C4 **Butare** Rwanda
8C4 **Bute** *I* Scotland
26F2 **Butha Qi** China
65D2 **Butler** USA
32B1 **Buton** *I* Indonesia
48C4 **Butta** Togo
56B2 **Butte** USA
30C4 **Butterworth** Malaysia
47D3 **Butterworth** South Africa
10B2 **Butt of Lewis** *C* Scotland
55M3 **Button Is** Canada
66C3 **Buttonwillow** USA
27F6 **Butuan** Philippines
21G5 **Buturlinovka** Russian Federation
43E3 **Butwal** Nepal
13E2 **Butzbach** Germany
50E3 **Buulobarde** Somalia
50E3 **Buurhakaba** Somalia
7D3 **Buxton** England
20G4 **Buy** Russian Federation
31B1 **Buyant Ovoo** Mongolia
21H7 **Buynaksk** Russian Federation
25N5 **Buyr Nuur** *L* Mongolia
21G8 **Büyük Ağrı Dağı** *Mt* Turkey
40A2 **Büyük Menderes** *R* Turkey
17F1 **Buzău** Romania
17F1 **Buzău** *R* Romania
75D3 **Búzios, Ponta dos** *Pt* Brazil
20J5 **Buzuluk** Russian Federation
68E2 **Buzzards B** USA
17F2 **Byala** Bulgaria
17E2 **Byala Slatina** Bulgaria
54H2 **Byam Martin Channel** Canada
54H2 **Byam Martin I** Canada
45C1 **Byblos** *Hist site* Lebanon
19D2 **Bydgoszcz** Poland
60C3 **Byers** USA
12F7 **Bygland** Norway
19G2 **Bykhov** Belarus
55L2 **Bylot I** Canada
34C2 **Byrock** Australia
66B2 **Byron** USA
34D1 **Byron** *C* Australia
25P3 **Bytantay** *R* Russian Federation
19D2 **Bytom** Poland

C

74E3 **Caacupú** Paraguay
75A4 **Caaguazú** Paraguay
51B5 **Caála** Angola
75A4 **Caapucú** Paraguay
75B3 **Caarapó** Brazil
74E3 **Caazapá** Paraguay
15C1 **Caballería, Cabo de** *C* Spain
62A2 **Caballo Res** USA
27F5 **Cabanatuan** Philippines
65F1 **Cabano** Canada
73M5 **Cabedelo** Brazil
15A2 **Cabeza del Buey** Spain
72D1 **Cabimas** Venezuela
50B4 **Cabinda** Angola
50B4 **Cabinda** *Province* Angola
58C1 **Cabinet Mts** USA
75D3 **Cabo Frio** Brazil
55L5 **Cabonga,Réservoire** Canada
34D1 **Caboolture** Australia
51D5 **Cabora Bassa Dam** Mozambique
70A1 **Caborca** Mexico
55M5 **Cabot Str** Canada
15B2 **Cabra** Spain
75D2 **Cabral, Serra do** *Mts* Brazil
15A1 **Cabreira** *Mt* Portugal
15C2 **Cabrera** *I* Spain
15B2 **Cabriel** *R* Spain
17E2 **Čačak** Serbia, Yugoslavia
68A3 **Cacapon** *R* USA
73G7 **Cáceres** Brazil
15A2 **Cáceres** Spain
63D1 **Cache** *R* USA
66A1 **Cache Creek** *R* USA
58D2 **Cache Peak** *Mt* USA
74C3 **Cachi** Argentina
73G5 **Cachimbo** Brazil
73G5 **Cachimbo, Serra do** *Mts* Brazil
73L6 **Cachoeira** Brazil
75B2 **Cachoeira Alta** Brazil
73L5 **Cachoeira de Paulo Afonso** *Waterfall* Brazil
74F4 **Cachoeira do Sul** Brazil
73K8 **Cachoeiro de Itapemirim** Brazil
66C3 **Cachuma,L** USA
51B5 **Cacolo** Angola
51B5 **Caconda** Angola
62B1 **Cactus** USA
75B2 **Caçu** Brazil
75D1 **Caculé** Brazil
51B5 **Caculuvar** *R* Angola
19D3 **Čadca** Slovakia
7C3 **Cader Idris** *Mt* Wales
57E2 **Cadillac** USA
15A2 **Cádiz** Spain
15A2 **Cádiz, Golfo de** *G* Spain
14B2 **Caen** France
7B3 **Caernarfon** Wales
7B3 **Caernarfon B** Wales
7C4 **Caerphilly** Wales
45C2 **Caesarea** *Hist Site* Israel
75D1 **Caetité** Brazil
74C3 **Cafayate** Argentina
40B2 **Caga Tepe** *Mt* Turkey
27F6 **Cagayan de Oro** Philippines
16B3 **Cagliari** Sardinia, Italy
16B3 **Cagliari, G di** Sardinia, Italy
69D3 **Caguas** Puerto Rico
67A2 **Cahaba** *R* USA
9C3 **Cahir** Irish Republic
9C3 **Cahore Pt** Irish Republic
14C3 **Cahors** France
51D5 **Caia** Mozambique
73G6 **Caiabis, Serra dos** *Mts* Brazil
51C5 **Caianda** Angola
75B2 **Caiapó** *R* Brazil
75B2 **Caiapônia** Brazil
75B2 **Caiapó, Serra do** *Mts* Brazil
73L5 **Caicó** Brazil
69C2 **Caicos Is** Caribbean Sea
57F4 **Caicos Pass** The Bahamas
8D3 **Cairngorms** *Mts* Scotland
8C4 **Cairnryan** Scotland
32D2 **Cairns** Australia
40B3 **Cairo** Egypt
57E3 **Cairo** USA
8D2 **Caithness** Scotland
34B1 **Caiwarro** Australia
72C5 **Cajabamba** Peru
72C5 **Cajamarca** Peru
48C4 **Calabar** Nigeria
69D5 **Calabozo** Venezuela

17E2 **Calafat** Romania
74B8 **Calafate** Argentina
15B1 **Calahorra** Spain
14C1 **Calais** France
65F1 **Calais** USA
74C2 **Calama** Chile
72D3 **Calamar** Colombia
27E5 **Calamian Group** *Is* Philippines
51B4 **Calandula** Angola
27C6 **Calang** Indonesia
49E2 **Calanscio Sand Sea** Libya
27F5 **Calapan** Philippines
17F2 **Calarasi** Romania
15B1 **Calatayud** Spain
66B2 **Calaveras Res** USA
63D3 **Calcasieu L** USA
43F4 **Calcutta** India
15A2 **Caldas da Rainha** Portugal
73J7 **Caldas Novas** Brazil
74B3 **Caldera** Chile
56B2 **Caldwell** USA
47B3 **Caledon** South Africa
47D3 **Caledon** *R* South Africa
64A2 **Caledonia** Minnesota, USA
68B1 **Caledonia** New York, USA
74C7 **Caleta Olivia** Argentina
56B3 **Calexico** USA
54G4 **Calgary** Canada
67B2 **Calhoun** USA
67B2 **Calhoun Falls** USA
72C3 **Cali** Colombia
66C3 **Caliente** California, USA
56B3 **Caliente** Nevada, USA
62A1 **Caliente** New Mexico, USA
56A3 **California** *State* USA
66C3 **California Aqueduct** USA
70A1 **California, G de** Mexico
44B3 **Calimera,Pt** India
59C4 **Calipatria** USA
47C3 **Calitzdorp** South Africa
34B1 **Callabonna** *R* Australia
34A1 **Callabonna,L** Australia
65D1 **Callander** Canada
8C3 **Callander** Scotland
72C6 **Callao** Peru
68C2 **Callicoon** USA
67B3 **Caloosahatchee** *R* USA
34D1 **Caloundra** Australia
16C3 **Caltanissetta** Sicily, Italy
51B4 **Caluango** Angola
51B5 **Calulo** Angola
51B5 **Caluquembe** Angola
50F2 **Caluula** Somalia
16B2 **Calvi** Corsica, France
47B3 **Calvinia** South Africa
13E3 **Calw** Germany
75E1 **Camacari** Brazil
70E2 **Camagüey** Cuba
70E2 **Camagüey,Arch de** *Is* Cuba
75E1 **Camamu** Brazil
72D7 **Camaná** Peru
75B2 **Camapuã** Brazil
72E8 **Camargo** Bolivia
66C3 **Camarillo** USA
74C6 **Camarones** Argentina
58B1 **Camas** USA
51B4 **Camaxilo** Angola
51B4 **Cambatela** Angola
30C3 **Cambodia** *Republic* SE Asia
7B4 **Camborne** England
14C1 **Cambrai** France
66B3 **Cambria** USA
7C3 **Cambrian Mts** Wales
64C2 **Cambridge** Canada
7E3 **Cambridge** England
69H1 **Cambridge** Jamaica
65D3 **Cambridge** Maryland, USA
65E2 **Cambridge** Massachussets, USA
61E1 **Cambridge** Minnesota, USA
35C1 **Cambridge** New Zealand
64C2 **Cambridge** Ohio, USA
7D3 **Cambridge** *County* England
54H3 **Cambridge Bay** Canada
27F8 **Cambridge G** Australia
21F7 **Cam Burun** *Pt* Turkey
57D3 **Camden** Arkansas, USA
34D2 **Camden** Australia
65E3 **Camden** New Jersey, USA
68C1 **Camden** New York, USA
67B2 **Camden** South Carolina, USA
61E3 **Cameron** Missouri, USA
63C2 **Cameron** Texas, USA
54H2 **Cameron I** Canada
35A3 **Cameron Mts** New Zealand
50B3 **Cameroon** *Federal Republic* Africa
48C4 **Cameroun, Mt** Cameroon
73J4 **Cametá** Brazil
67B2 **Camilla** USA
66B1 **Camino** USA
72F8 **Camiri** Bolivia
51C4 **Camissombo** Angola
73K4 **Camocim** Brazil
32C2 **Camooweal** Australia
44E4 **Camorta** *I* Nicobar Is, Indian Ocean
74A7 **Campana** *I* Chile
47C2 **Campbell** South Africa
35B2 **Campbell,C** New Zealand
37K7 **Campbell I** New Zealand
54E3 **Campbell,Mt** Canada
42C2 **Campbellpore** Pakistan
54F5 **Campbell River** Canada
64B3 **Campbellsville** USA
55M5 **Campbellton** Canada
34D2 **Campbelltown** Australia
8C4 **Campbeltown** Scotland
70C3 **Campeche** Mexico
70C2 **Campeche, B de** Mexico
34B3 **Camperdown** Australia
73L5 **Campina Grande** Brazil
73J8 **Campinas** Brazil
75C2 **Campina Verde** Brazil
66C2 **Camp Nelson** USA
48C4 **Campo** Cameroon
16C2 **Campobasso** Italy
75C3 **Campo Belo** Brazil
75C2 **Campo Florido** Brazil
74D3 **Campo Gallo** Argentina
74F2 **Campo Grande** Brazil
73K4 **Campo Maior** Brazil
74F2 **Campo Mourão** Brazil
75D3 **Campos** Brazil
75C2 **Campos Altos** Brazil
59D4 **Camp Verde** USA
30D3 **Cam Ranh** Vietnam
54G4 **Camrose** Canada
51B5 **Camucuio** Angola
69K1 **Canaan** Tobago
68D1 **Canaan** USA
51B5 **Canacupa** Angola
53F3 **Canada** *Dominion* N America
74D4 **Cañada de Gómez** Argentina
68C2 **Canadensis** USA
62B1 **Canadian** USA
56C3 **Canadian** *R* USA
21D7 **Çanakkale** Turkey
68B1 **Canandaigua** USA
68B1 **Canandaigua L** USA
70A1 **Cananea** Mexico
75C4 **Cananeia** Brazil
Canarias, Islas = Canary Islands
52G3 **Canary Basin** Atlantic Ocean
48A2 **Canary Is** *Atlantic Ocean*
75C3 **Canastra, Serra da** *Mts* Brazil
70B2 **Canatlán** Mexico
57E4 **Canaveral,C** USA
73L7 **Canavieiras** Brazil
32D4 **Canberra** Australia
58B2 **Canby** California, USA
61D2 **Canby** Minnesota, USA
17F3 **Çandarlı Körfezi** *B* Turkey
68D2 **Candlewood,L** USA
60D1 **Cando** USA
68B1 **Candor** USA
74E4 **Canelones** Uruguay
63C1 **Caney** USA
51C5 **Cangamba** Angola
51C5 **Cangombe** Angola
31D2 **Cangzhou** China
55M4 **Caniapiscau** *R* Canada
55M4 **Caniapiscau, Réservoir** *Res* Canada
16C3 **Canicatti** Sicily, Italy
73L4 **Canindé** Brazil
68B1 **Canisteo** USA
68B1 **Canisteo** *R* USA
62A1 **Canjilon** USA
40B1 **Çankırı** Turkey
8B3 **Canna** *I* Scotland
44B3 **Cannanore** India
14D3 **Cannes** France
7C3 **Cannock** England
60C1 **Cannonball** *R* USA
34C3 **Cann River** Australia
74F3 **Canõas** Brazil
75B4 **Canoinhas** Brazil
60B3 **Canon City** USA
34B2 **Canopus** Australia
54H4 **Canora** Canada
34C2 **Canowindra** Australia
15B1 **Cantabria** *Region* Spain
14A3 **Cantabrica, Cord** *Mts* Spain
7E4 **Canterbury** England
35B2 **Canterbury Bight** *B* New Zealand
35B2 **Canterbury Plains** New Zealand
30D4 **Can Tho** Vietnam
66D3 **Cantil** USA
Canton = Guangzhou
63E2 **Canton** Mississippi, USA
64A2 **Canton** Missouri, USA
57E2 **Canton** Ohio, USA
68B2 **Canton** Pensylvania, USA
61D2 **Canton** S Dakota, USA
33H1 **Canton** *I* Phoenix Islands
75B3 **Cantu, Serra do** *Mts* Brazil
62B2 **Canyon** USA
58C2 **Canyon City** USA
58D1 **Canyon Ferry L** USA
59E3 **Canyonlands Nat Pk** USA
58B2 **Canyonville** USA
51C4 **Canzar** Angola
30D1 **Cao Bang** Vietnam
28B2 **Caoshi** China
73J4 **Capanema** Brazil
75C3 **Capão Bonito** Brazil
75D3 **Caparaó, Serra do** *Mts* Brazil
14B3 **Capbreton** France
16B2 **Cap Corse** *C* Corsica, France
14B2 **Cap de la Hague** *C* France
65E1 **Cap-de-la-Madeleine** Canada
15C2 **Capdepera** Spain
34C4 **Cape Barren I** Australia
52J6 **Cape Basin** Atlantic Ocean
55N5 **Cape Breton I** Canada
Cape, Cabo etc: see also individual cape names
48B4 **Cape Coast** Ghana
65E2 **Cape Cod B** USA
55M3 **Cape Dyer** Canada
76F7 **Cape Evans** *Base* Antarctica
67C2 **Cape Fear** *R* USA
63E1 **Cape Girardeau** USA
74C8 **Cape Horn** Chile
36H4 **Cape Johnson Depth** Pacific Ocean
75D2 **Capelinha** Brazil
54B3 **Cape Lisburne** USA
51B5 **Capelongo** Angola
65E3 **Cape May** USA
54F5 **Cape Mendocino** USA
51B4 **Capenda Camulemba** Angola
54F2 **Cape Parry** Canada
47B3 **Cape Town** South Africa
52G4 **Cape Verde** *Is* Atlantic Ocean
52G4 **Cape Verde Basin** Atlantic Ocean
32D2 **Cape York Pen** Australia
69C3 **Cap-Haïtien** Haiti
73J4 **Capim** *R* Brazil
75A3 **Capitán Bado** Paraguay
59E3 **Capitol Reef Nat Pk** USA
75A2 **Capivari** *R* Brazil
9C3 **Cappoquin** Irish Republic
69P2 **Cap Pt** St Lucia
16C2 **Capri** *I* Italy
51C5 **Caprivi Strip** *Region* Namibia
72D4 **Caquetá** *R* Colombia
17E2 **Caracal** Romania
72F3 **Caracaraí** Brazil
72E1 **Caracas** Venezuela
75A3 **Caracol** Brazil
75C3 **Caraguatatuba** Brazil
74B5 **Carahue** Chile
75D2 **Caraí** Brazil
75D3 **Carandaí** Brazil
75A2 **Carandazal** Brazil
73K8 **Carangola** Brazil
17E1 **Caransebeş** Romania
69A3 **Caratasca** Honduras
70D3 **Caratasca, L de** *Lg* Honduras
75D2 **Caratinga** Brazil
15B2 **Caravaca de la Cruz** Spain
75E2 **Caravelas** Brazil
16B3 **Carbonara, C** Sardinia, Italy
64B3 **Carbondale** Illinois, USA
68C2 **Carbondale** Pennsylvania, USA
55N5 **Carbonear** Canada
16B3 **Carbonia** Sardinia, Italy
54G4 **Carcajou** Canada
50E2 **Carcar Mts** Somalia
14C3 **Carcassonne** France
54E3 **Carcross** Canada
30C3 **Cardamomes, Chaîne des** *Mts* Cambodia
70D2 **Cardenas** Cuba
7C4 **Cardiff** Wales
7B3 **Cardigan** Wales
7B3 **Cardigan B** Wales
75C4 **Cardoso, Ilha do** Brazil
17E1 **Carei** Romania
73G4 **Careiro** Brazil
64C2 **Carey** USA
14B2 **Carhaix-Plouguer** France
74D5 **Carhué** Argentina
73K8 **Cariacíca** Brazil
71C2 **Caribbean S** Central America
54J4 **Caribou** Canada
65F1 **Caribou** USA
54G4 **Caribou Mts** Alberta, Canada
54F4 **Caribou Mts** British Columbia, Canada
13C3 **Carignan** France
75D1 **Carinhanha** Brazil
75D1 **Carinhanha** *R* Brazil
72F1 **Caripito** Venezuela
65D1 **Carleton Place** Canada
47D2 **Carletonville** South Africa
58C2 **Carlin** USA
9C2 **Carlingford, L** Northern Ireland
64B3 **Carlinville** USA
6C2 **Carlisle** England
65D2 **Carlisle** USA
75D2 **Carlos Chagas** Brazil
9C3 **Carlow** Irish Republic
9C3 **Carlow** *County* Irish Republic
59C4 **Carlsbad** California, USA
56C3 **Carlsbad** New Mexico, USA
62B2 **Carlsbad Caverns Nat Pk** USA
36E4 **Carlsberg Ridge** Indian Ocean
54H5 **Carlyle** Canada
54E3 **Carmacks** Canada
7B4 **Carmarthen** Wales
7B4 **Carmarthen B** Wales
66B2 **Carmel** California, USA
68D2 **Carmel** New York, USA
7B3 **Carmel Hd** *Pt* Wales
45C2 **Carmel,Mt** Israel
66B2 **Carmel Valley** USA
56B4 **Carmen** *I* Mexico
74D6 **Carmen de Patagones** Argentina
64B3 **Carmi** USA
59B3 **Carmichael** USA
75C2 **Carmo do Paranaiba** Brazil
15A2 **Carmona** Spain
75E2 **Carnacá** Brazil
32A3 **Carnarvon** Australia
47C3 **Carnarvon** South Africa
9C2 **Carndonagh** Irish Republic
32B3 **Carnegie,L** Australia
44E4 **Car Nicobar** *I* Nicobar Is, Indian Ocean
50B3 **Carnot** Central African Republic
8D3 **Carnoustie** Scotland
9C3 **Carnsore Pt** Irish Republic
67B3 **Carol City** USA
73J5 **Carolina** Brazil
47E2 **Carolina** South Africa
67C2 **Carolina Beach** USA
27H6 **Caroline Is** Pacific Ocean
19F3 **Carpathian Mts** Romania
21C6 **Carpathians** *Mts* E Europe
32C2 **Carpentaria,G of** Australia
39H5 **Carpenter Ridge** Indian Ocean
14D3 **Carpentras** France
16C2 **Carpi** Italy
66C3 **Carpinteria** USA
67B3 **Carrabelle** USA
16C2 **Carrara** Italy
10B3 **Carrauntoohill** *Mt* Irish Republic
8C4 **Carrick** Scotland
9D2 **Carrickfergus** Northern Ireland
9C3 **Carrickmacross** Irish Republic
9C3 **Carrick-on-Suir** Irish Republic
34A2 **Carrieton** Australia
54J5 **Carrington** USA
15B1 **Carrión** *R* Spain
62C3 **Carrizo Springs** USA
62A2 **Carrizozo** USA
57D2 **Carroll** USA
67A2 **Carrollton** Georgia, USA
64B3 **Carrollton** Kentucky, USA
61E3 **Carrollton** Missouri, USA
9B2 **Carrowmore,L** *Irish Republic*
63E1 **Carruthersville** USA
21F7 **Carşamba** Turkey
21E8 **Carşamba** *R* Turkey
56B3 **Carson City** USA
64C2 **Carsonville** USA
8D4 **Carstairs** Scotland
69B4 **Cartagena** Colombia
15B2 **Cartagena** Spain
72C3 **Cartago** Colombia
70D4 **Cartago** Costa Rica
66C2 **Cartago** USA
35C2 **Carterton** New Zealand
63D1 **Carthage** Missouri, USA
65D2 **Carthage** New York, USA
63D2 **Carthage** Texas, USA
32B2 **Cartier I** Timor Sea
55N4 **Cartwright** Canada
73L5 **Caruaru** Brazil
72F1 **Carúpano** Venezuela
13B2 **Carvin** France
15A2 **Carvoeiro, Cabo** *C* Portugal
67C1 **Cary** USA
48B1 **Casablanca** Morocco
75C3 **Casa Branca** Brazil
56B3 **Casa Grande** USA
16B1 **Casale Monferrato** Italy
58D1 **Cascade** USA
35A2 **Cascade Pt** New Zealand
56A2 **Cascade Range** *Mts* USA
58C2 **Cascade Res** USA
74F2 **Cascavel** Brazil
16C2 **Caserta** Italy
76G9 **Casey** *Base* Antarctica
9C3 **Cashel** Irish Republic
33E3 **Casino** Australia
72C5 **Casma** Peru
66B3 **Casmalia** USA
15C1 **Caspe** Spain
56C2 **Casper** USA
21H6 **Caspian Depression** *Region* Kazakhstan
21H7 **Caspian S** Asia/Europe
65D3 **Cass** USA
51C5 **Cassamba** Angola
13B2 **Cassel** France
61D1 **Casselton** USA
54E3 **Cassiar Mts** Canada
75B2 **Cassilândia** Brazil
16C2 **Cassino** Italy
61E1 **Cass Lake** USA
66C3 **Castaic** USA
14D3 **Castellane** France
16C2 **Castello, Città di** Italy
15C1 **Castellón de la Plana** Spain
73K5 **Castelo** Brazil
15A2 **Castelo Branco** Portugal
14C3 **Castelsarrasin** France
16C3 **Castelvetrano** Sicily, Italy
34B3 **Casterton** Australia
15B2 **Castilla la Mancha** *Region* Spain
15B1 **Castilla y León** *Region* Spain
10B3 **Castlebar** Irish Republic
8B3 **Castlebay** Scotland
9C2 **Castleblayney** Irish Republic
59D3 **Castle Dale** USA
8D4 **Castle Douglas** Scotland
6D3 **Castleford** England
58C1 **Castlegar** Canada
34B3 **Castlemaine** Australia
66B3 **Castle Mt** USA
58D2 **Castle Peak** *Mt* USA
34C2 **Castlereagh** *R* Australia
60C3 **Castle Rock** USA
6B2 **Castletown** England
9B4 **Castletown Bere** Irish Republic
14C3 **Castres-sur-l'Agout** France
69P2 **Castries** St Lucia
74B6 **Castro** Argentina
74F2 **Castro** Brazil
73L6 **Castro Alves** Brazil
16D3 **Castrovillari** Italy
66B2 **Castroville** USA
35A2 **Caswell Sd** New Zealand
70E2 **Cat** *I* The Bahamas
72B5 **Catacaos** Peru
75D3 **Cataguases** Brazil
63D2 **Catahoula L** USA
75C2 **Catalão** Brazil
15C1 **Cataluña** *Region* Spain
74C3 **Catamarca** Argentina
74C3 **Catamarca** *State* Argentina
51D5 **Catandica** Mozambique
27F5 **Catanduanes** *I* Philippines
74G2 **Catanduva** Brazil
75B4 **Catanduvas** Brazil
16D3 **Catania** Sicily, Italy
16D3 **Catanzaro** Italy
62C3 **Catarina** USA
27F5 **Catarman** Philippines
69C5 **Catatumbo** *R* Venezuela
68B2 **Catawissa** USA
27F5 **Catbalogan** Philippines
16B2 **Cateraggio** Corsica, France
51B4 **Catete** Angola
47D3 **Cathcart** South Africa
48A3 **Catio** Guinea-Bissau
55J4 **Cat Lake** Canada
33E3 **Cato** *I* Australia
70D2 **Catoche,C** Mexico
68B3 **Catoctin Mt** USA
65D3 **Catonsville** USA
65E2 **Catskill** USA
65E2 **Catskill Mts** USA
72D2 **Cauca** *R* Colombia
73L4 **Caucaia** Brazil
72C2 **Caucasia** Colombia
21G7 **Caucasus** *Mts* Georgia
13B2 **Caudry** France
51B4 **Caungula** Angola
74B5 **Cauquenes** Chile
65F1 **Causapscal** Canada
44B3 **Cauvery** *R* India
14D3 **Cavaillon** France
75C1 **Cavalcante** Brazil
61D1 **Cavalier** USA
48B4 **Cavally** *R* Liberia
9C3 **Cavan** Irish Republic
9C3 **Cavan** *County* Irish Republic
72D4 **Caxias** Brazil

73K4 **Caxias** Brazil
74F3 **Caxias do Sul** Brazil
51B4 **Caxito** Angola
67B2 **Cayce** USA
40D1 **Çayeli** Turkey
73H3 **Cayenne** French Guiana
70E3 **Cayman Brac** *I* Cayman Is, Caribbean Sea
69A3 **Cayman Is** Caribbean Sea
69A3 **Cayman Trench** Caribbean Sea
50E3 **Caynabo** Somalia
70E2 **Cayo Romano** *I* Cuba
70D3 **Cayos Miskito** *Is* Nicaragua
69A2 **Cay Sal** *I* Caribbean Sea
66B3 **Cayucos** USA
68B1 **Cayuga L** USA
68C1 **Cazenovia** USA
51C5 **Cazombo** Angola
Ceará = Fortaleza
73K5 **Ceará** *State* Brazil
27F5 **Cebu** Philippines
27F5 **Cebu** *I* Philippines
68C3 **Cecilton** USA
16C2 **Cecina** Italy
61E2 **Cedar** *R* USA
56B3 **Cedar City** USA
63C2 **Cedar Creek Res** USA
61E2 **Cedar Falls** USA
54H4 **Cedar L** Canada
66D1 **Cedar Mts** USA
57D2 **Cedar Rapids** USA
67A2 **Cedartown** USA
70A2 **Cedros** *I* Mexico
56B4 **Cedros, Isla de** Mexico
32C4 **Ceduna** Australia
50E3 **Ceelbuur** Somalia
50E2 **Ceerigaabo** Somalia
16C3 **Cefalù** Sicily, Italy
19D3 **Cegléd** Hungary
51B5 **Cela** Angola
70B2 **Celaya** Mexico
Celebes = Sulawesi
27F6 **Celebes S** SE Asia
64C2 **Celina** USA
16D1 **Celje** Slovenia
18C2 **Celle** Germany
7A4 **Celtic S** British Islands
7B3 **Cemmaes Hd** *Pt* Wales
27G7 **Cendrawasih** *Pen* Indonesia
63D2 **Center** USA
67A1 **Center Hill L** USA
68D2 **Center Moriches** USA
67A2 **Center Point** USA
62A2 **Central** USA
8C3 **Central** *Region* Scotland
50B3 **Central African Republic** Africa
61D2 **Central City** Nebraska, USA
68A2 **Central City** Pennsylvania, USA
68E2 **Central Falls** USA
64B3 **Centralia** Illinois, USA
56A2 **Centralia** Washington, USA
47C1 **Central Kalahari Game Res** Botswana
42A3 **Central Makran Ra** *Mts* Pakistan
58B2 **Central Point** USA
27H7 **Central Range** *Mts* Papua New Guinea
68B1 **Central Square** USA
67A2 **Centreville** Alabama, USA
68B3 **Centreville** Maryland, USA
Ceram = Seram
Ceram Sea = Seram Sea
73J7 **Ceres** Brazil
47B3 **Ceres** South Africa
66B2 **Ceres** USA
14C2 **Cergy-Pontoise** France
16D2 **Cerignola** Italy
21D7 **Cernavodă** Romania
13D4 **Cernay** France
56C4 **Cerralvo** *I* Mexico
72C6 **Cerro de Pasco** Peru
69D3 **Cerro de Punta** *Mt* Puerto Rico
69C4 **Cerron** *Mt* Venezuela
74C5 **Cerros Colorados, Embalse** *Res* Argentina
16C2 **Cesena** Italy
20D4 **Cēsis** Latvia
18C3 **České Budějovice** Czech Republic
18D3 **Českomoravská Vyosina** *Region* Czech Republic
17F3 **Çeşme** Turkey
32E4 **Cessnock** Australia
16D2 **Cetina** *R* Croatia
15A2 **Ceuta** NW Africa
40C2 **Ceyhan** Turkey
40C2 **Ceyhan** *R* Turkey
40C2 **Ceylanpınar** Turkey
44C4 **Ceylon** *I* Indian Oc
Ceylon *Republic* **= Sri Lanka**
25L4 **Chaa-Khol** Russian Federation
14C2 **Chaâteaudun** France
13B4 **Chablis** France
72C5 **Chachapoyas** Peru
42C3 **Chachran** Pakistan
42C3 **Chachro** Pakistan
74D3 **Chaco** *State* Argentina
50B2 **Chad** *Republic* Africa
50B2 **Chad, L** C Africa
56C2 **Chadron** USA
28B3 **Chaeryŏng** N Korea
63E1 **Chaffee** USA
42A3 **Chagai** Pakistan
25P4 **Chagda** Russian Federation
42B2 **Chaghcharan** Afghanistan
36E5 **Chagos Arch** Indian Ocean
69L1 **Chaguanas** Trinidad
38E3 **Chāh Bahār** Iran
28A2 **Ch'aho** N Korea
30C2 **Chai Badan** Thailand
43F4 **Chāībāsa** India
30C2 **Chaiyaphum** Thailand
42C2 **Chakwal** Pakistan
72D7 **Chala** Peru
51D5 **Chalabesa** Zambia
42A2 **Chalap Dalam** *Mts* Afghanistan
57G2 **Chaleurs, B des** Canada
13C4 **Chalindrey** France
31C4 **Chaling** China
42D4 **Chālisgaon** India
27H5 **Challenger Deep** Pacific Ocean
13C3 **Challerange** France
58D2 **Challis** USA
13C3 **Châlons-sur-Marne** France
14C2 **Chalon sur Saône** France
28B2 **Chaluhe** China
18C3 **Cham** Germany
62A1 **Chama** USA
42B2 **Chaman** Pakistan
42D2 **Chamba** India
42D3 **Chambal** *R* India
60D2 **Chamberlain** USA
65D3 **Chambersburg** USA
14D2 **Chambéry** France
13B3 **Chambly** France
65E1 **Chambord** Canada
42A3 **Chambor Kalat** Pakistan
41F3 **Chamgordan** Iran
43E4 **Chāmpa** India
14C2 **Champagne** *Region* France
47D2 **Champagne Castle** *Mt* Lesotho
57E2 **Champaign** USA
43N2 **Champaran** *District* India
30D3 **Champassak** Laos
57F2 **Champlain,L** USA
44B3 **Chāmrājnagar** India
74B3 **Chañaral** Chile
54D3 **Chandalar** USA
54D3 **Chandalar** *R* USA
63E3 **Chandeleur Is** USA
42D2 **Chandīgarh** India
59D4 **Chandler** USA
43G4 **Chandpur** Bangladesh
42D5 **Chandrapur** India
47E1 **Changane** *R* Mozambique
51D5 **Changara** Mozambique
28B2 **Changbai** China
28B2 **Changbai Shan** *Mts* China
28B2 **Changchun** China
31C4 **Changde** China
28A3 **Changdo** N Korea
28A3 **Changhai** China
28A3 **Changhang** S Korea
28A3 **Changhowan** S Korea
26E4 **Changhua** Taiwan
28A4 **Changhŭng** S Korea
30D2 **Changjiang** China
31D3 **Chang Jiang** *R* China
28B2 **Changjin** N Korea
28A2 **Changjin** *R* N Korea
28A2 **Changjin Res** N Korea
28B3 **Changnyŏn** N Korea
31C4 **Changsha** China
31E3 **Changshu** China
31B2 **Changwu** China
28A3 **Changyŏn** N Korea
31C2 **Changzhi** China
31E3 **Changzhou** China
14B2 **Channel Is** British Isles
56B3 **Channel Is** USA
55N5 **Channel Port-aux-Basques** Canada
30C3 **Chanthaburi** Thailand
13B3 **Chantilly** France
55J3 **Chantrey Inlet** *B* Canada
63C1 **Chanute** USA
24J4 **Chany, Ozero** *L* Russian Federation
31D5 **Chao'an** China
31D3 **Chao Hu** *L* China
30C3 **Chao Phraya** *R* Thailand
15A2 **Chaouen** Morocco
31E1 **Chaoyang** China
73K6 **Chapada Diamantina** *Mts* Brazil
73K4 **Chapadinha** Brazil
70B2 **Chapala, L de** Mexico
21J5 **Chapayevo** Kazakhstan
74F3 **Chapecó** Brazil
7D3 **Chapel-en-le-Frith** England
67C1 **Chapel Hill** USA
69H1 **Chapeltown** Jamaica
55K5 **Chapleau** Canada
25U3 **Chaplino, Mys** *C* Russian Federation
20G5 **Chaplygin** Russian Federation
60C2 **Chappell** USA
76G3 **Charcot I** Antarctica
7C4 **Chard** England
38E2 **Chardzhou** Turkmenistan
14C2 **Charente** *R* France
50B2 **Chari** *R* Chad
50B2 **Chari Baguirmi** *Region* Chad
42B1 **Charikar** Afghanistan
61E2 **Chariton** *R* USA
73G2 **Charity** Guyana
42D3 **Charkhāri** India
13C2 **Charleroi** Belgium
57F3 **Charles,C** USA
64B3 **Charleston** Illinois, USA
63E1 **Charleston** Missouri, USA
57F3 **Charleston** S Carolina, USA
57E3 **Charleston** W Virginia, USA
59C3 **Charleston Peak** *Mt* USA
68B3 **Charles Town** USA
68D1 **Charlestown** USA
50C4 **Charlesville** Zaïre
32D3 **Charleville** Australia
14C2 **Charleville-Mézières** France
64B1 **Charlevoix** USA
64C2 **Charlotte** Michigan, USA
57E3 **Charlotte** N Carolina, USA
67B3 **Charlotte Harbor** *B* USA
57F3 **Charlottesville** USA
55M5 **Charlottetown** Canada
69K1 **Charlotteville** Tobago
34B3 **Charlton** Australia
57F1 **Charlton I** Canada
13D3 **Charmes** France
42C2 **Charsadda** Pakistan
32D3 **Charters Towers** Australia
14C2 **Chartres** France
74E5 **Chascomús** Argentina
28B2 **Chasong** N Korea
14B2 **Châteaubriant** France
14B2 **Châteaulin** France
13B4 **Châteauneuf-sur-Loire** France
14C2 **Châteauroux** France
13D3 **Château-Salins** France
14C2 **Château-Thierry** France
13C2 **Châtelet** Belgium
14C2 **Châtellerault** France
61E2 **Chatfield** USA
7F6 **Chatham** England
68E2 **Chatham** Massachusetts, USA
55M5 **Chatham** New Brunswick, Canada
68D1 **Chatham** New York, USA
64C2 **Chatham** Ontario, Canada
65D3 **Chatham** Virginia, USA
33H5 **Chatham Is** New Zealand
54E4 **Chatham Str** USA
14C2 **Châtillon** France
13B4 **Châtillon-Coligny** France
13C4 **Châtillon-sur-Seine** France
43E5 **Chatrapur** India
68C3 **Chatsworth** USA
67B2 **Chattahoochee** USA
67A2 **Chattahoochee** *R* USA
57E3 **Chattanooga** USA
30A1 **Chauk** Burma
43L2 **Chauka** *R* India
14D2 **Chaumont** France
13B3 **Chauny** France
30D3 **Chau Phu** Vietnam
44E4 **Chaura** *I* Nicobar Is, Indian Ocean
15A1 **Chaves** Portugal
20J4 **Chaykovskiy** Russian Federation
18C2 **Cheb** Czech Republic
20H4 **Cheboksary** Russian Federation
57E2 **Cheboygan** USA
19G2 **Chechersk** Belarus
28B3 **Chech'on** S Korea
63C1 **Checotah** USA
7C4 **Cheddar** England
30A2 **Cheduba I** Burma
34B1 **Cheepie** Australia
48B2 **Chegga** Mauritius
51D5 **Chegutu** Zimbabwe
58B1 **Chehalis** USA
28B4 **Cheju** S Korea
28B4 **Cheju Do** *I* S Korea
28B4 **Cheju Haehyŏp** *Str* S Korea
25P4 **Chekunda** Russian Federation
58B1 **Chelan,L** USA
21J8 **Cheleken** Turkmenistan
16B3 **Chélia, Dj** *Mt* Algeria
15C2 **Cheliff** *R* Algeria
38D1 **Chelkar** Kazakhstan
19E2 **Chełm** Poland
19D2 **Chełmno** Poland
7E4 **Chelmsford** England
7C4 **Cheltenham** England
20L4 **Chelyabinsk** Russian Federation
25M2 **Chelyuskin, Mys** *C* Russian Federation
51D5 **Chemba** Mozambique
18C2 **Chemnitz** Germ
68B1 **Chemung** *R* USA
42D2 **Chenab** *R* India/Pakistan
48B2 **Chenachen** Algeria
68C1 **Chenango** *R* USA
58C1 **Cheney** USA
63C1 **Cheney Res** USA
31D1 **Chengde** China
31A3 **Chengdu** China
31E2 **Chengshan Jiao** *Pt* China
28A3 **Chengzitan** China
31C4 **Chenxi** China
31C4 **Chen Xian** China
31D3 **Cheo Xian** China
72C5 **Chepén** Peru
7C4 **Chepstow** Wales
64A1 **Chequamegon B** USA
14C2 **Cher** *R* France
67C2 **Cheraw** USA
14B2 **Cherbourg** France
15C2 **Cherchell** Algeria
20K3 **Cherdyn** Russian Federation
25M4 **Cheremkhovo** Russian Federation
20F4 **Cherepovets** Russian Federation
21E6 **Cherkassy** Ukraine
21G7 **Cherkessk** Russian Federation
21E5 **Chernigov** Ukraine
19G2 **Chernobyl** Ukraine
21D6 **Chernovtsy** Ukraine
20K4 **Chernushka** Russian Federation
20C5 **Chernyakhovsk** Russian Federation
21H6 **Chernyye Zemli** *Region* Russian Federation
61D2 **Cherokee** Iowa, USA
62C1 **Cherokee** Oklahoma, USA
63D1 **Cherokees,L o'the** USA
43G3 **Cherrapunji** India
33F2 **Cherry** *I* Solomon Islands
25S3 **Cherskiy** Russian Federation
25Q3 **Cherskogo, Khrebet** *Mts* Russian Federation
20D5 **Cherven'** Belarus
19E2 **Chervonograd** Ukraine
65D3 **Chesapeake** USA
65D3 **Chesapeake B** USA
7D4 **Chesham** England
68D1 **Cheshire** USA
7C3 **Cheshire** *County* England
20H2 **Chëshskaya Guba** *B* Russian Federation
59B2 **Chester** California, USA
7C3 **Chester** England
64B3 **Chester** Illinois, USA
68D1 **Chester** Massachusets, USA
58D1 **Chester** Montana, USA
65D3 **Chester** Pennsylvania, USA
67B2 **Chester** S Carolina, USA
68D1 **Chester** Vermont, USA
68B3 **Chester** *R* USA
7D3 **Chesterfield** England
33E2 **Chesterfield, Îles** Nouvelle Calédonie
55J3 **Chesterfield Inlet** Canada
68B3 **Chestertown** USA
65F1 **Chesuncook L** USA
70D3 **Chetumal** Mexico
35B2 **Cheviot** New Zealand
10C2 **Cheviots** *Hills* England/Scotland
60C2 **Cheyenne** USA
60C2 **Cheyenne** *R* USA
60C3 **Cheyenne Wells** USA
43E3 **Chhapra** India
43G3 **Chhātak** Bangladesh
42D4 **Chhatarpur** India
42D4 **Chhindwāra** India
43F3 **Chhukha** Bhutan
51B5 **Chiange** Angola
30C2 **Chiang Kham** Thailand
30B2 **Chiang Mai** Thailand
31E5 **Chiayi** Taiwan
29E3 **Chiba** Japan
51B5 **Chibia** Angola
55L4 **Chibougamau** Canada
28B3 **Chiburi-jima** *I* Japan
47E1 **Chibuto** Mozambique
57E2 **Chicago** USA
64B2 **Chicago Heights** USA
54E4 **Chichagof I** USA
7D4 **Chichester** England
29C3 **Chichibu** Japan
26H4 **Chichi-jima** *I* Japan
57E3 **Chickamauga L** USA
63E2 **Chickasawhay** *R* USA
56D3 **Chickasha** USA
54D3 **Chicken** USA
72B5 **Chiclayo** Peru
56A3 **Chico** USA
74C6 **Chico** *R* Argentina
51D5 **Chicoa** Mozambique
65E2 **Chicopee** USA
55L5 **Chicoutimi** Canada
51D6 **Chicualacuala** Mozambique
44B3 **Chidambaram** India
55M3 **Chidley,C** Canada
67B3 **Chiefland** USA
48B4 **Chiehn** Liberia
51C4 **Chiengi** Zambia
13C3 **Chiers** *R* France
16C2 **Chieti** Italy
31D1 **Chifeng** China
73K7 **Chifre, Serra do** *Mts* Brazil
54C3 **Chigmit Mts** USA
47E1 **Chigubo** Mozambique
70B2 **Chihuahua** Mexico
62A3 **Chihuahua** *State* Mexico
44B3 **Chik Ballāpur** India
44B3 **Chikmagalūr** India
51D5 **Chikwawa** Malawi
30A1 **Chi-kyaw** Burma
44C2 **Chilakalūrupet** India
44B4 **Chilaw** Sri Lanka
34D1 **Childers** Australia
62B2 **Childress** USA
71C6 **Chile** *Republic* S America
51C5 **Chililabombwe** Zambia
43F5 **Chilka L** India
54F4 **Chilko L** Canada
74B5 **Chillán** Chile
61E3 **Chillicothe** Missouri, USA
64C3 **Chillicothe** Ohio, USA
43G3 **Chilmari** India
74B6 **Chiloé, Isla de** Chile
51D5 **Chilongozi** Zambia
58B2 **Chiloquin** USA
70C3 **Chilpancingo** Mexico
7D4 **Chiltern Hills** *Upland* England
64B2 **Chilton** USA
51D5 **Chilumba** Malawi
Chi-lung = Keelung
51D5 **Chilwa, L** Malawi
51D5 **Chimanimani** Zimbabwe
13C2 **Chimay** Belgium
24G5 **Chimbay** Uzbekistan
72C4 **Chimborazo** *Mt* Ecuador
72C5 **Chimbote** Peru
24H5 **Chimkent** Kazakhstan
51D5 **Chimoio** Mozambique
22F4 **China** *Republic* Asia
66D3 **China L** USA
66D3 **China Lake** USA
China, National Republic of = Taiwan
70D3 **Chinandega** Nicaragua
62B3 **Chinati Peak** *Mt* USA
72C6 **Chincha Alta** Peru
34D1 **Chinchilla** Australia
51D5 **Chinde** Mozambique
28A4 **Chindo** S Korea
43G4 **Chindwin** *R* Burma
51C5 **Chingola** Zambia
51B5 **Chinguar** Angola
48A2 **Chinguetti** Mauritius
28B3 **Chinhae** S Korea
51D5 **Chinhoyi** Zimbabwe
42C2 **Chiniot** Pakistan
28B3 **Chinju** S Korea
50C3 **Chinko** *R* Central African Republic
29C3 **Chino** Japan
51D5 **Chinsali** Zambia
16C1 **Chioggia** Italy
51D5 **Chipata** Zambia
51D6 **Chipinge** Zimbabwe
44A2 **Chiplūn** India
7C4 **Chippenham** England
64A1 **Chippewa** *R* USA
57D2 **Chippewa Falls** USA
64A1 **Chippewa,L** USA
7D4 **Chipping Norton** England
7C4 **Chipping Sodbury** England
72B4 **Chira** *R* Peru
44C2 **Chīrāla** India
51D6 **Chiredzi** Zimbabwe
50B1 **Chirfa** Niger
59E4 **Chiricahua Peak** *Mt* USA
70D4 **Chiriquí, G de** Panama
72B2 **Chiriquí, Lago de** Panama
17F2 **Chirpan** Bulgaria
72B2 **Chirripó Grande** *Mt* Costa Rica
51C5 **Chirundu** Zimbabwe
51C5 **Chisamba** Zambia
55L4 **Chisasibi** Canada

61E1 **Chisholm** USA
31B4 **Chishui He** *R* China
Chisimaio = Kismaayo
Chişinău = Kishinev
20H4 **Chistopol** Russian Federation
26E1 **Chita** Russian Federation
51B5 **Chitado** Angola
51B5 **Chitembo** Angola
29D2 **Chitose** Japan
44B3 **Chitradurga** India
42C1 **Chitral** Pakistan
72B2 **Chitré** Panama
43G4 **Chittagong** Bangladesh
42C4 **Chittaurgarh** India
44B3 **Chittoor** India
51C5 **Chiume** Angola
74D4 **Chivilcoy** Argentina
51D5 **Chivu** Zimbabwe
29B3 **Chizu** Japan
28A3 **Choch'iwŏn** S Korea
72D2 **Chocontá** Colombia
28A4 **Ch'o-do** *I* S Korea
74C5 **Choele Choel** Argentina
33E1 **Choiseul** *I* Solomon Islands
70B2 **Choix** Mexico
19D2 **Chojnice** Poland
29D3 **Chokai-san** *Mt* Japan
50D2 **Choke Mts** Ethiopia
25Q2 **Chokurdakh** Russian Federation
66B3 **Cholame** USA
66B3 **Cholame Creek** *R* USA
14B2 **Cholet** France
72A1 **Choluteca** Honduras
51C5 **Choma** Zambia
28A3 **Chŏmch'ŏn** S Korea
43F3 **Chomo Yummo** *Mt* China/India
18C2 **Chomutov** Czech Republic
25M3 **Chona** *R* Russian Federation
28B3 **Ch'ŏnan** S Korea
30C3 **Chon Buri** Thailand
28A2 **Chonchon** N Korea
72C4 **Chone** Ecuador
74B6 **Chones, Archipiélago de las** Chile
28A3 **Chongdo** S Korea
28B2 **Ch'ŏngjin** N Korea
28B3 **Chŏngju** N Korea
28B3 **Ch'ŏngju** S Korea
51B5 **Chongoroi** Angola
28A3 **Chongpyong** N Korea
31B4 **Chongqing** China
28A3 **Chŏngsŏn** S Korea
28B3 **Chŏngŭp** S Korea
28B3 **Ch'ŏnju** S Korea
43F3 **Cho Oyu** *Mt* China/Nepal
75B4 **Chopim** *R* Brazil
6C3 **Chorley** England
19F3 **Chortkov** Ukraine
28B3 **Ch'ŏrwŏn** S Korea
19D2 **Chorzów** Poland
28A2 **Chosan** N Korea
29E3 **Chōshi** Japan
18D2 **Choszczno** Poland
43E4 **Chotanāgpur** *Region* India
58D1 **Choteau** USA
48C1 **Chott ech Chergui** *L* Algeria
15C2 **Chott El Hodna** *L* Algeria
48C1 **Chott Melrhir** *L* Algeria
66B2 **Chowchilla** USA
25N5 **Choybalsan** Mongolia
7D4 **Christchurch** England
35B2 **Christchurch** New Zealand
47D2 **Christiana** South Africa
55M2 **Christian,C** Canada
55N3 **Christianshåb** Greenland
27D8 **Christmas I** Indian Ocean
24J5 **Chu** Kazakhstan
24J5 **Chu** *R* Kazakhstan
58D2 **Chubbuck** USA
74C6 **Chubut** *R* Argentina
74C6 **Chubut** *State* Argentina
20E4 **Chudovo** Russian Federation
54D3 **Chugach Mts** USA
28B3 **Chūgoku-sanchi** *Mts* Japan
60C2 **Chugwater** USA
74F4 **Chui** Uruguay
30C5 **Chukai** Malaysia
26G1 **Chukchagirskoye, Ozero** *L* Russian Federation
25T3 **Chukotskiy Khrebet** *Mts* Russian Federation
25U3 **Chukotskiy Poluostrov** *Pen* Russian Federation
30D2 **Chu Lai** Vietnam
59C4 **Chula Vista** USA
26F1 **Chulman** Russian Federation
72B5 **Chulucanas** Peru
72E7 **Chulumani** Bolivia
24K4 **Chulym** Russian Federation
25K4 **Chulym** *R* Russian Federation
25L4 **Chuma** *R* Russian Federation
42D2 **Chumar** India
25P4 **Chumikan** Russian Federation
30B3 **Chumphon** Thailand
28B3 **Ch'unch'ŏn** S Korea
43F4 **Chunchura** India
28B3 **Ch'ungju** S Korea
Chungking = Chongqing
28A4 **Ch'ungmu** S Korea
28B3 **Chŭngsan** N Korea
28A3 **Chungwa** N Korea
28C2 **Chunhua** China
51D4 **Chunya** Tanzania
25M3 **Chunya** *R* Russian Federation
28B2 **Chunyang** China
28A3 **Ch'unyang** S Korea
69L1 **Chupara Pt** Trinidad
74C2 **Chuquicamata** Chile
16B1 **Chur** Switzerland
43G4 **Churāchāndpur** India
25P3 **Churapcha** Russian Federation
55J4 **Churchill** Canada
55M4 **Churchill** *R* Labrador, Canada
55J4 **Churchill** *R* Manitoba, Canada
55J4 **Churchill,C** Canada
55M4 **Churchill Falls** Canada
54H4 **Churchill L** Canada
42C3 **Chūru** India
20K4 **Chusovoy** Russian Federation
20H4 **Chuvash Republic** Russian Federation
26D4 **Chuxiong** China
30D3 **Chu Yang Sin** *Mt* Vietnam
75B3 **Cianorte** Brazil
19E2 **Ciechanów** Poland
70E2 **Ciego de Ávila** Cuba
72D1 **Ciénaga** Colombia
70D2 **Cienfuegos** Cuba
19D3 **Cieszyn** Poland
15B2 **Cieza** Spain
40B2 **Cihanbeyli** Turkey
15B2 **Cijara, Embalse de** *Res* Spain
27D7 **Cilacap** Indonesia
62B1 **Cimarron** USA
62C1 **Cimarron** *R* USA
16C2 **Cimone, Monte** *Mt* Italy
17F1 **Cîmpina** Romania
15C1 **Cinca** *R* Spain
16D2 **Cincer** *Mt* Bosnia-Herzegovina
57E3 **Cincinnati** USA
17E1 **Cindrelu** *Mt* Romania
17F3 **Cine** *R* Turkey
13C2 **Ciney** Belgium
16B2 **Cinto, Monte** *Mt* Corsica, France
54D3 **Circle** Alaska, USA
60B1 **Circle** Montana, USA
64C3 **Circleville** USA
27D7 **Cirebon** Indonesia
7D4 **Cirencester** England
62C2 **Cisco** USA
70C3 **Citlaltepetl** *Vol* Mexico
47B3 **Citrusdal** South Africa
70B2 **Ciudad Acuña** Mexico
72F2 **Ciudad Bolívar** Venezuela
70B2 **Ciudad Camargo** Mexico
70C3 **Ciudad del Carmen** Mexico
15C2 **Ciudadela** Spain
72F2 **Ciudad Guayana** Venezuela
70B3 **Ciudad Guzman** Mexico
70B1 **Ciudad Juárez** Mexico
56C4 **Ciudad Lerdo** Mexico
70C2 **Ciudad Madero** Mexico
70B2 **Ciudad Obregon** Mexico
69C4 **Ciudad Ojeda** Venezuela
72F2 **Ciudad Piar** Venezuela
15B2 **Ciudad Real** Spain
15A1 **Ciudad Rodrigo** Spain
70C2 **Ciudad Valles** Mexico
70C2 **Ciudad Victoria** Mexico
16C2 **Civitavecchia** Italy
40D2 **Cizre** Turkey
7E4 **Clacton-on-Sea** England
54G4 **Claire,L** Canada
65D2 **Clairton** USA
67A2 **Clanton** USA
47B3 **Clanwilliam** South Africa
9C3 **Clara** Irish Republic
64C2 **Clare** USA
65E2 **Claremont** USA
63C1 **Claremore** USA
34D1 **Clarence** *R* Australia
35B2 **Clarence** *R* New Zealand
32C2 **Clarence Str** Australia
63D2 **Clarendon** USA
55N5 **Clarenville** Canada
54G4 **Claresholm** Canada
61D2 **Clarinda** USA
61E2 **Clarion** Iowa, USA
65D2 **Clarion** Pennsylvania, USA
70A3 **Clarión** *I* Mexico
65D2 **Clarion** *R* USA
37M4 **Clarion Fracture Zone** Pacific Ocean
57E3 **Clark Hill Res** USA
59C3 **Clark Mt** USA
64C2 **Clark,Pt** Canada
64C3 **Clarksburg** USA
57D3 **Clarksdale** USA
58C1 **Clarkston** USA
63D1 **Clarksville** Arkansas, USA
67A1 **Clarksville** Tennessee, USA
75B2 **Claro** *R* Brazil
74E5 **Claromecó** Argentina
61D3 **Clay Center** USA
8E2 **Claymore** *Oilfield* N Sea
56C3 **Clayton** New Mexico, USA
65D2 **Clayton** New York, USA
10B3 **Clear, C** Irish Republic
68A2 **Clearfield** Pennsylvania, USA
58D2 **Clearfield** Utah, USA
59B3 **Clear L** USA
61E2 **Clear Lake** USA
58B2 **Clear Lake Res** USA
60B2 **Clearmont** USA
57E4 **Clearwater** USA
58C1 **Clearwater Mts** USA
56D3 **Cleburne** USA
7D3 **Cleethorpes** England
6E2 **Cleeton** *Oilfield* N Sea
66B1 **Clements** USA
32D3 **Clermont** Australia
13B3 **Clermont** France
13C3 **Clermont-en-Argonne** France
14C2 **Clermont-Ferrand** France
13D2 **Clervaux** Luxembourg
63D2 **Cleveland** Mississippi, USA
57E2 **Cleveland** Ohio, USA
67B1 **Cleveland** Tennessee, USA
63C2 **Cleveland** Texas, USA
6D2 **Cleveland** *County* England
75B4 **Clevelândia** Brazil
58D1 **Cleveland,Mt** USA
10B3 **Clew B** Irish Republic
59E4 **Clifton** Arizona, USA
34D1 **Clifton** Australia
68C2 **Clifton** New Jersey, USA
34A1 **Clifton Hills** Australia
67B1 **Clinch** *R* USA
67B1 **Clinch Mts** USA
63D1 **Clinton** Arkansas, USA
54F4 **Clinton** Canada
68D2 **Clinton** Connecticut, USA
64A2 **Clinton** Iowa, USA
68E1 **Clinton** Massachusetts, USA
63D2 **Clinton** Mississippi, USA
63D1 **Clinton** Missouri, USA
67C2 **Clinton** N Carolina, USA
68C2 **Clinton** New Jersey, USA
62C1 **Clinton** Oklahoma, USA
54H3 **Clinton-Colden L** Canada
70B3 **Clipperton I** Pacific Ocean
6C3 **Clitheroe** England
72E7 **Cliza** Bolivia
9C3 **Clogher Hd** *Pt* Irish Republic
9B4 **Clonakilty B** Irish Republic
32D3 **Cloncurry** Australia
9C3 **Clones** Irish Republic
9C3 **Clonmel** Irish Republic
13E1 **Cloppenburg** Germany
57D2 **Cloquet** USA
75A4 **Clorinda** Argentina
60B2 **Cloud Peak** *Mt* USA
66A1 **Cloverdale** USA
66C2 **Clovis** California, USA
56C3 **Clovis** New Mexico, USA
21C6 **Cluj** Romania
17E1 **Cluj-Napoca** Romania
35A3 **Clutha** *R* New Zealand
7C3 **Clwyd** *County* Wales
7C3 **Clwyd** *R* Wales
55M2 **Clyde** Canada
35A3 **Clyde** New Zealand
6F1 **Clyde** *Oilfield* N Sea
68B1 **Clyde** USA
8C4 **Clyde** *R* Scotland
8C4 **Clydebank** Scotland
59C4 **Coachella** USA
62B3 **Coahuila** *State* Mexico
59C3 **Coaldale** USA
59B3 **Coalinga** USA
7D3 **Coalville** England
58D2 **Coalville** USA
75E1 **Coaraci** Brazil
72F5 **Coari** *R* Brazil
67A2 **Coastal Plain** USA
54E4 **Coast Mts** Canada
56A2 **Coast Ranges** *Mts* USA
8C4 **Coatbridge** Scotland
68C3 **Coatesville** USA
65E1 **Coaticook** Canada
55K3 **Coats I** Canada
76F1 **Coats Land** *Region* Antarctica
70C3 **Coatzacoalcas** Mexico
55L5 **Cobalt** Canada
70C3 **Cobán** Guatemala
32D4 **Cobar** Australia
34C3 **Cobargo** Australia
72E6 **Cobija** Bolivia
68C1 **Cobleskill** USA
55L5 **Cobourg** Canada
32C2 **Cobourg Pen** Australia
18C2 **Coburg** Germany
72C4 **Coca** Ecuador
75B1 **Cocalinho** Brazil
72E7 **Cochabamba** Bolivia
13D2 **Cochem** Germany
55K5 **Cochrane** Ontario, Canada
74B7 **Cochrane, Lago** Argentina/Chile
34B2 **Cockburn** Australia
6C2 **Cockermouth** England
68B3 **Cockeysville** USA
69H1 **Cockpit Country,The** Jamaica
47C3 **Cockscomb** *Mt* South Africa
70D3 **Coco** *R* Honduras/Nicaragua
67B3 **Cocoa** USA
48C4 **Cocobeach** Equatorial Guinea
44E3 **Coco Channel** Andaman Is/Burma
53K8 **Coco, Isla del** Costa Rica
75D1 **Côcos** Brazil
69L1 **Cocos B** Trinidad
27C8 **Cocos Is** Indian Ocean
37P4 **Cocos Ridge** Pacific Ocean
57F2 **Cod,C** USA
35A3 **Codfish I** New Zealand
55M4 **Cod I** Canada
15C1 **Codi, Sierra del** *Mts* Spain
73K4 **Codó** Brazil
56C2 **Cody** USA
27H8 **Coen** Australia
18C2 **Coesfeld** Germany
56B2 **Coeur d'Alene** USA
58C1 **Coeur d'Alene L** USA
13D1 **Coevorden** Netherlands
56D3 **Coffeyville** USA
34D2 **Coff's Harbour** Australia
47D3 **Cofimvaba** South Africa
16B2 **Coghinas, Lago del** Sardinia, Italy
14B2 **Cognac** France
68B1 **Cohocton** USA
68B1 **Cohocton** *R* USA
65E2 **Cohoes** USA
34B3 **Cohuna** Australia
72B2 **Coiba, Isla** Panama
74B7 **Coihaique** Chile
44B3 **Coimbatore** India
15A1 **Coimbra** Portugal
72B3 **Cojimies** Ecuador
58D2 **Cokeville** USA
32D4 **Colac** Australia
73K7 **Colatina** Brazil
76F6 **Colbeck,C** Antarctica
14B2 **Colby** USA
7E4 **Colchester** England
68D2 **Colchester** USA
8D4 **Coldstream** Scotland
64C2 **Coldwater** USA
58D1 **Coleman** Canada
64C2 **Coleman** Michigan, USA
62C2 **Coleman** Texas, USA
47D2 **Colenso** South Africa
9C2 **Coleraine** Northern Ireland
35B2 **Coleridge,L** New Zealand
47D3 **Colesberg** South Africa
72D7 **Coles, Puerta** Peru
66C1 **Coleville** USA
59B3 **Colfax** California, USA
63D2 **Colfax** Louisiana, USA
58C1 **Colfax** Washington, USA
74C7 **Colhué Huapí, Lago** Argentina
70B3 **Colima** Mexico
8B3 **Coll** *I* Scotland
34C1 **Collarenebri** Australia
67B2 **College Park** Georgia, USA
68B3 **College Park** Washington DC, USA
63C2 **College Station** USA
32A4 **Collie** Australia
32B2 **Collier B** Australia
13A2 **Collines de l'Artois** *Hills* France
13B3 **Collines de la Thiérache** *Hills* France
64C2 **Collingwood** Canada
35B2 **Collingwood** New Zealand
63E2 **Collins** Mississippi, USA
68A1 **Collins** New York, USA
54H2 **Collinson Pen** Canada
32D3 **Collinsville** Australia
64B3 **Collinsville** Illinois, USA
63C1 **Collinsville** Oklahoma, USA
14D2 **Colmar** France
6C3 **Colne** England
56B3 **Colnett, Cabo** *C* Mexico
18B2 **Cologne** Germany
75C3 **Colômbia** Brazil
65D3 **Colombia** USA
72D3 **Colombia** *Republic* S America
44B4 **Colombo** Sri Lanka
74E4 **Colón** Argentina
70D2 **Colon** Cuba
72C2 **Colón** Panama
Colón, Arch. de = Galapagos Islands
74E4 **Colonia** Uruguay
74C7 **Colonia Las Heras** Argentina
65D3 **Colonial Heights** USA
8B3 **Colonsay** *I* Scotland
69E5 **Coloradito** Venezuela
74D5 **Colorado** *R* Buenos Aires, Argentina
56D3 **Colorado** *R* Texas, USA
56B3 **Colorado** *R* Mexico/USA
56C3 **Colorado** *State* USA
62B2 **Colorado City** USA
56B3 **Colorado Plat** USA
56C3 **Colorado Springs** USA
68B3 **Columbia** Maryland, USA
63E2 **Columbia** Mississippi, USA
57D3 **Columbia** Missouri, USA
65D2 **Columbia** Pennsylvania, USA
57E3 **Columbia** S Carolina, USA
57E3 **Columbia** Tennessee, USA
56A2 **Columbia** *R* USA
58D1 **Columbia Falls** USA
54G4 **Columbia,Mt** Canada
58C1 **Columbia Plat** USA
47B3 **Columbine,C** South Africa
15C2 **Columbretes, Islas** Spain
57E3 **Columbus** Georgia, USA
64B3 **Columbus** Indiana, USA
57E3 **Columbus** Mississippi, USA
58E1 **Columbus** Montana, USA
56D2 **Columbus** Nebraska, USA
62A2 **Columbus** New Mexico, USA
57E2 **Columbus** Ohio, USA
63C3 **Columbus** Texas, USA
64B2 **Columbus** Wisconsin, USA
58C1 **Colville** USA
54C3 **Colville** *R* USA
35C1 **Colville,C** New Zealand
54F3 **Colville L** Canada
7C3 **Colwyn Bay** Wales
62C2 **Comanche** USA
66B1 **Comanche Res** USA
76G2 **Comandante Ferraz** *Base* Antarctica
70D3 **Comayagua** Honduras
13C4 **Combeaufontaine** France
9D2 **Comber** Northern Ireland
43G5 **Combermere B** Burma
9C3 **Comeragh Mts** Irish Republic
62C2 **Comfort** USA
43G4 **Comilla** Bangladesh
70C3 **Comitán** Mexico
13C3 **Commercy** France
55K3 **Committee B** Canada
16B1 **Como** Italy
74C7 **Comodoro Rivadavia** Argentina
16B1 **Como, L di** Italy
44B4 **Comorin,C** India
51E5 **Comoros** *Is, Republic* Indian Ocean
14C2 **Compiègne** France
75C3 **Comprida, Ilha** Brazil
15B2 **Comunidad Valenciana** *Region* Spain
43G3 **Cona** China
48A4 **Conakry** Guinea
14B2 **Concarneau** France
75E2 **Conceiçao da Barra** Brazil
73J5 **Conceição do Araguaia** Brazil
75D2 **Conceiçao do Mato Dentro** Brazil
74E4 **Concepción** Argentina
75A3 **Concepción** Brazil/Paraguay
74B5 **Concepción** Chile
74E2 **Concepción** Paraguay
70B2 **Concepción del Oro** Mexico
47A1 **Conception B** Namibia
56A3 **Conception,Pt** USA
75C3 **Conchas** Brazil
62B1 **Conchas L** USA
56C4 **Conchos** *R* Mexico
59B3 **Concord** California, USA
57F2 **Concord** New Hampshire, USA
67B1 **Concord** North Carolina, USA
74E4 **Concordia** Argentina
56D3 **Concordia** USA
58B1 **Concrete** USA

34D1 **Condamine** Australia
75D1 **Condeuba** Brazil
32D4 **Condobolin** Australia
58B1 **Condon** USA
13C2 **Condroz** *Mts* Belgium
67A2 **Conecuh** *R* USA
68B1 **Conesus L** USA
75A3 **Confuso** *R* Paraguay
7C3 **Congleton** England
46F8 **Congo** *R* W Africa
46F8 **Congo** *Republic* Africa
Congo,R = Zaire
64C1 **Coniston** Canada
64C2 **Conneaut** USA
65E2 **Connecticut** *R* USA
57F2 **Connecticut** *State* USA
65D2 **Connellsville** USA
64B3 **Connersville** USA
10B3 **Conn, Lough** *L* Irish Republic
34B2 **Conoble** Australia
58D1 **Conrad** USA
63C2 **Conroe** USA
75D3 **Conselheiro Lafaiete** Brazil
6D2 **Consett** England
30D4 **Con Son** *Is* Vietnam
21D7 **Constanța** Romania
16B3 **Constantine** Algeria
74B5 **Constitución** Chile
58D2 **Contact** USA
73K6 **Contas** *R* Brazil
13C3 **Contrexéville** France
54H3 **Contwoyto L** Canada
57D3 **Conway** Arkansas, USA
65E2 **Conway** New Hampshire, USA
67C2 **Conway** South Carolina, USA
7C3 **Conwy** Wales
7C3 **Conwy** *R* Wales
32C3 **Coober Pedy** Australia
67A1 **Cookeville** USA
54C3 **Cook Inlet** *B* USA
37L5 **Cook Is** Pacific Ocean
35B2 **Cook,Mt** New Zealand
9C2 **Cookstown** Northern Ireland
33G5 **Cook Str** New Zealand
32D2 **Cooktown** Australia
34C2 **Coolabah** Australia
34C1 **Cooladdi** Australia
34C2 **Coolah** Australia
34C2 **Coolamon** Australia
32B4 **Coolgardie** Australia
59D4 **Coolidge** USA
34C3 **Cooma** Australia
34C2 **Coonabarabran** Australia
34C2 **Coonambie** Australia
34B2 **Coonbah** Australia
44A3 **Coondapoor** India
34C1 **Coongoola** Australia
44B3 **Coonoor** India
34B1 **Cooper Basin** Australia
32C3 **Cooper Creek** Australia
34B1 **Cooper Creek** *R* Australia
67C3 **Cooper's Town** Bahamas
68C1 **Cooperstown** New York, USA
61D1 **Cooperstown** North Dakota, USA
34A3 **Coorong,The** Australia
34D1 **Cooroy** Australia
58B2 **Coos B** USA
58B2 **Coos Bay** USA
32D4 **Cootamundra** Australia
9C2 **Cootehill** Irish Republic
60C3 **Cope** USA
18C1 **Copenhagen** Denmark
74B3 **Copiapó** Chile
54D3 **Copper Center** USA
64C1 **Copper Cliff** Canada
64B1 **Copper Harbor** USA
54G3 **Coppermine** Canada
54G3 **Coppermine** *R* Canada
64C1 **Coppermine Pt** Canada
Coquilhatville = Mbandaka
74B3 **Coquimbo** Chile
17E2 **Corabia** Romania
67B3 **Coral Gables** USA
55K3 **Coral Harbour** Canada
32E2 **Coral S** Australia/Papua New Guinea
36J5 **Coral Sea Basin** Pacific Ocean
32E2 **Coral Sea Island Territories** Australia
34B3 **Corangamite,L** Australia
73G3 **Corantijn** *R* Guyana/Surinam
13B3 **Corbeil-Essonnes** France
64C3 **Corbin** USA
6D2 **Corbridge** England
7D3 **Corby** England
66C2 **Corcoran** USA
74B6 **Corcovado, Golfo** *G* Chile
15A1 **Corcubíon** Spain
57E3 **Cordele** USA
15A1 **Cordillera Cantabrica** *Mts* Spain
69C3 **Cordillera Central** *Mts* Dominican Republic/Haiti
75A4 **Cordillera de Caaguazú** Paraguay
70D3 **Cordillera Isabelia** *Mts* Nicaragua
72C2 **Cordillera Occidental** *Mts* Colombia
72C3 **Cordillera Oriental** *Mts* Colombia
34B1 **Cordillo Downs** Australia
74D4 **Córdoba** Argentina
70C3 **Córdoba** Mexico
15B2 **Córdoba** Spain
74D4 **Córdoba** *State* Argentina
54D3 **Cordova** USA
17D3 **Corfu** Greece
17D3 **Corfu** *I* Greece
75D1 **Coribe** Brazil
34D2 **Coricudgy,Mt** Australia
16D3 **Corigliano Calabro** Italy
32E2 **Coringa Is** Australia
17E3 **Corinth** Greece
57E3 **Corinth** Mississippi, USA
68D1 **Corinth** New York, USA
17E3 **Corinth, Gulf of** Greece
73K7 **Corinto** Brazil
10B3 **Cork** Irish Republic
40A1 **Çorlu** Turkey
73K7 **Cornel Fabriciano** Brazil
75B3 **Cornélio Procópio** Brazil
55N5 **Corner Brook** Canada
34C3 **Corner Inlet** *B* Australia
13D4 **Cornimont** France
65D2 **Corning** USA
16C2 **Corno, Monte** *Mt* Italy
55L5 **Cornwall** Canada
7B4 **Cornwall** *County* England
7B4 **Cornwall,C** England
54H2 **Cornwall I** Canada
55J2 **Cornwallis I** Canada
72E1 **Coro** Venezuela
73K4 **Coroatá** Brazil
72E7 **Coroico** Bolivia
75C2 **Coromandel** Brazil
44C3 **Coromandel Coast** India
35C1 **Coromandel Pen** New Zealand
35C1 **Coromandel Range** *Mts* New Zealand
66D4 **Corona** California, USA
62A2 **Corona** New Mexico, USA
72B2 **Coronado, B. de** Costa Rica
54G3 **Coronation G** Canada
74B5 **Coronel** Chile
75D2 **Coronel Fabriciano** Brazil
74E3 **Coronel Oviedo** Paraguay
74D5 **Coronel Pringles** Argentina
72D7 **Coropuna** *Mt* Peru
34C3 **Corowa** Australia
14D3 **Corps** France
56D4 **Corpus Christi** USA
63C3 **Corpus Christi,L** USA
9B3 **Corraun Pen** Irish Republic
27F5 **Corregidor** *I* Philippines
75D1 **Corrente** *R* Bahia, Brazil
75C1 **Corrente** *R* Goias, Brazil
75B2 **Corrente** *R* Mato Grosso, Brazil
75D1 **Correntina** Brazil
10B3 **Corrib, Lough** *L* Irish Republic
74E3 **Corrientes** Argentina
74E3 **Corrientes** *State* Argentina
72C2 **Corrientes, Cabo** *C* Colombia
70B2 **Corrientes, Cabo** *C* Mexico
63D2 **Corrigan** USA
32A4 **Corrigin** Australia
34C3 **Corryong** Australia
Corse = Corsica
8C4 **Corsewall Pt** Scotland
16B2 **Corsica** *I* Medit Sea
56D3 **Corsicana** USA
55O3 **Cort Adelaer, Kap** *C* Greenland
16B2 **Corte** Corsica, France
56C3 **Cortez** USA
16C1 **Cortina d'Ampezzo** Italy
65D2 **Cortland** USA
21G7 **Çoruh** *R* Turkey
21F7 **Çorum** Turkey
73G7 **Corumbá** Brazil
75C2 **Corumbá** *R* Brazil
75C2 **Corumbaiba** Brazil
58B2 **Corvallis** USA
48A1 **Corvo** *I* Azores
7C3 **Corwen** Wales
16D3 **Cosenza** Italy
51E5 **Cosmoledo Is** Seychelles
66D2 **Coso Junction** USA
15B2 **Costa Blanca** *Region* Spain
15C1 **Costa Brava** *Region* Spain
15B2 **Costa Calída** *Region* Spain
15B2 **Costa de Almería** *Region* Spain
15A2 **Costa de la Luz** *Region* Spain
15B2 **Costa del Sol** *Region* Spain
15C1 **Costa Dorada** *Region* Spain
66D4 **Costa Mesa** USA
70D3 **Costa Rica** *Republic* Central America
27F6 **Cotabato** Philippines
72E8 **Cotagaita** Bolivia
14D3 **Côte d'Azur** *Region* France
Côte D'Ivoire = Ivory Coast
13C4 **Côte-d'Or** *Department* France
13C3 **Côtes de Meuse** *Mts* France
7B4 **Cothi** *R* Wales
48C4 **Cotonou** Benin
72C4 **Cotopaxi** *Mt* Ecuador
7C4 **Cotswold Hills** *Upland* England
58B2 **Cottage Grove** USA
18C2 **Cottbus** Germany
59D4 **Cottonwood** USA
62C3 **Cotulla** USA
68A2 **Coudersport** USA
13B3 **Coulommiers** France
65D1 **Coulonge** *R* Canada
66B2 **Coulterville** USA
54B3 **Council** USA
56D2 **Council Bluffs** USA
8D3 **Coupar Angus** Scotland
19E1 **Courland Lagoon** *Lg* Lithuania/Russian Federation
Courtrai = Kortrijk
14B2 **Coutances** France
7D3 **Coventry** England
15A1 **Covilhã** Portugal
67B2 **Covington** Georgia, USA
64C3 **Covington** Kentucky, USA
63D2 **Covington** Louisiana, USA
65D3 **Covington** Virginia, USA
34C2 **Cowal,L** Australia
34B3 **Cowangie** Australia
65E1 **Cowansville** Canada
8D3 **Cowdenbeath** Scotland
34C3 **Cowes** Australia
7D4 **Cowes** England
58B1 **Cowichan L** Canada
58B1 **Cowlitz** *R* USA
34C2 **Cowra** Australia
73H7 **Coxim** Brazil
75B2 **Coxim** *R* Brazil
68D1 **Coxsackie** USA
43G4 **Cox's Bazar** Bangladesh
66B2 **Coyote** USA
60D2 **Cozad** USA
70D2 **Cozumel, Isla de** Mexico
34D1 **Cracow** Australia
19D2 **Cracow** Poland
47D3 **Cradock** South Africa
56C2 **Craig** USA
9C2 **Craigavon** Northern Ireland
18C3 **Crailsheim** Germany
17E2 **Craiova** Romania
65E2 **Cranberry L** USA
54G5 **Cranbrook** Canada
58C2 **Crane** Oregon, USA
62B2 **Crane** Texas, USA
68E2 **Cranston** USA
58B2 **Crater L** USA
58B2 **Crater Lake Nat Pk** USA
73K5 **Crateús** Brazil
73L5 **Crato** Brazil
60C2 **Crawford** USA
64B2 **Crawfordsville** USA
67B2 **Crawfordville** USA
7D4 **Crawley** England
58D1 **Crazy Mts** USA
7C4 **Crediton** England
54H4 **Cree L** Canada
13B3 **Creil** France
16C1 **Cremona** Italy
13B3 **Crépy-en-Valois** France
16C2 **Cres** *I* Croatia
58B2 **Crescent** USA
56A2 **Crescent City** USA
61E2 **Cresco** USA
61E2 **Creston** USA
67A2 **Crestview** USA
34B3 **Creswick** Australia
61D2 **Crete** USA
17E3 **Crete** *I* Greece
17E3 **Crete,S of** Greece
15C1 **Creus, Cabo de** *C* Spain
14C2 **Creuse** *R* France
7C3 **Crewe** England
8C3 **Crianlarich** Scotland
7B3 **Criccieth** Wales
74G3 **Criciuma** Brazil
8D3 **Crieff** Scotland
21E6 **Crimea** *Pen* Ukraine
75C2 **Cristalina** Brazil
75B1 **Cristalina** *R* Brazil
75C1 **Crixás** Brazil
75C1 **Crixás Acu** *R* Brazil
75B1 **Crixás Mirim** *R* Brazil
16D1 **Croatia** *Republic* Europe
63C2 **Crockett** USA
61D2 **Crofton** USA
32C2 **Croker I** Australia
8D3 **Cromarty** Scotland
7E3 **Cromer** England
35A3 **Cromwell** New Zealand
6D2 **Crook** England
57F4 **Crooked** *I* The Bahamas
56D2 **Crookston** USA
34C2 **Crookwell** Australia
34D1 **Croppa Creek** Australia
7C3 **Crosby** England
61E1 **Crosby** USA
47A1 **Cross,C** Namibia
57D3 **Crossett** USA
54E4 **Cross Sd** USA
67A1 **Crossville** USA
16D3 **Crotone** Italy
63D2 **Crowley** USA
66C2 **Crowley,L** USA
69K1 **Crown Pt** Tobago
34D1 **Crows Nest** Australia
32D2 **Croydon** Australia
7D4 **Croydon** England
36E6 **Crozet Basin** Indian Ocean
36D7 **Crozet, Îles** *Is* Indian Ocean
54F2 **Crozier Chan** Canada
74F3 **Cruz Alta** Brazil
69B3 **Cruz, Cabo** *C* Cuba
74D4 **Cruz del Eje** Argentina
75D3 **Cruzeiro** Brazil
72D5 **Cruzeiro do Sul** Brazil
34A2 **Crystal Brook** Australia
63D1 **Crystal City** Missouri, USA
62C3 **Crystal City** Texas, USA
64B1 **Crystal Falls** USA
51D5 **Cuamba** Mozambique
51C5 **Cuando** *R* Angola
51B5 **Cuangar** Angola
Cuango,R = Kwango,R
70B2 **Cuauhtémoc** Mexico
68A1 **Cuba** USA
70D2 **Cuba** *Republic* Caribbean Sea
51B5 **Cubango** *R* Angola
51B5 **Cuchi** Angola
51B5 **Cuchi** *R* Angola
7D4 **Cuckfield** England
72E3 **Cucuí** Brazil
72D2 **Cúcuta** Colombia
44B3 **Cuddalore** India
44B3 **Cuddapah** India
66D3 **Cuddeback L** USA
32A3 **Cue** Australia
72C4 **Cuenca** Ecuador
15B1 **Cuenca** Spain
70C3 **Cuernavaca** Mexico
63C3 **Cuero** USA
73G7 **Cuiabá** Brazil
75A1 **Cuiabá** *R* Brazil
75D2 **Cuieté** *R* Brazil
8B3 **Cuillin Hills** Scotland
51B4 **Cuilo** *R* Angola/Zaïre
51B5 **Cuito** *R* Angola
51B5 **Cuito Cuanavale** Angola
30D3 **Cu Lao Hon** *I* Vietnam
60C1 **Culbertson** Montana, USA
60C2 **Culbertson** Nebraska, USA
34C3 **Culcairn** Australia
34C1 **Culgoa** *R* Australia
70B2 **Culiacán** Mexico
67A2 **Cullman** USA
65D3 **Culpeper** USA
75B1 **Culuene** *R* Brazil
35B2 **Culverden** New Zealand
72F1 **Cumaná** Venezuela
57F3 **Cumberland** Maryland, USA
64A1 **Cumberland** Wisconsin, USA
57E3 **Cumberland** *R* USA
55M3 **Cumberland Pen** Canada
64C3 **Cumberland Plat** USA
55M3 **Cumberland Sd** Canada
8C4 **Cumbernauld** Scotland
6C2 **Cumbria** *County* England
59B3 **Cummings** USA
8C4 **Cumnock** Scotland
51B5 **Cunene** *R* Angola/Namibia
16B2 **Cuneo** Italy
32D3 **Cunnamulla** Australia
8D3 **Cupar** Scotland
17E2 **Ćuprija** Serbia, Yugoslavia
69D4 **Curaçao** *I* Caribbean Sea
74B4 **Curicó** Chile
75B1 **Curisevo** *R* Brazil
74G3 **Curitiba** Brazil
34A2 **Curnamona** Australia
51B5 **Curoca** *R* Angola
73K7 **Curvelo** Brazil
68A2 **Curwensville** USA
63C1 **Cushing** USA
58E1 **Custer** Montana, USA
60C2 **Custer** S Dakota, USA
58D1 **Cut Bank** USA
67B2 **Cuthbert** USA
67B3 **Cutler Ridge** USA
43F4 **Cuttack** India
51B5 **Cuvelai** Angola
18B2 **Cuxhaven** Germany
64C2 **Cuyahoga Falls** USA
66C3 **Cuyama** *R* USA
72D6 **Cuzco** Peru
7C4 **Cwmbran** Wales
50C4 **Cyangugu** Zaïre
17E3 **Cyclades** *Is* Greece
40B3 **Cyprus** *Republic* Medit Sea
55M3 **Cyrus Field B** Canada
19C3 **Czech Republic** Europe
19D2 **Częstochowa** Poland

D

30C1 **Da** *R* Vietnam
26F2 **Da'an** China
45D3 **Dab'a** Jordan
45C3 **Dabab, Jebel ed** *Mt* Jordan
69C4 **Dabajuro** Venezuela
48B4 **Dabakala** Ivory Coast
50E3 **Dabaro** Somalia
31B3 **Daba Shan** *Mts* China
50D2 **Dabat** Ethiopia
42C4 **Dabhoi** India
31C3 **Dabie Shan** *U* China
48A3 **Dabola** Guinea
48B4 **Dabou** Ivory Coast
19D2 **Dabrowa Górn** Poland
Dacca = Dhākā
18C3 **Dachau** Germany
16C1 **Dachstein** *Mt* Austria
31A3 **Dada He** *R* China
67B3 **Dade City** USA
42B3 **Dadhar** Pakistan
42B3 **Dadu** Pakistan
26D3 **Dadu He** *R* China
27F5 **Daet** Philippines
31B4 **Dafang** China
30B2 **Daga** *R* Burma
48A3 **Dagana** Senegal
21H7 **Daghestan Republic** Russian Federation
27F5 **Dagupan** Philippines
43G3 **Dagzê** China
40B4 **Dahab** Egypt
25O5 **Da Hinggan Ling** *Mts* China
67B2 **Dahlonega** USA
42C4 **Dāhod** India
28A2 **Dahongqi** China
15C2 **Dahra** *Region* Algeria
21G8 **Dahuk** Iraq
28A2 **Dahushan** China
43E3 **Dailekh** Nepal
Dairen = Lüda
40B4 **Dairût** Egypt
26G4 **Daitō Is** Pacific Ocean
32C3 **Dajarra** Australia
48A3 **Dakar** Senegal
48A2 **Dakhla** Morocco
49E2 **Dakhla Oasis** Egypt
48C3 **Dakoro** Niger
61D2 **Dakota City** USA
17E2 **Dakovica** Serbia, Yugoslavia
17D1 **Dakovo** Croatia
20B3 **Dal** *R* Sweden
51C5 **Dala** Angola
48A3 **Dalaba** Guinea
31D1 **Dalai Nur** *L* China
26D2 **Dalandzadgad** Mongolia
30D3 **Da Lat** Vietnam
31A1 **Dalay** Mongolia
8D4 **Dalbeattie** Scotland
32E3 **Dalby** Australia
67A1 **Dale Hollow L** USA
12F7 **Dalen** Norway
6C2 **Dales,The** *Upland* England
67A2 **Daleville** USA
56C3 **Dalhart** USA
65F1 **Dalhousie** Canada
54E2 **Dalhousie,C** Canada
26D4 **Dali** China
31E2 **Dalian** China
8D4 **Dalkeith** Scotland
56D3 **Dallas** USA
58B1 **Dalles,The** USA
54E4 **Dall I** USA
43E4 **Dalli Rajhara** India
48C3 **Dallol** *Watercourse* Niger
8C3 **Dalmally** Scotland
16D2 **Dalmatia** *Region* Croatia
8C4 **Dalmellington** Scotland
26G2 **Dal'nerechensk** Russian Federation
48B4 **Daloa** Ivory Coast
31B4 **Dalou Shan** *Mts* China
8C4 **Dalry** Scotland
43E4 **Dāltenganj** India
6C2 **Dalton** England
67B2 **Dalton** Georgia, USA
68D1 **Dalton** Massachusetts, USA
55Q3 **Dalton, Kap** *C* Greenland

32C2 **Daly** *R* Australia
59B3 **Daly City** USA
32C2 **Daly Waters** Australia
42C4 **Damān** India
40B3 **Damanhûr** Egypt
32B1 **Damar** *I* Indonesia
50B3 **Damara** Central African Republic
32B1 **Damar, Kepulauan** *Is* Indonesia
40C3 **Damascus** Syria
68B3 **Damascus** USA
48D3 **Damaturu** Nigeria
41F2 **Damavand** Iran
51B4 **Damba** Angola
44C4 **Dambulla** Sri Lanka
41F2 **Damghan** Iran
Damietta = Dumyât
42D4 **Damoh** India
50E3 **Damot** Ethiopia
45C2 **Damour** Lebanon
32A3 **Dampier** Australia
45C3 **Danā** Jordan
66C2 **Dana,Mt** USA
48B4 **Danané** Liberia
30D2 **Da Nang** Vietnam
27C6 **Danau Toba** *L* Indonesia
27F7 **Danau Towuti** *L* Indonesia
31A3 **Danba** China
65E2 **Danbury** USA
68D1 **Danby** USA
43E3 **Dandeldhura** Nepal
44A2 **Dandeli** India
34C3 **Dandenong** Australia
28A2 **Dandong** China
47B3 **Danger Pt** *C* South Africa
50D2 **Dangila** Ethiopia
58D2 **Daniel** USA
55N4 **Daniel's Harbour** Canada
47C2 **Danielskuil** South Africa
55P3 **Dannebrogs Øy** *I* Greenland
35C2 **Dannevirke** New Zealand
68B1 **Dansville** USA
44C2 **Dantewāra** India
17F2 **Danube** *R* E Europe
57E2 **Danville** Illinois, USA
57E3 **Danville** Kentucky, USA
68B2 **Danville** Pennsylvania, USA
57F3 **Danville** Virginia, USA
Danzig = Gdańsk
31C4 **Dao Xian** China
31B4 **Daozhen** China
43H3 **Dapha Bum** *Mt* India
45B3 **Daphnae** *Hist Site* Egypt
26C3 **Da Qaidam** China
26F2 **Daqing** China
45D2 **Dar'a** Syria
40C3 **Dar'ā** Syria
41F4 **Dārāb** Iran
49D1 **Daraj** Libya
41F3 **Dārān** Iran
43F3 **Darbhanga** India
66C1 **Dardanelle** USA
63D1 **Dardanelle,L** USA
Dar-el-Beida = Casablanca
51D4 **Dar es Salaam** Tanzania
35B1 **Dargaville** New Zealand
67B2 **Darien** USA
69B5 **Darién, G of** Colombia/Panama
Darjeeling = Dārjiling
43F3 **Dārjiling** India
32D4 **Darling** *R* Australia
34C1 **Darling Downs** Australia
55L1 **Darling Pen** Canada
34B2 **Darlington** Australia
6D2 **Darlington** England
67C2 **Darlington** USA
18B3 **Darmstadt** Germany
49E1 **Darnah** Libya
34B2 **Darnick** Australia
54F3 **Darnley B** Canada
76G10 **Darnley,C** Antarctica
15B1 **Daroca** Spain
50C3 **Dar Rounga** *Region* Central African Republic
7C4 **Dart** *R* England
7C4 **Dartmoor** England
55M5 **Dartmouth** Canada
7C4 **Dartmouth** England
32D1 **Daru** Papua New Guinea
16D1 **Daruvar** Croatia
6C3 **Darwen** England
32C2 **Darwin** Australia
41F4 **Daryācheh-ye Bakhtegan** *L* Iran
41F4 **Daryācheh-ye Mahārlū** *L* Iran
41F3 **Daryācheh-ye Namak** *Salt Flat* Iran
21H8 **Daryācheh-ye Orūmīyeh** *L* Iran
41F4 **Daryācheh-ye Tashk** *L* Iran
41G4 **Dārzīn** Iran
41F4 **Dās** *I* UAE
31C3 **Dashennongjia** *Mt* China
41G2 **Dasht** Iran
41F3 **Dasht-e-Kavir** *Salt Desert* Iran
41G3 **Dasht-e Lut** *Salt Desert* Iran
29D2 **Date** Japan
42D3 **Datia** India
31A2 **Datong** China
31C1 **Datong** China
31A2 **Datong He** *R* China
27D6 **Datuk, Tanjung** *C* Indonesia
19E1 **Daugava** *R* Latvia
20D4 **Daugavpils** Latvia
55M1 **Dauguard Jensen Land** *Region* Canada
42A1 **Daulatabad** Afghanistan
42B2 **Daulat Yar** Afghanistan
42D3 **Daulpur** India
13D2 **Daun** Germany
44A2 **Daund** India
54H4 **Dauphin** Canada
68B2 **Dauphin** USA
14D3 **Dauphiné** *Region* France
63E2 **Dauphin I** USA
48C3 **Daura** Nigeria
42D3 **Dausa** India
44B3 **Dāvangere** India
27F6 **Davao** Philippines
27F6 **Davao G** Philippines
66A2 **Davenport** California, USA
57D2 **Davenport** Iowa, USA
7D3 **Daventry** England
72B2 **David** Panama
54D3 **Davidson Mts** USA
59B3 **Davis** USA
76G10 **Davis** *Base* Antarctica
55M4 **Davis Inlet** Canada
55N3 **Davis Str** Canada/Greenland
20K5 **Davlekanovo** Russian Federation
28A2 **Dawa** China
50E3 **Dawa** *R* Ethiopia
31A4 **Dawan** China
41F4 **Dawḩat Salwah** *B* Qatar/Saudi Arabia
30B2 **Dawna Range** *Mts* Burma/Thailand
54E3 **Dawson** Canada
67B2 **Dawson** Georgia, USA
60D1 **Dawson** N Dakota, USA
32D3 **Dawson** *R* Australia
54F4 **Dawson Creek** Canada
31A3 **Dawu** China
31C3 **Dawu** China
14B3 **Dax** France
31B3 **Daxian** China
31B5 **Daxin** China
31A3 **Daxue Shan** *Mts* China
31C4 **Dayong** China
45D2 **Dayr 'Alī** Syria
45D1 **Dayr 'Aṭīyah** Syria
40D2 **Dayr az Zawr** Syria
45D1 **Dayr Shumayyil** Syria
57E2 **Dayton** Ohio, USA
67A1 **Dayton** Tennessee, USA
63D3 **Dayton** Texas, USA
58C1 **Dayton** Washington, USA
57E4 **Daytona Beach** USA
31C4 **Dayu** China
31D2 **Da Yunhe** *R* China
58C2 **Dayville** USA
31B3 **Dazhu** China
47C3 **De Aar** South Africa
69C2 **Deadman's Cay** The Bahamas
40C3 **Dead S** Israel/Jordan
60C2 **Deadwood** USA
7E4 **Deal** England
47D2 **Dealesville** South Africa
64C2 **Dearborn** USA
54F3 **Dease Arm** *B* Canada
54E4 **Dease Lake** Canada
56B3 **Death V** USA
66D2 **Death Valley Nat Mon** USA
14C2 **Deauville** France
69L1 **Débé** Trinidad
19E2 **Dębica** Poland
19E2 **Dęblin** Poland
48B3 **Débo,L** Mali
50D3 **Debre Birhan** Ethiopia
19E3 **Debrecen** Hungary
50D2 **Debre Mark'os** Ethiopia
50D2 **Debre Tabor** Ethiopia
57E3 **Decatur** Alabama, USA
67B2 **Decatur** Georgia, USA
57E3 **Decatur** Illinois, USA
64C2 **Decatur** Indiana, USA
14C3 **Decazeville** France
65D1 **Decelles, Réservoir** Canada
47C1 **Deception** *R* Botswana
31A4 **Dechang** China
61E2 **Decorah** USA
48B3 **Dedougou** Burkina
51D5 **Dedza** Malawi
8C4 **Dee** *R* Dumfries and Galloway, Scotland
7C3 **Dee** *R* England/Wales
8D3 **Dee** *R* Grampian, Scotland
65D1 **Deep River** Canada
68D2 **Deep River** USA
66D2 **Deep Springs** USA
34D1 **Deepwater** Australia
55N5 **Deer Lake** Canada
56B2 **Deer Lodge** USA
58C2 **Deeth** USA
67A2 **De Funiak Springs** USA
26C3 **Dêgê** China
50E3 **Degeh Bur** Ethiopia
32A3 **De Grey** *R* Australia
50E2 **Dehalak Arch** *Is* Eritrea
41F3 **Deh Bīd** Iran
42B1 **Dehi** Afghanistan
48D1 **Dehibat** Tunisia
44B4 **Dehiwala-Mt Lavinia** Sri Lanka
41E3 **Dehlorān** Iran
42D2 **Dehra Dūn** India
43E4 **Dehri** India
50C3 **Deim Zubeir** Sudan
45C2 **Deir Abu Sa'id** Jordan
45D1 **Deir el Ahmar** Lebanon
21C6 **Dej** Romania
64B2 **De Kalb** Illinois, USA
63D2 **De Kalb** Texas, USA
25Q4 **De Kastri** Russian Federation
50C4 **Dekese** Zaïre
50B3 **Dekoa** Central African Republic
56B3 **Delano** USA
59D3 **Delano Peak** *Mt* USA
47D2 **Delareyville** South Africa
64C2 **Delaware** USA
65D2 **Delaware** *R* USA
57F3 **Delaware** *State* USA
57F3 **Delaware B** USA
34C3 **Delegate** Australia
13C1 **Delft** Netherlands
13D1 **Delfzijl** Netherlands
51E5 **Delgado, C** Mozambique
62B1 **Delhi** Colorado, USA
42D3 **Delhi** India
65E2 **Delhi** New York, USA
40B1 **Delice** Turkey
70B2 **Delicias** Mexico
41F3 **Delījān** Iran
61D2 **Dell Rapids** USA
15C2 **Dellys** Algeria
66D4 **Del Mar** USA
12F8 **Delmenhorst** Germany
25R2 **De-Longa, Ostrova** *Is* Russian Federation
54B3 **De Long Mts** USA
34C4 **Deloraine** Australia
54H5 **Deloraine** Canada
67B3 **Delray Beach** USA
56C4 **Del Rio** USA
56B3 **Delta** USA
68C1 **Delta Res** USA
50D3 **Dembī Dolo** Ethiopia
13C2 **Demer** *R* Belgium
19G1 **Demidov** Russian Federation
62A2 **Deming** USA
17F2 **Demirköy** Turkey
63E2 **Demopolis** USA
24H4 **Dem'yanskoye** Russian Federation
14C1 **Denain** France
39E2 **Denau** Uzbekistan
7C3 **Denbigh** Wales
13C2 **Dendermond** Belgium
50D3 **Dendi** *Mt* Ethiopia
13B2 **Dèndre** *R* Belgium
31B1 **Dengkou** China
31C3 **Deng Xian** China
Den Haag = The Hague
69H1 **Denham,Mt** Jamaica
18A2 **Den Helder** Netherlands
15C2 **Denia** Spain
32D4 **Deniliquin** Australia
58C2 **Denio** USA
61D2 **Denison** Iowa, USA
56D3 **Denison** Texas, USA
21D8 **Denizli** Turkey
12F7 **Denmark** *Kingdom* Europe
76C1 **Denmark Str** Greenland/Iceland
69P2 **Dennery** St Lucia
8D2 **Dennis Head** *Pt* Scotland
27E7 **Denpasar** Indonesia
68C3 **Denton** Maryland, USA
56D3 **Denton** Texas, USA
32E1 **D'Entrecasteaux Is** Papua New Guinea
56C3 **Denver** USA
50B3 **Déo** *R* Cameroon
48D4 **Déo** *R* Cameroon/Nigeria
43F4 **Deoghar** India
42C5 **Deolāli** India
43M2 **Deoria** *District* India
42D1 **Deosai Plain** India
68A1 **Depew** USA
68C1 **Deposit** USA
25P3 **Deputatskiy** Russian Federation
63D2 **De Queen** USA
42B3 **Dera Bugti** Pakistan
42C3 **Dera Ghazi Khan** Pakistan
42C2 **Dera Ismail Khan** Pakistan
21H7 **Derbent** Russian Federation
32B2 **Derby** Australia
68D2 **Derby** Connecticut, USA
7D3 **Derby** England
63C1 **Derby** Kansas, USA
7D3 **Derby** *County* England
21F5 **Dergachi** Ukraine
10B3 **Derg, Lough** *L* Irish Republic
63D2 **De Ridder** USA
Derna = Darnah
9C3 **Derravaragh, L** Irish Republic
50E3 **Derri** Somalia
68E1 **Derry** USA
50D2 **Derudeb** Sudan
47C3 **De Rust** South Africa
68C1 **De Ruyter** USA
6D3 **Derwent** *R* England
34C4 **Derwent Bridge** Australia
72E7 **Desaguadero** *R* Bolivia
59C4 **Descanso** Mexico
58B2 **Deschutes** *R* USA
50D2 **Desē** Ethiopia
74C7 **Deseado** Argentina
74C7 **Deseado** *R* Argentina
48A1 **Deserta Grande** *I* Madeira
59C4 **Desert Center** USA
59D2 **Desert Peak** *Mt* USA
63D1 **Desloge** USA
57D2 **Des Moines** Iowa, USA
62B1 **Des Moines** New Mexico, USA
61E2 **Des Moines** *R* USA
21E5 **Desna** *R* Russian Federation
74B8 **Desolación** *I* Chile
64B2 **Des Plaines** USA
18C2 **Dessau** Germany
54E3 **Destruction Bay** Canada
17E1 **Deta** Romania
51C5 **Dete** Zimbabwe
13E2 **Detmold** Germany
57E2 **Detroit** USA
61D1 **Detroit Lakes** USA
30D3 **Det Udom** Thailand
17E1 **Deva** Romania
18B2 **Deventer** Netherlands
8D3 **Deveron** *R* Scotland
42C3 **Devikot** India
66C2 **Devil Postpile Nat Mon** USA
66C3 **Devils Den** USA
66C1 **Devils Gate** *P* USA
6E1 **Devil's Hole** *Region* N Sea
Devil's Island = Diable, Isla du
60D1 **Devils L** N Dakota, USA
62B3 **Devils L** Texas, USA
56D2 **Devils Lake** USA
7D4 **Devizes** England
42D3 **Devli** India
17E2 **Devoll** *R* Albania
7B4 **Devon** *County* England
55J2 **Devon I** Canada
32D5 **Devonport** Australia
43G3 **Dewangiri** Bhutan
42D4 **Dewās** India
47D2 **Dewetsdorp** South Africa
57E3 **Dewey Res** USA
63D2 **De Witt** USA
6D3 **Dewsbury** England
63E1 **Dexter** Missouri, USA
62B2 **Dexter** New Mexico, USA
31A3 **Deyang** China
41G3 **Deyhuk** Iran
41E3 **Dezfūl** Iran
31D2 **Dezhou** China
41E2 **Dezh Shāhpūr** Iran
45D3 **Dhab'i, Wadi edh** Jordan
41F4 **Dhahran** Saudi Arabia
43G4 **Dhākā** Bangladesh
45B1 **Dhali** Cyprus
44B3 **Dhamavaram** India
43E4 **Dhamtari** India
43F4 **Dhanbād** India
43E3 **Dhangarhi** Nepal
43M1 **Dhang Range** *Mts* Nepal
43F3 **Dhankuta** Nepal
42D4 **Dhār** India
44B3 **Dharmapuri** India
42D2 **Dharmsāla** India
48B3 **Dhar Oualata** *Desert Region* Mauritius
43E3 **Dhaulagiri** *Mt* Nepal
43F4 **Dhenkānāl** India
45C3 **Dhībān** Jordan
17F3 **Dhíkti Óri** *Mt* Greece
Dhodhekánisos = Dodecanese
17E3 **Dhomokós** Greece
44B2 **Dhone** India
42C4 **Dhoraji** India
42C4 **Dhrāngadhra** India
43F3 **Dhuburi** India
42C4 **Dhule** India
73H2 **Diable, Isle du** French Guiana
66B2 **Diablo,Mt** USA
59B3 **Diablo Range** *Mts* USA
73K7 **Diamantina** Brazil
32D3 **Diamantina** *R* Australia
75A1 **Diamantino** Brazil
43F4 **Diamond Harbour** India
66B1 **Diamond Springs** USA
58D2 **Diamondville** USA
41G4 **Dibā** UAE
51C4 **Dibaya** Zaïre
43G3 **Dibrugarh** India
62B2 **Dickens** USA
56C2 **Dickinson** USA
67A1 **Dickson** USA
65D2 **Dickson City** USA
21G8 **Dicle** *R* Turkey
42C3 **Dīdwāna** India
47E2 **Die Berg** *Mt* South Africa
48B3 **Diébougou** Burkina
13E3 **Dieburg** Germany
74C9 **Diego Ramírez, Islas** Chile
Diégo Suarez = Antsirañana
13D3 **Diekirch** Luxembourg
48B3 **Diéma** Mali
30C1 **Dien Bien Phu** Vietnam
18B2 **Diepholz** Germany
14C2 **Dieppe** France
13C2 **Diest** Belgium
13D3 **Dieuze** France
48D3 **Diffa** Niger
43H3 **Digboi** India
55M5 **Digby** Canada
14D3 **Digne-les-B.** France
14C2 **Digoin** France
27F6 **Digos** Philippines
32C1 **Digul** *R* Indonesia
43G3 **Dihang** *R* China/India
Dijlah = Tigris
14C2 **Dijon** France
50B3 **Dik** Chad
50E2 **Dikhil** Djibouti
45A3 **Dîkirnis** Egypt
13B2 **Diksmuide** Belgium
24K2 **Dikson** Russian Federation
38E2 **Dilaram** Afghanistan
27F7 **Dili** Indonesia
30D3 **Di Linh** Vietnam
13E2 **Dillenburg** Germany
62C3 **Dilley** USA
50C2 **Dilling** Sudan
54C4 **Dillingham** USA
56B2 **Dillon** USA
68B2 **Dillsburg** USA
51C5 **Dilolo** Zaïre
43G3 **Dimāpur** India
Dimashq = Damascus
50C4 **Dimbelenge** Zaïre
48B4 **Dimbokro** Ivory Coast
17F2 **Dimitrovgrad** Bulgaria
20H5 **Dimitrovgrad** Russian Federation
45C3 **Dīmona** Israel
27F5 **Dinagat** *I* Philippines
43F3 **Dinajpur** India
14B2 **Dinan** France
13C2 **Dinant** Belgium
40B2 **Dinar** Turkey
50D2 **Dinder** *R* Sudan
44B3 **Dindigul** India
31B2 **Dingbian** China
43F3 **Dinggyê** China
10A3 **Dingle** Irish Republic
10A3 **Dingle B** Irish Republic
48A3 **Dinguiraye** Guinea
8C3 **Dingwall** Scotland
31A2 **Dingxi** China
31D2 **Ding Xian** China
30D1 **Dinh Lap** Vietnam
60B2 **Dinosaur** USA
66C2 **Dinuba** USA
48A3 **Diouloulou** Senegal
43G3 **Diphu** India
50E3 **Dirē Dawa** Ethiopia
32A3 **Dirk Hartog** *I* Australia
50B2 **Dirkou** Niger
34C1 **Dirranbandi** Australia
74J8 **Disappointment,C** South Georgia
58B1 **Disappointment,C** USA
32B3 **Disappointment,L** Australia
34B3 **Discovery B** Australia
27E5 **Discovery Reef** S China Sea
52J7 **Discovery Tablemount** Atlantic Ocean
40B4 **Dishna** Egypt
55N3 **Disko** *I* Greenland
55N3 **Disko Bugt** *B* Greenland
55N3 **Diskofjord** Greenland
65D3 **Dismal Swamp** USA
19F1 **Disna** *R* Belarus
67B3 **Disney World** USA
75C2 **Distrito Federal** Brazil
42C4 **Diu** India
73K8 **Divinópolis** Brazil
21G6 **Divnoye** Russian Federation
40C2 **Divriği** Turkey
66B1 **Dixon** California, USA
64B2 **Dixon** Illinois, USA
58D1 **Dixon** Montana, USA
54E4 **Dixon Entrance** *Sd* Canada/USA
41E3 **Diyālā** *R* Iraq

21G8 **Diyarbakır** Turkey
41E3 **Diz** *R* Iran
50B3 **Dja** *R* Cameroon
50B1 **Djado,Plat du** Niger
50B4 **Djambala** Congo
48C2 **Djanet** Algeria
48C1 **Djedi** *Watercourse* Algeria
48C1 **Djelfa** Algeria
50C3 **Djéma** Central African Republic
48B3 **Djenné** Mali
48B3 **Djibo** Burkina
50E2 **Djibouti** Djibouti
50E2 **Djibouti** *Republic* E Africa
50C3 **Djolu** Zaïre
48C4 **Djougou** Benin
50B2 **Djourab, Erg du** *Desert Region* Chad
50D3 **Djugu** Zaïre
12C2 **Djúpivogur** Iceland
15C2 **Djurdjura** *Mts* Algeria
25P2 **Dmitriya Lapteva, Proliv** *Str* Russian Federation
20F4 **Dmitrov** Russian Federation
Dnepr *R* Ukraine = **Dnieper**
21E6 **Dneprodzerzhinsk** Ukraine
21F6 **Dnepropetrovsk** Ukraine
20D5 **Dneprovskaya Nizmennost'** *Region* Belarus
21C6 **Dnestr** *R* Ukraine = **Dniester**
21E6 **Dnieper** *R* Ukraine
21C6 **Dniester** *R* Ukraine
20E4 **Dno** Russian Federation
50B3 **Doba** Chad
19E1 **Dobele** Latvia
32C1 **Dobo** Indonesia
17D2 **Doboj** Bosnia-Herzegovina
17F2 **Dobrich** Bulgaria
21E5 **Dobrush** Belarus
73K7 **Doce** *R* Brazil
74D2 **Doctor P P Peña** Paraguay
44B3 **Dod** India
44B3 **Doda Betta** *Mt* India
17F3 **Dodecanese** *Is* Greece
56C3 **Dodge City** USA
64A2 **Dodgeville** USA
50D4 **Dodoma** Tanzania
64B1 **Dog L** Canada
64C1 **Dog L** Canada
29B3 **Dōgo** *I* Japan
48C3 **Dogondoutchi** Niger
41D2 **Doğubayazit** Turkey
41F4 **Doha** Qatar
43G3 **Doilungdêqên** China
13D1 **Dokkum** Netherlands
29F2 **Dokuchayevo, Mys** *C* Russian Federation
32C1 **Dolak** *I* Indonesia
61D2 **Doland** USA
55L5 **Dolbeau** Canada
14D2 **Dole** France
7C3 **Dolgellau** Wales
68C1 **Dolgeville** USA
20K2 **Dolgiy, Ostrov** *I* Russian Federation
50E3 **Dolo Odo** Ethiopia
74E5 **Dolores** Argentina
60B3 **Dolores** *R* USA
54G3 **Dolphin and Union Str** Canada
74E8 **Dolphin,C** Falkland Islands
27G7 **Dom** *Mt* Indonesia
21K5 **Dombarovskiy** Russian Federation
12F6 **Dombås** Norway
13D3 **Dombasle-sur-Meurthe** France
17D1 **Dombóvár** Hungary
14B2 **Domfront** France
69E3 **Dominica** *I* Caribbean Sea
69C3 **Dominican Republic** Caribbean Sea
55L3 **Dominion,C** Canada
55N4 **Domino** Canada
26E1 **Domna** Russian Federation
16B1 **Domodossola** Italy
74B5 **Domuyo, Vol** Argentina
34D1 **Domville,Mt** Australia
8D3 **Don** *R* Scotland
21G6 **Don** *R* Russian Federation
9C2 **Donaghadee** Northern Ireland
Donau *R* Bulgaria = **Danube**
Donau *R* Austria/ Germany = **Danube**
13E4 **Donaueschingen** Germany
18C3 **Donauwörth** Germany
15A2 **Don Benito** Spain
7D3 **Doncaster** England
51B4 **Dondo** Angola
51D5 **Dondo** Mozambique
44C4 **Dondra Head** *C* Sri Lanka
10B3 **Donegal** Irish Republic
9C2 **Donegal** *County* Irish Republic
10B3 **Donegal B** Irish Republic
9C2 **Donegal Mts** Irish Republic
9B3 **Donegal Pt** Irish Republic
21F6 **Donetsk** Ukraine
31C4 **Dong'an** China
32A3 **Dongara** Australia
31A4 **Dongchuan** China
30D2 **Dongfang** China
28B2 **Dongfeng** China
32A1 **Donggala** Indonesia
26C3 **Donggi Cona** *L* China
28A3 **Donggou** China
31C5 **Donghai Dao** *I* China
31A1 **Dong He** *R* China
30D2 **Dong Hoi** Vietnam
31C5 **Dong Jiang** *R* China
28A2 **Dongliao He** *R* China
28C2 **Dongning** China
50D2 **Dongola** Sudan
31D5 **Dongshan** China
26E4 **Dongsha Qundao** *I* China
31C2 **Dongsheng** China
31E3 **Dongtai** China
31C4 **Dongting Hu** *L* China
31B5 **Dongxing** China
31D3 **Dongzhi** China
63D1 **Doniphan** USA
16D2 **Donji Vakuf** Bosnia-Herzegovina
12G5 **Dönna** *I* Norway
59B3 **Donner P** USA
13D3 **Donnersberg** *Mt* Germany
47D2 **Donnybrook** South Africa
Donostia = San Sebatián
66B2 **Don Pedro Res** USA
8C4 **Doon, Loch** *L* Scotland
31A3 **Do Qu** *R* China
14D2 **Dorbirn** Austria
7C4 **Dorchester** England
55L3 **Dorchester,C** Canada
14C2 **Dordogne** *R* France
18A2 **Dordrecht** Netherlands
47D3 **Dordrecht** South Africa
68D1 **Dorest Peak** *Mt* USA
48B3 **Dori** Burkina
47B3 **Doring** *R* South Africa
7D4 **Dorking** England
13B3 **Dormans** France
18B3 **Dornbirn** Austria
8C3 **Dornoch** Scotland
8D3 **Dornoch Firth** *Estuary* Scotland
12H6 **Dorotea** Sweden
34D2 **Dorrigo** Australia
58B2 **Dorris** USA
7C4 **Dorset** *County* England
55L3 **Dorset, Cape** Canada
13D2 **Dorsten** Germany
18B2 **Dortmund** Germany
50C3 **Doruma** Zaïre
25N4 **Dosatuy** Russian Federation
42B1 **Doshi** Afghanistan
66B2 **Dos Palos** USA
48C3 **Dosso** Niger
24G5 **Dossor** Kazakhstan
57E3 **Dothan** USA
14C1 **Douai** France
50A3 **Douala** Cameroon
34D1 **Double Island Pt** Australia
62B2 **Double Mountain Fork** *R* USA
66C3 **Double Mt** USA
14D2 **Doubs** *R* France
35A3 **Doubtful Sd** New Zealand
48B3 **Douentza** Mali
56C3 **Douglas** Arizona, USA
67B2 **Douglas** Georgia, USA
6B2 **Douglas** Isle of Man, British Islands
47C2 **Douglas** South Africa
56C2 **Douglas** Wyoming, USA
67B1 **Douglas L** USA
13C2 **Doulevant-le-Château** France
13B2 **Doullens** France
75B2 **Dourada, Serra** *Mts* Brazil
75C1 **Dourada, Serra** *Mts* Brazil
73H8 **Dourados** Brazil
75B3 **Dourados** *R* Brazil
75B3 **Dourados, Serra dos** *Mts* Brazil
13B3 **Dourdan** France
15A1 **Douro** *R* Portugal
7D3 **Dove** *R* England
62A1 **Dove Creek** USA
65D3 **Dover** Delaware, USA
7E4 **Dover** England
65E2 **Dover** New Hampshire, USA
68C2 **Dover** New Jersey, USA
64C2 **Dover** Ohio, USA
7E4 **Dover,Str of** England/ France
19G2 **Dovsk** Belarus
9C2 **Down** *County* Northern Ireland
68C3 **Downingtown** USA
9D2 **Downpatrick** Northern Ireland
68C1 **Downsville** USA
68C2 **Doylestown** USA
28B3 **Dōzen** *I* Japan
65D1 **Dozois, Réservoir** Canada
48A2 **Dr'aa** *Watercourse* Morocco
75B3 **Dracena** Brazil
13D1 **Drachten** Netherlands
68E1 **Dracut** USA
14D3 **Draguignan** France
60C1 **Drake** USA
51D6 **Drakensberg** *Mts* South Africa
47D2 **Drakensberg** *Mt* South Africa
52E7 **Drake Passage** Atlantic O/ Pacific Ocean
17E2 **Dráma** Greece
12G7 **Drammen** Norway
12A1 **Drangajökull** *Ice cap* Iceland
16D1 **Drava** *R* Slovenia
13D1 **Drenthe** *Province* Netherlands
18C2 **Dresden** Germany
14C2 **Dreux** France
58C2 **Drewsey** USA
68A2 **Driftwood** USA
17E2 **Drin** *R* Albania
17D2 **Drina** *R* Bosnia-Herzegovina/Serbia, Yugoslavia
19F1 **Drissa** *R* Belarus
9C3 **Drogheda** Irish Republic
19E3 **Drogobych** Ukraine
9C3 **Droihead Nua** Irish Republic
7C3 **Droitwich** England
9C2 **Dromore** Northern Ireland
76F12 **Dronning Maud Land** *Region* Antarctica
54G4 **Drumheller** Canada
58D1 **Drummond** USA
64C1 **Drummond I** USA
65E1 **Drummondville** Canada
8C3 **Drumochter Pass** Scotland
19E2 **Druskininkai** Lithuania
25Q3 **Druzhina** Russian Federation
61E1 **Dryberry L** Canada
55J5 **Dryden** Canada
68B1 **Dryden** USA
69H1 **Dry Harbour Mts** Jamaica
30B3 **Duang** *I* Burma
40C4 **Dubā** Saudi Arabia
41G4 **Dubai** UAE
54H3 **Dubawnt** *R* Canada
54H3 **Dubawnt L** Canada
32D4 **Dubbo** Australia
9C3 **Dublin** Irish Republic
67B2 **Dublin** USA
9C3 **Dublin** *County* Irish Republic
20F4 **Dubna** Russian Federation
21D5 **Dubno** Ukraine
58D2 **Dubois** Idaho, USA
65D2 **Du Bois** USA
58E2 **Dubois** Wyoming, USA
19F3 **Dubossary** Moldavia
19F2 **Dubrovica** Ukraine
17D2 **Dubrovnik** Croatia
57D2 **Dubuque** USA
59D2 **Duchesne** USA
67A1 **Duck** *R* USA
66C3 **Ducor** USA
13D3 **Dudelange** Luxembourg
24K3 **Dudinka** Russian Federation
7C3 **Dudley** England
25L2 **Dudypta** *R* Russian Federation
48B4 **Duekoué** Ivory Coast
15B1 **Duero** *R* Spain
33F1 **Duff Is** Solomon Islands
8D3 **Dufftown** Scotland
16C2 **Dugi Otok** *I* Croatia
18B2 **Duisburg** Germany
47E1 **Duiwelskloof** South Africa
41E3 **Dūkan** Iraq
50D3 **Duk Faiwil** Sudan
41F4 **Dukhān** Qatar
31A4 **Dukou** China
26C3 **Dulan** China
70D4 **Dulce, Golfo** Costa Rica
43G4 **Dullabchara** India
13D2 **Dülmen** Germany
57D2 **Duluth** USA
7C4 **Dulverton** England
45D2 **Dūmā** Syria
27D6 **Dumai** Indonesia
56C3 **Dumas** USA
45D2 **Ḑumayr** Syria
8C4 **Dumbarton** Scotland
48B1 **Dumer Rbia** Morocco
8D4 **Dumfries** Scotland
8C4 **Dumfries and Galloway** *Region* Scotland
43F4 **Dumka** India
65D1 **Dumoine,L** Canada
76G8 **Dumont d'Urville** *Base* Antarctica
49F1 **Dumyat** Egypt
Dunărea *R* Romania = **Danube**
9C3 **Dunary Head** *Pt* Irish Republic
Dunav *R* Bulgaria = **Danube**
Dunav *R* Croatia/Serbia = **Danube**
28C2 **Dunay** Russian Federation
19F3 **Dunayevtsy** Ukraine
8D4 **Dunbar** Scotland
63C2 **Duncan** USA
68B2 **Duncannon** USA
44E3 **Duncan Pass** *Chan* Andaman Islands
8D2 **Duncansby Head** *Pt* Scotland
9C2 **Dundalk** Irish Republic
68B3 **Dundalk** USA
9C3 **Dundalk B** Irish Republic
55M2 **Dundas** Greenland
54G2 **Dundas Pen** Canada
27G8 **Dundas Str** Australia
47E2 **Dundee** South Africa
8D3 **Dundee** Scotland
68B1 **Dundee** USA
34B1 **Dundoo** Australia
9D2 **Dundrum B** Northern Ireland
43M2 **Dundwa Range** *Mts* Nepal
33G5 **Dunedin** New Zealand
67B3 **Dunedin** USA
34C2 **Dunedoo** Australia
8D3 **Dunfermline** Scotland
9C2 **Dungannon** Northern Ireland
42C4 **Dūngarpur** India
9C3 **Dungarvan** Irish Republic
7E4 **Dungeness** *Pen* England
34D2 **Dungog** Australia
50C3 **Dungu** Zaïre
50D1 **Dungunab** Sudan
28B2 **Dunhua** China
26C2 **Dunhuang** China
8D3 **Dunkeld** Scotland
Dunkerque = Dunkirk
13B2 **Dunkirk** France
57F2 **Dunkirk** USA
50D2 **Dunkur** Ethiopia
48B4 **Dunkwa** Ghana
10B3 **Dun Laoghaire** Irish Republic
9B4 **Dunmanus** Irish Republic
68C2 **Dunmore** USA
69B1 **Dunmore Town** The Bahamas
67C1 **Dunn** USA
8D2 **Dunnet Head** *Pt* Scotland
60C2 **Dunning** USA
8C4 **Dunoon** Scotland
8D4 **Duns** Scotland
60C1 **Dunseith** USA
58B2 **Dunsmuir** USA
35A2 **Dunstan Mts** New Zealand
13C3 **Dun-sur-Meuse** France
31D1 **Duolun** China
60C1 **Dupree** USA
64B3 **Du Quoin** USA
45C3 **Dura** Israel
14D3 **Durance** *R* France
64A2 **Durand** USA
70B2 **Durango** Mexico
15B1 **Durango** Spain
56C3 **Durango** USA
56D3 **Durant** USA
45D1 **Duraykīsh** Syria
74E4 **Durazno** Uruguay
47E2 **Durban** South Africa
13D2 **Duren** Germany
43E4 **Durg** India
43F4 **Durgapur** India
6D2 **Durham** England
57F3 **Durham** N Carolina, USA
68E1 **Durham** New Hampshire, USA
6D2 **Durham** *County* England
34B1 **Durham Downs** Australia
17D2 **Durmitor** *Mt* Montenegro, Yugoslavia
8C2 **Durness** Scotland
17D2 **Durrës** Albania
34B1 **Durrie** Australia
17F3 **Dursunbey** Turkey
35B2 **D'Urville I** New Zealand
41H2 **Dushak** Turkmenistan
31B4 **Dushan** China
39E2 **Dushanbe** Tajikistan
68B2 **Dushore** USA
35A3 **Dusky Sd** New Zealand
18B2 **Düsseldorf** Germany
59D3 **Dutton,Mt** USA
31B4 **Duyun** China
40B1 **Düzce** Turkey
20F2 **Dvinskaya Guba** *B* Russian Federation
42B4 **Dwārka** India
58C1 **Dworshak Res** USA
57E3 **Dyersburg** USA
7B3 **Dyfed** *County* Wales
21G7 **Dykh Tau** *Mt* Russian Federation
34B1 **Dynevor Downs** Australia
26C2 **Dzag** Mongolia
26E2 **Dzamïn Üüd** Mongolia
51E5 **Dzaoudzi** Mayotte, Indian Ocean
26C2 **Dzavhan Gol** *R* Mongolia
20G4 **Dzerzhinsk** Russian Federation
25O4 **Dzhalinda** Russian Federation
24J5 **Dzhambul** Kazakhstan
21E6 **Dzhankoy** Ukraine
24H5 **Dzhezkazgan** Kazakhstan
42B1 **Dzhilikul'** Tajikistan
25P4 **Dzhugdzhur, Khrebet** *Mts* Russian Federation
24J5 **Dzhungarskiy Alatau** *Mts* Kazakhstan
18D2 **Dzierzoniów** Poland
39G1 **Dzungaria Basin** China
25L5 **Dzüyl** Mongolia

E

55K4 **Eabamet L** Canada
60B3 **Eagle** Colorado, USA
60C1 **Eagle Butte** USA
58B2 **Eagle L** California, USA
65F1 **Eagle L** Maine, USA
65F1 **Eagle Lake** USA
63C2 **Eagle Mountain L** USA
56C4 **Eagle Pass** USA
62A2 **Eagle Peak** *Mt* USA
54E3 **Eagle Plain** Canada
59C3 **Earlimart** USA
8D3 **Earn** *R* Scotland
8C3 **Earn, Loch** *L* Scotland
59D4 **Earp** USA
62B2 **Earth** USA
6D2 **Easingwold** England
67B2 **Easley** USA
65D2 **East Aurora** USA
63E2 **East B** USA
7E4 **Eastbourne** England
68C1 **East Branch Delaware** *R* USA
33G4 **East C** New Zealand
64B2 **East Chicago** USA
26F3 **East China Sea** China/ Japan
7E3 **East Dereham** England
37O6 **Easter I** Pacific Ocean
51C7 **Eastern Cape** *Province* South Africa
43E5 **Eastern Ghats** *Mts* India
51C6 **Eastern Transvaal** *Province* South Africa
74E8 **East Falkland** *Is* Falkland Islands
59C3 **Eastgate** USA
61D1 **East Grand Forks** USA
7D4 **East Grinstead** England
68D1 **Easthampton** USA
68D2 **East Hampton** USA
8C4 **East Kilbride** Scotland
64B2 **East Lake** USA
7D4 **Eastleigh** England
64C2 **East Liverpool** USA
47D3 **East London** South Africa
55L4 **Eastmain** Canada
55L4 **Eastmain** *R* Canada
67B2 **Eastman** USA
64A2 **East Moline** USA
65D3 **Easton** Maryland, USA
65D2 **Easton** Pennsylvania, USA
68C2 **East Orange** USA
37O5 **East Pacific Ridge** Pacific Ocean
37O4 **East Pacific Rise** Pacific Ocean
67B2 **East Point** USA
65F2 **Eastport** USA
7D3 **East Retford** England
67A1 **East Ridge** USA
57D3 **East St Louis** USA
25R2 **East Siberian S** Russian Federation
7E4 **East Sussex** *County* England
65D3 **Eastville** USA
66C1 **East Walker** *R* USA
67B2 **Eatonton** USA
61E2 **Eau Claire** USA
27H6 **Eauripik** *I* Pacific Ocean
7C4 **Ebbw Vale** Wales
50B3 **Ebebiyin** Equatorial Guinea
68A2 **Ebensburg** USA
13E3 **Eberbach** Germany
18C2 **Eberswalde** Germany
29D2 **Ebetsu** Japan
31A4 **Ebian** China
24K5 **Ebinur** *L* China

16D2 **Eboli** Italy
50B3 **Ebolowa** Cameroon
15B1 **Ebro** *R* Spain
40A1 **Eceabat** Turkey
15C2 **Ech Cheliff** Algeria
31D2 **Eching** China
58C1 **Echo** USA
54G3 **Echo Bay** Canada
13D3 **Echternach** Luxembourg
34B3 **Echuca** Australia
15A2 **Ecija** Spain
55K2 **Eclipse Sd** Canada
72C4 **Ecuador** *Republic* S America
50E2 **Ed** Eritrea
8D2 **Eday** *I* Scotland
50C2 **Ed Da'ein** Sudan
50D2 **Ed Damer** Sudan
50D2 **Ed Debba** Sudan
8C2 **Eddrachillis B** Scotland
50D2 **Ed Dueim** Sudan
34C4 **Eddystone Pt** Australia
13C1 **Ede** Netherlands
50A3 **Edea** Cameroon
34C3 **Eden** Australia
62C2 **Eden** Texas, USA
58E2 **Eden** Wyoming, USA
6C2 **Eden** *R* England
47D2 **Edenburg** South Africa
35A3 **Edendale** New Zealand
9C3 **Edenderry** Irish Republic
13D3 **Edenkoben** Germany
13E2 **Eder** *R* Germany
60D1 **Edgeley** USA
55M3 **Edgell I** Canada
60C2 **Edgemont** USA
24D2 **Edgeøya** *I* Svalbard, Norway
68B3 **Edgewood** USA
45C3 **Edh Dhahiriya** Israel
17E2 **Edhessa** Greece
62C3 **Edinburg** USA
8D3 **Edinburgh** Scotland
21D7 **Edirne** Turkey
66C3 **Edison** USA
67B2 **Edisto** *R* USA
58B1 **Edmonds** USA
54G4 **Edmonton** Canada
60D1 **Edmore** USA
55M5 **Edmundston** Canada
63C3 **Edna** USA
16C1 **Edolo** Italy
45C3 **Edom** *Region* Jordan
21D8 **Edremit** Turkey
17F3 **Edremit Körfezi** *B* Turkey
26C2 **Edrengiyn Nuruu** *Mts* Mongolia
54G4 **Edson** Canada
34B3 **Edward** *R* Australia
50C4 **Edward,L** Uganda/Zaïre
66D3 **Edwards** USA
56C3 **Edwards Plat** USA
64B3 **Edwardsville** USA
13B2 **Eeklo** Belgium
33F2 **Efate** *I* Vanuatu
57E3 **Effingham** USA
16C3 **Egadi,I** Sicily, Italy
59D3 **Egan Range** *Mts* USA
55N3 **Egedesminde** Greenland
54C4 **Egegik** USA
19E3 **Eger** Hungary
12F7 **Egersund** Norway
13E2 **Eggegebirge** *Mts* Germany
68C3 **Egg Harbor City** USA
54G2 **Eglinton I** Canada
35B1 **Egmont,C** New Zealand
35B1 **Egmont,Mt** New Zealand
6C2 **Egremont** England
40B2 **Eğridir Gölü** *L* Turkey
6D2 **Egton** England
75C1 **Eguas** *R* Brazil
25U3 **Egvekinot** Russian Federation
49E2 **Egypt** *Republic* Africa
15B1 **Eibar** Spain
34D1 **Eidsvold** Australia
13D2 **Eifel** *Region* Germany
8B3 **Eigg** *I* Scotland
39F5 **Eight Degree Chan** Indian Ocean
32B2 **Eighty Mile Beach** Australia
34C3 **Eildon,L** Australia
18B2 **Eindhoven** Netherlands
45C3 **Ein Yahav** Israel
18C2 **Eisenach** Germany
18C3 **Eisenerz** Austria
13D2 **Eitorf** Germany
31A1 **Ejin qi** China
60C1 **Ekalaka** USA
35C2 **Eketahuna** New Zealand
24J4 **Ekibastuz** Kazakhstan
25P4 **Ekimchan** Russian Federation
12H7 **Eksjö** Sweden
57E1 **Ekwan** *R* Canada
45A3 **El Abbâsa** Egypt
40A3 **El'Alamein** Egypt
47D2 **Elands** *R* South Africa
47C3 **Elands Berg** *Mt* South Africa
40B3 **El'Arîsh** Egypt
40B4 **Elat** Israel
50C2 **El' Atrun Oasis** Sudan
21F8 **Elazığ** Turkey
40C3 **El Azraq** Jordan
16C2 **Elba** *I* Italy
49F2 **El Balyana** Egypt
72D2 **El Banco** Colombia
17E2 **Elbasan** Albania
69D5 **El Baúl** Venezuela
18C2 **Elbe** *R* Germany
45D1 **El Beqa'a** *R* Lebanon
64B2 **Elberta** USA
56C3 **Elbert,Mt** USA
67B2 **Elberton** USA
14C2 **Elbeuf** France
40C2 **Elbistan** Turkey
19D2 **Elblag** Poland
74B6 **El Bolsón** Argentina
61D1 **Elbow Lake** USA
21G7 **Elbrus** *Mt* Russian Federation
Elburz Mts = Reshteh-ye Alborz
59C4 **El Cajon** USA
63C3 **El Campo** USA
59C4 **El Centro** USA
15B2 **Elche** Spain
74C5 **El Chocón, Embalse** *Res* Argentina
15B2 **Elda** Spain
25P3 **El'dikan** Russian Federation
72C3 **El Diviso** Colombia
48B2 **El Djouf** *Desert Region* Mauritius
63D1 **Eldon** USA
75B4 **Eldorado** Argentina
57D3 **El Dorado** Arkansas, USA
75C3 **Eldorado** Brazil
56D3 **El Dorado** Kansas, USA
70B2 **El Dorado** Mexico
62B2 **Eldorado** Texas, USA
72F2 **El Dorado** Venezuela
50D3 **Eldoret** Kenya
68A2 **Eldred** USA
45C1 **Elea, C** Cyprus
66C1 **Eleanor,L** USA
58D2 **Electric Peak** *Mt* USA
48B2 **El Eglab** *Region* Algeria
62A2 **Elephant Butte Res** USA
40D2 **Eleşkirt** Turkey
16B3 **El Eulma** Algeria
57F4 **Eleuthera** *I* The Bahamas
40B4 **El Faiyûm** Egypt
48B2 **El Farsia** *Well* Morocco
50C2 **El Fasher** Sudan
40B4 **El Fashn** Egypt
15A1 **El Ferrol** Spain
45B3 **El Firdân** Egypt
50C2 **El Fula** Sudan
48C1 **El Gassi** Algeria
50D2 **El Geteina** Sudan
50D2 **El Gezīra** *Region* Sudan
45C3 **El Ghor** *V* Israel/Jordan
57E2 **Elgin** Illinois, USA
60C1 **Elgin** N Dakota, USA
8D3 **Elgin** Scotland
40B3 **El Gîza** Egypt
48C1 **El Golea** Algeria
59D4 **El Golfo de Santa Clara** Mexico
50D3 **Elgon,Mt** Kenya/Uganda
50E3 **El Goran** Ethiopia
48B2 **El Guettara** *Well* Mali
48B2 **El Hank** *Region* Mauritius
48B2 **El Haricha** *Desert Region* Mali
40A4 **El Harra** Egypt
15C2 **El Harrach** Algeria
50D2 **El Hawata** Sudan
40B4 **El'Igma** *Desert Region* Egypt
Elisabethville = Lubumbashi
12K6 **Elisenvaara** Russian Federation
El Iskandarîya = Alexandria
21G6 **Elista** Russian Federation
32C4 **Elizabeth** Australia
65E2 **Elizabeth** USA
47B2 **Elizabeth B** Namibia
57F3 **Elizabeth City** USA
68E2 **Elizabeth Is** USA
67B1 **Elizabethton** Tennessee, USA
64B3 **Elizabethtown** Kentucky, USA
67C2 **Elizabethtown** N Carolina, USA
68B2 **Elizabethtown** Pennsylvania, USA
48B1 **El Jadida** Morocco
40C3 **El Jafr** Jordan
45D3 **El Jafr** *L* Jordan
50D2 **El Jebelein** Sudan
48D1 **El Jem** Tunisia
19E2 **Ełk** Poland
68C3 **Elk** *R* Maryland/Penn, USA
64C3 **Elk** *R* W Virginia, USA
61E2 **Elkader** USA
16B3 **El Kala** Algeria
50D2 **El Kamlin** Sudan
48C1 **El Kef** Tunisia
66B1 **Elk Grove** USA
El Khalil = Hebron Israel
45A3 **El Khânka** Egypt
40B4 **El Khârga** Egypt
40B4 **El-Khârga Oasis** Egypt
64B2 **Elkhart** USA
48B2 **El Khenachich** *Desert Region* Mali
61D2 **Elkhorn** *R* USA
17F2 **Elkhovo** Bulgaria
65D3 **Elkins** USA
68B2 **Elkland** USA
60B2 **Elk Mt** USA
58C1 **Elko** Canada
56B2 **Elko** USA
16B3 **El Kroub** Algeria
68C3 **Elkton** USA
45B3 **El Kûbri** Egypt
40B3 **El Kuntilla** Egypt
50C2 **El Lagowa** Sudan
54H2 **Ellef Ringnes I** Canada
60D1 **Ellendale** USA
59D3 **Ellen,Mt** USA
56A2 **Ellensburg** USA
68C2 **Ellenville** USA
55K2 **Ellesmere I** Canada
35B2 **Ellesmere,L** New Zealand
7C3 **Ellesmere Port** England
68B3 **Ellicott City** USA
47D3 **Elliot** South Africa
55K5 **Elliot Lake** Canada
58D2 **Ellis** USA
45C3 **El Lisān** *Pen* Jordan
47D1 **Ellisras** South Africa
65F2 **Ellsworth** USA
76F3 **Ellsworth Land** *Region* Antarctica
45A4 **El Ma'âdi** Egypt
49E1 **El Maghra** *L* Egypt
40B3 **El Mahalla el Kubra** Egypt
40B3 **El Mansûra** Egypt
45A3 **El Manzala** Egypt
45B3 **El Matarîya** Egypt
68C3 **Elmer** USA
48B3 **El Merejé** *Desert Region* Mali/Mauritius
16B3 **El Milia** Algeria
45C1 **El Mīna** Lebanon
40B4 **El Minya** Egypt
66B1 **Elmira** California, USA
57F2 **Elmira** New York, USA
59D4 **El Mirage** USA
62B3 **El Moral** Mexico
48B2 **El Mreiti** *Well* Mauritius
18B2 **Elmshorn** Germany
50C2 **El Muglad** Sudan
48B2 **El Mzereb** *Well* Mali
50D2 **El Obeid** Sudan
48C1 **El Oued** Algeria
59D4 **Eloy** USA
56C3 **El Paso** USA
59B3 **El Portal** USA
62A2 **El Porvenir** Mexico
15A2 **El Puerto del Sta Maria** Spain
El Qâhira = Cairo
45B3 **El Qantara** Egypt
El Quds = Jerusalem
45C3 **El Quseima** Egypt
45C4 **El Quwetra** Jordan
56D3 **El Reno** USA
54E3 **Elsa** Canada
45A4 **El Saff** Egypt
45B3 **El Sâlhîya** Egypt
70D3 **El Salvador** *Republic* Central America
59C4 **El Sauzal** Mexico
45B3 **El Shallûfa** Egypt
45B4 **El Shatt** Egypt
45A3 **El Simbillâwein** Egypt
66D4 **Elsinore L** USA
18C2 **Elsterwerde** Germany
62A3 **El Sueco** Mexico
El Suweis = Suez
45A4 **El Tabbin** Egypt
15A1 **El Teleno** *Mt* Spain
35B1 **Eltham** New Zealand
45C4 **El Thamad** Egypt
72F2 **El Tigre** Venezuela
40B4 **El Tîh** *Desert Region* Egypt
45B3 **El Tîna** Egypt
58C1 **Eltopia** USA
40B4 **El Tûr** Egypt
44C2 **Elūru** India
15A2 **Elvas** Portugal
72D5 **Elvira** Brazil
54H2 **Elvira,C** Canada
64B2 **Elwood** USA
7E3 **Ely** England
57D2 **Ely** Minnesota, USA
56B3 **Ely** Nevada, USA
64C2 **Elyria** USA
45A3 **El Zarqa** Egypt
41G2 **Emāmrūd** Iran
42B1 **Emām Sāheb** Afghanistan
18D1 **Eman** *R* Sweden
21K6 **Emba** Kazakhstan
21K6 **Emba** *R* Kazakhstan
Embalse de Ricobayo = Esla, Embalse
74D2 **Embarcación** Argentina
54G4 **Embarras Portage** Canada
50D4 **Embu** Kenya
18B2 **Emden** Germany
31A4 **Emei** China
32D3 **Emerald** Australia
54J5 **Emerson** Canada
58C2 **Emigrant P** USA
50B1 **Emi Koussi** *Mt* Chad
40B2 **Emirdağ** Turkey
68C2 **Emmaus** USA
18B2 **Emmen** Netherlands
13D3 **Emmendingen** Germany
13D2 **Emmerich** Germany
58C2 **Emmett** USA
68B3 **Emmitsburg** USA
56C4 **Emory Peak** *Mt* USA
70A2 **Empalme** Mexico
47E2 **Empangeni** South Africa
74E3 **Empedrado** Argentina
37K2 **Emperor Seamount Chain** Pacific Ocean
63C1 **Emporia** Kansas, USA
65D3 **Emporia** Virginia, USA
68A2 **Emporium** USA
18B2 **Ems** *R* Germany
28B2 **Emu** China
8C2 **Enard B** Scotland
74E3 **Encarnación** Paraguay
48B4 **Enchi** Ghana
62C3 **Encinal** USA
66D4 **Encinitas** USA
75D2 **Encruzilhada** Brazil
32B1 **Endeh** Indonesia
76G11 **Enderby Land** *Region* Antarctica
61D1 **Enderlin** USA
65D2 **Endicott** USA
54C3 **Endicott Mts** USA
16C3 **Enfida** Tunisia
67C1 **Enfield** USA
27F5 **Engaño, C** Philippines
29D2 **Engaru** Japan
45C3 **En Gedi** Israel
21H5 **Engel's** Russian Federation
27D7 **Enggano** *I* Indonesia
10C3 **England** UK
55N4 **Englee** Canada
67C1 **Englehard** USA
65D1 **Englehart** Canada
60C3 **Englewood** USA
10C3 **English Channel** England/France
63C1 **Enid** USA
29D2 **Eniwa** Japan
48B3 **Enji** *Well* Mauritius
13C1 **Enkhuizen** Netherlands
12H7 **Enköping** Sweden
16C3 **Enna** Sicily, Italy
50C2 **En Nahud** Sudan
50C2 **Ennedi** *Desert Region* Chad
9C3 **Ennell, L** Irish Republic
34C1 **Enngonia** Australia
60C2 **Enning** USA
10B3 **Ennis** Irish Republic
58D1 **Ennis** Montana, USA
63C2 **Ennis** Texas, USA
9C3 **Enniscorthy** Irish Republic
9C2 **Enniskillen** Northern Ireland
45C2 **Enn Nâqoûra** Lebanon
18C3 **Enns** *R* Austria
12F8 **Enschede** Netherlands
70A1 **Ensenada** Mexico
31B3 **Enshi** China
13D4 **Ensisheim** France
50D4 **Entebbe** Uganda
67A2 **Enterprise** Alabama, USA
58C1 **Enterprise** Oregon, USA
74E4 **Entre Ríos** *State* Argentina
48C4 **Enugu** Nigeria
13E3 **Enz** *R* Germany
29C3 **Enzan** Japan
14C2 **Epernay** France
40A2 **Ephesus** Turkey
59D3 **Ephraim** USA
68B2 **Ephrata** Pennsylvania, USA
58C1 **Ephrata** Washington, USA
33F2 **Epi** *I* Vanuatu
14D2 **Épinal** France
45B1 **Episkopi** Cyprus
45B1 **Episkopi B** Cyprus
7E4 **Epping** England
13E3 **Eppingen** Germany
7D4 **Epsom** England
47B1 **Epukiro** Namibia
41F3 **Eqlid** Iran
46D7 **Equator**
48C4 **Equatorial Guinea** *Republic* W Africa
68D1 **Equinox Mt** USA
68C2 **Equinunk** USA
13E3 **Erbach** Germany
13D3 **Erbeskopf** *Mt* Germany
41D2 **Erciş** Turkey
21F8 **Erciyas Dağları** *Mt* Turkey
28B2 **Erdaobaihe** China
28B2 **Erdao Jiang** *R* China
31C1 **Erdene** Mongolia
26D2 **Erdenet** Mongolia
50C2 **Erdi** *Desert Region* Chad
74F3 **Erechim** Brazil
40B1 **Ereğli** Turkey
40B2 **Ereğli** Turkey
26E2 **Erenhot** China
15B1 **Eresma** *R* Spain
13D2 **Erft** *R* Germany
18C2 **Erfurt** Germany
40C2 **Ergani** Turkey
48B2 **Erg Chech** *Desert Region* Algeria/Mali
48D3 **Erg du Ténéré** *Desert Region* Niger
40A1 **Ergene** *R* Turkey
48B2 **Erg Iguidi** *Region* Algeria/Mauritania
19F1 **Ērgli** Latvia
50B2 **Erguig** *R* Chad
25N4 **Ergun'** *R* China/Russian Federation
26E1 **Ergun** *R* China/Russian Federation
25O4 **Ergun Zuoqi** China
50D2 **Eriba** Sudan
8C2 **Eriboll, Loch** *Inlet* Scotland
8C3 **Ericht, Loch** *L* Scotland
57F2 **Erie** USA
57E2 **Erie,L** Canada/USA
29D2 **Erimo-misaki** *C* Japan
8B3 **Eriskay** *I* Scotland
50D2 **Eritrea** *Republic* Africa
13D2 **Erkelenz** Germany
18C3 **Erlangen** Germany
63D2 **Erling,L** USA
47D2 **Ermelo** South Africa
44B4 **Ernākulam** India
9C2 **Erne, L** Northern Ireland
44B3 **Erode** India
34B1 **Eromanga** Australia
47B1 **Erongoberg** *Mt* Namibia
48B1 **Er Rachidia** Morocco
50D2 **Er Rahad** Sudan
51D5 **Errego** Mozambique
10B2 **Errigal** *Mt* Irish Republic
10A3 **Erris Head** *Pt* Irish Republic
33F2 **Erromanga** *I* Vanuatu
50D2 **Er Roseires** Sudan
45C2 **Er Rummān** Jordan
61D1 **Erskine** USA
13D3 **Erstein** France
18C2 **Erzgebirge** *Upland* Germany
21F8 **Erzincan** Turkey
21G8 **Erzurum** Turkey
29D2 **Esan-misaki** *C* Japan
29D2 **Esashi** Japan
18B1 **Esbjerg** Denmark
59D3 **Escalante** USA
56C4 **Escalón** Mexico
57E2 **Escanaba** USA
70C3 **Escárcega** Mexico
13C3 **Esch** Luxembourg
59C4 **Escondido** USA
70B2 **Escuinapa** Mexico
70C3 **Escuintla** Guatemala
50B3 **Eséka** Cameroon
13D1 **Esens** Germany
14C3 **Esera** *R* Spain
15C1 **Esera** *R* Spain
41F3 **Eşfahān** Iran
47E2 **Eshowe** South Africa
45C3 **Esh Sharā** *Upland* Jordan
8D4 **Esk** *R* Scotland
35C1 **Eskdale** New Zealand
12C1 **Eskifjörður** Iceland
12H7 **Eskilstuna** Sweden
54E3 **Eskimo Lakes** Canada
55J3 **Eskimo Point** Canada
21E8 **Eskişehir** Turkey
15A1 **Esla** *R* Spain
15A1 **Esla, Embalse del** *Res* Spain
69B2 **Esmeralda** Cuba
74A7 **Esmeralda** *I* Chile
72C3 **Esmeraldas** Ecuador
14C3 **Espalion** France
64C1 **Espanola** Canada
62A1 **Espanola** USA
32B4 **Esperance** Australia
76G2 **Esperanza** *Base* Antarctica
15A2 **Espichel, Cabo** *C* Portugal
75D2 **Espinhaço, Serra do** *Mts* Brazil
75D2 **Espírito Santo** *State* Brazil
33F2 **Espiritu Santo** *I* Vanuatu
51D6 **Espungabera** Mozambique
74B6 **Esquel** Argentina
58B1 **Esquimalt** Canada
45D2 **Es Samrā** Jordan
48B1 **Essaouira** Morocco
18B2 **Essen** Germany
73G3 **Essequibo** *R* Guyana
7E4 **Essex** *County* England

64C2 **Essexville** USA
18B3 **Esslingen** Germany
13B3 **Essonne** *Department* France
13C3 **Essoyes** France
74D8 **Estados, Isla de los** Argentina
73L6 **Estância** Brazil
47D2 **Estcourt** South Africa
72A1 **Esteí** Nicaragua
13B3 **Esternay** France
66B3 **Estero B** USA
74D2 **Esteros** Paraguay
60B2 **Estes Park** USA
54H5 **Estevan** Canada
61E2 **Estherville** USA
67B2 **Estill** USA
13B3 **Estissac** France
20C4 **Estonia** *Republic* Europe
66B3 **Estrella** *R* USA
15A2 **Estremoz** Portugal
19D3 **Esztergom** Hungary
34A1 **Etadunna** Australia
55L2 **Etah** Canada
43K2 **Etah** India
13C3 **Etam** France
14C2 **Étampes** France
34A1 **Etamunbanie,L** Australia
42D3 **Etāwah** India
50D3 **Ethiopia** *Republic* Africa
8C3 **Etive, Loch** *Inlet* Scotland
16C3 **Etna** *Vol* Sicily, Italy
51B5 **Etosha Nat Pk** Namibia
51B5 **Etosha Pan** *Salt L* Namibia
67B2 **Etowah** *R* USA
13C3 **Ettelbruck** Luxembourg
33H3 **Eua** *I* Tonga
34C2 **Euabalong** Australia
17E3 **Euboea** *I* Greece
64C2 **Euclid** USA
34C3 **Eucumbene,L** Australia
34A2 **Eudunda** Australia
63C1 **Eufala L** USA
67A2 **Eufaula** USA
56A2 **Eugene** USA
70A2 **Eugenia, Punta** *Pt* Mexico
34C1 **Eulo** Australia
63D2 **Eunice** Louisiana, USA
62B2 **Eunice** New Mexico, USA
13D2 **Eupen** Germany
40D3 **Euphrates** *R* Iraq/Syria
63E2 **Eupora** USA
14C2 **Eure** *R* France
58B2 **Eureka** California, USA
55K1 **Eureka** Canada
58C1 **Eureka** Montana, USA
56B3 **Eureka** Nevada, USA
60D1 **Eureka** S Dakota, USA
59D3 **Eureka** Utah, USA
55K2 **Eureka Sd** Canada
66D2 **Eureka V** USA
34C3 **Euroa** Australia
34C1 **Eurombah** *R* Australia
51E6 **Europa** *I* Mozambique Channel
13C2 **Europoort** Netherlands
18B2 **Euskirchen** Germany
63E2 **Eutaw** USA
55K1 **Evans,C** Canada
55L4 **Evans,L** Canada
60B3 **Evans,Mt** Colorado, USA
58D1 **Evans,Mt** Montana, USA
55K3 **Evans Str** Canada
64B2 **Evanston** Illinois, USA
56B2 **Evanston** Wyoming, USA
57E3 **Evansville** Indiana, USA
60B2 **Evansville** Wyoming, USA
47D2 **Evaton** South Africa
32C4 **Everard,L** Australia
39G3 **Everest,Mt** China/Nepal
68A2 **Everett** Pennsylvania, USA
56A2 **Everett** Washington, USA
68D1 **Everett,Mt** USA
57E4 **Everglades,The** *Swamp* USA
67A2 **Evergreen** USA
7D3 **Evesham** England
50B3 **Evinayong** Equatorial Guinea
12F7 **Evje** Norway
15A2 **Évora** Portugal
14C2 **Evreux** France
Évvoia = Euboea
8C3 **Ewe, Loch** *Inlet* Scotland
50B4 **Ewo** Congo
66C1 **Excelsior Mt** USA
66C1 **Excelsior Mts** USA
61E3 **Excelsior Springs** USA
7C4 **Exe** *R* England
59C3 **Exeter** California, USA
7C4 **Exeter** England
65E2 **Exeter** New Hampshire, USA
7C4 **Exmoor** England
7C4 **Exmouth** England
15A2 **Extremadura** *Region* Spain
70E2 **Exuma Sd** The Bahamas
50D4 **Eyasi, L** Tanzania
8D4 **Eyemouth** Scotland
50E3 **Eyl** Somalia
32B4 **Eyre** Australia
32C3 **Eyre Creek** *R* Australia
32C3 **Eyre,L** Australia
32C4 **Eyre Pen** Australia
17F3 **Ezine** Turkey

F

54G3 **Faber L** Canada
12F7 **Fåborg** Denmark
16C2 **Fabriano** Italy
50B2 **Fachi** Niger
50C2 **Fada** Chad
48C3 **Fada N'Gourma** Burkina
25Q2 **Faddeyevskiy, Ostrov** *I* Russian Federation
16C2 **Faenza** Italy
55N3 **Færingehavn** Greenland
12D3 **Faeroes** *Is* N Atlantic Oc
50B3 **Fafa** *R* Central African Republic
50E3 **Fafan** *R* Ethiopia
17E1 **Făgăraş** Romania
13C2 **Fagnes** *Region* Belgium
48B3 **Faguibine,L** Mali
41G5 **Fahūd** Oman
48A1 **Faiol** *I* Azores
62A2 **Fairacres** USA
54D3 **Fairbanks** USA
64C3 **Fairborn** USA
56D2 **Fairbury** USA
68B3 **Fairfax** USA
59B3 **Fairfield** California, USA
68D2 **Fairfield** Connecticut, USA
58D2 **Fairfield** Idaho, USA
58D1 **Fairfield** Montana, USA
64C3 **Fairfield** Ohio, USA
9C2 **Fair Head** *Pt* Northern Ireland
10C2 **Fair Isle** *I* Scotland
35B2 **Fairlie** New Zealand
61E2 **Fairmont** Minnesota, USA
64C3 **Fairmont** W Virginia, USA
68B1 **Fairport** USA
62C1 **Fairview** USA
54E4 **Fairweather,Mt** USA
27H6 **Fais** *I* Pacific Ocean
42C2 **Faisalabad** Pakistan
60C1 **Faith** USA
8E1 **Faither,The** *Pen* Scotland
33H1 **Fakaofo** *I* Tokelau Islands
7E3 **Fakenham** England
32C1 **Fakfak** Indonesia
28A2 **Faku** China
43G4 **Falam** Burma
70C2 **Falcon Res** Mexico/USA
48A3 **Falémé** *R* Mali/Senegal/Guinea
62C3 **Falfurrias** USA
12G7 **Falkenberg** Sweden
8D4 **Falkirk** Scotland
74D8 **Falkland Is** *Dependency* S Atlantic
74E8 **Falkland Sd** Falkland Islands
12G7 **Falköping** Sweden
66D4 **Fallbrook** USA
56B3 **Fallon** USA
65E2 **Fall River** USA
60B2 **Fall River P** USA
61D2 **Falls City** USA
7B4 **Falmouth** England
69H1 **Falmouth** Jamaica
65E2 **Falmouth** Maine, USA
68E2 **Falmouth** Massachusetts, USA
7B4 **Falmouth Bay** England
47B3 **False B** South Africa
70A2 **Falso,C** Mexico
18C2 **Falster** *I* Denmark
17F1 **Fălticeni** Romania
12H6 **Falun** Sweden
40B2 **Famagusta** Cyprus
45B1 **Famagusta B** Cyprus
13C2 **Famenne** *Region* Belgium
66C3 **Famoso** USA
30B2 **Fang** Thailand
50D3 **Fangak** Sudan
31E5 **Fangliao** Taiwan
8C3 **Fannich, L** Scotland
16C2 **Fano** Italy
45A3 **Fâqûs** Egypt
76G3 **Faraday** *Base* Antarctica
50C3 **Faradje** Zaïre
51E6 **Farafangana** Madagascar
49E2 **Farafra Oasis** Egypt
38E2 **Farah** Afghanistan
27H5 **Farallon de Medinilla** *I* Pacific Ocean
26H4 **Farallon de Pajaros** *I* Marianas
48A3 **Faranah** Guinea
50E2 **Farasan Is** Saudi Arabia
27H6 **Faraulep** *I* Pacific Ocean
55J5 **Farbault** USA
7D4 **Fareham** England
55O4 **Farewell,C** Greenland
33G5 **Farewell,C** New Zealand
35B2 **Farewell Spit** *Pt* New Zealand
56D2 **Fargo** USA
45C2 **Fari'a** *R* Israel
57D2 **Faribault** USA
43F4 **Faridpur** Bangladesh
41G2 **Farīmān** Iran
45A3 **Fâriskûr** Egypt
65E2 **Farmington** Maine, USA
63D1 **Farmington** Missouri, USA
68E1 **Farmington** New Hampshire, USA
56C3 **Farmington** New Mexico, USA
58D2 **Farmington** Utah, USA
66B2 **Farmington Res** USA
6D2 **Farne Deep** N Sea
15A2 **Faro** Portugal
12H7 **Fårö** *I* Sweden
46K9 **Farquhar Is** Indian Ocean
8C3 **Farrar** *R* Scotland
64C2 **Farrell** USA
43K2 **Farrukhabad** *District* India
17E3 **Fársala** Greece
75B4 **Fartura, Serra de** *Mts* Brazil
62B2 **Farwell** USA
41F4 **Fasā** Iran
21D5 **Fastov** Ukraine
43K2 **Fatehgarh** India
43E3 **Fatehpur** India
73H7 **Fatima du Sul** Brazil
58C1 **Fauquier** Canada
47D2 **Fauresmith** South Africa
12H5 **Fauske** Norway
7E4 **Faversham** England
55K4 **Fawn** *R* Canada
12H6 **Fax** *R* Sweden
12A2 **Faxaflói** *B* Iceland
50B2 **Faya** Chad
63E2 **Fayette** USA
57D3 **Fayetteville** Arkansas, USA
57F3 **Fayetteville** N Carolina, USA
67A1 **Fayetteville** Tennessee, USA
45B3 **Fâyid** Egypt
41E4 **Faylakah** *I* Kuwait
42C2 **Fāzilka** India
48A2 **Fdérik** Mauritius
57F3 **Fear,C** USA
66B1 **Feather** *R* USA
59B3 **Feather Middle Fork** *R* USA
14C2 **Fécamp** France
18C2 **Fehmarn** *I* Germany
75D3 **Feia, Lagoa** Brazil
72D5 **Feijó** Brazil
31C5 **Feilai Xai Bei Jiang** *R* China
35C2 **Feilding** New Zealand
51D5 **Feira** Zambia
73L6 **Feira de Santan** Brazil
40C2 **Feke** Turkey
13D4 **Feldberg** *Mt* Germany
18B3 **Feldkirch** Austria
10D3 **Felixstowe** England
12G6 **Femund** *L* Norway
28A2 **Fengcheng** China
31B4 **Fengdu** China
31B3 **Fengjie** China
31D1 **Fengning** China
31B3 **Feng Xian** China
31C1 **Fengzhen** China
31C2 **Fen He** *R* China
51E5 **Fenoarivo Atsinanana** Madagascar
21F7 **Feodosiya** Ukraine
41G3 **Ferdow** Iran
13B3 **Fère-Champenoise** France
39F1 **Fergana** Uzbekistan
61D1 **Fergus Falls** USA
48B4 **Ferkessedougou** Ivory Coast
9C2 **Fermanagh** *County* Northern Ireland
67B2 **Fernandina Beach** USA
73M4 **Fernando de Noronha, Isla** Brazil
75B3 **Fernandópolis** Brazil
Fernando Poo *I* **=Bioko**
58B1 **Ferndale** USA
58C1 **Fernie** Canada
59C3 **Fernley** USA
16C2 **Ferrara** Italy
15B2 **Ferrat, Cap** *C* Algeria
72C5 **Ferreñafe** Peru
63D2 **Ferriday** USA
13B3 **Ferrières** France
48B1 **Fès** Morocco
63D1 **Festus** USA
17F2 **Feteşti** Romania
9C3 **Fethard** Irish Republic
40A2 **Fethiye** Turkey
21J7 **Fetisovo** Kazakhstan
8E1 **Fetlar** *I* Scotland
55L4 **Feuilles, Rivière aux** *R* Canada
24J6 **Feyzabad** Afghanistan
7C3 **Ffestiniog** Wales
51E6 **Fianarantsoa** Madagascar
50D3 **Fichē** Ethiopia
47D2 **Ficksburg** South Africa
45C3 **Fidan, Wadi** Jordan
17D2 **Fier** Albania
8D3 **Fife** *Region* Scotland
8D3 **Fife Ness** *Pen* Scotland
14C3 **Figeac** France
15A1 **Figueira da Foz** Portugal
Figueres = Figueras
15C1 **Figueras** Spain
48B1 **Figuig** Morocco
33G2 **Fiji** *Is* Pacific Ocean
15B2 **Filabres, Sierra de los** *Mts* Spain
73G8 **Filadelfia** Paraguay
6D2 **Filey** England
17E2 **Filiaşi** Romania
17E3 **Filiatrá** Greece
16C3 **Filicudi** *I* Italy
59C4 **Fillmore** California, USA
59D3 **Fillmore** Utah, USA
8C3 **Findhorn** *R* Scotland
57E2 **Findlay** USA
65D2 **Finger Lakes** USA
51D5 **Fingoè** Mozambique
21E8 **Finike** Turkey
15A1 **Finisterre, Cabo** *C* Spain
32C3 **Finke** *R* Australia
20C3 **Finland** *Republic* N Europe
12J7 **Finland,G of** N Europe
54F4 **Finlay** *R* Canada
54F4 **Finlay Forks** Canada
34C3 **Finley** Australia
9C2 **Finn** *R* Irish Republic
12H5 **Finnsnes** Norway
27H7 **Finschhafen** Papua New Guinea
12H7 **Finspång** Sweden
18C2 **Finsterwalde** Germany
9C2 **Fintona** Northern Ireland
35A3 **Fiordland Nat Pk** New Zealand
45C2 **Fiq** Syria
21F8 **Firat** *R* Turkey
66B2 **Firebaugh** USA
Firenze = Florence
42D3 **Firozābād** India
42C2 **Firozpur** India
8C4 **Firth of Clyde** *Estuary* Scotland
8D3 **Firth of Forth** *Estuary* Scotland
8B3 **Firth of Lorn** *Estuary* Scotland
10C2 **Firth of Tay** *Estuary* Scotland
41F4 **Firūzābād** Iran
47B2 **Fish** *R* Namibia
47C3 **Fish** *R* South Africa
66C2 **Fish Camp** USA
68D2 **Fishers I** USA
55K3 **Fisher Str** Canada
7B4 **Fishguard** Wales
55N3 **Fiskenæsset** Greenland
13B3 **Fismes** France
65E2 **Fitchburg** USA
8E2 **Fitful Head** *Pt* Scotland
67B2 **Fitzgerald** USA
32B2 **Fitzroy** *R* Australia
32B2 **Fitzroy Crossing** Australia
64C1 **Fitzwilliam I** Canada
Fiume = Rijeka
50C4 **Fizi** Zaïre
47D3 **Flagstaff** South Africa
56B3 **Flagstaff** USA
65E1 **Flagstaff L** USA
6D2 **Flamborough Head** *C* England
56C2 **Flaming Gorge Res** USA
27G7 **Flamingo, Teluk** *B* Indonesia
13B2 **Flandres, Plaine des** Belgium/France
8B2 **Flannan Isles** Scotland
56B2 **Flathead L** USA
63D1 **Flat River** USA
27H8 **Flattery,C** Australia
56A2 **Flattery,C** USA
6C3 **Fleetwood** England
12F7 **Flekkefjord** Norway
26H4 **Fleming Deep** Pacific Ocean
68C2 **Flemington** USA
18B2 **Flensburg** Germany
32C4 **Flinders** *I* Australia
32D5 **Flinders** *I* Australia
32D2 **Flinders** *R* Australia
32C4 **Flinders Range** *Mts* Australia
54H4 **Flin Flon** Canada
57E2 **Flint** USA
7C3 **Flint** Wales
57E3 **Flint** *R* USA
13B2 **Flixecourt** France
64A1 **Floodwood** USA
67A2 **Florala** USA
57E3 **Florence** Alabama, USA
59D4 **Florence** Arizona, USA
60B3 **Florence** Colorado, USA
16C2 **Florence** Italy
63C1 **Florence** Kansas, USA
58B2 **Florence** Oregon, USA
57F3 **Florence** S Carolina, USA
66C2 **Florence L** USA
72C3 **Florencia** Colombia
74C6 **Florentine Ameghino, Embalse** *Res* Argentina
13C3 **Florenville** Belgium
70D3 **Flores** Guatemala
48A1 **Flores** *I* Azores
32B1 **Flores** *I* Indonesia
27E7 **Flores S** Indonesia
73K5 **Floriano** Brazil
74G3 **Florianópolis** Brazil
74E4 **Florida** Uruguay
70D2 **Florida** *State* USA
67B3 **Florida B** USA
67B3 **Florida City** USA
33E1 **Florida Is** Solomon Islands
57E4 **Florida Keys** *Is* USA
57E4 **Florida,Strs of** USA
17E2 **Flórina** Greece
12F6 **Florø** Norway
62B2 **Floydada** USA
32D1 **Fly** *R* Papua New Guinea
17F1 **Focşani** Romania
16D2 **Foggia** Italy
48A4 **Fogo** *I* Cape Verde
14C3 **Foix** France
64C1 **Foleyet** Canada
55L3 **Foley I** Canada
16C2 **Foligno** Italy
7E4 **Folkestone** England
67B2 **Folkston** USA
16C2 **Follonica** Italy
66B1 **Folsom** USA
68C1 **Fonda** USA
54H4 **Fond-du-Lac** Canada
57E2 **Fond du Lac** USA
70D3 **Fonseca, G de** Honduras
14C2 **Fontainbleau** France
14B2 **Fontenay-le-Comte** France
17D1 **Fonyód** Hungary
Foochow = Fuzhou
54C3 **Foraker, Mt** USA
13D3 **Forbach** France
34C2 **Forbes** Australia
48C4 **Forcados** Nigeria
66C3 **Ford City** USA
12F6 **Førde** Norway
7D4 **Fordingbridge** England
34C1 **Fords Bridge** Australia
63D2 **Fordyce** USA
48A4 **Forécariah** Guinea
55P3 **Forel,Mt** Greenland
58D1 **Foremost** Canada
64C2 **Forest** Canada
63E2 **Forest** USA
61E2 **Forest City** Iowa, USA
68C2 **Forest City** Pennsylvania, USA
7C4 **Forest of Dean** England
67B2 **Forest Park** USA
66A1 **Forestville** USA
13B3 **Forêt d'Othe** France
8D3 **Forfar** Scotland
62B1 **Forgan** USA
58B1 **Forks** USA
16C2 **Forli** Italy
7C3 **Formby** England
15C2 **Formentera** *I* Spain
15C1 **Formentor, Cabo** *C* Spain
16C2 **Formia** Italy
48A1 **Formigas** *I* Azores
Formosa = Taiwan
74E3 **Formosa** Argentina
73J7 **Formosa** Brazil
74D2 **Formosa** *State* Argentina
Formosa Channel = Taiwan Str
73G6 **Formosa, Serra** *Mts* Brazil
75C1 **Formoso** Brazil
75C1 **Formoso** *R* Brazil
8D3 **Forres** Scotland
32B4 **Forrest** Australia
57D3 **Forrest City** USA
32D2 **Forsayth** Australia
12J6 **Forssa** Finland
34D2 **Forster** Australia
63D1 **Forsyth** Missouri, USA
60B1 **Forsyth** Montana, USA
42C3 **Fort Abbas** Pakistan
55K4 **Fort Albany** Canada
73L4 **Fortaleza** Brazil
8C3 **Fort Augustus** Scotland
47D3 **Fort Beaufort** South Africa
58D1 **Fort Benton** USA
59B3 **Fort Bragg** USA
62C1 **Fort Cobb Res** USA
56C2 **Fort Collins** USA
65D1 **Fort Coulonge** Canada
62B2 **Fort Davis** USA
69E4 **Fort-de-France** Martinique
67A2 **Fort Deposit** USA

Fort Dodge **Gennargentu, Monti del**

57D2 **Fort Dodge** USA
32A3 **Fortescue** *R* Australia
57D2 **Fort Frances** Canada
54F3 **Fort Franklin** Canada
54F3 **Fort Good Hope** Canada
34B1 **Fort Grey** Australia
8C3 **Forth** *R* Scotland
62A2 **Fort Hancock** USA
55K4 **Fort Hope** Canada
8F3 **Forties** *Oilfield* N Sea
65F1 **Fort Kent** USA
48C1 **Fort Lallemand** Algeria
Fort Lamy = Ndjamena
60C2 **Fort Laramie** USA
57E4 **Fort Lauderdale** USA
54F3 **Fort Liard** Canada
54G4 **Fort Mackay** Canada
54G5 **Fort Macleod** Canada
54G4 **Fort McMurray** Canada
54E3 **Fort McPherson** Canada
64A2 **Fort Madison** USA
56C2 **Fort Morgan** USA
57E4 **Fort Myers** USA
54F4 **Fort Nelson** Canada
54F3 **Fort Norman** Canada
67A2 **Fort Payne** USA
60B1 **Fort Peck** USA
56C2 **Fort Peck Res** USA
57E4 **Fort Pierce** USA
60C2 **Fort Pierre** USA
68C1 **Fort Plain** USA
54G3 **Fort Providence** Canada
54G3 **Fort Resolution** Canada
50B4 **Fort Rousset** Congo
54F4 **Fort St James** Canada
54F4 **Fort St John** Canada
63D1 **Fort Scott** USA
54E3 **Fort Selkirk** Canada
55K4 **Fort Severn** Canada
21J7 **Fort Shevchenko** Kazakhstan
54F3 **Fort Simpson** Canada
54G3 **Fort Smith** Canada
57D3 **Fort Smith** USA
54F3 **Fort Smith** *Region* Canada
56C3 **Fort Stockton** USA
62B2 **Fort Sumner** USA
62C1 **Fort Supply** USA
58B2 **Fortuna** California, USA
60C1 **Fortuna** N Dakota, USA
54G4 **Fort Vermilion** Canada
67A2 **Fort Walton Beach** USA
57E2 **Fort Wayne** USA
8C3 **Fort William** Scotland
62A1 **Fort Wingate** USA
56D3 **Fort Worth** USA
54D3 **Fort Yukon** USA
31C5 **Foshan** China
55K2 **Fosheim Pen** Canada
61D1 **Fosston** USA
50B4 **Fougamou** Gabon
14B2 **Fougères** France
8D1 **Foula** *I* Scotland
7E4 **Foulness I** England
35B2 **Foulwind,C** New Zealand
50B3 **Foumban** Cameroon
48B2 **Foum el Alba** *Region* Mali
14C1 **Fourmies** France
17F3 **Foúrnoi** *I* Greece
48A3 **Fouta Djallon** *Mts* Guinea
33F5 **Foveaux Str** New Zealand
7B4 **Fowey** England
62B1 **Fowler** USA
64B2 **Fox** *R* USA
55K3 **Foxe Basin** *G* Canada
55K3 **Foxe Chan** Canada
55L3 **Foxe Pen** Canada
60B2 **Foxpark** USA
35C2 **Foxton** New Zealand
10B2 **Foyle, Lough** *Estuary* Irish Republic/Northern Ireland
51B5 **Foz do Cuene** Angola
74F3 **Foz do Iguaçu** Brazil
68B2 **Frackville** USA
15C1 **Fraga** Spain
68E1 **Framingham** USA
73J8 **Franca** Brazil
14C2 **France** *Republic* Europe
14D2 **Franche Comté** *Region* France
47D1 **Francistown** Botswana
58E2 **Francs Peak** *Mt* USA
13E2 **Frankenberg** Germany
64B2 **Frankfort** Indiana, USA
57E3 **Frankfort** Kentucky, USA
68C1 **Frankfort** New York, USA
47D2 **Frankfort** South Africa
18B2 **Frankfurt am Main** Germany
18C2 **Frankfurt an-der-Oder** Germany
18C3 **Fränkischer Alb** *Upland* Germany
58D2 **Franklin** Idaho, USA
64B3 **Franklin** Indiana, USA
63D3 **Franklin** Louisiana, USA
68E1 **Franklin** Massachusetts, USA
67B1 **Franklin** N Carolina, USA
68E1 **Franklin** New Hampshire, USA
68C2 **Franklin** New Jersey, USA
65D2 **Franklin** Pennsylvania, USA
67A1 **Franklin** Tennessee, USA
65D3 **Franklin** Virginia, USA
54F2 **Franklin B** Canada
58C1 **Franklin D Roosevelt** *L* USA
54F3 **Franklin Mts** Canada
54J2 **Franklin Str** Canada
68A1 **Franklinville** USA
35B2 **Franz Josef Glacier** New Zealand
Franz-Josef-Land = Zemlya Frantsa Josifa
54F5 **Fraser** *R* Canada
47C3 **Fraserburg** South Africa
8D3 **Fraserburgh** Scotland
34D1 **Fraser I** Australia
68C3 **Frederica** USA
18B1 **Fredericia** Denmark
65D3 **Frederick** Maryland, USA
62C2 **Frederick** Oklahoma, USA
62C2 **Fredericksburg** Texas, USA
65D3 **Fredericksburg** Virginia, USA
64A3 **Fredericktown** USA
55M5 **Fredericton** Canada
55N3 **Frederikshåp** Greenland
12G7 **Frederikshavn** Denmark
65D2 **Fredonia** USA
12G7 **Fredrikstad** Norway
68C2 **Freehold** USA
66C1 **Freel Peak** *Mt* USA
61D2 **Freeman** USA
64B2 **Freeport** Illinois, USA
63C3 **Freeport** Texas, USA
69B1 **Freeport** The Bahamas
62C3 **Freer** USA
48A4 **Freetown** Sierra Leone
18B3 **Freiburg** Germany
13D3 **Freiburg im Breisgau** Germany
18C3 **Freistadt** Austria
32A4 **Fremantle** Australia
66B2 **Fremont** California, USA
61D2 **Fremont** Nebraska, USA
64C2 **Fremont** Ohio, USA
73H3 **French Guiana** *Dependency* S America
60B1 **Frenchman** *R* USA
34C4 **Frenchmans Cap** *Mt* Australia
37M5 **French Polynesia** *Is* Pacific Ocean
15C2 **Frenda** Algeria
70B2 **Fresnillo** Mexico
56B3 **Fresno** USA
66C2 **Fresno** *R* USA
58D1 **Fresno Res** USA
13E3 **Freudenstadt** Germany
13B2 **Frévent** France
34C4 **Freycinet Pen** Australia
48A3 **Fria** Guinea
66C2 **Friant** USA
66C2 **Friant Dam** USA
16B1 **Fribourg** Switzerland
13E2 **Friedberg** Germany
18B3 **Friedrichshafen** Germany
13C1 **Friesland** *Province* Netherlands
62C3 **Frio** *R* USA
75D3 **Frio, Cabo** *C* Brazil
62B2 **Friona** USA
55M3 **Frobisher B** Canada
55M3 **Frobisher Bay** Canada
54H4 **Frobisher L** Canada
21G6 **Frolovo** Russian Federation
7C4 **Frome** England
7C4 **Frome** *R* England
32C4 **Frome,L** Australia
63D1 **Frontenac** USA
70C3 **Frontera** Mexico
65D3 **Front Royal** USA
16C2 **Frosinone** Italy
60B3 **Fruita** USA
31C5 **Fuchuan** China
31E4 **Fuding** China
70B2 **Fuerte** *R* Mexico
75A3 **Fuerte Olimpo** Brazil
74E2 **Fuerte Olimpo** Paraguay
48A2 **Fuerteventura** *I* Canary Islands
31C2 **Fugu** China
26B2 **Fuhai** China
41G4 **Fujairah** UAE
29C3 **Fuji** Japan
31D4 **Fujian** *Province* China
26G2 **Fujin** China
29C3 **Fujinomiya** Japan
29D3 **Fuji-san** *Mt* Japan
29C3 **Fujisawa** Japan
29C3 **Fuji-Yoshida** Japan
29D2 **Fukagawa** Japan
24K5 **Fukang** China
29D3 **Fukuchiyama** Japan
28A4 **Fukue** Japan
28A4 **Fukue** *I* Japan
29D3 **Fukui** Japan
28C4 **Fukuoka** Japan
29E3 **Fukushima** Japan
29C4 **Fukuyama** Japan
61D2 **Fulda** USA
18B2 **Fulda** Germany
18B2 **Fulda** *R* Germany
31B4 **Fuling** China
69L1 **Fullarton** Trinidad
66D4 **Fullerton** USA
6F1 **Fulmar** *Oilfield* N Sea
64A2 **Fulton** Illinois, USA
64B3 **Fulton** Kentucky, USA
65D2 **Fulton** New York, USA
13C2 **Fumay** France
29D3 **Funabashi** Japan
33G1 **Funafuti** *I* Tuvalu
48A1 **Funchal** Madeira
75D2 **Fundão** Brazil
55M5 **Fundy,B of** Canada
51D6 **Funhalouro** Mozambique
31B5 **Funing** China
31D3 **Funing** China
48C3 **Funtua** Nigeria
31D4 **Fuqing** China
51D5 **Furancungo** Mozambique
29D2 **Furano** Japan
41G4 **Fūrg** Iran
75B2 **Furnas, Serra das** *Mts* Brazil
32D5 **Furneaux Group** *Is* Australia
13D1 **Furstenau** Germany
18C2 **Fürstenwalde** Germany
18C3 **Fürth** Germany
29D2 **Furubira** Japan
29E3 **Furukawa** Japan
55K3 **Fury and Hecla Str** Canada
28A2 **Fushun** China
31A4 **Fushun** Sichuan, China
28B2 **Fusong** China
18C3 **Füssen** Germany
31E2 **Fu Xian** China
31E1 **Fuxin** China
31D3 **Fuyang** China
31E1 **Fuyuan** Liaoning, China
31A4 **Fuyuan** Yunnan, China
26B2 **Fuyun** China
31D4 **Fuzhou** China
28A3 **Fuzhoucheng** China
18C1 **Fyn** *I* Denmark
8C3 **Fyne, Loch** *Inlet* Scotland

G

50E3 **Gaalkacyo** Somalia
59C3 **Gabbs** USA
66C1 **Gabbs Valley Range** *Mts* USA
51B5 **Gabela** Angola
48D1 **Gabès, G de** Tunisia
66B2 **Gabilan Range** *Mts* USA
50B4 **Gabon** *Republic* Africa
47D1 **Gaborone** Botswana
15A1 **Gabriel y Galán, Embalse** *Res* Spain
17F2 **Gabrovo** Bulgaria
41F3 **Gach Sārān** Iran
44B2 **Gadag** India
67A2 **Gadsden** Alabama, USA
59D4 **Gadsden** Arizona, USA
16C2 **Gaeta** Italy
27H6 **Gaferut** *I* Pacific Ocean
67B1 **Gaffney** USA
45A3 **Gafra, Wadi el** Egypt
48C1 **Gafsa** Tunisia
20E4 **Gagarin** Russian Federation
55M4 **Gagnon** Canada
21G7 **Gagra** Georgia
43F3 **Gaibanda** Bangladesh
74C6 **Gaimán** Argentina
67B3 **Gainesville** Florida, USA
67B2 **Gainesville** Georgia, USA
63C2 **Gainesville** Texas, USA
7D3 **Gainsborough** England
32C4 **Gairdner, L** Australia
8C3 **Gairloch** Scotland
68B3 **Gaithersburg** USA
28A2 **Gai Xian** China
44B2 **Gajendragarh** India
31D4 **Ga Jiang** *R* China
47C2 **Gakarosa** *Mt* South Africa
50D4 **Galana** *R* Kenya
72N **Galapagos Is** Pacific Ocean
Gálápagos, Islas = Galapagos Islands
8D4 **Galashiels** Scotland
17F1 **Galaţi** Romania
64C3 **Galax** USA
62A2 **Galeana** Mexico
54C3 **Galena** Alaska, USA
64A2 **Galena** Illinois, USA
63D1 **Galena** Kansas, USA
69L1 **Galeota Pt** Trinidad
69L1 **Galera Pt** Trinidad
64A2 **Galesburg** USA
68B2 **Galeton** USA
20G4 **Galich** Russian Federation
15A1 **Galicia** *Region* Spain
Galilee,S of = Tiberias,L
69J1 **Galina Pt** Jamaica
50D2 **Gallabat** Sudan
67A1 **Gallatin** USA
58D1 **Gallatin** *R* USA
44C4 **Galle** Sri Lanka
62A3 **Gallego** Mexico
15B1 **Gállego** *R* Spain
72D1 **Gallinas, Puerta** Colombia
Gallipolī = Gelibolu
17D2 **Gallipoli** Italy
20C2 **Gällivare** Sweden
8C4 **Galloway** *District* Scotland
8C4 **Galloway,Mull of** *C* Scotland
62A1 **Gallup** USA
66B1 **Galt** USA
9B3 **Galty Mts** Irish Republic
70C2 **Galveston** USA
57D4 **Galveston B** USA
10B3 **Galway** Irish Republic
10B3 **Galway B** Irish Republic
43F3 **Gamba** China
48B3 **Gambaga** Ghana
54A3 **Gambell** USA
48A3 **Gambia** *R* Senegal/The Gambia
48A3 **Gambia,The** *Republic* Africa
37N6 **Gambier, Îles** Pacific Ocean
50B4 **Gamboma** Congo
51B5 **Gambos** Angola
44C4 **Gampola** Sri Lanka
59E3 **Ganado** USA
50E3 **Ganale Dorya** *R* Ethiopia
65D2 **Gananoque** Canada
Gand = Gent
51B5 **Ganda** Angola
51C4 **Gandajika** Zaïre
43N2 **Gandak** *R* India/Nepal
43M2 **Gandak Dam** Nepal
42B3 **Gandava** Pakistan
55N5 **Gander** Canada
42B4 **Gāndhīdhām** India
42C4 **Gāndhīnagar** India
42D4 **Gāndhi Sāgar** *L* India
15B2 **Gandia** Spain
75E1 **Gandu** Brazil
Ganga *R* **=Ganges**
42C3 **Gangānagar** India
43G4 **Gangaw** Burma
31A2 **Gangca** China
39G2 **Gangdise Shan** *Mts* China
22F4 **Ganges** *R* India
43F4 **Ganges, Mouths of the** Bangladesh/India
28B2 **Gangou** China
43F3 **Gangtok** India
31B3 **Gangu** China
58E2 **Gannett Peak** *Mt* USA
31B2 **Ganquan** China
12K8 **Gantsevichi** Belarus
31D4 **Ganzhou** China
48C3 **Gao** Mali
31A2 **Gaolan** China
31C2 **Gaoping** China
48B3 **Gaoua** Burkina
48A3 **Gaoual** Guinea
31D3 **Gaoyou Hu** *L* China
31C5 **Gaozhou** China
14D3 **Gap** France
42D2 **Gar** China
9C3 **Gara,L** Irish Republic
34C1 **Garah** Australia
73L5 **Garanhuns** Brazil
59B2 **Garberville** USA
75C3 **Garça** Brazil
15A2 **Garcia de Sola, Embalse de** *Res* Spain
75B3 **Garcias** Brazil
16C1 **Garda, L di** Italy
62B1 **Garden City** USA
64B1 **Garden Pen** USA
42B2 **Gardez** Afghanistan
58D1 **Gardiner** USA
68D2 **Gardiners I** USA
68E1 **Gardner** USA
33H1 **Gardner** *I* Phoenix Islands
66C1 **Gardnerville** USA
16D2 **Gargano, Monte** *Mt* Italy
16D2 **Gargano, Prom. del** Italy
42D4 **Garhākota** India
43K1 **Garhmuktesar** India
20L4 **Gari** Russian Federation
47B3 **Garies** South Africa
50D4 **Garissa** Kenya
63C2 **Garland** USA
18C3 **Garmisch-Partenkirchen** Germany
41F2 **Garmsar** Iran
63C1 **Garnett** USA
56B2 **Garnett Peak** *Mt* USA
14C3 **Garonne** *R* France
49D4 **Garoua** Cameroon
49D4 **Garoua Boulai** Cameroon
60C1 **Garrison** USA
9D2 **Garron** *Pt* Northern Ireland
8C3 **Garry** *R* Scotland
54H3 **Garry L** Canada
43E4 **Garwa** India
64B2 **Gary** USA
39G2 **Garyarsa** China
63C2 **Garza-Little Elm** *Res* USA
41F2 **Gasan Kuli** Turkmenistan
14B3 **Gascogne** *Region* France
63D1 **Gasconade** *R* USA
32A3 **Gascoyne** *R* Australia
50B3 **Gashaka** Nigeria
48D3 **Gashua** Nigeria
57G2 **Gaspé** Canada
57G2 **Gaspé,C de** Canada
57G2 **Gaspé, Peninsule de** Canada
67B1 **Gastonia** USA
67C1 **Gaston,L** USA
45B1 **Gata, C** Cyprus
15B2 **Gata, Cabo de** *C* Spain
20D4 **Gatchina** Russian Federation
8C4 **Gatehouse of Fleet** Scotland
6D2 **Gateshead** England
63C2 **Gatesville** USA
13B3 **Gâtinais** *Region* France
65D1 **Gatineau** Canada
65D1 **Gatineau** *R* Canada
67B1 **Gatlinburg** USA
34D1 **Gatton** Australia
33F2 **Gaua** *I* Vanuatu
43G3 **Gauhāti** India
19E1 **Gauja** *R* Latvia
43E3 **Gauri Phanta** India
17E4 **Gávdhos** *I* Greece
75D1 **Gavião** *R* Brazil
66B3 **Gaviota** USA
12H6 **Gävle** Sweden
32C4 **Gawler Ranges** *Mts* Australia
31A1 **Gaxun Nur** *L* China
43E4 **Gaya** India
48C3 **Gaya** Niger
48C3 **Gaya** Nigeria
28B2 **Gaya He** *R* China
64C1 **Gaylord** USA
34D1 **Gayndah** Australia
20J3 **Gayny** Russian Federation
19F3 **Gaysin** Ukraine
40B3 **Gaza** Israel
40C2 **Gaziantep** Turkey
48B4 **Gbaringa** Liberia
48D1 **Gbbès** Tunisia
19D2 **Gdańsk** Poland
19D2 **Gdańsk,G of** Poland
12K7 **Gdov** Russian Federation
19D2 **Gdynia** Poland
45A4 **Gebel el Galâla el Baharîya** *Desert* Egypt
50D2 **Gedaref** Sudan
17F3 **Gediz** *R* Turkey
18C2 **Gedser** Denmark
13C2 **Geel** Belgium
34B3 **Geelong** Australia
34C4 **Geeveston** Australia
48D3 **Geidam** Nigeria
13D2 **Geilenkirchen** Germany
50D4 **Geita** Tanzania
31A5 **Gejiu** China
16C3 **Gela** Italy
50E3 **Geladī** Ethiopia
13D2 **Geldern** Germany
17F2 **Gelibolu** Turkey
40B2 **Gelidonya Burun** Turkey
13E2 **Gelnhausen** Germany
13D2 **Gelsenkirchen** Germany
12F8 **Gelting** Germany
30C5 **Gemas** Malaysia
13C2 **Gembloux** Belgium
50B3 **Gemena** Zaïre
40C2 **Gemerek** Turkey
40A1 **Gemlik** Turkey
16C1 **Gemona** Italy
47C2 **Gemsbok Nat Pk** Botswana
50C2 **Geneina** Sudan
74C5 **General Alvear** Argentina
76F2 **General Belgrano** *Base* Antarctica
76G2 **General Bernardo O'Higgins** *Base* Antarctica
74B7 **General Carrera, Lago** Chile
74D2 **General Eugenio A Garay** Paraguay
66C2 **General Grant Grove Section** *Region* USA
74C3 **General Manuel Belgrano** *Mt* Argentina
74D5 **General Pico** Argentina
74C5 **General Roca** Argentina
27F6 **General Santos** Philippines
65D2 **Genesee** *R* USA
65D2 **Geneseo** USA
61D2 **Geneva** Nebraska, USA
68B1 **Geneva** New York, USA
16B1 **Geneva** Switzerland
Geneva,L of = Léman, L
Genève = Geneva
15B2 **Genil** *R* Spain
16B2 **Gennargentu, Monti del** *Mt* Sardinia, Italy

34C3 **Genoa** Australia
16B2 **Genoa** Italy
Genova = Genoa
16B2 **Genova, G di** Italy
13B2 **Gent** Belgium
27D7 **Genteng** Indonesia
18C2 **Genthin** Germany
21H7 **Geokchay** Azerbaijan
47C3 **George** South Africa
55M4 **George** *R* Canada
34C2 **George,L** Australia
67B3 **George,L** Florida, USA
65E2 **George,L** New York, USA
35A2 **George Sd** New Zealand
34C4 **George Town** Australia
66B1 **Georgetown** California, USA
65D3 **Georgetown** Delaware, USA
73G2 **Georgetown** Guyana
64C3 **Georgetown** Kentucky, USA
30C4 **George Town** Malaysia
69N2 **Georgetown** St Vincent
67C2 **Georgetown** S Carolina, USA
63C2 **Georgetown** Texas, USA
48A3 **Georgetown** The Gambia
76G8 **George V Land** *Region* Antarctica
62C3 **George West** USA
21G7 **Georgia** *Republic* Europe
76F12 **Georg Forster** *Base* Antarctica
67B2 **Georgia** *State* USA
64C1 **Georgian B** Canada
54F5 **Georgia, Str of** Canada
32C3 **Georgina** *R* Australia
21F5 **Georgiu-Dezh** Russian Federation
21G7 **Georgiyevsk** Russian Federation
76F1 **Georg von Neumayer** *Base* Antarctica
18C2 **Gera** Germany
13B2 **Geraardsbergen** Belgium
75C1 **Geral de Goiás, Serra** *Mts* Brazil
35B2 **Geraldine** New Zealand
75C2 **Geral do Paraná, Serra** *Mts* Brazil
32A3 **Geraldton** Australia
57E2 **Geraldton** Canada
75D2 **Geral, Serra** *Mts* Bahia, Brazil
75B4 **Geral, Serra** *Mts* Paraná, Brazil
45C3 **Gerar** *R* Israel
13D3 **Gérardmer** France
54C3 **Gerdine,Mt** USA
30C4 **Gerik** Malaysia
60C2 **Gering** USA
21C6 **Gerlachovsky** *Mt* Poland
47D2 **Germiston** South Africa
13D2 **Gerolstein** Germany
15C1 **Gerona** Spain
13E2 **Geseke** Germany
50E3 **Gestro** *R* Ethiopia
15B1 **Getafe** Spain
68B3 **Gettysburg** Pennsylvania, USA
60D1 **Gettysburg** S Dakota, USA
41D2 **Gevaş** Turkey
17E2 **Gevgeliija** Macedonia, Yugoslavia
45D2 **Ghabāghib** Syria
45D3 **Ghadaf, Wadi el** Jordan
48C1 **Ghadamis** Libya
41F2 **Ghaem Shahr** Iran
43E3 **Ghāghara** *R* India
48B4 **Ghana** *Republic* Africa
47C1 **Ghanzi** Botswana
48C1 **Ghardaïa** Algeria
49D1 **Gharyān** Libya
49D2 **Ghāt** Libya
15B2 **Ghazaouet** Algeria
42D3 **Ghāziābād** India
42B2 **Ghazni** Afghanistan
17F1 **Gheorgheni** Romania
40D3 **Ghudāf, Wadi al** *Watercourse* Iraq
16D3 **Giarre** Sicily, Italy
60D2 **Gibbon** USA
47B2 **Gibeon** Namibia
15A2 **Gibraltar** *Colony* SW Europe
7E7 **Gibraltar** *Pt* England
15A2 **Gibraltar,Str of** Africa/Spain
32B3 **Gibson Desert** Australia
58B1 **Gibsons** Canada
44B2 **Giddalūr** India
45B3 **Giddi, Gebel el** *Mt* Egypt
45B3 **Giddi Pass** Egypt
50D3 **Gīdolē** Ethiopia
13B4 **Gien** France
18B2 **Giessen** Germany
8D4 **Gifford** Scotland
67B3 **Gifford** USA
29D3 **Gifu** Japan
8C4 **Gigha** *I* Scotland
16C2 **Giglio** *I* Italy
15A1 **Gijón** Spain
59D4 **Gila** *R* USA
59D4 **Gila Bend** USA
59D4 **Gila Bend Mts** USA
32D2 **Gilbert** *R* Australia
33G1 **Gilbert Is** Pacific Ocean
58D1 **Gildford** USA
51D5 **Gilé** Mozambique
45C2 **Gilead** *Region* Jordan
49E2 **Gilf Kebir Plat** Egypt
34C2 **Gilgandra** Australia
42C1 **Gilgit** Pakistan
42C1 **Gilgit** *R* Pakistan
34C2 **Gilgunnia** Australia
55J4 **Gillam** Canada
60B2 **Gillette** USA
7E4 **Gillingham** England
64B1 **Gills Rock** USA
64B2 **Gilman** USA
66B2 **Gilroy** USA
69P2 **Gimie, Mont** St Lucia
45B3 **Gineifa** Egypt
47E2 **Gingindlovu** South Africa
50E3 **Gīnīr** Ethiopia
17E3 **Gióna** *Mt* Greece
34C3 **Gippsland** *Mts* Australia
64C2 **Girard** USA
72D3 **Girardot** Colombia
8D3 **Girdle Ness** *Pen* Scotland
40C1 **Giresun** Turkey
40B4 **Girga** Egypt
42C4 **Gīr Hills** India
50B3 **Giri** *R* Zaïre
43F4 **Girīdīh** India
42A2 **Girishk** Afghanistan
13D4 **Giromagny** France
Girona = Gerona
14B2 **Gironde** *R* France
8C4 **Girvan** Scotland
35C1 **Gisborne** New Zealand
50C4 **Gitega** Burundi
Giuba,R = Juba,R
17F2 **Giurgiu** Romania
13C2 **Givet** France
25S3 **Gizhiga** Russian Federation
19E2 **Gizycko** Poland
17E2 **Gjirokastër** Albania
54J3 **Gjoatlaven** Canada
12G6 **Gjøvik** Norway
55M5 **Glace Bay** Canada
58B1 **Glacier Peak** *Mt* USA
55K2 **Glacier Str** Canada
32E3 **Gladstone** Queensland, Australia
34A2 **Gladstone** S Aust, Australia
34C4 **Gladstone** Tasmania, Australia
64B1 **Gladstone** USA
12A1 **Gláma** *Mt* Iceland
12G6 **Glåma** *R* Norway
13D3 **Glan** *R* Germany
61D3 **Glasco** USA
64B3 **Glasgow** Kentucky, USA
60B1 **Glasgow** Montana, USA
8C4 **Glasgow** Scotland
68C3 **Glassboro** USA
66C2 **Glass Mt** USA
7C4 **Glastonbury** England
20J4 **Glazov** Russian Federation
18D3 **Gleisdorf** Austria
35C1 **Glen Afton** New Zealand
9D2 **Glenarm** Northern Ireland
68B3 **Glen Burnie** USA
47E2 **Glencoe** South Africa
59D4 **Glendale** Arizona, USA
66C3 **Glendale** California, USA
60C1 **Glendive** USA
60C2 **Glendo Res** USA
9C2 **Glengad Hd** *Pt* Irish Republic
34D1 **Glen Innes** Australia
8C4 **Glenluce** Scotland
34C1 **Glenmorgan** Australia
34D2 **Glenreagh** Australia
68B3 **Glen Rock** USA
63C2 **Glen Rose** USA
8D3 **Glenrothes** Scotland
68D1 **Glens Falls** USA
63D2 **Glenwood** Arkansas, USA
61D1 **Glenwood** Minnesota, USA
62A2 **Glenwood** New Mexico, USA
60B3 **Glenwood Springs** USA
64A1 **Glidden** USA
12F6 **Glittertind** *Mt* Norway
19D2 **Gliwice** Poland
59D4 **Globe** USA
18D2 **Głogów** Poland
12G5 **Glomfjord** Norway
51E5 **Glorieuses, Isles** Madagascar
7C3 **Glossop** England
34D2 **Gloucester** Australia
7C4 **Gloucester** England
68E1 **Gloucester** USA
7C4 **Gloucester** *County* England
68C1 **Gloversville** USA
19F1 **Glubokoye** Belarus
13E1 **Glückstadt** Germany
21E5 **Glukhov** Ukraine
18D3 **Gmünd** Austria
18C3 **Gmunden** Austria
19D2 **Gniezno** Poland
44A2 **Goa, Daman and Diu** *Union Territory* India
47B2 **Goageb** Namibia
43G3 **Goālpāra** India
50D3 **Goba** Ethiopia
47B1 **Gobabis** Namibia
31B1 **Gobi** *Desert* China/Mongolia
29C4 **Gobo** Japan
19G1 **Gobza** *R* Russian Federation
47B1 **Gochas** Namibia
7D4 **Godalming** England
44C2 **Godāvari** *R* India
66C2 **Goddard,Mt** USA
64C2 **Goderich** Canada
55N3 **Godhavn** Greenland
42C4 **Godhra** India
57D1 **Gods L** Canada
55N3 **Godthåb** Greenland
Godwin Austen *Mt* **=K2**
68E1 **Goffstown** USA
64C1 **Gogama** Canada
13E1 **Gohfeld** Germany
75C2 **Goiandira** Brazil
75C2 **Goianésia** Brazil
75C2 **Goiânia** Brazil
75B2 **Goiás** Brazil
73J6 **Goiás** *State* Brazil
75B3 **Goio-Erê** Brazil
50D3 **Gojab** *R* Ethiopia
17F2 **Gökçeada** *I* Turkey
17F3 **Gökova Körfezi** *B* Turkey
21F8 **Goksu** *R* Turkey
40C2 **Göksun** Turkey
43G3 **Golāghāt** India
9B2 **Gola, I** Irish Republic
40C2 **Gölbaşı** Turkey
24K2 **Gol'chikha** Russian Federation
58C2 **Golconda** USA
68B2 **Gold** USA
58B2 **Gold Beach** USA
34D1 **Gold Coast** Australia
35B2 **Golden B** New Zealand
58B1 **Goldendale** USA
66A2 **Golden Gate** *Chan* USA
63D3 **Golden Meadow** USA
59C3 **Goldfield** USA
66D2 **Gold Point** USA
67C1 **Goldsboro** USA
62C2 **Goldthwaite** USA
18C2 **Goleniów** Poland
66C3 **Goleta** USA
26C3 **Golmud** China
50E3 **Gololcha** Ethiopia
29F2 **Golovnino** Russian Federation
50C4 **Goma** Zaïre
43L2 **Gomati** India
48D3 **Gombe** Nigeria
19G2 **Gomel** Belarus
48A2 **Gomera** *I* Canary Islands
70B2 **Gómez Palacio** Mexico
25O4 **Gonam** *R* Russian Federation
69C3 **Gonâve, Isla de la** Cuba
41G2 **Gonbad-e Kāvūs** Iran
43E3 **Gonda** India
42C4 **Gondal** India
50D2 **Gonder** Ethiopia
43E4 **Gondia** India
40A1 **Gönen** Turkey
17F3 **Gonen** *R* Turkey
31A4 **Gongga Shan** *Mt* China
31A2 **Gonghe** China
75D1 **Gongogi** *R* Brazil
48D3 **Gongola** *R* Nigeria
66B2 **Gonzales** California, USA
63C3 **Gonzales** Texas, USA
47B3 **Good Hope,C of** South Africa
58D2 **Gooding** USA
60C3 **Goodland** USA
34C1 **Goodooga** *R* Australia
7D3 **Goole** England
34C2 **Goolgowi** Australia
34A3 **Goolwa** Australia
32A4 **Goomalling** Australia
34C2 **Goombalie** Australia
34D1 **Goomeri** Australia
34D1 **Goondiwindi** Australia
55N4 **Goose Bay** Canada
67C2 **Goose Creek** USA
58B2 **Goose L** USA
44B2 **Gooty** India
32D1 **Goraka** Papua New Guinea
43E3 **Gorakhpur** India
20K3 **Gora Koyp** *Mt* Russian Federation
25M4 **Gora Munku Sardyk** *Mt* Mongolia/Russian Federation
20K3 **Gora Narodnaya** *Mt* Russian Federation
20L2 **Gora Pay-Yer** *Mt* Russian Federation
20K3 **Gora Telpos-Iz** *Mt*
17D2 **Goražde** Bosnia-Herzegovina
54D2 **Gordon** USA
65D3 **Gordonsville** USA
50B3 **Goré** Chad
50D3 **Gorē** Ethiopia
35A3 **Gore** New Zealand
25P4 **Gore Topko** *Mt* Russian Federation
9C3 **Gorey** Irish Republic
41F2 **Gorgān** Iran
13C2 **Gorinchem** Netherlands
41E2 **Goris** Armenia
16C1 **Gorizia** Italy
19G2 **Gorki** Belarus
20M2 **Gorki** Russian Federation
Gorki = Novgorod
20G4 **Gor'kovskoye Vodokhranilishche** *Res* Russian Federation
7E3 **Gorleston** England
18C2 **Görlitz** Germany
21F6 **Gorlovka** Ukraine
66C3 **Gorman** USA
17F2 **Gorna Orjahovica** Bulgaria
26B1 **Gorno-Altaysk** Russian Federation
26H2 **Gornozavodsk** Russian Federation
20K3 **Goro Denezhkin Kamen'** *Mt* Russian Federation
20G4 **Gorodets** Russian Federation
19G2 **Gorodnya** Ukraine
19F1 **Gorodok** Belarus
19E3 **Gorodok** Ukraine
19F3 **Gorodok** Ukraine
27H7 **Goroka** Papua New Guinea
51D5 **Gorongosa** Mozambique
27F6 **Gorontalo** Indonesia
20L4 **Goro Yurma** *Mt* Russian Federation
75D2 **Gorutuba** *R* Brazil
25M4 **Goryachinsk** Russian Federation
21J7 **Gory Akkyr** *Upland* Turkmenistan
25L2 **Gory Byrranga** *Mts* Russian Federation
19F3 **Goryn'** *R* Ukraine
25L3 **Gory Putorana** *Mts* Russian Federation
19E2 **Góry Świętokrzyskie** *Upland* Poland
12H8 **Gorzów Wielkopolski** Poland
66C2 **Goshen** USA
29E2 **Goshogawara** Japan
16D2 **Gospić** Croatia
7D4 **Gosport** England
17E2 **Gostivar** Macedonia, Yugoslavia
19D2 **Gostynin** Poland
12G7 **Göteborg** Sweden
50B3 **Gotel Mts** Nigeria
60C2 **Gothenburg** USA
12H7 **Gotland** *I* Sweden
28B4 **Gotō-rettō** *Is* Japan
12H7 **Gotska Sandön** *I* Sweden
28C4 **Gōtsu** Japan
18B2 **Göttingen** Germany
28A2 **Goubangzi** China
13C2 **Gouda** Netherlands
50B2 **Goudoumaria** Niger
52H7 **Gough I** Atlantic Ocean
55L5 **Gouin, Réservoire** Canada
34C2 **Goulburn** Australia
48B3 **Goumbou** Mali
48B3 **Goundam** Mali
50B2 **Gouré** Niger
48B3 **Gourma Rharous** Mali
50B2 **Gouro** Chad
58E1 **Govenlock** Canada
27G8 **Gove Pen** Australia
21C6 **Goverla** *Mt* Ukraine
75D2 **Governador Valadares** Brazil
43E4 **Govind Ballabh Paht Sāgar** *L* India
42B3 **Gowārān** Afghanistan
7B4 **Gower** Wales
74E3 **Goya** Argentina
50C2 **Goz-Beïda** Chad
16C3 **Gozo** *I* Malta
50D2 **Goz Regeb** Sudan
47C3 **Graaff-Reinet** South Africa
65D1 **Gracefield** Canada
69A4 **Gracias à Dios, Cabo** Honduras
34D1 **Grafton** Australia
61D1 **Grafton** N Dakota, USA
64C3 **Grafton** W Virginia, USA
54E4 **Graham I** Canada
59E4 **Graham,Mt** USA
47D3 **Grahamstown** South Africa
73J5 **Grajaú** Brazil
19E2 **Grajewo** Poland
17E2 **Grámmos** *Mt* Albania/Greece
8C3 **Grampian** *Mts* Scotland
8D3 **Grampian** *Region* Scotland
72D3 **Granada** Colombia
72A1 **Granada** Nicaragua
15B2 **Granada** Spain
65E1 **Granby** Canada
60B2 **Granby** USA
48A2 **Gran Canaria** *I* Canary Islands
74D3 **Gran Chaco** *Region* Argentina
64B2 **Grand** *R* Michigan, USA
61E2 **Grand** *R* Missouri, USA
69Q2 **Grand B** Dominica
57F4 **Grand Bahama** *I* The Bahamas
13D4 **Grand Ballon** *Mt* France
55N5 **Grand Bank** Canada
52F2 **Grand Banks** Atlantic Ocean
48B4 **Grand Bassam** Ivory Coast
59D3 **Grand Canyon** USA
59D3 **Grand Canyon Nat Pk** USA
69A3 **Grand Cayman** *I* Cayman Is, Caribbean Sea
58C1 **Grand Coulee** USA
73K6 **Grande** *R* Bahia, Brazil
75C2 **Grande** *R* Minas Gerais/São Paulo, Brazil
55L4 **Grande 2, Rēservoir de la** Canada
55L4 **Grande 3, Rēservoir de la** Canada
55L4 **Grande 4, Rēservoir de la** Canada
74C8 **Grande, Bahía** *B* Argentina
51E5 **Grande Comore** *I* Comoros
75D3 **Grande, Ilha** Brazil
63C2 **Grande Prairie** USA
50B2 **Grand Erg de Bilma** *Desert Region* Niger
48C1 **Grand Erg Occidental** *Desert* Algeria
48C2 **Grand Erg Oriental** *Desert* Algeria
55L4 **Grande Rivière de la Baleine** *R* Canada
58C1 **Grande Ronde** *R* USA
59D4 **Gran Desierto** USA
55M5 **Grand Falls** New Brunswick, Canada
55N5 **Grand Falls** Newfoundland, Canada
58C1 **Grand Forks** Canada
61D1 **Grand Forks** USA
68C1 **Grand Gorge** USA
64B2 **Grand Haven** USA
60D2 **Grand Island** USA
63E2 **Grand Isle** USA
60B3 **Grand Junction** USA
63D3 **Grand L** USA
64A1 **Grand Marais** USA
65E1 **Grand Mère** Canada
15A2 **Grândola** Portugal
54G4 **Grand Prairie** Canada
54J4 **Grand Rapids** Canada
64B2 **Grand Rapids** Michigan, USA
64A1 **Grand Rapids** Minnesota, USA
16B1 **Grand St Bernard, Col du** *P* Italy/Switzerland
56B2 **Grand Teton** *Mt* USA
58D2 **Grand Teton Nat Pk** USA
60B3 **Grand Valley** USA
58C1 **Grangeville** USA
58E1 **Granite Peak** *Mt* Montana, USA
59D2 **Granite Peak** *Mt* Utah, USA
15C1 **Granollérs** Spain
16B1 **Gran Paradiso** *Mt* Italy
7D3 **Grantham** England
66C1 **Grant,Mt** USA
8D3 **Grantown-on-Spey** Scotland
62A1 **Grants** USA
58B2 **Grants Pass** USA
14B2 **Granville** France
68D1 **Granville** USA
54H4 **Granville L** Canada
75D2 **Grão Mogol** Brazil
66C3 **Grapevine** USA
66D2 **Grapevine Mts** USA
47E1 **Graskop** South Africa
54G3 **Gras, Lac de** Canada
14D3 **Grasse** France
6D2 **Grassington** England
58E1 **Grassrange** USA
59B3 **Grass Valley** USA
74F4 **Gravatai** Brazil
54H5 **Gravelbourg** Canada

13B2 **Gravelines** France
51D6 **Gravelotte** South Africa
65D2 **Gravenhurst** Canada
58D1 **Grave Peak** *Mt* USA
34D1 **Gravesend** Australia
7E4 **Gravesend** England
58B1 **Grays Harbour** *B* USA
58D2 **Grays L** USA
64C3 **Grayson** USA
64B3 **Grayville** USA
18D3 **Graz** Austria
69H1 **Great** *R* Jamaica
57F4 **Great Abaco** *I* The Bahamas
32B4 **Great Australian Bight** *G* Australia
68E1 **Great B** New Hampshire, USA
68C3 **Great B** New Jersey, USA
70E2 **Great Bahama Bank** The Bahamas
35C1 **Great Barrier I** New Zealand
32D2 **Great Barrier Reef** *Is* Australia
68D1 **Great Barrington** USA
59C2 **Great Basin** USA
54F3 **Great Bear L** Canada
62C1 **Great Bend** USA
45B3 **Great Bitter L** Egypt
68A3 **Great Cacapon** USA
44E3 **Great Coco I** Burma
32D3 **Great Dividing Range** *Mts* Australia
6D2 **Great Driffield** England
68C3 **Great Egg Harbor** *B* USA
76F10 **Greater Antarctica** *Region* Antarctica
69B2 **Greater Antilles** *Is* Caribbean Sea
7D4 **Greater London** *Metropolitan County* England
7C3 **Greater Manchester** *Metropolitan County* England
70E2 **Great Exuma** *I* The Bahamas
58D1 **Great Falls** USA
47D3 **Great Fish** *R* South Africa
8C3 **Great Glen** *V* Scotland
43F3 **Great Himalayan Range** *Mts* Asia
57F4 **Great Inagua** *I* The Bahamas
47C3 **Great Karoo** *Mts* South Africa
47D3 **Great Kei** *R* South Africa
34C4 **Great L** Australia
7C3 **Great Malvern** England
51B6 **Great Namaland** *Region* Namibia
44E4 **Great Nicobar** *I* Indian Ocean
7C3 **Great Ormes Head** *C* Wales
68E2 **Great Pt** USA
57F4 **Great Ragged** *I* The Bahamas
51D4 **Great Ruaha** *R* Tanzania
65E2 **Great Sacandaga L** USA
58D2 **Great Salt L** USA
58D2 **Great Salt Lake Desert** USA
49E2 **Great Sand Sea** Egypt/Libya
32B3 **Great Sandy Desert** Australia
56A2 **Great Sandy Desert** USA
Great Sandy I = Fraser I
54G3 **Great Slave L** Canada
67B1 **Great Smoky Mts** USA
67B1 **Great Smoky Mts Nat Pk** USA
68D2 **Great South B** USA
47C3 **Great Tafelberg** *Mt* South Africa
32B3 **Great Victoria Desert** Australia
31B2 **Great Wall** China
7E3 **Great Yarmouth** England
48C2 **Gréboun, Mont** Niger
45C1 **Greco, C** Cyprus
15A1 **Gredos, Sierra de** *Mts* Spain
65D2 **Greece** USA
17E3 **Greece** *Republic* Europe
60C2 **Greeley** USA
55K1 **Greely Fjord** Canada
24H1 **Greem Bell, Ostrov** *I* Russian Federation
64B3 **Green** *R* Kentucky, USA
59D3 **Green** *R* Utah, USA
64B1 **Green B** USA
64B2 **Green Bay** USA
64B3 **Greencastle** Indiana, USA
68B3 **Greencastle** Pennsylvania, USA
68C1 **Greene** USA
67B1 **Greeneville** USA
66B2 **Greenfield** California, USA
66C3 **Greenfield** California, USA
68D1 **Greenfield** Massachusetts, USA
64B2 **Greenfield** Wisconsin, USA
55O2 **Greenland** *Dependency* N Atlantic Ocean
52F1 **Greenland** *I* Atlantic Ocean
52H1 **Greenland Basin** Greenland Sea
76B1 **Greenland Sea** Greenland
8D4 **Greenlaw** Scotland
8C4 **Greenock** Scotland
68D2 **Greenport** USA
59D3 **Green River** Utah, USA
58E2 **Green River** Wyoming, USA
68C3 **Greensboro** Maryland, USA
67C1 **Greensboro** N Carolina, USA
62C1 **Greensburg** Kansas, USA
64B3 **Greensburg** Kentucky, USA
65D2 **Greensburg** Pennsylvania, USA
8C3 **Greenstone Pt** Scotland
64B3 **Greenup** USA
59D4 **Green Valley** USA
67A2 **Greenville** Alabama, USA
48B4 **Greenville** Liberia
63D2 **Greenville** Mississippi, USA
67C1 **Greenville** N Carolina, USA
68E1 **Greenville** N Hampshire, USA
64C2 **Greenville** Ohio, USA
67B2 **Greenville** S Carolina, USA
63C2 **Greenville** Texas, USA
67B2 **Greenville** Florida, USA
27H8 **Greenville,C** Australia
7E4 **Greenwich** England
68D2 **Greenwich** USA
68C3 **Greenwood** Delaware, USA
63D2 **Greenwood** Mississippi, USA
67B2 **Greenwood** S Carolina, USA
63D1 **Greers Ferry L** USA
60D2 **Gregory** USA
34A1 **Gregory,L** Australia
32D2 **Gregory Range** *Mts* Australia
18C2 **Greifswald** Germany
20F2 **Gremikha** Russian Federation
18C1 **Grenå** Denmark
63E2 **Grenada** USA
69E4 **Grenada** *I* Caribbean Sea
69E4 **Grenadines,The** *Is* Caribbean Sea
34C2 **Grenfell** Australia
14D2 **Grenoble** France
69M2 **Grenville** Grenada
32D2 **Grenville,C** Australia
58B1 **Gresham** USA
63D3 **Gretna** USA
35B2 **Grey** *R* New Zealand
58E2 **Greybull** USA
55N4 **Grey Is** Canada
68D1 **Greylock,Mt** USA
35B2 **Greymouth** New Zealand
32D3 **Grey Range** *Mts* Australia
9C3 **Greystones** Irish Republic
47E2 **Greytown** South Africa
67B2 **Griffin** USA
34C2 **Griffith** Australia
32D5 **Grim,C** Australia
65D2 **Grimsby** Canada
7D3 **Grimsby** England
12B1 **Grimsey** *I* Iceland
12F7 **Grimstad** Norway
61E2 **Grinnell** USA
55J2 **Grinnell Pen** Canada
55K2 **Grise Fjord** Canada
20J3 **Griva** Russian Federation
12J7 **Grobina** Latvia
47D2 **Groblersdal** South Africa
19E2 **Grodno** Belarus
43E3 **Gromati** *R* India
13D1 **Gronan** Germany
18B2 **Groningen** Netherlands
13D1 **Groningen** *Province* Netherlands
62B1 **Groom** USA
47C3 **Groot** *R* South Africa
32C2 **Groote Eylandt** *I* Australia
51B5 **Grootfontein** Namibia
47B2 **Groot-Karasberge** *Mts* Namibia
47C1 **Groot Laagte** *R* Botswana/Namibia
47C2 **Groot Vloer** *Salt L* South Africa
69P2 **Gros Islet** St Lucia
13E2 **Grosser Feldberg** *Mt* Germany
16C2 **Grosseto** Italy
13E3 **Gross-Gerau** Germany
18C3 **Grossglockner** *Mt* Austria
58D2 **Gros Ventre Range** *Mts* USA
61D1 **Groton** USA
64C1 **Groundhog** *R* Canada
63E2 **Grove Hill** USA
66B2 **Groveland** USA
66B3 **Grover City** USA
65E2 **Groveton** USA
21H7 **Groznyy** Russian Federation
19D2 **Grudziądz** Poland
47B2 **Grünau** Namibia
8E2 **Grutness** Scotland
21G5 **Gryazi** Russian Federation
20G4 **Gryazovets** Russian Federation
74J8 **Grytviken** South Georgia
69B2 **Guacanayabo, G de** Cuba
75D3 **Guaçuí** Brazil
70B2 **Guadalajara** Mexico
15B1 **Guadalajara** Spain
33E1 **Guadalcanal** *I* Solomon Islands
15B2 **Guadalimar** *R* Spain
15B1 **Guadalope** *R* Spain
15B2 **Guadalqivir** *R* Spain
70B2 **Guadalupe** Mexico
66B3 **Guadalupe** USA
53G6 **Guadalupe** *I* Mexico
62C3 **Guadalupe** *R* USA
62B2 **Guadalupe Mtns Nat Pk** USA
62B2 **Guadalupe Peak** *Mt* USA
15A2 **Guadalupe, Sierra de** *Mts* Spain
15B1 **Guadarrama, Sierra de** *Mts* Spain
69E3 **Guadeloupe** *I* Caribbean Sea
15B2 **Guadian** *R* Spain
15A2 **Guadiana** *R* Portugal
15B2 **Guadiana** *R* Spain
15B2 **Guadix** Spain
75B3 **Guaíra** Brazil
72E6 **Guajará Mirim** Brazil
72D1 **Guajira,Pen de** Colombia
69C4 **Guajiri, Península de la** Colombia
72C4 **Gualaceo** Ecuador
27H5 **Guam** *I* Pacific Ocean
74D5 **Guaminí** Argentina
30C5 **Gua Musang** Malaysia
69A2 **Guanabacoa** Cuba
75D1 **Guanambi** Brazil
72E2 **Guanare** Venezuela
28B2 **Guandi** China
70D2 **Guane** Cuba
31C5 **Guangdong** *Province* China
31A3 **Guanghan** China
31C3 **Guanghua** China
31A4 **Guangmao Shan** *Mt* China
31A5 **Guangnan** China
31B5 **Guangxi** *Province* China
31B3 **Guangyuan** China
31D4 **Guangze** China
31C5 **Guangzhou** China
75D2 **Guanhães** Brazil
72E3 **Guania** *R* Colombia/Venezuela
69E5 **Guanipa** *R* Venezuela
69B2 **Guantánamo** Cuba
31D1 **Guanting Shuiku** *Res* China
31A3 **Guan Xian** China
72C2 **Guapá** Colombia
72F6 **Guaporé** *R* Bolivia/Brazil
72E7 **Guaquí** Bolivia
75D1 **Guará** *R* Brazil
72C4 **Guaranda** Ecuador
75B4 **Guarapuava** Brazil
75C4 **Guaraqueçaba** Brazil
15B1 **Guara, Sierra de** *Mts* Spain
75C3 **Guaratinguetá** Brazil
75C4 **Guaratuba, B** Brazil
15A1 **Guarda** Portugal
75C2 **Guarda Mor** Brazil
56C4 **Guasave** Mexico
70C3 **Guatemala** Guatemala
70C3 **Guatemala** *Republic* Central America
72D3 **Guaviare** *R* Colombia
75C3 **Guaxupé** Brazil
69L1 **Guayaguayare** Trinidad
72B4 **Guayaquil** Ecuador
72B4 **Guayaquil, Golfo de** Ecuador
70A2 **Guaymas** Mexico
51C5 **Guba** Zaïre
25P2 **Guba Buorkhaya** *B* Russian Federation
50E3 **Guban** *Region* Somalia
18C2 **Gubin** Poland
15B1 **Gudar, Sierra de** *Mts* Spain
44B3 **Gūdūr** India
13D4 **Guebwiller** France
16B3 **Guelma** Algeria
64C2 **Guelph** Canada
48A2 **Guelta Zemmur** Morocco
50C2 **Guéréda** Chad
14C2 **Guéret** France
60C2 **Guernsey** USA
14B2 **Guernsey** *I* Channel Islands
50D3 **Gughe** *Mt* Ethiopia
25O4 **Gugigu** China
27H5 **Guguan** *I* Pacific Ocean
49D4 **Guider** Cameroon
31C4 **Guidong** China
48B4 **Guiglo** Ivory Coast
47E1 **Guijá** Mozambique
31C5 **Gui Jiang** *R* China
7D4 **Guildford** England
31C4 **Guilin** China
31A2 **Guinan** China
66A1 **Guinda** USA
48A3 **Guinea** *Republic* Africa
52H4 **Guinea Basin** Atlantic Ocean
48A3 **Guinea-Bissau** *Republic* Africa
48C4 **Guinea,G of** W Africa
69A2 **Güines** Cuba
48B3 **Guir** *Well* Mali
75B2 **Guiratinga** Brazil
72F1 **Güiria** Venezuela
6D2 **Guisborough** England
13B3 **Guise** France
27F5 **Guiuan** Philippines
31B5 **Gui Xian** China
31B4 **Guiyang** China
31B4 **Guizhou** *Province* China
42C4 **Gujarāt** *State* India
42C2 **Gujranwala** Pakistan
42C2 **Gujrat** Pakistan
34C2 **Gulargambone** Australia
44B2 **Gulbarga** India
19F1 **Gulbene** Latvia
44B2 **Guledagudda** India
63E2 **Gulfport** USA
Gulf,The = Persian Gulf
34C2 **Gulgong** Australia
31B4 **Gulin** China
17F3 **Güllük Körfezi** *B* Turkey
50D3 **Gulu** Uganda
34C1 **Guluguba** Australia
48C3 **Gumel** Nigeria
43E4 **Gumla** India
13D2 **Gummersbach** Germany
40C1 **Gümüşhane** Turkey
42D4 **Guna** India
50D2 **Guna** *Mt* Ethiopia
34C3 **Gundagai** Australia
50B4 **Gungu** Zaïre
55Q3 **Gunnbjørn Fjeld** *Mt* Greenland
34D2 **Gunnedah** Australia
60B3 **Gunnison** USA
60B3 **Gunnison** *R* USA
44B2 **Guntakal** India
67A2 **Guntersville** USA
67A2 **Guntersville L** USA
44C2 **Guntūr** India
30C5 **Gunung Batu Puteh** *Mt* Malaysia
30C5 **Gunung Tahan** *Mt* Malaysia
51B5 **Gunza** Angola
31D3 **Guoyang** China
42D2 **Gurdāspur** India
42D3 **Gurgaon** India
72F2 **Guri, Embalse de** *Res* Venezuela
43E3 **Gurkha** Nepal
40C2 **Gürün** Turkey
73J4 **Gurupi** *R* Brazil
51D5 **Guruve** Zimbabwe
31A1 **Gurvan Sayhan Uul** *Upland* Mongolia
21J6 **Gur'yev** Kazakhstan
48C3 **Gusau** Nigeria
19E2 **Gusev** Russian Federation
28A3 **Gushan** China
20G4 **Gus' Khrustalnyy** Russian Federation
55P3 **Gustav Holm, Kap** *C* Greenland
54E4 **Gustavus** USA
66B2 **Gustine** USA
57E3 **Guston** USA
18B2 **Gütersloh** Germany
64B3 **Guthrie** Kentucky, USA
63C1 **Guthrie** Oklahoma, USA
62B2 **Guthrie** Texas, USA
61E2 **Guttenberg** USA
73G3 **Guyana** *Republic* S America
52F4 **Guyana Basin** Atlantic Ocean
31C1 **Guyang** China
14B3 **Guyenne** *Region* France
62B1 **Guymon** USA
34D2 **Guyra** Australia
31B2 **Guyuan** China
62A2 **Guzmán, Laguna** *L* Mexico
43G5 **Gwa** Burma
34C2 **Gwabegar** Australia
38E3 **Gwadar** Pakistan
42D3 **Gwalior** India
47D1 **Gwanda** Zimbabwe
50C3 **Gwane** Zaïre
7C4 **Gwent** *County* Wales
51C5 **Gweru** Zimbabwe
34C1 **Gwydir** *R* Australia
7C3 **Gwynedd** Wales
21H7 **Gyandzha** Azerbaijan
43F3 **Gyangzê** China
26C3 **Gyaring Hu** *L* China
24J2 **Gydanskiy Poluostrov** *Pen* Russian Federation
43F3 **Gyirong** China
55O3 **Gyldenløves Fjord** Greenland
34D1 **Gympie** Australia
19D3 **Gyöngyös** Hungary
19D3 **Györ** Hungary

H

33H2 **Ha'apai Group** *Is* Tonga
12K6 **Haapajärvi** Finland
20C4 **Haapsalu** Estonia
18A2 **Haarlem** Netherlands
13D2 **Haarstrang** *Region* Germany
Habana, La = Havana
43G4 **Habiganj** Bangladesh
29D4 **Hachijō-jima** *I* Japan
29C3 **Hachiman** Japan
29E2 **Hachinohe** Japan
29C3 **Hachioji** Japan
68C2 **Hackettstown** USA
34A2 **Hack** *Mt* Australia
8D4 **Haddington** Scotland
34B1 **Haddon Corner** Australia
34B1 **Haddon Downs** Australia
48D3 **Hadejia** Nigeria
48C3 **Hadejia** *R* Nigeria
45C2 **Hadera** Israel
18B1 **Haderslev** Denmark
38D4 **Hadībọh** Socotra
54H2 **Hadley B** Canada
28A3 **Hadong** S Korea
31B5 **Hadong** Vietnam
38C4 **Ḥaḍramawt** *Region* Yemen
18C1 **Hadsund** Denmark
28B3 **Haeju** N Korea
28A3 **Haeju-man** *B* N Korea
28A4 **Haenam** S Korea
41E4 **Hafar al Bātin** Saudi Arabia
55M2 **Haffners Bjerg** *Mt* Greenland
42C2 **Hafizabad** Pakistan
43G3 **Hāflong** India
12A2 **Hafnarfjörður** Iceland
18B2 **Hagen** Germany
68B3 **Hagerstown** USA
28B4 **Hagi** Japan
31A5 **Ha Giang** Vietnam
13D3 **Hagondange** France
13D3 **Haguenan** France
48A2 **Hagunia** *Well* Morocco
26H4 **Haha-jima** *I* Japan
26C3 **Hah Xil Hu** *L* China
28A2 **Haicheng** China
30D1 **Hai Duong** Vietnam
45C2 **Haifa** Israel
45C2 **Haifa,B of** Israel
31D2 **Hai He** *R* China
31C5 **Haikang** China
30E1 **Haikou** China
40D4 **Hā'il** Saudi Arabia
43G4 **Hailākāndi** India
25N5 **Hailar** China
28B2 **Hailong** China
26F2 **Hailun** China
12J5 **Hailuoto** *I* Finland
30D2 **Hainan** *I* China
54E4 **Haines** USA
54E3 **Haines Junction** Canada
18D3 **Hainfeld** Austria
31B5 **Haiphong** Vietnam
28A2 **Haisgai** China
69C3 **Haiti** *Republic* Caribbean Sea
66D2 **Haiwee Res** USA
50D2 **Haiya** Sudan
31A2 **Haiyan** China
31B2 **Haiyuan** China
19E3 **Hajdúböszörmény** Hungary
29C3 **Hajiki-saki** *Pt* Japan
43G4 **Haka** Burma
66E5 **Hakalau** Hawaiian Islands
41D2 **Hakkâri** Turkey
29E2 **Hakodate** Japan
29C3 **Hakui** Japan
29C3 **Haku-san** *Mt* Japan
Ḥalab = Aleppo
41E2 **Halabja** Iraq
50D1 **Halaib** Egypt
45B3 **Halâl, Gebel** *Mt* Egypt
45D1 **Halba** Lebanon
26C2 **Halban** Mongolia
18C2 **Halberstadt** Germany
12G7 **Halden** Norway
43F4 **Haldia** India
42D3 **Haldwāni** India

55M5 **Halifax** Canada
6D3 **Halifax** England
65D3 **Halifax** USA
45D1 **Halīmah, Jabal** *Mt* Lebanon/Syria
8D2 **Halkirk** Scotland
28A4 **Halla-san** *Mt* S Korea
55M1 **Hall Basin** *Sd* Canada/Greenland
55K3 **Hall Beach** Canada
13C2 **Halle** Belgium
18C2 **Halle** Germany
76F1 **Halley** *Base* Antarctica
65D1 **Halleybury** Canada
60C1 **Halliday** USA
12F6 **Hallingdal** *R* Norway
61D1 **Hallock** USA
55M3 **Hall Pen** Canada
32B2 **Hall's Creek** Australia
68C2 **Hallstead** USA
27F6 **Halmahera** *Is* Indonesia
12G7 **Halmstad** Sweden
16C3 **Halq el Qued** Tunisia
18B2 **Haltern** Germany
20C2 **Halti** *Mt* Finland/Norway
8D4 **Haltwhistle** England
41F4 **Halul** *I* Qatar
45C3 **Haluza** *Hist Site* Israel
28B4 **Hamada** Japan
48C2 **Hamada de Tinrhert** *Desert Region* Algeria
48B2 **Hamada du Dra** *Upland* Algeria
41E3 **Hamadān** Iran
48B2 **Hamada Tounassine** *Region* Algeria
21F8 **Ḩamāh** Syria
29C4 **Hamamatsu** Japan
12G6 **Hamar** Norway
40C5 **Hamâta, Gebel** *Mt* Egypt
29D1 **Hama-Tombetsu** Japan
44C4 **Hambantota** Sri Lanka
63D2 **Hamburg** Arkansas, USA
61D2 **Hamburg** Iowa, USA
68A1 **Hamburg** New York, USA
68C2 **Hamburg** Pennsylvania, USA
18B2 **Hamburg** Germany
68D2 **Hamden** USA
12J6 **Hämeenlinna** Finland
13E1 **Hameln** Germany
32A3 **Hamersley Range** *Mts* Australia
28B2 **Hamgyong Sanmaek** *Mts* N Korea
28B3 **Hamhŭng** N Korea
26C2 **Hami** China
45C1 **Ḩamīdīyah** Syria
63E2 **Hamilton** Alabama, USA
34B3 **Hamilton** Australia
65D2 **Hamilton** Canada
58D1 **Hamilton** Montana, USA
68C1 **Hamilton** New York, USA
35C1 **Hamilton** New Zealand
64C3 **Hamilton** Ohio, USA
8C4 **Hamilton** Scotland
66B2 **Hamilton,Mt** USA
12K6 **Hamina** Finland
43E3 **Hamīrpur** India
28A3 **Hamju** N Korea
18B2 **Hamm** Germany
49D2 **Hammādāh al Hamrā** *Upland* Libya
16C3 **Hammamet** Tunisia
16C3 **Hammamet, Golfe de** Tunisia
12H6 **Hammerdal** Sweden
12J4 **Hammerfest** Norway
64B2 **Hammond** Illinois, USA
63D2 **Hammond** Louisiana, USA
60C1 **Hammond** Montana, USA
68C3 **Hammonton** USA
35B3 **Hampden** New Zealand
7D4 **Hampshire** *County* England
63D2 **Hampton** Arkansas, USA
61E2 **Hampton** Iowa, USA
68E1 **Hampton** New Hampshire, USA
65D3 **Hampton** Virginia, USA
38D3 **Hāmūn-e-Jāz-Mūrīān** *L* Iran
42B3 **Hamun-i-Lora** *Salt L* Pakistan
28A3 **Han** *R* S Korea
66E5 **Hana** Hawaiian Islands
66E5 **Hanalei** Hawaiian Islands
29E3 **Hanamaki** Japan
13E2 **Hanau** Germany
31C2 **Hancheng** China
31C3 **Hanchuan** China
65D3 **Hancock** Maryland, USA
64B1 **Hancock** Michigan, USA
68C2 **Hancock** New York, USA
29C4 **Handa** Japan
8C2 **Handa, I** Scotland
31C2 **Handan** China
50D4 **Handeni** Tanzania
66C2 **Hanford** USA
31B2 **Hanggin Qi** China
12J7 **Hangö** Finland
31E3 **Hangzhou** China
31E3 **Hangzhou Wan** *B* China
61D1 **Hankinson** USA
59D3 **Hanksville** USA
35B2 **Hanmer Springs** New Zealand
54G4 **Hanna** Canada
61E3 **Hannibal** USA
18B2 **Hannover** Germany
12G7 **Hanöbukten** *B* Sweden
30D1 **Hanoi** Vietnam
47C3 **Hanover** South Africa
68B3 **Hanover** USA
74B8 **Hanover** *I* Chile
31C3 **Han Shui** *R* China
42D3 **Hānsi** India
26D2 **Hantay** Mongolia
31B3 **Hanzhong** China
43F4 **Hāora** India
12J5 **Haparanda** Sweden
28A3 **Hapch'on** S Korea
43G3 **Hāpoli** India
43J1 **Hapur** India
40C4 **Ḩaql** Saudi Arabia
41E5 **Ḩaradh** Saudi Arabia
45C4 **Harad, Jebel el** *Mt* Jordan
50E3 **Hara Fanna** Ethiopia
29D3 **Haramachi** Japan
51D5 **Harare** Zimbabwe
50C2 **Harazé** Chad
26F2 **Harbin** China
64C2 **Harbor Beach** USA
42D4 **Harda** India
12F6 **Hardangerfjord** *Inlet* Norway
13D1 **Härdenberg** Netherlands
13C1 **Harderwijk** Netherlands
60B1 **Hardin** USA
43L2 **Hardoi** India
13D3 **Hardt** *Region* Germany
63D1 **Hardy** USA
45C3 **Hareidin, Wadi** Egypt
50E3 **Harēr** Ethiopia
50E3 **Hargeysa** Somalia
45C3 **Har Hakippa** *Mt* Israel
26C3 **Harhu** *L* China
27D7 **Hari** *R* Indonesia
29B4 **Harima-nada** *B* Japan
64C3 **Harlan** USA
7B3 **Harlech** Wales
58E1 **Harlem** USA
7E3 **Harleston** England
18B2 **Harlingen** Netherlands
63C3 **Harlingen** USA
7E4 **Harlow** England
58E1 **Harlowtown** USA
45C2 **Har Meron** *Mt* Israel
58C2 **Harney Basin** USA
58C2 **Harney L** USA
12H6 **Härnösand** Sweden
48B4 **Harper** Liberia
66D3 **Harper L** USA
65D3 **Harpers Ferry** USA
13E1 **Harpstedt** Germany
45C3 **Har Ramon** *Mt* Israel
40C4 **Harrāt al 'Uwayrid** *Region* Saudi Arabia
40D5 **Ḩarrāt Kishb** *Region* Saudi Arabia
55L4 **Harricanaw** *R* Canada
67B1 **Harriman** USA
68D1 **Harriman Res** USA
68C3 **Harrington** USA
55N4 **Harrington Harbour** Canada
8B3 **Harris** *District* Scotland
64B3 **Harrisburg** Illinois, USA
68B2 **Harrisburg** Pennsylvania, USA
47D2 **Harrismith** South Africa
63D1 **Harrison** USA
65D3 **Harrisonburg** USA
55N4 **Harrison,C** Canada
61E3 **Harrisonville** USA
8B3 **Harris,Sound of** *Chan* Scotland
64C2 **Harrisville** USA
6D2 **Harrogate** England
45C3 **Har Saggi** *Mt* Israel
45D2 **Ḩarsīr, Wadi al** Syria
12H5 **Harstad** Norway
28A2 **Hartao** China
47C2 **Hartbees** *R* South Africa
12F6 **Hårteigen** *Mt* Norway
68D2 **Hartford** Connecticut, USA
64B2 **Hartford** Michigan, USA
61D2 **Hartford** S Dakota, USA
12G6 **Hartkjølen** *Mt* Norway
65F1 **Hartland** Canada
7B4 **Hartland** England
7B4 **Hartland Pt** England
6D2 **Hartlepool** England
62B1 **Hartley** USA
67A2 **Hartselle** USA
63C2 **Hartshorne** USA
67B2 **Hartwell Res** USA
47C2 **Hartz** *R* South Africa
45C3 **Hārūn, Jebel** *Mt* Jordan
25L5 **Har Us Nuur** *L* Mongolia
38E2 **Harut** *R* Afghanistan
60B3 **Harvard,Mt** USA
60C1 **Harvey** USA
7E4 **Harwich** England
42D3 **Haryāna** *State* India
45C3 **Hāsā** Jordan
45B3 **Hasana, Wadi** Egypt
45C3 **Hāsā, Wadi el** Jordan
45C2 **Hāsbaiya** Lebanon
13E1 **Hase** *R* Germany
13D1 **Haselünne** Germany
29C4 **Hashimoto** Japan
41E2 **Hashtpar** Iran
41E2 **Hashtrūd** Iran
62C2 **Haskell** USA
7D4 **Haslemere** England
44B3 **Hassan** India
18B2 **Hasselt** Belgium
48C2 **Hassi Inifel** Algeria
48B2 **Hassi Mdakane** *Well* Algeria
48C1 **Hassi Messaoud** Algeria
12G7 **Hässleholm** Sweden
34C3 **Hastings** Australia
7E4 **Hastings** England
61E2 **Hastings** Minnesota, USA
56D2 **Hastings** Nebraska, USA
35C1 **Hastings** New Zealand
63E1 **Hatchie** *R* USA
34B2 **Hatfield** Australia
42D3 **Hāthras** India
30D2 **Ha Tinh** Vietnam
34B2 **Hattah** Australia
57F3 **Hatteras,C** USA
63E2 **Hattiesburg** USA
19D3 **Hatvan** Hungary
30D3 **Hau Bon** Vietnam
50E3 **Haud** *Region* Ethiopia
12F7 **Haugesund** Norway
35C1 **Hauhungaroa Range** *Mts* New Zealand
35B1 **Hauraki G** New Zealand
35A3 **Hauroko,L** New Zealand
48B1 **Haut Atlas** *Mts* Morocco
50C3 **Haute Kotto** *Region* Central African Republic
13C3 **Haute-Marne** *Department* France
13D4 **Haute-Saône** *Department* France
13C2 **Hautes Fagnes** *Mts* Belgium/Germany
65F2 **Haut, Isle au** USA
13C2 **Hautmont** France
13D4 **Haut-Rhin** *Department* France
42A2 **Hauz Qala** Afghanistan
70D2 **Havana** Cuba
64A2 **Havana** USA
44B4 **Havankulam** Sri Lanka
59D4 **Havasu L** USA
67C2 **Havelock** USA
35C1 **Havelock North** New Zealand
7E3 **Haverhill** England
68E1 **Haverhill** USA
44B3 **Hāveri** India
68D2 **Haverstraw** USA
18D3 **Havlíčkův Brod** Czech Republic
58E1 **Havre** USA
68B3 **Havre de Grace** USA
55M4 **Havre-St-Pierre** Canada
17F2 **Havsa** Turkey
66E5 **Hawaii** *Is, State* Pacific Ocean
66E5 **Hawaii Volcanoes Nat Pk** Hawaiian Islands
35A2 **Hawea,L** New Zealand
35B1 **Hawera** New Zealand
66E5 **Hawi** Hawaiian Islands
8D4 **Hawick** Scotland
35A2 **Hawkdun Range** *Mts* New Zealand
35C1 **Hawke B** New Zealand
34D2 **Hawke,C** Australia
34A2 **Hawker** Australia
68C2 **Hawley** USA
30B1 **Hawng Luk** Burma
41D3 **Hawr al Habbaniyah** *L* Iraq
41E3 **Hawr al Hammár** *L* Iraq
40D3 **Ḩawrān, Wadi** *R* Iraq
66C1 **Hawthorne** USA
34B2 **Hay** Australia
7C3 **Hay** England
54G3 **Hay** *R* Canada
13C3 **Hayange** France
54B3 **Haycock** USA
59D4 **Hayden** Arizona, USA
60B2 **Hayden** Colorado, USA
55J4 **Hayes** *R* Canada
55M2 **Hayes Halvø** *Region* Greenland
54D3 **Hayes, Mt** USA
7B4 **Hayle** England
7D4 **Hayling** *I* England
68B3 **Haymarket** USA
54G3 **Hay River** Canada
60D3 **Hays** USA
63C1 **Haysville** USA
66A2 **Hayward** California, USA
64A1 **Hayward** Wisconsin, USA
7D4 **Haywards Heath** England
42A2 **Hazarajat** *Region* Afghanistan
64C3 **Hazard** USA
43F4 **Hazārībāg** India
13B2 **Hazebrouck** France
63D2 **Hazelhurst** USA
54F4 **Hazelton** Canada
54B3 **Hazen B** USA
55L1 **Hazen L** Canada
54G2 **Hazen Str** Canada
45C3 **Hazeva** Israel
68C2 **Hazleton** USA
66A1 **Healdsburg** USA
34C3 **Healesville** Australia
36E7 **Heard I** Indian Ocean
63C2 **Hearne** USA
57E2 **Hearst** Canada
60C1 **Heart** *R* USA
62C3 **Hebbronville** USA
31D2 **Hebei** *Province* China
34C1 **Hebel** Australia
58D2 **Heber City** USA
58D2 **Hebgen L** USA
31C2 **Hebi** China
31C2 **Hebian** China
55M4 **Hebron** Canada
45C3 **Hebron** Israel
60C1 **Hebron** N Dakota, USA
61D2 **Hebron** Nebraska, USA
54E4 **Hecate Str** Canada
31B5 **Hechi** China
13E3 **Hechingen** Germany
54G2 **Hecla and Griper B** Canada
35C2 **Hector,Mt** New Zealand
12G6 **Hede** Sweden
12H6 **Hedemora** Sweden
58C1 **He Devil Mt** USA
18B2 **Heerenveen** Netherlands
13C2 **Heerlen** Netherlands
Hefa = Haifa
31D3 **Hefei** China
31B4 **Hefeng** China
26G2 **Hegang** China
29C3 **Hegura-jima** *I* Japan
30B1 **Heho** Burma
45C3 **Heidan** *R* Jordan
18B2 **Heide** Germany
47C3 **Heidelberg** Cape Province, South Africa
47D2 **Heidelberg** Transvaal, South Africa
18B3 **Heidelberg** Germany
18C3 **Heidenheim** Germany
25O4 **Heihe** China
47D2 **Heilbron** South Africa
18B3 **Heilbronn** Germany
18C2 **Heiligenstadt** Germany
12K6 **Heinola** Finland
28A2 **Heishan** China
31B4 **Hejiang** China
55R3 **Hekla** *Mt* Iceland
30C1 **Hekou** Vietnam
31A5 **Hekou Yaozou Zizhixian** China
31B2 **Helan** China
31B2 **Helan Shan** *Mt* China
63D2 **Helena** Arkansas, USA
58D1 **Helena** Montana, USA
66D3 **Helendale** USA
27G6 **Helen Reef** Pacific Ocean
8C3 **Helensburgh** Scotland
45A3 **Heliopolis** Egypt
41F4 **Helleh** *R* Iran
15B2 **Hellín** Spain
58C1 **Hells Canyon** *R* USA
13D2 **Hellweg** *Region* Germany
66B2 **Helm** USA
38E2 **Helmand** *R* Afghanistan/Iran
47B2 **Helmeringhausen** Namibia
13C2 **Helmond** Netherlands
8D2 **Helmsdale** Scotland
51F5 **Helodrano Antongila** *B* Madagascar
28B2 **Helong** China
12G7 **Helsingborg** Sweden
Helsingfors = Helsinki
18C1 **Helsingør** Denmark
12J6 **Helsinki** Finland
7B4 **Helston** England
9C3 **Helvick Hd** *Pt* Irish Republic
40B4 **Helwân** Egypt
7D4 **Hemel Hempstead** England
63C2 **Hempstead** USA
12H7 **Hemse** Sweden
31A3 **Henan** China
31C3 **Henan** *Province* China
35B1 **Hen and Chickens Is** New Zealand
29C2 **Henashi-zaki** *C* Japan
64B3 **Henderson** Kentucky, USA
67C1 **Henderson** N Carolina, USA
59D3 **Henderson** Nevada, USA
63D2 **Henderson** Texas, USA
67B1 **Hendersonville** N Carolina, USA
67A1 **Hendersonville** Tennessee, USA
47D3 **Hendrik Verwoerd Dam** South Africa
31E5 **Hengchun** Taiwan
26C4 **Hengduan Shan** *Mts* China
18B2 **Hengelo** Netherlands
31B2 **Hengshan** China
31D2 **Hengshui** China
30D1 **Heng Xian** China
31C4 **Hengyang** China
30A4 **Henhoaha** Nicobar Is, India
7D4 **Henley-on-Thames** England
68C3 **Henlopen,C** USA
68E1 **Henniker** USA
62C2 **Henrietta** USA
55K4 **Henrietta Maria,C** Canada
59D3 **Henrieville** USA
63C1 **Henryetta** USA
55M3 **Henry Kater Pen** Canada
47A1 **Henties Bay** Namibia
26D2 **Hentiyn Nuruu** *Mts* Mongolia
30B2 **Henzada** Burma
31B5 **Hepu** China
38E2 **Herat** Afghanistan
54H4 **Herbert** Canada
35C2 **Herbertville** New Zealand
13E2 **Herborn** Germany
69A4 **Heredia** Costa Rica
7C3 **Hereford** England
62B2 **Hereford** USA
7C3 **Hereford & Worcester** *County* England
13C2 **Herentals** Belgium
13E1 **Herford** Germany
61D3 **Herington** USA
35A3 **Heriot** New Zealand
68C1 **Herkimer** USA
8E1 **Herma Ness** *Pen* Scotland
47B3 **Hermanus** South Africa
34C2 **Hermidale** Australia
35B2 **Hermitage** New Zealand
32D1 **Hermit Is** Papua New Guinea
45C2 **Hermon, Mt** Lebanon/Syria
70A2 **Hermosillo** Mexico
75B4 **Hernandarias** Paraguay
68B2 **Herndon** USA
66C2 **Herndon** USA
13D2 **Herne** Germany
7E4 **Herne Bay** England
18B1 **Herning** Denmark
41E2 **Herowābad** Iran
75A4 **Herradura** Argentina
15B2 **Herrera del Duque** Spain
68B2 **Hershey** USA
7D4 **Hertford** England
7D4 **Hertford** *County* England
45C2 **Herzliyya** Israel
13C2 **Hesbaye** Region, Belgium
13A2 **Hesdin** France
31B2 **Heshui** China
66D3 **Hesperia** USA
18B2 **Hessen** *State* Germany
66C2 **Hetch Hetchy Res** USA
60C1 **Hettinger** USA
48B1 **Heuts Plateaux** Algeria/Morocco
7E3 **Hewett** *Oilfield* N Sea
6C2 **Hexham** England
31C5 **He Xian** China
6C2 **Heysham** England
47D2 **Heystekrand** South Africa
31C5 **Heyuan** China
34B3 **Heywood** Australia
31D2 **Heze** China
67B3 **Hialeah** USA
61E1 **Hibbing** USA
67B1 **Hickory** USA
35C1 **Hicks Bay** New Zealand
34C3 **Hicks,Pt** Australia
63C2 **Hico** USA
29D2 **Hidaka-sammyaku** *Mts* Japan
70B2 **Hidalgo del Parral** Mexico
75C2 **Hidrolândia** Brazil
48A2 **Hierro** *I* Canary Islands
29D3 **Higashine** Japan
28B4 **Higashi-suidō** *Str* Japan
45B3 **Higâyib, Wadi el** Egypt
58B2 **High Desert** USA
63D3 **High Island** USA
66D3 **Highland** USA
8C3 **Highland** *Region* Scotland
8E2 **Highlander** *Oilfield* N Sea
66C1 **Highland Peak** *Mt* USA
68C2 **Highland Falls** USA
67B1 **High Point** USA
54G4 **High Prairie** Canada
54G4 **High River** Canada
67B3 **High Springs** USA
68C2 **Hightstown** USA
7D4 **High Wycombe** England
12J7 **Hiiumaa** *I* Estonia
40C4 **Hijaz** *Region* Saudi Arabia

29C4 **Hikigawa** Japan
59C3 **Hiko** USA
29C3 **Hikone** Japan
35B1 **Hikurangi** New Zealand
56C4 **Hildago del Parral** Mexico
18B2 **Hildesheim** Germany
69R2 **Hillaby,Mt** Barbados
60D3 **Hill City** USA
18C1 **Hillerød** Denmark
61D1 **Hillsboro** N Dakota, USA
68E1 **Hillsboro** New Hampshire, USA
62A2 **Hillsboro** New Mexico, USA
64C3 **Hillsboro** Ohio, USA
58B1 **Hillsboro** Oregon, USA
63C2 **Hillsboro** Texas, USA
34C2 **Hillston** Australia
64C3 **Hillsville** USA
8E1 **Hillswick** Scotland
66E5 **Hilo** Hawaiian Islands
6C2 **Hilpsford** *Pt* England
68B1 **Hilton** USA
40C2 **Hilvan** Turkey
18B2 **Hilversum** Netherlands
42D2 **Himāchal Pradesh** *State* India
Himalaya = Great Himalayan Range
39G3 **Himalaya** *Mts* Asia
43N1 **Himalchuli** *Mt* Nepal
42C4 **Himatnagar** India
29C4 **Himeji** Japan
29D3 **Himi** Japan
45D1 **Ḩimş** Syria
7D3 **Hinckley** England
61E1 **Hinckley** Minnesota, USA
68C1 **Hinckley Res** USA
42D3 **Hindaun** India
42B1 **Hindu Kush** *Mts* Afghanistan
44B3 **Hindupur** India
54G4 **Hines Creek** Canada
42D4 **Hinganghāt** India
42B3 **Hingol** *R* Pakistan
42D5 **Hingoli** India
66D3 **Hinkley** USA
12H5 **Hinnøya** *I* Norway
68D1 **Hinsdale** USA
62C1 **Hinton** USA
28A4 **Hirado** Japan
28A4 **Hirado-shima** *I* Japan
43E4 **Hirakud Res** India
40B2 **Hirfanli Baraji** *Res* Turkey
44B3 **Hirihar** India
29D2 **Hiroo** Japan
29E2 **Hirosaki** Japan
28C4 **Hiroshima** Japan
13C3 **Hirson** France
17F2 **Hîrşova** Romania
18B1 **Hirtshals** Denmark
42D3 **Hisār** India
69C3 **Hispaniola** *I* Caribbean Sea
45D1 **Ḩisyah** Syria
40D3 **Hīt** Iraq
29E3 **Hitachi** Japan
29D3 **Hitachi-Ota** Japan
7D4 **Hitchin** England
28C4 **Hitoyoshi** Japan
12F6 **Hitra** *I* Norway
29B4 **Hiuchi-nada** *B* Japan
29B4 **Hiwasa** Japan
45C3 **Hiyon** *R* Israel
18B1 **Hjørring** Denmark
30B1 **Hka** *R* Burma
48C4 **Ho** Ghana
30D1 **Hoa Binh** Vietnam
30D3 **Hoa Da** Vietnam
34C4 **Hobart** Australia
62C2 **Hobart** USA
62B2 **Hobbs** USA
18B1 **Hobro** Denmark
50E3 **Hobyo** Somalia
30D3 **Ho Chi Minh City** Vietnam
18C3 **Hochkonig** *Mt* Austria
28A2 **Hochon** N Korea
13E3 **Hockenheim** Germany
Hodeida = Al Ḩudaydah
17E1 **Hódmezö'hely** Hungary
15C2 **Hodna, Monts du** Algeria
18D3 **Hodonin** Czech Republic
13C2 **Hoek van Holland** Netherlands
28A3 **Hoengsŏng** S Korea
28B2 **Hoeryŏng** N Korea
28A3 **Hoeyang** N Korea
18C2 **Hof** Germany
55R3 **Höfn** Iceland
12B2 **Hofsjökull** *Mts* Iceland
28C4 **Hōfu** Japan
48C2 **Hoggar** *Upland* Algeria
13D2 **Hohe Acht** *Mt* Germany
13E2 **Hohes Gras** *Mts* Germany
31C1 **Hohhot** China
26C3 **Hoh Sai Hu** *L* China
39G2 **Hoh Xil Shan** *Mts* China
50D3 **Hoima** Uganda
43G3 **Hojāi** India
28B4 **Hojo** Japan
35B1 **Hokianga Harbour** *B* New Zealand
35B2 **Hokitika** New Zealand
26H2 **Hokkaidō** *I* Japan
41G2 **Hokmābād** Iran
29D3 **Hokota** Japan
7E3 **Holbeach** England
34C3 **Holbrook** Australia
59D4 **Holbrook** USA
59D3 **Holden** USA
63C1 **Holdenville** USA
60D2 **Holdrege** USA
44B3 **Hole Narsipur** India
69Q2 **Holetown** Barbados
69B2 **Holguín** Cuba
18D3 **Hollabrunn** Austria
64B2 **Holland** USA
68A2 **Hollidaysburg** USA
62C2 **Hollis** USA
66B2 **Hollister** USA
63E2 **Holly Springs** USA
66C3 **Hollywood** California, USA
67B3 **Hollywood** Florida, USA
54G2 **Holman Island** Canada
12J6 **Holmsund** Sweden
45C2 **Holon** Israel
18B1 **Holstebro** Denmark
61D2 **Holstein** USA
55N3 **Holsteinsborg** Greenland
67B1 **Holston** *R* USA
64C2 **Holt** USA
61D3 **Holton** USA
54C3 **Holy Cross** USA
7B3 **Holyhead** Wales
6D3 **Holy I** England
7B3 **Holy I** Wales
60C2 **Holyoke** Colorado, USA
68D1 **Holyoke** Massachusetts, USA
9D2 **Holywood** Northern Ireland
13E2 **Holzminden** Germany
43G4 **Homalin** Burma
13E2 **Homburg** Germany
55M3 **Home B** Canada
63D2 **Homer** Louisiana, USA
54C4 **Homer** USA
35A2 **Homer Tunnel** New Zealand
67B2 **Homerville** USA
67B3 **Homestead** USA
67A2 **Homewood** USA
44B2 **Homnābād** India
51D6 **Homoine** Mozambique
Homs = Al Khums
Homs = Ḩimş
47B3 **Hondeklip B** South Africa
62A2 **Hondo** New Mexico, USA
62C3 **Hondo** Texas, USA
70D3 **Hondo** *R* Mexico
70D3 **Honduras** *Republic* Central America
70D3 **Honduras,G of** Honduras
12G6 **Hønefoss** Norway
68C2 **Honesdale** USA
59B2 **Honey L** USA
Hong *R* **= Nui Con Voi**
30C1 **Hong** *R* Vietnam
30D1 **Hon Gai** Vietnam
28A3 **Hongchŏn** S Korea
31A4 **Hongguo** China
31C4 **Hong Hu** *L* China
31B2 **Honghui** China
31C4 **Hongjiang** China
31C5 **Hong Kong** *Colony* SE Asia
26E2 **Hongor** Mongolia
31B5 **Hongshui He** *R* China
28A3 **Hongsong** S Korea
28A3 **Hongwon** N Korea
31A3 **Hongyuan** China
31D3 **Hongze Hu** *L* China
33E1 **Honiara** Solomon Islands
7C4 **Honiton** England
29D3 **Honjō** Japan
30C4 **Hon Khoai** *I* Cambodia
30D3 **Hon Lan** *I* Vietnam
12K4 **Honnigsvåg** Norway
20D1 **Honningsvåg** Norway
66E5 **Honokaa** Hawaiian Islands
66E5 **Honolulu** Hawaiian Islands
30C4 **Hon Panjang** *I* Vietnam
26G3 **Honshū** *I* Japan
58B1 **Hood,Mt** USA
58B1 **Hood River** USA
13D1 **Hoogeveen** Netherlands
62B1 **Hooker** USA
9C3 **Hook Head** *C* Irish Republic
54E4 **Hoonah** USA
54B3 **Hooper Bay** USA
47D2 **Hoopstad** South Africa
18A2 **Hoorn** Netherlands
68D1 **Hoosick Falls** USA
56B3 **Hoover Dam** USA
63D2 **Hope** Arkansas, USA
55M4 **Hopedale** Canada
24D2 **Hopen** *I* Svalbard
55M3 **Hopes Advance,C** Canada
34B3 **Hopetoun** Australia
47C2 **Hopetown** South Africa
68A2 **Hopewell** Pennsylvania, USA
65D3 **Hopewell** Virginia, USA
64B3 **Hopkinsville** USA
58B1 **Hoquiam** USA
40D2 **Horasan** Turkey
13E3 **Horb** Germany
50E2 **Hordiyo** Somalia
31B1 **Hörh Uul** *Mt* Mongolia
37L6 **Horizon Depth** Pacific Ocean
41G4 **Hormuz,Str of** Oman/Iran
18D3 **Horn** Austria
55Q3 **Horn** *C* Iceland
12H5 **Hornavan** *L* Sweden
63D2 **Hornbeck** USA
58B2 **Hornbrook** USA
35B2 **Hornby** New Zealand
7D3 **Horncastle** England
68B1 **Hornell** USA
55K5 **Hornepayne** Canada
63E2 **Horn I** USA
33H2 **Horn, Îles de** Pacific Ocean
54F3 **Horn Mts** Canada
74C9 **Hornos, Cabo de** *C* Chile
6D3 **Hornsea** England
28A2 **Horqin Zuoyi Houqi** China
74E2 **Horqueta** Paraguay
68B1 **Horseheads** USA
18C1 **Horsens** Denmark
58B1 **Horseshoe Bay** Canada
58C2 **Horseshoe Bend** USA
34B3 **Horsham** Australia
7D4 **Horsham** England
12G7 **Horten** Norway
54F3 **Horton** *R* Canada
27E6 **Hose Mts** Borneo
42D4 **Hoshangābād** India
42D2 **Hoshiārpur** India
62C1 **Hosington** USA
44B2 **Hospet** India
74C9 **Hoste** *I* Chile
39F2 **Hotan** China
47C2 **Hotazel** South Africa
63D2 **Hot Springs** Arkansas, USA
60C2 **Hot Springs** S Dakota, USA
54G3 **Hottah L** Canada
69C3 **Hotte, Massif de la** *Mts* Haiti
47A2 **Hottentot Pt** Namibia
64B1 **Houghton** USA
65F1 **Houlton** USA
31C2 **Houma** China
63D3 **Houma** USA
8C3 **Hourn, Loch** *Inlet* Scotland
68D2 **Housatonic** *R* USA
63E2 **Houston** Mississippi, USA
63C3 **Houston** Texas, USA
32A3 **Houtman** *Is* Australia
68A2 **Houtzdale** USA
26C2 **Hovd** Mongolia
26D1 **Hövsgol Nuur** *L* Mongolia
34D1 **Howard** Australia
64B2 **Howard City** USA
50C2 **Howa, Wadi** *Watercourse* Chad/Sudan
34C3 **Howe,C** Australia
58B1 **Howe Sd** Canada
47E2 **Howick** South Africa
65F1 **Howland** USA
9C3 **Howth** Irish Republic
13E2 **Höxter** Germany
8D2 **Hoy** *I* Scotland
12F6 **Høyanger** Norway
61E1 **Hoyt Lakes** USA
18D2 **Hradec-Králové** Czech Republic
19D3 **Hranice** Czech Republic
19D3 **Hron** *R* Slovakia
31E5 **Hsinchu** Taiwan
30B1 **Hsipaw** Burma
31E5 **Hsüeh Shan** *Mt* Taiwan
47A1 **Huab** *R* Namibia
31B2 **Huachi** China
72C6 **Huacho** Peru
31C1 **Huade** China
28B2 **Huadian** China
31D3 **Huaibei** China
31D3 **Huaibin** China
28A2 **Huaide** China
28A2 **Huaidezhen** China
31D3 **Huai He** *R* China
31C4 **Huaihua** China
31C5 **Huaiji** China
31D3 **Huainan** China
59D3 **Hualapai Peak** *Mt* USA
26F4 **Hualien** Taiwan
72C5 **Huallaga** *R* Peru
72C5 **Huallanca** Peru
72C5 **Huamachuco** Peru
51B5 **Huambo** Angola
72E7 **Huanay** Bolivia
72C5 **Huancabamba** Peru
72C6 **Huancavelica** Peru
72C6 **Huancayo** Peru
31D3 **Huangchuan** China
Huang Hai = Yellow Sea
31D2 **Huang He** *R* China
31B2 **Huangling** China
30D2 **Huangliu** China
28B2 **Huangnihe** China
31C3 **Huangpi** China
31D3 **Huangshi** China
31D4 **Huangshan** China
31E4 **Huangyan** China
28B2 **Huanren** China
72C5 **Huānuco** Peru
74C1 **Huanuni** Bolivia
31B2 **Huan Xian** China
72C5 **Huaráz** Peru
72C6 **Huarmey** Peru
72C5 **Huascarán** *Mt* Peru
74B3 **Huasco** Chile
31C2 **Hua Xian** China
70B2 **Huayapan** *R* Mexico
31C3 **Hubei** *Province* China
44B2 **Hubli** India
28B2 **Huch'ang** N Korea
7D3 **Hucknell Torkard** England
7D3 **Huddersfield** England
13E1 **Hude** Germany
12H6 **Hudiksvall** Sweden
67B3 **Hudson** Florida, USA
64C2 **Hudson** Michigan, USA
68D1 **Hudson** New York, USA
68D1 **Hudson** *R* USA
55K4 **Hudson B** Canada
54H4 **Hudson Bay** Canada
68D1 **Hudson Falls** USA
55L3 **Hudson Str** Canada
30D2 **Hue** Vietnam
15A2 **Huelva** Spain
15B2 **Húercal Overa** Spain
15B1 **Huesca** Spain
32D3 **Hughenden** Australia
54C3 **Hughes** USA
43F4 **Hugli** *R* India
63C2 **Hugo** USA
62B1 **Hugoton** USA
31D4 **Hui'an** China
35C1 **Huiarau Range** *Mts* New Zealand
47B2 **Huib Hochplato** *Plat* Namibia
28B2 **Hŭich'ŏn** N Korea
72C3 **Huila** *Mt* Colombia
31D5 **Huilai** China
31A4 **Huili** China
28B2 **Huinan** China
70C3 **Huixtla** Mexico
31A4 **Huize** China
31C5 **Huizhou** China
40D4 **Ḩulayfah** Saudi Arabia
26G2 **Hulin** China
65D1 **Hull** Canada
6D3 **Hull** England
33H1 **Hull** *I* Phoenix Islands
18D1 **Hultsfred** Sweden
25N5 **Hulun Nur** *L* China
72F5 **Humaitá** Brazil
47C3 **Humansdorp** South Africa
7D3 **Humber** *R* England
6D3 **Humberside** *County* England
54H4 **Humboldt** Canada
61E2 **Humboldt** Iowa, USA
63E1 **Humboldt** Tennessee, USA
58C2 **Humboldt** *R* USA
58B2 **Humboldt B** USA
55M2 **Humboldt Gletscher** *Gl* Greenland
59C3 **Humboldt L** USA
34C1 **Humeburn** Australia
34C3 **Hume,L** Australia
13D1 **Hümmling** *Hill* Germany
51B5 **Humpata** Angola
66C2 **Humphreys** USA
66C2 **Humphreys,Mt** California, USA
59D3 **Humphreys Peak** *Mt* Arizona, USA
12A1 **Húnaflóri** *B* Iceland
31C4 **Hunan** *Province* China
28C2 **Hunchun** China
17E1 **Hunedoara** Romania
19D3 **Hungary** *Republic* Europe
34B1 **Hungerford** Australia
28B3 **Hŭngnam** N Korea
58D1 **Hungry Horse Res** USA
28B2 **Hunjiang** China
47B2 **Hunsberge** *Mts* Namibia
13D3 **Hunsrück** *Mts* Germany
7E3 **Hunstanton** England
13E1 **Hunte** *R* Germany
34D2 **Hunter** *R* Australia
34C4 **Hunter Is** Australia
64B3 **Huntingburg** USA
7D3 **Huntingdon** England
64B2 **Huntingdon** Indiana, USA
68A2 **Huntingdon** Pennsylvania, USA
64C3 **Huntington** USA
66C4 **Huntington Beach** USA
66C2 **Huntington L** USA
35C1 **Huntly** New Zealand
8D3 **Huntly** Scotland
54F3 **Hunt, Mt** Canada
67A2 **Huntsville** Alabama, USA
65D1 **Huntsville** Canada
63C2 **Huntsville** Texas, USA
30D2 **Huong Khe** Vietnam
27H7 **Huon Peninsula** Papua New Guinea
34C4 **Huonville** Australia
64C1 **Hurd,C** Canada
28A2 **Hure Qi** China
40B4 **Hurghada** Egypt
64A1 **Hurley** USA
66B2 **Huron** California, USA
61D2 **Huron** S Dakota, USA
64C1 **Huron,L** Canada/USA
35B2 **Hurunui** *R* New Zealand
12B1 **Húsavík** Iceland
17F1 **Huşi** Romania
12G7 **Huskvarna** Sweden
45C2 **Husn** Jordan
18B2 **Husum** Germany
56D3 **Hutchinson** USA
63C1 **Hutchinson** USA
34C1 **Hutton,Mt** Australia
31D2 **Hutuo He** *R* China
13C2 **Huy** Belgium
31A2 **Huzhu** China
16D2 **Hvar** *I* Croatia
28A2 **Hwadae** N Korea
51C5 **Hwange** Zimbabwe
51C5 **Hwange Nat Pk** Zimbabwe
28A2 **Hwapyong** N Korea
68E2 **Hyannis** Massachusetts, USA
60C2 **Hyannis** Nebraska, USA
26C2 **Hyargas Nuur** *L* Mongolia
54E4 **Hydaburg** USA
68D2 **Hyde Park** USA
44B2 **Hyderābād** India
42B3 **Hyderabad** Pakistan
14D3 **Hyères** France
14D3 **Hyères, Iles d'** *Is* France
28B2 **Hyesan** N Korea
68A3 **Hyndman** USA
56B2 **Hyndman Peak** *Mt* USA
20D3 **Hyrynsalmi** Finland
7E4 **Hythe** England
12J6 **Hyvinkää** Finland

I

73K6 **Iaçu** Brazil
17F2 **Ialomiţa** *R* Romania
17F1 **Iaşi** Romania
48C4 **Ibadan** Nigeria
72C3 **Ibagué** Colombia
17E2 **Ibar** *R* Montenegro/ Serbia, Yugoslavia
72C3 **Ibarra** Ecuador
13D1 **Ibbenbüren** Germany
75C2 **Ibiá** Brazil
75E1 **Ibicaraí** Brazil
74E3 **Ibicuí** *R* Brazil
74E4 **Ibicuy** Argentina
15C2 **Ibiza** Spain
15C2 **Ibiza** *I* Spain
51E5 **Ibo** Mozambique
73K6 **Ibotirama** Brazil
50C2 **Ibra, Wadi** *Watercourse* Sudan
41G5 **'Ibrī** Oman
72C6 **Ica** Peru
72E4 **Içá** *R* Brazil
72E3 **Içana** Brazil
12A1 **Iceland** *Republic* N Atlantic Ocean
25R4 **Icha** Russian Federation
44A2 **Ichalkaranji** India
29C3 **Ichinomiya** Japan
29E3 **Ichinosek** Japan
54B2 **Icy C** USA
63D2 **Idabell** USA
61D2 **Ida Grove** USA
58D2 **Idaho** State, USA
58C2 **Idaho City** USA
58D2 **Idaho Falls** USA
60B3 **Idaho Springs** USA
45B1 **Idalion** *Hist Site* Cyprus
58B2 **Idanha** USA
13D3 **Idar Oberstein** Germany
49D2 **Idehan Marzūg** *Desert* Libya
49D2 **Idehan Ubari** *Desert* Libya
48C2 **Idelès** Algeria
26C2 **Ideriym Gol** *R* Mongolia
40B5 **Idfu** Egypt
17E3 **Ídhi Óros** *Mt* Greece
17E3 **Ídhra** *I* Greece
50B4 **Idiofa** Zaïre
40C2 **Idlib** Syria
12K7 **Idritsa** Russian Federation
47D3 **Idutywa** South Africa
13B2 **Ieper** Belgium
17F3 **Ierápetra** Greece
25N4 **Iet Oktyob'ya** Russian Federation
51D4 **Ifakara** Tanzania
27H6 **Ifalik** *I* Pacific Ocean
51E6 **Ifanadiana** Madagascar
48C4 **Ife** Nigeria
48C3 **Iférouane** Niger
27E6 **Igan** Malaysia
75C3 **Igarapava** Brazil

24K3 **Igarka** Russian Federation
75A3 **Igatimi** Paraguay
41E2 **Igdir** Iran
12H6 **Iggesund** Sweden
16B3 **Iglesias** Sardinia, Italy
55K3 **Igloolik** Canada
57D2 **Ignace** Canada
40A1 **Iğneada Burun** *Pt* Turkey
48C1 **Ignil-Izane** Algeria
44E3 **Ignoitijala** Andaman Islands
17E3 **Igoumenítsa** Greece
20J4 **Igra** Russian Federation
20L3 **Igrim** Russian Federation
74F3 **Iguaçu, Quedas do** *Falls* Argentina/Brazil
70C3 **Iguala** Mexico
74G2 **Iguape** Brazil
75C3 **Iguatama** Brazil
75B3 **Iguatemi** Brazil
75A3 **Iguatemi** *R* Brazil
73L5 **Iguatu** Brazil
50A4 **Iguéla** Gabon
51E6 **Ihosy** Madagascar
29D3 **Iida** Japan
29C3 **Iide-san** *Mt* Japan
12K6 **Iisalmi** Finland
28B4 **Iisuka** Japan
48C4 **Ijebu** Nigeria
13C1 **Ijmuiden** Netherlands
13C1 **Ijssel** *R* Netherlands
18B2 **Ijsselmeer** *S* Netherlands
17F3 **Ikaría** *I* Greece
29E2 **Ikeda** Japan
50C4 **Ikela** Zaïre
17E2 **Ikhtiman** Bulgaria
28A4 **Iki** *I* Japan
51E5 **Ikopa** *R* Madagascar
27F5 **Ilagan** Philippines
41E3 **Ilām** Iran
26C1 **Ilanskiy** Russian Federation
50C4 **Ilebo** Zaïre
13B3 **Île De France** *Region* France
65E1 **Ile d'Orleans** Canada
21K5 **Ilek** *R* Russian Federation
7B4 **Ilfracombe** England
40B1 **Ilgaz Dağları** *Mts* Turkey
73H6 **Ilha do Bananal** *Region* Brazil
75D3 **Ilha Grande, B de** Brazil
73H8 **Ilha Grande, Reprêsa** Brazil/Paraguay
75B3 **Ilha Solteira Dam** Brazil
73L6 **Ilhéus** Brazil
54C4 **Iliamna L** USA
25M4 **Ilim** *R* Russian Fed
25M4 **Ilimsk** Russian Federation
25M4 **Ilin** *R* Russian Federation
26H2 **Il'inskiy** Russian Federation
17E3 **Iliodhrómia** *I* Greece
68C1 **Ilion** USA
6D3 **Ilkley** England
74B4 **Illapel** Chile
48C3 **Illéla** Niger
64A3 **Illinois** *R* USA
64B2 **Illinois** *State* USA
48C2 **Illizi** Algeria
20E4 **Il'men, Ozero** *L* Russian Federation
72D7 **Ilo** Peru
27F5 **Iloilo** Philippines
12L6 **Ilomantsi** Finland
48C4 **Ilorin** Nigeria
19G1 **Il'yino** Russian Federation
28B4 **Imabari** Japan
29C3 **Imaichi** Japan
12L5 **Imandra, Ozero** *L* Russian Federation
28A4 **Imari** Japan
20D3 **Imatra** Finland
74G3 **Imbituba** Brazil
75B4 **Imbituva** Brazil
50E3 **Imi** Ethiopia
28A3 **Imjin** *R* N Korea
58C2 **Imlay** USA
16C2 **Imola** Italy
73J5 **Imperatriz** Brazil
16B2 **Imperia** Italy
60C2 **Imperial** USA
59C4 **Imperial V** USA
50B3 **Impfondo** Congo
43G4 **Imphāl** India
29C3 **Ina** Japan
48C2 **In Afaleleh** *Well* Algeria
29C4 **Inamba-jima** *I* Japan
48C2 **In Amenas** Algeria
12K5 **Inari** Finland
12K5 **Inarijärvi** *L* Finland
29D3 **Inawashiro-ko** *L* Japan
48C2 **In Belbel** Algeria
21F7 **Ince Burun** *Pt* Turkey
40B2 **Incekum Burnu** *Pt* Turkey
8C2 **Inchnadamph** Scotland
28B3 **Inch'on** S Korea
8B4 **Indaal, Loch** *Inlet* Scotland
48B2 **In Dagouber** *Well* Mali
75C2 **Indaiá** *R* Brazil
12H6 **Indals** *R* Sweden
66C2 **Independence** California, USA
61E2 **Independence** Iowa, USA
63C1 **Independence** Kansas, USA
61E3 **Independence** Missouri, USA
58C2 **Independence Mts** USA
21J6 **Inderborskiy** Kazakhstan
39F3 **India** *Federal Republic* Asia
65D2 **Indiana** USA
64B2 **Indiana** *State* USA
36F7 **Indian-Antarctic Basin** Indian Ocean
36F7 **Indian-Antarctic Ridge** Indian Ocean
64B3 **Indianapolis** USA
Indian Desert = Thar Desert
55N4 **Indian Harbour** Canada
36E5 **Indian O**
61E2 **Indianola** Iowa, USA
63D2 **Indianola** Mississippi, USA
75C2 **Indianópolis** Brazil
59C3 **Indian Springs** USA
20H2 **Indiga** Russian Federation
25Q3 **Indigirka** *R* Russian Federation
30D2 **Indo-China** *Region* SE Asia
27F7 **Indonesia** *Republic* SE Asia
42D4 **Indore** India
14C2 **Indre** *R* France
42B3 **Indus** *R* Pakistan
42B4 **Indus, Mouths of the** Pakistan
48C2 **In Ebeggi** *Well* Algeria
21E7 **Inebolu** Turkey
48C2 **In Ecker** Algeria
40A1 **Inegöl** Turkey
48D2 **In Ezzane** Algeria
47C3 **Infantta, C** South Africa
70B3 **Infiernillo, Pico del** *Mt* Mexico
48C3 **Ingal** Niger
64C2 **Ingersoll** Canada
32D2 **Ingham** Australia
55M2 **Inglefield Land** *Region* Greenland
35B1 **Inglewood** New Zealand
34D1 **Inglewood** Queensland, Australia
66C4 **Inglewood** USA
34B3 **Inglewood** Victoria, Australia
12B2 **Ingólfshöfdi** *I* Iceland
18C3 **Ingolstadt** Germany
43F4 **Ingrāj Bāzār** India
48C3 **In Guezzam** *Well* Algeria
47E2 **Inhaca** *I* Mozambique
47E2 **Inhaca Pen** Mozambique
51D6 **Inhambane** Mozambique
51D6 **Inharrime** Mozambique
75C2 **Inhumas** Brazil
72E3 **Inirida** *R* Colombia
9C2 **Inishowen** *District* Irish Republic
9C2 **Inishtrahull Sd** Irish Republic
34C1 **Injune** Australia
34B1 **Innamincka** Australia
8D4 **Innerleithen** Scotland
31B1 **Inner Mongolia Aut. Region** China
32D2 **Innisfail** Australia
18C3 **Innsbruck** Austria
50B4 **Inongo** Zaïre
19D2 **Inowrocław** Poland
48C2 **In Salah** Algeria
28A3 **Insil** S Korea
20L2 **Inta** Russian Federation
16B1 **Interlaken** Switzerland
33H3 **International Date Line**
61E1 **International Falls** USA
29D3 **Inubo-saki** *C* Japan
55L4 **Inukjuak** Canada
54E3 **Inuvik** Canada
54E3 **Inuvik** *Region* Canada
8C3 **Inveraray** Scotland
8D3 **Inverbervie** Scotland
35A3 **Invercargill** New Zealand
34D1 **Inverell** Australia
8C3 **Invergordon** Scotland
8C3 **Inverness** Scotland
8D3 **Inverurie** Scotland
32C4 **Investigator Str** Australia
26B1 **Inya** Russian Federation
25Q3 **Inya** *R* Russian Federation
51D5 **Inyanga** Zimbabwe
66D3 **Inyokern** USA
66C2 **Inyo Mts** USA
50B4 **Inzia** *R* Zaïre
17E3 **Ioánnina** Greece
63C1 **Iola** USA
8B3 **Iona** *I* Scotland
51B5 **Iôna Nat Pk** Angola
58C1 **Ione** USA
17E3 **Ionian Is** Greece
17D3 **Ionian S** Greece/Italy
Iónioi Nísoi *Is* **= Ionian Islands**
17F3 **Íos** *I* Greece
20J3 **Iosser** Russian Federation
61E2 **Iowa** *R* USA
61E3 **Iowa** *State* USA
64A2 **Iowa City** USA
61E2 **Iowa Falls** USA
75C2 **Ipameri** Brazil
75D2 **Ipanema** Brazil
21G6 **Ipatovo** Russian Federation
72C3 **Ipiales** Colombia
75E1 **Ipiaú** Brazil
75B4 **Ipiranga** Brazil
30C5 **Ipoh** Malaysia
73H7 **Iporá** Brazil
17F2 **Ipsala** Turkey
34D1 **Ipswich** Australia
7E3 **Ipswich** England
68E1 **Ipswich** USA
19G2 **Iput** *R* Russian Federation
75C3 **Iquape** Brazil
74B2 **Iquique** Chile
72D4 **Iquitos** Peru
17F3 **Iráklion** Greece
38D2 **Iran** *Republic* SW Asia
70B2 **Irapuato** Mexico
40D3 **Iraq** *Republic* SW Asia
75B4 **Irati** Brazil
49D2 **Irāwan** *Watercourse* Libya
45C2 **Irbid** Jordan
20L4 **Irbit** Russian Federation
10B3 **Ireland, Republic of** NW Europe
73G3 **Ireng** *R* Guyana
28B3 **Iri** S Korea
27G7 **Irian Jaya** *Province* Indonesia
50C2 **Iriba** Chad
51D4 **Iringa** Tanzania
26F4 **Iriomote** *I* Ryukyu Is, Japan
69A3 **Iriona** Honduras
73H5 **Iriri** *R* Brazil
10B3 **Irish S** England/Ire
25M4 **Irkutsk** Russian Federation
32C4 **Iron Knob** Australia
64B1 **Iron Mountain** USA
32D2 **Iron Range** Australia
64B1 **Iron River** USA
64C3 **Irontown** USA
64A1 **Ironwood** USA
57E2 **Iroquois Falls** Canada
29C4 **Iro-zaki** *C* Japan
30B2 **Irrawaddy** *R* Burma
30A2 **Irrawaddy,Mouths of the** Burma
24H4 **Irtysh** *R* Russian Federation
15B1 **Irún** Spain
8C4 **Irvine** Scotland
8C4 **Irvine** *R* Scotland
63C2 **Irving** USA
66C3 **Isabella Res** USA
54H2 **Isachsen** Canada
54H2 **Isachsen,C** Canada
55Q3 **Ísafjörður** Iceland
28C4 **Isahaya** Japan
50C3 **Isangi** Zaïre
8E1 **Isbister** Scotland
16C2 **Ischia** *I* Italy
29C4 **Ise** Japan
13D2 **Iserlohn** Germany
16C2 **Isernia** Italy
29C4 **Ise-wan** *B* Japan
Isfahan = Esfahan
26F4 **Ishigaki** *I* Ryukyu Is, Japan
29E2 **Ishikari** *R* Japan
29E2 **Ishikari-wan** *B* Japan
24H4 **Ishim** Russian Federation
24H4 **Ishim** *R* Kazakhstan
29E3 **Ishinomaki** Japan
29D3 **Ishioka** Japan
42C1 **Ishkashim** Afghanistan
64B1 **Ishpeming** USA
24J4 **Isil'kul'** Russian Federation
50D3 **Isiolo** Kenya
50C3 **Isiro** Zaïre
40C2 **Iskenderun** Turkey
40C2 **Iskenderun Körfezi** *B* Turkey
40B1 **İskilip** Turkey
24K4 **Iskitim** Russian Federation
17E2 **Iskur** *R* Bulgaria
42C2 **Islamabad** Pakistan
67B4 **Islamorada** USA
57D1 **Island L** Canada
9D2 **Island Magee** Northern Ireland
58D2 **Island Park** USA
35B1 **Islands,B of** New Zealand
Islas Baleares = Balearic Islands
Islas Malvinas = Falkland Islands
8B4 **Islay** *I* Scotland
14C2 **Isle** *R* France
Isle, Island, Isola etc : see also individual island names
7D4 **Isle of Wight** *County* England
64B1 **Isle Royale Nat Pk** USA
7A5 **Isles of Scilly** England
66B1 **Isleton** USA
40B3 **Ismâ'ilîya** Egypt
40B4 **Isna** Egypt
51E6 **Isoanala** Madagascar
51D5 **Isoka** Zambia
16D3 **Isola de Correnti, C** Sicily, Italy
29C3 **Isosaki** Japan
40B2 **İsparta** Turkey
45C2 **Israel** *Republic* SW Asia
15C2 **Isser** *R* Algeria
14C2 **Issoire** France
14C2 **Issoudun** France
39F1 **Issyk Kul', Ozero** *L* Kirgizia
40A1 **İstanbul** Turkey
17E3 **Istiáia** Greece
67B3 **Istokpoga,L** USA
16C1 **Istra** *Pen* Croatia
75C2 **Itaberai** Brazil
75D2 **Itabira** Brazil
75D3 **Itabirito** Brazil
75E1 **Itabuna** Brazil
75E1 **Itacaré** Brazil
73G4 **Itacoatiara** Brazil
75A3 **Itacurubí del Rosario** Paraguay
75C1 **Itaguari** *R* Brazil
72C2 **Itagui** Colombia
75B4 **Itaipu, Reprêsa** *Res* Brazil/Paraguay
73G4 **Itaituba** Brazil
74G3 **Itajaí** Brazil
75C3 **Itajuba** Brazil
16C2 **Italy** *Republic* Europe
75E2 **Itamaraju** Brazil
75D2 **Itamarandiba** Brazil
75D2 **Itambacuri** Brazil
75D2 **Itambé** Brazil
75D2 **Itambé** *Mt* Brazil
43G3 **Itānagar** India
75C3 **Itanhaém** Brazil
75D2 **Itanhém** Brazil
75D2 **Itanhém** *R* Brazil
75D2 **Itaobím** Brazil
75C1 **Itapaci** Brazil
75C3 **Itapecerica** Brazil
75D3 **Itaperuna** Brazil
73K7 **Itapetinga** Brazil
75C3 **Itapetininga** Brazil
75C3 **Itapeva** Brazil
73L4 **Itapipoca** Brazil
75C2 **Itapuranga** Brazil
74E3 **Itaqui** Brazil
75D2 **Itarantim** Brazil
75C3 **Itararé** Brazil
75C3 **Itararé** *R* Brazil
75D3 **Itaúna** Brazil
72F6 **Iténez** *R* Bolivia/Brazil
65D2 **Ithaca** USA
45D3 **Ithrīyat, Jebel** *Mt* Jordan
50C3 **Itimbiri** *R* Zaïre
75D2 **Itinga** Brazil
75A2 **Itiquira** *R* Brazil
55N3 **Itivdleq** Greenland
29C4 **Ito** Japan
29D3 **Itoigawa** Japan
72F6 **Itonomas** *R* Bolivia
75C3 **Itu** Brazil
75E1 **Ituberá** Brazil
75C2 **Ituiutaba** Brazil
75C2 **Itumbiara** Brazil
75B2 **Iturama** Brazil
74C2 **Iturbe** Argentina
26H2 **Iturup** *I* Russian Federation
18B2 **Itzehoe** Germany
25U3 **Iul'tin** Russian Federation
19F2 **Ivacevichi** Belarus
75B3 **Ivai** *R* Brazil
12K5 **Ivalo** Finland
17D2 **Ivangrad** Montenegro, Yugoslavia
34B2 **Ivanhoe** Australia
19E3 **Ivano-Frankovsk** Ukraine
20G4 **Ivanovo** Russian Federation
20L3 **Ivdel'** Russian Federation
50B3 **Ivindo** *R* Gabon
75B3 **Ivinhema** Brazil
75B3 **Ivinhema** *R* Brazil
51E6 **Ivohibe** Madagascar
51E5 **Ivongo Soanierana** Madagascar
48B4 **Ivory Coast** *Republic* Africa
16B1 **Ivrea** Italy
55L3 **Ivujivik** Canada
29E3 **Iwaki** Japan
29D2 **Iwaki** *R* Japan
29D2 **Iwaki-san** *Mt* Japan
28C4 **Iwakuni** Japan
29D2 **Iwamizawa** Japan
29E2 **Iwanai** Japan
48C4 **Iwo** Nigeria
26H4 **Iwo Jima** *I* Japan
70C3 **Ixtepec** Mexico
28B4 **Iyo** Japan
28B4 **Iyo-nada** *B* Japan
24G4 **Izhevsk** Russian Federation
20J2 **Izhma** Russian Federation
20J2 **Izhma** *R* Russian Federation
41G5 **Izkī** Oman
19F3 **Izmail** Ukraine
40A2 **İzmir** Turkey
17F3 **İzmir Körfezi** *B* Turkey
40A1 **İzmit** Turkey
40A1 **İznik** Turkey
17F2 **Iznik Golü** *L* Turkey
45D2 **Izra'** Syria
28A4 **Izuhara** Japan
29C4 **Izumi-sano** Japan
28B3 **Izumo** Japan

J

41F5 **Jabal aẓ Ẓannah** UAE
43E4 **Jabalpur** India
40D4 **Jabal Shammar** *Region* Saudi Arabia
45C1 **Jablah** Syria
18D2 **Jablonec nad Nisou** Czech Republic
73L5 **Jaboatão** Brazil
75C3 **Jaboticabal** Brazil
15B1 **Jaca** Spain
73G5 **Jacareacanga** Brazil
73H8 **Jacarezinho** Brazil
75C3 **Jacarie** Brazil
74C4 **Jáchal** Argentina
75B2 **Jaciara** Brazil
75D2 **Jacinto** Brazil
65E1 **Jackman Station** USA
62C2 **Jacksboro** USA
68B2 **Jacks Mt** USA
67A2 **Jackson** Alabama, USA
34C1 **Jackson** Australia
66B1 **Jackson** California, USA
64C2 **Jackson** Michigan, USA
61E2 **Jackson** Minnesota, USA
63D2 **Jackson** Mississippi, USA
64B3 **Jackson** Missouri, USA
64C3 **Jackson** Ohio, USA
63E2 **Jackson** Tennessee, USA
58D2 **Jackson** Wyoming, USA
35B2 **Jackson,C** New Zealand
35A2 **Jackson Head** *Pt* New Zealand
58D2 **Jackson L** USA
63D2 **Jacksonville** Arkansas, USA
67B2 **Jacksonville** Florida, USA
64A3 **Jacksonville** Illinois, USA
67C2 **Jacksonville** N Carolina, USA
63C2 **Jacksonville** Texas, USA
67B2 **Jacksonville Beach** USA
69C3 **Jacmel** Haiti
42B3 **Jacobabad** Pakistan
73K6 **Jacobina** Brazil
Jadotville = Likasi
72C5 **Jaén** Peru
15B2 **Jaén** Spain
Jaffa = Tel Aviv-Yafo
34A3 **Jaffa,C** Australia
44B4 **Jaffna** Sri Lanka
68D1 **Jaffrey** USA
43F4 **Jagannathganj Ghat** Bangladesh
44C2 **Jagdalpur** India
41G4 **Jagin** *R* Iran
44B2 **Jagtial** India
75E1 **Jaguaquara** Brazil
74F4 **Jaguarão** *R* Brazil/Uruguay
75C3 **Jaguariaiva** Brazil
21H8 **Jahan Dāgh** *Mt* Iran
41F4 **Jahrom** Iran
31A2 **Jainca** China
42D3 **Jaipur** India
42C3 **Jaisalmer** India
41G2 **Jajarm** Iran
16D2 **Jajce** Bosnia-Herzegovina
27D7 **Jakarta** Indonesia
55N3 **Jakobshavn** Greenland
12J6 **Jakobstad** Finland
62B2 **Jal** USA
42C2 **Jalalabad** Afghanistan
70C3 **Jalapa** Mexico
75B3 **Jales** Brazil
43F3 **Jaleswar** Nepal
42D4 **Jalgaon** India
48D4 **Jalingo** Nigeria
42D5 **Jālna** India
15B1 **Jalón** *R* Spain
49E2 **Jalo Oasis** Libya
42C3 **Jālor** India
43F3 **Jalpāiguri** India
49E2 **Jālū Oasis** Libya
72B4 **Jama** Ecuador
50E3 **Jamaame** Somalia
69B3 **Jamaica** *I* Caribbean Sea
69B3 **Jamaica Chan** Haiti/Jamaica
43F4 **Jamalpur** Bangladesh
27D7 **Jambi** Indonesia

42C4 **Jambusar** India
60D1 **James** *R* N Dakota, USA
65D3 **James** *R* Virginia, USA
55K4 **James B** Canada
34A2 **Jamestown** Australia
60D1 **Jamestown** N Dakota, USA
65D2 **Jamestown** New York, USA
68E2 **Jamestown** Rhode Island, USA
47D3 **Jamestown** South Africa
54J5 **Jamestown** USA
44B2 **Jamkhandi** India
42C2 **Jammu** India
42D2 **Jammu and Kashmīr** *State* India
42B4 **Jāmnagar** India
42C3 **Jampur** Pakistan
20C3 **Jämsä** Finland
43F4 **Jamshedpur** India
45D3 **Janab, Wadi el** Jordan
43F3 **Janakpur** Nepal
75D2 **Janaúba** Brazil
41F3 **Jandaq** Iran
34D1 **Jandowae** Australia
64B2 **Janesville** USA
76B1 **Jan Mayen** *I* Norwegian Sea
75D2 **Januária** Brazil
42D4 **Jaora** India
26G3 **Japan, S of** Japan
36J3 **Japan Trench** Pacific Ocean
72E4 **Japurá** *R* Brazil
40C2 **Jarābulus** Syria
75C2 **Jaraguá** Brazil
75B3 **Jaraguari** Brazil
15B1 **Jarama** *R* Spain
45C2 **Jarash** Jordan
75A3 **Jardim** Brazil
69B2 **Jardines de la Reina** *Is* Cuba
Jargalant = Hovd
73H3 **Jari** *R* Brazil
43G3 **Jaria Jhānjail** Bangladesh
13C3 **Jarny** France
18D2 **Jarocin** Poland
19E2 **Jarosław** Poland
12G6 **Järpen** Sweden
31B2 **Jartai** China
42C4 **Jasdan** India
48C4 **Jasikan** Ghana
41G4 **Jāsk** Iran
19E3 **Jasło** Poland
74D8 **Jason Is** Falkland Islands
63E2 **Jasper** Alabama, USA
63D1 **Jasper** Arkansas, USA
54G4 **Jasper** Canada
67B2 **Jasper** Florida, USA
64B3 **Jasper** Indiana, USA
63D2 **Jasper** Texas, USA
18D2 **Jastrowie** Poland
75B2 **Jataí** Brazil
15B2 **Játiva** Spain
75C3 **Jau** Brazil
72C6 **Jauja** Peru
43E3 **Jaunpur** India
44B3 **Javadi Hills** India
27D7 **Java,I** Indonesia
Javari *R* **= Yavari**
27D7 **Java S** Indonesia
32A2 **Java Trench** Indonesia
Jawa = Java
27G7 **Jaya, Pk** Indonesia
27H7 **Jayapura** Indonesia
45D2 **Jayrūd** Syria
63D3 **Jeanerette** USA
48C4 **Jebba** Nigeria
50C2 **Jebel Abyad** *Desert Region* Sudan
Jebel esh Sheikh = Hermon, Mt
8D4 **Jedburgh** Scotland
Jedda = Jiddah
19E2 **Jędrzejów** Poland
61E2 **Jefferson** Iowa, USA
63D2 **Jefferson** Texas, USA
58D1 **Jefferson** *R* USA
57D3 **Jefferson City** USA
56B3 **Jefferson,Mt** USA
64B3 **Jeffersonville** USA
45C3 **Jeib, Wadi el** Israel/ Jordan
75A3 **Jejui-Guazú** *R* Paraguay
20D4 **Jekabpils** Latvia
18D2 **Jelena Góra** Poland
20C4 **Jelgava** Latvia
27E7 **Jember** Indonesia
62A1 **Jemez Pueblo** USA
18C2 **Jena** Germany
16B3 **Jendouba** Tunisia
45C2 **Jenin** Israel
63D2 **Jennings** USA
55O3 **Jensen Nunatakker** *Mt* Greenland
55K3 **Jens Munk** *I* Canada
34B3 **Jeparit** Australia
73L6 **Jequié** Brazil
75D2 **Jequitai** *R* Brazil
75D2 **Jequitinhonha** Brazil
73K7 **Jequitinhonha** *R* Brazil
48D1 **Jerba, I de** Tunisia
15A2 **Jerez de la Frontera** Spain
15A2 **Jerez de los Caballeros** Spain
45C3 **Jericho** Israel
34C3 **Jerilderie** Australia
58D2 **Jerome** USA
14B2 **Jersey** *I* Channel Islands
57F2 **Jersey City** USA
65D2 **Jersey Shore** USA
64A3 **Jerseyville** USA
40C3 **Jerusalem** Israel
34D3 **Jervis B** Australia
16C1 **Jesenice** Slovenia
18D2 **Jeseníky** *Upland* Czech Republic
43F4 **Jessore** Bangladesh
57E3 **Jesup** USA
62C1 **Jetmore** USA
13D1 **Jever** Germany
68E2 **Jewett City** USA
44C2 **Jeypore** India
17D2 **Jezerce** *Mt* Albania
19E2 **Jezioro Mamry** *L* Poland
19E2 **Jezioro Śniardwy** *L* Poland
45C2 **Jezzine** Lebanon
42C4 **Jhābua** India
42D4 **Jhālāwār** India
42C2 **Jhang Maghiana** Pakistan
42D3 **Jhānsi** India
43E4 **Jhārsuguda** India
42C2 **Jhelum** Pakistan
42C2 **Jhelum** *R* Pakistan
42D3 **Jhunjhunūn** India
31B3 **Jialing Jiang** *R* China
26G2 **Jiamusi** China
28B2 **Ji'an** China
31C4 **Ji'an** Jiangxi, China
31D4 **Jiande** China
31B4 **Jiang'an** China
31D4 **Jiangbiancun** China
31A5 **Jiangcheng** China
31C5 **Jiangmen** China
31D3 **Jiangsu** *Province* China
31C4 **Jiangxi** *Province* China
31A3 **Jiangyou** China
31D1 **Jianping** China
31A5 **Jianshui** China
31D4 **Jian Xi** *R* China
31D4 **Jianyang** China
28B2 **Jiaohe** China
31E2 **Jiaonan** China
31E2 **Jiao Xian** China
31E2 **Jiaozhou Wan** *B* China
31C2 **Jiaozuo** China
31E3 **Jiaxiang** China
26C3 **Jiayuguan** China
75C2 **Jibão, Serra do** *Mts* Brazil
50D1 **Jiddah** Saudi Arabia
31D3 **Jieshou** China
31C2 **Jiexiu** China
31A3 **Jigzhi** China
18D3 **Jihlava** Czech Republic
16B3 **Jijel** Algeria
50E3 **Jilib** Somalia
28B2 **Jilin** China
28B2 **Jilin** *Province* China
15B1 **Jiloca** *R* Spain
50D3 **Jima** Ethiopia
62B3 **Jiménez** Coahuila, Mexico
31D2 **Jinan** China
42D3 **Jind** India
31B2 **Jingbian** China
31D4 **Jingdezhen** China
30C1 **Jinghong** China
31C3 **Jingmen** China
31B2 **Jingning** China
31B4 **Jing Xian** China
28B2 **Jingyu** China
31D4 **Jinhua** China
31C1 **Jining** Inner Mongolia, China
31D2 **Jining** Shandong, China
50D3 **Jinja** Uganda
30C1 **Jinping** China
31A4 **Jinsha Jiang** *R* China
31C4 **Jinshi** China
31E1 **Jinxi** China
28A2 **Jin Xian** China
31E1 **Jinzhou** China
72F5 **Jiparaná** *R* Brazil
72B4 **Jipijapa** Ecuador
41G4 **Jīroft** Iran
50E3 **Jirriiban** Somalia
31B4 **Jishou** China
40C2 **Jisr ash Shughūr** Syria
17E2 **Jiu** *R* Romania
31D4 **Jiujiang** China
31C4 **Jiuling Shan** *Hills* China
31A4 **Jiulong** China
31D4 **Jiulong Jiang** *R* China
26G2 **Jixi** China
45C3 **Jiza** Jordan
50E2 **Jīzān** Saudi Arabia
48A3 **Joal** Senegal
75D2 **João Monlevade** Brazil
73M5 **João Pessoa** Brazil
73J7 **João Pinheiro** Brazil
42C3 **Jodhpur** India
12K6 **Joensuu** Finland
13C3 **Joeuf** France
43F3 **Jogbani** India
44A3 **Jog Falls** India
47D2 **Johannesburg** South Africa
59C3 **Johannesburg** USA
55L2 **Johan Pen** Canada
58C2 **John Day** USA
58B1 **John Day** *R* USA
57F3 **John H Kerr L** USA
65D3 **John H. Kerr Res** USA
62B1 **John Martin Res** USA
8D2 **John o'Groats** Scotland
63C1 **John Redmond Res** USA
68A2 **Johnsonburg** USA
68C1 **Johnson City** New York, USA
67B1 **Johnson City** Tennessee, USA
67B2 **Johnston** USA
69N2 **Johnston Pt** St Vincent
68C1 **Johnstown** New York, USA
65D2 **Johnstown** Pennsylvania, USA
30C5 **Johor Bharu** Malaysia
14C2 **Joigny** France
74G3 **Joinville** Brazil
13C3 **Joinville** France
20J5 **Jok** *R* Russian Federation
12H5 **Jokkmokk** Sweden
21H8 **Jolfa** Iran
57E2 **Joliet** USA
55L5 **Joliette** Canada
27F6 **Jolo** Philippines
27F6 **Jolo** *I* Philippines
39H2 **Joma** *Mt* China
19E1 **Jonava** Lithuania
31A3 **Jonê** China
57D3 **Jonesboro** Arkansas, USA
63D2 **Jonesboro** Louisiana, USA
55K2 **Jones Sd** Canada
19E1 **Joniškis** Lithuania
12G7 **Jönköping** Sweden
65E1 **Jonquière** Canada
57D3 **Joplin** USA
60B1 **Jordan** Montana, USA
68B1 **Jordan** New York, USA
40C3 **Jordan** *Kingdom* SW Asia
45C2 **Jordan** *R* Israel
58C2 **Jordan Valley** USA
75B4 **Jordão** *R* Brazil
43G3 **Jorhāt** India
20C2 **Jörn** Sweden
12F7 **Jørpeland** Norway
48C3 **Jos** Nigeria
32B2 **Joseph Bonaparte G** Australia
59D3 **Joseph City** USA
55M4 **Joseph, Lac** Canada
24B3 **Jotunheimen** *Mt* Norway
45C2 **Jouai'ya** Lebanon
45C2 **Jounié** Lebanon
43G3 **Jowai** India
50E3 **Jowhar** Somalia
54F5 **Juan de Fuca,Str of** Canada/USA
51E5 **Juan de Nova** *I* Mozambique Channel
72Q **Juan Fernández, Islas** Pacific Ocean
73K5 **Juàzeiro** Brazil
73L5 **Juàzeiro do Norte** Brazil
50D3 **Juba** Sudan
50E3 **Juba** *R* Somalia
45C1 **Jubail** Lebanon
76G2 **Jubany** *Base* Antarctica
40D4 **Jubbah** Saudi Arabia
15B2 **Júcar** *R* Spain
18C3 **Judenburg** Austria
13D1 **Juist** *I* Germany
73K8 **Juiz de Fora** Brazil
74C2 **Jujuy** *State* Argentina
60C2 **Julesburg** USA
72E7 **Juli** Peru
72D7 **Juliaca** Peru
73G3 **Julianatop** *Mt* Surinam
55O3 **Julianehåb** Greenland
13D2 **Jülich** Germany
42D2 **Jullundur** India
43E3 **Jumla** Nepal
45C3 **Jum Suwwāna** *Mt* Jordan
42C4 **Jūnāgadh** India
31D2 **Junan** China
62C2 **Junction** Texas, USA
59D3 **Junction** Utah, USA
56D3 **Junction City** USA
74G2 **Jundiaí** Brazil
54E4 **Juneau** USA
32D4 **Junee** Australia
66C2 **June Lake** USA
16B1 **Jungfrau** *Mt* Switzerland
68B2 **Juniata** *R* USA
74D4 **Junín** Argentina
66B2 **Junipero Serra Peak** *Mt* USA
31A4 **Junlian** China
75D2 **Juparanã, Lagoa** Brazil
74G2 **Juquiá** Brazil
50C3 **Jur** *R* Sudan
8C4 **Jura** *I* Scotland
14D2 **Jura** *Mts* France
8C3 **Jura,Sound of** *Chan* Scotland
45C3 **Jurf ed Darāwīsh** Jordan
24K4 **Jurga** Russian Federation
20C4 **Jūrmala** Latvia
72E4 **Juruá** *R* Brazil
73G6 **Juruena** *R* Brazil
45D1 **Jūsīyah** Syria
72E4 **Jutaí** *R* Brazil
70D3 **Juticalpa** Honduras
Jutland *Pen* **= Jylland**
69A2 **Juventud, Isla de la** Cuba
41G3 **Jūymand** Iran
18B1 **Jylland** *Pen* Denmark
12K6 **Jyväskyla** Finland

K

39F2 **K2** *Mt* China/India
41G2 **Kaakhka** Turkmenistan
47E2 **Kaapmuiden** South Africa
27F7 **Kabaena** Indonesia
32B1 **Kabaena** *I* Indonesia
48A4 **Kabala** Sierra Leone
50D4 **Kabale** Uganda
50C4 **Kabalo** Zaïre
50C4 **Kabambare** Zaïre
50D3 **Kabarole** Uganda
64C1 **Kabinakagami L** Canada
50C4 **Kabinda** Zaïre
45C1 **Kabīr** *R* Syria
41E3 **Kabir Kuh** *Mts* Iran
51C5 **Kabompo** Zambia
51C5 **Kabompo** *R* Zambia
51C4 **Kabongo** Zaïre
42B2 **Kabul** Afghanistan
42B4 **Kachchh,G of** India
20K4 **Kachkanar** Russian Federation
25M4 **Kachug** Russian Federation
30B3 **Kadan** *I* Burma
42C4 **Kadi** India
40B2 **Kadınhanı** Turkey
44B3 **Kadiri** India
21F6 **Kadiyevka** Ukraine
60C2 **Kadoka** USA
51C5 **Kadoma** Zimbabwe
50C2 **Kadugli** Sudan
48C3 **Kaduna** Nigeria
48C3 **Kaduna** *R* Nigeria
44B3 **Kadūr** India
43H3 **Kadusam** *Mt* China
20K3 **Kadzherom** Russian Federation
28A3 **Kaechon** N Korea
48A3 **Kaédi** Mauritius
66E5 **Kaena Pt** Hawaiian Islands
28B3 **Kaesŏng** N Korea
48C4 **Kafanchan** Nigeria
48A3 **Kaffrine** Senegal
45D1 **Kafr Behum** Syria
45A3 **Kafr Sa'd** Egypt
45A3 **Kafr Saqv** Egypt
45D1 **Kafrūn Bashūr** Syria
51C5 **Kafue** Zambia
51C5 **Kafue** *R* Zambia
51C5 **Kafue Nat Pk** Zambia
29D3 **Kaga** Japan
24H6 **Kagan** Uzbekistan
21G7 **Kağızman** Turkey
19F3 **Kagul** Moldavia
41G2 **Kāhak** Iran
50D4 **Kahama** Tanzania
42B3 **Kahan** Pakistan
51B4 **Kahemba** Zaïre
13E2 **Kahler Asten** *Mt* Germany
41G4 **Kahnūj** Iran
64A2 **Kahoka** USA
66E5 **Kahoolawe** *I* Hawaiian Islands
40C2 **Kahramanmaraş** Turkey
66E5 **Kahuku Pt** Hawaiian Islands
66E5 **Kahului** Hawaiian Islands
35B2 **Kaiapoi** New Zealand
59D3 **Kaibab Plat** USA
73G2 **Kaieteur Falls** Guyana
31C3 **Kaifeng** China
27G7 **Kai, Kepulauan** *Arch* Indonesia
35B1 **Kaikohe** New Zealand
33G5 **Kaikoura** New Zealand
35B2 **Kaikoura Pen** New Zealand
35B2 **Kaikoura Range** *Mts* New Zealand
31B4 **Kaili** China
28A2 **Kailu** China
66E5 **Kailua** Hawaii
66E5 **Kailua** Oahu, Hawaiian Islands
27G7 **Kaimana** Indonesia
35C1 **Kaimenawa Mts** New Zealand
29C4 **Kainan** Japan
48C3 **Kainji Res** Nigeria
35B1 **Kaipara Harbour** *B* New Zealand
31C5 **Kaiping** China
16C3 **Kairouan** Tunisia
66C2 **Kaiser Peak** *Mt* USA
14D2 **Kaiserslautern** Germany
28B2 **Kaishantun** China
19E2 **Kaisiadorys** Lithuania
35B1 **Kaitaia** New Zealand
35A3 **Kaitangata** New Zealand
42D3 **Kaithal** India
66E5 **Kaiwi Chan** Hawaiian Islands
31B3 **Kai Xian** China
28A2 **Kaiyuan** Liaoning, China
31A5 **Kaiyuan** Yunnan, China
12K6 **Kajaani** Finland
42B2 **Kajaki** Afghanistan
50D4 **Kajiado** Kenya
42B2 **Kajrān** Afghanistan
50D2 **Kaka** Sudan
64B1 **Kakabeka Falls** Canada
50D3 **Kakamega** Kenya
28B4 **Kake** Japan
21E6 **Kakhovskoye Vodokhranilishche** *Res* Ukraine
41F4 **Kākī** Iran
44C2 **Kākināda** India
29B4 **Kakogawa** Japan
54D2 **Kaktovik** USA
29D3 **Kakuda** Japan
16B3 **Kalaat Khasba** Tunisia
17E3 **Kalabáka** Greece
51C5 **Kalabo** Zambia
21G5 **Kalach** Russian Federation
21G6 **Kalach-na-Donu** Russian Federation
43G4 **Kaladan** *R* Burma/India
66E5 **Ka Lae** *C* Hawaiian Islands
51C6 **Kalahari Desert** Botswana
47C2 **Kalahari Gemsbok Nat Pk** South Africa
20C3 **Kalajoki** Finland
25N4 **Kalakan** Russian Federation
27C6 **Kalakepen** Indonesia
42C1 **Kalam** Pakistan
17E3 **Kalámai** Greece
57E2 **Kalamazoo** USA
66E5 **Kalapana** Hawaiian Islands
19F3 **Kalarash** Moldavia
42B3 **Kalat** Pakistan
66E5 **Kalaupapa** Hawaiian Islands
40B1 **Kalecik** Turkey
50C4 **Kalémié** Zaïre
20E2 **Kalevala** Russian Federation
43G4 **Kalewa** Burma
32B4 **Kalgoorlie** Australia
43E3 **Kali** *R* India/Nepal
50C4 **Kalima** Zaïre
27E7 **Kalimantan** *Terr* Indonesia
17F3 **Kálimnos** *I* Greece
43F3 **Kālimpang** India
43K1 **Kali Nadi** *R* India
12J8 **Kaliningrad** Russian Federation
21D5 **Kalinkovichi** Belarus
19F3 **Kalinovka** Ukraine
56B2 **Kalispell** USA
19D2 **Kalisz** Poland
50D4 **Kaliua** Tanzania
12J5 **Kalix** *R* Sweden
51B6 **Kalkfeld** Namibia
47C1 **Kalkfontein** Botswana
12K6 **Kallavesi** *L* Finland
17F3 **Kallonis Kólpos** *B* Greece
12H7 **Kalmar** Sweden
21H6 **Kalmyk Republic** Russian Federation
51C5 **Kalomo** Zambia
64A2 **Kalona** USA
44A3 **Kalpeni** *I* India
42D3 **Kālpi** India
20F5 **Kaluga** Russian Federation
12G7 **Kalundborg** Denmark
19E3 **Kalush** Ukraine
44A2 **Kalyān** India
44B3 **Kalyandurg** India
20F4 **Kalyazin** Russian Federation
20J3 **Kama** *R* Russian Federation
29E3 **Kamaishi** Japan
42C2 **Kamalia** Pakistan
51B5 **Kamanjab** Namibia
25O4 **Kamara** China
42D2 **Kamat** *Mt* China/India
44B4 **Kambam** India
20J4 **Kambarka** Russian Federation
48A4 **Kambia** Sierra Leone
25S4 **Kamchatka** *Pen* Russian Federation
19F3 **Kamenets Podolskiy** Ukraine
20G5 **Kamenka** Russian Federation

24K4 **Kamen-na-Obi** Russian Federation
25S3 **Kamenskoya** Russian Federation
20L4 **Kamensk-Ural'skiy** Russian Federation
47B3 **Kamieskroon** South Africa
54H3 **Kamilukuak L** Canada
51C4 **Kamina** Zaïre
55J3 **Kaminak L** Canada
29D3 **Kaminoyama** Japan
54F4 **Kamloops** Canada
41E1 **Kamo** Armenia
29D3 **Kamogawa** Japan
50D3 **Kampala** Uganda
30C5 **Kampar** Malaysia
18B2 **Kampen** Netherlands
30B2 **Kamphaeng Phet** Thailand
30C3 **Kampot** Cambodia
20K4 **Kamskoye Vodokhranilishche** *Res* Russian Federation
42D4 **Kāmthi** India
21H5 **Kamyshin** Russian Federation
20L4 **Kamyshlov** Russian Federation
55L4 **Kanaaupscow** *R* Canada
59D3 **Kanab** USA
50C4 **Kananga** Zaïre
20H4 **Kanash** Russian Federation
29C3 **Kanayama** Japan
29D3 **Kanazawa** Japan
44B3 **Kānchipuram** India
20E2 **Kandagan** Indonesia
42B2 **Kandahar** Afghanistan
20E2 **Kandalaksha** Russian Federation
12L5 **Kandalakshskaya Guba** *B* Russian Federation
13D3 **Kandel** *Mt* Germany
48C3 **Kandi** Benin
34C2 **Kandos** Australia
44C4 **Kandy** Sri Lanka
65D2 **Kane** USA
55L1 **Kane Basin** *B* Canada
50B2 **Kanem** *Desert Region* Chad
66E5 **Kaneohe** Hawaiian Islands
20F2 **Kanevka** Russian Federation
47C1 **Kang** Botswana
48B3 **Kangaba** Mali
40C2 **Kangal** Turkey
55N3 **Kangâmiut** Greenland
41F4 **Kangān** Iran
30C4 **Kangar** Malaysia
32C4 **Kangaroo I** Australia
55N3 **Kangâtsiaq** Greenland
41E3 **Kangavar** Iran
31C1 **Kangbao** China
39G3 **Kangchenjunga** *Mt* China/Nepal
31A4 **Kangding** China
32A1 **Kangean** *Is* Indonesia
55P3 **Kangerdlugssuaq** *B* Greenland
55P3 **Kangerdlugssuatsaiq** *B* Greenland
50D3 **Kangetet** Kenya
28B2 **Kanggye** N Korea
28B3 **Kanghwa** S Korea
55M4 **Kangiqsualujjuaq** Canada
55L3 **Kangiqsujuak** Canada
55L3 **Kangirsuk** Canada
28B3 **Kangnŭng** S Korea
50B3 **Kango** Gabon
28A2 **Kangping** China
26C4 **Kangto** *Mt* China/India
31B3 **Kang Xian** China
51C4 **Kaniama** Zaïre
44B2 **Kani Giri** India
20G2 **Kanin, Poluostrov** *Pen* Russian Federation
12J6 **Kankaanpää** Finland
64B2 **Kankakee** USA
64B2 **Kankakee** *R* USA
48B3 **Kankan** Guinea
43E4 **Kānker** India
67B1 **Kannapolis** USA
44B4 **Kanniyākumari** India
48C3 **Kano** Nigeria
60C3 **Kanorado** USA
43E3 **Kānpur** India
61D3 **Kansas** *R* USA
56D3 **Kansas** *State* USA
57D3 **Kansas City** USA
31D5 **Kanshi** China
25L4 **Kansk** Russian Federation
28A3 **Kansŏng** S Korea
48C3 **Kantchari** Burkina
48C4 **Kanté** Togo
43F4 **Kanthi** India
54C3 **Kantishna** USA
9B3 **Kanturk** Irish Republic
47D1 **Kanye** Botswana
26E4 **Kaohsiung** Taiwan
51B5 **Kaoka Veld** *Plain* Namibia
48A3 **Kaolack** Senegal
51C5 **Kaoma** Zambia
66E5 **Kapaa** Hawaiian Islands
66E5 **Kapaau** Hawaiian Islands
51C4 **Kapanga** Zaïre
12H7 **Kapellskär** Sweden
Kap Farvel = Farewell, C
51C5 **Kapiri** Zambia
63D2 **Kaplan** USA
18C3 **Kaplice** Czech Republic
30B4 **Kapoe** Thailand
51C4 **Kapona** Zaïre
17D1 **Kaposvár** Hungary
55L2 **Kap Parry** *C* Greenland
28A2 **Kapsan** N Korea
27E6 **Kapuas** *R* Indonesia
34A2 **Kapunda** Australia
42D2 **Kapurthala** India
55K5 **Kapuskasing** Canada
64C1 **Kapuskasing** *R* Canada
34D2 **Kaputar** *Mt* Australia
21H8 **Kapydzhik** *Mt* Armenia
28A3 **Kapyŏng** S Korea
21G8 **Kara** *R* Turkey
40B1 **Karabük** Turkey
17F2 **Karacabey** Turkey
42B4 **Karachi** Pakistan
44A2 **Karād** India
21F7 **Kara Dağları** *Mt* Turkey
21D7 **Karadeniz Boğazi** *Str* Turkey
26E1 **Karaftit** Russian Federation
24J5 **Karaganda** Kazakhstan
24J5 **Karagayly** Kazakhstan
25S4 **Karaginskiy, Ostrov** *I* Russian Federation
44B3 **Kāraikāl** India
41F2 **Karaj** Iran
40C3 **Karak** Jordan
24G5 **Karakalpak Republic** Uzbekistan
42D1 **Karakax He** *R* China
27F6 **Karakelong** *I* Indonesia
42D1 **Karakoram** *Mts* India
42D1 **Karakoram P** China/India
48A3 **Karakoro** *Watercourse* Mali/Mauritius
24G6 **Karakumy** *Desert* Turkmenistan
45C3 **Karama** Jordan
21E8 **Karaman** Turkey
24K5 **Karamay** China
35B2 **Karamea** New Zealand
35B2 **Karamea Bight** *B* New Zealand
42D4 **Kāranja** India
21E8 **Karanlik** *R* Turkey
40B2 **Karapınar** Turkey
24J2 **Kara S** Russian Federation
47B2 **Karasburg** Namibia
12K5 **Karasjok** Norway
24J4 **Karasuk** Russian Federation
40C2 **Karataş** Turkey
24H5 **Kara Tau** *Mts* Kazakhstan
30B3 **Karathuri** Burma
28B4 **Karatsu** Japan
24K2 **Karaul** Russian Federation
45B1 **Karavostasi** Cyprus
41F4 **Karāz** Iran
41D3 **Karbalā'** Iraq
19E3 **Karcag** Hungary
17E3 **Kardhítsa** Greece
20E3 **Karelian Republic** Russian Federation
44E3 **Karen** Andaman Islands
20K3 **Karepino** Russian Federation
12J5 **Karesvando** Sweden
48B2 **Karet** *Desert Region* Mauritius
24K4 **Kargasok** Russian Federation
20F3 **Kargopol'** Russian Federation
48D3 **Kari** Nigeria
51C5 **Kariba** Zimbabwe
51C5 **Kariba Dam** Zambia/Zimbabwe
51C5 **Kariba, L** Zambia/Zimbabwe
47B1 **Karibib** Namibia
50D2 **Karima** Sudan
27D7 **Karimata** *I* Indonesia
43G4 **Karīmganj** India
44B2 **Karīmnagar** India
50E2 **Karin** Somalia
12J6 **Karis** Finland
50C4 **Karisimbe** *Mt* Zaïre
17E3 **Káristos** Greece
44A3 **Kārkal** India
27H7 **Karkar** *I* Papua New Guinea
41E3 **Karkheh** *R* Iran
21E6 **Karkinitskiy Zaliv** *B* Ukraine
25L5 **Karlik Shan** *Mt* China
18D2 **Karlino** Poland
16D2 **Karlobag** Croatia
16D1 **Karlovac** Croatia
17E2 **Karlovo** Bulgaria
18C2 **Karlovy Vary** Czech Republic
12G7 **Karlshamn** Sweden
12G7 **Karlskoga** Sweden
12H7 **Karlskrona** Sweden
18B3 **Karlsruhe** Germany
12G7 **Karlstad** Sweden
61D1 **Karlstad** USA
54C4 **Karluk** USA
43G4 **Karnafuli Res** Bangladesh
42D3 **Karnāl** India
44A2 **Karnātaka** *State* India
17F2 **Karnobat** Bulgaria
51C5 **Karoi** Zimbabwe
51D4 **Karonga** Malawi
50D2 **Karora** Sudan
17F3 **Kárpathos** *I* Greece
55N2 **Karrats Fjord** Greenland
47C3 **Karree Berge** *Mts* South Africa
21G7 **Kars** Turkey
24H5 **Karsakpay** Kazakhstan
19F1 **Kārsava** Latvia
38E2 **Karshi** Uzbekistan
24G2 **Karskiye Vorota, Proliv** *Str* Russian Federation
12J6 **Karstula** Finland
45C1 **Kartaba** Lebanon
17F2 **Kartal** Turkey
20L5 **Kartaly** Russian Federation
68A2 **Karthaus** USA
41E3 **Kārūn** *R* Iran
19D3 **Karviná** Czech Republic
43E3 **Karwa** India
44A3 **Kārwār** India
26E1 **Karymskoye** Russian Federation
50B4 **Kasai** *R* Zaïre
51C5 **Kasaji** Zaïre
51D5 **Kasama** Zambia
51D4 **Kasanga** Tanzania
44A3 **Kāsaragod** India
54H3 **Kasba L** Canada
51C5 **Kasempa** Zambia
51C5 **Kasenga** Zaïre
50D3 **Kasese** Uganda
43K2 **Kasganj** India
41F3 **Kāshān** Iran
39F2 **Kashi** China
28B4 **Kashima** Japan
42D3 **Kāshipur** India
29D3 **Kashiwazaki** Japan
41G2 **Kāshmar** Iran
22E4 **Kashmir** *State* India
20G5 **Kasimov** Russian Federation
64B3 **Kaskaskia** *R* USA
12J6 **Kaskinen** Finland
20L4 **Kasli** Russian Federation
54G5 **Kaslo** Canada
50C4 **Kasongo** Zaïre
51B4 **Kasongo-Lunda** Zaïre
17F3 **Kásos** *I* Greece
21H6 **Kaspiyskiy** Russian Federation
50D2 **Kassala** Sudan
18B2 **Kassel** Germany
48C1 **Kasserine** Tunisia
51B5 **Kassinga** Angola
40B1 **Kastamonu** Turkey
17E3 **Kastélli** Greece
40A2 **Kastellorizon** *I* Greece
17E2 **Kastoría** Greece
17F3 **Kástron** Greece
29D3 **Kasugai** Japan
29B3 **Kasumi** Japan
51D5 **Kasungu** Malawi
42C2 **Kasur** Pakistan
51C5 **Kataba** Zambia
65F1 **Katahdin,Mt** USA
50C4 **Katako-kombe** Zaïre
54D3 **Katalla** USA
25Q4 **Katangli** Russian Federation
32A4 **Katanning** Australia
44E4 **Katchall** *I* Nicobar Is, Indian Ocean
17E2 **Kateríni** Greece
54E4 **Kates Needle** *Mt* Canada/USA
40B4 **Katharîna, Gebel** *Mt* Egypt
32C2 **Katherine** Australia
42C4 **Kāthiāwār** *Pen* India
45B3 **Kathib el Henu** *Hill* Egypt
43F3 **Kathmandu** Nepal
42D2 **Kathua** India
43F3 **Katihār** India
51C5 **Katima Mulilo** Namibia
48B4 **Katiola** Ivory Coast
54C4 **Katmai,Mt** USA
43E4 **Katni** India
34D2 **Katoomba** Australia
19D2 **Katowice** Poland
12H7 **Katrineholm** Sweden
8C3 **Katrine, Loch** *L* Scotland
48C3 **Katsina** Nigeria
48C4 **Katsina** *R* Cameroon/Nigeria
48C4 **Katsina Ala** Nigeria
29D3 **Katsuta** Japan
29D3 **Katsuura** Japan
29C3 **Katsuyama** Japan
24H6 **Kattakurgan** Uzbekistan
12G7 **Kattegat** *Str* Denmark/Sweden
13E3 **Katzenbuckel** *Mt* Germany
66E5 **Kauai** *I* Hawaiian Islands
66E5 **Kauai Chan** Hawaiian Islands
66E5 **Kaulakahi Chan** Hawaiian Islands
66E5 **Kaunakakai** Hawaiian Islands
20C5 **Kaunas** Lithuania
48C3 **Kaura Namoda** Nigeria
12J5 **Kautokeino** Norway
17E2 **Kavadarci** Macedonia, Yugoslavia
17D2 **Kavajë** Albania
44B3 **Kavali** India
17E2 **Kavála** Greece
42B4 **Kāvda** India
32E1 **Kavieng** Papua New Guinea
29C3 **Kawagoe** Japan
29C3 **Kawaguchi** Japan
66E5 **Kawaihae** Hawaiian Islands
35B1 **Kawakawa** New Zealand
51C4 **Kawambwa** Zambia
43E4 **Kawardha** India
65D2 **Kawartha Lakes** Canada
29D3 **Kawasaki** Japan
66C2 **Kaweah** *R* USA
35C1 **Kawerau** New Zealand
35B1 **Kawhia** New Zealand
48B3 **Kaya** Burkina
27E6 **Kayan** *R* Indonesia
44B4 **Kāyankulam** India
60B2 **Kaycee** USA
59D3 **Kayenta** USA
48A3 **Kayes** Mali
21F8 **Kayseri** Turkey
25P2 **Kazach'ye** Russian Federation
41E1 **Kazakh** Azerbaijan
24G5 **Kazakhstan** *Republic* Asia
20H4 **Kazan'** Russian Federation
17F2 **Kazanlŭk** Bulgaria
26H4 **Kazan Retto** *Is* Japan
19F3 **Kazatin** Ukraine
21G7 **Kazbek** *Mt* Georgia
41F4 **Kāzerūn** Iran
20J3 **Kazhim** Russian Federation
41E1 **Kazi Magomed** Azerbaijan
19E3 **Kazincbarcika** Hungary
20M3 **Kazym** *R* Russian Federation
20M3 **Kazymskaya** Russian Federation
17E3 **Kéa** *I* Greece
9C2 **Keady** Northern Ireland
66E5 **Kealaikahiki Chan** Hawaiian Islands
56D2 **Kearney** USA
59D4 **Kearny** USA
40C2 **Keban Baraji** *Res* Turkey
48A3 **Kébémer** Senegal
48C1 **Kebili** Tunisia
45D1 **Kebīr** *R* Lebanon/Syria
12H5 **Kebnekaise** *Mt* Sweden
19D3 **Kecskemét** Hungary
19E1 **Kedainiai** Lithuania
65F1 **Kedgwick** Canada
27E7 **Kediri** Indonesia
48A3 **Kédougou** Senegal
20J3 **Kedva** Russian Federation
54E3 **Keele Pk** *Mt* Canada
59C3 **Keeler** USA
27C8 **Keeling Is** Indian Ocean
26F4 **Keelung** Taiwan
66C3 **Keene** California, USA
65E2 **Keene** New Hampshire, USA
47B2 **Keetmanshoop** Namibia
64B2 **Keewanee** USA
64A1 **Keewatin** USA
55J3 **Keewatin** *Region* Canada
17E3 **Kefallinía** *I* Greece
45C2 **Kefar Sava** Israel
48C4 **Keffi** Nigeria
12A2 **Keflavík** Iceland
54G4 **Keg River** Canada
30B1 **Kehsi Mansam** Burma
48C3 **Keita** Niger
34B3 **Keith** Australia
8D3 **Keith** Scotland
54F3 **Keith Arm** *B* Canada
6C3 **Keithley** England
55M3 **Kekertuk** Canada
42D3 **Kekri** India
30C5 **Kelang** Malaysia
30C4 **Kelantan** *R* Malaysia
16C3 **Kelibia** Tunisia
42B1 **Kelif** Turkmenistan
40C1 **Kelkit** *R* Turkey
50B4 **Kellé** Congo
54F2 **Kellett,C** Canada
58C1 **Kellogg** USA
24D3 **Kelloselka** Finland
33B9 **Kells** Irish Republic
8C4 **Kells Range** *Hills* Scotland
19E1 **Kelme** Lithuania
54G5 **Kelowna** Canada
54F4 **Kelsey Bay** Canada
8D4 **Kelso** Scotland
58B1 **Kelso** USA
20E3 **Kem'** Russian Federation
20E3 **Kem'** *R* Russian Federation
48B3 **Ke Macina** Mali
24K4 **Kemerovo** Russian Federation
12J5 **Kemi** Finland
12K5 **Kemi** *R* Finland
12K5 **Kemijärvi** Finland
58D2 **Kemmerer** USA
13C2 **Kempen** *Region* Belgium
62C2 **Kemp,L** USA
69B2 **Kemps Bay** The Bahamas
34D2 **Kempsey** Australia
18C3 **Kempten** Germany
65E1 **Kempt,L** Canada
54C3 **Kenai** USA
54C3 **Kenai Pen** USA
50D3 **Kenamuke Swamp** Sudan
6C2 **Kendal** England
34D2 **Kendall** Australia
32B1 **Kendari** Indonesia
27E7 **Kendawangan** Indonesia
43F4 **Kendrāpāra** India
58C1 **Kendrick** USA
63C3 **Kenedy** USA
48A4 **Kenema** Sierra Leone
50B4 **Kenge** Zaïre
30B1 **Kengtung** Burma
47C2 **Kenhardt** South Africa
48A3 **Kéniéba** Mali
48B1 **Kenitra** Morocco
60C1 **Kenmare** USA
62B2 **Kenna** USA
65F1 **Kennebec** *R* USA
68E1 **Kennebunk** USA
63D3 **Kenner** USA
63E1 **Kennett** USA
68C3 **Kennett Square** USA
58C1 **Kennewick** USA
54F4 **Kenny Dam** Canada
55J5 **Kenora** Canada
57E2 **Kenosha** USA
62B2 **Kent** Texas, USA
58B1 **Kent** Washington, USA
7E4 **Kent** *County* England
64B2 **Kentland** USA
64C2 **Kenton** USA
54H3 **Kent Pen** Canada
64C3 **Kentucky** *R* USA
57E3 **Kentucky** *State* USA
57E3 **Kentucky L** USA
63D2 **Kentwood** Louisiana, USA
64B2 **Kentwood** Michigan, USA
50D3 **Kenya** *Republic* Africa
Kenya,Mt = Kirinyaga
64A2 **Keokuk** USA
43E4 **Keonchi** India
43F4 **Keonjhargarh** India
19D2 **Kępno** Poland
44B3 **Kerala** *State* India
34B3 **Kerang** Australia
12K6 **Kerava** Finland
21F6 **Kerch'** Ukraine
20J3 **Kerchem'ya** Russian Federation
32D1 **Kerema** Papua New Guinea
58C1 **Keremeos** Canada
50D2 **Keren** Eritrea
36E7 **Kerguelen** *Is* Indian Ocean
36E7 **Kerguelen Ridge** Indian Ocean
50D4 **Kericho** Kenya
27D7 **Kerinci** *Mt* Indonesia
50D3 **Kerio** *R* Kenya
48D1 **Kerkenna, Îles** Tunisia
38E2 **Kerki** Turkmenistan
Kérkira = Corfu
33H3 **Kermadec Is** Pacific Ocean
33H4 **Kermadec Trench** Pacific Ocean
41G3 **Kermān** Iran
66B2 **Kerman** USA
41E3 **Kermānshāh** Iran
62B2 **Kermit** USA
59C3 **Kern** *R* USA
66C3 **Kernville** USA
20J3 **Keros** Russian Federation
62C2 **Kerrville** USA
9B3 **Kerry Hd** Irish Republic
67B2 **Kershaw** USA
25N5 **Kerulen** *R* Mongolia
48B2 **Kerzaz** Algeria
17F2 **Keşan** Turkey
43N2 **Kesariya** India
29E3 **Kesennuma** Japan
21G7 **Kesir Dağları** *Mt* Turkey
12L5 **Kesten'ga** Russian Federation
6C2 **Keswick** England
48C4 **Kéta** Ghana
27E7 **Ketapang** Indonesia
54E4 **Ketchikan** USA

42B4 **Keti Bandar** Pakistan
19E2 **Kętrzyn** Poland
7D3 **Kettering** England
64C3 **Kettering** USA
58C1 **Kettle** *R* Canada
66C2 **Kettleman City** USA
58C1 **Kettle River Range** *Mts* USA
55L3 **Kettlestone B** Canada
68B1 **Keuka L** USA
41G3 **Kevir-i-Namak** *Salt Flat* Iran
64B2 **Kewaunee** USA
64B1 **Keweenaw B** USA
64B1 **Keweenaw Pen** USA
64C1 **Key Harbour** Canada
67B3 **Key Largo** USA
57E4 **Key West** USA
25M4 **Kezhma** Russian Federation
45D2 **Khabab** Syria
26G2 **Khabarovsk** Russian Federation
21G8 **Khabūr, al** *R* Syria
42B3 **Khairpur** Pakistan
42B3 **Khairpur** *Division* Pakistan
47C1 **Khakhea** Botswana
45B3 **Khalig el Tîna** *B* Egypt
38D4 **Khalīj Maşīrah** *G* Oman
17F3 **Khálki** *I* Greece
17E2 **Khalkidhíki** *Pen* Greece
17E3 **Khalkís** Greece
20L2 **Khal'mer-Yu** Russian Federation
20H4 **Khalturin** Russian Federation
42C4 **Khambhāt,G of** India
42D4 **Khāmgaon** India
30C2 **Kham Keut** Laos
44C2 **Khammam** India
45B3 **Khamsa** Egypt
41E2 **Khamseh** *Mts* Iran
30C2 **Khan** *R* Laos
42B1 **Khanabad** Afghanistan
41E3 **Khānaqīn** Iraq
42D4 **Khandwa** India
42C2 **Khanewal** Pakistan
45D3 **Khan ez Zabīb** Jordan
30D4 **Khanh Hung** Vietnam
17E3 **Khaniá** Greece
26G2 **Khanka, Ozero** *L* China/Russian Federation
Khankendy = Stepanakert
42C3 **Khanpur** Pakistan
45D1 **Khān Shaykhūn** Syria
24H3 **Khanty-Mansiysk** Russian Federation
45C3 **Khan Yunis** Israel
42D1 **Khapalu** India
26E2 **Khapcheranga** Russian Federation
21H6 **Kharabali** Russian Federation
43F4 **Kharagpur** India
42B3 **Kharan** Pakistan
41G4 **Khārān** *R* Iran
41F3 **Kharānaq** Iran
41F4 **Khārg** *I* Iran
49F2 **Khârga Oasis** Egypt
42D4 **Khargon** India
45B3 **Kharîm, Gebel** *Mt* Egypt
21F6 **Khar'kov** Ukraine
20F2 **Kharlovka** Russian Federation
17F2 **Kharmanli** Bulgaria
20G4 **Kharovsk** Russian Federation
50D2 **Khartoum** Sudan
50D2 **Khartoum North** Sudan
28C2 **Khasan** Russian Federation
50D2 **Khashm el Girba** Sudan
43G3 **Khasi-Jaīntīa Hills** India
17F2 **Khaskovo** Bulgaria
25M2 **Khatanga** Russian Federation
25N2 **Khatangskiy Zaliv** *Estuary* Russian Federation
25T3 **Khatyrka** Russian Federation
30B3 **Khawsa** Burma
40C4 **Khaybar** Saudi Arabia
40B5 **Khazzan an-Nasr** *L* Egypt
30C2 **Khe Bo** Vietnam
42C4 **Khed Brahma** India
15C2 **Khemis** Algeria
16B3 **Khenchela** Algeria
48B1 **Khenifra** Morocco
43L1 **Kheri** *District* India
15D2 **Kherrata** Algeria
21E6 **Kherson** Ukraine
25N4 **Khilok** Russian Federation
17F3 **Khíos** Greece
17F3 **Khíos** *I* Greece
21D6 **Khmel'nitskiy** Ukraine
19E3 **Khodorov** Ukraine
42B1 **Kholm** Afghanistan
19G1 **Kholm** Russian Federation
47B1 **Khomas Hochland** *Mts* Namibia
30D3 **Khong** Laos
41F4 **Khonj** Iran
26G2 **Khor** Russian Federation
41F5 **Khōr Duwayhin** *B* UAE
42C1 **Khorog** Tajikistan
41E3 **Khorramābad** Iran
41E3 **Khorramshahr** Iran
41G3 **Khosf** Iran
42B2 **Khost** Pakistan
21D6 **Khotin** Ukraine
21D5 **Khoyniki** Belarus
41G2 **Khrebet Kopet Dag** *Mts* Iran/Turkmenistan
20L2 **Khrebet Pay-khoy** *Mts* Russian Federation
45B1 **Khrysokhou B** Cyprus
39E1 **Khudzhand** Tajikistan
20L3 **Khulga** *R* Russian Federation
43F4 **Khulna** Bangladesh
42D1 **Khunjerāb P** China/India
41F3 **Khunsar** Iran
41E4 **Khurays** Saudi Arabia
43F4 **Khurda** India
42D3 **Khurja** India
42C2 **Khushab** Pakistan
45C2 **Khushnīyah** Syria
45D4 **Khush Shah, Wadi el** Jordan
19E3 **Khust** Ukraine
50C2 **Khuwei** Sudan
42B3 **Khuzdar** Pakistan
21H5 **Khvalynsk** Russian Federation
41G3 **Khvor** Iran
41F4 **Khvormūj** Iran
21G8 **Khvoy** Iran
42C1 **Khwaja Muhammad Ra** *Mts* Afghanistan
42C2 **Khyber P** Afghanistan/Pakistan
51C4 **Kiambi** Zaïre
63C2 **Kiamichi** *R* USA
50B4 **Kibangou** Congo
50D4 **Kibaya** Tanzania
50C4 **Kibombo** Zaïre
50D4 **Kibondo** Tanzania
50D4 **Kibungu** Rwanda
17E2 **Kicevo** Macedonia, Yugoslavia
54G4 **Kicking Horse P** Canada
48C3 **Kidal** Mali
7C3 **Kidderminster** England
48A3 **Kidira** Senegal
35C1 **Kidnappers,C** New Zealand
18C2 **Kiel** Germany
19E2 **Kielce** Poland
6C2 **Kielder Res** England
18C2 **Kieler Bucht** *B* Germany
21E5 **Kiev** Ukraine
38E2 **Kifab** Uzbekistan
48A3 **Kiffa** Mauritius
50D4 **Kigali** Rwanda
50C4 **Kigoma** Tanzania
66E5 **Kiholo** Hawaiian Islands
29C4 **Kii-sanchi** *Mts* Japan
29C4 **Kii-suidō** *Str* Japan
25R4 **Kikhchik** Russian Federation
17E1 **Kikinda** Serbia, Yugoslavia
Kikládhes = Cyclades
32D1 **Kikon** Papua New Guinea
29D2 **Kikonai** Japan
27H7 **Kikori** Papua New Guinea
50B4 **Kikwit** Zaïre
66E5 **Kilauea Crater** *Vol* Hawaiian Islands
8C4 **Kilbrannan Sd** Scotland
54C3 **Kilbuck Mts** USA
28B2 **Kilchu** N Korea
34D1 **Kilcoy** Australia
9C3 **Kildare** Irish Republic
9C3 **Kildare** *County* Irish Republic
63D2 **Kilgore** USA
50E4 **Kilifi** Kenya
50D4 **Kilimanjaro** *Mt* Tanzania
51D4 **Kilindoni** Tanzania
40C2 **Kilis** Turkey
19F3 **Kiliya** Ukraine
9D2 **Kilkeel** Northern Ireland
9C3 **Kilkenny** Irish Republic
9C3 **Kilkenny** *County* Irish Republic
17E2 **Kilkís** Greece
34D1 **Killarney** Australia
10B3 **Killarney** Irish Republic
63C2 **Killeen** USA
8C3 **Killin** Scotland
17E3 **Killíni** *Mt* Greece
9B3 **Killorglin** Irish Republic
9D2 **Killyleagh** Northern Ireland
8C4 **Kilmarnock** Scotland
20J4 **Kil'mez** Russian Federation
9C3 **Kilmichael Pt** Irish Republic
51D4 **Kilosa** Tanzania
10B3 **Kilrush** Irish Republic
8C4 **Kilsyth** Scotland
51C4 **Kilwa** Zaïre
51D4 **Kilwa Kisiwani** Tanzania
51D4 **Kilwa Kivinje** Tanzania
60C2 **Kimball** USA
54G5 **Kimberley** Canada
47C2 **Kimberley** South Africa
32B2 **Kimberley Plat** Australia
28B2 **Kimch'aek** N Korea
28B3 **Kimch'ŏn** S Korea
28A3 **Kimhae** S Korea
17E3 **Kími** Greece
28A3 **Kimje** S Korea
20F4 **Kimry** Russian Federation
28A3 **Kimwha** N Korea
27E6 **Kinabalu** *Mt* Malaysia
8D2 **Kinbrace** Scotland
64C2 **Kincardine** Canada
63D2 **Kinder** USA
48A3 **Kindia** Guinea
50C4 **Kindu** Zaïre
20J5 **Kinel'** Russian Federation
20G4 **Kineshma** Russian Federation
34D1 **Kingaroy** Australia
59B3 **King City** USA
54F4 **Kingcome Inlet** Canada
63C1 **Kingfisher** USA
76H4 **King George I** Antarctica
55L4 **King George Is** Canada
32D5 **King I** Australia
32B2 **King Leopold Range** *Mts* Australia
56B3 **Kingman** USA
50C4 **Kingombe** Zaïre
66C2 **Kingsburg** USA
59C3 **Kings Canyon Nat Pk** USA
32B2 **King Sd** Australia
64B1 **Kingsford** USA
67B2 **Kingsland** USA
7E3 **King's Lynn** England
33G1 **Kingsmill Group** *Is* Kiribati
68D2 **Kings Park** USA
66C2 **Kings Peak** *Mt* USA
67B1 **Kingsport** USA
32C4 **Kingston** Australia
55L5 **Kingston** Canada
70E3 **Kingston** Jamaica
65E2 **Kingston** New York, USA
35A3 **Kingston** New Zealand
68C2 **Kingston** Pennsylvania, USA
69N2 **Kingstown** St Vincent
56D4 **Kingsville** USA
7C3 **Kington** England
8C3 **Kingussie** Scotland
54J3 **King William I** Canada
47D3 **King William's Town** South Africa
50B4 **Kinkala** Congo
12G7 **Kinna** Sweden
8D3 **Kinnairds Head** *Pt* Scotland
29C3 **Kinomoto** Japan
8D3 **Kinross** Scotland
50B4 **Kinshasa** Zaïre
62C1 **Kinsley** USA
67C1 **Kinston** USA
27E7 **Kintap** Indonesia
8C4 **Kintyre** *Pen* Scotland
50D3 **Kinyeti** *Mt* Sudan
17E3 **Kiparissía** Greece
17E3 **Kiparissiakós Kólpos** *G* Greece
65D1 **Kipawa,L** Canada
51D4 **Kipili** Tanzania
9C3 **Kippure** *Mt* Irish Republic
51C5 **Kipushi** Zaïre
25M4 **Kirensk** Russian Federation
24J5 **Kirghizia** *Republic* Asia
39F1 **Kirgizskiy Khrebet** *Mts* Kirgizia
50B4 **Kiri** Zaïre
33G1 **Kiribati** *Is, Republic* Pacific Ocean
40B2 **Kırıkkale** Turkey
50D4 **Kirinyaga, Mt** Kenya
20E4 **Kirishi** Russian Federation
42B3 **Kirithar Range** *Mts* Pakistan
17F3 **Kirkağaç** Turkey
21H8 **Kirk Bulāg Dāgh** *Mt* Iran
6C2 **Kirkby** England
8D3 **Kirkcaldy** Scotland
8C4 **Kirkcudbright** Scotland
12K5 **Kirkenes** Norway
6C3 **Kirkham** England
55K5 **Kirkland Lake** Canada
40A1 **Kırklareli** Turkey
6C2 **Kirkoswald** England
76E7 **Kirkpatrick,Mt** Antarctica
57D2 **Kirksville** USA
41D2 **Kirkūk** Iraq
8D2 **Kirkwall** Scotland
47D3 **Kirkwood** South Africa
61E3 **Kirkwood** USA
20E5 **Kirov** Russian Federation
20H4 **Kirov** Russian Federation
41D1 **Kirovakan** Armenia
20K4 **Kirovgrad** Russian Federation
21E6 **Kirovograd** Ukraine
20E2 **Kirovsk** Russian Federation
25R4 **Kirovskiy** Kamchatka, Russian Federation
8D3 **Kirriemuir** Scotland
20J4 **Kirs** Russian Federation
40B2 **Kırşehir** Turkey
18C2 **Kiruna** Sweden
29C3 **Kiryū** Japan
50C3 **Kisangani** Zaïre
29C3 **Kisarazu** Japan
43F3 **Kishanganj** India
42C3 **Kishangarh** India
19F3 **Kishinev** Moldavia
29C4 **Kishiwada** Japan
50D4 **Kisii** Kenya
51D4 **Kisiju** Tanzania
17D1 **Kiskunfélegyháza** Hungary
19D3 **Kiskunhalas** Hungary
21G7 **Kislovodsk** Russian Federation
50E4 **Kismaayo** Somalia
29C3 **Kiso-sammyaku** *Mts* Japan
48B4 **Kissidougou** Guinea
67B3 **Kissimmee,L** USA
50D4 **Kisumu** Kenya
19E3 **Kisvárda** Hungary
48B3 **Kita** Mali
24H6 **Kitab** Uzbekistan
29D3 **Kitakami** Japan
29D3 **Kitakami** *R* Japan
29D3 **Kitakata** Japan
28C4 **Kita-Kyūshū** Japan
50D3 **Kitale** Kenya
26H4 **Kitalo** *I* Japan
29E2 **Kitami** Japan
29D2 **Kitami-Esashi** Japan
60C3 **Kit Carson** USA
55K5 **Kitchener** Canada
50D3 **Kitgum** Uganda
17E3 **Kíthira** *I* Greece
17E3 **Kíthnos** *I* Greece
45B1 **Kiti, C** Cyprus
54G2 **Kitikmeot** *Region* Canada
54F4 **Kitimat** Canada
12K5 **Kitinen** *R* Finland
28B4 **Kitsuki** Japan
65D2 **Kittanning** USA
65E2 **Kittery** USA
12J5 **Kittilä** Finland
67C1 **Kitty Hawk** USA
51D4 **Kitunda** Tanzania
51C5 **Kitwe** Zambia
18C3 **Kitzbühel** Austria
18C3 **Kitzingen** Germany
50C4 **Kiumbi** Zaïre
54B3 **Kivalina** USA
19F2 **Kivercy** Ukraine
50C4 **Kivu,L** Rwanda/Zaïre
54B3 **Kiwalik** USA
Kiyev = Kiev
19G2 **Kiyevskoye Vodokhranilishche** *Res* Ukraine
20K4 **Kizel** Russian Federation
20G3 **Kizema** Russian Federation
40C2 **Kizil** *R* Turkey
38D2 **Kizyl'-Arvat** Turkmenistan
21J8 **Kizyl-Atrek** Turkmenistan
18C2 **Kladno** Czech Republic
18C3 **Klagenfurt** Austria
20C4 **Klaipēda** Lithuania
58B2 **Klamath** *R* USA
56A2 **Klamath Falls** USA
58B2 **Klamath Mts** USA
18C3 **Klatovy** Czech Republic
45C1 **Kleiat** Lebanon
47B2 **Kleinsee** South Africa
47D2 **Klerksdorp** South Africa
19G2 **Kletnya** Russian Federation
13D2 **Kleve** Germany
19G2 **Klimovichi** Belarus
20F4 **Klin** Russian Federation
19D1 **Klintehamn** Sweden
21E5 **Klintsy** Russian Federation
47C3 **Klipplaat** South Africa
16D2 **Ključ** Bosnia-Herzegovina
18D2 **Kłodzko** Poland
54D3 **Klondike Plat** Canada/USA
18D3 **Klosterneuburg** Austria
19D2 **Kluczbork** Poland
6D2 **Knaresborough** England
7C3 **Knighton** Wales
16D2 **Knin** Croatia
32A4 **Knob,C** Australia
9B3 **Knockmealdown Mts** Irish Republic
13B2 **Knokke-Heist** Belgium
76G9 **Knox Coast** Antarctica
61E2 **Knoxville** Iowa, USA
57E3 **Knoxville** Tennessee, USA
55Q3 **Knud Rasmussens Land** *Region* Greenland
7C3 **Knutsford** England
47C3 **Knysna** South Africa
55O3 **Kobberminebugt** *B* Greenland
29D4 **Kōbe** Japan
København = Copenhagen
18B2 **Koblenz** Germany
19E2 **Kobrin** Belarus
27G7 **Kobroör** *I* Indonesia
54B3 **Kobuk** *R* USA
17E2 **Kočani** Macedonia, Yugoslavia
28B3 **Kochang** S Korea
28B3 **Koch'ang** S Korea
30C3 **Ko Chang** *I* Thailand
43F3 **Koch Bihār** India
55L3 **Koch I** Canada
44B4 **Kochi** India
29C4 **Kōchi** Japan
54C4 **Kodiak** USA
54C4 **Kodiak I** USA
44B3 **Kodikkarai** India
50D3 **Kodok** Sudan
29D2 **Kodomari-misaki** *C* Japan
19F3 **Kodyma** Ukraine
66D3 **Koehn L** USA
47B2 **Koes** Namibia
47D2 **Koffiefontein** South Africa
48B4 **Koforidua** Ghana
29D3 **Kofu** Japan
29C3 **Koga** Japan
12G7 **Køge** Denmark
42C2 **Kohat** Pakistan
42B2 **Koh-i-Baba** *Mts* Afghanistan
42B1 **Koh-i-Hisar** *Mts* Afghanistan
42B2 **Koh-i-Khurd** *Mt* Afghanistan
43G3 **Kohīma** India
42B2 **Koh-i-Mazar** *Mt* Afghanistan
42B3 **Kohlu** Pakistan
20D4 **Kohtla Järve** Estonia
28A4 **Kohung** S Korea
28A4 **Kohyon** S Korea
29C3 **Koide** Japan
30A4 **Koihoa** Nicobar Is, India
28A2 **Koin** N Korea
28B4 **Koje Dŏ** *I* S Korea
29C2 **Ko-jima** *I* Japan
24H4 **Kokchetav** Kazakhstan
12J6 **Kokemäki** *L* Finland
12J6 **Kokkola** Finland
32D1 **Kokoda** Papua New Guinea
64B2 **Kokomo** USA
27G7 **Kokonau** Indonesia
26B2 **Kokpekty** Kazakhstan
28A3 **Koksan** N Korea
55M4 **Koksoak** *R* Canada
28A3 **Koksŏng** S Korea
47D3 **Kokstad** South Africa
30C3 **Ko Kut** *I* Thailand
20E2 **Kola** Russian Federation
27F7 **Kolaka** Indonesia
30B4 **Ko Lanta** *I* Thailand
44B3 **Kolār** India
44B3 **Kolār Gold Fields** India
48A3 **Kolda** Senegal
12F7 **Kolding** Denmark
20H2 **Kolguyev, Ostrov** *I* Russian Federation
44A2 **Kolhāpur** India
18D2 **Kolín** Czech Republic
44B4 **Kollam** India
Köln = Cologne
19D2 **Koło** Poland
66E5 **Koloa** Hawaiian Islands
18D2 **Kołobrzeg** Poland
48B3 **Kolokani** Mali
20F4 **Kolomna** Russian Federation
21D6 **Kolomyya** Ukraine
25R4 **Kolpakovskiy** Russian Federation
24K4 **Kolpashevo** Russian Federation
17F3 **Kólpos Merabéllou** *B* Greece
17E2 **Kólpos Singitikós** *G* Greece
17E2 **Kólpos Strimonikós** *G* Greece
17E2 **Kólpos Toronaíos** *G* Greece
20F2 **Kol'skiy Poluostrov** *Pen* Russian Federation
20K2 **Kolva** *R* Russian Federation
12G6 **Kolvereid** Norway
51C5 **Kolwezi** Zaïre
25R3 **Kolyma** *R* Russian Federation
25R3 **Kolymskaya Nizmennost'** *Lowland* Russian Federation
25S3 **Kolymskoye Nagor'ye** *Mts* Russian Federation
17E2 **Kom** *Mt* Bulgaria/Serbia, Yugoslavia
50D3 **Koma** Ethiopia
29D3 **Koma** Japan

48D3 **Komadugu Gana** *R* Nigeria
29D2 **Komaga take** *Mt* Japan
25S4 **Komandorskiye Ostrova** *Is* Russian Federation
19D3 **Komárno** Slovakia
47E2 **Komati** *R* South Africa/ Swaziland
47E2 **Komati Poort** South Africa
29D3 **Komatsu** Japan
29B4 **Komatsushima** Japan
20J3 **Komi Republic** Russian Federation
26B1 **Kommunar** Russian Federation
27E7 **Komodo** *I* Indonesia
27G7 **Komoran** *I* Indonesia
29C3 **Komoro** Japan
17F2 **Komotiní** Greece
47C3 **Kompasberg** *Mt* South Africa
30D3 **Kompong Cham** Cambodia
30C3 **Kompong Chhnang** Cambodia
30C3 **Kompong Som = Sihanoukville**
30D3 **Kompong Thom** Cambodia
30D3 **Kompong Trabek** Cambodia
19F3 **Komrat** Moldavia
47C3 **Komsberg** *Mts* South Africa
25L1 **Komsomolets, Ostrov** *I* Russian Federation
20L2 **Komsomol'skiy** Russian Federation
25P4 **Komsomol'sk na Amure** Russian Federation
24H4 **Konda** *R* Russian Federation
43E5 **Kondagaon** India
50D4 **Kondoa** Tanzania
20E3 **Kondopoga** Russian Federation
44B2 **Kondukūr** India
20F3 **Konevo** Russian Federation
55P3 **Kong Christian IX Land** *Region* Greenland
55O3 **Kong Frederik VI Kyst** *Region* Greenland
28A3 **Kongju** S Korea
24D2 **Kong Karls Land** *Is* Svalbard
50C4 **Kongolo** Zaïre
12F7 **Kongsberg** Norway
12G6 **Kongsvinger** Norway
Königsberg = Kaliningrad
19D2 **Konin** Poland
17D2 **Konjic** Bosnia-Herzegovina
20G3 **Konosha** Russian Federation
29C3 **Konosu** Japan
21E5 **Konotop** Ukraine
19E2 **Końskie** Poland
18B3 **Konstanz** Germany
48C3 **Kontagora** Nigeria
30D3 **Kontum** Vietnam
21E8 **Konya** Turkey
58C1 **Kootenay L** Canada
42C5 **Kopargaon** India
55R3 **Kópasker** Iceland
12A2 **Kópavogur** Iceland
16C1 **Koper** Slovenia
38D2 **Kopet Dag** *Mts* Iran/ Turkmenistan
20L4 **Kopeysk** Russian Federation
30C4 **Ko Phangan** *I* Thailand
30B4 **Ko Phuket** *I* Thailand
12H7 **Köping** Sweden
28A3 **Kopo-ri** S Korea
44B2 **Koppal** India
16D1 **Koprivnica** Croatia
42B4 **Korangi** Pakistan
44C2 **Koraput** India
43E4 **Korba** India
18B2 **Korbach** Germany
17E2 **Korçë** Albania
16D2 **Korčula** *I* Croatia
31E2 **Korea B** China/Korea
28B2 **Korea, North** *Republic* Asia
28B3 **Korea, South** *Republic* Asia
26F3 **Korea Strait** Japan/Korea
19F2 **Korec** Ukraine
25S3 **Korf** Russian Federation
40B1 **Körğlu Tepesi** *Mt* Turkey
48B4 **Korhogo** Ivory Coast
42B4 **Kori Creek** India
Kórinthos = Corinth
29E3 **Kōriyama** Japan
20L5 **Korkino** Russian Federation
25R3 **Korkodon** Russian Federation
25R3 **Korkodon** *R* Russian Federation
40B2 **Korkuteli** Turkey
39G1 **Korla** China
45B1 **Kormakiti, C** Cyprus
16D2 **Kornat** *I* Croatia
21E7 **Köroğlu Tepesi** *Mt* Turkey
50D4 **Korogwe** Tanzania
34B3 **Koroit** Australia
27G6 **Koror** Palau, Pacific Ocean
19E3 **Körös** *R* Hungary
21D5 **Korosten** Ukraine
19F2 **Korostyshev** Ukraine
50B2 **Koro Toro** Chad
26H2 **Korsakov** Russian Federation
12G7 **Korsør** Denmark
20J3 **Kortkeros** Russian Federation
18A2 **Kortrijk** Belgium
25S3 **Koryakskoye Nagor'ye** *Mts* Russian Federation
28A3 **Koryong** S Korea
17F3 **Kós** *I* Greece
30C4 **Ko Samui** *I* Thailand
28A3 **Kosan** N Korea
19D2 **Kościerzyna** Poland
63E2 **Kosciusko** USA
32D4 **Kosciusko** *Mt* Australia
43J2 **Kosi** India
43K1 **Kosi** *R* India
19E3 **Košice** Slovakia
20J2 **Kosma** *R* Russian Federation
28B3 **Kosŏng** N Korea
17E2 **Kosovo** *Region* Serbia, Yugoslavia
17E2 **Kosovska Mitrovica** Serbia, Yugoslavia
48B4 **Kossou** *L* Ivory Coast
47D2 **Koster** South Africa
50D2 **Kosti** Sudan
19F2 **Kostopol'** Ukraine
20G4 **Kostroma** Russian Federation
18C2 **Kostrzyn** Poland
20K2 **Kos'yu** *R* Russian Federation
12H8 **Koszalin** Poland
42D3 **Kota** India
30C4 **Kota Baharu** Malaysia
42C2 **Kot Addu** Pakistan
27E6 **Kota Kinabalu** Malaysia
44C2 **Kotapad** India
20H4 **Kotel'nich** Russian Federation
21G6 **Kotel'nikovo** Russian Federation
25P2 **Kotel'nyy, Ostrov** *I* Russian Federation
12K6 **Kotka** Finland
20H3 **Kotlas** Russian Federation
54B3 **Kotlik** USA
17D2 **Kotor** Montenegro, Yugoslavia
21D6 **Kotovsk** Ukraine
42B3 **Kotri** Pakistan
44C2 **Kottagūdem** India
44B4 **Kottayam** India
50C3 **Kotto** *R* Central African Republic
44B3 **Kottūru** India
25L3 **Kotuy** *R* Russian Federation
54B3 **Kotzebue** USA
54B3 **Kotzebue Sd** USA
48C3 **Kouandé** Benin
50C3 **Kouango** Central African Republic
48B3 **Koudougou** Burkina
47C3 **Kougaberge** *Mts* South Africa
50B4 **Koulamoutou** Gabon
48B3 **Koulikoro** Mali
48B3 **Koupéla** Burkina
73H2 **Kourou** French Guiana
48B3 **Kouroussa** Guinea
50B2 **Kousséri** Cameroon
12K6 **Kouvola** Finland
12L5 **Kovdor** Russian Federation
12L5 **Kovdozero, Ozero** *L* Russian Federation
19E2 **Kovel** Ukraine
Kovno = Kaunas
20G4 **Kovrov** Russian Federation
20G5 **Kovylkino** Russian Federation
20F3 **Kovzha** *R* Russian Federation
30C4 **Ko Way** *I* Thailand
31C5 **Kowloon** Hong Kong
28A3 **Kowŏn** N Korea
42B2 **Kowt-e-Ashrow** Afghanistan
40A2 **Köyceğğiz** Turkey
20G2 **Koyda** Russian Federation
44A2 **Koyna Res** India
20H3 **Koynas** Russian Federation
54C3 **Koyukuk** USA
40C2 **Kozan** Turkey
17E2 **Kozańi** Greece
44B3 **Kozhikode** India
20K2 **Kozhim** Russian Federation
20H4 **Koz'modemyansk** Russian Federation
29C4 **Kōzu-shima** *I* Japan
48C4 **Kpalimé** Togo
47D3 **Kraai** *R* South Africa
12F7 **Kragerø** Norway
17E2 **Kragujevac** Serbia, Yugoslavia
30B3 **Kra,Isthmus of** Burma/ Malaysia
45D1 **Krak des Chevaliers** *Hist Site* Syria
Kraków = Cracow Poland
17E2 **Kraljevo** Serbia, Yugoslavia
21F6 **Kramatorsk** Ukraine
12H6 **Kramfors** Sweden
16C1 **Kranj** Slovenia
20H3 **Krasavino** Russian Federation
20J1 **Krasino** Russian Federation
28C2 **Kraskino** Russian Federation
19E2 **Kraśnik** Poland
21H5 **Krasnoarmeysk** Russian Federation
21F6 **Krasnodar** Russian Federation
20K4 **Krasnokamsk** Russian Federation
20L4 **Krasnotur'insk** Russian Federation
20K4 **Krasnoufimsk** Russian Federation
20K5 **Krasnousol'skiy** Russian Federation
20K3 **Krasnovishersk** Russian Federation
21J7 **Krasnovodsk** Turkmenistan
25L4 **Krasnoyarsk** Russian Federation
19E2 **Krasnystaw** Poland
21H5 **Krasnyy Kut** Russian Federation
21F6 **Krasnyy Luch** Ukraine
21H6 **Krasnyy Yar** Russian Federation
30D3 **Kratie** Cambodia
55N2 **Kraulshavn** Greenland
18B2 **Krefeld** Germany
21E6 **Kremenchug** Ukraine
21E6 **Kremenchugskoye Vodokhranilische** *Res* Ukraine
19F2 **Kremenets** Ukraine
60B2 **Kremming** USA
48C4 **Kribi** Cameroon
20E5 **Krichev** Belarus
44B2 **Krishna** *R* India
44B3 **Krishnagiri** India
43F4 **Krishnanagar** India
12F7 **Kristiansand** Norway
12G7 **Kristianstad** Sweden
24B3 **Kristiansund** Norway
12J6 **Kristiinankaupunki** Finland
12G7 **Kristinehamn** Sweden
Kríti = Crete
21E6 **Krivoy Rog** Ukraine
16C1 **Krk** *I* Croatia
47D1 **Krokodil** *R* South Africa
25S4 **Kronotskaya Sopka** *Mt* Russian Federation
25S4 **Kronotskiy, Mys** *C* Russian Federation
55P3 **Kronprins Frederik Bjerge** *Mts* Greenland
12K7 **Kronshtadt** Russian Federation
47D2 **Kroonstad** South Africa
21G6 **Kropotkin** Russian Federation
47E1 **Kruger Nat Pk** South Africa
47D2 **Krugersdorp** South Africa
17D2 **Kruje** Albania
Krung Thep = Bangkok
19F2 **Krupki** Belarus
17E2 **Kruševac** Serbia, Yugoslavia
12K7 **Krustpils** Latvia
Krym = Crimea
21F7 **Krymsk** Russian Federation
18D2 **Krzyz** Poland
15C2 **Ksar El Boukhari** Algeria
15A2 **Ksar-el-Kebir** Morocco
48C1 **Ksour, Mts des** Algeria
27C6 **Kuala** Indonesia
30C5 **Kuala Dungun** Malaysia
30C4 **Kuala Kerai** Malaysia
30C5 **Kuala Kubu Baharu** Malaysia
30C5 **Kuala Lipis** Malaysia
30C5 **Kuala Lumpur** Malaysia
30C4 **Kuala Trengganu** Malaysia
27F6 **Kuandang** Indonesia
28A2 **Kuandian** China
30C5 **Kuantan** Malaysia
21H7 **Kuba** Azerbaijan
27H7 **Kubor** *Mt* Papua New Guinea
27E6 **Kuching** Malaysia
27E6 **Kudat** Malaysia
20J4 **Kudymkar** Russian Federation
18C3 **Kufstein** Austria
41G3 **Kuh Duren** *Upland* Iran
41F3 **Kūh-e Dinar** *Mt* Iran
41G2 **Kūh-e-Hazār Masjed** *Mts* Iran
41G4 **Kūh-e Jebāl Barez** *Mts* Iran
41F3 **Kūh-e Karkas** *Mts* Iran
41G4 **Kūh-e Laleh Zar** *Mt* Iran
41E2 **Kūh-e Sahand** *Mt* Iran
38E3 **Kuh-e-Taftān** *Mt* Iran
21H9 **Kūhhaye Alvand** *Mts* Iran
21H8 **Kūhhaye Sabalan** *Mts* Iran
41E3 **Kūhhā-ye Zāgros** *Mts* Iran
12K6 **Kuhmo** Finland
41F3 **Kūhpāyeh** Iran
41G3 **Kūhpāyeh** *Mt* Iran
41G4 **Kūh-ye Bashākerd** *Mts* Iran
41E2 **Kūh-ye Sabalan** *Mt* Iran
47B2 **Kuibis** Namibia
47B1 **Kuiseb** *R* Namibia
51B5 **Kuito** Angola
28A3 **Kujang** N Korea
29E2 **Kuji** Japan
28B4 **Kuju-san** *Mt* Japan
17E2 **Kukës** Albania
30C5 **Kukup** Malaysia
41G4 **Kūl** *R* Iran
17F3 **Kula** Turkey
21K6 **Kulakshi** Kazakhstan
50D3 **Kulal,Mt** Kenya
17E2 **Kulata** Bulgaria
20C4 **Kuldīga** Latvia
20G2 **Kulov** *R* Russian Federation
21J6 **Kul'sary** Kazakhstan
42D2 **Kulu** India
40B2 **Kulu** Turkey
24J4 **Kulunda** Russian Federation
34B2 **Kulwin** Australia
21H7 **Kuma** *R* Russian Federation
29C3 **Kumagaya** Japan
27E7 **Kumai** Indonesia
21L5 **Kumak** Russian Federation
28C4 **Kumamoto** Japan
29C4 **Kumano** Japan
17E2 **Kumanovo** Macedonia, Yugoslavia
48B4 **Kumasi** Ghana
21G7 **Kumayri** Armenia
48C4 **Kumba** Cameroon
44B3 **Kumbakonam** India
28A3 **Kŭmch'ŏn** N Korea
20K5 **Kumertau** Russian Federation
28A3 **Kumgang** N Korea
12H7 **Kumla** Sweden
28A4 **Kŭmnyŏng** S Korea
28A4 **Kŭmo-do** *I* S Korea
44A3 **Kumta** India
39G1 **Kumüx** China
28B3 **Kumwha** S Korea
42C2 **Kunar** *R* Afghanistan
29F2 **Kunashir, Ostrov** *I* Russian Federation
12K7 **Kunda** Estonia
42C4 **Kundla** India
42B1 **Kunduz** Afghanistan
Kunene *R* **= Cunene R**
12G7 **Kungsbacka** Sweden
20K4 **Kungur** Russian Federation
30B1 **Kunhing** Burma
39G2 **Kunlun Shan** *Mts* China
31A4 **Kunming** China
20M3 **Kunovat** *R* Russian Federation
28B3 **Kunsan** S Korea
12K6 **Kuopio** Finland
16D1 **Kupa** *R* Bosnia-Herzegovina/Croatia
32B2 **Kupang** Indonesia
32D2 **Kupiano** Papua New Guinea
54E4 **Kupreanof I** USA
21F6 **Kupyansk** Ukraine
39G1 **Kuqa** China
21H8 **Kura** *R* Azerbaijan
29C3 **Kurabe** Japan
29C4 **Kurashiki** Japan
29B3 **Kurayoshi** Japan
41E2 **Kurdistan** *Region* Iran
17F2 **Kŭrdzhali** Bulgaria
28C4 **Kure** Japan
20C4 **Kuressaare** Estonia
25L3 **Kureyka** *R* Russian Federation
24H4 **Kurgan** Russian Federation
12J6 **Kurikka** Finland
25Q5 **Kuril Is** Russian Federation
Kuril'skiye Ostrova *Is* **= Kuril Islands**
36J2 **Kuril Trench** Pacific Ocean
21H8 **Kurinskaya Kosa** *Sand Spit* Azerbaijan
44B2 **Kurnool** India
29D2 **Kuroishi** Japan
29D3 **Kuroiso** Japan
35B2 **Kurow** New Zealand
34D2 **Kurri Kurri** Australia
21F5 **Kursk** Russian Federation
26B2 **Kuruktag** *R* China
47C2 **Kuruman** South Africa
47C2 **Kuruman** *R* South Africa
28C4 **Kurume** Japan
44C3 **Kurunegala** Sri Lanka
24K5 **Kurunktag** *R* China
20K3 **Kur'ya** Russian Federation
20K4 **Kusa** Russian Federation
17F3 **Kuşadası Körfezi** *B* Turkey
17F2 **Kus Golü** *L* Turkey
29D4 **Kushimoto** Japan
29E2 **Kushiro** Japan
38E2 **Kushka** Afghanistan
43F4 **Kushtia** Bangladesh
21J5 **Kushum** *R* Kazakhstan
20K4 **Kushva** Russian Federation
54B3 **Kuskokwim** *R* USA
54C3 **Kuskokwim Mts** USA
43E3 **Kusma** Nepal
28B3 **Kusŏng** N Korea
24H4 **Kustanay** Kazakhstan
27E7 **Kuta** *R* Indonesia
21D8 **Kütahya** Turkey
21G7 **Kutaisi** Georgia
29D2 **Kutchan** Japan
29E2 **Kutcharo-ko** *L* Japan
18D3 **Kutná Hora** Czech Republic
19D2 **Kutno** Poland
50B4 **Kutu** Zaïre
43G4 **Kutubdia I** Bangladesh
50C2 **Kutum** Sudan
55M4 **Kuujjuaq** Canada
55L4 **Kuujjuarapik** Canada
12K5 **Kuusamo** Finland
21K5 **Kuvandyk** Russian Federation
41E4 **Kuwait** Kuwait
38C3 **Kuwait** *Sheikhdom* SW Asia
29C3 **Kuwana** Japan
24J4 **Kuybyshev** Russian Federation
Kuybyshev = Samara
20H5 **Kuybyshevskoye Vodokhranilishche** *Res* Russian Federation
20E2 **Kuyto, Ozero** *L* Russian Federation
25M4 **Kuytun** Russian Federation
21F7 **Kuzey Anadolu Dağları** *Mts* Turkey
20F2 **Kuzomen** Russian Federation
20C2 **Kvænangen** *Sd* Norway
12G5 **Kvigtind** *Mt* Norway
20B2 **Kvikkjokk** Sweden
50D4 **Kwale** Kenya
28B3 **Kwangju** S Korea
50B4 **Kwango** *R* Zaïre
28A3 **Kwangyang** S Korea
28A2 **Kwanmo-bong** *Mt* N Korea
51D6 **KwaZulu Natal** *Province* South Africa
51C5 **Kwekwe** Zimbabwe
19D2 **Kwidzyn** Poland
54B4 **Kwigillingok** USA
27G7 **Kwoka** *Mt* Indonesia
34C3 **Kyabram** Australia
30B2 **Kyaikkami** Burma
30B2 **Kyaikto** Burma
26D1 **Kyakhta** Russian Federation
30B1 **Kyaukme** Burma
30B1 **Kyauk-padaung** Burma
30A2 **Kyaukpyu** Burma
20G2 **Kychema** Russian Federation
10B2 **Kyle of Lochalsh** Scotland
13D2 **Kyll** *R* Germany
34B3 **Kyneton** Australia
50D3 **Kyoga, L** Uganda
34D1 **Kyogle** Australia
28B3 **Kyŏngju** S Korea
28A3 **Kyongsang Sanmaek** *Mts* S Korea
28A2 **Kyŏngsŏng** N Korea
29D3 **Kyōto** Japan
45B1 **Kyrenia** Cyprus
20K3 **Kyrta** Russian Federation
20L4 **Kyshtym** Russian Federation
45B1 **Kythrea** Cyprus

28B4 **Kyūshū** *I* Japan
36H4 **Kyushu-Palau Ridge** Pacific Ocean
17E2 **Kyustendil** Bulgaria
25O2 **Kyusyur** Russian Federation
26C1 **Kyzyl** Russian Federation
24H5 **Kyzylkum** *Desert* Uzbekistan
24H5 **Kzyl Orda** Kazakhstan

L

50E3 **Laascaanood** Somalia
50E2 **Laas Dawaco** Somalia
13E2 **Laasphe** Germany
50E2 **Laasqoray** Somalia
72F1 **La Asunción** Venezuela
48A2 **Laâyoune** Morocco
58D2 **La Barge** USA
48A3 **Labé** Guinea
18D2 **Labe** *R* Czech Republic
65E1 **Labelle** Canada
67B3 **La Belle** USA
21G7 **Labinsk** Russian Federation
45D1 **Laboué** Lebanon
55M4 **Labrador** *Region* Canada
55M4 **Labrador City** Canada
55N4 **Labrador S** Canada/Greenland
72F5 **Lábrea** Brazil
27E6 **Labuk B** Malaysia
30A2 **Labutta** Burma
20M2 **Labytnangi** Russian Federation
13B2 **La Capelle** France
Laccadive Is = Lakshadweep
39F4 **Laccadive Is** India
70D3 **La Ceiba** Honduras
34A3 **Lacepede B** Australia
14C2 **La Châtre** France
45C3 **Lachish** *Hist Site* Israel
32D4 **Lachlan** *R* Australia
72C2 **La Chorrera** Panama
65E1 **Lachute** Canada
65D2 **Lackawanna** USA
54G4 **Lac la Biche** Canada
55L4 **Lac L'eau Claire** Canada
65E1 **Lac Mégantic** Canada
54G4 **Lacombe** Canada
65E2 **Laconia** USA
15A1 **La Coruña** Spain
57D2 **La Crosse** USA
63D1 **La Cygne** USA
42D2 **Ladākh Range** *Mts* India
27E6 **Ladd Reef** S China Sea
42C3 **Lādnūn** India
20E3 **Ladoga, L** Russian Federation
31B5 **Ladong** China
Ladozhskoye Oz *L* = **Ladoga, L**
55K2 **Lady Ann Str** Canada
34C4 **Lady Barron** Australia
47D2 **Ladybrand** South Africa
47D2 **Ladysmith** South Africa
64A1 **Ladysmith** USA
32D1 **Lae** Papua New Guinea
30C3 **Laem Ngop** Thailand
18C1 **Laesø** *I* Denmark
60B3 **Lafayette** Colorado, USA
57E2 **Lafayette** Indiana, USA
57D3 **Lafayette** Louisiana, USA
13B3 **La Fère** France
13B3 **La-Ferté-sous-Jouarre** France
48C4 **Lafia** Nigeria
48C4 **Lafiagi** Nigeria
14B2 **La Flèche** France
16B3 **La Galite** *I* Tunisia
18C1 **Lagan** *R* Sweden
73L6 **Lagarto** Brazil
8C3 **Laggan, L** Scotland
48C1 **Laghouat** Algeria
72C4 **Lago Agrio** Ecuador
48C4 **Lagos** Nigeria
15A2 **Lagos** Portugal
70B2 **Lagos de Moreno** Mexico
56B2 **La Grande** USA
32D3 **Lagrange** Australia
57E3 **La Grange** Georgia, USA
64B3 **La Grange** Kentucky, USA
67C1 **La Grange** N Carolina, USA
63C3 **La Grange** Texas, USA
72F2 **La Gran Sabana** *Mts* Venezuela
62A2 **Laguna** USA
59C4 **Laguna Beach** USA
56C4 **Laguna Seca** Mexico
28B2 **Lagusha** N Korea
27E6 **Lahad Datu** Malaysia
41F2 **Lāhījān** Iran
13D2 **Lahn** *R* Germany
13D2 **Lahnstein** Germany
42C2 **Lahore** Pakistan
13D3 **Lahr** Germany
12K6 **Lahti** Finland
50B3 **Lai** Chad
31B5 **Laibin** China
30C1 **Lai Chau** Vietnam
13C4 **Laignes** France
12J6 **Laihia** Finland
47C3 **Laingsburg** South Africa
8C2 **Lairg** Scotland
31E2 **Laiyang** China
31D2 **Laizhou Wan** *B* China
74B5 **Laja, Lago de la** Chile
74F3 **Lajes** Brazil
66D4 **La Jolla** USA
56C3 **La Junta** USA
60D2 **Lake Andes** USA
34C2 **Lake Cargelligo** Australia
57D3 **Lake Charles** USA
67B2 **Lake City** Florida, USA
61E2 **Lake City** Minnesota, USA
67C2 **Lake City** S Carolina, USA
6C2 **Lake District** *Region* England
66D4 **Lake Elsinore** USA
32C3 **Lake Eyre Basin** Australia
65D2 **Lakefield** Canada
64B2 **Lake Geneva** USA
68D1 **Lake George** USA
55M3 **Lake Harbour** Canada
59D4 **Lake Havasu City** USA
66C3 **Lake Hughes** USA
68C2 **Lakehurst** USA
66C3 **Lake Isabella** USA
63C3 **Lake Jackson** USA
67B3 **Lakeland** USA
55J5 **Lake of the Woods** Canada
58B1 **Lake Oswego** USA
12K7 **Lake Peipus** Estonia/Russian Federation
59B3 **Lakeport** USA
63D2 **Lake Providence** USA
35B2 **Lake Pukaki** New Zealand
34C3 **Lakes Entrance** Australia
66C2 **Lakeshore** USA
34B1 **Lake Stewart** Australia
65D1 **Lake Traverse** Canada
56A2 **Lakeview** USA
58B1 **Lakeview Mt** Canada
63D2 **Lake Village** USA
67B3 **Lake Wales** USA
66C4 **Lakewood** California, USA
60B3 **Lakewood** Colorado, USA
68C2 **Lakewood** New Jersey, USA
64C2 **Lakewood** Ohio, USA
67B3 **Lake Worth** USA
43E3 **Lakhīmpur** India
42B4 **Lakhpat** India
62B1 **Lakin** USA
42C2 **Lakki** Pakistan
17E3 **Lakonikós Kólpos** *G* Greece
48B4 **Lakota** Ivory Coast
12K4 **Laksefjord** *Inlet* Norway
12K4 **Lakselv** Norway
44A3 **Lakshadweep** *Is, Union Territory* India
72B4 **La Libertad** Ecuador
15A2 **La Linea** Spain
42D4 **Lalitpur** India
54H4 **La Loche** Canada
13C2 **La Louvière** Belgium
69A4 **La Luz** Nicaragua
55L5 **La Malbaie** Canada
56C3 **Lamar** Colorado, USA
63D1 **Lamar** Missouri, USA
63C3 **La Marque** USA
50B4 **Lambaréné** Gabon
72B5 **Lambayeque** Peru
76F10 **Lambert Glacier** Antarctica
47B3 **Lamberts Bay** South Africa
68C2 **Lambertville** USA
54F2 **Lambton,C** Canada
30C2 **Lam Chi** *R* Thailand
15A1 **Lamego** Portugal
72C6 **La Merced** Peru
62B2 **Lamesa** USA
59C4 **La Mesa** USA
17E3 **Lamía** Greece
8D4 **Lammermuir Hills** Scotland
12G7 **Lammhult** Sweden
61E2 **Lamoni** USA
66C3 **Lamont** California, USA
60B2 **Lamont** Wyoming, USA
27H6 **Lamotrek** *I* Pacific Ocean
13B4 **Lamotte-Beuvron** France
60D1 **La Moure** USA
62C2 **Lampasas** USA
7B3 **Lampeter** Wales
50E4 **Lamu** Kenya
66E5 **Lanai** *I* Hawaiian Islands
66E5 **Lanai City** Hawaiian Islands
27F6 **Lanao, L** Philippines
8D4 **Lanark** Scotland
30B3 **Lanbi** *I* Burma
30C1 **Lancang** *R* China
6C3 **Lancashire** *County* England
59C4 **Lancaster** California, USA
6C2 **Lancaster** England
61E2 **Lancaster** Missouri, USA
65E2 **Lancaster** New Hampshire, USA
68A1 **Lancaster** New York, USA
64C3 **Lancaster** Ohio, USA
57F3 **Lancaster** Pennsylvania, USA
67B2 **Lancaster** S Carolina, USA
55K2 **Lancaster Sd** Canada
13E3 **Landan** Germany
18C3 **Landeck** Austria
56C2 **Lander** USA
14B3 **Landes, Les** *Region* France
67B1 **Landrum** USA
18C3 **Landsberg** Germany
54F2 **Lands End** *C* Canada
7B4 **Land's End** *Pt* England
18C3 **Landshut** Germany
12G7 **Làndskrona** Sweden
67A2 **Lanett** USA
43E2 **La'nga Co** *L* China
60D1 **Langdon** USA
47C2 **Langeberg** *Mts* South Africa
18B2 **Langenhagen** Germany
13D1 **Langeoog** *I* Germany
8D4 **Langholm** Scotland
12A2 **Langjökull** *Mts* Iceland
30B4 **Langkawi** *I* Malaysia
34C1 **Langlo** *R* Australia
6B2 **Langness** *Pt* England
14B3 **Langon** France
14D2 **Langres** France
13C4 **Langres, Plateau de** France
27C6 **Langsa** Indonesia
26D2 **Lang Shan** *Mts* China
30D1 **Lang Son** Vietnam
62B3 **Langtry** USA
14C3 **Languedoc** *Region* France
74B5 **Lanin, Vol** Argentina
68C2 **Lansdale** USA
55K4 **Lansdowne House** Canada
68C2 **Lansford** USA
57E2 **Lansing** USA
48A2 **Lanzarote** *I* Canary Islands
31A2 **Lanzhou** China
27F5 **Laoag** Philippines
30C1 **Lao Cai** Vietnam
31D1 **Laoha He** *R* China
9C3 **Laois** *County* Irish Republic
28A2 **Laoling** China
13B3 **Laon** France
72C6 **La Oroya** Peru
30C2 **Laos** *Republic* SE Asia
75C4 **Lapa** Brazil
14C2 **Lapalisse** France
72C2 **La Palma** Panama
48A2 **La Palma** *I* Canary Islands
74C5 **La Pampa** *State* Argentina
66B3 **La Panza Range** *Mts* USA
72F2 **La Paragua** Venezuela
74E4 **La Paz** Argentina
72E7 **La Paz** Bolivia
70A2 **La Paz** Mexico
26H2 **La Perouse Str** Japan/Russian Federation
58B2 **La Pine** USA
45B1 **Lapithos** Cyprus
63D2 **Laplace** USA
60C1 **La Plant** USA
74E4 **La Plata** Argentina
64B2 **La Porte** USA
68B2 **Laporte** USA
12K6 **Lappeenranta** Finland
12H5 **Lappland** *Region* Finland/Sweden
62C3 **La Pryor** USA
25O2 **Laptev S** Russian Federation
12J6 **Lapua** Finland
56B4 **La Purísima** Mexico
50C1 **Laqiya Arbain** *Well* Sudan
74C2 **La Quiaca** Argentina
16C2 **L'Aquila** Italy
41F4 **Lār** Iran
15A2 **Larache** Morocco
56C2 **Laramie** USA
60B2 **Laramie Mts** USA
56C2 **Laramie Range** *Mts* USA
75B4 **Laranjeiras do Sul** Brazil
56D4 **Laredo** USA
41F4 **Larestan** *Region* Iran
Largeau = Faya
67B3 **Largo** USA
8C4 **Largs** Scotland
41E2 **Lārī** Iran
74C3 **La Rioja** Argentina
15B1 **La Rioja** *Region* Spain
74C3 **La Rioja** *State* Argentina
17E3 **Lárisa** Greece
42B3 **Larkana** Pakistan
40B3 **Larnaca** Cyprus
45B1 **Larnaca B** Cyprus
9C2 **Larne** Northern Ireland
62C1 **Larned** USA
15A1 **La Robla** Spain
13C2 **La Roche-en-Ardenne** Belgium
14B2 **La Rochelle** France
14B2 **La Roche-sur-Yon** France
15B2 **La Roda** Spain
69D3 **La Romana** Dominican Republic
54H4 **La Ronge** Canada
12F7 **Larvik** Norway
24J3 **Laryak** Russian Federation
15B2 **La Sagra** *Mt* Spain
65E1 **La Salle** Canada
64B2 **La Salle** USA
62B1 **Las Animas** USA
55L5 **La Sarre** Canada
62A2 **Las Cruces** USA
69C3 **La Selle** *Mt* Haiti
31B2 **Lasengmiao** China
74B3 **La Serena** Chile
74E5 **Las Flores** Argentina
30B1 **Lashio** Burma
16D3 **La Sila** *Mts* Italy
41F2 **Lāsjerd** Iran
42A2 **Laskar Gāh** Afghanistan
15A2 **Las Marismas** *Marshland* Spain
48A2 **Las Palmas de Gran Canaria** Canary Islands
16B2 **La Spezia** Italy
74C6 **Las Plumas** Argentina
58B2 **Lassen Peak** *Mt* USA
58B2 **Lassen Volcanic Nat Pk** USA
50B4 **Lastoursville** Gabon
16D2 **Lastovo** *I* Croatia
70B2 **Las Tres Marias** *Is* Mexico
56B3 **Las Vegas** USA
40C2 **Latakia** Syria
16C2 **Latina** Italy
69D4 **La Tortuga, I** Venezuela
34C4 **Latrobe** Australia
45C3 **Latrun** Israel
55L5 **La Tuque** Canada
44B2 **Lātūr** India
20C4 **Latvia** *Republic* Europe
8D4 **Lauder** Scotland
18B2 **Lauenburg** Germany
33H2 **Lau Group** *Is* Fiji
32D5 **Launceston** Australia
7B4 **Launceston** England
74B6 **La Unión** Chile
70D3 **La Unión** El Salvador
72C5 **La Unión** Peru
32D2 **Laura** Australia
65D3 **Laurel** Delaware, USA
68B3 **Laurel** Maryland, USA
57E3 **Laurel** Mississippi, USA
58E1 **Laurel** Montana, USA
67B2 **Laurens** USA
67C2 **Laurinburg** USA
16B1 **Lausanne** Switzerland
27E7 **Laut** *I* Indonesia
74B7 **Lautaro** Chile
13E2 **Lauterbach** Germany
13D3 **Lauterecken** Germany
65E1 **Laval** Canada
14B2 **Laval** France
66B2 **Laveaga Peak** *Mt* USA
58E1 **Lavina** USA
13C3 **La Vôge** *Region* France
73K8 **Lavras** Brazil
54A3 **Lavrentiya** Russian Federation
47E2 **Lavumisa** Swaziland
30B1 **Lawksawk** Burma
61D3 **Lawrence** Kansas, USA
65E2 **Lawrence** Massachusetts, USA
35A3 **Lawrence** New Zealand
63E1 **Lawrenceburg** USA
64B3 **Lawrenceville** Illinois, USA
68B2 **Lawrenceville** Pennsylvania, USA
56D3 **Lawton** USA
40C4 **Lawz, Jebel al** *Mt* Saudi Arabia
6B2 **Laxey** England
38C3 **Layla'** Saudi Arabia
50D3 **Laylo** Sudan
70B3 **Lázaro Cardenas** Mexico
29C2 **Lazo** Russian Federation
56C2 **Lead** USA
60B3 **Leadville** USA
63E2 **Leaf** *R* USA
62C3 **Leakey** USA
7D5 **Leamington Spa, Royal** England
61E3 **Leavenworth** USA
19D2 **Łeba** Poland
60D3 **Lebanon** Kansas, USA
63D1 **Lebanon** Missouri, USA
58B2 **Lebanon** Oregon, USA
65D2 **Lebanon** Pennsylvania, USA
64B3 **Lebanon** Tennessee, USA
40C3 **Lebanon** *Republic* SW Asia
66C3 **Lebec** USA
51D6 **Lebombo Mts** Mozambique/South Africa/Swaziland
19D2 **Lębork** Poland
74B5 **Lebu** Chile
13B2 **Le Cateau** France
17D2 **Lecce** Italy
16B1 **Lecco** Italy
13D3 **Le Champ du Feu** *Mt* France
14C2 **Le Creusot** France
7C3 **Ledbury** England
43H3 **Ledo** India
68D1 **Lee** USA
61E1 **Leech L** USA
10C3 **Leeds** England
7C3 **Leek** England
18B2 **Leer** Germany
67B3 **Leesburg** Florida, USA
68B3 **Leesburg** Virginia, USA
63D2 **Leesville** USA
34C2 **Leeton** Australia
47C3 **Leeugamka** South Africa
18B2 **Leeuwarden** Netherlands
32A4 **Leeuwin,C** Australia
66C2 **Lee Vining** USA
69E3 **Leeward Is** Caribbean Sea
45B1 **Lefka** Cyprus
45B1 **Lefkara** Cyprus
45B1 **Lefkoniko** Cyprus
27F5 **Legazpi** Philippines
18D2 **Legnica** Poland
73G2 **Leguan Island** Guyana
72D4 **Leguizamo** Peru
42D2 **Leh** India
14C2 **Le Havre** France
59D2 **Lehi** USA
68C2 **Lehigh** *R* USA
68C2 **Lehighton** USA
13D3 **Le Hohneck** *Mt* France
42C2 **Leiah** Pakistan
18D3 **Leibnitz** Austria
7D3 **Leicester** England
7D3 **Leicester** *County* England
32C2 **Leichhardt** *R* Australia
18A2 **Leiden** Netherlands
13B2 **Leie** *R* Belgium
32C4 **Leigh Creek** Australia
7E4 **Leigh on Sea** England
7D4 **Leighton Buzzard** England
18B2 **Leine** *R* Germany
9C3 **Leinster** *Region* Irish Republic
18C2 **Leipzig** Germany
15A2 **Leiria** Portugal
12F7 **Leirvik** Norway
8D4 **Leith** Scotland
31C4 **Leiyang** China
31B5 **Leizhou Bandao** *Pen* China
31C5 **Leizhou Wan** *B* China
18A2 **Lek** *R* Netherlands
16B3 **Le Kef** Tunisia
63D2 **Leland** USA
17D2 **Lelija** *Mt* Bosnia-Herzegovina
16B1 **Léman, Lac** France/Switzerland
14C2 **Le Mans** France
61D2 **Le Mars** USA
13E1 **Lemgo** Germany
58D2 **Lemhi Range** *Mts* USA
55M3 **Lemieux Is** Canada
56C2 **Lemmon** USA
59D4 **Lemmon,Mt** USA
59C3 **Lemoore** USA
14C2 **Lempdes** France
43G4 **Lemro** *R* Burma
16D2 **Le Murge** *Region* Italy
25O3 **Lena** *R* Russian Federation
20E3 **Lendery** Russian Federation
13D1 **Lengerich** Germany
31C4 **Lengshuijiang** China
Leningrad = St Petersburg
76F7 **Leningradskaya** *Base* Antarctica
20J5 **Leninogorsk** Russian Federation
26B1 **Leninogorsk** Kazakhstan
24K4 **Leninsk-Kuznetskiy** Russian Federation
26G2 **Leninskoye** Russian Federation
21H8 **Lenkoran'** Azerbaijan
13E2 **Lenne** *R* Germany
67B1 **Lenoir** USA
68D1 **Lenox** USA
13B2 **Lens** France
25N3 **Lensk** Russian Federation
16C3 **Lentini** Sicily, Italy
30B3 **Lenya** *R* Burma
16C1 **Leoben** Austria
7C3 **Leominster** England
68E1 **Leominster** USA
70B2 **León** Mexico
72A1 **León** Nicaragua
15A1 **León** Spain
47B1 **Leonardville** Namibia

45C1 **Leonarisso** Cyprus
32B3 **Leonora** Australia
75D3 **Leopoldina** Brazil
Léopoldville = Kinshasa
20D5 **Lepel** Belarus
31D4 **Leping** China
14C2 **Le Puy-en-Velay** France
50B3 **Léré** Chad
47D2 **Leribe** Lesotho
15C1 **Lérida** Spain
17F3 **Léros** *I* Greece
68B1 **Le Roy** USA
10C1 **Lerwick** Scotland
69C3 **Les Cayes** Haiti
65F1 **Les Escoumins** Canada
31A4 **Leshan** China
17E2 **Leskovac** Serbia, Yugoslavia
47D2 **Leslie** South Africa
20J4 **Lesnoy** Russian Federation
25L4 **Lesosibirsk** Russian Federation
47D2 **Lesotho** *Kingdom* South Africa
26G2 **Lesozavodsk** Russian Federation
14B2 **Les Sables-d'Olonne** France
76E4 **Lesser Antarctica** *Region* Antarctica
69E3 **Lesser Antilles** *Is* Caribbean Sea
21G7 **Lesser Caucasus** *Mts* Azerbaijan/Georgia
17F3 **Lésvos** *I* Greece
18D2 **Leszno** Poland
47E1 **Letaba** *R* South Africa
43G4 **Letha Range** *Mts* Burma
54G5 **Lethbridge** Canada
73G3 **Lethem** Guyana
19F3 **Letichev** Ukraine
72E4 **Letícia** Colombia
32B1 **Leti, Kepulauan** *I* Indonesia
47D1 **Letlhakeng** Botswana
7E4 **le Touquet-Paris-Plage** France
30B2 **Letpadan** Burma
25N4 **Let Oktyabr'ya** Russian Federation
14C1 **Le Tréport** France
9C2 **Letterkenny** Irish Republic
27C6 **Leuser** *Mt* Indonesia
18A2 **Leuven** Belgium
17E3 **Levádhia** Greece
12G6 **Levanger** Norway
62B2 **Levelland** USA
8D3 **Leven** Scotland
8D3 **Leven, Loch** *L* Scotland
27F8 **Lévèque,C** Australia
13D2 **Leverkusen** Germany
19D3 **Levice** Slovakia
35C2 **Levin** New Zealand
55L5 **Lévis** Canada
65E2 **Levittown** USA
17E3 **Lévka Óri** *Mt* Greece
17E3 **Levkás** Greece
17E3 **Levkás** *I* Greece
32B2 **Lévêque,C** Australia
17F2 **Levski** Bulgaria
7E4 **Lewes** England
62C1 **Lewis** USA
10B2 **Lewis** *I* Scotland
68B2 **Lewisburg** USA
35B2 **Lewis P** New Zealand
56B2 **Lewis Range** *Mts* USA
67A2 **Lewis Smith,L** USA
56B2 **Lewiston** Idaho, USA
57F2 **Lewiston** Maine, USA
56C2 **Lewistown** Montana, USA
65D2 **Lewistown** Pennsylvania, USA
63D2 **Lewisville** USA
57E3 **Lexington** Kentucky, USA
61E3 **Lexington** Missouri, USA
67B1 **Lexington** N Carolina, USA
60D2 **Lexington** Nebraska, USA
65D3 **Lexington** Virginia, USA
65D3 **Lexington Park** USA
6D2 **Leyburn** England
27F5 **Leyte** *I* Philippines
17D2 **Lezhe** Albania
39H3 **Lhasa** China
43F3 **Lhazê** China
27C6 **Lhokseumawe** Indonesia
43G3 **Lhozhag** China
26C4 **Lhunze** China
Liancourt Rocks = Tok-do
28B2 **Liangbingtai** China
31B3 **Liangdang** China
31C5 **Lianjiang** China
31C5 **Lianping** China
31C5 **Lian Xian** China
31D3 **Lianyungang** China
31E1 **Liaodong Bandao** *Pen* China
31E1 **Liaodong Wan** *B* China
31E1 **Liao He** *R* China
28A2 **Liaoning** *Province* China
31E1 **Liaoyang** China
28A2 **Liaoyangwopu** China
31E1 **Liaoyuan** China
28A2 **Liaozhong** China
54F3 **Liard** *R* Canada
54F4 **Liard River** Canada
13C3 **Liart** France
45C2 **Liban, Jebel** *Mts* Lebanon
58C1 **Libby** USA
50B3 **Libenge** Zaïre
56C3 **Liberal** USA
18C2 **Liberec** Czech Republic
48A4 **Liberia** *Republic* Africa
61E3 **Liberty** Missouri, USA
65E2 **Liberty** New York, USA
68B2 **Liberty** Pennsylvania, USA
63D2 **Liberty** Texas, USA
45B3 **Libni, Gebel** *Mt* Egypt
14B3 **Libourne** France
48C4 **Libreville** Equatorial Guinea
49D2 **Libya** *Republic* Africa
49E2 **Libyan Desert** Egypt/Libya/Sudan
49E1 **Libyan Plat** Egypt
16C3 **Licata** Sicily, Italy
7D3 **Lichfield** England
51D5 **Lichinga** Mozambique
47D2 **Lichtenburg** South Africa
64C3 **Licking** *R* USA
66B2 **Lick Observatory** USA
16C2 **Licosa, Punta** *Pt* Italy
66D2 **Lida** USA
20D5 **Lida** Belarus
12G7 **Lidköping** Sweden
16C2 **Lido di Ostia** Italy
16B1 **Liechtenstein** *Principality* Europe
18B2 **Liège** Belgium
19E1 **Lielupe** *R* Latvia
50C3 **Lienart** Zaïre
18C3 **Lienz** Austria
12J7 **Liepāja** Latvia
13C2 **Lier** Belgium
65E1 **Lièvre** *R* Canada
18C3 **Liezen** Austria
9C3 **Liffey** *R* Irish Republic
9C2 **Lifford** Irish Republic
33F3 **Lifu** *I* Nouvelle Calédonie
34C1 **Lightning Ridge** Australia
13C3 **Ligny-en-Barrois** France
51D5 **Ligonha** *R* Mozambique
16B2 **Ligurian S** Italy
33E1 **Lihir Group** *Is* Papua New Guinea
66E5 **Lihue** Hawaiian Islands
51C5 **Likasi** Zaïre
14C1 **Lille** France
12G6 **Lillehammer** Norway
13B2 **Lillers** France
12G7 **Lillestrøm** Norway
51D5 **Lilongwe** Malawi
17D2 **Lim** *R* Montenegro/Serbia, Yugoslavia
72C6 **Lima** Peru
57E2 **Lima** USA
15A1 **Lima** *R* Portugal
58D2 **Lima Res** USA
40B3 **Limassol** Cyprus
9C2 **Limavady** Northern Ireland
48C4 **Limbe** Cameroon
51D5 **Limbe** Malawi
18B2 **Limburg** Germany
73J8 **Limeira** Brazil
10B3 **Limerick** Irish Republic
18B1 **Limfjorden** *L* Denmark
32C2 **Limmen Bight** *B* Australia
17F3 **Límnos** *I* Greece
73L5 **Limoeiro** Brazil
14C2 **Limoges** France
70D4 **Limón** Costa Rica
56C3 **Limon** USA
14C2 **Limousin** *Region* France
14C2 **Limousin, Plateaux de** France
47E1 **Limpopo** *R* Mozambique
74B5 **Linares** Chile
56D4 **Linares** Mexico
15B2 **Linares** Spain
26C4 **Lincang** China
74D4 **Lincoln** Argentina
7D3 **Lincoln** England
64B2 **Lincoln** Illinois, USA
65F1 **Lincoln** Maine, USA
56D2 **Lincoln** Nebraska, USA
65E2 **Lincoln** New Hampshire, USA
35B2 **Lincoln** New Zealand
7D3 **Lincoln** *County* England
58B2 **Lincoln City** USA
64C2 **Lincoln Park** USA
76A2 **Lincoln Sea** Greenland
16B2 **L'Incudine** *Mt* Corsica, France
18B3 **Lindau** Germany
73G2 **Linden** Guyana
12F7 **Lindesnes** *C* Norway
51D4 **Lindi** Tanzania
50C3 **Lindi** *R* Zaïre
47D2 **Lindley** South Africa
17F3 **Lindos** Greece
66C2 **Lindsay** California, USA
65D2 **Lindsay** Canada
60B1 **Lindsay** Montana, USA
37M4 **Line Is** Pacific Ocean
31C2 **Linfen** China
30D2 **Lingao** China
27F5 **Lingayen** Philippines
18B2 **Lingen** Germany
27D7 **Lingga** *I* Indonesia
60C2 **Lingle** USA
31C4 **Lingling** China
31B5 **Lingshan** China
31C2 **Lingshi** China
48A3 **Linguère** Senegal
31E4 **Linhai** Zhejiang, China
73L7 **Linhares** Brazil
31B1 **Linhe** China
28B2 **Linjiang** China
28A2 **Linjiatai** China
12H7 **Linköping** Sweden
8C3 **Linnhe, Loch** *Inlet* Scotland
31D2 **Linqing** China
75C3 **Lins** Brazil
31A2 **Lintao** China
60C1 **Linton** USA
26E2 **Linxi** China
31A2 **Linxia** China
18C3 **Linz** Austria
14C3 **Lion, Golfe du** *G* France
16C3 **Lipari** *I* Italy
16C3 **Lipari, Isole** *Is* Italy
21F5 **Lipetsk** Russian Federation
17E1 **Lipova** Romania
18B2 **Lippe** *R* Germany
13E2 **Lippstadt** Germany
50D3 **Lira** Uganda
50B4 **Liranga** Congo
50C3 **Lisala** Zaïre
Lisboa = Lisbon
15A2 **Lisbon** Portugal
61D1 **Lisbon** USA
9C2 **Lisburn** Northern Ireland
31D4 **Lishui** China
31C4 **Li Shui** *R* China
21F6 **Lisichansk** Ukraine
14C2 **Lisieux** France
21F5 **Liski** Russian Federation
13B3 **L'Isle-Adam** France
33E3 **Lismore** Australia
9C3 **Lismore** Irish Republic
31B5 **Litang** China
45C2 **Līṭāni** *R* Lebanon
73H3 **Litani** *R* Surinam
64B3 **Litchfield** Illinois, USA
61E1 **Litchfield** Minnesota, USA
32E4 **Lithgow** Australia
20C4 **Lithuania** *Republic* Europe
68B2 **Lititz** USA
26G2 **Litovko** Russian Federation
63C2 **Little** *R* USA
57F4 **Little Abaco** *I* The Bahamas
44E3 **Little Andaman** *I* Andaman Islands
67C3 **Little Bahama Bank** Bahamas
35C1 **Little Barrier I** New Zealand
58D1 **Little Belt Mts** USA
45B3 **Little Bitter L** Egypt
70D3 **Little Cayman** *I* Cayman Is, Caribbean Sea
68C3 **Little Egg Harbor** *B* USA
61E1 **Little Falls** Minnesota, USA
68C1 **Little Falls** New York, USA
62B2 **Littlefield** USA
61E1 **Littlefork** USA
61E1 **Little Fork** *R* USA
8E2 **Little Halibut Bank** *Sand-bank* Scotland
7D4 **Littlehampton** England
69C2 **Little Inagua** *I* The Bahamas
47C3 **Little Karoo** *Mts* South Africa
66D3 **Little Lake** USA
60C1 **Little Missouri** *R* USA
30A4 **Little Nicobar** *I* Nicobar Is, India
57D3 **Little Rock** USA
66D3 **Littlerock** USA
68B3 **Littlestown** USA
60B3 **Littleton** Colorado, USA
65E2 **Littleton** New Hampshire, USA
28B2 **Liuhe** China
31B2 **Liupan Shan** *Upland* China
31B5 **Liuzhou** China
17E3 **Livanátais** Greece
19F1 **Līvāni** Latvia
67B2 **Live Oak** USA
59B3 **Livermore** USA
62B2 **Livermore,Mt** USA
55M5 **Liverpool** Canada
7C3 **Liverpool** England
54E2 **Liverpool B** Canada
7C3 **Liverpool B** England
55L2 **Liverpool,C** Canada
34D2 **Liverpool Range** *Mts* Australia
56B2 **Livingston** Montana, USA
67A1 **Livingston** Tennessee, USA
63D2 **Livingston** Texas, USA
8D4 **Livingstone** Scotland
51C5 **Livingstone** Zambia
63C2 **Livingston,L** USA
16D2 **Livno** Bosnia-Herzegovina
21F5 **Livny** Russian Federation
64C2 **Livonia** USA
16C2 **Livorno** Italy
75D1 **Livramento do Brumado** Brazil
51D4 **Liwale** Tanzania
7B5 **Lizard Pt** England
16C1 **Ljubljana** Slovenia
12G6 **Ljungan** *R* Sweden
12G7 **Ljungby** Sweden
12H6 **Ljusdal** Sweden
20B3 **Ljusnan** *R* Sweden
7C4 **Llandeilo** Wales
7C4 **Llandovery** Wales
7C3 **Llandrindod Wells** Wales
7C3 **Llandudno** Wales
7D4 **Llanelli** Wales
7C3 **Llangollen** Wales
62C2 **Llano** USA
62C2 **Llano** *R* USA
56C3 **Llano Estacado** *Plat* USA
72D2 **Llanos** *Region* Colombia/Venezuela
72F7 **Llanos de Chiquitos** *Region* Bolivia
7C4 **Llantrisant** Wales
7C3 **Llanwrst** Wales
Lleida = Lérida
15A2 **Llerena** Spain
7B3 **Lleyn** *Pen* Wales
54F4 **Lloyd George,Mt** Canada
54H4 **Lloydminster** Canada
74C2 **Llullaillaco** *Mt* Argentina/Chile
74C2 **Loa** *R* Chile
50B4 **Loange** *R* Zaïre
47D2 **Lobatse** Botswana
50B3 **Lobaye** *R* Central African Republic
51B5 **Lobito** Angola
8B3 **Lochboisdale** Scotland
8C3 **Lochearnhead** Scotland
14C2 **Loches** France
8C3 **Lochgoilhead** Scotland
8C2 **Lochinver** Scotland
8D4 **Lochmaben** Scotland
8B3 **Lochmaddy** Scotland
8D3 **Lochnagar** *Mt* Scotland
8C3 **Loch Ness** Scotland
58C1 **Lochsa** *R* USA
8C3 **Lochy, Loch** *L* Scotland
8D4 **Lockerbie** Scotland
65D2 **Lock Haven** USA
65D2 **Lockport** USA
30D3 **Loc Ninh** Vietnam
16D3 **Locri** Italy
45C3 **Lod** Israel
34B3 **Loddon** *R* Australia
20E3 **Lodeynoye Pole** Russian Federation
58E1 **Lodge Grass** USA
42C3 **Lodhran** Pakistan
16B1 **Lodi** Italy
59B3 **Lodi** USA
50C4 **Lodja** Zaïre
50D3 **Lodwar** Kenya
19D2 **Łódź** Poland
47B3 **Loeriesfontein** South Africa
12G5 **Lofoten** *Is* Norway
6D2 **Loftus** England
62B1 **Logan** New Mexico, USA
56B2 **Logan** Utah, USA
54D3 **Logan,Mt** Canada
64B2 **Logansport** Indiana, USA
15D3 **Logansport** Louisiana, USA
68B2 **Loganton** USA
50B2 **Logone** *R* Cameroon/Chad
15B1 **Logroño** Spain
43E4 **Lohārdaga** India
12J6 **Lohja** Finland
30B2 **Loikaw** Burma
12J6 **Loimaa** Finland
13B3 **Loing** *R* France
14C2 **Loir** *R* France
14C2 **Loire** *R* France
13B4 **Loiret** *Department* France
72C4 **Loja** Ecuador
15B2 **Loja** Spain
12K5 **Lokan Tekojärvi** *Res* Finland
13B2 **Lokeren** Belgium
27F7 **Lokialaki, G** *Mt* Indonesia
50D3 **Lokitaung** Kenya
19F1 **Loknya** Russian Federation
50C4 **Lokolo** *R* Zaïre
50C4 **Lokoro** *R* Zaïre
55M3 **Loks Land** *I* Canada
18C2 **Lolland** *I* Denmark
58D1 **Lolo P** USA
17E2 **Lom** Bulgaria
51C4 **Lomami** *R* Zaïre
48A4 **Loma Mts** Guinea/Sierra Leone
27F7 **Lomblen** *I* Indonesia
27E7 **Lombok** *I* Indonesia
48C4 **Lomé** Togo
50C4 **Lomela** Zaïre
50C4 **Lomela** *R* Zaïre
8C3 **Lomond, Loch** *L* Scotland
20D4 **Lomonosov** Russian Federation
59B4 **Lompoc** USA
19E2 **Łomza** Poland
44A2 **Lonāvale** India
74B5 **Loncoche** Chile
55K5 **London** Canada
7D4 **London** England
64C3 **London** USA
9C2 **Londonderry** Northern Ireland
9C2 **Londonderry** *County* Northern Ireland
74B9 **Londonderry** *I* Chile
32B2 **Londonderry,C** Australia
74C3 **Londres** Argentina
74F2 **Londrina** Brazil
66D1 **Lone Mt** USA
66C2 **Lone Pine** USA
27H7 **Long** *I* Papua New Guinea
57F4 **Long** *I* The Bahamas
25T2 **Longa, Proliv** *Str* Russian Federation
69H2 **Long B** Jamaica
67C2 **Long B** USA
56B3 **Long Beach** California, USA
65E2 **Long Beach** New York, USA
65E2 **Long Branch** USA
31D5 **Longchuan** China
58C2 **Long Creek** USA
7D3 **Long Eaton** England
34C4 **Longford** Australia
9C3 **Longford** Irish Republic
9C3 **Longford** *County* Irish Republic
8E3 **Long Forties** *Region* N Sea
28B2 **Longgang Shan** *Mts* China
31D1 **Longhua** China
57F4 **Long I** Bahamas
55L4 **Long I** Canada
32D1 **Long I** Papua New Guinea
57F2 **Long I** USA
68D2 **Long Island Sd** USA
28B2 **Longjing** China
64B1 **Long L** Canada
60C1 **Long L** USA
55K4 **Longlac** Canada
31B5 **Longlin** China
8C3 **Long, Loch** *Inlet* Scotland
7E3 **Long Melford** England
56C2 **Longmont** USA
13C3 **Longny** France
61E1 **Long Prairie** USA
32D3 **Longreach** Australia
31A2 **Longshou Shan** *Upland* China
60B2 **Longs Peak** *Mt* USA
7E3 **Long Sutton** England
6C2 **Longtown** England
65E1 **Longueuil** Canada
13C3 **Longuyon** France
57D3 **Longview** Texas, USA
56A2 **Longview** Washington, USA
14D2 **Longwy** France
31A3 **Longxi** China
30D3 **Long Xuyen** Vietnam
31D4 **Longyan** China
31B5 **Longzhou** China
13D1 **Löningen** Germany
74B5 **Lonquimay** Chile
14D2 **Lons-le-Saunier** France
7B4 **Looe** England
57F3 **Lookout,C** USA
50D4 **Loolmalasin** *Mt* Tanzania
25R4 **Lopatka, Mys** *C* Russian Federation
30C3 **Lop Buri** Thailand
26C2 **Lop Nur** *L* China
15A2 **Lora del Rio** Spain
57E2 **Lorain** USA
42B2 **Loralai** Pakistan
15B2 **Lorca** Spain
41F3 **Lordegān** Iran
33E4 **Lord Howe** *I* Australia
37K6 **Lord Howe Rise** Pacific Ocean
55J3 **Lord Mayor B** Canada
56C3 **Lordsburg** USA
75C3 **Lorena** Brazil
14B2 **Lorient** France

34B3 Lorne Australia
18B3 Lörrach Germany
13C3 Lorraine Region France
56C3 Los Alamos USA
66B3 Los Alamos USA
74B5 Los Angeles Chile
56B3 Los Angeles USA
66C3 Los Angeles Aqueduct USA
59B3 Los Banos USA
59B3 Los Gatos USA
16C2 Lošinj I Croatia
74B5 Los Lagos Chile
62A2 Los Lunas USA
70B2 Los Mochis Mexico
66B3 Los Olivos USA
72E1 Los Roques, Islas Venezuela
8D3 Lossie R Scotland
8D3 Lossiemouth Scotland
69E4 Los Testigos Is Venezuela
66C3 Lost Hills USA
58D1 Lost Trail P USA
74B4 Los Vilos Chile
14C3 Lot R France
8D4 Lothian Region Scotland
50D3 Lotikipi Plain Kenya/Sudan
50C4 Loto Zaïre
47D1 Lotsane R Botswana
12K5 Lotta R Finland/Russian Federation
14B2 Loudéac France
48A3 Louga Senegal
7D3 Loughborough England
54H2 Lougheed I Canada
64C3 Louisa USA
27E6 Louisa Reef S China Sea
33E2 Louisiade Arch Papua New Guinea
57D3 Louisiana State USA
47D1 Louis Trichardt South Africa
67B2 Louisville Georgia, USA
57E3 Louisville Kentucky, USA
63E2 Louisville Mississippi, USA
20E2 Loukhi Russian Federation
61D2 Loup R USA
14B3 Lourdes France
Lourenço Marques = Maputo
34C2 Louth Australia
7D3 Louth England
9C3 Louth County Irish Republic
Louvain = Leuven
14C2 Louviers France
20E4 Lovat R Russian Federation
17E2 Lovech Bulgaria
60B2 Loveland USA
60B3 Loveland P USA
58E2 Lovell USA
59C2 Lovelock USA
16C1 Lóvere Italy
62B2 Lovington USA
20F2 Lovozero Russian Federation
55K3 Low,C Canada
57F2 Lowell Massachusetts, USA
58B2 Lowell Oregon, USA
68E1 Lowell USA
58C1 Lower Arrow L Canada
35B2 Lower Hutt New Zealand
66A1 Lower Lake USA
61D1 Lower Red L USA
7E3 Lowestoft England
19D2 Łowicz Poland
34B2 Loxton Australia
47C3 Loxton South Africa
68B2 Loyalsock Creek R USA
33F3 Loyalty Is New Caledonia
17D2 Loznica Serbia, Yugoslavia
24H3 Lozva R Russian Federation
51C5 Luacano Angola
51C4 Luachimo Angola
50C4 Lualaba R Zaïre
51C5 Luampa Zambia
51C5 Luân Angola
31D3 Lu'an China
51B4 Luanda Angola
51B5 Luando R Angola
51C5 Luanginga R Angola
30C1 Luang Namtha Laos
30C2 Luang Prabang Laos
51B4 Luangue R Angola
51D5 Luangwa R Zambia
31D1 Luan He R China
31D1 Luanping China
51C5 Luanshya Zambia
51C5 Luapula R Zaïre
15A1 Luarca Spain
51B4 Lubalo Angola
19F2 L'uban Belarus
51B5 Lubango Angola
56C3 Lubbock USA
18C2 Lübeck Germany
50C4 Lubefu Zaïre
50C4 Lubefu R Zaïre
50C3 Lubero Zaïre
51C4 Lubilash R Zaïre
19E2 Lublin Poland
21E5 Lubny Ukraine
51C4 Lubudi Zaïre
51C4 Lubudi R Zaïre
27D7 Lubuklinggau Indonesia
51C5 Lubumbashi Zaïre
50C4 Lubutu Zaïre
75A1 Lucas Brazil
67C3 Lucaya Bahamas
16C2 Lucca Italy
8C4 Luce B Scotland
63E2 Lucedale USA
19D3 Lucenec Slovakia
Lucerne = Luzern
62A2 Lucero Mexico
31C5 Luchuan China
66B2 Lucia USA
18C2 Luckenwalde Germany
47C2 Luckhoff South Africa
43E3 Lucknow India
51C5 Lucusse Angola
13D2 Lüdenscheid Germany
47B2 Lüderitz Namibia
42D2 Ludhiana India
64B2 Ludington USA
59C4 Ludlow California, USA
7C3 Ludlow England
68D1 Ludlow Vermont, USA
17F2 Ludogorie Upland Bulgaria
67B2 Ludowici USA
17E1 Luduş Romania
12H6 Ludvika Sweden
18B3 Ludwigsburg Germany
18B3 Ludwigshafen Germany
18C2 Ludwigslust Germany
50C4 Luebo Zaïre
50C4 Luema R Zaïre
51C4 Luembe R Angola
51B5 Luena Angola
51C5 Luene R Angola
31B3 Lüeyang China
31D5 Lufeng China
57D3 Lufkin USA
20D4 Luga Russian Federation
20D4 Luga R Russian Federation
16B1 Lugano Switzerland
51D5 Lugela Mozambique
51D5 Lugenda R Mozambique
9C3 Lugnaquillia,Mt Irish Republic
15A1 Lugo Spain
17E1 Lugoj Romania
45D2 Luhfi, Wadi Jordan
31A3 Luhuo China
51B4 Lui R Angola
51C5 Luiana Angola
51C5 Luiana R Angola
Luichow Peninsula = Leizhou Bandao
20D2 Luiro R Finland
51C5 Luishia Zaïre
26C4 Luixi China
51C4 Luiza Zaïre
31D3 Lujiang China
50B4 Lukenie R Zaïre
59D4 Lukeville USA
51C5 Lukolela Zaïre
19E2 Łuków Poland
50C4 Lukuga R Zaïre
51C5 Lukulu Zambia
20C2 Lule R Sweden
12J5 Luleå Sweden
17F2 Lüleburgaz Turkey
31C2 Lüliang Shan Mts China
63C3 Luling USA
50C3 Lulonga R Zaïre
Luluabourg = Kananga
51C5 Lumbala Kaquengue Angola
57F3 Lumberton USA
20G2 Lumbovka Russian Federation
43G3 Lumding India
51C5 Lumeje Angola
35A3 Lumsden New Zealand
12G7 Lund Sweden
51D5 Lundazi Zambia
51D6 Lundi R Zimbabwe
7B4 Lundy I England
18C2 Lüneburg Germany
13D3 Lunéville France
51C5 Lunga R Zambia
43G4 Lunglei India
51B5 Lungue Bungo R Angola
19F2 Luninec Belarus
66C1 Luning USA
50B4 Luobomo Congo
31B5 Luocheng China
31C5 Luoding China
31C3 Luohe China
31C3 Luo He R Henan, China
31B2 Luo He R Shaanxi, China
31C4 Luoxiao Shan Hills China
31C3 Luoyang China
50B4 Luozi Zaïre
51C5 Lupane Zimbabwe
51D5 Lupilichi Mozambique
Lu Qu R = Tao He
74E3 Luque Paraguay
13D4 Lure France
9C2 Lurgan Northern Ireland
51D5 Lurio R Mozambique
41E3 Luristan Region Iran
51C5 Lusaka Zambia
50C4 Lusambo Zaïre
17D2 Lushnjë Albania
50D4 Lushoto Tanzania
26C4 Lushui China
31E2 Lüshun China
60C2 Lusk USA
7D4 Luton England
21D5 Lutsk Ukraine
50E3 Luuq Somalia
61D2 Luverne USA
51C4 Luvua R Zaïre
51D4 Luwegu R Tanzania
51D5 Luwingu Zambia
27F7 Luwuk Indonesia
14D2 Luxembourg Luxembourg
13D3 Luxembourg Grand Duchy NW Europe
13D4 Luxeuil-les-Bains France
31A5 Luxi China
49F2 Luxor Egypt
20H3 Luza Russian Federation
20H3 Luza R Russian Federation
16B1 Luzern Switzerland
68D1 Luzerne USA
31B5 Luzhai China
31B4 Luzhi China
31B4 Luzhou China
75C2 Luziânia Brazil
27F5 Luzon I Philippines
27F5 Luzon Str Philippines
19E3 L'vov Ukraine
8D2 Lybster Scotland
12H6 Lycksele Sweden
7E4 Lydd England
51C6 Lydenburg South Africa
56B3 Lyell,Mt USA
68B2 Lykens USA
58D2 Lyman USA
7C4 Lyme B England
7C4 Lyme Regis England
7D4 Lymington England
57F3 Lynchburg USA
34A2 Lyndhurst Australia
65E2 Lynn USA
67A2 Lynn Haven USA
54H4 Lynn Lake Canada
7C4 Lynton England
54H3 Lynx L Canada
14C2 Lyon France
67B2 Lyons Georgia, USA
68B1 Lyons New York, USA
32A3 Lyons R Australia
20K4 Lys'va Russian Federation
6C3 Lytham St Anne's England
35B2 Lyttelton New Zealand
66A1 Lytton USA
19F2 Lyubeshov Ukraine
20F4 Lyublino Russian Federation

M

30C1 Ma R Laos/Vietnam
45C2 Ma'agan Jordan
45C2 Ma'alot Tarshīhā Israel
40C3 Ma'ān Jordan
31D3 Ma'anshan China
45D1 Ma'arrat an Nu'mān Syria
13C2 Maas R Netherlands
13C2 Maaseik Belgium
18B2 Maastricht Netherlands
47E1 Mabalane Mozambique
73G2 Mabaruma Guyana
7E3 Mablethorpe England
51D6 Mabote Mozambique
19E2 Mabrita Belarus
75D3 Macaé Brazil
56D3 McAlester USA
56D4 McAllen USA
51D5 Macaloge Mozambique
73H3 Macapá Brazil
75D2 Macarani Brazil
72C4 Macas Ecuador
73L5 Macaú Brazil
31C5 Macau Dependency SE Asia
75D1 Macaúbas Brazil
50C3 M'Bari R Central African Republic
58C2 McCall USA
62B2 McCamey USA
58D2 McCammon USA
7C3 Macclesfield England
55K1 McClintock B Canada
54H2 McClintock Chan Canada
68B2 McClure USA
66B2 McClure,L USA
54G2 McClure Str Canada
63D2 McComb USA
60C2 McConaughy,L USA
68B3 McConnellsburg USA
56C2 McCook USA
55L2 Macculloch,C Canada
54F4 McDame Canada
58C2 McDermitt USA
58D1 McDonald Peak Mt USA
32C3 Macdonnell Ranges Mts Australia
8D3 MacDuff Scotland
15A1 Macedo de Cavaleiros Portugal
17E2 Macedonia Republic Europe
73L5 Maceió Brazil
48B4 Macenta Guinea
16C2 Macerata Italy
63D2 McGehee USA
59D3 McGill USA
54C3 McGrath USA
58D1 McGuire,Mt USA
75C3 Machado Brazil
51D6 Machaíla Mozambique
50D4 Machakos Kenya
72C4 Machala Ecuador
51D6 Machaze Mozambique
44B2 Mācherla India
45C2 Machgharab Lebanon
65F2 Machias USA
44C2 Machilīpatnam India
72D1 Machiques Venezuela
72D6 Machu-Picchu Hist Site Peru
7C3 Machynlleth Wales
51D6 Macia Mozambique
Macias Nguema I = Bioko
60C1 McIntosh USA
34C1 MacIntyre R Australia
60B3 Mack USA
32D3 Mackay Australia
58D2 Mackay USA
32B3 Mackay,L Australia
33H1 McKean I Phoenix Islands
65D2 McKeesport USA
54F3 Mackenzie R Canada
54E3 Mackenzie B Canada
54G2 Mackenzie King I Canada
54E3 Mackenzie Mts Canada
64C1 Mackinac,Str of USA
64C1 Mackinaw City USA
54C3 McKinley, Mt USA
63C2 McKinney USA
55L2 Mackinson Inlet B Canada
66C3 McKittrick USA
34D2 Macksville Australia
60C1 McLaughlin USA
34D1 Maclean Australia
47D3 Maclear South Africa
54G4 McLennan Canada
54G3 McLeod B Canada
32A3 McLeod,L Australia
58B2 McLoughlin,Mt USA
54E3 Macmillan R Canada
62B2 McMillan,L USA
58B1 McMinnville Oregon, USA
67A1 McMinnville Tennessee, USA
76F7 McMurdo Base Antarctica
59E4 McNary USA
64A2 Macomb USA
16B2 Macomer Sardinia, Italy
51D5 Macomia Mozambique
14C2 Mâcon France
57E3 Macon Georgia, USA
61E3 Macon Missouri, USA
51C5 Macondo Angola
63C1 McPherson USA
34C2 Macquarie R Australia
34C4 Macquarie Harbour B Australia
36J7 Macquarie Is Australia
34D2 Macquarie,L Australia
67B2 McRae USA
76F11 Mac Robertson Land Region Antarctica
54G3 McTavish Arm B Canada
54F3 McVicar Arm B Canada
45C3 Mādabā Jordan
50C2 Madadi Well Chad
46J9 Madagascar I Indian Ocean
36D6 Madagascar Basin Indian Ocean
50B1 Madama Niger
32D1 Madang Papua New Guinea
48C3 Madaoua Niger
43G4 Madaripur Bangladesh
41F2 Madau Turkmenistan
65D1 Madawaska R Canada
48A1 Madeira I Atlantic Ocean
72F5 Madeira R Brazil
19F2 M'adel Belarus
55M5 Madeleine Îles de la Canada
61E2 Madelia USA
70B2 Madera Mexico
59B3 Madera USA
44A2 Madgaon India
43F3 Madhubani India
43E4 Madhya Pradesh State India
44B3 Madikeri India
50B4 Madimba Zaïre
50B4 Madingo Kayes Congo
50B4 Madingou Congo
57E3 Madison Indiana, USA
61D1 Madison Minnesota, USA
61D2 Madison Nebraska, USA
61D2 Madison S Dakota, USA
57E2 Madison Wisconsin, USA
58D1 Madison R USA
64B3 Madisonville Kentucky, USA
63C2 Madisonville Texas, USA
50D3 Mado Gashi Kenya
44C3 Madras India
58B2 Madras USA
74A8 Madre de Dios I Chile
72E6 Madre de Dios R Bolivia
70C2 Madre, Laguna Mexico
63C3 Madre, Laguna USA
15B1 Madrid Spain
15B2 Madridejos Spain
27E7 Madura I Indonesia
44B4 Madurai India
29C3 Maebashi Japan
30B3 Mae Khlong R Thailand
30B4 Mae Luang R Thailand
30C2 Mae Nam Mun R Thailand
30B2 Mae Nam Ping R Thailand
28A3 Maengsan N Korea
51E5 Maevatanana Madagascar
33F2 Maewo I Vanuatu
47D2 Mafeteng Lesotho
34C3 Maffra Australia
51D4 Mafia I Tanzania
47D2 Mafikeng South Africa
74G3 Mafra Brazil
40C3 Mafraq Jordan
25R4 Magadan Russian Federation
74B8 Magallanes, Estrecho de Str Chile
72D2 Magangué Colombia
56B3 Magdalena Mexico
62A2 Magdalena USA
72D2 Magdalena R Colombia
70A2 Magdalena, Bahía Mexico
70A2 Magdalena, Isla Mexico
18C2 Magdeburg Germany
73K8 Magé Brazil
16B1 Maggiore, L Italy
40B4 Maghâgha Egypt
45B3 Maghâra, Gebel Mt Egypt
9C2 Maghera Northern Ireland
9C2 Magherafelt Northern Ireland
17D2 Maglie Italy
20K5 Magnitogorsk Russian Federation
63D2 Magnolia USA
51D5 Magoé Mozambique
65E1 Magog Canada
66D2 Magruder Mt USA
73J4 Maguarinho, Cabo C Brazil
47E2 Magude Mozambique
55J3 Maguse River Canada
Magway = Magwe
30B1 Magwe Burma
21H8 Mahābād Iran
43F3 Mahabharat Range Mts Nepal
44A2 Mahād India
42D4 Mahadeo Hills India
68A2 Mahaffey USA
51E5 Mahajamba, Baie de B Madagascar
51E5 Mahajanga Madagascar
47D1 Mahalapye Botswana
43E4 Mahānadi R India
51E5 Mahanoro Madagascar
68B2 Mahanoy City USA
44A2 Mahārāshtra State India
43E4 Māhāsamund India
30C2 Maha Sarakham Thailand
51E5 Mahavavy R Madagascar
44B2 Mahbūbnagar India
48D1 Mahdia Tunisia
44B3 Mahe India
51D4 Mahenge Tanzania
42C4 Mahesāna India
35C1 Mahia Pen New Zealand
61D1 Mahnomen USA
42D3 Mahoba India
15C2 Mahón Spain
48D1 Mahrès Tunisia
42C4 Mahuva India
72D1 Maicao Colombia
7D4 Maidenhead England
7E4 Maidstone England
50B2 Maiduguri Nigeria
43E4 Maihar India
43G4 Maijdi Bangladesh
43E4 Maikala Range Mts India
42A1 Maimana Afghanistan
64C1 Main Chan Canada
50B4 Mai-Ndombe, L Zaïre
57G2 Maine State, USA
8D2 Mainland I Scotland
42D3 Mainpuri India

51E5 **Maintirano** Madagascar
18B2 **Mainz** Germany
48A4 **Maio** *I* Cape Verde
74C4 **Maipó, Vol** Argentina/ Chile
72E1 **Maiquetía** Venezuela
43G3 **Mairābāri** India
43G4 **Maiskhal I** Bangladesh
32E4 **Maitland** New South Wales, Australia
76F12 **Maitri** *Base* Antarctica
70D3 **Maíz, Isla del** Caribbean Sea
29D3 **Maizuru** Japan
32A1 **Majene** Indonesia
72D7 **Majes** *R* Peru
50D3 **Maji** Ethiopia
31D2 **Majia He** *R* China
15C2 **Majorca** *I* Balearic Is, Spain
Majunga = Mahajanga
27E7 **Makale** Indonesia
43F3 **Makalu** *Mt* China/Nepal
50B3 **Makanza** Zaïre
20K2 **Makarikha** Russian Federation
16D2 **Makarska** Croatia
20G4 **Makaryev** Russian Federation
Makassar = Ujung Pandang
27E7 **Makassar Str** Indonesia
21J6 **Makat** Kazakhstan
48A4 **Makeni** Sierra Leone
13C1 **Makerwaard** *Polder* Netherlands
21F6 **Makeyevka** Ukraine
51C6 **Makgadikgadi** *Salt Pan* Botswana
21H7 **Makhachkala** Russian Federation
50D4 **Makindu** Kenya
Makkah = Mecca Saudi Arabia
55N4 **Makkovik** Canada
19E3 **Makó** Hungary
50B3 **Makokou** Gabon
35C1 **Makorako,Mt** New Zealand
50B3 **Makoua** Congo
42C3 **Makrāna** India
42A3 **Makran Coast Range** *Mts* Pakistan
16B3 **Makthar** Tunisia
21G8 **Mākū** Iran
50C4 **Makumbi** Zaïre
48C4 **Makurdi** Nigeria
44B3 **Malabar Coast** India
48C4 **Malabo** Equatorial Guinea
Malacca = Melaka
30C5 **Malacca,Str of** SE Asia
58D2 **Malad City** USA
72D2 **Málaga** Colombia
15B2 **Málaga** Spain
62B2 **Malaga** USA
51E6 **Malaimbandy** Madagascar
33F1 **Malaita** *I* Solomon Islands
50D3 **Malakal** Sudan
42C2 **Malakand** Pakistan
27F6 **Malanbang** Philippines
27E7 **Malang** Indonesia
51B4 **Malanje** Angola
48C3 **Malanville** Benin
25S3 **Mal Anyuy** *R* Russian Federation
12H7 **Mälaren** *L* Sweden
65D1 **Malartic** Canada
21F8 **Malatya** Turkey
51D5 **Malawi** *Republic* Africa
Malawi,L = Nyasa,L
41E3 **Malāyer** Iran
27D6 **Malaysia** *Federation* SE Asia
40D2 **Malazgirt** Turkey
19D2 **Malbork** Poland
18C2 **Malchin** Germany
63E1 **Malden** USA
39F5 **Maldives** *Is* Indian Ocean
36E4 **Maldives Ridge** Indian Ocean
7E4 **Maldon** England
74F4 **Maldonado** Uruguay
42C4 **Malegaon** India
18D3 **Malé Karpaty** *Upland* Slovakia
33F2 **Malekula** *I* Vanuatu
51D5 **Malema** Mozambique
20F3 **Malen'ga** Russian Federation
13B3 **Malesherbes** France
42B2 **Mālestān** Afghanistan
12H5 **Malgomaj** *L* Sweden
20B3 **Malgomaj** *R* Sweden
50C2 **Malha** *Well* Sudan
58C2 **Malheur L** USA
48B3 **Mali** *Republic* Africa
30B3 **Mali Kyun** *I* Burma
19F2 **Malin** Ukraine
27E6 **Malinau** Indonesia
50E4 **Malindi** Kenya
Malines = Mechelen
10B2 **Malin Head** *Pt* Irish Republic
42D4 **Malkāpur** India
17F2 **Malkara** Turkey
17F2 **Malko Tŭrnovo** Bulgaria
8C3 **Mallaig** Scotland
49F2 **Mallawi** Egypt
Mallorca *I* **= Majorca**
12G6 **Malm** Norway
12J5 **Malmberget** Sweden
13D2 **Malmédy** Germany
7C4 **Malmesbury** England
47B3 **Malmesbury** South Africa
12G7 **Malmö** Sweden
20J4 **Malmyzh** Russian Federation
65E2 **Malone** USA
47D2 **Maloti Mts** Lesotho
12F6 **Måloy** Norway
20J2 **Malozemel'skaya Tundra** *Plain* Russian Federation
71B3 **Malpelo** *I* Colombia
42D3 **Mālpura** India
58D2 **Malta** Idaho, USA
56C2 **Malta** Montana, USA
16C3 **Malta** *I and Republic* Medit Sea
16C3 **Malta Chan** Italy/Malta
47B1 **Maltahöhe** Namibia
6D2 **Malton** England
45D2 **Ma'lūlā, Jabal** *Mt* Syria
12G6 **Malung** Sweden
44A2 **Mālvan** India
63D2 **Malvern** USA
47E1 **Malvérnia** Mozambique
Malvinas, Islas = Falkland Islands
42D4 **Malwa Plat** India
25Q2 **Malyy Lyakhovskiy, Ostrov** *I* Russian Federation
25M2 **Malyy Taymyr, Ostrov** *I* Russian Federation
21H6 **Malyy Uzen'** *R* Kazakhstan
25N4 **Mama** Russian Federation
20J4 **Mamadysh** Russian Federation
50C3 **Mambasa** Zaïre
32C1 **Mamberamo** *R* Australia
27G7 **Mamberamo** *R* Indonesia
50B3 **Mambéré** *R* Central African Republic
48C4 **Mamfé** Cameroon
59D4 **Mammoth** USA
64B3 **Mammoth Cave Nat Pk** USA
66C2 **Mammoth Pool Res** USA
72E6 **Mamoré** *R* Bolivia/Brazil
48A3 **Mamou** Guinea
51E5 **Mampikony** Madagascar
48B4 **Mampong** Ghana
45C3 **Mamshit** *Hist Site* Israel
27E7 **Mamuju** Indonesia
47C1 **Mamuno** Botswana
48B4 **Man** Ivory Coast
66E5 **Mana** Hawaiian Islands
51E6 **Manabo** Madagascar
72F4 **Manacapuru** Brazil
15C2 **Manacor** Spain
27F6 **Manado** Indonesia
72A1 **Managua** Nicaragua
70D3 **Managua, L de** Nicaragua
51E6 **Manakara** Madagascar
32D1 **Manam** *I* Papua New Guinea
51E5 **Mananara** Madagascar
51E6 **Mananjary** Madagascar
35A3 **Manapouri** New Zealand
35A3 **Manapouri,L** New Zealand
39G1 **Manas** China
43G3 **Manas** *R* Bhutan
24K5 **Manas Hu** *L* China
43E3 **Manaslu** *Mt* Nepal
68C2 **Manasquan** USA
73G4 **Manaus** Brazil
21E8 **Manavgat** Turkey
40C2 **Manbij** Syria
6B2 **Man,Calf of** *I* Isle of Man, British Islands
64B2 **Mancelona** USA
44B2 **Mancherāl** India
65E2 **Manchester** Connecticut, USA
7C3 **Manchester** England
64C3 **Manchester** Kentucky, USA
57F2 **Manchester** New Hampshire, USA
68B2 **Manchester** Pennsylvania, USA
67A1 **Manchester** Tennessee, USA
68D1 **Manchester** Vermont, USA
26F2 **Manchuria** *Division* China
41F4 **Mand** *R* Iran
51D5 **Manda** Tanzania
75B3 **Mandaguari** Brazil
12F7 **Mandal** Norway
27G7 **Mandala, Peak** *Mt* Indonesia
30B1 **Mandalay** Burma
26D2 **Mandalgovĭ** Mongolia
56C2 **Mandan** USA
50E3 **Mandera** Ethiopia
69H1 **Mandeville** Jamaica
42D2 **Mandi** India
51D5 **Mandimba** Mozambique
75A2 **Mandiore, Lagoa** Brazil
43E4 **Mandla** India
51E5 **Mandritsara** Madagascar
42D4 **Mandsaur** India
17D2 **Manduria** Italy
42B4 **Māndvi** India
44B3 **Mandya** India
43E4 **Manendragarh** India
19F2 **Manevichi** Ukraine
40B4 **Manfalût** Egypt
16D2 **Manfredonia** Italy
75D1 **Manga** Brazil
50B2 **Manga** *Desert Region* Niger
35C1 **Mangakino** New Zealand
17F2 **Mangalia** Romania
50C2 **Mangalmé** Chad
44A3 **Mangalore** India
43H4 **Mangin Range** *Mts* Burma
26C3 **Mangnai** China
48C3 **Mango** Togo
51D5 **Mangoche** Malawi
51E6 **Mangoky** *R* Madagascar
27F7 **Mangole** *I* Indonesia
42B4 **Māngral** India
75B4 **Mangueirinha** Brazil
25O4 **Mangui** China
62C2 **Mangum** USA
21J7 **Mangyshlak, Poluostrov** *Pen* Kazakhstan
56D3 **Manhattan** USA
47E2 **Manhica** Mozambique
73K8 **Manhuacu** Brazil
51E5 **Mania** *R* Madagascar
51D5 **Manica** Mozambique
55M5 **Manicouagan** *R* Canada
55M5 **Manicouagan, Réservoir** Canada
41E4 **Manifah** Saudi Arabia
27F5 **Manila** Philippines
58E2 **Manila** USA
34D2 **Manilla** Australia
48B3 **Maninian** Ivory Coast
43G4 **Manipur** *R* Burma/India
43G4 **Manipur** *State* India
21D8 **Manisa** Turkey
10C3 **Man,Isle of** Irish Sea
64B2 **Manistee** USA
64B2 **Manistee** *R* USA
64B1 **Manistique** USA
54J4 **Manitoba** *Province* Canada
54J4 **Manitoba,L** Canada
60D1 **Manitou** Canada
64B1 **Manitou Is** USA
55K5 **Manitoulin** *I* Canada
60C3 **Manitou Springs** USA
64C1 **Manitowik L** Canada
64B2 **Manitowoc** USA
65D1 **Maniwaki** Canada
72C2 **Manizales** Colombia
51E6 **Manja** Madagascar
32A4 **Manjimup** Australia
44B2 **Mānjra** *R* India
57D2 **Mankato** USA
48B4 **Mankono** Ivory Coast
35B1 **Manly** New Zealand
42C4 **Manmād** India
34A2 **Mannahill** Australia
44B4 **Mannar** Sri Lanka
44B4 **Mannār,G of** India
44B3 **Mannārgudi** India
18B3 **Mannheim** Germany
67B2 **Manning** USA
34A2 **Mannum** Australia
48A4 **Mano** Sierra Leone
32C1 **Manokwari** Indonesia
51C4 **Manono** Zaïre
30B3 **Manoron** Burma
55L4 **Manouane, Lac** Canada
29C3 **Mano-wan** *B* Japan
28B2 **Manp'o** N Korea
42D2 **Mānsa** India
51C5 **Mansa** Zambia
55K3 **Mansel I** Canada
63D1 **Mansfield** Arkansas, USA
34C3 **Mansfield** Australia
7D3 **Mansfield** England
63D2 **Mansfield** Louisiana, USA
68E1 **Mansfield** Massachusetts, USA
57E2 **Mansfield** Ohio, USA
65D2 **Mansfield** Pennsylvania, USA
75B2 **Manso** *R* Brazil
27H5 **Mansyu Deep** Pacific Ocean
72B4 **Manta** Ecuador
28A2 **Mantap-san** *Mt* N Korea
72C6 **Mantaro** *R* Peru
66B2 **Manteca** USA
67C1 **Manteo** USA
14C2 **Mantes** France
59D3 **Manti** USA
75C3 **Mantiqueira, Serra da** *Mts* Brazil
16C1 **Mantova** Italy
12J6 **Mäntta** Finland
Mantua = Mantova
20G4 **Manturovo** Russian Federation
62B3 **Manuel Benavides** Mexico
75B3 **Manuel Ribas** Brazil
27F6 **Manukan** Philippines
33G4 **Manukau** New Zealand
27H7 **Manus** *I* Pacific Ocean
15B2 **Manzanares** Spain
70E2 **Manzanillo** Cuba
70B3 **Manzanillo** Mexico
25N5 **Manzhouli** China
45D3 **Manzil** Jordan
51D6 **Manzini** Swaziland
50B2 **Mao** Chad
27G7 **Maoke, Pegunungan** *Mts* Indonesia
31A2 **Maomao Shan** *Mt* China
31C5 **Maoming** China
51D6 **Mapai** Mozambique
43E2 **Mapam Yumco** *L* China
27G6 **Mapia** *Is* Pacific Ocean
27E6 **Mapin** *I* Philippines
54H5 **Maple Creek** Canada
47E1 **Mapulanguene** Mozambique
47E2 **Maputo** Mozambique
47E2 **Maputo** *R* Mozambique
47E2 **Maputo, Baia de** *B* Mozambique
Ma Qu = Huang He
31A3 **Maqu** China
43F3 **Maquan He** *R* China
50B4 **Maquela do Zombo** Angola
74C6 **Maquinchao** Argentina
73J5 **Marabá** Brazil
72D1 **Maracaibo** Venezuela
72D2 **Maracaibo, Lago de** Venezuela
73H3 **Maracá, Ilha de** *I* Brazil
75A3 **Maracaju** Brazil
75A3 **Maracaju, Serra de** *Mts* Brazil
75D1 **Máracás** Brazil
72E1 **Maracay** Venezuela
49D2 **Marādah** Libya
48C3 **Maradi** Niger
21H8 **Marāgheh** Iran
73J4 **Marajó, Baia de** *B* Brazil
73H4 **Marajó, Ilha de** *I* Brazil
28E5 **Marakech** Morocco
50D3 **Maralal** Kenya
33F1 **Maramasike** *I* Solomon Islands
Maramba = Livingstone
59D4 **Marana** USA
21H8 **Marand** Iran
75C1 **Maranhão** *R* Brazil
73J4 **Maranhão** *State* Brazil
34C1 **Maranoa** *R* Australia
72C4 **Marañón** *R* Peru
21F8 **Maras** Turkey
55K5 **Marathon** Canada
67B4 **Marathon** Florida, USA
68B1 **Marathon** New York, USA
62B2 **Marathon** Texas, USA
75E1 **Maraú** Brazil
27F6 **Marawi** Philippines
15B2 **Marbella** Spain
32A3 **Marble Bar** Australia
59D3 **Marble Canyon** USA
47D2 **Marble Hall** South Africa
68E1 **Marblehead** USA
18B2 **Marburg** Germany
Mar Cantabrico = Biscay, B of
51B5 **Marca, Punta da** *Pt* Angola
18B2 **Marche** Belgium
13C2 **Marche-en-Famenne** Belgium
15A2 **Marchena** Spain
74D4 **Mar Chiquita, Lagoa** *L* Argentina
67B3 **Marco** USA
65E2 **Marcy,Mt** USA
42C2 **Mardan** Pakistan
74E5 **Mar del Plata** Argentina
21G8 **Mardin** Turkey
33F3 **Maré** *I* New Caledonia
50D2 **Mareb** *R* Eritrea/Ethiopia
27H8 **Mareeba** Australia
8C3 **Maree, Loch** *L* Scotland
50E3 **Mareeq** Somalia
62B2 **Marfa** USA
68C1 **Margaretville** USA
69E4 **Margarita, Isla** Venezuela
72F1 **Margarita, Islas de** Venezuela
29C2 **Margaritovo** Russian Federation
7E4 **Margate** England
17E1 **Marghita** Romania
34C4 **Maria I** Australia
27H5 **Marianas** *Is* Pacific Ocean
36J4 **Mariana Trench** Pacific Ocean
43G3 **Mariāni** India
63D2 **Marianna** Arkansas, USA
67A2 **Marianna** Florida, USA
72B2 **Mariato, Puerta** Panama
57G4 **Maria Van Diemen,C** New Zealand
18D3 **Mariazell** Austria
16D1 **Maribor** Slovenia
47D1 **Marico** *R* Botswana/ South Africa
66C3 **Maricopa** USA
50C3 **Maridi** Sudan
76F5 **Marie Byrd Land** *Region* Antarctica
69E3 **Marie Galante** *I* Caribbean Sea
12H6 **Mariehamn** Finland
13C2 **Mariembourg** Belgium
73H2 **Marienburg** Surinam
47B1 **Mariental** Namibia
12G7 **Mariestad** Sweden
67B2 **Marietta** Georgia, USA
64C3 **Marietta** Ohio, USA
63C2 **Marietta** Oklahoma, USA
69Q2 **Marigot** Dominica
74G2 **Marilia** Brazil
20C5 **Marijampole** Lithuania
51B4 **Marimba** Angola
57E2 **Marinette** USA
74F2 **Maringá** Brazil
50C3 **Maringa** *R* Zaïre
63D1 **Marion** Arkansas, USA
64B3 **Marion** Illinois, USA
57E2 **Marion** Indiana, USA
57E2 **Marion** Ohio, USA
67C2 **Marion** S Carolina, USA
57E3 **Marion,L** USA
33E2 **Marion Reef** Australia
59C3 **Mariposa** USA
66B2 **Mariposa** *R* USA
66B2 **Mariposa Res** USA
20H4 **Mari Republic** Russian Federation
21D7 **Marista** *R* Bulgaria
21F6 **Mariupol'** Ukraine
45C2 **Marjayoun** Lebanon
19F2 **Marjina Gorki** Belarus
45C3 **Marka** Jordan
50E3 **Marka** Somalia
18C1 **Markaryd** Sweden
7C3 **Market Drayton** England
7D3 **Market Harborough** England
6D3 **Market Weighton** England
76E7 **Markham,Mt** Antarctica
66C1 **Markleeville** USA
25T3 **Markovo** Russian Federation
68E1 **Marlboro** Massachusetts, USA
68D1 **Marlboro** New Hampshire, USA
32D3 **Marlborough** Australia
7D4 **Marlborough** England
13B3 **Marle** France
63C2 **Marlin** USA
68D1 **Marlow** USA
14C3 **Marmande** France
17F2 **Marmara Adasi** *I* Turkey
40A1 **Marmara,S of** Turkey
17F3 **Marmaris** Turkey
60C1 **Marmarth** USA
64C3 **Marmet** USA
61E1 **Marmion L** Canada
16C1 **Marmolada** *Mt* Italy
13C3 **Marne** *Department* France
13B3 **Marne** *R* France
50B3 **Maro** Chad
51E5 **Maroantsetra** Madagascar
51D5 **Marondera** Zimbabwe
73H3 **Maroni** *R* French Guiana
34D1 **Maroochydore** Australia
50B2 **Maroua** Cameroon
51E5 **Marovoay** Madagascar
57E4 **Marquesas Keys** *Is* USA
57E2 **Marquette** USA
37N5 **Marquises, Îles** Pacific Ocean
34C2 **Marra** *R* Australia
47E2 **Marracuene** Mozambique
50C2 **Marra, Jebel** *Mt* Sudan
48B1 **Marrakech** Morocco
32C3 **Marree** Australia
63D3 **Marrero** USA
51D5 **Marromeu** Mozambique
51D5 **Marrupa** Mozambique
40B4 **Marsa Alam** Egypt
50D3 **Marsabit** Kenya
16C3 **Marsala** Sicily, Italy
13E2 **Marsberg** Germany
14D3 **Marseilles** France
75D3 **Mar, Serra do** *Mts* Brazil
64B3 **Marshall** Illinois, USA
64C2 **Marshall** Michigan, USA
61D2 **Marshall** Minnesota, USA
61E3 **Marshall** Missouri, USA

57D3 **Marshall** Texas, USA
68B3 **Marshall** Virginia, USA
37K4 **Marshall Is** Pacific Ocean
61E2 **Marshalltown** USA
63D1 **Marshfield** Missouri, USA
64A2 **Marshfield** Wisconsin, USA
69B1 **Marsh Harbour** The Bahamas
63D3 **Marsh I** USA
30B2 **Martaban,G of** Burma
65E2 **Martha's Vineyard** *I* USA
14D2 **Martigny** Switzerland
14D3 **Martigues** France
19D3 **Martin** Slovakia
60C2 **Martin** S Dakota, USA
63E1 **Martin** Tennessee, USA
35C2 **Martinborough** New Zealand
69E4 **Martinique** *I* Caribbean Sea
67A2 **Martin,L** USA
65D3 **Martinsburg** USA
64C2 **Martins Ferry** USA
65D3 **Martinsville** USA
52G6 **Martin Vaz** *I* Atlantic Ocean
35C2 **Marton** New Zealand
15B2 **Martos** Spain
54G3 **Martre, Lac la** Canada
42B2 **Maruf** Afghanistan
29B4 **Marugame** Japan
59D3 **Marvine,Mt** USA
42C3 **Mārwār** India
24H6 **Mary** Turkmenistan
33E3 **Maryborough** Queensland, Australia
34B3 **Maryborough** Victoria, Australia
54F4 **Mary Henry,Mt** Canada
57F3 **Maryland** *State* USA
6C2 **Maryport** England
59B3 **Marysville** California, USA
61D3 **Marysville** Kansas, USA
58B1 **Marysville** Washington, USA
57D2 **Maryville** Iowa, USA
61D2 **Maryville** Missouri, USA
67B1 **Maryville** Tennessee, USA
49D2 **Marzuq** Libya
45A3 **Masabb Dumyât** *C* Egypt
Masada = Mezada
45C2 **Mas'adah** Syria
50D4 **Masai Steppe** *Upland* Tanzania
50D4 **Masaka** Uganda
41E2 **Masally** Azerbaijan
28B3 **Masan** S Korea
51D5 **Masasi** Tanzania
70D3 **Masaya** Nicaragua
27F5 **Masbate** Philippines
27F5 **Masbate** *I* Philippines
15C2 **Mascara** Algeria
36D5 **Mascarene Ridge** Indian Ocean
75E2 **Mascote** Brazil
47D2 **Maseru** Lesotho
42B2 **Mashaki** Afghanistan
41G2 **Mashhad** Iran
50B4 **Masi-Manimba** Zaïre
50D3 **Masindi** Uganda
38D3 **Maşīrah** *I* Oman
50C4 **Masisi** Zaïre
41E3 **Masjed Soleyman** Iran
51F5 **Masoala, C** Madagascar
66C1 **Mason** Nevada, USA
62C2 **Mason** Texas, USA
57D2 **Mason City** USA
Masqat = Muscat
16C2 **Massa** Italy
57F2 **Massachusetts** *State* USA
65E2 **Massachusetts B** USA
50B2 **Massakori** Chad
51D6 **Massangena** Mozambique
50D2 **Massawa** Eritrea
65E2 **Massena** USA
50B2 **Massénya** Chad
64C1 **Massey** Canada
14C2 **Massif Central** *Mts* France
51E6 **Massif de l'Isalo** *Upland* Madagascar
51E5 **Massif du Tsaratanana** *Mts* Madagascar
64C2 **Massillon** USA
48B3 **Massina** *Region* Mali
51D6 **Massinga** Mozambique
47E1 **Massingir** Mozambique
21J6 **Masteksay** Kazakhstan
33G5 **Masterton** New Zealand
28C4 **Masuda** Japan
50B4 **Masuku** Gabon
40C2 **Maşyāf** Syria
64C1 **Matachewan** Canada
62A3 **Matachie** Mexico
50B4 **Matadi** Zaïre
72A1 **Matagalpa** Nicaragua
55L5 **Matagami** Canada
56D4 **Matagorda B** USA
63C3 **Matagorda I** USA
35C1 **Matakana I** New Zealand
51B5 **Matala** Angola
44C4 **Matale** Sri Lanka
48A3 **Matam** Senegal
48C3 **Matameye** Niger
70C2 **Matamoros** Mexico
49E2 **Ma'tan as Sarra** *Well* Libya
55M5 **Matane** Canada
70D2 **Matanzas** Cuba
65F1 **Matapedia** *R* Canada
44C4 **Matara** Sri Lanka
32A1 **Mataram** Indonesia
72D7 **Matarani** Peru
75E1 **Mataripe** Brazil
15C1 **Mataró** Spain
47D3 **Matatiele** South Africa
35A3 **Mataura** New Zealand
70B2 **Matehuala** Mexico
69L1 **Matelot** Trinidad
16D2 **Matera** Italy
19E3 **Mátészalka** Hungary
16B3 **Mateur** Tunisia
66C2 **Mather** USA
64C1 **Matheson** Canada
63C3 **Mathis** USA
42D3 **Mathura** India
7D3 **Matlock** England
73G6 **Mato Grosso** *State* Brazil
73G7 **Mato Grosso do Sul** *State* Brazil
47E2 **Matola** Mozambique
49E1 **Matrûh** Egypt
28C3 **Matsue** Japan
29E2 **Matsumae** Japan
29D3 **Matsumoto** Japan
29D4 **Matsusaka** Japan
28C4 **Matsuyama** Japan
55K5 **Mattagami** *R* Canada
65D1 **Mattawa** Canada
16B1 **Matterhorn** *Mt* Italy/Switzerland
58C2 **Matterhorn** *Mt* USA
69C2 **Matthew Town** The Bahamas
68D2 **Mattituck** USA
64B3 **Mattoon** USA
42B2 **Matun** Afghanistan
69L1 **Matura B** Trinidad
72F2 **Maturín** Venezuela
43E3 **Mau** India
51D5 **Maúa** Mozambique
14C1 **Maubeuge** France
34B2 **Maude** Australia
52J8 **Maud Seamount** Atlantic Ocean
26H4 **Maug Is** Marianas
66E5 **Maui** *I* Hawaiian Islands
64C2 **Maumee** USA
64C2 **Maumee** *R* USA
51C5 **Maun** Botswana
66E5 **Mauna Kea** *Vol* Hawaiian Islands
66E5 **Mauna Loa** *Vol* Hawaiian Islands
54F3 **Maunoir,L** Canada
14C2 **Mauriac** France
48A2 **Mauritania** *Republic* Africa
46K10 **Mauritius** *I* Indian Ocean
64A2 **Mauston** USA
51C5 **Mavinga** Angola
47E1 **Mavue** Mozambique
43G4 **Mawlaik** Burma
Mawlamyine = Moulmein
76G10 **Mawson** *Base* Antarctica
60C1 **Max** USA
47E1 **Maxaila** Mozambique
27D7 **Maya** *I* Indonesia
25P4 **Maya** *R* Russian Federation
40D2 **Mayādīn** Syria
57F4 **Mayaguana** *I* The Bahamas
69D3 **Mayagüez** Puerto Rico
48C3 **Mayahi** Niger
50B4 **Mayama** Congo
41G2 **Mayamey** Iran
8C4 **Maybole** Scotland
57F3 **May,C** USA
34C4 **Maydena** Australia
13D2 **Mayen** Germany
14B2 **Mayenne** France
59D4 **Mayer** USA
64B3 **Mayfield** USA
62A2 **Mayhill** USA
21G7 **Maykop** Russian Federation
30B1 **Maymyo** Burma
54E3 **Mayo** Canada
68B3 **Mayo** USA
15C2 **Mayor** *Mt* Spain
35C1 **Mayor I** New Zealand
74D1 **Mayor P Lagerenza** Paraguay
51E5 **Mayotte** *I* Indian Ocean
69H2 **May Pen** Jamaica
68C3 **May Point,C** USA
68C3 **Mays Landing** USA
64C3 **Maysville** USA
50B4 **Mayumba** Gabon
61D1 **Mayville** USA
60C2 **Maywood** USA
51C5 **Mazabuka** Zambia
42D1 **Mazar** China
45C3 **Mazār** Jordan
16C3 **Mazara del Vallo** Sicily, Italy
42B1 **Mazar-i-Sharif** Afghanistan
15B2 **Mazarrón, Golfo de** *G* Spain
70B2 **Mazatlán** Mexico
20C4 **Mazeikiai** Lithuania
45C3 **Mazra** Jordan
51D6 **Mbabane** Swaziland
50B3 **Mbaïki** Central African Republic
51D4 **Mbala** Zambia
51C6 **Mbalabala** Zimbabwe
50D3 **Mbale** Uganda
50B3 **Mbalmayo** Cameroon
50B3 **Mbam** *R* Cameroon
51D5 **Mbamba Bay** Tanzania
50B3 **Mbandaka** Zaïre
50B4 **Mbanza Congo** Angola
50B4 **Mbanza-Ngungu** Zaïre
50D4 **Mbarara** Uganda
50C3 **M'Bari,R** Central African Republic
50B3 **Mbèndza** Congo
50B3 **Mbére** *R* Cameroon/Central African Republic/Chad
51D4 **Mbeya** Tanzania
50B4 **Mbinda** Congo
48A3 **Mbout** Mauritius
50C4 **Mbuji-Mayi** Zaïre
50D4 **Mbulu** Tanzania
48B2 **Mcherrah** *Region* Algeria
51D5 **Mchinji** Malawi
30D3 **Mdrak** Vietnam
62B1 **Meade** USA
56B3 **Mead,L** USA
54H4 **Meadow Lake** Canada
64C2 **Meadville** USA
29D2 **Me-akan dake** *Mt* Japan
55N4 **Mealy Mts** Canada
34C1 **Meandarra** Australia
54G4 **Meander River** Canada
9C3 **Meath** Irish Republic
14C2 **Meaux** France
50E1 **Mecca** Saudi Arabia
59C4 **Mecca** USA
68D1 **Mechanicville** USA
24G2 **Mechdusharskiy, O** *I* Russian Federation
18A2 **Mechelen** Belgium
48B1 **Mecheria** Algeria
18C2 **Meckenburg-Vorpommern** *State* Germany
18C2 **Mecklenburger Bucht** *B* Germany
51D5 **Meconta** Mozambique
51D5 **Mecuburi** Mozambique
51E5 **Mecufi** Mozambique
51D5 **Mecula** Mozambique
27C6 **Medan** Indonesia
74C7 **Médanosa, Puerta** *Pt* Argentina
15C2 **Médéa** Algeria
72C2 **Medellín** Colombia
13C1 **Medemblik** Netherlands
48D1 **Medenine** Tunisia
56A2 **Medford** USA
17F2 **Medgidia** Romania
17E1 **Mediaş** Romania
58C1 **Medical Lake** USA
60B2 **Medicine Bow** USA
60B2 **Medicine Bow Mts** USA
60B2 **Medicine Bow Peak** *Mt* USA
54G5 **Medicine Hat** Canada
62C1 **Medicine Lodge** USA
75D2 **Medina** Brazil
60D1 **Medina** N Dakota, USA
68A1 **Medina** New York, USA
40C5 **Medina** Saudi Arabia
15B1 **Medinaceli** Spain
15A1 **Medina del Campo** Spain
15A1 **Medina de Rioseco** Spain
62C3 **Medina L** USA
43F4 **Medinīpur** India
46E4 **Mediterranean S** Europe
16B3 **Medjerda** *R* Algeria/Tunisia
16B3 **Medjerda, Mts de la** Algeria/Tunisia
21K5 **Mednogorsk** Russian Federation
25S4 **Mednyy, Ostrov** *I* Russian Federation
43H3 **Mêdog** China
50B3 **Medouneu** Gabon
21G5 **Medvedista** *R* Russian Federation
25S2 **Medvezh'i Ova** *Is* Russian Federation
20E3 **Medvezh'yegorsk** Russian Federation
32A3 **Meekatharra** Australia
60B2 **Meeker** USA
42D3 **Meerut** India
58E2 **Meeteetse** USA
50D3 **Mēga** Ethiopia
17E3 **Megalópolis** Greece
17E3 **Mégara** Greece
43G3 **Meghālaya** *State* India
43G4 **Meghna** *R* Bangladesh
45C2 **Megiddo** *Hist Site* Israel
42D4 **Mehekar** India
43M2 **Mehndawal** India
41F4 **Mehrān** *R* Iran
41F3 **Mehriz** Iran
75C2 **Meia Ponte** *R* Brazil
50B3 **Meiganga** Cameroon
30B1 **Meiktila** Burma
31A4 **Meishan** China
18C2 **Meissen** Germany
31D5 **Mei Xian** China
31D5 **Meizhou** China
72D8 **Mejillones** Chile
50B3 **Mekambo** Gabon
50D2 **Mek'elē** Ethiopia
48B1 **Meknès** Morocco
30D3 **Mekong** *R* Cambodia
30D4 **Mekong, Mouths of the** Vietnam
48C3 **Mekrou** *R* Benin
30C5 **Melaka** Malaysia
36J5 **Melanesia** *Region* Pacific Ocean
32D4 **Melbourne** Australia
57E4 **Melbourne** USA
56C4 **Melchor Múzquiz** Mexico
20K5 **Meleuz** Russian Federation
50B2 **Melfi** Chad
54H4 **Melfort** Canada
15B2 **Melilla** NW Africa
74B6 **Melimoyu** *Mt* Chile
60C1 **Melita** Canada
21F6 **Melitopol'** Ukraine
50D3 **Melka Guba** Ethiopia
13E1 **Melle** Germany
16B3 **Mellégue** *R* Algeria/Tunisia
47E2 **Melmoth** South Africa
74F4 **Melo** Uruguay
75A3 **Melo** *R* Brazil
66B2 **Melones Res** USA
8D4 **Melrose** Scotland
61E1 **Melrose** USA
7D3 **Melton Mowbray** England
14C2 **Melun** France
54H4 **Melville** Canada
55M2 **Melville Bugt** *B* Greenland
69Q2 **Melville,C** Dominica
54F3 **Melville Hills** Canada
32C2 **Melville I** Australia
54G2 **Melville I** Canada
55N4 **Melville,L** Canada
55K3 **Melville Pen** Canada
51E5 **Memba** Mozambique
32A1 **Memboro** Indonesia
18C3 **Memmingen** Germany
57E3 **Memphis** Tennessee, USA
62B2 **Memphis** Texas, USA
63D2 **Mena** USA
19G2 **Mena** Ukraine
7B3 **Menai Str** Wales
48C3 **Ménaka** Mali
64B2 **Menasha** USA
27E7 **Mendawai** *R* Indonesia
14C3 **Mende** France
50D3 **Mendebo Mts** Ethiopia
32D1 **Mendi** Papua New Guinea
7C4 **Mendip Hills** *Upland* England
58B2 **Mendocino,C** USA
37M3 **Mendocino Seascarp** Pacific Ocean
66B2 **Mendota** California, USA
64B2 **Mendota** Illinois, USA
74C4 **Mendoza** Argentina
74C5 **Mendoza** *State* Argentina
17F3 **Menemen** Turkey
13B2 **Menen** Belgium
31D3 **Mengcheng** China
30B1 **Menghai** China
31A5 **Mengla** China
30B1 **Menglian** China
31A5 **Mengzi** China
32D4 **Menindee** Australia
34B2 **Menindee L** Australia
34A3 **Meningie** Australia
64B1 **Menominee** USA
64B2 **Menomonee Falls** USA
64A2 **Menomonie** USA
51B5 **Menongue** Angola
Menorca *I* **= Minorca**
27C7 **Mentawi, Kepulauan** *Is* Indonesia
62A1 **Mentmore** USA
27D7 **Mentok** Indonesia
64C2 **Mentor** USA
27E6 **Menyapa** *Mt* Indonesia
31A2 **Menyuan** China
16B3 **Menzel** Tunisia
20J4 **Menzelinsk** Russian Federation
13D1 **Meppel** Netherlands
18B2 **Meppen** Germany
15B1 **Mequinenza, Embalse de** *Res* Spain
63D1 **Meramec** *R* USA
16C1 **Merano** Italy
27E7 **Meratus, Pegunungan** *Mts* Indonesia
32D1 **Merauke** Indonesia
56A3 **Merced** USA
66B2 **Merced** *R* USA
74B4 **Mercedario** *Mt* Argentina
74E4 **Mercedes** Buenos Aires, Argentina
74E3 **Mercedes** Corrientes, Argentina
74C4 **Mercedes** San Luis, Argentina
74E4 **Mercedes** Uruguay
35C1 **Mercury B** New Zealand
35C1 **Mercury Is** New Zealand
54F2 **Mercy B** Canada
55M3 **Mercy,C** Canada
62B1 **Meredith,L** USA
30B3 **Mergui** Burma
30B3 **Mergui Arch** Burma
70D2 **Mérida** Mexico
15A2 **Mérida** Spain
72D2 **Mérida** Venezuela
72D2 **Mérida, Cordillera de** Venezuela
57E3 **Meridian** USA
34C3 **Merimbula** Australia
34B2 **Meringur** Australia
27G6 **Merir** *I* Pacific Ocean
62B2 **Merkel** USA
50D2 **Merowe** Sudan
32A4 **Merredin** Australia
8C4 **Merrick** *Mt* Scotland
64B1 **Merrill** USA
64B2 **Merrillville** USA
68E1 **Merrimack** *R* USA
60C2 **Merriman** USA
67B3 **Merritt Island** USA
34D2 **Merriwa** Australia
50E3 **Mersa Fatma** Eritrea
7E4 **Mersea** *I* England
15B2 **Mers el Kebir** Algeria
7C3 **Mersey** *R* England
7C3 **Merseyside** *Metropolitan County* England
21E8 **Mersin** Turkey
30C5 **Mersing** Malaysia
42C3 **Merta** India
7C4 **Merthyr Tydfil** Wales
15A2 **Mertola** Portugal
13B3 **Méru** France
50D4 **Meru** *Mt* Tanzania
21F7 **Merzifon** Turkey
13D3 **Merzig** Germany
56B3 **Mesa** USA
62A1 **Mesa Verde Nat Pk** USA
13E2 **Meschede** Germany
40D1 **Mescit Dağ** *Mt* Turkey
50C3 **Meshra'er Req** Sudan
17E3 **Mesolóngion** Greece
59D3 **Mesquite** Nevada, USA
63C2 **Mesquite** Texas, USA
51D5 **Messalo** *R* Mozambique
47D1 **Messina** South Africa
16D3 **Messina** Sicily, Italy
16D3 **Messina, Stretto de** *Str* Italy/Sicily
17E3 **Messini** Greece
17E3 **Messiniakós Kólpos** *G* Greece
Mesta *R* **= Néstos**
17E2 **Mesta** *R* Bulgaria
16C1 **Mestre** Italy
72D3 **Meta** *R* Colombia/Venezuela
20E4 **Meta** *R* Russian Federation
55M3 **Meta Incognita Pen** Canada
63D3 **Metairie** USA
58C1 **Metaline Falls** USA
74D3 **Metán** Argentina
51D5 **Metangula** Mozambique
16D2 **Metaponto** Italy
8D3 **Methil** Scotland
68E1 **Methuen** USA
35B2 **Methven** New Zealand
54E4 **Metlakatla** USA
64B3 **Metropolis** USA
44B3 **Mettūr** India
14D2 **Metz** France
27C6 **Meulaboh** Indonesia
13D3 **Meurthe** *R* France
13D3 **Meurthe-et-Moselle** *Department* France
13C3 **Meuse** *Department* France
13C2 **Meuse** *R* Belgium
14D2 **Meuse** *R* France
7D3 **Mexborough** England
63C2 **Mexia** USA
70A1 **Mexicali** Mexico
59E3 **Mexican Hat** USA
70C3 **México** Mexico
61E3 **Mexico** USA
70B2 **Mexico** *Federal Republic* Central America
70C2 **Mexico,G of** Central America
24H6 **Meymaneh** Afghanistan
45C3 **Mezada** *Hist Site* Israel

20G2 **Mezen'** Russian Federation
20H3 **Mezen'** *R* Russian Federation
14C3 **Mézenc, Mount** France
19G1 **Mezha** *R* Russian Federation
20J1 **Mezhdusharskiy, Ostrov** *I* Russian Federation
42D4 **Mhow** India
59D4 **Miami** Arizona, USA
57E4 **Miami** Florida, USA
63D1 **Miami** Oklahoma, USA
57E4 **Miami Beach** USA
21H8 **Miandowāb** Iran
51E5 **Miandrivazo** Madagascar
21H8 **Mīāneh** Iran
42C2 **Mianwali** Pakistan
31A3 **Mianyang** China
31C3 **Mianyang** China
31A3 **Mianzhu** China
31E2 **Miaodao Qundao** *Arch* China
31B4 **Miao Ling** *Upland* China
20L5 **Miass** Russian Federation
19E3 **Michalovce** Slovakia
58D1 **Michel** Canada
69D3 **Miches** Dominican Republic
57E2 **Michigan** *State* USA
64B2 **Michigan City** USA
57E2 **Michigan,L** USA
64C1 **Michipicoten** Canada
55K5 **Michipicoten I** Canada
17F2 **Michurin** Bulgaria
21G5 **Michurinsk** Russian Federation
36J4 **Micronesia, Fed. States of** *Is* Pacific Ocean
36J4 **Micronesia** *Region* Pacific Ocean
52F4 **Mid Atlantic Ridge** Atlantic Ocean
47C3 **Middelburg** Cape Province, South Africa
13B2 **Middelburg** Netherlands
47D2 **Middelburg** Transvaal, South Africa
58B2 **Middle Alkali L** USA
37O4 **Middle America Trench** Pacific Ocean
44E3 **Middle Andaman** *I* Indian Ocean
68E2 **Middleboro** USA
68B2 **Middleburg** Pennsylvania, USA
68B3 **Middleburg** Virginia, USA
68C1 **Middleburgh** USA
65E2 **Middlebury** USA
57E3 **Middlesboro** USA
6D2 **Middlesbrough** England
68D2 **Middletown** Connecticut, USA
68C3 **Middletown** Delaware, USA
65E2 **Middletown** New York, USA
64C3 **Middletown** Ohio, USA
68B2 **Middletown** Pennsylvania, USA
68C1 **Middleville** USA
7C3 **Middlewich** England
48B1 **Midelt** Morocco
7C4 **Mid Glamorgan** *County* Wales
50E2 **Mīdī** Yemen
36E5 **Mid Indian Basin** Indian Ocean
36E5 **Mid Indian Ridge** Indian Ocean
55L5 **Midland** Canada
64C2 **Midland** Michigan, USA
56C3 **Midland** Texas, USA
9B4 **Midleton** Irish Republic
51E6 **Midongy Atsimo** Madagascar
37K4 **Mid Pacific Mts** Pacific Ocean
58C2 **Midvale** USA
37L3 **Midway Is** Pacific Ocean
60B2 **Midwest** USA
63C1 **Midwest City** USA
40D2 **Midyat** Turkey
17E2 **Midžor** *Mt* Serbia, Yugoslavia
19E2 **Mielec** Poland
17F1 **Miercurea-Ciuc** Romania
15A1 **Mieres** Spain
68B2 **Mifflintown** USA
13B4 **Migennes** France
28B4 **Mihara** Japan
17E2 **Mikhaylovgrad** Bulgaria
21G5 **Mikhaylovka** Russian Federation
28C2 **Mikhaylovka** Russian Federation
24J4 **Mikhaylovskiy** Russian Federation
45C4 **Mikhrot Timna** Israel
12K6 **Mikkeli** Finland
17F3 **Míkonos** *I* Greece
18D3 **Mikulov** Czech Republic
51D4 **Mikumi** Tanzania
20J3 **Mikun** Russian Federation
29D3 **Mikuni-sammyaku** *Mts* Japan
29C4 **Mikura-jima** *I* Japan
61E1 **Milaca** USA
72C4 **Milagro** Ecuador
16B1 **Milan** Italy
63E1 **Milan** USA
51D5 **Milange** Mozambique
Milano = Milan
21D8 **Milas** Turkey
61D1 **Milbank** USA
32D4 **Mildura** Australia
31A5 **Mile** China
41D3 **Mileh Tharthār** *L* Iraq
32E3 **Miles** Australia
56C2 **Miles City** USA
16C2 **Miletto, Monte** *Mt* Italy
68D2 **Milford** Connecticut, USA
65D3 **Milford** Delaware, USA
61D2 **Milford** Nebraska, USA
68E1 **Milford** New Hampshire, USA
68C2 **Milford** Pennsylvania, USA
59D3 **Milford** Utah, USA
7B4 **Milford Haven** Wales
7B4 **Milford Haven** *Sd* Wales
61D3 **Milford L** USA
35A2 **Milford Sd** New Zealand
15C2 **Miliana** Algeria
54G4 **Milk** *R* Canada/USA
60B1 **Milk** *R* USA
25R4 **Mil'kovo** Russian Federation
50C2 **Milk, Wadi el** *Watercourse* Sudan
14C3 **Millau** France
68D2 **Millbrook** USA
67B2 **Milledgeville** USA
61E1 **Mille Lacs L** USA
61E1 **Mille Lacs, Lac des** Canada
60D2 **Miller** USA
21G6 **Millerovo** Russian Federation
68B2 **Millersburg** USA
68D1 **Millers Falls** USA
68D2 **Millerton** USA
66C2 **Millerton L** USA
65E2 **Millford** Massachusetts, USA
34B3 **Millicent** Australia
63E1 **Millington** USA
65F1 **Millinocket** USA
34D1 **Millmerran** Australia
6C2 **Millom** England
8C4 **Millport** Scotland
9B3 **Millstreet** Irish Republic
65F1 **Milltown** Canada
58D1 **Milltown** USA
66A2 **Mill Valley** USA
65E3 **Millville** USA
55Q2 **Milne Land** *I* Greenland
66E5 **Milolii** Hawaiian Islands
17E3 **Milos** *I* Greece
32D3 **Milparinka** Australia
68B2 **Milroy** USA
67A2 **Milton** Florida, USA
35A3 **Milton** New Zealand
68B2 **Milton** Pennsylvania, USA
7D3 **Milton Keynes** England
57E2 **Milwaukee** USA
29D2 **Mimmaya** Japan
66C1 **Mina** USA
15C2 **Mina** *R* Algeria
41E4 **Mīnā' al Aḥmadī** Kuwait
41G4 **Mīnāb** Iran
74E4 **Minas** Uruguay
73J7 **Minas Gerais** *State* Brazil
75D2 **Minas Novas** Brazil
70C3 **Minatitlán** Mexico
30A1 **Minbu** Burma
30A1 **Minbya** Burma
8B3 **Minch,Little** *Sd* Scotland
8B2 **Minch,North** *Sd* Scotland
10B2 **Minch,The** *Sd* Scotland
27F6 **Mindanao** *I* Philippines
63D2 **Minden** Louisiana, USA
66C1 **Minden** Nevada, USA
18B2 **Minden** Germany
34B2 **Mindona L** Australia
27F5 **Mindoro** *I* Philippines
27F5 **Mindoro Str** Philippines
7C4 **Minehead** England
73H7 **Mineiros** Brazil
63C2 **Mineola** USA
62C2 **Mineral Wells** USA
68B2 **Minersville** USA
34B2 **Mingary** Australia
21H7 **Mingechaurskoye Vodokhranilische** *Res* Azerbaijan
8B3 **Mingulay, I** Scotland
31A2 **Minhe** China
44A4 **Minicoy** *I* India
31D4 **Min Jiang** *R* Fujian, China
31A4 **Min Jiang** *R* Sichuan, China
66C2 **Minkler** USA
34A2 **Minlaton** Australia
31A2 **Minle** China
48C4 **Minna** Nigeria
57D2 **Minneapolis** USA
54J4 **Minnedosa** Canada
61D2 **Minnesota** *R* USA
57D2 **Minnesota** *State* USA
15A1 **Miño** *R* Spain
15C1 **Minorca** *I* Spain
56C2 **Minot** USA
31A2 **Minqin** China
31A3 **Min Shan** *Upland* China
20D5 **Minsk** Belarus
19E2 **Mińsk Mazowiecki** Poland
54G2 **Minto Inlet** *B* Canada
55L4 **Minto,L** Canada
60B3 **Minturn** USA
26C1 **Minusinsk** Russian Federation
31A3 **Min Xian** China
45A3 **Minya el Qamn** Egypt
55N5 **Miquelon** *I* France
66D3 **Mirage L** USA
40D3 **Mīrah, Wadi al** *Watercourse* Iraq/Saudi Arabia
44A2 **Miraj** India
74E5 **Miramar** Argentina
42B2 **Miram Shah** Pakistan
75A3 **Miranda** Brazil
75A2 **Miranda** *R* Brazil
15B1 **Miranda de Ebro** Spain
75B3 **Mirante, Serra do** *Mts* Brazil
42B2 **Mīr Bachchen Kūt** Afghanistan
13C3 **Mirecourt** France
27E6 **Miri** Malaysia
48A3 **Mirik,C** Mauritius
74F4 **Mirim, Lagoa** *L* Brazil/ Uruguay
25K3 **Mirnoye** Russian Federation
25N3 **Mirnyy** Russian Federation
76G9 **Mirnyy** *Base* Antarctica
19G3 **Mironovka** Ukraine
42C2 **Mirpur** Pakistan
42B3 **Mirpur Khas** Pakistan
17E3 **Mirtoan S** Greece
28B3 **Miryang** S Korea
43E3 **Mirzāpur** India
42C1 **Misgar** Pakistan
64B2 **Mishawaka** USA
28B4 **Mi-shima** *I* Japan
43H3 **Mishmi Hills** India
33E2 **Misima** *I* Papua New Guinea
74F3 **Misiones** *State* Argentina
19E3 **Miskolc** Hungary
45D2 **Mismīyah** Syria
27G7 **Misoöl** *I* Indonesia
49D1 **Misrātah** Libya
55K5 **Missinaibi** *R* Canada
64C1 **Missinaibi L** Canada
60C2 **Mission** S Dakota, USA
62C3 **Mission** Texas, USA
58B1 **Mission City** Canada
65D2 **Mississauga** Canada
57D3 **Mississippi** *R* USA
57D3 **Mississippi** *State* USA
63E3 **Mississippi Delta** USA
56B2 **Missoula** USA
48B1 **Missour** Morocco
57D3 **Missouri** *R* USA
57D3 **Missouri** *State* USA
61D2 **Missouri Valley** USA
57F1 **Mistassini,Lac** Canada
72D7 **Misti** *Mt* Peru
34C1 **Mitchell** Australia
56D2 **Mitchell** USA
32D2 **Mitchell** *R* Australia
57E3 **Mitchell,Mt** USA
27H8 **Mitchell River** Australia
45A3 **Mīt el Nasâra** Egypt
45A3 **Mīt Ghamr** Egypt
42C3 **Mithankot** Pakistan
17F3 **Mitilíni** Greece
45B3 **Mitla Pass** Egypt
29E3 **Mito** Japan
33G2 **Mitre** *I* Solomon Islands
Mits'iwa = Massawa
13D1 **Mittel Land Kanal** Germany
72D3 **Mitú** Colombia
51C4 **Mitumba, Chaine des** *Mts* Zaïre
50C4 **Mitumbar Mts** Zaïre
51C4 **Mitwaba** Zaïre
50B3 **Mitzic** Gabon
29C3 **Miura** Japan
31C3 **Mi Xian** China
26G3 **Miyake** *I* Japan
29C4 **Miyake-jima** *I* Japan
29E3 **Miyako** Japan
26F4 **Miyako** *I* Ryukyu Is, Japan
29C3 **Miyazu** Japan
28C4 **Miyoshi** Japan
31D1 **Miyun** China
31D1 **Miyun Shuiku** *Res* China
29D2 **Mi-zaki** *Pt* Japan
50D3 **Mīzan Teferī** Ethiopia
49D1 **Mizdah** Libya
17F1 **Mizil** Romania
43G4 **Mizo Hills** India
43G4 **Mizoram** *Union Territory* India
45C3 **Mizpe Ramon** Israel
29E3 **Mizusawa** Japan
12H7 **Mjölby** Sweden
51C5 **Mkushi** Zambia
47E2 **Mkuzi** South Africa
18C2 **Mladá Boleslav** Czech Republic
19E2 **Mława** Poland
17D2 **Mljet** *I* Croatia
47D2 **Mmabatho** South Africa
48A4 **Moa** *R* Sierra Leone
56C3 **Moab** USA
45C3 **Moab** *Region* Jordan
47E2 **Moamba** Mozambique
50B4 **Moanda** Congo
50B4 **Moanda** Gabon
9C3 **Moate** Irish Republic
51C4 **Moba** Zaïre
29D3 **Mobara** Japan
50C3 **Mobaye** Central African Republic
50C3 **Mobayi** Zaïre
57D3 **Moberly** USA
57E3 **Mobile** USA
57E3 **Mobile B** USA
63E2 **Mobile Pt** USA
56C2 **Mobridge** USA
51E5 **Moçambique** Mozambique
Moçâmedes = Namibe
30C1 **Moc Chau** Vietnam
Mocha = Al Mukhā
47D1 **Mochudi** Botswana
51E5 **Mocimboa da Praia** Mozambique
72C3 **Mocoa** Colombia
75C3 **Mococa** Brazil
51D5 **Mocuba** Mozambique
47D2 **Modder** *R* South Africa
16C2 **Modena** Italy
13D3 **Moder** *R* France
56A3 **Modesto** USA
66B2 **Modesto Res** USA
16C3 **Modica** Sicily,
18D3 **Mödling** Austria
8D4 **Moffat** Scotland
42D2 **Moga** India
50E3 **Mogadishu** Somalia
75C3 **Mogi das Cruzes** Brazil
19G2 **Mogilev** Belarus
21D6 **Mogilev Podol'skiy** Ukraine
75C3 **Mogi-Mirim** Brazil
51E5 **Mogincual** Mozambique
26E1 **Mogocha** Russian Federation
24K4 **Mogochin** Russian Federation
47D1 **Mogol** *R* South Africa
15A2 **Moguer** Spain
35C1 **Mohaka** *R* New Zealand
47D3 **Mohale's Hoek** Lesotho
60C1 **Mohall** USA
15C2 **Mohammadia** Algeria
43G4 **Mohanganj** Bangladesh
59D3 **Mohave,L** USA
68C1 **Mohawk** USA
65E2 **Mohawk** *R* USA
51E5 **Mohéli** *I* Comoros
51D4 **Mohoro** Tanzania
24J5 **Mointy** Kazakhstan
12G5 **Mo i Rana** Norway
14C3 **Moissac** France
59C3 **Mojave** USA
66D3 **Mojave** *R* USA
56B3 **Mojave Desert** USA
43F3 **Mokama** India
35B1 **Mokau** *R* New Zealand
66B1 **Mokelumne** *R* USA
66B1 **Mokelumne Aqueduct** USA
66B1 **Mokelumne Hill** USA
47D2 **Mokhotlong** Lesotho
16C3 **Moknine** Tunisia
43G3 **Mokokchūng** India
50B2 **Mokolo** Cameroon
28B4 **Mokp'o** S Korea
20G5 **Moksha** *R* Russian Federation
17E3 **Moláoi** Greece
7C3 **Mold** Wales
Moldavia = Moldova
12F6 **Molde** Norway
21D6 **Moldova** *Republic* Europe
17E1 **Moldoveanu** *Mt* Romania
47D1 **Molepolole** Botswana
13D3 **Molesheim** France
16D2 **Molfetta** Italy
72D7 **Mollendo** Peru
20D5 **Molodechno** Belarus
76G11 **Molodezhnaya** *Base* Antarctica
66E5 **Molokai** *I* Hawaiian Islands
20H4 **Moloma** *R* Russian Federation
34C2 **Molong** Australia
47C2 **Molopo** *R* Botswana/ South Africa
50B3 **Molounddu** Cameroon
56D1 **Molson L** Canada
32B1 **Molucca S** Indonesia
27F7 **Moluccas** *Is* Indonesia
51D5 **Moma** Mozambique
73K5 **Mombaça** Brazil
50D4 **Mombasa** Kenya
29D2 **Mombetsu** Japan
75B2 **Mombuca, Serra da** *Mts* Brazil
50C3 **Mompono** Zaïre
18C2 **Mon** *I* Denmark
8B3 **Monach Is** Scotland
14D3 **Monaco** *Principality* Europe
8C3 **Monadhliath Mts** Scotland
9C2 **Monaghan** Irish Republic
9C2 **Monaghan** *County* Irish Republic
62B2 **Monahans** USA
69D3 **Mona Pass** Caribbean Sea
60B3 **Monarch P** USA
54G4 **Monashee Mts** Canada
10B3 **Monastereven** Irish Republic
16C3 **Monastir** Tunisia
29D2 **Monbetsu** Japan
73J4 **Monção** Brazil
12L5 **Monchegorsk** Russian Federation
18B2 **Mönchen-gladbach** Germany
70B2 **Monclova** Mexico
55M5 **Moncton** Canada
15A1 **Mondego** *R* Portugal
16B2 **Mondovi** Italy
69H1 **Moneague** Jamaica
65D2 **Monessen** USA
63D1 **Monett** USA
16C1 **Monfalcone** Italy
15A1 **Monforte de Lemos** Spain
50C3 **Monga** Zaïre
50C3 **Mongala** *R* Zaïre
50D3 **Mongalla** Sudan
30D1 **Mong Cai** Vietnam
50B2 **Mongo** Chad
26C2 **Mongolia** *Republic* Asia
51C5 **Mongu** Zambia
8D4 **Moniaive** Scotland
59C3 **Monitor Range** *Mts* USA
50C4 **Monkoto** Zaïre
64A2 **Monmouth** USA
7C4 **Monmouth** Wales
48C4 **Mono** *R* Benin/Togo
59C3 **Mono L** USA
17D2 **Monopoli** Italy
15B1 **Monreal del Campo** Spain
63D2 **Monroe** Louisiana, USA
64C2 **Monroe** Michigan, USA
67B2 **Monroe** N Carolina, USA
58B1 **Monroe** Washington, USA
64B2 **Monroe** Wisconsin, USA
61E3 **Monroe City** USA
48A4 **Monrovia** Liberia
66D3 **Monrovia** USA
18A2 **Mons** Belgium
68D1 **Monson** USA
18D1 **Mönsterås** Sweden
47C3 **Montagu** South Africa
54D4 **Montague I** USA
14B2 **Montaigu** France
16D3 **Montallo** *Mt* Italy
56B2 **Montana** *State* USA
15A1 **Montañas de León** *Mts* Spain
14C2 **Montargis** France
14C3 **Montauban** France
65E2 **Montauk** USA
65E2 **Montauk Pt** USA
13C4 **Montbard** France
14D2 **Montbéliard** France
Montblanc = Montblanch
16B1 **Mont Blanc** France/Italy
15C1 **Montblanch** Spain
14C2 **Montceau-les-Mines** France
16B1 **Mont Cenis, Col du** *P* France/Italy
15C1 **Montceny** *Mt* Spain
13C3 **Montcornet** France
14B3 **Mont-de-Marsan** France
14C2 **Montdidier** France
72F7 **Monteagudo** Bolivia
73H4 **Monte Alegre** Brazil
75D2 **Monte Azul** Brazil
65D1 **Montebello** Canada
32A3 **Monte Bello Is** Australia
14D3 **Monte Carlo** Monaco
75C2 **Monte Carmelo** Brazil
69C3 **Montecristi** Dominican Republic
16C2 **Montecristo** *I* Italy
69H1 **Montego Bay** Jamaica
14C3 **Montélimar** France
75A3 **Montelindo** *R* Paraguay
70C2 **Montemorelos** Mexico
15A2 **Montemor-o-Novo** Portugal

17D2 **Montenegro** *Republic* Yugoslavia
51D5 **Montepuez** Mozambique
13B3 **Montereau-Faut-Yonne** France
56A3 **Monterey** California, USA
65D3 **Monterey** Virginia, USA
56A3 **Monterey B** USA
72C2 **Montería** Colombia
72F7 **Montero** Bolivia
70B2 **Monterrey** Mexico
73K7 **Montes Claros** Brazil
15B2 **Montes de Toledo** *Mts* Spain
74E4 **Montevideo** Uruguay
61D2 **Montevideo** USA
62A1 **Monte Vista** USA
62B1 **Montezuma** USA
66D2 **Montezuma Peak** *Mt* USA
57E3 **Montgomery** Alabama, USA
68B2 **Montgomery** Pennsylvania, USA
7C3 **Montgomery** Wales
66C2 **Montgomery P** USA
13C3 **Monthermé** France
63D2 **Monticello** Arkansas, USA
64A2 **Monticello** Iowa, USA
61E1 **Monticello** Minnesota, USA
68C2 **Monticello** New York, USA
56C3 **Monticello** Utah, USA
13C3 **Montier-en-Der** France
55L5 **Mont-Laurier** Canada
14C2 **Montluçon** France
55L5 **Montmagny** Canada
13C3 **Montmédy** France
13B3 **Montmirail** France
Mont, Monte : see also individual mt. names
65E1 **Montmorency** Canada
15B2 **Montoro** Spain
68B2 **Montoursville** USA
58D2 **Montpelier** Idaho, USA
64C2 **Montpelier** Ohio, USA
57F2 **Montpelier** Vermont, USA
14C3 **Montpellier** France
55L5 **Montréal** Canada
14C1 **Montreuil** France
16B1 **Montreux** Switzerland
56C3 **Montrose** Colorado, USA
68C2 **Montrose** Pennsylvania, USA
10C2 **Montrose** Scotland
8F3 **Montrose** *Oilfield* N Sea
14B2 **Mont-St-Michel** France
69E3 **Montserrat** *I* Caribbean Sea
57F1 **Monts Otish** Canada
56B3 **Monument V** USA
50C3 **Monveda** Zaïre
30B1 **Monywa** Burma
16B1 **Monza** Italy
51C5 **Monze** Zambia
47E2 **Mooi** *R* South Africa
47D2 **Mooi River** South Africa
34B1 **Moomba** Australia
34D2 **Moonbi Range** *Mts* Australia
34B1 **Moonda L** Australia
34D1 **Moonie** Australia
34C1 **Moonie** *R* Australia
34A2 **Moonta** Australia
32A4 **Moora** Australia
34B1 **Mooraberree** Australia
60C2 **Moorcroft** USA
32A3 **Moore,L** Australia
8D4 **Moorfoot Hills** Scotland
56D2 **Moorhead** USA
66C3 **Moorpark** USA
47B3 **Moorreesburg** South Africa
55K4 **Moose** *R* Canada
65F1 **Moosehead L** USA
54H4 **Moose Jaw** Canada
61E1 **Moose Lake** USA
54H4 **Moosomin** Canada
55K4 **Moosonee** Canada
68E2 **Moosup** USA
51D5 **Mopeia** Mozambique
48B3 **Mopti** Mali
72D7 **Moquegua** Peru
12G6 **Mora** Sweden
61E1 **Mora** USA
42D3 **Morādābād** India
73L5 **Morada Nova** Brazil
75C2 **Morada Nova de Minas** Brazil
51E5 **Morafenobe** Madagascar
51E5 **Moramanga** Madagascar
58D2 **Moran** USA
69J2 **Morant Bay** Jamaica
69J2 **Morant Pt** Jamaica
8C3 **Morar, Loch** *L* Scotland
44B4 **Moratuwa** Sri Lanka
18D3 **Morava** *R* Austria/Czechoslovakia
17E2 **Morava** *R* Serbia, Yugoslavia
41G2 **Moraveh Tappeh** Iran
10C2 **Moray Firth** *Estuary* Scotland
42C4 **Morbi** India
41D2 **Mor Dağ** *Mt* Turkey
54J5 **Morden** Canada
20G5 **Mordovian Republic** Russian Federation
60C1 **Moreau** *R* USA
7C2 **Morecambe** England
7C2 **Morecambe B** England
32D3 **Moree** Australia
64C3 **Morehead** USA
67C2 **Morehead City** USA
70B3 **Morelia** Mexico
42D3 **Morena** India
15A2 **Morena, Sierra** *Mts* Spain
54E4 **Moresby I** Canada
34D1 **Moreton I** Australia
13B3 **Moreuil** France
63D3 **Morgan City** USA
66B2 **Morgan Hill** USA
66C2 **Morgan,Mt** USA
67B1 **Morganton** USA
65D3 **Morgantown** USA
47D2 **Morgenzon** South Africa
13D3 **Morhange** France
29E2 **Mori** Japan
69K1 **Moriah** Tobago
62A2 **Moriarty** USA
29E3 **Morioka** Japan
34D2 **Morisset** Australia
25N3 **Morkoka** *R* Russian Federation
14B2 **Morlaix** France
69Q2 **Morne Diablotin** *Mt* Dominica
34B1 **Morney** Australia
32C2 **Mornington** *I* Australia
42B3 **Moro** Pakistan
32D1 **Morobe** Papua New Guinea
48B1 **Morocco** *Kingdom* Africa
27F6 **Moro G** Philippines
51D4 **Morogoro** Tanzania
51E6 **Morombe** Madagascar
69B2 **Morón** Cuba
51E6 **Morondava** Madagascar
15A2 **Moron de la Frontera** Spain
51E5 **Moroni** Comoros
27F6 **Morotai** *I* Indonesia
50D3 **Moroto** Uganda
21G6 **Morozovsk** Russian Federation
6D2 **Morpeth** England
45B1 **Morphou** Cyprus
45B1 **Morphou B** Cyprus
60C2 **Morrill** USA
63D1 **Morrilton** USA
75C2 **Morrinhos** Brazil
35C1 **Morrinsville** New Zealand
61D1 **Morris** Canada
61D1 **Morris** USA
68C2 **Morristown** New Jersey, USA
65D2 **Morristown** New York, USA
67B1 **Morristown** Tennessee, USA
68C1 **Morrisville** New York, USA
68C2 **Morrisville** Pennsylvania, USA
66B3 **Morro Bay** USA
51D5 **Morrumbala** Mozambique
51D6 **Morrumbene** Mozambique
20G5 **Morshansk** Russian Federation
Mortes *R* **= Manso**
73H6 **Mortes** *R* Mato Grosso, Brazil
75D3 **Mortes** *R* Minas Gerais, Brazil
34B3 **Mortlake** Australia
62B2 **Morton** USA
69L1 **Moruga** Trinidad
34D3 **Moruya** Australia
34C1 **Morven** Australia
8C3 **Morvern** *Pen* Scotland
34C3 **Morwell** Australia
13E3 **Mosbach** Germany
30B3 **Moscos Is** Burma
58C1 **Moscow** Idaho, USA
68C2 **Moscow** Pennsylvania, USA
42F4 **Moscow** Russian Federation
18B2 **Mosel** *R* Germany
47C2 **Moselebe** *R* Botswana
13D3 **Moselle** *Department* France
13D3 **Moselle** *R* France
58C1 **Moses Lake** USA
35B3 **Mosgiel** New Zealand
50D4 **Moshi** Tanzania
64B2 **Mosinee** USA
12G5 **Mosjøen** Norway
25Q4 **Moskal'vo** Russian Federation
Moskva = Moscow
62B1 **Mosquero** USA
75D2 **Mosquito** *R* Brazil
72B2 **Mosquitos, Golfo de los** Panama
12G7 **Moss** Norway
50B4 **Mossaka** Congo
Mossâmedes = Namibe
47C3 **Mossel Bay** South Africa
50B4 **Mossendjo** Congo
34B2 **Mossgiel** Australia
73L5 **Mossoró** Brazil
18C2 **Most** Czech Republic
15C2 **Mostaganem** Algeria
17D2 **Mostar** Bosnia-Herzegovina
19E2 **Mosty** Belarus
41D2 **Mosul** Iraq
12H7 **Motala** Sweden
8D4 **Motherwell** Scotland
43E3 **Motihāri** India
15B2 **Motilla del Palancar** Spain
47D1 **Motloutse** *R* Botswana
15B2 **Motril** Spain
60C1 **Mott** USA
35B2 **Motueka** New Zealand
35B2 **Motueka** *R* New Zealand
50B4 **Mouila** Gabon
34B2 **Moulamein** Australia
54G2 **Mould Bay** Canada
69P2 **Moule à Chique, Cap** St Lucia
14C2 **Moulins** France
30B2 **Moulmein** Burma
48B1 **Moulouya** *R* Morocco
67B2 **Moultrie** USA
67C2 **Moultrie,L** USA
64B3 **Mound City** Illinois, USA
61D2 **Mound City** Missouri, USA
50B3 **Moundou** Chad
64C3 **Moundsville** USA
67A2 **Mountain Brook** USA
63D1 **Mountain Grove** USA
63D1 **Mountain Home** Arkansas, USA
58C2 **Mountain Home** Idaho, USA
66A2 **Mountain View** USA
54B3 **Mountain Village** USA
68B3 **Mount Airy** Maryland, USA
67B1 **Mount Airy** N Carolina, USA
47D3 **Mount Ayliff** South Africa
68B2 **Mount Carmel** USA
65F2 **Mount Desert I** USA
47D3 **Mount Fletcher** South Africa
34B3 **Mount Gambier** Australia
32D1 **Mount Hagen** Papua New Guinea
68C3 **Mount Holly** USA
68B2 **Mount Holly Springs** USA
32C3 **Mount Isa** Australia
68A3 **Mount Jackson** USA
68A2 **Mount Jewett** USA
34A2 **Mount Lofty Range** *Mts* Australia
32A3 **Mount Magnet** Australia
34B2 **Mount Manara** Australia
9C3 **Mountmellick** Irish Republic
32E3 **Mount Morgan** Australia
68B1 **Mount Morris** USA
34D1 **Mount Perry** Australia
63D2 **Mount Pleasant** Texas, USA
59D3 **Mount Pleasant** Utah, USA
68C2 **Mount Pocono** USA
58B1 **Mount Rainier Nat Pk** USA
7B4 **Mounts B** England
58B2 **Mount Shasta** USA
68B2 **Mount Union** USA
63E2 **Mount Vernon** Alabama, USA
64B3 **Mount Vernon** Illinois, USA
63D1 **Mount Vernon** Missouri, USA
58B1 **Mount Vernon** Washington, USA
50C2 **Mourdi, Dépression du** *Desert Region* Chad
9C2 **Mourne Mts** Northern Ireland
50B2 **Moussoro** Chad
48C2 **Mouydir, Mts du** Algeria
50B4 **Mouyondzi** Congo
13C3 **Mouzon** France
18D3 **M'óvár** Hungary
9C2 **Moville** Irish Republic
9B2 **Moy** *R* Irish Republic
50D3 **Moyale** Kenya
48A4 **Moyamba** Sierra Leone
48B1 **Moyen Atlas** *Mts* Morocco
47D3 **Moyeni** Lesotho
25M3 **Moyero** *R* Russian Federation
50D3 **Moyo** Uganda
72C5 **Moyobamba** Peru
42D1 **Moyu** China
51D6 **Mozambique** *Republic* Africa
51D6 **Mozambique Chan** Madagascar/Mozambique
20J4 **Mozhga** Russian Federation
12K8 **Mozyr'** Belarus
50D4 **Mpanda** Tanzania
51D5 **Mpika** Zambia
51D4 **Mporokosa** Zambia
51C5 **Mposhi** Zambia
48B4 **Mpraeso** Ghana
51D4 **Mpulungu** Zambia
50D4 **Mpwapwa** Tanzania
16C3 **M'saken** Tunisia
15C2 **M'Sila** Algeria
19G2 **Mstislavl'** Belarus
20F5 **Mtsensk** Russian Federation
47E2 **Mtubatuba** South Africa
51E5 **Mtwara** Tanzania
30C2 **Muang Chainat** Thailand
30C2 **Muang Chiang Rai** Thailand
30C2 **Muang Kalasin** Thailand
30C2 **Muang Khon Kaen** Thailand
30B2 **Muang Lampang** Thailand
30B2 **Muang Lamphun** Thailand
30C2 **Muang Loei** Thailand
30C2 **Muang Lom Sak** Thailand
30C2 **Muang Nakhon Phanom** Thailand
30B2 **Muang Nakhon Sawan** Thailand
30C2 **Muang Nan** Thailand
30C2 **Muang Phayao** Thailand
30C2 **Muang Phetchabun** Thailand
30C2 **Muang Phichit** Thailand
30C2 **Muang Phitsanulok** Thailand
30C2 **Muang Phrae** Thailand
30C2 **Muang Roi Et** Thailand
30C2 **Muang Sakon Nakhon** Thailand
30C3 **Muang Samut Prakan** Thailand
30C2 **Muang Uthai Thani** Thailand
30C2 **Muang Yasothon** Thailand
30C5 **Muar** Malaysia
27D7 **Muara** Indonesia
30A2 **Muaungmya** Burma
50D3 **Mubende** Uganda
49D3 **Mubi** Nigeria
45C3 **Mubrak, Jebel** *Mt* Jordan
51D5 **Muchinga Mts** Zambia
7C3 **Much Wenlock** England
8B3 **Muck** *I* Scotland
34C1 **Muckadilla** Australia
9B2 **Muckros Hd,** *Pt* Irish Republic
51C5 **Muconda** Angola
75E2 **Mucuri** Brazil
75D2 **Mucuri** *R* Brazil
51C5 **Mucusso** Angola
26F2 **Mudanjiang** China
60B2 **Muddy Gap P** USA
45D3 **Mudeisisat, Jebel** *Mt* Jordan
34C2 **Mudgee** Australia
66D2 **Mud L** USA
30B2 **Mudon** Burma
20F3 **Mud'yuga** Russian Federation
51D5 **Mueda** Mozambique
33F3 **Mueo** New Caledonia (Nouvelle Calédonie)
51C5 **Mufulira** Zambia
31C4 **Mufu Shan** *Hills* China
40C4 **Mughayra** Saudi Arabia
40A2 **Muğla** Turkey
21K5 **Mugodzhary** *Mts* Kazakhstan
43E3 **Mugu** Nepal
31A3 **Muguaping** China
40D3 **Muhaywir** Iraq
13E3 **Mühlacker** Germany
18C3 **Mühldorf** Germany
18C2 **Mühlhausen** Germany
12K6 **Muhos** Finland
30C4 **Mui Bai Bung** *C* Cambodia
9C3 **Muine Bheag** Irish Republic
45C3 **Mujib, Wadi** Jordan
51C5 **Mujimbeji** Zambia
19E3 **Mukachevo** Ukraine
27E6 **Mukah** Malaysia
29D2 **Mukawa** Japan
26H4 **Muko-jima** *I* Japan
43E3 **Muktinath** Nepal
42B2 **Mukur** Afghanistan
63D1 **Mulberry** USA
18C2 **Mulde** *R* Germany
60C2 **Mule Creek** USA
62B2 **Muleshoe** USA
27H8 **Mulgrave I** Australia
15B2 **Mulhacén** *Mt* Spain
13D2 **Mülheim** Germany
13D4 **Mulhouse** France
31A4 **Muli** China
8C3 **Mull** *I* Scotland
44C4 **Mullaittvu** Sri Lanka
34C2 **Mullaley** Australia
27E6 **Muller, Pegunungan** *Mts* Indonesia
9A2 **Mullet, The** *Pt* Irish Republic
32A3 **Mullewa** Australia
13D4 **Müllheim** Germany
68C3 **Mullica** *R* USA
9C3 **Mullingar** Irish Republic
8C4 **Mull of Kintyre** *Pt* Scotland
8B4 **Mull of Oa** *C* Scotland
34D1 **Mullumbimby** Australia
51C5 **Mulobezi** Zambia
42C2 **Multan** Pakistan
51C5 **Mumbwa** Zambia
21H6 **Mumra** Russian Federation
27F7 **Muna** Indonesia
München = Munich
28A3 **Munchŏn** N Korea
64B2 **Muncie** USA
34A1 **Muncoonie,L** Australia
68B2 **Muncy** USA
18B2 **Münden** Germany
34D1 **Mundubbera** Australia
34C1 **Mungallala** Australia
34C1 **Mungallala** *R* Australia
50C3 **Mungbere** Zaïre
43E4 **Mungeli** India
43F3 **Munger** India
34C1 **Mungindi** Australia
18C3 **Munich** Germany
64B1 **Munising** USA
74B8 **Muñoz Gamero,Pen** Chile
28A3 **Munsan** S Korea
13D3 **Munster** France
18B2 **Münster** Germany
13D2 **Münsterland** *Region* Germany
17E1 **Munţii Apuseni** *Mts* Romania
17E1 **Munţii Călimani** *Mts* Romania
17E1 **Munţii Carpaţii Meridionali** *Mts* Romania
17E1 **Munţii Rodnei** *Mts* Romania
17E1 **Munţii Zarandului** *Mts* Romania
40C2 **Munzur Silsilesi** *Mts* Turkey
30C1 **Muong Khoua** Laos
30D3 **Muong Man** Vietnam
30D2 **Muong Nong** Laos
30C1 **Muong Ou Neua** Laos
30C1 **Muong Sai** Laos
30C2 **Muong Sen** Vietnam
30C1 **Muong Sing** Laos
30C1 **Muong Son** Laos
12J5 **Muonio** Finland
12J5 **Muonio** *R* Finland/Sweden
28A3 **Muping** China
Muqdisho = Mogadishu
16C1 **Mur** *R* Austria
29D3 **Murakami** Japan
74B7 **Murallón** *Mt* Argentina/Chile
20H4 **Murashi** Russian Federation
40D2 **Murat** *R* Turkey
16B3 **Muravera** Sardinia, Italy
29D3 **Murayama** Japan
41F3 **Murcheh Khvort** Iran
35B2 **Murchison** New Zealand
32A3 **Murchison** *R* Australia
15B2 **Murcia** Spain
15B2 **Murcia** *Region* Spain
60C2 **Murdo** USA
17E1 **Mureş** *R* Romania
67C1 **Murfreesboro** N Carolina, USA
67A1 **Murfreesboro** Tennessee, USA
13E3 **Murg** *R* Germany
24H6 **Murgab** *R* Turkmenistan
42A1 **Murghab** *R* Afghanistan
42B2 **Murgha Kibzai** Pakistan
34D1 **Murgon** Australia
43F4 **Muri** India
75D3 **Muriaé** Brazil
51C4 **Muriege** Angola
20E2 **Murmansk** Russian Federation
20G4 **Murom** Russian Federation
29E2 **Muroran** Japan
15A1 **Muros** Spain
29C4 **Muroto** Japan
29B4 **Muroto-zaki** *C* Japan
58C2 **Murphy** Idaho, USA
67B1 **Murphy** N Carolina, USA
66B1 **Murphys** USA
64B3 **Murray** Kentucky, USA
58D2 **Murray** Utah, USA

34B2 **Murray** *R* Australia
34A3 **Murray Bridge** Australia
27H7 **Murray,L** Papua New Guinea
67B2 **Murray,L** USA
47C3 **Murraysburg** South Africa
37M3 **Murray Seacarp** Pacific Ocean
34B2 **Murrumbidgee** *R* Australia
34C2 **Murrumburrah** Australia
34D2 **Murrurundi** Australia
34B3 **Murtoa** Australia
28A2 **Muruin Sum** *R* China
35C1 **Murupara** New Zealand
43E4 **Murwāra** India
34D1 **Murwillimbah** Australia
27E7 **Muryo** *Mt* Indonesia
40D2 **Muş** Turkey
17E2 **Musala** *Mt* Bulgaria
28B2 **Musan** N Korea
41G4 **Musandam Pen** Oman
38D3 **Muscat** Oman
61E2 **Muscatine** USA
32C3 **Musgrave Range** *Mts* Australia
50B4 **Mushie** Zaïre
68E2 **Muskeget Chan** USA
64B2 **Muskegon** USA
64B2 **Muskegon** *R* USA
63C1 **Muskogee** USA
65D2 **Muskoka,L** Canada
50D2 **Musmar** Sudan
50D4 **Musoma** Tanzania
32D1 **Mussau** *I* Papua New Guinea
58E1 **Musselshell** *R* USA
51B5 **Mussende** Angola
14C3 **Mussidan** France
17F2 **Mustafa-Kemalpasa** Turkey
43E3 **Mustang** Nepal
74C7 **Musters, Lago** Argentina
28A2 **Musu-dan** *C* N Korea
34D2 **Muswellbrook** Australia
49E2 **Mut** Egypt
75E1 **Mutá, Ponta do** *Pt* Brazil
51D5 **Mutarara** Mozambique
51D5 **Mutare** Zimbabwe
20K2 **Mutnyy Materik** Russian Federation
51D5 **Mutoko** Zimbabwe
51E5 **Mutsamudu** Comoros
51C5 **Mutshatsha** Zaïre
29E2 **Mutsu** Japan
29E2 **Mutsu-wan** *B* Japan
75C1 **Mutunópolis** Brazil
31B2 **Mu Us Shamo** *Desert* China
51B4 **Muxima** Angola
25N4 **Muya** Russian Federation
20E3 **Muyezerskiy** Russian Federation
50D4 **Muyinga** Burundi
51C4 **Muyumba** Zaïre
39E1 **Muyun Kum** *Desert* Kazakhstan
42C2 **Muzaffarābād** Pakistan
42C2 **Muzaffargarh** Pakistan
42D3 **Muzaffarnagar** India
43F3 **Muzaffarpur** India
24H3 **Muzhi** Russian Federation
39G2 **Muzlag** *Mt* China
39F2 **Muztagala** *Mt* China
51D5 **Mvuma** Zimbabwe
50D4 **Mwanza** Tanzania
51C4 **Mwanza** Zaïre
50C4 **Mweka** Zaïre
51C4 **Mwene Ditu** Zaïre
51D6 **Mwenezi** Zimbabwe
47E1 **Mwenezi** *R* Zimbabwe
50C4 **Mwenga** Zaïre
51C4 **Mweru, L** Zaïre/Zambia
51C5 **Mwinilunga** Zambia
30B2 **Myanaung** Burma
Myanmar = Burma
18D3 **M'yaróvár** Hungary
30B1 **Myingyan** Burma
30B3 **Myinmoletkat** *Mt* Burma
30B3 **Myitta** Burma
43G4 **Mymensingh** Bangladesh
7C3 **Mynydd Eppynt** Wales
26G3 **Myojin** *I* Japan
28A2 **Myongchon** N Korea
28A2 **Myonggan** N Korea
12F6 **Myrdal** Norway
12B2 **Myrdalsjökull** *Mts* Iceland
67C2 **Myrtle Beach** USA
58B2 **Myrtle Creek** USA
12G7 **Mysen** Norway
20G2 **Mys Kanin Nos** *C* Russian Federation
19D3 **Myślenice** Poland
18C2 **Myśliborz** Poland
44B3 **Mysore** India
21E7 **Mys Sarych** *C* Ukraine
25U3 **Mys Shmidta** Russian Federation
20F2 **Mys Svyatoy Nos** *C* Russian Federation
68E2 **Mystic** USA
21J7 **Mys Tyub-Karagan** *Pt* Kazakhstan
24H2 **Mys Zhelaniya** *C* Russian Federation
30D3 **My Tho** Vietnam
58B2 **Mytle Point** USA
51D5 **Mzimba** Malawi
51D5 **Mzuzú** Malawi

N

66E5 **Naalehu** Hawaiian Islands
12J6 **Naantali** Finland
9C3 **Naas** Irish Republic
29C4 **Nabari** Japan
20J4 **Naberezhnyye Chelny** Russian Federation
16C3 **Nabeul** Tunisia
75A3 **Nabileque** *R* Brazil
45C2 **Nablus** Israel
51E5 **Nacala** Mozambique
58B1 **Naches** USA
51D5 **Nachingwea** Tanzania
66B3 **Nacimiento** *R* USA
66B3 **Nacimiento Res** USA
63D2 **Nacogdoches** USA
70B1 **Nacozari** Mexico
13E2 **Nadel** *Mt* Germany
42C4 **Nadiād** India
15B2 **Nador** Morocco
41F3 **Nadūshan** Iran
20E3 **Nadvoitsy** Russian Federation
19E3 **Nadvornaya** Ukraine
18C1 **Naestved** Denmark
49E2 **Nafoora** Libya
27F5 **Naga** Philippines
28B4 **Nagahama** Japan
43H3 **Naga Hills** India
29C3 **Nagai** Japan
43G3 **Nāgāland** *State* India
29D3 **Nagano** Japan
29D3 **Nagaoka** Japan
44B3 **Nāgappattinam** India
42C4 **Nagar Parkar** Pakistan
28B4 **Nagasaki** Japan
29C4 **Nagashima** Japan
28B4 **Nagato** Japan
42C3 **Nāgaur** India
44B4 **Nāgercoil** India
42B3 **Nagha Kalat** Pakistan
42D3 **Nagīna** India
13E3 **Nagold** Germany
29D3 **Nagoya** Japan
42D4 **Nāgpur** India
39H2 **Nagqu** China
18D3 **Nagykanizsa** Hungary
19D3 **Nagykörös** Hungary
26F4 **Naha** Okinawa, Japan
42D2 **Nāhan** India
54F3 **Nahanni Butte** Canada
45C2 **Nahariya** Israel
41E3 **Nahāvand** Iran
13D3 **Nahe** *R* Germany
31D2 **Nahpu** China
74B6 **Nahuel Haupí, Lago** Argentina
31E1 **Naimen Qi** China
55M4 **Nain** Canada
41F3 **Nā'īn** Iran
42D3 **Naini Tal** India
43E4 **Nainpur** India
8D3 **Nairn** Scotland
50D4 **Nairobi** Kenya
41F3 **Najafābād** Iran
40C4 **Najd** *Region* Saudi Arabia
28C2 **Najin** N Korea
50E2 **Najrān** Saudi Arabia
28A3 **Naju** S Korea
28A4 **Nakadori-jima** Japan
28B4 **Nakama** Japan
29E3 **Nakaminato** Japan
28B4 **Nakamura** Japan
29C3 **Nakano** Japan
29B3 **Nakano-shima** *I* Japan
28C4 **Nakatsu** Japan
29C3 **Nakatsu-gawa** Japan
50D2 **Nak'fa** Eritrea
21H8 **Nakhichevan** Azerbaijan
45B4 **Nakhl** Egypt
28C2 **Nakhodka** Russian Federation
30C3 **Nakhon Pathom** Thailand
30C3 **Nakhon Ratchasima** Thailand
30C4 **Nakhon Si Thammarat** Thailand
55K4 **Nakina** Ontario, Canada
54C4 **Naknek** USA
12G8 **Nakskov** Denmark
28A3 **Naktong** *R* S Korea
50D4 **Nakuru** Kenya
21G7 **Nal'chik** Russian Federation
44B2 **Nalgonda** India
44B2 **Nallamala Range** *Mts* India
49D1 **Nālūt** Libya
47E2 **Namaacha** Mozambique
24G6 **Namak** *L* Iran
41G3 **Namakzar-e Shadad** *Salt Flat* Iran
24J5 **Namangan** Uzbekistan
51D5 **Namapa** Mozambique
51B7 **Namaqualand** *Region* South Africa
34D1 **Nambour** Australia
34D2 **Nambucca Heads** Australia
30D4 **Nam Can** Vietnam
39H2 **Nam Co** *L* China
30D1 **Nam Dinh** Vietnam
51D5 **Nametil** Mozambique
47A1 **Namib Desert** Namibia
51B5 **Namibe** Angola
51B6 **Namibia** *Republic* Africa
27F7 **Namlea** Indonesia
43F3 **Namling** China
34C2 **Namoi** *R* Australia
58C2 **Nampa** USA
48B3 **Nampala** Mali
30C2 **Nam Phong** Thailand
28B3 **Namp'o** N Korea
51D5 **Nampula** Mozambique
12G6 **Namsos** Norway
30B1 **Namton** Burma
25O3 **Namtsy** Russian Federation
51D5 **Namuno** Mozambique
13C2 **Namur** Belgium
51B5 **Namutoni** Namibia
56A2 **Nanaimo** Canada
28B2 **Nanam** N Korea
34D1 **Nanango** Australia
29D3 **Nanao** Japan
29C3 **Nanatsu-jima** *I* Japan
31B3 **Nanbu** China
31D4 **Nanchang** China
31B3 **Nanchong** China
44E4 **Nancowry** *I* Nicobar Is, Indian Ocean
14D2 **Nancy** France
43E2 **Nanda Devi** *Mt* India
44B2 **Nānded** India
34D2 **Nandewar Range** *Mts* Australia
42C4 **Nandurbār** India
44B2 **Nandyāl** India
50B3 **Nanga Eboko** Cameroon
42C1 **Nanga Parbat** *Mt* Pakistan
27E7 **Nangapinon** Indonesia
13B3 **Nangis** France
28A2 **Nangnim** N Korea
28B2 **Nangnim Sanmaek** *Mts* N Korea
43G3 **Nang Xian** China
44B3 **Nanjangūd** India
31D3 **Nanjing** China
Nanking = Nanjing
29B4 **Nankoku** Japan
31C4 **Nan Ling** *Region* China
30D1 **Nanliu** *R* China
31B5 **Nanning** China
55O3 **Nanortalik** Greenland
31A5 **Nanpan Jiang** *R* China
43E3 **Nānpāra** India
31D4 **Nanping** China
28B2 **Nanping** China
55J1 **Nansen Sd** Canada
27E5 **Nanshan** *I* S China Sea
50D4 **Nansio** Tanzania
14B2 **Nantes** France
68C2 **Nanticoke** USA
31E3 **Nantong** China
68E2 **Nantucket** USA
68E2 **Nantucket I** USA
68E2 **Nantucket Sd** USA
7C3 **Nantwich** England
33G1 **Nanumanga** *I* Tuvalu
33G1 **Nanumea** *I* Tuvalu
75D2 **Nanuque** Brazil
31C3 **Nanyang** China
31D2 **Nanyang Hu** *L* China
50D3 **Nanyuki** Kenya
28A2 **Nanzamu** China
15C2 **Nao, Cabo de la** *C* Spain
29D3 **Naoetsu** Japan
42B4 **Naokot** Pakistan
66A1 **Napa** USA
65D2 **Napanee** Canada
24K4 **Napas** Russian Federation
55N3 **Napassoq** Greenland
30D2 **Nape** Laos
35C1 **Napier** New Zealand
67B3 **Naples** Florida, USA
16C2 **Naples** Italy
68B1 **Naples** New York, USA
63D2 **Naples** Texas, USA
31B5 **Napo** China
72D4 **Napo** *R* Ecuador/Peru
60D1 **Napoleon** USA
Napoli = Naples
41E2 **Naqadeh** Iran
45C3 **Naqb Ishtar** Jordan
29C4 **Nara** Japan
48B3 **Nara** Mali
32D4 **Naracoorte** Australia
44B2 **Narasarāopet** India
30C4 **Narathiwat** Thailand
43G4 **Narayanganj** Bangladesh
44B2 **Nārāyenpet** India
14C3 **Narbonne** France
30A3 **Narcondam** *I* Indian Ocean
42D2 **Narendranagar** India
55L2 **Nares Str** Canada
19E2 **Narew** *R* Poland
28B2 **Narhong** China
29D3 **Narita** Japan
42C4 **Narmada** *R* India
42D3 **Nārnaul** India
20F4 **Naro Fominsk** Russian Federation
50D4 **Narok** Kenya
19F2 **Narovl'a** Belarus
42C2 **Narowal** Pakistan
32D4 **Narrabri** Australia
34C1 **Narran** *R* Australia
34C2 **Narrandera** Australia
34C1 **Narran L** Australia
32A4 **Narrogin** Australia
34C2 **Narromine** Australia
64C3 **Narrows** USA
68C2 **Narrowsburg** USA
42D4 **Narsimhapur** India
44C2 **Narsīpatnam** India
55O3 **Narssalik** Greenland
55O3 **Narssaq** Greenland
55O3 **Narssarssuaq** Greenland
47B2 **Narubis** Namibia
29D3 **Narugo** Japan
29B4 **Naruto** Japan
20D4 **Narva** Russian Federation
12H5 **Narvik** Norway
42D3 **Narwāna** India
20J2 **Nar'yan Mar** Russian Federation
34B1 **Narylico** Australia
24J5 **Naryn** Kirgizia
48C4 **Nasarawa** Nigeria
52D6 **Nasca Ridge** Pacific Ocean
68E1 **Nashua** USA
63D2 **Nashville** Arkansas, USA
67A1 **Nashville** Tennessee, USA
17D1 **Našice** Croatia
42C4 **Nāsik** India
50D3 **Nasir** Sudan
69B1 **Nassau** The Bahamas
68D1 **Nassau** USA
49F2 **Nasser,L** Egypt
12G7 **Nässjö** Sweden
55L4 **Nastapoka Is** Canada
51C6 **Nata** Botswana
73L5 **Natal** Brazil
27C6 **Natal** Indonesia
36C6 **Natal Basin** Indian Ocean
41F3 **Natanz** Iran
55M4 **Natashquan** Canada
55M4 **Natashquan** *R* Canada
63D2 **Natchez** USA
63D2 **Natchitoches** USA
34C3 **Nathalia** Australia
55Q2 **Nathorsts Land** *Region* Greenland
59C4 **National City** USA
29D3 **Natori** Japan
50D4 **Natron, L** Tanzania
40A3 **Natrun, Wadi el** *Watercourse* Egypt
32A4 **Naturaliste,C** Australia
18C2 **Nauen** Germany
68D2 **Naugatuck** USA
18C2 **Naumburg** Germany
45C3 **Naur** Jordan
33F1 **Nauru** *I, Republic* Pacific Ocean
25M4 **Naushki** Russian Federation
47B2 **Naute Dam** *Res* Namibia
56C3 **Navajo Res** USA
15A2 **Navalmoral de la Mata** Spain
25T3 **Navarin, Mys** *C* Russian Federation
74C9 **Navarino** *I* Chile
15B1 **Navarra** *Province* Spain
63C2 **Navasota** USA
63C2 **Navasota** *R* USA
8C2 **Naver, L** Scotland
15A1 **Navia** *R* Spain
42C4 **Navlakhi** India
21E5 **Navlya** Russian Federation
70B2 **Navojoa** Mexico
17E3 **Návpaktos** Greece
17E3 **Návplion** Greece
42C4 **Navsāri** India
45D2 **Nawá** Syria
42B3 **Nawabshah** Pakistan
43F4 **Nawāda** India
42B2 **Nawah** Afghanistan
31B4 **Naxi** China
17F3 **Náxos** *I* Greece
41F4 **Nāy Band** Iran
41G3 **Nāy Band** Iran
29E2 **Nayoro** Japan
75E1 **Nazaré** Brazil
45C2 **Nazareth** Israel
72D6 **Nazca** Peru
40A2 **Nazilli** Turkey
25L4 **Nazimovo** Russian Federation
50D3 **Nazrēt** Ethiopia
41G5 **Nazwa'** Oman
24J4 **Nazyvayevsk** Russian Federation
51B4 **Ndalatando** Angola
50C3 **Ndélé** Central African Republic
50B4 **Ndendé** Gabon
33F2 **Ndende** *I* Solomon Islands
50B2 **Ndjamena** Chad
50B4 **Ndjolé** Gabon
51C5 **Ndola** Zambia
34C1 **Neabul** Australia
10B3 **Neagh, Lough** *L* Northern Ireland
17E3 **Neápolis** Greece
7C4 **Neath** Wales
34C1 **Nebine** *R* Australia
24G6 **Nebit Dag** Turkmenistan
56C2 **Nebraska** *State* USA
61D2 **Nebraska City** USA
16C3 **Nebrodi, Monti** *Mts* Sicily, Italy
63C2 **Neches** *R* USA
74E5 **Necochea** Argentina
43G3 **Nêdong** China
7E3 **Needham Market** England
59D4 **Needles** USA
7D4 **Needles** *Pt* England
64B2 **Neenah** USA
54J4 **Neepawa** Canada
13C2 **Neerpelt** Belgium
25M4 **Neftelensk** Russian Federation
50D3 **Negelē** Ethiopia
45C3 **Negev** *Desert* Israel
75A3 **Negla** *R* Paraguay
21C6 **Negolu** *Mt* Romania
44B4 **Negombo** Sri Lanka
30A2 **Negrais,C** Burma
72B4 **Negritos** Peru
72F4 **Negro** *R* Amazonas, Brazil
74D5 **Negro** *R* Argentina
74F4 **Negro** *R* Brazil/Uruguay
75A2 **Negro** *R* Mato Grosso do Sul, Brazil
75A3 **Negro** *R* Paraguay
15A2 **Negro, Cap** *C* Morocco
27F6 **Negros** *I* Philippines
17F2 **Negru Vodă** Romania
31B4 **Neijiang** China
64A2 **Neillsville** USA
Nei Monggol Zizhiqu = Inner Mongolia Aut. Region
72C3 **Neiva** Colombia
50D3 **Nejo** Ethiopia
50D3 **Nek'emte** Ethiopia
20E4 **Nelidovo** Russian Federation
61D2 **Neligh** USA
44B3 **Nellore** India
26G2 **Nel'ma** Russian Federation
54G5 **Nelson** Canada
6C3 **Nelson** England
35B2 **Nelson** New Zealand
34B3 **Nelson,C** Australia
47E2 **Nelspruit** South Africa
48B3 **Néma** Mauritius
31A1 **Nemagt Uul** *Mt* Mongolia
16B3 **Nementcha, Mts Des** Algeria
17F1 **Nemira** *Mt* Romania
13B3 **Nemours** France
19E1 **Nemunas** *R* Lithuania
29F2 **Nemuro** Japan
29F2 **Nemuro-kaikyō** *Str* Japan/Russian Federation
25O5 **Nen** *R* China
10B3 **Nenagh** Irish Republic
54D3 **Nenana** USA
7D3 **Nene** *R* England
26F2 **Nenjiang** China
63C1 **Neodesha** USA
63D1 **Neosho** USA
25M4 **Nepa** Russian Federation
39G3 **Nepal** *Kingdom* Asia
43E3 **Nepalganj** Nepal
59D3 **Nephi** USA
45C3 **Neqarot** *R* Israel
26E1 **Nerchinsk** Russian Federation
17D2 **Neretva** *R* Bosnia-Herzegovina/Croatia
27H5 **Nero Deep** Pacific Ocean
20G2 **Nes'** Russian Federation
12C1 **Neskaupstaður** Iceland
13B3 **Nesle** France
62C1 **Ness City** USA
8C3 **Ness, Loch** *L* Scotland
17E2 **Néstos** *R* Greece
45C2 **Netanya** Israel
68C2 **Netcong** USA
18B2 **Netherlands** *Kingdom* Europe
53M7 **Netherlands Antilles** *Is* Caribbean Sea
43G4 **Netrakona** Bangladesh
55L3 **Nettilling L** Canada
18C2 **Neubrandenburg** Germany
16B1 **Neuchâtel** Switzerland
13C3 **Neufchâteau** Belgium

13C3 **Neufchâteau** France
14C2 **Neufchâtel** France
18B2 **Neumünster** Germany
16D1 **Neunkirchen** Austria
13D3 **Neunkirchen** Germany
74C5 **Neuquén** Argentina
74C5 **Neuquén** *R* Argentina
74B5 **Neuquén** *State* Argentina
18C2 **Neuruppin** Germany
67C1 **Neuse** *R* USA
13D2 **Neuss** Germany
18C2 **Neustadt** Germany
13E3 **Neustadt an der Weinstrasse** Germany
13E1 **Neustadt a R** Germany
13E4 **Neustadt im Schwarzwald** Germany
18C2 **Neustrelitz** Germany
13E1 **Neuwerk** *I* Germany
13D2 **Neuwied** Germany
63D1 **Nevada** USA
56B3 **Nevada** *State* USA
15B2 **Nevada, Sierra** *Mts* Spain
45C3 **Nevatim** Israel
20D4 **Nevel'** Russian Federation
14C2 **Nevers** France
34C2 **Nevertire** Australia
Nevis = St Kitts-Nevis
40B2 **Nevşehir** Turkey
20L4 **Nev'yansk** Russian Federation
64C3 **New** *R* USA
51D5 **Newala** Tanzania
64B3 **New Albany** Indiana, USA
63E2 **New Albany** Mississippi, USA
73G2 **New Amsterdam** Guyana
34C1 **New Angledool** Australia
65D3 **Newark** Delaware, USA
57F2 **Newark** New Jersey, USA
68B1 **Newark** New York, USA
64C2 **Newark** Ohio, USA
7D3 **Newark-upon-Trent** England
65E2 **New Bedford** USA
58B1 **Newberg** USA
67C1 **New Bern** USA
67B2 **Newberry** USA
47C3 **New Bethesda** South Africa
69B2 **New Bight** The Bahamas
64C3 **New Boston** USA
62C3 **New Braunfels** USA
68D2 **New Britain** USA
32E1 **New Britain** *I* Papua New Guinea
32E1 **New Britain Trench** Papua New Guinea
68C2 **New Brunswick** USA
55M5 **New Brunswick** *Province* Canada
68C2 **Newburgh** USA
7D4 **Newbury** England
68E1 **Newburyport** USA
33F3 **New Caledonia** *I* SW Pacific Ocean
68D2 **New Canaan** USA
34D2 **Newcastle** Australia
64B3 **New Castle** Indiana, USA
9D2 **Newcastle** Northern Ireland
64C2 **New Castle** Pennsylvania, USA
47D2 **Newcastle** South Africa
60C2 **Newcastle** Wyoming, USA
8D4 **New Castleton** Scotland
7C3 **Newcastle under Lyme** England
6D2 **Newcastle upon Tyne** England
32C2 **Newcastle Waters** Australia
66C3 **New Cuyama** USA
42D3 **New Delhi** India
34D2 **New England Range** *Mts* Australia
68A1 **Newfane** USA
7D4 **New Forest,The** England
55N5 **Newfoundland** *I* Canada
55M4 **Newfoundland** *Province* Canada
52F2 **Newfoundland Basin** Atlantic Ocean
61E3 **New Franklin** USA
8C4 **New Galloway** Scotland
33E1 **New Georgia** *I* Solomon Islands
55M5 **New Glasgow** Canada
32D1 **New Guinea** *I* SE Asia
66C3 **Newhall** USA
57F2 **New Hampshire** *State* USA
61E2 **New Hampton** USA
47E2 **New Hanover** South Africa
32E1 **New Hanover** *I* Papua New Guinea
7E4 **Newhaven** England
65E2 **New Haven** USA
33F3 **New Hebrides Trench** Pacific Ocean
63D2 **New Iberia** USA
32E1 **New Ireland** *I* Papua New Guinea
57F2 **New Jersey** *State* USA
62B2 **Newkirk** USA
55L5 **New Liskeard** Canada
68D2 **New London** USA
32A3 **Newman** Australia
66B2 **Newman** USA
7E3 **Newmarket** England
65D3 **New Market** USA
58C2 **New Meadows** USA
56C3 **New Mexico** *State* USA
68D2 **New Milford** Connecticut, USA
68C2 **New Milford** Pennsylvania, USA
67B2 **Newnan** USA
34C4 **New Norfolk** Australia
57D3 **New Orleans** USA
68C2 **New Paltz** USA
64C2 **New Philadelphia** USA
35B1 **New Plymouth** New Zealand
63D1 **Newport** Arkansas, USA
7D4 **Newport** England
64C3 **Newport** Kentucky, USA
68D1 **Newport** New Hampshire, USA
58B2 **Newport** Oregon, USA
68B2 **Newport** Pennsylvania, USA
65E2 **Newport** Rhode Island, USA
65E2 **Newport** Vermont, USA
7C4 **Newport** Wales
58C1 **Newport** Washington, USA
66D4 **Newport Beach** USA
57F3 **Newport News** USA
69B1 **New Providence** *I* The Bahamas
7B4 **Newquay** England
7B3 **New Quay** Wales
55L3 **New Quebec Crater** Canada
7C3 **New Radnor** Wales
7E4 **New Romney** England
9C3 **New Ross** Irish Republic
9C2 **Newry** Northern Ireland
New Siberian Is = Novosibirskye Ostrova
67B3 **New Smyrna Beach** USA
32D4 **New South Wales** *State* Australia
61E2 **Newton** Iowa, USA
63C1 **Newton** Kansas, USA
68E1 **Newton** Massachusetts, USA
63E2 **Newton** Mississippi, USA
68C2 **Newton** New Jersey, USA
9D2 **Newtonabbey** Northern Ireland
7C4 **Newton Abbot** England
9C2 **Newton Stewart** Northern Ireland
8C4 **Newton Stewart** Scotland
60C1 **New Town** USA
7C3 **Newtown** Wales
9D2 **Newtownards** Northern Ireland
61E2 **New Ulm** USA
68B2 **Newville** USA
54F5 **New Westminster** Canada
57F2 **New York** USA
57F2 **New York** *State* USA
33G5 **New Zealand** *Dominion* SW Pacific Ocean
37K7 **New Zealand Plat** Pacific Ocean
20G4 **Neya** Russian Federation
41F4 **Neyrīz** Iran
41G2 **Neyshābūr** Iran
21E5 **Nezhin** Ukraine
50B4 **Ngabé** Congo
51C6 **Ngami, L** Botswana
49D4 **Ngaoundéré** Cameroon
30A1 **Ngape** Burma
35C1 **Ngaruawahia** New Zealand
35C1 **Ngaruroro** *R* New Zealand
35C1 **Ngauruhoe,Mt** New Zealand
50B4 **Ngo** Congo
30D2 **Ngoc Linh** *Mt* Vietnam
50B3 **Ngoko** *R* Cameroon/ Central African Republic/Congo
26C3 **Ngoring Hu** *L* China
50D4 **Ngorongoro Crater** Tanzania
50B4 **N'Gounié** *R* Gabon
50B2 **Nguigmi** Niger
27G6 **Ngulu** *I* Pacific Ocean
48D3 **Nguru** Nigeria
30D3 **Nha Trang** Vietnam
75A2 **Nhecolandia** Brazil
34B3 **Nhill** Australia
47E2 **Nhlangano** Swaziland
30D2 **Nhommarath** Laos
32C2 **Nhulunbuy** Australia
48B3 **Niafounké** Mali
64B1 **Niagara** USA
65D2 **Niagara Falls** Canada
65D2 **Niagara Falls** USA
27E6 **Niah** Malaysia
48B4 **Niakaramandougou** Ivory Coast
48C3 **Niamey** Niger
50C3 **Niangara** Zaïre
50C3 **Nia Nia** Zaïre
27E6 **Niapa** *Mt* Indonesia
27C6 **Nias** *I* Indonesia
70D3 **Nicaragua** *Republic* Central America
70D3 **Nicaragua, L de** Nicaragua
16D3 **Nicastro** Italy
14D3 **Nice** France
69B1 **Nicholl's Town** The Bahamas
68C2 **Nicholson** USA
39H5 **Nicobar Is** India
45B1 **Nicosia** Cyprus
72A2 **Nicoya, Golfo de** Costa Rica
70D3 **Nicoya,Pen de** Costa Rica
6D2 **Nidd** *R* England
13E2 **Nidda** *R* Germany
19E2 **Nidzica** Poland
13D3 **Niederbronn** France
18B2 **Niedersachsen** *State* Germany
50C4 **Niemba** Zaïre
18B2 **Nienburg** Germany
13D2 **Niers** *R* Germany
48B4 **Niete,Mt** Liberia
73G2 **Nieuw Amsterdam** Surinam
73G2 **Nieuw Nickerie** Surinam
47B3 **Nieuwoudtville** South Africa
13B2 **Nieuwpoort** Belgium
40B2 **Niğde** Turkey
48B3 **Niger** *R* W Africa
48C3 **Niger** *Republic* Africa
48C4 **Nigeria** *Federal Republic* Africa
48C4 **Niger, Mouths of the** Nigeria
43L1 **Nighasan** India
64C1 **Nighthawk L** Canada
17E2 **Nigríta** Greece
29D3 **Nihommatsu** Japan
29D3 **Niigata** Japan
29C4 **Niihama** Japan
29C4 **Nii-jima** *I* Japan
29B4 **Niimi** Japan
29D3 **Niitsu** Japan
45C3 **Nijil** Jordan
18B2 **Nijmegen** Netherlands
20E2 **Nikel'** Russian Federation
48C4 **Nikki** Benin
29D3 **Nikko** Japan
21E6 **Nikolayev** Ukraine
21H6 **Nikolayevsk** Russian Federation
25Q4 **Nikolayevsk-na-Amure** Russian Federation
20H5 **Nikol'sk** Penza, Russian Federation
20H4 **Nikol'sk** Russian Federation
21E6 **Nikopol** Ukraine
40C1 **Niksar** Turkey
17D2 **Nikšić** Montenegro, Yugoslavia
33G1 **Nikunau** *I* Kiribati
27F7 **Nila** *I* Indonesia
38B3 **Nile** *R* NE Africa
64B2 **Niles** USA
44B3 **Nilgiri Hills** India
42C4 **Nimach** India
14C3 **Nîmes** France
34C3 **Nimmitabel** Australia
50D3 **Nimule** Sudan
39F5 **Nine Degree Chan** Indian Ocean
36F5 **Ninety-East Ridge** Indian Ocean
34C3 **Ninety Mile Beach** Australia
31D4 **Ningde** China
31D4 **Ningdu** China
26C3 **Ningjing Shan** *Mts* China
30D1 **Ningming** China
31A4 **Ningnan** China
31B2 **Ningxia** *Province* China
31B2 **Ning Xian** China
31B5 **Ninh Binh** Vietnam
32D1 **Ninigo Is** Papua New Guinea
75A3 **Nioaque** Brazil
60C2 **Niobrara** *R* USA
50B4 **Nioki** Zaïre
48B3 **Nioro du Sahel** Mali
14B2 **Niort** France
54H4 **Nipawin** Canada
55K5 **Nipigon** Canada
64B1 **Nipigon B** Canada
55K5 **Nipigon,L** Canada
64C1 **Nipissing,L** Canada
66B3 **Nipomo** USA
59C3 **Nipton** USA
75C1 **Niquelândia** Brazil
44B2 **Nirmal** India
43F3 **Nirmāli** India
17E2 **Niš** Serbia, Yugoslavia
38C4 **Nişāb** Yemen
26H4 **Nishino-shima** *I* Japan
28C3 **Nishino-shima** *I* Japan
28A4 **Nishi-suidō** *Str* S Korea
29B4 **Nishiwaki** Japan
33E1 **Nissan Is** Papua New Guinea
55L4 **Nitchequon** Canada
73K8 **Niterói** Brazil
8D4 **Nith** *R* Scotland
19D3 **Nitra** Slovakia
64C3 **Nitro** USA
33J2 **Niue** *I* Pacific Ocean
33G2 **Niulakita** *I* Tuvalu
27E6 **Niut** *Mt* Indonesia
33G1 **Niutao** *I* Tuvalu
28A2 **Niuzhuang** China
13C2 **Nivelles** Belgium
14C2 **Nivernais** *Region* France
12L5 **Nivskiy** Russian Federation
44B2 **Nizāmābād** India
45C3 **Nizana** *Hist Site* Israel
26C1 **Nizhneudinsk** Russian Federation
20K4 **Nizhniye Sergi** Russian Federation
20G5 **Nizhniy Lomov** Russian Federation
20G4 **Nizhniy Novgorod** Russian Federation
20J3 **Nizhniy Odes** Russian Federation
20K4 **Nizhniy Tagil** Russian Federation
25L3 **Nizhnyaya Tunguska** *R* Russian Federation
20G2 **Nizhnyaya Zolotitsa** Russian Federation
40C2 **Nizip** Turkey
12C1 **Njarðvik** Iceland
51C5 **Njoko** *R* Zambia
51D4 **Njombe** Tanzania
50B3 **Nkambé** Cameroon
51D5 **Nkhata Bay** Malawi
50B3 **Nkongsamba** Cameroon
48C3 **N'Konni** Niger
43G4 **Noakhali** Bangladesh
54B3 **Noatak** USA
54B3 **Noatak** *R* USA
28C4 **Nobeoka** Japan
29D2 **Noboribetsu** Japan
75A1 **Nobres** Brazil
63C2 **Nocona** USA
70A1 **Nogales** Sonora, Mexico
59D4 **Nogales** USA
28B4 **Nogata** Japan
13C3 **Nogent-en-Bassigny** France
13B3 **Nogent-sur-Seine** France
20F4 **Noginsk** Russian Federation
42C3 **Nohar** India
29D2 **Noheji** Japan
14B2 **Noirmoutier, Ile de** *I* France
47C1 **Nojane** Botswana
29C4 **Nojima-zaki** *C* Japan
50B3 **Nola** Central African Republic
20H4 **Nolinsk** Russian Federation
68E2 **Nomans Land** *I* USA
54B3 **Nome** USA
13D3 **Nomeny** France
31B1 **Nomgon** Mongolia
28A4 **Nomo-saki** *Pt* Japan
54H3 **Nonacho L** Canada
30C2 **Nong Khai** Thailand
47E2 **Nongoma** South Africa
33G1 **Nonouti** *I* Kiribati
28A3 **Nonsan** S Korea
13C1 **Noord Holland** *Province* Netherlands
47B2 **Noordoewer** Namibia
13C1 **Noordoost Polder** Netherlands
13C1 **Noordzeekanal** Netherlands
54B3 **Noorvik** USA
50B4 **Noqui** Angola
55L5 **Noranda** Canada
13B2 **Nord** *Department* France
24D2 **Nordaustlandet** *I* Svalbard
13D1 **Norden** Germany
13E1 **Nordenham** Germany
13D1 **Norderney** *I* Germany
12F6 **Nordfjord** *Inlet* Norway
12F8 **Nordfriesische** *Is* Germany
18C2 **Nordhausen** Germany
13D1 **Nordhorn** Germany
18B2 **Nordrhein Westfalen** *State* Germany
12J4 **Nordkapp** *C* Norway
55N3 **Nordre Strømfyord** *Fyord* Greenland
12G5 **Nord Storfjället** *Mt* Sweden
25N2 **Nordvik** Russian Federation
9C3 **Nore** *R* Irish Republic
61D2 **Norfolk** Nebraska, USA
65D3 **Norfolk** Virginia, USA
7E3 **Norfolk** *County* England
33F3 **Norfolk I** Pacific Ocean
37K6 **Norfolk I Ridge** Pacific Ocean
63D1 **Norfolk L** USA
25K3 **Noril'sk** Russian Federation
64B2 **Normal** USA
63C1 **Norman** USA
14B2 **Normandie** *Region* France
67B1 **Norman,L** USA
32D2 **Normanton** Australia
54F3 **Norman Wells** Canada
20B2 **Norra Storfjället** *Mt* Sweden
67B1 **Norris L** USA
65D2 **Norristown** USA
12H7 **Norrköping** Sweden
12H6 **Norrsundet** Sweden
12H7 **Norrtälje** Sweden
32B4 **Norseman** Australia
26F1 **Norsk** Russian Federation
75A1 **Nortelândia** Brazil
6D2 **Northallerton** England
32A4 **Northam** Australia
47D2 **Northam** South Africa
52E3 **North American Basin** Atlantic Ocean
32A3 **Northampton** Australia
7D3 **Northampton** England
65E2 **Northampton** USA
7D3 **Northampton** *County* England
44E3 **North Andaman** *I* Indian Ocean
54G3 **North Arm** *B* Canada
67B2 **North Augusta** USA
55M4 **North Aulatsivik** *I* Canada
54H4 **North Battleford** Canada
55L5 **North Bay** Canada
58B2 **North Bend** USA
8D3 **North Berwick** Scotland
68E1 **North Berwick** USA
55M5 **North,C** Canada
62B1 **North Canadian** *R* USA
57E3 **North Carolina** *State* USA
58B1 **North Cascades Nat Pk** USA
64C1 **North Chan** Canada
6B2 **North Chan** Ire/Scotland
56C2 **North Dakota** *State* USA
7E4 **North Downs** England
65D2 **North East** USA
52H2 **North East Atlantic Basin** Atlantic Ocean
54B3 **Northeast C** USA
51C6 **Northern Cape** *Province* South Africa
10B3 **Northern Ireland** UK
61E1 **Northern Light L** Canada/USA
27H5 **Northern Mariana Is** Pacific Ocean
69L1 **Northern Range** *Mts* Trinidad
32C2 **Northern Territory** Australia
51C6 **Northern Transvaal** *Province* South Africa
8D3 **North Esk** *R* Scotland
68D1 **Northfield** Massachusetts, USA
61E2 **Northfield** Minnesota, USA
7E4 **North Foreland** England
35B1 **North I** New Zealand
28B3 **North Korea** *Republic* SE Asia
North Land = Severnaya Zemlya
63D2 **North Little Rock** USA
60C2 **North Loup** *R* USA
76B4 **North Magnetic Pole** Canada
67B3 **North Miami** USA
67B3 **North Miami Beach** USA
66C2 **North Palisade** *Mt* USA
60C2 **North Platte** USA
56C2 **North Platte** *R* USA
76A **North Pole** Arctic
69R3 **North Pt** Barbados
64C1 **North Pt** USA
61E2 **North Raccoon** *R* USA
10B2 **North Rona** *I* Scotland
8D2 **North Ronaldsay** *I* Scotland
52F7 **North Scotia Ridge** Atlantic Ocean
10D2 **North Sea** NW Europe
44E3 **North Sentinel** *I* Andaman Islands
54D3 **North Slope** *Region* USA

34D1 North Stradbroke I Australia
68B1 North Syracuse USA
35B1 North Taranaki Bight *B* New Zealand
68A1 North Tonawanda USA
56C3 North Truchas Peak *Mt* USA
8B3 North Uist *I* Scotland
6C2 Northumberland *County* England
32E3 Northumberland Is Australia
55M5 Northumberland Str Canada
58B1 North Vancouver Canada
68C1 Northville USA
7E3 North Walsham England
54D3 Northway USA
51C6 North West *Province* South Africa
32A3 North West C Australia
42C2 North West Frontier Province Pakistan
55M4 North West River Canada
54G3 North West Territories Canada
61D1 Northwood USA
6D2 North York Moors England
6D2 North Yorkshire *County* England
60D3 Norton *R* USA
54B3 Norton Sd USA
76F1 Norvegia,C Antarctica
68D2 Norwalk Connecticut, USA
64C2 Norwalk Ohio, USA
12F6 Norway *Kingdom* Europe
54J4 Norway House Canada
55J2 Norwegian B Canada
52H1 Norwegian Basin Norwegian Sea
24B3 Norwegian S NW Europe
68D2 Norwich Connecticut, USA
7E3 Norwich England
68C1 Norwich New York, USA
68E1 Norwood Massachusetts, USA
64C3 Norwood Ohio, USA
17F2 Nos Emine *C* Bulgaria
29E2 Noshiro Japan
17F2 Nos Kaliakra *C* Bulgaria
47B1 Nosob *R* Namibia
20J2 Nosovaya Russian Federation
19G2 Nosovka Ukraine
8E1 Noss *I* Scotland
8D2 Noss Head, Pt Scotland
51E5 Nosy Barren *I* Madagascar
51E5 Nosy Bé *I* Madagascar
51F5 Nosy Boraha *I* Madagascar
51E6 Nosy Varika Madagascar
18D2 Notéc *R* Poland
54G4 Notikewin Canada
16D3 Noto Italy
12F7 Notodden Norway
29C3 Noto-hantō *Pen* Japan
55N5 Notre Dame B Canada
48C4 Notsé Togo
7D3 Nottingham England
7D3 Nottingham *County* England
55L3 Nottingham Canada
55L3 Nottingham Island Canada
48A2 Nouadhibou Mauritius
48A3 Nouakchott Mauritius
33F3 Nouméa New Caledonia
48B3 Nouna Burkina
8D2 Noup Head, Pt Scotland
47C3 Noupoort South Africa
55L3 Nouvelle-France, Cap de *C* Canada
75C2 Nova América Brazil
51B4 Nova Caipemba Angola
75B3 Nova Esperança Brazil
75D3 Nova Friburgo Brazil
51B5 Nova Gaia Angola
75C3 Nova Granada Brazil
75C3 Nova Horizonte Brazil
75D3 Nova Lima Brazil
Nova Lisboa = Huambo
75B3 Nova Londrina Brazil
51D6 Nova Mambone Mozambique
16B1 Novara Italy
75C1 Nova Roma Brazil
73K4 Nova Russas Brazil
55M5 Nova Scotia *Province* Canada
66A1 Novato USA
75D2 Nova Venécia Brazil
21E6 Novaya Kakhovka Ukraine
25R2 Novaya Sibir, Ostrov *I* Russian Federation
24G2 Novaya Zemlya *I* Russian Federation
17F2 Nova Zagora Bulgaria
19D3 Nové Zámky Slovakia
20E4 Novgorod Russian Federation
16B2 Novi Ligure Italy
17F2 Novi Pazar Bulgaria
17E2 Novi Pazar Serbia, Yugoslavia
17D1 Novi Sad Serbia, Yugoslavia
21K5 Novoalekseyevka Kazakhstan
21G5 Novoanninskiy Russian Federation
21F6 Novocherkassk Russian Federation
20G3 Novodvinsk Russian Federation
21D5 Novograd Volynskiy Ukraine
19F2 Novogrudok Belarus
74F3 Novo Hamburgo Brazil
24H5 Novokazalinsk Kazakhstan
24K4 Novokuznetsk Russian Federation
76F12 Novolazarevskaya *Base* Antarctica
16D1 Novo Mesto Slovenia
19G3 Novomirgorod Ukraine
20F5 Novomoskovsk Russian Federation
Novo Redondo = Sumbe
21F7 Novorossiysk Russian Federation
25M2 Novorybnoye Russian Federation
24K4 Novosibirsk Russian Federation
25P2 Novosibirskye Ostrova *Is* Russian Federation
21K5 Novotroitsk Russian Federation
21H5 Novo Uzensk Russian Federation
19E2 Novovolynsk Ukraine
20H4 Novo Vyatsk Russian Federation
21E5 Novozybkov Russian Federation
24J3 Novyy Port Russian Federation
19E2 Novy Dwór Mazowiecki Poland
20L4 Novyy Lyalya Russian Federation
20N2 Novyy Port Russian Federation
21J7 Novyy Uzen Kazakhstan
18D2 Nowa Sól Poland
63C1 Nowata USA
43G3 Nowgong India
34D2 Nowra Australia
41F2 Now Shahr Iran
42C2 Nowshera Pakistan
19E3 Nowy Sącz Poland
13B3 Noyon France
14B2 Nozay France
48B4 Nsawam Ghana
47E1 Nuanetsi Zimbabwe
50D2 Nuba Mts Sudan
50D1 Nubian Desert Sudan
56D4 Nueces *R* USA
54J3 Nueltin L Canada
28A2 Nü'erhe China
70B1 Nueva Casas Grandes Mexico
75A3 Nueva Germania Paraguay
69A2 Nueva Gerona Cuba
70B2 Nueva Rosita Mexico
69B2 Nuevitas Cuba
70B1 Nuevo Casas Grandes Mexico
70C2 Nuevo Laredo Mexico
50E3 Nugaal *Region* Somalia
55N2 Nûgâtsiaq Greenland
55N2 Nûgussuaq *I* Greenland
55N2 Nûgussuaq *Pen* Greenland
33G1 Nui *I* Tuvalu
31A5 Nui Con Voi *R* Vietnam
13C4 Nuits France
40D3 Nukhayb Iraq
33G1 Nukufetau *I* Tuvalu
33G1 Nukulaelae *I* Tuvalu
33H1 Nukunon *I* Tokelau Islands
24G5 Nukus Uzbekistan
54C3 Nulato USA
32B4 Nullarbor Plain Australia
48D4 Numan Nigeria
29C3 Numata Japan
50C3 Numatinna *R* Sudan
29D3 Numazu Japan
27G7 Numfoor *I* Indonesia
34C3 Numurkah Australia
68A1 Nunda USA
7D3 Nuneaton England
42D2 Nunkun *Mt* India
16B2 Nuoro Sicily, Italy
41F3 Nurābād Iran
34A2 Nuriootpa Australia
42C1 Nuristan *Region* Afghanistan
20J5 Nurlat Russian Federation
12K6 Nurmes Finland
18C3 Nürnberg Germany
34C2 Nurri,Mt Australia
40D2 Nusaybin Turkey
45D1 Nuşayrīyah, Jabalan *Mts* Syria
42B3 Nushki Pakistan
55M4 Nutak Canada
Nuuk = Godthåb
43E3 Nuwakot Nepal
44C4 Nuwara-Eliya Sri Lanka
47C3 Nuweveldreeks *Mts* South Africa
55L3 Nuyukjuak Canada
54C3 Nyac USA
68D2 Nyack USA
50D3 Nyahururu Falls Kenya
34B3 Nyah West Australia
26C3 Nyainqentanglha Shan *Mts* Tibet, China
50D4 Nyakabindi Tanzania
20L3 Nyaksimvol' Russian Federation
50C2 Nyala Sudan
43F3 Nyalam China
50C3 Nyamlell Sudan
51D6 Nyanda Zimbabwe
20G3 Nyandoma Russian Federation
50B4 Nyanga *R* Gabon
51D5 Nyasa, L Malawi/Mozambique
30B2 Nyaunglebin Burma
20K4 Nyazepetrovsk Russian Federation
12G7 Nyborg Denmark
12H7 Nybro Sweden
24J3 Nyda Russian Federation
55M1 Nyeboes Land *Region* Canada
50D4 Nyeri Kenya
51D5 Nyimba Zambia
39H2 Nyingchi China
19E3 Nyíregyháza Hungary
50D3 Nyiru,Mt Kenya
12J6 Nykarleby Finland
12F7 Nykøbing Denmark
12G8 Nykøbing Denmark
12H7 Nyköping Sweden
47D1 Nyl *R* South Africa
47D1 Nylstroom South Africa
34C2 Nymagee Australia
12H7 Nynäshamn Sweden
34C2 Nyngan Australia
50B3 Nyong *R* Cameroon
28A3 Nyongwol S Korea
28A3 Nyongwon N Korea
14D3 Nyons France
18D2 Nysa Poland
58C2 Nyssa USA
20H3 Nyukhcha Russian Federation
26F1 Nyukzha *R* Russian Federation
25N3 Nyurba Russian Federation
50D4 Nzega Tanzania
48B4 Nzérékoré Guinea
51B4 N'zeto Angola

O

60D2 Oacoma USA
60C2 Oahe,L *Res* USA
66E5 Oahu *I* Hawaiian Islands
34B2 Oakbank Australia
66B2 Oakdale USA
61D1 Oakes USA
34D1 Oakey Australia
59B3 Oakland California, USA
61D2 Oakland Nebraska, USA
58B2 Oakland Oregon, USA
64B3 Oakland City USA
64B2 Oak Lawn USA
66B2 Oakley California, USA
60C3 Oakley Kansas, USA
67B1 Oak Ridge USA
58B2 Oakridge USA
65D2 Oakville Canada
35B3 Oamaru New Zealand
66D2 Oasis California, USA
58D2 Oasis Nevada, USA
76F7 Oates Land *Region* Antarctica
34C4 Oatlands Australia
70C3 Oaxaca Mexico
24H3 Ob' *R* Russian Federation
29C3 Obama Japan
35A3 Oban New Zealand
8C3 Oban Scotland
29D3 Obanazawa Japan
13D2 Oberhausen Germany
60C3 Oberlin USA
13E3 Obernburg Germany
27F7 Obi *I* Indonesia
73G4 Obidos Brazil
29E2 Obihiro Japan
26G2 Obluch'ye Russian Federation
50C3 Obo Central African Republic
50E2 Obock Djibouti
18D2 Oborniki Poland
21F5 Oboyan' Russian Federation
58B2 O'Brien USA
21J5 Obshchiy Syrt *Mts* Russian Federation
24J3 Obskaya Guba *B* Russian Federation
48B4 Obuasi Ghana
67B3 Ocala USA
72D2 Ocaña Colombia
15B2 Ocaña Spain
65D3 Ocean City Maryland, USA
68C3 Ocean City New Jersey, USA
54F4 Ocean Falls Canada
Ocean I = Banaba
66B3 Oceano USA
66D4 Oceanside USA
63E2 Ocean Springs USA
20J4 Ocher Russian Federation
8D3 Ochil Hills Scotland
67B2 Ochlockonee *R* USA
69H1 Ocho Rios Jamaica
67B2 Ocmulgee *R* USA
67B2 Oconee *R* USA
64B2 Oconto USA
70B2 Ocotlán Mexico
48B4 Oda Ghana
28B3 Oda Japan
12B2 Ódáðahraun *Region* Iceland
28A2 Ŏdaejin N Korea
50D1 Oda, Jebel *Mt* Sudan
29E2 Odate Japan
29D3 Odawara Japan
12F6 Odda Norway
48C4 Ode Nigeria
63C3 Odem USA
15A2 Odemira Portugal
17F3 Ödemiş Turkey
47D2 Odendaalsrus South Africa
12G7 Odense Denmark
18C2 Oder *R* Germany/Poland
62B2 Odessa Texas, USA
21E6 Odessa Ukraine
58C1 Odessa Washington, USA
48B4 Odienné Ivory Coast
Odra = Oder
19D2 Odra *R* Poland
73K5 Oeiras Brazil
60C2 Oelrichs USA
61E2 Oelwein USA
16D2 Ofanto *R* Italy
45C3 Ofaqim Israel
9C3 Offaly *County* Irish Republic
13E2 Offenbach Germany
13D3 Offenburg Germany
29D3 Ofunato Japan
29D3 Oga Japan
50E3 Ogaden *Region* Ethiopia
29D3 Ōgaki Japan
60C2 Ogallala USA
26H4 Ogasawara Gunto *Is* Japan
48C4 Ogbomosho Nigeria
61E2 Ogden Iowa, USA
58D2 Ogden Utah, USA
65D2 Ogdensburg USA
67B2 Ogeechee *R* USA
54E3 Ogilvie Mts Canada
67B2 Oglethorpe,Mt USA
48C4 Ogoja Nigeria
19E1 Ogre Latvia
48B2 Oguilet Khenachich *Well* Mali
16D1 Ogulin Croatia
68E1 Ogunquit USA
21J8 Ogurchinskiy, Ostrov *I* Turkmenistan
35A3 Ohai New Zealand
35C1 Ohakune New Zealand
48C2 Ohanet Algeria
29D2 Ōhata Japan
35A2 Ohau,L New Zealand
74B7 O'Higgins, Lago Chile
64B3 Ohio *R* USA
57E2 Ohio *State* USA
13E2 Ohm *R* Germany
51B5 Ohopoho Namibia
18C2 Ohre *R* Czech Republic
17E2 Ohrid Macedonia, Yugoslavia
17E2 Ohridsko Jezero *L* Albania/Macedonia, Yugoslavia
35B1 Ohura New Zealand
73H3 Oiapoque French Guiana
65D2 Oil City USA
66C3 Oildale USA
13B3 Oise *Department* France
14C2 Oise *R* France
28C4 Ōita Japan
66C3 Ojai USA
70B2 Ojinaga Mexico
29C3 Ojiya Japan
74C3 Ojos del Salado *Mt* Argentina
20F5 Oka *R* Russian Federation
47B1 Okahandja Namibia
58C1 Okanagan Falls Canada
58C1 Okanogan USA
58C1 Okanogan *R* USA
58B1 Okanogan Range *Mts* Canada/USA
42C2 Okara Pakistan
47B1 Okasise Namibia
51B5 Okavango *R* Angola/Namibia
51C5 Okavango Delta *Marsh* Botswana
29D3 Okaya Japan
29C4 Okayama Japan
29C4 Okazaki Japan
67B3 Okeechobee USA
67B3 Okeechobee,L USA
67B2 Okefenokee Swamp USA
48C4 Okene Nigeria
42B4 Okha India
43F3 Okhaldunga Nepal
25Q4 Okhotsk Russian Federation
25Q4 Okhotsk, S of Russian Federation
26F4 Okinawa *I* Japan
26F4 Okinawa gunto *Arch* Japan
28C3 Oki-shotō *Is* Japan
28A2 Okkang-dong N Korea
56D3 Oklahoma *State* USA
63C1 Oklahoma City USA
63C1 Okmulgee USA
48C4 Okoja Nigeria
47B1 Okombahe Namibia
50B4 Okondja Gabon
29D2 Okoppe Japan
50B4 Okoyo Congo
48C4 Okpara *R* Benin/Nigeria
20A2 Okstindan *Mt* Norway
21K6 Oktyabr'sk Kazakhstan
20J5 Oktyabr'skiy Bashkirskaya, Russian Federation
26J1 Oktyabr'skiy Kamchatka, Russian Federation
20M3 Oktyabr'skoye Russian Federation
25L2 Oktyabrskoy Revolyutsii, Ostrov *I* Russian Federation
29D2 Okushiri-tō Japan
47C1 Okwa *R* Botswana
12B1 Olafsjorðr Iceland
66D2 Olancha USA
66C2 Olancha Peak *Mt* USA
12H7 Öland *I* Sweden
34B2 Olary Australia
61E3 Olathe USA
74D5 Olavarría Argentina
16B2 Olbia Sicily, Italy
68A1 Olcott USA
54E3 Old Crow Canada
18B2 Oldenburg Niedersachsen, Germany
18C2 Oldenburg Schleswig-Holstein, Germany
68C2 Old Forge USA
7C3 Oldham England
10B3 Old Head of Kinsale *C* Irish Republic
68D2 Old Lyme USA
8D3 Oldmeldrum Scotland
54G4 Olds Canada
65F2 Old Town USA
31B1 Öldziyt
68A1 Olean USA
25O4 Olekma *R* Russian Federation
25O3 Olekminsk Russian Federation
20E2 Olenegorsk Russian Federation
25N3 Olenek Russian Federation
25O2 Olenek *R* Russian Federation
19F2 Olevsk Ukraine
29D2 Ol'ga Russian Federation
47C3 Olifants *R* Cape Province, South Africa
47B1 Olifants *R* Namibia
47E1 Olifants *R* Transvaal, South Africa
47C2 Olifantshoek South Africa
17E2 Ólimbos *Mt* Greece
75C3 Olímpia Brazil
73M5 Olinda Brazil
74C4 Olivares *Mt* Argentina/Chile
75D3 Oliveira Brazil
61E2 Olivia USA
74C2 Ollagüe Chile
74C2 Ollagüe, Vol Bolivia
7D3 Ollerton England
64B3 Olney Illinois, USA
62C2 Olney Texas, USA

26E1 **Olochi** Russian Federation
12G7 **Olofström** Sweden
50B4 **Olombo** Congo
18D3 **Olomouc** Czech Republic
20E3 **Olonets** Russian Federation
14B3 **Oloron-Ste-Marie** France
26E1 **Olovyannaya** Russian Federation
13D2 **Olpe** Germany
19E2 **Olsztyn** Poland
16B1 **Olten** Switzerland
17E2 **Olt** *R* Romania
58B1 **Olympia** USA
58B1 **Olympic Nat Pk** USA
Olympus *Mt* = **Ólimbos**
45B1 **Olympus,Mt** Cyprus
58B1 **Olympus,Mt** USA
25T4 **Olyutorskiy, Mys** *C* Russian Federation
29C3 **Omachi** Japan
29C4 **Omae-zaki** *C* Japan
9C2 **Omagh** Northern Ireland
61D2 **Omaha** USA
58C1 **Omak** USA
38D4 **Oman** *Sultanate* Arabian Pen
38D3 **Oman,G of** UAE
47B1 **Omaruru** Namibia
47A1 **Omaruru** *R* Namibia
29D2 **Ōma-saki** *C* Japan
50A4 **Omboué** Gabon
50D2 **Omdurman** Sudan
50D2 **Om Häjer** Eritrea
29D2 **Ōminato** Japan
54F4 **Omineca Mts** Canada
29C3 **Omiya** Japan
54H2 **Ommanney B** Canada
50D3 **Omo** *R* Ethiopia
16B2 **Omodeo, L** Sardinia, Italy
25R3 **Omolon** *R* Russian Federation
25P3 **Omoloy** *R* Russian Federation
29D3 **Omono** *R* Japan
24J4 **Omsk** Russian Federation
29D2 **Ōmu** Japan
28C4 **Omura** Japan
47C1 **Omuramba Eiseb** *R* Botswana
28C4 **Ōmuta** Japan
20J4 **Omutninsk** Russian Federation
64A2 **Onalaska** USA
65D3 **Onancock** USA
43K1 **Onandausi** India
64C1 **Onaping L** Canada
61D2 **Onawa** USA
51B5 **Oncócua** Angola
51B5 **Ondangua** Namibia
19E3 **Ondava** *R* Slovakia
48C4 **Ondo** Nigeria
26E2 **Öndörhaan** Mongolia
39F5 **One and Half Degree Chan** Indian Ocean
42F3 **Onega** Russian Federation
20F3 **Onega** *R* Russian Federation
20F3 **Onega, L** Russian Federation
68C1 **Oneida** USA
68B1 **Oneida L** USA
60D2 **O'Neill** USA
26J2 **Onekotan** *I* Kuril Is, Russian Federation
50C4 **Onema** Zaïre
68C1 **Oneonta** USA
17F1 **Oneşti** Romania
20F3 **Onezhskaya Guba** *B* Russian Federation
Onezhskoye, Oz *L* = **Onega, L**
47C3 **Ongers** *R* South Africa
51B5 **Ongiva** Angola
28B3 **Ongjin** N Korea
31D1 **Ongniud Qi** China
44C2 **Ongole** India
51E6 **Onilahy** *R* Madagascar
48C4 **Onitsha** Nigeria
26D2 **Onjüül** Mongolia
29C3 **Ono** Japan
29C4 **Ōnohara-jima** *I* Japan
29C4 **Onomichi** Japan
33G1 **Onotoa** *I* Kiribati
32A3 **Onslow** Australia
67C2 **Onslow B** USA
29C3 **Ontake-san** *Mt* Japan
66D3 **Ontario** California, USA
58C2 **Ontario** Oregon, USA
55J4 **Ontario** *Province* Canada
65D2 **Ontario,L** Canada/USA
15B2 **Onteniente** Spain
33E1 **Ontong Java Atoll** Solomon Islands
28A3 **Onyang** S Korea
66C3 **Onyx** USA
32C3 **Oodnadatta** Australia
32C4 **Ooldea** Australia
63C1 **Oologah L** USA
13C1 **Oostelijk Flevoland** *Polder* Netherlands
13B2 **Oostende** Belgium
13B2 **Oosterschelde** *Estuary* Netherlands
44B3 **Ootacamund** India
25R4 **Opala** Russian Federation
50C4 **Opala** Zaïre
44C4 **Opanake** Sri Lanka
20H4 **Oparino** Russian Federation
19D3 **Opava** Czech Republic
67A2 **Opelika** USA
63D2 **Opelousas** USA
60B1 **Opheim** USA
19F1 **Opochka** Russian Federation
19D2 **Opole** Poland
15A1 **Oporto** Portugal
35C1 **Opotiki** New Zealand
67A2 **Opp** USA
12F6 **Oppdal** Norway
35B1 **Opunake** New Zealand
17E1 **Oradea** Romania
12B2 **Öræfajökull** *Mts* Iceland
42D3 **Orai** India
15B2 **Oran** Algeria
72F8 **Orán** Argentina
28A2 **Orang** N Korea
34C2 **Orange** Australia
66D4 **Orange** California, USA
14C3 **Orange** France
63D2 **Orange** Texas, USA
47B2 **Orange** *R* South Africa
67B2 **Orangeburg** USA
73H3 **Orange, Cabo** *C* Brazil
61D2 **Orange City** USA
47D2 **Orange Free State** *Province* South Africa
67B2 **Orange Park** USA
64C2 **Orangeville** Canada
18C2 **Oranienburg** Germany
47B2 **Oranjemund** Namibia
47D1 **Orapa** Botswana
27F5 **Oras** Philippines
17E1 **Orăştie** Romania
17E1 **Oraviţa** Romania
16C2 **Orbetello** Italy
68B2 **Orbisonia** USA
34C3 **Orbost** Australia
13B2 **Orchies** France
66B3 **Orcutt** USA
60D2 **Ord** USA
32B2 **Ord** *R* Australia
59D3 **Orderville** USA
32B2 **Ord,Mt** Australia
25M6 **Ordos** *Desert* China
40C1 **Ordu** Turkey
62B1 **Ordway** USA
12H7 **Örebro** Sweden
64C2 **Oregon** USA
56A2 **Oregon** *State* USA
58B1 **Oregon City** USA
12H6 **Öregrund** Sweden
20F4 **Orekhovo Zuyevo** Russian Federation
21F5 **Orel** Russian Federation
59D2 **Orem** USA
21J5 **Orenburg** Russian Federation
15A1 **Orense** Spain
18C1 **Oresund** *Str* Denmark/Sweden
35A3 **Oreti** *R* New Zealand
19F3 **Orgeyev** Moldavia
17F3 **Orhaneli** *R* Turkey
26D2 **Orhon Gol** *R* Mongolia
34B1 **Orientos** Australia
15B2 **Orihuela** Spain
65D2 **Orillia** Canada
72F2 **Orinoco** *R* Venezuela
68C1 **Oriskany Falls** USA
43E4 **Orissa** *State* India
16B3 **Oristano** Sicily, Italy
16B3 **Oristano, G. di** Sardinia, Italy
12K6 **Orivesi** *L* Finland
73G4 **Oriximiná** Brazil
70C3 **Orizaba** Mexico
75C2 **Orizona** Brazil
8D2 **Orkney** *Is, Region* Scotland
75C3 **Orlândia** Brazil
67B3 **Orlando** USA
14C2 **Orléanais** *Region* France
14C2 **Orléans** France
68E2 **Orleans** USA
25L4 **Orlik** Russian Federation
67B3 **Ormond Beach** USA
7C3 **Ormskirk** England
13C3 **Ornain** *R* France
14B2 **Orne** *R* France
12H6 **Örnsköldsvik** Sweden
28A2 **Oro** N Korea
72D3 **Orocué** Colombia
58C1 **Orofino** USA
45C3 **Oron** Israel
8B3 **Oronsay, I** Scotland
Orontes = **Asi**
19E3 **Orosháza** Hungary
25R3 **Orotukan** Russian Federation
59B3 **Oroville** California, USA
58C1 **Oroville** Washington, USA
19G2 **Orsha** Belarus
21K5 **Orsk** Russian Federation
12F6 **Ørsta** Norway
14B3 **Orthez** France
15A1 **Ortigueira** Spain
14E2 **Ortles** *Mt* Italy
69L1 **Ortoire** *R* Trinidad
61D1 **Ortonville** USA
25O3 **Orulgan, Khrebet** *Mts* Russian Federation
72E7 **Oruro** Bolivia
7E3 **Orwell** *R* England
20K4 **Osa** Russian Federation
61E2 **Osage** Iowa, USA
60C2 **Osage** Wyoming, USA
63D1 **Osage** *R* USA
29D4 **Ōsaka** Japan
70D4 **Osa,Pen de** Costa Rica
63E1 **Osceola** Arkansas, USA
61E2 **Osceola** Iowa, USA
58C2 **Osgood Mts** USA
29D2 **Oshamambe** Japan
65D2 **Oshawa** Canada
29D4 **Ō-shima** *I* Japan
60C2 **Oshkosh** Nebraska, USA
55K5 **Oshkosh** USA
64B2 **Oshkosh** Wisconsin, USA
21H8 **Oshnovīyeh** Iran
48C4 **Oshogbo** Nigeria
50B4 **Oshwe** Zaïre
17D1 **Osijek** Croatia
24K4 **Osinniki** Russian Federation
19F2 **Osipovichi** Belarus
61E2 **Oskaloosa** USA
20B4 **Oskarshamn** Sweden
12G6 **Oslo** Norway
40C2 **Osmaniye** Turkey
18B2 **Osnabrück** Germany
74B6 **Osorno** Chile
15B1 **Osorno** Spain
58C1 **Osoyoos** Canada
32D5 **Ossa,Mt** Australia
64A2 **Osseo** USA
68D2 **Ossining** USA
25S4 **Ossora** Russian Federation
20E4 **Ostashkov** Russian Federation
13E1 **Oste** *R* Germany
Ostend = **Oostende**
12G6 **Østerdalen** *V* Norway
13E1 **Osterholz-Scharmbeck** Germany
12G6 **Östersund** Sweden
13D1 **Ostfriesland** *Region* Germany
12H6 **Östhammär** Sweden
16C2 **Ostia** Italy
19D3 **Ostrava** Czech Republic
19D2 **Ostróda** Poland
19E2 **Ostrołęka** Poland
20D4 **Ostrov** Russian Federation
19D2 **Ostrów Wlkp** Poland
19E2 **Ostrowiec** Poland
19E2 **Ostrów Mazowiecka** Poland
15A2 **Osuna** Spain
65D2 **Oswego** USA
68B1 **Oswego** *R* USA
7C3 **Oswestry** England
19D3 **Oświęcim** Poland
29C3 **Ota** Japan
35B3 **Otago Pen** New Zealand
35C2 **Otaki** New Zealand
29E2 **Otaru** Japan
72C3 **Otavalo** Ecuador
51B5 **Otavi** Namibia
29D3 **Otawara** Japan
68C1 **Otego** USA
58C1 **Othello** USA
17E3 **Óthris** *Mt* Greece
60C2 **Otis** Colorado, USA
68D1 **Otis** Massachusetts, USA
68C2 **Otisville** USA
47B1 **Otjimbingwe** Namibia
51B6 **Otjiwarongo** Namibia
6D3 **Otley** England
31B2 **Otog Qi** China
29D2 **Otoineppu** Japan
35C1 **Otorohanga** New Zealand
12F7 **Otra** *R* Norway
17D2 **Otranto** Italy
17D2 **Otranto,Str of** *Chan* Albania/Italy
64B2 **Otsego** USA
68C1 **Otsego L** USA
29C3 **Ōtsu** Japan
12F6 **Otta** Norway
65D1 **Ottawa** Canada
64B2 **Ottawa** Illinois, USA
63C1 **Ottawa** Kansas, USA
65D1 **Ottawa** *R* Canada
55K4 **Ottawa Is** Canada
13E1 **Otterndorf** Germany
55K4 **Otter Rapids** Canada
55K1 **Otto Fjord** Canada
47D2 **Ottosdal** South Africa
64A2 **Ottumwa** USA
13D3 **Ottweiler** Germany
48C4 **Oturkpo** Nigeria
72C5 **Otusco** Peru
34B3 **Otway,C** Australia
19E2 **Otwock** Poland
30C1 **Ou** *R* Laos
63D2 **Ouachita** *R* USA
63D2 **Ouachita,L** USA
63D2 **Ouachita Mts** USA
48A2 **Ouadane** Mauritius
50C3 **Ouadda** Central African Republic
50C2 **Ouaddai** *Desert Region* Chad
48B3 **Ouagadougou** Burkina
48B3 **Ouahigouya** Burkina
50C3 **Ouaka** *R* Central African Republic
48C3 **Oualam** Niger
48C2 **Ouallen** Algeria
50C3 **Ouanda Djallé** Central African Republic
13B4 **Ouanne** *R* France
48A2 **Ouarane** *Region* Mauritius
48C1 **Ouargla** Algeria
48B2 **Ouarkziz, Jbel** *Mts* Morocco
50C3 **Ouarra** *R* Central African Republic
15C2 **Ouarsenis, Massif de l'** *Mts* Algeria
48B1 **Ouarzazate** Morocco
15C2 **Ouassel** *R* Algeria
50B3 **Oubangui** *R* Central African Republic/Congo/Zaïre
13B2 **Oudenaarde** Belgium
47C3 **Oudtshoorn** South Africa
15B2 **Oued Tlělat** Algeria
48B1 **Oued Zem** Morocco
40B4 **Ouena, Wadi** *Watercourse* Egypt
14A2 **Ouessant, Ile d'** *I* France
50B3 **Ouesso** Congo
48B1 **Ouezzane** Morocco
9C2 **Oughter, L** Irish Republic
50B3 **Ouham** *R* Chad
48C4 **Ouidah** Benin
48B1 **Oujda** Morocco
12J6 **Oulainen** Finland
15C3 **Ouled Nail, Monts des** Algeria
12K5 **Oulu** Finland
12K6 **Oulu** *R* Finland
12K6 **Oulujärvi** *L* Finland
50C2 **Oum Chalouba** Chad
16B3 **Oumel Bouaghi** Algeria
50B2 **Oum Hadjer** Chad
50C2 **Oum Haouach** *Watercourse* Chad
12K5 **Ounas** *R* Finland
20C2 **Ounastunturi** *Mt* Finland
50C2 **Ounianga Kebir** Chad
13D2 **Our** *R* Germany
62A1 **Ouray** USA
13C3 **Ource** *R* France
13B3 **Ourcq** *R* France
Ourense = **Orense**
73K5 **Ouricurí** Brazil
75C3 **Ourinhos** Brazil
75D3 **Ouro Prêto** Brazil
13C2 **Ourthe** *R* Belgium
7E3 **Ouse** *R* Norfolk, England
6D2 **Ouse** *R* N Yorks, England
10B2 **Outer Hebrides** *Is* Scotland
66C4 **Outer Santa Barbara** *Chan* USA
51B6 **Outjo** Namibia
12K6 **Outokumpu** Finland
34B3 **Ouyen** Australia
16B2 **Ovada** Italy
74B4 **Ovalle** Chile
51B5 **Ovamboland** *Region* Namibia
13D1 **Overijssel** *Province* Netherlands
59D3 **Overton** USA
12J5 **Övertorneå** Sweden
60C2 **Ovid** Colorado, USA
68B1 **Ovid** New York, USA
15A1 **Oviedo** Spain
12F6 **Øvre** Norway
21D5 **Ovruch** Ukraine
25O4 **Ovsyanka** Russian Federation
35A3 **Owaka** New Zealand
68B1 **Owasco L** USA
29C4 **Owase** Japan
61E2 **Owatonna** USA
68B1 **Owego** USA
66C2 **Owens** *R* USA
64B3 **Owensboro** USA
66D2 **Owens L** USA
64C2 **Owen Sound** Canada
32D1 **Owen Stanley Range** *Mts* Papua New Guinea
48C4 **Owerri** Nigeria
58E2 **Owl Creek Mts** USA
48C4 **Owo** Nigeria
64C2 **Owosso** USA
58C2 **Owyhee** USA
58C2 **Owyhee** *R* USA
58C2 **Owyhee Mts** USA
72C6 **Oxapampa** Peru
12H7 **Oxelösund** Sweden
7D3 **Oxford** England
68E1 **Oxford** Massachusetts, USA
63E2 **Oxford** Mississippi, USA
68C1 **Oxford** New York, USA
7D4 **Oxford** *County* England
66C3 **Oxnard** USA
29D3 **Oyama** Japan
50B3 **Oyen** Gabon
8C3 **Oykel** *R* Scotland
25Q3 **Oymyakon** Russian Federation
34C4 **Oyster B** Australia
27F6 **Ozamiz** Philippines
19F2 **Ozarichi** Belarus
67A2 **Ozark** USA
63D1 **Ozark Plat** USA
63D1 **Ozarks,L of the** USA
19E3 **Ózd** Hungary
62B2 **Ozona** USA
40D1 **Ozurgety** Georgia

P

47B3 **Paarl** South Africa
8B3 **Pabbay** *I* Scotland
19D2 **Pabianice** Poland
43F4 **Pabna** Bangladesh
19F1 **Pabrade** Lithuania
72F3 **Pacaraima, Serra** *Mts* Brazil/Venezuela
72C5 **Pacasmayo** Peru
70C2 **Pachuca** Mexico
66B1 **Pacific** USA
37N7 **Pacific-Antarctic Ridge** Pacific Ocean
66B2 **Pacific Grove** USA
37L4 **Pacific O**
75D2 **Pacuí** *R* Brazil
27D7 **Padang** Indonesia
20E3 **Padany** Russian Federation
18B2 **Paderborn** Germany
54J3 **Padlei** Canada
43G4 **Padma** *R* Bangladesh
16C1 **Padova** Italy
50B4 **Padrão, Ponta do** *Pt* Angola
56D4 **Padre I** USA
7B4 **Padstow** England
34B3 **Padthaway** Australia
Padua = **Padova**
64B3 **Paducah** Kentucky, USA
62B2 **Paducah** Texas, USA
12L5 **Padunskoye More** *L* Russian Federation
28A2 **Paegam** N Korea
35C1 **Paeroa** New Zealand
47E1 **Pafuri** Mozambique
16C2 **Pag** *I* Croatia
27D7 **Pagai Selatan** *I* Indonesia
27C7 **Pagai Utara** *I* Indonesia
27H5 **Pagan** *I* Pacific Ocean
59D3 **Page** USA
27F8 **Pago Mission** Australia
17F3 **Pagondhas** Greece
62A1 **Pagosa Springs** USA
66E5 **Pahala** Hawaiian Islands
35C2 **Pahiatua** New Zealand
66E5 **Pahoa** Hawaiian Islands
67B3 **Pahokee** USA
12K6 **Päijänne** *L* Finland
66E5 **Pailola Chan** Hawaiian Islands
64C2 **Painesville** USA
59D3 **Painted Desert** USA
64C3 **Paintsville** USA
8C4 **Paisley** Scotland
15B1 **País Vasco** *Region* Spain
72B5 **Paita** Peru
12J5 **Pajala** Sweden
38E3 **Pakistan** *Republic* Asia
30C2 **Pak Lay** Laos
43H4 **Pakokku** Burma
16D1 **Pakrac** Croatia
17D1 **Paks** Hungary
30C2 **Pak Sane** Laos
30D2 **Pakse** Laos
50D3 **Pakwach** Uganda
50B3 **Pala** Chad
16D2 **Palagruža** *I* Croatia
13B3 **Palaiseau** France
47D1 **Palala** *R* South Africa
44E3 **Palalankwe** Andaman Islands
25S4 **Palana** Russian Federation
27E7 **Palangkaraya** Indonesia
44B3 **Palani** India
42C4 **Pālanpur** India
47D1 **Palapye** Botswana
67B3 **Palatka** USA
36H4 **Palau** *USA Dependency* Pacific Ocean
30B3 **Palaw** Burma
27E6 **Palawan** *I* Philippines
44B4 **Palayankottai** India
12J7 **Paldiski** Estonia
27D7 **Palembang** Indonesia
15B1 **Palencia** Spain
45B1 **Paleokhorio** Cyprus
16C3 **Palermo** Sicily, Italy
63C2 **Palestine** USA

43G4 Paletwa Burma
44B3 Pālghāt India
42C3 Pāli India
60B3 Palisade USA
42C4 Pālitāna India
44B4 Palk Str India/Sri Lanka
21H5 Pallasovka Russian Federation
12J5 Pallastunturi *Mt* Finland
35B2 Palliser B New Zealand
35C2 Palliser,C New Zealand
51E5 Palma Mozambique
15C2 Palma de Mallorca Spain
73L5 Palmares Brazil
69A5 Palmar Sur Costa Rica
75B4 Palmas Brazil
48B4 Palmas,C Liberia
75D1 Palmas de Monte Alto Brazil
69B2 Palma Soriano Cuba
67B3 Palm Bay USA
67B3 Palm Beach USA
66C3 Palmdale USA
59C4 Palm Desert California, USA
75C4 Palmeira Brazil
73L5 Palmeira dos Indos Brazil
54D3 Palmer USA
76G3 Palmer *Base* Antarctica
76G3 Palmer Arch Antarctica
76F3 Palmer Land *Region* Antarctica
35B3 Palmerston New Zealand
35C2 Palmerston North New Zealand
68C2 Palmerton USA
67B3 Palmetto USA
16D3 Palmi Italy
72C3 Palmira Colombia
32D2 Palm Is Australia
59C4 Palm Springs USA
64A3 Palmyra Missouri, USA
68B1 Palmyra New York, USA
68B2 Palmyra Pennsylvania, USA
43F4 Palmyras Pt India
66A2 Palo Alto USA
27D6 Paloh Indonesia
50D2 Paloích Sudan
59C4 Palomar Mt USA
27F7 Palopo Indonesia
15B2 Palos, Cabo de *C* Spain
27E7 Palu Indonesia
40C2 Palu Turkey
42D3 Palwal India
48C3 Pama Burkina
27E7 Pamekasan Indonesia
14C3 Pamiers France
39F2 Pamir *Mts* Tajikistan
67C1 Pamlico *R* USA
67C1 Pamlico Sd USA
62B1 Pampa USA
74C4 Pampa de la Salinas *Plain* Argentina
74D5 Pampas *Plains* Argentina
72D2 Pamplona Colombia
15B1 Pamplona Spain
64B3 Pana USA
59D3 Panaca USA
17E2 Panagyurishte Bulgaria
44A2 Panaji India
72C2 Panamá Panama
72B2 Panama *Republic* Central America
69B5 Panama Canal Panama
67A2 Panama City USA
70E4 Panamá, G de Panama
59C3 Panamint Range *Mts* USA
66D2 Panamint V USA
27F5 Panay *I* Philippines
17E2 Pancevo Serbia, Yugoslavia
27F5 Pandan Philippines
44B2 Pandharpur India
34A1 Pandie Pandie Australia
19E1 Panevežys Lithuania
24K5 Panfilov Kazakhstan
30B1 Pang *R* Burma
50D4 Pangani Tanzania
50D4 Pangani *R* Tanzania
50C4 Pangi Zaïre
27D7 Pangkalpinang Indonesia
55M3 Pangnirtung Canada
30B1 Pangtara Burma
59D3 Panguitch USA
62B1 Panhandle USA
42D3 Pānīpat India
42B2 Panjao Afghanistan
28B3 P'anmunjom S Korea
43E4 Panna India
75B3 Panorama Brazil
28A2 Panshan China
28B2 Panshi China
75A2 Pantanal de São Lourenço *Swamp* Brazil
75A2 Pantanal do Rio Negro *Swamp* Brazil
75A2 Pantanal do Taquari *Swamp* Brazil
16C3 Pantelleria *I* Italy
31A4 Pan Xian China
16D3 Paola Italy
63D1 Paola USA
64B3 Paoli USA
18D3 Pápa Hungary
72A1 Papagaya, Golfo del Nicaragua
70D3 Papagayo, G de Costa Rica
66E5 Papaikou Hawaiian Islands
35B1 Papakura New Zealand
70C2 Papantla Mexico
8E1 Papa Stour *I* Scotland
35B1 Papatoetoe New Zealand
8D2 Papa Westray *I* Scotland
13D1 Papenburg Germany
45B1 Paphos Cyprus
8B4 Paps of Jura Scotland
32D1 Papua,G of Papua New Guinea
32D1 Papua New Guinea *Republic* SE Asia
30B2 Papun Burma
73J4 Pará *R* Brazil
73H4 Pará *State* Brazil
32A3 Paraburdoo Australia
72C6 Paracas,Pen de Peru
75C2 Paracatu Brazil
75C2 Paracatu *R* Brazil
30E2 Paracel Is SE Asia
34A2 Parachilna Australia
42C2 Parachinar Pakistan
17E2 Paracin Serbia, Yugoslavia
75D2 Pará de Minas Brazil
59B3 Paradise California, USA
59D3 Paradise Nevada, USA
66D1 Paradise Peak *Mt* USA
63D1 Paragould USA
72F6 Paraguá *R* Bolivia
72F2 Paragua *R* Venezuela
75D1 Paraguaçu *R* Brazil
73G7 Paraguai *R* Brazil
75A4 Paraguarí Paraguay
74E2 Paraguay *R* Paraguay
74E2 Paraguay *Republic* S America
75C3 Paraíba *R* Brazil
73L5 Paraíba *State* Brazil
75D3 Paraíba do Sul *R* Brazil
48C4 Parakou Benin
44B4 Paramakkudi India
73G2 Paramaribo Surinam
75D1 Paramirim Brazil
26J1 Paramushir *I* Russian Federation
74D4 Paraná Argentina
74E4 Paraná *R* Argentina
75B3 Paraná *R* Brazil
73J6 Paranã *R* Brazil
74F2 Paraná *State* Brazil
75C4 Paranaguá Brazil
75B2 Paranaíba Brazil
75B2 Paranaíba *R* Brazil
75B3 Paranapanema *R* Brazil
75C3 Paranapiacaba, Serra do *Mts* Brazil
75B3 Paranavaí Brazil
75D2 Paraope *R* Brazil
35B2 Paraparaumu New Zealand
75D1 Paratinga Brazil
44B2 Parbhani India
45C2 Pardes Hanna Israel
75E2 Pardo *R* Bahia, Brazil
75B3 Pardo *R* Mato Grosso do Sul, Brazil
75C2 Pardo *R* Minas Gerais, Brazil
75C3 Pardo *R* São Paulo, Brazil
18D2 Pardubice Czech Republic
26G4 Parece Vela *Reef* Pacific Ocean
75A1 Parecis Brazil
72F6 Parecis, Serra dos *Mts* Brazil
57F2 Parent Canada
65D1 Parent,L Canada
32A1 Parepare Indonesia
69E4 Paria, G de Trinidad/Venezuela
27D7 Pariaman Indonesia
69E4 Paria, Península de Venezuela
72F3 Parima, Serra *Mts* Brazil
14C2 Paris France
64C3 Paris Kentucky, USA
63E1 Paris Tennessee, USA
63C2 Paris Texas, USA
59D4 Parker USA
64C3 Parkersburg USA
34C2 Parkes Australia
68C3 Parkesburg USA
64A1 Park Falls USA
66B3 Parkfield USA
64B2 Park Forest USA
61D1 Park Rapids USA
61D2 Parkston USA
58B1 Parksville Canada
58D2 Park Valley USA
44C2 Parlākimidi India
44B2 Parli India
16C2 Parma Italy
64C2 Parma USA
73K4 Parnaiba Brazil
73K4 Parnaiba *R* Brazil
17E3 Párnon Óros *Mts* Greece
20C4 Pärnu Estonia
43F3 Paro Bhutan
34B1 Paroo *R* Australia
34B2 Paroo Channel *R* Australia
17F3 Páros *I* Greece
59D3 Parowan USA
34D2 Parramatta Australia
56C4 Parras Mexico
55K3 Parry B Canada
54G2 Parry Is Canada
55L2 Parry, Kap *C* Canada
55L5 Parry Sound Canada
18C3 Parsberg Germany
54F4 Parsnip *R* Canada
63C1 Parsons Kansas, USA
65D3 Parsons West Virginia, USA
14B2 Parthenay France
16C3 Partinico Italy
28C2 Partizansk Russian Federation
9B3 Partry *Mts* Irish Republic
73H4 Paru *R* Brazil
44C2 Parvatipuram India
47D2 Parys South Africa
63C3 Pasadena Texas, USA
66C3 Pasadena USA
30B2 Pasawing Burma
63E2 Pascagoula USA
17F1 Paşcani Romania
58C1 Pasco USA
75E2 Pascoal, Monte Brazil
Pascua, Isla de = Easter I
13B2 Pas-de-Calais *Department* France
12G8 Pasewalk Germany
41G4 Pashū'īyeh Iran
32B4 Pasley,C Australia
74E3 Paso de los Libres Argentina
74E4 Paso de los Toros Uruguay
74B6 Paso Limay Argentina
66B3 Paso Robles USA
68C2 Passaic USA
18C3 Passau Germany
74F3 Passo Fundo Brazil
75C3 Passos Brazil
72C4 Pastaza *R* Peru
72C3 Pasto Colombia
19E1 Pasvalys Lithuania
74B8 Patagonia *Region* Argentina
42C4 Pātan India
43F3 Patan Nepal
43J1 Patandi India
34B3 Patchewollock Australia
35B1 Patea New Zealand
35B2 Patea *R* New Zealand
6D2 Pateley Bridge England
16C3 Paterno Sicily, Italy
68C2 Paterson USA
35A3 Paterson Inlet *B* New Zealand
42D2 Pathankot India
60B2 Pathfinder Res USA
42D2 Patiāla India
72C6 Pativilca Peru
17F3 Pátmos *I* Greece
43F3 Patna India
40D2 Patnos Turkey
25N4 Patomskoye Nagor'ye *Upland* Russian Federation
73L5 Patos Brazil
75C2 Patos de Minas Brazil
74F4 Patos, Lagoa dos *Lg* Brazil
17E3 Pátrai Greece
20L3 Patrasuy Russian Federation
75C2 Patrocínio Brazil
50E4 Patta I Kenya
30C4 Pattani Thailand
30C3 Pattaya Thailand
66B2 Patterson California, USA
63D3 Patterson Louisiana, USA
66C2 Patterson Mt USA
68A2 Patton USA
73L5 Patu Brazil
43G4 Patuakhali Bangladesh
70D3 Patuca *R* Honduras
14B3 Pau France
54F3 Paulatuk Canada
73K5 Paulistana Brazil
47E2 Paulpietersburg South Africa
63C2 Pauls Valley USA
30B2 Paungde Burma
42D2 Pauri India
75D2 Pavão Brazil
16B1 Pavia Italy
24J4 Pavlodar Kazakhstan
20K4 Pavlovka Russian Federation
20G4 Pavlovo Russian Federation
21G5 Pavlovsk Russian Federation
63C1 Pawhuska USA
68A3 Paw Paw USA
68E2 Pawtucket USA
60C2 Paxton USA
58C2 Payette USA
55L4 Payne,L Canada
61E1 Paynesville USA
74E4 Paysandú Uruguay
17E2 Pazardzhik Bulgaria
54G4 Peace *R* Canada
67B3 Peace *R* USA
54G4 Peace River Canada
59D3 Peach Springs USA
7D3 Peak District Nat Pk England
65F1 Peaked Mt USA
34C2 Peak Hill Australia
7D3 Peak,The *Mt* England
59E3 Peale,Mt USA
63D2 Pearl *R* USA
66E5 Pearl City Hawaiian Islands
66E5 Pearl Harbor Hawaiian Islands
62C3 Pearsall USA
47D3 Pearston South Africa
54H2 Peary Chan Canada
51D5 Pebane Mozambique
17E2 Peć Serbia, Yugoslavia
75D2 Peçanha Brazil
63D3 Pecan Island USA
12L5 Pechenga Russian Federation
20K2 Pechora Russian Federation
20J2 Pechora *R* Russian Federation
20J2 Pechorskaya Guba *G* Russian Federation
20J2 Pechorskoye More *S* Russian Federation
16D3 Pecoraro *Mt* Italy
62B2 Pecos USA
62B2 Pecos *R* USA
19D3 Pécs Hungary
45B1 Pedhoulas Cyprus
75D2 Pedra Azul Brazil
75C3 Pedregulho Brazil
69B3 Pedro Cays *Is* Caribbean Sea
74C2 Pedro de Valdivia Chile
75B2 Pedro Gomes Brazil
75A3 Pedro Juan Caballero Paraguay
44C4 Pedro,Pt Sri Lanka
34B2 Peebinga Australia
8D4 Peebles Scotland
67C2 Pee Dee *R* USA
68D2 Peekskill USA
6B2 Peel Isle of Man, British Islands
54E3 Peel *R* Canada
54J2 Peel Sd Canada
Pefos = Paphos
27G7 Peg Arfak *Mt* Indonesia
35B2 Pegasus B New Zealand
30B2 Pegu Burma
32C1 Pegunungan Maoke *Mts* Indonesia
30B2 Pegu Yoma *Mts* Burma
74D5 Pehuajó Argentina
Peipsi Järv = Lake Peipus
75B1 Peixe *R* Mato Grosso, Brazil
75B3 Peixe *R* São Paulo, Brazil
31D3 Pei Xian China
30C5 Pekan Malaysia
27D6 Pekanbaru Indonesia
64B2 Pekin USA
Peking = Beijing
30C5 Pelabohan Kelang Malaysia
14D3 Pelat, Mont France
17E1 Peleaga *Mt* Romania
25N4 Peleduy Russian Federation
64C2 Pelee I Canada
32B1 Peleng *I* Indonesia
61E1 Pelican L USA
47A1 Pelican Pt South Africa
17D2 Pelješac *Pen* Croatia
12J5 Pello Finland
55K3 Pelly Bay Canada
54E3 Pelly Mts Canada
74F4 Pelotas Brazil
74F3 Pelotas *R* Brazil
45B3 Pelusium *Hist Site* Egypt
14D2 Pelvoux, Massif du *Mts* France
20L3 Pelym *R* Russian Federation
51E5 Pemba Mozambique
51E5 Pemba, Baiá de *B* Mozambique
50D4 Pemba I Tanzania
61D1 Pembina USA
65D1 Pembroke Canada
67B2 Pembroke USA
7B4 Pembroke Wales
68E1 Penacook USA
75B3 Penápolis Brazil
15A2 Peñarroya Spain
15B1 Peñarroya *Mt* Spain
7C4 Penarth Wales
15A1 Peñas, Cabo de *C* Spain
74B7 Penas, Golfo de *G* Chile
15A1 Peña Trevinca *Mt* Spain
50B3 Pende *R* Central African Republic/Chad
58C1 Pendleton USA
58C1 Pend Oreille *R* USA
73L6 Penedo Brazil
42D5 Penganga *R* India
31D5 Pengho Lieh Tao *Is* Taiwan
31E2 Penglai China
31B4 Pengshui China
8D4 Penicuik Scotland
30C5 Peninsular Malaysia Malaysia
7D3 Penistone England
44B3 Penner *R* India
6C2 Pennine Chain *Mts* England
68C3 Penns Grove USA
57F2 Pennsylvania *State* USA
68B1 Penn Yan USA
55M3 Penny Highlands *Mts* Canada
65F1 Penobscot *R* USA
65F2 Penobscot B USA
34B3 Penola Australia
32C4 Penong Australia
69A5 Penonomé Panama
6C2 Penrith England
63E2 Pensacola USA
76E2 Pensacola Mts Antarctica
33F2 Pentecost *I* Vanuatu
54G5 Penticton Canada
8D2 Pentland Firth *Chan* Scotland
8D4 Pentland Hills Scotland
6C2 Pen-y-ghent *Mt* England
20H5 Penza Russian Federation
7B4 Penzance England
25S3 Penzhina *R* Russian Federation
25S3 Penzhinskaya Guba *B* Russian Federation
64B2 Peoria USA
30C5 Perak *R* Malaysia
75A3 Perdido *R* Brazil
72C3 Pereira Colombia
75B3 Pereira Barreto Brazil
21G6 Perelazovskiy Russian Federation
19G2 Pereyaslav Ukraine
74D4 Pergamino Argentina
40B2 Perge Turkey
55L4 Péribonca *R* Canada
14C2 Périgueux France
72C2 Perlas, Archipiélago de las Panama
69A4 Perlas, Laguna de Nicaragua
20K4 Perm' Russian Federation
Pernambuco = Recife
73L5 Pernambuco *State* Brazil
17E2 Pernik Bulgaria
13B3 Péronne France
14C3 Perpignan France
66D4 Perris USA
67B2 Perry Florida, USA
67B2 Perry Georgia, USA
68A1 Perry New York, USA
63C1 Perry Oklahoma, USA
54H3 Perry River Canada
64C2 Perrysburg USA
62B1 Perryton USA
63E1 Perryville Missouri, USA
Persia = Iran
38D3 Persian Gulf SW Asia
32A4 Perth Australia
65D2 Perth Canada
8D3 Perth Scotland
68C2 Perth Amboy USA
64B2 Peru USA
72D6 Peru *Republic* S America
37P5 Peru Basin Pacific Ocean
52E6 Peru-Chile Trench Pacific Ocean
16C2 Perugia Italy
16D2 Perušic Croatia
40D2 Pervari Turkey
20G5 Pervomaysk Russian Federation
21E6 Pervomaysk Ukraine
20K4 Pervoural'sk Russian Federation
16C2 Pesaro Italy
66A2 Pescadero USA
Pescadores = Pengho Lieh Tao
16C2 Pescara Italy
42C2 Peshawar Pakistan
17E2 Peshkopi Albania
64B1 Peshtigo USA
20F4 Pestovo Russian Federation
70B3 Petacalco, B de Mexico
45C2 Petah Tiqwa Israel
59B3 Petaluma USA
13C3 Pétange Luxembourg

51D5 **Petauke** Zambia
64B2 **Petenwell L** USA
34A2 **Peterborough** Australia
65D2 **Peterborough** Canada
7D3 **Peterborough** England
68E1 **Peterborough** USA
8E3 **Peterhead** Scotland
55M1 **Petermann Gletscher** *Gl* Greenland
32B3 **Petermann Range** *Mts* Australia
74B5 **Peteroa, Vol** Argentina/ Chile
76G4 **Peter 1 Øy** *I* Antarctica
54E4 **Petersburg** USA
65D3 **Petersburg** Virginia, USA
7D4 **Petersfield** England
16B3 **Petite Kabylie** *Hills* Algeria
55M4 **Petit Mècatina, Rivière du** *R* Canada
42C4 **Petlād** India
70D2 **Peto** Mexico
64C1 **Petoskey** USA
45C3 **Petra** *Hist Site* Jordan
25N2 **Petra, Ostrova** *Is* Russian Federation
28C2 **Petra Velikogo, Zaliv** *B* Russian Federation
59E3 **Petrified Forest Nat Pk** USA
73K5 **Petrolina** Brazil
24H4 **Petropavlovsk** Kazakhstan
26J1 **Petropavlovsk-Kamchatskiy** Russian Federation
75D3 **Petrópolis** Brazil
21H5 **Petrovsk** Russian Federation
25M4 **Petrovsk Zabaykal'skiy** Russian Federation
20E3 **Petrozavodsk** Russian Federation
47D2 **Petrusburg** South Africa
47D2 **Petrus Steyn** South Africa
47C3 **Petrusville** South Africa
25T3 **Pevek** Russian Federation
20H2 **Peza** *R* Russian Federation
13E2 **Pfälzer Wald** *Region* Germany
18B3 **Pforzheim** Germany
42D2 **Phagwara** India
47E1 **Phalaborwa** South Africa
42C3 **Phalodī** India
13D3 **Phalsbourg** France
44A2 **Phaltan** India
30B4 **Phangnga** Thailand
30C3 **Phanom Dang** *Mts* Cambodia/Thailand
30D3 **Phan Rang** Vietnam
30D3 **Phan Thiet** Vietnam
62C3 **Pharr** USA
67C1 **Phelps L** USA
67A2 **Phenix City** USA
30B3 **Phet Buri** Thailand
30D3 **Phiafay** Laos
63E2 **Philadelphia** Mississippi, USA
68C2 **Philadelphia** Pennsylvania, USA
60C2 **Philip** USA
Philippeville = Skikda
13C2 **Philippeville** Belgium
27F5 **Philippine S** Pacific Ocean
27F5 **Philippines** *Republic* SE Asia
36H4 **Philippine Trench** Pacific Ocean
47D3 **Philippolis** South Africa
58D1 **Philipsburg** Montana, USA
65D2 **Philipsburg** Pennsylvania, USA
54D3 **Philip Smith Mts** USA
47C3 **Philipstown** South Africa
55K1 **Phillips B** Canada
60D3 **Phillipsburg** Kansas, USA
68C2 **Phillipsburg** New Jersey, USA
55K2 **Philpots Pen** Canada
30C3 **Phnom Penh** Cambodia
59D4 **Phoenix** Arizona, USA
68B1 **Phoenix** New York, USA
33H1 **Phoenix Is** Pacific Ocean
68C2 **Phoenixville** USA
30C1 **Phong Saly** Laos
30C3 **Phra Nakhon** Thailand
30C2 **Phu Bia** *Mt* Laos
30D3 **Phu Cuong** Vietnam
30B4 **Phuket** Thailand
43E4 **Phulbāni** India
30C2 **Phu Miang** *Mt* Thailand
30C2 **Phu Set** *Mt* Laos
30D1 **Phu Tho** Vietnam
30D4 **Phu Vinh** Vietnam
16B1 **Piacenza** Italy
34D1 **Pialba** Australia
34C2 **Pian** *R* Australia
16C2 **Pianosa** *I* Italy
16D2 **Pianosa** *I* Italy
19E2 **Piaseczno** Poland
75D1 **Piatā** Brazil
17F1 **Piatra-Neamţ** Romania
73K5 **Piauí** *State* Brazil
16C1 **Piave** *R* Italy
50D3 **Pibor** *R* Sudan
50D3 **Pibor Post** Sudan
13B3 **Picardie** *Region* France
63E2 **Picayune** USA
74B4 **Pichilemu** Chile
6D2 **Pickering** England
55J4 **Pickle Lake** Canada
48A1 **Pico** *I* Azores
69C5 **Pico Bolivar** *Mt* Venezuela
15A1 **Pico de Almanzor** *Mt* Spain
15C1 **Pico de Aneto** *Mt* Spain
69C3 **Pico Duarte** *Mt* Dominican Republic
73K5 **Picos** Brazil
15B1 **Picos de Europa** *Mt* Spain
34D2 **Picton** Australia
35B2 **Picton** New Zealand
50B1 **Pic Toussidé** *Mt* Chad
75C3 **Piedade** Brazil
66C2 **Piedra** USA
66B3 **Piedras Blancas,Pt** USA
70B2 **Piedras Negras** Mexico
64B1 **Pie I** Canada
12K6 **Pieksämäki** Finland
12K6 **Pielinen** *L* Finland
47D2 **Pienaar's River** South Africa
60C2 **Pierre** USA
19D3 **Piešťany** Slovakia
47E2 **Pietermaritzburg** South Africa
47D1 **Pietersburg** South Africa
47E2 **Piet Retief** South Africa
17F1 **Pietrosul** *Mt* Romania
27H6 **Pigailoe** *I* Pacific Ocean
63D1 **Piggott** USA
28A3 **Pihyŏn** N Korea
55J4 **Pikangikum L** Canada
60B3 **Pikes Peak** USA
47B3 **Piketberg** South Africa
64C3 **Pikeville** USA
55O3 **Pikiutaleq** Greenland
39F2 **Pik Kommunizma** *Mt* Tajikistan
50B3 **Pikounda** Congo
39G1 **Pik Pobedy** *Mt* China/ Kirgizia
18D2 **Piła** Poland
74E3 **Pilar** Paraguay
74D2 **Pilcomayo** *R* Argentina/ Bolivia/Paraguay
47E1 **Pilgrim's Rest** South Africa
42D3 **Pīlībhīt** India
19D2 **Pilica** *R* Poland
34C4 **Pillar,C** Australia
75C2 **Pilões, Serra dos** *Mts* Brazil
17E3 **Pílos** Greece
58C1 **Pilot Knob** *Mt* USA
66D1 **Pilot Peak** *Mt* USA
63E3 **Pilottown** USA
73G4 **Pimenta** Brazil
30C4 **Pinang** *I* Malaysia
69A2 **Pinar del Rio** Cuba
13C2 **Pinche** Belgium
73J4 **Pindaré** *R* Brazil
17E3 **Píndhos** *Mts* Greece
63D2 **Pine Bluff** USA
60C2 **Pine Bluffs** USA
61E1 **Pine City** USA
32C2 **Pine Creek** Australia
68B2 **Pine Creek** *R* USA
66C1 **Pinecrest** USA
66C2 **Pinedale** California, USA
58E2 **Pinedale** Wyoming, USA
66C2 **Pine Flat Res** USA
20G3 **Pinega** Russian Federation
20H3 **Pinega** *R* Russian Federation
68B2 **Pine Grove** USA
67B3 **Pine Hills** USA
67C1 **Pinehurst** USA
67B3 **Pine I** USA
63D2 **Pineland** USA
67B3 **Pinellas Park** USA
66B3 **Pine Mt** USA
54G3 **Pine Point** Canada
60C2 **Pine Ridge** USA
63D2 **Pines,L. o'the** USA
63D2 **Pineville** USA
31C3 **Pingdingshan** China
31B5 **Pingguo** China
31B2 **Pingliang** China
31B2 **Pingluo** China
31D4 **Pingtan Dao** *I* China
31E5 **Pingtung** Taiwan
31A3 **Pingwu** China
31B5 **Pingxiang** Guangxi, China
31C4 **Pingxiang** Jiangxi, China
73J4 **Pinheiro** Brazil
27C6 **Pini** *I* Indonesia
17E3 **Piniós** *R* Greece
32A4 **Pinjarra** Australia
66B2 **Pinnacles Nat. Mon.** USA
34B3 **Pinnaroo** Australia
Pinos,I de = Juventud, Isla de la
66C3 **Pinos,Mt** USA
59B3 **Pinos,Pt** USA
27E7 **Pinrang** Indonesia
33F3 **Pins, Île des** New Caledonia
21D5 **Pinsk** Belarus
20H3 **Pinyug** Russian Federation
59D3 **Pioche** USA
16C2 **Piombino** Italy
58D1 **Pioneer Mts** USA
25K2 **Pioner, Ostrov** *I* Russian Federation
20L3 **Pionerskiy** Russian Federation
19D2 **Piotrków Trybunalski** Poland
8F2 **Piper** *Oilfield* N Sea
66D2 **Piper Peak** *Mt* USA
61D2 **Pipestone** USA
57F2 **Pipmuacan, Rés** *Res* Canada
64C2 **Piqua** USA
75B4 **Piquiri** *R* Brazil
75C2 **Piracanjuba** Brazil
75C3 **Piracicaba** Brazil
75C3 **Piraçununga** Brazil
75C3 **Piraí do Sul** Brazil
17E3 **Piraiévs** Greece
75C3 **Pirajuí** Brazil
75B2 **Piranhas** Brazil
75D2 **Pirapora** Brazil
75C2 **Pirenópolis** Brazil
75C2 **Pires do Rio** Brazil
17E3 **Pírgos** Greece
14B3 **Pirineos** *Mts* France/ Spain
73K4 **Piripiri** Brazil
13D3 **Pirmasens** Germany
17E2 **Pirot** Serbia, Yugoslavia
42C2 **Pīr Panjāl Range** *Mts* Pakistan
27F7 **Piru** Indonesia
66C3 **Piru Creek** *R* USA
16C2 **Pisa** Italy
72C6 **Pisco** Peru
68C1 **Piseco** USA
18C3 **Písek** Czech Republic
42B2 **Pishin** Pakistan
66B3 **Pismo Beach** USA
74C3 **Pissis** *Mt* Argentina
16C2 **Pistoia** Italy
15B1 **Pisuerga** *R* Spain
58B2 **Pit** *R* USA
72C3 **Pitalito** Colombia
37N6 **Pitcairn** *I* Pacific Ocean
12H5 **Pite** *R* Sweden
12J5 **Piteå** Sweden
17E2 **Piteşti** Romania
25L4 **Pit Gorodok** Russian Federation
13B3 **Pithiviers** France
20E3 **Pitkyaranta** Russian Federation
8D3 **Pitlochry** Scotland
20M2 **Pitlyar** Russian Federation
33H5 **Pitt** *I* New Zealand
54F4 **Pitt I** Canada
66B1 **Pittsburg** California, USA
63D1 **Pittsburg** Kansas, USA
65D2 **Pittsburgh** USA
64A3 **Pittsfield** Illinois, USA
68D1 **Pittsfield** Massachusetts, USA
68C2 **Pittston** USA
34D1 **Pittsworth** Australia
72B5 **Piura** Peru
66C3 **Piute Peak** *Mt* USA
43E3 **Piuthan** Nepal
66C3 **Pixley** USA
12B2 **Pjórsá** *R* Iceland
55N5 **Placentia B** Canada
66B1 **Placerville** USA
13C3 **Plaine Lorraine** *Region* France
62B1 **Plains** USA
61D2 **Plainview** Nebraska, USA
62B2 **Plainview** Texas, USA
66B2 **Planada** USA
73H7 **Planalto de Mato Grosso** *Plat* Brazil
73L5 **Planalto do Borborema** *Plat* Brazil
33E1 **Planet Deep** Papua New Guinea
60D2 **Plankinton** USA
63C2 **Plano** USA
67B3 **Plantation** USA
67B3 **Plant City** USA
15A1 **Plasencia** Spain
20L5 **Plast** Russian Federation
26G2 **Plastun** Russian Federation
74E5 **Plata, Río de la** Argentina/ Uruguay
13D2 **Plateau Lorrain** France
69C5 **Plato** Colombia
45B1 **Platres** Cyprus
60D2 **Platte** USA
60C2 **Platte** *R* USA
64A2 **Platteville** USA
65E2 **Plattsburgh** USA
61D2 **Plattsmouth** USA
18C2 **Plauen** Germany
20F5 **Plavsk** Russian Federation
72B4 **Playas** Ecuador
66B2 **Pleasanton** California, USA
62C3 **Pleasanton** Texas, USA
68C3 **Pleasantville** USA
64B3 **Pleasure Ridge Park** USA
30D3 **Pleiku** Vietnam
35C1 **Plenty,B of** New Zealand
60C1 **Plentywood** USA
20G3 **Plesetsk** Russian Federation
19D2 **Pleszew** Poland
55L4 **Pletipi,L** Canada
17E2 **Pleven** Bulgaria
17D2 **Pljevlja** Montenegro, Yugoslavia
17D2 **Ploče** Bosnia-Herzegovina
19D2 **Płock** Poland
14B2 **Ploërmel** France
17F2 **Ploieşti** Romania
13D4 **Plombières-les-Bains** France
20C5 **Płońsk** Poland
17E2 **Plovdiv** Bulgaria
58C1 **Plummer** USA
51C6 **Plumtree** Zimbabwe
66B1 **Plymouth** California, USA
7B4 **Plymouth** England
64B2 **Plymouth** Indiana, USA
68E2 **Plymouth** Massachusetts, USA
68C2 **Plymouth** Pennsylvania, USA
68E2 **Plymouth B** USA
7B4 **Plymouth Sd** England
7C3 **Plynlimon** *Mt* Wales
18C3 **Plzeň** Czech Republic
18D2 **Pniewy** Poland
48B3 **Po** Burkina
16C2 **Po** *R* Italy
48C4 **Pobé** Benin
26H2 **Pobedino** Russian Federation
58D2 **Pocatello** USA
19G2 **Pochinok** Russian Federation
75D1 **Poções** Brazil
65D3 **Pocomoke City** USA
75A2 **Poconé** Brazil
75C3 **Poços de Caldas** Brazil
17D2 **Podgorica** Montenegro, Yugoslavia
25L3 **Podkamennaya Tunguska** *R* Russian Federation
20F4 **Podol'sk** Russian Federation
19F3 **Podol'skaya Vozvyshennost'** *Upland* Ukraine
20E3 **Podporozh'ye** Russian Federation
20G3 **Podyuga** Russian Federation
47B2 **Pofadder** South Africa
42A2 **Poghdar** Afghanistan
28B3 **P'ohang** S Korea
76G9 **Poinsett,C** Antarctica
34C2 **Point** Australia
69E3 **Pointe-à-Pitre** Guadeloupe
50B4 **Pointe Noire** Congo
34B3 **Point Fairy** Australia
69L1 **Point Fortin** Trinidad
54B3 **Point Hope** USA
54G3 **Point L** Canada
54B3 **Point Lay** USA
68C2 **Point Pleasant** New Jersey, USA
64C3 **Point Pleasant** W Virginia, USA
14C2 **Poitiers** France
14B2 **Poitou** *Region* France
13A3 **Poix** France
42C3 **Pokaran** India
34C1 **Pokataroo** Australia
43E3 **Pokhara** Nepal
25O3 **Pokrovsk** Russian Federation
59D3 **Polacca** USA
68C1 **Poland** USA
19D2 **Poland** *Republic* Europe
40B2 **Polatlı** Turkey
49D4 **Poli** Cameroon
16D3 **Policastro, G di** Italy
27F5 **Polillo Is** Philippines
25P4 **Poliny Osipenko** Russian Federation
45B1 **Polis** Cyprus
17E2 **Políyiros** Greece
44B3 **Pollāchi** India
16D3 **Pollino, Monte** *Mt* Italy
19F2 **Polonnye** Ukraine
19F1 **Polotsk** Belarus
58D1 **Polson** USA
21E6 **Poltava** Ukraine
16D1 **Pölten** Austria
20L3 **Polunochoye** Russian Federation
12L5 **Poluostrov Rybachiy** *Pen* Russian Federation
62A2 **Polvadera** USA
20E2 **Polyarnyy** Murmansk, Russian Federation
25Q2 **Polyarnyy** Yakutskaya, Russian Federation
20L2 **Polyarnyy Ural** *Mts* Russian Federation
37L4 **Polynesia** *Region* Pacific Ocean
72C5 **Pomabamba** Peru
75D3 **Pomba** *R* Brazil
9C2 **Pomeroy** Northern Ireland
66D3 **Pomona** USA
61D3 **Pomona Res** USA
67B3 **Pompano Beach** USA
68C2 **Pompton Lakes** USA
63C1 **Ponca City** USA
69D3 **Ponce** Puerto Rico
67B3 **Ponce de Leon B** USA
44B3 **Pondicherry** India
55L2 **Pond Inlet** Canada
15A1 **Ponferrada** Spain
48C4 **Pongara, Pte** Equatorial Guinea
50C3 **Pongo** *R* Sudan
47E2 **Pongola** *R* South Africa
44B3 **Ponnāni** India
43G4 **Ponnyadoung Range** *Mts* Burma
24F3 **Ponoy** Russian Federation
20G2 **Ponoy** *R* Russian Federation
14B2 **Pons** France
48A1 **Ponta Delgada** Azores
75B4 **Ponta Grossa** Brazil
75C3 **Pontal** Brazil
13C3 **Pont-à-Mousson** France
75A3 **Ponta Pora** Brazil
14D2 **Pontarlier** France
63D2 **Pontchartrain,L** USA
75A1 **Ponte de Pedra** Brazil
16C2 **Pontedera** Italy
7D3 **Pontefract** England
16B2 **Ponte Leccia** Corsica, France
15A1 **Pontevedra** Spain
64B2 **Pontiac** Illinois, USA
64C2 **Pontiac** Michigan, USA
27D7 **Pontianak** Indonesia
14B2 **Pontivy** France
13B3 **Pontoise** France
63E2 **Pontotoc** USA
13B3 **Pont-sur-Yonne** France
7C4 **Pontypool** Wales
7C4 **Pontypridd** Wales
16C2 **Ponziane, I** Italy
7D4 **Poole** England
Poona = Pune
34B2 **Pooncarie** Australia
34B2 **Poopelloe,L** Australia
72E7 **Poopó, Lago** Bolivia
54C3 **Poorman** USA
72C3 **Popayán** Colombia
13B2 **Poperinge** Belgium
34B2 **Popilta L** Australia
60B1 **Poplar** USA
63D1 **Poplar Bluff** USA
63E2 **Poplarville** USA
70C3 **Popocatepetl** *Vol* Mexico
50B4 **Popokabaka** Zaïre
27H7 **Popondetta** Papua New Guinea
17F2 **Popovo** Bulgaria
75C1 **Porangatu** Brazil
42B4 **Porbandar** India
75C1 **Porcos** *R* Brazil
54D3 **Porcupine** *R* Canada/ USA
16C1 **Poreč** Croatia
75B3 **Porecatu** Brazil
12J6 **Pori** Finland
35B2 **Porirua** New Zealand
12H5 **Porjus** Sweden
69E4 **Porlamar** Venezuela
26H2 **Poronaysk** Russian Federation
20E3 **Porosozero** Russian Federation
12K4 **Porsangen** *Inlet* Norway
12F7 **Porsgrunn** Norway
9C2 **Portadown** Northern Ireland
9D2 **Portaferry** Northern Ireland
64B2 **Portage** USA
60C1 **Portal** USA
54F5 **Port Alberni** Canada
15A2 **Portalegre** Portugal
62B2 **Portales** USA
47D3 **Port Alfred** South Africa
54F4 **Port Alice** Canada
68A2 **Port Allegany** USA
63D2 **Port Allen** USA
58B1 **Port Angeles** USA
69B3 **Port Antonio** Jamaica
9C3 **Portarlington** Irish Republic
63D3 **Port Arthur** USA
8B4 **Port Askaig** Scotland
32C4 **Port Augusta** Australia
69C3 **Port-au-Prince** Haiti

64C2 **Port Austin** USA
44E3 **Port Blair** Andaman Islands
34B3 **Port Campbell** Australia
43F4 **Port Canning** India
55M5 **Port Cartier** Canada
35B3 **Port Chalmers** New Zealand
67B3 **Port Charlotte** USA
68D2 **Port Chester** USA
64C2 **Port Clinton** USA
65D2 **Port Colborne** Canada
34C4 **Port Davey** *B* Australia
69C3 **Port-de-Paix** Haiti
30C5 **Port Dickson** Malaysia
47E3 **Port Edward** South Africa
75D2 **Porteirinha** Brazil
64C2 **Port Elgin** Canada
47D3 **Port Elizabeth** South Africa
8B4 **Port Ellen** Scotland
6B2 **Port Erin** Isle of Man, British Islands
69N2 **Porter Pt** St Vincent
66C2 **Porterville** USA
32D4 **Port Fairy** Australia
50A4 **Port Gentil** Gabon
63D2 **Port Gibson** USA
58B1 **Port Hammond** Canada
48C4 **Port Harcourt** Nigeria
54F4 **Port Hardy** Canada
55M5 **Port Hawkesbury** Canada
7C4 **Porthcawl** Wales
32A3 **Port Hedland** Australia
7B3 **Porthmadog** Wales
55N4 **Port Hope Simpson** Canada
66C3 **Port Hueneme** USA
64C2 **Port Huron** USA
15A2 **Portimão** Portugal
34D2 **Port Jackson** *B* Australia
68D2 **Port Jefferson** USA
68C2 **Port Jervis** USA
34D2 **Port Kembla** Australia
7C4 **Portland** England
64C2 **Portland** Indiana, USA
65E2 **Portland** Maine, USA
34C2 **Portland** New South Wales, Australia
58B1 **Portland** Oregon, USA
34B3 **Portland** Victoria, Australia
69H2 **Portland Bight** *B* Jamaica
7C4 **Portland Bill** *Pt* England
34C4 **Portland,C** Australia
35C1 **Portland I** New Zealand
69H2 **Portland Pt** Jamaica
9C3 **Port Laoise** Irish Republic
63C3 **Port Lavaca** USA
32C4 **Port Lincoln** Australia
48A4 **Port Loko** Sierra Leone
51F6 **Port Louis** Mauritius
34B3 **Port MacDonnell** Australia
34D2 **Port Macquarie** Australia
68A2 **Port Matilda** USA
32D1 **Port Moresby** Papua New Guinea
47B2 **Port Nolloth** South Africa
68C3 **Port Norris** USA
Porto = Oporto
74F4 **Pôrto Alegre** Brazil
Porto Alexandre = Tombua
69A5 **Porto Armuelles** Panama
75A1 **Pôrto Artur** Brazil
75B3 **Pôrto 15 de Novembro** Brazil
75B1 **Pôrto dos Meinacos** Brazil
74F2 **Pôrto E Cunha** Brazil
75A2 **Pôrto Esperança** Brazil
16C2 **Portoferraio** Italy
69L1 **Port of Spain** Trinidad
75A2 **Pôrto Jofre** Brazil
75B3 **Pôrto Mendez** Brazil
75A3 **Pôrto Murtinho** Brazil
48C4 **Porto Novo** Benin
75B3 **Pôrto Primavera, Represa** *Res* Brazil
58B1 **Port Orchard** USA
58B2 **Port Orford** USA
75B3 **Pôrto Santa Helena** Brazil
48A1 **Porto Santo** *I* Madeira
75B3 **Pôrto São José** Brazil
73L7 **Pôrto Seguro** Brazil
16B2 **Porto Torres** Sardinia, Italy
75B4 **Pôrto União** Brazil
16B2 **Porto Vecchio** Corsica, France
72F5 **Pôrto Velho** Brazil
8C4 **Portpatrick** Scotland
35A3 **Port Pegasus** *B* New Zealand
34B3 **Port Phillip B** Australia
34A2 **Port Pirie** Australia
8B3 **Portree** Scotland
58B1 **Port Renfrew** Canada
69J2 **Port Royal** Jamaica
67B2 **Port Royal Sd** USA
9C2 **Portrush** Northern Ireland
45B3 **Port Said** Egypt
67A3 **Port St Joe** USA
47D3 **Port St Johns** South Africa
55N4 **Port Saunders** Canada
47E3 **Port Shepstone** South Africa
69Q2 **Portsmouth** Dominica
7D4 **Portsmouth** England
68E1 **Portsmouth** New Hampshire, USA
64C3 **Portsmouth** Ohio, USA
65D3 **Portsmouth** Virginia, USA
34D2 **Port Stephens** *B* Australia
9C2 **Portstewart** Northern Ireland
50D2 **Port Sudan** Sudan
63E3 **Port Sulphur** USA
12K5 **Porttipahdan Tekojärvi** *Res* Finland
15A2 **Portugal** *Republic* Europe
9B3 **Portumna** Irish Republic
68A1 **Portville** USA
64B2 **Port Washington** USA
30C5 **Port Weld** Malaysia
72E6 **Porvenir** Bolivia
12K6 **Porvoo** Finland
74E3 **Posadas** Argentina
15A2 **Posadas** Spain
41G3 **Posht-e Badam** Iran
27F7 **Poso** Indonesia
28A4 **Posŏng** S Korea
20M2 **Pos Poluy** Russian Federation
75C1 **Posse** Brazil
62B2 **Post** USA
19F1 **Postavy** Belarus
47C2 **Postmasburg** South Africa
16C1 **Postojna** Slovenia
28C2 **Pos'yet** Russian Federation
47D2 **Potchefstroom** South Africa
63D1 **Poteau** USA
16D2 **Potenza** Italy
47D1 **Potgietersrus** South Africa
62C3 **Poth** USA
21G7 **Poti** Georgia
48D3 **Potiskum** Nigeria
58C1 **Potlatch** USA
47C3 **Potloer** *Mt* South Africa
58C1 **Pot Mt** USA
65D3 **Potomac** *R* USA
72E7 **Potosí** Bolivia
74C3 **Potrerillos** Chile
18C2 **Potsdam** Germany
60C2 **Potter** USA
68C2 **Pottstown** USA
68B2 **Pottsville** USA
68D2 **Poughkeepsie** USA
75C3 **Pouso Alegre** Brazil
35C1 **Poverty B** New Zealand
20F3 **Povonets** Russian Federation
21G5 **Povorino** Russian Federation
55L4 **Povungnituk** Canada
60B1 **Powder** *R* USA
60B2 **Powder River** USA
58E2 **Powell** USA
32C2 **Powell Creek** Australia
59D3 **Powell,L** USA
54F5 **Powell River** Canada
7C3 **Powys** *County* Wales
75B2 **Poxoréo** Brazil
31D4 **Poyang Hu** *L* China
40C2 **Pozantı** Turkey
70C2 **Poza Rica** Mexico
18D2 **Poznań** Poland
74E2 **Pozo Colorado** Paraguay
16C2 **Pozzuoli** Italy
48B4 **Pra** *R* Ghana
30C3 **Prachin Buri** Thailand
30B3 **Prachuap Khiri Khan** Thailand
18D2 **Praděd** *Mt* Czech Republic
14C3 **Pradelles** France
75E2 **Prado** Brazil
18C2 **Prague** Czech Republic
Praha = Prague
48A4 **Praia** Cape Verde
75A1 **Praia Rica** Brazil
72F5 **Prainha** Brazil
62B2 **Prairie Dog Town Fork** *R* USA
64A2 **Prairie du Chien** USA
61E3 **Prairie Village** USA
30C3 **Prakhon Chai** Thailand
75C2 **Prata** Brazil
75C2 **Prata** *R* Brazil
Prates *I* **= Dongsha Qundao**
16C2 **Prato** Italy
68C1 **Prattsville** USA
67A2 **Prattville** USA
14B1 **Prawle Pt** England
25L4 **Predivinsk** Russian Federation
25Q3 **Predporozhnyy** Russian Federation
19E2 **Pregolyu** *R* Russian Federation
30D3 **Prek Kak** Cambodia
64A1 **Prentice** USA
18C2 **Prenzlau** Germany
44E3 **Preparis I** Burma
18D3 **Přerov** Czech Republic
59D4 **Prescott** Arizona, USA
63D2 **Prescott** Arkansas, USA
65D2 **Prescott** Canada
60C2 **Presho** USA
74D3 **Presidencia Roque Sáenz Peña** Argentina
75B3 **Presidente Epitácio** Brazil
75B2 **Presidente Murtinho** Brazil
75B3 **Presidente Prudente** Brazil
75B3 **Presidente Venceslau** Brazil
62B3 **Presidio** USA
19E3 **Prešov** Slovakia
65F1 **Presque Isle** USA
6C3 **Preston** England
56B2 **Preston** Idaho, USA
61E2 **Preston** Minnesota, USA
63D1 **Preston** Missouri, USA
8C4 **Prestwick** Scotland
73J8 **Prêto** Brazil
75C2 **Prêto** *R* Brazil
47D2 **Pretoria** South Africa
17E3 **Préveza** Greece
30D3 **Prey Veng** Cambodia
59D3 **Price** USA
63E2 **Prichard** USA
21E6 **Prichernomorskaya Nizmennost'** *Lowland* Ukraine
69M2 **Prickly Pt** Grenada
19F3 **Pridneprovskaya Vozvyshennost'** *Upland* Ukraine
19E1 **Priekule** Lithuania
47C2 **Prieska** South Africa
58C1 **Priest L** USA
58C1 **Priest River** USA
17E2 **Prilep** Albania/Macedonia, Yugoslavia/Greece
21E5 **Priluki** Ukraine
76G3 **Primavera** *Base* Antarctica
12K6 **Primorsk** Russian Federation
21F6 **Primorsko-Akhtarsk** Russian Federation
54H4 **Prince Albert** Canada
47C3 **Prince Albert** South Africa
54F2 **Prince Albert,C** Canada
54G2 **Prince Albert Pen** Canada
54G2 **Prince Albert Sd** Canada
55L3 **Prince Charles I** Canada
76F10 **Prince Charles Mts** Antarctica
55M5 **Prince Edward I** *Province* Canada
36C7 **Prince Edward Is** Indian Ocean
54F4 **Prince George** Canada
54H2 **Prince Gustaf Adolf Sea** Canada
27H8 **Prince of Wales I** Australia
54H2 **Prince of Wales I** Canada
54E4 **Prince of Wales I** USA
54G2 **Prince of Wales Str** Canada
54G2 **Prince Patrick I** Canada
55J2 **Prince Regent Inlet** *Str* Canada
54E4 **Prince Rupert** Canada
32D2 **Princess Charlotte B** Australia
69L1 **Princes Town** Trinidad
54F5 **Princeton** Canada
64B2 **Princeton** Illinois, USA
64B3 **Princeton** Kentucky, USA
61E2 **Princeton** Missouri, USA
68C2 **Princeton** New Jersey, USA
64C3 **Princeton** W Virginia, USA
54D3 **Prince William Sd** USA
48C4 **Príncipe** *I* Sao Tome & Principe
58B2 **Prineville** USA
55O3 **Prins Christian Sund** Greenland
76F12 **Prinsesse Astrid Kyst** *Region* Antarctica
76F12 **Prinsesse Ragnhild Kyst** *Region* Antarctica
24C2 **Prins Karls Forland** *I* Svalbard, Norway
70D3 **Prinzapolca** Nicaragua
20E3 **Priozersk** Russian Federation
19F2 **Pripet** *R* Belarus
Pripyat' *R* Belarus = **Pripet**
17E2 **Prispansko Jezero** *L* Albania/Macedonia, Yugoslavia/Greece
17E2 **Priština** Serbia, Yugoslavia
18C2 **Pritzwalk** Germany
20G5 **Privolzhskaya Vozvyshennost'** *Upland* Russian Federation
17E2 **Prizren** Serbia, Yugoslavia
27E7 **Probolinggo** Indonesia
61E1 **Proctor** USA
44B3 **Proddatūr** India
70D2 **Progreso** Mexico
58B2 **Project City** USA
21G7 **Prokhladnyy** Russian Federation
24K4 **Prokop'yevsk** Russian Federation
21G6 **Proletarskaya** Russian Federation
Prome = Pyè
75A2 **Promissão** Brazil
19G2 **Pronya** *R* Belarus
73L6 **Propriá** Brazil
32D3 **Proserpine** Australia
68C1 **Prospect** New York, USA
58B2 **Prospect** Oregon, USA
18D3 **Prostějov** Czech Republic
55N2 **Prøven** Greenland
14D3 **Provence** *Region* France
68E2 **Providence** USA
69A4 **Providencia, Isla de** Caribbean Sea
25U3 **Provideniya** Russian Federation
68E1 **Provincetown** USA
13B3 **Provins** France
59D2 **Provo** USA
54G4 **Provost** Canada
75B4 **Prudentópolis** Brazil
54D2 **Prudhoe Bay** USA
55M2 **Prudhoe Land** *Region* Greenland
19E2 **Pruszkow** Poland
19F3 **Prut** *R* Moldavia/ Romania
21D6 **Prutul** *R* Romania
19E2 **Pruzhany** Belarus
63C1 **Pryor** USA
19E3 **Przemyśl** Poland
17F3 **Psará** *I* Greece
20D4 **Pskov** Russian Federation
19F2 **Ptich** *R* Belarus
17E2 **Ptolemaïs** Greece
28A3 **Puan** S Korea
72D5 **Pucallpa** Peru
31D4 **Pucheng** China
12K5 **Pudasjärvi** Finland
20F3 **Pudozh** Russian Federation
44B3 **Pudukkottai** India
70C3 **Puebla** Mexico
15A1 **Puebla de Sanabria** Spain
15A1 **Puebla de Trives** Spain
62B1 **Pueblo** USA
73L5 **Puerta do Calcanhar** *Pt* Brazil
47E2 **Puerta do Oro** *Pt* South Africa
75B3 **Puerto Adela** Brazil
74B7 **Puerto Aisén** Chile
70D4 **Puerto Armuelles** Panama
73G6 **Puerto Artur** Brazil
72C3 **Puerto Asis** Colombia
72E2 **Puerto Ayacucho** Venezuela
70D3 **Puerto Barrios** Guatemala
72D2 **Puerto Berrio** Colombia
72E1 **Puerto Cabello** Venezuela
70D3 **Puerto Cabezas** Nicaragua
72E2 **Puerto Carreño** Colombia
75A3 **Puerto Casado** Brazil
75A3 **Puerto Cooper** Brazil
70D4 **Puerto Cortés** Costa Rica
70D3 **Puerto Cortés** Honduras
48A2 **Puerto del Rosario** Canary Islands
73H8 **Puerto E. Cunha** Brazil
72D1 **Puerto Fijo** Venezuela
73J5 **Puerto Franco** Brazil
75A3 **Puerto Guarani** Brazil
72E6 **Puerto Heath** Bolivia
70D2 **Puerto Juárez** Mexico
72F1 **Puerto la Cruz** Venezuela
15B2 **Puertollano** Spain
69C4 **Puerto López** Colombia
74D6 **Puerto Madryn** Argentina
72E6 **Puerto Maldonado** Peru
74B6 **Puerto Montt** Chile
73G8 **Puerto Murtinho** Brazil
74B8 **Puerto Natales** Chile
70A1 **Puerto Peñasco** Mexico
75A3 **Puerto Pinasco** Brazil
74D6 **Puerto Pirámides** Argentina
69C3 **Puerto Plata** Dominican Republic
74F3 **Puerto Presidente Stroessner** Brazil
27E6 **Puerto Princesa** Philippines
72C3 **Puerto Rico** Colombia
69D3 **Puerto Rico** *I* Caribbean Sea
69D3 **Puerto Rico Trench** Caribbean Sea
73H4 **Puerto Santana** Brazil
75A3 **Puerto Sastre** Brazil
74E1 **Puerto Suárez** Bolivia
70B2 **Puerto Vallarta** Mexico
74B6 **Puerto Varas** Chile
72F7 **Puerto Villarroel** Bolivia
21H5 **Pugachev** Russian Federation
42C3 **Pūgal** India
15C1 **Puigcerdá** Spain
28A2 **Pujŏn** N Korea
28A2 **Pujŏn Res** N Korea
35B2 **Pukaki,L** *L* New Zealand
28A2 **Pukchin** N Korea
28B2 **Pukch'ŏng** N Korea
35B1 **Pukekohe** New Zealand
35B2 **Puketeraki Range** *Mts* New Zealand
20G3 **Puksoozero** Russian Federation
16C2 **Pula** Croatia
65D2 **Pulaski** New York, USA
67A1 **Pulaski** Tennessee, USA
64C3 **Pulaski** Virginia, USA
27G7 **Pulau Kolepom** *I* Indonesia
27C7 **Pulau Pulau Batu** *Is* Indonesia
Pulau Pulau Macan - Kepulauan = Takabonerate
19E2 **Puławy** Poland
44C3 **Pulicat L** India
42B1 **Pul-i-Khumri** Afghanistan
44B4 **Puliyangudi** India
58C1 **Pullman** USA
27G6 **Pulo Anna** *I* Pacific Ocean
12L5 **Pulozero** Russian Federation
19E2 **Pułtusk** Poland
74C3 **Puna de Atacama** Argentina
72B4 **Puná, Isla** Ecuador
43F3 **Punakha** Bhutan
42C2 **Pūnch** Pakistan
47E1 **Punda Milia** South Africa
44A2 **Pune** India
28A2 **Pungsan** N Korea
28A2 **Pungso** N Korea
50C4 **Punia** Zaïre
74B4 **Punitaqui** Chile
42C2 **Punjab** *Province* Pakistan
42D2 **Punjab** *State* India
72D7 **Puno** Peru
74D5 **Punta Alta** Argentina
74B8 **Punta Arenas** Chile
59C4 **Punta Banda, Cabo** *C* Mexico
74F4 **Punta del Este** Uruguay
70D3 **Punta Gorda** Belize
67B3 **Punta Gorda** USA
72B1 **Puntarenas** Costa Rica
31C4 **Puqi** China
24J3 **Pur** *R* Russian Federation
72C3 **Purace, Vol** Colombia
63C1 **Purcell** USA
62B1 **Purgatoire** *R* USA
43F5 **Puri** India
44B2 **Pūrna** India
43F3 **Pūrnia** India
30C3 **Pursat** Cambodia
72F4 **Purus** *R* Brazil
63E2 **Purvis** USA
27D7 **Purwokerto** Indonesia
28B2 **Puryŏng** N Korea
42D5 **Pusad** India
28B3 **Pusan** S Korea
20E4 **Pushkin** Russian Federation
20F3 **Pushlakhta** Russian Federation
19F1 **Pustoshka** Russian Federation
43H3 **Putao** Burma
35C1 **Putaruru** New Zealand
31D4 **Putian** China
27E7 **Puting, Tanjung** *C* Indonesia
68E2 **Putnam** USA
68D1 **Putney** USA
44B4 **Puttalam** Sri Lanka
18C2 **Puttgarden** Germany
72C4 **Putumayo** *R* Colombia/ Ecuador/Peru
27E6 **Putussiban** Indonesia
12K6 **Puulavesi** *L* Finland
58B1 **Puyallup** USA
35A3 **Puysegur Pt** New Zealand
51C4 **Pweto** Zaïre
7B3 **Pwllheli** Wales
51C6 **PWV** *Province* South Africa
20F3 **Pyal'ma** Russian Federation
20E2 **Pyaozero, Ozero** *L* Russian Federation
30B2 **Pyapon** Burma
25K2 **Pyasina** *R* Russian Federation

21G7 **Pyatigorsk** Russian Federation
43H5 **Pyè** Burma
12K6 **Pyhäselkä** *L* Finland
30B2 **Pyinmana** Burma
28A2 **Pyŏktong** N Korea
28A3 **Pyonggang** N Korea
28A3 **Pyŏnggok-dong** S Korea
28A3 **P'yŏngsan** N Korea
28A3 **P'yŏngt'aek** S Korea
28B3 **P'yŏngyang** N Korea
34B3 **Pyramid Hill** Australia
59C2 **Pyramid L** USA
35A2 **Pyramid,Mt** New Zealand
14B3 **Pyrénées** *Mts* France/Spain
19F1 **Pytalovo** Russian Federation
30B2 **Pyu** Burma

Q

45D4 **Qa'ash Shubyk, Wadi** Jordan
45C2 **Qabatiya** Israel
45D3 **Qā'el Hafīra** *Mud Flats* Jordan
45D3 **Qa'el Jinz** *Mud Flats* Jordan
55O3 **Qagssimiut** Greenland
26C3 **Qaidam Pendi** *Salt Flat* China
45D2 **Qa Khanna** *Salt Marsh* Jordan
50D2 **Qala'en Nahl** Sudan
42B2 **Qalat** Afghanistan
45D1 **Qal'at al Ḥiṣn** Syria
45C1 **Qal'at al Marqab** *Hist Site* Syria
50E2 **Qal'at Bīshah** Saudi Arabia
41E3 **Qal'at Sālih** Iraq
26C3 **Qamdo** Tibet, China
Qaqortoq = Julianehåb
50E2 **Qandala** Somalia
49E2 **Qara** Egypt
50E3 **Qardho** Somalia
21H8 **Qareh Dāgh** *Mts* Iran
41E4 **Qaryat al Ulyā** Saudi Arabia
45C3 **Qasr ed Deir, Jebel** *Mt* Jordan
45D3 **Qasr el Kharana** Jordan
41E3 **Qāşr e Shīrīn** Iran
49E2 **Qasr Farâfra** Egypt
45D2 **Qaṭanā** Syria
41F4 **Qatar** *Emirate* Arabian Pen
45C4 **Qatim, Jebel** *Mt* Jordan
45D3 **Qatrāna** Jordan
49E2 **Qattâra Depression** Egypt
41G3 **Qāyen** Iran
41F2 **Qazvīn** Iran
40B4 **Qena** Egypt
Qeqertarsuaq = Julianehåb
41E2 **Qeydār** Iran
41F4 **Qeys** *I* Iran
21H8 **Qezel Owzan** *R* Iran
45C3 **Qeziot** Israel
31B5 **Qian Jiang** *R* China
31E1 **Qian Shan** *Upland* China
31E3 **Qidong** China
31B4 **Qijiang** China
26C2 **Qijiaojing** China
42B2 **Qila Saifullah** Pakistan
31A2 **Qilian** China
26C3 **Qilian Shan** China
25L6 **Qilian Shan** *Mts* China
31B3 **Qin'an** China
31E2 **Qingdao** China
28A3 **Qingduizi** China
31A2 **Qinghai** *Province* China
26C3 **Qinghai Hu** *L* China
31D3 **Qingjiang** Jiangsu, China
31D4 **Qingjiang** Jiangxi, China
31B3 **Qing Jiang** *R* China
31C2 **Qingshuihe** China
31B2 **Qingshui He** *R* China
31B2 **Qingtongxia** China
31B2 **Qingyang** China
28A2 **Qingyuan** China
31D4 **Qingyuan** Zhejiang, China
39G2 **Qing Zang** *Upland* China
31B5 **Qingzhou** China
31D2 **Qinhuangdao** China
31B3 **Qin Ling** *Mts* China
30D1 **Qinzhou** China
30E2 **Qionghai** China
31A3 **Qionglai Shan** *Upland* China
30D1 **Qiongzhou Haixia** *Str* China
26F2 **Qiqihar** China
45C3 **Qiraîya, Wadi** Egypt
45C2 **Qiryat Ata** Israel
45C3 **Qiryat Gat** Israel
45C2 **Qiryat Shemona** Israel
45C2 **Qiryat Yam** Israel
45C2 **Qishon** *R* Israel
25K5 **Qitai** China
31C4 **Qiyang** China
31B1 **Qog Qi** China
41F2 **Qolleh-ye Damavand** *Mt* Iran
41F3 **Qom** Iran
41F3 **Qomisheh** Iran
Qomolangma Feng *Mt* **= Everest,Mt**
45D1 **Qornet es Saouda** *Mt* Lebanon
55N3 **Qôrnoq** Greenland
41E2 **Qorveh** Iran
41G4 **Qotbābad** Iran
21H8 **Qotur** *R* Iran
68D1 **Quabbin Res** USA
47C2 **Quaggablat** South Africa
13D1 **Quakenbrück** Germany
68C2 **Quakertown** USA
30C3 **Quam Phu Quoc** *I* Vietnam
62C2 **Quanah** USA
30D2 **Quang Ngai** Vietnam
30D2 **Quang Tri** Vietnam
30D4 **Quan Long** Vietnam
31D5 **Quanzhou** Fujian, China
31C4 **Quanzhou** Guangxi, China
54H4 **Qu' Appelle** *R* Canada
59D4 **Quartzsite** USA
41G2 **Quchan** Iran
34C3 **Queanbeyan** Australia
65E1 **Québec** Canada
55L4 **Quebec** *Province* Canada
75C2 **Quebra-Anzol** *R* Brazil
74F3 **Quedas do Iguaçu** *Falls* Argentina/Brazil
68C3 **Queen Anne** USA
54E4 **Queen Charlotte Is** Canada
54F4 **Queen Charlotte Sd** Canada
54F4 **Queen Charlotte Str** Canada
54H1 **Queen Elizabeth Is** Canada
76F9 **Queen Mary Land** *Region* Antarctica
54H3 **Queen Maud G** Canada
76E6 **Queen Maud Mts** Antarctica
68D2 **Queens** *Borough* New York, USA
27F8 **Queen's Ch** Australia
34B3 **Queenscliff** Australia
32D3 **Queensland** *State* Australia
34C4 **Queenstown** Australia
35A3 **Queenstown** New Zealand
47D3 **Queenstown** South Africa
68B3 **Queenstown** USA
51B4 **Quela** Angola
51D5 **Quelimane** Mozambique
62A2 **Quemado** USA
70B2 **Querétaro** Mexico
42B2 **Quetta** Pakistan
70C3 **Quezaltenango** Guatemala
27F5 **Quezon City** Philippines
51B5 **Quibala** Angola
51B4 **Quibaxe** Angola
72C2 **Quibdó** Colombia
14B2 **Quiberon** France
51B4 **Quicama Nat Pk** Angola
75A4 **Quiindy** Paraguay
72D6 **Quillabamba** Peru
72E7 **Quillacollo** Bolivia
14C3 **Quillan** France
54H4 **Quill Lakes** Canada
74B4 **Quillota** Chile
34B1 **Quilpie** Australia
51B4 **Quimbele** Angola
14B2 **Quimper** France
14B2 **Quimperlé** France
59B3 **Quincy** California, USA
64A3 **Quincy** Illinois, USA
68E1 **Quincy** Massachusetts, USA
30D3 **Qui Nhon** Vietnam
15B2 **Quintanar de la Orden** Spain
51B5 **Quirima** Angola
34D2 **Quirindi** Australia
51E5 **Quissanga** Mozambique
51D6 **Quissico** Mozambique
72C4 **Quito** Ecuador
73L4 **Quixadá** Brazil
31A4 **Qujing** China
47D3 **Qumbu** South Africa
32C4 **Quorn** Australia
40B4 **Qus** Egypt
40B4 **Quseir** Egypt
55N3 **Qutdligssat** Greenland
Quthing = Moyeni
31B3 **Qu Xian** Sichuan, China
31D4 **Qu Xian** Zhejiang, China
30D2 **Quynh Luu** Vietnam
31C2 **Quzhou** China
43G3 **Qüzü** China

R

12J6 **Raahe** Finland
8B3 **Raasay** *I* Scotland
8B3 **Raasay,Sound of** *Chan* Scotland
50F2 **Raas Caseyr** Somalia
16C2 **Rab** *I* Croatia
27E7 **Raba** Indonesia
18D3 **Rába** *R* Hungary
48B1 **Rabat** Morocco
32E1 **Rabaul** Papua New Guinea
45C3 **Rabba** Jordan
40C5 **Rābigh** Saudi Arabia
55N5 **Race,C** Canada
68E1 **Race Pt** USA
45C2 **Rachaya** Lebanon
18C3 **Rachel** *Mt* Germany
30D3 **Rach Gia** Vietnam
64B2 **Racine** USA
19F3 **Rădăuţi** Romania
64B3 **Radcliff** USA
64C3 **Radford** USA
42C4 **Radhanpur** India
69L1 **Radix,Pt** Trinidad
19E2 **Radom** Poland
19D2 **Radomsko** Poland
19F2 **Radomyshl'** Ukraine
18C3 **Radstad** Austria
19E1 **Radviliškis** Lithuania
54G3 **Rae** Canada
43E3 **Rāe Bareli** India
55K3 **Rae Isthmus** Canada
54G3 **Rae L** Canada
35C1 **Raetihi** New Zealand
74D4 **Rafaela** Argentina
45C3 **Rafah** Egypt
50C3 **Rafai** Central African Republic
41D3 **Rafhā** Saudi Arabia
41G3 **Rafsanjān** Iran
50C3 **Raga** Sudan
69Q2 **Ragged Pt** Barbados
16C3 **Ragusa** Sicily, Italy
50D2 **Rahad** *R* Sudan
42C3 **Rahimyar Khan** Pakistan
41F3 **Rāhjerd** Iran
44B2 **Rāichur** India
43E4 **Raigarh** India
34B3 **Rainbow** Australia
67A2 **Rainbow City** USA
58B1 **Rainier** USA
58B1 **Rainier,Mt** USA
61E1 **Rainy** *R* Canada/USA
55J5 **Rainy L** Canada
61E1 **Rainy L** Canada/USA
61E1 **Rainy River** Canada
43E4 **Raipur** India
44C2 **Rājahmundry** India
27E6 **Rajang** *R* Malaysia
42C3 **Rajanpur** Pakistan
44B4 **Rājapālaiyam** India
42C3 **Rājasthān** *State* India
42D4 **Rājgarh** Madhya Pradesh, India
42D3 **Rājgarh** Rājasthān, India
42C4 **Rājkot** India
43F4 **Rājmahāl Hills** India
43E4 **Raj Nāndgaon** India
42C4 **Rājpīpla** India
43F4 **Rajshahi** Bangladesh
42D4 **Rājur** India
35B2 **Rakaia** *R* New Zealand
39G3 **Raka Zangbo** *R* China
19E3 **Rakhov** Ukraine
42A3 **Rakhshan** *R* Pakistan
47C1 **Rakops** Botswana
19F2 **Rakov** Belarus
67C1 **Raleigh** USA
45C4 **Ram** Jordan
45C2 **Rama** Israel
75D1 **Ramalho, Serra do** *Mts* Brazil
45C3 **Ramallah** Israel
44B4 **Rāmanāthapuram** India
26H3 **Ramapo Deep** Pacific Ocean
45C2 **Ramat Gan** Israel
13D3 **Rambervillers** France
14C2 **Rambouillet** France
43F4 **Rāmgarh** Bihār, India
42C3 **Rāmgarh** Rājasthān, India
41E3 **Rāmhormoz** Iran
45C4 **Ram, Jebel** *Mt* Jordan
45C3 **Ramla** Israel
59C4 **Ramona** USA
42D3 **Rāmpur** India
42D4 **Rāmpura** India
43G5 **Ramree I** Burma
21J8 **Rāmsar** Iran
6B2 **Ramsey** Isle of Man, British Islands
68C2 **Ramsey** USA
7B4 **Ramsey I** Wales
7E4 **Ramsgate** England
45D2 **Ramtha** Jordan
32D1 **Ramu** *R* Papua New Guinea
27E6 **Ranau** Malaysia
74B4 **Rancagua** Chile
60B2 **Ranchester** USA
43F4 **Rānchi** India
43E4 **Rānchi Plat** India
74B6 **Ranco, Lago** Chile
47D2 **Randburg** South Africa
12F7 **Randers** Denmark
47D2 **Randfontein** South Africa
65E2 **Randolph** Vermont, USA
66D3 **Randsburg** USA
35B3 **Ranfurly** New Zealand
43G4 **Rangamati** Bangladesh
60B2 **Rangely** USA
35B2 **Rangiora** New Zealand
35C1 **Rangitaiki** *R* New Zealand
35B2 **Rangitata** *R* New Zealand
35C1 **Rangitikei** *R* New Zealand
30B2 **Rangoon** Burma
43F3 **Rangpur** Bangladesh
44B3 **Rānībennur** India
43F4 **Rānīganj** India
55J3 **Rankin Inlet** Canada
34C2 **Rankins Springs** Australia
8C3 **Rannoch, Loch** *L* Scotland
42B4 **Rann of Kachchh** *Flood Area* India
30B4 **Ranong** Thailand
27C6 **Rantauparapat** Indonesia
27F7 **Rantekombola, G** *Mt* Indonesia
64B2 **Rantoul** USA
75B1 **Ranuro** *R* Brazil
13D3 **Raon-l'Etape** France
33H3 **Raoul** *I* Pacific Ocean
16B2 **Rapallo** Italy
55M3 **Raper,C** Canada
60C2 **Rapid City** USA
64B1 **Rapid River** USA
65D3 **Rappahannock** *R* USA
43M2 **Rapti** *R* India
68C2 **Raritan B** USA
40C5 **Ras Abû Dâra** *C* Egypt
40C5 **Ra's Abu Madd** *C* Saudi Arabia
50D1 **Ras Abu Shagara** *C* Sudan
40D2 **Ra's al 'Ayn** Syria
41G4 **Ras al Khaimah** UAE
38D4 **Ra's al Madrakah** *C* Oman
50E2 **Ras Andadda** *C* Eritrea
41E4 **Ra's az Zawr** *C* Saudi Arabia
40C5 **Râs Banâs** *C* Egypt
45B3 **Râs Burûn** *C* Egypt
50D2 **Ras Dashan** *Mt* Ethiopia
41E3 **Ra's-e Barkan** *Pt* Iran
45A3 **Râs el Barr** *C* Egypt
16B3 **Ras El Hadid** Algeria
40A3 **Râs el Kenâyis** *Pt* Egypt
45C4 **Râs el Nafas** *Mt* Egypt
45B4 **Râs el Sudr** *C* Egypt
45C4 **Ras en Naqb** *Upland* Jordan
38D4 **Ra's Fartak** *C* Yemen
40B4 **Râs Ghârib** Egypt
50D2 **Rashad** Sudan
45C3 **Rashādīya** Jordan
40B3 **Rashîd** Egypt
41E2 **Rasht** Iran
45C1 **Ra's ibn Hāni'** *C* Syria
50E2 **Ras Khanzira** *C* Somalia
42B3 **Ras Koh** *Mt* Pakistan
45B4 **Râs Matarma** *C* Egypt
40B4 **Râs Muhammad** *C* Egypt
48A2 **Ras Nouadhibou** *C* Mauritius/Morocco
26J2 **Rasshua** *I* Kuril Is, Russian Federation
21G5 **Rasskazovo** Russian Federation
41E4 **Ra's Tanāqib** *C* Saudi Arabia
41F4 **Ra's Tannūrah** Saudi Arabia
18B3 **Rastatt** Germany
Ras Uarc = Tres Forcas, Cabo
45C4 **Ras Um Seisabān** *Mt* Jordan
50E2 **Ras Xaafuun** *C* Somalia
42C3 **Ratangarh** India
30B3 **Rat Buri** Thailand
42D3 **Rāth** India
18C2 **Rathenow** Germany
9C2 **Rathfriland** Northern Ireland
9C2 **Rathlin I** Northern Ireland
9C2 **Rathmelton** Irish Republic
45D4 **Ratiyah, Wadi** Jordan
42C4 **Ratlām** India
44A2 **Ratnāgiri** India
44C4 **Ratnapura** Sri Lanka
19E2 **Ratno** Ukraine
62B1 **Raton** USA
12H6 **Rättvik** Sweden
35C1 **Raukumara Range** *Mts* New Zealand
75D3 **Raul Soares** Brazil
12J6 **Rauma** Finland
43E4 **Raurkela** India
41E3 **Ravānsar** Iran
41G3 **Rāvar** Iran
19E2 **Rava Russkaya** Ukraine
68D1 **Ravena** USA
16C2 **Ravenna** Italy
18B3 **Ravensburg** Germany
32D2 **Ravenshoe** Australia
6E2 **Ravenspurn** *Oilfield* N Sea
42C2 **Ravi** *R* Pakistan
55Q3 **Ravn Kap** *C* Greenland
42C2 **Rawalpindi** Pakistan
41D2 **Rawāndiz** Iraq
18D2 **Rawicz** Poland
32B4 **Rawlinna** Australia
56C2 **Rawlins** USA
74D6 **Rawson** Argentina
6C3 **Rawtenstall** England
44B3 **Rāyadurg** India
44C2 **Rāyagada** India
45D2 **Rayak** Lebanon
55N5 **Ray,C** Canada
41G4 **Rāyen** Iran
66C2 **Raymond** California, USA
58D1 **Raymond** Canada
68E1 **Raymond** New Hampshire, USA
58B1 **Raymond** Washington, USA
34D2 **Raymond Terrace** Australia
63C3 **Raymondville** USA
41E2 **Razan** Iran
19G3 **Razdel'naya** Ukraine
28C2 **Razdol'noye** Russian Federation
17F2 **Razgrad** Bulgaria
17F2 **Razim** *L* Romania
7D4 **Reading** England
68C2 **Reading** USA
54G3 **Read Island** Canada
68D1 **Readsboro** USA
49E2 **Rebiana** *Well* Libya
49E2 **Rebiana Sand Sea** Libya
12L6 **Reboly** Russian Federation
29E1 **Rebun-tō** *I* Japan
32B4 **Recherche,Arch of the** *Is* Australia
19G2 **Rechitsa** Belarus
73M5 **Recife** Brazil
47D3 **Recife,C** South Africa
75E2 **Recifes da Pedra Grande** *Arch* Brazil
33F2 **Récifs d'Entrecasteaux** New Caledonia
13D2 **Recklinghausen** Germany
74E3 **Reconquista** Argentina
61D1 **Red** *R* Canada/USA
63D2 **Red** *R* USA
30C4 **Redang** *I* Malaysia
68C2 **Red Bank** New Jersey, USA
67A1 **Red Bank** Tennessee, USA
59B2 **Red Bluff** USA
62B2 **Red Bluff L** USA
6D2 **Redcar** England
34D1 **Redcliffe** Australia
34B2 **Red Cliffs** Australia
60D2 **Red Cloud** USA
54G4 **Red Deer** Canada
54G4 **Red Deer** *R* Canada
58B2 **Redding** USA
7D3 **Redditch** England
60D2 **Redfield** USA
7D4 **Redhill** England
62C1 **Red Hills** USA
57D2 **Red L** USA
55J4 **Red Lake** Canada
61D1 **Red Lake** *R* USA
66D3 **Redlands** USA
68B3 **Red Lion** USA
58E1 **Red Lodge** USA
58B2 **Redmond** USA
66D3 **Red Mountain** USA
61D2 **Red Oak** USA
14B2 **Redon** France
66C4 **Redondo Beach** USA
31B5 **Red River Delta** Vietnam
7B4 **Redruth** England
38B3 **Red Sea** Africa/Arabian Pen
54G4 **Redwater** Canada
61E2 **Red Wing** USA
66A2 **Redwood City** USA
61D2 **Redwood Falls** USA
64B2 **Reed City** USA
66C2 **Reedley** USA
58B2 **Reedsport** USA
65D3 **Reedville** USA
35B2 **Reefton** New Zealand
10B3 **Ree, Lough** *L* Irish Republic
6D2 **Reeth** England
40C2 **Refahiye** Turkey
63C3 **Refugio** USA
75E2 **Regência** Brazil
18C3 **Regensburg** Germany
48C2 **Reggane** Algeria
16D3 **Reggio di Calabria** Italy
16C2 **Reggio nell'Emilia** Italy
17E1 **Reghin** Romania
54H4 **Regina** Canada
42A2 **Registan** *Region* Afghanistan
47B1 **Rehoboth** Namibia
65D3 **Rehoboth Beach** USA
45C3 **Rehovot** Israel

67C1 Reidsville USA
7D4 Reigate England
14B2 Ré, Ile de I France
13B3 Reims France
74B8 Reina Adelaida, Archipiélago de la Chile
61E2 Reinbeck USA
54H4 Reindeer L Canada
15B1 Reinosa Spain
68B3 Reisterstown USA
47D2 Reitz South Africa
54H3 Reliance Canada
58E2 Reliance USA
15C2 Relizane Algeria
34A2 Remarkable,Mt Australia
27E7 Rembang Indonesia
13D3 Remiremont France
13D2 Remscheid Germany
68C1 Remsen USA
12G6 Rena Norway
64B3 Rend L USA
18B2 Rendsburg Germany
65D1 Renfrew Canada
8C4 Renfrew Scotland
27D7 Rengat Indonesia
19F3 Reni Ukraine
50D2 Renk Sudan
55Q2 Renland Pen Greenland
34B2 Renmark Australia
33F2 Rennell I Solomon Islands
14B2 Rennes France
59C3 Reno USA
16C2 Reno R Italy
68B2 Renovo USA
68D1 Rensselaer USA
58B1 Renton USA
27F7 Reo Indonesia
19G2 Repki Ukraine
75C3 Reprêsa de Furnas Dam Brazil
75C2 Reprêsa Três Marias Dam Brazil
58C1 Republic USA
60D2 Republican R USA
55K3 Repulse Bay Canada
41F2 Reshteh-ye Alborz Mts Iran
31A2 Reshui China
74E3 Resistencia Argentina
17E1 Reşiţa Romania
55J2 Resolute Canada
35A3 Resolution I New Zealand
55M3 Resolution Island Canada
47E2 Ressano Garcia Mozambique
13C3 Rethel France
17E3 Réthimnon Greece
36D6 Réunion I Indian Ocean
15C1 Reus Spain
18B3 Reutlingen Germany
20K4 Revda Russian Federation
54G4 Revelstoke Canada
13C3 Revigny-sur-Ornain France
70A3 Revillagigedo Is Mexico
37O4 Revilla Gigedo, Islas Pacific Ocean
13C3 Revin France
45C3 Revivim Israel
43E4 Rewa India
42D3 Rewāri India
58D2 Rexburg USA
12A2 Reykjavik Iceland
70C2 Reynosa Mexico
14B2 Rezé France
19F1 Rezekne Latvia
20L4 Rezh Russian Federation
7C3 Rhayader Wales
45C1 Rhazīr Lebanon
13E2 Rheda Wiedenbrück Germany
18B2 Rhein R W Europe
18B2 Rheine Germany
14D2 Rheinland Pfalz Region Germany
Rhine R = Rhein
68D2 Rhinebeck USA
64B1 Rhinelander USA
65E2 Rhode Island State USA
68E2 Rhode Island Sd USA
17F3 Rhodes Greece
17F3 Rhodes I Greece
47D1 Rhodes Drift Ford Botswana/South Africa
58D1 Rhodes Peak Mt USA
7C4 Rhondda Wales
14C3 Rhône R France
7C3 Rhyl Wales
73L6 Riachão do Jacuipe Brazil
75D1 Riacho de Santana Brazil
15A1 Ria de Arosa B Spain
15A1 Ria de Betanzos B Spain
15A1 Ria de Corcubion B Spain
15A1 Ria de Lage B Spain
15A1 Ria de Sta Marta B Spain
15A1 Ria de Vigo B Spain
42C2 Riāsi Pakistan
27D6 Riau, Kepulauan Is Indonesia
15A1 Ribadeo Spain
75B3 Ribas do Rio Pardo Brazil
51D5 Ribauè Mozambique
6C3 Ribble R England
75C3 Ribeira Brazil
75C3 Ribeirão Prêto Brazil
72E6 Riberalta Bolivia
65D2 Rice L Canada
64A1 Rice Lake USA
47E2 Richard's Bay South Africa
63C2 Richardson USA
54E3 Richardson Mts Canada
59D3 Richfield USA
68C1 Richfield Springs USA
66C3 Richgrove USA
58C1 Richland USA
64C3 Richlands USA
66A2 Richmond California, USA
47C3 Richmond Cape Province, South Africa
6D2 Richmond England
64C3 Richmond Kentucky, USA
47E2 Richmond Natal, South Africa
34D2 Richmond New South Wales, Australia
35B2 Richmond New Zealand
32D3 Richmond Queensland, Australia
65D3 Richmond Virginia, USA
35B2 Richmond Range Mts New Zealand
68C1 Richmondville USA
7D4 Rickmansworth England
65D2 Rideau Lakes Canada
67B2 Ridgeland USA
68A2 Ridgway USA
69D4 Riecito Venezuela
18C2 Riesa Germany
74B8 Riesco I Chile
47C2 Riet R South Africa
16C2 Rieti Italy
15B2 Rif Mts Morocco
48B1 Rif R Morocco
60B3 Rifle USA
19E1 Riga Latvia
11H2 Riga,G of Estonia/Latvia
Rīgas Jūrās Līcis = Gulf of Riga
58D2 Rigby USA
58C1 Riggins USA
55N4 Rigolet Canada
Riia Laht = Gulf of Riga
12J6 Riihimaki Finland
16C1 Rijeka Croatia
29D3 Rikuzen-Tanaka Japan
12H7 Rimbo Sweden
16C2 Rimini Italy
17F1 Rîmnicu Sărat Romania
17E1 Rîmnicu Vîlcea Romania
57G2 Rimouski Canada
12F7 Ringkøbing Denmark
27E7 Rinjani Mt Indonesia
8B4 Rinns Point Scotland
13E1 Rinteln Germany
72C4 Riobamba Ecuador
48C4 Rio Benito Equatorial Guinea
72E5 Rio Branco Brazil
75C4 Rio Branco do Sul Brazil
62C3 Rio Bravo Mexico
70B1 Rio Bravo del Norte R Mexico/USA
75B3 Rio Brilhante Brazil
75C3 Rio Claro Brazil
69L1 Rio Claro Trinidad
74D4 Ríocuarto Argentina
75D3 Rio de Janeiro Brazil
75D3 Rio de Janeiro State Brazil
48A2 Rio de Oro, Bahia de B Morocco
74C8 Río Gallegos Argentina
74C8 Río Grande Argentina
74F4 Rio Grande Brazil
69A4 Rio Grande Nicaragua
70B2 Rio Grande R Mexico/USA
70D3 Rio Grande R Nicaragua
62C3 Rio Grande City USA
70B2 Rio Grande de Santiago R Mexico
73L5 Rio Grande do Norte State Brazil
74F3 Rio Grande Do Sul State Brazil
52G6 Rio Grande Rise Atlantic Ocean
69C4 Ríohacha Colombia
14C2 Riom France
72E7 Rio Mulatos Bolivia
75C4 Rio Negro Brazil
74C5 Río Negro State Argentina
74E4 Rio Negro, Embalse de Res Uruguay
74F3 Rio Pardo Brazil
74B8 Rio Turbio Argentina
75B2 Rio Verde Brazil
75B2 Rio Verde de Mato Grosso Brazil
7D3 Ripley England
64C3 Ripley Ohio, USA
63E1 Ripley Tennessee, USA
64C3 Ripley West Virginia, USA
6D2 Ripon England
66B2 Ripon USA
29E1 Rishiri-tō I Japan
45C3 Rishon le Zion Israel
68B3 Rising Sun USA
12F7 Risør Norway
44E3 Ritchie's Arch Is Andaman Islands
55N2 Ritenbenk Greenland
66C2 Ritter,Mt USA
58C1 Ritzville USA
74B3 Rivadavia Chile
72A1 Rivas Nicaragua
74E4 Rivera Uruguay
66B2 Riverbank USA
48B4 River Cess Liberia
66C2 Riverdale USA
68D2 Riverhead USA
34B3 Riverina Region Australia
35A3 Riversdale New Zealand
47C3 Riversdale South Africa
66D4 Riverside USA
35A3 Riverton New Zealand
58E2 Riverton USA
67B3 Riviera Beach USA
65F1 Riviére-du-Loup Canada
28A2 Riwon N Korea
41E5 Rīyadh Saudi Arabia
40D1 Rize Turkey
31D2 Rizhao China
45C1 Rizokaipaso Cyprus
16D3 Rizzuto, C Italy
12F7 Rjukan Norway
8B2 Roag, Loch Inlet Scotland
55K2 Roanes Pen Canada
14C2 Roanne France
67A2 Roanoke Alabama, USA
65D3 Roanoke Virginia, USA
65D3 Roanoke R USA
67C1 Roanoke Rapids USA
59D3 Roan Plat USA
58D2 Roberts USA
59C3 Roberts Creek Mt USA
12J6 Robertsfors Sweden
63D1 Robert S Kerr Res USA
47B3 Robertson South Africa
48A4 Robertsport Liberia
55L5 Roberval Canada
6D2 Robin Hood's Bay England
34B2 Robinvale Australia
63C3 Robstown USA
15A2 Roca, Cabo de C Portugal
70A3 Roca Partida I Mexico
73M4 Rocas I Brazil
74F4 Rocha Uruguay
7C3 Rochdale England
75B2 Rochedo Brazil
14B2 Rochefort France
64B2 Rochelle USA
54G3 Rocher River Canada
34B3 Rochester Australia
55L5 Rochester Canada
7E4 Rochester England
61E2 Rochester Minnesota, USA
68E1 Rochester New Hampshire, USA
68B1 Rochester New York, USA
64B2 Rock R USA
52H2 Rockall I UK
64B2 Rockford USA
67B2 Rock Hill USA
67C2 Rockingham USA
64A2 Rock Island USA
64B1 Rockland Michigan, USA
34B3 Rocklands Res Australia
67B3 Rockledge USA
63C3 Rockport USA
61D2 Rock Rapids USA
60B2 Rock River USA
60B1 Rock Springs Montana, USA
62B2 Rocksprings Texas, USA
58E2 Rock Springs Wyoming, USA
35B2 Rocks Pt New Zealand
34C3 Rock,The Australia
68D2 Rockville Connecticut, USA
64B3 Rockville Indiana, USA
68B3 Rockville Maryland, USA
65F1 Rockwood USA
62B1 Rocky Ford USA
64C1 Rocky Island L Canada
67C1 Rocky Mount USA
60B2 Rocky Mountain Nat Pk USA
56B1 Rocky Mts Canada/USA
18C2 Rødbyhavn Denmark
14C3 Rodez France
Ródhos = Rhodes
16D2 Rodi Garganico Italy
17E2 Rodopi Planina Mts Bulgaria
32A3 Roebourne Australia
47D1 Roedtan South Africa
13D2 Roer R Netherlands
13C2 Roermond Netherlands
13B2 Roeselare Belgium
55K3 Roes Welcome Sd Canada
19F2 Rogachev Belarus
72E6 Rogaguado, Lago Bolivia
63D1 Rogers USA
64C1 Rogers City USA
66D3 Rogers L USA
64C3 Rogers,Mt USA
58D2 Rogerson USA
47B3 Roggeveldberge Mts South Africa
58B2 Rogue R USA
42B3 Rohri Pakistan
42D3 Rohtak India
19E1 Roja Latvia
70C2 Rojo, Cabo C Mexico
75B3 Rolândia Brazil
63D1 Rolla USA
58D1 Rollins USA
Roma = Rome
34C1 Roma Australia
67C2 Romain,C USA
17F1 Roman Romania
52H5 Romanche Gap Atlantic Ocean
27F7 Romang I Indonesia
21C6 Romania Republic E Europe
67B3 Romano,C USA
14D2 Romans-sur-Isère France
27F5 Romblon Philippines
67A2 Rome Georgia, USA
16C2 Rome Italy
68C1 Rome New York, USA
65D2 Rome USA
14C2 Romilly-sur-Seine France
65D3 Romney USA
21E5 Romny Ukraine
18B1 Rømø I Denmark
14C2 Romorantin France
8C3 Rona, I Scotland
8B3 Ronay, I Scotland
75B1 Roncador, Serra do Mts Brazil
15A2 Ronda Spain
15A2 Ronda, Sierra de Mts Spain
72F6 Rondônia Brazil
72F6 Rondônia State Brazil
75B2 Rondonópolis Brazil
31B4 Rong'an China
31B4 Rongchang China
31E2 Rongcheng China
54H4 Ronge, Lac la Canada
31B4 Rongjiang China
31B4 Rong Jiang R China
30A1 Rongklang Range Mts Burma
12G7 Rønne Denmark
12H7 Ronneby Sweden
76F2 Ronne Ice Shelf Antarctica
13B2 Ronse Belgium
13D1 Roodeschool Netherlands
56C3 Roof Butte Mt USA
42D3 Roorkee India
13C2 Roosendaal Netherlands
59D2 Roosevelt USA
76E6 Roosevelt I Antarctica
61E2 Root R USA
32C2 Roper R Australia
8D2 Rora Head Pt Scotland
72F2 Roraima Mt Brazil/Guyana/Venezuela
72F3 Roraima State Brazil
12G6 Røros Norway
12G6 Rørvik Norway
19G3 Ros' R Ukraine
69Q2 Rosalie Dominica
66C3 Rosamond USA
66C3 Rosamond L USA
74D4 Rosario Argentina
73K4 Rosário Brazil
75A3 Rosario Paraguay
75A1 Rosário Oeste Brazil
68C2 Roscoe USA
14B2 Roscoff France
10B3 Roscommon Irish Republic
9C3 Roscrea Irish Republic
69Q2 Roseau Dominica
34C4 Rosebery Australia
60B1 Rosebud USA
58B2 Roseburg USA
63C3 Rosenberg USA
18C3 Rosenheim Germany
54H4 Rosetown Canada
66B1 Roseville USA
12G7 Roskilde Denmark
20E5 Roslavl' Russian Federation
20G4 Roslyatino Russian Federation
17E2 Roşorii de Vede Romania
35B2 Ross New Zealand
16D3 Rossano Italy
10B3 Rossan Pt Irish Republic
63E2 Ross Barnett Res USA
65D1 Rosseau L Canada
33E2 Rossel I Papua New Guinea
76E6 Ross Ice Shelf Antarctica
58B1 Ross L USA
9C3 Rosslare Irish Republic
35C2 Ross,Mt New Zealand
48A3 Rosso Mauritius
16B2 Rosso, C Corsica, France
7C4 Ross-on-Wye England
21F5 Rossosh Russian Federation
54E3 Ross River Canada
76F6 Ross S Antarctica
41F4 Rostāq Iran
18C2 Rostock Germany
20F4 Rostov Russian Federation
21F6 Rostov-na-Donu Russian Federation
67B2 Roswell Georgia, USA
62B2 Roswell New Mexico, USA
27H5 Rota I Pacific Ocean
27F8 Rote I Indonesia
18B2 Rotenburg Niedersachsen, Germany
13E2 Rothaar-Geb Region Germany
6D2 Rothbury England
76G3 Rothera Base Antarctica
7D3 Rotherham England
8C4 Rothesay Scotland
8D3 Rothes-on-Spey Scotland
34C2 Roto Australia
35B2 Rotoiti,L New Zealand
35B2 Rotoroa,L New Zealand
35C1 Rotorua New Zealand
35C1 Rotorua,L New Zealand
13E3 Rottenburg Germany
18A2 Rotterdam Netherlands
13E3 Rottweil Germany
33G2 Rotuma I Fiji
13B2 Roubaix France
14C2 Rouen France
6E3 Rough Oilfield N Sea
Roulers = Roeselare
51F6 Round I Mauritius
66D1 Round Mountain USA
34D2 Round Mt Australia
58E1 Roundup USA
8D2 Rousay I Scotland
14C3 Roussillon Region France
47D3 Rouxville South Africa
65D1 Rouyn Canada
12K5 Rovaniemi Finland
16C1 Rovereto Italy
16C1 Rovigo Italy
16C1 Rovinj Croatia
19F2 Rovno Ukraine
41E2 Row'ān Iran
34C1 Rowena Australia
55L3 Rowley I Canada
32A2 Rowley Shoals Australia
27F5 Roxas Philippines
67C1 Roxboro USA
35A3 Roxburgh New Zealand
58E1 Roy USA
9C3 Royal Canal Irish Republic
64B1 Royale, Isle USA
7D3 Royal Leamington Spa England
64C2 Royal Oak USA
7E4 Royal Tunbridge Wells England
14B2 Royan France
13B3 Roye France
7D3 Royston England
19E3 Rožňava Slovakia
13B3 Rozoy France
21G5 Rtishchevo Russian Federation
7C3 Ruabon Wales
51D4 Ruaha Nat Pk Tanzania
35C1 Ruahine Range Mts New Zealand
35C1 Ruapehu,Mt New Zealand
38C4 Rub' al Khālī Desert Saudi Arabia
8B3 Rubha Hunish C Scotland
8C3 Rubha Réidh Pt Scotland
75B3 Rubinéia Brazil
24K4 Rubtsovsk Russian Federation
54C3 Ruby USA
59C2 Ruby Mts USA
41G4 Rudan Iran
43L2 Rudanli India
41E2 Rūdbār Iran
29F2 Rudnaya Russian Federation
26G2 Rudnaya Pristan' Russian Federation
19G2 Rudnya Russian Federation
17E2 Rudoka Planina Mt Macedonia, Yugoslavia
24G1 Rudol'fa, Ostrov I Russian Federation
31E3 Rudong China
64C1 Rudyard USA
14C2 Ruffec France
51D4 Rufiji R Tanzania
74D4 Rufino Argentina
48A3 Rufisque Senegal
51C5 Rufunsa Zambia

7D3 **Rugby** England
60C1 **Rugby** USA
12G8 **Rügen** *I* Germany
13D2 **Ruhr** *R* Germany
31D4 **Ruijin** China
17E2 **Rujen** *Mt* Bulgaria/ Macedonia, Yugoslavia
51D4 **Rukwa, L** Tanzania
8B3 **Rum** *I* Scotland
17D1 **Ruma** Serbia, Yugoslavia
41E4 **Rumāh** Saudi Arabia
50C3 **Rumbek** Sudan
69C2 **Rum Cay** *I* The Bahamas
65E2 **Rumford** USA
32C2 **Rum Jungle** Australia
29D2 **Rumoi** Japan
51D5 **Rumphi** Malawi
35B2 **Runanga** New Zealand
35C1 **Runaway,C** New Zealand
7C3 **Runcorn** England
51B5 **Rundu** Namibia
51D4 **Rungwa** Tanzania
51D4 **Rungwa** *R* Tanzania
51D4 **Rungwe** *Mt* Tanzania
39G2 **Ruoqiang** China
26D2 **Ruo Shui** *R* China
17F1 **Rupea** Romania
58D2 **Rupert** USA
55L4 **Rupert** *R* Canada
13D2 **Rur** *R* Germany
72E6 **Rurrenabaque** Bolivia
51D5 **Rusape** Zimbabwe
17F2 **Ruse** Bulgaria
64A2 **Rushville** Illinois, USA
60C2 **Rushville** Nebraska, USA
34B3 **Rushworth** Australia
63C2 **Rusk** USA
67B3 **Ruskin** USA
35B1 **Russell** New Zealand
60D3 **Russell** USA
63E2 **Russellville** Alabama, USA
63D1 **Russellville** Arkansas, USA
64B3 **Russellville** Kentucky, USA
59B3 **Russian** *R* USA
20F4 **Russian Federation** *Republic* Asia/Europe
25L2 **Russkiy, Ostrov** *I* Russian Federation
41E1 **Rustavi** Georgia
47D2 **Rustenburg** South Africa
63D2 **Ruston** USA
50C4 **Rutana** Burundi
27F7 **Ruteng** Indonesia
47E1 **Rutenga** Zimbabwe
59C3 **Ruth** USA
13E2 **Rüthen** Germany
65E2 **Rutland** USA
44E3 **Rutland** *I* Andaman Islands
42D2 **Rutog** China
Ruvu = Pangani
51E5 **Ruvuma** *R* Mozambique/ Tanzania
45D4 **Ruweila, Wadi** Jordan
50D3 **Ruwenzori Range** *Mts* Uganda/Zaïre
51D5 **Ruya** *R* Zimbabwe
19D3 **Ružomberok** Slovakia
50C4 **Rwanda** *Republic* Africa
8C4 **Ryan, L** Scotland
20F5 **Ryazan'** Russian Federation
20G5 **Ryazhsk** Russian Federation
20F4 **Rybinsk** Russian Federation
20F4 **Rybinskoye Vodokhranilishche** *Res* Russian Federation
19F3 **Rybnitsa** Moldavia
7D4 **Ryde** England
7E4 **Rye** England
58C2 **Rye Patch Res** USA
21E5 **Ryl'sk** Russian Federation
21H6 **Ryn Peski** *Desert* Kazakhstan
28A3 **Ryoju** S Korea
29D3 **Ryōtsu** Japan
19F3 **Ryskany** Moldavia
26F4 **Ryūkyū Is** Japan
19E2 **Rzeszów** Poland
20E4 **Rzhev** Russian Federation

S

41F3 **Sa'ādatābād** Iran
40B5 **Saad el Aali** *Dam* Egypt
18C2 **Saale** *R* Germany
13D3 **Saar** *R* Germany
13D3 **Saarbrücken** Germany
13D3 **Saarburg** Germany
12J7 **Saaremaa** *I* Estonia
13D3 **Saarland** *State* Germany
13D3 **Saarlouis** Germany
45B3 **Saba'a** Egypt
17D2 **Šabac** Serbia, Yugoslavia
15C1 **Sabadell** Spain
29C3 **Sabae** Japan
27E6 **Sabah** *State* Malaysia
69C4 **Sabanalarga** Colombia
27C6 **Sabang** Indonesia
44C2 **Sabari** *R* India
45C2 **Sabastiya** Israel
72E7 **Sabaya** Bolivia
40C3 **Sab'Bi'ār** Syria
45D2 **Sabhā** Jordan
49D2 **Sabhā** Libya
51D6 **Sabi** *R* Zimbabwe
47E2 **Sabie** *R* South Africa
70B2 **Sabinas** Mexico
70B2 **Sabinas Hidalgo** Mexico
63C2 **Sabine** *R* USA
63D3 **Sabine L** USA
41F5 **Sabkhat Maṭṭī** *Salt Marsh* UAE
45B3 **Sabkhet el Bardawîl** *Lg* Egypt
55M5 **Sable,C** Canada
67B3 **Sable,C** USA
55M5 **Sable I** Canada
50E2 **Şabyā** Saudi Arabia
41G2 **Sabzevār** Iran
58C1 **Sacajawea Peak** USA
68C1 **Sacandaga Res** USA
61E2 **Sac City** USA
57D1 **Sachigo** *R* Canada
28A3 **Sach'on** S Korea
18C2 **Sachsen** *State* Germany
18C2 **Sachsen-Anhalt** *State* Germany
54F2 **Sachs Harbour** Canada
65E2 **Saco** Maine, USA
60B1 **Saco** Montana, USA
66B1 **Sacramento** USA
66B1 **Sacramento** *R* USA
59B2 **Sacramento V** USA
62A2 **Sacramento Mts** USA
50E2 **Şa'dah** Yemen
17E2 **Sadanski** Bulgaria
43H3 **Sadiya** India
15A2 **Sado** *R* Portugal
29D3 **Sado-shima** *I* Japan
42C3 **Sādri** India
Safad = Zefat
42A2 **Safed Koh** *Mts* Afghanistan
12G7 **Säffle** Sweden
59E4 **Safford** USA
7E3 **Saffron Walden** England
40C3 **Safi** Jordan
48B1 **Safi** Morocco
45D1 **Şāfītā** Syria
19G1 **Safonovo** Russian Federation
20H2 **Safonovo** Russian Federation
41E3 **Safwān** Iraq
43F3 **Saga** China
28B4 **Saga** Japan
30B1 **Sagaing** Burma
29C4 **Sagami-nada** *B* Japan
42D4 **Sāgar** India
68D2 **Sag Harbor** USA
64C2 **Saginaw** USA
64C2 **Saginaw B** USA
55M4 **Saglek B** Canada
28A3 **Sagŏ-ri** S Korea
62A1 **Saguache** USA
69B2 **Sagua de Tánamo** Cuba
69B2 **Sagua la Grande** Cuba
57F2 **Saguenay** *R* Canada
48A2 **Saguia el Hamra** *Watercourse* Morocco
15B2 **Sagunto** Spain
45D3 **Sahāb** Jordan
15A1 **Sahagún** Spain
48C2 **Sahara** *Desert* N Africa
42D3 **Sahāranpur** India
43K1 **Sahaswan** India
45B4 **Saheira, Wadi el** Egypt
42C2 **Sahiwal** Pakistan
41D3 **Şahrā al Hijārah** *Desert Region* Iraq
40B4 **Sahra esh Sharqiya** *Desert Region* Egypt
70B2 **Sahuayo** Mexico
45D1 **Sahyūn** *Hist Site* Syria
32D1 **Saibai I** Australia
Saïda = Sidon
41G4 **Sa'īdābad** Iran
15B2 **Saïdia** Morocco
43F3 **Saidpur** Bangladesh
42C2 **Saidu** Pakistan
29B3 **Saigō** Japan
Saigon = Ho Chi Minh City
43G4 **Saiha** India
26E2 **Saihan Tal** China
29B4 **Saijo** Japan
28C4 **Saiki** Japan
12K6 **Saimaa** *L* Finland
8D4 **St Abb's Head** *Pt* Scotland
7D4 **St Albans** England
65E2 **St Albans** Vermont, USA
64C3 **St Albans** West Virginia, USA
7C4 **St Albans Head** *C* England
13B2 **St Amand-les-Eaux** France
14C2 **St Amand-Mont Rond** France
67A3 **St Andrew B** USA
8D3 **St Andrews** Scotland
67B2 **St Andrew Sd** USA
61D1 **Ste Anne** Canada
65E1 **Ste Anne de Beaupré** Canada
69H1 **St Ann's Bay** Jamaica
55N4 **St Anthony** Canada
58D2 **St Anthony** USA
34B3 **St Arnaud** Australia
51E6 **St Augustin, Baie de** *B* Madagascar
67B3 **St Augustine** USA
7B4 **St Austell** England
7B4 **St Austell Bay** England
13D3 **St-Avold** France
6C2 **St Bees Head** *Pt* England
7B4 **St Brides B** Wales
14B2 **St-Brieuc** France
65D2 **St Catharines** Canada
69M2 **St Catherine,Mt** Grenada
67B2 **St Catherines I** USA
7D4 **St Catherines Pt** England
14C2 **St-Chamond** France
58D2 **St Charles** Idaho, USA
61E3 **St Charles** Missouri, USA
64C2 **St Clair** USA
64C2 **St Clair,L** Canada/USA
64C2 **St Clair Shores** USA
14D2 **St Claude** France
61E1 **St Cloud** USA
69E3 **St Croix** *I* Caribbean Sea
65F1 **St Croix** *R* Canada/USA
64A1 **St Croix** *R* USA
64A1 **St Croix Falls** USA
7B4 **St Davids Head** *Pt* Wales
13B3 **St Denis** France
51F6 **St Denis** Réunion
13D3 **St-Dié** France
13C3 **St-Dizier** France
54D3 **St Elias, Mt** USA
54E3 **St Elias Mts** Canada
14B2 **Saintes** France
14C2 **St-Étienne** France
65E1 **St-Félicien** Canada
16B2 **St Florent, G de** Corsica, France
13B3 **St-Florentin** France
60C3 **St Francis** USA
63D1 **St Francis** *R* USA
47C3 **St Francis B** South Africa
47C3 **St Francis,C** South Africa
16B1 **St Gallen** Switzerland
14C3 **St-Gaudens** France
34C1 **St George** Australia
67B2 **St George** South Carolina, USA
59D3 **St George** Utah, USA
67B3 **St George I** Florida, USA
13E3 **St Georgen im Schwarzwald** Germany
58B2 **St George,Pt** USA
65E1 **St-Georges** Canada
69M2 **St George's** Grenada
7A4 **St George's Chan** Irish Republic/Wales
33E1 **St George's Chan** Papua New Guinea
16B1 **St Gotthard** *Pass* Switzerland
7B4 **St Govans Head** *Pt* Wales
66A1 **St Helena** USA
52H5 **St Helena** *I* Atlantic Ocean
47B3 **St Helena B** South Africa
67B2 **St Helena Sd** USA
34C4 **St Helens** Australia
7C3 **St Helens** England
58B1 **St Helens** USA
58B1 **St Helens,Mt** USA
14B2 **St Helier** Jersey, Channel Islands
13C2 **St-Hubert** Belgium
55L5 **St-Hyacinthe** Canada
64C1 **St Ignace** USA
64B1 **St Ignace I** Canada
7D3 **St Ives** Cambs, England
7B4 **St Ives** Cornwall, England
61E2 **St James** Minnesota, USA
63D1 **St James** Missouri, USA
54E4 **St James, C** Canada
65E1 **St-Jean** Canada
14B2 **St Jean-d'Angely** France
65E1 **St-Jean,L** Canada
65E1 **St-Jérôme** Canada
58C1 **St Joe** *R* USA
55M5 **Saint John** Canada
65F1 **St John** *R* Canada/USA
59E4 **St Johns** Arizona, USA
55N5 **St John's** Canada
64C2 **St Johns** Michigan, USA
67B3 **St Johns** *R* USA
65E2 **St Johnsbury** USA
6C2 **St John's Chapel** England
9D2 **St John's** *Pt* Northern Ireland
68C1 **St Johnsville** USA
65E1 **St-Joseph** Canada
63D2 **St Joseph** Louisiana, USA
64B2 **St Joseph** Michigan, USA
61E3 **St Joseph** Missouri, USA
69L1 **St Joseph** Trinidad
64C2 **St Joseph** *R* USA
64C1 **St Joseph I** Canada
63C3 **St Joseph I** USA
55J4 **St Joseph,L** Canada
14C2 **St-Junien** France
13B3 **St-Just-en-Chaussée** France
8A3 **St Kilda** *I* Scotland
69E3 **St Kitts-Nevis** *Is* Caribbean Sea
55M5 **St Lawrence** *R* Canada
55M5 **St Lawrence,G of** Canada
54B3 **St Lawrence I** USA
65D2 **St Lawrence Seaway** Canada/USA
65F1 **St Leonard** Canada
7E4 **St Leonards** England
14B2 **St-Lô** France
48A3 **St-Louis** Senegal
64A3 **St Louis** USA
13D4 **St-Loup-sur-Semouse** France
69E4 **St Lucia** *I* Caribbean Sea
47E2 **St Lucia,L** South Africa
8E1 **St Magnus B** Scotland
14B2 **St-Malo** France
14B2 **St-Malo, Golfe de** *B* France
13D3 **Ste-Marie-aux-Mines** France
58C1 **St Maries** USA
69E3 **St Martin** *I* Caribbean Sea
32D1 **St Mary,Mt** Papua New Guinea
34A2 **St Mary Peak** *Mt* Australia
34C4 **St Marys** Australia
65D2 **St Marys** USA
7A5 **St Marys** *I* England
67B2 **St Marys** *R* USA
32E1 **Saint Mathias Group** *Is* Papua New Guinea
65E1 **St Maurice** *R* Canada
13C3 **Ste-Menehould** France
54B3 **St Michael** USA
68B3 **St Michaels** USA
13C3 **St-Mihiel** France
16B1 **St Moritz** Switzerland
14B2 **St-Nazaire** France
7D3 **St Neots** England
13C2 **St-Niklaas** Belgium
13B2 **St-Omer** France
65F1 **St-Pascal** Canada
54G4 **St Paul** Canada
61E2 **St Paul** Minnesota, USA
60D2 **St Paul** Nebraska, USA
36E6 **St Paul** *I* Indian Ocean
48A4 **St Paul** *R* Liberia
61E2 **St Peter** USA
20E4 **St Petersburg** Russian Federation
67B3 **St Petersburg** USA
55N5 **St Pierre** *I* France
65E1 **St Pierre,L** Canada
13B2 **St-Pol-sur-Ternoise** France
18D3 **St Pölten** Austria
13B3 **St-Quentin** France
14D3 **St Raphaël** France
65F1 **St-Siméon** Canada
67B2 **St Simons I** USA
67B2 **St Stephen** USA
64C2 **St Thomas** Canada
14D3 **St Tropez** France
13C2 **St Truiden** Belgium
61D1 **St Vincent** USA
69E4 **St Vincent and The Grenadines** *Is* Caribbean Sea
34A2 **St Vincent,G** Australia
13D2 **St-Vith** Germany
13D3 **St Wendel** Germany
27H5 **Saipan** *I* Pacific Ocean
42B2 **Sajydabad** Afghanistan
72E7 **Sajama** *Mt* Bolivia
47C3 **Sak** *R* South Africa
29D4 **Sakai** Japan
29B4 **Sakaidi** Japan
28B3 **Sakaiminato** Japan
40D4 **Sakākah** Saudi Arabia
60C1 **Sakakawea,L** USA
57F1 **Sakami,L** Canada
51C5 **Sakania** Zaïre
51E6 **Sakaraha** Madagascar
21E7 **Sakarya** *R* Turkey
19E1 **Sakasleja** Latvia
29D3 **Sakata** Japan
48C4 **Sakété** Benin
26H1 **Sakhalin** *I* Russian Federation
26F4 **Sakishima guntō** *Is* Japan
47C3 **Sakrivier** South Africa
48A4 **Sal** *I* Cape Verde
21G6 **Sal** *R* Russian Federation
12H7 **Sala** Sweden
59C4 **Salada, Laguna** *L* Mexico
74D3 **Salado** *R* Sante Fe, Argentina
48B4 **Salaga** Ghana
30C3 **Sala Hintoun** Cambodia
50B2 **Salal** Chad
38D4 **Şalālah** Oman
15A1 **Salamanca** Spain
68A1 **Salamanca** USA
50B3 **Salamat** *R* Chad
27H7 **Salamaua** Papua New Guinea
45B1 **Salamis** *Hist Site* Cyprus
12H5 **Salangen** Norway
74C2 **Salar de Arizaro** *Salt Pan* Argentina
74C2 **Salar de Atacama** *Salt Pan* Chile
72E7 **Salar de Coipasa** *Salt Pan* Bolivia
72E8 **Salar de Uyuni** *Salt Pan* Bolivia
20K5 **Salavat** Russian Federation
32C1 **Salawati** *I* Indonesia
37O6 **Sala y Gómez** *I* Pacific Ocean
14C2 **Salbris** France
47B3 **Saldanha** South Africa
19E1 **Saldus** Latvia
34C3 **Sale** Australia
20M2 **Salekhard** Russian Federation
64B3 **Salem** Illinois, USA
44B3 **Salem** India
68E1 **Salem** Massachusetts, USA
68C3 **Salem** New Jersey, USA
68D1 **Salem** New York, USA
58B2 **Salem** Oregon, USA
64C3 **Salem** Virginia, USA
12G6 **Sälen** Sweden
16C2 **Salerno** Italy
7C3 **Salford** England
17D1 **Salgót** Hungary
19D3 **Salgótarján** Hungary
73L5 **Salgueiro** Brazil
60B3 **Salida** USA
17F3 **Salihli** Turkey
51D5 **Salima** Malawi
61D3 **Salina** Kansas, USA
59D3 **Salina** Utah, USA
16C3 **Salina** *I* Italy
70C3 **Salina Cruz** Mexico
75D2 **Salinas** Brazil
66B2 **Salinas** USA
66B2 **Salinas** *R* USA
15C2 **Salinas, Cabo de** *C* Spain
74D3 **Salinas Grandes** *Salt Pans* Argentina
62A2 **Salinas Peak** *Mt* USA
63D2 **Saline** *R* Arkansas, USA
60C3 **Saline** *R* Kansas, USA
69M2 **Salines,Pt** Grenada
66D2 **Saline V** USA
73J4 **Salinópolis** Brazil
Salisbury = Harare
7D4 **Salisbury** England
65D3 **Salisbury** Maryland, USA
67B1 **Salisbury** North Carolina, USA
55L3 **Salisbury I** Canada
7D4 **Salisbury Plain** England
45D2 **Şalkhad** Syria
12K5 **Salla** Finland
63D1 **Sallisaw** USA
55L3 **Salluit** Canada
43E3 **Sallyana** Nepal
41D2 **Salmas** Iran
12L6 **Salmi** Russian Federation
58C1 **Salmo** Canada
58D1 **Salmon** USA
58C1 **Salmon** *R* USA
54G4 **Salmon Arm** Canada
58C1 **Salmon River Mts** USA
12J6 **Salo** Finland
14D3 **Salon-de-Provence** France
Salonica = Thessaloníki
17E1 **Salonta** Romania
12K6 **Salpausselkä** *Region* Finland
21G6 **Sal'sk** Russian Federation
45C2 **Salt** Jordan
47C3 **Salt** *R* South Africa
59D4 **Salt** *R* USA
74C2 **Salta** Argentina
74C2 **Salta** *State* Argentina
7B4 **Saltash** England
9C3 **Saltee, I** Irish Republic
70B2 **Saltillo** Mexico
58D2 **Salt Lake City** USA
72D3 **Salto Angostura** *Waterfall* Colombia
75E2 **Salto da Divisa** Brazil
75B3 **Salto das Sete Quedas** Brazil
72F2 **Salto del Angel** *Waterfall* Venezuela
74E2 **Salto del Guaíra** *Waterfall* Brazil
72D4 **Salto Grande** *Waterfall* Colombia
59C4 **Salton S** USA
75B4 **Saltos do Iguaçu** *Waterfall* Argentina
74E4 **Salto Tacuarembó** Uruguay
42C2 **Salt Range** *Mts* Pakistan
69H2 **Salt River** Jamaica
67B2 **Saluda** USA

44C2 **Sālūr** India
73L6 **Salvador** Brazil
63D3 **Salvador,L** USA
41F5 **Salwah** Qatar
30B1 **Salween** *R* Burma
21H8 **Sal'yany** Azerbaijan
64C3 **Salyersville** USA
18C3 **Salzburg** Austria
18C2 **Salzgitter** Germany
18C2 **Salzwedel** Germany
26C1 **Samagaltay** Russian Federation
69D3 **Samaná** Dominican Republic
40C2 **Samandağı** Turkey
42B1 **Samangan** Afghanistan
29D2 **Samani** Japan
45A3 **Samannûd** Egypt
27F5 **Samar** *I* Philippines
20J5 **Samara** Russian Federation
32E2 **Samarai** Papua New Guinea
27E7 **Samarinda** Indonesia
38E2 **Samarkand** Uzbekistan
41D3 **Sāmarrā'** Iraq
43E4 **Sambalpur** India
27D6 **Sambas** Indonesia
51F5 **Sambava** Madagascar
42D3 **Sambhal** India
19E3 **Sambor** Ukraine
13B2 **Sambre** *R* France
28B3 **Samch'ŏk** S Korea
28A4 **Samch'ŏnp'o** S Korea
28A3 **Samdŭng** N Korea
50D4 **Same** Tanzania
51C5 **Samfya** Zambia
30B1 **Samka** Burma
30C1 **Sam Neua** Laos
33H2 **Samoan Is** Pacific Ocean
17F3 **Sámos** *I* Greece
17F2 **Samothráki** *I* Greece
27E7 **Sampit** Indonesia
63D2 **Sam Rayburn Res** USA
30C3 **Samrong** Cambodia
18C1 **Samsø** *I* Denmark
28A2 **Samsu** N Korea
40C1 **Samsun** Turkey
48B3 **San** Mali
30D3 **San** *R* Cambodia
19E2 **San** *R* Poland
50E2 **San'ā** Yemen
50B3 **Sanaga** *R* Cameroon
74C4 **San Agustín** Argentina
52D6 **San Ambrosia, Isla** Pacific Ocean
41E2 **Sanandaj** Iran
66B1 **San Andreas** USA
69A4 **San Andres, Isla de** Caribbean Sea
62A2 **San Andres Mts** USA
70C3 **San Andrés Tuxtla** Mexico
62B2 **San Angelo** USA
16B3 **San Antioco** Sardinia, Italy
16B3 **San Antioco** *I* Sardinia, Italy
56B4 **San Antonia, Pt** Mexico
74B4 **San Antonio** Chile
62A2 **San Antonio** New Mexico, USA
62C3 **San Antonio** Texas, USA
66B2 **San Antonio** *R* California, USA
63C3 **San Antonio** *R* Texas, USA
15C2 **San Antonio Abad** Spain
69A2 **San Antonio, Cabo** *C* Cuba
62B2 **San Antonio de Bravo** Mexico
69A2 **San Antonio de los Banos** Cuba
66D3 **San Antonio,Mt** USA
74D6 **San Antonio Oeste** Argentina
66B3 **San Antonio Res** USA
66B2 **San Ardo** USA
42D4 **Sanāwad** India
70A3 **San Benedicto** *I* Mexico
63C3 **San Benito** USA
66B2 **San Benito** *R* USA
66B2 **San Benito Mt** USA
66D3 **San Bernardino** USA
74B4 **San Bernardo** Chile
59C4 **San Bernardo Mts** USA
67A3 **San Blas,C** USA
70E4 **San Blas, Puerta** *Pt* Panama
74E3 **San Borja** Brazil
74B5 **San Carlos** Chile
72B1 **San Carlos** Nicaragua
59D4 **San Carlos** USA
74B6 **San Carlos de Bariloche** Argentina
20H4 **Sanchursk** Russian Federation
66D4 **San Clemente** USA
59C4 **San Clemente I** USA
70C3 **San Cristóbal** Mexico
72D2 **San Cristóbal** Venezuela
33F2 **San Cristobal** *I* Solomon Islands
70E2 **Sancti Spíritus** Cuba
14C2 **Sancy, Puy de** *Mt* France
47D1 **Sand** *R* South Africa
8C4 **Sanda, I** Scotland
27E6 **Sandakan** Malaysia
8D2 **Sanday** *I* Scotland
62B2 **Sanderson** USA
7E4 **Sandgate** England
59C4 **San Diego** USA
74C8 **San Diego, Cabo** Argentina
40B2 **Sandıklı** Turkey
43E3 **Sandīla** India
12F7 **Sandnes** Norway
12G5 **Sandnessjøen** Norway
51C4 **Sandoa** Zaïre
19E2 **Sandomierz** Poland
43G5 **Sandoway** Burma
7D4 **Sandown** England
12D3 **Sandoy** *I* Faeroes
58C1 **Sandpoint** USA
63C1 **Sand Springs** USA
32A3 **Sandstone** Australia
61E1 **Sandstone** USA
31C4 **Sandu** China
64C2 **Sandusky** USA
12H6 **Sandviken** Sweden
68E2 **Sandwich** USA
55J4 **Sandy L** Canada
75A3 **San Estanislao** Paraguay
56B3 **San Felipe** Baja Cal, Mexico
74B4 **San Felipe** Chile
69D4 **San Felipe** Venezuela
15C1 **San Felíu de Guixols** Spain
52D6 **San Felix, Isla** Pacific Ocean
74B4 **San Fernando** Chile
27F5 **San Fernando** Philippines
15A2 **San Fernando** Spain
69L2 **San Fernando** Trinidad
66C3 **San Fernando** USA
72E2 **San Fernando** Venezuela
67B3 **Sanford** Florida, USA
65E2 **Sanford** Maine, USA
67C1 **Sanford** N Carolina, USA
57E4 **Sanford** USA
54D3 **Sanford, Mt** USA
74D4 **San Francisco** Argentina
69C3 **San Francisco** Dominican Republic
66A2 **San Francisco** USA
66A2 **San Francisco B** USA
70B2 **San Francisco del Oro** Mexico
66D3 **San Gabriel Mts** USA
42C5 **Sangamner** India
64B3 **Sangamon** *R* USA
25O3 **Sangar** Russian Federation
44B2 **Sangāreddi** India
66C2 **Sanger** USA
31C2 **Sanggan He** *R* China
27E6 **Sanggau** Indonesia
50B3 **Sangha** *R* Congo
42B3 **Sanghar** Pakistan
27F6 **Sangir** *I* Indonesia
27F6 **Sangir, Kepulauan** *Is* Indonesia
30B3 **Sangkhla Buri** Thailand
27E6 **Sangkulirang** Indonesia
44A2 **Sāngli** India
50B3 **Sangmélima** Cameroon
56B3 **San Gorgonio Mt** USA
62A1 **Sangre de Cristo Mts** USA
66A2 **San Gregorio** USA
42D2 **Sangrūr** India
47E1 **Sangutane** *R* Mozambique
74E3 **San Ignacio** Argentina
72D2 **San Jacinto** Colombia
59C4 **San Jacinto Peak** *Mt* USA
28A2 **Sanjiangkou** China
29D3 **Sanjō** Japan
74H2 **San João del Rei** Brazil
66B2 **San Joaquin** *R* USA
66B2 **San Joaquin Valley** USA
62B1 **San Jon** USA
74C7 **San Jorge, Golfo** *G* Argentina
15C1 **San Jorge, Golfo de** *G* Spain
72B1 **San José** Costa Rica
70C3 **San José** Guatemala
66B2 **San Jose** USA
56B4 **San José** *I* Mexico
72F7 **San José de Chiquitos** Bolivia
56C4 **San José del Cabo** Mexico
74G2 **San José do Rio Prêto** Brazil
70B2 **San Joseé del Cabo** Mexico
28A3 **Sanju** S Korea
74C4 **San Juan** Argentina
69D3 **San Juan** Puerto Rico
69L1 **San Juan** Trinidad
72E2 **San Juan** Venezuela
69B2 **San Juan** *Mt* Cuba
66B3 **San Juan** *R* California, USA
70D3 **San Juan** *R* Costa Rica/ Nicaragua
59D3 **San Juan** *R* Utah, USA
74C4 **San Juan** *State* Argentina
74E3 **San Juan Bautista** Paraguay
66B2 **San Juan Bautista** USA
70D3 **San Juan del Norte** Nicaragua
69D4 **San Juan de los Cayos** Venezuela
70D3 **San Juan del Sur** Nicaragua
58B1 **San Juan Is** USA
62A1 **San Juan Mts** USA
74C7 **San Julián** Argentina
50C4 **Sankuru** *R* Zaïre
66A2 **San Leandro** USA
40C2 **Sanliurfa** Turkey
72C3 **San Lorenzo** Colombia
72B4 **San Lorenzo, Cabo** *C* Ecuador
15B1 **San Lorenzo de Escorial** Spain
66B2 **San Lucas** USA
74C4 **San Luis** Argentina
59D4 **San Luis** USA
74C4 **San Luis** *State* Argentina
66B2 **San Luis Canal** USA
66B3 **San Luis Obispo** USA
66B3 **San Luis Obispo B** USA
70B2 **San Luis Potosí** Mexico
66B2 **San Luis Res** USA
16B3 **Sanluri** Sardinia, Italy
72E2 **San Maigualida** *Mts* Venezuela
63C3 **San Marcos** USA
76G3 **San Martin** *Base* Antarctica
74B7 **San Martin, Lago** Argentina/Chile
66A2 **San Mateo** USA
73G7 **San Matías** Bolivia
74D6 **San Matías, Golfo** *G* Argentina
31C3 **Sanmenxia** China
70D3 **San Miguel** El Salvador
66B3 **San Miguel** USA
66B3 **San Miguel** *I* USA
74C3 **San Miguel de Tucumán** Argentina
74F3 **San Miguel d'Oeste** Brazil
31D4 **Sanming** China
74D4 **San Nicolas** Argentina
56B3 **San Nicolas** *I* USA
47D2 **Sannieshof** South Africa
48B4 **Sanniquellie** Liberia
19E3 **Sanok** Poland
69B5 **San Onofore** Colombia
66D4 **San Onofre** USA
27F5 **San Pablo** Philippines
66A1 **San Pablo B** USA
48B4 **San Pédro** Ivory Coast
74D2 **San Pedro** Jujuy, Argentina
74E2 **San Pedro** Paraguay
59D4 **San Pedro** *R* USA
66C4 **San Pedro Chan** USA
56C4 **San Pedro de los Colonias** Mexico
70D3 **San Pedro Sula** Honduras
16B3 **San Pietro** *I* Sardinia, Italy
8D4 **Sanquar** Scotland
70A1 **San Quintin** Mexico
74C4 **San Rafael** Argentina
66A2 **San Rafael** USA
66C3 **San Rafael Mts** USA
16B2 **San Remo** Italy
62C2 **San Saba** *R* USA
71B2 **San Salvador** El Salvador
69C2 **San Salvador** *I* The Bahamas
74C2 **San Salvador de Jujuy** Argentina
15B1 **San Sebastián** Spain
16D2 **San Severo** Italy
66B3 **San Simeon** USA
72E7 **Santa Ana** Bolivia
70C3 **Santa Ana** Guatemala
66D4 **Santa Ana** USA
66D4 **Santa Ana Mts** USA
62C2 **Santa Anna** USA
70B2 **Santa Barbara** Mexico
66C3 **Santa Barbara** USA
66C4 **Santa Barbara** *I* USA
66B3 **Santa Barbara Chan** USA
66C3 **Santa Barbara Res** USA
66C4 **Santa Catalina** *I* USA
66C4 **Santa Catalina,G of** USA
74F3 **Santa Catarina** *State* Brazil
74G3 **Santa Catarina, Isla de** Brazil
69B2 **Santa Clara** Cuba
66B2 **Santa Clara** USA
66C3 **Santa Clara** *R* USA
74C8 **Santa Cruz** Argentina
72F7 **Santa Cruz** Bolivia
27F5 **Santa Cruz** Philippines
66A2 **Santa Cruz** USA
66C4 **Santa Cruz** *I* USA
59D4 **Santa Cruz** *R* USA
74B7 **Santa Cruz** *State* Argentina
75E2 **Santa Cruz Cabrália** Brazil
66C3 **Santa Cruz Chan** USA
48A2 **Santa Cruz de la Palma** Canary Islands
69B2 **Santa Cruz del Sur** Cuba
48A2 **Santa Cruz de Tenerife** Canary Islands
51C5 **Santa Cruz do Cuando** Angola
75C3 **Santa Cruz do Rio Pardo** Brazil
33F2 **Santa Cruz Is** Solomon Islands
66A2 **Santa Cruz Mts** USA
72F3 **Santa Elena** Venezuela
74D4 **Santa Fe** Argentina
62A1 **Santa Fe** USA
74D3 **Santa Fe** *State* Argentina
75B2 **Santa Helena de Goiás** Brazil
31B3 **Santai** China
74B8 **Santa Inés** *I* Chile
33E1 **Santa Isabel** *I* Solomon Islands
66B2 **Santa Lucia Range** *Mts* USA
48A4 **Santa Luzia** *I* Cape Verde
66B3 **Santa Margarita** USA
66D4 **Santa Margarita** *R* USA
70A2 **Santa Margarita, Isla** Mexico
74F3 **Santa Maria** Brazil
66B3 **Santa Maria** USA
48A1 **Santa Maria** *I* Azores
62A2 **Santa María** *R* Chihuahua, Mexico
47E2 **Santa Maria, Cabo de** *C* Mozambique
75D1 **Santa Maria da Vitória** Brazil
17D3 **Santa Maria di Leuca, Capo** *C* Italy
62A2 **Santa María Laguna de** *L* Mexico
69C4 **Santa Marta** Colombia
72D1 **Santa Marta, Sierra Nevada de** *Mts* Colombia
66C3 **Santa Monica** USA
66C4 **Santa Monica B** USA
75D1 **Santana** Brazil
74E4 **Santana do Livramento** Brazil
72C3 **Santander** Colombia
15B1 **Santander** Spain
15C2 **Santañy** Spain
66C3 **Santa Paula** USA
73K4 **Santa Quitéria** Brazil
73H4 **Santarém** Brazil
15A2 **Santarém** Portugal
75B2 **Santa Rita do Araguaia** Brazil
74D5 **Santa Rosa** Argentina
66A1 **Santa Rosa** California, USA
70D3 **Santa Rosa** Honduras
62B2 **Santa Rosa** New Mexico, USA
66B3 **Santa Rosa** *I* USA
70A2 **Santa Rosalía** Mexico
58C2 **Santa Rosa Range** *Mts* USA
73L5 **Santa Talhada** Brazil
75D2 **Santa Teresa** Brazil
16B2 **Santa Teresa di Gallura** Sardinia, Italy
66B3 **Santa Ynez** *R* USA
66B3 **Santa Ynez Mts** USA
67C2 **Santee** *R* USA
74B4 **Santiago** Chile
69C3 **Santiago** Dominican Republic
72B2 **Santiago** Panama
72C4 **Santiago** *R* Peru
15A1 **Santiago de Compostela** Spain
69B2 **Santiago de Cuba** Cuba
74D3 **Santiago del Estero** Argentina
74D3 **Santiago del Estero** *State* Argentina
66D4 **Santiago Peak** *Mt* USA
33F2 **Santo** Vanuatu
75C3 **Santo Amaro, Ilha** Brazil
75B3 **Santo Anastatácio** Brazil
74F3 **Santo Angelo** Brazil
48A4 **Santo Antão** *I* Cape Verde
75B3 **Santo Antônio da Platina** Brazil
75E1 **Santo Antônio de Jesus** Brazil
75A2 **Santo Antônio do Leverger** Brazil
69D3 **Santo Domingo** Dominican Republic
75C3 **Santos** Brazil
75D3 **Santos Dumont** Brazil
59C4 **Santo Tomas** Mexico
74E3 **Santo Tomé** Argentina
74B7 **San Valentin** *Mt* Chile
16C3 **San Vito, C** Sicily, Italy
28B2 **Sanyuanpu** China
51B4 **Sanza Pomba** Angola
75C3 **São Carlos** Brazil
75C1 **São Domingos** Brazil
73H5 **São Félix** Mato Grosso, Brazil
75D3 **São Fidélis** Brazil
75D2 **São Francisco** Brazil
73L5 **São Francisco** *R* Brazil
74G3 **São Francisco do Sul** Brazil
75C4 **São Francisco, Ilha de** Brazil
75C2 **São Gotardo** Brazil
51D4 **Sao Hill** Tanzania
75A2 **São Jerônimo, Serra de** *Mts* Brazil
75D3 **São João da Barra** Brazil
75C3 **São João da Boa Vista** Brazil
75C1 **São João d'Aliança** Brazil
75D2 **São João da Ponte** Brazil
75D3 **São João del Rei** Brazil
75D2 **São João do Paraíso** Brazil
75C3 **São Joaquim da Barra** Brazil
48A1 **São Jorge** *I* Azores
75C3 **São José do Rio Prêto** Brazil
75C3 **São José dos Campos** Brazil
75C4 **São José dos Pinhais** Brazil
75A2 **São Lourenço** *R* Brazil
73K4 **São Luís** Brazil
75C2 **São Marcos** *R* Brazil
73K4 **São Marcos, Baia de** *B* Brazil
75D2 **São Maria do Suaçui** Brazil
75E2 **São Mateus** Brazil
75D2 **São Mateus** *R* Brazil
48A1 **São Miguel** *I* Azores
75B1 **São Miguel de Araguaia** Brazil
14C2 **Saône** *R* France
48A4 **São Nicolau** *I* Cape Verde
75D1 **São Onofre** *R* Brazil
75C3 **São Paulo** Brazil
75B3 **São Paulo** *State* Brazil
71H3 **São Pedro e São Paulo** *Is* Atlantic Ocean
73K5 **São Raimundo Nonato** Brazil
75C2 **São Romão** Brazil
75C3 **São Sebastia do Paraíso** Brazil
75C3 **São Sebastião, Ilha de** Brazil
75B2 **São Simão,Barragem de** Brazil
75B2 **São Simão** Goias, Brazil
75C3 **São Simão** São Paulo, Brazil
48A4 **São Tiago** *I* Cape Verde
48C4 **São Tomé** *I* W Africa
48C4 **Sao Tome and Principe** *Republic* W Africa
75D3 **São Tomé, Cabo de** *C* Brazil
48B2 **Saoura** *Watercourse* Algeria
75A1 **Saouriuiná** *R* Brazil
75C3 **São Vicente** Brazil
15A2 **São Vicente, Cabo de** *C* Portugal
48A4 **São Vincente** *I* Cape Verde
17F2 **Sápai** Greece
48C4 **Sapele** Nigeria
29E2 **Sapporo** Japan
16D2 **Sapri** Italy
63C1 **Sapulpa** USA
41E2 **Saqqez** Iran
21H8 **Sarāb** Iran
17D2 **Sarajevo** Bosnia-Herzegovina
21K5 **Saraktash** Russian Federation
25K4 **Sarala** Russian Federation
65E2 **Saranac Lake** USA
17E3 **Sarandë** Albania
20L3 **Saranpaul'** Russian Federation
20H5 **Saransk** Russian Federation
20J4 **Sarapul** Russian Federation
67B3 **Sarasota** USA
17F1 **Sărat** Romania
19F3 **Sarata** Ukraine
60B2 **Saratoga** USA
68D1 **Saratoga Springs** USA

21H5 **Saratov** Russian Federation
21H5 **Saratovskoye Vodokhranilishche** *Res* Russian Federation
30D2 **Saravane** Laos
27E6 **Sarawak** *State* Malaysia
40A2 **Saraykoy** Turkey
49D2 **Sardalas** Libya
41E2 **Sar Dasht** Iran
Sardegna = Sardinia
16B2 **Sardinia** *I* Medit Sea
12H5 **Sarektjåkkå** *Mt* Sweden
42C2 **Sargodha** Pakistan
50B3 **Sarh** Chad
48B1 **Sarhro, Jbel** *Mt* Morocco
41F2 **Sārī** Iran
45C2 **Sarida** *R* Israel
27H5 **Sarigan** *I* Pacific Ocean
40D1 **Sarıkamış** Turkey
32D3 **Sarina** Australia
42B1 **Sar-i-Pul** Afghanistan
49E2 **Sarīr** Libya
49D2 **Sarir Tibesti** *Desert* Libya
28B3 **Sariwŏn** N Korea
14B2 **Sark** *I* Channel Islands
40C2 **Şarkışla** Turkey
27G7 **Sarmi** Indonesia
74C7 **Sarmiento** Argentina
12G6 **Särna** Sweden
64C2 **Sarnia** Canada
19F2 **Sarny** Ukraine
42B2 **Sarobi** Afghanistan
17E3 **Saronikós Kólpos** *G* Greece
17F2 **Saros Körfezi** *B* Turkey
20M2 **Saroto** Russian Federation
12G7 **Sarpsborg** Norway
55N2 **Sarqaq** Greenland
13D3 **Sarralbe** France
13D3 **Sarrebourg** France
13D3 **Sarreguemines** France
13D3 **Sarre-Union** France
15B1 **Sarrion** Spain
42B3 **Sartanahu** Pakistan
16B2 **Sartène** Corsica, France
14B2 **Sarthe** *R* France
45D1 **Sārūt** *R* Syria
21J6 **Sarykamys** Kazakhstan
24H5 **Sarysu** *R* Kazakhstan
43E4 **Sasarām** India
28B4 **Sasebo** Japan
54H4 **Saskatchewan** *Province* Canada
54H4 **Saskatchewan** *R* Canada
54H4 **Saskatoon** Canada
25N2 **Saskylakh** Russian Federation
47D2 **Sasolburg** South Africa
20G5 **Sasovo** Russian Federation
48B4 **Sassandra** Ivory Coast
48B4 **Sassandra** *R* Ivory Coast
16B2 **Sassari** Sardinia, Italy
18C2 **Sassnitz** Germany
28A4 **Sasuna** Japan
44A2 **Sātāra** India
54G2 **Satellite B** Canada
12H6 **Säter** Sweden
67B2 **Satilla** *R* USA
20K4 **Satka** Russian Federation
42D2 **Satluj** *R* India
43E4 **Satna** India
42C4 **Sātpura Range** *Mts* India
17E1 **Satu Mare** Romania
12B1 **Sauðárkrókur** Iceland
12F7 **Sauda** Norway
38C3 **Saudi Arabia** *Kingdom* Arabian Pen
13D3 **Sauer** *R* Germany/Luxembourg
13D2 **Sauerland** *Region* Germany
64B2 **Saugatuck** USA
68D1 **Saugerties** USA
61E1 **Sauk Center** USA
64B2 **Sauk City** USA
64C1 **Sault Ste Marie** Canada
64C1 **Sault Ste Marie** USA
27G7 **Saumlaki** Indonesia
14B2 **Saumur** France
51C4 **Saurimo** Angola
69M2 **Sauteurs** Grenada
17D2 **Sava** *R* Serbia, Yugoslavia
33H2 **Savai'i** *I* Western Samoa
48C4 **Savalou** Benin
67B2 **Savannah** Georgia, USA
63E1 **Savannah** Tennessee, USA
67B2 **Savannah** *R* USA
30C2 **Savannakhet** Laos
69G1 **Savanna la Mar** Jamaica
55J4 **Savant Lake** Canada
48C4 **Savé** Benin
51D6 **Save** *R* Mozambique
41F3 **Sāveh** Iran
13D3 **Saverne** France
13B3 **Savigny** France
20G3 **Savinskiy** Russian Federation
14D2 **Savoie** *Region* France
16B2 **Savona** Italy
12K6 **Savonlinna** Finland
54A3 **Savoonga** USA
32B2 **Savu** *I* Indonesia
12K5 **Savukoski** Finland
27F7 **Savu S** Indonesia
30A1 **Saw** Burma
42D3 **Sawai Mādhopur** India
30C2 **Sawankhalok** Thailand
29D3 **Sawara** Japan
60B3 **Sawatch Mts** USA
49D2 **Sawdā', Jabal as** *Mts* Libya
58C2 **Sawtooth Range** *Mts* USA
27F8 **Sawu** *I* Indonesia
7E3 **Saxmundham** England
68A2 **Saxton** USA
48C3 **Say** Niger
42B1 **Sayghan** Afghanistan
38D4 **Sayhūt** Yemen
21H6 **Saykhin** Kazakhstan
26D2 **Saynshand** Mongolia
62C1 **Sayre** Oklahoma, USA
68B2 **Sayre** Pennsylvania, USA
21J7 **Say-Utes** Kazakhstan
68D2 **Sayville** USA
18C3 **Sázava** *R* Czech Republic
15C2 **Sbisseb** *R* Algeria
6C2 **Scafell Pike** *Mt* England
8E1 **Scalloway** Scotland
8C3 **Scalpay, I** Scotland
8D2 **Scapa Flow** *Sd* Scotland
65D2 **Scarborough** Canada
6D2 **Scarborough** England
69K1 **Scarborough** Tobago
8B2 **Scarp** *I* Scotland
16B1 **Schaffhausen** Switzerland
18C3 **Schärding** Austria
13E1 **Scharhörn** *I* Germany
13D2 **Scharteberg** *Mt* Germany
55M4 **Schefferville** Canada
13B2 **Schelde** *R* Belgium
59D3 **Schell Creek Range** *Mts* USA
68D1 **Schenectady** USA
62C3 **Schertz** USA
13C2 **Schiedam** Netherlands
13D1 **Schiermonnikoog** *I* Netherlands
13D2 **Schleiden** Germany
18B2 **Schleswig** Germany
18B2 **Schleswig Holstein** *State* Germany
68C1 **Schoharie** USA
32D1 **Schouten Is** Papua New Guinea
13E3 **Schramberg** Germany
55K5 **Schreiber** Canada
9B4 **Schull** Irish Republic
59C3 **Schurz** USA
68C2 **Schuylkill** *R* USA
68B2 **Schuylkill Haven** USA
18B3 **Schwabische Alb** *Upland* Germany
27E7 **Schwaner, Pegunungan** *Mts* Indonesia
47B2 **Schwarzrand** *Mts* Namibia
13E3 **Schwarzwald** *Mts* Germany
18C2 **Schweinfurt** Germany
47D2 **Schweizer Reneke** South Africa
18C2 **Schwerin** Germany
16B1 **Schwyz** Switzerland
16C3 **Sciacca** Italy
7A5 **Scilly, Isles of** England
64C3 **Scioto** *R* USA
60B1 **Scobey** USA
34D2 **Scone** Australia
55Q2 **Scoresby Sd** Greenland
52F7 **Scotia Sea** Atlantic Ocean
8C3 **Scotland** U K
76F7 **Scott** *Base* Antarctica
47E3 **Scottburgh** South Africa
62B1 **Scott City** USA
76G6 **Scott I** Antarctica
55L2 **Scott Inlet** *B* Canada
58B2 **Scott,Mt** USA
32B2 **Scott Reef** Timor Sea
60C2 **Scottsbluff** USA
67A2 **Scottsboro** USA
34C4 **Scottsdale** Australia
59D4 **Scottsdale** USA
68C2 **Scranton** USA
61D2 **Scribner** USA
7D3 **Scunthorpe** England
Scutari = Shkodër
47C3 **Seacow** *R* South Africa
7E4 **Seaford** England
54J4 **Seal** *R* Canada
34B3 **Sea Lake** Australia
59D3 **Searchlight** USA
63D1 **Searcy** USA
66D3 **Searles** USA
66B2 **Seaside** California, USA
58B1 **Seaside** Oregon, USA
68C3 **Seaside Park** USA
58B1 **Seattle** USA
65E2 **Sebago L** USA
70A2 **Sebastian Vizcaino, B** Mexico
66A1 **Sebastopol** USA
50D2 **Sebderat** Eritrea
19F1 **Sebez** Russian Federation
65F1 **Seboomook L** USA
67B3 **Sebring** USA
35A3 **Secretary I** New Zealand
61E3 **Sedalia** USA
13C3 **Sedan** France
6C2 **Sedbergh** England
35B2 **Seddonville** New Zealand
45C3 **Sede Boqer** Israel
45C3 **Sederot** Israel
48A3 **Sédhiou** Senegal
45C3 **Sedom** Israel
59D4 **Sedona** USA
47B2 **Seeheim** Namibia
76E4 **Seelig,Mt** Antarctica
35B2 **Sefton,Mt** New Zealand
30C5 **Segamat** Malaysia
20E3 **Segezha** Russian Federation
15B2 **Segorbe** Spain
48B3 **Ségou** Mali
Segovia = Coco
15B1 **Segovia** Spain
15C1 **Segre** *R* Spain
48B4 **Séguéla** Ivory Coast
63C3 **Seguin** USA
15B2 **Segura** *R* Spain
15B2 **Segura, Sierra de** *Mts* Spain
42B3 **Sehwan** Pakistan
62C1 **Seiling** USA
13D3 **Seille** *R* France
12J6 **Seinäjoki** Finland
61E1 **Seine** *R* Canada
14C2 **Seine** *R* France
13B3 **Seine-et-Marne** *Department* France
50D4 **Sekenke** Tanzania
48B4 **Sekondi** Ghana
50D2 **Sek'ot'a** Ethiopia
58B1 **Selah** USA
27G7 **Selaru** *I* Indonesia
27D6 **Selatan** *I* Indonesia
27G7 **Selat Dampier** *Str* Indonesia
27E7 **Selat Lombok** *Chan* Indonesia
27D7 **Selat Sunda** *Str* Indonesia
27F7 **Selat Wetar** *Chan* Indonesia
54C3 **Selawik** USA
32B1 **Selayar** *I* Indonesia
6D3 **Selby** England
60C1 **Selby** USA
17F3 **Selçuk** Turkey
47D1 **Selebi Pikwe** Botswana
25Q3 **Selennyakh** *R* Russian Federation
13D3 **Selestat** France
55Q3 **Selfoss** Iceland
60C1 **Selfridge** USA
50C1 **Selima Oasis** Sudan
19G1 **Selizharovo** Russian Federation
54J4 **Selkirk** Canada
8D4 **Selkirk** Scotland
54G4 **Selkirk Mts** Canada/USA
67A2 **Selma** Alabama, USA
66C2 **Selma** California, USA
63E1 **Selmer** USA
15B2 **Selouane** Morocco
72D5 **Selvas** *Region* Brazil
48A2 **Selvegens, Ilhas** *Is* Atlantic Ocean
58C1 **Selway** *R* USA
32D3 **Selwyn** Australia
54E3 **Selwyn Mts** Canada
27E7 **Semarang** Indonesia
20G4 **Semenov** Russian Federation
21F5 **Semiluki** Russian Federation
60B2 **Seminoe Res** USA
63C1 **Seminole** Oklahoma, USA
62B2 **Seminole** Texas, USA
67B2 **Seminole,L** USA
24K4 **Semipalatinsk** Kazakhstan
41F3 **Semirom** Iran
41F2 **Semnān** Iran
13C3 **Semois** *R* Belgium
72E5 **Sena Madureira** Brazil
51C5 **Senanga** Zambia
63E2 **Senatobia** USA
29E3 **Sendai** Japan
42D4 **Sendwha** India
68B1 **Seneca Falls** USA
68B1 **Seneca L** USA
62A2 **Senecu** Mexico
48A3 **Sénégal** *R* Mauritius/Senegal
48A3 **Senegal** *Republic* Africa
47D2 **Senekal** South Africa
73L6 **Senhor do Bonfim** Brazil
16C2 **Senigallia** Italy
16D2 **Senj** Croatia
26F4 **Senkaku Gunto** *Is* Japan
13B3 **Senlis** France
50D2 **Sennar** Sudan
55L5 **Senneterre** Canada
13D3 **Senones** France
13B3 **Sens** France
17D1 **Senta** Serbia, Yugoslavia
50C4 **Sentery** Zaïre
42D4 **Seoni** India
28B3 **Seoul** S Korea
35B2 **Separation Pt** New Zealand
75D3 **Sepetiba, B de** Brazil
27H7 **Sepik** *R* Papua New Guinea
28A3 **Sep'o** N Korea
30D2 **Sepone** Laos
75A2 **Sepotuba** *R* Brazil
55M4 **Sept-Iles** Canada
50B1 **Séquédine** Niger
66C2 **Sequoia Nat Pk** USA
45C1 **Serai** Syria
27F7 **Seram** *I* Indonesia
27F7 **Seram Sea** Indonesia
17D2 **Serbia** *Republic* Yugoslavia
21G5 **Serdobsk** Russian Federation
13B4 **Serein** *R* France
30C5 **Seremban** Malaysia
50D4 **Serengeti Nat Pk** Tanzania
51D5 **Serenje** Zambia
19F3 **Seret** *R* Ukraine
20H4 **Sergach** Russian Federation
28C2 **Sergeyevka** Russian Federation
24H3 **Sergino** Russian Federation
73L6 **Sergipe** *State* Brazil
20F4 **Sergiyev Posad** Georgia
27E6 **Seria** Brunei
27E6 **Serian** Malaysia
17E3 **Sérifos** *I* Greece
49E2 **Serir Calanscio** *Desert* Libya
13C3 **Sermaize-les-Bains** France
32B1 **Sermata** *I* Indonesia
55P3 **Sermilik** *Fjord* Greenland
20J5 **Sernovodsk** Russian Federation
20L4 **Serov** Russian Federation
47D1 **Serowe** Botswana
15A2 **Serpa** Portugal
20F5 **Serpukhov** Russian Federation
15A1 **Serra da Estrela** *Mts* Portugal
73H3 **Serra do Navio** Brazil
17E2 **Sérrai** Greece
70D3 **Serrana Bank** *Is* Caribbean Sea
15B1 **Serraná de Cuenca** *Mts* Spain
75B2 **Serranópolis** Brazil
16B3 **Serrat, C** Tunisia
13B3 **Serre** *R* France
73L6 **Serrinha** Brazil
75D2 **Serro** Brazil
15C2 **Sersou, Plateau du** Algeria
75B3 **Sertanópolis** Brazil
31A3 **Sêrtar** China
47D1 **Serule** Botswana
51B5 **Sesfontein** Namibia
51C5 **Sesheke** Zambia
29D2 **Setana** Japan
14C3 **Sète** France
75D2 **Sete Lagoas** Brazil
15C2 **Sétif** Algeria
29C3 **Seto** Japan
28B4 **Seto Naikai** *S* Japan
48B1 **Settat** Morocco
6C2 **Settle** England
15A2 **Setúbal** Portugal
55J4 **Seul, Lac** Canada
21H7 **Sevan, Ozero** *L* Armenia
21E7 **Sevastopol'** Ukraine
7E4 **Sevenoaks** England
55K4 **Severn** *R* Canada
7C3 **Severn** *R* England
20G3 **Severnaya Dvina** *R* Russian Federation
25L1 **Severnaya Zemlya** *I* Russian Federation
20L3 **Severnyy Sos'va** *R* Russian Federation
20K3 **Severnyy Ural** *Mts* Russian Federation
25M4 **Severo Baykal'skoye Nagor'ye** *Mts* Russian Federation
21F6 **Severo Donets** *R* Ukraine
20F3 **Severodvinsk** Russian Federation
24H3 **Severo Sos'va** *R* Russian Federation
20L3 **Severoural'sk** Russian Federation
59D3 **Sevier** *R* USA
59D3 **Sevier Desert** USA
59D3 **Sevier L** USA
Sevilla = Seville
15A2 **Seville** Spain
17F2 **Sevlievo** Bulgaria
48A4 **Sewa** *R* Sierra Leone
61D2 **Seward** Nebraska, USA
54D3 **Seward** USA
54B3 **Seward Pen** USA
46K8 **Seychelles** *Is, Republic* Indian Ocean
40C2 **Seyhan** *R* Turkey
12C1 **Seyðisfjörður** Iceland
21F5 **Seym** *R* Russian Federation
25R3 **Seymchan** Russian Federation
34C3 **Seymour** Australia
68D2 **Seymour** Connecticut, USA
64B3 **Seymour** Indiana, USA
62C2 **Seymour** Texas, USA
13B3 **Sézanne** France
48D1 **Sfax** Tunisia
17F1 **Sfînto Gheorghe** Romania
's-Gravenhage = The Hague
8C3 **Sgúrr na Lapaich,** *Mt* Scotland
31B3 **Shaanxi** *Province* China
50E3 **Shabeelle** *R* Ethiopia/Somalia
50C4 **Shabunda** Zaïre
39F2 **Shache** China
76G9 **Shackleton Ice Shelf** Antarctica
42B3 **Shadadkot** Pakistan
41F3 **Shādhām** *R* Iran
66C3 **Shafter** USA
7C4 **Shaftesbury** England
28A2 **Shagang** China
74J8 **Shag Rocks** *Is* South Georgia
44B2 **Shāhābād** India
41E3 **Shāhābād** Iran
45D2 **Shahbā** Syria
41G3 **Shahdāb** Iran
43E4 **Shahdol** India
41E2 **Shāhīn Dezh** Iran
41G3 **Shāh Kūh** *Mt* Iran
41G3 **Shahr-e Bābak** Iran
Shahresa = Qomisheh
41F3 **Shahr Kord** Iran
21J8 **Shahsavār** Iran
20L3 **Shaim** Russian Federation
45C4 **Sha'îra, Gebel** *Mt* Egypt
40B5 **Sha'it, Wadi** *Watercourse* Egypt
42D3 **Shājahānpur** India
42D4 **Shājāpur** India
21G6 **Shakhty** Russian Federation
20H4 **Shakhun'ya** Russian Federation
48C4 **Shaki** Nigeria
61E2 **Shakopee** USA
29D2 **Shakotan-misaki** *C* Japan
20K4 **Shamary** Russian Federation
50D3 **Shambe** Sudan
68B2 **Shamokin** USA
62B1 **Shamrock** USA
68C1 **Shandaken** USA
66B3 **Shandon** USA
31D2 **Shandong** *Province* China
31C5 **Shangchuan Dao** *I* China
31C1 **Shangdu** China
31E3 **Shanghai** China
31C3 **Shangnan** China
51C5 **Shangombo** Zambia
31D3 **Shangqiu** China
31D4 **Shangrao** China
31B5 **Shangsi** China
31C3 **Shang Xian** China
7D4 **Shanklin** England
9B3 **Shannon** *R* Irish Republic
28B2 **Shansonggang** China
26G1 **Shantarskiye Ostrova** *I* Russian Federation
31D5 **Shantou** China
31C2 **Shanxi** *Province* China
31D3 **Shan Xian** China
31C5 **Shaoguan** China
31E4 **Shaoxing** China
31C4 **Shaoyang** China
8D2 **Shapinsay** *I* Scotland
45D2 **Shaqqā** Syria
41E4 **Shaqra'** Saudi Arabia
31A1 **Sharhulsan** Mongolia
29D2 **Shari** Japan
41G2 **Sharifābād** Iran
41G4 **Sharjah** UAE
32A3 **Shark B** Australia
41G2 **Sharlauk** Turkmenistan
45C2 **Sharon,Plain of** Israel
68B3 **Sharpsburg** USA
40C3 **Sharqi, Jebel esh** *Mts* Lebanon/Syria
20H4 **Sharya** Russian Federation
50D3 **Shashamenē** Ethiopia
47D1 **Shashani** *R* Zimbabwe
47D1 **Shashe** *R* Botswana

31C3 **Shashi** China
58B2 **Shasta L** USA
58B2 **Shasta,Mt** USA
45D1 **Shaṭḥah at Taḥtā** Syria
41E3 **Shaṭṭ al Gharraf** *R* Iraq
45C3 **Shaubak** Jordan
66C2 **Shaver L** USA
68C2 **Shawangunk Mt** USA
64B2 **Shawano** USA
65E1 **Shawinigan** Canada
63C1 **Shawnee** Oklahoma, USA
60B2 **Shawnee** Wyoming, USA
31D4 **Sha Xian** China
32B3 **Shay Gap** Australia
45D2 **Shaykh Miskīn** Syria
50E2 **Shaykh 'Uthmān** Yemen
21F5 **Shchigry** Russian Federation
21E5 **Shchors** Ukraine
24J4 **Shchuchinsk** Kazakhstan
50E3 **Shebele** *R* Ethiopia
64B2 **Sheboygan** USA
50B3 **Shebshi Mts** Nigeia
9C3 **Sheelin, L** Irish Republic
9C2 **Sheep Haven** *Estuary* Irish Republic
7E4 **Sheerness** England
45C2 **Shefar'am** Israel
63E2 **Sheffield** Alabama, USA
7D3 **Sheffield** England
62B2 **Sheffield** Texas, USA
8C3 **Sheil, Loch** *L* Scotland
42C2 **Shekhupura** Pakistan
25T2 **Shelagskiy, Mys** *C* Russian Federation
68D1 **Shelburne Falls** USA
64B2 **Shelby** Michigan, USA
58D1 **Shelby** Montana, USA
67B1 **Shelby** N Carolina, USA
64B3 **Shelbyville** Indiana, USA
67A1 **Shelbyville** Tennessee, USA
61D2 **Sheldon** USA
54C4 **Shelikof Str** USA
58D2 **Shelley** USA
34D2 **Shellharbour** Australia
35A3 **Shelter Pt** New Zealand
58B1 **Shelton** USA
41E1 **Shemakha** Azerbaijan
61D2 **Shenandoah** USA
65D3 **Shenandoah** *R* USA
65D3 **Shenandoah Nat Pk** USA
48C4 **Shendam** Nigeria
50D2 **Shendi** Sudan
20G3 **Shenkursk** Russian Federation
31C2 **Shenmu** China
31E1 **Shenyang** China
31C5 **Shenzhen** China
42D3 **Sheopur** India
19F2 **Shepetovka** Ukraine
68B3 **Shepherdstown** USA
34C3 **Shepparton** Australia
7E4 **Sheppey** *I* England
55K2 **Sherard,C** Canada
7C4 **Sherborne** England
48A4 **Sherbro I** Sierra Leone
65E1 **Sherbrooke** Canada
68C1 **Sherburne** USA
42C3 **Shergarh** India
63D2 **Sheridan** Arkansas, USA
60B2 **Sheridan** Wyoming, USA
7E3 **Sheringham** England
63C2 **Sherman** USA
18B2 **'s-Hertogenbosch** Netherlands
10C1 **Shetland** *Is* Scotland
21J7 **Shevchenko** Kazakhstan
60D1 **Sheyenne** USA
60D1 **Sheyenne** *R* USA
41F4 **Sheyk Sho'eyb** *I* Iran
8B3 **Shiant, Sd of** Scotland
26J2 **Shiashkotan** *I* Kuril Is, Russian Federation
42B1 **Shibarghan** Afghanistan
29D3 **Shibata** Japan
29D2 **Shibetsu** Japan
49F1 **Shibîn el Kom** Egypt
45A3 **Shibîn el Qanâtir** Egypt
29C3 **Shibukawa** Japan
68B2 **Shickshinny** USA
28A3 **Shidao** China
31C2 **Shijiazhuang** China
42B3 **Shikarpur** Pakistan
26G3 **Shikoku** *I* Japan
29B4 **Shikoku-sanchi** *Mts* Japan
26H2 **Shikotan** *I* Russian Federation
29D2 **Shikotsu-ko** *L* Japan
20G3 **Shilega** Russian Federation
43F3 **Shiliguri** India
26E1 **Shilka** Russian Federation
26E1 **Shilka** *R* Russian Federation
68C2 **Shillington** USA
43G3 **Shillong** India
20G5 **Shilovo** Russian Federation
28B4 **Shimabara** Japan
29C4 **Shimada** Japan
26F1 **Shimanovsk** Russian Federation
29D3 **Shimizu** Japan
29C4 **Shimoda** Japan
44B3 **Shimoga** India
28C4 **Shimonoseki** Japan
29C3 **Shinano** *R* Japan
41G5 **Shināş** Oman
38E2 **Shindand** Afghanistan
68A2 **Shinglehouse** USA
29D4 **Shingū** Japan
29D3 **Shinjō** Japan
8C2 **Shin, Loch** *L* Scotland
29D3 **Shinminato** Japan
45D1 **Shinshār** Syria
50D4 **Shinyanga** Tanzania
29E3 **Shiogama** Japan
29C4 **Shiono-misaki** *C* Japan
31A5 **Shiping** China
68B2 **Shippensburg** USA
62A1 **Shiprock** USA
31B3 **Shiquan** China
29D3 **Shirakawa** Japan
29C3 **Shirane-san** *Mt* Japan
41F4 **Shīraz** Iran
45A3 **Shirbîn** Egypt
29F2 **Shiretoko-misaki** *C* Japan
29D2 **Shiriya-saki** *C* Japan
41F3 **Shīr Kūh** *Mt* Iran
29C3 **Shirotori** Japan
41G2 **Shirvān** Iran
54B3 **Shishmaref** USA
31B2 **Shitanjing** China
64B3 **Shively** USA
42D3 **Shivpuri** India
45C3 **Shivta** *Hist Site* Israel
59D3 **Shivwits Plat** USA
51D5 **Shiwa Ngandu** Zambia
31C3 **Shiyan** China
31B2 **Shizuishan** China
29C3 **Shizuoka** Japan
17D2 **Shkodër** Albania
19G2 **Shkov** Belarus
25L1 **Shmidta, Ostrov** *I* Russian Federation
34D2 **Shoalhaven** *R* Australia
28B4 **Shobara** Japan
44B3 **Shoranūr** India
44B2 **Shorāpur** India
59C3 **Shoshone** California, USA
58D2 **Shoshone** Idaho, USA
58E2 **Shoshone** *R* USA
58D2 **Shoshone L** USA
59C3 **Shoshone Mts** USA
58E2 **Shoshoni** USA
21E5 **Shostka** Ukraine
59D4 **Show Low** USA
63D2 **Shreveport** USA
7C3 **Shrewsbury** England
7C3 **Shropshire** *County* England
31E1 **Shuangliao** China
28B2 **Shuangyang** China
26G2 **Shuangyashan** China
21K6 **Shubar-Kuduk** Kazakhstan
20N2 **Shuga** Russian Federation
31D2 **Shu He** *R* China
31A4 **Shuicheng** China
42C3 **Shujaabad** Pakistan
42D4 **Shujālpur** India
26C2 **Shule He** *R* China
17F2 **Shumen** Bulgaria
20H4 **Shumerlya** Russian Federation
31D4 **Shuncheng** China
54C3 **Shungnak** USA
31C2 **Shuo Xian** China
38D3 **Shūr Gaz** Iran
51C5 **Shurugwi** Zimbabwe
20G4 **Shuya** Russian Federation
30B1 **Shwebo** Burma
30B2 **Shwegyin** Burma
42A2 **Siah Koh** *Mts* Afghanistan
42C2 **Sialkot** Pakistan
Sian = Xi'an
27F6 **Siargao** *I* Philippines
27F6 **Siaton** Philippines
19E1 **Šiauliai** Lithuania
20K5 **Sibay** Russian Federation
47E2 **Sibayi L** South Africa
16D2 **Šibenik** Croatia
25L5 **Siberia** Russian Federation
27C7 **Siberut** *I* Indonesia
42B3 **Sibi** Pakistan
50B4 **Sibiti** Congo
50D4 **Sibiti** *R* Tanzania
17E1 **Sibiu** Romania
61D2 **Sibley** USA
27C6 **Sibolga** Indonesia
43G3 **Sibsāgar** India
27E6 **Sibu** Malaysia
50B3 **Sibut** Central African Republic
31A3 **Sichuan** *Province* China
Sicilia = Sicily
16C3 **Sicilian Chan** Italy/Tunisia
16C3 **Sicily** *I* Medit Sea
72D6 **Sicuani** Peru
42C4 **Siddhapur** India
44B2 **Siddipet** India
43E4 **Sidhi** India
49E1 **Sidi Barrani** Egypt
15B2 **Sidi-bel-Abbès** Algeria
48B1 **Sidi Kacem** Morocco
8D3 **Sidlaw Hills** Scotland
76F5 **Sidley,Mt** Antarctica
7C4 **Sidmouth** England
58B1 **Sidney** Canada
60C1 **Sidney** Montana, USA
60C2 **Sidney** Nebraska, USA
68C1 **Sidney** New York, USA
64C2 **Sidney** Ohio, USA
67B2 **Sidney Lanier,L** USA
45C2 **Sidon** Lebanon
75B3 **Sidrolândia** Brazil
19E2 **Siedlce** Poland
13D2 **Sieg** *R* Germany
13D2 **Siegburg** Germany
13D2 **Siegen** Germany
30C3 **Siem Reap** Cambodia
16C2 **Siena** Italy
19D2 **Sierpc** Poland
62A2 **Sierra Blanca** USA
70B2 **Sierra de los Alamitos** *Mts* Mexico
48A4 **Sierra Leone** *Republic* Africa
48A4 **Sierra Leone,C** Sierra Leone
70B3 **Sierra Madre del Sur** Mexico
66B3 **Sierra Madre Mts** USA
70B2 **Sierra Madre Occidental** *Mts* Mexico
70B2 **Sierra Madre Oriental** *Mts* Mexico
56C4 **Sierra Mojada** Mexico
59B3 **Sierra Nevada** *Mts* USA
59D4 **Sierra Vista** USA
75A3 **Siete Puntas** *R* Paraguay
17E3 **Sífnos** *I* Greece
15B2 **Sig** Algeria
20E2 **Sig** Russian Federation
19E3 **Sighetu Marmaţiei** Romania
17E1 **Sighişoara** Romania
12B1 **Siglufjörður** Iceland
72A1 **Siguatepeque** Honduras
15B1 **Sigüenza** Spain
48B3 **Siguiri** Guinea
30C3 **Sihanoukville** Cambodia
42D4 **Sihora** India
40D2 **Siirt** Turkey
43J1 **Sikandarabad** India
42D3 **Sīkar** India
42B2 **Sikaram** *Mt* Afghanistan
48B3 **Sikasso** Mali
63E1 **Sikeston** USA
26G2 **Sikhote-Alin'** *Mts* Russian Federation
17F3 **Síkinos** *I* Greece
17E3 **Sikionía** Greece
43F3 **Sikkim** *State* India
25O3 **Siktyakh** Russian Federation
15A1 **Sil** *R* Spain
43G4 **Silchar** India
48C2 **Silet** Algeria
43E3 **Silgarhi** Nepal
40B2 **Silifke** Turkey
45D1 **Şilinfah** Syria
39G2 **Siling Co** *L* China
17F2 **Silistra** Bulgaria
20A3 **Siljan** *L* Sweden
12F7 **Silkeborg** Denmark
6C2 **Silloth** England
63D1 **Siloam Springs** USA
63D2 **Silsbee** USA
50B2 **Siltou** *Well* Chad
19E1 **Šilute** Lithuania
40D2 **Silvan** Turkey
75C2 **Silvania** Brazil
42C4 **Silvassa** India
61E1 **Silver Bay** USA
59C3 **Silver City** Nevada, USA
62A2 **Silver City** New Mexico, USA
58B2 **Silver Lake** USA
66D2 **Silver Peak Range** *Mts* USA
68B3 **Silver Spring** USA
34B2 **Silverton** Australia
62A1 **Silverton** USA
27E6 **Simanggang** Malaysia
30C1 **Simao** China
65D1 **Simard,L** Canada
41E3 **Simareh** *R* Iran
17F3 **Simav** Turkey
17F3 **Simav** *R* Turkey
65D2 **Simcoe,L** Canada
27C6 **Simeulue** *I* Indonesia
21E7 **Simferopol'** Ukraine
17F3 **Sími** *I* Greece
43E3 **Simikot** Nepal
42D2 **Simla** India
60C3 **Simla** USA
13D2 **Simmern** Germany
66C3 **Simmler** USA
47B3 **Simonstown** South Africa
14D2 **Simplon** *Mt* Switzerland
16B1 **Simplon** *Pass* Italy/Switzerland
54C2 **Simpson,C** USA
32C3 **Simpson Desert** Australia
55K3 **Simpson Pen** Canada
12G7 **Simrishamn** Sweden
26J2 **Simushir** *I* Kuril Is, Russian Federation
50E3 **Sina Dhaga** Somalia
40B4 **Sinai** *Pen* Egypt
72C2 **Sincelejo** Colombia
67B2 **Sinclair,L** USA
75D1 **Sincora, Serra do** *Mts* Brazil
42D3 **Sind** *R* India
42B3 **Sindh** *Province* Pakistan
17F3 **Sindirği** Turkey
43F4 **Sindri** India
15A2 **Sines** Portugal
15A2 **Sines, Cabo de** *C* Portugal
50D2 **Singa** Sudan
30C5 **Singapore** *Republic* SE Asia
30C5 **Singapore,Str of** SE Asia
27E7 **Singaraja** Indonesia
13E4 **Singen** Germany
50D4 **Singida** Tanzania
43H3 **Singkaling Hkamti** Burma
27D6 **Singkawang** Indonesia
27D7 **Singkep** *I* Indonesia
34D2 **Singleton** Australia
30B1 **Singu** Burma
47E1 **Singuédeze** *R* Mozambique
28A3 **Sin'gye** N Korea
28A2 **Sinhŭng** N Korea
16B2 **Siniscola** Sardinia, Italy
40D2 **Sinjár** Iraq
42B2 **Sinkai Hills** *Mts* Afghanistan
50D2 **Sinkat** Sudan
39G1 **Sinkiang** *Autonomous Region* China
43K2 **Sinkobabad** India
73H2 **Sinnamary** French Guiana
45B4 **Sinn Bishr, Gebel** *Mt* Egypt
28A3 **Sinnyong** S Korea
40C1 **Sinop** Turkey
28A2 **Sinpa** N Korea
28A2 **Sinp'o** N Korea
28A3 **Sinp'yong** N Korea
17E1 **Sîntana** Romania
27E6 **Sintang** Indonesia
63C3 **Sinton** USA
15A2 **Sintra** Portugal
72C2 **Sinú** *R* Colombia
28A2 **Sinŭiju** N Korea
19D3 **Siófok** Hungary
16B1 **Sion** Switzerland
61D2 **Sioux City** USA
61D2 **Sioux Falls** USA
69L1 **Siparia** Trinidad
28A2 **Siping** China
76F3 **Siple** *Base* Antarctica
76F5 **Siple I** Antarctica
27C7 **Sipora** *I* Indonesia
63E2 **Sipsey** *R* USA
45B4 **Sîq, Wadi el** Egypt
44B3 **Sira** India
Siracusa = Syracuse
43F4 **Sirajganj** Bangladesh
41F5 **Şir Banī Yās** *I* UAE
32C2 **Sir Edward Pellew Group** *Is* Australia
17F1 **Siret** *R* Romania
40C3 **Sirhān, Wādi as** *V* Jordan/Saudi Arabia
40D2 **Şirnak** Turkey
42C4 **Sirohi** India
44C2 **Sironcha** India
42D4 **Sironj** India
17E3 **Síros** *I* Greece
66C3 **Sirretta Peak** *Mt* USA
41F4 **Sīrrī** *I* Iran
42C3 **Sirsa** India
44A3 **Sirsi** India
49D1 **Sirt** Libya
49D1 **Sirte Desert** Libya
49D1 **Sirte,G of** Libya
21H9 **Sirvan** *R* Iran
16D1 **Sisak** Croatia
30C2 **Sisaket** Thailand
30C3 **Sisophon** Cambodia
66B3 **Sisquoc** USA
66C3 **Sisquoc** *R* USA
61D1 **Sisseton** USA
13B3 **Sissonne** France
14D3 **Sisteron** France
25L4 **Sistig Khem** Russian Federation
43E3 **Sītāpur** India
17F3 **Sitía** Greece
75C1 **Sítio d'Abadia** Brazil
54E4 **Sitka** USA
30B2 **Sittang** *R* Burma
13C2 **Sittard** Netherlands
43G4 **Sittwe** Burma
40C2 **Sivas** Turkey
40C2 **Siverek** Turkey
40B2 **Sivrihisar** Turkey
25S4 **Sivuchiy, Mys** *C* Russian Federation
49E2 **Siwa** Egypt
42D2 **Siwalik Range** *Mts* India
43E3 **Siwalik Range** *Mts* Nepal
20G3 **Siya** Russian Federation
31D3 **Siyang** China
18C1 **Sjaelland** *I* Denmark
12G7 **Skagen** Denmark
12F7 **Skagerrak** *Str* Denmark/Norway
58B1 **Skagit** *R* USA
58B1 **Skagit Mt** Canada
54E4 **Skagway** USA
68B1 **Skaneateles** USA
68B1 **Skaneateles L** USA
12G7 **Skara** Sweden
19E2 **Skarzysko-Kamienna** Poland
54F4 **Skeena** *R* Canada
54F4 **Skeene Mts** Canada
54D3 **Skeenjek** *R* USA
7E3 **Skegness** England
20B2 **Skellefte** *R* Sweden
12J6 **Skellefteå** Sweden
9C3 **Skerries** Irish Republic
17E3 **Skíathos** *I* Greece
54E4 **Skidegate** Canada
19E2 **Skiemiewice** Poland
12F7 **Skien** Norway
16B3 **Skikda** Algeria
6D3 **Skipton** England
17E3 **Skíros** *I* Greece
12F7 **Skive** Denmark
18B1 **Skjern** Denmark
55O3 **Skjoldungen** Greenland
64B2 **Skokie** USA
17E3 **Skópelos** *I* Greece
17E2 **Skopje** Macedonia, Yugoslavia
12G7 **Skövde** Sweden
25O4 **Skovorodino** Russian Federation
65F2 **Skowhegan** USA
47E1 **Skukuza** South Africa
54C3 **Skwentna** USA
18D2 **Skwierzyna** Poland
10B2 **Skye** *I* Scotland
12G7 **Slagelse** Denmark
27D7 **Slamet** *Mt* Indonesia
9C3 **Slaney** *R* Irish Republic
17E2 **Slatina** Romania
54G3 **Slave** *R* Canada
19G2 **Slavgorod** Belarus
24J4 **Slavgorod** Russian Federation
19F2 **Slavuta** Ukraine
21F6 **Slavyansk** Ukraine
18D2 **Sławno** Poland
7D3 **Sleaford** England
8C3 **Sleat,Sound of** *Chan* Scotland
54C3 **Sleetmute** USA
63E2 **Slidell** USA
68C2 **Slide Mt** USA
9B3 **Slieve Aughty Mts** Irish Republic
9C3 **Slieve Bloom** *Mts* Irish Republic
10B3 **Sligo** Irish Republic
10B3 **Sligo B** Irish Republic
17F2 **Sliven** Bulgaria
59C3 **Sloan** USA
17F2 **Slobozia** Romania
19F2 **Slonim** Belarus
7D4 **Slough** England
66B2 **Slough** *R* USA
19D3 **Slovakia** *Republic* Europe
16C1 **Slovenia** *Republic* Europe
18C2 **Słubice** Poland
19F2 **Sluch'** *R* Ukraine
18D2 **Słupsk** Poland
19F2 **Slutsk** Belarus
19F2 **Slutsk** *R* Belarus
10A3 **Slyne Head** *Pt* Irish Republic
25M4 **Slyudyanka** Russian Federation
55M4 **Smallwood Res** Canada
48A2 **Smara** Morocco
17E2 **Smederevo** Serbia, Yugoslavia
17E2 **Smederevska Palanka** Serbia, Yugoslavia
21E6 **Smela** Ukraine
68A2 **Smethport** USA
66C1 **Smith** USA
54F3 **Smith Arm** *B* Canada
54F4 **Smithers** Canada
67C1 **Smithfield** N Carolina, USA
47D3 **Smithfield** South Africa
58D2 **Smithfield** Utah, USA
55L3 **Smith I** Canada
65D2 **Smiths Falls** Canada
34C4 **Smithton** Australia
60C3 **Smoky** *R* USA
34D2 **Smoky C** Australia
60D3 **Smoky Hills** USA
58D2 **Smoky Mts** USA
12F6 **Smøla** *I* Norway
20E5 **Smolensk** Russian Federation
17E2 **Smólikas** *Mt* Greece
17E2 **Smolyan** Bulgaria

19F2 **Smorgon'** Belarus
Smyrna = Izmir
68C3 **Smyrna** Delaware, USA
67B2 **Smyrna** Georgia, USA
12B2 **Snæfell** *Mt* Iceland
6B2 **Snaefell** *Mt* Isle of Man, British Islands
58C1 **Snake** *R* USA
56B2 **Snake River Canyon** USA
58D2 **Snake River Plain** USA
33F5 **Snares Is** New Zealand
18B2 **Sneek** Netherlands
66B2 **Snelling** USA
18D2 **Sněžka** *Mt* Czech Republic/Poland
8B3 **Snizort, Loch** *Inlet* Scotland
12F6 **Snøhetta** *Mt* Norway
58B1 **Snohomish** USA
58B1 **Snoqualmie P** USA
30D3 **Snoul** Cambodia
7B3 **Snowdon** *Mt* Wales
7B3 **Snowdonia Nat Pk** Wales
54G3 **Snowdrift** Canada
59D4 **Snowflake** USA
54H4 **Snow Lake** Canada
68B2 **Snow Shoe** USA
34A2 **Snowtown** Australia
58D2 **Snowville** USA
34C3 **Snowy Mts** Australia
62B2 **Snyder** USA
28B4 **Soan Kundo** *Is* S Korea
8B3 **Soay, I** Scotland
28A3 **Sobaek Sanmaek** *Mts* S Korea
50D3 **Sobat** *R* Sudan
73K4 **Sobral** Brazil
19E2 **Sochaczew** Poland
21F7 **Sochi** Russian Federation
28A3 **Sŏch'on** S Korea
37M5 **Société, Îles de la** Pacific Ocean
49D2 **Socna** Libya
62A2 **Socorro** USA
70A3 **Socorro** *I* Mexico
38D4 **Socotra** *I* Yemen
66C3 **Soda L** USA
12K5 **Sodankylä** Finland
58D2 **Soda Springs** USA
50D3 **Soddo** Ethiopia
12H6 **Söderhamn** Sweden
12H7 **Södertälje** Sweden
50C2 **Sodiri** Sudan
50D3 **Sodo** Ethiopia
68B1 **Sodus Point** USA
13E2 **Soest** Germany
51D5 **Sofala** Mozambique
17E2 **Sofia** Bulgaria
Sofiya = Sofia
20E2 **Sofporog** Russian Federation
26H4 **Sofu Gan** *I* Japan
72D2 **Sogamoso** Colombia
12F6 **Sognefjorden** *Inlet* Norway
28A4 **Sŏgwi-ri** S Korea
39H2 **Sog Xian** China
40B4 **Sohâg** Egypt
33E1 **Sohano** Papua New Guinea
13B2 **Soignies** Belgium
13B3 **Soissons** France
42C3 **Sojat** India
28A3 **Sokcho** S Korea
40A2 **Söke** Turkey
19E2 **Sokołka** Poland
48C4 **Sokodé** Togo
20G4 **Sokol** Russian Federation
48B3 **Sokolo** Mali
55Q3 **Søkongens Øy** *I* Greenland
48C3 **Sokoto** Nigeria
48C3 **Sokoto** *R* Nigeria
35A3 **Solander I** New Zealand
44B2 **Solāpur** India
69C4 **Soledad** Colombia
66B2 **Soledad** USA
7D4 **Solent** *Sd* England
13B2 **Solesmes** France
19F2 **Soligorsk** Belarus
20K4 **Solikamsk** Russian Federation
21J5 **Sol'lletsk** Russian Federation
72D4 **Solimões** Peru
13D2 **Solingen** Germany
47B1 **Solitaire** Namibia
12H6 **Sollefteå** Sweden
27D7 **Solok** Indonesia
33E1 **Solomon Is** Pacific Ocean
64A1 **Solon Springs** USA
20F2 **Solovetskiye, Ostrova** *I* Russian Federation
12F8 **Soltau** Germany
66B3 **Solvang** USA
68B1 **Solvay** USA
8D4 **Solway Firth** *Estuary* England/Scotland
51C5 **Solwezi** Zambia
29D3 **Sōma** Japan
17F3 **Soma** Turkey
38C5 **Somalia** *Republic* E Africa
36D4 **Somali Basin** Indian Ocean
17D1 **Sombor** Serbia, Yugoslavia
44E4 **Sombrero Chan** Nicobar Is, Indian Ocean
32D2 **Somerset** Australia
64C3 **Somerset** Kentucky, USA
68E2 **Somerset** Massachusetts, USA
65D2 **Somerset** Pennsylvania, USA
7C4 **Somerset** *County* England
47D3 **Somerset East** South Africa
55J2 **Somerset I** Canada
68D1 **Somerset Res** USA
68C3 **Somers Point** USA
68E1 **Somersworth** USA
68C2 **Somerville** USA
63C2 **Somerville Res** USA
17E1 **Someş** *R* Romania
13B3 **Somme** *Department* France
13B3 **Somme** *R* France
13C3 **Sommesous** France
72A1 **Somoto** Nicaragua
43E4 **Son** *R* India
28A3 **Sŏnch'ŏn** N Korea
47D3 **Sondags** *R* South Africa
12F8 **Sønderborg** Denmark
55N3 **Søndre Strømfjord** Greenland
55N2 **Søndre Upernavik** Greenland
14D2 **Sondrio** Italy
30D3 **Song Ba** *R* Vietnam
30D3 **Song Cau** Vietnam
28A3 **Sŏngch'on** N Korea
51D5 **Songea** Tanzania
28A2 **Songgan** N Korea
26F2 **Songhua** *R* China
31E3 **Songjiang** China
28A3 **Songjŏng** S Korea
30C4 **Songkhla** Thailand
30C5 **Sông Pahang** *R* Malaysia
31A3 **Songpan** China
28A4 **Sŏngsan-ni** S Korea
31C1 **Sonid Youqi** China
42D3 **Sonīpat** India
30C1 **Son La** Vietnam
42B3 **Sonmiani** Pakistan
42B3 **Sonmiani Bay** Pakistan
59D4 **Sonoita** Mexico
66A1 **Sonoma** USA
66B2 **Sonora** California, USA
62B2 **Sonora** Texas, USA
70A2 **Sonora** *R* Mexico
59D4 **Sonora** *State* Mexico
56B3 **Sonoran Desert** USA
66C1 **Sonora P** USA
70D3 **Sonsonate** El Salvador
27G6 **Sonsorol** *I* Pacific Ocean
57E2 **Soo Canals** Canada/USA
19D2 **Sopot** Poland
18D3 **Sopron** Hungary
66B2 **Soquel** USA
16C2 **Sora** Italy
45C3 **Sored** *R* Israel
65E1 **Sorel** Canada
34C4 **Sorell** Australia
40C2 **Sorgun** Turkey
15B1 **Soria** Spain
24C2 **Sørkapp** *I* Barents Sea
12J5 **Sørkjosen** Norway
21J6 **Sor Mertvyy Kultuk** *Plain* Kazakhstan
75C3 **Sorocaba** Brazil
20J5 **Sorochinsk** Moldavia
19F3 **Soroki** Russian Federation
27H6 **Sorol** *I* Pacific Ocean
29D2 **Soroma-ko** *L* Japan
27G7 **Sorong** Indonesia
50D3 **Soroti** Uganda
12J4 **Sørøya** *I* Norway
16C2 **Sorrento** Italy
12K5 **Sorsatunturi** *Mt* Finland
12H5 **Sorsele** Sweden
20E3 **Sortavala** Russian Federation
28B3 **Sŏsan** S Korea
19D2 **Sosnowiec** Poland
20L4 **Sos'va** Russian Federation
50B3 **Souanké** Congo
48B4 **Soubré** Ivory Coast
68C2 **Souderton** USA
69P2 **Soufrière** St Lucia
69N2 **Soufrière** *Mt* St Vincent
14C3 **Souillac** France
16B3 **Souk Ahras** Algeria
Sŏul = Seoul
15C2 **Soummam** *R* Algeria
Sour = Tyre
47D2 **Sources,Mt aux** Lesotho
60C1 **Souris** Manitoba, Canada
60C1 **Souris** *R* Canada/USA
73L5 **Sousa** Brazil
16C3 **Sousse** Tunisia
51C7 **South Africa** *Republic* Africa
68C2 **S Amboy** USA
64C2 **Southampton** Canada
7D4 **Southampton** England
68D2 **Southampton** USA
55K3 **Southampton I** Canada
44E3 **South Andaman** *I* Indian Ocean
55M4 **South Aulatsivik I** Canada
32C3 **South Australia** *State* Australia
36H6 **South Australian Basin** Indian Ocean
63E2 **Southaven** USA
62A2 **South Baldy** *Mt* USA
67B3 **South Bay** USA
64C1 **South Baymouth** Canada
64B2 **South Bend** Indiana, USA
58B1 **South Bend** Washington, USA
65D3 **South Boston** USA
68E1 **Southbridge** USA
South Cape = Ka Lae
57E3 **South Carolina** *State* USA
27E5 **South China S** SE Asia
56C2 **South Dakota** *State* USA
68D1 **South Deerfield** USA
7D4 **South Downs** England
34C4 **South East C** Australia
37O7 **South East Pacific Basin** Pacific Ocean
54H4 **Southend** Canada
7E4 **Southend-on-Sea** England
35A2 **Southern Alps** *Mts* New Zealand
32A4 **Southern Cross** Australia
54J4 **Southern Indian L** Canada
67C1 **Southern Pines** USA
69H2 **Southfield** Jamaica
37K6 **South Fiji Basin** Pacific Ocean
7E4 **South Foreland** *Pt* England
62A1 **South Fork** USA
66B1 **South Fork** *R* California, USA
66B1 **South Fork American** *R* USA
66C3 **South Fork Kern** *R* USA
71G9 **South Georgia** *I* S Atlantic Ocean
7C4 **South Glamorgan** *County* Wales
64B2 **South Haven** USA
54J3 **South Henik L** Canada
65D3 **South Hill** USA
36J3 **South Honshu Ridge** Pacific Ocean
35A2 **South I** New Zealand
68D2 **Southington** USA
28B3 **South Korea** *Republic* S Korea
59B3 **South Lake Tahoe** USA
36D6 **South Madagascar Ridge** Indian Ocean
76G8 **South Magnetic Pole** Antarctica
67B3 **South Miami** USA
68B3 **South Mt** USA
54F3 **South Nahanni** *R* Canada
69G1 **South Negril Pt** Jamaica
52F8 **South Orkney Is** Atlantic Ocean
71B5 **South Pacific O**
60C2 **South Platte** *R* USA
76E **South Pole** Antarctica
64C1 **South Porcupine** Canada
7C3 **Southport** England
69Q2 **South Pt** Barbados
68C2 **South River** USA
8D2 **South Ronaldsay** *I* Scotland
52G7 **South Sandwich Trench** Atlantic Ocean
66A2 **South San Francisco** USA
54H4 **South Saskatchewan** *R* Canada
6D2 **South Shields** England
35B1 **South Taranaki Bight** *B* New Zealand
8B3 **South Uist** *I* Scotland
South West Africa = Namibia
32D5 **South West C** Australia
36D6 **South West Indian Ridge** Indian Ocean
37M6 **South West Pacific Basin** Pacific Ocean
52D5 **South West Peru Ridge** Pacific Ocean
7E3 **Southwold** England
7D3 **South Yorkshire** *County* England
47D1 **Soutpansberg** *Mts* South Africa
19E1 **Sovetsk** Russian Federation
20H4 **Sovetsk** Russian Federation
26G2 **Sovetskaya Gavan'** Russian Federation
20L3 **Sovetskiy** Russian Federation
47D2 **Soweto** South Africa
29D1 **Sōya-misaki** *C* Japan
51B4 **Soyo Congo** Angola
19G2 **Sozh** *R* Belarus
13C2 **Spa** Belgium
15 **Spain** *Kingdom* SW Europe
Spalato = Split
7D3 **Spalding** England
64C1 **Spanish** *R* Canada
59D2 **Spanish Fork** USA
69J1 **Spanish Town** Jamaica
59C3 **Sparks** USA
64A2 **Sparta** USA
67B2 **Spartanburg** USA
17E3 **Spartí** Greece
16D3 **Spartivento, C** Italy
26G2 **Spassk Dal'niy** Russian Federation
60C2 **Spearfish** USA
62B1 **Spearman** USA
69R2 **Speightstown** Barbados
54D3 **Spenard** USA
55J3 **Spence Bay** Canada
64B3 **Spencer** Indiana, USA
61D2 **Spencer** Iowa, USA
32C4 **Spencer G** Australia
55L3 **Spencer Is** Canada
35B2 **Spenser Mts** New Zealand
9C2 **Sperrin Mts** Northern Ireland
8D3 **Spey** *R* Scotland
18B3 **Speyer** Germany
69K1 **Speyside** Tobago
58C1 **Spirit Lake** USA
54G4 **Spirit River** Canada
24C2 **Spitsbergen** *I* Svalbard, Norway
Spitsbergen *Is* **= Svalbard**
18C3 **Spittal** Austria
13D1 **Spjekeroog** *I* Germany
12F6 **Spjelkavik** Norway
16D2 **Split** Croatia
58C1 **Spokane** USA
64A1 **Spooner** USA
Sporádhes *Is* **= Dodecanese**
27E6 **Spratly** *I* S China Sea
27E6 **Spratly Is** S China Sea
58C2 **Spray** USA
18C2 **Spree** *R* Germany
47B2 **Springbok** South Africa
63D1 **Springdale** USA
62B1 **Springer** USA
59E4 **Springerville** USA
62B1 **Springfield** Colorado, USA
64B3 **Springfield** Illinois, USA
68D1 **Springfield** Massachusetts, USA
61E2 **Springfield** Minnesota, USA
63D1 **Springfield** Missouri, USA
64C3 **Springfield** Ohio, USA
58B2 **Springfield** Oregon, USA
67A1 **Springfield** Tennessee, USA
65E2 **Springfield** Vermont, USA
47D3 **Springfontein** South Africa
59C3 **Spring Mts** USA
47D2 **Springs** South Africa
68A1 **Springville** New York, USA
59D2 **Springville** Utah, USA
68B1 **Springwater** USA
58D2 **Spruce Mt** USA
7E3 **Spurn Head** *C* England
58B1 **Spuzzum** Canada
16D3 **Squillace, G di** Italy
25S4 **Sredinnyy Khrebet** *Mts* Russian Federation
25R3 **Srednekolymsk** Russian Federation
20F5 **Sredne-Russkaya Vozvyshennost'** *Upland* Russian Federation
25M3 **Sredne Sibirskoye Ploskogorye** *Tableland* Russian Federation
20K4 **Sredniy Ural** *Mts* Russian Federation
30D3 **Srepok** *R* Cambodia
26E1 **Sretensk** Russian Federation
30C3 **Sre Umbell** Cambodia
44C2 **Srīkākulam** India
44B3 **Sri Kālahasti** India
39G5 **Sri Lanka** *Republic* S Asia
42C2 **Srīnagar** Pakistan
44A2 **Srīvardhan** India
18D2 **Środa Wlk.** Poland
8C2 **Stack Skerry** *I* Scotland
13E1 **Stade** Germany
13E1 **Stadthagen** Germany
8B3 **Staffa** *I* Scotland
7C3 **Stafford** England
7C3 **Stafford** *County* England
68D2 **Stafford Springs** USA
Stalingrad = Volgograd
47B3 **Stallberg** *Mt* South Africa
55J1 **Stallworthy,C** Canada
19E2 **Stalowa Wola** Poland
68D2 **Stamford** Connecticut, USA
7D3 **Stamford** England
68C1 **Stamford** New York, USA
62C2 **Stamford** Texas, USA
47B1 **Stampriet** Namibia
47D2 **Standerton** South Africa
64C2 **Standish** USA
58D1 **Stanford** USA
47E2 **Stanger** South Africa
6C2 **Stanhope** England
66B2 **Stanislaus** *R* USA
17E2 **Stanke Dimitrov** Bulgaria
34C4 **Stanley** Australia
74E8 **Stanley** Falkland Islands
58D2 **Stanley** Idaho, USA
60C1 **Stanley** N Dakota, USA
44B3 **Stanley Res** India
Stanleyville = Kisangani
70D3 **Stann Creek** Belize
26F1 **Stanovoy Khrebet** *Mts* Russian Federation
34D1 **Stanthorpe** Australia
8A3 **Stanton Banks** *Sand-bank* Scotland
60C2 **Stapleton** USA
19E2 **Starachowice** Poland
17E2 **Stara Planiná** *Mts* Bulgaria
20E4 **Staraya Russa** Russian Federation
17F2 **Stara Zagora** Bulgaria
18D2 **Stargard Szczecinski** Poland
63E2 **Starkville** USA
18C3 **Starnberg** Germany
19D2 **Starogard Gdański** Poland
19F3 **Starokonstantinov** Ukraine
7C4 **Start Pt** England
21F5 **Staryy Oskol** Russian Federation
68B2 **State College** USA
68C2 **Staten I** USA
67B2 **Statesboro** USA
67B1 **Statesville** USA
65D3 **Staunton** USA
12F7 **Stavanger** Norway
13C2 **Stavelot** Belgium
13C1 **Stavoren** Netherlands
21G6 **Stavropol'** Russian Federation
34B3 **Stawell** Australia
58B2 **Stayton** USA
60B2 **Steamboat Springs** USA
68B2 **Steelton** USA
58C2 **Steens Mt** USA
55N2 **Steenstrups Gletscher** *Gl* Greenland
13D1 **Steenwijk** Netherlands
54H2 **Stefansson I** Canada
47E2 **Stegi** Swaziland
61D1 **Steinbach** Canada
12G6 **Steinkjer** Norway
47B2 **Steinkopf** South Africa
47C2 **Stella** South Africa
47B3 **Stellenbosch** South Africa
13C3 **Stenay** France
18C2 **Stendal** Germany
21H8 **Stepanakert** Azerbaijan
61D1 **Stephen** USA
35B2 **Stephens,C** New Zealand
34B2 **Stephens Creek** Australia
64B1 **Stephenson** USA
55N5 **Stephenville** Canada
62C2 **Stephenville** USA
47D3 **Sterkstroom** South Africa
60C2 **Sterling** Colorado, USA
64B2 **Sterling** Illinois, USA
62C1 **Sterling** Kansas, USA
60C1 **Sterling** N Dakota, USA
62B2 **Sterling City** USA
64C2 **Sterling Heights** USA
20K5 **Sterlitamak** Russian Federation
54G4 **Stettler** Canada
64C2 **Steubenville** USA
7D4 **Stevenage** England
64B2 **Stevens Point** USA
54D3 **Stevens Village** USA
54F4 **Stewart** Canada
59C3 **Stewart** USA
54E3 **Stewart** *R* Canada
35A3 **Stewart I** New Zealand
33F1 **Stewart Is** Solomon Islands
8C4 **Stewarton** Scotland
54E3 **Stewart River** Canada
68B3 **Stewartstown** USA
61E2 **Stewartville** USA
47D3 **Steynsburg** South Africa
18C3 **Steyr** Austria
47C3 **Steytlerville** South Africa

54F4 **Stikine** *R* Canada
61E1 **Stillwater** Minnesota, USA
63C1 **Stillwater** Oklahoma, USA
59C3 **Stillwater Range** *Mts* USA
62B1 **Stinnett** USA
34A2 **Stirling** Australia
8D3 **Stirling** Scotland
12G6 **Stjørdal** Norway
13E4 **Stockach** Germany
68D1 **Stockbridge** USA
18D3 **Stockerau** Austria
12H7 **Stockholm** Sweden
7C3 **Stockport** England
66B2 **Stockton** California, USA
6D2 **Stockton** England
67D3 **Stockton** Kansas, USA
63D1 **Stockton L** USA
7C3 **Stoke-on-Trent** England
12G5 **Stokmarknes** Norway
25P2 **Stolbovoy, Ostrov** *I* Russian Federation
12K8 **Stolbtsy** Russian Federation
19F2 **Stolin** Belarus
7C3 **Stone** England
68C3 **Stone Harbor** USA
8D3 **Stonehaven** Scotland
63C2 **Stonewall** USA
7D3 **Stony Stratford** England
12H5 **Storavan** *L* Sweden
12G6 **Støren** Norway
34C4 **Storm B** Australia
61D2 **Storm Lake** USA
8B2 **Stornoway** Scotland
19F3 **Storozhinets** Ukraine
68D2 **Storrs** USA
12G6 **Storsjön** *L* Sweden
12H5 **Storuman** Sweden
60B2 **Story** USA
68E1 **Stoughton** USA
7E4 **Stour** *R* England
7C3 **Stourbridge** England
7C3 **Stourport** England
7E3 **Stowmarket** England
9C2 **Strabane** Northern Ireland
34C4 **Strahan** Australia
18C2 **Stralsund** Germany
47B3 **Strand** South Africa
12F6 **Stranda** Norway
9D2 **Strangford Lough** *L* Irish Republic
12H7 **Strängnäs** Sweden
8C4 **Stranraer** Scotland
14D2 **Strasbourg** France
65D3 **Strasburg** USA
66C2 **Stratford** California, USA
64C2 **Stratford** Canada
68D2 **Stratford** Connecticut, USA
35B1 **Stratford** New Zealand
62B1 **Stratford** Texas, USA
7D3 **Stratford-on-Avon** England
34A3 **Strathalbyn** Australia
8C4 **Strathclyde** *Region* Scotland
65E1 **Stratton** USA
64B2 **Streator** USA
8D2 **Stroma, I** Scotland
16D3 **Stromboli** *I* Italy
8D2 **Stromness** Scotland
61D2 **Stromsburg** USA
12H6 **Stromsund** Sweden
12G6 **Ströms Vattudal** *L* Sweden
8D2 **Stronsay** *I* Scotland
7C4 **Stroud** England
68C2 **Stroudsburg** USA
17E2 **Struma** *R* Bulgaria
7B3 **Strumble Head** *Pt* Wales
17E2 **Strumica** Macedonia, Yugoslavia
19E3 **Stryy** Ukraine
19E3 **Stryy** *R* Ukraine
34B1 **Strzelecki Creek** *R* Australia
67B3 **Stuart** Florida, USA
60D2 **Stuart** Nebraska, USA
54F4 **Stuart L** Canada
12G8 **Stubice** Poland
30D3 **Stung Sen** *R* Cambodia
30D3 **Stung Treng** Cambodia
16B2 **Stura** *R* Italy
76G7 **Sturge I** Antarctica
64B2 **Sturgeon Bay** USA
65D1 **Sturgeon Falls** Canada
64B3 **Sturgis** Kentucky, USA
64B2 **Sturgis** Michigan, USA
60C2 **Sturgis** S Dakota, USA
32B2 **Sturt Creek** *R* Australia
34B1 **Sturt Desert** Australia
47D3 **Stutterheim** South Africa
63D2 **Stuttgart** USA
18B3 **Stuttgart** Germany
12A1 **Stykkishólmur** Iceland
19F2 **Styr'** *R* Ukraine
75D2 **Suaçuí Grande** *R* Brazil
50D2 **Suakin** Sudan
28A3 **Suan** N Korea
31E5 **Suao** Taiwan
17D1 **Subotica** Serbia, Yugoslavia
21D6 **Suceava** Romania
72E7 **Sucre** Bolivia
75B2 **Sucuriú** *R* Brazil
50C2 **Sudan** *Republic* Africa
64C1 **Sudbury** Canada
7E3 **Sudbury** England
50C3 **Sudd** *Swamp* Sudan
73G2 **Suddie** Guyana
45B4 **Sudr** Egypt
50C3 **Sue** *R* Sudan
40B4 **Suez** Egypt
40B3 **Suez Canal** Egypt
40B4 **Suez,G of** Egypt
68C2 **Suffern** USA
65D3 **Suffolk** USA
7E3 **Suffolk** *County* England
65E2 **Sugarloaf Mt** USA
34D2 **Sugarloaf Pt** Australia
25R3 **Sugoy** *R* Russian Federation
41G5 **Suḩār** Oman
26D1 **Sühbaatar** Mongolia
42B3 **Sui** Pakistan
31C2 **Suide** China
28C2 **Suifen He** *R* China
26F2 **Suihua** China
31B3 **Suining** China
13C3 **Suippes** France
10B3 **Suir** *R* Irish Republic
31C3 **Sui Xian** China
31E1 **Suizhong** China
42C3 **Sujāngarh** India
27D7 **Sukadana** Indonesia
29E3 **Sukagawa** Japan
26C3 **Sukai Hu** *L* China
28B3 **Sukch'ŏn** N Korea
20F5 **Sukhinichi** Russian Federation
20G4 **Sukhona** *R* Russian Federation
21G7 **Sukhumi** Georgia
55N3 **Sukkertoppen** Greenland
55N3 **Sukkertoppen Isflade** *Ice field* Greenland
12L6 **Sukkozero** Russian Federation
42B3 **Sukkur** Pakistan
44C2 **Sukma** India
51B6 **Sukses** Namibia
28B4 **Sukumo** Japan
21F5 **Sula** *R* Russian Federation
42B3 **Sulaiman Range** *Mts* Pakistan
32B1 **Sula, Kepulauan** *I* Indonesia
8B2 **Sula Sgeir** *I* Scotland
27E7 **Sulawesi** *Is* Indonesia
41E2 **Sulaymānīyah** Iraq
8C2 **Sule Skerry** *I* Scotland
17F1 **Sulina** Romania
13E1 **Sulingen** Germany
12H5 **Sulitjelma** Norway
72B4 **Sullana** Peru
63D1 **Sullivan** USA
13B4 **Sully-sur-Loire** France
16C2 **Sulmona** Italy
63D2 **Sulphur** Louisiana, USA
63C2 **Sulphur** Oklahoma, USA
63C2 **Sulphur Springs** USA
21E8 **Sultan Dağları** *Mts* Turkey
43E3 **Sultānpur** India
27F6 **Sulu Arch** *Is* Philippines
27E6 **Sulu S** Philippines
13E3 **Sulz** Germany
74D3 **Sumampa** Argentina
27C6 **Sumatera** *I* Indonesia
27E8 **Sumba** *I* Indonesia
27E7 **Sumbawa** *I* Indonesia
27E7 **Sumbawa Besar** Indonesia
51D4 **Sumbawanga** Tanzania
51B5 **Sumbe** Angola
8E2 **Sumburgh Head** *Pt* Scotland
43N2 **Sumesar Ra** *Mts* Nepal
21H7 **Sumgait** Azerbaijan
26H3 **Sumisu** *I* Japan
54F4 **Summit Lake** Canada
59C3 **Summit Mt** USA
35B2 **Sumner,L** New Zealand
29B4 **Sumoto** Japan
67B2 **Sumter** USA
21E5 **Sumy** Ukraine
58D1 **Sun** *R* USA
29D2 **Sunagawa** Japan
28A3 **Sunan** N Korea
8C3 **Sunart, Loch** *Inlet* Scotland
68B2 **Sunbury** USA
28B3 **Sunch'ŏn** N Korea
28B4 **Sunch'ŏn** S Korea
60C2 **Sundance** USA
43E4 **Sundargarh** India
43F4 **Sunderbans** *Swamp* Bangladesh/India
6D2 **Sunderland** England
65D1 **Sundridge** Canada
12H6 **Sundsvall** Sweden
58C1 **Sunnyside** USA
59B3 **Sunnyvale** USA
64B2 **Sun Prairie** USA
25N3 **Suntar** Russian Federation
58D2 **Sun Valley** USA
48B4 **Sunyani** Ghana
20E3 **Suojarvi** Russian Federation
28B4 **Suō-nada** *B* Japan
12K6 **Suonenjoki** Finland
43F3 **Supaul** India
59D4 **Superior** Arizona, USA
61D2 **Superior** Nebraska, USA
64A1 **Superior** Wisconsin, USA
64B1 **Superior,L** Canada/USA
30C3 **Suphan Buri** Thailand
40D2 **Süphan Dağ** *Mt* Turkey
27G7 **Supiori** *I* Indonesia
41E3 **Sūq ash Suyūkh** Iraq
45D1 **Şuqaylibīyah** Syria
31D3 **Suqian** China
Suqutra = Socotra
38D3 **Sūr** Oman
20H5 **Sura** *R* Russian Federation
27E7 **Surabaya** Indonesia
29C4 **Suraga-wan** *B* Japan
27E7 **Surakarta** Indonesia
45D1 **Şūrān** Syria
34C1 **Surat** Australia
42C4 **Sūrat** India
42C3 **Sūratgarh** India
30B4 **Surat Thani** Thailand
42C4 **Surendranagar** India
68C3 **Surf City** USA
24J3 **Surgut** Russian Federation
44B2 **Suriāpet** India
27F6 **Surigao** Philippines
30C3 **Surin** Thailand
73G3 **Surinam** *Republic* S America
66B2 **Sur,Pt** USA
7D4 **Surrey** *County* England
49D1 **Surt** Libya
12A2 **Surtsey** *I* Iceland
16B1 **Susa** Italy
28B4 **Susa** Japan
29B4 **Susaki** Japan
59B2 **Susanville** USA
68C2 **Susquehanna** USA
68B3 **Susquehanna** *R* USA
68C2 **Sussex** USA
7D4 **Sussex West** England
47C3 **Sutherland** South Africa
60C2 **Sutherland** USA
42C2 **Sutlej** *R* Pakistan
59B3 **Sutter Creek** USA
64C3 **Sutton** USA
29D2 **Suttsu** Japan
29D3 **Suwa** Japan
19E2 **Suwałki** Poland
67B3 **Suwannee** *R* USA
45C2 **Suweilih** Jordan
28B3 **Suwŏn** S Korea
31D3 **Su Xian** China
29C3 **Suzaka** Japan
31E3 **Suzhou** China
29D3 **Suzu** Japan
29C4 **Suzuka** Japan
29C3 **Suzu-misaki** *C* Japan
24C2 **Svalbard** *Is* Barents Sea
19E3 **Svalyava** Ukraine
55N2 **Svartenhuk Halvø** *Region* Greenland
12G5 **Svartisen** *Mt* Norway
30D3 **Svay Rieng** Cambodia
12G6 **Sveg** Sweden
12G7 **Svendborg** Denmark
Sverdlovsk = Yekaterinburg
55J1 **Sverdrup Chan** Canada
54H2 **Sverdrup Is** Canada
26G2 **Svetlaya** Russian Federation
19E2 **Svetlogorsk** Russian Federation
12K6 **Svetogorsk** Russian Federation
17E2 **Svetozarevo** Serbia, Yugoslavia
17F2 **Svilengrad** Bulgaria
19F2 **Svir'** Belarus
20E3 **Svir'** *R* Russian Federation
18D3 **Švitavy** Czech Republic
26F1 **Svobodnyy** Russian Federation
12G5 **Svolvær** Norway
7E3 **Swaffam** England
33E3 **Swain Reefs** Australia
67B2 **Swainsboro** USA
33H2 **Swains I** American Samoa
47B1 **Swakop** *R* Namibia
47A1 **Swakopmund** Namibia
6D2 **Swale** *R* England
27E6 **Swallow Reef** S China Sea
44B3 **Swāmihalli** India
70D3 **Swan** *I* Honduras
7D4 **Swanage** England
34B3 **Swan Hill** Australia
69A3 **Swan I** Caribbean Sea
54H4 **Swan River** Canada
7C4 **Swansea** Wales
7C4 **Swansea B** Wales
47C3 **Swartberge** *Mts* South Africa
47D2 **Swartruggens** South Africa
Swatow = Shantou
47E2 **Swaziland** *Kingdom* South Africa
12G7 **Sweden** *Kingdom* N Europe
58B2 **Sweet Home** USA
62B2 **Sweetwater** USA
60B2 **Sweetwater** *R* USA
47C3 **Swellendam** South Africa
18D2 **Świdnica** Poland
18D2 **Świdwin** Poland
18D2 **Świebodzin** Poland
19D2 **Świecie** Poland
54H4 **Swift Current** Canada
9C2 **Swilly, Lough** *Estuary* Irish Republic
7D4 **Swindon** England
18C2 **Świnoujście** Poland
14D2 **Switzerland** Europe
9C3 **Swords** Irish Republic
43M1 **Syang** Nepal
9A3 **Sybil Pt** Irish Republic
34D2 **Sydney** Australia
20H3 **Syktyvkar** Russian Federation
67A2 **Sylacauga** USA
12G6 **Sylarna** *Mt* Sweden
43G4 **Sylhet** Bangladesh
18B1 **Sylt** *I* Germany
64C2 **Sylvania** USA
76G11 **Syowa** *Base* Antarctica
16D3 **Syracuse** Italy
62B1 **Syracuse** Kansas, USA
68B1 **Syracuse** New York, USA
65D2 **Syracuse** USA
24H5 **Syr Darya** *R* Kazakhstan
40C2 **Syria** *Republic* SW Asia
20L4 **Sysert'** Russian Federation
20H5 **Syzran'** Russian Federation
18C2 **Szczecin** Poland
18D2 **Szczecinek** Poland
19E2 **Szczytno** Poland
19E3 **Szeged** Hungary
19D3 **Székesfehérvár** Hungary
19D3 **Szekszárd** Hungary
19D3 **Szolnok** Hungary
18D3 **Szombathely** Hungary
18D2 **Szprotawa** Poland

T

47D3 **Tabankulu** South Africa
32E1 **Tabar Is** Papua New Guinea
16B3 **Tabarka** Tunisia
41G3 **Tabas** Iran
72E4 **Tabatinga** Brazil
48B2 **Tabelbala** Algeria
30C3 **Tabeng** Cambodia
54G5 **Taber** Canada
47B3 **Table Mt** South Africa
63D1 **Table Rock Res** USA
18C3 **Tábor** Czech Republic
50D4 **Tabora** Tanzania
20L4 **Tabory** Russian Federation
48B4 **Tabou** Ivory Coast
41E2 **Tabrīz** Iran
40C4 **Tabūk** Saudi Arabia
39G1 **Tacheng** China
27F5 **Tacloban** Philippines
72D7 **Tacna** Peru
59D4 **Tacna** USA
56A2 **Tacoma** USA
68D1 **Taconic Range** USA
75A3 **Tacuatí** Paraguay
48C2 **Tademait, Plateau du** Algeria
50E2 **Tadjoura** Djibouti
65F1 **Tadoussac** Canada
44B3 **Tādpatri** India
28B3 **Taebaek Sanmaek** *Mts* N Korea/S Korea
28B3 **T'aech'ŏn** N Korea
28A3 **Taech'on** S Korea
28A3 **Taedasa-Do** N Korea
28A3 **Taedong** *R* N Korea
28A3 **Taegang-got** *Pen* N Korea
28B3 **Taegu** S Korea
28A2 **Taehung** N Korea
28B3 **Taejŏn** S Korea
15B1 **Tafalla** Spain
48C2 **Tafasaset** *Watercourse* Algeria
7C4 **Taff** *R* Wales
45C3 **Tafila** Jordan
66C3 **Taft** USA
21F6 **Taganrog** Russian Federation
48A3 **Tagant** *Region* Mauritius
48B2 **Taguenout Hagguerete** *Well* Mali
33E2 **Tagula** *I* Papua New Guinea
Tagus = Tejo
48C2 **Tahat** *Mt* Algeria
37M5 **Tahiti** *I* Pacific Ocean
63C1 **Tahlequah** USA
59B3 **Tahoe City** USA
59B3 **Tahoe,L** USA
62B2 **Tahoka** USA
48C3 **Tahoua** Niger
40B4 **Tahta** Egypt
27F6 **Tahuna** Indonesia
31D2 **Tai'an** China
28A2 **Tai'an** China
31B3 **Taibai Shan** *Mt* China
31D1 **Taibus Qi** China
31E5 **Taichung** Taiwan
35B3 **Taieri** *R* New Zealand
31C2 **Taihang Shan** *Upland* China
35C1 **Taihape** New Zealand
31E3 **Tai Hu** *L* China
29D2 **Taiki** Japan
34A3 **Tailem Bend** Australia
8C3 **Tain** Scotland
31E5 **Tainan** Taiwan
75D2 **Taiobeiras** Brazil
31E5 **Taipei** Taiwan
30C5 **Taiping** Malaysia
29D3 **Taira** Japan
28B3 **Taisha** Japan
74B7 **Taitao,Pen de** Chile
31E5 **Taitung** Taiwan
12K5 **Taivalkoski** Finland
26F4 **Taiwan** *Republic* China
31D5 **Taiwan Str** China/Taiwan
45C3 **Taiyiba** Jordan
31C2 **Taiyuan** China
31D3 **Taizhou** China
50E2 **Ta'izz** Yemen
39E2 **Tajikistan** *Republic* Asia
15B1 **Tajo** *R* Spain
30B2 **Tak** Thailand
32B1 **Takabonerate, Kepulauan** *Is* Indonesia
29D3 **Takada** Japan
29B4 **Takahashi** Japan
35B2 **Takaka** New Zealand
29C4 **Takamatsu** Japan
29D3 **Takaoka** Japan
35B1 **Takapuna** New Zealand
29D3 **Takasaki** Japan
29C3 **Takayama** Japan
29D3 **Takefu** Japan
27C6 **Takengon** Indonesia
30C3 **Takeo** Cambodia
28B4 **Takeo** Japan
Take-shima = Tok-do
41E2 **Takestān** Iran
28B4 **Taketa** Japan
29D2 **Takikawa** Japan
29D2 **Takinoue** Japan
54G3 **Takiyvak L** Canada
50D2 **Takkaze** *R* Eritrea/Ethiopia
48B4 **Takoradi** Ghana
42C2 **Talagang** Pakistan
44B4 **Talaimannar** Sri Lanka
48C3 **Talak** *Desert Region* Niger
72B4 **Talara** Peru
32E1 **Talasea** Papua New Guinea
45B3 **Talata** Egypt
27F6 **Talaud, Kepulauan** *Is* Indonesia
15B2 **Talavera de la Reina** Spain
74B5 **Talca** Chile
74B5 **Talcahuano** Chile
43F4 **Tālcher** India
39F1 **Taldy Kurgan** Kazakhstan
27F7 **Taliabu** *I* Indonesia
42B1 **Taligan** Afghanistan
50D3 **Tali Post** Sudan
27E7 **Taliwang** Indonesia
54D3 **Talkeetna** USA
45A3 **Talkha** Egypt
67A2 **Talladega** USA
40D2 **Tall 'Afar** Iraq
67B2 **Tallahassee** USA
45D1 **Tall Bīsah** Syria
20C4 **Tallinn** Estonia
40C3 **Tall Kalakh** Syria
63D2 **Tallulah** USA
26B1 **Tal'menka** Russian Federation
21E6 **Tal'noye** Ukraine
19E2 **Talpaki** Russian Federation
74B3 **Taltal** Chile
34C1 **Talwood** Australia
61E2 **Tama** USA
27E6 **Tamabo Ra** *Mts* Borneo
48B4 **Tamale** Ghana
29C4 **Tamano** Japan
48C2 **Tamanrasset** Algeria
48C2 **Tamanrasset** *Watercourse* Algeria
68C2 **Tamaqua** USA
7B4 **Tamar** *R* England
Tamatave = Toamasina
48A3 **Tambacounda** Senegal

21G5 Tambov Russian Federation
15A1 Tambre R Spain
50C3 Tambura Sudan
48A3 Tamchaket Mauritius
15A1 Tamega R Portugal
70C2 Tamiahua, L de Lg Mexico
44B3 Tamil Nādu State India
17E1 Tamiş R Romania
30D2 Tam Ky Vietnam
67B3 Tampa USA
67B3 Tampa B USA
12J6 Tampere Finland
70C2 Tampico Mexico
26E2 Tamsagbulag Mongolia
31E4 Tamsui Taiwan
43G4 Tamu Burma
34D2 Tamworth Australia
7D3 Tamworth England
20D1 Tana Norway
12K5 Tana R Finland/Norway
50E4 Tana R Kenya
29C4 Tanabe Japan
12K4 Tanafjord Inlet Norway
27E7 Tanahgrogot Indonesia
27G7 Tanahmerah Indonesia
50D2 Tana, L Ethiopia
54C3 Tanana USA
54C3 Tanana R USA
Tananarive = Antananarivo
28B2 Tanch'ŏn N Korea
74E5 Tandil Argentina
27G7 Tandjung d'Urville C Indonesia
27G7 Tandjung Vals C Indonesia
42B3 Tando Adam Pakistan
42B3 Tando Muhammad Khan Pakistan
34B2 Tandou L Australia
44B2 Tāndūr India
35C1 Taneatua New Zealand
30B2 Tanen Range Mts Burma/Thailand
48B2 Tanezrouft Desert Region Algeria
50D4 Tanga Tanzania
33E1 Tanga Is Papua New Guinea
50C4 Tanganyika,L Tanzania/Zaïre
Tanger = Tangiers
39H2 Tanggula Shan Mts China
15A2 Tangiers Morocco
28A3 Tangjin S Korea
39G2 Tangra Yumco L China
31D2 Tangshan China
26D1 Tanguy Russian Federation
27G7 Tanimbar, Kepulauan Arch Indonesia
51E6 Tanjona Ankaboa C Madagascar
51E5 Tanjona Anorontany C Madagascar
51E5 Tanjona Bobaomby C Madagascar
51E5 Tanjona Vilanandro C Madagascar
51E6 Tanjona Vohimena C Madagascar
27C6 Tanjungbalai Indonesia
27D7 Tanjungpandan Indonesia
27D7 Tanjung Priok Indonesia
27E6 Tanjungredeb Indonesia
32A1 Tanjung Selatan Pt Indonesia
27E6 Tanjungselor Indonesia
32C1 Tanjung Vals Pt Indonesia
42C2 Tank Pakistan
33F2 Tanna I Vanuatu
26C1 Tannu Ola Mts Russian Federation
48B4 Tano R Ghana
48C3 Tanout Niger
43E3 Tansing Nepal
49F1 Tanta Egypt
48A2 Tan-Tan Morocco
54B3 Tanunak USA
28A3 Tanyang S Korea
50D4 Tanzania Republic Africa
31A3 Tao He R China
31B2 Taole China
62A1 Taos USA
48B1 Taourirt Morocco
20D4 Tapa Estonia
70C3 Tapachula Mexico
73G4 Tapajós R Brazil
27D7 Tapan Indonesia
35A3 Tapanui New Zealand
72E5 Tapauá R Brazil
42D4 Tāpi R India
43F3 Taplejung Nepal
65D3 Tappahannock USA
35B2 Tapuaenuku Mt New Zealand
75C3 Tapuaritinga Brazil
72F4 Tapurucuara Brazil
75B2 Taquaral, Serra do Mts Brazil
75B2 Taquari R Brazil
34D1 Tara Australia
24J4 Tara Russian Federation
24J4 Tara R Russian Federation
17D2 Tara R Bosnia-Herzegovina
48D4 Taraba R Nigeria
72F7 Tarabuco Bolivia
Tarābulus = Tripoli (Libya)
35C1 Taradale New Zealand
27E6 Tarakan Indonesia
Taranaki, Mt = Egmont, Mt
15B1 Tarancón Spain
8B3 Taransay I Scotland
16D2 Taranto Italy
16D2 Taranto, G di Italy
72C5 Tarapoto Peru
14C2 Tarare France
35C2 Tararua Range Mts New Zealand
20H2 Tarasovo Russian Federation
48C2 Tarat Algeria
35C1 Tarawera New Zealand
15B1 Tarazona Spain
39G1 Tarbagatay, Khrebet Mts Russian Federation
8D3 Tarbat Ness Pen Scotland
42C2 Tarbela Res Pakistan
8C4 Tarbert Strathclyde, Scotland
8B3 Tarbert Western Isles, Scotland
14B3 Tarbes France
67C1 Tarboro USA
32C4 Tarcoola Australia
34C2 Tarcoon Australia
34D2 Taree Australia
48A2 Tarfaya Morocco
58D2 Targhee P USA
49D1 Tarhūnah Libya
41F5 Tarīf UAE
72F8 Tarija Bolivia
44B3 Tarikere India
38C4 Tarīm Yemen
50D4 Tarime Tanzania
39G1 Tarim He R China
39G2 Tarim Pendi Basin China
42B2 Tarin Kut Afghanistan
47D3 Tarkastad South Africa
61D2 Tarkio USA
27F5 Tarlac Philippines
72C6 Tarma Peru
14C3 Tarn R France
19E2 Tarnobrzeg Poland
19E3 Tarnów Poland
16B2 Taro R Italy
32D3 Taroom Australia
48B1 Taroudannt Morocco
15C1 Tarragona Spain
34C4 Tarraleah Australia
15C1 Tarrasa Spain
68D2 Tarrytown USA
40B2 Tarsus Turkey
8E2 Tartan Oilfield N Sea
26H2 Tartarskiy Proliv Str Russian Federation
20D4 Tartu Estonia
40C3 Tartūs Syria
75D2 Tarumirim Brazil
27C6 Tarutung Indonesia
16C1 Tarvisio Italy
65D1 Taschereau Canada
38D1 Tashauz Turkmenistan
43G3 Tashigang Bhutan
39E1 Tashkent Uzbekistan
24K4 Tashtagol Russian Federation
25K4 Tashtyp Russian Federation
45C2 Tasīl Syria
55N2 Tasiussaq Greenland
50B2 Tasker Well Niger
35B2 Tasman B New Zealand
32D5 Tasmania I Australia
35B2 Tasman Mts New Zealand
34C4 Tasman Pen Australia
33E4 Tasman S Australia/New Zealand
40C1 Taşova Turkey
48C2 Tassili du Hoggar Desert Region Algeria
48C2 Tassili N'jjer Desert Region Algeria
48B2 Tata Morocco
19D3 Tatabánya Hungary
48D1 Tataouine Tunisia
24J4 Tatarsk Russian Federation
20J4 Tatarstan Republic Russian Federation
29C3 Tateyama Japan
54G3 Tathlina L Canada
55J4 Tatnam, Cape Canada
19D3 Tatry Mts Poland/Slovakia
29B4 Tatsuno Japan
42B4 Tatta Pakistan
75C3 Tatuí Brazil
62B2 Tatum USA
40D2 Tatvan Turkey
33H2 Ta'u I American Samoa
73K5 Tauá Brazil
75C3 Taubaté Brazil
13E2 Taufstein Mt Germany
35C1 Taumarunui New Zealand
47C2 Taung South Africa
30B2 Taungdwingyi Burma
30B1 Taung-gyi Burma
30A2 Taungup Burma
42C2 Taunsa Pakistan
7C4 Taunton England
68E2 Taunton USA
40B2 Taunus Mts Turkey
13E2 Taunus Region Germany
35C1 Taupo New Zealand
35C1 Taupo,L New Zealand
19E1 Taurage Lithuania
35C1 Tauranga New Zealand
35C1 Tauranga Harbour B New Zealand
35B1 Tauroa Pt New Zealand
40B2 Taurus Mts Turkey
55J3 Tavani Canada
24H4 Tavda Russian Federation
24H4 Tavda R Russian Federation
33H2 Taveuni I Fiji
15A2 Tavira Portugal
7B4 Tavistock England
30B3 Tavoy Burma
30B3 Tavoy Pt Burma
40A2 Tavşanlı Turkey
7C4 Taw R England
35B2 Tawa New Zealand
63C2 Tawakoni,L USA
64C2 Tawas City USA
27E6 Tawau Malaysia
50C2 Taweisha Sudan
27F6 Tawitawi I Philippines
70C3 Taxco Mexico
8D3 Tay R Scotland
27E7 Tayan Indonesia
50E3 Tayeeglow Somalia
8C3 Tay, Loch L Scotland
64C2 Taylor Michigan, USA
63C2 Taylor Texas, USA
54B3 Taylor USA
62A1 Taylor,Mt USA
64B3 Taylorville USA
40C4 Taymā' Saudi Arabia
25L3 Taymura R Russian Federation
25M2 Taymyr, Ozero L Russian Federation
25L2 Taymyr, Poluostrov Pen Russian Federation
30D3 Tay Ninh Vietnam
25L4 Tayshet Russian Federation
26C2 Tayshir Mongolia
8D3 Tayside Region Scotland
27E5 Taytay Philippines
48B1 Taza Morocco
29D3 Tazawako Japan
29D3 Tazawa-ko L Japan
49E2 Tāzirbū Libya
24J3 Tazovskiy Russian Federation
21G7 Tbilisi Georgia
50B4 Tchibanga Gabon
50B1 Tchigai,Plat du Niger
48C3 Tchin Tabaradene Niger
50B3 Tcholliré Cameroon
19D2 Tczew Poland
35A3 Te Anau New Zealand
35A3 Te Anua,L New Zealand
35C1 Te Aroha New Zealand
35C1 Te Awamutu New Zealand
16B3 Tébessa Algeria
16B3 Tébessa, Mts De Algeria/Tunisia
16B3 Téboursouk Tunisia
59C4 Tecate Mexico
20L4 Techa R Russian Federation
70B3 Tecomán Mexico
70B3 Tecpan Mexico
17F1 Tecuci Romania
61D2 Tecumseh USA
24H6 Tedzhen Turkmenistan
24H6 Tedzhen R Turkmenistan
6D2 Tees R England
72F4 Tefé Brazil
70D3 Tegucigalpa Honduras
66C3 Tehachapi USA
66C3 Tehachapi Mts USA
59C3 Tehachapi P USA
54J3 Tehek L Canada
41F2 Tehrān Iran
70C3 Tehuacán Mexico
70C3 Tehuantepec Mexico
70C3 Tehuantepec, G de Mexico
70C3 Tehuantepec, Istmo de isthmus Mexico
7B3 Teifi R Wales
7C4 Teignmouth England
15A2 Tejo R Portugal
66C3 Tejon P USA
61D2 Tekamah USA
35B2 Tekapo,L New Zealand
39F1 Tekeli Kazakhstan
40A1 Tekirdağ Turkey
17F2 Tekir Dağları Mts Turkey
43G4 Teknaf Bangladesh
35C1 Te Kuiti New Zealand
70D3 Tela Honduras
21H7 Telavi Georgia
45C2 Tel Aviv Yafo Israel
54E4 Telegraph Creek Canada
74C5 Telén Argentina
59C3 Telescope Peak Mt USA
73G5 Teles Pires R Brazil
7C3 Telford England
25K4 Teli Russian Federation
45C3 Tell el Meise Mt Jordan
54B3 Teller USA
44B3 Tellicherry India
30C5 Telok Anson Malaysia
20K3 Tel'pos-iz, Gory Mt Russian Federation
19E1 Telšiai Lithuania
27D7 Telukbetung Indonesia
27F7 Teluk Bone B Indonesia
27G7 Teluk Cendrawasih B Indonesia
27E6 Teluk Darvel B Malaysia
27F7 Teluk Tolo B Indonesia
27F6 Teluk Tomini B Indonesia
27F6 Teluk Weda B Indonesia
64C1 Temagami,L Canada
69E5 Temblador Venezuela
66B3 Temblor Range Mts USA
7C3 Teme R England
30C5 Temerloh Malaysia
24G5 Temir Kazakhstan
24J4 Temirtau Kazakhstan
65D1 Temiscaming Canada
65F1 Témiscouata,L Canada
34C2 Temora Australia
59D4 Tempe USA
63C2 Temple USA
9C3 Templemore Irish Republic
66B3 Templeton USA
74B5 Temuco Chile
35B2 Temuka New Zealand
72C4 Tena Ecuador
44C2 Tenāli India
30B3 Tenasserim Burma
7B4 Tenby Wales
50E3 Tendaho Ethiopia
16B2 Tende, Colle de P France/Italy
44E4 Ten Degree Chan Indian Ocean
29E3 Tendo Japan
50B2 Ténéré, Erg du Desert Region Niger
48A2 Tenerife I Canary Islands
15C2 Ténès Algeria
30B1 Teng R Burma
31A2 Tengger Shamo Desert China
24H4 Tengiz, Ozero L Kazakhstan
76G2 Teniente Rodolfo Marsh Base Antarctica
44B4 Tenkāsi India
51C5 Tenke Zaïre
48B3 Tenkodogo Burkina
32C2 Tennant Creek Australia
63E1 Tennessee R USA
57E3 Tennessee State USA
60B3 Tennesse P USA
27E6 Tenom Malaysia
70C3 Tenosique Mexico
34D1 Tenterfield Australia
67B3 Ten Thousand Is USA
75D2 Teófilo Otôni Brazil
70B2 Tepehuanes Mexico
70B2 Tepic Mexico
18C2 Teplice Czech Republic
35C1 Te Puke New Zealand
15C1 Ter R Spain
48C3 Téra Niger
29C3 Teradomari Japan
16C2 Teramo Italy
48A1 Terceira I Azores
19F3 Terebovlya Ukraine
75B3 Terenos Brazil
73K5 Teresina Brazil
75D3 Teresópolis Brazil
44E4 Teressa I Nicobar Is, Indian Ocean
40C1 Terme Turkey
38E2 Termez Uzbekistan
70C3 Términos, L de Lg Mexico
16C2 Termoli Italy
27F6 Ternate Indonesia
16C2 Terni Italy
19F3 Ternopol Ukraine
26H2 Terpeniya, Zaliv B Russian Federation
66C3 Terra Bella USA
64B1 Terrace Bay Canada
16C2 Terracina Italy
51C6 Terrafirma South Africa
76G8 Terre Adélie Region Antarctica
63D3 Terre Bonne B USA
64B3 Terre Haute USA
63C2 Terrell USA
60B1 Terry USA
18B2 Terschelling I Netherlands
15B1 Teruel Spain
54C2 Teshekpuk Lake USA
29D2 Teshikaga Japan
29E2 Teshio R Japan
29D2 Teshio dake Mt Japan
25L5 Tesiyn Gol R Mongolia
54E3 Teslin Canada
75B2 Tesouro Brazil
48C2 Tessalit Mali
48C3 Tessaoua Niger
7D4 Test R England
51D5 Tete Mozambique
19F2 Teterev R Ukraine
58D1 Teton R USA
58D2 Teton Range Mts USA
48B1 Tetouan Morocco
20H5 Tetyushi Russian Federation
72F8 Teuco R Argentina
74D2 Teuco R Paraguay
16B3 Teulada, C Sardinia, Italy
27F7 Teun I Indonesia
29D2 Teuri-tō I Japan
13E1 Teutoburger Wald Hills Germany
16C2 Tevere R Italy
8D4 Teviot R Scotland
24J4 Tevriz Russian Federation
35A3 Te Waewae B New Zealand
34D1 Tewantin Australia
7C3 Tewkesbury England
31A3 Têwo China
63D2 Texarkana USA
63D2 Texarkana,L USA
34D1 Texas Australia
56C3 Texas State USA
63D3 Texas City USA
18A2 Texel I Netherlands
62B1 Texhoma USA
63C2 Texoma,L USA
47D2 Teyateyaneng Lesotho
42A2 Teyvareh Afghanistan
43G3 Tezpur India
30C1 Tha R Laos
47D2 Thabana Ntlenyana Mt Lesotho
47D2 Thaba Putsoa Mt Lesotho
47D1 Thabazimbi South Africa
30B3 Thagyettaw Burma
30D1 Thai Binh Vietnam
30C2 Thailand Kingdom SE Asia
30C3 Thailand,G of Thailand
30D1 Thai Nguyen Vietnam
30D2 Thakhek Laos
42C2 Thal Pakistan
30C4 Thale Luang L Thailand
34C1 Thallon Australia
35C1 Thames New Zealand
7E4 Thames R England
21G8 Thamhar, Wadi ath R Iraq
44A2 Thāne India
30D2 Thanh Hoa Vietnam
44B3 Thanjāvūr India
13D4 Thann France
42C3 Thar Desert India
34B1 Thargomindah Australia
17E2 Thásos I Greece
30B2 Thaton Burma
30A2 Thayetmyo Burma
7E3 The Broads England
54F5 The Dalles USA
60C2 Thedford USA
48A3 The Gambia Republic W Africa
41F4 The Gulf SW Asia
18A2 The Hague Netherlands
54H3 Thelon R Canada
7E4 The Naze Pt England
32E3 Theodore Australia
59D4 Theodore Roosevelt L USA
72F6 Theodore Roosevelt, R Brazil
54H4 The Pas Canada
17E2 Thermaïkós Kólpos G Greece
58E2 Thermopolis USA
54F2 Thesiger B Canada
64C1 Thessalon Canada
17E2 Thessaloníki Greece
7E3 Thetford England
65E1 Thetford Mines Canada
47D2 Theunissen South Africa
63D3 Thibodaux USA
54J4 Thicket Portage Canada
61D1 Thief River Falls USA
58B2 Thielsen,Mt USA
14C2 Thiers France
48A3 Thiès Senegal
50D4 Thika Kenya
43F3 Thimphu Bhutan
14D2 Thionville France
17F3 Thíra I Greece

6D2 **Thirsk** England
44B4 **Thiruvananthapuram** India
12F7 **Thisted** Denmark
27E5 **Thitu** S China Sea
17E3 **Thívai** Greece
14C2 **Thiviers** France
66C2 **Thomas A Edison,L** USA
67B2 **Thomaston** Georgia, USA
65F2 **Thomaston** Maine, USA
9C3 **Thomastown** Irish Republic
63E2 **Thomasville** Alabama, USA
67B2 **Thomasville** Georgia, USA
67C1 **Thomasville** N Carolina, USA
55J2 **Thom Bay** Canada
54J4 **Thompson** Canada
61E2 **Thompson** *R* USA
58C1 **Thompson Falls** USA
54G3 **Thompson Landing** Canada
68D2 **Thompsonville** USA
67B2 **Thomson** USA
32D3 **Thomson** *R* Australia
30C3 **Thon Buri** Thailand
30B2 **Thongwa** Burma
62A1 **Thoreau** USA
6D2 **Thornaby** England
7D3 **Thorne** England
8D4 **Thornhill** Scotland
14B2 **Thouars** France
65D2 **Thousand Is** Canada/USA
58D1 **Three Forks** USA
64B1 **Three Lakes** USA
30B2 **Three Pagodas P** Thailand
48B4 **Three Points, C** Ghana
66C2 **Three Rivers** California, USA
64B2 **Three Rivers** Michigan, USA
62C3 **Three Rivers** Texas, USA
58B2 **Three Sisters** *Mt* USA
55M2 **Thule** Greenland
16B1 **Thun** Switzerland
64B1 **Thunder Bay** Canada
30B4 **Thung Song** Thailand
18C2 **Thüringen** *State* Germany
18C2 **Thüringer Wald** *Upland* Germany
9C3 **Thurles** Irish Republic
8D2 **Thurso** Scotland
76F4 **Thurston I** Antarctica
34B1 **Thylungra** Australia
31B5 **Tiandong** China
31B5 **Tian'e** China
31D2 **Tianjin** China
31B5 **Tianlin** China
28B2 **Tianqiaoling** China
24J5 **Tian Shan** *Mts* China/Kirgizia
31B3 **Tianshui** China
31A2 **Tianzhu** China
15C2 **Tiaret** Algeria
75B3 **Tibagi** *R* Brazil
48D4 **Tibati** Cameroon
45C2 **Tiberias** Israel
45C2 **Tiberias,L** Israel
Tiber,R = Tevere,R
58D1 **Tiber Res** USA
50B1 **Tibesti** *Mountain Region* Chad
39G2 **Tibet** *Autonomous Region* China
34B1 **Tibooburra** Australia
43E3 **Tibrikot** Nepal
70A2 **Tiburón** *I* Mexico
48B3 **Tichitt** Mauritius
48A2 **Tichla** Morocco
65E2 **Ticonderoga** USA
70D2 **Ticul** Mexico
48C2 **Tidikelt, Plaine du** *Desert Region* Algeria
48A3 **Tidjikja** Mauritius
48A3 **Tidra, Isla** Mauritius
13C2 **Tiel** Netherlands
28A2 **Tieling** China
13B2 **Tielt** Belgium
13C2 **Tienen** Belgium
13E4 **Tiengen** Germany
Tientsin = Tianjin
12H6 **Tierp** Sweden
62A1 **Tierra Amarilla** USA
70C3 **Tierra Blanca** Mexico
71C9 **Tierra del Fuego** *I* Argentina/Chile
74C8 **Tierra del Fuego** *Territory* Argentina
74C8 **Tierra del Fuego, Isla Grande de** Argentina/Chile
75C3 **Tietê** Brazil
75B3 **Tiete** *R* Brazil
64C2 **Tiffin** USA
67B2 **Tifton** USA
25R4 **Tigil** Russian Federation
72C4 **Tigre** *R* Peru
72F2 **Tigre** *R* Venezuela
50D2 **Tigre** *Region* Ethiopia
41E3 **Tigris** *R* Iraq
45B4 **Tīh, Gebel el** *Upland* Egypt
59C4 **Tijuana** Mexico
42D4 **Tikamgarh** India
21G6 **Tikhoretsk** Russian Federation
20E4 **Tikhvin** Russian Federation
33F2 **Tikopia** *I* Solomon Islands
41D3 **Tikrīt** Iraq
25O2 **Tiksi** Russian Federation
13C2 **Tilburg** Netherlands
7E4 **Tilbury** England
74C2 **Tilcara** Argentina
34B1 **Tilcha** Australia
48C3 **Tilemis, Vallée du** Mali
43K2 **Tilhar** India
30A1 **Tilin** Burma
48C3 **Tillabéri** Niger
58B1 **Tillamook** USA
44E4 **Tillanchong** *I* Nicobar Is, Indian Ocean
48C3 **Tillia** Niger
6D2 **Till, R** England
17F3 **Tílos** *I* Greece
34B2 **Tilpa** Australia
8D3 **Tilt** *R* Scotland
20H2 **Timanskiy Kryazh** *Mts* Russian Federation
35B2 **Timaru** New Zealand
21F6 **Timashevsk** Russian Federation
17E3 **Timbákion** Greece
63D3 **Timbalier B** USA
48B3 **Timbédra** Mauritius
Timbuktu = Tombouctou
48B3 **Timétrine Monts** *Mts* Mali
48C3 **Timia** Niger
17E1 **Timiş** *R* Romania
48C2 **Timimoun** Algeria
17E1 **Timişoara** Romania
64C1 **Timmins** Canada
32B1 **Timor** *I* Indonesia
32B2 **Timor** *S* Australia/Indonesia
45B3 **Timsâh,L** Egypt
67A1 **Tims Ford L** USA
27F6 **Tinaca Pt** Philippines
69D5 **Tinaco** Venezuela
44B3 **Tindivanam** India
48B2 **Tindouf** Algeria
66C2 **Tinemaha Res** USA
48B2 **Tinfouchy** Algeria
48C2 **Tin Fouye** Algeria
55O3 **Tingmiarmiut** Greenland
72C5 **Tingo María** Peru
48B3 **Tingrela** Ivory Coast
43F3 **Tingri** China
75E1 **Tinharé, Ilha de** Brazil
27H5 **Tinian** Pacific Ocean
74C3 **Tinogasta** Argentina
17F3 **Tínos** *I* Greece
43H3 **Tinsukia** India
7B4 **Tintagel Head** *Pt* England
48C2 **Tin Tarabine** *Watercourse* Algeria
34B3 **Tintinara** Australia
48C2 **Tin Zaouaten** Algeria
60C1 **Tioga** USA
68B2 **Tioga** *R* USA
66C2 **Tioga P** USA
30C5 **Tioman** *I* Malaysia
68B1 **Tioughnioga** *R* USA
10B3 **Tipperary** Irish Republic
9C3 **Tipperary** *County* Irish Republic
66C2 **Tipton** California, USA
61E3 **Tipton** Missouri, USA
44B3 **Tiptūr** India
17D2 **Tiranë** Albania
19F3 **Tiraspol** Moldavia
45A3 **Tir'at el Ismâilîya** *Canal* Egypt
17F3 **Tire** Turkey
40C1 **Tirebolu** Turkey
8B3 **Tiree** *I* Scotland
17F2 **Tîrgovişte** Romania
17E1 **Tîrgu Jiu** Romania
17E1 **Tîrgu Mureş** Romania
42C1 **Tirich Mir** *Mt* Pakistan
48A2 **Tiris** *Region* Morocco
20K5 **Tirlyanskiy** Russian Federation
17E1 **Tîrnăveni** Romania
17E3 **Tírnavos** Greece
42D4 **Tirodi** India
16B2 **Tirso** *R* Sardinia, Italy
44B4 **Tiruchchendūr** India
44B3 **Tiruchchirāppalli** India
44B4 **Tirunelveli** India
44B3 **Tirupati** India
44B3 **Tiruppattūr** India
44B3 **Tiruppur** India
44B3 **Tiruvannāmalai** India
63C2 **Tishomingo** USA
45D2 **Tisīyah** Syria
19E3 **Tisza** *R* Hungary
72E7 **Titicaca, Lago** Bolivia/Peru
43E4 **Titlagarh** India
17E2 **Titov Veles** Macedonia, Yugoslavia
50C3 **Titule** Zaïre
67B3 **Titusville** USA
8B2 **Tiumpan Head** *Pt* Scotland
7C4 **Tiverton** England
16C2 **Tivoli** Italy
70D2 **Tizimín** Mexico
15C2 **Tizi Ouzou** Algeria
48B2 **Tiznit** Morocco
48B1 **Tlemcen** Algeria
51E5 **Toamasina** Madagascar
29C4 **Toba** Japan
42B2 **Toba and Kakar Ranges** *Mts* Pakistan
69E4 **Tobago** *I* Caribbean Sea
27F6 **Tobelo** Indonesia
64C1 **Tobermory** Canada
8B3 **Tobermory** Scotland
27G6 **Tobi** *I* Pacific Ocean
59C2 **Tobin,Mt** USA
29C3 **Tobi-shima** *I* Japan
27D7 **Toboah** Indonesia
24H4 **Tobol** *R* Russian Federation
27F7 **Toboli** Indonesia
24H4 **Tobol'sk** Russian Federation
Tobruk = Tubruq
20J2 **Tobseda** Russian Federation
73J4 **Tocantins** *R* Brazil
73J6 **Tocantins** *State* Brazil
67B2 **Toccoa** USA
74B2 **Tocopilla** Chile
74C2 **Tocorpuri** Bolivia/Chile
72E1 **Tocuyo** *R* Venezuela
42D3 **Toda** India
28B3 **Todong** S Korea
73L6 **Todos os Santos, Baia de** *B* Brazil
56B4 **Todos Santos** Mexico
59C4 **Todos Santos,B de** Mexico
33H2 **Tofua** *I* Tonga
32B1 **Togian, Kepulauan** *I* Indonesia
48C4 **Togo** *Republic* W Africa
31C1 **Togtoh** China
62A1 **Tohatchi** USA
29E2 **Tokachi** *R* Japan
29C3 **Tokamachi** Japan
50D2 **Tokar** Sudan
26F4 **Tokara Retto** *Arch* Japan
40C1 **Tokat** Turkey
28B3 **Tok-do** *I* S Korea
33H1 **Tokelau Is** Pacific Ocean
39F1 **Tokmak** Kirgizia
35C1 **Tokomaru Bay** New Zealand
26F4 **Tokuno** *I* Ryukyu Is, Japan
29C4 **Tokushima** Japan
28B4 **Tokuyama** Japan
29D3 **Tōkyō** Japan
35C1 **Tolaga Bay** New Zealand
51E6 **Tôlañaro** Madagascar
73H8 **Toledo** Brazil
15B2 **Toledo** Spain
64C2 **Toledo** USA
63D2 **Toledo Bend Res** USA
51E6 **Toliara** Madagascar
72C2 **Tolina** *Mt* Colombia
19F2 **Toločhin** Belarus
15B1 **Tolosa** Spain
28A4 **Tolsan-do** *I* S Korea
74B5 **Toltén** Chile
70C3 **Toluca** Mexico
20H5 **Tol'yatti** Russian Federation
64A2 **Tomah** USA
64B1 **Tomahawk** USA
29E2 **Tomakomai** Japan
15A2 **Tomar** Portugal
19E2 **Tomaszów Mazowiecka** Poland
63E2 **Tombigbee** *R* USA
51B4 **Tomboco** Angola
75D3 **Tombos** Brazil
48B3 **Tombouctou** Mali
59E4 **Tombstone** USA
51B5 **Tombua** Angola
47D1 **Tomburke** South Africa
74B5 **Tomé** Chile
15B2 **Tomelloso** Spain
28A4 **Tomie** Japan
8D3 **Tomintoul** Scotland
32B3 **Tomkinson Range** *Mts* Australia
25O4 **Tommot** Russian Federation
17E2 **Tomorrit** *Mt* Albania
24K4 **Tomsk** Russian Federation
68C3 **Toms River** USA
70C3 **Tonalá** Mexico
58C1 **Tonasket** USA
7E4 **Tonbridge** England
33H3 **Tonga** *Is, Kingdom* Pacific Ocean
47E2 **Tongaat** South Africa
33H3 **Tongatapu** *I* Tonga
33H3 **Tongatapu Group** *Is* Tonga
33H3 **Tonga Trench** Pacific Ocean
28A2 **Tongchang** N Korea
31D3 **Tongcheng** China
31B2 **Tongchuan** China
31A2 **Tongde** China
13C2 **Tongeren** Belgium
30E2 **Tonggu Jiao** *I* China
31A5 **Tonghai** China
28B2 **Tonghua** China
28B3 **Tongjosŏn-Man** *S* N Korea
30D1 **Tongkin,G of** China/Vietnam
31E1 **Tongliao** China
31D3 **Tongling** China
28A3 **Tongnae** S Korea
34B2 **Tongo** Australia
31B4 **Tongren** Guizhou, China
31A2 **Tongren** Qinghai, China
43G3 **Tongsa** Bhutan
30B1 **Tongta** Burma
26C3 **Tongtian He** *R* China
8C2 **Tongue** Scotland
60B1 **Tongue** *R* USA
31D2 **Tong Xian** China
31B2 **Tongxin** China
28A2 **Tongyuanpu** China
31B4 **Tongzi** China
25L5 **Tonhil** Mongolia
56C4 **Tónichi** Mexico
50C3 **Tonj** Sudan
42D3 **Tonk** India
63C1 **Tonkawa** USA
30C3 **Tonle Sap** *L* Cambodia
13C4 **Tonnerre** France
29D3 **Tono** Japan
59C3 **Tonopah** USA
58D2 **Tooele** USA
34D1 **Toogoolawah** Australia
34B1 **Toompine** Australia
34D1 **Toowoomba** Australia
66C1 **Topaz L** USA
61D3 **Topeka** USA
59D4 **Topock** USA
56C4 **Topolobampo** Mexico
20E2 **Topozero, Ozero** *L* Russian Federation
58B1 **Toppenish** USA
68E1 **Topsfield** USA
50D3 **Tor** Ethiopia
17F3 **Torbalı** Turkey
41G2 **Torbat-e-Heydarīyeh** Iran
15A1 **Tordesillas** Spain
18C2 **Torgau** Germany
13B2 **Torhout** Belgium
26H3 **Tori** *I* Japan
Torino = Turin
50D3 **Torit** Sudan
75B2 **Torixoreu** Brazil
15A1 **Tormes** *R* Spain
12J5 **Torne** *R* Sweden
12H5 **Torneträsk** *L* Sweden
55M4 **Torngat** *Mts* Canada
12J5 **Tornio** Finland
74C3 **Toro, Cerro del** *Mt* Argentina/Chile
65D2 **Toronto** Canada
20E4 **Toropets** Russian Federation
50D3 **Tororo** Uganda
Toros, Dağlari = Taurus Mts
7C4 **Torquay** England
66C4 **Torrance** USA
15A2 **Torrão** Portugal
15C1 **Torreblanca** Spain
16C2 **Torre del Greco** Italy
15B1 **Torrelavega** Spain
15B2 **Torremolinos** Spain
32C4 **Torrens, L** Australia
56C4 **Torreón** Mexico
33F2 **Torres Is** Vanuatu
32D2 **Torres Str** Australia
15A2 **Torres Vedras** Portugal
7B4 **Torridge** *R* England
8C3 **Torridon, Loch** *Inlet* Scotland
68D2 **Torrington** Connecticut, USA
60C2 **Torrington** Wyoming, USA
12D3 **Tórshavn** Faeroes
15C1 **Tortosa** Spain
15C1 **Tortosa, Cabo de** *C* Spain
72C3 **Tortugas, Golfo de** Colombia
41G2 **Torūd** Iran
19D2 **Toruń** Poland
10B2 **Tory I** Irish Republic
9B2 **Tory Sol** Irish Republic
20E4 **Torzhok** Russian Federation
29B4 **Tosa** Japan
28C4 **Tosashimizu** Japan
29C4 **Tosa-Wan** *B* Japan
29C4 **To-shima** *I* Japan
12L7 **Tosno** Russian Federation
28B4 **Tosu** Japan
40B1 **Tosya** Turkey
15B2 **Totana** Spain
20G4 **Tot'ma** Russian Federation
7C4 **Totnes** England
73G2 **Totness** Surinam
34C2 **Tottenham** Australia
29C3 **Tottori** Japan
48B4 **Touba** Ivory Coast
48A3 **Touba** Senegal
48B1 **Toubkal** *Mt* Morocco
13B4 **Toucy** France
48B3 **Tougan** Burkina
48C1 **Touggourt** Algeria
48A3 **Tougué** Guinea
13C3 **Toul** France
14D3 **Toulon** France
14C3 **Toulouse** France
48B4 **Toumodi** Ivory Coast
30B2 **Toungoo** Burma
13B2 **Tourcoing** France
48A2 **Tourine** Mauritius
13B2 **Tournai** Belgium
14C2 **Tours** France
47C3 **Touws River** South Africa
29E2 **Towada** Japan
29E2 **Towada-ko** *L* Japan
68B2 **Towanda** USA
66D2 **Towne P** USA
60C1 **Towner** USA
58D1 **Townsend** USA
32D2 **Townsville** Australia
68B3 **Towson** USA
7C4 **Towy** *R* Wales
62B2 **Toyah** USA
29D2 **Toya-ko** *L* Japan
29D3 **Toyama** Japan
29C3 **Toyama-wan** *B* Japan
29C4 **Toyohashi** Japan
29C4 **Toyonaka** Japan
29B3 **Toyooka** Japan
29D3 **Toyota** Japan
48C1 **Tozeur** Tunisia
13D3 **Traben-Trarbach** Germany
Trâblous = Tripoli
40C1 **Trabzon** Turkey
61D2 **Tracy** Minnesota, USA
66B2 **Tracy** USA
15A2 **Trafalgar, Cabo** *C* Spain
54G5 **Trail** Canada
10B3 **Tralee** Irish Republic
9C3 **Tramore** Irish Republic
12G7 **Tranås** Sweden
30B4 **Trang** Thailand
27G7 **Trangan** *I* Indonesia
34C2 **Trangie** Australia
76E3 **Transantarctic Mts** Antarctica
47D3 **Transkei** *Self-governing homeland* South Africa
Transylvanian Alps *Mts* **= Munţii Carpaţii Meridionali**
16C3 **Trapani** Italy
34C3 **Traralgon** Australia
48A3 **Trarza** *Region* Mauritius
30C3 **Trat** Thailand
34B2 **Traveller's L** Australia
18C2 **Travemünde** Germany
64B2 **Traverse City** USA
35B2 **Travers,Mt** New Zealand
62C2 **Travis,L** USA
18D3 **Třebíč** Czech Republic
17D2 **Trebinje** Bosnia-Herzegovina
18C3 **Trebon** Czech Republic
74F4 **Treinta y Tres** Uruguay
74C6 **Trelew** Argentina
12G7 **Trelleborg** Sweden
7B3 **Tremadog B** Wales
65E1 **Tremblant,Mt** Canada
16D2 **Tremiti, Is** Italy
68B2 **Tremont** USA
58D2 **Tremonton** USA
19D3 **Trenčín** Slovakia
74D5 **Trenque Lauquén** Argentina
7D3 **Trent** *R* England
16C1 **Trento** Italy
65D2 **Trenton** Canada
61E2 **Trenton** Missouri, USA
68C2 **Trenton** New Jersey, USA
55N5 **Trepassey** Canada
74D5 **Tres Arroyos** Argentina
75C3 **Três Corações** Brazil
15B2 **Tres Forcas, Cabo** *C* Morocco
75B2 **Três Irmãos, Représa** *Res* Brazil
74F2 **Três Lagoas** Brazil
66B2 **Tres Pinos** USA
74C7 **Tres Puntas, Cabo** Argentina
75D3 **Três Rios** Brazil
16C1 **Treviso** Italy
7B4 **Trevose Hd** *Pt* England
13E2 **Treysa** Germany
62B1 **Tribune** USA
44B3 **Trichūr** India
34C2 **Trida** Australia
13D3 **Trier** Germany
16C1 **Trieste** Italy

45B1 **Trikomo** Cyprus
9C3 **Trim** Irish Republic
44C4 **Trincomalee** Sri Lanka
52G6 **Trindade** *I* Atlantic Ocean
72F6 **Trinidad** Bolivia
74E4 **Trinidad** Uruguay
62B1 **Trinidad** USA
69E4 **Trinidad** *I* Caribbean Sea
69E4 **Trinidad & Tobago** *Is Republic* Caribbean Sea
63C2 **Trinity** USA
56D3 **Trinity** *R* USA
55N5 **Trinity B** Canada
67A2 **Trion** USA
45C1 **Tripoli** Lebanon
49D1 **Tripoli** Libya
17E3 **Trípolis** Greece
43G4 **Tripura** *State* India
52H6 **Tristan da Cunha** *Is* Atlantic Ocean
19D3 **Trnava** Slovakia
32E1 **Trobriand Is** Papua New Guinea
65F1 **Trois Pistoles** Canada
65E1 **Trois-Riviéres** Canada
20L5 **Troitsk** Russian Federation
20K3 **Troitsko Pechorsk** Russian Federation
12G7 **Trollhättan** Sweden
12F6 **Trollheimen** *Mt* Norway
46K9 **Tromelin** *I* Indian Ocean
47D3 **Trompsburg** South Africa
12H5 **Tromsø** Norway
66D3 **Trona** USA
12G6 **Trondheim** Norway
12G6 **Trondheimfjord** *Inlet* Norway
45B1 **Troödos Range** *Mts* Cyprus
8C4 **Troon** Scotland
52J3 **Tropic of Cancer**
52K6 **Tropic of Capricorn**
48B2 **Troudenni** Mali
55J4 **Trout L** Ontario, Canada
58E2 **Trout Peak** *Mt* USA
68B2 **Trout Run** USA
7C4 **Trowbridge** England
67A2 **Troy** Alabama, USA
58C1 **Troy** Montana, USA
68D1 **Troy** New York, USA
64C2 **Troy** Ohio, USA
68B2 **Troy** Pennsylvania, USA
17E2 **Troyan** Bulgaria
13C3 **Troyes** France
59C3 **Troy Peak** *Mt* USA
41F5 **Trucial Coast** *Region* UAE
59B3 **Truckee** *R* USA
70D3 **Trujillo** Honduras
72C5 **Trujillo** Peru
15A2 **Trujillo** Spain
72D2 **Trujillo** Venezuela
59D3 **Trumbull,Mt** USA
34C2 **Trundle** Australia
55M5 **Truro** Canada
7B4 **Truro** England
62A2 **Truth or Consequences** USA
26C2 **Tsagaan Nuur** *L* Mongolia
26C1 **Tsagan-Tologoy** Russian Federation
51E5 **Tsaratanana** Madagascar
51C6 **Tsau** Botswana
50D4 **Tsavo** Kenya
50D4 **Tsavo Nat Pk** Kenya
60C1 **Tschida,L** USA
24J4 **Tselinograd** Kazakhstan
47B2 **Tses** Namibia
26D2 **Tsetserleg** Mongolia
48C4 **Tsévié** Togo
47C2 **Tshabong** Botswana
47C1 **Tshane** Botswana
21F6 **Tshchikskoye Vdkhr** *Res* Russian Federation
50B4 **Tshela** Zaïre
51C4 **Tshibala** Zaïre
50C4 **Tshikapa** Zaïre
50C4 **Tshuapa** *R* Zaïre
21G6 **Tsimlyanskoye Vodokhranilishche** *Res* Russian Federation
Tsinan = Jinan
Tsingtao = Qingdao
51E6 **Tsiombe** Madagascar
51E5 **Tsiroanomandidy** Madagascar
19F2 **Tsna** *R* Belarus
31B1 **Tsogt Ovoo** Mongolia
47D3 **Tsomo** South Africa
26D2 **Tsomog** Mongolia
29C4 **Tsu** Japan
29C3 **Tsubata** Japan
29E3 **Tsuchiura** Japan
29E2 **Tsugarū-kaikyō** *Str* Japan
51B5 **Tsumeb** Namibia
51B6 **Tsumis** Namibia
29D3 **Tsuruga** Japan
29C3 **Tsurugi** Japan
29D3 **Tsuruoka** Japan
29C3 **Tsushima** Japan
28B4 **Tsushima** *Is* Japan
Tsushima-Kaikyō = Korea Str
29C3 **Tsuyama** Japan
15A1 **Tua** *R* Portugal
37M5 **Tuamotu, Îles** Pacific Ocean
21F7 **Tuapse** Russian Federation
35A3 **Tuatapere** New Zealand
59D3 **Tuba City** USA
37M6 **Tubai, Îles** Pacific Ocean
74G3 **Tubarão** Brazil
45C2 **Tubas** Israel
18B3 **Tübingen** Germany
49E1 **Tubruq** Libya
68C3 **Tuckerton** USA
59D4 **Tucson** USA
74C3 **Tucumán** *State* Argentina
62B1 **Tucumcari** USA
72F2 **Tucupita** Venezuela
15B1 **Tudela** Spain
40C3 **Tudmur** Syria
47E2 **Tugela** *R* South Africa
34D2 **Tuggerah L** Australia
27F5 **Tuguegarao** Philippines
25P4 **Tugur** Russian Federation
31D2 **Tuhai He** *R* China
27F7 **Tukangbesi, Kepulauan** *Is* Indonesia
54E3 **Tuktoyaktuk** Canada
19E1 **Tukums** Latvia
25O4 **Tukuringra, Khrebet** *Mts* Russian Federation
51D4 **Tukuyu** Tanzania
42B1 **Tukzar** Afghanistan
20F5 **Tula** Russian Federation
66C2 **Tulare** USA
66C2 **Tulare Lake Bed** USA
62A2 **Tularosa** USA
72C3 **Tulcán** Ecuador
21D6 **Tulcea** Romania
19F3 **Tul'chin** Ukraine
66C2 **Tule** *R* USA
51C6 **Tuli** Zimbabwe
47D1 **Tuli** *R* Zimbabwe
62B2 **Tulia** USA
45C2 **Tulkarm** Israel
67A1 **Tullahoma** USA
9C3 **Tullamore** Irish Republic
14C2 **Tulle** France
63D2 **Tullos** USA
9C3 **Tullow** Irish Republic
68B1 **Tully** USA
63C1 **Tulsa** USA
72C3 **Tuluá** Colombia
40C3 **Tulūl ash Shāmīyah** *Desert Region* Iran/Syria
25M4 **Tulun** Russian Federation
72C3 **Tumaco** Colombia
25R3 **Tumany** Russian Federation
34C3 **Tumbarumba** Australia
72B4 **Tumbes** Ecuador
28B2 **Tumen** China
28B2 **Tumen R** China/N Korea
44B3 **Tumkūr** India
30C4 **Tumpat** Malaysia
42D4 **Tumsar** India
48B3 **Tumu** Ghana
73H3 **Tumucumaque, Serra** *Mts* Brazil
34C3 **Tumut** Australia
34C3 **Tumut** *R* Australia
69L1 **Tunapuna** Trinidad
7E4 **Tunbridge Wells, Royal** England
40C2 **Tunceli** Turkey
51D4 **Tunduma** Zambia
51D5 **Tunduru** Tanzania
17F2 **Tundzha** *R* Bulgaria
44B2 **Tungabhadra** *R* India
26E4 **Tungkang** Taiwan
12B2 **Tungnafellsjökull** *Mts* Iceland
25M3 **Tunguska** *R* Russian Federation
44C2 **Tuni** India
16C3 **Tunis** Tunisia
16C3 **Tunis, G de** Tunisia
48C1 **Tunisia** *Republic* N Africa
72D2 **Tunja** Colombia
68C2 **Tunkhannock** USA
Tunxi = Huangshan
66C2 **Tuolumne Meadows** USA
75B3 **Tupã** Brazil
75C2 **Tupaciguara** Brazil
63E2 **Tupelo** USA
19G1 **Tupik** Russian Federation
72E8 **Tupiza** Bolivia
66C3 **Tupman** USA
65E2 **Tupper Lake** USA
74C4 **Tupungato** *Mt* Argentina
43L3 **Tura** India
25L3 **Tura** Russian Federation
20L4 **Tura** *R* Russian Federation
41G2 **Turān** Iran
25L4 **Turan** Russian Federation
40C3 **Turayf** Saudi Arabia
38E3 **Turbat** Pakistan
72C2 **Turbo** Colombia
17E1 **Turda** Romania
24K5 **Turfan Depression** China
24H5 **Turgay** Kazakhstan
25L5 **Turgen Uul** *Mt* Mongolia
40A2 **Turgutlu** Turkey
40C1 **Turhal** Turkey
12K7 **Türi** Estonia
15B2 **Turia** *R* Spain
16B1 **Turin** Italy
20L4 **Turinsk** Russian Federation
26G2 **Turiy Rog** Russian Federation
50D3 **Turkana, L** Ethiopia/Kenya
38E1 **Turkestan** *Region* C Asia
40C2 **Turkey** *Republic* W Asia
38D1 **Turkmenistan** *Republic* Asia
41F2 **Turkmenskiy Zaliv** *B* Turkmenistan
69C2 **Turks Is** Caribbean Sea
12J6 **Turku** Finland
50D3 **Turkwel** *R* Kenya
66B2 **Turlock** USA
66B2 **Turlock L** USA
35C2 **Turnagain,C** New Zealand
70D3 **Turneffe I** Belize
68D1 **Turners Falls** USA
13C2 **Turnhout** Belgium
17E2 **Turnu Măgurele** Romania
17E2 **Turnu-Severin** Romania
25K5 **Turpan** China
69B2 **Turquino** *Mt* Cuba
8D3 **Turriff** Scotland
38E1 **Turtkul'** Uzbekistan
61D3 **Turtle Creek Res** USA
25K3 **Turukhansk** Russian Federation
26D1 **Turuntayevo** Russian Federation
75B2 **Turvo** *R* Goias, Brazil
75C3 **Turvo** *R* São Paulo, Brazil
19E2 **Tur'ya** *R* Ukraine
63E2 **Tuscaloosa** USA
68B2 **Tuscarora Mt** USA
64B3 **Tuscola** Illinois, USA
62C2 **Tuscola** Texas, USA
63E2 **Tuscumbia** USA
41G3 **Tusharīk** Iran
68A2 **Tussey Mt** USA
Tutera = Tudela
44B4 **Tuticorin** India
17F2 **Tutrakan** Bulgaria
18B3 **Tuttlingen** Germany
33H2 **Tutuila** *I* American Samoa
26D2 **Tuul Gol** *R* Mongolia
25L4 **Tuva Republic** Russian Federation
33G1 **Tuvalu** *Is* Pacific Ocean
45C4 **Tuwayīlel Hāj** *Mt* Jordan
70B2 **Tuxpan** Mexico
70C2 **Tuxpan** Mexico
70C3 **Tuxtla Gutiérrez** Mexico
15A1 **Túy** Spain
30D3 **Tuy Hoa** Vietnam
40B2 **Tuz Gölü** *Salt L* Turkey
41D3 **Tuz Khurmātū** Iraq
17D2 **Tuzla** Bosnia-Herzegovina
20F4 **Tver'** Russian Federation
8D4 **Tweed** *R* England/Scotland
34D1 **Tweed Heads** Australia
8D4 **Tweedsmuir Hills** Scotland
59C4 **Twentynine Palms** USA
55N5 **Twillingate** Canada
58D1 **Twin Bridges** USA
62B2 **Twin Buttes Res** USA
58D2 **Twin Falls** USA
35B2 **Twins,The** *Mt* New Zealand
66B3 **Twitchell Res** USA
64A1 **Two Harbors** USA
58D1 **Two Medicine** *R* USA
64B2 **Two Rivers** USA
25O4 **Tygda** Russian Federation
63C2 **Tyler** USA
26H1 **Tymovskoye** Russian Federation
26F1 **Tynda** Russian Federation
6D2 **Tyne** *R* England
6D2 **Tyne and Wear** *Metropolitan County* England
6D2 **Tynemouth** England
12G6 **Tynset** Norway
Tyr = Tyre
45C2 **Tyre** Lebanon
62A2 **Tyrone** New Mexico, USA
68A2 **Tyrone** Pennsylvania, USA
9C2 **Tyrone** *County* Northern Ireland
34B3 **Tyrrell,L** Australia
16C2 **Tyrrhenian S** Italy
21J7 **Tyuleni, Ova** *Is* Kazakhstan
24H4 **Tyumen'** Russian Federation
25O3 **Tyung** *R* Russian Federation
7B3 **Tywyn** Wales
47E1 **Tzaneen** South Africa
17E3 **Tzoumérka** *Mt* Greece

U

75D3 **Ubá** Brazil
75D2 **Ubaí** Brazil
75E1 **Ubaitaba** Brazil
50B3 **Ubangi** *R* Central African Republic/Congo/Zaïre
40D3 **Ubayyid, Wadi al** *Watercourse* Iraq
28B4 **Ube** Japan
15B2 **Ubeda** Spain
55N2 **Ubekendt Ejland** *I* Greenland
75C2 **Uberaba** Brazil
75A2 **Uberaba, Lagoa** Brazil
75C2 **Uberlândia** Brazil
30D2 **Ubon Ratchathani** Thailand
19F2 **Ubort** *R* Belarus
50C4 **Ubundu** Zaïre
72D5 **Ucayali** *R* Peru
42C3 **Uch** Pakistan
25P4 **Uchar** *R* Russian Federation
29E2 **Uchiura-wan** *B* Japan
13E1 **Uchte** Germany
58A1 **Ucluelet** Canada
25L4 **Uda** *R* Russian Federation
42C4 **Udaipur** India
43F3 **Udaipur Garhi** Nepal
12G7 **Uddevalla** Sweden
12H5 **Uddjaur** *L* Sweden
44B2 **Udgir** India
42D2 **Udhampur** India
16C1 **Udine** Italy
20J4 **Udmurt Republic** Russian Federation
30C2 **Udon Thani** Thailand
25P4 **Udskaya Guba** *B* Russian Federation
44A3 **Udupi** India
25N2 **Udzha** Russian Federation
29C3 **Ueda** Japan
50C3 **Uele** *R* Zaïre
25U3 **Uelen** Russian Federation
18C2 **Uelzen** Germany
50C3 **Uere** *R* Zaïre
20K5 **Ufa** Russian Federation
20K4 **Ufa** *R* Russian Federation
51B6 **Ugab** *R* Namibia
50D4 **Ugaila** *R* Tanzania
50D3 **Uganda** *Republic* Africa
45C3 **'Ugeiqa, Wadi** Jordan
26H2 **Uglegorsk** Russian Federation
20F4 **Uglich** Russian Federation
28C2 **Uglovoye** Russian Federation
20F5 **Ugra** *R* Russian Federation
8B3 **Uig** Scotland
51B4 **Uige** Angola
28A3 **Üijŏngbu** S Korea
21J6 **Uil** Kazakhstan
58D2 **Uinta Mts** USA
28A3 **Üiryŏng** S Korea
28A3 **Uisŏng** S Korea
47D3 **Uitenhage** South Africa
19E3 **Újfehértó** Hungary
29C4 **Uji** Japan
50C4 **Ujiji** Tanzania
74C2 **Ujina** Chile
42D4 **Ujjain** India
32A1 **Ujung Pandang** Indonesia
50D4 **Ukerewe I** Tanzania
43G3 **Ukhrul** India
20J3 **Ukhta** Russian Federation
59B3 **Ukiah** California, USA
58C1 **Ukiah** Oregon, USA
56A3 **Ukiah** USA
19E1 **Ukmerge** Lithuania
21D6 **Ukraine** *Republic* Europe
28A4 **Uku-jima** *I* Japan
26D2 **Ulaanbaatar** Mongolia
26C2 **Ulaangom** Mongolia
31C1 **Ulaan Uul** Mongolia
Ulan Bator = Ulaanbaatar
39G1 **Ulangar Hu** *L* China
26F2 **Ulanhot** China
26D1 **Ulan Ude** Russian Federation
26C3 **Ulan Ul Hu** *L* China
25O3 **Ul'beya** *R* Russian Federation
28B3 **Ulchin** S Korea
17D2 **Ulcinj** Montenegro, Yugoslavia
26E2 **Uldz** Mongolia
26C2 **Uliastay** Mongolia
27G5 **Ulithi** *I* Pacific Ocean
19F1 **Ulla** Belarus
34D3 **Ulladulla** Australia
8C3 **Ullapool** Scotland
12H5 **Ullsfjorden** *Inlet* Norway
6C2 **Ullswater** *L* England
28C3 **Ullung-do** *I* Japan
18C3 **Ulm** Germany
34A1 **Uloowaranie,L** Australia
28B3 **Ulsan** S Korea
9C2 **Ulster** *Region* Northern Ireland
24K5 **Ulungur He** *R* China
24K5 **Ulungur Hu** *L* China
8B3 **Ulva** *I* Scotland
6C2 **Ulverston** England
34C4 **Ulverstone** Australia
25Q4 **Ulya** *R* Russian Federation
19G3 **Ulyanovka** Ukraine
20H5 **Ul'yanovsk** Russian Federation
62B1 **Ulysses** USA
21E6 **Uman'** Ukraine
55N2 **Umanak** Greenland
43E4 **Umaria** India
42B3 **Umarkot** Pakistan
58C1 **Umatilla** USA
20E2 **Umba** Russian Federation
50D4 **Umba** *R* Kenya/Tanzania
32D1 **Umboi I** Papua New Guinea
12H6 **Ume** *R* Sweden
12J6 **Umea** Sweden
45C2 **Um ed Daraj, Jebel** *Mt* Jordan
45C4 **Um el Hashīm, Jebel** *Mt* Jordan
47E2 **Umfolozi** *R* South Africa
54C3 **Umiat** USA
45C4 **Um Ishrīn, Jebel** *Mt* Jordan
47E3 **Umkomaas** *R* South Africa
41G4 **Umm al Qaiwain** UAE
50C2 **Umm Bell** Sudan
50C2 **Umm Keddada** Sudan
40C4 **Umm Lajj** Saudi Arabia
50D2 **Umm Ruwaba** Sudan
41F5 **Umm Sa'id** Qatar
51C5 **Umniaiti** *R* Zimbabwe
58B2 **Umpqua** *R* USA
42D4 **Umred** India
Umtali = Mutare
47D3 **Umtata** South Africa
75B3 **Umuarama** Brazil
47D3 **Umzimkulu** South Africa
47E3 **Umzimkulu** *R* South Africa
47D3 **Umzimvubu** *R* South Africa
47D1 **Umzingwane** *R* Zimbabwe
75E2 **Una** Brazil
16D1 **Una** *R* Bosnia-Herzegovina/Croatia
68C1 **Unadilla** USA
68C1 **Unadilla** *R* USA
75C2 **Unaí** Brazil
54B3 **Unalakleet** USA
41D4 **Unayzah** Saudi Arabia
68D2 **Uncasville** USA
60B3 **Uncompahgre Plat** USA
47D2 **Underberg** South Africa
60C1 **Underwood** USA
20E5 **Unecha** Russian Federation
45C3 **Uneisa** Jordan
55M4 **Ungava B** Canada
28C2 **Unggi** N Korea
74F3 **União de Vitória** Brazil
63D1 **Union** Missouri, USA
67B2 **Union** S Carolina, USA
65D2 **Union City** Pennsylvania, USA
63E1 **Union City** Tennessee, USA
47C3 **Uniondale** South Africa
67A2 **Union Springs** USA
65D3 **Uniontown** USA
41F5 **United Arab Emirates** Arabian Pen
4E3 **United Kingdom of Gt Britain & N Ireland** NW Europe
53H4 **United States of America**
55K1 **United States Range** *Mts* Canada
58C2 **Unity** USA
62A2 **University Park** USA
13D2 **Unna** Germany
43E3 **Unnão** India
28A2 **Unsan** N Korea
8E1 **Unst** *I* Scotland
40C1 **Ünye** Turkey
20G4 **Unzha** *R* Russian Federation
72F2 **Upata** Venezuela
51C4 **Upemba Nat Pk** Zaïre
55N2 **Upernavik** Greenland
47C2 **Upington** South Africa
66D3 **Upland** USA
33H2 **Upolu** *I* Western Samoa
35C2 **Upper Hutt** New Zealand
58B2 **Upper Klamath L** USA
58B2 **Upper L** USA
9C2 **Upper Lough Erne** *L* Northern Ireland

69L1 **Upper Manzanilla** Trinidad
61E1 **Upper Red L** USA
68B3 **Upperville** USA
12H7 **Uppsala** Sweden
61E1 **Upsala** Canada
60C2 **Upton** USA
40D4 **'Uqlat as Suqūr** Saudi Arabia
72C2 **Uraba, Golfo de** Colombia
31B1 **Urad Qianqi** China
41E4 **Urairah** Saudi Arabia
29D2 **Urakawa** Japan
21J5 **Ural** *R* Kazakhstan
34D2 **Uralla** Australia
20M4 **Ural Mts** Russian Federation
21J5 **Ural'sk** Kazakhstan
24G4 **Ural'skiy Khrebet** *Mts* Russian Federation
75D1 **Urandi** Brazil
54H4 **Uranium City** Canada
27G8 **Urapunga** Australia
60B3 **Uravan** USA
29C3 **Urawa** Japan
20L3 **Uray** Russian Federation
64B2 **Urbana** Illinois, USA
64C2 **Urbana** Ohio, USA
16C2 **Urbino** Italy
15B1 **Urbion, Sierra de** *Mt* Spain
6C2 **Ure** *R* England
20H4 **Uren'** Russian Federation
38E1 **Urgench** Uzbekistan
24J3 **Urengoy** Russian Federation
42B2 **Urgun** Afghanistan
17F3 **Urla** Turkey
17E2 **Uroševac** Serbia, Yugoslavia
75C1 **Uruaçu** Brazil
70B3 **Uruapan** Mexico
75C2 **Urucuia** *R* Brazil
74E3 **Uruguaiana** Brazil
74E4 **Uruguay** *R* Argentina/ Uruguay
74E4 **Uruguay** *Republic* S America
41E2 **Urumīyeh** Iran
39G1 **Ürümqi** China
26J2 **Urup** *I* Kuril Is, Russian Federation
24J1 **Urup, Ostrov** *I* Russian Federation
42B2 **Uruzgan** Afghanistan
29D2 **Uryū-ko** *L* Japan
21G5 **Uryupinsk** Russian Federation
20J4 **Urzhum** Russian Federation
17F2 **Urziceni** Romania
39G1 **Usa** China
28B4 **Usa** Japan
20L2 **Usa** *R* Russian Federation
40A2 **Uşak** Turkey
47B1 **Usakos** Namibia
24J1 **Ushakova, Ostrov** *I* Russian Federation
50D4 **Ushashi** Tanzania
24J5 **Ush Tobe** Kazakhstan
74C8 **Ushuaia** Argentina
25O4 **Ushumun** Russian Federation
7C4 **Usk** *R* Wales
40A1 **Üsküdar** Turkey
20H3 **Usogorsk** Russian Federation
25M4 **Usolye Sibirskoye** Russian Federation
26G2 **Ussuri** *R* China/Russian Federation
28C2 **Ussuriysk** Russian Federation
25T3 **Ust'-Belaya** Russian Federation
25R4 **Ust'Bol'sheretsk** Russian Federation
16C3 **Ustica** *I* Sicily, Italy
18C2 **Ústi-nad-Laben** Czech Republic
24J4 **Ust'Ishim** Russian Federation
18D2 **Ustka** Poland
25S4 **Ust'Kamchatsk** Russian Federation
24K5 **Ust'-Kamenogorsk** Kazakhstan
20L2 **Ust' Kara** Russian Federation
25L4 **Ust Karabula** Russian Federation
20K5 **Ust' Katav** Russian Federation
25M4 **Ust'-Kut** Russian Federation
21F6 **Ust Labinsk** Russian Federation
25P3 **Ust'Maya** Russian Federation
20K3 **Ust' Nem** Russian Federation
25Q3 **Ust'Nera** Russian Federation
25O4 **Ust'Nyukzha** Russian Federation
25M4 **Ust'Ordynskiy** Russian Federation
20J2 **Ust' Tsil'ma** Russian Federation
25P4 **Ust-'Umal'tu** Russian Federation
20G3 **Ust'ya** *R* Russian Federation
20M2 **Ust' Yuribey** Russian Federation
21J7 **Ustyurt Plateau** *Plat* Kazakhstan
28B4 **Usuki** Japan
70C3 **Usumacinta** *R* Guatemala/Mexico
47E2 **Usutu** *R* Swaziland
28A4 **Usuyŏng** S Korea
19G1 **Usvyaty** Russian Federation
56B3 **Utah** *State* USA
59D2 **Utah L** USA
19F1 **Utena** Lithuania
42B3 **Uthal** Pakistan
68C1 **Utica** USA
15B2 **Utiel** Spain
18B2 **Utrecht** Netherlands
47E2 **Utrecht** South Africa
15A2 **Utrera** Spain
12K5 **Utsjoki** Finland
29D3 **Utsonomiya** Japan
30C2 **Uttaradit** Thailand
43E3 **Uttar Pradesh** *State* India
7D3 **Uttoxeter** England
12J6 **Uusikaupunki** Finland
62C3 **Uvalde** USA
24H4 **Uvat** Russian Federation
33F3 **Uvéa** *I* New Caledonia
50D4 **Uvinza** Tanzania
50C4 **Uvira** Zaïre
55N2 **Uvkusigssat** Greenland
26C1 **Uvs Nuur** *L* Mongolia
28C4 **Uwajima** Japan
50C1 **Uweinat, Jebel** *Mt* Sudan
31B2 **Uxin Qi** China
25Q3 **Uyandina** *R* Russian Federation
25L4 **Uyar** Russian Federation
72E8 **Uyuni** Bolivia
45B4 **Uyûn Mûsa** *Well* Egypt
38E1 **Uzbekistan** *Republic* Asia
14C2 **Uzerche** France
19F2 **Uzh** *R* Ukraine
17D2 **Užice** Serbia, Yugoslavia
19E3 **Uzhgorod** Ukraine
20F5 **Uzlovaya** Russian Federation
40A1 **Uzunköprü** Turkey

V

47C2 **Vaal** *R* South Africa
47D2 **Vaal Dam** *Res* South Africa
47D1 **Vaalwater** South Africa
12J6 **Vaasa** Finland
19D3 **Vác** Hungary
74F3 **Vacaria** Brazil
75B3 **Vacaria** *R* Mato Grosso do, Brazil
75D2 **Vacaria** *R* Minas Gerais, Brazil
59B3 **Vacaville** USA
42C4 **Vadodara** India
12K4 **Vadsø** Norway
16B1 **Vaduz** Liechtenstein
20G3 **Vaga** *R* Russian Federation
19D3 **Váh** *R* Slovakia
45C3 **Vahel** Israel
44B3 **Vaigai** *R* India
8E1 **Vaila, I** Scotland
33G1 **Vaitupu** *I* Tuvalu
74C6 **Valcheta** Argentina
20E4 **Valday** Russian Federation
20E4 **Valdayskaya Vozvyshennost'** *Upland* Russian Federation
72E2 **Val de la Pascua** Venezuela
15B2 **Valdepeñas** Spain
54D3 **Valdez** USA
74B5 **Valdivia** Chile
13B3 **Val d'Oise** *Department* France
65D1 **Val-d'Or** Canada
67B2 **Valdosta** USA
58C2 **Vale** USA
75E1 **Valença** Bahia, Brazil
75D3 **Valença** Rio de Janeiro, Brazil
14C3 **Valence** France
15B2 **Valencia** Spain
72E1 **Valencia** Venezuela
Valencia *Region* = **Comunidad Valenciana**
15A2 **Valencia de Alcantara** Spain
15C2 **Valencia, Golfo de** *G* Spain
13B2 **Valenciennes** France
60C2 **Valentine** Nebraska, USA
62B2 **Valentine** Texas, USA
6D2 **Vale of Pickering** England
6D2 **Vale of York** England
72D2 **Valera** Venezuela
12K7 **Valga** Russian Federation
7E3 **Valiant** *Oilfield* N Sea
17D2 **Valjevo** Serbia, Yugoslavia
12J6 **Valkeakoski** Finland
70D2 **Valladolid** Mexico
15B1 **Valladolid** Spain
69D5 **Valle de la Pascua** Venezuela
72D1 **Valledupar** Colombia
72F7 **Valle Grande** Bolivia
66A1 **Vallejo** USA
74B3 **Vallenar** Chile
75D1 **Valle Pequeno** Brazil
61D1 **Valley City** USA
58B2 **Valley Falls** USA
65E1 **Valleyfield** Canada
15C1 **Valls** Spain
19F1 **Valmiera** Latvia
14B2 **Valognes** France
75B3 **Valparaíso** Brazil
74B4 **Valparaíso** Chile
67A2 **Valparaiso** USA
47D2 **Vals** *R* South Africa
42C4 **Valsād** India
21F5 **Valuyki** Russian Federation
15A2 **Valverde del Camino** Spain
12J6 **Vammala** Finland
41D2 **Van** Turkey
25M3 **Vanavara** Russian Federation
63D1 **Van Buren** Arkansas, USA
65F1 **Van Buren** Maine, USA
13C3 **Vancouleurs** France
54F5 **Vancouver** Canada
58B1 **Vancouver** USA
54F5 **Vancouver I** Canada
64B3 **Vandalia** Illinois, USA
64C3 **Vandalia** Ohio, USA
54F4 **Vanderhoof** Canada
27G8 **Van Diemen,C** Australia
32C2 **Van Diemen G** Australia
12G7 **Vänern** *L* Sweden
12G7 **Vänersborg** Sweden
68B1 **Van Etten** USA
51E6 **Vangaindrano** Madagascar
40D2 **Van Gölü** *Salt L* Turkey
29C2 **Vangou** Russian Federation
30C2 **Vang Vieng** Laos
62B2 **Van Horn** USA
65D1 **Vanier** Canada
33F2 **Vanikoro** *I* Solomon Islands
26G2 **Vanino** Russian Federation
25U3 **Vankarem** Russian Federation
12H6 **Vännäs** Sweden
14B2 **Vannes** France
47B3 **Vanrhynsdorp** South Africa
55K3 **Vansittart I** Canada
33F2 **Vanua Lava** *I* Vanuatu
33G2 **Vanua Levu** *I* Fiji
37K5 **Vanuatu** *Is, Republic* Pacific Ocean
64C2 **Van Wert** USA
47C3 **Vanwyksvlei** South Africa
14D3 **Var** *R* France
41F2 **Varāmīn** Iran
43E3 **Vārānasi** India
20K2 **Varandey** Russian Federation
12K4 **Varangerfjord** *Inlet* Norway
12L4 **Varangerhalvøya** *Pen* Norway
16D1 **Varazdin** Croatia
12G7 **Varberg** Sweden
12F7 **Varde** Denmark
12L4 **Vardø** Norway
13E1 **Varel** Germany
19E2 **Varéna** Lithuania
16B1 **Varese** Italy
75C3 **Varginha** Brazil
12K6 **Varkaus** Finland
17F2 **Varna** Bulgaria
12G7 **Värnamo** Sweden
20K2 **Varnek** Russian Federation
67B2 **Varnville** USA
75D2 **Várzea da Palma** Brazil
20H3 **Vashka** *R* Russian Federation
21E5 **Vasil'kov** Ukraine
64C2 **Vassar** USA
12H7 **Västerås** Sweden
12H7 **Västervik** Sweden
16C2 **Vasto** Italy
16C2 **Vaticano, Citta del** Italy
12B2 **Vatnajökull** *Mts* Iceland
17F1 **Vatra Dornei** Romania
12G7 **Vättern** *L* Sweden
62A2 **Vaughn** USA
72D3 **Vaupés** *R* Colombia
33H2 **Vava'u Group** *Is* Tonga
44C4 **Vavuniya** Sri Lanka
12G7 **Växjö** Sweden
20K1 **Vaygach, Ostrov** *I* Russian Federation
13D1 **Vecht** *R* Germany/ Netherlands
13E1 **Vechta** Germany
13D1 **Veendam** Netherlands
62B1 **Vega** USA
12G5 **Vega** *I* Norway
15A2 **Vejer de la Frontera** Spain
12F7 **Vejle** Denmark
47B3 **Velddrif** South Africa
16D2 **Velebit** *Mts* Croatia
16D1 **Velenje** Slovenia
75D2 **Velhas** *R* Brazil
25T3 **Velikaya** *R* Russian Federation
19F1 **Velikaya** *R* Russian Federation
12K7 **Velikaya** *R* Russian Federation
20E4 **Velikiye Luki** Russian Federation
20H3 **Velikiy Ustyug** Russian Federation
17F2 **Veliko Tŭrnovo** Bulgaria
48A3 **Vélingara** Senegal
19G1 **Velizh** Russian Federation
33E1 **Vella Lavella** *I* Solomon Islands
44B3 **Vellore** India
13E2 **Velmerstat** *Mt* Germany
20G3 **Vel'sk** Russian Federation
13C1 **Veluwe** *Region* Netherlands
60C1 **Velva** USA
44B4 **Vembanad L** India
74D4 **Venado Tuerto** Argentina
75C3 **Vençeslau Braz** Brazil
13C3 **Vendeuvre-sur-Barse** France
14C2 **Vendôme** France
Venezia = **Venice**
16C1 **Venezia, G di** Italy
72E2 **Venezuela** *Republic* S America
69C4 **Venezuela,G de** Venezuela
44A2 **Vengurla** India
16C1 **Venice** Italy
44B3 **Venkatagiri** India
18B2 **Venlo** Netherlands
19E1 **Venta** *R* Latvia
47D2 **Ventersburg** South Africa
7D4 **Ventnor** England
19E1 **Ventspils** Latvia
72E3 **Ventuarí** *R* Venezuela
66C3 **Ventura** USA
20E3 **Vepsovskaya Vozvyshennost'** *Upland* Russian Federation
74D3 **Vera** Argentina
15B2 **Vera** Spain
70C3 **Veracruz** Mexico
75A4 **Verá, L** Paraguay
42C4 **Verāval** India
16B1 **Vercelli** Italy
75A1 **Vérde** *R* Brazil
75B2 **Verde** *R* Goias, Brazil
75B2 **Verde** *R* Mato Grosso do Sul, Brazil
59D4 **Verde** *R* USA
Verde,C = **Cap Vert**
75D2 **Verde Grande** *R* Brazil
13E1 **Verden** Germany
14D3 **Verdon** *R* France
13C3 **Verdun** France
47D2 **Vereeniging** South Africa
20J4 **Vereshchagino** Russian Federation
48A3 **Verga,C** Guinea
15A1 **Verin** Spain
25N4 **Verkh Angara** *R* Russian Federation
20K5 **Verkhneural'sk** Russian Federation
25O3 **Verkhnevilyuysk** Russian Federation
20H3 **Verkhnyaya Toyma** Russian Federation
25P3 **Verkhoyansk** Russian Federation
25O3 **Verkhoyanskiy Khrebet** *Mts* Russian Federation
25K3 **Verkneimbatskoye** Russian Federation
20H3 **Verkola** Russian Federation
75B2 **Vermelho** *R* Brazil
13B4 **Vermenton** France
54G4 **Vermilion** Canada
61E1 **Vermilion L** USA
61D2 **Vermillion** USA
57F2 **Vermont** *State* USA
58E2 **Vernal** USA
66B2 **Vernalis** USA
47C3 **Verneuk Pan** *Salt L* South Africa
54G4 **Vernon** Canada
62C2 **Vernon** USA
67B3 **Vero Beach** USA
17E2 **Véroia** Greece
16C1 **Verona** Italy
13B3 **Versailles** France
48A3 **Vert, Cap** *C* Senegal
47E2 **Verulam** South Africa
13C2 **Verviers** Belgium
13B3 **Vervins** France
19G3 **Veselinovo** Ukraine
13C3 **Vesle** *R* France
14D2 **Vesoul** France
12G5 **Vesterålen** *Is* Norway
12G5 **Vestfjorden** *Inlet* Norway
12A2 **Vestmannaeyjar** Iceland
16C2 **Vesuvio** *Vol* Italy
19D3 **Veszprém** Hungary
12H7 **Vetlanda** Sweden
20G4 **Vetluga** *R* Russian Federation
13B2 **Veurne** Belgium
16B1 **Vevey** Switzerland
13C3 **Vézelise** France
Viangchan = **Vientiane**
15A1 **Viana do Castelo** Portugal
16C2 **Viareggio** Italy
12F7 **Viborg** Denmark
16D3 **Vibo Valentia** Italy
Vic = **Vich**
76G2 **Vice-commodoro Marambio** *Base* Antarctica
16C1 **Vicenza** Italy
15C1 **Vich** Spain
72E3 **Vichada** *R* Colombia/ Venezuela
20G4 **Vichuga** Russian Federation
14C2 **Vichy** France
63D2 **Vicksburg** USA
75D3 **Vicosa** Brazil
32C4 **Victor Harbor** Australia
63C3 **Victoria** USA
32C2 **Victoria** *R* Australia
34B3 **Victoria** *State* Australia
69B2 **Victoria de las Tunas** Cuba
51C5 **Victoria Falls** Zambia/ Zimbabwe
54G2 **Victoria I** Canada
34B2 **Victoria,L** Australia
50D4 **Victoria,L** C Africa
76F7 **Victoria Land** *Region* Antarctica
43G4 **Victoria,Mt** Burma
27H7 **Victoria,Mt** Papua New Guinea
50D3 **Victoria Nile** *R* Uganda
35B2 **Victoria Range** *Mts* New Zealand
32C2 **Victoria River Downs** Australia
54H3 **Victoria Str** Canada
65E1 **Victoriaville** Canada
47C3 **Victoria West** South Africa
59C4 **Victorville** USA
67B2 **Vidalia** USA
17F2 **Videle** Romania
17E2 **Vidin** Bulgaria
42D4 **Vidisha** India
19F1 **Vidzy** Belarus
74D6 **Viedma** Argentina
74B7 **Viedma, Lago** Argentina
69A4 **Viejo** Costa Rica
Vielha = **Viella**
15C1 **Viella** Spain
18D3 **Vienna** Austria
64B3 **Vienna** Illinois, USA
64C3 **Vienna** W Virginia, USA
14C2 **Vienne** France
14C2 **Vienne** *R* France
30C2 **Vientiane** Laos
14C2 **Vierzon** France
16D2 **Vieste** Italy
27D5 **Vietnam** *Republic* SE Asia
30D1 **Vietri** Vietnam
69P2 **Vieux Fort** St Lucia
27F5 **Vigan** Philippines
14B3 **Vignemale** *Mt* France/ Spain
15A1 **Vigo** Spain
44C2 **Vijayawāda** India
17D2 **Vijosë** *R* Albania
17E2 **Vikhren** *Mt* Bulgaria
12G6 **Vikna** *I* Norway
51D5 **Vila da Maganja** Mozambique
51D5 **Vila Machado** Mozambique
51D6 **Vilanculos** Mozambique
Vilanova i la Geltrú = **Villanueva-y-Geltrú**
15A1 **Vila Real** Portugal
51D5 **Vila Vasco da Gama** Mozambique
75D3 **Vila Velha** Brazil

19F2 **Vileyka** Belarus
12H6 **Vilhelmina** Sweden
73G6 **Vilhena** Brazil
19F2 **Viliya** Belarus
20D4 **Viljandi** Estonia
47D2 **Viljoenskroon** South Africa
25L2 **Vilkitskogo, Proliv** *Str* Russian Federation
19F3 **Vilkovo** Ukraine
62A2 **Villa Ahumada** Mexico
15A1 **Villaba** Spain
16C1 **Villach** Austria
74C4 **Villa Dolores** Argentina
74E5 **Villa Gesell** Argentina
75A4 **Villa Hayes** Paraguay
70C3 **Villahermosa** Mexico
74D4 **Villa Huidobro** Argentina
74D4 **Villa María** Argentina
72F8 **Villa Montes** Bolivia
15A1 **Villa Nova de Gaia** Portugal
15A2 **Villanueva de la Serena** Spain
15C1 **Villanueva-y-Geltrú** Spain
15B2 **Villarreal** Spain
74E3 **Villarrica** Paraguay
15B2 **Villarrobledo** Spain
62B3 **Villa Unión** Coahuila, Mexico
72D3 **Villavicencio** Colombia
14C2 **Villefranche** France
55L5 **Ville-Marie** Canada
15B2 **Villena** Spain
13B3 **Villeneuve-St-Georges** France
14C3 **Villeneuve-sur-Lot** France
13B3 **Villeneuve-sur-Yonne** France
63D2 **Ville Platte** USA
13B3 **Villers-Cotterêts** France
14C2 **Villeurbanne** France
47D2 **Villiers** South Africa
13E3 **Villingen-Schwenningen** Germany
44B3 **Villupuram** India
19F2 **Vilnius** Lithuania
25N3 **Vilyuy** *R* Russian Federation
25O3 **Vilyuysk** Russian Federation
15C1 **Vinaroz** Spain
64B3 **Vincennes** USA
12H5 **Vindel** *R* Sweden
42D4 **Vindhya Range** *Mts* India
68C3 **Vineland** USA
68E2 **Vineyard Haven** USA
30D2 **Vinh** Vietnam
30D3 **Vinh Cam Ranh** *B* Vietnam
30D4 **Vinh Loi** Vietnam
30D3 **Vinh Long** Vietnam
63C1 **Vinita** USA
17D1 **Vinkovci** Croatia
19F3 **Vinnitsa** Ukraine
76F3 **Vinson Massif** *Upland* Antarctica
61E2 **Vinton** USA
74B4 **Viõna del Mar** Chile
51B5 **Virei** Angola
75D2 **Virgem da Lapa** Brazil
59D3 **Virgin** *R* USA
47D2 **Virginia** South Africa
61E1 **Virginia** USA
57F3 **Virginia** *State* USA
65D3 **Virginia Beach** USA
59C3 **Virginia City** USA
69E3 **Virgin Is** Caribbean Sea
64A2 **Viroqua** USA
16D1 **Virovitica** Croatia
13C3 **Virton** Belgium
44B4 **Virudunagar** India
16D2 **Vis** *I* Croatia
66C2 **Visalia** USA
12H7 **Visby** Sweden
54H2 **Viscount Melville Sd** Canada
17D2 **Višegrad** Bosnia-Herzegovina
15A1 **Viseu** Portugal
44C2 **Vishākhapatnam** India
20K3 **Vishera** *R* Russian Federation
16B2 **Viso, Monte** *Mt* Italy
59C4 **Vista** USA
Vistula *R* = **Wisla**
44A2 **Vite** India
19G1 **Vitebsk** Belarus
16C2 **Viterbo** Italy
15A1 **Vitigudino** Spain
25N4 **Vitim** *R* Russian Federation
73K8 **Vitória** Brazil
15B1 **Vitoria** Spain
73K6 **Vitória da Conquista** Brazil
14B2 **Vitré** France
13C3 **Vitry-le-François** France
12J5 **Vittangi** Sweden
13C3 **Vittel** France
16C3 **Vittoria** Sicily, Italy
26J2 **Vityaz Depth** Pacific Ocean
Viviero = **Vivero**
15A1 **Vivero** Spain
25L3 **Vivi** *R* Russian Federation
15B1 **Vizcaya, Golfo de** Spain
25M4 **Vizhne-Angarsk** Russian Federation
44C2 **Vizianagaram** India
20J3 **Vizinga** Russian Federation
17E1 **Vlădeasa** *Mt* Romania
21G7 **Vladikavkaz** Russian Federation
20G4 **Vladimir** Russian Federation
19E2 **Vladimir Volynskiy** Ukraine
28C2 **Vladivostok** Russian Federation
18A2 **Vlieland** *I* Netherlands
13B2 **Vlissingen** Netherlands
47B2 **Vloosdrift** South Africa
17D2 **Vlorë** Albania
18C3 **Vltara** *R* Czech Republic
18C3 **Vöcklabruck** Austria
30D3 **Voeune Sai** Cambodia
13E2 **Vogelsberg** *Region* Germany
Vohemar = **Vohimarina**
Vohibinany = **Ampasimanolotra**
51F5 **Vohimarina** Madagascar
50D4 **Voi** Kenya
48B4 **Voinjama** Liberia
14D2 **Voiron** France
17D1 **Vojvodina** *Region* Serbia, Yugoslavia
60B1 **Volborg** USA
69A5 **Volcán Barú** *Mt* Panama
Volcano Is = **Kazan Retto**
20K4 **Volchansk** Russian Federation
21H6 **Volga** *R* Russian Federation
21G6 **Volgodonsk** Russian Federation
21G6 **Volgograd** Russian Federation
21H5 **Volgogradskoye Vodokhranilishche** *Res* Russian Federation
20E4 **Volkhov** Russian Federation
20E4 **Volkhov** *R* Russian Federation
19E2 **Volkovysk** Belarus
47D2 **Volksrust** South Africa
25L2 **Volochanka** Russian Federation
20G4 **Vologda** Russian Federation
17E3 **Vólos** Greece
21H5 **Vol'sk** Russian Federation
66B2 **Volta** USA
48B3 **Volta Blanche** *R* Burkina/Ghana
48B4 **Volta, L** Ghana
48B3 **Volta Noire** *R* W Africa
75D3 **Volta Redonda** Brazil
48B3 **Volta Rouge** *R* Burkina/Ghana
21G6 **Volzhskiy** Russian Federation
20F3 **Vonguda** Russian Federation
55R3 **Vopnafjörður** Iceland
18C1 **Vordingborg** Denmark
21C8 **Voriái** *I* Greece
20L2 **Vorkuta** Russian Federation
12G6 **Vorma** *R* Norway
21F5 **Voronezh** Russian Federation
12M5 **Voron'ya** *R* Russian Federation
21F6 **Voroshilovgrad** Ukraine
12K7 **Võru** Estonia
13D3 **Vosges** *Department* France
14D2 **Vosges** *Mts* France
12F6 **Voss** Norway
25L4 **Vostochnyy Sayan** *Mts* Russian Federation
76F9 **Vostok** *Base* Antarctica
20J4 **Votkinsk** Russian Federation
13C3 **Vouziers** France
61E1 **Voyageurs Nat Pk** USA
20K3 **Voy Vozh** Russian Federation
21E6 **Voznesensk** Ukraine
17E2 **Vranje** Serbia, Yugoslavia
17E2 **Vratsa** Bulgaria
17D1 **Vrbas** Serbia, Yugoslavia
16D2 **Vrbas** *R* Bosnia-Herzegovina
16C1 **Vrbovsko** Croatia
47D2 **Vrede** South Africa
47B3 **Vredendal** South Africa
73G2 **Vreed en Hoop** Guyana
44B3 **Vriddhāchalam** India
17E1 **Vršac** Serbia, Yugoslavia
16D2 **Vrtoče** Bosnia-Herzegovina
47C2 **Vryburg** South Africa
47E2 **Vryheid** South Africa
17D1 **Vukovar** Croatia
20K3 **Vuktyl'** Russian Federation
7F3 **Vulcan** *Oilfield* N Sea
16C3 **Vulcano** *I* Italy
30D3 **Vung Tau** Vietnam
12J5 **Vuollerim** Sweden
20E3 **Vyartsilya** Russian Federation
20J4 **Vyatka** *R* Russian Federation
26G2 **Vyazemskiy** Russian Federation
20E4 **Vyaz'ma** Russian Federation
20G4 **Vyazniki** Russian Federation
20D3 **Vyborg** Russian Federation
20F3 **Vygozero, Ozero** *L* Russian Federation
20J3 **Vym** *R* Russian Federation
7C3 **Vyrnwy** *R* Wales
20E4 **Vyshniy-Volochek** Russian Federation
18D3 **Vyškov** Czech Republic
20F3 **Vytegra** Russian Federation

W

48B3 **Wa** Ghana
13C2 **Waal** *R* Netherlands
54G4 **Wabasca** *R* Canada
64B2 **Wabash** USA
64B3 **Wabash** *R* USA
64C1 **Wabatongushi L** Canada
54J4 **Wabowden** Canada
55M4 **Wabush** Canada
67B3 **Waccasassa B** USA
68E1 **Wachusett Res** USA
63C2 **Waco** USA
42B3 **Wad** Pakistan
49D2 **Waddān** Libya
13C1 **Waddenzee** *S* Netherlands
54F4 **Waddington,Mt** Canada
7B4 **Wadebridge** England
61D1 **Wadena** USA
45C3 **Wadi es Sir** Jordan
50D1 **Wadi Halfa** Sudan
45C3 **Wādi Mūsā** Jordan
50D2 **Wad Medani** Sudan
28A3 **Waegwan** S Korea
28A2 **Wafang** China
41E4 **Wafra** Kuwait
13C2 **Wageningen** Netherlands
55K3 **Wager B** Canada
55J3 **Wager Bay** Canada
34C3 **Wagga Wagga** Australia
32A4 **Wagin** Australia
61D2 **Wagner** USA
66E5 **Wahiawa** Hawaiian Islands
61D2 **Wahoo** USA
61D1 **Wahpeton** USA
44A2 **Wai** India
66E5 **Waialua** Hawaiian Islands
35B2 **Waiau** New Zealand
35B2 **Waiau** *R* New Zealand
27G6 **Waigeo** *I* Indonesia
35C1 **Waihi** New Zealand
35C1 **Waikaremoana,L** New Zealand
35C1 **Waikato** *R* New Zealand
34A2 **Waikerie** Australia
35B3 **Waikouaiti** New Zealand
66E5 **Wailuku** Hawaiian Islands
35B2 **Waimakariri** *R* New Zealand
35B2 **Waimate** New Zealand
66E5 **Waimea** Hawaiian Islands
32B1 **Waingapu** Indonesia
54G4 **Wainwright** Canada
54B2 **Wainwright** USA
35C1 **Waioura** New Zealand
35B2 **Waipara** New Zealand
35C2 **Waipukurau** New Zealand
35C2 **Wairarapa,L** New Zealand
35B2 **Wairau** *R* New Zealand
35C1 **Wairoa** New Zealand
35C1 **Wairoa** *R* New Zealand
35B2 **Waitaki** *R* New Zealand
35B1 **Waitara** New Zealand
35C1 **Waitomo** New Zealand
35B1 **Waiuku** New Zealand
29C3 **Wajima** Japan
50E3 **Wajir** Kenya
29C3 **Wakasa-wan** *B* Japan
35A3 **Wakatipu,L** New Zealand
29D4 **Wakayama** Japan
60D3 **Wa Keeney** USA
7D3 **Wakefield** England
69H1 **Wakefield** Jamaica
64B1 **Wakefield** Michigan, USA
68E2 **Wakefield** Rhode Island, USA
30B2 **Wakema** Burma
29E1 **Wakkanai** Japan
34B3 **Wakool** *R* Australia
18D2 **Wałbrzych** Poland
34D2 **Walcha** Australia
18D2 **Wałcz** Poland
13D2 **Waldbröl** Germany
68C2 **Walden** USA
13E4 **Waldshut** Germany
54B3 **Wales** USA
7C3 **Wales** *Principality* U K
55K3 **Wales I** Canada
34C2 **Walgett** Australia
76F4 **Walgreen Coast** *Region* Antarctica
50C4 **Walikale** Zaïre
61E1 **Walker** USA
66C1 **Walker L** USA
66C3 **Walker Pass** USA
64C2 **Walkerton** Canada
60C2 **Wall** USA
58C1 **Wallace** USA
32C4 **Wallaroo** Australia
34C3 **Walla Walla** Australia
58C1 **Walla Walla** USA
68D2 **Wallingford** USA
37K5 **Wallis and Futuna** *Is* Pacific Ocean
33H2 **Wallis, Îles** Pacific Ocean
58C1 **Wallowa** USA
58C1 **Wallowa Mts** USA
34C1 **Wallumbilla** Australia
6C2 **Walney** *I* England
63D1 **Walnut Ridge** USA
68D1 **Walpole** USA
7D3 **Walsall** England
62B1 **Walsenburg** USA
67B2 **Walterboro** USA
67A2 **Walter F George Res** USA
62C2 **Walters** USA
68E1 **Waltham** USA
68C1 **Walton** USA
7E4 **Walton-on-the Naze** England
47A1 **Walvis Bay** Namibia
52J6 **Walvis Ridge** Atlantic Ocean
48C4 **Wamba** Nigeria
50B4 **Wamba** *R* Zaïre
61D3 **Wamego** USA
58E2 **Wamsutter** USA
42B2 **Wana** Pakistan
34B1 **Wanaaring** Australia
35A2 **Wanaka** New Zealand
35A2 **Wanaka,L** New Zealand
64C1 **Wanapitei L** Canada
28A4 **Wando** S Korea
34C1 **Wandoan** Australia
34B3 **Wanganella** Australia
35B1 **Wanganui** New Zealand
35C1 **Wanganui** *R* New Zealand
34C3 **Wangaratta** Australia
13D1 **Wangerooge** *I* Germany
28B2 **Wangqing** China
28A3 **Wanjialing** China
Wankie = **Hwange**
50E3 **Wanleweyne** Somalia
30E2 **Wanning** China
44B2 **Wanparti** India
6D2 **Wansbeck, R** England
7D4 **Wantage** England
31B3 **Wanxian** China
31B3 **Wanyuan** China
63D1 **Wappapello,L** USA
68D2 **Wappingers Falls** USA
61E2 **Wapsipinicon** *R* USA
44B2 **Warangal** India
34C4 **Waratah** Australia
34C3 **Waratah B** Australia
13E2 **Warburg** Germany
34C3 **Warburton** Australia
34C1 **Ward** *R* Australia
47D2 **Warden** South Africa
42D4 **Wardha** India
35A3 **Ward,Mt** New Zealand
54F4 **Ware** Canada
68D1 **Ware** USA
7C4 **Wareham** England
68E2 **Wareham** USA
13D2 **Warendorf** Germany
34D1 **Warialda** Australia
30D2 **Warin Chamrap** Thailand
47B2 **Warmbad** Namibia
51C6 **Warmbad** South Africa
7C4 **Warminster** England
68C2 **Warminster** USA
59C3 **Warm Springs** USA
18C2 **Warnemünde** Germany
58B2 **Warner Mts** USA
67B2 **Warner Robins** USA
34B3 **Warracknabeal** Australia
32D3 **Warrego** *R* Australia
63D2 **Warren** Arkansas, USA
34C2 **Warren** Australia
61D1 **Warren** Minnesota, USA
64C2 **Warren** Ohio, USA
65D2 **Warren** Pennsylvania, USA
68E2 **Warren** Rhode Island, USA
9C2 **Warrenpoint** Northern Ireland
61E3 **Warrensburg** USA
47C2 **Warrenton** South Africa
65D3 **Warrenton** USA
48C4 **Warri** Nigeria
7C3 **Warrington** England
63E2 **Warrington** USA
34B3 **Warrnambool** Australia
61D1 **Warroad** USA
19E2 **Warsaw** Poland
68A1 **Warsaw** USA
50E3 **Warshiikh** Somalia
Warszawa = **Warsaw**
19D2 **Warta** *R* Poland
34D1 **Warwick** Australia
7D3 **Warwick** England
68C2 **Warwick** New York, USA
68E2 **Warwick** Rhode Island, USA
7D3 **Warwick** *County* England
59D3 **Wasatch Range** *Mts* USA
47E2 **Wasbank** South Africa
66C3 **Wasco** USA
61E2 **Waseca** USA
64A1 **Washburn** USA
54H2 **Washburn L** Canada
58D2 **Washburn,Mt** USA
42D4 **Wāshīm** India
57F3 **Washington** District of Columbia, USA
67B2 **Washington** Georgia, USA
64B3 **Washington** Indiana, USA
61E2 **Washington** Iowa, USA
61E3 **Washington** Missouri, USA
67C1 **Washington** N Carolina, USA
68C2 **Washington** New Jersey, USA
64C2 **Washington** Pennsylvania, USA
59D3 **Washington** Utah, USA
56A2 **Washington** *State* USA
64C3 **Washington Court House** USA
55M1 **Washington Land** *Region* Canada
65E2 **Washington,Mt** USA
62C1 **Washita** *R* USA
7E3 **Wash,The** *B* England
42A3 **Washuk** Pakistan
51L4 **Waskaganish** Canada
69A4 **Waspán** Nicaragua
66C1 **Wassuk Range** *Mts* USA
13C3 **Wassy** France
27F7 **Watampone** Indonesia
47D3 **Waterberge** *Mts* South Africa
68D2 **Waterbury** USA
10B3 **Waterford** Irish Republic
9C3 **Waterford** *County* Irish Republic
9C3 **Waterford Harbour** Irish Republic
13C2 **Waterloo** Belgium
61E2 **Waterloo** USA
64B1 **Watersmeet** USA
58D1 **Waterton-Glacier International Peace Park** USA
65D2 **Watertown** New York, USA
61D2 **Watertown** S Dakota, USA
64B2 **Watertown** Wisconsin, USA
47E2 **Waterval-Boven** South Africa
65F2 **Waterville** Maine, USA
68C1 **Waterville** New York, USA
68D1 **Watervliet** USA
54G4 **Waterways** Canada
7D4 **Watford** England
60C1 **Watford City** USA
68B1 **Watkins Glen** USA
62C1 **Watonga** USA
56C1 **Watrous** Canada
62B1 **Watrous** USA
50C3 **Watsa** Zaïre
54F3 **Watson Lake** Canada
66B2 **Watsonville** USA
27H7 **Wau** Papua New Guinea
50C3 **Wau** Sudan
34D2 **Wauchope** Australia
67B3 **Wauchula** USA
64B2 **Waukegan** USA
64B2 **Waukesha** USA
64B2 **Waupaca** USA
64B2 **Waupun** USA
63C2 **Waurika** USA
64B2 **Wausau** USA
64B2 **Wauwatosa** USA
32C2 **Wave Hill** Australia
7E3 **Waveney** *R* England
60E2 **Waverly** Iowa, USA
68B1 **Waverly** New York, USA
64C3 **Waverly** Ohio, USA
13C2 **Wavre** Belgium
64C1 **Wawa** Canada
49D2 **Wāw Al Kabīr** Libya
49D2 **Wāw an Nāmūs** *Well* Libya

66C2 **Wawona** USA
63C2 **Waxahachie** USA
67B2 **Waycross** USA
61D2 **Wayne** USA
67B2 **Waynesboro** Georgia, USA
63E2 **Waynesboro** Mississippi, USA
68B3 **Waynesboro** Pennsylvania, USA
65D3 **Waynesboro** Virginia, USA
63D1 **Waynesville** Missouri, USA
67B1 **Waynesville** N Carolina, USA
42B2 **Wazi Khwa** Afghanistan
8E1 **W Burra** *I* Scotland
7E4 **Weald,The** *Upland* England
6C2 **Wear** *R* England
62C1 **Weatherford** Oklahoma, USA
63C2 **Weatherford** Texas, USA
58B2 **Weaverville** USA
64C1 **Webbwood** Canada
68B1 **Webster** New York, USA
61D1 **Webster** S Dakota, USA
68E1 **Webster** USA
61E2 **Webster City** Massachusetts, USA
64A3 **Webster Groves** USA
74D8 **Weddell** *I* Falkland Islands
76G2 **Weddell Sea** Antarctica
58B2 **Weed** USA
68A2 **Weedville** USA
47E2 **Weenen** South Africa
34C2 **Wee Waa** Australia
31D1 **Weichang** China
18C3 **Weiden** Germany
31D2 **Weifang** China
31E2 **Weihai** China
31C3 **Wei He** *R* Henan, China
31C2 **Wei He** *R* Shaanxi, China
34C1 **Weilmoringle** Australia
13E3 **Weinheim** Germany
31A4 **Weining** China
32D2 **Weipa** Australia
64C2 **Weirton** USA
58C2 **Weiser** USA
31D3 **Weishan Hu** *L* China
18C2 **Weissenfels** Germany
67A2 **Weiss L** USA
64C3 **Welch** USA
50E3 **Weldiya** Ethiopia
66C3 **Weldon** USA
47D2 **Welkom** South Africa
65D2 **Welland** Canada
7D3 **Welland** *R* England
32C2 **Wellesley Is** Australia
68E2 **Wellfleet** USA
7D3 **Wellingborough** England
34C2 **Wellington** Australia
60C2 **Wellington** Colorado, USA
7C4 **Wellington** England
63C1 **Wellington** Kansas, USA
66C1 **Wellington** Nevada, USA
35B2 **Wellington** New Zealand
47B3 **Wellington** South Africa
62B2 **Wellington** Texas, USA
55J2 **Wellington Chan** Canada
74B7 **Wellington, Isla** Chile
7C4 **Wells** England
58D2 **Wells** Nevada, USA
68C1 **Wells** New York, USA
68B2 **Wellsboro** USA
35B1 **Wellsford** New Zealand
32B3 **Wells,L** Australia
7E3 **Wells-next-the-Sea** England
68B1 **Wellsville** USA
18C3 **Wels** Austria
7C3 **Welshpool** Wales
7D4 **Welwyn Garden City** England
55L4 **Wemindji** Canada
58B1 **Wenatchee** USA
58C1 **Wenatchee** *R* USA
48B4 **Wenchi** Ghana
31E2 **Wendeng** China
58D2 **Wendover** USA
31E4 **Wenling** China
31A5 **Wenshan** China
6D2 **Wensleydale** England
7E3 **Wensum** *R* England
34B2 **Wentworth** Australia
31A3 **Wen Xian** China
31E4 **Wenzhou** China
31C4 **Wenzhu** China
47D2 **Wepener** South Africa
47C2 **Werda** Botswana
50E3 **Werder** Ethiopia
18C2 **Werra** *R* Germany
34D2 **Werris Creek** Australia
13D2 **Wesel** Germany
18B2 **Weser** *R* Germany
60C3 **Weskan** USA
63C3 **Weslaco** USA
55N5 **Wesleyville** Canada
32C2 **Wessel Is** Australia
60D2 **Wessington Springs** USA
64B2 **West Allis** USA
36F5 **West Australian Basin** Indian Ocean
36F6 **West Australian Ridge** Indian Ocean
63E3 **West B** USA
43F4 **West Bengal** *State* India
68C1 **West Branch Delaware** *R* USA
68A2 **West Branch Susquehanna** *R* USA
7D3 **West Bromwich** England
65E2 **Westbrook** USA
64A2 **Westby** USA
68C3 **West Chester** USA
67C3 **West End** Bahamas
66D3 **Westend** USA
13D2 **Westerburg** Germany
18B2 **Westerland** Germany
68E2 **Westerly** USA
32B3 **Western Australia** *State* Australia
51B7 **Western Cape** *Province* South Africa
44A2 **Western Ghats** *Mts* India
8B3 **Western Isles** *Region* Scotland
48A2 **Western Sahara** *Region* Morocco
33H2 **Western Samoa** *Is* Pacific Ocean
13B2 **Westerschelde** *Estuary* Netherlands
13D1 **Westerstede** Germany
13D2 **Westerwald** *Region* Germany
14D1 **Westfalen** *Region* Germany
74D8 **West Falkland** *Is* Falkland Islands
68D1 **Westfield** Massachusetts, USA
65D2 **Westfield** New York, USA
68B2 **Westfield** Pennsylvania, USA
64B3 **West Frankfort** USA
34C1 **Westgate** Australia
7C4 **West Glamorgan** *County* Wales
65F1 **West Grand L** USA
52E3 **West Indies** *Is* Caribbean Sea
64C3 **West Liberty** USA
64C2 **West Lorne** Canada
9C3 **Westmeath** *County* Irish Republic
63D1 **West Memphis** USA
7D3 **West Midlands** *County* England
7D4 **Westminster** England
68B3 **Westminster** Maryland, USA
67B2 **Westminster** S Carolina, USA
47D1 **West Nicholson** Zimbabwe
27E6 **Weston** Malaysia
64C3 **Weston** USA
7C4 **Weston-super-Mare** England
67B3 **West Palm Beach** USA
63D1 **West Plains** USA
66B1 **West Point** California, USA
63E2 **West Point** Mississippi, USA
61D2 **West Point** Nebraska, USA
68D2 **West Point** New York, USA
35B2 **Westport** New Zealand
10C2 **Westray** *I* Scotland
6E3 **West Sole** *Oilfield* N Sea
57E3 **West Virginia** *State* USA
66C1 **West Walker** *R* USA
34C2 **West Wyalong** Australia
58D2 **West Yellowstone** USA
7D3 **West Yorkshire** *County* England
27F7 **Wetar** *I* Indonesia
54G4 **Wetaskiwin** Canada
50D4 **Wete** Tanzania
13E2 **Wetter** *R* Germany
13E2 **Wetzlar** Germany
Wevok = Lisburne, Cape
32D1 **Wewak** Papua New Guinea
63C1 **Wewoka** USA
9C3 **Wexford** Irish Republic
9C3 **Wexford** *County* Irish Republic
7D4 **Weybridge** England
54H5 **Weyburn** Canada
7C4 **Weymouth** England
68E1 **Weymouth** USA
35C1 **Whakatane** New Zealand
35C1 **Whakatane** *R* New Zealand
8E1 **Whalsay** *I* Scotland
35B1 **Whangarei** New Zealand
6D3 **Wharfe** *R* England
63C3 **Wharton** USA
60B2 **Wheatland** USA
68B3 **Wheaton** Maryland, USA
61D1 **Wheaton** Minnesota, USA
59D3 **Wheeler Peak** *Mt* Nevada, USA
62A1 **Wheeler Peak** *Mt* New Mexico, USA
66C3 **Wheeler Ridge** USA
64C2 **Wheeling** USA
65D2 **Whitby** Canada
6D2 **Whitby** England
7C3 **Whitchurch** England
63D1 **White** *R* Arkansas, USA
60B2 **White** *R* Colorado, USA
64B3 **White** *R* Indiana, USA
60C2 **White** *R* S Dakota, USA
55N4 **White B** Canada
60C1 **White Butte** *Mt* USA
34B2 **White Cliffs** Australia
10C2 **White Coomb** *Mt* Scotland
58D1 **Whitefish** USA
64B1 **Whitefish Pt** USA
55M4 **Whitegull L** Canada
65E2 **Whitehall** New York, USA
68C2 **Whitehall** Pennsylvania, USA
64A2 **Whitehall** Wisconsin, USA
6C2 **Whitehaven** England
54E3 **Whitehorse** Canada
35C1 **White I** New Zealand
63D3 **White L** USA
34C4 **Whitemark** Australia
59C3 **White Mountain Peak** *Mt* USA
66C2 **White Mts** California, USA
65E2 **White Mts** New Hampshire, USA
50D2 **White Nile** *R* Sudan
68D2 **White Plains** USA
55K5 **White River** Canada
60C2 **White River** USA
65E2 **White River Junction** USA
White Russia = Belarus
58B1 **White Salmon** USA
20F2 **White Sea** Russian Federation
58D1 **White Sulphur Springs** USA
67C2 **Whiteville** USA
48B4 **White Volta** W Africa
64B2 **Whitewater** USA
8C4 **Whithorn** Scotland
67B2 **Whitmire** USA
66C2 **Whitney,Mt** USA
66C4 **Whittier** California, USA
7D3 **Whittlesey** England
54H3 **Wholdaia** Canada
32C4 **Whyalla** Australia
64C2 **Wiarton** Canada
8B3 **Wiay, I** Scotland
60C1 **Wibaux** USA
63C1 **Wichita** USA
62C2 **Wichita** *R* USA
62C2 **Wichita Falls** USA
62C2 **Wichita Mts** USA
8D2 **Wick** Scotland
59D4 **Wickenburg** USA
9C3 **Wicklow** Irish Republic
9C3 **Wicklow** *County* Irish Republic
9C3 **Wicklow Hd** *Pt* Irish Republic
9C3 **Wicklow Mts** Irish Republic
34C1 **Widgeegoara** *R* Australia
7C3 **Widnes** England
13D2 **Wied** *R* Germany
19D2 **Wielun** Poland
Wien = Vienna
18D3 **Wiener Neustadt** Austria
19E2 **Wieprz** *R* Poland
13E2 **Wiesbaden** Germany
13D4 **Wiese** *R* Germany
7C3 **Wigan** England
63E2 **Wiggins** USA
7D4 **Wight, I of** *County* England
6C2 **Wigton** England
8C4 **Wigtown** Scotland
8C4 **Wigtown B** Scotland
58C1 **Wilbur** USA
34B2 **Wilcannia** Australia
59C3 **Wildcat Peak** *Mt* USA
13E1 **Wildeshausen** Germany
16C1 **Wildspitze** *Mt* Austria
67B3 **Wildwood** Florida, USA
68C3 **Wildwood** New Jersey, USA
62B1 **Wiley** USA
47D2 **Wilge** *R* South Africa
32D1 **Wilhelm,Mt** Papua New Guinea
18B2 **Wilhelmshaven** Germany
68C2 **Wilkes-Barre** USA
76F8 **Wilkes Land** *Region* Antarctica
58B2 **Willamette** *R* USA
34B2 **Willandra** *R* Australia
58B1 **Willapa B** USA
59E4 **Willcox** USA
69D4 **Willemstad** Curaçao
34B3 **William,Mt** Australia
59D3 **Williams** Arizona, USA
59B3 **Williams** California, USA
65D3 **Williamsburg** USA
54F4 **Williams Lake** Canada
64C3 **Williamson** USA
68B2 **Williamsport** USA
67C1 **Williamston** USA
68D1 **Williamstown** Massachusetts, USA
64C3 **Williamstown** W Virginia, USA
68D2 **Willimantic** USA
68C2 **Willingboro** USA
32E2 **Willis Group** *Is* Australia
67B3 **Williston** Florida, USA
60C1 **Williston** N Dakota, USA
47C3 **Williston** South Africa
61D1 **Willmar** USA
34A3 **Willoughby,C** Australia
60B1 **Willow Bunch** Canada
47C3 **Willowmore** South Africa
58B2 **Willow Ranch** USA
59B3 **Willows** USA
63D1 **Willow Springs** USA
34A2 **Wilmington** Australia
68C3 **Wilmington** Delaware, USA
67C2 **Wilmington** N Carolina, USA
68D1 **Wilmington** Vermont, USA
60D3 **Wilson** Kansas, USA
67C1 **Wilson** N Carolina, USA
68A1 **Wilson** New York, USA
57F3 **Wilson** USA
34B1 **Wilson** *R* Australia
55K3 **Wilson,C** Canada
60D3 **Wilson L** USA
66C3 **Wilson,Mt** California, USA
62A1 **Wilson,Mt** Colorado, USA
58B1 **Wilson,Mt** Oregon, USA
34C3 **Wilson's Promontory** *Pen* Australia
13E1 **Wilstedt** Germany
7D4 **Wiltshire** *County* England
13C3 **Wiltz** Luxembourg
32B3 **Wiluna** Australia
64B2 **Winamac** USA
47D2 **Winburg** South Africa
7C4 **Wincanton** England
68D1 **Winchendon** USA
65D1 **Winchester** Canada
7D4 **Winchester** England
64C3 **Winchester** Kentucky, USA
68D1 **Winchester** New Hampshire, USA
65D3 **Winchester** Virginia, USA
58E2 **Wind** *R* USA
60C2 **Wind Cave Nat Pk** USA
6C2 **Windermere** England
6C2 **Windermere** *L* England
47B1 **Windhoek** Namibia
61D2 **Windom** USA
32D3 **Windorah** Australia
58E2 **Wind River Range** *Mts* USA
34D2 **Windsor** Australia
68D2 **Windsor** Connecticut, USA
7D4 **Windsor** England
67C1 **Windsor** N Carolina, USA
55M5 **Windsor** Nova Scotia, Canada
64C2 **Windsor** Ontario, Canada
65E1 **Windsor** Quebec, Canada
67B2 **Windsor Forest** USA
68D2 **Windsor Locks** USA
69E4 **Windward Is** Caribbean Sea
69C3 **Windward Pass** Caribbean Sea
63E2 **Winfield** Alabama, USA
63C1 **Winfield** Kansas, USA
34D2 **Wingham** Australia
55K4 **Winisk** *R* Canada
55K4 **Winisk L** Canada
30B2 **Winkana** Burma
58B1 **Winlock** USA
48B4 **Winneba** Ghana
61E2 **Winnebago** USA
64B2 **Winnebago,L** USA
58C2 **Winnemucca** USA
60D2 **Winner** USA
63D2 **Winnfield** USA
61E1 **Winnibigoshish L** USA
54J4 **Winnipeg** Canada
54J4 **Winnipeg,L** Canada
54J4 **Winnipegosis** Canada
65E2 **Winnipesaukee,L** USA
61E2 **Winona** Minnesota, USA
63E2 **Winona** Mississippi, USA
55J5 **Winona** USA
65E2 **Winooski** USA
13D1 **Winschoten** Netherlands
59D4 **Winslow** USA
68D2 **Winsted** USA
67B1 **Winston-Salem** USA
13E2 **Winterberg** Germany
67B3 **Winter Garden** USA
67B3 **Winter Park** USA
66B1 **Winters** USA
13D2 **Winterswijk** Netherlands
16B1 **Winterthur** Switzerland
61E2 **Winthrop** USA
32D3 **Winton** Australia
35A3 **Winton** New Zealand
7E3 **Wisbech** England
64A2 **Wisconsin** *R* USA
57E2 **Wisconsin** *State* USA
64B2 **Wisconsin Dells** USA
55K5 **Wisconsin Rapids** USA
54C3 **Wiseman** USA
19D2 **Wisła** *R* Poland
18C2 **Wismar** Germany
13D3 **Wissembourg** France
73G2 **Witagron** Surinam
47D2 **Witbank** South Africa
56D3 **Witchita Falls** USA
7E3 **Witham** England
7D3 **Witham** *R* England
6E3 **Withernsea** England
7D4 **Witney** England
13D2 **Witten** Germany
18C2 **Wittenberg** Germany
16B1 **Wittenberg** France/Italy
18C2 **Wittenberge** Germany
32A3 **Wittenoom** Australia
13D2 **Wittlich** Germany
47B1 **Witvlei** Namibia
19D2 **Władysławowo** Poland
19D2 **Włocławek** Poland
19E2 **Włodawa** Poland
34C3 **Wodonga** Australia
27G7 **Wokam** *I* Indonesia
7D4 **Woking** England
68B1 **Wolcott** USA
27H6 **Woleai** *I* Pacific Ocean
64B1 **Wolf** *R* USA
13E3 **Wolfach** Germany
58B2 **Wolf Creek** USA
62A1 **Wolf Creek P** USA
60B1 **Wolf Point** USA
18C3 **Wolfsberg** Austria
18C2 **Wolfsburg** Germany
74C9 **Wollaston, Islas** Chile
54H4 **Wollaston L** Canada
54H4 **Wollaston Lake** Canada
54G3 **Wollaston Pen** Canada
34D2 **Wollongong** Australia
47D2 **Wolmaransstad** South Africa
18D2 **Wołow** Poland
34B3 **Wolseley** Australia
7C3 **Wolverhampton** England
7D3 **Wolverton** England
68B2 **Womelsdorf** USA
34D1 **Wondai** Australia
28B3 **Wŏnju** S Korea
28B3 **Wŏnsan** N Korea
34C3 **Wonthaggi** Australia
68C3 **Woodbine** USA
7E3 **Woodbridge** England
65D3 **Woodbridge** USA
54G4 **Wood Buffalo Nat. Pk** Canada
34D1 **Woodburn** Australia
58B1 **Woodburn** USA
68C3 **Woodbury** USA
54D3 **Woodchopper** USA
66C1 **Woodfords** USA
66C2 **Woodlake** USA
59B3 **Woodland** California, USA
66B1 **Woodland** USA
58B1 **Woodland** Washington, USA
33E1 **Woodlark** *I* Papua New Guinea
32C3 **Woodroffe,Mt** Australia
61E1 **Woods,L of the** Canada/USA
64B2 **Woodstock** Illinois, USA
65F1 **Woodstock** New Brunswick, Canada
64C2 **Woodstock** Ontario, Canada
68A3 **Woodstock** Virginia, USA
68C3 **Woodstown** USA
35C2 **Woodville** New Zealand
63D2 **Woodville** USA
62C1 **Woodward** USA
6D2 **Wooler** England
32C4 **Woomera** Australia
65E2 **Woonsocket** USA
64C2 **Wooster** USA
7D4 **Wootton Bassett** England
7C3 **Worcester** England
47B3 **Worcester** South Africa
68E1 **Worcester** USA
6C2 **Workington** England
7D3 **Worksop** England
58E2 **Worland** USA
13E3 **Worms** Germany
7B4 **Worms Head** *Pt* Wales
7D4 **Worthing** England
61D2 **Worthington** USA
64C2 **Worthington** USA
60C2 **Wounded Knee** USA
27F7 **Wowoni** Indonesia
25T2 **Wrangel I** Russian Federation
54E4 **Wrangell** USA
54D3 **Wrangell Mts** USA

10B2 Wrath,C Scotland
60C2 Wray USA
7C3 Wrexham Wales
59D4 Wrightson, Mt USA
67B2 Wrightsville USA
66D3 Wrightwood USA
54F3 Wrigley Canada
18D2 Wrocław Poland
19D2 Września Poland
26F2 Wuchang China
30E1 Wuchuan China
31E2 Wuda China
31C2 Wuding He R China
31A3 Wudu China
31C4 Wugang China
31B2 Wuhai China
31C3 Wuhan China
31D3 Wuhu China
31D5 Wuhua China
42D2 Wūjang China
31B1 Wujia He R China
31B4 Wu Jiang R China
48C4 Wukari Nigeria
31B4 Wuling Shan Mts China
31A4 Wumeng Shan Upland China
13E1 Wümme R Germany
13E1 Wunstorf Germany
43H4 Wuntho Burma
13D2 Wuppertal Germany
31B2 Wuqi China
31D2 Wuqing China
18B3 Würzburg Germany
18C2 Wurzen Germany
31C2 Wutai Shan Mt China
27H7 Wuvulu I Pacific Ocean
31A2 Wuwei China
31E3 Wuxi China
31E3 Wuxing China
31C2 Wuyang China
31D4 Wuyi Shan Mts China
31B1 Wuyuan China
30D2 Wuzhi Shan Mts China
31B2 Wuzhong China
31C5 Wuzhou China
64C2 Wyandotte USA
34C1 Wyandra Australia
7C4 Wye R England
7C4 Wylye R England
7E3 Wymondham England
32B2 Wyndham Australia
63D1 Wynne USA
54G2 Wynniatt B Canada
34C4 Wynyard Australia
64B2 Wyoming USA
56C2 Wyoming State USA
58D2 Wyoming Peak Mt USA
58D2 Wyoming Range Mts USA
34D2 Wyong Australia
64C3 Wytheville USA

X

42D1 Xaidulla China
47E2 Xai Xai Mozambique
51B5 Xangongo Angola
13D2 Xanten Germany
17E2 Xánthi Greece
31D1 Xar Moron He R China
47C1 Xau,L Botswana
64C3 Xenia USA
Xiaguan = Dali
31A2 Xiahe China
31D5 Xiamen China
31B3 Xi'an China
31B4 Xianfeng China
31C3 Xiangfan China
31C4 Xiang Jiang R China
31C4 Xiangtan China
31C4 Xianning China
31B3 Xianyang China
26F2 Xiao Hinggan Ling Region China
31C4 Xiao Shui R China
31D4 Xiapu China
31A4 Xichang China
30C2 Xieng Khouang Laos
31B4 Xifeng China
28A2 Xifeng China
43F3 Xigazê China
31A1 Xi He R China
28A2 Xi He R China
31B2 Xiji China
31C5 Xi Jiang R China
31E1 Xiliao He R China
31B5 Xilin China
28A2 Xinbin China
28A2 Xinchengzi China
31D4 Xinfeng China
31C1 Xinghe China
31D5 Xingning China
31B4 Xingren China
31C2 Xingtai China
73H4 Xingu R Brazil
26C2 Xingxingxia China
31A4 Xingyi China
31A2 Xining China
31E2 Xinjin Liaoning, China
31A3 Xinjin Sichuan, China
28A2 Xinlitun China
28A2 Xinmin China
31D2 Xinwen China
31C2 Xin Xian China
31C2 Xinxiang China
31C3 Xinyang China
31C5 Xinyi Guangdong, China
31D3 Xinyi Jiangsu, China
28B2 Xinzhan China
28A2 Xiongyuecheng China
31D1 Xi Ujimqin Qi China
28A2 Xiuyan China
31D3 Xuancheng China
31B3 Xuanhan China
31D1 Xuanhua China
31A4 Xuanwei China
31C3 Xuchang China
50E3 Xuddur Somalia
28A2 Xujiatun China
31A2 Xunhua China
31C5 Xun Jiang R China
26F2 Xunke China
31D5 Xunwu China
31C4 Xupu China
43N1 Xurgru China
30E1 Xuwen China
31B4 Xuyong China
31D3 Xuzhou China

Y

31A4 Ya'an China
34B3 Yaapeet Australia
50B3 Yabassi Cameroon
26D1 Yablonovyy Khrebet Mts Russian Federation
45D2 Yabrūd Syria
58B2 Yachats USA
72F8 Yacuiba Bolivia
44B2 Yādgīr India
49D1 Yafran Libya
29D2 Yagishiri-tō I Japan
19G2 Yagotin Ukraine
50C3 Yahuma Zaïre
29C3 Yaita Japan
29C4 Yaizu Japan
31A4 Yajiang China
54D3 Yakataga USA
58B1 Yakima USA
58B1 Yakima R USA
48B3 Yako Burkina
50C3 Yakoma Zaïre
29E2 Yakumo Japan
25O3 Yakut Republic Russian Federation
54E4 Yakutat USA
54E4 Yakutat B USA
25O3 Yakutsk Russian Federation
30C4 Yala Thailand
58B1 Yale Canada
50C3 Yalinga Central African Republic
34C3 Yallourn Australia
26C3 Yalong R China
31A4 Yalong Jiang R China
17F2 Yalova Turkey
21E7 Yalta Ukraine
28B2 Yalu Jiang R China/N Korea
29D3 Yamada Japan
29E3 Yamagata Japan
28C4 Yamaguchi Japan
24J2 Yamal, Poluostrov Pen Russian Federation
26E1 Yamarovka Russian Federation
34D1 Yamba New S Wales, Australia
34B2 Yamba S Australia, Australia
50C3 Yambio Sudan
17F2 Yambol Bulgaria
27G7 Yamdena I Indonesia
30B1 Yamethin Burma
Yam Kinneret = Tiberias,L
34B1 Yamma Yamma,L Australia
48B4 Yamoussoukro Ivory Coast
60B2 Yampa R USA
25R4 Yamsk Russian Federation
42D3 Yamuna R India
43G3 Yamzho Yumco L China
25P3 Yana R Russian Federation
34B3 Yanac Australia
28B4 Yanagawa Japan
44C2 Yanam India
31B2 Yan'an China
40C5 Yanbu'al Baḩr Saudi Arabia
34B2 Yancannia Australia
31E3 Yancheng China
31B2 Yanchi China
34B1 Yandama R Australia
50C3 Yangambi Zaïre
28A3 Yanggu S Korea
31C1 Yang He R China
31C5 Yangjiang China
Yangon = Rangoon
31C2 Yangquan China
28A3 Yangsan S Korea
31C5 Yangshan China
31C3 Yangtze Gorges China
31E3 Yangtze,Mouths of the China
28A3 Yangyang S Korea
31D3 Yangzhou China
31B4 Yanhe China
28B2 Yanji China
34C3 Yanko Australia
61D2 Yankton USA
26B2 Yanqqi China
39G1 Yanqqi China
31D1 Yan Shan Hills
25P2 Yanskiy Zaliv B Russian Federation
34B1 Yantabulla Australia
31E2 Yantai China
28B2 Yantongshan China
31D2 Yanzhou China
50B3 Yaoundé Cameroon
27G6 Yap I Pacific Ocean
27G7 Yapen I Indonesia
70B2 Yaqui R Mexico
20H4 Yaransk Russian Federation
7E3 Yare R England
20H3 Yarenga Russian Federation
20H3 Yarensk Russian Federation
72D3 Yari R Colombia
29D3 Yariga-take Mt Japan
39F2 Yarkant He R China
43G3 Yarlung Zangbo Jiang R China
55M5 Yarmouth Canada
45C2 Yarmūk R Jordan/Syria
20F4 Yaroslavl' Russian Federation
45C2 Yarqon R Israel
34C3 Yarram Australia
34D1 Yarraman Australia
34C3 Yarrawonga Australia
20N2 Yar Sale Russian Federation
20E4 Yartsevo Russian Federation
25L3 Yartsevo Russian Federation
72C2 Yarumal Colombia
48C3 Yashi Nigeria
48C4 Yashikera Nigeria
21G6 Yashkul' Russian Federation
42C1 Yasin Pakistan
19E3 Yasinya Ukraine
34C2 Yass Australia
34C2 Yass R Australia
28B3 Yasugi Japan
63C1 Yates Center USA
54J3 Yathkyed L Canada
50C3 Yatolema Zaïre
45C3 Yatta Israel
72D4 Yavari Peru
42D4 Yavatmāl India
28C4 Yawatahama Japan
30D2 Ya Xian China
41F3 Yazd Iran
41F3 Yazd-e Khvāst Iran
63D2 Yazoo R USA
63D2 Yazoo City USA
30B2 Ye Burma
19F3 Yedintsy Moldavia
20F5 Yefremov Russian Federation
21G6 Yegorlyk R Russian Federation
50D3 Yei Sudan
20L4 Yekaterinburg Russian Federation
21F5 Yelets Russian Federation
25Q4 Yelizavety, Mys C Russian Federation
10C1 Yell I Scotland
44C2 Yellandu India
56B1 Yellowhead P Canada
54G3 Yellowknife Canada
34C2 Yellow Mt Australia
Yellow R = Huang He
26F3 Yellow Sea China Korea
56C2 Yellowstone R USA
58D2 Yellowstone L USA
58D2 Yellowstone Nat Pk USA
8E1 Yell Sd Scotland
19G2 Yel'nya Russian Federation
19F2 Yel'sk Belarus
55K1 Yelverton B Canada
48C3 Yelwa Nigeria
38C4 Yemen Republic Arabian Pen
30C1 Yen Bai Vietnam
48B4 Yendi Ghana
30B1 Yengan Burma
24K3 Yenisey R Russian Federation
25L4 Yeniseysk Russian Federation
25L3 Yeniseyskiy Kryazh Ridge Russian Federation
24J2 Yeniseyskiy Zaliv B Russian Federation
7C4 Yeo R England
34C2 Yeoval Australia
7C4 Yeovil England
25M3 Yerbogachen Russian Federation
21G7 Yerevan Armenia
59C3 Yerington USA
20J2 Yermitsa Russian Federation
59C4 Yermo USA
25O4 Yerofey-Pavlovich Russian Federation
45C3 Yeroham Israel
25S3 Yeropol Russian Federation
21H5 Yershov Russian Federation
Yerushalayim = Jerusalem
40C1 Yeşil R Turkey
25M3 Yessey Russian Federation
45C2 Yesud Hama'ala Israel
34D1 Yetman Australia
48B2 Yetti Mauritius
43H4 Yeu Burma
14B2 Yeu, Ile d' I France
21H7 Yevlakh Azerbaijan
21E6 Yevpatoriya Ukraine
31E2 Ye Xian China
21F6 Yeysk Russian Federation
45B3 Yi'allaq, Gebel Mt Egypt
45C1 Yialousa Cyprus
17E2 Yiannitsá Greece
31A4 Yibin China
31C3 Yichang China
26F2 Yichun China
31B2 Yijun China
17F2 Yıldız Dağları Upland Turkey
40C2 Yıldızeli Turkey
31A5 Yiliang China
31B2 Yinchuan China
31D3 Ying He R China
28A2 Yingkou China
31D3 Yingshan Hubei, China
31B3 Yingshan Sichuan, China
31D4 Yingtan China
39G1 Yining China
31B1 Yin Shan Upland China
50D3 Yirga' Alem Ethiopia
50D3 Yirol Sudan
25N5 Yirshi China
31B5 Yishan China
31D2 Yishui China
17E3 Yíthion Greece
28B2 Yitong China
28A2 Yi Xian China
31C4 Yiyang China
20D2 Yli-Kitka L Finland
12J5 Ylitornio Sweden
12J6 Ylivieska Finland
63C3 Yoakum USA
27E7 Yogyakarta Indonesia
50B3 Yokadouma Cameroon
29C4 Yokkaichi Japan
29D3 Yokobori Japan
29C3 Yokohama Japan
29C3 Yokosuka Japan
29D3 Yokote Japan
48D4 Yola Nigeria
29C3 Yonago Japan
28A3 Yŏnan N Korea
29E3 Yonezawa Japan
28A4 Yongam S Korea
31D4 Yong'an China
31A2 Yongchang China
28B3 Yŏngch'ŏn S Korea
31B4 Yongchuan China
31A2 Yongdeng China
31D5 Yongding China
31D2 Yongding He R China
28B3 Yŏngdŏk S Korea
28A3 Yŏnggwang S Korea
28B3 Yŏnghŭng N Korea
28A3 Yŏnghŭng-man I N Korea
28A3 Yŏngil-man B S Korea
28B2 Yongji China
28B3 Yongju S Korea
31B2 Yongning China
28A3 Yŏngsanp'o S Korea
28A3 Yŏngyang S Korea
68D2 Yonkers USA
13B4 Yonne Department France
14C2 Yonne R France
6D3 York England
61D2 York Nebraska, USA
68B3 York Pennsylvania, USA
32D2 York,C Australia
55J4 York Factory Canada
55M2 York, Kap C Greenland
27F8 York Sd Australia
6C4 Yorkshire Dales Nat Pk England
10C3 Yorkshire Moors England
7D2 Yorkshire Wolds Upland England
56C1 Yorkton Canada
65D3 Yorktown USA
68E1 York Village USA
66B2 Yosemite L USA
66C1 Yosemite Nat Pk USA
29B3 Yoshii R Japan
29B4 Yoshino R Japan
20H4 Yoshkar Ola Russian Federation
28B4 Yŏsu S Korea
45C4 Yotvata Israel
10B3 Youghal Irish Republic
31B5 You Jiang R China
34C2 Young Australia
35A2 Young Range Mts New Zealand
68A1 Youngstown New York, USA
64C2 Youngstown Ohio, USA
66A1 Yountville USA
31B4 Youyang China
40B2 Yozgat Turkey
75A3 Ypané R Paraguay
58B2 Yreka USA
12G7 Ystad Sweden
7C3 Ystwyth R Wales
8D3 Ythan R Scotland
31C4 Yuan Jiang R Hunan, China
31A5 Yuan Jiang R Yunnan, China
31A4 Yuanmu China
31C2 Yuanping China
59B3 Yuba City USA
29E2 Yūbari Japan
48A2 Yubi,C Morocco
70D3 Yucatan Pen Mexico
70D2 Yucatan Chan Cuba/Mexico
59D4 Yucca USA
31C2 Yuci China
25P4 Yudoma R Russian Federation
31D4 Yudu China
31A4 Yuexi China
31C4 Yueyang China
20L2 Yugorskiy Poluostrov Pen Russian Federation
17D2 Yugoslavia Federal Republic Europe
31B5 Yu Jiang R China
54D3 Yukon R Canada/USA
54E3 Yukon Territory Canada
30E1 Yulin Guangdong, China
31C5 Yulin Guangxi, China
31B2 Yulin Shaanxi, China
59D4 Yuma USA
26C3 Yumen China
31C5 Yunkai Dashan Hills China
34A2 Yunta Australia
31C3 Yunxi China
31C3 Yun Xian China
31B3 Yunyang China
72C5 Yurimaguas Peru
31E5 Yu Shan Mt Taiwan
20E3 Yushkozero Russian Federation
39H2 Yushu Tibet, China
31D2 Yutian China
75A4 Yuty Paraguay
31A5 Yuxi China
29D3 Yuzawa Japan
19F3 Yuzhnyy Bug R Ukraine
26H2 Yuzhno-Sakhalinsk Russian Federation
20K5 Yuzh Ural Mts Russian Federation

Z

13C1 Zaandam Netherlands
18A2 Zaanstad Netherlands
21G8 Zab al Asfal R Iraq
41D2 Zāb al Babīr R Iraq
41D2 Zāb aş Şaghīr R Iraq
26E2 Zabaykal'sk Russian Federation
18D3 Zabreh Czech Republic
19D2 Zabrze Poland
70B2 Zacatecas Mexico
16D2 Zadar Croatia
30B4 Zadetkyi I Burma
15A2 Zafra Spain
49F1 Zagazig Egypt
16C3 Zaghouan, Dj Mt Tunisia
48B1 Zagora Morocco
16D1 Zagreb Croatia
Zagros Mts = Kūhhā-ye Zāgros
38E3 Zāhedān Iran
45C2 Zahle Lebanon
15C2 Zahrez Chergui Marshland Algeria
20J4 Zainsk Russian Federation
50B4 Zaïre R Congo/Zaïre
50C4 Zaïre Republic Africa
17E2 Zaječār Serbia, Yugoslavia
26D1 Zakamensk Russian Federation
21H7 Zakataly Azerbaijan
40D2 Zakho Iraq
17E3 Zákinthos I Greece
19D3 Zakopane Poland
18D3 Zalaegerszeg Hungary
17E1 Zalău Romania
18C2 Zalew Szczeciński Lg Poland
40D5 Zalim Saudi Arabia
50C2 Zalingei Sudan

25P4 **Zaliv Akademii** *B* Russian Federation
25M2 **Zaliv Faddeya** *B* Russian Federation
21J7 **Zaliv Kara-Bogaz-Gol** *B* Turkmenistan
25R3 **Zaliv Shelikhova** *B* Russian Federation
49D2 **Zaltan** Libya
51C5 **Zambezi** Zambia
51C5 **Zambezi** *R* Africa
51C5 **Zambia** *Republic* Africa
27F6 **Zamboanga** Philippines
19E2 **Zambrów** Poland
72C4 **Zamora** Ecuador
70B2 **Zamora** Mexico
15A1 **Zamora** Spain
66B1 **Zamora** USA
19E2 **Zamość** Poland
31A3 **Zamtang** China
50B4 **Zanaga** Congo
15B2 **Záncara** *R* Spain
42D2 **Zanda** China
64C3 **Zanesville** USA
42D2 **Zangla** India
41E2 **Zanjān** Iran
Zante = Zákinthos
50D4 **Zanzibar** Tanzania
50D4 **Zanzibar** *I* Tanzania
48C2 **Zaouatallaz** Algeria
31D3 **Zaozhuang** China
41D2 **Zap** *R* Turkey
19G1 **Zapadnaya Dvina** Russian Federation
20L3 **Zapadno-Sibirskaya Nizmennost'** Lowland, Russian Federation
25L4 **Zapadnyy Sayan** *Mts* Russian Federation
74C5 **Zapala** Argentina
62C3 **Zapata** USA
20E2 **Zapolyarnyy** Russian Federation
21F6 **Zaporozh'ye** Ukraine
40C2 **Zara** Turkey
15B1 **Zaragoza** Spain
41F2 **Zarand** Iran
41G3 **Zarand** Iran
38E2 **Zaranj** Afghanistan
72E2 **Zarara** Venezuela
19F1 **Zarasai** Lithuania
41E3 **Zard Kuh** *Mt* Iran
42B2 **Zarghun Shahr** Afghanistan
42B2 **Zargun** *Mt* Pakistan
48C3 **Zaria** Nigeria
40C3 **Zarqa** Jordan
45C2 **Zarqa** *R* Jordan
72C4 **Zaruma** Ecuador
18D2 **Zary** Poland
48D1 **Zarzis** Tunisia
42D2 **Zāskār** *R* India
42D2 **Zāskār Mts** India
47D3 **Zastron** South Africa
45D2 **Zatara** *R* Jordan
Zatoka Gdańska = Gdańsk,G of
26F1 **Zavitinsk** Russian Federation
19D2 **Zawiercie** Poland
45D1 **Zāwīyah, Jabal az** *Upland* Syria
25M4 **Zayarsk** Russian Federation
45D2 **Zaydī, Wadi az** Syria
24K5 **Zaysan** Kazakhstan
24K5 **Zaysan, Ozero** Kazakhstan
43H3 **Zayü** China
26C4 **Zayü** China
19D2 **Zduńska Wola** Poland
13B2 **Zeebrugge** Belgium
45C3 **Zeelim** Israel
47D2 **Zeerust** South Africa
45C2 **Zefat** Israel
48C3 **Zegueren** *Watercourse* Mali
50E2 **Zeila** Somalia
18C2 **Zeitz** Germany
31A2 **Zêkog** China
20E2 **Zelenoborskiy** Russian Federation
20H4 **Zelenodol'sk** Russian Federation
12K6 **Zelenogorsk** Russian Federation
50C3 **Zemio** Central African Republic
24F1 **Zemlya Aleksandry** *I* Russian Federation
24F2 **Zemlya Frantsa Iosifa** *Is* Russian Federation
24F1 **Zemlya Georga** *I* Russian Federation
24H1 **Zemlya Vil'cheka** *I* Russian Federation
17D2 **Zenica** Bosnia-Herzegovina
45C3 **Zenifim** *R* Israel
31B4 **Zenning** China
21G7 **Zestafoni** Georgia
13E1 **Zeven** Germany
45B1 **Zevgari, C** Cyprus
25O4 **Zeya** Russian Federation
25O4 **Zeya Res** Russian Federation
15A1 **Zêzere** *R* Portugal
45C1 **Zghorta** Lebanon
19D2 **Zgierz** Poland
31D1 **Zhangjiakou** China
31D4 **Zhangping** China
31D2 **Zhangwei He** *R* China
31E1 **Zhangwu** China
31A2 **Zhangye** China
31D5 **Zhangzhou** China
31C5 **Zhanjiang** China
31A4 **Zhanyi** China
31C5 **Zhaoqing** China
31A4 **Zhaotong** China
31D2 **Zhaoyang Hu** *L* China
21K6 **Zharkamys** Kazakhstan
19G1 **Zharkovskiy** Russian Federation
19G3 **Zhashkov** Ukraine
25O3 **Zhatay** Russian Federation
31D4 **Zhejiang** *Province* China
20J3 **Zheleznodorozhnyy** Russian Federation
31C3 **Zhengzhou** China
31D3 **Zhenjiang** China
31A4 **Zhenxiong** China
31B4 **Zhenyuan** China
21G5 **Zherdevka** Russian Federation
31C3 **Zhicheng** China
26D1 **Zhigalovo** Russian Federation
25O3 **Zhigansk** Russian Federation
31B4 **Zhijin** China
19F2 **Zhitkovichi** Belarus
19F2 **Zhitomir** Ukraine
19F2 **Zhlobin** Belarus
19F3 **Zhmerinka** Ukraine
42B2 **Zhob** Pakistan
19F2 **Zhodino** Belarus
43E3 **Zhongba** China
31B2 **Zhongning** China
31C5 **Zhongshan** China
76F10 **Zhongshan** *Base* Antarctica
31B2 **Zhongwei** China
26C4 **Zhougdian** China
31E3 **Zhoushan Qundao** *Arch* China
19G3 **Zhovten'** Ukraine
31E2 **Zhuanghe** China
31A3 **Zhugqu** China
31C3 **Zhushan** China
31C4 **Zhuzhou** China
31D2 **Zibo** China
32C3 **Ziel,Mt** Australia
18D2 **Zielona Góra** Poland
45A3 **Zifta** Egypt
30A1 **Zigaing** Burma
31A4 **Zigong** China
48A3 **Ziguinchor** Senegal
45C2 **Zikhron Ya'aqov** Israel
19D3 **Žilina** Slovakia
19F1 **Zilupe** Latvia
25M4 **Zima** Russian Federation
47D1 **Zimbabwe** *Republic* Africa
45C3 **Zin** *R* Israel
48C3 **Zinder** Niger
59D3 **Zion Nat Pk** USA
31C4 **Zi Shui** *R* China
18C2 **Zittau** Germany
31D2 **Ziya He** *R* China
31A3 **Ziyang** China
20K4 **Zlatoust** Russian Federation
19D3 **Zlin** Czech Republic
24K4 **Zmeinogorsk** Russian Federation
19D2 **Znin** Poland
18D3 **Znojmo** Czech Republic
47D1 **Zoekmekaar** South Africa
31A3 **Zoigê** China
19E3 **Zolochev** Ukraine
19G3 **Zolotonosha** Ukraine
51D5 **Zomba** Malawi
50B3 **Zongo** Zaïre
40B1 **Zonguldak** Turkey
48B4 **Zorzor** Liberia
48A2 **Zouerate** Mauritius
13D1 **Zoutkamp** Netherlands
17E1 **Zrenjanin** Serbia, Yugoslavia
16B1 **Zug** Switzerland
21G7 **Zugdidi** Georgia
13C1 **Zuidelijk Flevoland** *Polder* Netherlands
15A2 **Zújar** *R* Spain
51D5 **Zumbo** Mozambique
61E2 **Zumbrota** USA
48C4 **Zungeru** Nigeria
62A1 **Zuni** USA
62A1 **Zuni Mts** USA
31B4 **Zunyi** China
30D1 **Zuo** *R* China
31B5 **Zuo Jiang** *R* China
14D2 **Zürich** Switzerland
13D1 **Zutphen** Netherlands
49D1 **Zuwārah** Libya
49D2 **Zuwaylah** Libya
20J4 **Zuyevka** Russian Federation
19G3 **Zvenigorodka** Ukraine
51C6 **Zvishavane** Zimbabwe
19D3 **Zvolen** Slovakia
17D2 **Zvornik** Bosnia-Herzegovina
26G1 **Zvoron, Ozero** *L* Russian Federation
13D3 **Zweibrücken** Germany
18C2 **Zwickau** Germany
18B2 **Zwolle** Netherlands
19E2 **Zyrardów** Poland
25R3 **Zyryanka** Russian Federation
24K5 **Zyryanovsk** Kazakhstan
19D3 **Żywiec** Poland
45B1 **Zyyi** Cyprus

ACKNOWLEDGEMENTS

PICTURE CREDITS

The sources for the photographs and illustrations appearing in the atlas are listed below.

page	
48-61	Physical maps by Duncan Mackay, copyright © Times Books., London
62	*Mercury* NSSDC/NASA *Venus* NASA/Science Photo Library *Mars* NASA/Science Photo Library *Neptune* NASA/Science Photo Library *Uranus* Jet Propulsion Laboratory/NASA *Saturn* NASA
63	*Rock and Hydrological Cycles* Encyclopaedia Universalis Editeur, Paris
90	*Manhattan* Adapted from map by Nicholson Publications Ltd.
94-99	Robert Harding Picture Library Ltd.
Rear Endpaper	G.L. Fitzpatrick and M.J. Modlin: *Direct Line Distances. International Edition* Metuchen N.J. and London, 1986

ABU DHABI	5167	3260	14244	4975	5142	5972	4637	2003	10735	5158	13534	2367	3471	7498	11688	4845	2317	4903	4892	6071	13865	2987	2043	5478
AMSTERDAM		2164	18728	9185	1237	7841	577	6864	5575	174	11424	3282	7620	9647	6628	623	6368	690	367	9300	11676	2213	3350	359
ATHENS			16775	7933	1822	7633	1803	5179	7639	2092	11677	1120	6325	7979	8765	2136	5019	1710	2026	8560	13439	562	1256	2394
AUCKLAND				9566	19204	10388	17743	12294	14478	18279	10372	16573	11176	11796	13181	17525	12482	18609	17813	9121	7052	17042	16287	18330
BANGKOK					9692	3291	8613	3010	13733	9263	16885	7279	1610	10144	13789	8628	2917	9249	8824	1723	10634	7477	6895	9544
BARCELONA						8822	1500	7044	5881	1063	10447	2897	8084	8502	7101	1760	6782	624	1473	10087	12766	2238	3122	1138
BEIJING							7375	4760	10860	7983	19265	7557	3271	12947	10626	7218	3788	8223	7492	1972	8171	7072	7135	8160
BERLIN								6298	6098	654	11890	2891	7045	9588	7103	355	5791	876	255	8770	11782	1739	2903	934
BOMBAY									12275	6891	14937	4363	1664	8216	12976	6430	1156	6725	6544	4311	12928	4818	4017	7205
BOSTON										5598	8619	8737	12517	12411	1369	5904	11504	5929	5843	12831	8191	7783	8884	5280
BRUSSELS											11282	3212	7689	9490	6679	769	6427	533	491	9416	11825	2185	3302	320
BUENOS AIRES												11811	16535	6891	8978	12046	15800	11045	11773	18463	12160	12235	12236	11105
CAIRO													5708	7208	9881	3206	4436	2816	3125	8158	14239	1234	426	3513
CALCUTTA														9684	12861	7083	1307	7651	7264	2654	11357	5867	5314	7978
CAPE TOWN															13658	9942	9284	8958	9725	11867	18562	8367	7481	9635
CHICAGO																6860	12047	7069	6850	12560	6849	8834	9978	6371
COPENHAGEN																	5857	1145	289	8688	11428	2021	3191	958
DELHI																		6363	6020	3770	11930	4560	4032	6724
GENEVA																			862	9544	12358	1921	2959	748
HAMBURG																				8934	11629	1988	3150	723
HONG KONG																					8945	8034	7740	9646
HONOLULU																						13068	13969	11653
ISTANBUL																							1170	2504
JERUSALEM																								3615

	ABU DHABI	AMSTERDAM	ATHENS	AUCKLAND	BANGKOK	BARCELONA	BEIJING	BERLIN	BOMBAY	BOSTON	BRUSSELS	BUENOS AIRES	CAIRO	CALCUTTA	CAPE TOWN	CHICAGO	COPENHAGEN	DELHI	GENEVA	HAMBURG	HONG KONG	HONOLULU	ISTANBUL	JERUSALEM	LONDON	LOS ANGELES
AMSTERDAM	3211																									
ATHENS	2026	1345																								
AUCKLAND	8851	11637	10424																							
BANGKOK	3091	5707	4930	5944																						
BARCELONA	3195	769	1132	11933	6023																					
BEIJING	3711	4872	4743	6455	2045	5482																				
BERLIN	2881	358	1120	11025	5352	932	4583																			
BOMBAY	1245	4265	3218	7639	1870	4377	2958	3914																		
BOSTON	6671	3464	4747	8996	8534	3654	6748	3789	7628																	
BRUSSELS	3205	108	1300	11358	5756	661	4961	406	4282	3479																
BUENOS AIRES	8410	7099	7256	6445	10492	6492	11971	7388	9282	5356	7011															
CAIRO	1471	2039	696	10298	4523	1800	4696	1796	2711	5429	1996	7339														
CALCUTTA	2157	4735	3930	6945	1000	5023	2033	4378	1034	7778	4778	10275	3547													
CAPE TOWN	4659	5995	4958	7330	6303	5283	8045	5958	5105	7712	5897	4282	4479	6018												
CHICAGO	7263	4119	5447	8191	8568	4413	6603	4414	8063	851	4150	5579	6140	7992	8487											
COPENHAGEN	3011	387	1327	10890	5361	1094	4485	221	3996	3669	478	7485	1992	4401	6178	4263										
DELHI	1440	3957	3119	7756	1813	4214	2354	3599	718	7148	3994	9818	2757	812	5769	7486	3640									
GENEVA	3047	429	1063	11563	5747	388	5110	544	4179	3684	331	6863	1750	4754	5566	4393	712	3954								
HAMBURG	3040	228	1259	11069	5483	915	4655	159	4066	3631	305	7291	1942	4514	6043	4257	180	3741	536							
HONG KONG	3772	5779	5319	5668	1071	6268	1225	5450	2679	7973	5851	11473	5069	1649	7374	7805	5399	2343	5931	5552						
HONOLULU	8616	7255	8351	4382	6608	7933	5077	7321	8033	5090	7348	7556	8848	7057	11534	4256	7101	7413	7679	7226	5558					
ISTANBUL	1856	1375	349	10590	4646	1391	4394	1081	2994	4836	1358	7603	767	3646	5199	5489	1256	2834	1194	1235	4992	8120				
JERUSALEM	1270	2082	781	10121	4285	1940	4434	1804	2496	5520	2052	7603	265	3302	4649	6200	1983	2505	1839	1957	4810	8680	727			
LONDON	3404	223	1488	11390	5931	707	5071	580	4477	3281	199	6901	2183	4957	5987	3959	595	4178	465	449	5994	7241	1556	2246		
LOS ANGELES	8377	5570	6909	6512	8276	6013	6265	5799	8713	2597	5627	6107	7595	8166	9976	1746	5609	8005	5915	5653	7254	2563	6862	7587	5455	
	3500	921	1475	12174	6336	314	5744	1163	4688	3410	818	6229	2085	5337	5304	4191	1289	4529	637	1111	6562	7874	1705	2238	785	5833
	7263	10280	9289	1634	4573	10458	5650	9924	6096	10521	10325	7226	8678	5547	6424	9673	9930	6333	10271	10057	4593	5507	9090	8521	10503	7930
	8932	5739	7024	6802	9739	5909	7754	6056	9739	2279	5757	4577	7700	9504	8515	1691	5921	9121	5962	5898	8796	3789	7114	7800	5560	1549
	2893	514	910	11482	5614	452	5031	523	4029	3838	434	6943	1599	4619	5493	4542	720	3816	155	560	5823	7764	1041	1685	597	6051
	6616	3428	4737	8935	8337	3677	6518	3740	7522	251	3451	5593	5427	7615	7919	744	3606	7013	3677	3581	7744	4918	4803	5502	3256	2469
	2321	1337	1386	10063	4393	1873	3610	1002	3129	4498	1404	8365	1801	3443	6277	4984	971	2702	1504	1109	4672	7048	1091	1660	1557	6085
	2126	4133	2828	8678	4485	3652	5727	3948	2816	7190	4066	6472	2186	3839	2542	8010	4155	3373	3764	4080	5449	10741	2952	2276	4229	9664
	6860	3654	4937	8816	8668	3842	6843	3979	7808	191	3669	5276	5618	7936	7799	713	3857	7319	3874	3820	8068	4969	5026	5711	3471	2451
	4808	5742	5797	5532	2615	6421	1110	5494	3956	6871	5840	9786	5796	2955	8906	6500	5363	3415	6036	5541	1549	4104	5448	5535	5919	5724
	6692	3512	4825	8835	8353	3772	6509	3820	7582	313	3536	5612	5516	7649	8010	645	3682	7061	3766	3661	7734	4819	4887	5588	3342	2366
	3260	266	1306	11521	5877	517	5118	547	4365	3446	163	6853	1998	4892	5783	4143	639	4102	257	464	5996	7449	1405	2075	212	5658
	5614	8779	7628	3312	3301	8788	4944	8427	4514	11621	8793	7839	6992	4163	5416	10979	8499	4877	8660	8579	3728	6777	7467	6850	8989	9337
	7310	5937	6033	7636	9993	5294	10766	6207	8338	4829	5844	1223	6141	9372	3775	5284	6321	8749	5673	6147	11005	8291	6380	6405	5750	6294
	2674	804	655	11433	5494	534	5061	735	3845	4102	729	6919	1327	4495	5230	4821	951	3684	433	813	5779	8038	857	1435	891	6346
	8145	5468	6792	6517	7930	5963	5918	567	8405	2699	5532	6453	7466	7828	10245	1859	5474	7693	5833	5533	6910	4261	672	7436	5369	347
	9097	7452	7797	6021	10968	6923	11842	7772	9984	5217	7375	705	7954	10961	4946	5294	7835	10518	7274	7677	11607	6861	8136	2005	7240	5578
	7527	6077	6221	7483	10196	5452	10933	6356	8558	4795	5985	1044	6345	9592	3949	5209	6462	8967	5826	6290	11221	8090	6567	6610	5885	6149
	4299	5332	5305	5963	2312	5982	595	5064	3488	6815	5425	12073	5284	2514	8519	6546	4948	2920	5601	5123	1303	4549	4956	5023	5519	5968
	4068	5530	5318	5815	1784	6119	669	5233	3131	7314	5616	12190	5199	2113	8053	7081	5143	2640	5753	5310	755	4955	4973	4934	5731	6507
	3669	6526	5629	5227	887	6767	2775	6169	2428	9410	6566	9873	5139	1794	6009	9375	6195	2574	6525	6306	1600	6726	5376	4924	6748	8784
	2978	701	1497	10565	5143	1417	4179	505	3878	3753	799	7793	2115	4204	6421	4286	325	3467	1032	505	5122	6872	1352	2064	892	5531
	6085	2875	9523	1343	4675	10677	5545	9998	6305	10092	10404	7345	8957	5668	6856	9242	9963	6472	10422	10111	4566	5065	9286	8778	10557	7497
	5018	5788	5922	5475	2865	6487	1307	5556	4195	6718	5888	11412	5957	3200	9157	6311	5415	3640	6101	5594	1798	3858	5574	5699	5956	5486
	6905	3728	5044	8624	8480	3989	6594	4035	7777	431	3754	5545	5734	7810	8134	437	3896	7243	3985	3877	7815	4659	5103	5806	3560	2176
	2635	582	797	11094	5251	1026	4647	326	3721	4045	570	7328	1480	4262	5653	4698	541	3465	500	462	5437	7634	794	1504	769	6116
	7063	3858	5141	8621	8806	4044	6941	4181	8002	395	3873	5194	5822	8102	7892	595	4058	7501	4075	4023	8163	4838	5231	5915	3676	2300

MILES